WHO WAS WHO

IN THE THEATRE:

1912-1976

A Biographical Dictionary of Actors, Actresses, Directors, Playwrights, and Producers of the English-Speaking Theatre

Compiled from *Who's Who in the Theatre*, Volumes 1-15 (1912-1972)

Volume 3

I-P

An Omnigraphics Book

Gale Composite Biographical Dictionary Series
Number 3

GALE RESEARCH COMPANY
BOOK TOWER
DETROIT, MICHIGAN 48226

BIBLIOGRAPHIC NOTE

The 4,100 biographical entries in this work represent the latest sketches on the deceased or inactive individuals included in the original series, *Who's Who in the Theatre.* The series, edited by John Parker, was published in 15 editions between 1912 and 1972 by Pitman Publishing Limited, London, England. Updating through 1976 has been added for death dates.

The 16th edition of *Who's Who in the Theatre,* covering currently active persons, is also published by Pitman, and is distributed in the United States by Gale Research Company.

Original editions copyright 1961, 1967, 1972
Pitman Publishing Ltd.

Copyright © 1978 by Omnigraphics

Library of Congress Cataloging in Publication Data

Main entry under title:

Who was who in the theatre, 1912-1976.

(Gale composite biographical dictionary series ; no. 3) (An Omnigraphics book)
Includes index.
1. Theater--Great Britain--Biography. 2. Theater--United States--Biography. I. Who's who in the theatre. II. Series. III. Series: An Omnigraphics book.
PN2597.W52   792'.028'0922 [B]   78-9634
ISBN 0-8103-0406-6
UK ISBN 273 01313 0

IDEN, Rosalind, actress; *b.* Manchester, 29 July, 1911; *d.* of Ben Iden Payne and his wife Mary Charlotte Louise (Gadney); *e.* Margaret Morris School of Dancing and Education; *m.* (Sir) Donald Wolfit; made her first appearance on the stage at the Everyman Theatre, Hampstead, 27 Dec., 1920, as Toby in "Through the Crack"; subsequently, for many years, appeared in ballet; appeared at the Kingsway, with Donald Wolfit's company, 12 Feb., 1940, as Bianca in "Othello," and subsequently played Nerissa in "The Merchant of Venice," Olivia in "Twelfth Night," Ophelia in "Hamlet," Hero in "Much Ado About Nothing," and Bianca in "The Taming of the Shrew"; at the Strand, Dec., 1940–Jan., 1941, played Mistress Quickly in "The Merry Wives of Windsor," Desdemona in "Othello," Lady Anne in "Richard III," Annabella in "'Tis Pity She's a Whore," Titania in "A Midsummer Night's Dream," Portia in "The Merchant of Venice"; St. James's, Mar., 1942, Celia in "Volpone"; Dec., 1942, Ada Ingot in "The Romance of David Garrick"; Jan., 1943, Cordelia in "King Lear" and Viola in "Twelfth Night"; toured, 1943, in Garrison Theatres; Westminster, June, 1943, Toinette in "The Imaginary Invalid" and Hilda Wangel in "The Master Builder"; Scala, Feb., 1944, Rosalind in "As You Like It," and Winter Garden, Feb., 1945, Lady Macduff in "Macbeth" and Beatrice in "Much Ado About Nothing"; during the ensuing tour, played Mistress Quickly in "The Merry Wives of Windsor," and at the Winter Garden, Feb., 1946, Imogen in "Cymbeline"; Wimbledon, June, 1946, played Lisa Protasova in "Redemption"; made her first appearance in New York at the Century Theatre, 18 Feb., 1947, as Cordelia in "King Lear," subsequently playing Rosalind, Portia, Ophelia, and Celia in "Volpone"; appeared at the Savoy, London, Apr.– May, 1947, in these same parts, also as Desdemona, and Viola in "Twelfth Night"; Westminster, May, 1948, again played Hilda Wangel in "The Master Builder"; Winter Garden, Nov., 1948, Stella in "The Solitary Lover"; also, 1948, appeared in a season of Shakespeare at the Bedford Theatre, Camden Town; Fortune, Dec., 1949, Mrs. Hawkins in "Treasure Island"; Richmond, May, 1950, appeared as Lady Allworth in "A New Way to Pay Old Debts"; appeared at the Malvern Festival, 1950, when she played Katherine in "The Taming of the Shrew" for the first time; at Middle Temple Hall, 1951, appeared as Viola in "Twelfth Night"; at the Old Vic, Dec., 1951, played Miss Sterling in "The Clandestine Marriage"; Vaudeville, Apr., 1952, played Clarissa Brumfit in "Lords of Creation"; Court, July, 1952, Rosalind in "Bernard Shaw in Heaven"; at the King's Theatre, Hammersmith, 1953, appeared in a season of Shakespearean and other classical plays; Lyric, Hammersmith, Feb., 1957, played Tia Campanita in "The Master of Santiago"; toured, Sept., 1958, as the Midwife in "The Broken Jug"; with Sir Donald Wolfit, 1959–60, toured in Australia, New Zealand, Ethiopia, Uganda, Kenya, India, Malay, Canada, and the United States, in Shakespeare Recitals; since 1954 has broadcast in many radio productions. *Favourite parts:* Viola, Ophelia, and Desdemona. *Recreations:* Gardening and painting. *Address:* Swift Cottage, Ibthorpe, Andover, Hants.

IDZIKOWSKI, Stanislas, dancer; *b.* Warsaw, Poland; studied dancing in his native city under Gilbert, Wiltzak, and Cecchetti; first appeared in London, at the Empire, Leicester Square, 1912; joined Anna Pavlova's company, 1913, and appeared with her at the Palace Theatre, 1913; joined Diaghileff's company at Lausanne, 1914, and toured in the United States, 1915; in 1918, appeared at the Coliseum, and in the following year at the Coliseum, Alhambra, and Empire; Covent Garden, 1920; Prince's and Alhambra, 1921; Coliseum, 1924; also appeared at the Coliseum, 1924, with Lydia Lopokova in "The Soldier and the Grizette," and in 1925, with his own company, in "Les Roses"; rejoined Diaghileff, 1926, and remained with him until the latter's death in 1929; he then toured through

Great Britain, producing "The White Mask," "Spring's Ecstasy," etc.; appeared for a short time with the Vic.-Wells company at Sadler's Wells; danced with outstanding success in "Le Lac des Cygnes," "The Sleeping Princess," "Le Carnaval," "Petrouchka," "The Good Humoured Ladies," "Les Contes Russes," "La Boutique Fantasque," "The Three-Cornered Hat," "Pulcinella," "Jack in the Box," "The Triumph of Neptune," "Children's Tales," "Le Train Bleu," "Cimarosiana," etc.

ILLING, Peter, actor; *b.* Vienna, 4 Mar., 1905; *e.* Vienna; *m.* Maxine Wolpert; studied for the stage with Professor Ernst Arndt at the Academy of Acting, Vienna; appeared for 13 years on the stage in Berlin, Germany, before coming to England in 1937; B.B.C. European Service, 1939–1945, when he broadcast "Churchill's Voice" in German, a translation of the speeches of Sir Winston Churchill; made his first appearance in London at the Phoenix Theatre, Aug., 1943, as Napoleon I in an adaptation of Tolstoy's "War and Peace"; first appeared in the United States at the Bellevue Theatre, Boston, Mass., Mar., 1950, as Jussuf in "The Heart of the Matter"; Duchess, London, Mar., 1952, played Mr. Miller in "The Deep Blue Sea"; Manchester Opera House, July, 1955, played the Russian delegate in "The Delegate" by Roger MacDougal; Globe, Feb., 1958, appeared as Dr. Kreuzer in "The Potting Shed"; Comedy, Oct., 1961, and Wyndham's, Feb., 1962, played The Croupier in "La Bonne Soupe"; Westminster, Dec., 1963, played M. Zenofors in "The Diplomats"; Queen's, July, 1964, Juror No. 11 in "12 Angry Men"; Royal Court, Apr., 1965, played The Man at the End in "Spring Awakening"; has appeared in numerous films, including "I Accuse," "Fire Down Below," and "Bhowani Junction"; made his first appearance on television, 1955, and appearances include: "A Bouquet For the President," "Dr. Kabil," etc. *Recreations:* Reading history.
(Died 29 Oct., 1966; age 61)

ILLINGTON, Margaret, actress; *b.* Bloomington, Ill., U.S.A., 23 July, 1881; *d.* of I. H. Light and his wife Mary Ellen; *e.* at Illinois Wesleyan University; *m.* (1) Daniel Frohman (mar. dis. 1909); (2) Edward J. Bowes; for two years she was a pupil at Conway's Dramatic School, Chicago, where she was the winner of the Jefferson Diamond Medal for Shakespearean work; she then came to New York, where she was immediately engaged by Daniel Frohman, and made her first appearance at the Criterion Theatre, 3 Sept., 1900, as Michel in "The Pride of Jennico"; at Daly's Theatre, in 1902, appeared as Victorine in "Frocks and Frills," and Fleur-de-Lys in "Notre Dame," and subsequently went to Richmond, Virginia, to play lead in a "stock" company; she was then engaged by E. H. Sothern, and appeared with that actor in "If I were King"; returning to New York, she appeared at Daly's Theatre, 19 Nov., 1903, as Yuki, in "A Japanese Nightingale," in which she gained an instantaneous success; she was married to Daniel Frohman during the same month; at the New Amsterdam Theatre, 28 Mar., 1904, she played Henriette in the "all-star" cast of "The Two Orphans," and at the Knickerbocker Theatre, 13 May, 1904, she was seen as Yvette in the play of that name; at the Criterion Theatre, New York, 19 Dec., 1904, she played Mrs. Rippingill in "The Wife Without a Smile"; at the Savoy, New York, 11 Jan., 1905, was Mrs. Leffingwell in "Mrs. Leffingwell's Boots"; at the Broadway, in Apr., 1905, played in "In the Eyes of the World"; and at the Lyceum, New York, 21 Aug., 1905, was Edith in "A Maker of Men"; at South Bend, 2 Feb., 1906, she appeared as Shirley Rossmore in "The Lion and the Mouse," and it was in this part that she made her first appearance in London at the Duke of York's Theatre, on 22 May, 1906; at the Empire Theatre, New York, 3 Sept., 1906, she played the part of Nina Jesson in "His House in Order"; at the Lyceum, New York, 9 Sept., 1907, played Marie Louise Voysin in "The Thief," with great success, the play running fourteen months; at Tacoma, Washington, Aug., 1910, she played in " U til Eternity "; at Los Ángeles, Oct., 1910, appeared as Helene Brechebel in " The Whirlwind "; at Louisville, Jan., 1911, played Louise Arnold in " The Encounter "; at New Haven, Apr., 1911, played in " Mrs. Maxwell's Mistake "; at Los Angeles, July, 1911, played Maggie Schultz in " Kindling "; in Sept., 1911, appeared there as Juliet in " Romeo and Juliet "; at Daly's, New York, Dec., 1911, appeared as Maggie in " Kindling," toured in this play throughout 1912-13; during 1913-14, toured as Mary Turner in " Within the Law "; at the Harris Theatre, New York, Dec., 1914, played Elinore Shale in " The Lie "; at the Harris Theatre, Nov., 1916, " Dodo " Warren in " Our Little Wife "; at the Forty-eighth Street Theatre, Nov., 1917, Sophy Fullgarney in " The Gay Lord Quex "; at the Princess, Chicago, Aug., 1918, Gina Ashling in " The Eyes of Youth "; at the Harris Theatre, New York, Apr., 1919, Ruth Brant in " A Good Bad Woman." *Recreations :* Riding and driving.

(Died 11 Mar., 1934; age 52)

ILLINGTON, Marie, actress ; *d.* of Edward Frederick Inman ; *m.* Gordon Maddick ; first appeared on stage at Edinburgh in 1874 ; she became very well known in Scotland, where she played Fanny Power in " Arrah-Na-Pogue," Julia Latimer in " The Flying Scud," Arte O'Neale in " The Shaughraun," Blue Peter in a burlesque of " Black Eyed Susan," etc. ; made her first appearance in London, 18 Sept., 1875, at Haymarket, in " Red Tape "; in 1876, was at the Princess's, with Miss Heath, in " Jane Shore "; in 1877, appeared there in " Guinea Gold "; for three years a prominent member of the Vaudeville Theatre Company under David James and Thomas Thorne, 1878-1880 ; appeared at Drury Lane, 1884 in " The World " and in 1885, in " Human Nature "; also appeared at Gaiety, Princess's, Criterion, etc. ; toured in " Aunt Jack " and " The

Late Lamented," 1891 ; Covent Garden, 1892, " The Prodigal Daughter "; from 1896-8 lived in retirement; reappeared on tour, under George Edwardes ; at the Princess's, Aug., 1899, played Anna Townshend in " Going the Pace "; at Wyndham's, Oct., 1900, appeared as Mrs. Bulsom-Porter in " Mrs. Dane's Defence "; at the Shaftesbury, Sept., 1901, played Mrs. Caroline Bloodgood in " Are You a Mason ? "; at Wyndham's, May, 1903, played Mrs. Jardine in " Mrs. Gorringe's Necklace "; at the Criterion, Jan., 1904, appeared as Mrs. Mulholland in " The Duke of Killicrankie "; at Wyndham's, Oct., 1904, appeared in " A Wife Without a Smile "; at the Royalty, Feb., 1905, appeared as Mrs. Prothero in " The Diplomatists "; at the Criterion, July, 1905, as Lady Ventry in " The Axis "; at the Apollo, Nov., 1905, played Mrs. Doring in " Mr. Popple (of Ippleton) "; at Drury Lane, Sept., 1906, appeared as Mrs. Fairbrother in " The Bondman "; at the Apollo, Jan., 1907, played Mrs. Van Garkerken in " The Stronger Sex," and at the Vaudeville, June, 1907, Mrs. Ponderbury in " Mrs. Ponderbury's Past "; at the Court, Mar., 1908, played Mrs. Wilbraham in " Mrs. Bill," and at the Comedy, Apr., 1908, Lady Sellenger in " Mrs, Dot "; at the Criterion, Jan., 1909, again appeared in " Mrs. Gorringe's Necklace "; at the Garrick, Feb., 1909, played the Marquise d'Andeline in " Samson," and in May, 1909, the Gentlewoman in " Macbeth "; at the Criterion, June, 1910, played Lady Darby in " The Case of Rebellious Susan "; subsequently went to Australia, to play the Hon. Mrs. Beamish in " The Whip "; on her return, appeared at the Gala performance, at His Majesty's Theatre, 27 June, 1911, as Mrs. Smith in Act II of " David Garrick "; at the Criterion, July, 1911, played Mrs. Huegall in " The Girl Who Couldn't Lie "; at the Criterion, Feb., 1912, played Mrs. Anne Delphy in " 98.9 "; at the New, May, 1912, Mrs. Bulsom-Porter in " Mrs. Dane's Defence "; went to New York, Nov., 1912, and in that month appeared at the Manhattan

Opera House, as the Hon. Mrs. Beamish in " The Whip " ; on returning to London, appeared at the Playhouse, June, 1914, as Mrs. Mulholland in " The Duke of Killicrankie " ; at the Comedy, Feb., 1915, as Mrs. Bloodgood in " Are You a Mason ? " ; at Drury Lane, Apr., 1915, Mrs. O'Mara in " Sealed Orders " ; at the New Theatre, Oct , 1915, Mrs. Carr in " Stop Thief ! " ; at the Savoy, Mar., 1916, Lady Marshall in " The Barton Mystery " ; at Wyndham's, Aug., 1916, Caroline Bawtrey in " The Sister-in-Law " ; Aug., 1918, Mrs. Gaythorne in " The Law Divine " ; at the Apollo, July, 1919, Lady Marian Mainwaring in " Tilly of Bloomsbury " ; at the Garrick, Apr., 1921, Lady Bax in " Count X " ; at the Apollo, Nov., 1921, Mrs. Franklyn in " Thank You, Phillips ! "

(Died 3 Feb., 1927; age 71)

NESCORT, Elaine (*née* Charlotte Elizabeth Ihle), actress ; *b.* London ; *e.* in London and Dresden (Saxony), Germany, and studied principally for grand opera; *m.* (1) John Wightman (mar. dis.); (2) Capt. Harry de Windt; she played a number of leading parts for the Philosophical Dramatic Society at Edinburgh; her first appearance professionally was made on tour with George Edwardes's Company, and in 1899-1900, she was touring in " San Toy " ; her first London engagement was with H. Beerbohm Tree, at His Majesty's Theatre, in 1903, where she played many parts and understudied for a period of two years ; she first appeared as " Nu," the singing girl in the " Darling of the Gods," 28 Dec., 1903, and during her connection with His Majesty's played in " Richard II," " The Last of the Dandies," " The Man who Was," " The Merry Wives of Windsor," " Twelfth Night," " Business is Business," " Much Ado About Nothing," " Julius Caesar," etc. ; in 1905 she was selected by Sir Charles Wyndham to follow Miss Lena Ashwell in the title-*rôle* of " Leah Kleschna " ; was afterwards engaged by H. B. Irving to play important parts in his *répertoire*

company, in which she toured the English provinces and America, appearing in " Paola and Francesca," " Mauricette," " The Bells," " The Lyons Mail," " Charles I," " King René's Daughter," etc. ; on returning from the United States in 1907, she played Mrs. Vidal in " Raffles " with Leonard Boyne on tour, being re-engaged by that gentleman until her appearance in Oct., 1907, at the Criterion with Sir Charles Wyndham and Miss Mary Moore in H. H. Davies's comedy, " The Mollusc " ; at the Playhouse, May, 1908, played Triamour in " Lanval," and at the New and Haymarket Theatres, Pierrette in " Pierrette's Birthday " ; at the Court, Nov., 1908, appeared as Margaret Ramsden in " Into the Light " ; at Wyndham's, Jan., 1909, played Maggie Brown in " An Englishman's Home " ; at the Apollo, Apr., 1910, appeared as Georgina in " The Islander " ; at the Garrick, Sept., 1910, played Mona Mylrea in " The Bishop's Son " ; at the Globe, Nov., 1910, played Mrs. Verney in " A Woman's Way " ; at the Court, May, 1911, played Gwendolen in " The Remedy " ; at the Prince of Wales's, July, 1911, appeared as Mrs. Durlacher in " Sally Bishop " ; at the Pier Pavilion, Hastings, Sept., 1911, appeared as Sylvia in " Down Stream " ; at Buffalo, U.S.A., Apr., 1912, played in " The Law and the Lawless " ; next played a " stock " season at Los Angeles, with J. K. Hackett ; at the Little Theatre, New York, Nov., 1912, played Queen Brangomar in " Snow White " ; at Baltimore, Apr., 1913, played a " stock " season with Miss Percy Haswell ; at the Eltinge Theatre, New York, Jan., 1914, played Margery Seaton in " The Yellow Ticket " ; in Sept., 1914, toured in " The Secret " ; at the Comedy, New York, Feb., 1915, played Miriam Leigh in " The White Feather " (" The Man Who Stayed at Home ") ; on returning to London, appeared at His Majesty's Dec., 1915, as Lady Arlington in " Mavourneen " ; during 1917, appeared in Miss Horniman's company, at the Gaiety, Manchester ; at the Strand, Dec., 1917, played Mrs. Smithers in " The Happy Family " ;

at the Gaiety, May, 1918, Mrs. Douglas in "Going-Up"; at the Lyric, Apr., 1919, appeared as Chorus to Doris Keane's revival of "Romeo and Juliet"; subsequently again returned to New York, and at the Broadhurst Theatre, Dec., 1919, played the Mother of the Girl and Mary Clare in "Smilin' Through"; during 1922-23, toured in South Africa and Australia with Gertrude Elliott; on returning to London, appeared at the Haymarket, June, 1923, when she succeeded Lilian Braithwaite as Isabel in "Isabel, Edward, and Anne"; after a lengthy absence from the stage, reappeared at the Everyman, May, 1929, as Princess Baharodi in "Smoke Persian"; His Majesty's, July, 1929, played Mrs. Millick in "Bitter Sweet;" Arts, Oct, 1931, Lady Metroland in "Vile Bodies." *Hobbies:* Walking, Travelling, and music. *Club:* Arts Theatre. *(Died 7 July, 1964; age 86)*

INESCORT, Frieda, actress; *b.* Edinburgh, Scotland, 28 June, 1901; *d.* of John Wightman and his wife Elaine (Inescort); *m.* Ben Ray Redman; made her first appearance on the stage at the Theatre Royal, Colchester, 1917, as Miss Roberts in "The Mollusc," deputizing for her mother, whom she understudied; made her first appearance on the New York stage, at the Booth Theatre, 14 Mar., 1922, as Septima Blayds Conway in "The Truth About Blayds"; at the Belmont Theatre, Feb., 1923, appeared as Veronica Duane in "You and I"; next appeared at the Eltinge, Aug., 1923, as Marion Masters in "The Woman on the Jury"; at the Garrick (for the Theatre Guild), Oct., 1923, played Mary March in "Windows"; Hudson, Oct., 1924, Mavis Stanton in "The Fake"; at the Garrick (for the Theatre Guild), Feb., 1925, Janet Ingleby in "Ariadne"; at Maxine Elliott's, Oct., 1925, Sorel Bliss in "Hay Fever"; at the Gaiety, Apr., 1926, Sydney Rose Wynne in "Love in a Mist"; at the Music Box, Nov., 1926, Marie-Anne in "Mozart"; at the New Amsterdam, Jan., 1927, Clara de Foenix in "Trelawny of the Wells";

at the Booth, Oct., 1927, The Shingled Lady in "Escape"; during 1928-9, toured with George Arliss, as Portia in "The Merchant of Venice"; during the season, 1929-30, toured for the Theatre Guild, as Barbara in "Major Barbara," and Eliza Doolittle in "Pygmalion"; at the Longacre Theatre, Mar., 1931, played the Empress Josephine in "Napi"; Lyceum, Apr., 1931, Mrs. Janney in "Company's Coming"; during the summer of 1931, at Newport and Stockbridge, played as guest star in the leading parts of "The Constant Wife," "Alice Sit-by-the-Fire," "The Second Man," etc.; at the Bijou Theatre, Dec., 1931, played Julia Jelliwell in "Springtime for Henry"; in the autumn of 1932, toured in the same part; Royale, Oct., 1932, played Mary Howard in "When Ladies Meet"; Little, Jan., 1934, Faith Baldy in "False Dreams, Farewell"; Plymouth, Sept., 1934, Sybil Kingdom in "Lady Jane"; Curran, San Francisco, Jan., 1935, appeared in "Merrily We Roll Along"; spent the next nine years, 1935-44, in films in Hollywood, appearing successfully in numerous pictures; reappeared in New York, at the Golden Theatre, Oct., 1944, as Florence Lane in "Soldier's Wife"; Empire, Nov., 1945, played Mrs. Matthews in "The Mermaids Singing"; Martin Beck, Mar., 1948, Mrs. Clandon in "You Never Can Tell." *Address:* c/o Actors' Equity Association, 45 West 47th Street, New York City, U.S.A.

INGE, William, dramatic author; *b.* Independence, Kansas, 3 May, 1913; *s.* of Luther Clayton Inge and his wife Maude Sarah (Gibson); *e.* University of Kansas, and Peabody Teachers' College, Nashville; formerly a teacher, journalist and actor; was drama critic for the *St. Louis Star Times*, 1943-6; is the author of "Farther Off from Heaven," 1947; "Come Back, Little Sheba," 1950; "Picnic" (which won the New York Drama Critics award, the Donaldson award, and the Pulitzer Prize), 1953; "Bus Stop," 1955; "The Dark at the Top of the Stairs," 1957; "Tiny Closet" (Spoleto Festival, Italy), 1958; "A Loss of Roses," 1959;

"Summer Brave," "Natural Affection," 1962; "Hot September" (based on his play "Picnic"), 1965; "Where's Daddy?" 1966; "Bad Breath," "Don't Go Gentle," 1967; "The Last Pad," 1970; received the Academy Award for his screen-play "Splendor in the Grass," 1962. *Recreations:* Drawing, collecting pictures, swimming.

INGLESBY, Mona, dancer, choreographer, and founder of the International Ballet; *b.* London, 3 May, 1918; *d.* of J. C. Vredenburg and his wife Van Reede de Matalha Bal; *e.* Dunluce, Queen's Gate, London; *m.* E. G. Derrington; studied dancing in London and Paris, under Egorova, Nicolas Legat, Kshesinskaya, Judith Espinosa; made her first appearance on the stage at the King's Theatre, Hammersmith, 1923; appeared with the Ballet Rambert, 1932–5, including seasons at the Ballet Club and Duke of York's Theatre; appeared at Covent Garden, 1937, with Colonel de Basil's "Monte Carlo Ballets Russes"; was responsible for the choreography of "Endymion" at the Cambridge, 1938; "Amoras" at a season of ballet at the same theatre, 1939; the first performance of her International Ballet was given at the Alhambra, Glasgow, May, 1941; was responsible for the scenario and choreography for "Planetomania," Theatre Royal, Birmingham, 1941; produced the ballet, "Twelfth Night," at the Court Theatre, Liverpool, 1942; responsible for the choreography of "Everyman," at the Lyric, London, 1943; her *rôles* include Giselle, Odette-Odile in "Swan Lake," the Bride in "Amoras," Good Deeds in "Everyman," Swanilda in "Coppelia," Princess Aurora in "The Sleeping Princess," the Glove-seller in "Gaieté Parisienne"; has played seasons in London at the Lyric, Adelphi, His Majesty's, Savoy, London Coliseum and Prince's; was responsible for the choreography of "Comus," Opera House, Blackpool, Apr., 1946, and appeared in this as Cotytto, at the London Coliseum, Sept., 1946; appeared with the International Ballet Company at the Adelphi, Mar., 1947, and at the Casino, Oct., 1948; presented the first season of ballet to be given at the Royal Festival Hall, July-Sept., 1951; has presented seasons and danced as *prima ballerina* with her International Ballet Company at Zürich, Verona, Palermo, Trieste, Turin, San Remo, Brescia and Barcelona; in Spain, 1953, appeared in a film of "Swan Lake." *Recreations:* An active interest in all the Arts, and sailing. *Address:* 9 Thurloe Close, London, S.W.3.

INGRAM, Rex, actor; *b.* on board the "Robert E. Lee," a Mississippi river boat, 20 Oct., 1895; *s.* of Mack Ingram and his wife Mamie (Hicks); *e.* Auburn Military Academy; *m.* Lauwaune Kennard; made his first appearance in silent pictures in 1919, in which he appeared for eight years; made his first appearance on the regular stage at the Curran Theatre, San Francisco, Oct., 1928, as Clarence in "Lulu Belle"; first appeared on the New York stage at the Forrest Theatre, 31 Jan., 1934, as Hatu in "Theodora the Quean"; Civic Repertory, Apr., 1934, played Blacksnake in "Stevedore"; Mansfield, Oct., 1934, Maître Livers in "Dance With Your Gods"; Aug., 1935, the Nubian Sentinel in "Caesar and Cleopatra"; 48th Street, Nov., 1935, Buttinhead Adams in "Stick-in-the-Mud"; at the County Theatre, Suffern, N.Y., Aug., 1936, the title-*rôle* in "The Emperor Jones"; Baye's, New York, Feb., 1937, Lucky Johnson in "Marching Song"; Ann Arbor, Mich., May, 1937, the Prince of Morocco in "The Merchant of Venice"; 49th Street, New York, Sept., 1937, Big Boy, in "How Come, Lawd?"; Lafayette, Mar., 1938, Christophe in "Haiti"; Music Box, Sept., 1938, appeared in "Sing Out the News"; Martin Beck, Oct., 1940, played the Head Man in "Cabin in the Sky"; at Cambridge, Mass., Aug., 1943, again played "The Emperor Jones"; Martin Beck, Mar., 1946, Biglow Brown in "St. Louis Woman"; Belasco, Oct., 1946, President of the Senate in "Lysistrata"; has also appeared in several films; is a director of the Screen Actors' Guild and an officer of the Negro Actors' Guild. *Recreation:* Photography.

(Died 19 Sept., 1969; age 73)

IRELAND, Anthony, actor; *b.* Peru, 5 Feb., 1902; *s.* of Sidney Richard Ireland and his wife Hilda Margarita (Rowlatt); *e.* Cheltenham College; formerly engaged in a commercial career; studied for the stage at the Royal Academy of Dramatic Art; made his first appearance on the stage at the Lyric, Hammersmith, May, 1925, when he succeeded Douglas Burbidge as Jack Absolute in "The Rivals"; in Aug., 1925, toured with Phyllis Neilson-Terry, as Jack Druce in "The Folly of Youth"; at Barnes, Feb.–Mar., 1926, played Alexy Fedotik in "The Three Sisters" and Toropetz in "Katerina"; Garrick, July, 1926, Gaston de Rieux in "The Lady of the Camellias"; Strand, (for the Repertory Players), Mar., 1927, and Royalty, May, 1927, Leonard Mercier in "The Combined Maze"; Everyman, Mar., 1927, and St. Martin's, Apr., 1927, Barrington in "The White Château"; Apollo, Sept., 1927, Beverley Cruger in "The Music Master"; Lyric, Jan., 1928, José Vallejo in "Sauce for the Gander"; New, June, 1928, Father Estrella in "Spread Eagle"; Court, Oct., 1928, Nicolas in "The Lady from Alfaqueque"; Arts, Dec., 1928, Viscomte des Ardrets in "The Lion Tamer"; Court, Feb., 1929, Camille in "Thérèse Raquin"; Strand (for Repertory Players), Mar., 1929, and Ambassadors', Apr., 1929, Charles Granillo in "Rope"; subsequently toured as Sir John Chadwick in "Her Past"; Arts, Apr., 1930, played Dr. Fessler in "Jitta's Atonement"; Lyric, Hammersmith, July–Oct., 1930, Algernon Moncrieff in "The Importance of Being Earnest," and Rhodophil in "Marriage à la Mode"; Royalty, Dec., 1930, Gilbert Fordyce in "No. 17"; New, Jan., 1931, Nicholas Fleete in "To Account Rendered"; Embassy, Sept., 1931, Richard Fayre in "The Nelson Touch"; made his first appearance in New York, at the Henry Miller Theatre, 20 Oct., 1931, as Philippe Leroy-Gomez in "The Sex Fable"; Phoenix (for the Repertory Players), Jan., 1932, and Prince of Wales's, Feb., 1932, Lt.-Commander Cramer in "Below the Surface"; New, June, 1932, Thomas Mowbray in "Richard of Bordeaux"; Duke of York's, Oct., 1932, Paul in

"Cold Blood"; Embassy, Jan., 1933, and Haymarket, Feb., 1933, Philip Sevilla in "Ten Minute Alibi," which he played for nearly two years; Arts, Apr., 1934, John in "Secret Orchard"; Arts, Mar., 1935, Derek Bryce in "Short Circuit"; Westminster, May, 1935, Iago in "Othello"; Apollo, June, 1935, Keith Flaxman in "Duet in Floodlight"; Royalty, Sept., 1935, Mardsen in "Closing at Sunrise"; Ambassadors', Feb., 1936, Maurice Armstrong in "Out of the Dark"; Criterion, July, 1936, Vicente Alcantara in "The Lady of La Paz"; Phoenix, Oct., 1936, Esteban in "Hell for Leather"; Wyndham's, Feb., 1937, Hugh Greatorex in "Because We Must"; New, Mar., 1937, Tranio in "The Taming of the Shrew"; St. Martin's, June, 1937, the Spanish Ambassador in "The King's Pirate"; Vaudeville, Dec., 1937, Georgi in "A Lady's Gentleman"; Gate, Feb., 1938, Vincent in "Frozen Glory"; Lyric, Sept., 1938, Lieut.-Commander Peter Brissing in "The Flashing Stream," and at the Biltmore, New York, Apr., 1939, played the same part; at the "Q" Theatre, Dec., 1939, played Julian Savage in "To Whom We Belong"; Apollo, Feb., 1940, Robert in "The Light of Heart"; during the War, served in the R.A.F., 1940–5; reappeared on London stage, at the Embassy, May, 1946, as Stephen Proctor in "Guest in the House"; Comedy, Aug., 1946, appeared as Major Aubrac in "The Other Side"; Savoy, Nov., 1946, Capt. Montgomerie in "Lady Frederick"; Embassy, Sept., 1947, Mortimer Quinn in "Point Valaine"; Lyric, Hammersmith, Dec., 1947, appeared as Loveless in "The Relapse," and played the same part at the Phoenix, Jan., 1948; Westminster, May, 1949, Dr. Bennett Hawkins in "Black Chiffon"; 48th Street Theatre, New York, Sept., 1950, again appeared as Dr. Hawkins in "Black Chiffon"; Arts, London, Sept., 1951, played James Blenkinsop in a revival of "Mrs. Dot"; Westminster, Jan., 1952, Claud Pickering in "Sunset in Knightsbridge"; Comedy, Oct., 1952, Insp. William Burnett in "The Apples of Eve"; St. James's, Aug., 1953, appeared as Prince Bounine in

"Anastasia"; Westminster, June, 1954 played Stephen Hodgson in "It's Never Too Late"; joined the Shakespeare Memorial Theatre Company which toured the Continent, 1955, and with this company appeared at the Palace, London, July, 1955, as Don Pedro in "Much Ado About Nothing," and the Duke of Cornwall in "King Lear"; he has also appeared in many television plays and in films. *Recreations:* Golf, tennis, and swimming. *Club:* Stage Golfing Society.
(Died 4 Dec., 1957; age 55)

IRISH, Annie, actress; *b.* Warloys, Hunts, 21 Apr., 1865; *m.* W. F. Fladgate; made her first appearance on the stage at the Theatre Royal, Nottingham, in 1880, under the management of the late W. H. Vernon; first appeared on the London stage, at the Adelphi Theatre, Mar., 1887, when she succeeded Mary Rorke as Lena Nelson in "The Harbour Lights"; she also appeared at the Adelphi, 28 July, 1887, as Mary Northcote in "The Bells of Haslemere"; in 1889, she went to the Vaudeville Theatre, and appeared there, 4 Jan., as Kitty Ferriby in "The Poet," and 4 Mar., as Kate Constant in "That Doctor Cupid"; in July, 1889, she succeeded Maude Millett as Minnie Gilfillian in "Sweet Lavender," at Terry's Theatre; the following year, at the Haymarket, she appeared as Julie de Noirville in "A Man's Shadow," and at the St. James's, in June, 1890, under Arthur Bourchier's management, she appeared as Lucy in "Your Wife," Alice in "Old Friends," and Nan in "Kit Marlowe"; in 1891, she was engaged by the late Sir Henry Irving for the Lyceum, and appeared there 5 Jan., 1891, as Hero in "Much Ado About Nothing," subsequently playing Lady Eleanor in "Charles I," Sophia in "Olivia," and Emilie in "The Corsican Brothers"; she then joined Charles Hawtrey at the Comedy, and in Oct. played Mrs. St. Germain in "Godpapa," and subsequently Julia Maxwell in "The Grey Mare"; at the Royalty, in June, 1892, she played Belle Dori-

court in "Moses and Son"; in the autumn of that year she joined the Kendals on tour, and played Lady Ingram in "A Scrap of Paper," Mrs. Macdonald in "Impulse," the Baronne de Préfont in "The Iron-master," Lady Molyneux in "A White Lie," Mrs. Bellamy Ives in "The Senator's Wife"; at the Avenue, 7 Jan., 1893, she played Lady Molyneux in "A White Lie," and also appeared in "The Ironmaster," and as Lady Armitage in "The Silver Shell"; at Leicester, in Aug., 1893, she played Ellean in "The Second Mrs. Tanqueray," and in Sept. she accompanied the Kendals to the United States; she made her first appearance on the American stage at the Star Theatre, New York, 9 Oct., 1893, in the last-mentioned part; since that date she has appeared in America in the following parts and plays: Grace in "The District Attorney," 1895; Helen in "The Two Vagrants," 1896; Marian in "Tess of the D'Urbervilles," 1897; Constance in "A Virginia Courtship," 1898; Lucilla in "His Honor the Mayor," 1898; Rosamund in "The Liars," 1898; Martha West in "Her Atonement," 1899; Gertrude West in "Because She Loved Him So," 1899; Miss Hunter in "The Climbers," 1900; Nerissa in "The Merchant of Venice," 1901; "Miranda of the Balcony," 1901; Lina Thurston in "The Unwelcome Mrs. Hatch," 1901; "Life," 1902; "An American Invasion," 1902; Comtesse de Linières in "The Two Orphans," 1904; Ann Cruger in "The Charity Ball," 1905; Duchess of Queensbury in "The Crossways," 1905; has since retired from the stage.
(Died 20 May, 1947; age 82)

IRVINE, Robin, actor; *b.* London, 21 Dec., 1901; *s.* of William Joseph Irvine and his wife Lillian Anne (Robins); *e.* Aldenham and Mill Hill School; *m.* Ursula Jeans; made his first appearance on the stage at Ipswich 26 Dec., 1918, as Captain D'Arcy in "My Lady Frayle"; made his first appearance on the London stage, at the Kingsway, 31 Mar., 1923, as Mr. Carhampton in "Love in Pawn";

Shaftesbury, Dec., 1923, Warwick Entwhistle in "The Rising Generation"; Savoy, Sept., 1924, Joe Purdie in "The Sport of Kings"; at the Ambassadors', 1925, succeeded Robert Andrews as Simon in "Hay Fever"; Prince's, May, 1926, Wilfred Varney in "Secret Service"; Savoy, June-July, 1926, Hector Burrows in "What Might Happen," and Lord Vere in "The Truth About the Russian Dancers," and understudied Seymour Hicks in "Sleeping Partners"; Adelphi, Dec., 1926, played Mr. Darling in "Peter Pan"; during 1927-8, was engaged in various films; at His Majesty's, Jan., 1929, played Digby in "Beau Geste"; Prince of Wales's, Dec., 1929, 2nd Lt. Raleigh in "Journey's End"; Prince of Wales's (for the Stage Society), Feb., 1930, Hickson in "Forty-seven"; Little, Dec., 1930, played in "Caviare"; commenced film career 1927, and has appeared in "Downhill," "Easy Virtue," "Confetti," "Land of Hope and Glory," "The Rising Generation," "Keepers of Youth," "Young Woodley," "Leave It to Me," "A Knight in London," "Palais de Dance," "Above Rubies," "The Ship of Lost Men," since 1931 has been general manager of the St. George Film Productions, and has devoted himself to production. *Recreations :* Swimming, motoring, fishing, and all mechanical pastimes. *Clubs :* Green Room and Stage Golfing Society. *Address :* 2 Adam Street, W.1. *Telephone No. :* Welbeck 7141.

(Died 28 Apr., 1933; age 31)

IRVING, Daisy, actress and vocalist ; *b.* Ireland ; *m.* Lieut.-Col. J. Sargent, Lancashire Fusiliers ; appeared at Daly's, 8 June, 1907, as Frou-Frou in "The Merry Widow"; in Sept., 1907, played Lo-Lo and during 1909, succeeded Lily Elsie as Sonia in the same piece ; during 1909-12, toured with George Edwardes's company, as Alice in "The Dollar Princess," Angèle Didier in "The Count of Luxembourg," and Ilona in "Gipsy Love"; appeared at Daly's, during 1911, as Angèle in "The Count of Luxembourg"; at the New Theatre, Oct., 1913, played Hella Brückner in "The Laughing Husband"; at the

Adelphi, Apr., 1915, appeared as Agatha in "Véronique"; subsequently went to America ; at Hartford, Conn., Jan., 1916, played in "The Beautiful Unknown"; at Atlantic City, Mar., 1916, played Madeleine D'Orsay in "Come to Bohemia"; at the Winter Garden, New York, Oct., 1916, appeared in "The Show of Wonders"; on returning to England, toured during 1918 as Pamela in the play of that name ; appeared at the Coliseum, Mar., 1919, in a repertory of songs ; subsequently toured in variety theatres. *(Died 10 Apr., 1938)*

IRVING, Elizabeth, actress ; *b.* London, 14 Apr., 1904 ; *d.* of H. B. Irving and his wife Dorothea (Baird); *m.* Sir Felix Brunner, Bart.; made her first appearance on the stage at the Savoy Theatre, 22 Apr., 1917, when she walked on in her father's revival of "The Bells"; made her first professional appearance at the Court Theatre, 4 Dec., 1920, as Titania in "A Midsummer Night's Dream"; at Canterbury, Aug., 1921, with the Old Stagers, appeared as Trilby O'Ferrall in "Trilby"; in 1922, appeared with the O.U.D.S., as Margrete in "The Pretenders," and with the Old Stagers, at Canterbury, as Olivia in the play of that name ; at the St. James's, Nov., 1922, played Joan Cradock in "The Happy Ending"; at the Comedy, Jan., 1924, Amy in "Alice Sit-by-the-Fire." *Address :* 2 Ilchester Place, W.14. *Telephone No. :* Western 0364.

IRVING, Ethel, actress; *b.* 5 Sept., 1869; *d.* of the late Joseph Irving, actor, who died in 1870; *m.* Gilbert Porteous; she made her first appearance on the stage at the Gaiety Theatre, 8 Aug., 1885, as a Peasant in "The Vicar of Wideawakefield," appearing under the name of Birdie Irving; next appeared, 23 Dec., 1886, as Valentine in "Monte Cristo, Jr."; she then went to the Prince of Wales's Theatre, 1887, and played Lady Betty in "Dorothy," also appearing there in May, 1887, as Genevra Jones in "Jubilation" and June, 1888, as

L'Arlésienne in "The Love that Kills," in which she danced the *Fandavole* ; in 1889, she danced in "Ruy Blas, or the Blasé Roué" at the Gaiety, and in "The Red Hussar" at the Lyric ; she then went to America, making her first appearance there, at Palmer's Theatre, New York, 6 Oct., 1890, in "The Red Hussar" ; she remained in America six years; returning to England in 1898, toured as Molly Seamore in "The Geisha" ; at Christmas, 1899, appeared at the Coronet, as Maid Marion in "The Babes in the Wood" ; at Daly's, London, July, 1900, she played Dudley in "San Toy," and Jan., 1902, she played Madame Sophie in "A Country Girl" ; at the Apollo, Nov., 1902, was highly successful as Winnie Harborough in "The Girl from Kay's" ; at the Strand, June, 1904, played Lady Bickenhall in "Sergeant Brue" ; at the Royalty, Nov., 1904, made an enormous hit when she appeared as Mrs. Millamant in a revival of Congreve's old comedy "The Way of the World" ; at the Avenue, Dec., 1904, played Alma Molyneux in "Ladyland" ; at the King's Hall, Covent Garden, Mar., 1905, she made another hit when she played Julie in "The Three Daughters of Monsieur Dupont," and then went into management on her own account at the Criterion, opening on 22 Apr., 1905, as Pamela Tuckwell in "What Pamela Wanted" ; in May, 1905, she again scored heavily when she played Clarice in "Comedy and Tragedy" ; in July, 1905, played La Villette in "Where the Crows Gathered," and in Aug., 1905, played Acacia Dean in "Lucky Miss Dean" ; she was then engaged at the Apollo, Nov., 1905, when she played La Bolero in "Mr. Popple (of Ippleton)" ; at the Apollo, Aug., 1907, played the Countess di Ravogli in "The Three Kisses," and at the Court, Oct., 1907, Lady Frederick Berolles in "Lady Frederick" ; in the last-mentioned play she scored a huge success, and played the piece continuously for over a year, at five different theatres ; at the Haymarket, Nov., 1908, played Mrs. Harry Telfer in "Dolly Reforming Herself" ; in Feb.,

1909, played Kate Hardcastle in "She Stoops to Conquer" ; at the Garrick, Sept., 1909, appeared as the Baroness Von Ritzen in "Making a Gentleman" ; she then produced at the same theatre, Jan., 1910, "Dame Nature," in which she appeared as Lolotte ; subsequently toured in the same play ; at the St. James's Theatre, Feb., 1911, played Stella Ballantyne in "The Witness for the Defence" ; in May, 1911, took her own company to Australia, opening in Melbourne in July ; during her Australian tour she also appeared as Nina Jesson in "His House in Order" ; on her return, appeared at the Hippodrome, July, 1912, in "Dolly's Little Bills" ; she next appeared at the St. James's, Oct., 1912, as Monique Felt in "The Turning Point" ; at the Strand, Feb., 1913, as Beatrice Wishaw in "The Son and Heir" ; entered on the management of the Globe Theatre, Apr., 1913, when she played Vanity in a piece of that name ; subsequently revived "Lady Frederick" at the same theatre ; Sept., 1913, appeared as Mrs. Farrell Howard in "Years of Discretion" ; at the Comedy Theatre, Feb., 1914, played Mrs. Parbury in "The Tyranny of Tears" ; at the Golder's Green Hippodrome, Mar., 1915, appeared as Antoinette de Latour in "The Call" ; subsequently toured in leading variety theatres, in the same piece ; in Nov., 1915, sailed for South Africa, where she appeared during 1916, in "The Witness for the Defence," "Dame Nature," "Lady Frederick," and "The Ware Case" ; returning to England in the same year, toured in variety theatres in "The Hotel de Waterloo" ; at the Queen's Theatre, Feb., 1917, played Evelyn Swizel in "The Double Event" ; at the Ambassadors', June, 1917, Julie in a revival of "The Three Daughters of M. Dupont" ; at the Royalty, Mar., 1918, Margaret Schiller in "The Prime Minister" ; at the New Theatre, July, 1918, Naomi Melsham in "The Chinese Puzzle" ; at the King's Hall, Covent Garden, Jan., 1919, played Lady Fanciful in "The Provoked Wife" ; during 1920, toured as Floria Tosca in "La Tosca" ; at the St. Martin's, July, 1920, played

Liubor (Mdme. Ranevskala) in " The Cherry Orchard " ; at the Aldwych, Sept., 1920, Floria Tosca in " La Tosca " ; at the Garrick, Jan., 1921, again appeared as Julie in a revival of " The Three Daughters of M. Dupont " ; at the Empire, July, 1921, played Rose Hart in " Some Detective " ; at the St. James's, Nov., 1922, Mildred Cradock in " The Happy Ending " ; during 1924–5 toured in " Mrs. Dane's Defence," " La Locandiera," and " East Lynne " ; appeared at the Little, Feb., 1926, as Signora de Grasso in " The Forcing House "; Garrick, Apr., 1926, played Marguerite in " Enchantress "; again visited South Africa, 1926; after returning to London, appeared at the Grand, Croydon, Feb., 1927, as Elsie Lindtner in " The White Villa "; at " Q," July, 1927, played Ruth Ayrton in " The Pagans," and Sept., 1927, Helen Vereker in " The Lonely Road " ; at the Fortune, Nov., 1927, for a time succeeded Ellis Jeffreys as Mrs. Wislack in " On Approval "; in June, 1928, toured as Mrs. Vexted in " Thunder in the Air " ; appeared at the Queen's, Oct., 1928, succeeding Leonore Harris as Mrs. Rice in " The Trial of Mary Dugan "; Wyndham's, Jan., 1929, played Lady Belting in " Living Together "; Royalty, May, 1929, Susan Rakonitz in " The Matriarch."
(Died 3 May, 1963; age 93)

IRVING, H. B. (Henry Brodribb Irving), actor-manager and author ; *b.* London, 5 Aug., 1870 ; *e.s.* of the late Sir Henry Irving, and brother to Laurence Irving ; *e.* Marlborough and Oxford University ; M.A. honour school of modern history ; *m.* Dorothea Baird ; originally studied for the Law and was called to the Bar, Inner Temple, 1894 ; he made his first appearance on the stage at the Garrick Theatre, under John Hare, on 19 Sept., 1891, when he played Lord Beaufoy in " School," and he also appeared at that theatre, Jan., 1892, as Philip Selwyn in " A Fool's Paradise " ; he then retired for a time ; re-appeared on the stage in 1894, since which date he has been continuously before the public ; fulfilled successful engagements with Sir

George Alexander (1896-1900), Charles Frohman (1902-4), and other prominent West End managements ; organised his own company in 1906, appearing in a number of his famous father's plays, including " The Bells," " Louis XI," " Charles I," " The Lyons Mail," etc., has, at various times, assumed the management of the Shaftesbury, Queen's, and Savoy Theatres; he made his first appearance on the variety stage, at the Palace Theatre, 26 Jan., 1914, as Arthur Blair Woldingham in " The Van Dyck," subsequently touring in the leading provincial halls in the same piece ; at the Palace, Manchester, Nov., 1914, played Corporal Gregory Brewster in " A Story of Waterloo," appearing for the first time in London in the same part at the Coliseum, Dec., 1914,; was Commanded by the late King Edward to appear at Windsor Castle, 19 Nov., 1909, in " The Lyons Mail " ; he is the author of the " Life of Judge Jeffreys," 1898 ; a volume of criminal studies, " French Criminals of the Nineteenth Century," 1901 ; " Occasional Papers," 1906 ; " Trials of Franz Muller and Mrs. Maybrick— Notable English Trials," 1911-12. *Address :* 7 Gordon Place W.C., and The Mill, Whitstable, Kent. *Telephone :* 3360 Central. *Clubs :* Athenaeum, Garrick, Beefsteak, and Green Room. *(Died 17 Oct., 1919; age 49)*

IRVING, Isabel, actress ; *b.* Bridgeport, Conn., U.S.A., 28 Feb., 1871 ; *d.* of Charles Washington and Isabella Irving ; *e.* Bridgeport ; *m.* W. H. Thompson (dec.) ; made her first appearance on the stage at the Standard Theatre, New York, 7 Dec., 1886, as Gwendoline in " The Schoolmistress," under the management of Rosina Vokes ; she subsequently toured as Bessy Smith in " Gwynne's Oath," and appeared at the Windsor Theatre, New York, in that part, on 15 Aug., 1887 ; she then returned to Rosina Vokes, and at Daly's Theatre, New York, in Apr., 1888, played in " A Pantomime Rehearsal," " A Game of Cards," and subsequently in " A Double Lesson " ; she was then engaged by the late Augustin

Daly, and from 1888 until 1893 remained a member of his company; made her first appearance under his management on 18 Dec., 1888, as Caroline in "Needles and Pins"; during her long engagement she played the following, among other parts: Jenny in "An International Match," Pansy in "The Great Unknown," Audrey in "As You Like It," Suzette in "A Priceless Paragon," Faith Rutherell in "The Last Word," Virginie in "The Prodigal Son" (" L'Enfant Prodigue"), Katherine in "Love's Labour's Lost," Imogene in "The Cabinet Minister," Daisy Griffing in "Nancy and Co.," Sabina in "A Test Case," Helen in "The Hunchback," Susan in "A Night Off," Oberon in "A Midsummer Night's Dream," etc., etc.; she made her first appearance on the London stage at the Lyceum Theatre, 24 June, 1890, as Daisy in "Nancy and Co."; on leaving the Daly company, she joined Daniel Frohman's company at the Lyceum, New York; she first appeared there, on 7 June, 1894, as Lady Neoline Belturbet in "The Amazons," and during this engagement she was also seen as Dorothea March in "A Woman's Silence," Susan in "The Case of Rebellious Susan," Lady Chiltern in "An Ideal Husband," Ruth in "Fortune," Rhoda Trendel in "The Home Secretary," Theophila Fraser in "The Benefit of the Doubt," and the Princess Flavia in "The Prisoner of Zenda"; she next became leading lady with John Drew, and in that capacity appeared with him at the Empire, New York, 8 Nov., 1897, as the Comtesse de Candale in "A Marriage of Convenience"; Jessica in "The Liars," 26 Sept., 1898, and Mrs. Parbury in "The Tyranny of Tears," 11 Sept., 1899; she also played with him at Wallack's Theatre, 14 Feb., 1898, as Maysie in "One Summer's Day"; at Hoyt's Theatre, 8 Sept., 1900, appeared as Leontine in "The Husbands of Leontine," and 8 Oct., 1900, as Josephine Furet in "Self and Lady"; at the Knickerbocker Theatre, 4 Mar., 1901, she played the part of Jocelyn Leigh in

"To Have and to Hold," and in Oct., 1901, she succeeded Blanche Bates as Cigarette in "Under Two Flags"; she was next seen with Charles Hawtrey, playing Minnie Templar in "A Message from Mars," and subsequently appeared in "The Fantasticks"; she was then seen as Marita in "A Royal Rival," and in 1903 toured as Virginia Carvel in "The Crisis"; at Proctor's, in Nov., 1904, she played Eugenia in "Six Persons," and at Boston, 23 Jan., 1905, played Louise in the "all-star" cast of "The Two Orphans"; at the New Amsterdam, 17 Apr., 1905, she played Constance Neville in the "all-star" revival of "She Stoops to Conquer," and later in the year toured as Mistress Roxana in "The Toast of the Town," appearing in New York, at Daly's, on 27 Nov., 1905, in the same part; at the Liberty Theatre, 20 Nov., 1906, she appeared as Robina in "Susan in Search of a Husband"; and 4 Dec., 1906, as Ruth Carney in "The Girl Who has Everything"; during 1907, "starred" as Susan Gambett in "Susan in Search of a Husband," and Sylvia Lang in "The Girl Who Has Everything"; at the Savoy, Sept., 1908, appeared as Mater in a play of that name; at the Criterion, New York, 30 Aug., 1909, played Mrs, Cameron in "The Flag Lieutenant". at the Savoy, New York, 27 Dec.; 1909, appeared as Floyd Carroll in "The Commanding Officer"; at the Empire, New York, 5 Sept., 1910, played Mrs. Dallas-Baker in "Smith"; in Sept., 1911, started on a tour with Kyrle Bellew, playing Mrs. Baxter in "The Mollusc"; at the Lyceum, New York, 27 Feb., 1912, played Dulcie Anstice in "Preserving Mr. Panmure"; at the Belasco, 16 Sept., 1912, Helen Arany in "The Concert"; at the same theatre, 4 Sept., 1913, played Delphine in "The Temperamental Journey"; at the Little Theatre, New York, 13 Apr., 1914, Eve Lindon in "The Truth"; at the Grand Theatre, Chicago, 31 Aug., 1914, appeared as Ethel Cartwright in "Under Cover"; at Syracuse, N.Y., Oct. 1915, played Bianca Sonino in "$2,000 a Night" ("The Great Lover"), during 1916, toured as Mistress Page in " The Merry Wives of Windsor," and played the same part at the Park Theatre, New York, Jan., 1917 ; at the Playhouse, New York, Aug., 1918, played Serena Lenox in " She Walked in Her Sleep " ; at the Morosco Theatre, Sept., 1919, Mrs. Lanham in " Civilian Clothes " ; at the Park Theatre, Oct., 1921, Mrs. Jarvis in " A Bachelor's Night " ; at the Liberty, Feb., 1922, Mrs. Kincaid in " To the Ladies " ; at the Gaiety, New York, March, 1924, Katherine Sundale in " We Moderns " ; at the Thirty-ninth Street Theatre, May, 1924, Henrietta Travers in " The Bride " ; Bijou, Nov., 1925, Mrs. Lucas in " A Lady's Virtue " ; during 1926-7, toured as Mrs. Craig in " Craig's Wife " ; Little, Feb., 1928, played Madre Superior in " La Gringa " ; Empire, Nov., 1928, Mrs. Henry van der Luyden in " The Age of Innocence" ; Cort, May, 1930, Madame Voinitskaya in " Uncle Vanya." *Address :* Siasconset, Nantucket Island, Mass., U.S.A.

(Died 1 Sept., 1944; age 73)

IRVING, K. Ernest, Hon. R.A.M., composer and conductor ; *b.* Godalming, Surrey, 6 Nov., 1878 ; his first engagement was at Maidenhead, 1895 ; has composed and arranged the music for several plays, including " The Circle of Chalk," 1931 ; " The Two Bouquets," 1936 ; " An Elephant in Arcady," 1938 ; eight Shakespearean productions, and much incidental music ; has been at one time or another Musical Director at all the West End theatres in London, except the Phoenix, also of the Mogador, Paris, and Comedia, Madrid ; member of the Honorary Committee of Management of the Royal Philharmonic Society for over thirty years ; as Musical Director composed or arranged music for over thirty films at Ealing Film Studios ; is an Hon. R.A.M. *Recreations :* Music and chess. *Club :* Savage. *Address :* The Lawn, Ealing, W.5. *Telephone No. :* Ealing 2110.

IRVING, Laurence Henry ˟ **Forster,** O.B.E., R.D.I., artist, designer, and author ; *b.* London, 11 Apr., 1897 ;

o.s. of the late H. B. Irving and his wife Dorothea (Baird) ; grandson of the late Sir Henry Irving ; *e.* Wellington College ; *m.* Rosalind Woolner ; served in the R.N.A.S., and R.A.F., 1914–19 ; France, 1916 (Croix de Guerre) ; studied Art at the Byam Shaw School, and later at R.A. schools ; has held four exhibitions of his pictures in London ; designed settings, and, in most cases, costumes for "Vaudeville Vanities," 1926 ; "The Five o'Clock Girl," 1929 ; "Heat Wave," 1929 ; was art-director in Hollywood to Douglas Fairbanks, for "The Man in the Iron Mask," 1928, and "The Taming of the Shrew," 1929 ; "The Circle," "The Painted Veil," "The Nelson Touch," "The Good Companions," "There's Always Juliet," 1931 ; "Punchinello," "Never Come Back," "Evensong," 1932 ; **"Clive of India," 1934** ; **"Murder in the Cathedral," 1935** ; **"Bees on the Boatdeck," 1936** ; **"I Have Been Here Before,"** "People at Sea," "Yes and No," 1937 ; "Mary Goes to See," "Banana Ridge," "The Sun Never Sets," 1938 ; rejoined the R.A.F., 1939–45 ; served in France, 1940 (mentioned in Dispatches) ; France and Belgium, 1944 (O.B.E. Military) ; has since designed "She Follows Me About," 1943 ; "Desert Rats," "The First Gentleman," 1945 ; "Marriage à la Mode," 1946 ; "Hamlet," for the Old Vic, 1950 ; "Man and Superman," 1951 ; "Sweet Peril," 1952 ; "The Happy Marriage," "Out of the Whirlwind," "Pygmalion," 1953 ; "The Shadow of Doubt," "The Wild Duck," 1955 ; "The Broken Jug," 1958 ; "Wolf's Clothing," 1959 ; "A Stranger in the Tea," 1960 ; designed the film production of "Pygmalion," 1937 ; designed and produced the film of Lefanu's "Uncle Silas," 1947 ; has published "Windmills and Waterways" ; edited and illustrated "Hakluyt's Voyages," "Bligh's Journal of the Voyage of the Bounty" ; illustrated Masefield's " Philip the King" ; illustrated the edition of Conrad's "Mirror of the Seas," 1935 ; author of "Henry Irving : The Actor and His World," 1951 ; edited and illustrated "The Maid of Athens," 1952 ; illustrated Overbury's "A

Theatre of Natures," and St.-Exupéry's "Flight to Arras," 1955; is a Director of the Times Publishing Company; is a Governor of the Shakespeare Memorial Theatre, Stratford-on-Avon, and of the Royal Academy of Dramatic Art; Chairman of the British Theatre Museum, 1957–66. *Club:* Garrick. *Address:* The Lea, Wittersham, Kent. *(Died 29 May, 1914; age 42)*

IRVING, Laurence Sidney, actor and dramatist; *b.* London, 21 Dec., 1871; *y.s.* of the late Sir Henry Irving; *m.* Mabel Hackney; was intended for the diplomatic profession, and was for a short time at the British Embassy, St. Petersburg; made his professional *début* on the stage, Aug., 1891, as a member of F. R. Benson's company, at the Theatre Royal, Dundee, as Snug in " A Midsummer Night's Dream "; first appeared in London, at Toole's Theatre, 26 Mar., 1892, as Augustus Caddell in " Daisy's Escape "; subsequently toured with Toole as Andrew McPhail in " Walker, London "; he also appeared at Toole's in " Dot," " Homburg," etc.; then toured in " A Bunch of Violets " and " Trilby " (as Svengali); appeared at the Lyceum, Jan., 1898, as Peter in his own play, (owing to his father's illness), " Peter the Great "; as Tallien in " Robespierre " (1899), Junius Brutus in " Coriolanus," Colonel Midwinter in " Waterloo," Fouché in " Madame Sans-Gêne," Courriol in " The Lyons Mail," Antonio in " The Merchant of Venice," De Nemours in " Louis XI," and Valentine in " Faust "; toured as Colonel Hawley and as Lovelace in " Richard Lovelace," 1904, and appeared at the Comedy Theatre as Crawshay in " Raffles," May, 1906; during 1907 played in " The Phœnix " and " The Incubus," at the Coronet and Court Theatres; during 1908, appeared at various music halls, in " Peg Woffington," " Feed the Brute," " The Dog Between," and a version of " The Ballad Monger "; visited America in 1909, and appeared at the New York Theatre, Mar., 1909, played Louis XI in " The King and the Vagabond " (" The

Ballad Monger "); and at the Hackett Theatre, New York, Apr., 1909, Pierre in " The Incubus "; at the Comedy, New York, Apr., 1910, appeared as M. Dupont in " The Three Daughters of M. Dupont "; appeared at the Prince of Wales's, Birmingham, July, 1910, as John Luff in " Margaret Catchpole," and at the Gaiety, Manchester, Aug., 1910, as Rodion Raskolnikoff in his own play " The Unwritten Law "; produced the last mentioned play at the Garrick, London, on 14 Nov., 1910, when it met with instantaneous success; at the Kingsway Theatre, 23 Feb., 1911, he produced " The Lily," and appeared in it as the Comte de Maigny, with great success; at the Duke of York's, Apr., 1911, appeared as The Governor in his own play " The Terrorist "; at the Command performance at Drury Lane, 17 May, 1911, appeared as Mr. Sharp in " Money "; at the Duke of York's, May, 1911, appeared as John Luff in " Margaret Catchpole "; at the Gala performance at His Majesty's, 27 June, 1911, played the Earl of Leicester in " The Critic," subsequently toured in " The Lily," and " The Unwritten Law "; at the Lyceum, Edinburgh, 9 Nov., 1911, appeared as Hamlet; he is the author of " Time, Hunger, and the Law," " Uncle Silas " (with Seymour Hicks), " Gedefroi and Yolande," " A Christmas Story," " Peter the Great," " Bonnie Dundee," " Richard Lovelace," " The Phœnix," and " The Fool hath said in his Heart," the latter produced by Mr. E. H. Sothern at Chicago, 23 Sept., 1907. Translated " Robespierre " and " Dante " from the French of Sardou, both produced by the late Sir Henry Irving, and " Les Hannetons " (" The Incubus "). *Address :* 10 Gilston Road, The Boltons, S W *Club :* Garrick

IRWIN, Edward, actor and dramatic author; *b.* Leeds, 7 Mar., 1867; *s.* of Sir George Irwin and his wife Flora (Smith); *e.* University College School; *m.* Minnie Florence Knight; made his first appearance on the stage at the Londesborough Theatre, Scarborough, 22 Aug., 1887, as Desmoulins in " The

Lady of Lyons," with Wilson Barrett's company ; he made his first appearance on the London Stage, at the old Globe Theatre, 22 Dec., 1887, as the Turnkey in " The Golden Ladder "; he remained a member of Barrett's company until that manager died, in 1904 ; he played in all his London seasons at the Globe, Princess's, New Olympic, Lyric, Lyceum, and Adelphi toured with him in America (four times), Australia and South Africa · he appeared at New Olympic, Dec., 1890, as Mr. Dolroyd in " The People's Idol " ; Feb., 1891, Trotters in " The Lights o' London " ; Mar., 1891, General Morivart in " Father Buonaparte " ; Apr., 1891, General Pouffière in " The Acrobat"; at the Lyric, Jan., 1896, Licinius in " The Sign of the Cross," subsequently appearing as Nero; Feb., 1897, Ahira in " The Daughters of Babylon "; May, 1897, Icilius in " Virginius "; May, 1897, Montano in " Othello " ; at the Lyceum, Oct., 1899, he played in " Man and his Makers "; at the Adelphi, Dec., 1902, Guthrum in " The Christian King "; after the death of Wilson Barrett, he appeared under the management of Sir Herbert Tree, Granville-Barker, Frank Curson, Oscar Asche, Frederick Harrison ; has toured in several leading parts, notably as Joe Quinney in "Quinney's," Hornblower in " The Skin Game," etc. ; at the Apollo, Dec., 1922, played Augustus Percival Hawley in " Hawley's of the High Street "; at the St. Martin's, Feb., 1924, Robert Beton in " The Forest " ; at the Apollo, Sept., 1924, Charlie Benfield in " The Fool " ; at the " Q," Jan., 1926, played Silas Comber in " The Tame Cat "; Lyric, Mar., 1926, the Waiter in " The Best People "; May, 1927, Durand in " The Garden of Eden "; during 1928-9 toured as the Doctor in " The Crooked Billet "; Wyndham's, June, 1929, played Hodgkin in " Exiled "; July, 1929, the Auctioneer in " The Skin Game," subsequently playing Hornblower in the same piece; Adelphi, Dec., 1930, appeared in "Ever Green "; Garrick, June, 1931, played Augustus Percival-Hawley in "What Woman Wants"; Globe, Apr., 1932, Sir Humphrey Haliburton in "Wings Over Europe"; Everyman, June, 1932, Beckford in "The Marvellous Boy"; Arts, Oct., 1932, Manulah in "The Gates of Ur"; Westminster, Jan., 1934, Mr. Clark in "Saturday's Children"; Little, May, 1934, the Duke of Leftsbury in "Once Upon a Time"; Duchess, Sept., 1934, Dr. Kirby in "Eden End"; again went to America, 1935, and played the same part at the Masque Theatre, New York, Oct., 1935; is part-author of several plays, including "Sunday," "The Bargain," "The Man Who Came Home," etc. *(Died 25 Feb., 1937; age 70)*

IRWIN, May, actress ; *b.* at Whitby, Ontario, 27 June, 1862 ; *d.* of Robert E. Campbell and his wife Jane (Draper); *m.* (1) Frederick W. Keller (*d.* 1886); (2) Kurt Eisfeldt; *e.* at High School, Whitby ; made her first appearance on the stage at the Theatre Comique, Rochester, New York, singing in " vaudeville," 8 Feb., 1875; in 1877 she joined Tony Pastor's company at the Old Metropolitan Theatre, New York, and continued under his management at that theatre, and at Pastor's Fourteeth Street Theatre, until 1883 ; at the latter theatre, 8 Feb., 1881, she played in " The Pie Rats of Penn Yan," and 23 Jan., 1883, as Lady Angela in " Patience "; in 1883 she joined the late Augustin Daly's company, with which she remained until 1886 ; during this period she played, among other parts, the following : Lucy in " The Recruiting Officer," Susan in " A Night Off," Betsy in " Nancy and Co.," the Maid in " A Woman's Won't," Popham in " The Magistrate," Angolina in " After Business Hours," etc. ; she made her first appearance on the London stage, with the Daly company, at Toole's Theatre, 1 Aug., 1884 in " Dollars and Sense " ; in 1887-8, appeared in " vaudeville "; subsequently played for some time in " The City Directory," and in " The Junior Partner "; during 1892-3 toured with John T. Powers in " A Straight Tip "; at the Garden Theatre, New York, 3 Apr., 1893, she played Lottie Singleton in "His Wedding Day," and in Sept. of the same year appeared

in "The Poet and the Puppets"; she then "starred" under Rich and Harris, and appeared at the Bijou Theatre in the following parts: Elizabeth Alwright in "A Country Sport," 1893, Beatrice Byke in "The Widow Jones," 1895, Dottie Dimple in "Courted in Court," 1896, Countess de Cagiac in "The Swell Miss Fitzswell," 1897, Kate Kip in "Kate Kip, Buyer," 1898, Alice in "Sister Mary," 1899, Madge Smith in "Madge Smith, Attorney," 1900, and Mrs. Black in "Mrs. Black is Back," 1904; at Plainfield, New Jersey, 21 Sept., 1906, she played the part of Mrs. Wilson in "Mrs. Wilson, That's All"; subsequently appearing in the same part at the Bijou, New York, 5 Nov., when the title of the play was reduced to "Mrs. Wilson"; during 1907 also appeared as Mrs. Peckham in "Mrs. Peckham's Carouse"; in Dec., 1908 toured as Mrs. Baxter in "The Mollusc"; at Detroit, Mar., 1910, appeared as Mrs. Jim in a play of that name; at Wallack's, New York, Nov., 1910, appeared in the same part, the play being re-named "Getting a Polish"; in Nov., 1911, toured in "She Knows Better Now"; from 1894 to 1908, was playing under her own management; at the George M. Cohan Theatre, 24 Feb., 1913, appeared as Gloria Grey in "A Widow by Proxy"; during 1914, appeared in "vaudeville," in "She Just Wouldn't"; at White Plains, N.J., Apr., 1915, appeared in "No. 13 Washington Square," and played the same piece at the Park Theatre, New York, Aug., 1915; toured in the same play during 1916-17; in 1919-20, toured in "On the Hiring Line"; at the Punch and Judy Theatre, Nov., 1922, played in "The '49ers."
Address: May Irwin Farms, Clayton 1000 Islands, New York, U.S.A.
(Died 22 Oct., 1938; age 76)

ISAACS, Edith J. R., *b.* Milwaukee, Wis., U.S.A., 27 Mar., 1878; *d.* of Adolph Walter Rich and his wife Rose (Sidenberg); *e.* Milwaukee High School and Downer College; *m.* Lewis M. Isaacs; was dramatic critic for *Ainslee's Magazine,* 1913; editor of *Theatre Arts Monthly,* 1918 to 1945;

editor of *Essays on the Arts of the Theatre,* 1928, and *Plays of American Life and Fantasy,* 1929; during the War (1916–18), was chief of the Woman's Publicity Dept. (Liberty Loans). *Recreation:* Gardening. *Clubs:* Cosmopolitan, and MacDowell Association. *Address:* Hotel Elysée, 60 East 54th Street, New York City, U.S.A. *Telephone No.:* Plaza 3-1066.
(Died 10 Jan., 1956; age 77)

ISHAM, Sir Gyles (Bart.) actor; *b.* Lamport, Northampton, 31 Oct., 1903; *s.* of the late Sir Vere Isham, Bart., and his wife Millicent (Vaughan); *e.* Rugby and Magdalen College, Oxford, where he took Secondclass Honours in Modern History; while at Oxford was a member of the O.U.D.S., and appeared with success as Hamlet and Hotspur, among other parts; was President of the O.U.D.S., 1924-5; President of the Oxford Union, 1926; made his first appearance on the professional stage at the Theatre Royal, Huddersfield, 14 Feb., 1927, as King Charles II in "And So To Bed"; made his first appearance on the London stage, at the Strand, 27 June, 1927, as Baron Skanskorg in "The Spook Sonata"; appeared with J. B. Fagan's Repertory Company at the Playhouse, Oxford, Aug., 1927, in "Uncle Vanya" and several other plays; accompanied J. B. Fagan to New York, in the autumn, making his first appearance there at the Shubert Theatre, 9 Nov., 1927, as Prodgers in "And So To Bed"; at the Playhouse, New York, Jan., 1928, played Frederick Granton in "The Queen's Husband"; at the Bijou, Mar., 1928, Simenoff Pishtshik in "The Cherry Orchard"; on his return to England, appeared at the Duke of York's, Sept., 1928, as The Czarevitch in "Such Men Are Dangerous"; in 1929 toured as Trino in "One Hundred Years Old," and subsequently with the Masque Players in "Misalliance," "Berkeley Square," "On Approval," and "The Sea-Gull"; joined the company of the Old Vic., Sept., 1929, and appeared as Mercutio, Bassanio, Thomas in "The Imaginary Invalid," Horatio, etc.; at the Arts Theatre, July, 1930, played Albert

Gregor in "The Macropulos Secret"; in Feb., 1931, toured with Matheson Lang in "General Crack" and "Jew Süss"; subsequently joined the Stratford-on-Avon Festival company, and toured in U.S.A. and Canada, 1931; at the opening of the New Memorial Theatre, Stratford-on-Avon, Apr., 1932, played Prince Henry in "Henry IV" (part I); subsequently played Brutus, Antony, Oberon, etc.; at the Garrick, Sept., 1932, played Hector Frome in "Justice"; Oct., 1932, Vladimir Blok in "The Bear Dances"; Royalty, Dec., 1932, Jonathan Berry in "A Cup of Happiness"; Lyric, Hammersmith, June, 1933, Straforel in "The Fantasticks"; Lyric, Oct., 1933, Richard Burbage in "This Side Idolatry"· Wyndham's, Dec., 1933, Colonel Maitland in "What Happened to George"; at the Vaudeville, Feb., 1934, appeared as Henry VIII in "A Rose Without a Thorn"; "Q," Mar., 1934, Lieut. Hartmann in "Dance Macabre"; Strand, Mar., 1934, Rev. Sanderson Albaugh in "The Bride"; Lyceum, May, 1934, Convict Q 83 in "King of the Damned"; Ambassadors', Aug., 1934, Sydney in "Family Affairs"; Savoy, Oct., 1934, De Silva in "Two Kingdoms"; Westminster (for the Charta Theatre), Feb., 1935, George Lorrimer in "Our Ostriches"; then went to Hollywood; on returning to London, appeared at the Embassy, Oct., 1935, as Crichton in "The Admirable Crichton"; Westminster, Jan., 1936, Chorus in "The Dog Beneath the Skin"; Globe (for New "G" Club), Mar., 1936, Oliver Cromwell in "Stubble Before Swords"; Savoy, May, 1936, Hsieh Ping-Kuei in "Lady Precious Stream," and Playhouse in "My Son's My Son"; Open Air Theatre, June–Sept., 1936, Buckingham in "Henry VIII," Antonio in "The Tempest," Orlando, Theseus in "A Midsummer Night's Dream," Ferdinand in "Love's Labour's Lost"; Sir Toby Belch in "Twelfth Night"; Little, Nov., 1936, Edward IV in "The King and Mistress Shore"; toured in South Africa, Jan.–Apr., 1937, in "The Frog" and "The Amazing Doctor Clitterhouse"; St. James's, London, Aug., 1937, Edward Tresham in "Old Music"; Old Vic., Dec., 1937,

again played Theseus; Stratford-on-Avon, 1938 season, played Orsino, Henry VIII, Macduff, Mercutio, and Prospero in "The Tempest"; Garrick, Nov., 1938, Emperor Franz Josef in "Elizabeth of Austria"; Winter Garden (for English School Theatre), May, 1939, Macduff in "Macbeth"; Old Vic., June, 1939, Sir James Ransom in "The Ascent of F.6"; at the Tewkesbury Festival, July, 1939, played Saul in "The Boy David"; joined the Territorial Association before the commencement of the late War, was called up as Sergeant in T.A., Aug., 1940, in the London Irish Rifles; commissioned into the King's Royal Rifles, Feb., 1941; Captain, Apr., 1941; Major, July, 1942; Lieut.-Colonel, Apr., 1943; served throughout the War in the Western Desert Campaign, May, 1940–July, 1942; later held Staff appointments in Egypt, Syria, the War Office, and Palestine; demobilized, Dec., 1946, with the rank of Lieut.-Colonel; unsuccessfully contested the Kettering Division of Northamptonshire (Conservative), Feb., 1950; having resumed amateur status, appeared for the Old Stagers, during Canterbury Cricket Week, 1948–50; first appeared in films, 1933; succeeded his father as 12th Baronet, Feb., 1941. *Club:* Garrick. *Address:* Lamport Hall, Northampton. *Telephone No.:* Maidwell 272.

ISHERWOOD, Christopher, dramatic author and novelist; *b.* Disley, Cheshire, 26 Aug., 1904; *s.* of Lt.-Col. Francis B. Isherwood and his wife Kathleen (Machell-Smith); *e.* Repton and Corpus Christi College, Cambridge; has collaborated with W. H. Auden in the following plays: "The Dog Beneath The Skin," 1935; "The Ascent of F.6.," 1936; "On the Frontier," 1938; also collaborated with Auden in the book, "Journey to a War," 1939; author of the novels, "All the Conspirators," "The Memorial," "Mr. Norris Changes Trains," "Goodbye to Berlin," "Prater Violet" (semi-autobiographical); his autobiography, "Lions and Shadows," was published, 1938. *Address:* 333 East Rustic Road, Santa Monica, Calif., U.S.A.

1275

IVOR, Frances, actress ; *b.* Scotland ; *y.d.* of the late William Nathaniel Forbes, J.P., D.L. of Dunnottar, Auchernach, Netherley, N.B., etc. ; *m.* Herbert Thomas ; made her first appearance in London at the Princess's Theatre, 24 May, 1888, as Mathilde in "Midnight, or the Woodcarver of Bruges" ; was then engaged by the late Sir Henry Irving for the Lyceum, and Dec., 1888, played Hecate in "Macbeth," also understudying Miss Ellen Terry ; in a revival of W. G. Will's "Juana," at the Opéra Comique, Apr., 1890, played the title-*rôle* ; at the Adelphi, May, 1890, played in "The Bride of Love" ; at the Lyric, July, 1890, in "Sweet Nancy" ; at the Princess's, Nov., 1890, played Octavia in "Antony and Cleopatra" ; returned to the Lyceum, Feb., 1891, to play Jeannette in "The Lyons Mail" ; at the New Olympic, Mar., 1891, appeared in "Father Buonaparte" ; at the Avenue, 1891, played in "A Mighty Error," and "The Fiat of the Gods" ; at the Globe, Apr., 1892, appeared in "Beata" in the title-*rôle* ; during 1893, at the Opéra Comique, appeared in "Rosmersholm" and "Brand" ; subsequently toured with the late Wilson Barrett, playing Lady Eva Glendale in "Our Pleasant Sins," also appearing in "Pharaoh," "Othello," "Virginius," "Hamlet," and "The Lady of Lyons" ; at the Prince of Wales's, Feb., 1894, played Rosalind in "As You Like It" ; appeared at the Gaiety, Apr., 1894, in "Miss Rutland" ; at the Strand, May, 1894, in "Gentle Ivy" ; subsequently toured as Mrs. Rennick in "The New Boy" ; accompanied H. Beerbohm Tree to America, Jan., 1895, playing in "Hamlet," "The Merry Wives of Windsor," and "Captain Swift" ; on her return, toured as Lady Marchant in "A Bunch of Violets," with Tree ; at the Haymarket, Oct., 1895, appeared as Mrs. Bagot in "Trilby" ; at the Prince of Wales's, May, 1896, played Lady Capulet in "Romeo and Juliet" ; toured with Beerbohm Tree, 1896, as Mistress Quickly in "King Henry IV" (part I), and in the United States, 1897, in *répertoire* ; on her return, appeared at the Lyric, with Wilson Barrett, May, 1897, as Emilia in "Othello," and Servia in "Virginius" ; at Her Majesty's, Aug., 1897, appeared as the Queen in "Hamlet" ; in Nov., 1897, played Curtis in "Katherine and Petruchio" ; at the Duke of York's, Dec., 1897, played Mrs. Smith in "The Happy Life" ; appeared at the Garrick, Oct., 1898, as Lady Margaret Pleydell in "Brother Officers" ; during 1899, toured with Mrs. Patrick Campbell in "The Second Mrs. Tanqueray" and "Carlyon Sahib" ; at the Royalty, 1900, appeared as Augusta in "Magda," and Mrs. Buxton in "Mr. and Mrs. Daventry" ; at the Avenue, Jan., 1904, appeared in "The Perils of Flirtation" ; at the Shaftesbury, Nov. 1904, played Countess Feldershay in "The Flute of Pan" ; at the Court, appeared as Margaret Granger in "A Little Brown Branch," Dec., 1904 ; Mrs. Barthwick in "The Silver Box," Sept., 1906 ; Mrs. Heriot in "Votes for Women," Apr., 1907 ; at the Kingsway, Oct., 1907, played Lady Wycherley in "Irene Wycherley," and Nov., 1907, Aunt Sarah in "A Stroke of Business" ; during 1908, appeared there in "Diana of Dobson's," "The Sway Boat," "Grit," and "The Truants" ; at the Haymarket, Oct., 1909, appeared as Mrs. Bonnington in "Don" ; June, 1910, played Lady Shuttleworth in "Priscilla Runs Away" ; at the Duke of York's, Feb., 1911, appeared as Lady Sophia Spratte in "Loaves and Fishes" ; at the Haymarket, May, 1911, played Mrs. O'Farrell in "Lady Patricia." Apr., 1912, the Duchess of Glastonbury in "Pitch and Soap" ; at the Playhouse, May, 1912, Mrs. Burden senior in "Love—and What Then ?" ; Jan., 1913, the Hon. Cornelia Grantley in "The Headmaster" ; at the New Theatre, Aug., 1913, played Mrs. Grimshaw in "The Big Game" ; at the Haymarket, Nov., 1914, appeared as Lady Dugdale in "The Flag Lieutenant" ; at the St. James's, Jan., 1915, as Queen Elizabeth in "Kings and Queens" ; at the Prince of Wales's, May, 1915, as Mrs. Grieg in "The Laughter of Fools" ; at the Royalty, Apr. 1916, played the Duchess of Glastonbury in "Disraeli" ;

at the Haymarket, Feb., 1917, Mrs. Twentyman in " Felix Gets a Month " ; at the Ambassadors', Jan., 1918, Mrs. Ford and Frau Hartzmann in " Out of Hell " ; during 1919, toured in the same play ; at the Kingsway Theatre, Mar., 1920, played Rose Hutchings in " Sinners Both ; " at the Ambassadors', Feb., 1922, played Mary Holloway in " My Son " ; during 1923 toured as Freda Draycott in " The Law of Moses " ; during 1923, also toured with Mrs. Patrick Campbell ; Ambassadors', Nov., 1925, played Katherine Huxtable in " The Madras House " ; Savoy, May, 1926, Mrs. Archdale in " Intimate Enemies." *Address :* Mazemore, Hailsham, Sussex. *Telephone No. :* Hailsham 97.

JACK and EVELYN, duettists (Jack and Evelyn O'Connor); *b.* Liverpool, in 1886 and 1888, respectively; made their first appearance together on the variety stage in 1903, since which date they have played at all the principal variety theatres in London and the provinces, with the utmost success. *Address:* 134 Loughborough Road, Brixton, S.W. *Telephone No.:* Brixton 1749.

JACKSON, Sir Barry Vincent (cr. 1925), M.A., LL.D., D.Litt., theatre director and dramatic author; *b.* Birmingham, 6 Sept., 1879; *s.* of George Jackson and his wife Jane (Spreadborough); *e.* privately; is the founder and director of the Birmingham Repertory Company, which first commenced operations 13 Feb., 1913, and during the first season of just over four months, produced over twenty plays, including " Twelfth Night," " King John," " The Merry Wives of Windsor," and " The Merchant of Venice " ; Bernard Shaw's " Candida " and " Press Cuttings " ; Galsworthy's " The Pigeon," " The Silver Box " ; Wilde's " The Importance of Being Earnest " ; Masefield's " Tragedy of Nan " ; St. John Hankin's " The Cassilis Engagement " and " The Constant Lover " ; Ibsen's " An Enemy of the People " ; Lady Gregory's " The White Cockade " ; W. B. Yeats's " Countess Cathleen " ; Rostand's " The Fantasticks," etc. ; although serving in the Navy during the war, 1914-18, he continued to direct the Repertory Theatre in its work, and in 1919 John Drinkwater's " Abraham Lincoln " was first produced there ; the play was subsequently, in 1920, produced at the Lyric, Hammersmith, where it ran over a year ; in Oct., 1922, he produced " The Immortal Hour " at the Regent, subsequently producing " Romeo and Juliet " ; in 1924, he took over the Court Theatre, where he produced Bernard Shaw's " Back to Methuselah," followed by " The Farmer's Wife " ; " The Farmer's Wife " ran nearly three years, from Mar., 1924, to Jan., 1927 ; took over the Kingsway, 1925, and during 1925-6 produced there " Caesar and Cleopatra," " The New Morality,"

" Hamlet " (in modern dress), " The Immortal Hour," " The Marvellous History of St. Bernard," " Rosmersholm " ; produced " Yellow Sands " at Haymarket, Nov., 1926, which ran until 1928; at the Court, Feb. to Apr., 1928, produced " Macbeth " (in modern dress), revived " Back to Methuselah " and " The Farmer's Wife," and produced " Harold," and " The Taming of the Shrew " (in modern dress); produced " Bird in Hand," at the Royalty, Apr., 1928; " Six Characters in Search of an Author," Globe, May, 1928; at the Queen's, Sept., 1929, produced Bernard Shaw's play " The Apple Cart"; Queen's, Sept., 1930, " The Barretts of Wimpole Street"; St. James's, Sept., 1931, " A Trip to Scarborough"; Queen's, Apr., 1932, " Caravan"; Queen's, June, 1932, " Evensong"; New, Sept., 1932, " Too True to be Good"; Globe, Nov., 1932, " For Services Rendered"; Globe, " Marriage is No Joke," 1934; New, " A Man's House," 1934; Strand, " 1066 and All That," 1935; in 1922 was awarded the Gold Medal of the Birmingham Civic Society; in 1923 received the Honorary Degree of M.A., at Birmingham University; Hon. LL.D., St. Andrews, 1937, and Hon. D.Litt., Birmingham, 1950, Hon. D.Litt., Manchester; received the Honorary Freedom of the City of Birmingham, 1955; since its foundation, the Birmingham Repertory Theatre Company has produced some 750 plays and operas to Dec., 1955; in 1950, the Company visited Holland with "The Importance of Being Earnest"; in 1952, "Henry VI" (Part II), was presented at the Old Vic; the Company again appeared at the Old Vic in 1953, in "Henry VI" (Parts I, II, and III); the Company appeared at the Paris Festival in 1956 in "Caesar and Cleopatra"; Edinburgh Festival, 1959, in "Gammer Gurton's Needle" and "Fratricide Punished"; in 1935, he handed over the theatre to the public, under the Sir Barry Jackson Trust; he remains Governing Director; Governing Trustee of the Birmingham Repertory Trust Company; resumed active direction of the theatre, Nov., 1942; appointed Director of the

Stratford Memorial Theatre, Stratford-on-Avon, 1945, and remained in that capacity until the end of the 1948 season; also a director of the Royal Opera House, Covent Garden, 1949–55; he is the author of "Fifinella" (with Basil Dean), first produced in 1911; "Ser Taldo's Bride" (with John Drinkwater), 1911; "The Christmas Party," 1913; "The Marvellous History" of St. Bernard" (translation), 1925; "The Marriage of Figaro" (new adaptation), 1926; "He Who Gets Slapped" (from the Russian, with Gertrude Schurhoff), 1926; "Demos, King and Slave" (adaptation), 1931; "The Swiss Family Robinson" (with R. H. Baptist), 1938; "Backward and Forward" (with John Ellison), 1939; "Doctor's Delight," (Molière), 1944; "Jonathan Wild" (Fielding), 1948; "The Bears of Bay-Rum" (Scribe), 1948; "The Gay Invalid" (adaptation, with Robert Brenon), 1950; "Emmy" (translation), 1952, and a work entitled "The Theatre and Civic Life," 1922; was also the founder of The Pilgrim Players, 1907; was Founder and Director of the Malvern Summer Festivals, 1929–37. *Recreations:* Travelling, gardening and painting. *Address:* Birmingham Repertory Theatre, Birmingham, 5. *Telephone No.:* Midland 2472. (*Died* 3 Apr., 1961; *age 81*)

JACKSON, Ethel, actress and vocalist; *b.* New York City, 1 Nov., 1877; *d.* of Francis Wyatt Jackson and his wife Hart; *e.* in Paris, Dresden, and Vienna; *m.* (1) J. Fred Zimmerman; (2) Benoni Lockwood, Jr. (mar. dis.); was originally intended to follow the profession of a pianist, and studied at the Vienna Conservatoire; made her first appearance on the stage at the Savoy Theatre, London, Aug., 1897, in the chorus of "The Yeomen of the Guard"; Jan., 1898, played Wanda in "The Grand Duchess"; Mar., 1898, Fiametta in "The Gondoliers"; May, 1898, Barbe in "The Beauty Stone"; went to America, Aug., 1898, under the management of Charles Frohman, to play Elsie Crockett in "Little Miss Nobody"; subsequently appeared at Madison Square Theatre, New York, in "On and Off"; she next appeared at Daly's, in "The Runaway Girl," at the Casino, in "Little Red Riding Hood," etc.; at the Broadway Theatre 1902, appeared in "Vienna Life," and at Philadelphia, in "Miss Bob White"; she then retired from the stage for four years, and made her reappearance in Aug., 1906, as Chandra Nil in "The Blue Moon," appearing in this part at the Casino, New York, Nov., 1906; at the New Amsterdam Theatre, Oct., 1907, appeared as Sonia in "The Merry Widow"; reappeared, after some years absence from the stage, at the Lyric, Philadelphia, Apr., 1912, in "A Wild Goose"; in Mar., 1913, toured in "The Purple Road"; at the Longacre Theatre, New York, May, 1914, played Mrs. Nettleton in "A Pair of Sixes"; at the Eltinge Theatre, Dec., 1922, Madame Montebel in "The Masked Woman"; at the Jolson Theatre, Dec., 1923, appeared as Mummy Tyl in "The Blue Bird"; at the Morosco, Mar., 1924, played Mrs. Kennedy in "The Lady Killer"; after many years absence, reappeared, at the Booth Theatre, Dec., 1932, as the Countess Kernitz in "Girls in Uniform"; Shubert, Feb., 1934, Mrs. Pearson in "Dodsworth"; 46th Street, Sept., 1936, Mrs. Thornton in "So Proudly We Hail"; Ethel Barrymore, Dec., 1936, Mrs. Wagstaff in "The Women," which she played to July, 1938; Longacre, Feb., 1939, Mrs. Long in "I Must Love Someone"; Ethel Barrymore, Nov., 1939, Mrs. Wheeler in "Key Largo." *Recreations:* Riding, reading, and painting (*Died 23 Nov., 1957; age 80*)

JACKSON, Frederic, dramatic author; *b.* Pittsburg, Pa., U.S.A., 21 Sept., 1886; *e.* Washington and Jefferson University, and Columbia University; *m.* Florence Howe; has written the following plays: "A Full House," 1915; "Losing Eloise" ("The Naughty Wife"), 1917; "Baa-Baa, Black Sheep," 1917; "La, La, Lucille," 1919; "One a Minute," 1919; "The Hole in the Wall," 1920; "Two Little Girls in Blue," 1921; "For Goodness' Sake," ("Stop Flirting"), 1922; "Cold Feet" (with Pierre Grendron), 1923; "Beginners' Luck," 1925; "The Duchess Decides,"

1926; " Just a Kiss " (from the French) 1926; " Peg o' Mine " (from " Peg o' My Heart "), " Telling the Tale," 1927; " Her Past " (from the French), "Open Your Eyes," 1929; "The King's Messenger," "Her First Affaire" (with Merril Rogers), "A Pair of Trousers," 1930; "The Cannibal," "The Ninth Man," "Widows Might," 1931; "Your Money or Your Wife," "The Iron Woman," "The School for Husbands," 1932; "A Night of Nights" (with Merril Rogers), 1933; "Wife Insurance," "The Bishop Misbehaves," "By Appointment," 1934; "The Naked Man," "Road to Paradise," "Murder with Pen and Ink," "The Closed Door," "The Ascending Dragon," 1935; "The Long Night," 1937; "Don't Mention It," 1943; "Slightly Scandalous," 1944; "Song Without Words," 1945; has also written books and plays under the name of Victor Thorne.

(Died 22 May, 1953; age 66)

JACKSON, Nelson, entertainer at the piano; *b.* Liverpool, 24 Sept, 1870; *s.* of John Jackson and his wife Mary (Pattison); *e.* York Institute, Liverpool; *m.* Margaret Winterbottom; formerly engaged as secretary in a merchant's office; made his first appearance at the Hope Hall, Liverpool, 10 Apr., 1891, giving a sketch at the piano; first appeared in London at the Queen's Hall, 10 Nov., 1893; has fulfilled engagements at the Palace, Coliseum, Palladium, Tivoli, Oxford, and London Pavilion, etc.; has toured the Moss and Stoll tours, Macnaghten, London Theatre of Varieties and Variety Theatres controlling circuits; has also appeared at several London theatres; among many popular songs which he has introduced, may be mentioned "When father laid the Carpet on the Stairs "; "When Richard the First sat on the Throne "; "Bargains "; "Father's Photographs "; "In the Future "; "Nursery Rhymes grown up "; "Our New Flat "; "Since Angelina joined a cooking class "; "When Uncle sings the only song he knows "; "Let's have a song about father "; "The

New Roundabout Papers "; "Society Snap Shots "; has written and composed over eighty different songs. *Recreations :* Golf and photography. *Clubs :* Savage, Wigwam and London Sketch. *Address :* 58 Lonsdale Road, Barnes, S.W. *Telephone No. :* Hammersmith 1173.

JACOB, Naomi, actress and author; *b.* Ripon, Yorks, 1 July, 1889; *d.* of Nina Ellington Collinson (Nina Abbott, novelist); *e.* privately and Middlesbrough High School; was formerly engaged as a school-teacher at Middlesbrough, and was also, for a time, engaged in secretarial work; during the first World War, was an officer in the Women's Legion and also engaged in a munitions factory; made her first appearance on the stage at the Devonshire Park Theatre, 1920, as Brownie in "Scandal"; first appeared in London, at the Comedy Theatre, 25 June, 1920, as Julia in "The 'Ruined' Lady"; Savoy, Feb., 1923, played Julia Cragworthy in "The Young Idea"; Duke of York's, June, 1923, Lady Pennybroke in "Eliza Comes to Stay"; played in "Outward Bound"; Wyndham's, May, 1926, Mrs. Hackitt in "The Ringer"; Winter Garden, Mar., 1928, Mrs. Wimble in "The Spider"; Playhouse, May, 1928, Maw Benson in "The Barker"; Playhouse, Sept., 1928, Madame Bernoux in "Excelsior"; St. James's, Feb., 1929, Mrs. Keene in "Fame"; then retired from the stage to devote herself to writing; reappeared, at the Lyric, Oct., 1941, when she played Ma Gennochio in "The Nutmeg Tree"; Phoenix, Apr., 1943, played the Nurse in "Love for Love"; first appeared in films in "The First Born"; her first novel, "Jacob Ussher," was published in 1926; has written, among other works, "Rock and Sand," 1929; "That Wild Lie—," 1930; "Roots," 1931; "Props" and "Young Emmanuel," 1932; "Four Generations," 1934; "Founder of the House," 1935; a series of autobiographical books, "Me," "Me Again," "More About Me," "Me, in the Kitchen," "Me in Wartime", "Me in the Mediterranean"; "Our Marie" (Marie Lloyd), 1936; "Private Gollantz,"etc.;

on the outbreak of War, 1939, joined the staff of E.N.S.A.; went overseas in 1943, North Africa, Sicily, and Italy; was Public Relations Officer for Italy, working for E.N.S.A. *Hobby:* Work. *Club:* Sesame.
(Died 26 Aug., 1964; age 80)

JACOBS, William Wymark, dramatic author and novelist; *b.* London, 8 Sept., 1863; *s.* of William Gage Jacobs; *e.* privately; *m.* Agnes Eleanor Williams; was engaged in the Civil Service for sixteen years, from 1883; author of the following plays: " Beauty and the Barge " (with Louis N. Parker), 1903; his story, " The Monkey's Paw," was dramatised by Louis N. Parker, and produced, 1903; " A Boatswain's Mate " (with H. C. Sargent), 1907; " Admiral Peters " (with Horace Mills), 1909; " Keeping Up Appearances," 1915; also " Establishing Relations," " The Warming-Pan," " Master Mariners," " Matrimonial Openings," " Dixon's Return," " A Distant Relative," " Double Dealing "; is the author of several humorous books, including " Many Cargoes," " The Skipper's Wooing," " A Master of Craft," " Light Freights," " The Lady of the Barge," " Odd Craft," " Captains All," " Short Cruises," " Deep Waters," " Sea Whispers," etc. *Club:* Garrick.
(Died 1 Sept., 1943; age 79)

JAGGER, Dean, actor; *b.* Columbus Grove, Lima, Ohio, U.S.A., 7 Nov., 1904; *s.* of Albert Jagger and his wife Lillie Mayberry; *e.* Collins, Ind., and Wabash College, Crawfordsville, Ind.; at the Masque Theatre, 4 Dec., 1933, appeared as Lov Bensey in " Tobacco Road "; Royale, Feb., 1934, played Russell Evans in " They Shall Not Die "; returned to Hollywood and appeared exclusively in films for four years; reappeared on the New York stage, at the Empire, Sept., 1938, as Thomas Howard in " Missouri Legend "; National, Dec., 1938, played The Man in " Everywhere I Roam "; Lyceum, May, 1939, Ernest Hammaka in " Brown Danube"; Cort, Nov., 1939, Jan Gerart in " Farm of Three Echoes"; Biltmore, Feb., 1940, An-

drei Taganov in " The Unconquered"; again returned to Hollywood, 1940; Booth, Feb., 1948, Dr. Norman Farrar in " Doctor Social"; first appeared in films, in Hollywood, 1927, and in England, 1944, in " I Lived in Grosvenor Square."

JALLAND, Henry, business manager; *b.* Horncastle, Lincs., 7 Aug., 1861; *s.* of Robert Jalland; *e.* Horncastle Grammar School; was formerly a civil engineer; first entered the dramatic profession under Mat Robson's management at Sadler's Wells Theatre, 1881; in 1889, was business manager with F. R. Benson at the old Globe Theatre, and has fulfilled similar engagements with Violet Melnotte, Royalty, 1890; Arthur Bourchier, St. James's, 1890; F. R Benson, Lyceum, 1900; was associated for nineteen years with F. R. Benson, and for seven years with Olga Nethersole; has also been business manager at various times for Marie Tempest, Frank Curzon, Charles Kenyon, Sir Charles Wyndham and Miss Mary Moore. *Favourite play:* " Much Ado About Nothing." *Hobby:* Horticulture. *Address:* Rolleston House, Horncastle, Lincs.

JAMES, Daisy, comedienne; *b.* London; *m.* Harry Villiers (*d.* 1906); made her first appearance, under the name of Daisy Martin, at Kilburn Town Hall, as a singer and skipping-rope dancer; made her first professional appearance, under her own name, at the Standard Music Hall, July, 1895; at Christmas, 1895, fulfilled a pantomime engagement with the late Ernest Carpenter, as Dolly Varden in " Little Red Riding Hood "; her first " hit " was " Her Eyes that shine like Diamonds "; has appeared at all the leading London and provincial halls, and has played all the leading tours and circuits; among her more popular songs may be mentioned " Go Easy "; " Tramway Tickets "; " Mine's a better one than yours "; " Young men specially invited "; " The Gibson Girl "; " Oh ! Hamlet, what have you done for me ? ";

" Come with me, down Regent Street";
" Snooky Ookums "; " There's a
good time coming by-and-by ";
" Won't you tell me the lady's name ? "
Address : 65 Sudbourne Road, Brixton Hill, S.W. *Telephone No. :*
Brixton 2115.

JAMES, Francis, actor; *b.* Melbourne, Australia, 18 Aug., 1907; *s.*
of Louis Philip Jacobs and his wife
Elizabeth (Jacobs); *e.* Leighton Park
School, Reading, and Balliol College,
Oxford; *m.* Alice Darch; studied
for the stage at the Royal Academy
of Dramatic Art; made his first
appearance on the stage at the Theatre Royal, Morecambe, Aug., 1927,
as John Freeman in "The Fanatics";
he played a season with the Bath
repertory, followed by a tour in
"Charley's Aunt"; toured in Canada,
1928, with Baliol Holloway in a repertory of Shaw's plays; on returning to
England, made his first appearance in
London, at the Royalty, 8 May, 1929,
as Felix Rakonitz in "The Matriarch";
joined the company of the Old Vic. for
the season Sept., 1929–May, 1930, and
appeared there as Benvolio in "Romeo
and Juliet," Bonnefoi in "The Imaginary Invalid," Aumerle in "Richard
II," Soothsayer in "Julius Caesar,"
Silvius in "As You Like It," Lentulus
in "Androcles and the Lion," Malcolmi
in "Macbeth," Laertes in "Hamlet,"
etc.; at the Arts, May, 1930, played
Chretien de Laferte in "The Ugly
Duchess"; Queen's, May, 1930, Laertes
in "Hamlet"; in the autumn of 1930,
toured with Sybil Thorndike in "The
Squall," "Granite," "Ghosts," and
"The Matchmaker's Arms"; Everyman, Mar., 1931, played Richard Carter
in "Phoenix"; Arts, May, 1931,
Sebastien in "Make Up Your Mind";
Embassy, June, 1931, Peter in
"Strange Orchestra"; Arts, Nov.,
1931, Roderigo in "Othello"; St.
Martin's, Apr., 1932, Johnny in
"Cloudy With Showers"; Globe, Apr.,
1932, Francis Lightfoot in "Wings
Over Europe"; Duke of York's, Oct.,
1932, Antony Carver in "Cold Blood";
Arts, Nov., 1932, Arnold Waite in
"Other People's Lives"; Mar., 1933,
Oswald Alving in "Ghosts"; Shaftesbury, Apr., 1933, Anthony Field in

"Crime on the Hill"; Duchess, Nov.,
1933, Harold Russ in "Laburnum
Grove"; Westminster, Oct., 1934,
Edmund in "King Lear"; Shaftesbury, Nov., 1934, Guido in "For
Ever"; Royalty, Sept., 1935, Tony
in "Closing at Sunrise"; Embassy,
Dec., 1935, Pepe in "Goosefeather
Bed"; Shaftesbury, Feb., 1936, Toni
in "Promise"; Westminster, Nov.,
1936, the Herald in "Agamemnon";
Little, Nov., 1936, Marquis of Dorset
in "The King and Mistress Shore";
Ambassadors', Feb., 1937, Alceste in
"The Misanthrope"; Mercury, Apr.,
1937, the Author in "In Theatre
Street"; Vaudeville, Feb., 1938, M.
de Fletange in "Mirabelle"; Stratford-on-Avon, 1938 season, Romeo, Oberon, Buckingham in "Henry VIII,"
Proteus in "The Two Gentlemen of
Verona," Malcolm in "Macbeth" and
Ferdinand in "The Tempest"; Arts,
Oct., 1938, Louis Dijon in "Oscar
Wilde"; Playhouse, Feb., 1939, Josephus in "Jerusalem"; Old Vic., June,
1939, the Abbot in "The Ascent
of F.6"; directed several productions
at the "Q" Theatre, 1943–4, and
appeared there, May, 1944, as John
Tanner in "Man and Superman";
author of the play, "Belle View,"
1940; has also appeared for the
Stage Society, Group Theatre, etc., in
various productions. *Recreations :* Tennis, squash, motoring, and writing.
Clubs : Savage, Arts Theatre, and
O.U.D.S. *Address :* 67 Meadowside,
Twickenham, Middlesex. *Telephone
No. :* Popesgrove 6175.

JAMES, Julia, actress; *b.* London,
28 Dec., 1890 ; *m.* Maurice Dollfus ; was
originally in the chorus at the Aldwych
Theatre, under Seymour Hicks, and on
23 Dec., 1905, appeared there as Supper
Belle in "Blue Bell"; she then
went to the Gaiety Theatre in small
parts, appearing there, May, 1907,
as Lina in "The Girls of Gottenburg"; Apr., 1908, in "Havana";
Jan., 1909, as Lady Sybil in "Our
Miss Gibbs "; in Aug., 1909, succeeded
Miss Denise Orme as Lady Elizabeth
Thanet in the same piece ; appeared at
the Knickerbocker Theatre, New York,
29 Aug., 1910, as Lady Elizabeth in

the same play; appeared at Drury Lane, Christmas, 1910, as Princess Dorothy in "Jack and the Beanstalk"; at the Whitney Theatre, Sept., 1911, played Annamiri in "The Spring Maid"; at the Garrick, June, 1912, appeared as Perwinkle in "Improper Peter"; during 1913, appeared at Olympia, Paris, as Sombra in "The Arcadians," and subsequently in "La Revue Merveilleuses"; at the Vaudeville, Aug., 1913, played Sybil Vane in "The Picture of Dorian Gray"; at the London Hippodrome, Dec., 1913, played in "Hullo, Tango!"; at the New Theatre, Feb., 1914, Fleurette de Verdier in "The Joy-Ride Lady"; at the Ambassadors', May, 1914, Lord St. John in "Plantons les Capucines"; at the Lyceum, June, 1914, appeared as Fifi Fricot in "The Belle of New York"; at the Aldwych, Dec., 1914, as Cinderella in the pantomime; at the Lyric, Feb., 1914, played Angela Gilfain in "Florodora"; at the Gaiety, Apr., 1914, Beatrice Carraway in "To-Night's the Night"; Sept., 1916, the Hon. Sapphire Blissett in "Theodore and Co."; at the Prince of Wales's, Dec., 1917, Mabel Mannering in "Yes, Uncle"; at the Royalty, Jan., 1920, appeared as Lady Mary Lasenby in "The Admirable Crichton"; at the Shaftesbury, Oct., 1920, succeeded Miss Virginia Brooks as Ethel Warren in "The Great Lover."

(Died July, 1964; age 73)

JAMES, Wilson (Lakeman), comedian; *b.* London, 1872; *m.* Ruby Wilson; previous to appearing on the variety stage, was favourably known in the Bohemian Concert world and at seaside resorts; made his first appearance on the variety stage at the Empire, Chatham, 1913, with his company "The Gaieties"; was immediately engaged for the Coliseum, and other Stoll halls; among his more successful "original" songs, may be mentioned "The English Language"; "Since then I've used no other"; "Voila!" etc. *Address*: 99 Adelaide Road, N.W. *Telephone No.*: Hampstead, 1222.

JANIS, Elsie (Bierbower), actress and author; *b.* Columbus, Franklin Co., O., U.S.A., 16 Mar., 1889; *d.* of John E. Bierbower and his wife Jane Elizabeth (Cockrell); *m.* Gilbert Wilson; made her first appearance on the stage at Columbus, Ohio, 24 Dec., 1897, as Cain (a boy) in "The Charity Ball"; during 1898, appeared in the Cincinnati "stock" company in "Little Lord Fauntleroy," "East Lynne," and "The Galley Slave"; made her first appearance in New York, at the Casino Theatre Roof Garden, June, 1900, on the "vaudeville" stage, as "Little Elsie," under the management of E. E. Rice; for the next three years toured all over the United States; in 1904, at Washington, appeared as Fifi Fricot in "The Belle of New York," and as Little Miss Muffet in "Jack and the Beanstalk"; during 1905 toured in "The Fortune Teller" and "The Little Duchess"; made her first substantial "hit" when she appeared at the New York Theatre Roof Garden, in the summer of 1905, in "When We were Forty-one," in which her imitations of popular artistes created quite a furore; was next engaged by Liebler and Co., and appeared as Dorothy Willetts in "The Vanderbilt Cup," first seen in New York, at the Broadway Theatre, 16 Jan., 1906; this ran throughout the season, and was followed by a long tour; her next appearance in New York was made at the Knickerbocker Theatre, 14 Oct., 1907, when she scored another success as Joan Talbot in "The Hoyden"; in Sept., 1908, toured as Cynthia Bright in "The Fair Co-Ed."; appeared in the same part at the Knickerbocker Theatre, New York, 1 Feb., 1909; during 1910, toured as Princess Kalora in "The Slim Princess," appearing in the same part at the Globe Theatre, New York, 2 Jan., 1911; at the same theatre, 30 Mar., 1911, appeared as Martha Farnum in a play written by herself, entitled, "A Star for a Night"; subsequently toured in "The Slim Princess"; at the Globe, New York, 28 Oct., 1912, appeared as Cinderella in "The Lady of the Slipper"; made her first appearance in London, at the Palace, 20 Apr., 1914, as Kitty

O'Hara in " The Passing Show," and scoring an instantaneous success; subsequently returned to America; reappeared at the Palace, London, 1915, in a new edition of " The Passing Show " ; on returning to America, appeared at the George M. Cohan Theatre, Oct., 1915, as Dot in " Miss Information " ; at the Century Theatre, Nov., 1916, played in " The Century Girl," and Dec., 1917, in "Miss 1917"; went to France, 1918, and entertained troops of the A.E.F. for some months; at the Palace, London, Sept., 1918, played in "Hullo! America " ; at the Academy of Music, Baltimore, Nov., 1919, played in " Elsie Janis and Her Gang " ; entered on the management of the Queen's Theatre, London, Dec., 1920, opening with " It's All Wrong," of which she was author and part-composer; made her first appearance in Paris, at the Théâtre Apollo, 1921, in "La Revue de Elsie Janis," with great success; at the Gaiety, New York, Jan., 1922, appeared in a new version of " Elsie Janis and Her Gang " ; during 1924, appeared at the Queen's Theatre, London, in her own entertainment; at the Fulton, New York, Feb., 1925, played in " Puzzles of 1925," of which she was also the author; during 1927 toured as Kay in " Oh, Kay! " ; reappeared in London at the Adelphi Sept., 1928, when she played for a short period in " Clowns in Clover " ; at the Music Box, New York, Jan., 1939, gave a series of Sunday night performances of songs and impersonations; and at the 44th Street, Mar., 1939, appeared in "Frank Fay Vaudeville"; author of "Love Letters of an Actress," "If I Know What I Mean," and an autobiography, "So Far So Good," 1932; is the author and composer of over fifty songs; appeared in films in 1920, and appeared in " A Merry Madcap," "A Regular Girl," "Nearly a Lady," "'Twas Ever Thus," etc.; author of the film "Close Harmony," etc.; staged "New Faces," 1934. *Recreation:* Physical exercise.
Died 28 Feb., 1956; age 66)

JANNEY, Russell, manager; *b.* Wilmington, Ohio, U.S.A., 14 Apr.,

1884; *s.* of Reynold Janney and his wife Ella (Dixon); *e.* public schools and Yale University; has been a manager for nearly twenty years, having made his first production at the Broad Street Theatre, Newark, N.J., in 1909; for some years ran his own company as the "Russell Janney Players "; his first big production in New York, was " Sancho Panza," 1923; subsequently produced " The Vagabond King," 1925; " Ballyhoo," 1927, " White Eagle," 1927; " The Vagabond King," was produced at the Winter Garden, London, Apr., 1927; in June, 1928, produced " Marjolaine," at the Gaiety, London; produced "The O'Flynn," New York, 1934. *Favourite play:* "If I Were King."
(Died 14 July, 1963; age 79)

JARDINE, Betty (*née* Elizabeth McKittrick Jardine), actress; *b.* Heaton Moor, Manchester; *d.* of William James Jardine and his wife Meta Elizabeth (Clarke); *e.* Penrhos College, Colwyn Bay; after leaving school, for a time, taught elocution; had amateur experience before making her first appearance on the professional stage, with the Rusholme Repertory company, Manchester, 12 Apr., 1926, as Evadne in "The New Religion"; she remained with this company for seven years; made her first appearance in London at the Fortune Theatre, 25 Sept., 1933, as Louise in "Disharmony"; Wyndham's, Dec., 1933, played Annie in "What Happened to George"; Phoenix (for Repertory Players), Sept., 1934, Lady Newberry in "The Bishop Misbehaves"; Savoy, Dec., 1934, again played in "What Happened to George"; Duchess, May, 1935, Dora Parkoe in "Night Must Fall "; made her first appearance in New York at the Ethel Barrymore Theatre, 28 Sept., 1936, in the same part; after returning to London, appeared at the Queen's, May, 1937, as Prissy Dell in "He Was Born Gay"; New, Sept., 1937, played Carola Withers in "Bonnet Over the Windmill"; King's, Hammersmith, Jan., 1938, Ariel Forbes in "Gaily We Set Out"; Duchess, Sept., 1938, Bessie Watty in "The Corn is Green"; entered films, 1937, and has appeared in "Oh! Mr. Porter," "Almost a Honeymoon," "Inspector Hornleigh on Holiday," etc.; appeared in Cabaret at the Players' Theatre. *Favourite part:* Bessie in "The Corn is Green." *Recreations:* Photography and studying dialects. *(Died 28 Feb., 1945)*

JARMAN, Herbert, actor; *b.* Aug., 1871; made his first appearance on the stage, in 1889, as Sam Thorpe in "A Ring of Iron"; toured the provinces for many years in numerous parts, among others George Benson in "Shadows of a Great City," Prince Zouroff in "Moths," Dick Phenyl in "Sweet Lavender," Poskett in "The Magistrate," etc.; Tigellinus and Glabrio in "The Sign of the Cross," the Ghost in "Hamlet," Dogberry in "Much Ado About Nothing," Prince of Morocco in "The Merchant of Venice," Dromio of Syracuse in "The Comedy of Errors," Touchstone in "As You Like It," Quince in "A Midsummer Night's Dream," Clown in "Twelfth Night," Mercutio in "Romeo and Juliet," Autolycus in "A Winter's Tale," etc.; toured in Australia, New Zealand, and Africa in a round of comedy parts; assisted Mr. Lewis Waller in various productions at the Lyric, has also appeared at that theatre as Little John in "Robin Hood," Cobbledick in "The Little Admiral," "Scum" Goodman in "Clancarty," Beau Nash in "Monsieur Beaucaire," Cocardasse in "The Duke's Motto," Williams in "King Henry V," Porthos in "The Three Musketeers," the Chevalier Du Pré in "The Conquest," Owen Glendower in "King Henry IV" (Part I), James Longbowe in "Sir Walter Ralegh," Fag in "The Rivals," Mr. Valentine in "Miss Elizabeth's Prisoner"; at the Theatre Royal, Birmingham, Aug., 1910, played Louis XIII in "Bardelys the Magnificent"; at the Gaiety, 4 Mar., 1911, played Montague Bartle in "Peggy"; rejoined Lewis Waller, in New York, and at Daly's, Sept., 1912, played Pistol in "Henry V"; at the Manhattan Opera House, New York, Nov., 1912, played the Marquis of Beverley in "The Whip";

at the New Theatre, Dec., 1913, played the Broker in "The Poor Little Rich Girl"; during 1914-5, toured with Lewis Waller, as Porthos in "The Three Musketeers," and Beau Nash in "Monsieur Beaucaire."
(Died 14 Nov., 1919; age 48)

JAY, Dorothy, actress and vocalist; *b.* London, 8 Apr., 1897; *d.* of Frank Jay and his wife Minnie Louise (Brazier); *e.* Stockwell College; *m.* Charles Claude Robinson; made her first appearance on the stage at the Wimbledon Theatre, Christmas, 1913, in the chorus of the pantomime "Cinderella"; at the Prince of Wales's Birmingham, Sept., 1915, played Lady Doris in "The Light Blues," and at Christmas, 1915, appeared at Edinburgh, as Lady Peggy in the same play; in 1916 toured as Vera de Vere in "My Lady Frayle"; at Daly's Theatre, Dec., 1916, appeared as Joan in "Young England," playing the same part when the piece was revived at Drury Lane, Feb., 1917; at the Prince's, Manchester, 1917, played Margaret Potts in "Oh! Caesar"; at the Empire, Dec., 1917, appeared in "Here and There"; at the London Hippodrome, Mar., 1918, in "Box o' Tricks"; during 1919 toured as Amy Lee in "Soldier Boy." *Recreations:* Poetry, music, needlework, and reading. *Address:* 505 Gladstone Avenue, Grand Rapids, Mich., U.S.A., or 21 Fircroft Road, Upper Tooting, S.W.17.

JAY, Ernest, actor; *b.* London, 18 Sept., 1893; *s.* of Harry Alberge and his wife Sarah (Schneiders); *m.* Catherine Mary Hay; during the War (1914-17) served with the H.A.C., invalided out; made his first appearance on the stage at the Empire, Penge, July, 1917, as Ernest Morrison in "Are You a Mason?"; toured in the provinces and played nearly a hundred parts in repertory seasons at Liverpool and Plymouth, 1917-26; made his first appearance in London at the Prince of Wales's Theatre, Apr., 1926, as Charles Murdoch in "The Ghost Train"; from 1926-9, toured in Newfoundland, Canada, British West Indies, etc., with Florence Glossop-Harris; reappeared in London at the Prince's, Sept., 1929, as Ponder in "The Flying Fool": Royalty, Mar., 1930, played Gerald Saunders in "Appearances"; Playhouse, June, 1930, The Coroner and Mr. Boot in "Cynara"; St. James's, May, 1931, Charlie Hammond in "Payment Deferred"; made his first appearance in New York at the 44th Street Theatre, 1 Oct., 1931, as Joby Jackson in "The Good Companions"; Garrick, London, May, 1932, the Landlord in "Man Overboard"; Shaftesbury, Aug., 1932, Private Slee in "Orders Are Orders"; Piccadilly, Apr., and Garrick, June, 1933, Lefty Williams in "Clear All Wires"; Lyric, Aug., 1933, Soldat Bolle in "The Ace"; Comedy, Dec., 1933, Herman Lefkowitz in "Whistling in the Dark"; Daly's, Apr., 1934, George Taylor in "Dark Horizon"; Shaftesbury, Aug., 1934, Mr. Stallybrass in "Admirals All"; His Majesty's, May, 1935, Mr. Stone in "Hervey House"; Embassy, Jan., 1936, Arthur Newstead in, "Golden Gander"; Strand, May, 1936, Harry Harper in "Aren't Men Beasts!" Hudson, New York, Mar., 1937, "Pal" Green in "The Amazing Dr. Clitterhouse"; Globe, London, Oct., 1937, Jackson in "Blondie White"; Gate, Feb., 1938, Crombie in "Frozen Glory"; Strand, Feb., 1939, Samuel Smithson in "Little Ladyship"; "Q" and Embassy, June, 1939, Mr. Moke in "Punch Without Judy"; Strand, July, 1939, Philip Anagnos in "The Gentle People"; New, Dec., 1939, again played Moke in "Punch Without Judy"; from 1940-4, was engaged broadcasting with the B.B.C. repertory company; "Q," June, 1944, played Corder Morris in "The Shop in Sly Street"; Arts Theatre, Oct.-Dec., 1944, played Alfred Granger in "The Breadwinner," Chris Christopherson in "Anna Christie," and the French Interpreter in "The Critic"; St. Martin's, Apr., 1945, Corder Morris in "The Shop at Sly Corner," which ran over a year New Lindsey, May, and Prince of Wales's, July; 1946, Judge Bentley in "Pick-Up Girl"; Arts, Nov., 1947, played Capt. Potts in "The Moon in the Yellow River";

People's Palace, Nov., 1948, appeared as Homer and Lenin in "These Mortals"; Apr., 1949, Dr. Paul Selder in "Max"; Lyric, Hammersmith, Jan., 1950, Sam Smith in "Shall We Join the Ladies?"; appeared at the Music Box, New York, Sept., 1950, as Mr. Gooch in "Daphne Laureola"; after returning to London he appeared at the New Boltons, Feb., 1951, playing Mr. Burgess in "Candida," and Mar., 1951, Polonius in "Hamlet"; Arts, July, 1951, played Jules Pasdelouoe in "Poor Judas"; Court, July, 1952, James Ruskin in "The Bride of Denmark Hill"; Mercury, Jan., 1953, King Agramor of Aquaraine in "The Princess and the Swineherd"; Duchess Nov., 1953, appeared as the Chaplain in "The Return"; has also played on numerous occasions for the Repertory Players, Arts Theatre Club, etc.; entered films, 1932, and has appeared in numerous pictures and in radio and television plays. *Recreations:* Walking and swimming. *Clubs:* Green Room, and Savage. *(Died 8 Feb., 1957; age 63)*

JAY, Harriett, dramatic author, novelist, and actress; author of the following, among other, plays: " The Queen of Connaught " (from her own novel), 1877; " Alone in London," 1885; " Fascination," 1887; " The Strange Adventures of Miss Brown," 1895; " The Romance of a Shopwalker," 1896; " A Wanderer from Venus," 1896; " The Mariners of England," 1897; " Two Little Maids from School," 1898, all in collaboration with her brother-in-law, the late Robert Buchanan; " When Knights were Bold," first produced in 1907 has been revived annually for many years; from 1895 wrote her plays under the *nom de plume* of Charles Marlowe; as an actress, made her first appearance on the stage in the provinces, in 1879; appeared at the Crystal Palace, 1880, as Kathleen, in a revival of " The Queen of Connaught "; made her first appearance on the London stage, at the Gaiety Theatre, 22 Nov., 1880, as Lady Jane Grey in " A Nine Day's Queen "; subsequently appeared in " The Madcap Prince," 1881; " The Exiles of Erin," 1881; " Lady Clan-

carty," 1882; "Lady Clare," 1883; "A Sailor and his Lass," 1883; "Alone in London," 1885; "Sapho," 1886; "The Blue Bells of Scotland" and "Fascination," 1887; "The Bride of Love" and "Sweet Nancy," 1890; author of the following novels: "The Dark Colleen," "Madge Dunraven," "My Connaught Cousins," "The Priest's Blessing," "Two Men and a Maid," "Through the Stage Door," also the author of the biography of Robert Buchanan.
(Died 21 Dec., 1932; age 79)

JAY, Isabel, actress and vocalist; *b.* London, 17 Oct., 1879; *d.* of John Wimburn Jay and his wife Isabelle Clara (Wicks); is a descendant of a famous musician of the eighteenth century, Dr. Jay, of the Royal Academy of Music; *m.* (1) H. S. H. Cavendish, the African explorer, 1902 (obtained dissolution in 1906); (2) Frank Curzon, 1910; prepared for the stage at Royal Academy of Music; studied under Mdme. Lemmens Sherrington and Miss Bateman; first appeared on the stage at Savoy Theatre, 12 July, 1897, as Elsie Maynard, in "The Yeomen of the Guard"; she then toured with the D'Oyly Carte company in "The Mikado," "Iolanthe," "The Sorcerer," and "The Pirates of Penzance"; returned to the Savoy, 1898, to play the Plaintiff in "Trial by Jury," and subsequently she appeared as Josephine in "H.M.S. Pinafore"; she also appeared at the Savoy as Tessa in "The Gondoliers," 1898; as Aloës in "The Lucky Star," Jan., 1899; as Blush-of-Morning in "The Rose of Persia," Nov., 1899, subsequently appearing in the same piece as the Sultana Zubeydeh; June, 1899, she played Mabel in "The Pirates of Penzance"; Nov., 1900, Patience in the opera of that name; Apr., 1901, she appeared as Lady Rose Pippin in "The Emerald Isle," Nov., 1901, as the Gipsy Woman in "Ib and Little Christina"; Dec., 1901, as Phyllis in "Iolanthe"; she was then absent from the stage for eighteen months, but reappeared, at Daly's, 24 Oct., 1903, as Nan in "A Country

Girl"; same theatre, 5 Mar., 1904, played Lady Patricia Vane in "The Cingalee"; at the Apollo, 22 Apr., 1905, appeared in the title-*rôle* of "Véronique"; at the Criterion, Aug., 1905, played Sybil Cunningham in "The White Chrysanthemum"; at Wyndham's, Apr., 1906, Winnie Willoughby in "The Girl Behind the Counter"; Olivia in "The Vicar of Wakefield," Prince of Wales's, Dec., 1906; Sally in "Miss Hook of Holland," Jan., 1907; Paulette in "My Mimosa Maid," Apr., 1908; Princess Marie in "King of Cadonia," Sept., 1908; Christine in "Dear Little Denmark," Sept., 1909; Princess Stephanie in "The Balkan Princess," Feb., 1910, all at the Prince of Wales's; in Dec., 1910, toured in the last-mentioned play; appeared for the last time at Kennington, 29 Apr., 1911, her retirement from the stage being announced earlier in the year; reappeared after twelve years' absence at Hastings, Feb., 1923, as Anne West in her own play "The Inevitable," and played the same part at the St. James's Theatre, Mar., 1923; won the first gold medal for operatic singing at R.A.M., 1897, and was created A.R.A.M. *Hobbies:* Motoring, piano, and painting. *(Died 26 Feb., 1927; age 47)*

JAY, John Herbert, manager; *b.* London, 19 Oct., 1871; *s.* of John Wimburn Jay and his wife Isabelle Clara (Wicks); brother of Isabel Jay; *e.* Shoreham and Brighton; *m.* Pauline Starck; was formerly engaged as clerk in the London School Board, and The Railway Companies' Association; became associated with the stage in 1903, as the first lessee and manager of the Royal Victoria Theatre, Ramsgate; first engaged as business manager in Sept., 1906, for tour of "The Girl Behind the Counter"; was engaged as business manager at Wyndham's Theatre, from Jan., 1907-15; in 1908, he started "The Rehearsal Theatre"; in 1910-11, was lessee and manager with Charlton Mann, of the Palace Pier Theatre, Brighton; built the Ambassadors' Theatre, which was opened in June, 1913, and is Managing Director of the

Syndicate controlling it; in Oct., 1915, started management in London for himself, producing, with Anthony Ellis, at the Criterion, " A Little Bit of Fluff," which ran nearly three years; produced " Tiger's Cub " and " Bluff " at the Garrick, 1916; " The Girl from Upstairs," at the Strand, 1916; in the same year purchased the Kingsway Theatre from Miss Lena Ashwell, and was Managing Director of the Syndicate controlling it until 1933; is now sole lessee and manager; in Aug., 1916, went to America, and produced "A Little Bit of Fluff" at the 39th Street, New York, remaining there until the end of the year; at the Haymarket, Mar., 1917, in conjunction with Percy Hutchison, produced "General Post"; has since produced

"The Pacifists" and "The Liars," at the St. James's, with Percy Hutchison, 1917; "Ghosts," at the Kingsway, with Victor Lewis, 1917; " One Hour of Life," with Anthony Ellis, at Kingsway, 1917; " Lot 79," at the Queen's, with Percy Hutchison, 1918; " A Temporary Gentleman," at the Oxford, with F. R. Littler, 1919; " In the Night," at the Kingsway, with F. R. Littler, 1919; " Such a Nice Young Man," at the Apollo, with F. R. Littler, 1920; " The Heart of a Child," at the Kingsway, with A. Hylton Allen, 1921; " Skittles," at the Apollo, with E. Taylor Platt, 1921 ; " The Limpet " and " I Serve," at the Kingsway, 1922 ; " Mr. Budd of Kennington, S.E.," at the Royalty with Frank Curzon, 1923 ; in 1923 with Sir George Dance, took a lease of the Court Theatre ; at the Criterion, 1923, produced " Three Birds," and with A. Hylton Allen, produced

" Dulcy "; at Wyndham's, 1928, associated with the production of " The Love Lorn-Lady "; at the Court, 1932, with Roy Limbert, produced " The School for Husbands"; "Glass Houses," Royalty, 1936; "Behind the Blinds," Winter Garden, 1938; "A Woman's Privilege," Kingsway, 1939; opened the Embassy Theatre, Swiss Cottage, 1928, and was Chairman of the Syndicate controlling it. *Club:* Green Room. *Address:* 82

Shaftesbury Avenue, W.1. *Telephone No.:* Gerrard 7144
(Died 19 Jan., 1942; age 70)

JEANS, Ronald, dramatic author ; *b.* Birkenhead, 10 May, 1887 ; *s.* of the late Sir Alexander Jeans, managing director of the *Liverpool Post and Mercury*; *e.* Loretto School; *m.* Margaret Wise ; from 1904–11 was engaged as a stockbroker ; in 1911 was largely responsible for the founding of the Liverpool Repertory Theatre ; is the author of " The Cage," 1913 ; " The Kiss Cure," 1914 ; " Pauline," 1914 ; " Hullo, Repertory," 1915 ; " No Reflection on the Wife," 1915; " Higgledy-Piggledy," 1915 ; " Oh, Law ! " 1916 ; " Give and Take," 1917 ; " Tabs," 1918 ; " Buzz-Buzz " (with Arthur Wimperis), 1918 ; " Bran Pie " (part-author), 1919 ; " Wild Geese " 1920 ; part-author of " Puss-Puss," 1921 ; " A. to Z.," 1921 ; " Pot Luck," 1921 ; " Snap," 1922 ; adapted " Dédé," 1922 ; author of " Rats," 1923 ; part-author of " London Calling," 1923 ; "Charlot's Revue," "By-the-Way," 1924 ; "Still Dancing," 1925 ; author of "Cochran's Revue," 1926 ; "The Charlot Show of 1926"; "Lido Lady," 1926 ; "One Dam Thing After Another," "Clowns in Clover," 1927 ; "The House that Jack Built," 1929 ; "Charlot's Masquerade," 1930 ; "Lean Harvest," "Can the Leopard . . .?" 1931 ; "Bow Bells," 1932 ; "After Dark," 1933 ; "Streamline" (with A. P. Herbert), 1934 ; "The Composite Man," "Follow the Sun" (with John Hastings Turner), 1935 ; "Ghost for Sale," 1938 ; "Lights Up," 1940 ; part-author of "Top of the World," 1940 ; from 1940–5 operated his own cinema, for the benefit of H.M. Forces; author of "Young Wives' Tale," 1949 ; "Count Your Blessings," 1951 ; "Grace and Favour," 1954 ; "The Goldfish Bowl," 1956 ; "Three-Way Switch," 1958 ; Director of the London Mask Theatre Co., 1938; he is also the author of the following books: "Vignettes from Vaudeville," "The Stage is Waiting," "Writing for the Theatre," etc. *Recreations:* Cinematography and country life. *Clubs:* Authors' and R.A.C.

Address: Flat 4, 85 Marine Parade, Brighton. *Telephone No.:* Brighton 62318.

JEANS, Ursula, actress; *b.* Simla, India, 5 May, 1906; *d.* of C. H. McMinn and his wife Margaret Ethel (Fisher); *e.* London; *m.* (1) Robin Irvine (dec.); (2) Roger Livesey; studied for the stage at the Royal Academy of Dramatic Art; made her first appearance on the stage at the Theatre Royal, Nottingham, 3 Aug., 1925, as Sophie Binner in "Cobra"; made her first appearance in London, at Wyndham's Theatre 8 Feb., 1926, as Angela in "The Firebrand"; next appeared at the Ambassadors', Aug., 1926, as The Girl of the Town in "Escape," and Mar., 1927, as Toby in "The Fanatics"; at the Arts Theatre, July, 1927, played Dagmar Krumbak in "Samson and Delilah"; at the Strand (for the Repertory Players), Sept., 1927, Jill Osborne in "Chance Acquaintance"; at the Playhouse, Jan., 1928, Monica Grey in "The Second Man"; Globe, May, 1928, Pearl Pretty in "Mud and Treacle"; Criterion, July, 1928, Miss Carruthers in "Passing Brompton Road"; in Sept., 1928, toured as Lady Hampton in "Virginia"; at the Strand, Nov., 1928, played Evelyn Seymour in "High Treason"; St. James's, Dec., 1928, Ilona Szabo in "The Play's The Thing"; at the London Hippodrome, Mar., 1929, Cora Wainwright in "The Five o'Clock Girl"; at the Haymarket, June, 1929, Elsie Fraser in "The First Mrs. Fraser"; Cambridge, Feb., 1931, Yung-Sa and Ker-A in "Kong"; Vaudeville, July, 1931, Barbara Olwell in "Apron Strings"; Adelphi, Sept., 1931, Flaemm-chen in "Grand Hotel"; Prince of Wales's, Mar., 1932, Glad in "I Lived With You"; St. Martin's (for Play-goers' League), Apr., 1932, Trudy Hanks in "The Multabello Road"; went to the United States, and made her first appearance on the New York stage at the Plymouth Theatre, 9 Jan., 1933, as Pauline Murray in "Late One Evening"; in Sept., 1933, joined the Old Vic.–Sadler's Wells Company, and during the season played Viola in "Twelfth Night," Anya in "The Cherry

Orchard," Anne Bullen in "Henry VIII," Mariana in "Measure for Measure," Cecily Cardew in "The Importance of Being Earnest," Angel-ica in "Love for Love," Miranda in "The Tempest"; at the Vaudeville, Oct., 1934, Sarah Traille in "Lovers' Leap"; Grafton (for Stage Society), Mar., 1935, The Sphinx in "The Machine of the Gods"; Arts, June, 1935, Olive Allingham in "The Benefit of the Doubt"; Victoria Palace, Aug., 1935, Nina Popinot in "Vintage Wine"; Queen's, Nov., 1935, Penelope Marsh in "Short Story"; Old Vic., Oct., 1936, Alithea in "The Country Wife"; Gate, Nov., 1936, Karen in "The Children's Hour"; Globe, July, 1937, Sally Grosvenor in "They Came by Night"; New, May, 1938, Shena March in "People of Our Class"; Old Vic., Jan.–Apr., 1939, Kate Hardcastle in "She Stoops to Con-quer," Petra in "The Enemy of the People," and Katherine in "The Taming of the Shrew"; Little The-atre, Apr., 1940, again played Alithea in "The Country Wife"; toured, June, 1940, as Mary of Magdala in "Family Portrait"; Globe, Jan., 1941, played Joanna in "Dear Brutus"; toured, 1942, as Elvira in "Blithe Spirit," and 1943, as Sara Müller in "Watch on the Rhine," and appeared in this part at the Aldwych, Aug., 1943; subse-quently, toured for E.N.S.A., in "Dear Brutus," "Watch on the Rhine," "Springtime for Henry," and "It De-pends What You Mean"; Wyndham's, Sept., 1944, played Frances in "The Banbury Nose"; New, June, 1947, Helen in "Ever Since Paradise"; Lyric, Hammersmith, Feb., 1950, Mary Bernard in "Man of the World"; at the reopening of the Old Vic, Nov., 1950, appeared as Olivia in "Twelfth Night," and later in the season as Dame Overdo in "Bartholomew Fair," Lady Cicely Waynflete in "Captain Brassbound's Conversion," and Mis-tress Ford in "The Merry Wives of Windsor"; Arts, Oct., 1951, played Jean Moreland in "Third Person," and appeared in this part at the Criterion, Jan., 195?; at the Citizen's Theatre, Glasgow, Oct., 1952, she played Lady Pounce-Pellott in "The Blaikie Chari-vari"; St. Martin's, London, Apr.,

1953, appeared as Margaret Bell in "The Teddy Bear"; at the 48th Street, New York, Nov., 1953, played Stella Hampden in "Escapade"; Court, London, Mar., 1955, Barbara Leigh in "Uncertain Joy"; Lyric, Hammersmith, Feb., 1956, played Mrs. Tarleton in "Misalliance"; toured Australia and New Zealand, with her husband, 1956–8, playing Sheila Broadbent in "The Reluctant Debutante," and also co-starring in "The Great Sebastians"; Old Vic, Sept., 1959, played Lady Touchwood in "The Double-Dealer"; Hampstead Theatre Club, Jan., 1962, played Juliette Dulac in "Head of the Family"; Oxford Playhouse, May, 1964, Irette in "The Twelfth Hour"; Nottingham Playhouse, Apr., 1965, Mrs. Pocock in "The Elephant's Foot," and subsequently toured with the production; Strand, Dec., 1965, Lady Markby in "An Ideal Husband"; toured South Africa, July, 1970, in "Oh, Clarence!"; commenced film career in "The Gypsy Cavalier," and has since appeared in numerous pictures. *Recreations:* Riding and swimming. *Address:* c/o I.F.A. Ltd., 11–12 Hanover Street, London, W.1.

JEAYES, Allan, actor; *b.* Finchley, 19 Jan., 1885; *s.* of Herbert Jeayes and his wife Mary (Hall); *e.* Merchant Taylors' School; *m.* Frances Hamerton; was formerly engaged in farming; made his first appearance on the stage at the Pleasure Gardens, Folkestone, 1906, as Trip in "The School for Scandal," with the Compton Comedy Company; made his first appearance in London at the Haymarket Theatre, 1910, succeeding to the part of Baron Osterman during the run of "Priscilla Runs Away"; next played several parts with The Play Actors at the Court Theatre, 1911–12; at the Haymarket, 1913, appeared in "The Pretenders" and "Typhoon"; at the St. James's, 1913, played in "Androcles and the Lion," "The Witch," etc.; toured as John Rhead in "Milestones"; at the Strand, May, 1915, played Charles IX in the revival of "Henry of Navarre"; subsequently toured as the Defendant in "On Trial"; at the

Playhouse, Sept., 1916, played Henry Tracey in "The Misleading Lady"; at the Savoy, Apr., 1917, First Player in "Hamlet": at the Royalty, June, 1917, Henry in "The Foundations"; next toured as Edward Smith in "General Post," and appeared in that part at the Haymarket, Jan., 1918; at the Royalty, Mar., 1918, played Sir Malcolm Clark in "The Prime Minister"; then toured as Captain Paul Chalfont in "By Pigeon Post"; at the Garrick, Mar., 1919, appeared as Captain Carbon de Castel-Jaloux in "Cyrano de Bergerac"; at the New Theatre, Dec., 1919, appeared as Captain Hook in "Peter Pan"; at the Holborn Empire, Mar., 1920, as Creon in "Medea"; at the Strand, June, 1920, played Sam Tullidge in "Tiger! Tiger!"; at the Prince of Wales's, Aug., 1920, Guy Néborg in "The Blue Lagoon"; during 1921 toured with Irene Vanbrugh as Durand in "Mis' Nell o' New Orleans," and George Marden in "Mr. Pim Passes By"; at the St. James's, Jan., 1922, played the Unknown Man in "The Bat"; Nov., 1922, Krasnocharkof in "The Beating on the Door"; at the Apollo, Jan., 1923, Lord Quihampton in "A Roof and Four Walls"; in June-July, 1923, at the Everyman Theatre, played Rev. James Mavor-Morrell in "Candida," Undershaft in "Major Barbara," and Juggins in "Fanny's First Play"; at the St. Martin's, Aug., 1923, George Miles in "The Likes of 'Er," and Mr. Devizes in "The Will"; at the Queen's, Nov., 1923, the Earl of Rintoul in "The Little Minister"; at the Apollo, Ernest Stanton, M.P., in "The Fake"; at the Little, Nov., 1924, Philip in "Falling Leaves"; at the New (for the Stage Society), Dec., 1924, the Nobleman in "The Man with a Load of Mischief"; at Drury Lane, Dec., 1924, Theseus in "A Midsummer Night's Dream"; Everyman, Mar. to Apr., 1925, Philip Jordan in "The Painted Swan," and Justice Plush in "Overture"; Queen's, June, 1925, Colonel Starbottle in "Salomy Jane"; Lyceum, July, 1925, again played Stanton in "The Fake"; Garrick, Oct., 1925, Lord Llanelly in "Cristilinda"; Ambassadors', Nov.,

1925, Constantine in "The Madras House"; New, Mar., 1926, Hadj Ismael in "Prince Fazil"; Adelphi, May, 1926, Summer Ridgley in "Aloma" Queen's, Sept., 1926, Charles II in "And So To Bed"; Royalty, Mar., 1927, Ludovico Nota in "Naked"; Globe, June, 1927, The Old Man in "The Spook Sonata"; went to New York, and at the Morosco, Sept., 1927, played Howard Joyce in "The Letter"; after returning to London, appeared at the Fortune, July, 1928, as Reginald Bringham in "Mischief"; Strand, Nov., 1928, Mark Tregesal in "Out of the Sea"; Court, Apr., 1929, Sir Henry Moore in "The Garey Hotel Case"; Globe, May, 1929, Judge Sewell in "The Black Ace"; Prince of Wales's (for the Sunday Players), June, 1929, Sir Edward Kane in "The Donkey's Nose"; Garrick, Oct., 1929, Oscar Beresford in "Happy Families"; Comedy, Nov., 1929, Lord Carleigh in "The Highwayman"; Criterion, Jan., 1930, John Rhead in "Milestones"; Aug., 1930, toured as James Fraser in "The First Mrs. Fraser"; Drury Lane, Jan., 1931, played The Ilkhani of Kahlek in "The Song of the Drum"; Globe, Nov., 1931, Charles II in "And So to Bed"; Feb., 1932, the Marquis of Partuga in "Punchinello"; at Wyndham's, Oct., 1932, played James Felton in "Service"; Little, Apr., 1933, Mr. Justice Plush in "Overture"; St. Martin's, Feb., 1935, William Lawrence in "Man of Yesterday"; Lyric, May, 1936, Lord Cottingley in "Bees on the Boatdeck" and Mar., 1939, Sir Ernest Shufflepenny in "The Jealous God"; toured, June, 1940, as Rabbi Samuel in "Family Portrait"; St. James's, Nov., 1943, played Sir Lawrence Wargrave in "Ten Little Niggers"; Wyndham's, Jan., 1945, Sir Ernest Foster in "The Years Between," which ran eighteen months; Wyndham's, July, 1947, Senator Ellsworth Langdon in "Deep Are the Roots"; Winter Garden, Oct., 1948, played the Manager and the Hon. Tchang in "Lute Song"; Lyric, Hammersmith, Apr., 1949, General Rosegger in "Royal Highness"; toured, Aug., 1949, as Dr. Sloper in "The Heiress"; Duchess, Oct., 1949,

Edouard Chardonne in "Gooseberry Fool"; Winter Garden, Apr., 1950, Counsellor Huld in "The Trial"; Scala, June, 1951, played George Mannering, K.C., in "Breach of Marriage"; Lyric, Hammersmith, Nov., 1951, played the Rev. Winemiller in "Summer and Smoke," and appeared in this part at the Duchess in Jan., 1952; New, Sept., 1952, appeared as the Foreman of the Jury in "The Hanging Judge"; toured, 1958, as the Judge in "The Chalk Garden"; Princes, Feb., 1960, Mr. Justice Tanyard in "The Girl on the Highway"; is the author of "So Proceed You," "Letters to an Actor," "Scenes for Audition," many short stories and talks for the B.B.C. and Canadian Broadcasting Co., as well as two plays; has appeared in films for many years; has also played on television regularly. *Recreations:* Writing and Walking. *Club:* Authors'. *Address:* c/o Al Parker, Ltd., 50 Mount Street, Park Lane, London, W.1.
(Died 20 Sept., 1963; age 78)

JECKS, Clara, actress; *d.* of Charles Albert Jecks, acting-manager, and his wife, the late Harriet Coveney; *e.* at London and Norfolk; *m.* W. C. Wigley; commenced acting as a young child, making her *début* as a baby in a play entitled "One Hundred and Two"; at the Opéra Comique, 12 July, 1873, played in "Kissi Kissi," this being her "grown up" *début*; appeared at Drury Lane in pantomime and drama; in 1877 appeared at the Adelphi, as Lord Eden in "Formosa," and remained at that theatre until 1883, playing among other parts, Sam Willoughby in "The Ticket-of-Leave Man," Josephs in "It's Never Too Late to Mend," etc.; during that year appeared at Drury Lane in "A Sailor and his Lass"; appeared at the Gaiety, 1884-5; returned to the Adelphi in 1886, and played in "The Harbour Lights," "The Bells of Haslemere," "The Union Jack," "The Silver Falls," "London Day by Day," "The Green Bushes," "The English Rose," "The Trumpet Call," "The White Rose," "The

Lights of Home," "The Lost Paradise" and "The Black Domino," remaining until 1893 ; at Toole's, Sept., 1894, played in "A Trip to Chinatown"; at the Prince of Wales's, Mar., 1895, appeared as William in "Gentleman Joe"; at Drury Lane, Christmas, 1896, played Saw-See in "Aladdin"; at the Royalty, Oct., 1897, played Tupper in "Oh! Susannah"; at the Prince of Wales's, 1898-9, appeared in "The Royal Star," and as Henri in "La Poupée"; since that date has appeared but rarely ; has played over 200 parts, and is an exceedingly competent and popular actress. *Address*: c/o *The Era*, or *The Stage*.

(Died 5 Jan., 1951; age 94)

JEFFERIES, Douglas, actor ; *b.* Hampstead, 21 Apr., 1884 ; *s.* of William Henry Jefferies and his wife Alice (Williams) ; *e.* London ; *m.* Nora Kathleen Wallis ; was formerly engaged as an architectural draughtsman ; made his first appearance on the stage at the Waldorf (now Strand) Theatre, 24 Apr., 1907, walking on in the Sothern-Marlowe production of "Jeanne D'Arc"; spent several years touring in the provinces ; played his first part in London, when he appeared at the Palace, 22 Jan., 1912, with Sir Herbert Tree, as Cyril Jackson in "The Man Who Was"; in 1913, went to America, where he toured as Richard Sibley in "Milestones"; from 1916-18, was engaged at Wyndham's, as understudy to Sir Gerald du Maurier, in "The Old Country," "London Pride" and "Dear Brutus," and also succeeded Sam Sothern as Mr. Purdie in the last-mentioned play, 1918 ; at the New Theatre, July, 1920, played Oliver in "I'll Leave it to You"; played in repertory at the Everyman Theatre, 1920-1 ; appeared at the Court, 1922, in "Justice" and "The Silver Box"; at the Everyman, 1922, played Morell in "Candida," Thomas Randolph in "Mary Stuart" and 1923, Dr. Paramore in "The Philanderer"; at His Majesty's, May, 1923, General Fairfax in "Oliver Cromwell"; at the Haymarket, Nov., 1923, Lane in "The Importance of Being Earnest";

during 1924 toured as Roddy Dunton in "Havoc"; during 1925-6 fulfilled several engagements at "Q" and Everyman Theatres; Barnes, Oct., 1926, played Lt.-Col. Vershinin in "The Three Sisters"; Duke of York's, Dec., 1926, Wolf in "Liliom"; Apollo, Jan., 1927, Dr. Burnham in "The Bend in the Road"; Everyman, Jan. to July, 1927, appeared in "The Square Peg," "Jazz Patterns," "The White Chateau," "This Year, Next Year," "Fire"; during 1928 toured as Sir John Marlay in "Interference"; Wyndham's, June, 1929, played George in "Exiled"; subsequently went to America, to play in "Bird in Hand"; after returning to London, appeared at the Everyman, Aug., 1930, as Paul in "The Bond"; Globe, Sept., 1930; played Steve Sankey in "Street Scene"; Haymarket, Feb., 1931, Mr. Blayne in "Supply and Demand"; St. Martin's, May, 1931, Duckit in "Lean Harvest"; with the Old Vic.-Sadler's Wells company, Sept., 1931–Apr., 1932; at the Lyric, Dec., 1932, Henry Hallam in "Another Language"; Arts and Westminster, Mar., 1933, Henry Surrege in "The Lake"; Lyric, Oct., 1933, Sir Fulke Greville in "This Side Idolatry"; Royalty, Feb., 1934, The Bishop in "Within the Gates"; Whitehall, May, 1934, Henry Pleydell in "No Way Back"; Lyric, June, 1934, Mr. Hudson in "Men in White"; Kingsway, Jan., 1935, Det.-Inspector Marshall in "Murder in Motley"; Duke of York's, Feb., 1935, Ralph Keeble and Mr. Justice Barrow in "For the Defence"; His Majesty's, May, 1935, Holden in "Hervey House"; Comedy, Mar., 1936, Walter Kent in "Dusty Ermine"; New, Mar., 1937, Vincentio in "The Taming of the Shrew"; Embassy, May, and Strand, June, 1937, Judge Vlora in "Judgment Day"; Lyric, June, 1937, Archbishop of Canterbury in "Victoria Regina"; St. James's, Nov., 1937, the Priest in "The Silent Knight"; Duke of York's, Apr., 1939, Rev. Herbert Sully in "Interlude"; St. James's, May, 1939, the Doctor in "Sixth Floor"; Phoenix, Nov., 1939, again played Vlora in "Judgment Day"; Queen's, Apr., 1940, Frith in "Rebecca," and at the Strand, May, 1942,

Colonel Julyan in the same play; Globe, Dec., 1942, played Mr. Chisholm in "The Petrified Forest," and Dec., 1943, Horton in "While the Sun Shines," which he played over a thousand times; Savoy, June, 1947, played the Rev. Doctor Lloyd in "Life With Father"; Cambridge, Nov., 1948, Sir George Surrey in "Home Is To-morrow"; "Q," Sept., 1949, Theo Ludlow in "By Adoption"; Arts, Jan,. 1950, Rev. Samuel Gardner in "Mrs. Warren's Profession"; Vaudeville, Apr., 1950, Thripp in "Cry Liberty"; Prince's, Mar., 1951, Dr. Kendal in "The Seventh Veil"; Arts, Sept., 1951, played Charles in a revival of "Mrs. Dot." *Favourite parts:* Morell in "Candida," and Cutler Walpole in "The Doctor's Dilemma." *Recreation:* Drawing in black and white. *Address:* 12 Hill Top, Hampstead, N.W.11. *Telephone No.:* Speedwell 2236.

(Died Dec., 1959; age 75)

JEFFREYS, Ellis (Minnie Gertrude Ellis Jeffreys), actress; *b.* Colombo, Ceylon, 17 May, 1872; *d.* of the late Captain Dodsworth Jeffreys; *m.* (1) Hon. Frederick Graham Curzon (mar. dis.); (2) Herbert Sleath (Skelton); made her first appearance on the stage, Oct., 1889, in the chorus of "The Yeomen of the Guard," at the Savoy; next appeared at Her Majesty's Theatre, Dec., 1889, as Butterfly in the pantomime "Cinderella"; subsequently appeared at the Lyric in 1890, as Polly in "The Sentry," and in "La Cigale," in which opera she played and sang nearly all the leading female *rôles* during its long run; appeared at the Prince of Wales's, Nov., 1891, as Priscilla B-Hives in "The Prancing Girl," and was then engaged by Sir Charles Wyndham for the Criterion, where she played in "The Bauble Shop," "The Fringe of Society," "The Headless Man," "Betsy," "Madame Favart," "La Mascotte," "The Wedding March," etc.; in 1894, she was seen at the Adelphi in "The Two Orphans"; at the Garrick, 1895, in "The Notorious Mrs. Ebbsmith," also accompanying John Hare to the United States to play in the same piece; on her return,

fulfilled an engagement with George Alexander at the St. James's and Royalty, subsequently appearing at the Criterion in "My Soldier Boy," at Terry's, in "Sweet Lavender," and at the Court in "The Vagabond King"; next appeared at the Vaudeville in "The Elixir of Youth," and "Kitty Grey"; returned to the Criterion to play in "The Noble Lord"; at the Haymarket in 1902, played in "Frocks and Frills"; and then at the Duke of York's, appeared in "The Marriage of Kitty"; at the Avenue in "Mrs. Willoughby's Kiss"; at the Criterion in "The Altar of Friendship"; at the Haymarket in "Cousin Kate," "Joseph Entangled," and "Lady Flirt"; went to the United States in 1905, and appeared at the New Amsterdam Theatre, New York, as Queen Sonia in "The Prince Consort" ("His Highness My Husband"), subsequently appearing as Lady Gay Spanker in "London Assurance"; reappeared in London, at the Haymarket, in "On the Love Path," 1905; again returned to New York, to create the part of Lady Clarice Howland in "The Fascinating Mr. Vanderveldt," at Daly's Theatre; reappeared at the Duke of York's in the revival of "The Marriage of Kitty," and again returning to New York, appeared at the Liberty Theatre as Mrs. Brooke in "The Dear Unfair Sex"; at Columbus, Ohio, Oct., 1906, appeared as Kate Hardcastle in "She Stoops to Conquer," with which play she toured the principal cities of the United States; on her return to England, appeared at His Majesty's, in May, 1907, as Mrs. Allonby in "A Woman of No Importance"; next appeared at the Queen's Theatre, 8 Oct., 1907, as Grace Pemberton in "The Sugar Bowl," under her husband's management; at the Apollo, Nov., 1907, appeared as Cynthia Karslake in "The New York Idea"; during 1908, toured in her husband's company in "A White Man"; appeared at the Palace, Jan., 1909, as She in "Number Two"; at His Majesty's, Apr., 1909, played Lady Sneerwell in "The School for Scandal"; at the

Garrick, July, 1909, played Margaret Rolfe in " A Woman in the Case " ; at the Criterion, June, 1910, played Mrs. Quesnel in " The Case of Rebellious Susan " ; Oct., 1910, Lady Rosamund Tatton in " The Liars " ; Jan., 1911, Madge Bolt in " Is Matrimony a Failure ? " ; at the Duke of York's, Feb., 1911, appeared as Mrs. Fitzgerald in " Loaves and Fishes"; at the Theatre Royal, Newcastle-on-Tyne, Nov., 1911, played Kitty Trevor in " Kit " ; at the Duke of York's, June, 1912, appeared as the Marchioness of Castlejordan in a revival of " The Amazons " ; at Wyndham's, Mar., 1913, played the Comtesse Zicka in a revival of " Diplomacy " ; at the Haymarket, Nov., 1914, played Mrs. Cameron in " The Flag Lieutenant " ; Apr., 1915, The Duchess of Wiltshire in " Five Birds in a Cage"; at the St. James's, May, 1916, the Duchess of Goring in " Pen " ; at the Haymarket, Sept., 1916, played Lady Angela Treve in " Mr. Jubilee Drax " ; Nov., 1916, Lady Deborah Carstairs in " The Widow's Might " ; at the St. James's, Sept., 1917, Susanna Peebody in " The Pacifists " ; at the Garrick, Oct., 1917, Mrs. Guildford in " The Saving Grace " ; at His Majesty's, Dec., 1917, appeared as Mrs. Montague Tidmarsh in the " all-star " revival of " The Man from Blankney's," given in aid of King George's Actors' Pension Fund ; at the Playhouse, Apr., 1918, played Nora Gail in " The Naughty Wife " ; at the Haymarket, Mar., 1920, Lady Tonbridge in " The Young Person in Pink " ; at the Globe, Oct., 1920, the Countess Olga in " Fédora " ; Feb., 1921, the Duchess of Rockingham in " The Hour and the Man " ; Mar., 1921, Emily Ladew in " Her Husband's Wife " ; at the St. James's, Aug., 1921, Amelia in " Threads " ; at the Strand, Jan., 1922, Lady Adela Boxgrove in " Me and My Diary " ; at Drury Lane, Apr., 1922, The Lady Violante in " Decameron Nights " ; at the Globe, Apr., 1923, Lady Frinton in " Aren't We All ? " ; at Drury Lane, Sept., 1923, Lady Patricia Wolseley in " Good Luck " ; in 1924, appeared in variety theatres in " Me and My Diary," and " Five

Birds in a Cage " ; at the St. James's, Sept., 1925, played Lady Frinton in " The Last of Mrs. Cheyney " ; Fortune, Apr., 1927, Mrs. Wislack in " On Approval " ; Mar., 1929, Lady Frinton in a revival of " Aren't We All? " Opera House, Blackpool, Nov., 1931, Lady Hylton in "Too Many Smiths"; Arts, Jan., 1932, Lady Rockstone in "Avalanche"; Haymarket, May, 1932, Lady Gorse in "Queer Cattle"; Phoenix, Oct., 1932, Lady Trench in "Never Come Back"; Criterion, Jan., 1933, Lady Mary Crabbe in "Fresh Fields"; Wyndham's, Sept., 1934, Mrs. Maria Townsend in "No More Ladies"; Queen's, Dec., 1934, Lady Groombridge in "Inside the Room"; commenced film career 1930, and since 1936 has appeared in "Sweet Devil," "Limelight," "Eliza Comes to Stay," "Return of a Stranger," etc. *Address:* Chobham Farm, Chobham, Surrey. *Telephone No.:* Chobham 48.
(Died 21 Jan., 1943; age 70)

JEFFRIES, Maud, actress ; *b.* in Mississippi, U.S.A., 14 Dec., 1869 ; *e.* Columbia, Tennessee ; *m.* James Nott Osbourne ; made her first appearance on the stage, at Daly's Theatre, New York, in 1889 ; she played small parts here for a year, and was then engaged by Wilson Barrett ; she made her first appearance on the London stage at the New Olympic Theatre, 4 Dec., 1890, as Lydia in " The People's Idol " ; she appeared at the same theatre as Annette in " The Stranger," Olive Skinner in " The Silver King," Annie in " The Lights o' London," Juno in " The Acrobat " ; subsequently she became leading lady with Wilson Barrett, and played, among other parts, Desdemona in " Othello," Nellie Denver in " The Silver King," Almida in " Claudian," Mona Mylrea in " Ben-My-Chree " ; Madeline in " The Acrobat," Ophelia, Pauline in " The Lady of Lyons," Latika in " Pharaoh," Greeba in " The Bondman," Kate Cregeen in " The Manxman," etc. ; she was the original Mercia in " The Sign of the Cross," at St. Louis, 28 Mar., 1895, and at the Lyric, London, 4 Jan., 1896 ; at the Lyric, Feb.,

1897, played Elna in " The Daughters of Babylon " ; May, 1897, played Virginia in " Virginius," and Desdemona in " Othello " ; in the same year accompanied Barrett to Australia; reappeared in London, at the Lyceum, 7 Oct., 1899, as Jane Humphries in " Man and His Makers " ; at Edinburgh May, 1900, played Lygia in " Quo Vadis ? " ; in Oct., 1900, joined Beerbohm Tree at Her Majesty's, and appeared as Marianne in " Herod " ; Feb., 1901, played Olivia in " Twelfth Night " ; toured 1903-4, as Donna Roma in " The Eternal City " ; returned to Australia in 1904, and in 1905-6 starred there with Julius Knight in, among other plays, " Resurrection," " The Eternal City," " Monsieur Beaucaire," " The Darling of the Gods," " If I were King," " His Majesty's Servant," " Comedy and Tragedy," " The Sign of the Cross," " The Silver King," " David Garrick," etc.; in 1904 married a wealthy Australian settler in Christchurch, N.Z., and retired from the stage in 1906; reappeared for a benefit in Aug., 1910, as Galatea in " Pygmalion and Galatea." *Address:* Bowlie, Gundraroo, N.S.W., Australia.
(Died 27 Sept., 1946; age 76)

JENKINS, R. Claud, producer and manager; *b.* Freckenham, Suffolk, 6 Nov., 1878; *s.* of George Frederick Jenkins and his wife Eliza Anne (Trundle); *e.* Holborn Estates Grammar School, St. Clement Danes; *m.* Elizabeth Florence Browne; started his career as limelight boy at Drury Lane Theatre, 1895; gained further experience with Imré Kiralfy at the Earl's Court Exhibitions, and was at the Savoy Theatre under D'Oyly Carte, 1896-1900; subsequently was travelling producer for the same management; was next engaged at Her Majesty's under Beerbohm Tree, and also at Covent Garden, 1900-8, on the production side of the International Grand Opera seasons; produced numerous plays in the provinces, and sketches in variety theatres; produced "Merrie England," Prince's, Sept., 1934; "The Rose of Persia," Prince's, Feb., 1935; "The

Grand Duchess," Daly's, Apr., 1937; toured a new version of "The Gipsy Baron," 1945; during the first World War, served in the Army, 1915-18; during the late War, was engaged in Civil Defence; produced several operettas for the entertainment of troops; is the author of "The Lotus Eaters," "Topsy-Turvey," "Man of Mettle," "Kiss Auntie," "Cupid and Parchment," etc. *Recreation:* Gardening, formerly cricket and boxing. *Address:* 127 Grand Buildings, Trafalgar Square, W.C.2. *Telephone No.:* Abbey, 1443.
(Died 12 Dec., 1967; age 88)

JENNER, Caryl (*née* Pamela Penelope Ripman), director and manager; *b.* London, 19 May, 1917; *d.* of Walter Ripman and his wife Constance (Brockwill Grier); *e.* Norland Place School and St. Paul's Girls' School; studied for the stage at the Central School of Speech Training and Dramatic Art, where she received, among several other awards, the Central School and London University diplomas in dramatic art; began her professional career at the Gate Theatre, 18 Sept., 1935, appearing as Marie's Sister in "Karl and Anna," and acting as assistant stage-manager; Westminster, Oct., 1935, played Clare Lesley in a revival of "Lady Patricia"; 1936-8, acted as stage manager for various managements in London and the provinces; in Dec., 1938, became resident director for Sally Latimer's Amersham Repertory Company, directing over 200 plays during the course of the next ten years; remained with this company until Mar., 1949, and during this period was appointed co-director of the Playhouse Theatre Training School and the Amersham Playhouse Schools Mobile Unit; in Nov., 1949, launched Mobile Theatre limited, developed from the Amersham Schools Mobile Unit, to play in isolated towns and villages lacking any form of theatrical activity; a second company was organized in 1951, and a third, for children only, in 1952; by 1960, one touring company for adults and four for children had been formed, under the title English Theatre for Children; Rudolf Steiner, London,

Dec., 1959, presented "Mango-Leaf Magic"; toured Northern Ireland, Jan., 1960, with one of the children's companies; toured Malta, May, 1960, with adult and children's companies; Rudolf Steiner, Dec., 1960, directed "The Coral King"; between 1961 and 1967 directed plays for Young People both for tours, and at the Lyric, Hammersmith, Yvonne Arnaud, Guildford, Belgrade, Coventry, Toynbee, Questors and Garrick Theatres intermittently and at the Arts Theatre with growing regularity; plays directed during this period included "The Circus Adventure," "Amelia's African Adventure," "The Three Wishes," "Lady Andley's Secret," "The Land of Green Ginger," "The Panther and the Unicorn," "The Thirteen Clocks," "The Tingalary Bird," "The Man Who Killed Time," "The Wappy Waterbus," "Mr. Punch—At Home," "The Midnight Child" and "Pierrot and Fat William"; in Oct., 1962, launched the Unicorn Theatre Club for Young People, and re-named her organization Caryl Jenner Productions Ltd., and the three remaining touring companies "The Unicorn Theatre for Young People"; in Oct., 1964, formed the permanent London Company of the Unicorn Theatre and began the process of phasing out the touring work; in July, 1967, the Arts Theatre was taken over on a 6 year lease to establish the first all the year round Young People's Theatre in this country; between then and Sep., 1970, she directed, amongst other plays, "Five Minutes to Morning," "The Snow Queen," "The Royal Pardon," "The Prince, the Wolf and the Firebird," "Parafinalia," "Wraggle Taggle Winter," "The Flight of the Princes," "The Flowers Shall Have a New Master"; apart from administering and directing the Unicorn Theatre Company she also organised performances for young audiences of visiting companies presenting dance-theatre and puppets, of films from this country and abroad and, with Sheridan Russell, instituted Chamber Music Concerts for 5 to 9 year olds; in addition, between 1950 and 1964, she operated Summer Theatre Seasons in Seaford, Southwold, Cornwall and Ayr; in 1970, appointed Chairman of the Young People's Theatre Executive of the Council of Repertory Theatres and representative of that body on the National Council of Theatre for Young People; British representative of the Association Internationale du Theatre pour L'Enfance et La Jeunesse; she served on the Young People's Theatre Panel of the Arts Council of Great Britain for two years from its inception in 1967. *Recreations:* Cooking, photography and doing nothing. *Address:* 4C Observatory Gardens, London, W.8. *Telephone No.:* 01-937 1919.

JENNINGS, Gertrude E., dramatic author; *y.d.* of Louis Jennings and his wife Madeleine (Henriques); her father was a former Editor of the *New York Times*, later M.P. for Stockport; was formerly an actress; has written the following plays: " Uncle Robert's Airship," 1910; " Between the Soup and the Savoury," 1910; " Our Nervous System," 1911; " The Girl Behind the Bar," 1912; " The ' Mind-the-Gates ' Girl," 1912; " Acid Drops," 1914; " The Rest Cure," 1914; " Five Birds in a Cage," 1915; " The Bathroom Door," 1916; " Elegant Edward " (with C. Boulton), 1916; " Poached Eggs and Pearls," 1916; " No Servants," 1917; " Waiting for the Bus," 1917; " The Lady in Red," 1917; also " After the War " (" Husbands for All "), 1918; " The Young Person in Pink," 1920; " Bobbie Settles Down," 1920; " Love Among the Paint Pots," 1921; " Me and My Diary," 1922 ; " Money Doesn't Matter," 1922 ; " Isabel, Edward, and Anne," 1923 ; " The Voice Outside," 1923; " Riquette " (adaptation), 1925 ; " Richmond Park," 1927; " These Pretty Things," 1928; " Scraps," 1929; " The Bride," 1931; " Pearly Gates," 1932; " Family Affairs," 1934; " Our Own Lives," 1935; " In the Fog," 1941; " Whiskers and Co.," 1942; " Sleeping Beauty," 1943; " Aladdin's Cave," 1944; " Bubble and Squeak," 1945; " The Olympian," 1954. *Address:* c/o Samuel French, Ltd., 26 Southampton Street, Strand, W.C.2. *(Died 28 Sept., 1958; age 81)*

JENOURE, Aïda, actress ; *b.* Hanwell, Middlesex ; *d.* of Oscar Ullithorne ; *m.* Howard Cochran ; *e.* in Brussels, Hanover, and Paris ; made her first appearance on the stage in the chorus of the D'Oyly Carte Opera Company in New York, then came to London, and first appeared at the Savoy, 28 May, 1887, in " Ruddigore " ; played her first part of importance at the Star Theatre, New York, 15 Oct., 1888, when she appeared as Penelope in a burlesque of that name, with the late Lydia Thompson ; subsequently played in " The Pearl of Pekin," and " The Babes in the Wood " ; at the Lyric, 4 Jan., 1892, made a pronounced success as Nita in " The Mountebanks " ; appeared at the same theatre in " Incognita," 1892, and " The Magic Opal," 1893 ; at the Prince of Wales's, in 1895, played Mrs. Ralli-Carr in " Gentleman Joe " ; at the Avenue, 1896, appeared in " Monte Carlo " ; has toured extensively in " Dandy Dan, the Lifeguardsman," " The Great Ruby," " Billy's Little Love Affair," " The Duke of Killicrankie," " Peggy Machree," " The Marriage of Kitty," " The March Hare," " The Mountaineers," etc. ; at the Liverpool Repertory Theatre, Nov., 1911, played the Countess of Brocklehurst in " The Admirable Crichton " ; during 1912-13, appeared there in several parts, including Mrs. Western in " The Bracelet," Lady Bracknell in " The Importance of Being Earnest," Fanny Silvain in " Iris," Fairy Queen in " Fifinella," Mrs. Walker in " Instinct," Mrs. Rolfe in " The Conynghams " ; appeared at the Gaiety, Manchester, Dec., 1913, as Mrs. Candour in " The School for Scandal " ; at the New Theatre, London, Feb., 1914, played Mdme. de Brys in " The " Joy-Ride Lady " ; at the Repertory Theatre, Liverpool, 1915, played Sarah in " Walker, London," Ruth Rolt in " Sweet Lavender," etc. ; during the war, spent two years in the Censorship Office at Liverpool ; subsequently acted in Camp Theatres, under the N.A.C.B., for eighteen months ; at the " Q," Feb. to May, 1925, appeared in " The Fraud," " The Round Table," " Adam and Eva," and " Idle Hands " ; Everyman, June, 1925, played Mrs.

Crosby in " Diff'rent," and Dec., 1925, the Grandmother in " Inheritors "; Little, Dec., 1927, Mrs. Bridgenorth in "Getting Married"; in 1928 toured as Mrs. Bewley-Thompson in "Mother's Brother" ; Kingsway, May, 1929, Lady Ferring in "The Autocrat"; subsequently toured in "The Girl in the Limousine."

JEROME, Daisy, comedienne ; *b.* New York, 1881 ; *d.* of J. Witkowski ; sister of Sadie Jerome ; made her first appearance on the stage at the Prince of Wales's Theatre, 8 Jan., 1897, in " A Pierrot's Life " ; subsequently went to the Continent to complete her education ; on her return was engaged for some time in Concert work ; appeared at the Comedy, Manchester, 1902, as Cinderella ; was then engaged for the Lyric Theatre, where she appeared, Apr., 1903, as Elsie in " The Medal and the Maid," subsequently, for a time, replacing Ada Reeve as Miss Ventnor in the same piece ; she made her first appearance on the variety stage, at the Palace Theatre, and has since appeared at most of the leading London and provincial halls ; among some of her successful songs may be mentioned " Starlight Sue " ; " The poor man never gets a chance."

JEROME, Helen, dramatic author; *b.* London, 10 May, 1883 ; *d.* of William Jerome and his wife Mary (Markby); *e.* Vincent's College, Sydney, N.S.W.; *m.* George D. Ali; contributed short stories to magazines and newspapers in Sydney and was subsequently dramatic critic of the Melbourne *Dramatic News*; while in Australia she also published two books, "Petals in the Wind" and "Japan of To-day"; is the author of the following plays; "Pride and Prejudice," 1935; "Limelight," 1936; "Jane Eyre," 1937; "Charlotte Corday," 1939; revised "All the Comforts of Home," 1942; author of the book "The Secret of Woman." *Address :* 995 Fifth Avenue, New York City; and 48 Shore Road, Old Greenwich, Conn., U.S.A.

JEROME, Jerome Klapka, dramatic author and novelist; *b.* Walsall, 2 May, 1859; *s.* of Rev. Jerome Clapp Jerome; *m.* Georgina Henrietta Stanley Nesza; was originally a clerk, then a schoolmaster, and subsequently, for two and a half years, was an actor, his experiences being related in " On the Stage and Off "; author of the following plays: " Barbara," 1886; " Fennel," 1888; " Sunset," 1888; " New Lamps for Old," 1890; " Ruth," 1890; " Woodbarrow Farm," 1891; " The Prude's Progress," 1895; " The Rise of Dick Halward," 1896; " Biarritz " (with Adrian Ross), 1896; " The Mac Haggis," 1898; " Miss Hobbs," 1900; " Tommy and Co.," 1904; " Susan in Search of a Husband," 1906; " The Passing of the Third Floor Back," 1907; " Fanny and the Servant Problem," 1908; " The Master of Mrs. Chilvers," 1911; " Esther Castways," 1913; " Poor Little Thing " (from the French), 1914; " The Great Gamble," 1914; " Cook," 1917; was founder and editor of *To-day*, and *The Idler*; has written several novels, including " Three Men in a Boat," " Idle Thoughts of An Idle Fellow," " John Ingerfield," " Paul Kelver," etc. *Address* : 41 Belsize Park, N.W. *Club* : National Liberal.

(Died 14 June, 1927; age 68)

JEROME, Rowena, actress; *b.* 12 Dec., 1890; *d.* of Jerome K. Jerome and his wife, Georgina Henrietta (Nesza); made her first appearance on the stage at the King's Theatre, Glasgow, Apr., 1911, as Mrs. Peekin in " The Master of Mrs. Chilvers," and made her first appearance in London, at the Royalty Theatre, 26 Apr., 1911, in the same part; at the Prince of Wales's Theatre, Jan., 1913, appeared as Virginia Grey in " Esther Castways "; at the Vaudeville, Dec., 1913, played Robina Pennicuique in " Robina in Search of a Husband "; at the Criterion, June, 1914, Pauline in " A Scrap of Paper "; at the St. James's, Sept., 1914, Dolly Tukes in " Those Who Sit in Judgment "; at the Queen's, Apr., 1917, Stasia in " The Passing of the Third Floor Back." *Address* : 41 Belsize Park, N.W.

JEROME, Sadie, actress; *b.* New York, 1876; *d.* of J. Witkowski, a cotton-planter before the American War, who later embarked in finance; *e.* at the Frederick Seminary, Frederick, Maryland; *m.* Albert Herzberg; made her first appearance on the stage, 1894; appeared at the Prince of Wales's, 1895, as Lalage Potts in " Gentleman Joe "; same theatre, 1896, played Niagara G. Wackett in " Biarritz "; appeared at the Opéra Comique, Aug., 1896, as Lady Ascotte in " Newmarket "; retired from the stage for nearly six years; reappeared in 1904, in South Africa, playing in " Cousin Kate "; subsequently toured there in " Just Like Callaghan," " When We were Twenty-one," " The Tyranny of Tears," " Twelfth Night," etc.; at the Garrick, London, Aug., 1906, played Mrs. McMurray in " The Morals of Marcus "; at the Duke of York's, June, 1907, played in " Divorçons "; at the Coronet, Dec., 1913, played the Emperor of Morocco in " Dick Whittington "; at the Opera House, Woolwich, Feb., 1914, Antinocris in " The Queen's Portrait "; at the King's Hall, Covent Garden, Feb., 1919, played Mrs. Peters in " Trifles." *Recreations* : Riding and painting. *(Died 30 Apr., 1950; age 76)*

JERROLD, Mary, actress; *b.* London, 4 Dec., 1877; *d.* of Philip F. Allen; *great g.-d.* of Douglas Jerrold, the famous journalist and dramatic author; *e.* Gower Street School; *m.* Hubert Harben; made her first appearance on the London stage at the St. James's Theatre, 14 Apr., 1896, as Prudence Dering in " Mary Pennington, Spinster," meeting with immediate success; at the same theatre, June, 1898, played Yolande Taylorson in " The Ambassador "; for three and a half years was engaged with Mr. and Mrs. Kendal, 1902-5; appeared at the St. James's, Sept.-Oct., 1905, with them, as Gwendolen Giles in " Dick Hope," and Cicely Blake in " The Housekeeper "; appeared at the Scala, Jan., 1906, as Stephanie de Beauharnais in " A Royal Divorce "; at the Lyric, Sept., 1907, with Maxine Elliott, played Peggy Ingledew in

" Under the Greenwood Tree " ; at the Royalty, May, 1908, appeared as Jenny Pargetter in " Nan " ; at the Aldwych Theatre, Mar., 1909, played Chenda Wren in " The Fountain " ; subsequently was engaged for repertory season at the Royalty, Glasgow, and appeared there as Barbara Morrison in " Barbara Grown Up," Madame Arcadina in " The Seagull," Zeolide in " The Palace of Truth," etc. ; from Mar.-May, 1910, was engaged during the repertory season at the Duke of York's Theatre, where she played Lyra in " The Sentimentalists," Marion Yates in " The Madras House," Sarah in " Trelawny of the Wells," and Lady Norah Mountliffey in " Helena's Path " ; at the New Theatre, Sept., 1910, played Enid Lowne in " Young Fernald " ; at the Playhouse, Nov., 1910, Isabella Worthington in " A Single Man " ; during 1911, appeared at the Aldwych, Jan., as Millie Brandon in " The Pride of Life " ; at the Court, Feb., as Jenny in " The Tragedy of Nan " ; toured in various music halls in " The Suffragette's Redemption " ; at the Playhouse, Apr., played Brenda Thompson in " Our Nervous System " ; at the Aldwych, May, Varia in " The Cherry Orchard " ; at the Little Theatre, Oct., 1911, Lyra in " The Sentimentalists," and Mrs. Uglow in " Rococo " ; at the Royalty, Mar., 1912, played Rose Sibley in " Milestones " ; at the Little Theatre, Dec., 1912, appeared as Myra Vale in " If We had Only Known "; at the Shaftesbury, Dec., 1913, as Eve Ripley in " In and Out " ; at the Little Theatre, June, 1914, Lady Ditcham of Drury in " Idle Women " ; at the Royalty, Oct., 1914, Rose in a revival of " Milestones " ; Dec., 1914, Fräulein Schroeder in " The Man Who Stayed at Home " ; at the Haymarket, May, 1915, Jehane de Pera in " The Royal Way " ; at the Royalty, Apr., 1916, played Lady Beaconsfield in " Disraeli " ; Oct., 1916, Mrs. Fletcher in " Home on Leave " ; at the Aldwych, Apr., 1917, Mrs. Frail in " Love for Love " ; at the Savoy, June, 1917, Mrs. Mott in " Humpty-Dumpty " ; at the Garrick, Oct., 1917, Mrs. Corbett in " The Saving

Grace " ; at the Haymarket, June, 1918, Lady Althea Gregory in " Marmaduke " ; at the Kennington, Mar., 1919, Mary Slade in " The Governor's Lady " ; at the Haymarket, Sept., 1919, Mrs. Audrey in " Daddies " ; at the Prince of Wales's, Feb., 1920, Ada in " The Young Person in Pink " ; at the Haymarket, Apr., 1920, Mrs. Morland in " Mary Rose " ; Aug., 1921, Susan Throssel in " Quality Street " ; at the St. James's, Nov., 1922, Princess Natalia Rosanova in " The Beating on the Door " ; at the New, Dec., 1922, Mrs. Challenor in " The Great Well " ; at the St. Martin's, Mar., 1923, Mrs. Broxopp in " The Great Broxopp " ; July, 1923, Kezia Spinfield in " Melloney Holtspur " ; Nov., 1923, Madame Hamelin in " The Fledglings " ; at the Apollo, Feb., 1924, Mrs. Star in " The Fairy Tale " ; at the Savoy, Feb., 1924, Mrs. Baird in " Lord O' Creation " ; Mar., 1924, Mrs. Merrytree in " Blinkers " ; at Drury Lane, June, 1924, Maria Blackshaw in " London Life " ; at the Savoy, Sept., 1924, Mrs. Purdie in " The Sport of Kings " ; New, July, 1925, Katherine Sundale in " We Moderns " ; Comedy, July, 1925, Rose Lavender in " The Lavender Ladies " ; during 1926–7, toured in Australia, with Dion Boucicault, playing in " Mary Rose," " Quality Street " and " What Every Woman Knows"; on returning to London, appeared at the Strand, Apr., 1927, as Mrs. Culver in " The Constant Wife"; Savoy, June, 1927, played Mrs. Price in " Wild-Cat Hetty"; Aug., 1927, Granny in " Barbara's Wedding"; Shaftesbury, Sept., 1927, Lady Minster in " The High Road"; Garrick, May, 1928, Mrs. Waterhen in " Call Me Georges"; went to New York, and appeared at the Henry Miller Theatre, Nov., 1928, as Mrs. Tabret in " The Sacred Flame"; returned to London to play the same part at the Playhouse, Feb., 1929; Playhouse, Feb., 1930, played Amy Widecombe in " Devonshire Cream"; Lyric, Apr., 1930, Mrs. Trevelyan in " Debonair "; Duke of York's, Oct., 1930, Jennie Pierce in " All that Glitters"; Criterion, Aug., 1931, Mrs. Wilder in " Those Naughty Nineties"; Embassy and St. Martin's,

Nov., 1931, Mrs. Bolton in "Britannia of Billingsgate"; Alhambra, Glasgow, Oct., 1932, Edith Black in "What Am I Bid?"; Lyric, Dec., 1932, Mrs. Hallam in "Another Language"; Strand, May, 1933, Lady Occleve in "Sally Who?"; Duchess, Nov., 1933, Mrs. Radfern in "Laburnum Grove"; Haymarket, Feb., 1935, Lucy Lannacott in "Barnet's Folly"; New, Apr., 1935, Lucy Amorest in "The Old Ladies"; Ambassadors', Mar., 1936, Clare Lawrence in "Children to Bless You!"; Strand, Apr., 1936, Janie Northorpe in "Baby Austin"; Shaftesbury, Dec., 1936, Lady Fenwick in "Heart's Content"; Phoenix, Apr., 1937, Mrs. Baker in "Climbing"; Ambassadors', Oct., 1937, Mrs. Jarrow in "Yes and No"; New, May, 1938, Lady March in "People of Our Class"; Richmond, June, 1939, Lady McLaren in "Summer Snow"; and Feb., 1940, Deborah Benton in "White Elephants"; Globe, Jan., 1941, played Mrs. Coade in "Dear Brutus"; Apollo, Nov., 1941, Cousin Irene Tree in "Ducks and Drakes"; Strand, Dec., 1942, Martha Brewster in "Arsenic and Old Lace," which she continued to play for nearly three-and-a-half years, and again for a short revival of the play, at the Cambridge Theatre, Apr., 1946; Apollo, May, 1946, played Nana in "The Wind is Ninety"; toured, July, 1946, as Emily in "But For the Grace of God," and played the same part at the St. James's, Sept., 1946; Duke of York's, May, 1947, Vera Whittaker in "We Proudly Present"; Duchess, Nov., 1948, Miss Mabel in the play of that name; Lyric, Hammersmith, Jan., 1950, Lady Wrathie in "Shall We Join the Ladies?" and Cuthman's Mother in "The Boy With a Cart"; Oct., 1950, Lucy Amorest in "The Old Ladies"; commenced film career, 1931, and has appeared in numerous pictures. *Address:* 1 Beaumanor Mansions, Queensway, W.2. *Telephone No.:* Bayswater 2091. *(Died 3 Mar., 1955; age 77)*

JESSE, F. Tennyson, dramatic author; *d.* of Rev. Eustace Tennyson Jesse; *m.* H. M. Harwood; author of "The Mask" (with H. M. Harwood),

1913; "Billeted" (with H. M. Harwood), 1917; "The Hotel Mouse" (with H. M. Harwood), 1921; "Quarantine," 1922; "The Pelican" (with H. M. Harwood), 1924; "Anyhouse," 1925; "How to be Healthy Though Married" (with H. M. Harwood), 1930; "Birdcage" (with Harold Dearden), 1950; "A Pin to See the Peepshow" (with H. M. Harwood), 1951. *Address:* 11 Melina Place, St. John's Wood, N.W.8. *Telephone No.:* Cunningham 5766. *(Died 6 Aug., 1958; age 69)*

JESSE, Stella, actress; *b.* Lowestoft, 6 Jan., 1897; *d.* of the Rev. Eustace Tennyson Jesse; *e.* Cheltenham and Paris; *m.* Eric Simpson; was a pupil at the Academy of Dramatic Art, 1914-5; made her first appearance on the stage, at the Apollo Theatre, 20 Mar., 1916, as Molly Preston in a revival of "The Man who Stayed at Home"; at the Royalty, Apr., 1916, succeeded to the part of Lady Cudworth in "Disraeli"; Oct., 1916, played Enid Fletcher in "Home on Leave"; Aug., 1917, Penelope Moon in "Billeted"; at the Haymarket, Sept., 1919, appeared as Bobbette Audrey in "Daddies"; at the Ambassadors', Mar., 1920, as Miss Fairchild in "Three Wise Fools"; at the New Theatre, July, 1920, as Sylvia Dermott in "I'll Leave it to You"; at the Royalty, Nov., 1920, as the Hon. Muriel Pym in "Milestones," and Feb., 1921, as Joyce Traill in "A Social Convenience." *Recreations:* Reading, travelling, and being in the open air. *Address:* 94 Addison Road, W.14. *Telephone No.:* Park 9358.

JESSEL, Patricia, actress; *b.* Hong Kong, China, 15 Oct., 1920; *d.* of Clement Edward Jessel, B.E.M., and his wife Ursula Theodora (Buckley); *e.* Convent of St. Philomena, and Storrington College, Westcliff; is a great-niece of Lillah McCarthy; *m.* J. C. Feinberg; studied for the stage under Italia Conti, from 1929; made her first appearance on the stage at the Lyceum Theatre, Sheffield, Dec., 1933, as Wendy in "Peter Pan"; in Nov., 1936, joined the Manchester Repertory

Theatre, Rusholme, and remained there three years, eventually playing leading parts; appeared at the Richmond Theatre, Sept., 1942, as Sybil Cartwright in "All This and To-Morrow"; joined the Shakespeare Memorial Theatre company, Stratford-on-Avon, 1943 season, and played Viola in "Twelfth Night," Goneril in "King Lear," Helena in "A Midsummer Night's Dream," Emilia in "Othello," and Paulina in "A Winter's Tale"; during the 1944 season appeared there as Lady Macbeth and as Katherine in "The Taming of the Shrew"; then toured in Donald Wolfit's company and, at the Winter Garden Theatre, Feb., 1945, played Lady Macbeth, and Goneril in "King Lear"; subsequently toured with the company, when she also appeared as Mistress Ford in "The Merry Wives of Windsor" and Maria in "Twelfth Night"; Winter Garden, Feb.–Mar., 1946, played Lady Macbeth; Torch, Sept., 1947, Miss Amesbury in "The Long Shadow"; in the spring of 1948 appeared in several productions at the "Q" Theatre; Winter Garden, Nov., 1948, played Vanessa in "The Solitary Lover"; at the Bedford Theatre, Camden Town, from Feb., 1949, again played with Donald Wolfit's company, as Lady Macbeth, Mistress Page, and Maria in "Twelfth Night"; "Q," Aug., 1949, Christine Carson in "Return, My Love"; Saville, Mar., 1950, Jayne Case in "The Platinum Set"; "Q," May, 1950, Pam in "Forsaking All Others"; at the Arts, between July and Dec., 1950, appeared as Lady Ariadne in "Heartbreak House," Savina Grazia in "The Mask and the Face," and the Princess of the Western Regions in "Lady Precious Stream"; Wyndham's, May, 1951, played Mrs. Breitenspiegel in "The Love of Four Colonels," in which she remained for nearly two years; next appeared at the Winter Garden, Oct., 1953, as Romaine in "Witness For the Prosecution," and played this part for a year; made her first appearance on the New York stage at the Henry Miller Theatre, 16 Dec., 1954, in the last-named part, for which performance she received the Antoinette Perry, the New York Drama Critics, the Lambs and the "Show Business" Awards; Golden, New York, Oct., 1957, Dr. Monique Rigaud in "Monique"; returned to London, where, at the Strand, Feb., 1958, she played Lisa Koletsky in "Verdict"; Royal Court, Sept., 1958, Mrs. Broadbent in "Lady on the Barometer"; Arts, Mar., 1959, Agata in "The Buskers"; Aldwych, Aug., 1959, Miss Forbes in "The Sound of Murder"; Duke of York's, May, 1960, Germaine Barnier in "It's in the Bag"; Shubert, Newhaven, Conn., Jan., 1961, played Julia in "Catstick"; Hudson, New York, Mar., 1961, took over the part of Albertine Prine in "Toys in the Attic," subsequently touring the U.S., Sept., 1961–Feb., 1962, when she played Carrie Berniers in the same production; joined the Old Vic Company, London, Mar., 1962, to play the following parts: Queen Margaret in "Richard III," Juno in "The Tempest," and Lady Macbeth in "Macbeth" (succeeding Maxine Audley in the last part); Goodman Theatre, Chicago, 1963, played Epifania in "The Millionairess"; Yvonne Arnaud Theatre, Guildford, England, May, 1965, played Lizaveta Bogdanovna in "A Month in the Country," and June, 1965, Chorus in "Samson Agonistes"; has appeared frequently in television plays, including: "He Who Gets Slapped" (New York), "Close Quarters" (New York), "Hamlet" (London), 1961, and "The Sound of Murder" (London), 1964. *Favourite parts:* Lady Macbeth, Katherine in "The Taming of the Shrew," Paulina, and Eliza in "Pygmalion." *Address:* 17 Old Church Street, Chelsea, S.W.3. *Telephone No.:* Flaxman 9517.
(Died 8 June, 1968; age 47)

JEWELL, Izetta (Kenney), actress; *b.* Hackettstown, N.Y., 24 Nov., 1883; *e.* East Greenwich Academy, Rhode Island; *m.* William G. Brown; studied for the stage at the American Academy of Dramatic Arts, New York; made her first appearance on the stage at Wilmington, North Carolina, 14 May, 1900, in "Tess," subsequently appearing as Lavender in "Sweet Lavender"; during the same year she toured as Poppœa in "Quo Vadis?"

and in 1901 toured the New England States, and then joined the "stock" company at the Castle Square Theatre, Boston; during 1903 she toured in "Near the Throne," "Paul Revere," etc.; the following season she played in various "stock" companies, and in 1905 appeared at Proctor's 125th Street Theatre, New York, with the "stock" company; in 1906 joined the Colonial Theatre company, San Francisco, and the following year appeared at Oakland, Cal., and Portland, Ore., where she made a great reputation by her performances of Salomé, Zaza, etc.; during 1908-9 appeared at San Francisco and Portland, and in Oct., 1909, joined Otis Skinner as leading lady, appearing with him as Margaret Druce in "Your Humble Servant"; she appeared in this part at the Garrick, New York, Jan., 1910; the following season she appeared with Otis Skinner, as Leonie Bouquet in "Sire," playing this part at the Criterion, New York, Jan., 1911; at Chicago, Oct., 1911, appeared in "The Girl in the Barracks"; subsequently touring with J. K. Hackett, in "The Grain of Dust"; at the Criterion, New York, Jan., 1912, played Dorothy Hallowell in "A Grain of Dust"; next played a "stock" engagement at Washington; in Nov., 1912, commenced a "stock" engagement at Los Angeles; during 1918, toured in "In a Net." *Recreation:* Riding. *Clubs:* Professional Woman's League, and Playgoers', New York.

JOB, Thomas, dramatic author; *b.* Conwil Elvet, Carmarthenshire, South Wales, 10 Aug., 1900; *s.* of Edwin Mansel Job and his wife Emma Augusta (Beard); *e.* University of Wales (B.A.); *m.* Edith Ann Robinson; went to the United States in 1924, and was engaged as a Professor of English Literature for ten years; he studied Drama at the Yale School, and subsequently at the Carnegie Technical College; is now a Professor of Dramatic Literature and Playwriting at the Carnegie Technical College, Pittsburgh; is the author of the following plays: "Barchester Towers" (adaptation), produced for the Theatre Guild, 1937; "Alas, Regardless," 1940; "Dawn in Lyonesse," 1940; "Uncle Harry," 1942; "Thérèse (adaptation of "Thérèse Raquin"), 1945; became a naturalized subject of the United States, 1940. *Address:* Carnegie Institute of Technology, Pittsburgh, Pa., U.S.A.
(Died 31 July, 1947; age 46)

JOEL, Clara, actress; *b.* Jersey City, New Jersey, U.S.A., 1890; *m.* William Boyd (mar. dis.); gained early experience in "stock" companies; at the Grand Street Theatre, New York, Oct., 1908, played Helen Cameron in "On Trial for his Life," and Ellen Neal in "Common Clay"; during 1913, toured as Mary Turner in "Within the Law"; during 1914-15, played lead with the Colonial Stock company, Cleveland; during 1916 toured as the Woman in "The Eternal Magdalene"; at the Eltinge, Aug., 1917, Rita Sismondi in "Business Before Pleasure"; at the Lyric, New York, Jan., 1920, Marna Lynd in "The Light of the World"; at the Greenwich Village, Jan., 1921, Mrs. Bill Trainor in "Near Santa Barbara"; at the Ritz, Feb., 1923, Eleanor Ainsworth in "The Sporting Thing To Do"; Times Square, Apr., 1925, Judy in "Mismates"; Aug., 1932, toured in the O'Neill triology, "Mourning Becomes Electra."

JOHANN, Zita, actress; *b.* in Hungary, 14 July, 1904; *m.* (1) John Haussman (mar. dis.); (2) John McCormick (mar. dis.); made her first appearance on the New York stage at the Garrick Theatre (for the Theatre Guild), 14 Apr., 1924, as the first Woman Prisoner in "Man and the Masses"; at the Sam H. Harris, Nov., 1924, played Judith in "Dawn"; Guild Theatre, Jan., 1926, Kruna in "The Goat Song"; Plymouth, Sept., 1928, the Young Woman in "Machinal"; Hudson, Apr., 1930, Natascha in "Troyka"; Booth, Sept., 1930, Sonia in "Uncle Vanya"; Henry Miller Theatre, Jan., 1931, Eve Redman in "To-Morrow and To-Morrow"; Masque, Oct., 1934, Lisl Heller in

"Waltz in Fire"; Imperial, Mar., 1935, Ione in "Panic"; National, for the Players, May, 1935, Mary Norton in "Seven Keys to Baldpate"; commenced film career 1932, and appeared in "The Struggle," "Tiger Shark," "The Mummy," "Luxury Liner," "The Man Who Dared," "The Sin of Nora Moran," "Grand Canary," etc. *Address:* c/o Actors' Equity Association, 45 West 47th Street, New York City, U.S.A.

JOHANSEN, Aud, actress, dancer and vocalist; *b.* Norway, 17 Jan., 1930; *d.* of Henry Johansen and his wife Aslaug (Rage); *e.* Kongsgard Skole, Stavanger, and at Bergen; studied for the ballet in Norway and London; first appeared as a child at Bergen, 1940, in a war-time *revue*; made her first appearance in London at the Cambridge, 1949, in the *revue* "Sauce Tartare"; His Majesty's, Nov., 1950, played Cora Pearl in "Music At Midnight"; later in the same month, at the same theatre, played Caprice in "Blue For a Boy," which ran for over eighteen months; Piccadilly, May, 1953, appeared in the *revue* "Over the Moon"; Criterion, Apr., 1954, played in the *revue* "Intimacy at 8.30"; has also appeared in cabaret in London and on the Continent. *Hobby:* Interior decorating. *Recreation:* Travelling abroad when possible. *Address:* 3 Kensington Park Gardens, London, W.11. *Telephone No.:* Bayswater 6308.

JOHN, Evan, actor, dramatic author and producer; *b.* London, 9 Apr., 1901; *s.* of Harry Butler Simpson and his wife Eva (Le Mesurier); *e.* Winchester and University College, Oxford; *m.* Dorothy Holmes-Gore; made his first appearance on the stage at the Playhouse, Liverpool, Jan., 1927, as Mackenzie in "Abraham Lincoln"; during the same year was engaged with the Lena Ashwell Players; during 1928, toured as Frush in "Thark"; made his first appearance in London at the Fortune Theatre, 24 Sept., 1928, as Concièrge in "Napoleon's Josephine"; during 1929–30, was engaged as stage-manager, producer and actor

at the Festival Theatre, Cambridge; in 1931, was producing and acting at the Huddersfield Repertory Theatre; at the New, June, 1931, played Piquoiseau in "Sea-Fever"; Westminster, Nov., 1931–July, 1932, was engaged acting and as stage-manager in "The Anatomist," "A Pair of Spectacles," "Tobias and the Angel," "Love's Labour's Lost," etc.; Shaftesbury, Apr., 1933, played Patrick Leary in "Crime on the Hill"; Sadler's Wells, Jan., 1934, Gonzalo in "The Tempest"; Westminster, Dec., 1934, Michael in "Three for Luck"; Playhouse, Apr.–May, 1935, Robert Cokeson in "Justice", and Harris in "A Family Man"; Old Vic., Sept., 1936, Holofernes in "Love's Labour's Lost"; Mercury, Feb., 1937, The Abbot in "The Ascent of F.6," which he also played at the Little, Apr., 1937; produced "Typhoon," 1929; "Tobias and the Angel," 1932; "Aureng-zebe," 1933; "Reverie of a Policeman," 1936; also wrote and produced "The Dark Path," 1928; "Two Kingdoms," 1934; "King-at-Arms," 1935; has also written several one-act plays and a life of Charles I; has arranged several stage-fights and has lectured on the history of sword-fighting. *Favourite part:* The Dauphin in "St. Joan." *Hobbies:* Carpentry and fencing. *Club:* Arts Theatre. *Address:* Neal's Farm, Wyfold, near Reading, Berks. *Telephone No.:* Checkenden 58. *(Died 1953)*

JOHN, Graham (*né* Graham John Colmer), dramatic author and lyrist; *b.* London, 13 July, 1887; *s.* of Joseph Grose Colmer, C.M.G., and his wife Margaret (Black); *e.* Rugby and Corpus Christi, Oxford; *m.* Bay O'Farrell Kelly; was a member of the O.U.D.S. and subsequently toured professionally; served in the Army, 1914–18, and was awarded the M.C.; was engaged on the Stock Exchange until 1925; contributed to "Nine o'Clock Revue," 1922; "Little Revue Starts at Nine," 1923; "Mercenary Mary," 1925; "Just a Kiss," 1926; "Ripples," 1931; "Gay Deceivers," 1935; wrote the lyrics of "By the Way," 1924; "Hearts and Diamonds,"

1926; "The Street Singer," New York, 1930; "Give Me a Ring," 1933; " Seeing Stars," 1935; "Swing Along," 1936; "Venus in Silk," 1937; author of "My Son John," 1926, and (with Guy Bolton) "Blue Eyes," 1928; adapted (with Hastings Turner) "Venus in Silk," 1937; contributed to "Up and Doing," 1941; "Fine and Dandy," 1942; " Jack and Jill," 1942; "Magic Carpet," 1943; edited "Panama Hattie," 1944; Army Liaison Officer to Department of National Service Entertainment, 1939–45; wrote and directed "Saturday Night Revues," for B.B.C., 1926; also engaged in motion picture work in Hollywood, 1931–33. *Recreations:* Reading, golf, and gardening. *Clubs:* Garrick and Stage Golfing ˙Society. *Address:* Meadow Cottage, Ferring, Sussex. *Telephone No.:* Goring-by-Sea 42085; or Sloane Avenue Mansions, S.W.3. *Telephone No.:* Kensington 7020.

JOHN, Rosamund (*née* Nora Rosamund Jones), actress; *b.* London, 19 Oct., 1913; *d.* of Frederick Henry Jones and his wife Edith Elizabeth (Elliott); *e.* Tottenham High School; *m.* (1) Hugh Russell Lloyd (mar. dis.); (2) Hon. John Silkin; made her first appearance, as a film actress, 1934, in "The Secret of the Loch"; made her first appearance on the regular stage, at the Shakespeare Memorial Theatre, Stratford-on-Avon, Apr., 1935, walking-on in "Antony and Cleopatra"; first appeared in London, at the New Theatre, 14 Oct., 1936, as the Attendant to Cleopatra in the same play; Adelphi, Feb., 1937, appeared in the Cochran *revue*, "Home and Beauty"; Saville, Feb., 1938, played Grace Whitson in "Welcome, Stranger"; Piccadilly, July, 1940, Judith Anderson in "The Devil's Disciple"; spent the next seven years in films; reappeared on the regular stage at Wyndham's, Oct., 1947, when she played Gloria Clandon in "You Never Can Tell"; Vaudeville, June, 1950, appeared as Bella Massingham in "Gaslight"; St. Martin's, Apr., 1951, appeared in "Shavings," a programme of one-act comedies by Bernard Shaw, when she played the Strange Lady in "The Man of Destiny" and "Z" in

"Village Wooing"; Winter Garden, May, 1952, played Harriet in "Dragon's Mouth"; "Q," Jan., 1953, Cleone Browne in "The Golden Thread"; toured, autumn, 1953, as Jane Baird in "A Chance of Happiness"; Westminster, June, 1959, Jane Palmer in "Murder on Arrival"; among her principal films, are "The First of the Few," "The Gentle Sex," "Tawny Pipit," "The Way to the Stars," "Fame is the Spur," etc. *Address:* 10 Hanover House, St. John's Wood, London, N.W.8. *Telephone No.:* Primrose 2728.

JOHNS, Eric, theatre critic and journalist; *b.* Chester, 9 Sept., 1907; *s.* of William Johns and his wife Nellie (Kelsall); *e.* University College of Wales, Swansea (B.A. Hon.); for a short period was an actor, and first appeared at the Everyman Theatre, 18 Mar., 1930, as the Lay Brother in "The Fire in the Opera House"; from 1931–8, engaged in theatre and film publicity, and travelled extensively in Europe, writing articles on the theatre in the countries he visited; during 1938–9, engaged in theatre publicity in London, with Robert Jorgensen; Air Ministry, 1940–5; appointed assistant editor of *The Stage,* July, 1945, and appointed editor in July, 1952; was a regular contributor to *Theatre World,* from 1932; with Anton Dolin, collaborated on a biography of Alicia Markova, 1950. *Recreations:* Exploring the theatrical past, and going to the ballet. *Clubs:* Arts Theatre and Green Room. *Address:* "The Stage," 19 Tavistock Street, London, WC2E 7PA or 253 New Church Road, Hove, Sussex, BN3 4EE. *Telephone Nos.:* 01-836 5213 or Brighton 49387.

JOHNSON, Bill, actor and vocalist; *b.* Baltimore, Md., U.S.A., 22 Mar., 1918; *s.* of Edward McKenna Johnson and his wife Lulu Mae (Nichols); *e.* University of Maryland (B.Sc.); *m.* Shirl Conway (Crosman); was formerly engaged in engineering; made his first appearance on the stage at the Pinebrook Theatre, Nichols, Conn., June, 1938, as Second Lieutenant Raleigh in

"Journey's End"; played numerous engagements in summer stock companies, appearing in the juvenile leads in "Having Wonderful Time," "You Can't Take It with You," "Boy Meets Girl," "Room Service," "Margin for Error," "Death Takes a Holiday," "The Tavern," "Of Thee I Sing," "The Pursuit of Happiness," "See my Lawyer," and "The Man Who Came to Dinner"; commenced his singing career as soloist with an orchestra; made his first appearance on the New York stage, at the Booth Theatre, Apr., 1940, in the *revue*, "Two for the Show"; Majestic, Dec., 1940, appeared in "All in Fun"; Hollywood Theatre, Dec., 1941, played Charlie in "Banjo Eyes"; Alvin, Jan., 1943, Rocky Fulton in "Something for the Boys"; National, Nov., 1945, Alex in "The Day Before Spring"; made his first appearance in London, at the Coliseum, 7 June, 1947, as Frank Butler in "Annie Get Your Gun," making an immediate success, and played the part throughout the long fun of the play, over 1300 performances; at the same theatre, Mar., 1951, played Fred Graham (Petruchio), in "Kiss Me, Kate," and was again a marked success; first appeared in films, 1945, in "It's a Pleasure." *Favourite parts:* Raleigh in "Journey's End," Rocky in "Something for the Boys," and Frank Butler in "Annie Get Your Gun." *Recreations:* Riding and sailing. *Hobby:* Raising chickens. *Clubs:* Lambs, New York; Green Room, London.
(Died 6 Mar., 1957; age 41)

JOHNSON, Chic (*né* Harold Ogden Johnson), actor; *b.* Chicago, Ill., U.S.A., 5 Mar., 1891; *e.* North Western University, Chicago; made his first appearance on the vaudeville stage, 1915, with his partner Ole Olsen, and appeared all over the United States. also visiting England and Australia; while in Australia, 1926, appeared in "Tip Toes," and "Tell Me More"; on returning to America, 1926, appeared on the Pacific Coast, at Los Angeles, and elsewhere, in "Monkey Business"; subsequently toured in "Atrocities of 1932" and "Everything Goes"; first appeared on the regular stage in New York, at the Apollo Theatre, June,

1933, when he succeeded Sid Silvers in "Take a Chance," subsequently touring all through the country in the same piece; in 1938, with Olsen, presented "Hellzapoppin," on the Pacific Coast, which was so successful that it was taken to New York and produced at the 46th Street Theatre, Sept., 1938; it again proved such an attraction, that it was performed there and at the Winter Garden over 1400 times in succession; at the Broadhurst Theatre, June, 1939, they presented "The Streets of Paris," without appearing in it; at the Golden Theatre, June, 1941, they presented "Snookie," but did not appear in this play; Winter Garden, Dec., 1941, appeared together in "Sons o' Fun," which was performed nearly 800 times; Ethel Barrymore, Oct., 1942, they presented "Count Me In," without appearing in it; Winter Garden, Dec., 1944, they appeared in "Laffing Room Only"; made their first appearance in London, at the Casino, 23 Feb., 1948, in "Hellzapoppin"; Madison Square Garden, July, 1949, appeared in "Funzapoppin"; Broadway, Sept., 1950, in "Pardon Our French"; they first appeared in films, 1930, in "Oh, Sailor Behave," and have since appeared in several pictures. *Club:* Lambs. *Address:* c/o Lambs Club, 128–30 West 44th Street, New York City, U.S.A.
(Died 25 Feb., 1962; age 70)

JOHNSON, Janet, actress; *b.* Adelaide, South Australia, 29 Nov., 1915; *d.* of Arthur George Johnson and his wife Jean (Ramsay); *e.* St. Catherine's, Toorak, Melbourne; made her first appearance on the stage at Wellington, New Zealand, 1934, as Ann Hargreaves in "The Wind and the Rain," and subsequently appeared in "Sixteen" and "The Shining Hour"; came to England, 1936, and made her first appearance on the London stage at the Criterion Theatre, 2 July, 1936, as Ana in "The Lady of La Paz"; Ambassadors', June, 1937, succeeded Vivien Leigh as Jessica Morton in "Bats in the Belfry"; Open Air, Aug.–Sept., 1937, played Miranda in "The Tempest" and Luciana in "The

Comedy of Errors"; Apollo, Mar., 1938, Mrs. Cherry in "Idiot's Delight"; Savoy (for Repertory Players), Oct., 1938, Joan Haviland in "A Room in Red and White"; His Majesty's, Oct., 1938, again played in "Idiot's Delight"; Aldwych (for Repertory Players), May, 1939, Isobel Castways in "The Admiral's Chair"; St. Martin's, Apr., 1940, Verity Winthrop in "A House in the Square"; entered films in Australia, 1935; in England has appeared in several pictures. *Recreation:* Music.

JOHNSON, Kay, actress; *b.* Mount Vernon, New York, U.S.A., *m.* John Cromwell; studied for the stage at the American Academy of Dramatic Art; made her first appearance on the stage at Chicago, 1923, as Helena, the Robot, in "R.U.R."; made her first appearance in New York, at the Punch and Judy Theatre, 12 Nov., 1923, as Laura Harper in "Go West, Young Man"; at the Broadhurst, Feb., 1924, played Cynthia Mason in "Beggar on Horseback," and appeared in the same part at the Shubert, Mar., 1925; Hudson July, 1925, Patsy Andrews in "The Morning After"; Eltinge, Sept., 1925, Eileen Stevens in "All Dressed Up"; 49th Street, Dec., 1925, Joyce Smith in "One of the Family"; Sam H. Harris, Sept., 1926, Zoe Galt in "No Trespassing"; Eltinge, Feb., 1927, Dorothy Palmer in "Crime"; Playhouse, Jan., 1928, Jan Ashe in "A Free Soul"; in 1929, toured in "The Little Accident," and appeared in Los Angeles as Christina in "The Silver Cord"; she then entered pictures; at the Belasco, Los Angeles, May, 1931, played Eve Redman in "To-Morrow and To-Morrow"; Columbia, San Francisco, Sept., 1931, Christina in "The Silver Cord"; Jan.-Feb., 1932, Roxane in "Cyrano de Bergerac"; Geary, San Francisco, Feb., 1933, appeared in "When Ladies Meet"; at Columbus, Ohio, Dec., 1937, played Lord Finch in "Y^r Obedient Husband," and at Pittsburg, in the same month, Mrs. Addison in the same play; commenced film career 1929, and appeared in numerous pictures to 1935; since 1936 has appeared in "White Banners." *Recreations:* Ten-

nis, swimming, riding, and the piano. *Address:* c/o Hallam Cooley Agency, 9111 Sunset Boulevard, Hollywood. Cal., U.S.A.

JOHNSON, Molly, actress and vocalist; *b.* London, 1903; *d.* of John Johnson and his wife Marie Louise Josephine (Arculler); *e.* Streatham College for Girls and Guildhall School of Music; originally intended to become an artist, and was the Winner of Gold and Bronze Stars at the Royal Drawing Society, for memory drawing, for all schools in England; studied for the stage under Paul Berton, Serafine Astafieva, etc.; made her first appearance on the stage, at the Grand Theatre, Croydon, 1922, as Edith in "The Private Secretary"; first appeared in the West-End, at the Haymarket, May, 1924, when she succeeded Norah Robinson as Tessie Dunton in "Havoc"; went to the United States, and made her first appearance in New York, at the Maxine Elliott Theatre, 1 Sept., 1924, as Tessie in "Havoc"; appeared at the Ritz Theatre, Dec., 1924, as Molly in "Old English," with George Arliss, in whose company she remained three seasons, 1924–7; at the Garrick, New York, Oct., 1927, played Bianca in "The Taming of the Shrew" (in modern dress); Selwyn Theatre, Dec., 1927, Julie Cavendish in "The Royal Family"; toured in repertory in Canada and New York State, 1928; returned to London, 1930; at the Arts and Apollo, Jan., 1930, played Gracie Abbott in "Nine Till Six"; Phoenix, June, 1931, the Telephone Operator in "Late Night Final"; Prince Edward Theatre, June, 1932, appeared in "Fanfare"; Alhambra, Aug., 1932, in "Over the Page"; Savoy, Nov., 1933, in "Please"; Wyndham's, Sept., 1934, played Jacquette in "No More Ladies"; Gate, Mar., 1935, Roxie Hart in "Chicago"; Ambassadors', Apr., 1936, Lady Anne in "The Future That Was"; Strand, Jan., 1937, Paula in "Behind Your Back"; Daly's, Apr., 1937, Amelie in "The Grand Duchess"; Open Air Theatre, Aug.–Sept., 1937, Ceres in "The Tempest," and the Courtesan in

"The Comedy of Errors"; toured, 1937, in "At the Silver Swan"; Wimbledon, Dec., 1937, played Fairy Heartsease in "The Sleeping Beauty"; toured, 1938, as Ilka in "Countess Maritza"; during 1941-3, toured for E.N.S.A.; toured, Sept., 1942, with Noel Coward in "Present Laughter," "This Happy Breed," and "Blithe Spirit"; Haymarket, Apr., 1943, played Miss Erikson in "Present Laughter" and Vi in "This Happy Breed"; during 1945-6, appeared with the B.B.C. repertory company. *Recreations:* Music and singing. *Address:* 57 Milner Road, Caterham, Surrey. *Telephone No.:* Caterham 2739.

JOHNSON, Orrin, actor; *b.* Louisville, Kentucky; *m.* (1) Katherine Grey (mar. dis.); (2) Isabel B. Smith; made one of his earliest appearances in New York at the People's Theatre, Apr., 1890, as Jack Rogers in "The Governess"; subsequently appeared at Proctor's, 23rd Street, Oct., 1890, as Edwin Seabury in "Men and Women," and Nov., 1891, as Ralph Standish in "The Lost Paradise"; was next seen as Jack Medbury in "The Councillor's Wife," at Madison Square; at the Empire, as Private Jones in "The Girl I Left Behind Me"; at Daly's, in "Peaceful Valley," and at the Star in "The Pacific Mail"; during 1895 appeared as Frank Hamilton in "My Wife's Father," and Frank Kennett in "The Great Diamond Robbery"; at Palmer's, in 1896, played Algy Bloomfield in "Mary Pennington, Spinster," and George Heathcote in "Squire Kate"; at the Garrick, 1897, played in "1 + 1 = 3, or the Sins of the Fathers"; at the Garden, 1897, in "A Bachelor's Romance"; at the Empire, 1898, appeared as George Nepean in "The Liars"; at the Academy of Music, 1899, as James Morton in "Her Atonement"; next appeared at the Lyceum, 1899-1901, as Percival Kingsearl in "Miss Hobbs," the Duke of Barascon in "A Royal Family," and George Buckingham in "The Girl and the Judge"; next toured as Mark Embury in "Mice and Men"; first

appeared as a "star" in Aug., 1903, as the Marquis de Roulerie in "Hearts Courageous," appearing in this part at the Broadway Theatre, New York, Oct. of the same year; at Daly's, in Nov., played Jack Bigelow in "A Japanese Nightingale"; at the Garrick, 1904, played Hawley Harwood in "The Ruling Power"; during 1905 toured in "Ben Hur" and "The Heart of Maryland"; in 1906 played in "The Plainsman"; at the Astor Theatre, Nov., 1906, played John Stedman in "The Daughters of Men," and at the Hudson, Dec., 1906, Valance in "Colombe's Birthday"; during 1907 appeared in "The Girl in White," and at Chicago as the Mayor in "The Man of the Hour"; at Boston, Sept., 1908, played Paul Normand in "The Richest Girl"; playing the same part at the Criterion, New York, Mar., 1909; during 1909, appeared in "The Gay Hussars"; at the Bijou, New York, Oct., 1909, played Edward Chard in "The Master Key"; at the Savoy, New York, Feb., 1910, appeared as Edwin Ford in "Children of Destiny"; at the Criterion, New York, Aug., 1910, played Larry Brice in "The Commuters"; at the Bijou, Oct., 1910, appeared as Oliver King in "New York"; at the Bijou, Mar., 1911, played the Rev. J. J. Bartlett in "The Confession"; at St. Louis, July, 1911, appeared in "Father Jerome"; at the Comedy, New York, Sept., 1911, played Edwin Wise Jessup in "Speed"; in Sept., 1912, played a "stock" season at Los Angeles; at the Comedy, New York, Oct., 1913, played Nevil Ingraham in "The Marriage Game"; at the Harris Theatre, Feb., 1914, Jack Henley in "The Rule of Three"; at the Majestic, Boston, Sept., 1914, William Graham in "The Trap"; at the Criterion, New York, Mar., 1916, Master Ford in "The Merry Wives of Windsor"; at Dayton, Ind., Sept., 1916, the Raggedy Man in "An Old Sweetheart of Mine"; at the Academy of Music, Baltimore, May, 1918, Major Edward Turner in "Peg of Peacock Alley"; at the Morosco Theatre, New York, Nov., 1919, Jules in "Remnant"; at the Standard, New York, Dec.,

1919, Captain Forrest in " The Whirlwind " ; at the Times Square Theatre, Oct., 1921, Dr. Duncan Pell in " Love Dreams " ; Comedy, Mar., 1925, George Lorrimer in " Ostriches." *Address:* Players' Club, 16 Gramercy Park, New York City, U.S.A.

JOHNSON, Philip, dramatic author; *b.* Congleton, Cheshire, 5 Oct., 1900; *s.* of Herbert James Johnson and his wife Mary Elizabeth (Stansfield) ; *e.* Macclesfield Grammar School; has written nearly one hundred one-act plays, sixteen of which have been produced at the Playhouse, Liverpool, by the Liverpool Repertory Company, and several at the Birmingham Repertory Theatre; his first three-act play produced in London was " Long Shadows," Everyman, 1930 ; also author of " Queer Cattle," 1931 ; " Lover's Leap," 1934 ; " One of Us," 1934 ; " Lovely to Look At," 1937 ; " Fish Out of Water," 1941 ; " Who Lies There ? " 1946 ; " The Door Opens," 1947. *Recreations:* Criminology, cats and country life. *Address:* The Owl Pen, West Hill, Ottery St. Mary, Devonshire. *Telephone No.:* Ottery St. Mary 203.

JOHNSTON, Denis (William), O.B.E., dramatic author; *b.* Dublin, Eire, 18 June, 1901; *s.* of the Hon. William John Johnston, Judge of the Supreme Court, and his wife Kathleen (King); *e.* St. Andrews College, Dublin, Merchiston Castle, Edinburgh, Christ's College, Cambridge (M.A.), and Harvard University, U.S.A.; Barrister-at-law (Inner Temple and King's Inns, and Northern Ireland); *m.* (1) Shelah Richards (mar. dis.), (2) Betty Chancellor; author of the following plays: " The Old Lady Says 'No' !," 1929; " The Moon in the Yellow River," 1931; " A Bride for the Unicorn," 1933; " Storm Song," 1934; " Blind Man's Buff " (adapted from Ernst Toller), 1936; " The Golden Cuckoo," 1938; " The Dreaming Dust," 1940, revived in 1946, as " Weep for the Cyclops"; " A Fourth for Bridge," 1948; " Strange Occurrence on Ireland's Eye" (re-written from " Blind Man's Buff "), 1956; " The Scythe and the Sunset," 1958; Director of the Dublin

Gate Theatre, 1931–6; appeared at the Westminster, London, Apr., 1936, as An-Lu-Shan in " Armlet of Jade"; co-directed " Ah, Wilderness," at the Westminster, May, 1936; joined the B.B.C., 1936, becoming a television producer at Alexandra Palace, in 1938; served as a B.B.C. War Correspondent, 1942–5; appointed Programme Director, B.B.C. Television Service, 1946–7; Director of the Provincetown Playhouse, New York, 1952; Professor of English at Mount Holyoke College, Mass., 1950–60; Head of Theatre Department, Smith College, Northampton, Mass., U.S.A., 1961; author of the autobiography "Nine Rivers from Jordan," 1953; "In Search of Swift" (biography), 1959. *Recreation:* Sailing. *Club:* Royal Irish Yacht. *Address:* 7 College Lane, Northampton, Mass., U.S.A.

JOHNSTON, Moffat, actor; *b.* Edinburgh, Scotland, 18 Aug., 1886; *s.* of John Moffat Johnston and his wife Margaret Parke (Boyd); *e.* Watson's School and University of Edinburgh; *m.* Winifred Durie Hodgson; was formerly engaged in the study of analytical chemistry; made his first appearance on the stage at the Theatre Royal, Manchester, Sept., 1905, with the F. R. Benson Shakespearean company, with which he remained several years, and played over two hundred parts; made his first appearance on the London stage at the Coronet Theatre, Notting Hill, 17 Feb., 1908, as the Sexton in "Much Ado About Nothing"; Mar., 1908, played Lopez in "Don Quixote"; at the Kingsway Theatre, 7 Sept., 1912, appeared as Peacey in "The Voysey Inheritance," and in Nov., 1912, played Dunning in "The Eldest Son"; at the Little, Feb., 1913, Herbert Coventry in "A Matter of Money"; in 1914, toured with his own company in Germany; during the War, served as Lieutenant of 8th Sherwood Foresters; after the War, appeared at the Court, Oct., 1918, as the Sea Captain and Fabian in "Twelfth Night"; Mar. 1919, Crabtree in "The School for Scandal"; June, 1919, Major White in "The Lost Leader"; Oct., 1919, Morocco in "The Merchant of Venice"; Feb., 1920,

Minnit in "The Young Visiters"; Dec., 1920, Ægeus in "A Midsummer Night's Dream"; Feb., 1921, Silence and Northumberland in "King Henry IV" (part II); subsequently he went to America and appeared with the Henry Jewett company at Boston, Mass.; made his first appearance on the New York stage at the Garrick Theatre (for the Theatre Guild), 27 Feb., 1922, as Conrad, Barnabas, and the He-Ancient in "Back to Methuselah"; May, 1922, played John Worgan in "What the Public Wants"; Oct., 1922, Dr. Hallemeire in "R.U.R."; Princess, Oct., 1922, The Father in "Six Characters in Search of an Author"; Earl Carroll, Mar., 1923, Earl of Kent in "King Lear"; Garrick (for the Guild), Apr., 1923, Anthony Anderson in "The Devil's Disciple"; Oct., 1923, Geoffrey March in "Windows"; Manhattan Opera House, Nov., 1923, Polonius in "Hamlet," with John Barrymore; 48th Street, Mar., 1924, Macduff in "Macbeth," with James K. Hackett; Frazee, Sept., 1924, Dr. Bornemissza in "The Little Angel"; 48th Street, Feb., 1925, Werle in "The Wild Duck"; Belasco, Sept., 1925, M. Lemercier in "Accused"; Lyceum, Dec., 1926, Pius in "What Never Dies"; Ritz, Mar., 1927, Mr. Justice Grim-Dyke in "The Legend of Leonora"; 48th Street, Jan., 1928, Julian Cleveland in "Cock Robin"; Hudson, Nov., 1928, Professor Eldridge in "To-Night at Twelve"; Lyceum, Feb., 1929, Simon Battersby in "To Meet the Prince"; Knickerbocker, June, 1929, Marquis of Steyne in "Becky Sharp"; Hampden, Nov., 1929, Pope Innocent XII in "Caponsacchi"; Dec., 1929, Baradas in "Richelieu"; Lyceum, Oct., 1930, Edward Garrison in "Solid South"; Broadhurst, Nov., 1930, Von Platz in "An Affair of State"; Guild, June, 1931, Petulant in "The Way of the World"; 48th Street, Oct., 1931, Gideon Bloodgood in "The Streets of New York," and Consul Bernick in "The Pillars of Society"; George M. Cohan, Dec., 1931, Prince Karl in "Berlin"; Booth, Feb., 1932, Dr. Sheppard in "The Fatal Alibi"; at Central City, Colorado, July, 1932, played M. Georges Duval in "Camille"; and appeared in the same part at the Morosco, New York, Oct., 1932; was engaged, for some time, teaching at the Royal Academy of Dramatic Art, London. *Recreations:* Gardening, carpentering, and yachting. *Club:* Players', New York, and Savage, London. *Address:* Narrow Rock Road, Westport, Conn., U.S.A. *Telephone No.:* Westport, Conn., 4278.
(Died 3 Nov., 1935; age 49)

JOHNSTONE, Justine, actress; *b.* Englewood, N.J., U.S.A., 1899; *e.* Englewood and Marchmont; *m.* Walter F. Wanger; made her first appearance on the stage at Long Branch, N.J., 13 Aug., 1914, in "Are You My Wife?"; in Sept., 1914, toured in "vaudeville" on the Keith Circuit; was next seen at Empire Theatre, Syracuse, 25 Nov., 1914, as Estelle in "Watch Your Step"; first appeared in New York, at the New Amsterdam Theatre, 8 Dec., 1914, in the same part; at the Winter Garden, June, 1915, played Columbia in "The Ziegfeld Follies of 1915"; at the Globe, Dec., 1915, played Mary Singer in "Stop! Look! Listen!"; at the New Amsterdam Theatre, June, 1916, appeared in "The Ziegfeld Follies of 1916"; at the Globe, New York, Oct., 1916, played Chiquette in "Betty"; at the Princess, New York, Feb., 1917, Polly Andrus in "Oh! Boy"; at the 44th Street Roof, Dec., 1917, appeared in "Over the Top"; in 1920 turned her attention to the cinema stage; made her first appearance on the London stage, at the Royalty Theatre, 5 Apr., 1924, as Polly Brown in "Polly Preferred"; in 1925 toured in "vaudeville" in the United States; at 49th Street Theatre, New York, Mar., 1926, played Kathleen Forrest in "Hush Money." *Address:* 150 East 55th Street, New York City, U.S.A. *Telephone No.:* Wickersham 2-5027.

JOLIVET, Rita, actress; *b.* New York; *e.* France; *m.* Count Beppi Cippiko; studied for the stage under Madame Thenard and Thérèse Kolb, of the Comédie Francaise, and Miss Bateman (Mrs. Crowe); made her first appearance on the stage, 1903, with the Elizabethan Stage Society, as Beatrice in "Much Ado About Nothing"; appeared at the Haymarket Theatre, 25 May, 1904, as Marie in "Lady Flirt"; at the New Theatre, 30 Aug., 1904, as Lucy Dallas in "Beauty and the Barge"; at the Avenue, May, 1905, as Catharine Hanway in "Jasper Bright"; at the Haymarket, June, 1905, as Angèle in "The Cabinet Minister"; at the Comedy, Aug., 1905, as Phyllis Wade in "The Duffer"; at the St. James's, Nov., 1909, appeared as the Grand Duchess Ina Drovinski in "Eccentric Lord Comberdene"; went to America in 1911, and at the Knickerbocker Theatre, New York, 25 Dec., 1911, played Marsinah in "Kismet," and continued in this play until 1913; at the Lyceum, New York, Sept., 1913, played Gertrude in "Where Ignorance is Bliss"; at the Shubert Theatre, New York, Jan., 1914, played Turandot in "A Thousand Years Ago"; at the Longacre Theatre, New York, Nov., 1914, Julia Grieves in "What it Means to a Woman"; returning from America in May, 1915, she was a passenger by the ss. *Lusitania*, torpedoed and sunk by a German submarine, but was, fortunately, rescued; in the same month went on tour with Seymour Hicks, playing Josie Richards in "Broadway Jones"; subsequently returned to America; at the Comedy Theatre, New York, Oct., 1915, played Boriska Boltay in "Mrs. Boltay's Daughters."

JOLSON, Albert, actor (Asa Yoelson); *b.* 26 May, 1886; *m.* (1) Henrietta Keller (mar. dis.); (2) Ethel Delmar (mar. dis.); (3) Ruby Keeler (mar. dis.); (4) Erle Chenault Galbraith; made his first appearance on the stage at the Herald Square Theatre, New York, 16 Oct., 1899, as one of the mob in "The Children of the Ghetto"; for several years appeared in various circus companies, also with Lew Dockstader's Minstrels; after appearing on the "vaudeville" stage for some time, was engaged for the Winter Garden, New York, and in Mar., 1911, appeared there as Erastus Sparkler in "La Belle Paree"; subsequently appeared there, Nov., 1911, as Claude in "Vera Violetta"; Mar., 1912, as Gus in "The Whirl of Society"; Feb., 1913, Gus in "The Honeymoon Express"; Oct., 1914, Gus in "Dancing Around"; Feb., 1916, Gus Jackson (Friday) in "Robinson Crusoe, Jun."; Feb., 1918, Sinbad in "Sinbad," and continued to play that part until 1920; at Jolson's Fifty-ninth Street Theatre, New York, Oct., 1921, played in "Bombo"; he toured in this play from 1922-4; at the Winter Garden, Jan., 1925, played Gus in "Big Boy"; at the Bayes Theatre, Mar., 1931, played Monsieur Al in "Wonder Bar"; reappeared on the New York stage at the Shubert Theatre, Sept., 1940, as Lone Rider in "Hold On to Your Hats"; commenced film career, 1927, when he appeared in the first "talkie," "The Jazz Singer"; has since appeared in numerous pictures. *Address:* Lambs Club, 130 West 44th Street, New York City, U.S.A.

(Died 23 Oct., 1950; age 64)

JONES, Barry, actor and manager; *b.* Guernsey, Channel Islands, 6 Mar., 1893; *s.* of William John Jones and his wife Amelia Hammond (Robilliard); *e.* Elizabeth College, Guernsey; on the outbreak of War, Aug., 1914, joined the Army, and served with the Royal Guernsey Light Infantry and Royal Irish Fusiliers until Feb., 1921; made his first appearance on the stage at the Grand Theatre, Leeds, with Sir Frank Benson's company, 29 Mar., 1921, as the Clerk of the Court in "Merchant of Venice"; next appeared at Stratford-on-Avon; subsequently again toured with the Benson company; went to America, 1923, played "stock" engagements at Toronto and Boston, and made his first appearance in New York, at the Garrick Theatre (for the Theatre Guild), 14 Apr., 1924, as the fifth Banker and an Officer in "Man and the Masses"; Hudson Theatre, Dec., 1924, played Stanley Winton in "The Bully"; subsequently played "stock" engagements at Boston and Toronto; at the Lyceum, New York, May, 1926, played Algernon Sprigge in "The Sport of Kings," and played the same part in Chicago; at the Selwyn, New York, Dec., 1926, played Robert Mainwaring in "The Constant Nymph"; Playhouse, New York, Jan., 1927, Mago in "The Road to Rome," and continued in this until July, 1928; at the end of 1928, entered partnership with Maurice Colbourne, and for the next three years they toured all over Canada and the United States; they appeared in "You Never Can Tell"; "John Bull's Other Island," "The Philanderer," "The Doctor's Dilemma," "Fanny's First Play," "Arms and the Man," "The Dover Road," "Candida," "Man and Superman," "The Importance of Being Earnest," "The Perfect Alibi," "The Applecart"; they undertook the management of the Ambassadors' Theatre, 6 Oct., 1931, when he made his first appearance in London as King Eric VIII in "The Queen's Husband"; toured in Canada, in this part, 1932, and returned to London to play the same part at the New Theatre, Mar., 1932; at the Haymarket, May, 1932, played The Man in "Queer Cattle"; Sept., 1932, again went to Canada, to play in "Too True to be Good," and "The Apple Cart"; Phoenix, Sept., 1933, Laurence Brooke in "Women Kind"; Nov., 1933, Jaques in "As You Like It"; returned to America, and at the Ritz, New York, Jan., 1934, played Laurence Brooke in "And Be My Love" ("Women Kind"); Apr., 1934, toured as Rudolph in "Reunion in Vienna"; on returning to London, appeared at the Queen's, Sept., 1934, as Charles Lankaster in "Moonlight is Silver"; Comedy, Feb., 1935, Anthony Lynton in "Mrs. Nobby Clark"; Drury Lane, May, 1935, King Stefan in "Glamorous Night"; Shaftesbury, Apr., 1936, succeeded Ralph Richardson as Emile Delbar in "Promise"; Lyric, Oct., 1936, Charles I in "Charles the King"; Embassy, June, 1937, Anthony Thorne in "Lovers' Meeting"; "Q," Nov., 1937, Dr. Mallaby in "The Switchback"; Haymarket, Feb., 1938, Stephen Davis in "Mary Goes to See," and June, 1938, Lord Bayfield in "Comedienne"; Westminster, Feb., 1939, Sir Colenso Ridgeon in "The

Doctor's Dilemma"; toured in Canada, under the auspices of the British Council, Oct., 1939, playing Charles in "Charles, the King," the Judge in "Geneva," and Tobias in "Tobias and the Angel"; at the Henry Miller Theatre, New York, Jan, 1940, played the Judge in "Geneva"; Hudson (for the Players' Club), June, 1940, Valentine in "Love for Love"; subsequently toured in "The Curtain Rises," and as Ilam Carve in "The Great Adventure"; in 1941, toured with Gertrude Lawrence, in "Private Lives" and "Behold We Live," for British War Charities; Shubert, New York, June, 1941, played Dr. Blenkinsopp in "The Doctor's Dilemma," subsequently touring in the same play until Dec., 1941; on his return to England, became a special constable in London; during 1942, toured as Frederick in "Home and Beauty," and appeared in this part at the Playhouse, Nov., 1942; subsequently joined the R.N.V.R., and was demobilized Oct., 1945; toured for E.N.S.A., 1945–6, in "The Apple Cart," in Austria, Italy and Germany; Covent Garden, July, 1948, appeared as Hopeful in "The Pilgrim's Progress"; Phoenix, Mar., 1949, succeeded Eric Portman as Andrew Crocker-Harris in "The Browning Version," and Arthur Gosport in "Harlequinade"; Savoy, Nov., 1950, Inspr. Howard Jones in "Mrs. Inspector Jones"; at the Martin Beck, New York, Oct., 1951, appeared as Socrates in "Barefoot in Athens"; New York City Center, Feb., 1953, Mr. Tarleton in "Misalliance," transferring with the production to the Ethel Barrymore in Mar., 1953; Bijou, New York, Oct., 1957, the King in "The Cave Dwellers"; Haymarket, Apr., 1959, Mackenzie Savage in "The Pleasure of His Company," which ran for one year; since 1950 has appeared in films, radio and television plays. *Recreations:* Painting and gardening. *Clubs:* R.N.V.R., and R.A.C. *Address:* 48 Campden Hill Square, London, W.8; or Le Catioroc, Perelle, Guernsey. *Telephone No.:* Park 4521; or St. Peter 3450.

JONES, Edward, musical conductor and composer; was musical director at the Princess's Theatre, 1881-6, during the late Wilson Barrett's management, and in that capacity composed the incidental music for the various productions which were made at the theatre, including " The Lights o' London," " The Romany Rye," " The Silver King," " Claudian," " Hamlet," " Junius," " Hoodman Blind," " The Lord Harry," " Clito," etc. ; has also officiated as conductor at other London theatres ; during the past few years has composed the music for " The Queen of the Fairies," 1909 ; " The Motor Chase," 1909 ; " Maid Marjorie," 1912 ; " Marusa," 1912 ; " A Pantomime Rehearsal," 1913 ; " Ma'm'selle Champagne," 1914 ; " England Expects," 1914 ; " Odds and Ends," 1914 ; " More," 1915 ; his music for Wilson Barrett's production of " The Sign of the Cross," which included the well-known " Shepherd of Souls," was familiar for several years. *Address :* Ambassadors' Theatre, West Street, Shaftesbury Avenue, W.C.

(Died 10 Aug., 1917)

JONES, Emrys, actor; *b.* Manchester, 22 Sept., 1915; *s.* of Edward Iorweth Jones and his wife Margaret Ellen (Davies) ; *e.* Manchester and in Wales; *m.* (1) Pauline Bentley (mar. dis.); (2) Anne Ridler; studied for the stage under James Bernard, of Manchester; made his first appearance on the stage at the Malvern Theatre, Oct., 1937, as Reynaldo in "Hamlet," in Donald Wolfit's company; from 1938–41, played in repertory at Southampton, Manchester, Swansea, and Peterborough; toured, 1942, as Bruce in "The Late Christopher Bean"; made his first appearance in London, at the Piccadilly, 8 July, 1942, as Malcolm in "Macbeth"; Arts, Dec., 1942, played Torquil in "Holy Isle"; Apollo, during 1943, appeared as Flight-Lt. Teddy Graham in "Flare-Path"; during 1944, toured in the Middle East with Emlyn Williams, playing in "Flare Path" and in "Night Must Fall"; Embassy, May, 1945, played Thomas Lennie in "Letters to a Lady"; Aldwych, Aug., 1945, Lachlen McLachlen in "The Hasty Heart"; St. Martin's,

Feb., 1948, Ned Hardlestone in "Gathering Storm"; "Q," Feb., 1949, Johnnie Lomax in "Jail-Break"; Theatre Royal, Stratford, Sept., 1949, Harry Brooks in "Let the Day Perish"; joined the Bristol Old Vic, Jan., 1950; at the Embassy, June, 1950, played John Featherstone in "Shepherd's Warning"; toured, Nov., 1950, in "Gathering Storm"; toured, 1951, as Tiger Reece in "Winter Sport"; Aldwych, Sept., 1951, played Capt. Ian Owen in "Ten Men and a Miss"; Westminster, June, 1952, appeared as Tony Wendice in "Dial 'M' For Murder," which he played for over a year at that theatre, subsequently touring in the same part, July, 1953–Dec., 1954; Arts, Mar., 1954, played the Supervisor in "The Enchanted"; toured South Africa, July–Dec., 1954, as Det.-Sergt. Trotter in "The Mousetrap," Major Carrington in "Carrington V.C.," and Tony Wendice in "Dial 'M' For Murder"; Her Majesty's, Brighton, Dec., 1954, appeared as the Beast in "Beauty and the Beast"; Arts, London, May, 1955, played André in "The Midnight Family"; Prince of Wales, Cardiff, Apr., 1956, Mac in "Albertine by Moonlight"; toured Australia, Apr.–Dec., 1957, as Julian/David in "Double Image"; Lyceum, Edinburgh, Mar., 1958, Stephen Craig in "The Last Word"; Lyric, Hammersmith, Sept., 1958, Alexander Matveyev in "The Russian"; Pembroke, Croydon, Oct., 1961, played Martin Careva in "The Winner"; Lyceum, Edinburgh, Feb., 1962, Ignatius Van Wyck in "Return to Mirredal"; Richmond, May, 1962, played Clostin in "The Clostin Case"; Comedy, Apr., 1964, Sir George Learoyd in "The Claimant"; toured, Oct., 1964, as Andreas Richeneau in "So Wise, So Young"; Richmond, Apr., 1965, again played Martin in "The Winner"; Arts, June, 1968, Lord William Dromondy M.P., in "The Foundations"; Whitehall, Mar., 1969, Sydney Oliver in "Dead Silence"; Alexandra, Birmingham, Oct., 1969, Winston Churchill in "A Man and His Wife"; has also appeared in television plays, including Mr. Polly in the serial "The History of Mr. Polly," and De Reval in the serial "The Scarlet and the Black," 1965; first appeared in films, 1941, in "One of Our Aircraft is Missing," and has since appeared frequently, recent performances include Robert Ross in "The Trials of Oscar Wilde," 1960. *Recreations:* Riding and golf. *Clubs:* Green Room and Stage Golfing Society. *Address:* c/o London Management, 235–241 Regent Street, London, W1A 2JT.

JONES, Hazel, actress ; *b.* Swarraton, Hants, 17 Oct., 1896; *m.* Harold Dimock Lee; made her first appearance on the stage, at the Savoy Theatre, 14 Nov., 1910, in " The Two Hunchbacks " ; at the Playhouse, June, 1911, played Angeline in " Pomander Walk " ; at the Savoy, Dec., 1911, played in " Where the Rainbow Ends" Jan., 1913, Antigone in " The Headmaster " ; at the Garrick, Sept., 1914, Princess Elizabeth in " Bluff King Hal " ; in the spring of 1916 toured with Matheson Lang as Ruth Harford in " The Mystery of John Wake," and as Jessica in " The Merchant of Venice " ; in 1917, toured as Louise in " The Aristocrat " ; at the Ambassadors', Dec., 1917, played Pandora in " Pandora," and Marygold in " Midas," in the Wonder Tales of Hawthorne ; at the Court, Aug., 1918, played The Wife in " Damaged Goods " ; at the Globe, Nov., 1918, appeared as Theresa de Loget in " L'Aiglon " ; at the Globe, Jan., 1919, played for Marie Löhr as Lady Gilian Dunsmore in " Nurse Benson," subsequently touring in the same part ; at the Ambassadors', Aug., 1919, played Eileen Chase in " Green Pastures and Piccadilly " ; at the Savoy, Sept., 1919, Alice Cook in " Too Many Cooks " ; at the St. Martin's, Oct., 1919, Edith Goodhue in " The Very Idea " ; at the Queen's, Oct., 1919, Margaret Wickham in " Napoleon " ; at Brighton, Nov., 1919, Janet Drage in " Just a Wife or Two " ; during the spring of 1920, again toured in " Nurse Benson " ; Sept., 1920, joined the repertory company of the Everyman Theatre, Hampstead, where she remained until Mar., 1922 ; she then toured as Eliza in " Eliza Comes to Stay " ; at the Little Theatre, Oct., 1922, played

Sada in " The Toils of Yoshitomo " ; in Dec., 1922, at the Comedie des Champs Elysées, Paris, played Juliet in " Romeo and Juliet " ; in Feb., 1923, went to Holland with the Everyman Theatre Company ; in Aug., 1923, toured with Ethel Irving, as Molly in " The Happy Ending " ; in Jan., 1924, toured with Harry Welchman, as Mistress Avery in " Sir Jackanapes " ; in June, 1924, toured as Anne in " The Dover Road " ; at the Everyman Theatre, Sept., 1924, played Judith Anderson in " The Devil's Disciple " ; at the Prince's, Dec., 1924, Liz Walker in " Alf's Button " ; Barnes, May, 1925, Summers in " Fatherhood " ; Aldwych (for the Phoenix), May, 1925, Serina in " The Orphan " ; " Q," May, 1925, Sally in " Idle Hands " ; went to America, Sept., 1925, and appeared at the Municipal Theatre, Northampton, Mass., in " Mr. Pim Passes By," " The Mollusc," " Smith," " Candida," etc.; on returning to London, appeared at " Q," Apr., 1926, as Carol in " Bongola " ; returned to America, Sept., 1926, again played repertory at Northampton; in Jan., 1927, was appointed a Director of the Repertory Co.; since her marriage in June, 1927, has not acted. *Recreations :* Gardening, motoring, and photography. *Address :* 20 Round Hill, Northampton, Mass, U.S.A.

JONES, Henry Arthur, dramatist ; *b.* Grandborough, Bucks, 20 Sept., 1851 ; *s.* of Silvanus Jones, farmer, father of Winifred, Gertrude, and Ethelwynne Arthur-Jones ; brother of Silvanus Dauncey ; *e.* at Winslow, Bucks ; commenced business life in Bradford and was for some time a commercial traveller ; commenced writing plays in 1878 ; his first play was produced at the Theatre Royal, Exeter, 11 Dec., 1878, and was entitled " Only Round the Corner " ; then followed " Hearts of Oak," Theatre Royal, Exeter, 1879 ; " Harmony Restored," Grand, Leeds, 1879 ; " Elopement," Theatre Royal, Oxford, 1879 ; " A Clerical Error," Court, 1879 ; " An Old Master," Princess's, 1880 ; " His Wife," Sadler's Wells, 1881 ; " Home Again," Theatre Royal, Oxford, 1881 ;

"A Bed of Roses," Globe, 1882 ; "The Silver King" (with Henry Herman), Princess's, 1882, which ran for twelve months, and brought him prominently before the public; "Breaking a Butterfly" (with Herman), Prince's, 1884 ; "Chatterton" (with Herman), Princess's, 1884 ; "Saints and Sinners," Vaudeville, 1884 ; "Hoodman Blind" (with Wilson Barrett), Princess's, 1885 ; "The Lord Harry" (with Barrett), Princess's, 1886 ; "The Noble Vagabond," Princess's, 1886 ; "Hard Hit," Haymarket, 1887 ; "Heart of Hearts," Vaudeville, 1887 ; "Wealth," Haymarket, 1889 ; "The Middleman," 1889, "Judah," 1890, "Sweet Will," 1890, and "The Deacon," 1890, all at the Shaftesbury; "The Dancing Girl," Haymarket, 1891 ; "The Crusaders," Avenue, 1891 ; "The Bauble Shop,"Criterion, 1893;"The Tempter," Haymarket, 1893 ; "The Masqueraders," St. James's, 1894 ; "The Case of Rebellious Susan," Criterion, 1894 ; "The Triumph of the Philistines," St. James's, 1895 ; "Michael and His Lost Angel," Lyceum, 1896 ; "The Rogue's Comedy," Garrick, 1896 ; "The Physician," Criterion, 1897 ; "The Liars," Criterion, 1897 ; "The Manoeuvres of Jane," Haymarket, 1898 ; "Carnac Sahib," Her Majesty's, 1899 ; "The Lackey's Carnival," Duke of York's, 1900 ; "Mrs. Dane's Defence," Wyndham's, 1900 ; "The Princess's Nose," Duke of York's, 1902 ; "Chance the Idol," Wyndham's, 1902 ; "Whitewashing Julia," Garrick, 1903 ; "Joseph Entangled," Haymarket, 1904 ; "The Chevaleer," Garrick, 1904 ; "The Heroic Stubbs," Terry's, 1906 ; "The Hypocrites," Hudson Theatre, New York, Aug., 1906, and Hicks Theatre, Aug., 1907 ; "The Goal," Chicago, 1907 ; "The Evangelist" (originally entitled "The Gallilean's Victory"), Knickerbocker Theatre, New York, 1907 ; "Dolly Reforming Herself," Haymarket, 1908 ; "We Can't Be as Bad as All That," Nazimova Theatre, New York, 1910 ; "The Ogre," St. James's, 1911 ; "Lydia Gilmore," Lyceum, New York, 1912 ; "Mary Goes First," Playhouse, London, 1913; "The Lie," Harris Theatre, New York, 1914 ;

"Cock o' the Walk," Cohan Theatre, New York, 1915 ; "The Pacifists," St. James's, 1917 ; author of "Patriotism and Popular Education," 1919 ; also wrote the music-hall sketches, "The Knife," 1909, and "Fall in Rookies !" 1910 ; in Nov., 1891, undertook the management of the Avenue Theatre, where he produced "The Crusaders" and revived "Judah"; wrote "The Divine Gift," published in 1913. *Address :* 19 Kidderpⁿre Avenue, Hampstead, N.W.3. *Telephone :* 3870 Hampstead. *Clubs :* Reform and Athenaeum. *(Died 7 Jan., 1929; age 77)*

JONES, Leslie Julian, composer and librettist; *b.* London, 9 May, 1910; *s.* of the late Julian Jones and his wife Elsie Hannah Barnett; *e.* Kingston-on-Thames Grammar School and Margate College; *m.* Virginia Winter; was engaged in stockbroking business from 1929–37; was part-author and composer of "Friends Romans . . .," "Les Folies de Paris et Londres," and "Copyright Reserved," 1937; "Come Out of Your Shell," 1940; "Rise Above It," 1941; "Whitehall Follies," 1942; "It's About Time," 1942; "Sweet and Low," "This Time It's Love," 1943; "That'll Be the Day," 1945; "Better Late," 1946; "Sugar and Spice," 1948; part-author and composer of "Latin Quarter," 1950; also wrote and composed several radio programmes, "Solitaire," for Ethel Revnell, "Vic Oliver Introduces," etc.; in 1945, entered into management with James Lavall, producing "That'll Be the Day"; during 1943, went to the Middle East, as staff-producer and writer for E.N.S.A. *Address :* 102 Dudley Court, Upper Berkeley Street, London, W.1. *Telephone No. :* Paddington 0072.

JONES, Margo, producing manager; *b.* Livingston, Texas, U.S.A., 12 Dec., 1913; *e.* Texas State College for Women (M.A.); since 1933, at Dallas, Pasadena Playhouse and elsewhere, has produced over 100 plays; in New York, was co-director of "The Glass Menagerie," 1945; directed "On Whitman Avenue" and "Joan of Lorraine," 1946; her first presentation in New York, was at the Music Box, Oct., 1948, "Summer and Smoke," by Tennessee Williams; Biltmore, Sept., 1950, presented and directed "Southern Exposure"; managing director of "Theatres 47, 48, and 49" at Dallas, Texas. *(Died 25 July, 1955; age 41)*

JONES, Robert Edmond, designer and producing manager; *b.* Milton, New Hampshire, U.S.A., 12 Dec., 1887; *s.* of Frederick Plumer Jones and his wife Emma Jane (Cowell); *e.* Harvard University; *m.* Margaret Carrington (Huston); began theatrical designing in 1911; designed the productions of "The Man Who Married a Dumb Wife," "The Jest," "Richard III," "Macbeth," "Redemption," "Hamlet," "Desire Under the Elms," "Mourning Becomes Electra," "The Lady With a Lamp," "The Passing Present," "Night Over Taos," "Lucrece," "Nine Pine Street," "Ah, Wilderness!"; "The Green Bay Tree," "Mary of Scotland," "The Joyous Season," "Othello," "The Seagull," "Everywhere I Roam," "The Philadelphia Story," "A Day in the Sun," "Summer Night," "Kindred," "Juno and the Paycock," "Without Love," "Othello," "Jackpot," "Helen Goes to Troy," "The Joyous Season," "Lute Song," "The Enchanted," etc.; associated with Kenneth MacGowan and Eugene O'Neill in the production of several plays at the Greenwich Village Playhouse, from 1925 onwards, and staged many of Eugene O'Neill's plays; also staged "Holiday" and "Mr. Moneypenny," 1928, and "Serena Blandish," 1929; "Camille," 1932; author (with Kenneth MacGowan) of "Continental Stagecraft." *Clubs:* Harvard, Century, and Players. *Address:* 760 Park Avenue, New York City, U.S.A. *Telephone No.* Butterfield 8–5958. *(Died 26 Nov., 1954; age 67)*

JONES, Samuel Major, actor and stage manager; *b.* Birkenhead, *e.* Ongar Grammar School; *m.* (1) Blanche Stanley; (2) Emily Foxcroft; made his first appearance on the stage, at the Comedy Theatre, Manchester, Easter, 1892, as the Lord Chamberlain in "The Sultan of Mocha"; made his first appearance in London, at the Princess's Theatre, 4 Oct., 1897, as Bill Mullins in "Two Little Vagabonds," which he also stage-managed; at the same theatre, succeeded Charles Warner as Happy Jack in "How London Lives," subsequently touring in the same part for two years; was for four years in South Africa with Leonard Rayne, stage-managing and playing a round of parts; in 1907, was engaged by Messrs. Smith and Carpenter to stage-manage and play parts, and was retained by Messrs. Melville, when they took over the house; remained nine years at the Lyceum Theatre, stage-managing over fifty plays; in 1916, was engaged by Gilbert Miller to stage-manage "Daddy Long-Legs," at the Duke of York's, and under the same management has stage-managed "The Willow Tree," Globe, 1917; "Nothing But the Truth," Savoy, 1918; "Too Many Cooks," Savoy, 1919; "Uncle Ned," St. James's, 1920; "His Lady Friends," St. James's 1920; has since fulfilled similar engagements with F. J. Nettlefold, Apollo, 1921; at the Royalty, 1922; Lyceum, 1922-3; Regent Theatre, 1923-4; Adelphi, 1924; Kingsway, 1926; Court, 1927; Royalty, 1928-29; Matheson Lang tours, 1930-31; he stage-managed twelve pantomimes at the Lyceum Theatre, to 1932; has appeared successfully as Bruno Rocco in "The Eternal City," Baillie Nicol Jarvie in "Rob Roy," Archdeacon Wealthy in "The Christian," the Messenger in "A Message from Mars," Athos in "The Three Musketeers," Seth Preene in "The Lights o' London," Jacques in "The Two Orphans," Taffy in "Trilby," The Sheriff in "A White Man," William in "Jane"; His Majesty's, May, 1933, played the Burgomaster in "Music in the Air"; Embassy, Nov., 1935, Blake in "Murder Gang"; New, Mar., 1936, Dr. Gribble in "Love from a Stranger"; Richmond, Jan., 1938, Matthew Holt in "Needs Must." *Club:* Savage. *Address:* 42 Knolly's House, Compton Street, W.C.1. *Telephone No.:* Euston 1905. *(Died 25 Aug., 1952; age 89)*

JONES, Sidney, composer; *b.* Leeds, 1869; *s.* of A. S. Jones, musician; *e.* at Leeds; where at an early age was well known as a conductor, before coming into prominence as a composer of the song "Linger Longer Loo," 1892; composer of the following, among other, works : " A Gaiety Girl," 1893 ; " An Artist's Model," 1895 ; "The Geisha," 1896 ; " A Greek Slave," 1898 ; " San Toy," 1899 ; " My Lady Molly," 1902 ; " See-See, ' 1906 ; " King of Cadonia," 1908 ; "A Persian Princess," 1909 ; " The Girl from Utah " (with Paul Rubens), 1913 ; " The Happy Day " (with Paul Rubens), 1916 ; was appointed musical director at the Empire, 1905, and composed several ballets for that house, notably " The Bugle Call," and " Cinderella." *Clubs :* Eccentric and Stage Golfing Society. *Address :* 17 Lichfield Road, Kew Gardens, Surrey. *Telephone No. :* Richmond 1737.

JONES, Trefor, actor and vocalist; *b.* Cymmer, Port Talbot, South Wales, 27 Aug., 1902; *s.* of David John Jones and his wife Mary (Jenkins); *m.* Florence Lincoln Fox; studied singing at the Royal College of Music; made his first appearance on the stage at the Lyric, Hammersmith, 16 Jan., 1931, as Hugh Heather in "Tantivy Towers"; St. Martin's, July, 1932, played Lieut. Launcelot Brown in "The Pride of the Regiment"; Drury Lane, May, 1935, Lorenti in "Glamorous Night"; Ambassadors', Sept., 1936, Julian Bromley in "The Two Bouquets," in which he toured, 1937; toured, 1946, in "Big Ben," and at the Adelphi, July, 1946, appeared as Henry Hope in this production; at the Open Air Theatre, Regent's Park, May, 1953, played Feste in "Twelfth Night"; Lyric, Hammersmith, Nov., 1956, played Tino in "Grab Me a Gondola," transferring to the Lyric, W.1, Dec., 1956; has appeared in Covent Garden opera seasons, and in "Hiawatha," at the Royal Albert Hall from 1930–5; has also appeared in films. *Club :* Savage. *(Died 22 Jan., 1965; age 62)*

JONES, Whitworth, actor; *b.* London, 13 Sept., 1873; *s.* of Henry Whitworth Jones and his wife Maria (Page) ; *e.* Radley College and Trinity Hall, Cambs. ; made his first appearance on the stage at Daly's Theatre, 1895, when, for a time, he succeeded Lawrence D'Orsay as the Earl of Thamesmead in " An Artist's Model " ; in 1896 toured as King Stephen in " For the Crown "; was subsequently with the Benson Company for a time ; also toured as the Duke of Buckingham and Fenton in " The Three Musketeers " ; at the Lyceum Theatre, Sept., 1897, played Fortinbras in Forbes-Robertson's revival of " Hamlet " ; subsequently played Douglas Cattermole in " The Private Secretary," and Jack Chesney in " Charley's Aunt," with Penley ; at the Comedy, Apr., 1900, played in " Tess " ; at the Lyceum, Dec., 1900, appeared as the Earl of Westmoreland in " Henry V " ; subsequently toured as Henry V with William Mollison ; at the Garrick, 1901, succeeded Charles Bryant as Lawrence Trenwith in " Iris " ; subsequently went to America, making his first appearance on the New York stage in 1904, at the Bijou Theatre, in " The American Invasion " ; he then left the stage for four years, and went to Egypt, where he was engaged under Lord Cromer ; was special correspondent for *The Daily Telegraph,* and also editor of *The Oriental Daily News ;* he returned to the stage in 1908, appearing with Louie Frear in " The Fortunes of Fan " ; again visited America, where he played a number of leading parts in Shakespeare and old comedy, also playing Mephistopheles in Marlowe's " Doctor Faustus," with Walker Whiteside in " The Melting Pot," Baroudi in " Bella Donna," etc. ; returned to England Jan., 1917, and reappeared in London, at the Duke of York's, where, for a time, he played Jervis Pendleton in " Daddy Long-Legs " ; at the Strand, July, 1917, played Prince Nicholas in " Three Weeks " ; at the Ambassadors', Dec., 1917, played in " Pandora," " Midas," and " Philemon and Baucis " in " The Wonder Tales " ; at the Globe, Jan., 1918, Sir Peter Ellingham in " Love in a Cottage." *Recreations :* Swimming, music, and gardening. *Address :* 3 Pall Mall Place, S.W.1.

JOOSS, Kurt, dancer and choreographer; *b.* Wurtemburg, Germany, 12 Jan., 1901; *m.* Aino Simola; studied music at Stuttgart, where in 1920 he entered the Dramatic School; made his first appearance at the National Theatre, Mannheim; in 1924, he was appointed general producer at the Stadt Theater, Münster, where he produced several ballets, including "A Persian Ballet," 1924; "A Spring Tale," 1925; "In Search of a Wife," 1925; "Dido and Aeneas," 1926; was appointed manager of the Opera House, Essen, 1929, and in 1930 became *maitre-de-ballet*; in 1931 composed the famous ballet "The Green Table," which has since been presented all over Europe, first at the Théâtre des Champs-Elysées, Paris, June 1932, and at the Savoy Theatre, London, June 1933; he formed his company, "Ballets Jooss," in Sept., 1933, and toured all over the world 1933–4, followed by further tours in 1935–6; has produced "Petrouchka," "Le Bal," "Coppélia," "Le Fils Prodigue," "Pulcinella," "Ball in Old Vienna," "The Seven Heroes," "Johann Strauss," "The Mirror," "Larven," "Gaukelei," "Chronica," "The Big City," "A Spring Tale," "Pavane Ball," etc.; presented "Ballets Jooss" at the Old Vic., May, 1938, and again in May, 1939; at the Haymarket, June, 1944, and at the Winter Garden, July, 1945; left for a tour of Canada and U.S.A., July, 1946; his next presentation in London was at Sadler's Wells, Apr., 1953.

JORDAN, Dorothy, actress; *b.* Clarkesville, Tenn., U.S.A., 9 Aug., 1908; *d.* of Edward P. Jordan and his wife Theresa (Harrison); *e.* Clarkesville, and South Western University, Memphis; *m.* Merian C. Cooper; studied for the stage at the American Academy of Dramatic Art; made her first appearance on the stage at the Garrick Theatre, New York (for the Theatre Guild), 10 May, 1926, in "Garrick Gaieties"; at the Liberty, Nov., 1926, danced in "Twinkle Twinkle"; Alvin Theatre, Nov., 1927, played the Bell Hop in "Funny Face"; Nov., 1928, Betty in "Treasure Girl"; commenced film career 1929, and has

appeared in "Black Magic," "The Taming of the Shrew," "The House of Troy," "Devil-May-Care," "In Gay Madrid" ("The Singer of Seville"), "The Call of the Flesh," "Love in the Rough," "Min and Bill," "A Tailor-Made Man," "Young Sinners," "Shipmates," "The Beloved Bachelor," "The Lost Squadron," "Hell Divers," "The Wet Parade," "The Roadhouse Murder," "70,000 Witnesses," "Down to Earth," "The Cabin in the Cotton," "That's My Boy," "Strictly Personal," "Bondage," "One Man's Journey," etc. *Recreations :* Riding and reading.

JORGENSEN, Robert, press representative and journalist; *b.* Copenhagen, Denmark, 30 Oct., 1903; *s.* of Carl Ernest Jorgensen and his wife Matilde Birgitte (Wenck); *e.* St. Josef's College, Copenhagen; *m.* Dora Barnes, actress; after leaving Copenhagen at the age of seventeen, went to New York, where he acted as newspaper correspondent; came to London, 1924, and became press representative to Carl Brisson; subsequently represented J. C. Williamson Ltd., Lee Ephraim, Julian Wylie, etc., in similar capacity; he also managed tours of "Wonder Bar" and "The Merry Widow"; after becoming a naturalized British subject, established his own theatre publicity organization and has acted as press representative, at various times, at the majority of West-End Theatres; acted in same capacity for tours of "Cavalcade," "The Miracle," etc.; was also responsible in a managerial capacity for production of "She Couldn't Say No," 1933, and tour of "The Rose Without a Thorn," 1934; since 1935, was Press representative for productions of Sydney W. Carroll, Jack Buchanan, André Charlot, Jack Waller, Sir Oswald Stoll at Coliseum and Alhambra, Howard Wyndham and Bronson Albery, National Theatre Appeal, etc.; Press representative Open Air Theatre since 1933; arranged the visit of the Old Vic. company in "Hamlet" at Kronborg Castle Elsinore, 1937, and John Gielgud and company in the same play, 1939; is a member of the Theatrical Managers

Association. *Recreations :* Sailing and gardening. *Club :* Press. *Address :* 24 Haymarket, London, S.W.1. *Telephone No. :* Whitehall 8351; and 28 Brook Green, W.6. *Telephone No. :* Riverside 5657.

JOSLYN, Allyn, actor; *b.* Milford, Pa., U.S.A., 21 July 1905; *e.* Philadelphia; *m.* Dorothy Yockel; made his first appearance on the stage in a "stock" company; first appeared in New York, at the Garrick Theatre (for the Theatre Guild), Jan., 1922, in "He Who Gets Slapped," and remained with the Guild for three seasons; at the Morosco, Oct., 1924, played Polverino in "The Firebrand"; Klaw, Dec., 1925, Tranio in "The Taming of the Shrew"; Playhouse, Mar., 1926, Tom in "The Moon is a Going"; Waldorf, Nov., 1926, Edwin Paris and Bubus in "Head or Tail"; Lyceum, Feb., 1927, Constant in "Lady in Love"; Greenwich Village, May, 1927, Eric Brent in "One For All"; Broadway (for Players' Club), June, 1932, Diomedes in "Troilus and Cressida"; Cort, Nov., 1935, Robert Law in "Boy Meets Girl," which he played for eighteen months; Biltmore, Jan., 1938, Morgan Williams in "All that Glitters"; Fulton, Jan., 1941, Mortimer Brewster in "Arsenic and Old Lace," which ran three-and-a-half years; entered films, 1937 and has appeared in innumerable pictures; was a highly popular radio artist, and has written many of the items he has broadcast. *Club:* Players. *Address:* 205 West 54th Street, New York City, U.S.A. *Telephone No.:* Circle 6–2730.

JOUVET, Louis, actor-manager; *b.* Crozon, Finistère, France, 24 Dec., 887; was formerly a chemist; he made his first appearance at a small theatre outside Paris in a melodrama; attempted entry to the Conservatoire on three occasions without success; appeared at the Théâtre des Arts, Paris, 1910, in "Les Frères Karamoff," and next appeared at the Odéon and Châtelet; in 1913, joined Jaques Copeau's company at the Théâtre du Vieux Colombier; served in the first World War from 1914–17; demobilized

in 1918, he went to New York, and remained there for 18 months; in 1922, he went to the Comédie des Champs-Elysées, as stage-director, and became director of the theatre in 1924; he remained until 1934, and made many notable productions there, among which may be mentioned, "La Trouhadec saisie par la débauche," "Le Mariage de la Trouhadec," "Knock," "Amédée ou messieurs en rang," "La Scintillante," "Démétrois," "Le Dictateur," "Malbrough s'en va-t'en guerre," "Jean de la lune," "Domino," "Petrus," "L'amour qui passe," "Madame Béliard," "Tripes d'Or," "Bava l'Africain," "Le coup du Deux Decembre," "Deux paires d'amis," "Au Grand Large," "Le Revisor," "Léopold le Bien-Aimé," "Siegfried," "Amphitryon 38," "Intermezzo," "Suzanne," "Le Prof. d'Anglais," "L'Eau Fraîche," "Un Taciturne," "Le Margrave," "La Machine Infernale," "La Jalousie de Barbouillé," "Le Carrosse du Saint-Sacrement," "La Folle Journée"; has been director of the Athénée, since 1934, where he has produced "Tessa" ("The Constant Nymph"), "Supplément au Voyage de Cook"; "La Guerre de Troie n'aura pas lieu," "L'Ecole des Femmes," "Electre," "Le Corsaire," "La Folle de Chaillot," "L'Apollon de Marsac," "Les Bonnes," "Don Juan," "Tartuffe," etc., in many of which he has played the leading part; has also supervised productions at the Comédie Française; is a professor of the Conservatoire; at the Edinburgh Festival, Sept., 1947, appeared in "L'Ecole des Femmes," and "Ondine"; received the Insignia of Commander of the Legion of Honour, 1950. *Address:* 20 Rue de Tournon, Paris (VI). *Telephone No. :* Dan. 99-08
(Died 16 Aug., 1951; age 63)

JOY, Nicholas, actor; *b.* Paris, France, 31 Jan., 1889; *s.* of Percy Frecknall Joy and his wife Louisa (Treble); *e.* Mercer's School, London, and Bancroft School, Woodford, Essex; *m.* Hildreth Sisson Riddle; studied for the stage at the Academy of Dramatic Art, London, 1910, and during this period "walked on" and understudied at the Lyric and Queen's Theatres; first appeared in a speaking part at the Queen's, Nov., 1910, when for a time he played Gervais McArthur in "A Butterfly on the Wheel"; toured during 1911; went to New York with Lewis Waller's company, and made his first appearance there, at Daly's Theatre, 30 Sept., 1912, as the Earl of Westmoreland in "Henry V"; at the Garden Theatre, Nov., 1912, played Rosencrantz in John E. Kellerd's revival of "Hamlet," subsequently appearing in "The Merchant of Venice," and "Œdipus"; at the 39th Street, Mar., 1913, played the Servant in "The Five Frankforters"; he then went to Australia, with Lewis Waller, in a repertory of plays; subsequently appeared there in "The Argyle Case," "Ready Money," "The Importance of Being Earnest," etc.; returned to New York, 1916, and appeared at the Shubert, Mar., 1916, as Benson in "The Great Pursuit"; from 1917–19, was engaged at the Copley Theatre, Boston, with the Jewett Players; toured, 1920, in "Everywoman"; Harris Theatre, New York, 1921, appeared in "Six Cylinder Love," and toured, 1922, in this play; Cort Theatre, New York, Dec., 1924, played Edmund in "Carnival"; toured in vaudeville, 1925; Henry Miller Theatre, Feb., 1926, Fournier in "Embers"; Sam H. Harris Theatre, Sept., 1926, Bob Hewett in "No Trespassing"; Jolson, Jan., 1927, Stephen Rutherford in "The Nightingale"; Martin Beck, Dec., 1928, Haliburton in "Wings Over Europe"; Music Box, Feb., 1930, Roger de Berville in "Topaze"; Booth, May, 1931, Richard Chiltern in "A Modern Virgin"; Fulton, Dec., 1931, Meredith Lane in "The Bride the Sun Shines On"; George M. Cohan Theatre, May, 1932, Clement Daudet in "The Cat and the Fiddle"; Alvin, Nov., 1932, Ernst Weber in "Music in the Air"; Booth, Apr., 1934, Anderson Townsend in "No More Ladies," and at the Morosco, Sept., 1934, the Earl of Moulton in the same play; Liberty, Dec., 1934, Barnaud in "Ode to Liberty"; Music Box, Feb., 1935, Dr. McPhail in "Rain"; Shubert,

Apr., 1935, General Metzger in "A Journey By Night"; Fulton, Nov., 1935, Henry Farraday in "The Ragged Edge"; Booth, Dec., 1935, Frank Glenn in "The Season Changes"; Golden, Feb., 1936, Zuard Takat in "Alice Takat"; Booth, Mar., 1936, Lord Farrington in "Sweet Aloes"; Guild, May, 1936, Sam Frothingham in "End of Summer"; Playhouse, Feb., 1937, Titus Jaywood in "Yes, My Darling Daughter"; Hudson, Nov., 1938, Lieut.-Col. Jervis in "Good Hunting"; Shubert, Mar., 1939, Seth Lord in "The Philadelphia Story"; Cort, Mar., 1941, Sir Francis Chesney in "Charley's Aunt"; Cort, Nov., 1941, Doctor Drew in "The Walrus and the Carpenter"; Longacre, May, 1942, Theodore Bender in "All the Comforts of Home"; Morosco, Sept., 1942, Sir Leo Alvers in "The Morning Star"; Morosco, Oct., 1942, Ambrose Godolphin in "Bird in Hand"; Longacre, Feb., 1943, Malcolm Stanley in "This Rock"; toured, 1943–4, as Brigadier-General Slade in "The Doughgirls"; Belasco, Mar., 1944, John Deacon January in "Mrs. January and Mr. Ex"; Broadhurst, June, 1944, General Mackenzie in "Ten Little Indians"; Biltmore, Jan., 1946, Arthur Barrington in "A Joy Forever"; Martin Beck, Oct., 1946, Cecil Lewis in "The Iceman Cometh"; National, Dec., 1949, Pothinus in "Caesar and Cleopatra"; Royale, Feb., 1952, played Mr. Fiske in "Dear Barbarians"; re-appeared on the English stage at the Opera House, Manchester, Sept., 1955, as Mr. Gans in "Anniversary Waltz," and played the same part at the Lyric, London, Nov., 1955; Ethel Barrymore, N.Y., Jan., 1957, played Major Clove in "Small War on Murray Hill"; Phoenix, N.Y., Oct., 1958, played the Hon. Gerald Piper in "The Family Reunion"; Shubert, New Haven, Mar., 1960, appeared as First Sea Lord Amory in "Goodwill Ambassador." *Favourite part:* Titus Jaywood in "Yes, My Darling Daughter." *Recreations:* Painting and cartooning. *Club:* Lambs. *Address:* 15 West 55th Street, New York City, 19 U.S.A. *Telephone No.:* CI. 5–9058

(Died 16 Mar., 1964; age 80)

JULLIEN, Jean, French dramatic author; *b.* Lyons, 4 Dec., 1854; *e.* Paris; *m.* Gladie Guinet; has written the following plays: " La Sérénade," 1887; " Le Maître," 1890; " La Mer," 1891; " La Poigne," 1900; " L'Ecollière," 1901; " L'Oasis," 1903; " La Mineure," 1904; " Les plumes du Geai," 1906; " Les Etoiles," 1907; among his literary works are " Trouble-coeur," " Le Vie sans lutte," " Le Théâtre Vivant," " Les petites Comédies," " Les Uns et les Autres " ; is a Chevalier of the Legion of Honour and a member of the Committee of the Society of Men of Letters. *Recreations:* Gardening and cycling. *Address:* 1 Chemin des Chalets, Ville-d'Avray, Seine-et-Oise.
(Died Sept., 1919; age 64)

JUNE (Howard Tripp), actress and vocalist; *b.* Blackpool, 11 June, 1901; *d.* of Walter Howard Tripp and his wife Ellen Kate (Sutherland); *e.* Paris and London; *m.* (1) Lord Inverclyde (mar. dis.); (2) Edward Hillman, Jr. (mar. dis.); made her first appearance on the stage at the Little, 27 Jan., 1911, as a Sea-Nymph in "The Goldfish"; then appeared professionally at the Palace Theatre, June, 1911, in the ballet "Snowflakes," with Anna Pavova; went to Paris, 1913, where she appeared at the Folies Bergère, Apr., 1914, in the *revue* "La Revue Galante"; appeared at the Palace, Dec., 1914, in "The Passing Show"; at the Empire, May, 1915, in "Watch Your Step"; at the Vaudeville, Dec., 1918, in "Buzz-Buzz"; then toured in variety theatres, with Nelson Keys; at the London Pavilion, Sept., 1920, played in "London, Paris, and New York"; Oct., 1921, in "Fun of the Fayre"; Aug., 1922, played Aspasia in "Phi-Phi";

at the New Oxford, July, 1923, Nellie Kelly in "Little Nellie Kelly"; at the Shaftesbury, May, 1924, Princess Stephanie in "Toni"; in Dec., 1924, went on tour, playing Daphne Drew in " Boodle," appearing at the Empire, in the same part, Mar., 1925; at the London Hippodrome, Oct., 1925, played June Somers in " Mercenary Mary " ; Prince of Wales's, Dec., 1926, June Willard in " Happy-Go-Lucky "; appeared at the Ambassadeurs, Paris, May, 1927, in *revue*; Adelphi, Dec., 1927, played in " Clowns in Clover "; went to New York, 1928, and appeared at the Lyric, 8 Jan., 1929, as Polly Shannon in " Polly "; at the conclusion of the run of that piece she married, and announced her intention of retiring from the stage; reappeared on the London stage at Prince Edward Theatre, June, 1932, in "Fanfare"; Alhambra, Aug., 1932, appeared in "Over the Page"; at the King's, Edinburgh, Oct., 1933, played Willa Hart in "No Surrender"; at the Palace, Manchester, Dec., 1933, appeared as Cinderella; at the Saville Theatre, Mar., 1934, succeeded Lily Damita as Mimi Lorraine in "Here's How!"; Comedy, Oct., 1934, appeared in "Hi-Diddle-Diddle"; Drury Lane, Dec., 1934, again played Cinderella in the pantomime; Comedy, May, 1935, appeared in "Shall We Reverse?"; Vaudeville, Mar., 1936, in "The Town Talks"; Prince of Wales's, Birmingham, Dec., 1936, Princess Marigold in "Humpty-Dumpty"; subsequently went to the United States; at the Civic Theatre, Santa Barbara, Cal., Mar., 1941, appeared in "Margin for Error"; made her first appearance in variety theatres, at the Palladium, July, 1935; published an autobiography, "The Whole Story," 1932. *Recreations:* Riding, reading, and drawing.

KAELRED, Katharine, actress ; *b.* in England, 9 May, 1882 ; *m.* J. H. Benrimo ; from 1903 to 1906 was engaged in England with F. R. Benson's company (two seasons), Cyril Maude's company and the Compton Comedy Company (two seasons) ; she then went to Australia in 1906, " co-starring " with Julius Knight under the management of J. C. Williamson, Ltd., succeeding Miss Maud Jeffries ; she remained in Australia until 1908, when she went to America and in the same year played Olga in " The Devil " ; and toured with Arnold Daly in " The Pickpockets " ; at Chicago, Jan., 1909, played Mrs. Payne-Allen in " The Renegade " ; during a " star stock " engagement at Milwaukee, played Mrs. Dane in " Mrs. Dane's Defence," Zira, etc. ; at the Liberty Theatre, New York, Mar., 1909, came into prominence by her performance of the part of the Woman in " A Fool there Was " ; at the New Theatre, New York, Feb., 1910, appeared as Alaine d'Estoile in " A Son of the People " ; subsequently played Judith Zaraine in the play of that name ; at the Nazimova Theatre, New York, Dec., 1910, played Mrs. Engaine in " We Can't be as Bad as All That " ; made her first appearance on the London stage at the Queen's Theatre, 21 Mar., 1911, in " A Fool there Was," repeating her former success ; at St. Louis, Mo., Apr., 1912, played Elinor Wyndham in " The Glass House " ; at the Lyric, New York, Sept., 1912, appeared as Edith Cortlandt in " The Ne'er do Well " ; made her reappearance in London, at His Majesty's Theatre, June, 1913, when she played Calpurnia in " Julius Caesar," during Sir Herbert Tree's Shakespearean festival ; at Chicago, Sept., 1914, appeared as Zuleika in " Joseph and his Brethren " ; at the Comedy, New York, Dec., 1914, as Mdme. de Semiano in " The Marriage of Kitty " ; at the Cort Theatre, Apr., 1916, played Mrs. St. Aubyn in " Beau Brummel " · at the Broadhurst, Sept., 1917, Lina Szezepanowska in " Misalliance " ; at the Forty-eighth Street Theatre, Apr., 1918, Miriam Lee in " The Man Who Stayed at Home " ; at the Harris Theatre, Apr., 1919, Dollie Bennett in " A Good Bad Woman " ; at the Garrick, Washington, Jan., 1920, played Mrs. Marchant in " Mamma's Affairs," appearing in the same part at the Little Theatre, New York, during the same month." *Address :* 368 Fifth Avenue, New York City, U.S.A.

KAHN, Florence, actress ; *b.* Memphis, Tenn., U.S.A., 3 Mar., 1878 ; *e.* Memphis ; *m.* Max Beerbohm ; was a student at the American Academy of Dramatic Arts, New York City, and made her first appearance on the stage in 1897, in " The Girl I left behind Me," on tour ; the following year she was identified with the Independent Theatre movement in New York, and played in Echegaray's " El Gran Galeoto," and in " Ties " ; subsequently she toured as Lady Winter in " The Three Musketeers " ; in 1900, she appeared with the late Richard Mansfield, as Chorus in " King Henry V," and next played Marita in " Don Cæsar's Return " ; in 1904, appeared with the Century Theatre company in " Rosmersholm," and " The Battle of the Butterflies " ; at the Knickerbocker Theatre, New York, she played the Strange Lady in " When We Dead Awaken," and then became leading lady at the Castle Square Theatre, Boston, where she played the Comtesse Zicka in " Diplomacy," Edith Varney in " Secret Service," Marian in " Tess " etc. ; at the Bijou Theatre, New York, Mar., 1907, she supported Alla Nazimova as Mrs. Elvsted in " Hedda Gabler " ; made her first appearance on the London stage, at Terry's Theatre, 10 Feb., 1908, as Rebecca West in " Rosmersholm " ; at the Aldwych, Mar., 1908, played Mary in " The Man on the Kerb." *Address :* 48 Upper Berkeley Street, W. *(Died 13 Jan.. 1951; age 74)*

KAISER, Georg, dramatic author; *b.* Magdeburg, Germany, 25 Nov., 1878 ; *s.* of Friedrich Kaiser and his wife Antonie (Anton) ; *e.* Magdeburg and Buenos Aires, Argentine ; *m.* Margarethe Habenicht ; is the author of the following among other plays : " Die Bürger von Calais," 1914 ; " Von

Morgens bis mitternachts" ("From Morn till Midnight"), 1916; "Die Koralle," 1917; "Gas," 1918; "Der Brand im Opernhaus," 1919; "Nebeneinander," 1923; "Kolportage" ("Melodrama"), 1924; "Der Protagonist," "Juana," "Zweimal Oliver," 1926; "Oktobertag," 1928; "Hellseherei," 1929; "Clairvoyance," "Mississippi," 1930; "Adrienne Ambrossat," 1935; "Der Gärtner von Toulouse," 1938. (*Died 5 June, 1945; age 67*)

KALICH, Bertha, actress; *b.* Lemberg, Galicia, 17 May, 1874; *m.* Leopold Spachner; at the age of fifteen entered the Lemberg Conservatoire, and studied singing; in 1890 made her *début* in a comic opera company; in 1891 she was singing at the Bucharest National Theatre; made her first appearance in New York as a singer in 1895, at the Thalia Theatre, appearing in "La Belle Hélène," "The Gipsy Baron," etc.; subsequently made a reputation by her performances in "A Doll's House," "Fédora," "Madame Sans-Gêne," "Magda," "Sapho," "The Orphan," "The Kreutzer Sonata," etc., all in Yiddish; made her *début* on the English-speaking stage, at the American Theatre, 22 May, 1905, as Fédora in Sardou's play of that name; at the Manhattan Theatre, 23 Oct., 1905, appeared in the title-*rôle* of "Monna Vanna"; during 1906 toured in "Thérèse Raquin"; at the Lyric, New York, Sept., 1906, appeared as Miriam Friedlander in "The Kreutzer Sonata"; and same theatre, Oct., 1907, played Sapho in "Sapho and Phaon"; subsequently toured in "Marta of the Lowlands" and, during 1908, in "Cora"; during 1909, she toured as Eva Fellanova in "The Unbroken Road"; at the New Theatre, New York, Feb., 1910, played Goodwife Joan Hathorne in "The Witch"; at New Haven, Oct., 1910, played in "A Woman of To-day"; in 1912, appeared in "vaudeville" as Toinette in "The Light of St. Agnes"; subsequently appeared in "Sapho"; at the Knickerbocker, New York, Dec., 1913, played Rachel in a play of that name; during 1914 toured in "Mari-

ana"; at the Palace, New York, Mar., 1915, appeared in "The Victim"; after an absence of three years, reappeared on the New York Stage at the Harris Theatre, Oct., 1918, as Lilla Olrik in "The Riddle: Woman," and toured in the same play during 1919-20; at the Comedy, New York, Jan., 1923, played Jitta Lenkheim in "Jitta's Atonement"; at the Frazee Theatre, May, 1924, again played Miriam in "The Kreutzer Sonata"; 49th Street Theatre, Jan., 1926, appeared as Magda in a revival of that play; in Oct., 1932, a testimonial performance was given in her honour at the Yiddish Art Theatre, to celebrate the fortieth anniversary of her first appearance on the stage, and a further performance was given in her honour, at the Vanderbilt, June, 1934.
(*Died 18 Apr., 1939; age 64*)

KALMAN, Emmerich, composer; *b.* 1882; has composed the scores of the following, among other musical plays: "The Gay Hussars," 1909; "Sari," 1914; "Miss Springtime," 1916; "Her Soldier Boy," 1917; "The Riviera Girl," 1917; "A Little Dutch Girl," 1920; "The Gipsy Princess," 1921; "The Nautch Girl" ("Die Bajadere"), 1922; "Countess Maritza," 1926; "The Circus Princess," 1927; "Golden Dawn" (with Herbert Stothard), 1927; "Paris in Spring," 1931; "The Devil Rider," 1932; "Marinka," 1945.

KALMAR, Bert, lyric writer, librettist and composer; is the author of "Arabian Knights," 1922; "Helen of Troy, New York," lyrics and music (with Harry Ruby), 1923; "Nifties of 1923," lyrics and music (with Ruby), 1923; "No Other Girl," lyrics and music (with Ruby), 1924; "Holka-Polka" (with Ruby), 1925; "The Ramblers" (part-author), 1926; contributed scenes and songs to "Twinkle Twinkle," 1926; part-author (with Otto Harbach) "Lucky," 1927; lyrics to "The Five o'Clock Girl," 1927; part-author (with Guy Bolton and Harry Ruby) "She's My Baby," 1927; "Top Speed" (with Bolton and Ruby), 1929; contributed lyrics to "Good

Boy," 1928, and "Animal Crackers," 1928; with Harry Ruby and George Jessel, contributed book and music of "High Kickers," 1941; contributed numbers to "8.40 Revue," 1944; with Ruby, has contributed to innumerable films; was formerly engaged in vaudeville as a magician; commenced his partnership with Harry Ruby in 1918, writing and publishing songs. *Address:* 1619 Broadway, New York City, U.S.A.
(Died 17 Sept., 1947; age 63)

KANE, Gail, actress; *b.* in England, 1887; *m.* Iden Ottmann; made her first appearance in New York, at the Lyceum, 19 Sept., 1910, as Madame Fauchel in "Decorating Clementine"; at the New (Repertory) Theatre, Jan., 1911, played Lady Gaunt in "Vanity Fair"; Nazimova, Mar., 1911, Miss Doane in "As a Man Thinks"; Grand Opera House, Feb., 1912, Patricia Boyer in "Macushla"; Harris, Aug., 1912, Louise in "The Model"; at the Little Theatre, Oct., 1912, Bianca in "The Affairs of Anatol"; at the Playhouse, Apr., 1913, Madame de Brionne in "Divorçons"; Astor, Sept., 1913, Myra Thornhill in "Seven Keys to Baldpate"; Sept., 1914, Helena Vail in "The Miracle Man"; Knickerbocker, Apr., 1915, Lili Buelow in "The Hyphen"; Globe, Nov., 1916, Zeila Vorona in "The Harp of Life"; for the next two years devoted herself to the cinema stage; reappeared on the regular stage at the Booth Theatre, Jan., 1919, when she played Edna Crane in "The Woman in Room 13"; at the Broadhurst, July, 1920, played Vistar Goino in "Come Seven"; Republic, Jan., 1922, Vivian Hepburn in "Lawful Larceny"; Klaw, Aug., 1923, Beverley in "The Breaking Point"; Thirty-ninth Street, Dec., 1923, Mrs. Dunsmore in "The Alarm Clock"; Punch and Judy, Apr., 1924, Helen Hessler in "Two Strangers from Nowhere"; Wallack's, Dec., 1924, Alice Huntingdon in "Artistic Temperament"; Cherry Lane, Feb., 1925, Ellen Halpin in "Loggerheads"; Booth, Nov., 1925, Mrs. John Ramsay in "Paid."

KANE, Whitford, actor; *b.* Larne, Ireland, 30 Jan., 1881; *s.* of John Kane and his wife Isabella (Whiteford); *e.* Royal Academical Institution, Belfast; is the son of a doctor; made his first appearance on the stage at the Theatre Royal, Belfast, 1903, as Maltby in "The Ticket-of-Leave Man"; subsequently toured with Mrs. Bandmann-Palmer, Osmond Tearle, Ian Maclaren, William Mollison, etc., mainly in Shakespearean repertory; in 1909 toured with Louis Calvert as Jackie in "Sunday"; made his first appearance in London, at the Duke of York's Theatre, 21 Feb., 1910, as O'Cleary in "Justice," at the commencement of Charles Frohman's Repertory Theatre season; subsequently appeared at the same theatre Apr.-May, 1910, as O'Dwyer in "Trelawny of the 'Wells'," the First Gardener in "Prunella," Mr. Peters in "Helena's Path"; he then joined Miss Horniman's Company at the Gaiety Theatre, Manchester, where he played an extensive round of parts; in Feb., 1911, became a member of the Liverpool Repertory Theatre Company; at the Royalty, Jan., 1912, played Christopher Wellwyn in "The Pigeon," and Feb., 1912, Daniel Murray in "The Drone," in which he scored a big success; he then went to America, making his first appearance at the Belasco, Washington, 16 Dec., 1912, in the last-mentioned part, in which he also made his first appearance in New York, at Daly's Theatre, 30 Dec., 1912; he then joined the company of the Fine Arts Theatre, Chicago, where, during 1913, he appeared in "Hindle Wakes," "The Master of the House," "Independent Means," etc.; at the Forty-eighth Street Theatre, New York, Apr., 1914, played Sam Horrocks in "Lonesome Like"; played a "stock" season at the Little Theatre, Philadelphia, in the autumn of 1914; at the Princess Theatre, New York, Jan., 1915, played Sir Walter Raleigh in "The Critic"; at the Bandbox Theatre, June, 1915, appeared as Martin Burke in "Red Turf" and Judas Iscariot in "Dust of the Road"; at the Princess Theatre, Nov., 1915, appeared as William Mossop in "Hobson's Choice"; during 1916 toured as Sam Horrocks in

"Lonesome Like"; at the Shubert, Boston, Apr., 1917, played Father Donovan in "The Woman Thou Gavest Me"; at the Comedy, New York, Apr., 1918, again played Sam in "Lonesome Like"; May, 1918, played Abraham Bentley in "The Rope"; at the Fulton, June, 1918, in "Muggins"; at the Belasco, Nov., 1918, Sam Tullidge in "Tiger! Tiger!"; at the Neighbourhood Theatre, Oct., 1920, William Banning in "The Mob"; at the Times Square Theatre, Feb., 1921, played the Doctor in "The Cradle Song"; at the Neighbourhood Theatre, May, 1921, appeared in "Harlequinade" and "A Night at an Inn"; at the Neighbourhood Playhouse, New York, Oct., 1921, played Henry Huxtable in "The Madras House"; at the Plymouth Theatre, New York, Dec., 1921, Schakne in "The Idle Man"; at the Greenwich Village, Feb., 1922, Christopher Wellwyn in "The Pigeon"; at the Vanderbilt, May, 1922, Christopher Hawthorn in "Fanny Hawthorn" ("Hindle Wakes"); at Daly's, New York, Oct., 1922, Mr. Swann in "Dolly Jordan"; at the Sam H. Harris Theatre, Nov., 1922, the First Gravedigger in "Hamlet"; at the Comedy, New York, Aug., 1923, Thomas in "The Children of the Moon"; at the Forty-ninth Street Theatre, Mar., 1924, Frederick Ladd in "The Outsider"; at the Shubert-Riviera, Sept., 1924, Rev. Frank Thompson in "Outward Bound"; Cherry Lane Theatre, Feb., 1925, Corny Halpin in "Loggerheads"; Neighbourhood Theatre, May, 1925, Dangle in "The Critic"; June, 1925, played in "Grand Street Follies"; 52nd Street Theatre, Dec., 1925, played Jasper in "The Devil to Pay"; he then went to the Goodman Theatre, Chicago, and during 1926 appeared there as Bottom in "A Midsummer Night's Dream"; at the Guild Theatre, New York, 1930, played Burbage in "Elizabeth the Queen"; at the Royale, Nov., 1931, with the Chicago Civic Shakespeare Society, played Launcelot Gobbo, First Gravedigger, etc.; New Amsterdam, New York, Dec., 1932, Ragueneau in "Cyrano de Bergerac"; subsequently toured in

"Hamlet," "Caponsacchi," etc., Masque, Nov., 1933, John Twohig in "Is Life Worth Living?"; Martin Beck, Mar., 1934, Dr. Finlay in "Yellow Jack"; 46th Street, Oct., 1934, the Right Rev. Monsignor Michael Carey in "The First Legion"; 58th Street, Feb., 1936, Fletch in "Searching for the Sun"; 48th Street, May, 1936, Michael Davitt in "Parnell"; Lyceum, Oct., 1936, Dr. O'Meara in "St. Helena"; St. James, Feb., 1937, the Gardener in "Richard II"; Vanderbilt, Apr., 1937, Obediah Rich in "Excursion"; 46th Street, Nov., 1937, Mike Fink in "Robin Landing"; Mercury, Jan., 1938, Simon Eyre in "The Shoemaker's Holiday"; St. James, Oct., 1938, First Gravedigger in "Hamlet"; Chestnut Street, Philadelphia, Dec., 1938, Canon Lavelle in "The White Steed"; toured, 1939, as the Gravedigger in "Hamlet" and Glendower in "Henry IV" (Part I); Longacre, Jan., 1940, played Samuel Cox in "The Man Who Killed Lincoln"; Booth, Oct., 1940, Andrew Boyd in "Boyd's Daughter"; Shubert, Mar., 1941, Sir Patrick Cullen in "The Doctor's Dilemma"; Martin Beck, Apr., 1942, Dr. Winter in "The Moon is Down"; Belasco, Nov., 1942, Jim Lloyd in "Lifeline," and Sept., 1943, The Wagon-Maker in "Land of Fame"; Mansfield, Mar., 1944, Hugo in "Thank You, Svoboda"; National, May, 1944, Brother Seraphim in "Career Angel"; Forrest, Oct., 1944, John MacGregor in "Meet a Body"; Playhouse, Mar., 1945, Rev. Mr. Endicott in "It's a Gift"; Cort, Jan., 1946, the Old Shepherd in "The Winter's Tale"; toured, Jan., 1948, as Host of the Garter Inn in "The Merry Wives of Windsor"; Mansfield, Feb., 1948, the Priest, and Father Keogh in "Kathleen"; at Stanford University, July, 1948, played Balthazar in "L'Arlésienne," and Sir Lucius O'Trigger in "The Rivals"; Cort, Jan., 1950, played Corin in "As You Like It," subsequently touring in the same part; at the Fair Park Auditorium, Dallas, June, 1953, appeared as Mr. Lundie in "Brigadoon"; at Ann Arbor, July, 1954, appeared as the First Gravedigger in "Hamlet"; Finch Playhouse, New York, Jan.,

1955, played Old Gobbo in "The Merchant of Venice"; has appeared regularly in television; first appeared in films, 1934; published a volume of reminiscences, "Are We All Met?" 1931; is part-author (with W. D. Hopenstall) of "Dark Rosaleen," first produced in 1917, and which secured a very lengthy run when produced at the Belasco Theatre, New York, Apr., 1919; part-author (with Milton Lomask) of "The Return of the Innocent," 1945. *Club:* Players'. *Address:* 325 West 14th Street, New York 14, U.S.A *(Died 17 Dec., 1956; age 75)*

KANN, Lilly, actress; *b.* Peitz, Spreewald, Germany; *d.* of Justizrat Berthold Kann and his wife Josephine (Manuel); *e.* Charlotten-Lyceum, Berlin; gained a scholarship to the Seebach School of the National Theatre, Berlin; made her first appearance on the stage as a student, at the age of 15, at the Goethe Festival Theatre, Düsseldorf, in "Penthesilea"; appeared at Lübeck, 1923; subsequently at the Municipal Theatre, Frankfurt am Main, played the Mother in "Cyankali," Queen Elizabeth in "Elizabeth of England," Queen Elizabeth in "Maria Stuart," Goetz's wife in Goethe's "Goetz von Berlichingen"; from 1923–32, was engaged at the National Theatre, Dresden, where she played a variety of parts, including Medea, Lady Macbeth, Judith, The Lady in "To Damascus," Clytemnestra in "The Oresteia" of Aeschylus, Brunhild in "Nibelungen," Rose Bernd, etc.; from 1933–9, played leading parts at the Jewish Theatre, Berlin, appearing in a number of plays by Ibsen, Strindberg, etc.; came to England, 1939; made her first appearance in London, at the Arts Theatre, 20 May, 1942, as Bessie Berger in "Awake and Sing"; Playhouse, Aug., 1943, played Grandmother Bossi in "Blow Your Own Trumpet"; Apollo, Jan., 1944, Mother Prioress in "The Cradle Song"; Aldwych, Aug., 1944, Frieda in "To-Morrow the World"; Arts, Apr., 1946, Mother in "Dutch Family"; Aldwych, Mar., 1948, Aunt Jenny in "I Remember Mama"; Embassy, Nov., 1948, the Nurse in "The Father," which she also played at the Duchess, Jan., 1949; Embassy,

Sept., 1949, Becky Felderman in "The Golden Door"; Westminster, May, 1950, Nanny Braun in "Background"; Saville, Oct., 1950, again played Bessie in "Awake and Sing"; Palace, Manchester, Apr., 1951, Mamma Birka in "Collector's Item"; Embassy, Nov., 1951, Milly Emmanuel in "Magnolia Street Story"; at the same theatre, Mar., 1952, played her old part of Becky Felderman in a revival of "The Golden Door"; Lyceum, Edinburgh, May, 1960, played Lotte Grossbek in "Stranger in the Tea"; has also appeared frequently on television, including "Enter Solly Gold," and "The Rabbi's Widow"; has appeared in films in Germany and England. *Recreations:* Reading, writing, swimming and sleeping. *Clubs:* Arts and Players. *Address:* Flat 1, Rivercourt, 21–23 Richmond Hill, Richmond, Surrey.

KARLOFF, Boris (*né* William Henry Pratt), actor; *b.* Dulwich, 23 Nov., 1887; *s.* of Edward Pratt and his wife Eliza Sara (Millard); *e.* Merchant Taylors' School and Uppingham; *m.* (1) Dorothy Stine (mar. dis.), (2) Evelyn Helmore; was originally intended for a diplomatic career; went to Canada, 1909; made his first appearance on the stage, 1910, at Kamloops, British Columbia, in a stock company, and appeared with various stock companies until 1916, when he entered films; appeared in over fifty films between 1916–58; at the Fulton Theatre, New York, 10 Jan., 1941, made a great success when he played Jonathan Brewster in "Arsenic and Old Lace"; at Hollywood and San Francisco, 1946, appeared as Gramps in "On Borrowed Time"; Music Box, Mar., 1948, Professor Linden in "The Linden Tree"; Booth, Jan., 1949, Decius Heiss in "The Shop at Sly Corner"; Imperial, Apr., 1950, Mr. Darling and Captain Hook in the record run of "Peter Pan" and toured in this production, 1951; Longacre, Nov., 1955, Cauchon in "The Lark"; has also given many notable television performances, including Colonel March of Scotland Yard and as the host and occasional star of the series "Thriller." *Club:* Garrick, London. *Address:*

641 Lexington Avenue, New York City, U.S.A. *(Died 2 Feb., 1969; age 81)*

KARLWEIS, Oscar, actor and vocalist; *b.* Vienna, Austria; *m.* Ninon Tallon; appeared in Vienna in the original versions of "Meet My Sister," "I Married an Angel" "The King with the Umbrella," "White Horse Inn," also in "Die Fledermaus" and many other light musical works; made his first appearance on the New York stage, at the Royale Theatre, 19 Dec., 1940, as Paul Albert Keppler in "Cue for Passion"; 44th Street, Oct., 1942, played Prince Orlofsky in "Rosalinda" ("Die Fledermaus"); Martin Beck (for the Theatre Guild), Mar., 1944, S. L. Jacobowsky in "Jacobowsky and the Colonel"; Golden, Mar., 1946, Willie Kringle in "I Like It Here"; Morosco, Dec., 1947, appeared as Topaze in the play of that name; subsequently returned to Vienna, where he played Elwood P. Dowd in "Harvey," and Garry Essendine in "Present Laughter," and also appeared at the State Opera House in "1001 Nights"; returned to New York and appeared at the Mansfield Theatre, Apr., 1950, as the Count in "The Cry of the Peacock"; Martin Beck, Nov., 1950, played Messerschmann in "Ring Round the Moon." *Address:* c/o Actors' Equity Association, 45 West 47th Street, New York City, U.S.A.

KARNO, Fred, comedian, author, and manager; *b.* Exeter, 26 Mar., 1866; *s.* of John Smith Wescott; made his first appearance on the stage about 1884; was originally a gymnast, and for some time appeared as one of the Karno Trio; after some years, made a speciality of sketch production on a somewhat larger scale than had hitherto been the custom; some of his sketches achieved immense popularity in the music halls; among the more notable of his productions being "His Majesty's Guests"; "Jail Birds"; "Hilarity"; "The Early Birds"; "The Mumming Birds"; "The Bailiff"; "Saturday to Monday"; "The Dandy Thieves"; "Perkins, M.P."; "Mr. Justice Perkins"; "Perkins the Punter"; "The

Hydro"; "G.P.O."; "Moses and Son"; "Parlez-vous Français"; "Hot and Cold"; "All Women," etc.; is the author or part-author of several of his own and other productions; for some time had more than half-a-dozen companies playing all the principal halls in London and the provinces. *Address:* 42 Cranbourn Street, W.C. *Telephone No.:* Regent 2551.

KARSAVINA, Tamara, Russian *danseuse*; *b.* Russia, 1885; *d.* of Platon Karsavin, dancer, and his wife Matoushka (Semenovna); *m.* (1) M. Mochin; (2) H. J. Bruce; was trained for dancing in the schools of the Imperial Ballet, St. Petersburg; after leaving the Imperial School, made her first appearance at the Marinsky Theatre, 1 May, 1902, in "Javotte"; in 1910, succeeded Anna Pavlova as *première danseuse* at the Imperial Opera House; made her first appearance in London, at the Coliseum, 22 Feb., 1909, under the name of La Tamara, when she danced in "The Firebird"; she appeared with the Imperial Russian ballet, on its first appearance, at Covent Garden, 21 June, 1911, as Armide in "Le Pavillon d'Armide"; subsequently she appeared in "Le Spectre de la Rose," "Scheherazade," "Les Sylphides," "Cléopatre," etc.; since 1911, has been a frequent visitor to England, appearing at Covent Garden, Drury Lane, Coliseum, Empire, etc., with the greatest success; at the Coliseum, Mar., 1920, appeared in "The Truth About the Russian Dancers," specially written for her by Sir James M. Barrie; again appeared at the Coliseum, 1921-2, and after three years absence, in Apr., 1925; at the Savoy, July, 1926, again played Karissima in "The Truth About the Russian Dancers"; again appeared at the Coliseum, Mar., 1927, and Feb., 1928; appeared in a selection of dances at the Arts Theatre, May 1930; published her reminiscences under the title of "Theatre Street," 1929.

KAUFMAN, George S., dramatic author and director; *b.* Pittsburgh,

Pa., U.S.A., 14 Nov., 1889; *s.* of Joseph Kaufman and his wife Nettie (Myers); *m.* (1) Beatrice Bakrow (mar. dis.); (2) Leueen MacGrath; was first engaged on the staff of the *Washington Times*, as a humorous writer, 1912–13; *New York Evening Mail*, 1914–15; was then engaged on the dramatic staff of the *New York Tribune*, and subsequently on the *New York Times*; in collaboration, has written the following plays: "Someone in the House" (with Larry Evans and Walter Percival), 1918; "Jacques Duval" (adaptation), 1919; with Marc Connelly has written "Dulcy," 1921; "To the Ladies," 1922; "The 49'ers," 1922; "Merton of the Movies," 1922; "Helen of Troy, New York," 1923, "The Deep Tangled Wildwood," 1923; "Beggar on Horseback," 1924; "Be Yourself," 1924; "Animal Crackers" (with Morris Ryskind), 1928; "June Moon" (with Ring Lardner), 1929; with Edna Ferber, wrote "Minick," 1924; "The Royal Family," 1927; "Dinner at Eight," 1932; sole author of "The Butter and Egg Man," "The Cocoanuts," 1925; "Strike Up the Band," 1927; "The Good Fellow" (with H. J. Mankiewicz), 1926; "The Channel Road" (with Alexander Woollcott), 1929; "Once in a Lifetime" (with Moss Hart), 1930; "The Band Wagon" (with Howard Dietz), "Of Thee I Sing" (with Ryskind), 1931; "Let 'Em Eat Cake" (with Ryskind), 1933; "The Dark Tower" (with Alexander Woollcott), 1933; "Merrily We Roll Along" (with Hart), "Bring on the Girls" (with Ryskind), 1934; "First Lady" (with Katherine Dayton), 1935; "Stage Door" (with Edna Ferber), 1936; with Moss Hart wrote "You Can't Take It With You," 1936, which gained the Pulitzer prize; "I'd Rather Be Right," 1937; "The Fabulous Invalid," 1938; "The American Way," 1939; "The Man Who Came to Dinner," 1939; "George Washington Slept Here," 1940; with Edna Ferber, wrote "The Land is Bright," 1941; with John P. Marquand, wrote "The Late George Apley," 1944; revised the book and lyrics of "Hollywood Pinafore," 1945; author of "Park Avenue" (with Nunnally Johnson),

1946; "Bravo !" (with Edna Ferber), 1948; "The Small Hours" (with Leueen McGrath), 1951; "Fancy Meeting You Again" (with Leueen McGrath), 1952; "The Solid Gold Cadillac" (with Howard Teichmann), 1953; "Silk Stockings" (with Leueen McGrath), 1955; was responsible for the staging of "The Front Page," 1928; "June Moon," 1929; "Joseph," "Once in a Lifetime," 1930; "Of Thee I Sing," 1931; "Here To-day," "Dinner at Eight," 1932; "Let 'Em Eat Cake," "The Dark Tower," 1933; "Merrily We Roll Along," "Bring on the Girls," 1934; "First Lady," 1935; "Stage Door," "You Can't Take It With You," 1936; "Of Mice and Men," "I'd Rather Be Right," 1937; "The Fabulous Invalid," 1938; "The American Way," 1939; "The Man Who Came to Dinner," 1939; "George Washington Slept Here," 1940; "My Sister Eileen," 1940; "Mr. Big," "The Land is Bright," 1941; "The Naked Genius," 1943; "Over Twenty-One," "While the Sun Shines," "The Late George Apley," 1944; "Hollywood Pinafore," "The Next Half-Hour," 1945; "Park Avenue," 1946; "Town House," "Bravo !," 1948; "Metropole," 1949; "The Enchanted," "Guys and Dolls," 1950; "The Small Hours," 1951; "Fancy Meeting You Again," and a revival of "Of Thee I Sing," 1952; "The Solid Gold Cadillac," 1953; "Romanoff and Juliet," 1957; has also written screen plays; played the part of Laurence Vail in "Once in a Lifetime," Music Box Theatre, Sept., 1930. *Clubs:* Lambs and Players'. *Address:* Players' Club, 16 Gramercy Park, New York City; or Holicong, Pa., U.S.A. *(Died 2 June, 1961; age 71)*

KAYE, Albert Patrick, actor; *b.* Ringwood, Hants., England, 1878; *s.* of Albert Joseph Kaye and his wife Janet Harriet (Brown); *e.* St. Anne's, Redhill, Surrey; *m.* Mary Scott Seton; began life by spending two years as a tea-taster in a Mincing Lane firm; made his first appearance on the stage at the Olympic Theatre, London, 19 Mar., 1896, in a minor part in "True Blue"; spent several years touring; in 1904 toured in Beerbohm Tree's company in "The Darling of the Gods"; at the Criterion, London, Apr., 1912, succeeded Edmund Gwenn as Henry Straker in "Man and Superman"; made his first appearance on the New York stage at the Hudson Theatre, 30 Sept., 1912, in the same part; Cohan and Harris, Aug., 1917, Jellicott in "A Tailor-Made Man"; Metropolitan Opera House, Oct., 1919, Admiral Maybridge in "The Luck of the Navy"; Longacre, Jan., 1921, The Mayor in "The Champion"; Garrick (for Theatre Guild), Feb., 1922, Joyce Burge, Burge-Lubin, the Envoy and Pygmalion in "Back to Methuselah"; Aug., 1922, in "He Who Gets Slapped"; Broadhurst, Dec., 1922, Mayor of Hammerpool in "The Lady Cristilinda"; Lyceum, Mar., 1923, Maillard in "The Comedian"; Belasco, Sept., 1923, Mr. Hobbs in "Mary, Mary, Quite Contrary"; 49th Street, Feb., 1924, Theodore Forsburg in "The Strong"; Garrick, Apr., 1924, First Banker in "Man and the Masses"; ·Henry Miller, Dec., 1924, Steward in "Quarantine"; Empire, Jan., 1925, Miteby in "Isabel" and Sam Smith in "Shall We Join the Ladies?"; Broadhurst, Sept., 1925, Dr. Masters in "The Green Hat"; Edyth Totten, Apr., 1927, Robert Benger in "Enchantment"; Charles Hopkins, Oct., 1927, Brand in "The Ivory Door"; New Amsterdam, Jan., 1928, Prince Rabisco in "Rosalie"; Guild, Nov., 1928, Peter Shirley in "Major Barbara"; Martin Beck, Dec., 1928, Rummel in "Wings Over Europe"; Forrest, Feb., 1929, Bird in "The Whispering Gallery"; St. James's, London, June, 1929, the Doctor in "Caprice"; Sam Harris, Sept., 1929, Sir Clive Heathcote in "Scotland Yard"; Assembly, Dec., 1929, Pompey in "The Novice and the Duke" ("Measure for Measure"); Selwyn, May, 1930, Harris in "Lost Sheep"; Henry Miller, Sept., 1930, the Producer-Manager in "The Violet"; 48th Street, Oct., 1931, Captain Fairweather in "The Streets of New York"; Morosco, Nov., 1931, Mr. Boot and the Coroner in "Cynara"; during 1933–4, toured all over the United States with Katherine Cornell; Guild, New York, Oct., 1934, played

Sir Douglas Todd-Walker in "A Sleeping Clergyman"; Morosco, Jan., 1935, Sir George Parker in "Living Dangerously"; Cort, Feb., 1935, Red Eagan in "The Bishop Misbehaves"; Hippodrome, Nov., 1935, Mr. Jellico in "Jumbo"; Mansfield, Nov., 1936, Williams in "Black Limelight"; New Amsterdam, Jan., 1937, Duke of Venice in "Othello"; Empire, Mar., 1937, Mr. Burgess in "Candida"; then toured as Martin Vanderhof in "You Can't Take It With You" and appeared at the St. James's, London, Dec., 1937, in the same part; Playhouse, New York, Sept., 1938, Chief-Inspector Wentworth in "Come Across"; Golden, Jan., 1939, Butler in "Where There's a Will." *Recreations:* Golf, gardening and painting. *Clubs:* Lambs, Automobile Assn. of America and Actors' Equity. *Address:* Lambs Club, 130 West 44th Street, New York City, U.S.A.
(Died 7 Sept., 1946; age 68)

KAYE, Frederick, actor; made his first appearance on the London Stage, at the Royalty Theatre. 23 Apr., 1883, as Sir Lothbury Jones in "The Merry Duchess," under the management of Miss Kate Santley; at the same theatre, Nov., 1883, played King René in "Gillette"; subsequently spent several years touring; in Feb., 1887, appeared at the Royalty, as Ulysses Simpkins in "The Professor's Wooing"; scored a great success when he appeared at Toole's Theatre, Oct., 1889, as Gregory Bell in "The Bungalow"; same theatre, July, 1890, played Colonel Sterndale in "The Solicitor," and Nov., 1890, Joe Gurgles in "Two Recruits"; at Terry's, Mar., 1891, played Sir Joseph Pendlecoop in "Culprits," and Joshua Morley in "Our Doctors"; at the Prince of Wales's, Oct., 1891, appeared as Donald MacHaddock in "The Planter"; at the Lyric, May, 1892, played James McGuinis in "An American Bride," and Oct., 1892, Dom Guzmano Grandi in "Incognita"; appeared at the Lyric, Jan., 1893, in "The Magic Opal"; the following year he joined George Edwardes' company at the Prince of Wales's

Theatre, first appearing there, Oct., 1893, as Major Barclay in " A Gaiety Girl " ; in 1894-5, went on a tour round the world under the same management ; at the Garrick, 1897, played in " My Friend the Prince," and " La Périchole " ; at the Gaiety, 1898, played in " A Runaway Girl " ; at Daly's, 1899-1908, played in " San Toy," " A Country Girl," " The Merry Widow," etc. ; during 1910, toured as Major McTurtle in " Mother-in-Law," and General Novakovitch in " The Merry Widow " ; at Daly's, May, 1911, appeared as the Registrar in " The Count of Luxembourg." *Address :* Daly's Theatre, Cranbourn Street, W.C.

KAZAN, Elia, actor and director; *b.* Istanbul, Turkey, 7 Sept., 1909; *s.* of George Kazan and his wife Athena (Sismanoglou); *e.* Williams' College, New York, and Yale University; *m.* Molly Day Thatcher (dec.); studied for the stage at the Yale Dramatic School; joined the Group Theatre, 1932, as assistant stage-manager, and made his first appearance at the Martin Beck Theatre, New York, 15 Nov., 1932, as Louis in "Chrysalis"; subsequently played for the Group at various New York theatres, as the Orderly in "Men in White," Sept., 1933; Polyzoides in "Gold-Eagle Guy," Nov., 1933; Agate Keller in " Waiting for Lefty," Mar., 1935; Kewpie in "Paradise Lost," Dec., 1935; Private Kearns in " Johnny Johnson," Nov., 1936; Eddie Fuselli in "Golden Boy," Nov., 1937; subsequently toured, 1938, as Joe Bonaparte in the last play; made his first appearance on the London stage, at the St. James's, 21 June, 1938, as Eddie Fuselli in the same play; on returning to New York, appeared for the Group, at the Belasco, Jan., 1939, as Eli Lieber in "The Gentle People"; Broadhurst, Feb., 1940, as Steve Takis in "Night Music"; 44th Street, Mar., 1940, Ficzur ("The Sparrow") in "Liliom"; Playhouse, Mar., 1941, Adam Boguris in "Five Alarm Waltz"; in 1946, presented (with Harold Clurman), "Truck-line Cafe"; has staged the following plays: "The Young Go First," 1935; "Casey Jones," 1938;

"Thunder Rock," 1939; "Café Crown," "The Strings, My Lord, Are False," "The Skin of Our Teeth," 1942; "Harriet," "One Touch of Venus," 1943; "Jacobowsky and the Colonel," 1944; "Deep Are the Roots," "Dunnigan's Daughter," 1945; "All My Sons," "A Streetcar Named Desire," 1947; "Sundown Beach," "Love Life," 1948; "Death of a Salesman," 1949; "Flight into Egypt," 1952; "Camino Real," "Tea and Sympathy," 1953; "Cat on a Hot Tin Roof," 1955; "The Dark at the Top of the Stairs," 1957; "J. B.," 1958, for which he received the Antoinette Perry (Tony) Award; "Sweet Bird of Youth," 1959, for which he received the New York Drama Critics Award; Director, with Robert Whitehead, of the Repertory Theatre of Lincoln Center for the Performing Arts, which presented, at the A.N.T.A. Washington Square Theatre, "After the Fall" (also directed), "Marco Millions," "But for Whom Charlie" (also directed), "The Changeling" (also directed), "Incident at Vichy," 1964; resigned in Dec., 1964; first appeared in films, 1940, in "City for Conquest"; in 1944, directed "A Tree Growns in Brooklyn"; has since directed "Boomerang," "Gentlemen's Agreement," "Pinky," "A Streetcar Named Desire," "Viva Zapata," "On the Waterfront," "East of Eden," "Baby Doll," "Wild River," "Splendor in the Grass," "America, America" (of which he was also the author), re-titled "The Anatolian Smile" in Great Britain, "The Arrangement" (also author, based on his novel), and "Face in the Crowd." *Address:* 1545 Broadway, New York City, U.S.A.

KEALY, Thomas J., Press representative; *b.* Co. Limerick, Ireland, 8 May, 1874 ; *s.* of Thomas Kealy and his wife Norah (O'Donnell) ; *e.* by Salesian and Jesuit Fathers ; *m.* Sophie Fetter ; well known as a journalist and theatrical press-agent ; part-founder and joint-editor of the *Catholic Review* ; was responsible for the publicity which led to the saving of " The Old Vic." for the nation; was business manager for Sybil Thorndike, 1920–9 ; of late years has been Press-representative for Emile Littler enterprises. *Favourite plays:* " Saint Joan," " The Trojan Women," " Jane Clegg." *Recreations:* Reading poetry and scribbling verse. *Club:* Interval. *Address:* 25 Salisbury Road, Worcester Park, Surrey. *Telephone No.:* Derwent 2956. *(Died 12 Feb., 1949; age 75)*

KEANE, Doris, actress ; *b.* Michigan, 12 Dec., 1881; *d.* of Joseph Keane and his wife Florence; *e.* privately in Chicago, New York, Paris, and Rome; *m.* Basil Sydney (mar. dis.); studied for a time at the American Academy of Dramatic Art, under Franklin Sargent; made her first appearance on the professional stage at the Garrick Theatre, New York, 2 Dec., 1903, as Rose in " Whitewashing Julia "; same theatre, 30 Dec., 1903, played Yvette in " Gypsy "; during 1904-5 toured in " The Other Girl "; at the Empire, New York, 4 Sept., 1905, appeared as Irene Millard in " De Lancey," subsequently touring in the same part; at St. Paul, Minn., June, 1906, played a " stock " engagement, appearing in " Friends," " A Social Highwayman," " The Middleman," " Peaceful Valley," etc.; at the Hudson Theatre, New York, 30 Aug., 1906, appeared as Rachel Neve in " The Hypocrites "; made her first appearance in London, at the Hicks Theatre, Aug., 1907, in the same part ; at the Garrick, New York, Sept., 1908, played Billy in " The Likes o' Me " ; at Wallack's, Oct., 1908, appeared as Margaret Ellen in " His Wife's Family " ; at the Garrick, New York, Apr., 1909, played Joan Thornton in " The Happy Marriage " ; at the Lyceum, New York, Aug., 1909, appeared as Sonia Kritchnofe in " Arséne Lupin "; same theatre, Sept., 1910, played Adrienne Morel in " Decorating Clementine " ; played the same part at the Globe Theatre, London, Nov., 1910 ; at the Garrick, New York, Feb., 1911, played Hope Summers in " Our World " ; at the Lyric, New York, May, 1911, appeared as Bess Marks in " The Lights o' London " ; at Boston, Oct., 1911, played Tress Conway in " The Warning " ; at the Fulton Theatre, Feb., 1912, played Deronda Deane in

" Making Good " ; at the Little Theatre, New York, Oct., 1912, Mimi in " The Affairs of Anatol " ; at the Maxine Elliott Theatre, Feb., 1913, became a " star," and scored a big success, when she played Margherita Cavallini in " Romance " ; she continued in this play until 1915, when she again came to London, and opened at the Duke of York's, 6 Oct., 1915, in the same part ; the play proved remarkably successful, was transferred to the Lyric, and ran 1,049 performances ; she subsequently appeared at the Lyric, Sept., 1918, as Roxana Clayton in " Roxana," and Apr., 1919, as Juliet in " Romeo and Juliet "; subsequently returned to America ; at the Playhouse, Feb., 1921, appeared as Cavallini in a revival of " Romance " ; at the Empire, New York, Jan., 1922, played the Czarina in a play of that name ; at the Thirty-ninth Street Theatre, Mar., 1924, Eleanor Owen in " Welded " ; at the Curran Theatre, San Francisco, Sept., 1924, Aurèlie in " Starlight," in which she also appeared at the Broadhurst, New York, Mar., 1925 ; reappeared in London, at the Playhouse, Oct., 1926, in a revival of " Romance," and toured in England in the same play, 1927 ; appeared at the Belasco, Los Angeles, Apr., 1929, as Elvira Moreno and Captain Veneno in " The Pirate." *Address:* c/o Brown Shipley & Co., 123 Pall Mall, S.W.1.
(Died 26 Nov., 1945; age 63)

KEANE, Robert Emmett, actor; *b.* New York City, U.S.A., 4 Mar., 1883; *m.* Muriel Window; made his first appearance on the stage at Keith and Proctor's, New York, 1900, in "Madame Sans-Gêne"; appeared at the Fourteenth Street Theatre, 7 Sept., 1908, as "Tod" in "The Star Bout"; during 1909, toured as Harling in " Via Wireless," and in " The Yankee-Doodle Detective " ; in 1910, toured in " What Money Couldn't Buy " ; he then appeared on the " vaudeville " stage for three years ; at the Winter Garden Theatre, New York, June, 1914, played Rip Van Winkle, Roosevelt, etc., in " The Passing Show of 1914 " ; he made his first appearance on the London stage at Drury Lane Theatre, 19 June, 1916, in " Razzle-Dazzle," and made an instantaneous success ; at the Prince of Wales's, Aug., 1916, succeeded Raymond Hitchcock as Mr. Manhattan in the piece of that name ; returning to America, he appeared at the Astor Theatre, New York, Apr., 1917, as Jack Grayson in " His Little Widows " : at the Cohan Theatre, Aug., 1917, as Anthony Squibbs in " Head Over Heels " ; at the Liberty Theatre, Dec., 1917, as Larry Doyle in " The Grass Widow " ; at the Fulton Theatre, May, 1920, played Henry Bird in " An Innocent Idea " ; during 1923 appeared at various London variety theatres ; at the Hudson Theatre, Mar., 1924, Kenneth Dodge in " Across the Street " ; Forrest, Feb. 1926, played Sonny Whitmore in " Mama Loves Papa " ; again appeared in London, at the Coliseum, Mar., 1928, in " The Gossipy Sex," subsequently touring in the same piece ; Hammerstein's, New York, Sept., 1929, played Dan Ward in " Sweet Adeline " ; Mayan Theatre, Los Angeles, Sept., 1930, appeared in " Temptations of 1930 " ; Biltmore, Los Angeles, June, 1931, played in " As Husbands Go " ; Bijou, New York, Aug., 1932, played John Coates in " Page Pygmalion " ; during 1932, played in " The Spider " at the Forty-fourth Street Theatre ; Jan., 1933, played Hal Reisman in " Face the Music " ; Royale, Jan., 1934, Roger Woods in " Hotel Alimony " ; Forrest, Apr., 1934, Grant Thompson in " Broadway Interlude " ; 44th Street May, 1934, Andrew McMurray in " The Only Girl " ; has appeared in films for several years, and since 1936 in " Jailbreak," " The Captain's Keel," " Down the Stretch," " Hot Money," " Under Suspicion," " Beware of Ladies," " Jim Hanvey—Detective," " Boys' Town," " The Chaser," " The Last Express," " Streets of New York," etc. *Address :* c/o Kingston and Mayers, 9120 Sunset Boulevard, Hollywood, Cal., U.S.A.

KEARNS, Allen, actor ; *b.* in Canada, 1893 ; made his first appearance on the stage in 1910, in " Tillie's Nightmare," with Marie Dressler ; subsequently appeared in vaudeville ; at Daly's, Nov., 1912, played the Miner in " The Red Petticoat " ; Shubert, Sept., 1914, Frederic in " Miss Daisy " ; Princess, 1916, succeeded Ernest Truex as Eddie Kettle in " Very Good Eddie " ; during the War, served two years in the navy ; after being demobilized in 1919, succeeded Charles King at the Shubert, as Hughie Cavanagh in " Good Morning, Judge " ; at Maxine Elliott's, Mar., 1920, played in " What's in a Name? " ; at the Selwyn, Aug., 1920, played Jack Barton in " Tickle Me " ; Globe, Jan., 1923, Billy Browning in " Lady Butterfly " ; Longacre, Aug., 1923, Tommy Tinker in " Little Jessie James " ; Apr., 1925, Jerry in " Mercenary Mary " ; Liberty, Dec., 1925, Steve Burton in " Tip-Toes " ; made his first appearance on the London stage, at the Winter Garden, 31 Aug., 1926, in the same part ; at the Shaftesbury, June, 1927, played Monty Blair in " Castles in the Air," and at the Adelphi, Aug., 1927, Freddy Van Bozer in " Up With the Lark " ; returning to New York, appeared at the Alvin Theatre, Nov., 1927, as Peter Thurston in " Funny Face " ; at the Broadhurst, May, 1928, played Billy Howe in " Here's Howe " ; at the Mansfield, Dec., 1928, Lawrence Tucker in " Hello, Daddy! " ; at the Alvin, Oct., 1930, Danny Churchill in " Girl Crazy " ; Vanderbilt, Jan., 1934, Boatswain Klatz in " A Divine Moment " ; reappeared in London at the London Hippodrome, June, 1935, when he played Tony Thornton in " Love Laughs ——."

(Died 20 Apr., 1956)

KEEN, Malcolm, actor ; *b.* Bristol, 8 Aug., 1887 ; *s.* of Malcolm Keen and his wife Elizabeth (Creed) ; *e.* Clifton, Bristol ; made his first appearance on the stage at His Majesty's Theatre, 1 Feb., 1902, walking on in " Ulysses " ; spent many years in the provinces playing a varied round of characters, including Krogstadt in " The Doll's House," Johann Tonneson in " The Pillars of Society," Pete in " The Manxman," John Storm in " The Christian," Dr. Meyer Isaacson in " Bella Donna," Rudolf Rassendyl in " The Prisoner of Zenda," Polignac in " The Glad Eye," Frank Taylor in " The Land of Promise," Will Mossop in " Hobson's Choice," Mr. Wu in the play of that name, Christopher Brent in " The Man who Stayed at Home," Terry Fielding in " Seven Days Leave, " etc.; appeared at the Old Vic., Jan., 1915, as Balthazar in " The Comedy of Errors "; spent two years with Martin Harvey, and appeared with him at the New Theatre, 1915, in " Armageddon," " The Corsican Brothers," etc.; at His Majesty's, with Martin Harvey, May, 1916, played Edward IV in " Richard III," Marcellus in " Hamlet," Vincentio in " The Taming of the Shrew," Williams in " King Henry V "; at the Palladium, Sept., 1916, played Harold in " The Moment Before "; at the Scala, Dec., 1919, the Dream Merchant in " Fifinella "; at the St. Martin's, Feb., 1920, Macaulay in " Over Sunday "; Apr., 1920, Charles in " The Skin Game "; Feb., 1921, Peter Jekyll in " The Wonderful Visit "; Mar., 1921, Hilary Fairfield in " A Bill of Divorcement "; at the Lyceum, Oct., 1921, Major Baron Von Rochow in " The Burgomaster of Stilemonde "; at the St. Martin's, Mar., 1922, Major Colford in " Loyalties," and Dolphin in " Shall We Join the Ladies ? "; at His Majesty's, Sept., 1922, Henry Anderson in " East of Suez "; Apr., 1923, Valma in " The Gay Lord Quex "; at the St. Martin's, Jane, 1923, succeeded Clifford Mollison as Jacob Berman in " R.U.R. "; July, 1923, played The Man in Armour in " Melloney Holtspur "; Aug., 1923, Philip Ross in " The Will "; at His Majesty's, Sept., 1923, The Caliph in " Hassan "; at the St. Martin's, Jan., 1924, Martin Potten in " A Magdalen's Husband," and the Envoy in " Gruach "; at the Queen's, Aug., 1924, the Butler in " Pansy's Arabian Night "; at His Majesty's, Sept., 1924, King John of Kurdania in " The Royal Visitor "; at the Criterion, Oct., 1924, Gabriel Fay in " Fata Morgana "; at the St. Martin's, Dec., 1924, Paul Parisot in " No Mans' Land "; Haymarket, Feb., 1925, Claudius in " Hamlet," with John Barrymore; Garrick, May, 1925, Rev. Alfred Davidson in " Rain "; Apr., 1926, Dr.

Fernay in " Enchantress "; Sept., 1926, Mr. Floyd in " After Dark "; Little, Nov., 1926, Sir Hugh Tremayne in " A House of Cards "; New (for the Stage Society), Feb., 1927, Gerald Mildmay in " One More River "; Coliseum, Feb., 1927, Lennox in " Packing Up "; New, Aug., 1927, Pierre Lachance in " The Wolves "; Globe, Nov., 1927, José Mendez in " The Squall "; Carlton, Feb., 1928, Li-San in " The Yellow Mask "; Arts, Apr., 1928, Richard Burbage in " The Making of an Immortal "; Palace (for King George's Pension Fund), May, 1928, the Prince of Wales in " The Scarlet Pimpernel "; Garrick, Dec., 1928, Captain Hook in " Peter Pan "; under his own management, appeared at the Lyric, Feb., 1929, as Daniel Everett in " Always Afternoon "; at the same theatre, Apr., 1929, appeared as James Hutton in " Paris Bound "; Garrick, June, 1929, played Simon Hardy in " The Stranger Within "; Arts Theatre, Oct., 1929, Dick Coverdale in "Time and the Hour"; Little, Oct., 1929, Jeff Stewart in "Conscience"; went to New York, and appeared at Erlanger's Theatre, 20 Jan., 1930, as Karl Alexander in " Josef Süss"; returned to England, and appeared at the Haymarket, Apr., 1930, as Claudius in the "all-star" cast of "Hamlet"; Comedy, Apr., 1930, played Austin Howard in "The Silent Witness"; Phoenix, Jan., 1931, Owen Brett in "Frailties"; Haymarket, Mar., 1931, Claudius in "Hamlet"; Prince of Wales's, July, 1931, David in "The Love Game"; St. Martin's, Dec., 1931, Abdullah in "The Nelson Touch"; Mar., 1932, Beguildy in "Precious Bane"; May, 1932, Sir Daniel Markby in "Somebody Knows"; Duchess, June, 1932, Anthony Redver; in "The Secret Woman"; in Sept., 1932, joined the company of the Old Vic.-Sadler's Wells, and played Caesar in "Caesar and Cleopatra," Iachimo in "Cymbeline," Touchstone in "As You Like It," Macbeth, Shylock, Old Hardcastle, Leontes, Mercutio, Sir Peter Teazle, Caliban, and Bothwell in "Mary Stuart"; at the Fortune, May, 1933, played the Counsel for the Defence in "Heritage"; Little, June, 1933, again played Von Rochow in "The Burgomaster of Stilemonde"; Queen's, Sept., 1933, Filippo Strozzi in "Night's Candles"; Daly's, Oct., 1933, Julien Brignac in "Maternité"; Playhouse, Apr., 1934, Sir Mark Loddon in "Libel"; Aldwych, Dec., 1934, Count Nicholas Povah in "Half-a-Crown"; "Q," Mar., 1935, Caesar in "Caesar and Cleopatra"; Playhouse, Apr., 1935, Mr. Justice Floyd in "Justice"; May, 1935, Hornblower in "The Skin Game"; Daly's, July, 1935, Colonel William Mason in "The Unguarded Hour"; St. Martin's, Apr., 1936, Herbert Calder in "The Great Experiment"; Empire, New York, Oct., 1936, Claudius and the Ghost in "Hamlet," with John Gielgud; Savoy, Dec., 1937, Long John Silver in "Treasure Island"; Garrick, Mar., 1938, Dr. Stanford in "Road to Gandahar," and June, 1938, Count von Ahlenfeld in "Trumpeter, Play!"; His Majesty's, Sept., 1938, Duke of Firth in "Paprika"; Old Vic., Oct., 1938, Ghost in "Hamlet" (in entirety and modern dress); Savoy, Dec., 1938, again played in "Treasure Island"; New, Mar., 1939, Dr. Ludwig Weisz in "The Man in Half-Moon Street"; Lyric, Aug., 1940, Hawkins in "The Body Was Well Nourished"; Coliseum, Apr., 1942, Baldasarre in "The Maid of the Mountains"; Duke of York's, May, 1943, Canon Skerritt in "Shadow and Substance"; Lyric, Mar., 1944, Ernest Motford in "A Murder for a Valentine"; Duke of York's, June, 1944, succeeded David Horne as Edward Strachan in "Pink String and Sealing Wax," and toured in the same part, 1945; toured, 1945, as Baldasarre in "The Maid of the Mountains"; went to Egypt, Jan., 1946, to appear at Cairo and elsewhere, as Edward Moulton Barrett in "The Barretts of Wimpole Street," and Sir Peter Teazle in "The School for Scandal"; at the Royale, New York, May, 1947, appeared as Sir Sampson Legend in "Love for Love"; Alvin, Oct., 1949, Roebuck Ramsden in "Man and Superman"; played the same part at the City Center, May, 1949; Lyceum, Jan., 1950, appeared as the Inspector in "The Enchanted"; Broadhurst, Mar., 1951, appeared as Capulet in "Romeo and Juliet"; Mark Hellinger,

Mar., 1952, played Shiel Harrigan in "Three Wishes For Jamie"; at the Westminster, London, May, 1954, appeared as Sir Percival Bastin in "The Bombshell"; Aldwych, Apr., 1955, Richard Bravo in "The Bad Seed"; Drury Lane, Jan., 1956, Papa Yoder in "Plain and Fancy"; Lunt-Fontanne, N.Y., Sept., 1959, Leonato in "Much Ado About Nothing"; Vaudeville, Sept., 1960, Charles Pine in "Horses in Midstream"; Haymarket, Apr., 1962, played Rowley in "The School for Scandal," subsequently appearing in the same production at the Majestic, New York, Jan., 1963; commenced film career, 1931, and has since appeared in numerous pictures, including: "Kind Lady," "Lorna Doone," and "Operation Amsterdam"; appeared on television as Marley's Ghost in "A Christmas Carol" (New York), 1951; Duncan in "Macbeth" (New York), 1961. President of Stage Golfing Society, 1960. *Recreations:* Riding and swimming. *Club:* Stage Golfing Society.
(Died 30 Jan., 1970; age 82)

KEENAN, Frank, actor; *b.* Dubuque, Iowa, U.S.A., 8 Apr., 1858; *s.* of Owen Keenan and his wife, Frances (Kelly); *e.* Boston; *m.* (1) Katherine Agnes Long (dec.); (2) Margaret White; made his first appearance on the stage at Boston, 1880, where for some time he was a member of the famous Boston Museum Stock Company; has been a prominent figure on the New York stage for over twenty-five years, and has appeared at the Standard, New York, Sept., 1895, as Herbert Garretson in "The Capitol"; at the Knickerbocker, Oct., 1898, as Brother Paul in "The Christian," and as John Storm in the same play, Nov., 1898; at the Belasco, Nov., 1905, played Jack Rance in "The Girl of the Golden West"; Dec., 1907, General Warren in "The Warrens of Virginia"; at the Hudson, Oct., 1909, appeared as Teploff in "On the Eve"; and was also general stage director for H. B. Harris, at that theatre; at the Savoy, New York, Jan., 1910, played Joe Moreau in "The Heights"; at the Lyric, New York, Nov., 1912, Cassius in "Julius Caesar"; at Daly's, New

York, Nov., 1914, Yosemite in the play of that name; at Chicago, Oct., 1920, John Ferguson in the play of that name; in 1921 toured in the same part; at San Francisco, June, 1921, appeared as Rip Van Winkle; at the Sam H. Harris Theatre, New York, Sept., 1923, played Peter Weston in a play of that name; of late years has mainly devoted himself to the cinema stage. *Address :* 1554 Poinsettia Place, Hollywood, Cal., U.S.A. *(Died 24 Feb., 1929; age 70)*

KEIGHTLEY, Cyril, actor; *b.* Wellington, New South Wales, Australia, 10 Nov., 1875; *s.* of Henry McCrummin Keightley, stipendiary magistrate, and his wife, Caroline M. (Rotton); *e.* at Albury Grammar School, New South Wales, and Geelong Grammar School, Victoria; studied for the Bar in Adelaide, South Australia; *m.* Ethel Dane; went straight into an engagement with a travelling company in Australia, first appearing in Seymour, Victoria, with Dan Barry, in *répertoire*; joined George Rignold at His Majesty's Theatre, Sydney, remaining about five years under his management; in 1896 he toured the colonies with Albert Norman, and in the following year visited New Zealand, playing lead in "The Land of the Moa"; he also had a short engagement with Brough and Boucicault in the same year, followed by a long engagement with J. C. Williamson; joined McKee Rankin, and after touring Western Australia, sailed for Africa, where he made his appearance in a round of leading parts, followed by a professional visit to Egypt; he arrived in England in 1902; made his first appearance on the London stage, at the Adelphi, 1 Sept., 1902, as Max in "Magda" with Nance O'Neil; subsequently appeared there as the Count de Varville in "Camille," and King James in "Elizabeth, Queen of England"; joined F. R. Benson as leading man, remaining with him till June, 1906; toured with his own company, 1906, in "She Stoops to Conquer," and "The School for Scandal"; during 1907, appeared at the Garrick Theatre under Mr. Arthur Bourchier, as Lord

Cray in "Mr. Sheridan," Sir Paul Forester in "The Duel," and Captain Villiers in "Simple Simon"; at the Haymarket, Jan., 1908, played Sir Claude Tremayne in "Her Father"; at Terry's, Apr., 1908, appeared as William Ashe in "The Marriage of William Ashe"; June, 1908, same theatre, as Louis Beresford in "The Three of Us"; subsequently went to America, and at the Lyceum, New York, Aug., 1908, appeared as Count André de Juvingy in "Love Watches"; on returning to England, Apr., 1909, appeared at Stratford-on-Avon, as Iachimo in "Cymbeline," and Cassius in "Julius Cæsar"; at Drury Lane, Sept., 1909, appeared as Captain Greville Sartoris in "The Whip"; appeared at the Empire, Dec., 1909, played in "Sanctuary"; at the Court, Feb., 1910, appeared as Bassanio in "The Merchant of Venice"; again visited America, and at the Comedy, New York, Sept., 1910, appeared as Recklaw Poole in "The Little Damozel"; subsequently played lead with Annie Russell in "The Backsliders"; at Drury Lane, Sept., 1911, played Harold, Earl of Norchester in "The Hope"; at the Playhouse, Feb., 1912, played Lieut.-Colonel Miles Anstruther in a revival of "The Second in Command"; at Wyndham's, Apr., 1912, James Palliser in "Jelf's"; then went to the United States, and in Sept., 1912, played Hilary Cutts in "The New Sin," appearing at Wallack's, New York, Oct., 1912, in the same part; at Philadelphia, Dec., 1912, and Empire, New York, Jan. 1913, played Colonel Felt in "The Spy" ("The Turning Point"); on his return, appeared at the Strand, Apr., 1913, as Hilary Chester in "The Chaperon"; at Eastbourne, Feb., 1914, played John Darchester in "Love and the Law"; at the Eltinge Theatre, New York, Dec., 1914, played Richard Laird in "The Song of Songs"; at the Eltinge Theatre, Aug., 1916, Tom Palmer in "Cheating Cheaters"; at the Fulton, Oct., 1917, Harry Wynn in "Broken Threads"; at the Playhouse, New York, Jan., 1918, Antonia in "The Heritage"; at the Empire, New

York, Feb., 1918, the Duke of Burchester in "The Off-Chance"; at the Cort Theatre, Mar., 1918, Cassius in "Julius Caesar"; at the Empire Theatre, New York, May, 1918, John Barrington in "Belinda"; at the Little Theatre, New York, Dec., 1918, Jim West in "A Little Journey"; at Greenwich Village, Dec., 1919, played in "Curiosity"; at the Little, Feb., 1920, Tom Herford in "He and She"; at Maxine Elliott's, May, 1920, Jim Heath in "All Soul's Eve"; at the La Salle, Chicago, Sept., 1920, Adam Smith in "Adam and Eva"; at the Booth Theatre, New York, Jan., 1921, Dr. Basil Traherne in "The Green Goddess"; at the Bijou, Mar., 1921, Dr. George Edwardes in "The Tyranny of Love"; at the Maxine Elliott Theatre, Aug., 1922, played Eric Brierly in "Fool's Errant"; at the Empire, New York, Nov., 1922, Steven Tillerton in "The Texas Nightingale"; at the Longacre, Feb., 1923, Daniel Farr, K.C., in "The Laughing Lady"; at Daly's, New York, Oct., 1923, Roger Carlyle in "Virginia Runs Away"; at the Plymouth Theatre, New York, Nov., 1923, Prince Peter in "A Royal Fandango." *Favourite parts :* Hotspur in "Henry IV" and Mercutio. *Recreations :* Fly-fishing, shooting, fencing, and billiards. *Clubs :* Green Room, London; Players', New York. *Address :* Green Room Club, 46 Leicester Square, W.C.2; or Players' Club, 16 Gramercy Park, New York City, U.S.A.
(Died 14 Aug., 1929; age 53)

KEIM, Adelaide, actress; *b.* New York City, 15 Feb., 1880; *d.* of Henry G. Keim; *e.* St. Joseph's Academy, New York; commenced her professional career at the Lyceum Theatre, New York, under the management of Daniel Frohman, being engaged as general understudy, 1898; during 1899, toured as Ottilie in "At the White Horse Tavern"; during 1900, was engaged at the Garden Theatre, New York, understudying Virginia Harned as Ophelia in "Hamlet," and eventually she succeeded that lady in the part; from 1901-3, played lead with the Fifth Avenue Theatre "stock" company, playing a great number of parts, including Peg Woffington, Camille, the Baroness in "The Last Word," and Mrs. Temple in "Mrs. Temple's Telegram"; in 1903, toured with Chauncey Olcott in "Terence"; subsequently in 1904, played a "stock" season at Baltimore, where among other parts she played Hamlet, with great success; in 1906, appeared at the Broadway Theatre, as the Princess Irene in "The Prince of India"; has since played various "stock" engagements; at the Bijou, New York, Jan., 1912, played Henriette Desclos in "The Right to Happiness." *Address :* c/o *New York Dramatic News,* 17 West 42nd Street, New York City, U.S.A.

KEITH, Ian, actor; *b.* Boston, Mass., U.S.A., 27 Feb., 1899; *s.* of William A. Ross and his wife Mahalah (Keith); *e.* New York City and Chicago; *m.* (1) Blanche Yurka (mar. dis.); (2) Ethel Clayton (mar. dis.); (3) Fern Andra (mar. dis.); (4) Hildegarde Pabst; studied for the stage at the American Academy of Dramatic Art; made his first appearance on the stage at the Comedy Theatre, New York, Oct., 1917, with the Washington Square Players, and remained there until Apr., 1918; appeared at Maxine Elliott's Theatre, New York, Sept., 1921, as Captain Douglas Belgrave in "The Silver Fox"; Empire, Jan., 1922, as the French Ambassador in "The Czarina"; Forty-fourth Street Theatre, Apr., 1923, Orlando in "As You Like It"; Belasco, Nov., 1923, Luigi Ravelli in "Laugh, Clown, Laugh" during 1924-5, toured in "He Who Gets Slapped"; Little, Dec., 1925, Toney Norton in "The Master of the Inn"; at San Francisco, 1926, played Benvenuto Cellini in "The Firebrand"; subsequently played in "An Ideal Husband," and "Monna Vanna"; at the Klaw, New York, Oct., 1928, Peter Kraditch and Prince Alexis in "The Command Performance"; Belmont, Nov., 1929, Gilbert Blake in "Queen Bee"; at Los Angeles, 1931, played Hamlet; subsequently toured as the Earl of Essex in "Elizabeth the Queen"; during 1932, toured in "Grand Hotel"; at the

Geary, San Francisco, May, 1932, appeared in "The Copperhead"; Empire, New York, Nov., 1932, Zoltan Balkanyi in "Firebird"; St. James, New York, Feb., 1933, Kurt von Eltz in "Hangman's Whip"; Morosco, May, 1933, Gilbert Marechal in "Best Sellers"; in May, 1933, toured as Bob Geldiss in "Hard Boiled Angel"; at Pasadena, Cal., 1933, played Charles Strickland in "The Moon and Sixpence"; in Aug., 1934, toured as Bothwell in "Mary of Scotland"· at Minneapolis, Oct., 1935, played Hamlet; St. James, New York, Feb., 1937, Bolingbroke in "King Richard II"; 46th Street, Nov., 1937, Grant Eaton in "Robin Landing"; National, Oct., 1938, Jeff Foster in "A Woman's a Fool——"; Blackstone, Chicago, Dec., 1938, Milt Shanks in "The Copperhead," and Apr., 1939, Hamlet and Iago in "Othello"; went to Australia, May, 1939, to play in "Robert's Wife" and "Yes, My Darling Daughter"; after returning to America, toured, 1941, in "Twentieth Century" and "To Live Again"; National, New York, Oct., 1948, played Gerald Marriott in "The Leading Lady"; in summer theatres, 1949, appeared in "The Winslow Boy"; at the Brattle Theatre, Harvard, 1949, appeared in "Henry of Canossa"; summer theatres, 1950, played in "Nothing Serious"; at the Brattle Theatre, Cambridge, Mass., May, 1951, played Armado in "Love's Labour's Lost," and Burgoyne in "The Devil's Disciple"; during 1952–53, appeared in "Pygmalion," "The Country Girl" and "Macbeth"; at the Music Box, New York, Feb., 1953, played Major Robert Spaulding in "Touchstone"; in summer theatres, 1955, appeared in "Dial 'M' For Murder"; commenced film career, 1924, in "Manhandled," and has since appeared in numerous pictures. *Address:* c/o Actors' Equity Association, 45 West 47th Street, New York City, U.S.A.
(Died 26 Mar., 1960; age 61)

KEITH, Robert, actor and dramatic author; *b.* Fowler, Indiana, U.S.A., 10 Feb., 1898; *s.* of James Howie Keith Richey and his wife May Dell

(Snyder); *e.* Fowler; *m.* Dorothy Tierney; commenced his career as a boy soprano, in his native town; made his first appearance on the stage at the Opera House, St. Charles, Ill., 25 Dec., 1914; first appeared in New York, at the Comedy Theatre, 24 Aug., 1921, as Ralph Armstrong in "The Triumph of X"; at the Fulton, Nov., 1924, played Thomas Bates Jun. in "New Brooms"; Greenwich Village, Jan., 1926, Dion Anthony in "The Great God Brown"; Music Box, Oct., 1926, Dick Cameron in "Gentle Grafters"; Mansfield, Nov., 1926, Robert Mayo in "Beyond the Horizon"; National, Feb., 1927, Charlie in "Fog"; from 1930–3, was in Hollywood, writing for films; Ambassador, Oct., 1933, played John Douglas in "Under Glass"; Civic Repertory, Nov., 1933, Peter Owens in "Peace on Earth"; Martin Beck, Mar., 1934, Jesse Lazear in "Yellow Jack"; Ritz, Oct., 1934, Jack in "Good-Bye, Please"; Maxine Elliott, Nov., 1934, Dr. Joseph Cardin in "The Children's Hour"; toured, 1936, as Iago in "Othello," with Walter Huston; Windsor, New York, Nov., 1937, Cornelius Prentiss in "Work Is for Horses"; Henry Miller, Jan., 1938, Pilon in "Tortilla Flat"; Windsor, Oct., 1938, Malcolm Eldred in "The Good"; Martin Beck, Oct., 1939, played Reynolds in "Ladies and Gentlemen," and toured in the same part, 1940; Playhouse, Dec., 1940, Charles Dickens in "Romantic Mr. Dickens"; Henry Miller, Nov., 1941, Dr. Lionel Carter in "Spring Again"; toured, 1942, for the Theatre Guild, in "Papa is All"; Biltmore, Mar., 1943, played Henry Archer in "Kiss and Tell"; Cort, Oct., 1944, produced and staged "No Way Out," in which he appeared as Dr. Miles Hilliard; Royale, Apr., 1945, played Charles Reddy in "A Place of Our Own"; toured, Sept., 1945, as Colonel Rainsford in "The Rugged Path"; Golden, Feb., 1946, played Herbert Gage in "January Thaw"; Alvin, Feb., 1948, Doc in "Mister Roberts," which he played for over two years; author of the plays: "The Tightwad," 1927; "Singapore," 1932; "Original Sinning," "Yellow Freight," "Into the Darkness," etc. *Recreations:*

Golf and writing plays. *Address* · 12 Wildwood Circle, Pryer Manor, Larchmont, N.Y., U.S.A.
(Died Dec., 1966; age 68)

KEITH-JOHNSTON, Colin, actor; *b.* London, 8 Oct., 1896; *s.* of Robert Keith-Johnston and his wife Jessy (Macfie); *e.* Felsted; *m.* (1) Mary Cooper (mar. dis.); (2) Rett Kitson; served in the B.E. Force, Infantry and Air Force, and was awarded the M.C., Aug., 1917; made his first appearance on the stage at Drury Lane Theatre, 2 July, 1919, walking-on in " The Daughter of Madame Angot "; in 1920-1 toured in " The Luck of the Navy," " Charley's Aunt," " Mr. Pim Passes By," and " Brown Sugar "; in Apr., 1921, joined the Birmingham Repertory Theatre Company, appearing as Geoffrey Cassilis in "The Cassilis Engagement," Eugene Marchbanks in " Candida," Oswald in " Ghosts," Bob Acres in " The Rivals," John Rhead in " Milestones," Rowland in " The Shoemaker's Holiday "; Randall Utterwood in " Heartbreak House," George Smerdon in " The Farmer's Wife," Adam and Pygmalion in " Back to Methuselah," etc.; he came to London with this company, and appeared at the Court, Feb., 1924, as Adam and Pygmalion in " Back to Methuselah "; Mar., 1924, played George Smerdon in " The Farmer's Wife "; after seventeen months in this part went to the Kingsway, Aug., 1925, to play the part of Hamlet in the modern dress revival of that play; returned to " The Farmer's Wife " for nine months, after which he appeared at Barnes Theatre, Sept., 1926, as Donald Farfrae in " The Mayor of Casterbridge "; again returned to " The Farmer's Wife," until Jan., 1927; at the Princes, Feb., 1927, played Vassili Pestoff in " The Greater Love "; at the same theatre (for the Venturers' Society), May, 1927, played He in " The Might-Have-Beens "; Shaftesbury, Sept., 1927, Lord Teylesmore in " The High Road ": at the Court, May, 1928, again played in " Back to Methuselah "; at the Queen's, Jan., 1929, played " Landolph " in " The Mock Emperor ";

Arts Theatre, Mar., 1929, Captain Stanhope in " Journey's End "; he then went to New York, making his first appearance there, at the Henry Miller Theatre, 22 Mar., 1929, in the same part; after returning to London, at the Duchess Theatre, Dec., 1930, played John Ford in " Jane's Legacy "; at the Players, July, 1931, and Garrick, Aug.,1931, the Young Man in " The Life Machine"; returned to New York, and at the Broadhurst, Nov., 1931, played Laertes in " Hamlet "; Morosco, Mar., 1932, Theseus in " The Warrior's Husband "; Empire, Oct., 1932, Robert Chatfield in "Dangerous Corner"; Vaudeville, London, Dec., 1933, Anthony Reading in " Angel"; Westminster, Jan., 1934, Robin O'Neill in "Saturday's Children"; Adelphi, Mar., 1934, John Cooper in "Magnolia Street"; Wyndham's, June, 1934, Clive in " Clive of India"; Shaftesbury, Mar., 1935, George West in "Ringmaster"; New, July, 1935, Ham in " Noah"; Music Box, New York, Nov., 1935, Mr. Darcy in "Pride and Prejudice"; Richmond, June, and Daly's, July, 1937, Rev. Mark Ahern, S.J., in "The First Legion"; Phoenix, Mar., 1938, John Egerton in "Floodtide"; Fortune, June, 1938, Otterleigh in "White Secrets"; Westminster, Sept., 1938, Hector in "Troilus and Cressida" (in modern dress); Apollo, Oct., 1938, Maurice Atkins in "Tree of Eden"; Old Vic., Feb., 1939, Hovstad in " An Enemy of the People"; Westminster, Mar., 1939, Hon. Gerald Piper in "The Family Reunion"; Playhouse, May, 1939, Marshall in "Only Yesterday"; Empire, Sept., 1939, played Stanhope in a revival of "Journey's End"; Biltmore, Dec., 1939, Ken Sutter in "The Woman Brown"; Ethel Barrymore, Mar., 1940, Captain English in "A Passenger to Bali"; toured, 1940, as Aubrey Tanqueray in "The Second Mrs. Tanqueray"; Shubert, Mar., 1941, played Dr. Blenkinsop in "The Doctor's Dilemma," and in May, 1941, succeeded Raymond Massey as Sir Colenso Ridgeon in the same play; Royale, May, 1942, played Bill Randall in "The Strings, My Lord, Are False"; Belasco, Nov., 1942, Peter Launder in "Lifeline"; returned to

England, Dec., 1942, joined the Army, was commissioned as Captain, and served as entertainments officer in the Middle East, 1943, to the end of hostilities, 1945; returned to America, and Sept., 1945, toured as Camillo in "The Winter's Tale," appearing at the Cort, New York, Jan., 1946, in the same part; Biltmore, June, 1946, played Aubrey Stewart in "The Dancer"; Booth, New York, Apr., 1948, Robin Claydon in "The Rats of Norway"; toured in summer theatres, 1950, as Arthur Winslow in "The Winslow Boy"; at Los Angeles and San Francisco, June–July, 1950, appeared as Father Soames in "Getting Married"; Coronet, New York, Mar., 1951, played Gen. Benjamin Griggs in "The Autumn Garden"; Alvin, Dec., 1951, Laurence Lovell in "Point of No Return"; toured, 1952–3, in the last-mentioned part; in summer theatres, 1955, appeared as Arthur Winslow in "The Winslow Boy"; Martin Beck, Oct., 1956, Peter Shirley in a revival of "Major Barbara"; has also appeared in films and many television plays in both the U.S.A. and England; also played on several occasions in special productions for the 300 Club, Renaissance Society, Play Actors, and at the Arts and "Q" Theatres. *Favourite parts:* Hamlet, and Stanhope in "Journey's End." *Recreations:* Golf, riding, reading, and entomology. *Club:* Stage Golfing Society. *Address:* c/o Actors Equity Association, 165 West 46th Street, New York City, N.Y. 10036, U.S.A.

KELCEY, Herbert (Lamb), actor; *b.* London, 10 Oct., 1856; made first appearance on the stage at Brighton, England, in 1877, in "Flirtation"; made his first appearance on the London stage at the Royalty Theatre, 4 Oct., 1880, when he played Fred Latham in "Bow Bells"; same theatre he appeared 14 Feb., 1881, as Lord Ronald Scoury in "Peggy"; he next appeared at Drury Lane, 6 Aug., 1881, when he played the part of Captain Lord Loverton in "Youth"; subsequently he was engaged to tour in "The Lights o' London"; he made his first ap-

pearance in New York, at Wallack's Theatre, 9 Sept., 1882, as Philip Radley in "Taken From Life," and 30 Sept., 1882, He played Charles Tracy in "The Parvenu"; 4 Dec., 1882, he appeared as Sergeant Sabretache in "The Queen's Shilling," and subsequently he played Captain Skinner ("The Spider") in "The Silver King," and Major Marsden in "The Cape Mail"; at Stetson's Fifth Avenue, in 1883-4, he played Smooth in "Money," Colonel Trevanion in "The Glass of Fashion," and Arthur Kenyon in "Called Back"; at Madison Square, 29 Sept., 1884, he played Douglas Cattermole in "The Private Secretary," and, returning to Wallack's in Nov., played in "Constance" and "A Sheep in Wolf's Clothing"; same theatre, Mar., 1885, he played Count Orloff in "Diplomacy," and in Apr. played Arthur Meredith in "Our Joan"; returning to the Madison Square Theatre, in the same month, he played in "Sealed Instructions," subsequently playing there in "Saints and Sinners," "Society," "Old Love Letters," and "Our Society"; at Wallack's, in Oct., 1886, he played Tressider in "Harvest," and later he appeared as Mark Helstone in "The Harbour Lights," also in "The Domine's Daughter"; in 1887 he joined Daniel Frohman's company at the Lyceum, New York, and he played the leading parts at that theatre until 1896; during this period he appeared in many notable plays, among them the following: "The Great Pink Pearl," "The Wife," "Sweet Lavender," "The Charity Ball," "The Idler," "Nerves," "Lady Bountiful," "Squire Kate," "The Grey Mare," "The Guardsman," "The Amazons," "A Woman's Silence," "The Case of Rebellious Susan," "An Ideal Husband," "The Home Secretary," "The Benefit of the Doubt," and "The Prisoner of Zenda"; at the Herald Square Theatre, 4 May, 1896, he played Alan Kendrick in "The Heart of Maryland," and at Wallack's, in Sept., 1897, he appeared in "A Coat of Many Colours"; at the Lyceum, 11 Apr., 1898, he was seen in New York for the first time as a "star" when,

in conjunction with Effie Shannon, he played in " The Moth and the Flame " ; since that date he has " starred " in " My Lady Dainty," " My Daughter-in-Law," " Her Lord and Master," " Sherlock Holmes," " Taps " (" Lights Out "), and " The Lightning Conductor " ; at the Astor Theatre, 19 Nov., 1906, he played Richard Milbank in " The Daughters of Men " ; at Herald Square, 7 Mar., 1907, played William De Burgh Cokane in " Widower's Houses," subsequently touring in the same piece ; during Oct., 1907, started a tour with a play entitled " Bridge," subsequently playing Jack Frobisher in " The Walls of Jericho " ; during 1908, toured as Richard Voysin in " The Thief " ; in 1909, toured as Raymonde in " The Thief " ; during 1911, played in " The Lady from Oklahoma " ; at the Lyric, New York, Nov., 1911, played Ariste in " The Learned Ladies," and James Mortimore in " The Thunderbolt " ; at the Belasco Theatre, Dec., 1912, played John Strong in " Years of Discretion " ; at the Alcazar, San Francisco, Mar., 1914, appeared in " Her Lord and Master," " Alice Sit-by-the-Fire," " The Moth and the Flame," and " The Idler " ; at the Booth Theatre, New York, Jan., 1915, played Aaron Barstow in " Children of Earth " ; at the Alhambra, New York, Mar., 1915, Colonel Fairfield in " At Sunrise " ; at the Detroit Opera House, Aug., 1915, played in " Polly-anna." *Address :* Lambs' Club, New York City, U.S.A.
(Died 10 July, 1917; age 60)

KELHAM, Avice, actress and vocalist ; *b.* London, 6 Nov., 1892 ; *d.* of Richard Phillips Kelham and his wife Amelia Catherine (Roberts) ; *e.* Hampstead ; *m.* Christopher Anstey ; made her first appearance on the stage at the Gaiety Theatre, 4 Mar., 1911, in the chorus of " Peggy " ; subsequently understudied Gabrielle Ray as Polly in this piece, and later appeared as Diamond in the same play ; in Feb., 1912, played Sybil in " The Sunshine Girl," and subsequently went to Daly's Theatre, succeeding Gertie Millar as Lady Babbie in " Gipsy

Love " ; at Daly's, May, 1913, played Emma in " The Marriage Market," and subsequently toured in both of these last-mentioned parts ; at the Princes, Manchester, Dec., 1914, played Estelle in " Betty " ; reappeared at the Gaiety, 1915, succeeding Moya Mannering, as Victoria in " To-Night's the Night " ; at the Strand, Nov., 1916, played Betty in " Buxell " ; at the London Pavilion, Feb., 1917, appeared in " Cheerio ! " ; and Dec., 1917, in " Any Old Thing " ; at the Winter Garden, May, 1919, played Zelie in " Kissing Time." *Recreations :* Motoring, tennis, walking, and dancing. *Address :* 9 Portsea Place, Hyde Park, W.1.

KELLERMANN, Annette, aquatic performer ; *b.* Australia ; *m.* J. R. Sullivan ; made her first appearance on the stage as a tank performer in Australia ; made her first appearance in London, at the London Hippodrome, 13 Nov., 1905, making an immediate success ; appeared at the Oxford, May, 1912, in " Undine " ; subsequently went to America, where she has taken part in several special productions introducing her swimming speciality ; is a very powerful swimmer and has won several important contests. *Address :* c/o *New York Dramatic Mirror,* 1493-1505 Broadway, New York City.

KELLOGG, Shirley, actress and vocalist ; *b.* 27 May, 1888 ; *m.* Albert P. de Courville (mar. dis.) ; made her earliest appearances in the United States ; at the New York Theatre, Nov., 1908, played Ella Lee in " Miss Innocence " ; in 1909 appeared with Montgommery and Stone as Ethel Trotter in " The Old Town," appeared at the Globe, New York, Jan., 1910, in the same part ; at the Jardin de Paris, New York, in June, 1910, played in " The Follies of 1910 " ; at the Globe, New York, Nov., 1911, appeared as Daisy Dean in " The Three Romeos " ; first appeared in London, at the Hippodrome, 28 Oct., 1912, as Cornelia Van Huyt in " The Blue House " ; in Dec., 1912, appeared there in the *revue* " Hullo, Ragtime ! " in which she made a big success ; at the Prince of Wales's Theatre, 1 Nov., 1913, appeared as Sylvia Lester in " Are You There ? " ; subsequently appeared at the Hippodrome in " Hullo, Tango ! " Dec., 1913 ; " Push and Go," May, 1915 ; " Joyland," Dec., 1915 ; at Drury Lane Theatre, June, 1916, played in " Razzle-Dazzle " ; at the Hippodrome, Jan., 1917, in " Zig-Zag " ; at the Strand Theatre, Feb., 1918, appeared as Nan Carey in " Cheating Cheaters " ; at the Hippodrome, Mar., 1918, in " Box o' Tricks " ; and Mar., 1919, in " Joy-Bells " ; went to Canada, 1921, opening at Quebec, Oct., 1921, in " Hullo, Canada ! " ; at the Palladium, Feb., 1924, appeared in " The Rainbow " ; later, during 1924, was touring in the English provinces in " The Little Fisher Maid," and " Happy Hours."

KELLY, E. H., actor ; b. Ireland ; made his first appearance on the stage at the Avenue Theatre, 25 Sept., 1890, as Stenne in " The Struggle for Life " ; was subsequently engaged at the Haymarket Theatre, 1891, in " The Dancing Girl," and at the Comedy Theatre, 1892, in " To-Day " ; appeared at the Court, Sept., 1893, in " The Other Fellow," and " Under the Clock," and, 1894, in " The Gay Widow " ; at Terry's, 1894, appeared in " King Kodak," and, 1895, in " Margate " ; at the Prince of Wales's, 1895, played Ralli Carr in " Gentleman Joe " ; at the Strand, Feb., 1896, De Haas in " On 'Change " ; at the Prince of Wales's, Oct., 1896, Lord Macready in " The White Silk Dress " ; at the Royalty, May, 1897, the Hon. Tom D'Arcy in " A Court of Honour " ; at the Gaiety, Nov., 1897, Lord Harold Craven in " Frolicsome Fanny " ; subsequently became acting manager at several theatres ; produced on his own account " The Lion Hunters," at Terry's, 1901 ; in 1904, toured as Lord Francis Hillyer in " A Man and his Wife " ; at Wyndham's, Dec., 1904, appeared as Sir Lawrence Borthwick in " Peggy Machree " ; at the Royalty, Feb., 1905, as Valentine Grayling in " The Diplomatists " ; in 1905, toured as Charles Beverley in " The Golden Girl " ; at the Apollo,

Dec., 1907, played the Mad Hatter in " Alice in Wonderland " ; in 1912, toured as Captain Gradinsk in " By Right of Sword " ; appeared at Drury Lane, Sept., 1913, as Bertie Hart in " Sealed Orders " ; at the Little, Sept., 1914, as Prince Maleotti in " Forget-Me-Not " ; at the Apollo, Jan., 1915, as the Marquis of Pentreath in " A Busy Day " ; at the Garrick, Mar., 1915, as Harold Wedgewood in " Excuse Me ! " ; at Drury Lane, Apr., 1915, as Bertie Hart in a revival of " Sealed Orders " ; in Aug., 1915, toured as Alaric Chichester in " Peg o' My Heart " ; at the Queen's, Mar., 1916, played Gerald Bostwick in " The Love Thief " ; during 1917, toured as Saunders in " Bootles' Baby " ; 1918, as Blinn Corbett in " The Saving Grace," and as Andrew Larkin in " Be Careful, Baby." *Address :* 19 Malvern Road, Southsea, Hants.

KELLY, Eva, actress and vocalist ; b. Lockhaven, Pa., U.S.A., 18 Sept., 1880 ; d. of James T. and Anna Kelly, actor and actress ; e. Lockhaven and New York Schools ; m. G. P. Huntley ; made her first appearance on the stage at California Theatre, San Francisco, in 1883, as a child of three, in McKee Rankin's company, as Mustard Seed in a revival of " A Midsummer Night's Dream " ; in 1894, was in the chorus of the Alice Neilson Opera Company ; appeared at the Casino, under George Lederer in " The Rounders " ; made her first appearance in London, at the Shaftesbury, 25 Apr., 1900, as Trotter in " An American Beauty " ; in July, 1909, played Lotta Rocks in " The Casino Girl " ; subsequently appeared at the Gaiety in " The Toreador " ; at the Apollo, Feb., 1901, played in " The Belle of Bohemia " ; Sept., 1901, appeared in " Kitty Grey," and in 1902, appeared in " Three Little Maids," and in " Naughty Nancy," at the Savoy ; subsequently toured through Australia and America with George Edwardes's company ; at the Apollo, 1906, played in " Mr. Popple (of Ippleton) " ; at the Prince of Wales's, 31 Jan., 1907, played Gretchen in " Miss Hook of Holland " ; Apr.,

1908, appeared as Mdme. de Pilaine in "My Mimosa Maid"; at the Hicks Theatre, Oct., 1908, appeared as Didine in "The Hon'ble Phil"; in Dec. sailed for America, to tour in "Kitty Grey"; in 1909-10, played lead in "stock" seasons; subsequently appeared, with her husband, in "Buying a Gun" and "Curios," in various variety theatres; at the Prince's, Manchester, Dec., 1914, played Rawlins in "Betty"; subsequently toured as Chicquette in the same piece; at Daly's, May, 1916, played Luna d'Etoile in "The Happy Day"; at the Coliseum, Nov., 1916, appeared with her husband in "Selling a Pup," of which she was part-author; toured in this 1917-18; at the Coliseum, June, 1918, played Dulcie Ducie in "A Change of Tactics," of which she was also part-author; in 1920, again went to the United States. *Recreations:* Ice skating, driving, motoring, and farming. *Address:* c/o J. Southern, 38 Bury Street, St. James's, S.W.1.
(Died 16 Mar., 1948; age 67)

KELLY, Gene, actor and dancer; *b.* Pittsburgh, Penn., U.S.A., 23 Aug., 1912; *s.* of James Patrick Joseph Kelly and his wife Harriet (Curran); *e.* State of Pennslyvania and University of Pittsburgh; *m.* Betsy Blair; was an instructor of dancing before making his first appearance on the stage, at the Imperial Theatre, 9 Nov., 1938, as a Secretary in "Leave It To Me"; Booth, Feb., 1939, appeared in the *revue,* "One for the Money," and Oct., 1939, played Harry in "The Time of Your Life"; during 1940, directed The Diamond Horseshoe Restaurant; Ethel Barrymore, Dec., 1940, Joey Evans in "Pal Joey"; at the same theatre, Oct., 1941, arranged the dances for "Best Foot Forward"; went to Hollywood, and first appeared in films, 1942, in "Me and My Gal"; has since appeared exclusively in films. *Recreations:* Sports and reading. *Address:* c/o M.C.A., Beverly Hills, Calif., U.S.A.

KELLY, George, actor, producer, and dramatic author; *b.* Philadelphia, Pa., U.S.A., 1890; *s.* of John Henry Kelly and his wife Mary (Costello); made his first appearance on the stage in 1911, and has appeared all over the United States; played juveniles on the regular stage for five years, and from 1915 appeared in vaudeville sketches for a further five years; among these may be mentioned "The Woman Proposes," "Finders Keepers," "Poor Aubrey," "The Flattering World"; has written "Mrs. Ritter Appears," 1917; "The Torch Bearers," 1922; "The Show-Off," 1924; "Craig's Wife," 1925 (which gained the Pulitzer prize of the year); "Daisy Mayme," 1926; "Behold the Bridegroom," 1927; sketches for "A La Carte," 1927; "Reflected Glory," 1929; "Maggie the Magnificent," 1929; "Philip Goes Forth," 1931; "The Deep Mrs. Sykes," 1945, which he also staged; "The Fatal Weakness," 1946, which he staged; has not acted in New York since he appeared at the Frazee Theatre, Aug., 1923, as Julian in "Tweedles." *Recreations:* Bridge, golf, and travel.

KELLY, Judy, actress; *b.* New South Wales, Australia, 1 Nov., 1913; *d.* of Gerald Eugene Kelly and his wife Blanche (Davies); *e.* Wagga Wagga, N.S.W.; *m.*: Eric Summer; formerly engaged as teacher in a school at Sydney; studied for the stage under Brunton Gibb and H. W. Varna; made her first appearance on the stage at the Arts Theatre, Sydney, 1930, as Vane in "The Rising Generation"; came to England, 1932, and appeared in films; made her first appearance on the London stage at the "Q." Theatre, 22 Oct., 1934, as Audrey Murray in "Courtship Dance" and played the same part at the Duke of York's, Nov., 1934, when the play was renamed "It Happened to Adam"; St. Martin's, May, 1937, played Mirabel in "A Ship Comes Home"; toured in South Africa, 1937, in "The Frog" and "The Amazing Dr. Clitterhouse"; on her return appeared at the Palace, Sept., 1937, as Vivien Gabriella in "Take It Easy"; Opera House, Blackpool, Nov., 1937, Eve Bentley in "Ring Off, Please"; Duke of York's (for London International Theatre), Jan., 1938, Julia de Biro in "Gentleman's Agreement"; Oct., 1938, toured as Nurse Appleby in "King of Nowhere"; Apollo, Dec., 1938, played Fay Larkin in "Windfall"; St. Martin's, June, 1939, Catherine, Empress of Russia in "Bridge of Sighs"; New, Jan., 1940, Janet Lawson in "Believe It or Not"; Strand, July, 1940, and Apr., 1941, Frankie in "Women Aren't Angels"; Garrick, Dec., 1941, Frances in "Warn That Man"; "Q," May, 1944, Margaret Foley in "The Crime of Margaret Foley"; Playhouse, Liverpool. Aug., 1944, Vanessa in "Violent Friendship," and appeared in the same play, at the "Q," Jan., 1945; St. James's, Apr., 1946, played Louise Dexter in "The Astonished Ostrich"; entered films, 1932, and has appeared in innumerable pictures since that date. *Recreations:* Tennis, horse-riding, and poetry.

KELLY, Paul, actor; *b.* Brooklyn, New York, U.S.A., 9 Aug., 1899; *e.* Brooklyn; *m.* (1) Dorothy Mackaye; (2) Claire Owen; made his first appearance on the stage at the age of eight in "A Grand Army Man"; toured and played in "stock" companies for several years; at the Booth, New York, Jan., 1918, played George Cooper in "Seventeen"; Globe, Sept., 1918, Robert Williams in "Penrod"; Times Square, Aug., 1921, Ralph Kingsland in "Honors Are Even"; Playhouse, Mar., 1922, John Allen in "Up the Ladder"; 49th Street, Aug., 1922, Barry McGill in "Whispering Wires"; Playhouse, Sept., 1923, Harry in "Chains"; Morosco, Mar., 1924, Jack Kennedy in "The Lady Killer"; Comedy, Sept., 1924, Ted Hill in "Nerves"; Hudson, Feb., 1925, Arthur Demarest in "Houses of Sand"; Little, Aug., 1925, Charlie Watts in "The Sea Woman"; Ritz, Mar., 1926, Larry Wood in "Find Daddy"; Cohan, Feb., 1930, played in "Nine-Fifteen Revue"; Hudson, Oct., 1930, Eddie in "Bad Girl"; Morosco, Feb., 1931, St. Louis Blackie in "Hobo"; Broadhurst, Sept., 1931, Jimmie Alden in "Just to Remind You"; Alvin, Jan., 1932, Matt in "Adam Had Two Sons"; Selwyn, Dec., 1932, Nicky in "The Great Magoo"; Coronet, Oct., 1945,

Frankie Madison in "Beggars Are Coming to Town"; Fulton, Oct., 1947, Brigadier Gen. K. C. Dennis in "Command Decision," which performance gained him three awards as the best actor of the 1947–8 season; Lyceum, Nov., 1950, Frank Elgin in "The Country Girl"; as a child acted in silent films; re-entered films, 1933, and has appeared in innumerable pictures since that date. *Address:* c/o Actors' Equity Association, 45 West 47th Street, New York City, U.S.A.
(Died 6 Nov., 1956; age 57)

KELLY, Renée, actress; *b.* London, 4 June, 1888; *d.* of Robert Kelly; *e.* London and in America; *m.* A. Hylton Allen; made her first appearance on the stage at Bridgeport, Conn., U.S.A., Nov., 1906, when she walked on in "The Genius," with Nat Goodwin; made her first appearance in New York, at the Garrick Theatre, 2 Mar., 1908, as Mamie Carter in "The Easterner"; appeared at Daly's, New York, Oct., 1908, when she played Mamie in "Myself-Bettina," with Maxine Elliott; remained in the same company till 1910, playing Kitty in "The Chaperon," at the opening of the Maxine Elliott Theatre, 30 Dec., 1908; toured in both these parts and as Violet in "Deborah of Tod's"; in 1911 joined the Drama Players at Chicago; appeared with that company at the Lyric Theatre, New York, Sept.-Nov., 1911, as Maisie Clifford in "Modern Marriage," Hilda Wangel in Ibsen's play, "The Lady from the Sea," and Henriette in an adaptation of Molière's play, "Les Femmes Savantes," entitled "The Learned Ladies"; appeared at the Casino, New York, Dec., 1911, as Peggy Barrison in "Peggy"; made her first appearance on the London Stage, at the Criterion, 18 June, 1912, as Ann in the play of that name; returned to America, and at the Fulton Theatre, N.Y., Sept., 1912, appeared as June Thornborough in "June Madness"; at Poughkeepsie, Oct., 1912, played Rachel in "The Five Frankforters"; in Nov., 1912, toured with Robert Loraine, as Ann Whitefield in "Man and Superman"; returning to London, appeared at the Comedy Theatre, Apr., 1913, as Eve Addison in "The Inferior Sex"; May, 1913, as Enid Underwood in "Strife," and June, 1913, as Agnes Ralston in "Jim the Penman"; returned to New York, 1913; at Maxine Elliott's Theatre, Jan., 1914, played Ethel Travis in "Don't Weaken"; at the Studebaker Theatre, Chicago, Feb., 1914, Enid Stonor in "The Speckled Band"; at the Davidson, Milwaukee, May, 1914, appeared in "The Call of Youth"; at the Park Theatre, New York, Nov., 1914, played the Queen of the Southland in "The Garden of Paradise"; at Toledo, Dec., 1914, appeared as Judy in "Daddy Long-Legs"; continued to tour in this part, 1915-16; she then returned to London, and at the Duke of York's, May, 1916, appeared in the same part, and continued throughout the run of over 500 performances; at the Globe, Oct., 1917, appeared as The Image and Mary Temple in "The Willow Tree"; at the Savoy, Feb., 1918, played Gwendolyn Ralston in "Nothing But the Truth"; at the Prince of Wales's, Apr., 1919, Blanche Wheeler in "Fair and Warmer": at the Queen's, June, 1919, Marjorie Caner in "The Cinderella Man"; at the Coliseum, Mar., 1920, Bobbie in "Bobbie Settles Down"; at the Globe, July, 1920, Mdlle. Juliette in "French Leave"; at the Kingsway, Mar., 1921, Sally Snape in "The Heart of a Child"; during 1922-3, appeared in variety theatres in playlets; at the Criterion, Nov., 1923, played Dulcinea in "Dulcy"; at the Savoy, Mar., 1924, Miranda in "Blinkers"; July, 1924, Lady O'Moy in "In the Snare"; in Oct., 1924, went to South Africa, playing lead in "Windows," "Outward Bound," "The Mask and the Face," "French Leave," "A Kiss for Cinderella," and "The Chinese Puzzle"; reappeared in London, at the Coliseum, Sept., 1925, in "Predestination"; during 1926-7 toured in Australia, playing "Polly with a Past," "The Mask and the Face," "Brown Sugar," "Daddy-Long-Legs," "The Naughty Wife," "The Last of Mrs. Cheyney"; returning to London, appeared at the Coliseum, Nov., 1927, in "Quits," and

"Selfishness"; appeared at the Everyman, Apr., 1928, as Jane in "The Dumb Man of Manchester"; next toured as Shirley Deane in "The House With Purple Stairs"; Everyman, Sept., 1928, played Ginevra in a play of that name; Wyndham's, Dec., 1928, Anne in "The Love-Lorn Lady"; during 1929 again appeared in variety theatres in sketches; subsequently toured in "Looking for a Wife"; Winter Garden, Oct., 1929, played Hania in "Miss Adventure"; Garrick, Feb., 1930, Rosalie Quilter in "Almost a Honeymoon"; June, 1931, Millicent in "What Woman Wants"; subsequently toured as Queenie Mellish in "The Meeker Sex," and Katherine Silverton in "The Marriage of Kitty"; during 1932, toured as Mary Marshall in "Mary's Other Husband"; Grand, Fulham, Feb., 1933, Mary Marshall in "Mary's Other Husband"; Victoria Palace, Dec., 1933, again played Judy Abbott in "Daddy Long-Legs"; during 1934, played a repertory season at Cairo and Alexandria; Little, Feb., 1937, Dorothy Williams in "Strange Barrier"; Arts, Mar., 1937, Fanny Burney in "Joy Will Come Back"; Richmond, May, 1938, Judy Campion in "Just Round the Corner"; Strand, Feb., 1939, Mrs. Jessup in "Little Ladyship"; reappeared on the stage after four years absence, 1943, when she toured as Fanny in "Watch on the Rhine"; Prince of Wales's, Apr., 1944, played Mrs. Smith in "The Rest is Silence"; St. James's, Sept., 1944, Mrs. Mainwaring in "Felicity Jasmine"; toured, Nov., 1944, as Janet Archer in "Kiss and Tell," and appeared in the same part at the Phoenix, Aug., 1945; Whitehall, Dec., 1946, Mrs. Hawkins in "Treasure Island"; Comedy and Embassy, Dec., 1947, Miss Pritchard in "Daddy Long-Legs"; "Q," Mar., 1948, Ruth Stafford in "Easy Money"; Boltons, May, 1948, Carrie Butterworth in "Third Cousin"; Wimbledon, Aug., 1949, Mrs. Robinson in "The Robinson Family." *Recreations:* Sewing and reading. *Address:* Manor Cottage, Brighton Road, Horley, Surrey. *Telephone No.:* Horley 875.
(Died 28 Aug., 1965; age 77)

1345

KELLY, W. W., J.P., C.C. ; *b.* in America, 16 Dec., 1853 ; manager ; *m.* Edith Cole ; prior to coming to England, was a prominent manager in the United States, and for some years managed W. J. Ferguson, Maud Granger, and Charlotte Thompson ; in 1883, he " discovered " Grace Hawthorne, whom he brought to London, opening at the old Olympic Theatre, Oct., 1886, with " The Governess," a revised version of " Miss Multon " and " East Lynne " ; subsequently produced " A Ring of Iron " ; from 1887-9, was manager of the Princess's Theatre, producing " Siberia," " Shadows of a Great City," " The Still Alarm," " Nowadays," " The Good Old Times," and " Theodora " ; in 1891, produced " A Royal Divorce " at the New Olympic Theatre, which he subsequently reproduced at the Princess's, and has been proprietor of this play ever since ; in 1897, he became Lessee and Manager of the Metropole Theatre and the New Theatre Royal, Birkenhead ; subsequently secured Queen's Theatre, Liverpool, which was renamed Kelly's, and in 1913 succeeded Mr. Wentworth Croke as Lessee and Manager of the Shakespeare Theatre, Liverpool ; he disposed of Kelly's, Liverpool in 1916, and the Theatre Royal, Birkenhead, in 1920 ; sat as Councillor for Argyle Ward, Birkenhead for over thirteen years, and was offered the Mayoralty of the Borough on three occasions, but pressure of business prevented his acceptance ; in 1916, elected City Councillor for Dingle Ward, Liverpool ; in 1918, was appointed a Justice of the Peace for the Borough of Birkenhead ; in 1928 disposed of his interest in the Shakespeare, Liverpool.
(Died 19 Sept., 1933; age 79)

KELLY, Walter C., actor ; *b.* Mineville, N.Y., U.S.A., 29 Oct., 1873 ; originally an engineer in the U.S. Navy for four years, and served in the Spanish-American War, 1896 ; made his first appearance on the stage in "vaudeville," 1899, as " The Virginia Judge," by which name he has become known all over the world ; in 1902, appeared on the regular stage as Mr. Doughton in "Huckleberry Finn," also in "The Office Boy"; in 1904, was with Marie Dressler in "Sweet Kitty Swellairs"; from 1904–12, in "vaudeville" in "The Virginia Judge," appearing all over the English-speaking world, including five engagements at the Palace Theatre, London; Winter Garden, New York, Jan., 1914, appeared in "The Whirl of the World"; 1914–16, in "vaudeville"; during 1917, appeared at the Winter Garden, in "The Show of Wonders"; 1918–24, again in "vaudeville"; again appeared in variety theatres in Great Britain, 1925; toured in "The Passing Show," 1927; again in "vaudeville," 1927–9; at the Cosmopolitan, New York, Oct., 1929, played Judge Totheridge in "The Great Day"; Royale (for Theatre Guild), Mar., 1933, Solomon Fitzmaurice in "Both Your Houses"; Cort, Nov., 1934, General Smallwood in "The Jayhawker"; entered films, 1935, and appeared in "McFadden's Flats" and "The Virginia Judge. *Address :* Elks Club, 110 West 43rd Street, New York City, U.S.A. *(Died 6 Jan., 1939; age 65)*

KELSO, Vernon, actor ; *b.* Southsea, Hants, 12 Aug., 1893 ; *s.* of John Edward Harry Kelso, M.D., and his wife Cecilia Emily (Dudingston) ; *e.* Eastman's Naval College and Sherborne ; *m.* Hazel Lawrence (mar. dis.) ; made his first appearance on the stage at the Grand Theatre, Blackpool, Aug., 1910, in the chorus of "The Girl in the Train"; toured for over six years and then went to the United States; made his first appearance on the New York stage at the Republic Theatre, 19 Apr., 1917, as Pasquier de la Marrière in "Peter Ibbetson"; spent two years in Shakespearean repertory with E. H. Sothern and Julia Marlowe; spent four years, 1923–6, in Jane Cowl's company, appearing with her at the Henry Miller Theatre, Jan., 1923, as Benvolio in "Romeo and Juliet," Lyceum, New York, Feb., 1924, as Octavius in "Antony and Cleopatra," Empire, Dec., 1925, Charles Burleigh in "Easy Virtue," and accompanying her to England, made his first appearance on the London stage, at the Duke of York's, 9 June, 1926, in the same part; appeared at the Charles Hopkins, New York, 1929–31, as Harry Price in "Michael and Mary," Willie Ragg in "Mrs. Moonlight," and Brice in "The Roof"; appeared at the Malvern Festival, Aug., 1932, in "The Alchemist" and "Tom Thumb"; on returning to London, appeared at the Ambassadors', Sept., 1932, as John Shelby in "The Left Bank"; at the Little and Kingsway, 1933–4, played Colonel Hammond in "While Parents Sleep"; Queen's, Mar., 1936, Captain Wilson in "Red Night"; New, Oct., 1936, Lepidus in "Antony and Cleopatra"; "Q," Nov., 1936, President Ruysdael in "Storm Over Europe"; Arts, Dec., 1936, Colonel Stacey in "Strange Incident"; Palace, Feb., 1937, Sergei in "On Your Toes"; Arts, June, 1937, Bronson Paget in "In the Best Families"; Duke of York's, Apr., 1939, Sir John Mapen in "Interlude"; Richmond, May, 1939, Frank Betterton in "Honeymoon for Three" (subsequently, "Is Your Honeymoon Really Necessary?"); St. Martin's, May, 1942, Clive Popkiss in "Rookery Nook"; Cambridge, Sept., 1942, Vladimir in "Waltz Without End," and Mar., 1943, Hector Hushabye in "Heartbreak House"; St. James's, June, 1943, Du Mesnil in "Parisienne"; toured, Feb., 1944, as Samson Appleby in "Staff Dance"; Duke of York's, Aug., 1944, Frank Betterton in "Is Your Honeymoon Really Necessary?", which then ran until 1946; Victoria Palace, Aug., 1946, played Mr. Vernon Cranford in "Sweetheart Mine"; toured, 1948, as Clive in "The Anonymous Lover." *Favourite part:* Feste in "Twelfth Night." *Recreations:* Golf and swimming. *Club:* Green Room. *Address:* 12 Queen Anne Mews, W.1. *Telephone No.:* Langham 1906.

KEMP, T. C. (Thos. Chas. Kemp), dramatic critic; *b.* Birmingham, 30 Apr., 1891; *s.* of Charles Henry Kemp and his wife Fanny Sophia (Ellis); *e.* King Edward's School, Birmingham, and Kelham College; *m.* Thelma Shwalbe; was formerly engaged as a schoolmaster and librarian; dramatic critic to *The*

Birmingham Post since 1935; was formerly Chairman of the Crescent Theatre, Birmingham; Lecturer and Tutor in English Literature and Drama to the Library Association of Great Britain; Lecturer for the British Council; a member of the Panel of Advisers to the British Council Centre of Shakespeare Studies, Stratford-on-Avon; drama and film critic B.B.C. (Midland Region) since 1945; is the author of a play "Supremacy," 1932, and of "Birmingham Repertory Theatre; the Playhouse and the Man," 1943; is a member of The Critics' Circle. *Recreation:* Walking. *Address:* 59 Cotton Lane, Moseley, Birmingham, 13. *Telephone No.:* (Birmingham) South 0601.
(Died 3 Jan., 1955; age 64)

KEMPER, Collin, American manager; *b.* Cincinnati, Ohio, U.S.A., 17 Feb., 1870; *e.* Cincinnati; *m.* Hope Latham; in conjunction with Lincoln Wagenhals, his partner, entered into management of Stone's Opera House, Binghampton, New York, where he founded a fine "stock" company in June, 1893; in the Sept. following, they presented Louis James and company in a Shakespearean repertory at the Grand Opera House, New York; since that date they have managed the following "stars": Louis James, Frederick Warde, Kathryn Kidder, Madame Modjeska, Henry Miller, Arthur Byron, Blanche Walsh, and Annie Russell; in the autumn of 1906 they opened the new Astor Theatre, New York, of which they were the sole lessees and managers; subsequently retired for some years, but re-entered the field as producing managers in 1918 with "Pack Up Your Troubles"; during 1920 they produced "Spanish Love," "The Bat," "Seeing Things," and "A Thief in the Night"; have since produced "Why Men Leave Home," 1922; "The Breaking Point," 1923; "Lovely Lady" and "The Joker," 1925; produced "The Bat," at the St. James's Theatre, London, Jan., 1922. *Recreations:* Athletics, music, and literature. *Address:* 1560 Broadway, New York City, U.S.A. *Telephone No.:* Bryant 9–0681. *(Died 27 Nov., 1955; age 85)*

KENDAL, Doris, actress ; made her first appearance on the stage in 1918, when she toured as Kitty in " Charley's Aunt " ; during 1919 toured as Lady Gillian Dunsmore in " Nurse Benson," and 1920, as Victoria in " Home and Beauty " ; she appeared at the Playhouse, Apr., 1921, as Martha Weldon in " Up in Mabel's Room " ; she then went to Australia, where she toured, under J. C. Williamson, Ltd. ; on returning to England, 1923, toured as Poppy in " Ambrose Applejohn's Adventure " and Ethel Warren in " The Great Lover " ; at the Haymarket, Nov., 1923, played the Hon. Gwendoline Fairfax in " The Importance of Being Earnest " ; at the Aldwych, Feb., 1924, Mary Grayson in " It Pays to Advertise."

KENDAL, Dame Madge (Margaret), G.C.B.E., actress ; *b.* at 58 Cleethorpes Road, Grimsby, Lincs, 15 Mar., 1848 ; *d.* of Margaretta (Marinus) and William Robertson, the twenty-second child of her parents ; sister of T. W. Robertson, the famous dramatist, E. Shafto Robertson, actor and Fanny Robertson, actress ; *m.* W. H. Kendal (Grimston) ; her parents were both in the theatrical profession, and from her childhood she was connected with the stage ; previous to her marriage she was known as Madge Robertson ; made her first appearance on the stage at the old Marylebone Theatre, 20 Feb., 1854, as the child Marie in " The Struggle for Gold," and " The Orphan of the Frozen Sea " ; at the same theatre she also played Jeannie in " The Seven Poor Travellers," 26 Feb., 1855 ; the child in " The Stranger," 26 Mar., 1855 ; Small Pica in " Tit-Tat-Toe," 26 Dec., 1856 ; Mary Fondlove in " Spare the Rod and Spoil the Child," 20 Apr., 1857 ; at the Theatre Royal, Bristol, 1855, she played Eva in " Uncle Tom's Cabin " ; from 1860-3, she was at this theatre, and in 1860, played in " Puss in Boots " ; in 1862, played Cinderella, and 1863, Little Goody Two-Shoes ; at the opening of the Theatre Royal, Bath, 4 Mar., 1863, she appeared as Alice in " Marriage at Any Price," and the second singing Fairy in " A Midsummer Night's Dream," in the latter piece

Ellen Terry appeared as Titania ; played Cinderella on 9 Mar., 1863, and returning to Bristol, remained there till 1865 ; she reappeared in London, at the Haymarket, 29 July, 1865, playing Ophelia in " Hamlet," Walter Montgommery playing Hamlet, and James Fernandez Laertes ; she also supported Montgommery there as Blanche in " King John " and Desdemona in " Othello " ; as a proof of her versatility, she played Cupid in " Ixion," on 29 Aug., 1865, and subsequently played Jessica in " The Merchant of Venice " ; she then toured with Montgommery, and subsequently appeared at Hull, where in 1866, she played Julie in " Richelieu " and Lady Macbeth with Samuel Phelps ; she then appeared at Liverpool and Nottingham as Juliet, Peg Woffington in " Masks and Faces," and Pauline in " The Lady of Lyons " ; at Drury Lane, 22 Apr., 1867, she played Edith Fairlam in " The Great City " ; at the Haymarket, Oct., 1867, she played Georgina in " Our American Cousin," with E. A. Sothern, also appearing with him as Alice in " Brother Sam," Ada Ingot in " David Garrick," Blanche Dumont in " A Hero of Romance," and also appeared as Marguerite in " A Wife Well Won " and Hypolita in " She Would and She Would Not " ; at the opening of the Gaiety Theatre, 21 Dec., 1868, she played Florence in " On the Cards " ; she also appeared there as Lady Clara Vere de Vere in " Dreams," 1869 ; she then rejoined the Haymarket comp ny on tour, and played Viola, Rosalind, Lady Teazle, Kate Hardcastle and Lydia Languish ; she remained at the Haymarket until the end of 1874, during which period she played Lilian Vavasour in " New Men and Old Acres," Ellen Petworth in " Barwise's Book," Lydia Languish in " The Rivals," Florence Marigold in " Uncle Will," Zeolide in " The Palace of Truth," Lady Teazle in " The School for Scandal," Rosalind in " As You Like It," Kate Hardcastle in " She Stoops to Conquer," Miranda in " The Busybody," Galatea in " Pygmalion and Galatea," Ada in " Faded Flowers," Ethel in " A Little Change," Selene in " The Wicked

World," Mrs. Whymper in " His Own Enemy," Mrs. Sebright in " The Overland Route," Lady Gay Spanker in " London Assurance," Madge in " Twenty Minutes Under An Umbrella," Jessy Meadows in " Single Life," Mrs. Van Brugh in " Charity," Mab in " Queen Mab," Elinor Vane in " A Madcap Prince," Mrs. Honeyton in " A Happy Pair " ; in Nov., 1874, she went on tour with her husband, then appeared at the Opéra Comique and Gaiety, 1875, and then appeared at the Court with John Hare in Mar., 1875, playing the name part in " Lady Flora " ; she also appeared at the Court, as Mrs. Fitzroy in " A Nine Days' Wonder," Lady Hilda in " Broken Hearts," and Susan Hartley in " A Scrap of Paper " ; during her engagement at the Court, her husband was a silent partner with John Hare ; she next appeared at the Prince of Wales's Theatre, Sept., 1876, under the Bancrofts, as Lady Ormond in " Peril," followed by Clara Douglas in " Money," Lady Gay Spanker in " London Assurance," and Dora in " Diplomacy " ; she then returned to the Court Theatre, Jan., 1879, appearing in a revival of " A Scrap of Paper " ; in Feb., 1879, she played the Countess D'Autreval in " The Ladies' Battle," and Apr., 1879, played Kate Greville in " The Queen's Shilling " ; her husband then publicly entered into partnership with John Hare at the St. James's, and this partnership existed from Oct., 1879, to July, 1888 ; during that period she appeared in the following parts : Kate Greville in " The Queen's Shilling," Lady Giovanna in " The Falcon," Mrs. Sternhold in " Still Waters Run Deep," Susan in " William and Susan," Isabel Ransome in " Good Fortune," Millicent Boycott in " The Money Spinner," Ann Carew in " A Sheep in Wolf's Clothing," Pauline in " The Lady of Lyons," Mrs. Pinchbeck in " Home," Mrs. Frank Preston in " The Cape Mail," Kate Verity in " The Squire," Mrs. Beresford in " Impulse," Nora Desmond in " Young Folks' Ways," Claire de Beaupré in " The Ironmaster," Rosalind in " As You Like It," Lilian Selkirk in " The Castaways," Agnes Roydant in " May-

fair," Antoinette Rigaud in the play of that name, the Countess de Moray in " The Wife's Sacrifice," Mrs. Spencer Jermyn in " The Hobby Horse," Lady Clancarty in the play of that name, and Lady Amyot in " The Wife's Secret " ; in the autumn of 1888 she toured with her husband, and her next appearance in London was at the Court Theatre, Mar., 1889, when she played Lady Vivash in " The Weaker Sex," and in May, 1889, she appeared as Kate Desmond in " A White Lie " ; the same year she went to America for the first time, making her first appearance in New York, at the Fifth Avenue Theatre, 7 Oct., 1889, as Susan Hartley in " A Scrap of Paper " ; further tours followed, and she added the parts of Lady Marsden in " All for Her," Helen Rutherford in " The Senator's Wife," Violet Huntley in " Marriage," 1892, and Katherine Vail in " Prince Karatoff" to her repertory ; reappeared in London, at the Avenue Theatre, Jan., 1893, in " A White Lie," followed by " The Ironmaster," " The Silver Shell " (" Prince Karatoff "), " A Scrap of Paper " ; again toured 1893-6 and played Paula in " The Second Mrs. Tanqueray," Miriam Chisholm in " The Fall of the Leaf," Mrs. Armitage in " The Greatest of These —," Lady Guilderoy in " Lord and Lady Guilderoy," etc. ; appeared at the Garrick Theatre, June, 1896, in " The Greatest of These — " ; again toured, 1896-8, playing Sara Lester in " A Flash in the Pan," Dorothy Blossom in " The Elder Miss Blossom," and Mrs. Grantham in " Not Wisely but too Well " ; appeared at the St. James's, Sept., 1898, as Dorothy in " The Elder Miss Blossom " ; on tour, 1899-1900, appeared as Margaret Hurlestone in " The Poverty of Riches " and Mildred Archerson in " The Likeness of the Night," playing the latter part at the Grand, Fulham, Nov., 1900 ; at the Tyne, Newcastle, Mar., 1901, played the Duchess of Cluny in " The Secret Orchard" ; reappeared at the St. James's, Sept., 1901, in " The Elder Miss Blossom," and in Oct. in " The Likeness of the Night " ; on tour, 1902, played Mrs. Trecarrel in " St. Martin's Summer," and Mrs.

Hamilton in "Conscience," subsequently called "Mrs. Hamilton's Silence"; appeared at His Majesty's Theatre, with Beerbohm Tree and Ellen Terry, June, 1902, as Mistress Ford in "The Merry Wives of Windsor"; on tour, 1903, played Anne McLeod in "One People," in which she appeared at the Coronet, May, 1903; on tour, 1903, played Marjorie Lyall in "Dick Hope," playing the same part at the Coronet, Dec., 1903; on tour, 1904, played Lady Audrey Whitby in "The Housekeeper," and played the same part at the Camden, Dec., 1904; on tour, 1905, played Nora in "The Bird at the Neck," appearing in the same part at the King's, Hammersmith, Mar., 1905; appeared at the St. James's, Sept., 1905, in "Dick Hope," and in Oct., in "The Housekeeper"; on tour, 1906, played Mrs. Hyacinth in "A Tight Corner," and 1907, Judith Carlusen in "The Melcombe Marriage"; at the Coronet, Apr., 1907, played in "A Tight Corner"; on tour, 1907, played Mrs. Stannas and Lady Marrable in "The Other Side," and played the same parts at the Grand, Fulham, Mar., 1908; on tour, 1908, played Constance Livingstone in "The Whirlpool," and played the same part at the Marlborough Theatre, Sept., 1908; also on tour, 1908, appeared as Madame Armiéres in "The House of Clay," in which she appeared at the Coronet, Oct., 1908; has since retired from the stage, her only appearance having been made at His Majesty's Theatre, on the occasion of the Gala performance, 27 June, 1911, when she played Mistress Ford in the letter scene from "The Merry Wives of Windsor"; received the honour of Dame Commander of the British Empire, 1926, and received the Grand Cross of the Order, 1927; received the honorary Freedom of Grimsby, July, 1932; was the recipient of her portrait, painted by Sir William Orpen, 1928; was Commanded by the late Queen Victoria to appear with her husband at Osborne, 1 Feb., 1887, in "Uncle's Will" and "Sweethearts." *Recreation*: Reading. *Address*: Dellcott, Chorley Wood, Herts.
(*Died 14 Sept., 1935; age 87*)

KENDAL, William Hunter (W. H. Grimston), actor and manager; *b.* London, 16 Dec., 1843; *e.* London; *m.* Margaret Robertson; made his first appearance on the stage at the Soho Theatre, 6 Apr., 1861, as Louis XIV in "A Life's Revenge"; he remained at that theatre, subsequently re-named the Royalty, for a year, and played there in "Atar Gull," "Matrimony," "A Chinese Romance," etc., others in the company being David James, Charles Wyndham, Ellen Terry, etc.; in 1862 he went to the Moore Street Theatre, Birmingham, and from thence to the Theatre Royal, Glasgow, where he remained four years, and where he played numerous parts with Mr. and Mrs. Charles Kean, Helen Faucit, G. V. Brooke, Dion Boucicault, Charles Mathews, etc.; returned to London in 1866, and was engaged for the Haymarket, where he appeared on 31 Oct., 1866, as Angus Mandeville in "A Dangerous Friend"; he remained a member of the Haymarket company until 1874, and played numerous leading parts, notably Sir Harry Lester in "A Game of Speculation," the Hon. Mr. Dacre in "A Lesson for Life," Charles Paragon in "Perfection," Master Waller in "The Love Chase," Charles Surface in "The School for Scandal," Harry Arncliffe in "An Unequal Match," Orlando in "As You Like It," Romeo, Captain Absolute in "The Rivals," the Marquis de Chamont in "A Wife Well Won," Don Octavio in "She Would and She Would Not," Rudolph in "Leah," Manfred in "Pietra," Bob Levitt in "Mary Warner," Charles Cashmore in "Uncle's Will," Prince Philamir in "The Palace of Truth," Young Marlow in "She Stoops to Conquer," Pygmalion in "Pygmalion and Galatea," Jeremy Diddler in "Raising the Wind," Ethais in "The Wicked World," Tom Dexter in "The Overland Route," Dazzle in "London Assurance," Frederick Smailey in "Charity," Gerald Carew in "Queen Mab," Harold Marjoribanks in "Mont Blanc," Harry Lisle in "A Madcap Prince"; his engagements have ever since been exactly the same as his wife's, and he appeared at the Opéra

Comique and Gaiety in " The Lady of Lyons," " As You Like It," and " She Stoops to Conquer " ; at the Court, 1875-6 entered into " silent " partnership with John Hare, with whom he played Harry Armytage in " Lady Flora," Christian Douglas in " A Nine Days' Wonder," Prince Florian in " Broken Hearts," and Colonel Blake in " A Scrap of Paper " ; at the Prince of Wales's, 1876-8, under the Bancrofts, he appeared as Dr. Thornton in " Peril," George Clarke in " The Vicarage," Charles Courtly in " London Assurance " and Julian Beauclerc in " Diplomacy " ; at the Court, 1879, played Colonel Blake in " A Scrap of Paper," Gustave de Grignon in " The Ladies' Battle," and Frank Maitland in " The Queen's Shilling " ; he then entered into open partnership with John Hare at the St. James's, commencing 4 Oct., 1879 ; at the St. James's, he played the following parts, Frank Maitland in " The Queen's Shilling," Count Alberighi in " The Falcon," John Mildmay in " Still Waters Run Deep," Sir Hugh de Brass in " A Regular Fix," William in " William and Susan," Charles Denis in " Good Fortune," Lord Kingussie in " The Money Spinner," Jasper Carew in " A Sheep in Wolf's Clothing," Claude Melnotte in " The Lady of Lyons," Captain Mainwaring in " Coralie," Colonel White in " Home," Lieutenant Thorndyke in " The Squire," Captain Crichton in " Impulse," Estabrook in " Young Folks' Ways," Philippe Derblay in " The Ironmaster," Orlando in " As You Like It," Geoffrey Roydant in " Mayfair," Henri de Tourvel in " Antoinette Rigaud," the Count de Moray in " The Wife's Sacrifice," Lord Clancarty in " Lady Clancarty," and Sir Walter Amyot in " The Wife's Secret " ; the partnership with John Hare terminated on 21 July, 1888, since which date he has appeared with his wife as Ira Lee in " The Weaker Sex," Sir John Molyneux in " A White Lie," Sir John Trevor in " All for Her," John Rutherford in " The Senator's Wife," Sir Rupert Huntley in " Marriage," 1892, Prince Karatoff in the play of that name, subsequently re-named " The Silver Shell," Aubrey Tanqueray in " The Second Mrs. Tanqueray," Sir John Frosdyke in " The Fall of the Leaf," Mr. Armitage in " The Greatest of These —," Lord Guilderoy in " Lord and Lady Guilderoy," Sir Everard Grey in " A Flash in the Pan," subsequently known as " A Cruel Heritage," Andrew Quick in " The Elder Miss Blossom," the Duke of Ayrshire in " Not Wisely but too Well," Anthony White in " The Poverty of Riches," Bernard Archerson in " The Likeness of the Night," Charles Henri Stuart in " The Secret Orchard," the Rev. Martin Verrian in " St. Martin's Summer," Henry Macdonald in " Conscience," Captain Sir James Stanley in " One People," Dick Hope in the play of that name, Colonel Lionel Trent in " The Housekeeper," Ulick Desmond in " The Bird at the Neck," Jack Hyacinth in " A Tight Corner," The Earl of Melcombe in " The Melcombe Marriage," Anthony Redwood in " The Other Side," Elijah D. Tillottson in " The Whirlpool," and Henri Armières in " The House of Clay." Since 1908 has practically retired from the stage, and has not appeared in London since that date ; with his wife, was honoured by Command of the late Queen Victoria, to appear at Osborne, 1 Feb., 1887, when they played in " Uncle's Will " and " Sweethearts." *Address :* 12 Portland Place, W., and The Lodge, Filey, Yorks. *Clubs :* Garrick, Arts, Beefsteak, Junior Carlton, etc. *(Died 6 Nov., 1917; age 73)*

KENDALL, Henry, actor and director; *b.* London, 28 May, 1897 ; *s.* of William Kendall and his wife Rebecca (Nathan); *e.* City of London School; made his first appearance on the stage at the Lyceum Theatre, Sept., 1914, as a "super" in "Tommy Atkins"; subsequently appeared in the chorus of " Business as Usual," at the Hippodrome, Dec., 1914 ; " Watch Your Step," Empire, 1915 ; spent nine months at the "Old Vic.," 1915, playing juvenile parts in Shakespearean repertory, including Claudio in " Much Ado About Nothing," Florizel in " The Winter's Tale," Sebastian in " Twelfth

Night," etc. ; served in the Royal Air Force, 1916-19, as Captain, gaining the Air Force Cross ; on being demobilized in 1919, appeared at the Garrick, Mar., 1919, as the Second Marquis in " Cyrano de Bergerac," and subsequently at Drury Lane, played Christian in the same play ; at the Little Theatre, Feb., 1920, played Guy in " Mumsee " ; at the Globe, July, 1920, scored a success when he appeared as Lieut. George Graham in " French Leave " ; at the Apollo, Dec., 1920, as St. George in " Where the Rainbow Ends " ; at the St. James's, Mar., 1921, as Harry Richardson in " Polly With a Past " ; at the Haymarket, May, 1921, succeeded Leon Quartermaine as Edward Luton in " The Circle " ; at the St. James's, Aug., 1921, played James in " Threads " ; at the Queen's, Oct., 1921, played the leading part of Barry Scarlett in " The Hotel Mouse " ; at the Royalty, Nov., 1921, Tom Godling in " Two Jacks and a Jill " ; at the Ambassadors', Mar., 1922, played in " The Curate's Egg " ; at the Everyman, July, 1922, played Bluntschli in " Arms and the Man " ; at His Majesty's, Sept., 1922, Harold Knox in " East of Suez " ; at the Ambassadors', Mar., 1923, John Wiltshire in " Marriage by Instalments " ; at the Shaftesbury, May, 1923, Geoffrey Dangerfield in " Stop Flirting " ; at the Regent (for the Repertory Players), Nov., 1923, Dick Chappell in " Havoc ", and the same part when the play was staged for a run at the Haymarket, Jan., 1924 ; at the Royalty, June, 1924, Billy Reynolds in " Bachelor Husbands " ; at the Regent (for the Fellowship of Players), July, 1924, Orlando in " As You Like It " ; at the Prince of Wales's, Sept., 1924, appeared in " Charlot's Revue " ; Prince's (for the Repertory Players), Mar., 1925, played Lieut. St. Aubyn in " Tunnel Trench " ; " Q," June, 1925, Count Alexei Czerny in " The Czarina " ; Savoy, July, 1925, Doctor Tom Pearson in " On 'Change " ; went to New York, and appeared at the Lyceum, Nov., 1925, as Gerald Gray in " Naughty Cinderella " ; at the Ritz, Dec., 1926, played Honey in " This Woman Business " ; after his return to London, appeared at the Comedy, June, 1927,

as Captain Philip Barty in " The Silent House " ; Strand, May, 1928, played Mago in " The Road to Rome " ; New, Aug., 1928, Reggie Higgins in " A Damsel in Distress " ; at the Strand (for the Repertory Players), Dec., 1928, Hugh Rawson in " Wrongs and Rights " ; New, Apr., 1929, Hugo Bonsor in " Baa, Baa, Black Sheep " ; Prince's, Sept., 1929, Vincent Floyd in " The Flying Fool " ; Lyric, Oct., 1929, Maxine de Bellencontre in " He's Mine " ; Comedy, Dec., 1929, Teddy Deakin in " The Ghost Train " ; Mar., 1930, John Strange in " Odd Numbers " ; Cambridge, Sept., 1930, played in " Charlot's Masquerade " ; Strand (for Repertory Players) and St. James's, Nov., 1930, Maurice Mullins in " A Murder has been Arranged " ; in the autumn of 1934, toured as Hugo Arnold in " Cut for Partners " ; at the Aldwych (for Repertory Players), Mar., 1935, and New, May, 1935, Ronnie Martin in " Someone at the Door " ; Aldwych (for Repertory Players), Sept., 1935, Kenneth Brice in " The World Waits " ; Ambassadors', Mar., 1937, Edward Morton in " Bats in the Belfry," and Jan., 1938, Gerald Esmond in " This Money Business " ; Comedy, Sept., 1938, Hubert Crone in " Room for Two " ; " Q," June, 1939, Micky Saunders in " Punch Without Judy," which he again played at the New Theatre, Dec., 1939 ; " Q," June, 1940, played Michael Drumley in " House Party " ; toured, July, 1940, in " Nap Hand," and Jan., 1941, in " High Temperature " ; Comedy, June, 1941, appeared in the *revue* " Rise Above It " ; Vaudeville, Apr., 1942, in " Scoop " ; Ambassadors', Feb., 1943, played John Ayers in " A Little Bit of Fluff " ; Comedy, June, 1943, Dominic Mallory in " The Fur Coat " ; Ambassadors', Jan., 1944, succeeded Walter Crisham in " Sweet and Low " ; Feb., 1944, appeared in " Sweeter and Lower," which ran until 1946 ; May, 1946, appeared in " Sweetest and Lowest " ; Savoy, June, 1948, appeared in the *revue* " A la Carte " ; Embassy, Apr., and Comedy, June, 1949, appeared as Harry Blacker in " On Monday Next . . ." ; Ambassadors', Aug., 1950, Lovewell in " For Love or Money " ; Vaudeville, Sept., 1950, for a time played Peter Perry in "The Dish Ran Away"; toured, Oct., 1950, in "Caprice"; is frequently engaged as a director, and since 1939 has directed "A Lass and a Lackey," 1940; "Rise Above It," "Other People's Houses," 1941; "Scoop," 1942; "Man from Heaven," 1943; "This Was a Woman," 1944; "Fly Away Peter," 1944; "See How They Run," "Great Day," "The Shop at Sly Corner," "Green Laughter," "Fit for Heroes," 1945; "On Monday Next . . ." (in association with Shaun Sutton), 1949; at the Aldwych, Mar., 1951, directed "Macadam and Eve"; Duchess, May, 1951, played Henry Lord in "The Happy Family"; Wimbledon, Nov., 1952, directed "The Nest Egg"; Savoy, Dec., 1953, directed "Down Came a Blackbird"; Stoll, Dec., 1953, directed "Where the Rainbow Ends"; Savoy, Feb., 1954, appeared as Sir Pomeroy Pomeroy-Jones in "Angels in Love"; Duke of York's, July, 1954, directed "Meet a Body"; at the "Q," Dec., 1954, played Montague Cloud, R.A., in "Portrait of a Woman," which he also directed; Royal, Brighton, Mar., 1955, directed "Tropical Fever"; Royal, Nottingham, May, 1955, played Oliver Charrington in "Beat the Panel," and appeared in this part at the Embassy, June, 1955, when the play was re-titled "The Lion in the Lighthouse," and which he directed in association with David Smith-Dorrien; Royal, Nottingham, Oct., 1955, played Julian Lassiter in "The Call of the Dodo"; Lyric, Feb., 1956, directed "Ring For Catty"; Victoria Palace, June, 1958, directed "You, Too, Can Have a Body"; New Victoria, Dec., 1958, directed, and played Joseph Flint in "Where the Rainbow Ends"; Cambridge, May, 1959, played Lord Whitehall in "Let Them Eat Cake"; Fortune, Nov., 1959, played the title part in "Aunt Edwina"; Aldwych, Feb., 1960, directed (with André van Gyseghem), "Watch It, Sailor!"; Piccadilly, May, 1960, directed "Bachelor Flat"; has also directed and played leading parts in television plays; has directed numerous plays at the "Q," and Embassy theatres; commenced film career, 1931, and has appeared in innumerable pictures; is one of the Founders of the Repertory Players; author of "I Remember Romano's" (autobiography). *Recreation:* Music: has composed several songs, and a musical comedy, "The New Poor." *Club:* Green Room. *Address:* Weatherall Lodge, Well Road, London, N.W.3. *(Died 9 June, 1962; age 65)*

KENDALL, John, dramatic author; *b.* London, 21 June, 1869; *s.* of the late Rev. E. K. Kendall, M.A., D.C.L., *e.* Portsmouth and Woolwich; *m.* Katherine Githa Sowerby; entered Royal Artillery in 1888; retired 1904, with rank of Captain; well known as a writer under his pseudonym of "Dum-Dum"; commenced writing in India, 1900; became a contributor to *Punch,* 1902; is the author of the following plays: "Mrs. Bill," Court, 1908; "Laughter in Court," Drury Lane, 1909; "Diul," Playhouse, 1911; "Bingo," New, 1923, is the author of several volumes of humorous verse, "Odd Creatures," "Odd Numbers," "A Fool's Paradise," "The Crackling of Thorns," "Rhymes of the East," "In the Hills," "At Odd Moments," "Oh, Helicon!" "The Seventh Hole," "Short Doses," "Says He" (prose); etc. *Recreations:* Golf and humorous literature. *Club:* Garrick. *Address:* 18 Kensington Square, W.8. *Telephone No.:* Western 6905.

KENDRICK, Alfred, actor; *b.* London, 5 Aug., 1869; *e.* at King's College; made his first appearance on the stage at the Grand, Islington, 20 Mar., 1890, as Lorenzo in "The Merchant of Venice," with Hermann Vezin; toured with Vezin in "Dan'l Druce," "The Love Chase," "Othello," etc.; subsequently appeared at Terry's, 1891, in "Culprits"; toured in "The Rocket," "The Magistrate," "In Chancery," "The Times," with Edward Terry; in 1894 toured as Jack Chesney in "Charley's Aunt"; subsequently appeared at the St. James's and toured with Ben Greet; in 1896, appeared at the Criterion in "A Blind Marriage"; during 1897-8 toured in the United States with Julia Marlowe, playing Romeo, Orlando,

Ingomar, Prince Charlie and the Marquis Von Sturmell in " The Countess Valeska " ; fulfilled long engagements with Sir Henry Irving, Sir Charles Wyndham, and Charles Frohman ; has appeared of late years with Fred Terry and Julia Neilson, at the New Theatre, Strand Theatre, and on tour in "The Scarlet Pimpernel," "The Popinjay," " Dorothy o' the Hall," " Matt o' Merrymount," " Henry of Navarre," "As You Like It," " The Duchess of Suds," " Mistress Wilful," " Sweet Nell of Old Drury," " The Argyle Case," " Much Ado About Nothing," " The Marlboroughs," etc. *Hobby :* Painting. *Club :* Green Room. *Address :* 43 Popesgrove, Twickenham. *Telephone No. :* Popesgrove 2479.

KENNEDY, Charles Rann, dramatic author ; *b.* Derby, 14 Feb., 1871 ; *s.* of Annie Leng (Fawcett) and Edmund Hall Kennedy ; *g.-s.* of Charles Rann Kennedy, the famous Greek scholar; *br.* of E. F. Kennedy : *br.-in-law* of Mrs. Harold E. Gorst, novelist ; *e.* College School, Saltley, Birmingham ; *m.* Edith Wynne Matthison ; formerly engaged in mercantile life, also as theatrical business manager, actor, etc. ; originally intended for holy orders ; made his first appearance on the stage at Her Majesty's Theatre, 28 April, 1897, as a starving Citizen in " The Seats of the Mighty " ; after touring as Lord Drelincourt in " Jim the Penman," became treasurer at the Metropole Theatre, Camberwell, under J. B. Mulholland, remaining two years ; next joined Ben Greet, first as business manager and subsequently as actor, appearing in the latter capacity as Prospero in " The Tempest," Duke Orsino in " Twelfth Night," Leonato in " Much Ado About Nothing," Oliver in " As You Like It," Doctor in " Everyman," etc., etc. ; made his first appearance in New York, 1903, as the Doctor and Messenger in " Everyman " ; author of " What Men Dare," " The Servant in the House," " The Winter-feast," " The Terrible Meek," " The Flower of the Palace of Han," " The Necessary Evil," " The Rib of

the Man," " The Army With Banners," " The Fool from the Hills," " The Chastening," " The Admiral," " The Salutation," " The Idol-Breaker," " Old Nobody," " Crumbs," " Flaming Ministers," " Face of God," " Beggar's Gift," etc. ; two pantomimes ; resumed acting at Chicago, May, 1913, when he appeared as John Heron in his own play " The Necessary Evil " ; at the Cort Theatre, New York, Jan., 1918, appeared in " Everyman " ; at the Vieux Colombier Theatre, New York, Apr., 1918, produced his own play, " The Army with Banners " ; has since produced and appeared in the annual Greek Play at Millbrook, New York, playing Herakles in " Alcestis," Creon in " Antigone," Theseus in " Hippolytus," Jason in " Medea," the Peasant in " Elektra," Talthybius in " The Trojan Women," also " The Fool from the Hills," etc. ; reappeared in London, June, 1924, when he played the Carpenter in " The Chastening," and the Sailor in " The Admiral " ; the Censor refused a licence for the first-named, which was performed at St. Paul's Church, and at the Mary Ward Settlement ; returned to America in Aug., 1924, and toured in " The Chastening," " The Admiral," " Old Nobody," and " The Salutation " ; again appeared in London, at the St. Pancras People's Theatre, July, 1926, as Dante Alighieri in " The " Salutation." *Club :* Players, New York. *Address :* The Bennett School, Millbrook, N.Y., U.S.A.
(Died 16 Feb., 1950; age 79)

KENNEDY, Edmund actor ; *b.* Derby, 8 Apr., 1873 ; *s.* of Edmund Hall Kennedy ; brother of C. Rann Kennedy ; *e.* Saltley College School, Birmingham ; *m.* Lilian Mason, actress ; was acting manager at Metropole, Camberwell, under J. B. Mulholland for some time ; made his first appearance on the stage in 1898, at Belfast ; toured as Colonel Anstruther in " The Second in Command " with Ben Greet's company, and as Prince Dimitri in " Resurrection," 1904 ; appeared in Wilson Barrett's drama, " The Never Never Land," and in the same author's " Lucky Durham," in which he played lead 1,500 times ;

visited America in 1908 and appeared in his brother's play, "The Servant in the House"; in 1911 toured as Harry Thresk in "The Witness for the Defence; in 1912, appeared at the Lyceum, as De Brissac in "The Women of France"; subsequently toured as Paul Sylvaine in "Leah Kleschna," Dexter in "Find the Woman," Brassbound in "Captain Brassbound's Conversion," and Jackson Ives in "Ready Money"; at the Booth Theatre, New York, Jan., 1914, played Sam Thatcher in "Change"; in 1914 toured in the English provinces as Prosper Couramont in "A Scrap of Paper"; during 1915-16 toured as Sir Berkeley Wynne in "The Flag Lieutenant"; 1917 toured as Harley Napier in "The Case of Lady Camber," and as Hyacinth Petaval in "The Angel in the House"; in 1918 toured as Yucca Len in "Inside the Lines"; also played various parts for the N.A.C.B., in English Garrison Theatres; during 1919-20 toured as Karl Pfeiffer in "Uncle Sam," The Beachcomber in "The Bird of Paradise," and Mr. Wu in the play of that name; at the Lyceum, 1921, played Big Wolf in "The Savage and the Woman"; at the St. James's, Aug., 1921, Barton in "Threads"; at the Kingsway, Mar., 1922, Tai Fah Min in "The Yellow Jacket"; Strand, July, 1922, Dr. Javelin in "The Risk"; at the Apollo, Sept., 1922, Veitel in "The Torch"; at the Strand, Dec., 1922, Dick and Supervisor Dance in "Treasure Island"; Dec., 1923, Blind Pew and Dick in the same play, and Dec., 1924, Blind Pew and Israel Hands in the same piece. *Address:* 38 Sydney Road, West Ealing, W.13. *Telephone No.:* Ealing 1699.

KENNEDY, Joyce, actress; *b.* London, 1 July, 1898; *d.* of Dr. Arthur Stoddard Kennedy and his wife, Katherine Stuart (Beane); *m.* Louis E. de Rouet (mar. dis.); was a pupil of the Royal Academy of Dramatic Art, where she gained a Gold Medal; made her first appearance on the stage at the St. James's Theatre, Jan., 1920, in "Julius Caesar"; she then toured with Henry Ainley

as Portia in "Julius Caesar"; Court, Dec., 1920, played Hippolyta in "A Midsummer Night's Dream"; at the Victoria Palace, Dec., 1921, played the Queen in "The Windmill Man"; at the Haymarket, June, 1922, appeared as a servant in "The Dover Road"; Mar., 1923, Alice in "Isabel, Edward and Anne"; June, 1923, Freda Mannock in "Success"; at the Apollo, Feb., 1924, Lesley Stanley in "The Fairy Tale"; at the Aldwych (for the Stage Society), Mar., 1924 and at the Queen's, Apr., 1924, Helen Thorburn in "The Conquering Hero"; at the Lyric, Hammersmith, May, 1924, succeeded Dorothy Green as Mrs. Marwood in "The Way of the World"; at the R.A.D.A. Theatre, May, 1924 (for the Three Hundred Club), Mrs. Richly in "The Discovery"; at the Ambassadors', Aug., 1924, Mrs. Blount in "Storm"; at the Scala, Nov., 1924 (for the Repertory Players), Löis in "Judas Iscariot." Haymarket, Apr., 1925, Janet Ingleby in "Ariadne"; June, 1925, The Lady's Maid in "The Man With a Load of Mischief"; Royalty, July, 1926, Josephine Trent in "The Awful Truth"; Everyman, Sept., 1926, Louka in "Arms and the Man"; Oct., 1926, Sheila in "The Rat Trap"; His Majesty's, Feb., 1927, Lois in "The Wicked Earl"; Criterion, Dec., 1927, Constance Drayton in "Quest"; Arts, Dec., 1928, Shirley Denham in "Wallflower"; Apollo (for the Stage Society), Feb., 1929, Countess Diana in "The Princess"; Arts, Mar., 1929, Mary in "The Tidings Brought to Mary"; Wyndham's, Apr., 1929, Moya Stacey in "The Moon Rides High"; Strand, May, 1929, Shirley Denham in "Why Drag In Marriage?" ("Wallflower"); Wyndham's, July, 1929, Chloe in "The Skin Game"; Daly's, Jan., 1930, Elinor Quarles in "This Way to Paradise"; New, May, 1930, Nan Fitzgerald in "The Last Chapter"; Ambassadors', Oct., 1930, Marjorie Corbett in "The Grain of Mustard Seed"; Wyndham's, Aug., 1931, Isla in "The Case of the Frightened Lady"; Sept., 1932, Veronica in "The Way to the Stars"; Oct., 1932, Isobel Service in "Service"; Prince's, May, 1933, the Comtesse Zicka in "Diplomacy"; Opera House,

Manchester, May, 1934, Myra Carton in "The Winding Journey"; Phoenix (for Repertory Players), Mar., 1935, Anna in "Family Group"; Ambassadors', Feb., 1936, Anne Felton in "Out of the Dark"; St. Martin's, May, 1936, Lady Oxford in "Bitter Harvest"; Lyric, Oct., 1936, Countess of Carlisle in "Charles, the King,"; commenced film career, 1930, and since 1936 has appeared in "Black Mask," "Twelve Good Men," "Debt of Honour," "Seven Sinners," "Hail and Farewell," "Big Fella," "The Nursemaid Who Disappeared," etc. *Address*: 23 Whitelands House, S.W.3. *Telephone No.*: Sloane 6894.
(Died 12 Mar., 1943; age 44)

KENNEDY, Madge, actress; *b.* Chicago, U.S.A.,; *d.* of Gordon Kennedy and his wife Carolyn (Warner); *e.* California and New York; *m.* (1) Harold Bolster; (2) William B. Hanley, Jun.; was a member of the Arts Students' League, and had had some experience as an amateur before making her first appearance on the professional stage in 1910, when she toured with Henry Woodruff in "The Genius"; in 1911 she followed Margaret Lawrence as Elsie Darling in "Over Night," and then played a "stock" engagement at the Colonial Theatre, Cleveland; at the Forty-eighth Street Theatre, New York, Aug., 1912, played the title-*rôle* in "Little Miss Brown," and continued in this part throughout 1912-13; at Poughkeepsie, New York, May, 1913, played Anne Grey in "The Co-respondent"; at the Fulton Theatre, New York, Aug., 1914, played Blanche Hawkins in "Twin Beds"; at the Eltinge Theatre, Nov., 1915, appeared as Barbara Wheeler in "Fair and Warmer," which she played throughout the long run of that play; she then turned her attention to the cinema stage, 1917, and appeared in "Nearly Married," "Baby Mine," "The Purple Highway," "Three Miles Out," "Bad Company," "Lying Wives," "Oh, Baby!""Strictly Confidential," etc.; and was not seen again on the regular stage until she appeared at the Astor Theatre, Dec., 1920, when she played the

dual *rôle* of Mary Brennan and Margaret Waring in "Cornered"; at the Little Theatre, New York, Sept., 1922, played Elizabeth Dean in "Spite Corner"; at the Apollo, New York, Sept., 1923, Poppy McGargle in "Poppy"; at the Forty-ninth Street Theatre, Dec., 1924, Miriam Holt in "Badges"; Elliott Theatre, Dec., 1925, Joyce Bragdon in "Beware of Widows"; Gaiety, Apr., 1926, Diana Wynne in "Love in a Mist"; Mansfield, Oct., 1927, Mary McVittey in "The Springboard"; Music Box, Dec., 1927, Mary Hutton in "Paris Bound"; during 1930, toured as Susan in "The Perfect Alibi," and as Mary in "Michael and Mary"; at Times Square Theatre, May, 1931, succeeded Gertrude Lawrence as Amanda Prynne in "Private Lives"; Cort, May, 1932, played Joyce Burroughs in "Bridal Wise"; at the Studebaker, Chicago, Jan., 1934, played Fanny Grey in "Autumn Crocus."

KENNEDY, Margaret, dramatic author and novelist; *b.* London, 23 Apr., 1896; *d.* of Charles Moore Kennedy and his wife Elinor; *e.* Cheltenham Ladies' College and Somerville College, Oxford; *m.* (His Honour Judge) David Davies, K.C.; author (with Basil Dean) of "The Constant Nymph," 1926, adapted from her novel; "Come With Me," 1928; "Escape Me Never," 1933; "Autumn" (with Gregory Ratoff), 1937; "Happy With Either," 1948; among her novels are "Ladies of Lyndon," "The Constant Nymph," "Red Sky at Morning," "The Fool of the Family," "Return I Dare Not," "A Long Time Ago," "The Oracles"; "The Heroes of Clone"; published her autobiography under the title of "Where Stands a Winged Sentry." *Address*: c/o Curtis Brown, Ltd., 6 Henrietta Street, London, W.C.2.
(Died 31 July, 1967; age 71)

KENNEDY, Mary, actress and dramatic author; *b.* Claxton, Ga., U.S.A.; *d.* of Foster Kennedy and his wife Josephine (McMahon); *m.* Deems Taylor; formerly engaged in newspaper work; made her first appearance in

New York, at the 39th Street Theatre, 3 Sept., 1917, as Nancy O'Dowd in "Lucky O'Shea"; subsequently she appeared at the Morosco Theatre, in "Lombardi Ltd"; Playhouse, Oct., 1919, played Miss Halsey in "A Young Man's Fancy"; Booth, May, 1920, Rosamond Gill in "Not So Long Ago"; Bijou, Mar., 1923, Marie in "The Love Habit"; Vanderbilt, Nov., 1923, Lorna Webster in "In the Next Room"; 52nd Street, Mar., 1925, Rosie Callaghan in "The Blue Peter"; Plymouth, Mar., 1927, Joan Shepperley in "Mariners"; George M. Cohan, Oct., 1927, Emmy Chase in "The Nineteenth Hole;" Garrick, Nov., 1928, Hesther Tobin in "A Man With Red Hair"; Martin Beck (for the Theatre Guild), Apr., 1929, Lilli Bojok in "The Camel Through the Needle's Eye"; Empire, Aug., 1931, Bella Hedley in "The Barretts of Wimpole Street"; Belasco, Jan., 1934, Edith Choate Farley in "The Joyous Season"; part author of "Mrs. Partridge Presents," 1925; "Captain Fury of the Holy Innocents"; and author of "Jordan," produced in London, 1928; appeared in films, with the Cosmopolitan Film Company, 1920. *Address :* Haviland Road, Stamford, Conn., U.S.A. *Telephone No.:* Stamford, Conn., 4–6813.

KENNY, Sean, designer; *b.* Portroe, Tipperary, Ireland, 23 Dec., 1932; *s.* of Thomas Joseph Kenny and his wife Nora (Gleeson); *e.* St. Flannan's College, Co. Clare, School of Architecture, Dublin, and Frank Lloyd Wright Foundation, U.S.A.; *m.* Jan Walker (mar. dis.); formerly an architect; he designed his first production at the Lyric Theatre, Hammersmith, Jan., 1957, "The Shadow of a Gunman"; has since designed the following productions: "The Hostage," "Bloomsday" (Oxford University Experimental Theatre Club), "Coriolanus" (Oxford Playhouse), 1958; "Sugar in the Morning," "Lock Up Your Daughters," "A Glimpse of the Sea" and "Last Day in Dreamland" (double-bill), "Cock-a-Doodle-Dandy," "Treasure Island," 1959; "The Lily-White Boys," "Henry V," "Great Expectations," "Bachelor Flat," "Laughing Academy," "Oliver!,"

"Chin-Chin," 1960; "The Devils," "The Miracle Worker," "Altona," "Stop the World—I Want to Get Off," "Romeo and Juliet" (Stratford-on-Avon), 1961; "Blitz!," "King Priam" (Coventry Festival and Covent Garden), "Uncle Vanya" (Chichester Festival), "Stop the World—I Want to Get Off" (New York), "End of Day" (Dublin Festival), 1962; "Oliver!" (New York), "Pickwick," "The Beggar's Opera," "Hamlet" (National Theatre), 1963; "Maggie May," 1964; "The Roar of the Grease Paint, the Smell of the Crowd" (New York), "Pickwick" (New York), 1965; "Oliver!" (tour), "The Flying Dutchman" (Covent Garden), 1966; "The Four Musketeers" (also designed the stage), 1967; "Gulliver's Travels" (also co-author and director), 1968; "Lock Up Your Daughters," "Anything You Say Will Be Twisted," "The Bandwagon," "I've Seen You Cut Lemons," 1969; "The Hallelujah Boy" (also lighting), "The Nuns" (Sussex University Art Centre), "Peer Gynt" (Chichester Festival), ' Here Are Ladies" (also directed), "Don't Let Summer Come" (Sussex), 1970; designed his first film production, Sept., 1961, with "I Thank a Fool"; first designed for television, Aug., 1959, and principal productions include: "Windmill Near a Frontier," "Juno and the Paycock," *Panorama* and *Monitor,* etc.; re-designed the Old Vic Theatre, for the National Theatre Company, 1963. *Recreation:* Sailing. *Address:* c/o Donald Langdon Agency Ltd., 24 Pembroke Place, London, W.1.

KENT, Keneth, actor, author, and director; *b.* Liverpool, 20 Apr., 1892; *s.* of Charles Kent and his wife Beatrice (Fox-Turner); *e.* Harrow (preparatory), Eastbourne College; the son of an actor, he studied for the stage at the Royal Academy of Dramatic Art; made his first appearance on the stage, at the Comedy Theatre, Nov., 1912, in "All Men Are Fools"; appeared at the same theatre, Feb., 1913, as Jimmy Cottenham in "Lady Noggs"; at the Duke of York's, 1914, understudied Donald Calthrop in "The Little Minister"; during 1915 was engaged with Miss Horniman's company, at the Gaiety, Manchester; at the Duke of York's, Sept., 1915, played Alan Jeffcoat in "Hindle Wakes"; at the St. James's, Oct., 1916, the Hon. James Parsons in "Lucky Jim"; subsequently toured with Irene Vanbrugh as Charles in "Rosalind"; at the Court, May, 1917, played Keith Allison in "Hush"; Dec., 1917, Lord Fancourt Babberley in "Charley's Aunt"; subsequently at the Duke of York's, played in "The Thirteenth Chair"; at the Strand, July, 1918, played Lieut. Stephen English in "The Hidden Hand"; he then toured as Lieutenant Clive Stanton in "The Luck of the Navy"; at the Garrick, Sept., 1920, "Tubbey" in "The Right to Strike"; at the Comedy, Dec., 1920, George Body in "The Charm School"; subsequently toured in the same part, and as Mr. Dipper in "The Dippers"; at the Lyceum, Feb., 1923, played Pierre in "The Orphans"; then toured as Nick in "The Way of an Eagle"; at the New Theatre, Mar., 1924, played the Soldier from Hell in "Saint Joan"; at the St. Martin's, Dec., 1924, Camille in "No Man's Land"; Comedy, May, 1925, Charles Lampeter in "The Crooked Friday"; Queen's, Aug., 1925, Lo-San in "The Man from Hong-Kong"; Comedy, Dec., 1925, Tom Turner in "9.45"; Mar., 1926, Alec Cameron in "Summer Lightning"; New, Sept., 1926, Jacob Birnbaum in "The Constant Nymph"; Dec., 1927, Chester Kyle in "The Wrecker"; Arts, May, 1928, Bob Farringdon in "Let's All Talk About Gerald"; Sept., 1928, Jim Culverwell in "Payment"; Garrick, Sept., 1928, again played Birnbaum in "The Constant Nymph"; Royalty, Mar., 1929, Herbert Alden in "Afraid of the Dark"; Globe, May, 1929, Uncle Ahab in "The Black Ace"; Strand, May, 1929, Arnold Dare in "Why Drag In, Marriage?"; subsequently toured as the Man in "Fast and Loose"; during 1930, toured as Carlo Caradini in "The Cheat"; New, June, 1931, played Panisse in "Sea Fever"; Vaudeville, Sept., 1931, Hoppy in "Blue Sky Beyond," of which he was the author; he is also the author of "The Cheat," and adapted "The Georgian House"

(from Swinnerton's novel); directed 'She Couldn't Say No," on tour, Sept., 1932; Duke of York's, Nov., 1932, played the Faithful Dog in "To-Night or Never"; Globe, June, 1933, Hyman in "Proscenium"; Comedy, Mar., 1935, Serge Bankieff in "Delusion"; in Sept., 1935, joined the Old Vic. Company, appearing in "Peer Gynt," "Julius Caesar," "The Three Sisters," "Macbeth," "The School for Scandal," "St. Helena"; the last-mentioned play was transferred to Daly's, Mar., 1936, when he again played Napoleon with great success; Daly's, Nov., 1936, Ludwig van Beethoven in "Muted Strings"; Haymarket, June, 1937, Brian Harding in "To Have and To Hold"; Comedy, Aug., 1938, Nicolai Szapary in "Give Me Yesterday"; at the "Q" and Embassy, 1939, played Tony Perelli in "On the Spot"; toured, 1941, as Napoleon in "Napoleon Couldn't Do It"; Palace, Apr., 1942, played Dr. Carlos in "Full Swing," which he played for over a year; toured, 1943, as Napoleon in "The Duchess of Dantzic," The Man in "The Man in Dark Glasses," and the Husband in "Parisienne"; "Q," June, 1944, Descius Heiss in "The Shop in Sly Street," which was revived at the St. Martin's, Apr., 1945, as "The Shop at Sly Corner," and which ran for over two years; toured during the spring, 1947, as Dr. Jekyll and Mr. Hyde in a play of that name; Wimbledon, Oct., and Embassy, Nov., 1947, played Reginald Wensley in ". . . Said the Spider!"; "Q," Apr., 1949, Paul Coryton in "House on the Sand"; Wimbledon, Oct., 1949, played Ralph Gordon, M.D., in "The Man They Acquitted," which he also directed; toured, 1950, as Professor Challenger in "The Poison Belt"; "Q," Aug., 1950, Nicolai Szapary in "Give Me Yesterday"; St. James's, Dec., 1950, Long John Silver in "Treasure Island"; toured, autumn, 1951, as Hercule Poirot in "Black Coffee"; directed "The Barton Mystery," and toured in this play during the spring of 1954; toured, autumn, 1954, in his original part of Descius Heiss in "The Shop at Sly Corner"; has made a number of appearances in television plays and has also frequently broadcast; was for a time, in 1934, a teacher at the R.A.D.A.; is currently teaching at the Webber-Douglas School of Drama; has taken part in numerous performances for The Repertory Players, Pioneers, etc., and in several productions at the "Q" and Embassy theatres; has also appeared in numerous films. *Recreations:* Bridge and theatre-going. *Address:* 8 Dorset Court, Dorset Street, London, W.1. *Telephone No.:* Welbeck 4601. *(Died 17 Nov., 1963; age 71)*

KENT, William, actor; *b.* St. Paul, Minn., U.S.A.; joined a minstrel show at the age of fourteen, making his first appearance at St. Paul, subsequently touring; made his first appearance on the New York stage, 1906, in "Chinatown Charlie," under A. H. Woods; was subsequently engaged by Charles Frohman for "Miss Hook of Holland"; for two years appeared in comedy parts with the Park Opera Company, St. Louis; in 1918, appeared in "Have a Heart"; was appearing at Hartford, Conn., in 1918, when he was seen and engaged by the late H. W. Savage; he made his first appearance on the New York Stage, at the Geo. M. Cohan Theatre, 11 Mar., 1918, as Hyperion Buncombe in "Toot! Toot!"; subsequently appeared at the Broadhurst Theatre in "Ladies First"; at the Winter Garden, July, 1919, played in "Shubert Gaieties of 1919"; at the Central, Dec., 1919, appeared as Sam Benton in "Somebody's Sweetheart"; Longacre, Sept., 1920, played Dick Crawford in "Pitter-Patter"; Globe, Nov., 1921, Steve Simmons in "Good Morning, Dearie"; Selwyn, Oct., 1923, Ernest Hozier in "Battling Butler"; Imperial, Sept., 1924, Hard-Boiled Herman in "Rose Marie"; made his first appearance in London, at the Empire, 14 Apr., 1926, as J. Watterson Watkins in "Lady Be Good"; appeared at the Victoria Palace, Apr., 1927, in "This Way Out"; after returning to New York, appeared at the Alvin Theatre, Nov., 1927, as Dugsie Gibbs in "Funny Face"; at the Shubert, Oct., 1928, played Montmorency Billings in "Ups-a-Daisy"; he then went to Australia,

appearing at the Empire Melbourne, Mar., 1929, in "Clowns in Clover," and in May, 1929, in "Whoopee"; after returning to New York, appeared at the Alvin, Oct., 1930, as Slick Fothergill in "Girl Crazy"; 44th Street, Jan., 1932, played Jay Slump in "A Little Racketeer"; during 1932–33, toured as Cap'n Andy in "Show Boat"; Majestic, New York, Dec., 1934, played Senator Belanqua in "Music Hath Charms"; New Amsterdam, Apr., 1935, succeeded Charles Winninger as Don Emilio in "Revenge With Music"; at Minneapolis, Oct., 1935, played the Rev. Doctor Moon in "Anything Goes," and the First Gravedigger in "Hamlet"; toured, 1938, in "Blossom Time"; is the author of several songs; in 1930, appeared in the film, "The King of Jazz"; subsequently in "The Scarlet Letter." *Recreations:* Riding, football, and music.

(Died 5 Oct., 1945; age 59)

KENTISH, Agatha, actress; *b.* London, 13 June, 1897; *d.* of Brigadier-General Horace J. J. Kentish and his wife Ethel Agatha, *2nd d.* of Sir Sanford Freeling, K.C.M.G.; *e.* in England, Germany and France; *m.* Captain E. D. B. McCarthy, R.N.; during the war was engaged in clerical work at the Air Ministry and the Intelligence branch of the War Office; made her first appearance on the stage at the Royalty Theatre, 14 Dec., 1919, as Amy Spettigue in "Charley's Aunt"; in Apr., 1920, was engaged at the Haymarket, as understudy to Fay Compton in "Mary Rose," and played the part on several occasions; at the Comedy, Apr., 1921, played Hilary Marlow in "A Matter of Fact"; June, 1921, Maud Builder in "A Family Man"; Aug., 1921, Myrtle Green in "By All Means, Darling"; at the Globe, Feb., 1922, succeeded Faith Celli as Septima Blayds in "The Truth About Blayds"; at the Ambassadors, Aug., 1922, played Joan Ripley in "Husbands are a Problem;" at the New, Dec., 1922, Annette Haverfield in "The Great Well"; at the Everyman, Mar., 1923, Cynthia in "The Alternative"; at the New, Aug., 1923, Chris Haversham in "The

Eye of Siva"; at the Adelphi, Mar., 1924, understudied Gladys Cooper as Dora in "Diplomacy," and played the part on several occasions; Dec., 1924, played the Second Twin in "Peter Pan"; Barnes, May, 1925, Marjorie Dale in "The Lavender Garden"; New Oxford, Dec., 1925, Lady Isobel in "Alf's Button"; Strand, Mar., 1926, Vivie Warren in "Mrs. Warren's Profession"; "Q," Aug., 1926, Muriel in "The Curate of St. Chad's"; Oct., 1927, Barbara Prout in "Bluff"; during 1929-30, played leading parts in Australia; after returning to England appeared with the Croydon Repertory company, 1931; Duchess, Nov., 1931, played Hilda Wangel and, subsequently, Kaia Tosti in "The Master Builder"; Duchess, 1932, played Katheryn Howard in "The Rose Without a Thorn"; Stage Guild, Jan., 1933, Marie in "Precious Safety"; Feb., 1933, Ellen in "Snowdrift"; Mar., 1933, Sybil Marshland in "The Shadow on the Earth"; May, 1933, Jenny in "Old Timber"; Westminster, Mar., 1934, Myra in "Private Room"; also played leading parts with the Old Stagers at Canterbury, 1931, and with the Windsor Strollers, 1932. *Favourite parts:* Mary Rose, Hilda in "The Master Builder," and the Lady in "A Man with a Load of Mischief." *Recreations:* Reading and country life. *Address:* "Three Elms," Horsell Rise, Woking. *Telephone No.:* Woking 635.

KENYON, Charles, actor; *b.* Bury, Lancs, 20 July, 1878; *s.* of Elise (Genth) and James Kenyon; *e.* Eton; first appeared in London with Sir Charles Wyndham, at the Criterion, 1909, playing David Cairn in "Mrs. Gorringe's Necklace"; subsequently played with Miss Horniman's repertory company, at Manchester; in 1910, with Miss Darragh, founded the Liverpool Repertory Theatre, and appeared there in "Strife," "The Choice," "Nan," "Cupid and the Styx," etc.; after playing at Kelly's, Liverpool, toured in 1911 with his own company in "The Prisoner of Zenda," and "Stephen Macquoid, M.P."; assumed the management of the Little Theatre, Jan., 1912, appearing as the Rev. Harry Pemberton in "The Blindness of Virtue"; subsequently produced "Rutherford and Son" at the same theatre, which was afterwards transferred to the Vaudeille Theatre; appeared at the New Theatre, May, 1912, as Lionel Carteret in "Mrs. Dane's Defence"; at the Little Theatre, Oct., 1912, played Alcides in "T e Sacrifice"; at the Theatre Royal, Bury, Dec., 1912, appeared as Lieutenant Alexis Petrovitch and Hamilton Tregethner in "By Right of Sword"; subsequently appeared in music-hall sketch, "Our Mutual Wife"; at the Comedy, May, 1913, layed Simon Harness in "Strife"; at the Aldwych, June, 1913, appeared as Charles Harvey in "The Duchess's Necklace"; at the Vaudeville, Aug., 1913, played Dr. Alan Campbell in "The Picture of Dorian Grey"; Sept., 1913, Basil Hallward in the same piece; at the Coronet, Dec., 1913, René in "Woman on her Own"; at the Vaudeville, Jan., 1914, George Latimer in "Mary Girl"; at the Lyceum, Feb., 1914, John Harrison in "You Made Me Love You"; from 1915-18 inclusive, was engaged on active service during the war; at the New Theatre, Jan., 1919, appeared as Sir Roger de la Haye in "The Chinese Puzzle"; at the Duke of York's, July, 1920, as George Edmondson in "Brown Sugar"; at the Garrick, Sept., 1920, in conjunction with Leon M. Lion, produced "The Right to Strike," in which he appeared as Dr. Wrigley; Jan., 1921, played Antonin Mairaut in "The Three Daughters of M. Dupont"; in June, 1921, toured with Iris Hoey in a sketch "The Evening Blast," subsequently touring as Captain Yeulatt in "The Wheel," with his own company; at the St. James's, May, 1923, played Vincent Helmore in "The Outsider," and in Aug., 1923, succeeded Leslie Faber as Anton Ragatzy in the same play; in Jan., 1924, toured in the last-mentioned part, with his own company; at the Prince's, Oct., 1924, played Edward Formby in "The Blue Peter," which he produced in conjunction with Alban Limpus; Aldwych (for the Interlude Players), Apr., 1925, played Adrian St. Clair in "The Passionate

Adventure"; Duke of York's, Sept., 1925, Hal Kendal in "De Luxe Annie"; Wyndham's, Dec., 1925, Paul Roland in "The Godless"; Scala (for Play-mates), July, 1926, Julian Hals in "The Strugglers." *Recreations :* Hunting, golf, tennis, etc. *Club :* Savage. *Address :* 15 Campden Hill Court, Kensington, W.8. *Telephone No. :* Western 4759.

KENYON, Doris, actress : *b.* Syracuse, New York, 5 Sept., 1897 ; *d.* of James Benjamin Kenyon and his wife Margaret Jane (Taylor) ; *e.* Packer Collegiate Institute, Barnard College ; *m.* (1) Milton Sills (dec.) ; (2) Arthur Hopkins ; (3) Albert D. Lasker ; made her first appearance on the stage at the Cort Theatre, New York, 29 Sept., 1915, as Coralie Bliss in "Princess Pat"; she then devoted herself to the cinema stage for three years, playing in several notable pictures; appeared with George Arliss in "The Love Chef"; at the Eltinge Theatre, Oct., 1919, played Betty Neville in "The Girl in the Limousine"; at the Eltinge, Feb., 1921, played Jeanne in "The White Villa"; at the Playhouse, New York, Mar., 1922, played Jane Smith in "Up the Ladder"; at the Greenwich Village, Jan., 1924, Yvonne Dubois in "The Gift"; subsequently returned to the cinema stage, where she remained until 1935 ; made her first appearance on the London stage, at His Majesty's Theatre, 5 Dec., 1935, as the Princess Sylvia in "A Royal Exchange"; since 1936 has appeared in the films "Girls' School," "The Man in the Iron Mask," etc. ; is the author of "Humorous Monologues" and, with her father, of "Spring Flowers and Rowen" (poems) ; also contributor of verse to numerous papers and magazines. *Recreations :* Riding and writing verse. *Address :* 315 Saltair Avenue, Brentwood Heights, Los Angeles, Cal., U.S.A.

KENYON, Neil (McKinnon), Scotch character actor ; *b.* Greenock, Renfrewshire ; was engaged on the regular stage for ten years, in farce, drama, old comedy, etc. ; played several " stock " seasons in the provinces ; made his

first appearance in London, at the Shakespeare Theatre, Clapham, 1897, with Osmond Tearle's Shakespearean Company ; his first pantomime engagement was at the Princess's Theatre, Glasgow, Christmas, 1901 ; made his first appearance on the London music-hall stage, at the London Pavilion 1904 ; he made a substantial success the following Christmas, at the Alexandra Theatre, Stoke Newington, in pantomime, and at Christmas, 1905, at the Prince's Theatre, Manchester ; has appeared at all the leading variety theatres in London, the provinces, Australia, South Africa, and the United States ; appeared also at Drury Lane Theatre, Christmas 1907, in pantomime, " Babes in the Wood " ; appeared at the Apollo Theatre, Apr., 1910, as Mirza Makh Ali Khan in "The Islander "; at the Aldwych, May, 1912, played Angus Macpherson in " Looking for Trouble "; at His Majesty's, Aberdeen, Sept., 1920, appeared as Hunky Dory in " What Fools Men Are "; at the Everyman, Sept., 1925, played Archie Sheepwell in " The Limpet "; has since appeared only on the variety stage and in films; first appeared in New York, at the Colonial Theatre, 5 Jan., 1914 ; has introduced several successful songs and scenas to the public, among which are " The Caddie," " The Ne'er-dae-Weel," " The Stationmaster of Dunrobin," " The Stoker," etc. *Address :* 6 Park Avenue, N.W.11. *Telephone No. :* Speedwell 2566.
(Died 1 June, 1946; age 73)

KEOWN, Eric (Eric Oliver Dilworth Keown), dramatic critic, journalist and author; *b.* London, 2 July, 1904; *s.* of Robert Keown and his wife Sarah (Gordon White) ; *e.* Highgate School, Pembroke College, Cambridge, and Grenoble University; *m.* Cicely Ritchie ; joined editorial staff of "Punch," 1928; first wrote dramatic criticism for this journal in 1932, and continued until 1940; was Parliamentary Correspondent, 1933–40; served with R.A.F.V.R., 1940–5; following his war service, re-joined staff of "Punch," and appointed Dramatic Critic, 1945; has broadcast in the B.B.C. series,

"The Critics," since 1948; is the author of "The Complete Dog's Dudgeon" (1938), "Peggy Ashcroft" (1955), "Margaret Rutherford" (1956), also author of the story on which the film "The Ghost Goes West" was based. *Recreations:* Fishing, *boules*, and snuff. *Club:* Royal Automobile. *Address:* Stringers Barn, Worplesdon, Surrey. *Telephone No.:* Guildford 3912. *(Died 15 Feb., 1963; age 58)*

KERIN, Nora, actress; *b.* London, 22 Oct., 1883; *d.* of Jeanne (Davis) and Charles J. W. Kerin; *e.* Queen's College, London, and Paris; cousin of Julia Neilson; *m.* Cyril Michael; made her first appearance on the stage, at the Court Theatre, Oct., 1899, in "A Royal Family"; during 1901 toured with George Alexander's *répertoire* company in "The Prisoner of Zenda," "Rupert of Hentzau," etc.; subsequently at Manchester, played Titania in "A Midsummer Night's Dream," and Anne Page in "The Merry Wives of Windsor"; at Drury Lane, Apr., 1902, played Esther in "Ben Hur"; at Manchester, Sept., 1902, appeared as Rosalind in "As You Like It"; in 1903 went to Australia with George Musgrove's company in Shakespearean *répertoire*; on her return to England in 1904, toured as Yo-San in "The Darling of the Gods"; at His Majesty's Theatre, Sept., 1904, appeared as Miranda in "The Tempest"; after her marriage, retired from the stage for two years; reappeared at Lyceum, Mar., 1907, as Princess Iris in "Her Love Against the World"; in June, 1907, played Princess Von Strelsburg, in "The Midnight Wedding"; Mar., 1908, Juliet in "Romeo and Juliet"; June, 1908, Princess Monica of Illyria in "The Prince and the Beggar Maid"; appeared in various music halls, 1909, as Winifred Warrener in "The Missing Hand"; at the Prince's Theatre, Apr., 1912, played the Queen Margaret of Slavonia in "The Apple of Eden"; at the Lyceum, June, 1912, Valerie de Brissac in "The Women of France"; at the Palladium, Sept., 1916, played the Duchess of Maldon in "The

Moment Before"; at the Lyceum, Feb., 1923, played the Countess de Linières in "The Orphans." *Recreations:* Swimming, walking, and bridge. *Favourite part:* Rosalind.

KERKER, Gustave Adolph, composer and conductor; *s.* of Gustave A. and Elizabeth Kerker, both in the musical profession; *b.* Herford, Germany, on 28 Feb., 1857; *e.* Germany and the United States; *m.* (1) Rose Keene (stage name, Rose Leighton), 14 Dec., 1884; (2) Mattie Rivenberg; his first opera, "Cadets," was written in 1879, and the following musical pieces also stand to his credit: "The Pearl of Pekin," 1888; "Castles in the Air," 1890; "Venus," 1893; "Little Christopher," 1894; "The Lady Slavey," 1895; "Kismet," 1895; "In Gay New York," 1896; "An American Beauty," 1896; "The Whirl of the Town," 1897; "The Belle of New York," 1897; "The Telephone Girl," 1897; "Yankee Doodle Dandy," 1898; "The Man in the Moon," 1899; "The Girl from Up There," 1900; "The Billionaire," 1902; "The Blonde in Black," 1903; "Winsome Winnie," 1903; "The Sambo Girl" ("The Blonde in Black"), 1904; "The Social Whirl," 1906; "The Tourists," 1906; "The White Hen," 1907; "Fascinating Flora," 1907; "The Lady from Lane's," 1907; "The Grand Mogul," 1907; "Two Little Brides" ("The Grass Widows"), 1912. *Clubs:* The Lambs' and Green Room, New York. *Address:* 115 Manhattan Avenue, New York City. *(Died 29 June, 1923; age 66)*

KERN, Jerome David, composer; *b.* New York, 27 Jan., 1885; *s.* of Henry Kern and his wife Fanny (Kakeles); *e.* Newark, N.J.; *m.* Eva Leale; studied music under his mother, also in Germany; commenced composing, 1903, while in England; has composed music for the following productions: "The Golden Widow," 1909; "A Polish Wedding," 1912; "The Red Petticoat," 1912; "The Laughing Husband," 1913; "The Girl from Utah," 1913; "Oh! I Say!", 1913; "Miss

Information," 1915 ; " Ninety in the Shade," 1915 ; " Nobody Home," 1915 ; " Cousin Lucy," 1915 ; " Very Good, Eddie," 1915 ; " The Ziegfeld Follies of 1916," 1916 ; " Girls Will be Girls," 1916 ; " Theodore and Co.," 1916 ; " Have a Heart," 1917 ; " Oh ! Boy," 1917 ; " Leave it to Jane," 1917 ; " Love o' Mike," 1917 ; " Houp-La," 1917 ; " Miss 1917," 1917 ; " Springtime," 1917 ; " Toot ! Toot ! ! " 1918 ; " Oh ! Lady, Lady," 1918 ; " Rock-a-bye, Baby," 1918 ; " Head Over Heels," 1918 ; " A New Girl," 1919 ; " She's a Good Fellow," 1919 ; "The Night Boat," 1919 ; "Night Boat," 1920 ; "Sally," 1920 ; "Good Morning, Dearie," 1921 ; " The Bunch and Judy," 1922 ; " The Cabaret Girl," 1922 ; " Stepping Stones," 1923 ; " The Beauty Prize," 1923 ; " Sitting Pretty," 1924 ; " Dear Sir," 1924 ; " Sunny," 1925 ; " The City Chap," 1925 ; " Criss-Cross," 1926 ; " Lucky," 1927 ; " Show Boat," 1927 ; " Blue Eyes," 1928 ; "Sweet Adeline," 1929 ; "The Cat and the Fiddle," 1931 ; " Music in the Air," 1932 ; "Roberta," 1933 ; "Three Sisters," 1934 ; also composed the music for the following films, "Men of the Sky," "I Dream Too Much," "Swing Time," "When You're In Love," etc. ; is vice-president of the music publishing firm of T. B. Harms & Co., New York. *Hobby :* Book-collecting. *Club :* Lambs. *Address :* c/o Chappell & Co., Rockefeller Center, New York City. U.S.A.

(Died 11 Nov., 1945; age 60)

KERR, Frederick (Frederick Grinham Keen), actor and stage director ; *b.* London, 11 Oct., 1858 ; *s.* of the late Grinham Keen, of Esher, solicitor ; *m.* Lucy H. Dowson ; *e.* Charterhouse and Caius College, Cambridge ; originally intended to follow his father's profession, but gave up the idea in 1881, in which year he sailed for America ; he made his first appearance on the stage at Wallack's Theatre, New York, 4 Jan., 1882, as Sir Toby in Lester Wallack's revival of " The School for Scandal," subsequently, at the same theatre, played the Detective in " Youth " ; he then went to the Bijou Opera House, under Selina Dolaro, and played there in

July, 1882, in " Olivette " and " The Snake Charmer " ; he returned to England the same year and made his first appearance on the London stage at the Gaiety Theatre, 6 Dec., 1882, as Sir Henry Harkaway in " My Life " ; the following year he toured with Miss Wallis, and was next engaged to support the late Ada Cavendish in " The New Magdalen," " Camille," " The Belle's Stratagem," " The Lady of Lyons " and " Broken Bonds " ; he appeared at the Novelty Theatre, 5 Jan., 1884, as Ignatius Wetzel in " The New Magdalen," subsequently playing in " Nita's First," " The Country Girl," " Lallah Rookh," " Reaping the Whirlwind," " The Scalded Back," etc. ; he then went to the Court Theatre, under John Clayton, and played there from 1884-7, appearing in " Young Mrs. Winthrop," " The Magistrate," " The Schoolmistress," " Dandy Dick " ; he appeared at Terry's, 1888, as Horace Bream in " Sweet Lavender " ; he went to America the following year to play Private Saunders in " Bootles' Baby," and on his return appeared at Terry's, 1890, as Postlethwaite in " New Lamps for Old " ; at the Shaftesbury, May, 1890, he played Juxon Prall in " Judah," and after appearing at the Avenue in " The Struggle for Life," joined Beerbohm Tree at the Haymarket, and played in " Called Back," " The Red Lamp " and " The Dancing Girl," appearing in the latter piece as the Hon. Reginald Slingsby ; at the Criterion, Oct., 1892, he played Charles Greythorne in " The Pink Dominos " ; at the Court, 1893, he played in " The Amazons " ; at the Haymarket, 1894, in " The Charlatan," and at the Criterion, Oct., 1894, played Ferguson Pybus in " The Case of Rebellious Susan " ; the following year he undertook the management of the Vaudeville Theatre, and on 26 June, 1895, appeared there as Captain Courtenay in " The Strange Adventures of Miss Brown," the piece was subsequently transferred to Terry's, and had an extensive run ; he also appeared at Terry's, 1896, as Christopher Jedbury in " Jedbury, Junior," and Sir John Quaill in " The Sunbury Scandal " ; subsequently toured with

John Hare (1896-7) playing Gerald Holmes in " A Bachelor's Romance," Hawtree in " Caste," etc. ; appeared at the Court, 1897, as Hawtree in " Caste," Pinching in " The Hobby Horse " ; at the Duke of York's, 1897, as Cyril Charteris in " The Happy Life," and at the Globe, 1898, as Gerald Holmes in " A Bachelor's Romance " and Major Hawkwood in "The Master"; again appeared at the Globe, 1899, in " Caste," and at the Criterion played George Gunning in " The Tyranny of Tears "; at the Royalty, Oct., 1900, played Mr. Daventry in "Mr. and Mrs. Daventry" ; appeared at the Garrick, Feb., 1901, as Sir Woodbine Grafton in " Peril " ; he then took the Court Theatre, and in May, 1901, produced " A Woman in the Case," playing Reggy Fairbairn, " Women are so Serious," in which he played Harold Twyford, " John Durnford, M.P.," in which he played the name part, and a revival of " The Strange Adventures of Miss Brown " ; at Wyndham's, 1902, played the Marquis de Neste in " Caesar's Wife " ; at the Comedy, Arthur Chandos in " The Lord of His House " and Sir George Langford in "Secret and Confidential " ; at the Avenue, 1903, played Jack Scarlet, in " The Little Countess," and at the Criterion, June, 1903, appeared as Manderberry in " Just Like Callaghan " ; at the Duke of York's, 1903, he played Bernard Mandeville in " Letty " ; at the Haymarket, May, 1904, played the Hon. Paul Harding in " Lady Flirt " ; at the Avenue, Feb., 1905, appeared as the Duke of Braceborough in " Mr. Hopkinson " ; at Wyndham's, Aug., 1905, played Spencer Traughton in " Public Opinion " ; at the Court, Feb., 1906, played in " A Question of Age," and in Mar. played Captain Brassbound in " Captain Brassbound's Conversion " ; at Wyndham's Sept., 1906, played John Crewys in " Peter's Mother " ; at the Criterion, Feb., 1907, appeared as Julian Shuckburgh in " Three Blind Mice " ; at the Haymarket, Apr., 1907, as Christopher Podmore in " The Palace of Puck," at the Queen's, in Oct., as Sir Basil Loring in " The Sugar Bowl " ; at the Apollo, Nov., 1907, as John

Karslake in " The New York Idea " ; same theatre, Feb., 1908, played Lord Linthorpe in " Stingaree " ; at the Comedy, Apr., 1908, appeared as James Blenkinsop in " Mrs. Dot " ; at Wyndham's, Aug., 1909, played Lord Emsworth in " The Best People "; at the Globe, Nov., 1909, appeared as Sir Charles Hewitt Gore in " The Great Mrs. Alloway " ; he then went to America, and at the Lyceum, New York, Jan., 1910, again appeared as James Blenkinsopp in " Mrs. Dot " ; in Oct., 1910, supported Maxine Elliott, on tour, in " The Inferior Sex " ; at the Garrick, Apr., 1912, played the Rt. Hon. Sir Walter Stancombe in " Improp r Peter " ; at the Duke of Y rk's, Oct., 1912, ap eared as the Visitor in " The Widow o Wasdale Head " ; at the Aldwych, Nov., 1912, as Professor Dama off in " T e Price "; at the Little Thea re, Apr., 1913, as the Earl of Chislehurst in " The Cap and Bells " ; at the Savoy, June, 1913, played Richard Farrant in " A Cardinal's Romance "; at the New Theatre, Aug., 1913, appeared as Edward Grimshaw in " The Big Game " ; at the Globe, Oct., 1913, as Sir Joseph Juttle in " People Like Ourselves "; at the Comedy, Feb., 1914, as George Gunning in a revival of " The Tyranny of Tears " ; at the Prince of Wales's, Jan., 1914, played the Rt. Hon. John Lamson in " The Bill " ; at the Playhouse, Sept., 1914, Major Claffenden in " Young Wisdom " ; at Drury Lane, Dec., 1914, Lord Amersham in " A Social Success " ; at the Metropolitan Music Hall, Feb., 1915, Alfred Critchett in " Who Wears the Breeches ? " ; at the Prince of Wales's, Mar., 1915, Pulsifer Witherton in " He Didn't Want to Do It " ; at the Comedy, June, 1915, Horatio Billington in " Mr. and Mrs. Ponsonby " ; in Aug., 1915, went on tour with Lewis Waller, playing Sir George Langworthy in " Gamblers All " ; at the Playhouse, Jan., 1916, played Sir Samuel Lethbridge in " Please Help Emily " ; at the Metropolitan, Aug., 1916, played in " The Beautiful Mrs. Blain," with which he subseq ently toured ; at the New Theatre, June, 1917, played Henry Carlton, M.P., in " His Excellency the Governor " ; Feb.,

1918, Sir Norton Ball-Jennings in "The Freaks"; at the Globe, June, 1918, Lord Messiger in "Nurse Benson"; Nov., 1918, Marshal Marmont in "L'Aiglon"; at the St. Martin's, Mar., 1919, appeared as the Husband in "Sleeping Partners"; Dec., 1919, as Colonel Saville in "A Dear Little Lady"; at the Queen's, Jan., 1920, as Martin Carrington in "Mr. Todd's Experiment"; at the Ambassadors', Apr., 1920, as the Rt. Hon. Lord Henry Markham, M.P., in "The Grain of Mustard Seed"; subsequently went to America, and at the Henry Miller Theatre, Nov., 1920, played the Marquis of Karnaby in "Just Suppose"; returned to England, 1921; at the Theatre Royal, Leamington, Oct., 1921, played Mr Lazarus in a play of that name; at the Empire, New York, Jan., 1922, The Chancellor in "The Czarina"; at the Times Square, Sept., 1922, Mr. Rackham in "The Exciters"; at the St. James's, London, Nov., 1922, Sir Anthony Fenwick in "The Happy Ending"; at His Majesty's, Feb., 1923, in aid of King George's Pension Fund for Actors, played Simon in "The Ballad Monger"; at the Prince of Wales's, Apr., 1923, Lord Worthing in "So This is London"; at the Ambassadors', Oct., 1924, General Sir John Heriot, Bart., in "The Pelican"; Nov., 1924, again played the Rt. Hon. Lord Henry Markham, M.P., in "The Grain of Mustard Seed"; again went to America, and in 1925 was supporting Bertha Kalish in "Magda"; at the Times Square, New York, Sept., 1925, played his original part in "The Pelican"; on returning to London, appeared at the Queen's, Apr., 1926, as Lord Bellingdon in "Conflict"; Savoy, June, 1926, played Lord Tottenham in "What Might Happen"; Lyric, Dec., 1926, James Blake in "The Gold Diggers"; Shaftesbury, Sept., 1927, Lord Trench in "The High Road"; again went to New York and at the Fulton, Sept., 1928, played the same part; at the Times Square, Oct., 1929, played Admiral Sir Hercules Hewitt in "The Middle Watch"; Fulton, Dec., 1930, Octave de Corquefou in "A Kiss of Importance"; has been frequently engaged as stage director at various theatres, making many productions in which he has taken no part; commenced film career, 1930, at the age of 72, and has appeared in "Raffles," "The High Road," "The Devil to Pay," "Born to Love," "Always Good-bye," "Waterloo Bridge," "The Honour of the Family," "Frankenstein," "Friends and Lovers," "Beauty and the Boss," "But the Flesh is Weak," "Lovers Courageous," "The Midshipmaid," "The Man from Toronto," etc.; published his reminiscences, 1931, under the title of "Recollections of a Defective Memory." *Clubs:* Devonshire, Garrick. *Address:* Russettings, Balcombe, Sussex. *Telephone No.:* Balcombe 60. *(Died 2 May, 1933; age 74)*

KERR, Geoffrey, actor; *b.* London, 26 Jan., 1895; *s.* of Fred Kerr (Keen) and his wife Lucy Houghton (Dowson); *e.* St. Andrew's, Eastbourne, and Charterhouse; *m.* (1) June Walker (mar. dis.); (2) Margot Kling; first appeared on the stage at the Savoy Theatre, 14 June, 1913, as Kenneth Lester in "A Cardinal's Romance"; at the Globe, 1913, played Lord Walter Sark in "People Like Ourselves"; at the Prince of Wales's, Dec., 1913, Charley Wyckham in "Charley's Aunt"; June, 1914, Pemberton in "The Bill," and at Wyndham's, Sept., 1914, Tony in "Outcast"; during the war served in the Army and with the Royal Air Force; reappeared on the stage at the Apollo, July, 1919, playing Richard in "Tilly of Bloomsbury"; in 1920 went to America and at the Henry Miller Theatre, New York, 1 Nov., 1920, appeared as the Marquis of Karnaby in "Just Suppose"; at the Apollo, London, July, 1921, played Lord Roftus in "Skittles"; at the Eltinge Theatre, New York, Sept., 1922, Harold Knox in "East of Suez"; at the Belmont, Feb., 1923, Roderick White in "You and I"; at the Henry Miller, Sept., 1923, Wicky Faber in "The Changelings"; at the Fulton, Oct., 1924, Ernest Fairleigh in "In His Arms"; at the Cort, Jan., 1925, Lionel Deport in "The Stork"; Booth, Nov., 1926, Jean in "First

Love"; Belasco, Feb., 1928, John Ashley in "The Bachelor Father," in which he continued, 1928-9; Little, Oct., 1930, played George Craft in "London Calling"; Plymouth, Nov., 1930, Joseph Gresham Jun. in "This is New York"; Gaiety, Feb., 1932, Dr. Gestzi in "Collision"; Booth, .Mar., 1932, Jean Servin in "We Are No Longer Children"; Playhouse, Aug., 1932, Cremone in "Domino"; Oct., 1932, toured as Dwight Houston in "There's Always Juliet"; Times Square, Jan., 1933, played Shakespeare in "Foolscap"; at Ann Arbor, June, 1933, played Leo in "Design for Living"; Martin Beck Theatre, New York, Mar., 1934, Stackpoole in "Yellow Jack"; during the war, served in the R.A.S.C., and in the Intelligence Corps; Shubert, Nov., 1949, Frederic Chanler in "I Know My Love"; returned to England and at the Comedy, Oct., 1952, appeared as Dr. John Kingsley in "The Apples of Eve"; Winter Garden, Feb., 1958, played Matthew in "Hunter's Moon"; Edinburgh Festival, Aug., 1958, played Lambert in "The Elder Statesman," subsequently appearing in the same production at the Cambridge, London, Sept., 1958; is the author of "Don't Play With Fire," 1927, "London Calling," 1930; "Till the Cows Come Home," 1936; "Oh! You Letty" (with Bert Lee and Clifford Grey), "Black Swans," 1937; "Cottage to Let," 1940; "The Man In the Street," 1947; "Welcome to Killoon," 1951; has also appeared in films, and written and collaborated in film scripts. *Recreations:* Photography and magic. *Address:* The Old Cottage, Frith End, Bordon, Hants. *Telephone No:* Bordon 318.

KERR. Molly, actress; *b.* Kensington, 28 May, 1904; *d.* of Fred Kerr and his wife Lucy Houghton (Dowson) : *e.* St. Paul's and Granville House, Eastbourne; made her first appearance on the stage at the St. James's Theatre, 23 Aug., 1921, as Chloe in "Threads"; next appeared at the Comedy, Nov., 1921, playing Diana Oughterson in "The Faithful Heart"; at the Playhouse, June, 1922, played Ellean in "The Se nd Mrs. Tan-

queray"; subsequently toured with Mrs. Patrick Campbell; at the Prince's, Oct., 1923, played Lady Frances Carfax in "The Return of Sherlock Holmes"; at the Everyman, Nov., 1924, and at the Royalty, Dec., 1924, played Bunty Mainwaring in "The Vortex"; went to New York, and at the Henry Miller, Sept., 1925, played the same part; at the Ritz, Nov., 1925, played Brenda Fallon in "Loose Ends"; returning to London, appeared at the Duke of York's, Apr., 1926, in the same part; Ambassadors', Aug., 1926, played the Shingled Lady in "Escape"; Everyman, Apr., 1927, Mavis Boycott in "Common People"; "Q," Aug., 1927, The Strange Lady in "The Intriguing Ladies"; Arts, Nov., 1927, Jennifer Gray in "The Peaceful Thief"; Ambassadors', Jan., 1928, Alison Liston in "Two White Arms"; Wyndham's, Aug., 1928, Margaret Orme in "Loyalties"; was responsible for the stage direction of "The Intriguing Ladies," "The Peaceful Thief," and of her own play "Requital," produced at the Everyman, April, 1929. *Favourite parts:* Juliet, Eliza Doolittle in "Pygmalion," and Peter Pan. *Address:* Russettings, Balcombe, Sussex. *Telephone No.:* Balcombe 60.

KERRIGAN, J. M., actor; *b.* Dublin, 4 Dec., 1885; *e.* Belvedere College, Dublin; was formerly a journalist; made his first appearance on the stage at the Abbey Theatre, Dublin, Jan., 1907, in "Deirdre," with Irish National Theatre Society, of which he remained a member for nine years, during which period he played over one hundred parts; made his first appearance on the London stage, at the Great Queen Street Theatre, 10 May, 1907, as Old Mahon in "The Playboy of the Western World"; at the end of 1916, he went to America, and at the Globe, New York, Mar., 1917, played the Irishman in "Out There"; at the Liberty, Nov., 1917, played Winch in "The Wooing of Eve"; at the Criterion, New York, Dec., 1917, Formoy McDonagh in "Happiness"; during 1918 toured in the same part; at the Playhouse, New York, Oct., 1919, appeared as Costigan in " A Young Man's Fancy"; at the Greenwich Village, New York, Nov., 1919, Peter Cooney in " The Lost Leader " ; on returning to London, appeared at the Lyric, Hammersmith, Feb., 1920, as James Caesar in " John Ferguson"; at the Abbey Theatre, Dublin, 1920, played Natty Murnaghan in " The King's Threshold " ; again visited New York, and at the Punch and Judy Theatre, Nov., 1920, played Horatio Webster in " Rollo's Wild Oat " ; at the Belmont, June, 1921, James Caesar in " John Ferguson " ; at the Thirty-ninth Street Theatre, Mar., 1922, Mr. McCann in " Broken Branches"; at the Klaw, Apr., 1922, Thomas Turtle in " The Shadow " ; at the Punch and Judy, Oct., 1922, Doody in " The Ever Green Lady " ; at the Comedy, New York, Nov., 1922, Master Susan in " The Romantic Age "; at the Forty-eighth Street Theatre, May, 1923, Sir Lucius O'Trigger in " The Rivals " ; at the Morosco, Oct., 1923, Polichinelle in " Scaramouche " ; at the Ritz, Jan., 1924, Scrubby in " Outward Bound "; 52nd Street, May, 1925, Ulric Brendel in " Rosmersholm "; June, 1925, Cheviot Hill in " Engaged "; George M. Cohan, Dec., 1925, Rodney Oneil in " Gypsy Fires "; Comedy, Mar., 1926, Jacob Engstrand in " Ghosts "; Bayes, Apr., 1926, Father Walter in " The Bells"; Knickerbocker, May, 1926, Silence in " King Henry IV "; Booth, Oct., 1926, Herbert in " White Wings"; New Amsterdam, Jan., 1927, O'Dwyer in " Trelawny of the Wells "; Strand, London, May, 1928, Fabius Maximus in " The Road to Rome "; Lyceum, New York, Feb., 1929, Dr. Ainslie in "Meet the Prince"; Martin Beck, Nov., 1937, The Archbishop in "Barchester Towers"; at the Gate Theatre, Hollywood, Sept., 1944, appeared in "Dr. Knock"; Booth, New York, Oct., 1946, Michael James Flaherty in "The Playboy of the Western World"; commenced film career, 1923, in "Little Old New York," and has since appeared in innumerable pictures. *Recreations:* Swimming, walking, and boxing. *Club:* Players', New York. *Address:* Players' Club, 16 Gramercy Park. *(Died 29 Apr., 1964; age 78)*

KERSHAW, Willette, actress, *b.* Clifton Heights, Mo., U.S.A., 17 June, 1890; *d.* of Harry W. Mansfield and his wife Mary (Noris); *e.* St. Louis; *m.* David Sturgis (mar. dis.); made her first appearance on the stage as a child, Feb., 1901, at St. Louis, in the Bernhardt-Coquelin Company, as a Page; made her first appearance in New York, at the Metropolitan Opera House 8 Apr., 1901, as a Page in " L'Aiglon," with Sarah Bernhardt and M. Coquelin; subsequently toured with Walker Whiteside, playing small parts in " Hamlet," " Othello," etc. ; subsequently toured in Canada with William S. Harkins ; about this period she played Little Eva and Topsy in "Uncle Tom's Cabin," Cedric in " Little Lord Fauntleroy," etc. ; made her next appearance in New York, at the Fourteenth Street Theatre, ın 1905, in " Marching Through Georgia"; was then engaged at the Princess Theatre, Apr., 1906, succeeding Laura Hope Crews as Evelyn Kenyon in " Brown of Harvard"; at the Knickerbocker, Sept., 1907, played Phoebe Ransford in " The Evangelist " ; at the Savoy, New York, 1909, succeeded Elsie Ferguson as Jenny Moran in " The Battle "; Jan., 1910, played Georgia Warren in " The Heights " ; at the Liberty, Aug., 1910, appeared as Ann Leroy in " The Country Boy," making her first substantial success ; appeared at the Hudson, Sept., 1911, as Nondas Parkyn in " Snobs " ; at the Princess Theatre (run by Holbrook Blinn on the " Grand Guignol " principle), Mar., 1913, played the Street-Walker in " Any Night," and Fancy in " Fancy Free," and Oct., 1913, Claire in " En Deshabille," and Sonia in " A Pair of White Gloves"; Dec., 1913, Madeline in "Hari-Kari," and Xenia in " Russia"; in 1914 was in Paris, where she acted on several occasions; returned to New York and at the Thirty-ninth Street Theatre, Oct., 1915, appeared as Emily Madden in " The Unchastened Woman " ; at the New Amsterdam Theatre, Mar., 1916, played Anne Bullen in " King Henry VIII," with Sir Herbert Tree ; at the A. H. Woods Theatre, Chicago, Oct., 1917, Mary Lawrence in " The Crowded Hour " ; returning to New

York, at the Forty-eighth Street Theatre, Dec., 1917, appeared as Margaret Vane in " Yes or No "; subsequently, at Philadelphia, appeared as Irene in " Irene O'Dare," and as Helen in " Whose Helen Are You ? "; appeared in " vaudeville," 1920, on the Keith Circuit, in " A Business Woman "; at the Playhouse, Chicago, Mar., 1921, played Deloryse in " Woman to Woman "; made her first appearance on the London stage at the Globe Theatre, 8 Sept., 1921, in the same year; at the Garrick, Jan., 1922, played Luana in " The Bird of Paradise "; at Drury Lane, Apr., 1922, Alatiel in " Decameron Nights "; in May, 1929, at the Théâtre des Champs-Elysées, Paris, produced " Maya," and played the name part, with great success; in Sept., 1930, appeared with her own company at the Potinière Theatre, Paris, where she produced "The Well of Loneliness"; at the Wharf, Provincetown, Mass., July, 1935, appeared in "Two's Company"; at various times has also played lengthy "stock" engagements at St. Louis, Milwaukee, Minneapolis, Denver, Baltimore, etc., where she has appeared as Desdemona, Lady Macbeth, Ophelia, Juliet, Portia, Zaza, Du Barry, and many other leading parts. *(Died 4 May, 1960; age 70)*

KESSELRING, Joseph O., dramatic author; *b.* New York City, U.S.A., 21 June, 1902; *s.* of Henry Kesselring and his wife Frances Langtry (Rudd); *m.* Charlotte Elsheimer; was a professor of Music, at Bethel College, Newton, Kansas, 1922–4; was, from 1925 until 1933, engaged as an actor, short-story writer, and producer of vaudeville sketches; author of the following plays: "Aggie Appleby, Maker of Men," 1933; "There's Wisdom in Women," 1935; "Cross Town," 1937; "Arsenic and Old Lace," 1941; "Maggie McGilligan," 1942; "Four Twelves Are 48," 1950; author of the films "Aggie Appleby, Maker of Men," 1933, and "Arsenic and Old Lace," 1944; member of the Dramatists' Guild, National Arts Club, British League of Dramatists, and Authors' League. *Address:* 1 Lexington Avenue, New York City, N.Y. 10010. *(Died 5 Nov., 1967; age 65)*

KESTER, Paul, dramatic author; *b.* Delaware, Ohio, 2 Nov., 1870; *s.* of Franklin C. Kester and his wife Harriet (Watkins); *e.* Mount Vernon, and Cleveland; has written the following plays, all of which have been seen in New York : " Countess Roudine " (with Mrs. Fiske), 1892; " Zamar," 1893; " Eugene Aram," 1896; " The Musketeers," 1898; " Guy Mannering," 1898; " What Dreams May Come," 1898; " Sweet Nell of Old Drury," 1900; " When Knighthood was in Flower," 1901; " Queen Fiametta," 1902; " The Cavalier " (adapted from Geo. W. Cable's novel), 1902; " Mademoiselle Mars," 1903; " Dorothy Vernon of Haddon Hall," 1903; " Friend Hannah," 1906; has also written " The Head of the Family " (with C. Haddon Chambers); " La Zulma "; " Don Quixote," 1908; " Lily, the Bill Topper," 1910; " The Lady in the Case," 1914; " The Desert Island " (re-named " Beverley's Balance "), 1915; " The Love of a King," 1917; " The Woman of Bronze," 1920; " Lady Dedlock " (on " Bleak House "), 1923; is also the author of the following books: " His Own Country," " Tales of the Real Gypsy," " Conservative Democracy," " The Course of True Love," " Diana Dauntless," " Sambo." *Address:* Mount Pleasant, Hague, Virginia, U.S.A. *(Died 21 June, 1933; age 62)*

KEYS, Nelson, actor ; *b.* 7 Aug.,1886 ; made his first appearance on the stage at the Grand Theatre, Hull, in 1906; toured for some time in George Edwardes' Company, and also as Sir Guy de Vere in " When Knights were Bold "; made his first appearance in London when he appeared at the Shaftesbury, 28 Apr., 1909, as Bobby in " The Arcadians " ; 9 Sept., 1911, as Lieutenant Makei in " The Mousmé "; at the Apollo, Dec., 1911, as Ginger in "Esther Waters"; at the Shaftesbury, May, 1912, as Ensign Pips in " Princess Caprice "; at the London Pavilion, Sept., 1912, as Jimmy Cann in " Oh ! Molly "; at the Lyric, Mar., 1913, succeeded Robert Averill as Hubert in " The Girl in the Taxi "; appeared at the Lyric, Sept., 1913, as Lieut. Skrydloff in " Love and Laughter " ; at the Empire, Jan., 1914, appeared in " Nuts and Wine " ; at the Palace, Apr., 1914, appeared in " The Passing Show," and Mar., 1915, in " The Passing Show of 1915 " ; Sept., 1915, played in " Bric-a-Brac " ; Nov., 1916, in " Vanity Fair " ; at the Alhambra, July, 1917, appeared in " Round the Map " ; at His Majesty's, Dec., 1917, played Mr. Poffley in the " all-star " performance of " The Man from Blankley's," given in aid of King George's Actors' Pension Fund ; at the Palace, May, 1918, played Eddie Kettle in " Very Good, Eddie " ; at the Vaudeville, Dec., 1918, played in " Buzz-Buzz " ; at the London Pavilion, Sept., 1920, appeared in " London, Paris, New York " ; in 1921 toured with his own company as Rex Van Zile in " Polly with a Past " ; entered on the management of the Ambassadors' Theatre, Mar., 1922, when he produced and played in " The Curate's Egg " ; went to New York, Feb., 1924, and appeared in " Ziegfeld Follies " ; at the Times Square Theatre, Apr., 1924, succeeded Jack Buchanan in " Charlot's Revue of 1924 " ; at Drury Lane, Mar., 1926, succeeded Billy Merson as Hard-Boiled Herman in " Rose Marie " ; reappeared on the stage, at Theatre Royal, Portsmouth, Nov., 1928, as Skid in " Burlesque," appearing in the same part at the Queen's Theatre, Dec., 1928 ; in the spring of 1930, toured as Basil Bath in " Making a Man " ; Piccadilly, Jan., 1931, played in " Folly to be Wise " ; Sept., 1931, in " Folly to be Wiser " ; London Hippodrome, Jan., 1932, appeared in " Bow Bells " ; Adelphi, Nov., 1932 (for King George's Pension Fund), played Derbyshire in " Bull-Dog Drummond " ; Vaudeville, July, 1933, appeared in " After Dark " ; Palace, Apr., 1934, appeared in " Why Not To-Night ? " ; commenced film career, 1927, and has also appeared in " Tiptoes," " Madame Pompadour," " Mumsee," " The Triumph of the Scarlet Pimpernel," " When Knights Were Bold," " Splinters," " A Yankee at the Court of King Arthur," " Almost a Divorce," " Send 'Em Back Half Dead," etc. *Club :* Stage Golfing Society. *Address :* 17 Stratton Street, W.1. *(Died 26 Apr., 1939; age 52)*

KIDDER, Kathryn, actress ; *b.* Newark, New Jersey, U.S.A., 23 Dec., 1867 ; *d.* of the late Colonel H. M. Kidder ; *e.* Evanstown, near Chicago ; *m.* Louis Kaufman Anspacher ; made her first appearance on the stage, in 1885, at Chicago, as Lucy Fairweather in " The Streets of London," with the late Frank Mayo, with whom she remained some years ; she made her first appearance in New York, at the Union Square Theatre, 18 May, 1885, when she appeared as the Countess Morynski in " Nordeck " ; at Madison Square Theatre, 16 Aug., 1886, she played Rachel McCreery in " Held by the Enemy " ; toured with the late Joseph Haworth in " Ruy Blas," " Saint Marc," " The Leavenworth Case," " The Soldier of Fortune," etc. ; and at the Broadway Theatre, 3 Dec., 1888, she appeared as Mrs. Errol in " Little Lord Fauntleroy " ; at Hermann's Theatre, 28 Feb., 1893, she played Dorothy in " Yesterday " ; and at the Broadway, 14 Jan., 1895, she made a big hit when she appeared as Catherine in " Madame Sans-Gêne " ; 1899-1902 was touring in Louis James's company in " The Winter's Tale," " Macbeth," " The Rivals," and " A Midsummer Night's Dream " ; played in " Molly Pitcher," 1902 ; " Françillon," Princesse Georges," 1903 ; in 1904 she was with Frederick Warde's company, playing Salambo in the play of that name, Hermione in " The Winter's Tale," Lady Macbeth in " Macbeth," Lady Teazle in " The School for Scandal," Desdemona, Portia, Rosalind, etc. ; in 1906 she appeared as Elizabeth Holt in " The Embarrassment of Riches " ; at Herald Square Theatre, Mar., 1909, played Leonora de Valera in " A Woman of Impulse " ; in May, 1911, played a " stock " engagement at Rochester, New York ; at St. Louis, Apr., 1912, played Geraldine Duquesne in " The Glass House " ; subsequently played in " vaudevill : " in " The Washerwoman Duchess " (" Madame Sans-Gêne ") ; at Los Angeles, May, 1915, played in " The Unchastened Woman " ; during 1917 appeared as Madame Cecile in a sketch of that name, and as Nora Cathleen in " The Shadow of the Glen " ; at the

Academy of Music, Baltimore, Oct., 1919, played Ruth Prescott in "All the King's Horses," written by her husband. *Address:* Rynstede, Ossining, N.Y., U.S.A.
(Died 7 Sept., 1939; age 71)

KIEPURA, Jan, actor and singer; *b.* Sosnowicz, Poland, 6 May, 1902; *s.* of Franciszek Kiepura and his wife Maria (Najman); *e.* Warsaw University; *m.* Marta Eggerth; made his first appearance on the stage, 1925, at the State Opera House, Warsaw, in "Faust"; in Vienna, played the leading part in "Turandot," and subsequently played at La Scala, Milan, for three years; subsequently went to the United States, and appeared in films for some years; appeared at the Metropolitan Opera House, New York, 1938, as Rodolfo in "La Bohême"; appeared at the Majestic, Aug., 1943, as Prince Danilo in "The Merry Widow"; Alvin, Oct., 1945, played General Thaddeus Kosciusko in "Polonaise"; at the Palace, London, May, 1955, again played Danilo in "The Merry Widow"; City Center, N.Y., Apr., 1957, Prince Danilo in "The Merry Widow"; appeared with Marta Eggerth in a concert programme, Theatre-in-the Park, N.Y., July, 1959; first appeared in films, 1933, in "Be Mine To-night," subsequent films include: "My Heart is Calling," "La Vie de Bohême," "Land of Smiles." *Address:* 17 East 96th Street, New York, N.Y. 10028, U.S.A.
(Died 15 Aug., 1966; age 62)

KILLICK, C. Egerton, manager; *b.* Southport, Lancs, 1 Dec., 1891; *s.* of Charles Killick and his wife Louise (Ashworth); *e.* Haileybury College; was formerly an accountant; was business manager for five years at the New Theatre for Sir Charles Wyndham and Mary Moore; fulfilled similar position at the Criterion Theatre, subsequently at the Garrick, Aldwych, etc.; in 1926, in conjunction with Victor Payne-Jennings acquired a lease of the Savoy Theatre until 1939; also acquired a lease of the Comedy Theatre from 1932; acquired, with Victor Payne-Jennings, various other leases, and in 1939, controlled the Comedy, Playhouse, Victoria Palace, Duke of York's, and Aldwych Theatres; during the War, took over Payne-Jennings' interest in the Comedy, in conjunction with Tom Arnold, subsequently acquired a licence of the Duke of York's Theatre; in 1946, was financially interested in seven West End Theatres; terminated his control of the Comedy Theatre, 1948; is an executive member of the Society of West End Theatre Managers, and is Chairman of the Finance Committee of the Society; is also on the Council of the Theatrical Managers' Association, and elected as its President in 1956; Chairman of the Theatres National Committee; Chairman of the Finance Committee of the Royal Academy of Dramatic Art; Chairman of North Kensington Advisory Committee of the National Assistance Board; Chairman of the West End local Employment Committee, Ministry of Labour. *Recreation:* Cricket. *Clubs:* M.C.C., R.A.C., and Royal Thames Yacht Club. *Address:* 19 Charing Cross Road, London, W.C.2. *Telephone No.:* Whitehall 2655. *(Died 31 May, 1967; age 75)*

KIMBALL, Grace, actress; *b.* Michigan, U.S.A., 18 Feb., 1870; *m.* M. D. McGuire; made her first appearance on the stage in 1888 in "Engaged"; subsequently appeared in "A Possible Case"; she then played Agnes in "Dr. Jekyll and Mr. Hyde," and other parts; at Palmer's, 17 June, 1890, played Florida Vervain in "A Foregone Conclusion"; at the Bijou 26 Jan., 1891, played Rose in "The Nominee" and Ethel Lydyard in "The Viper on the Hearth"; at Hermann's, 23 Mar., 1893, appeared as Elinor in "Hal o' the Hall"; in 1893 she was playing with E. H. Sothern, and also played in "The Harvest" and "The Squirrel Inn"; she then rejoined E. H. Sothern, and appeared with him as Fanny Hadden in "Captain Lettarblair"; at the Lyceum, with Sothern, she appeared, on 5 Sept., 1893, as Elizabeth Linley in "Sheridan; or the Maid of Bath"; 27 Aug., 1894, as Joan Strathallan in " The Victoria Cross " ; 26 Sept., 1894, as Madge Carruthers in " The Way to Win a Woman " ; and 29 Oct., 1894, in " Lord Chumley " ; 4 Sept., 1895, she was seen as Princess Flavia in " The Prisoner of Zenda " ; she then toured with Henry Miller, and at the Garden Theatre, 11 Jan., 1897, appeared as Miss Neville in " Heartsease " ; during 1902-3, was engaged with the Fawcett " stock " company at Baltimore ; at Madison Square, 19 Jan., 1904, she played Madame Santanay in " The Secret of Polichinelle " ; at Madison Square, Feb., 1905, appeared as Mrs. Jack Temple in " Mrs. Temple's Telegram," and in Sept., as Alice Travers in " The Prince Chap " ; at the Garrick, New York, Feb., 1906, played Mrs. Charles Galloway in " Gallops." *Address :* c/o *New York Dramatic News,* 17 West 42nd Street, New York City, U.S.A.

KIMBALL, Louis, actor ; *b.* Marshalltown, Iowa, U.S.A., 19 May, 1889 ; *s.* of William Kimball Conaughy and his wife Carmen Belmont (Daggett) ; *e.* Marshalltown ; *m.* Mary Stewart ; made his first appearance on the stage in 1909, at the Lyric Theatre, Minneapolis, as Brother Paul in " The Christian " ; after much " stock " experience, went to Australia in 1915, and remained there three years, playing a great number of parts ; made his first appearance on the New York stage, at the Republic Theatre, Nov., 1920, as Richard Watson in " Daddy Dumplins " ; at the same theatre, Aug., 1921, played Teddy Darling in " Getting Gertie's Garter " ; Selwyn, May, 1922, Dan Davis in " Partners Again " ; Longacre, May, 1923, Lawrence Banning in " For Value Received " ; subsequently appeared in " The Cat and the Canary " ; at the Klaw Theatre, Sept., 1924, played Tom Baxter in " The Green Beetle " ; Greenwich Village, Jan., 1926, Frank Beckwith in " Head First " ; Ritz., Mar., 1926, Serge Street in " Find Daddy " ; Morosco, Sept., 1926, Stanley Risdale in " The Shelf " ; made his first appearance on the London stage at the Queen's Theatre, 18 Oct., 1927, as Eugene Fenmore in

" Crime " ; at the Masque Theatre, New York, Aug., 1928, played " Duke " Kelton in " Gang War " ; Mansfield Theatre, Mar., 1929, Billy Noel in " Indiscretion." *Recreations :* Hunting, fishing, and racing. *Clubs :* Lambs' and Actors' Equity Association. *Address :* 130 West 44th Street, New York City, U.S.A.

(Died 29 Jan., 1936; age 46)

KIMMINS, Anthony, O.B.E., dramatic author ; *b.* Harrow-on-the-Hill, Middlesex, 10 Nov., 1901 ; *s.* of Charles William Kimmins, D.Sc., and his wife Grace Thyrza (Hannam) ; *e.* Osborne and Dartmouth R.N. Colleges ; *m.* Elizabeth Hodges ; formerly in the Royal Navy, becoming Lieut.-Commander, and a Pilot in the Fleet Air Arm ; author of "While Parents Sleep," 1932 ; "Night-club Queen," 1933 ; "Chase the Ace," 1935 ; "Winter Sport," 1951 ; "The Amorous Prawn," 1959 ; has written, directed, and acted in films ; rejoined the Navy during the War, serving in various theatres, and frequently broadcast commentaries on special operations ; awarded the O.B.E., 1946. *Recreations :* Fishing, tennis, and golf. *Clubs :* Garrick and Stage Golfing Society. *Address :* Acres Gate, Hurstpierpoint, Sussex. *Telephone No. :* Hurstpierpoint 2367.

(Died 19 May, 1964; age 62)

KING, Ada, actress ; in 1895, was touring with John D. Saunders's company in " The Lightning's Flash " ; in 1903, toured as Sal Parkins in " The Village Blacksmith " ; at the Lyric Theatre, Sept., 1907, appeared as the Gipsy Woman in " Under the Greenwood Tree " ; first came into prominence as a member of Miss Horniman's Repertory company at the Gaiety, Manchester, in 1908, and remained a member of the company until 1912 ; during this period she played a number of varied parts including Mrs. Ebton-Smith in " The Few and the Many," Lady Mendle-Parrish in " When the Devil was Ill," Caroline Parker in " Makeshifts," Mrs. Slater in " The Dear Departed," Mistress Merrythought in " The

Knight of the Burning Pestle," Ungild in " The Feud," Frau Orb in " The Vale of Content," Jane O'Gregory in " Independent Means," Mrs. Farrell in " Press Cuttings," Ursula in " Much Ado About Nothing," Arina in " Before the Dawn," Mrs. Gutterage in " The Tallyman," Mrs. Lilley in " The Choice," Mrs. Kennion in " The Younger Generation," Mrs. Frant in " Lords and Masters," Mrs. Timbrell in " Mary Broome," Mrs. Thompson in " Realities," Ellen Burtenshaw in " Our Little Fancies " and Mrs. Jones in " The Silver Box " ; at the Aldwych Theatre, June, 1912, played Mrs. Hawthorn in " Hindle Wakes," appearing in the same part when the play was reproduced at the Playhouse, July, 1912 ; at the Haymarket, Nov., 1912, played Mrs. Kennion in " The Younger Generation " ; at the Strand Theatre, Apr., 1913, appeared as Harriett Maxwell in " The Chaperon " ; at the Vaudeville, Oct., 1913, appeared as Mrs. Harris in " Between Sunset and Dawn " ; at His Majesty's, Dec., 1914, played Mrs. Gummidge in " David Copperfield " ; June, 1915, Sister Saint-Anatole in " Marie-Odile " ; in July, 1915, toured with Sir Herbert Tree in variety theatres as Mrs. Bagot in " Trilby " ; at Wyndham's, Dec., 1916, played Mrs. Tunks in " London Pride " ; at Prince of Wales's, May, 1917, Amelia Dobbin in " Penny Wise " ; at the Garrick, Mar., 1919, The Duenna in " Cyrano de Bergerac " ; at the Empire Theatre, New York, Dec., 1920, played Mrs. Otery in " Mary Rose " ; at the George M. Cohan Theatre, Oct., 1921, Hester Fairfield in " A Bill of Divorcement " ; at the St. Martin's, London, Apr., 1923, Emma in " R.U.R." ; July, 1923, Bethia Parkins in " Melloney Holtspur " ; Aug., 1923, Mrs. Pool in " The Likes of 'Er " ; Jan., 1924, Effie Draicott in " A Magdalen's Husband " ; at the Ambassadors', Feb., 1924, Mrs. Hanbury in " The Way Things Happen " ; at the Queen's, Sept., 1924, Anna Tunstall in " The Claimant " ; Wyndham's, May, 1925, Miss Williams-Williams in " The Round Table " ; Vaudeville, Aug., 1925, Mrs. Sparfoot in " Blessed Are the Rich " ; Empire, Dec., 1925, the Old Lady in " Henry VIII " ; St. Martin's, Aug., 1926, Miss Phipps in " The Queen was in the Parlour " ; Prince's, Feb., 1927, Tatiana Sergevna in " The Greater Love " ; Daly's, Nov., 1927, Miss Johnson in " Sirocco " ; New, Apr., 1928, Susan Luckin in " Come With Me " ; Arts, Feb., 1929, Mrs. Pool in a revival of " The Likes of 'Er." *Address* : c/o Williams Deacon's Bank, West End Office, 9 Pall Mall, S.W.1. *(Died 8 June, 1940; age 78)*

KING, Cecil, actor and stage-manager ; *b.* Fermoy ; co. Cork ; *m.* Phyllis Neilson-Terry ; made his first appearance on the stage at Her Majesty's Theatre, 6 Sept., 1900, walking on in " Julius Caesar " ; he remained at this theatre under Sir Herbert Tree for fourteen years ; at first played small parts, under the name of " Carlton Rex," and was then made assistant stage-manager ; in Feb., 1904, was appointed stage-manager at His Majesty's, a position he continued to occupy until 1914 ; during this period he was responsible for the stage management of " The Tempest," " Much Ado About Nothing," " Business is Business," " Oliver Twist," " Colonel Newcome," " Antony and Cleopatra," " The Merchant of Venice," " Faust," " The School for Scandal," " False Gods," " King Henry VIII," " Macbeth," " Othello," " Trilby," " Romeo and Juliet," " Joseph and his Brethren," " Drake," etc. ; also for the series of Shakespearean Festivals from 1905-13 ; toured in America, 1915, as Rev. Thomas Bagot in " Trilby," Rev. Mr. Blimboe in " The Adventure of Lady Ursula " ; subsequently he toured the English provinces in " Trilby," etc. ; at the Apollo, Jan., 1922, in conjunction with his wife, produced " The Wheel," followed in May, 1922, by a revival of " Trilby," in which he played the Rev. Thomas Bagot ; at the Apollo, Jan. 1923, produced " A Roof and Four Walls," and during the autumn played Mr. Bollon in this play on tour ; at the Theatre Royal, Brighton, Jan., 1924, produced " Stigmata," followed by a provincial tour of the same play ; at Opera House, Blackpool, Sept., 1924, revived "Bella Donna," in which he played Sir Henry Grebe; during 1926 toured as Watts in "Honour"; during 1929 toured with Leon M. Lion's Galsworthy Repertory Company; at the Prince of Wales's (for the Sunday Players), June, 1929, played Henry Parr in "The Donkey's Nose"; during 1930, toured as Cable in "The Limping Man"; of late years, has acted as producer of the various Christmas revivals of "Peter ·Pan." *Club:* Green Room. *Address:* Green Room Club, Whitcomb Street, London, S.W.1. *(Died 21 Sept., 1958; age 83)*

KING, Charles, actor and vocalist; *b.* New York City, U.S.A., 31 Oct., 1889; *e.* Fordham, N.Y.; *m.* Lila Rhodes; made his first appearance as a boy vocalist in 1905, at Miner's Bowery Theatre, and subsequently appeared in a minstrel show; made his first appearance on the regular stage, at the Knickerbocker Theatre, 20 Apr., 1908, in the chorus of "The Yankee Prince"; Casino, July, 1908, played Artie in "The Mimic World"; Globe, Jan., 1911, Tod Norcross in "The Slim Princess"; Moulin Rouge, Apr., 1912, Wilder Daly in "A Winsome Widow"; 44th Street, Mar., 1913, Dick Cunningham in "The Geisha"; Winter Garden, July, 1913, Broadway Jones in "The Passing Show of 1913"; in 1914, toured in "The Honeymoon Express"; New Amsterdam, Dec., 1914, played Algy Cuffs in "Watch Your Step"; then in "vaudeville"; at the Century, Nov., 1917, played in "Miss 1917"; during the War, served in the U.S. Navy; at the Shubert, Feb., 1919, played Hughie Cavanagh in "Good Morning, Judge"; subsequently appeared in "The Midnight Whirl"; then returned to "vaudeville" for some years; at the Globe, June, 1926, appeared in "No Foolin'"; Belasco, Apr., 1927, played Bilge in "Hit the Deck"; Mansfield, Apr., 1928, Chick Evans in "Present Arms"; at Chicago, Oct., 1933, appeared in "Crazy Quilt"; commenced film career 1928, and has appeared in "The Broadway Melody," "The Girl in the Show," "The Hollywood Revue," "Chasing Rainbows," "Oh, Sailor, Behave!" *Recreations:* Golf and riding. *Address:* Lambs' Club, 130 West 44th Street, New York City, U.S.A. *(Died 11 Jan., 1944; age 52)*

KING, Claude, actor; *b.* Northampton, 15 Jan., 1876; *s.* of Benjamin King; *m.* (1) Violet Luddington; (2) Evelyn Hall (mar. dis.); was originally intended for an artist; made his first appearance on the stage at the Theatre Royal, Richmond, 1895, as Frank Selwyn in "The Silver King"; made his first appearance on the London stage, at the Princess's Theatre, 16 Dec., 1901, in "The Boom of Big Ben"; from 1905-10, acted all over the English-speaking world, toured in Africa, America, Australia, Burmah, Ceylon, China, Egypt, Federated Malay States, India, Japan, and New Zealand; in 1910, appeared at the Adelphi. as Captain Jack Temperley in "The House of Temperley," Dr. Watson in "The Speckled Band," and James Ainslie in "A Pot of Caviare"; at the Court, 1911, with Lillah McCarthy, played in "The Witch," "Nan," and "The Master Builder"; at the Aldwych, Mar., 1911, in "Business"; at the Little Theatre, Apr., 1911, appeared as Mr. Trotter in "Fanny's First Play"; at the Kingsway, Feb , 1912, played Anthony Redvers in "The Secret Woman"; May, 1912, Boris in "A Double Game"; at the Duke of York's, Oct., 1912, played Gregory Lum in "Overruled"; at the Kingsway, Nov., 1912, appeared as Ronald Keith in "The Eldest Son," at the Savoy, 1913, played the Duke of Orsino in "Twelfth Night"; at the Kingsway, Mar., 1913, played Dr. Pascoe in "The Great Adventure"; at the Court, Sept., 1913, played George Dedmond in "The Fugitive"; at the Haymarket, Feb., 1914, Malège in "Au Petit Bonheur"; at various times has toured in "Arizona," "Old Heidelberg," "The Silver King," "Alice Sit-by-the-Fire," "Lady Clancarty," "The Admirable Crichton," "The Prodigal Daughter," etc.; on the outbreak of war, 1914, was granted a commission in the Royal Field Artillery; after being demobilised, appeared at the Kingsway, Apr., 1919, as Holofernes in "Judith"; June, 1919, as Edmund Copplestone in "St. George and the Dragons";

subsequently went to America; at the Empire Theatre, New York, Oct., 1919, played Rudolph Solomon in "Déclassée"; during 1920 turned his attention to the cinema stage; at Washington, May, 1921, appeared in " The Silver Fox " ; at the Republic, New York, Dec., 1921, Prince Mirza in " The Fair Circassian " ; at the Garrick, New York, Feb.-Mar., 1922, played Lubin, Confucius, Zozin and Martellus in " Back to Methuselah " ; May, 1922, Francis Worgan in " What the Public Wants " ; at the Hudson, Sept., 1923, Thomas Harvey in " The Crooked Square " ; at the Vanderbilt, Nov., 1923, Felix Armand and Colonel Pigott in " In the Next Room " ; at the Cort, Sept., 1924, Julian Marsh in " The Far Cry " ; Booth, Dec., 1924, Giovanni Malatesta in " Paolo and Francesca " ; appeared at the Knickerbocker, June, 1925, and played Tom Wrench in " Trelawny of the Wells " ; Booth, Aug., 1925, Herbert Craig in " The Fall of Eve " ; Playhouse, Hollywood, Apr., 1932, Barron in "Dinner is Served"; Belasco, Los Angeles, May, 1932, Maurice Klein in " The Mad Hopes "; commenced film career, 1920, in " Idols of Clay," and appeared in innumerable pictures; since 1936, has appeared in "It Couldn't Have Happened," "Love Under Fire," " Lancer Spy," "Four Men and a Prayer," "Booloo," etc. *Favourite part :* Crichton in "The Admirable Crichton." *Recreations :* Riding, driving, fishing, and shooting. *Clubs :* Green Room, London; and the Masquers, Hollywood. *(Died 18 Sept., 1941; age 65)*

KING, Dennis, actor and singer; *b.* Coventry, Warwickshire, 2 Nov., 1897; *s.* of John Pratt and his wife Elizabeth (King); *e.* Birmingham; *m.* Edith Wright (dec.); was call-boy, and, subsequently, assistant stage manager at the Birmingham Repertory Theatre, where he made his first appearance on the stage in 1916, as Dennis in "As You Like It"; made his first appearance on the London stage at the Palace Theatre, Sept., 1919, as Townbrake in "Monsieur Beaucaire"; he then went to America, and appeared at the Empire, New York, Apr., 1921, as the

Marquis de Trois Fleurs in "Clair de Lune"; at the Republic, Dec., 1921, played Hon. Claude Faulconhirst in "The Fair Circassian"; at the Garrick (for the Theatre Guild), Feb., 1922, Cain and Strephon in "Back to Methuselah"; at the Lyceum, 1922, Albert in "Bluebeard's Eighth Wife": Garrick (for the Theatre Guild), Nov., 1922, Gerald Farringdon in "The Lucky One"; Henry Miller Theatre, Jan., 1923, Mercutio in "Romeo and Juliet"; Lyceum, Feb., 1924, the Messenger in "Antony and Cleopatra"; Imperial, Sept., 1924, Jim Kenyon in "Rose Marie"; made a great success when he appeared at the Casino, Sept., 1925, as François Villon in "The Vagabond King," which he continued to play for over two years; at the Lyric, Mar., 1928, played D'Artagnan in the musical version of "The Three Musketeers"; reappeared in London, at Drury Lane, Mar., 1930, when he played the last-mentioned part; returned to New York, and at the Shubert Theatre, Apr., 1931, played Peter Ibbetson in a revival of the play of that name; Casino, May, 1932, played Gaylord Ravenal in a revival of "Show Boat"; Saville, London, Oct., 1933, Peter Mali in "Command Performance"; returned to New York, and at the Empire, Feb., 1934, appeared as Richard II in "Richard of Bordeaux," which he directed in conjunction with William Mollison; at the Chestnut, Philadelphia, Dec., 1934, played Dascom Dinsmore in "Petticoat Fever," appearing in the same part at the Ritz, New York, Mar., 1935; Chestnut, Philadelphia (for the Theatre Guild), Nov., 1935, Hans Angerer in "Love Is Not So Simple"; Daly's, London, Feb., 1936, Dinsmore in "Petticoat Fever"; 48th Street, New York, May, 1936, Parnell in the play of that name; Westport, Conn., June, 1936, Valentine in "Love for Love"; Imperial, New York, Feb., 1937, Goethe in "Frederika"; Central City, Col., July, 1937, Dr. Rank in "A Doll's House" and Morosco, New York, Dec., 1937, Thorwald Helmer in the same play; Shubert, May, 1938, Count Willy Palaffi in "I Married an Angel"; at the Longacre, Nov., 1938 (with Richard Aldrich), presented

"Lorelei"; in Chicago, 1942, played Charles Condamine in "Blithe Spirit"; Ethel Barrymore, New York, Dec., 1942, Colonel Vershinin in "The Three Sisters"; Fulton, Apr., 1944, Alexander Hazen in "The Searching Wind"; Golden (for the Guild), Dec., 1945, Clay Rainier in "Dunnigan's Daughter"; Booth (for the Guild), Mar. 1946, Funny in "He Who Gets Slapped"; National, Dec., 1947, succeeded John Gielgud as Jason in "Medea"; toured, 1948, from Coast to Coast, as Henry Higgins in "Pygmalion"; Martin Beck, Apr., 1949, succeeded Robert Morley as Arnold Holt in "Edward, My Son"; in summer theatres, 1949, played Sir Robert Morton in "The Winslow Boy," and also appeared in "The Second Man"; City Center, New York, Jan., and Royale, Feb., 1950, played General Burgoyne in "The Devil's Disciple"; in Los Angeles, June, 1950, played the Bishop in "Getting Married"; Falmouth, Mass., July, 1950, appeared as Reggie Pelham in "Travellers' Joy"; at the Biltmore New York, Feb., 1951, played Capt Edward Fairfax Vere, R.N., in "Billy Budd"; Ziegfeld, Oct., 1951, played Bruno Mahler in a revival of "Music in the Air"; Broadhurst, Sept., 1953, appeared as Don Pedro de Miura in "The Strong Are Lonely"; at the same theatre, Dec., 1954, played Judge Sullivan in "Lunatics and Lovers"; at the A.N.T.A. Playhouse, Sept., 1955, appeared as Dr. Farley in "A Day by the Sea"; Ethel Barrymore, Apr., 1956, Major Rogers in "Affair of Honor"; Winter Garden, June, 1956, Hugh Conway in "Shangri-La"; Playhouse, Jan., 1957, Daniel Monnerie in "The Hidden River"; Ethel Barrymore, May, 1957, Amos Benedict in "The Greatest Man Alive!"; Olympia, Dublin, Mar., 1959, Sir Robert Balchion in "Goodwill Ambassador"; Coconut Grove Playhouse, Miami, Dec., 1959, Nichols in "Come to the Dance"; Martin Beck, N.Y., Dec., 1960, Humphrey Cobbler in "Love and Libel"; Bucks County Playhouse, New Hope, Pa., Aug., 1962, Caleb Wendell in "Crazy Old Owl"; Brooks Atkinson, Feb., 1963, Sam Elderly in "Photo Finish"; Henry Miller's, Oct., 1965, Bishop O'Leary in "A Minor Miracle"; Helen Hayes, Oct., 1966, Mr. Ingram in "The Loves of Cass McGuire"; Henry Miller's, Feb., 1968, Benjamin Disraeli in "Portrait of a Queen"; New Theatre for Now, Los Angeles, July, 1969, Somerset Maugham in "Remembering Mr. Maugham"; Imperial, N.Y., Oct., 1969, Baron Von Epp in "A Patriot for Me"; elected President of The Players Club, 1965; commenced film career, 1930, in "The Vagabond King"; has appeared on television in "Dinner at Eight," 1948, and subsequently in "Babes in Toyland," "A Christmas Card," "The Devil's Disciple," "Twelfth Night," "The Mikado," etc. *Favourite parts:* Mercutio, Villon, General Burgoyne, Richard of Bordeaux, Vershinin, and D'Artagnan. *(Died May, 1971; age 73)*

KING, Edith (*née* Keck), actress; *b.* White Haven, Pa., U.S.A., 14 Nov., 1896; *d.* of John A. Keck and his wife Margaret (Tucker); *e.* East Orange, New Jersey, grammar and high schools; first appeared on the stage, at the Belasco, New York, Jan., 1915, in "Marie-Odile"; at the Shubert, Mar., 1916, played Lady Airdale in "The Great Pursuit"; Belasco, 1916, appeared in "The Boomerang"; Hudson, Nov., 1917, Esther in "The Pipes of Pan"; Belasco, Sept., 1918, Bobette in "Daddies"; Park, Oct., 1920, Lelia Archibald in "Bab"; Longacre, Oct., 1921, Diane in "Thank You"; Comedy, Feb., 1925, June Lawler in "A Good Bad Woman"; Wallack's, June, 1925, Belinda Perkins in "The Right to Love"; Morosco, Aug., 1933, Daisy Appleton in "Going Gay"; Masque, Feb., 1935, Leda in "Cross Ruff"; Vanderbilt, Feb., 1936, Amelia in "Halloween"; Lyceum, May, 1936, Julie Compton in "One Good Year"; Imperial, Feb., 1937, Mrs. Thorne in "Frederika"; in 1937, played a season in municipal opera at St. Louis; she then joined the Theatre Guild, and appeared at the Shubert Theatre, Nov., 1937, as Leda in "Amphitryon 38"; Mar., 1938, played Pauline in "The Seagull"; made her first appearance in London, at the Lyric Theatre, 17 May, 1938, as Leda in "Amphitryon 38"; on returning to the United States, toured during 1939, and at the Alvin, Feb., 1940, played The Widow and Curtis in "The Taming of the Shrew"; Maxine Elliott, Mar., 1940, appeared as Margaret Eaves in "The Burning Deck"; Playhouse, Feb., 1941, played Mary Tibbs in "Popsy"; Guild, Nov., 1941, Bertha Barnes in "Hope for a Harvest"; Music Box, Mar., 1942, the Godmother and Dr. Bodie in "A Kiss for Cinderella"; Shubert, Oct., 1943, Bianca in "Othello," and Mar., 1944, Emilia in the same play; toured, 1945, in the same play and part; Booth, Jan., 1946, Madame Jourdain in "The Would-Be Gentleman"; Coronet, 1946, took over the rôle of Lucy Allerton in "Dream Girl"; Actors, Hollywood, 1946, The Mother in "Euridice"; in summer theatres, 1947, appeared in "The Primrose Path," and "The Glass Menagerie"; toured Calif., 1948, in "Naughty Marietta"; at the Erlanger, Buffalo, Jan., 1951, played Mama in "The Guardsman"; Plymouth, New York, Dec., 1951, appeared as the Actress's Mother in "Legend of Lovers"; 46th Street, Feb., 1954, Eugenie in "Ondine"; Ethel Barrymore, Apr., 1956, Mrs. MacKenzie in "Affair of Honor"; Summer, Sea Cliff, New York, Aug., 1956, Prudence in "First Night"; Royale, New York, Dec., 1957, Mrs. Ling in "Miss Isobel"; Morosco, Oct., 1959, Charlotte Peloux in "Chéri"; Winter Garden, Dec., 1959, Mrs. Sophie Bellop in "Saratoga"; Alvin, Dec., 1960, Countess Emily O'Brien in "Wildcat"; toured, 1963, in "Wildcat" and "Showboat"; Morosco, Mar., 1964, Madame Maille in "A Murderer Among Us"; toured, summer, 1964, in "Bachelor's Wife"; has also played leading parts in the Jessie Bonstelle "stock" companies in Portland, Me., Pittsburgh, and Columbus, Ohio; entered films in 1945; first appeared on television when it was still in its experimental stage, and has since appeared in "Arms and the Man," "Man and Superman," "The Guardsman," "Dodsworth," "Cyrano de Bergerac," etc. *Favourite parts:* Emilia in "Othello" and Queen Leda in "Amphitryon 38." *Recreations:* Gardening and cooking.

Address: 3140 Avenue A, Riviera Beach, Florida, U.S.A. 33404, or c/o Actors' Equity Association, 165 West 46th Street, New York City, N.Y. 10036, U.S.A.

KING, Walter Woolf, actor and vocalist; *b.* San Francisco, California, U.S.A., 2 Nov., 1899; *s.* of Simon Woolf and his wife Matilda (Davis); *e.* High School, Salt Lake City, Utah; *m.* Ernestyne Bachrach; made his first appearance on the stage at the Potacello Theatre, Idaho, singing in "vaudeville"; made his first appearance in New York, at the Winter Garden, 23 Oct., 1919, as Bacchus and Dick in "The Passing Show of 1919"; at the Century, Apr., 1920, played Frank Abercoed in "Florodora"; Century Grove, July, 1920, appeared in "The Midnight Rounders"; Century, May, 1921, played Lieut. Jack Merrington in "The Last Waltz"; Ambassador, Oct., 1922, Colonel Belovar in "The Lady in Ermine"; Winter Garden, June, 1923, in "The Passing Show"; Ambassador, Aug., 1924, Jack Warren in "The Dream Girl"; Winter Garden, June, 1925, in "Artists and Models"; Shubert, Sept., 1926, Count Tassilo Enrody in "Countess Maritza"; Dec., 1928, Gil de Beraud in "The Red Robe"; Morosco, July, 1930, Bob Longworth in "Ladies All"; Ritz, Apr., 1931, Captain O'Malley in "The Great Man"; Longacre, Dec., 1931, Frank Cameron in "Experience Unnecessary"; June, 1932, toured in "Clowns in Clover"; Casino, Feb., 1933, George Richards in "Melody"; Belasco, Los Angeles, June, 1933, Bruno Mahler in "Music in the Air"; St. James, New York, Dec., 1935, Baron Kuno Adelhorst in "May Wine"; in 1930, appeared in picture, "Golden Dawn," and since 1936 has appeared in "Walking Down Broadway," "Swiss Miss," "Society Smugglers," "Big Town Czar," "The House of Fear," etc.; prior to 1933, appeared under the name of Walter Woolf. *Hobby:* Collecting pipes. *Recreations:* Golf, tennis, and playing with the children. *Club:* Lambs. *Address:* c/o William Morris Agency Inc., 8511 Sunset Boulevard, Hollywood, Cal., U.S.A.

KING-HALL, Sir Stephen (*cr.* Baron (Life Peer), 1966), dramatic author; *b.* 21 Jan., 1893; *s.* of Admiral Sir George Fowler King-Hall, K.C.B., C.V.O., and his wife Olga (Ker); *e.* Lausanne, Osborne, and Dartmouth; *m.* Kathleen Spencer (dec.); served with the Grand Fleet in H.M.S. *Southampton*, 1914–17; then with the Submarine Flotilla; retired from the Navy with rank of Commander, 1929, and joined the staff of the Royal Institute of International Affairs; has written the following plays: "The Middle Watch" (with Ian Hay), 1929; "B. J. One," 1930; "The Midshipmaid" (with Ian Hay), 1931; "Admirals All" (with Ian Hay), 1934; "Off the Record" (with Ian Hay), 1947; "No. 10, Downing Street," 1949; "Bunga-Bunga," 1951; founded the National News Letter, 1936; M.P. (Ind.) for Ormskirk, 1939–45; founded the Hansard Society, 1944; received the honour of Knighthood, 1954. *Recreations:* Writing and outdoor sports. *Club:* Athenaeum. *Address:* The Pent House, 162 Buckingham Palace Road, London, S.W.1.

(Died 2 June, 1966; age 73)

KINGSTON, Gertrude, actress and producer; *b.* London; *d.* of Hugo Konstam; *e.* London; studied painting in Berlin and Paris, under Carolus Duran, Henner and Goussot; *m.* Capt. Silver (dec.); had some experience as an amateur before joining Miss Sarah Thorne's company at Margate in 1887, with whom she played Ophelia in "Hamlet," Emilia in "Othello," Sophia in "The Road to Ruin," Zoë in "The Octoroon," etc.; she made her first appearance on the London stage at the Haymarket, 5 Jan., 1888, under Beerbohm Tree, as Mrs. Harkaway in "Partners"; she subsequently appeared at the Novelty in "Nita's First" and "Bonny Boy"; at the Olympic, 1888, played Enid Anstruther in "To the Death"; at the Comedy, June, 1889, she produced "Woodbarrow Farm," in which she appeared as Clara Dexter; at the Opéra Comique, Jan., 1889, she played Rachel Denison in "Tares," and at the Adelphi, Apr., 1889, appeared as Lina Nelson in

"The Harbour Lights"; she also appeared at the Gaiety, Feb., 1889, as Mrs. Selwyn in "A Fool's Paradise"; and at the Prince of Wales's, June, 1889, as Emily in "A Man's Love"; at Terry's, 1890, she played in "New Lamps for Old," and the following year at the St. James's, played Mrs. Glyn-Stanmore in "The Idler"; at the Adelphi, 1893, she played Mabel Wentworth in "A Woman's Revenge"; at the Haymarket, 1894, appeared as Madame Obnoskin in "The Charlatan"; at the Criterion, Oct., 1894, appeared as Mrs. Quesnel in "The Case of Rebellious Susan"; at Terry's, 1895 played Mrs. D'Arcy in "The Passport"; at the Duke of York's, 1895, appeared as Mrs. Field in "Her Advocate," and Ruth in "Tommy Atkins," in 1896 played Rose in "The Fool of the Family"; appeared at the Shaftesbury, 1896, as Mrs. Lane in "The Matchmaker"; in 1897 was engaged by Sir Henry Irving for the Lyceum, and appeared there, Apr., 1897, as the Queen of Naples in "Madame Sans-Gêne"; at the Haymarket, Oct., 1898, played Constantia Gage in "The Manœuvres of Jane"; at the St. James's, Feb., 1901, played Lady Margaret Staines in "The Awakening"; during the South African War, 1901-1902, she was with the Actors' and Actresses' Hospital Hut, and was specially mentioned in despatches for her services; on her return to England she was seen at the Duke of York's, Mar., 1902, as Mrs. Malpas in "The Princess's Nose"; at the Comedy, Sept., 1902, as Lady Langford in "Secret and Confidential," and Oct. as Mrs. Rose in "The Wisdom of Folly"; at Glasgow, Nov., 1903, she played Mrs. Le Mesurier in "The Peril's of Flirtation," appearing at the Avenue in the same part, Jan., 1904; at the New Theatre, Feb., 1904, appeared as Lady Prothero in "My Lady of Rosedale," at the Court, Jan., 1905, played Lady Raffin in "Good Friends"; at the Court, Apr., 1905, played Helen in "The Trojan Women" of Euripides; at the Comedy, Aug., 1905, appeared as Lady Amelia Cainshays in "The Duffer"; at Terry's, Jan., 1906, as Lady Hermione Candlish in "The

Heroic Stubbs," at the Savoy, March, 1906, as Œnone in "Paris and Œnone"; at the Duke of York's, Sept., 1906, played Lady Dover in "Toddles"; at the Royalty, Jan., 1908, appeared as Lady Corneston in "Susannah, and Some Others"; at the Royalty, May, 1908, as Mrs. Willbrough in "The Grey Stocking"; at the Court, Nov., 1908, played Lady Devenham in "A Bridge Tangle"; same theatre, June, 1909, played Lady Mary Wansley in "The Beetle"; at the Hicks Theatre, July, 1909, appeared as Angela Cranfield in "His Borrowed Plumes"; she then became lessee of the Little Theatre, and opened it on 11 Oct., 1910, with a revival of Aristophanes' old comedy "Lysistrata," in which she played the title part; in Nov., 1910, played Georgina Vicary in "Just to Get Married," and Dec., 1910, appeared in the title-*rôle* of "The Fotheringay"; at the Gala performance at His Majesty's, 27 June, 1911, played Harmony in "The Vision of Delight"; at the Comedy, July, 1911, appeared as Lady Warburton in "The Green Elephant"; at the Little Theatre, Mar., 1912, played Madame Arcádina in "The Seagull"; Oct., 1912, Lady Cecily Waynflete in "Captain Brassbound's Conversion"; Feb., 1913, Baroness Luisa Sangioyi in "Three"; at the Vaudeville, Nov., 1913, appeared as the Empress Catherine II in "Great Catherine"; at the Toy Theatre, Boston, Mass., Feb., 1915, appeared in "Great Catherine," "Over-ruled," "The Dark Lady of the Sonnets," and "Captain Brassbound's Conversion"; at the Repertory Theatre, Birmingham, Oct., 1916, played Ermyntrude in "The Inca of Perusalem"; returned to America, and at the Neighbourhood Playhouse Theatre, New York, Nov., 1916, played the same part; at Maxine Elliott's Theatre, Jan., 1917, appeared in "The Queen's Enemies," and "Great Katharine"; Feb., 1917, played Mrs. Juno in "Overruled"; after returning to England, appeared at the King's Hall, Covent Garden, Feb., 1919, as Mrs. Hale in "Trifles"; at the Everyman Theatre, Hampstead, Mar., 1922, played Mrs. George Collins in "Getting Married"; May, 1922,

Mrs. Clandon in "You Never Can Tell" · at the Ambassadors', June, 1923, Mrs. Rooke-Walter in "The Lilies of the Field"; Regent (for the Pioneers), Mar., 1925, Adelaide in "The Verge"; Scala, July, 1925, The Empress Dowager in "The Son of Heaven"; Lyric, Hammersmith, Nov., 1925, Miss Welcome in "Crossings"; Prince of Wales's (for the Venturers), Feb., 1926, Lady Kerandal in "Wet Paint"; Savoy, Mar., 1926, Mdme. du Parc in "The Snow Man"; went to New York, and appeared at the Maxine Elliott Theatre, Sept., 1926, as Lady Kerandal in "Red Blinds" ("Wet Paint"); Arts, London, July, 1927, Dowager Lady Rivers in "Nevertheless," which she also produced; Shaftesbury, Sept., 1927, Lady Trench in "The High Road"; Everyman, Jan., 1929, Old Mrs. Thurlow in "The Ship"; Arts, Oct., 1929, played Alice Pettigrew in "Time and the Hour"; during 1931, appeared with the Masque Theatre company, in Scotland, in "Great Catherine," etc.; at Wyndham's (for 1930 Players), May, 1932, played Queen Elizabeth in "When Essex Died." *Club* : Bath. *Address* : 73 Marsham Street, Westminster, S.W.1. *Telephone No. :* Victoria 0297. *(Died 7 Nov., 1937; age 71)*

KIRBY, John, actor; *b.* Dunedin, New Zealand, 24 Dec., 1894; *s.* of John Francis Kirby and his wife Agnes Julia (McCarthy); *e.* Otago Boys High School and Otago University; was formerly an articled clerk to a firm of solicitors; made his first appearance on the stage at the Theatre Royal, Brisbane, Queensland, 15 Feb., 1913, as Henri de Montrale in "The Monk and the Woman"; from 1913-15 was stage manager with Alban Wilkie's Shakespearean Company, and with Julius Knight's Company; from 1915-19, served in the War with the Australian Imperial Forces; from 1919-25, was producer for Sir Benjamin and John Fuller and Hugh J. Ward, Ltd., in Australia, also playing several important parts in numerous productions; came to London in 1925, and made his first appearance on the

London stage at the Lyceum, 2 Sept., 1925, in " The London Revue "; at the New Oxford, Oct., 1925, appeared in " Carry On, Sergeant"; at the Palladium, Feb., 1926, in " Palladium Pleasures "; at the Winter Garden, Aug., 1926, played Hen Kaye in " Tip-Toes "; Carlton, Apr., 1927, Ezra Pettyjohn in " Lady Luck "; London Hippodrome, July, 1927, appeared in " Shake Your Feet "; at His Majesty's, Sept., 1927, Shorty McGee in " Oh, Kay! "; Palace, Oct., 1928, Silas B. Hock in " Virginia "; June, 1929, Chubby in " Hold Everything." *Favourite parts :* Joe Horn in " Rain " and Silas in " Virginia." *Recreation :* Golf. *Clubs :* Eccentric, Green Room. *Address :* Eccentric Club, Ryder Street, St. James's, S.W.1.

KIRKLAND, Alexander, actor; *b.* Mexico City; *s.* of Robert G. Kirkland and his wife Charlotte Kirke (Meginn); *e.* privately and at Taft School, Water-town, Conn.; *m.* (1) Gypsy Rose Lee (mar. dis.); (2) Phyllis Anne Adams; studied for the stage under Jasper Deeter, Louis Calvert, and Rouben Mamoulian; made his first appearance on the stage, 1925, at the Ramshead Playhouse, Washington, D.C., in "L'Aiglon"; first appeared in New York, at 52nd Street Theatre, 3 Dec., 1925, as Nanning Storm in "The Devil to Pay"; 49th Street, Feb., 1926, played Stephen Bartan in "The Right Age to Marry"; Coburn, Nov., 1928, Wu-Hoo-Git in "The Yellow Jacket"; Martin Beck (for the Guild), Dec., 1928, Francis Lightfoot in "Wings Over Europe"; Guild Mar., 1930, Aleksei in "A Month in the Country"; Henry Miller, Nov., 1930, Marius in "Marseilles"; joined the Group Theatre, New York, 1933, and appeared at the Broadhurst, Sept., 1933, as Dr. Ferguson in "Men in White"; Morosco, Nov., 1934, Lon Firth in "Gold Eagle Guy"; Longacre, Mar., 1935, Ernst Taussig in "Till the Day I Die"; 46th Street, Nov., 1935, Danny Stowe in "Weep for the Virgins"; Barrymore, Mar., 1936, Clyde Griffiths in "The Case of Clyde Gr ffiths," and at the Mansfield, Nov., 1936, Peter Charrington in

"Black Limelight"; Biltmore, Oct., 1937, Peter Brent in "Many Mansions"; Playhouse, Dec., 1938, Henry in "Outward Bound"; at the Windsor Theatre, Feb., 1941, produced with William Deering, and directed "Out of the Frying Pan"; Golden Theatre, 1942, was co-producer of "The Strings, My Lord, Are False"; Lyceum, Nov., 1941, played Willis Reynolds in "Junior Miss," until 1943; Forty-eighth Street Theatre, Sept., 1943, directed "The Snark Was a Boojum"; Broadhurst, Mar., 1945, played Dr. Francis Gresham in "Lady in Danger," of which he was also part-author, with Max Afford; subsequently, 1945, toured overseas, in the European Theatre of Operations, for U.S.O., as Charles Considine in "Blithe Spirit"; in summer theatres, 1946, appeared in "To-Night or Never"; summer theatres, 1947, in "The Glass Menagerie," and "My Fair Lady"; founded the Berkshire Playhouse, Stockbridge, Mass., 1930, and was manager for three years; author of the "Naughty Nineties Cook Book," 1950; entered films, 1932, and appeared in numerous pictures. *Recreations :* Horses, writing, painting, boating, and farming. *Address :* c/o Garfield and Wrubel, 25 West 44th Street, New York City, U.S.A.

KIRKLAND, Jack, dramatic author and producer; *b.* St. Louis, Mo., U.S.A., 25 July, 1902; *s.* of William Thomas Kirkland and his wife Julia (Woodward); *e.* Columbia University; *m.* (1) Nancy Carroll (mar. dis.); (2) Jayne Shadduck (mar. dis.); (3) Julia Laird (mar. dis.); (4) Haila Stoddard (mar. dis.); (5) Nancy Hoadley; was formerly engaged in journalism and was on the staff of the New York *Daily News*; is the author of the following plays: "Frankie and Johnnie," 1928; "Tobacco Road," 1933, which ran continuously to 1941, the second longest run on record of any play in New York, 3,182 performances; "Tortilla Flat" (from a novel), 1938; "I Must Love Someone" (with Leyla Georgie), 1939; "Suds in Your Eye," 1944; "Georgia Boy," which he also directed and co-produced at the Copley Theatre,

Boston, Dec., 1945; "Mr. Adam," 1949, which he also produced; "The Man with the Golden Arm," 1956; "Mandingo," 1961; presented "Suzanna and the Elders," 1940; "Tanyard Street," 1941; "The Moon Vine," 1943; as co-producer was responsible for the production of "Forbidden Melody" and "Bright Honor," 1936; "Tortilla Flat," 1938; "I Must Love Someone" (with Leyla Georgie), 1939; is the author of several films since 1930, either alone or in collaboration. *Recreation:* Farming. *Clubs:* Columbia University; Tavern, Chicago; Racquet, Palm Springs.

KIRKLAND, Muriel, actress; *b.* Yonkers, New York, U.S.A., 19 Aug., 1903; *d.* of Charles B. Kirkland and his wife Margaret (Keith); *e.* Ursuline Convent, New Rochelle, New York; specially trained for the stage with Stuart Walker; *m.* Staats Cotsworth; made her first appearance on the New York stage at the Heckscher, 20 Feb., 1923, as Lady Ursula in the Strolling Players production "The Knave of Hearts"; at the National Theatre, Mar., 1923, played Maria in "The School for Scandal"; played in stock in "Smilin' Through" and "Peter Pan," 1923–5; played in stock companies throughout the 1920s, notably with Stuart Walker in Cincinnati and Indianapolis; at the Hudson, Jan., 1925, played Nettie in "Out of Step"; Bijou, Dec., 1927, Rosie Moore in "Brass Buttons"; 48th Street, Jan., 1928, Carlotta Maxwell in "Cock Robin"; Avon, Sept., 1929, Isabelle Parry in "Strictly Dishonorable"; Sam H. Harris, Sept., 1930, Polaire in "The Greeks Had a Word for It"; Times Square, Sept., 1931, Eva Sandor in "I Love an Actress"; Selwyn, Nov., 1931, Neila Anderson in "Fast Service"; at the Curran, San Francisco, Dec., 1933, appeared in "Sailor Beware"; Mansfield, New York, Mar., 1935, played Adelaide Willifer in "Lady of Letters"; Magnolia, Mass., July, 1935, played in "March Hares," "Private Lives." "The Curtain Rises," "Ariadne," "The Waltz," "There's Always Juliet," "After Such Plea-

sures"; toured, 1936–7, as Elizabeth Bennet in "Pride and Prejudice"; Lyceum, New York, Jan., 1938, Bessie Latimer in "Stop-Over"; toured, Feb.–Mar., 1938, in "Tonight at 8.30"; Plymouth, Oct., 1938, Mary Todd in "Abe Lincoln in Illinois"; toured in the same part, 1939–40; in 1941, at Stockbridge and Cohasset, played Mrs. Elvsted in "Hedda Gabler" and Louisa in "Ladies in Retirement"; in 1942, at Princeton, Maggie Wylie in "What Every Woman Knows"; Empire, New York, May, 1943, Vinnie in "Life with Father"; in summer theatres, 1947, played Elizabeth Barrett in "The Barretts of Wimpole Street"; at the Berkshire Playhouse, Stockbridge, Aug., 1952, played Lady Macbeth; in Dallas, Texas, 1954, appeared as Aunt Muriel in "A Dash of Bitters"; National, New York, Apr., 1955, played Mrs. Brady in "Inherit the Wind"; toured, 1958, as Big Mamma in "Cat on a Hot Tin Roof"; 54th Street, Feb., 1959, Abby Borden in "The Legend of Lizzie"; 1959–60, toured as Hannah Kennedy in "Mary Stuart," in which play she took over the part of Queen Elizabeth for several performances at the Shubert, Cincinnati, Ohio, Dec., 1959; Equity Library Theatre tour, 1962, played title-rôle in "Elizabeth the Queen"; Pocket, N.Y., Jan., 1969, Eugenia in "Tango"; entered films, 1933, in "The Cocktail Hour," "Nana," etc. and has appeared in numerous television productions in the U.S. and England. (*Died* 25 *Sept.,* 1971.)

KIRKLAND, Patricia, actress; *b.* New York City, U.S.A., 18 July, 1925; *d.* of Jack Kirkland and his wife Nancy (Carroll); *e.* Dwight Girls' School, Englewood, N.J.; made her first appearance on the stage, at the Bucks County Playhouse, 1942, in "Susan and God"; at Chicago, 1943, played Corliss Archer in "Kiss and Tell," in which she appeared for a year; first appeared in New York at the Henry Miller Theatre, 14 June, 1944, as Nancy Vanda in "For Keeps"; Biltmore, 1945, succeeded Arlene Joyce as Laura Jessup in "Snafu"; and May, 1945, played Virginia Albright in "Round Trip"; at the Bucks County Playhouse, July, 1946, Richardson in "Alice Sit-by-the-Fire"; Mansfield, Dec., 1946, Ruth Gordon Jones in "Years Ago"; Martin Beck, Mar., 1948, Dolly Clandon in "You Never Can Tell"; Fulton, Nov., 1948, Patty Morritt in "The Young and Fair." *Address:* c/o Actors' Equity Association, 45 West 47th Street, New York City, U.S.A.

KIRWAN, Patrick, actor and manager of "The Idyllic Players"; *b,* Ireland; *s.* of William Nicholas Kirwan, and Anna Maria (Byrne); *e.* Prior Park and University College, Gower Street; formerly occupied as a civil engineer; first appeared as a reciter at the Pavilion, Brighton, Oct., 1885; made his first appearance on the professional stage in "Cyrene," at the Avenue, 1890; was professor of stage training at the Lyric and Dramatic Academy, London; founded the Old Comedy Society; has given pastoral plays with his own company of Idyllic Players at the Botanic Gardens, Regent's Park, since the year 1904, producing "As You Like It," "A Midsummer Night's Dream," "The Tempest," "The Merry Wives of Windsor," "Much Ado About Nothing," "Twelfth Night," etc.; organised the Irish entertainments through the season of 1908 at the Franco-British Exhibition; appeared at His Majesty's, 1909, in "The Dancing Girl," and in the Shakespearean Festival; during 1910 played a seven weeks' season of open-air plays at the Crystal Palace; during 1912 presented a season of plays at the Elizabethan Exhibition at Earl's Court; at His Majesty's, May, 1913, played in "The Perfect Gentleman"; at the Strand, June, 1917, played the Mayor of Chevoche in "The Tidings Brought to Mary"; is founder of the Dilettanti Club, for artists and literary men and women. *Club:* Authors'. *Address:* 10 Berkeley Place, S.W.19. *Telephone No.:* Wimbledon 2713.
(Died 13 Feb., 1929; age 67)

KISTEMAECKERS, Henry, French dramatic author; *b.* Floreffe, 13 Oct., 1872; *e.* University of Brussels; *m.* Julie Carvès; has written the following, among other plays: "Pierrot amoureux," 1890; "Morale du Siècle," "Idylle Nocturne," 1891; "L'amour en jaune," "Accrochecœurs," "Le Ménage Quinquet," 1893; "Marthe," 1899; "La Blessure," 1900; "Œdipe," 1901; "Le Premier client," 1903; "L'Instinct," 1905; "La Rivale" (with Delard), 1907; "Le Marchand de Bonheur," 1910; "La Flambée," 1911; "Embuscade," 1913; "Exilée," 1913; "L'Occident," 1913; "La Belle Visite," 1918; "Un Soir au front," 1918; "Le Roi des Palaces," 1919; "La Passante," 1921; is an Officer of the Legion of Honour, and Vice-President of the Society of Men of Letters and Dramatic Authors; was decorated with the Croix de Guerre. *Recreations:* Fencing and motoring. *Address:* 4 Avenue du Colonel-Bonnet, Paris.

KLAUBER, Adolph, producing manager; *b.* Louisville, Ky., U.S.A., 29 Apr., 1879; *s.* of Edward Klauber and his wife Caroline (Brahms); *e.* Louisville and University of Virginia; *m.* Jane Cowl; was for some time on the staff of the New York *Commercial Advertiser,* and subsequently of the New York *Tribune*; was then appointed dramatic critic of the *New York Times,* a post he held from 1906-18 was a frequent contributor to the periodical press; has since devoted himself to theatrical production; produced "Nighty Night," 1919; "Scrambled Wives," "The Emperor Jones," "Diff'rent"; 1920; "Like a King," 1921; "The Charlatan," 1922; also associated with Jane Cowl in her productions of "Lilac Time," "Smilin' Through," and with Selwyn and Co. in "Romeo and Juliet," 1923; "Pelleas and Melisande," 1923; "Antony and Cleopatra," 1924, with Archibald Selwyn, produced "The Depths," 1925; produced "Diversion," 1928. *Address:* c/o Coudert Bros. 2 Rector Street, New York City, U.S.A.
(Died 7 Dec., 1933; age 54)

KLAW, Marc, manager ; b. Paducah, Kentucky, 29 May, 1858 ; s. of Leopold and Caroline Klaw ; e. at public and high schools, Louisville, Kentucky ; m. (1) Blanche Violet Day Harris ; (2) Antoinette M. Morris ; studied law and admitted to the Bar ; entered theatrical management on 26 Aug., 1881 ; was senior member of the firm of Klaw and Erlanger ; also member of the firms of Hayman, Klaw and Erlanger ; Hayman, Frohman, Klaw and Erlanger ; Nixon and Zimmerman ; his firms for years controlled the principal theatres in the United States ; was the founder of the Syndicate Booking Agency ; in Apr., 1907, his firm acquired the interests of the Shubert Bros.' various theatres, incorporating them under the title of the United States Amusement Co. ; this arrangement was not of long duration and the firms then worked entirely apart ; in 1920 severed the partnership with Abraham Erlanger, and became an independent producing manager ; produced " Dere Mable," " Sonya," " French Leave," 1920 ; " We Girls," " The Yellow Jacket," 1921 ; " The Shadow," " Hunky Dory," 1922 ; " Hell Bent Fer Heaven," " The Rising Son," 1924 ; built the Klaw Theatre, which opened in 1920 ; head of the firm of Marc Klaw (1921) Inc. ; President of the United Managers' Protective Association ; Trustee of the Actors' Fund of America. *Clubs :* Democratic, Green Room, Lambs' and Managers' Association of Greater New York. *Residence :* New Rochelle, New York. *(Died 14 June, 1936; age 78)*

KLEIN, Charles, playwright ; b. London, 7 Jan., 1867 ; m. Lilian Gottlieb ; formerly reader of plays to Charles Frohman ; has written the following, among other plays :— " A Mile a Minute," 1890 ; " By Proxy," 1892 ; " El Capitan," 1895 ; " The Merry Countess " (from the French, 1895) ; " The District Attorney " (with Harrison Grey Fiske, 1895) ; " Two Little Vagrants " (from the French, 1896) ; " Dr. Belgraff," 1897 ; " The Red Feather," 1897 ; " Heartsease," 1897 ; " The Charlatan," 1898 ; " A Royal Rogue," 1900 ; " The Auctioneer," 1901 ; " The Hon. John Grigsby," 1902 ; " Mr. Pickwick," 1903 ; " Truthful James " (with James Mortimer, 1903) ; " The Music Master," 1904 ; " The Lion and the Mouse," 1905 ; " The Daughters of Men," 1906 ; " The Step-Sister," 1907 ; " The Third Degree," 1908 ; " The Next of Kin," 1909 ; " The Gamblers," 1910 ; " Maggie Pepper," 1911 ; " The Outsiders," 1911 ; " The Ne'er do Well," 1912 ; also " A Paltry Million," " A Happy Little Home," " Willie," " Admitted to the Bar," and " The Cypher Code." *Address :* 3 Netherall Gardens, Hampstead, N.W. *(Died 7 May, 1915; age 48)*

KNIGHT, Julius, actor ; b. Dumfries, Scotland, 1863 ; made his first appearance on the stage at Llandudno, Sept., 1884, in " Called Back " ; for nearly two years played on tour in " The Private Secretary," subsequently touring with the late Alice Lingard as Captain Dyson in " Sister Mary," etc ; made his first appearance on the London stage, at the New Olympic Theatre, 1 Aug., 1891, as Andreas in " Theodora " ; at Drury Lane, Sept., 1892, played the Hon. Julian Belford in " The Prodigal Daughter " ; played a three years' engagement with Sir Henry Irving, appearing at the Lyceum, Apr., 1894, as Valentine in " Faust," also playing King Louis of France in " Becket," Sir Lavaine in " King Arthur," etc., etc. ; subsequently toured with Miss Fortescue, afterwards proceeding to Australia ; reappeared in England, at the Adelphi, Aug., 1899, in " With Flying Colours " ; appeared at the Lyric Club, 1902, as Praed in " Mrs. Warren's Profession," and at the Avenue, Jan., 1902, as Walter Orchard in " After All " ; subsequently toured with Mrs. Langtry as Napoleon in " Mademoiselle Mars " ; was then engaged by Beerbohm Tree for his Australian company to play the entire lead ; subsequently " starred " throughout Australia and New Zealand with Maud Jeffries, playing " The Sign of the Cross," " The Lady of Lyons," " Pygmalion and Galatea," " Monsieur Beaucaire," etc. ;

reappeared in London, at His Majesty's Theatre, Sept., 1906, as Polixines in " The Winter's Tale " ; subsequently again returned to Australia, and during 1910, played in " The Third Degree," " Henry of Navarre," " The Sign of the Cross," etc. ; at the Gaiety, Manchester, Mar., 1912, played John Tilford in " The Perfect Widow " ; at the Garrick, Aug., 1912, appeared as Richard Dexter in " Find the Woman " ; on returning to Australia, toured in " Milestones," as John Rhead, and in " Bella Donna," as Dr. Meyer Isaacson ; during 1915, played in " Monsieur Beaucaire," " The Lifeguardsman," " The Scarlet Pimpernel," etc. ; returned to London in 1917 ; at the Theatre Royal, Bradford, May, 1918, played Ronnay de Maurel in " The Legion of Honour " ; at the Devonshire Park Theatre, Nov., 1918, Ex-President Lanchester in " His Royal Happiness " ; at the Lyceum, Sheffield, Mar., 1919, Sir Robert Graham in " Uncle Ned," and subsequently toured in this ; at the Scala Theatre, Oct., 1919, played Sir Claude Petrie in " The Net " ; at the Prince's Manchester, Dec., 1919, played Sir Charles Pomander in " Our Peg." *Address :* 3 Mortimer Mansions, 73/5 Mortimer Street, W.1. *Telephone No. :* Museum 3640.

(Died 21 Feb., 1941; age 78)

KNIGHT, June (*née* Margaret Rose Valliquietto), actress and dancer; *b.* Hollywood, Ca., U.S.A., 22 Jan., 1911; *e.* Hollywood; *m.* (1) Paul S. Ames (mar. dis.); (2) Arthur Arden Cameron (mar. dis.); (3) Harry Packer; began her career as a dancer in cinemas; made her first appearance on the stage as a dancer in "Topsy and Eva," 1925; appeared in the chorus of several musical plays in Los Angeles; subsequently appeared in Cabaret on the Pacific Coast and in New York; first appeared on the regular stage in New York at the Lyric Theatre, 27 Nov., 1929, as a dancer in "Fifty Million Frenchmen"; subsequently was dancing-partner with John Holland; at San Francisco and Los Angeles, during 1931, appeared in "Girl Crazy" and "The Nine o'Clock Revue"; Ziegfeld, New York, Mar.,

1932, played Dorothy Maxwell in "Hot-Cha !"; Apollo, New York, Nov., 1932, Toni Ray in "Take a Chance"; Imperial, Oct., 1935, Karen O'Kane in "Jubilee"; made her first appearance in London, at the Savoy Theatre, 8 Oct., 1936, as Jeanne Laporte in "Going Places——"; Savoy, Apr., 1937, appeared in "And On We Go"; subsequently left the stage for several years; reappeared, at the Shubert Theatre, Boston, Apr., 1944, in "Dream with Music"; Booth Theatre, New York, Jan., 1946, played Dorimene in "The Would-be Gentleman"; Shubert, Jan., 1947, Liane in "Sweethearts"; first entered films in 1930.

KNOBLOCK, Edward, dramatic author ; *b.* New York City, 7 Apr., 1874 ; *s.* of Gertrude and Charles Knoblauch ; *e.* Harvard University ; naturalized British subject; spent some time on the stage as an actor, in order to gain experience of dramatic technique; appeared at the Royalty, 26 Nov., 1899, as Jo in " You Never Can Tell," with the Stage Society; at the Adelphi, Mar., 1900, played in " Bonnie Dundee " ; at the Vaudeville, Nov., 1900, played the Waiter in Ibsen's "The League of Youth"; is the author of the following plays: " The Club Baby " (with Lawrence Sterner), 1895 ; " The Partikler Pet " (from the French), 1905 ; " The Shulamite," adapted from Claude and Alice Askew's novel, 1906 ; " The Cottage in the Air," adapted from " Priscilla's Fortnight," 1909 ; " Sister Beatrice," translation of Maeterlinck's play, 1910 ; " The Faun," 1911 ; " Kismet," 1911 ; " Milestones " (with Arnold Bennett), 1912 ; " Discovering America," 1912 ; " The Headmaster " (with Wilfred T. Coleby), 1913 ; " My Lady's Dress," 1914 ; " England Expects " (with Seymour Hicks), 1914 ; " Hajj," 1915 ; " Marie-Odile," 1915 ; " The Way to Win," 1915 ; " A War Committee," 1915 ; " How to Get On," 1915 ; " Paganini," 1915 ; " Mouse," 1915 ; " The Hawk " (from the French), 1916 ; " Home on Leave," 1916 ; " Tiger! Tiger! " 1918 ; " Our Peg," 1919 ; " Mumsee," 1920; " Cherry," 1920 ; " One," 1920 ; " Lullaby,"

1923 ; " Conchita," 1924 ; " London Life " (with Arnold Bennett), 1924 ; " Simon; Called Peter " (with J. E. Goodman, from the novel), 1924 ; " Speak Easy " (with George Rosener), 1927 ; " The Mulberry Bush," 1927 ; " Mr. Prohack " (with Arnold Bennett), 1927 ; " The Good Companions " (with J. B. Priestley), 1931 ; " Grand Hotel " (adaptation), 1931 ; " Hatter's Castle " (from the novel), 1932 ; " Evensong " (with Beverley Nichols), 1932 ; " If a Body " (with George Rosener, from the French), 1935 ; " The Rolling Stone," 1936 ; " The Edwardians " (adaptation, from the novel), 1937 ; supervised the Irving Centenary _matinée_ at the Lyceum, 1938 ; with Mary Pickford and Douglas Fairbanks wrote the scenarios for the films of " The Three Musketeers," " Rosita," and " The Thief of Bagdad "; published his reminiscences, " Round the Room," 1939. _Favourite play :_ " As You Like It." _Clubs :_ Garrick and Beefsteak, London ; Century, University, New York. _Address :_ 21 Ashley Place, London, S.W.1. _Telephone No. :_ Victoria 2422. _Cable Address :_ Knoblock, London. _New York Address :_ c/o Charles Burlingham, 27 William Street, New York City, U.S.A.
(Died 19 July, 1945; age 71)

KNOTT, Roselle (Agnes Roselle), actress ; _b._ Hamilton, Ontario, 1870 ; _m._ Thomas Knott ; made her first appearance on the stage, in 1887, at Hamilton ; at Palmer's Theatre, New York, Nov., 1893, she appeared as Jacques de Bois in " As You Like It "; subsequently played Diane in " Paul Kauvar," and in 1896 she appeared as Nourmalle in " The Cherry Pickers," under Augustus Pitou ; during 1899 appeared with Richard Mansfield, and at the New York Theatre, Apr., 1900, played Lygia in " Quo Vadis ? "; during 1901 appeared as the Empress Josephine in " More Than Queen," and made her _début_ as a " star " as Katinka in " A Modern Magdalen "; for two seasons, 1902-3, toured as Mary Tudor in " When Knighthood Was In Flower," followed by a season as the heroine in " Cousin Kate "; this was

followed by a further tour in " When Knighthood Was In Flower," and then, in Oct., 1906, she appeared as the Lady Georgiana Spencer in " The Duchess of Devonshire " ; during 1906-7 she played Alice Grey in a tour of " Alice Sit-by-the-Fire " ; retired through ill-health during the autumn of 1907 ; at the New York Theatre, July, 1911, played Portia in " The Merchant of Venice " ; in 1912, toured in " The Awakening of Helena Ritchie " ; in 1914, toured with Ben Greet's Company ; in 1915, toured in " Sinners." _Address :_ c/o _New York Dramatic News,_ 75 West 44th Street, New York City, U.S.A.
(Died 28 Jan., 1948)

KNOWLES, Alex, dramatic critic and press representative ; _b._ Aberdeenshire, 23 Oct., 1850 ; _e._ privately ; has been a journalist since 1873 ; was dramatic critic to _The Lady's Pictorial,_ 1887-8 ; sub-editor and Editor of _The Bat, The Hawk,_ etc. ; was for seventeen years " Sir Affable " on the _Licensed Victualler's Mirror ;_ is a frequent contributor to the periodical and daily press ; since 1891 has served as Press Representative to many leading West End managements, including Sir Augustus Harris, Sir Charles Wyndham, Sir Henry Irving, Charles Hawtrey, Gatti and Frohman, Seymour Hicks, etc. ; from 1895-1913, was Press Representative of Drury Lane Theatre ; is an original member of the Institute of Journalists. _Address :_ 3 Macclesfield Chambers, Shaftesbury Avenue. _Clubs :_ Green Room and Eccentric.
(Died 15 Jan., 1917; age 66)

KOLB, Thérèse, French actress ; _b._ Atlkirch, 19 Jan., 1856 ; studied for the stage at the Paris Conservatoire, under M. Régnier ; made her first appearance at the Comédie Française, 9 Dec., 1898, as Dorine in " Tartuffe " ; has appeared at the Comédie Française, in the following, among other plays : " Cabotins," " Blanchette," " La Plus Faible," " Claudie," " Le Père Lebonnard," " Monsieur Alphonse," " L'Ame

des Héros," "L'Amour Veille," "Le Légataire Universal," "Simone," "Le Dépit amoureux," "Le Voyage de M. Perrichon," "Sapho," "Debureau," "La Robe Rouge," "Sire." "Paraître," "Le Prince D'Aurec," "Les Affaires sont les Affaires," "Les Soeurs d'Amour," "Le Voile Dechiré," "Turcaret,"; became a sociétaire of the Comédie Française, 1904. *Address :* 3 Rue Pierre-Haret, Paris.
(Died 19 Aug., 1935; age 79)

KOLKER, Henry, actor ; *b.* 13 Nov., 1874 ; *s.* of William Kolker and his wife Katherine (Dürjon) ; *e.* Quincy, Ill., U.S.A.; *m.* Margaret Bruenn; made his first appearance on the stage at Milwaukee, 1894, in the German Stock Company; in 1895 he made his first appearance on the English-speaking stage, with Robert Downing in "The Gladiator"; in 1897–8 toured with James O'Neill; made his first appearance on the New York stage, at Wallack's, 12 Nov., 1898, as Guiderius in "Cymbeline"; spent many years touring and in "stock" companies; at the Garrick, New York, Jan., 1903, played in "Harriet's Honeymoon," and Sept., 1903, in "Military Mad"; toured with Ada Rehan, in 1904; at the Hudson Theatre, New York, Feb., 1905, played Dick in "Strongheart," and subsequently was associated as leading man with Bertha Kalich in a number of productions ; during 1908–9 toured in Australia, as leading man, with Margaret Anglin ; later, in 1909, toured in the United States with Alla Nazimova ; during 1909–10 was a member of the New Theatre Company, where he appeared as Charles Surface in "The School for Scandal," Don in the play of that name, Leontes in "The Winter's Tale," etc. ; during 1910 - 11 toured as Hofer in "The Great Name"; at Daly's, New York, Nov., 1911, played Leofric in "The Lady of Coventry"; at Wallack's, Nov., 1912, Frank Bowers in "Our Wives," and toured in the same part, 1913; at Maxine Elliott's, Feb., 1914, played Jerrold R. Scott in "Help Wanted"; during 1915 toured as Willybald Engel in "Our Children"; at the Forty-eighth Street Theatre, Sept., 1917, The

Artist in "Over the 'Phone"; from 1925–30, played at San Francisco, Los Angeles, etc., in "The Wild Westcotts," "The Lion Tamer," "The Pleasure of Honesty," "Undertow," etc. ; during 1931, toured in "Topaze"; commenced film career 1915, and has played in innumerable pictures; since 1936 has appeared in "The Great Impersonation," "Collegiate" ("The Charm School"), "Romeo and Juliet," "Bullets or Ballots," "The Man Who Lived Twice," "Sitting on the Moon," "Theodora Goes Wild," "Under Cover of Night," "The Green Light," "Maid of Salem," "The Devil is Driving," "Thoroughbreds Don't Cry," "The Adventures of Marco Polo," "Free to Live" ("Holiday"), "Too Hot to Handle," "The Cowboy and the Lady," "Let Us Live," "Union Pacific," "Marie Antoinette," "The Jones Family," "The Higgins Family," "The Real Glory," etc. *Address:* c/o Alex Kempner, The Strips, Hollywood, Cal. *(Died 15 July, 1947; age 73)*

KOLLMAR, Richard, actor and manager; *b.* Ridgewood, New Jersey, U.S.A.; 31 Dec., 1910, *s.* of John Kollmar and his wife Christine (Smith); *e.* Tusculum College, Greenville, Tenn., Bard College, Columbia and Yale Universities (M.A.); *m.* Dorothy Kilgallen (dec.); while at Yale, he studied for a year at Professor Baker's "47" Workshop; made his first appearance on the stage in a summer "stock" season at Whitefield, New Hampshire, June, 1934, as Pierre in "The Two Orphans"; made his first appearance in New York, at the Ethel Barrymore Theatre, 19 Oct., 1938, as Brom Broeck in "Knickerbocker Holiday"; Imperial, Oct., 1939, played Clint Kelley in "Too Many Girls"; 44th Street, Jan., 1941, appeared in the *revue,* "Crazy with the Heat"; Broadhurst, June, 1943, played El Magnifico in "Early to Bed"; as a manager, presented (with Dwight Deere Wiman and Richard Rodgers), "By Jupiter," 1942; "Early to Bed," 1943; "Dream with Music," 1944, which he also staged; "Are You with It?" (with James W. Gardiner), 1945; "Windy City," 1946; "Plain and

Fancy" (with James W. Gardiner), 1955; "The Ziegfeld Follies" (with James W. Gardiner), 1956; "The Body Beautiful" (with Albert Selden), 1958. *Favourite part:* El Magnifico. *Hobby:* Collecting Americana. *Address:* 45 East 68th Street, New York City, U.S.A.

KOMISARJEVSKY, Theodore, producer, scenic and costume designer; *b.* Venice, Italy, 23 May, 1882; *s.* of Theodore Komisarjevsky and his wife the Princess Kourzevich; *e.* Imperial Institute of Architecture, and University, Petrograd, and in Germany; *m.* (1) Elfriede de Jarosy (mar. dis.); (2) Peggy Ashcroft (mar. dis.); (3) Ernestine Stodelle; made his first production at his sister's theatre, the Komisarjevsky, Petrograd, in 1907; during the management of his own theatre from 1910, and as director of the Imperial and State Theatres in Moscow, until 1919, produced more than twenty operas, besides many plays by Shakespeare, Molière, Shaw, and other authors; made his first production in London, at Covent Garden, Oct., 1919, when he produced Borodin's "Prince Igor"; since that date he has produced "The Government Inspector," Duke of York's, 1920; "Six Characters in Search of an Author," Kingsway, 1921; "The Love Thief," Comedy, 1921; "The Race With a Shadow," "Uncle Vanya," Court, 1921; "At the Gates of the Kingdom," Court, 1922; in New York, 1922-3, "The Lucky One," "The Tidings Brought to Mary," "Peer Gynt"; in Paris, he produced "The Dover Road" (in English), "The Duenna," "Le Club des Canards Mandarin," "Siegfried," "Walküre," and "La Maîtresse du Roy" (for Cecile Sorel); after returning to London he produced "The Bright Island," "Ivanoff," 1925; "Uncle Vanya," "The Three Sisters," "Hearts and Diamonds," "The Snow Man," "Katerina," "The Cherry Orchard," "Liliom," 1926; "Naked," "Paul I," "Mr. Prohack," 1927; "King Lear" and "The 14th of July," at Oxford, 1927; "A Man with Red Hair," "The Brass Paperweight" (of which he was the author), 1928; "Red Sunday,"

1929; "The Man with the Portfolio," 1930; "The Queen of Spades," "Take Two from One," "Musical Chairs," "Robin Hood," 1931; "The Heart Line," "Le Cocu Magnifique," "Fraulein Elsa," 1932; "Escape Me Never," 1933; "Magnolia Street," "The Maitlands," 1934; "Mesmer," "Further Outlook," 1935; "The Seagull," 1936; "Antony and Cleopatra," 1936; designed the costumes for both the last-mentioned productions; produced "The Boy David," 1936; subsequently went to the United States; he also produced "The Merchant of Venice," for the Shakespeare Memorial Theatre, 1932; and subsequently produced there "Macbeth," "The Merry Wives of Windsor," "King Lear," "The Comedy of Errors," and "The Taming of the Shrew"; he also produced "Hatter's Castle," Masque Theatre, Edinburgh, 1932; in Italy, he has produced Mozart's "Cosi fan tutte," and operas by Rossini, Alfano, etc.; in Paris, 1929, produced "The Fair of Sorotchin"; in Riga, "Mefistofele" and "The Wild Duck"; is the author of "Theatrical Preludes," "The Costume of the Theatre," "The Actor and the Theory of Stanislavsky," and "Myself and the Theatre," "The Theatre," etc.; adapted Schnitzler's "Fräulein Elsa," for the English production, 1932; part-author of the play, "Russian Bank," which he produced at the St. James Theatre, New York, May, 1940; at the National, Dec., 1947, produced "Crime and Punishment"; at the Open Air Theatre, Montreal, July, 1950, produced "Cymbeline"; became a naturalized British subject, Dec., 1932. *Club:* Authors'. *Recreations:* Tennis, painting, and music. *Address:* West Norwalk Road, Darien, U.S.A. *(Died 17 Apr., 1954; age 71)*

KONSTAM, Anna, actress; *b.* London, 22 Feb., 1914; *y.d.* of Alfred Kohnstamm and his wife Esther Violet (Sternberg); *e.* Godstowe (preparatory) School, High Wycombe, and Benenden School; *m.* Wilfred Marlowe; studied for the stage at the Royal Academy of Dramatic Art (Bronze Medallist); made her first appearance on the stage, at the

Theatre Royal, Margate, Apr., 1936, as Lady April Hannington in "Full House"; first appeared in London, at the Old Vic., 8 Dec., 1936, as Susan in "The Witch of Edmonton"; Embassy, Feb., and Daly's, Mar., 1937, played Celia in "Night Alone"; Comedy, Sept., 1937, Pamela Francis in "The Last Straw"; New, May, 1938, Agatha Penworthy in "People of Our Class"; Richmond, May, 1939, Rosemary Vining in "Honeymoon for Three" ("Is Your Honeymoon Really Necessary?"); Wyndham's, Nov.,1939, Ivy in "Saloon Bar"; Aldwych, Aug., 1940, Estelle Graham in "Once a Crook——"; "Q," Jan., 1941, Princess Adria in "The Velvet Touch"; New, Mar., 1941, again played Estelle in "Once a Crook——"; St. Martin's, Nov., 1941, Rose in "Love in a Mist"; Shakespeare Memorial Theatre, Stratford-on-Avon, Apr.–Sept., 1943, played Desdemona, Olivia in "Twelfth Night," Cordelia, Princess Catherine in "Henry V," Hermia in "A Midsummer Night's Dream," and Hermione in "A Winter's Tale"; at the Wimbledon, Sept., 1945, appeared as Olivia in "The Vicar of Wakefield"; first appeared in films, 1938, in "They Drive by Night." *Recreations:* Reading, writing, and cooking. *Address:* 6 Farm Street, London, W.1. *Telephone No.:* Grosvenor 3120.

KONSTAM, Phyllis, actress; *b.* London, 14 Apr., 1907; *d.* of Alfred Kohnstamm and his wife Esther Violet (Sternberg); *e.* Godstowe School and Bayford House School; *m.* H. W. Austin; studied for the stage in Paris; made her first appearance on the stage at the Haymarket, 24 July, 1925, as Abigail in "The Jew of Malta"; at the "Q," Nov., 1925, played Ruth Molyneux in "The Shingling of Jupiter"; Garrick, Apr., 1926, Alice Carter in "Enchantress"; "Q," June, 1926, Joyce Etherington in "Virginia's Husband"; Ambassadors', Aug., 1926, appeared in "Escape"; at the Strand (for the Repertory Players), Nov., 1926, played Anne in "The Three Barrows"; Lyric, Hammersmith, Jan., 1927, Dorinda in "The Beaux' Stratagem"; Wyndham's, Aug., 1927, Yoda Pazzi in "The

One-Eyed Herring"; Ambassadors', June, 1928, the Child of Joy in "The Man They Buried"; Wyndham's, Jan., 1929, Julia Bailey in "Living Together"; Feb., 1929, Rosie in "The Fanatics"; Royalty, May, 1929, Val Power in "The Matriarch"; in Aug., 1929, went to America, and at the Eltinge Theatre, New York, 11 Sept., 1929, played Sylvia Armitage in "Murder on the Second Floor"; returned to London, 1929; at the Garrick, July, 1932, played the Shingled Lady in a revival of "Escape"; Royalty, Oct., 1933, Mrs. Ballantine in "Up in the Air"; Adelphi, Mar., 1934, Rose Berman in "Magnolia Street"; "Q," Dec., 1934, Huguette du Hamel in "If I Were King"; during 1935, Lina in "Misalliance"; Dora in "Fanny's First Play," and Ann in "Man and Superman"; Wimbledon Mar., 1936, Florrie Sands in "Saturday's Children"; Duke of York's, June, 1936, Trixie Drew in "Miss Smith"; at Oxford, for O.U.D.S., June, 1937, Olivia in "Twelfth Night"; Strand, July, 1937, Margaret in "A Spot of Bother"; Westminster, Mimi in "A Farewell Supper" and Emily Ross in "The Will"; went to America, 1939; commenced film career, 1930, in "Escape."

KOSTA, Tessa, actress and vocalist: *b.* Chicago, Ill., U.S.A., 1893; first attracted attention when she appeared in "The Pink Lady"; made her first appearance in New York, when she appeared at the Astor Theatre, 13 Apr., 1914, as Anna Budd in "The Beauty Shop"; subsequently joined the Rochester "stock" company; at the Globe, Feb., 1916, succeeded Blossom Seeley as Lilla Kiliana in "Stop, Look and Listen!"; appeared at the Manhattan Opera House, 22 Oct., 1917, as Marjanah in "Chu-Chin-Chow"; at the Cohan and Harris Theatre, Feb., 1919, played Anitza Chefchek in "The Royal Vagabond"; at the Nora Bayes, Apr., 1920, Kitty Mackay in "Lassie"; at the Central, May, 1921, Lane Demarest in "Princess Virtue"; at the Century, Dec., 1921, Nadina Popoff in "The Chocolate Soldier"; Mar., 1922, Kondja Gul in "The Rose of Stamboul''; at the Ambassadors, Jan., 1923, Caroline Lee in '' Caroline''; Dec., 1924, April Daly in '' Princess April''; Shubert Theatre, Apr., 1925, Princess Ida in the opera of that name: 44th Street Theatre, Dec., 1925, Aniuta in ''Song of the Flame''; at Jolson's Theatre, Nov., 1929, played Musette, Irma, and Lieutenant Feodor in a revival of ''The Fortune Teller.''

KOUN, Karolos, director of the Greek Art Theatre; *b.* Broussa, Asia Minor, 13 Sept., 1908; *s.* of Henry Koun and his wife Melpomene (Papadopoulou); *e.* Robert College, Istanbul; formerly a college professor; directed his first production for the Art Theatre, Athens, Greece, in 1935, with ''Alcestis''; he has since directed the following productions: ''The Wild Duck'' (Greek Art Theatre), 1942; ''The Blood Wedding'' (Greek Art Theatre), 1948; ''A Streetcar Named Desire'' (Greek Art Theatre), 1949; ''Henry IV'' (Pirandello) (National Theatre, Greece), 1950; ''Death of a Salesman'' (Greek Art Theatre), 1950; ''The Three Sisters'' (National Theatre, Greece), 1951; and the following plays at the Greek Art Theatre: ''The Cherry Orchard,'' 1955; ''Twelfth Night,'' 1956; ''The Caucasian Chalk Circle,'' ''Plouto,'' 1957; ''The Birds,'' 1959; ''Arturo Ui,'' 1962; ''Rhinoceros,'' ''Exit the King,'' 1963; ''The Persians,'' 1965; at the Théâtre des Nations, Paris, June, 1962, directed ''The Birds''; directed his first London production, with the Greek Art Theatre Company, at the Aldwych, May, 1964, with ''The Birds''; returned to London with the same company to the Aldwych, Apr., 1965, where he again directed ''The Birds,'' followed by the world *première* of ''The Persians,'' in the World Theatre Season; Paris Festival, May, 1965, again directed ''The Persians''; Moscow, Leningrad and Warsaw, Oct., 1965, ''The Birds,'' and ''The Persians.'' *Address:* Art Theatre, Athens, Greece.

KOVE, Kenneth (John William Stevenson Bridgewater), actor; *b.* London, 1893; made his first appearance on the stage in 1912, and spent ten years touring all over the provinces; made his first appearance in London at the Finsbury Park Empire, 7 Nov., 1913, as Mr. Meeks in ''The Dandy Band''; at the Royalty, 3 Oct., 1922, appeared as Prince Karl in ''Mr. Budd (of Kennington, S.E.)''; at the Aldwych, Feb., 1924, played Ellery Clarke in ''It Pays to Advertise''; ''Q,'' Nov., 1925, Mr. Petwood in ''Punchinello''; Lyric, Mar., 1926, Lord Rockmere in ''The Best People''; returned to the Aldwych, July, 1927, and played Lionel Frush, in ''Thark,'' also appearing there, May, 1929, as Stanley Tutt in ''A Cup of Kindness,'' and Feb., 1930, as Aubrey Slo in ''A Night Like This''; at the Gaiety, Jan., 1931, played Egbert Parkinson in ''Blue Roses''; Vaudeville, July, 1931, Daniel Curtis in ''Apron Strings''; Alhambra, Nov., 1932, Henri in ''A Kiss in Spring''; Vaudeville, Feb., 1933, Wilfred in ''Half-a-Million''; Saville, Aug., 1934, Ambrose Pilkington in ''She Shall Have Music''; ''Q,'' May, 1935, Oswald Hope in ''A Spot of Bother''; Arts, June, 1935, Claude Emptage in ''The Benefit of the Doubt''; toured, Mar., 1936, as Clarence Townley in ''How Do, Princess!''; toured, 1937, as Count Bruzzi in ''Darling You''; Arts, June, 1937, Jim Paget in ''In the Best Families''; Theatre Royal, Glasgow, Dec., 1937, the Baron in ''Cinderella''; King's, Hammersmith, Dec., 1938, the Lord Chancellor in ''The Sleeping Beauty''; ''Q,'' May, 1939, Chumleigh in ''Wind Across the Tide''; Comedy, May, 1943, Hon. Richard Emsley in ''Vintage Wine''; Stoll, Dec., 1944, Gentleman Starkey in ''Peter Pan''; toured, 1945, in ''A Southern Maid,'' and from Apr., 1946, as Toto in ''Elusive Lady''; commenced film career, 1930. *Address:* 5 Cardozo Road, London, N.7. *Telephone.No.:* North 3492.

KRAUSS, Werner, actor; *b.* Gestungshausen, Coburg, Germany, 23 June, 1884; *s.* of Paul Emil Friedrich Krauss and his wife Lina (Wuest); *m.* Maria Bard; made his first appearance on the stage at the Stadt-Theater, Guben, Germany, 25 Dec., 1904; for many years has been one of the leading actors on the German and Austrian stages in Berlin and Vienna; has played all the leading classical *rôles*, and played leading parts in many modern plays; first appeared in New York, at the Century Theatre, 16 Jan., 1924, as the Crippled Piper in Rein-hardt's production of "The Miracle"; in Berlin, 1926, appeared in "Neidhart von Gneisenau," in 1927, as Napoleon in "Buonaparte," and in "Dorothea Angermann"; made his first appearance in London, at the Shaftesbury Theatre, 28 Sept., 1933, as Matthew Claussen in "Before Sunset"; in Berlin, 1933, played Napoleon in "Napoleon" ("The Hundred Days"); in Vienna, 1933, played Macbeth, Peer Gynt and Paul Lange; in 1934, Richard III, Falstaff in "The Merry Wives of Windsor," Julius Caesar, King Magnus in "The Apple Cart"; in 1935, King Lear; Burgtheater, Vienna, Sept., 1935, played in "Der Stärkere"; has appeared in films since 1920. *Address*: 43 Iglaseegasse, Vienna, Austria. *Telephone No.* Vienna B. 10041 *(Died 20 Oct., 1959; age 75)*

KREMER, Theodore, dramatic author; *b.* Cologne, Germany, 3 Mar., 1873; graduated at Bonn University; was originally intended for the Army, but left his native country for Australia where he made his *début* on the stage, ünder the management of Messrs. Brough and Boucicault, in "The Magistrate"; returned to Europe and played with the Burg Company at Vienna for eight months; again visited Australia, where he toured with the Wilson Forbes company; in 1896 went to San Francisco, and it was here that his first play, "The Nihilists," was first presented; the play was subsequently produced at the People's Theatre, New York, 9 Nov., 1896; since then he has proved a most prolific playwright, and he has been responsible for the following among other sensational dramas: "The Church and the Stage," "The Angel of the Valley," "The Slaves of the Orient," "The Triumph of an Empress," "The Fatal Wedding," "An Actor's Romance," "Wedded and Parted," "The Great Automobile Mystery," "A Race for Life," "A Desperate Chance," "Fast Life in New York," "Queen of the Convicts," "Secret Service Sam," "The Woman of Fire," "Bertha the Sewing Machine Girl," "The Outlaw's Christmas," "For Her Children's Sake," "The King of the Bigamists," "For Her Daily Bread," "The Kiss of Life," "Fallen by the Wayside," "A Fighting Chance," "The Millionaire and the Policeman's Wife," "The Power Behind the Throne," etc.

KRUGER, Alma, actress; *b.* Pittsburg, Pa.; *e.* Pittsburg, a graduate of the King's School of Oratory; for some years was a member of the Warde-James combination, playing the leading parts for some time in a repertory of standard plays; during 1903 toured successfully as Maryland Calvert in "The Heart of Maryland," and subsequently played Roxana in "Alexander the Great"; in 1905 appeared as Lady Babb in "Sweet Kitty Bellairs"; at the Academy of Music, Jan., 1906, played Kitty Bellairs in the same play; joined the Sothern-Marlowe company, and at the Lyric, New York, during Jan. and Feb., 1907, played Herodias in "John the Baptist," St. Margaret and Catherine of Rochelle in "Jeanne D'Arc," Magda in "The Sunken Bell," Lady Capulet in "Romeo and Juliet," the Queen in "Hamlet," Nerissa in "The Merchant of Venice," and Olivia in "Twelfth Night"; proceeded with the company to London, making her first appearance at the Waldorf Theatre, 22 Apr., 1907, as Magda in "The Sunken Bell," and fulfilling her old parts in the remainder of the plays presented during the season; on her return to America, went on tour with Blanche Walsh, playing in "The Straight Road"; during 1908 toured with Annie Russell in "The Stronger Sex," and appeared as Joan Forsythe in this play, at Weber's, New York, Nov., 1908; at Washington, Apr., 1909, played Mary Brereton in "The Whirlpool"; subsequently again toured with the Sothern-Marlowe company; in 1912 toured with Ben Greet's company, and subsequently with Henry Ludlowe's Shakespearean company: at the Fulton Theatre, New York, Mar., 1913, played Mrs. Winthrop in " What Happened to Mary "; during 1914 toured with Robert Mantell, and subsequently with E. H. Sothern, appearing with the latter in " Charlemagne," " If I Were King," etc.; at the Garrick, New York, Apr., 1915, played Ella Rentheim in " John Gabriel Borkman "; at Yale Bowl, Conn., May, 1915, played the Leader of the Chorus in " Iphigenia in Tauris "; at the Adolf Lewisohn Stadium, New York, May, 1915, the Leader of the Chorus in "The Trojan Women "; at the Cort Theatre, New York, Mar., 1918, played Portia in " Julius Caesar"; at the Republic, Nov., 1918, " A Voice " in " Roads of Destiny "; at the Shubert Theatre, Oct., 1919, Olivia in " Twelfth Night," and at the same theatre, Apr., 1920, appeared in the same part; at the Century Theatre, Oct.-Dec., 1921, played Olivia, Nerissa, the Widow in " The Taming of the Shrew," with the Sothern-Marlowe Co.; at the Klaw Theatre, May, 1922, played Herodias in " Salome "; at the Playhouse, Oct., 1926, played Mrs. Laura Fenner in " Daisy Mayne "; in Mar., 1927, joined the Civic Repertory Company, with which she remained until 1931, playing Kniertje in " The Good Hope," Mrs. Kluver in " 2 × 2 = 5," Minnie Barton in " The First Stone," Juliana Tesman in " Hedda Gabler," Madame Jourdain in " The Would-Be Gentleman," the Prioress in " The Cradle Song," Fernandita in " The Lady from Alfaqueque," Tatyana in " Katerina," Madame Bourat in "Mdlle. Bourat," Anna Pavlovna in" The Living Corpse," Lady Capulet in "Romeo and Juliet," Miss Agatha in "Alison's House," Doña Zurita in "Women Have Their Way," and Nanine in "Camille"; at the Selwyn Theatre, Jan., 1932, played Chorus in "Electra" of Sophocles; Guild, Feb., 1932, Aunt Columba in "The Moon in the Yellow River"; Lyceum, Oct., 1932, Madame Seward in "Men Must Fight "; at Newark, N.J., Sept., 1933, appeared in " He Knew Them All"; Ethel Barrymore, New York, Jan., 1934, played Mrs. John Brown in " John Brown"; Mansfield, Feb., 1935, Felisa in "Field of Ermine"; Music Box, Nov., 1935, Lady Catherine de Bourg in "Pride and Prejudice"; has since appeared only in films. *(Died 5 Apr., 1960; age 88)*

KRUGER, Otto, actor; *b.* Toledo, Ohio, U.S.A., 6 Sept., 1885; *s.* of Bernard Alvin Kruger and his wife Elizabeth (Winters); *e.* Toledo Public Schools, University of Michigan, and Columbia University; was formerly an electrician; *m.* Sue MacManamy; made his first appearance on the stage, Nov., 1900, at the Empire Theatre, Toledo, in "Quo Vadis?"; subsequently played sundry "stock" engagements at Milwaukee, Louisville, Columbus, Toledo, Kansas City, and Baltimore; toured in repertory company for a year; toured the Stair and Havilan circuit, playing "On the Swanee River," "Satan Sanderson," "Double-Dyed Deceiver," and "Old Heidelberg"; played in "vaudeville" for two years in sketches, "The Girl," "A Cup of Tea," etc.; in 1909, was with the Paycen Stock company; in 1911 toured in "The Lure"; subsequently toured in repertoire, "Dr. Jekyll and Mr. Hyde," "Hamlet," "Romeo and Juliet," etc.; at Brooklyn, Sept., 1914, appeared as Richard Ames in "The Stronger Magnet"; made his first appearance in New York at the Republic Theatre, 3 Apr., 1915, as Jack Bowling in "The Natural Law"; at the Astor, Aug., 1915, played Jack Doray in "Young America"; at the Cohan Theatre, Aug., 1916, Billy Meekin in "Seven Chances"; at the Cohan and Harris, Nov., 1916, Jim Anderson in "Captain Kidd, Jun."; at the Cohan Theatre, Sept., 1917, Frederick Tile in "Here Comes the Bride"; at the Cort, Chicago, played in "The Gypsy Trail," and toured in "Corsette"; at the Longacre Theatre, Sept., 1919, appeared as Adam Smith in "Adam and Eva"; at the Cort, Chicago, 1920, played in "I Love You"; at the Princess, Chicago, Nov., 1920, as the Crown Prince in "Sonya"; at the Hudson, New York, Jan., 1921, succeeded Geo. M. Cohan as Richard Clarke in

"The Meanest Man in the World"; at the Forty-eighth Street Theatre, Aug., 1921, played Prince Alexander in "Sonya"; at the Greenwich Village, Nov., 1921, Stephen Murray in "The Straw"; at the Gaiety, New York, Dec., 1921, Lee Randall in "Alias Jimmy Valentine"; at the Liberty, Feb., 1922, Leonard Beebe in "To the Ladies"; at the National, Jan., 1923, Will Shakespeare in the play of that name; at the Morosco, Mar., 1923, James Murray and Walter Allen in "The Wasp"; then toured in "Nobody's Money"; at the Sam H. Harris Theatre, Oct., 1923, Henry Williams in "The Nervous Wreck," continuing in this until the end of 1924; at the Cohan, Oct., 1925, played Dick Tain in "Easy Come, Easy Go"; New Amsterdam, Jan., 1927, Augustus Colpoys in "Trelawny of the Wells"; Selwyn, Dec., 1927, Anthony Cavendish in "The Royal Family," and continued in that part, 1928–9; at the Guild Theatre, Oct., 1929, played Karl in "Karl and Anna"; Nov., 1929, Claude Vallee in "The Game of Love and Death"; 44th Street, Feb., 1930, Allan Fenway in "The Boundary Line"; Masque, Apr., 1930, Andrew Ware in "They Never Grow Up"; Longacre, Sept., 1930, Dr. Tom Lovett in "The Long Road"; Times Square, Nov., 1930, Tom Banning in "As Good as New"; Avon, Feb., 1931, Prescott Barrington the 1st, in "The Great Barrington"; Times Square, May, 1931, succeeded Noel Coward as Elyot Chase in "Private Lives"; Selwyn, Chicago, Jan., 1932, played George Simon in "Counsellor-at-Law," and at the Plymouth Theatre, New York, May, 1932, succeeded Paul Muni in the same part; Alcazar, San Francisco, Mar., 1933, appeared as George Simon in "Counsellor-at-Law"; El Capitan, Hollywood, Apr., 1935, played Steven Gaye in "Accent on Youth," in which he subsequently appeared in leading cities; at the El Capitan, Hollywood, July, 1936, played Charles Stewart Parnell in "Parnell"; entered films, 1933, and has appeared in nearly eighty pictures; at the Alcazar, San Francisco, Sept., 1941, appeared in "The Male Animal"; Martin Beck,

New York, Apr., 1942, played Colonel Lanser in "The Moon is Down"; Wilmington, Apr., 1946, Waldo Lydecker in "Laura"; Henry Miller, Jan., 1947, Aaron Storm in "Little A"; Cort, June, 1947, Waldo Lydecker in "Laura"; Fulton, Sept., 1948, played Ed Davis in "Time for Elizabeth"; Lyceum, Jan., 1949, Justice Reuben Boulting in "The Smile of the World." *Favourite parts:* Karl Heinz in "Old Heidelberg" and Stephen Murray in "The Straw." *Club:* Players', New York. *Address:* 201 Woodruff Avenue, Los Angeles, Cal., U.S.A.

KRUTCH, Joseph Wood, dramatic critic, author, and editor; *b.* Knoxville, Tennessee, U.S.A., 25 Nov., 1893; *s.* of Edward Waldemore Krutch and his wife Adelaide (Wood); *e.* University of Tennessee (B.A.) and Columbia University (M.A. and Ph.D.); *m.* Marcelle Leguia; Instructor in English at Columbia University, 1917–18; dramatic critic and associate Editor of *The Nation,* 1924–32; dramatic critic 1937–52; has been Brander Matthews' Professor of Dramatic Literature at Columbia University 1943–52; President of the New York Drama Critics' Circle, 1940–1; is the author of many books on the drama and edited "The Plays of William Congreve," 1927; "Nine Plays of Eugene O'Neill," 1932; "Representative American Dramas," 1941, etc.; in June, 1965, narrated the television programme "The Grand Canyon with Joseph Wood Krutch." *Address:* 5041 East Grant Road, Tucson, Arizona.

KUMCHACHI, Madame, Japanese actress; *b.* Jan., 1843; *d.* of Saemon Uchiwada; *e.* at home; *m.* Morizumi, dramatic author; was trained as a dancer by a famous Japanese master of the art, named Kyo Bando, and made her first appearance on the stage in 1866, as a member of a troupe organized by Bando, at the Bushi Club, Sotokanda, Tokyo; was subsequently engaged by the famous Daimyo family; she was the first actress to appear on the stage in Japan, and has for many years held a high reputation, as an actress of considerable power; she now travels with her own company, and has established an Academy of Dramatic Art at Misakiza with over a hundred pupils. *Address :* Theatre Misukiya, Kauda, Tokyo, or No. 4. Sakuragicho Neno, Tokyo, Japan.

KUMMER, Clare (*née* Clare Rodman Beecher), dramatic author; *m.* (1) Frederick Arnold Kummer (mar. dis.); (2) Arthur Henry; is a cousin of William Gillette; first came into prominence as a song-writer, when, in 1906, she composed " Dearie "; her first play was " The Opera Ball " (with Sydney Rosenfeld), 1912; has since written " Good Gracious, Annabelle ! " 1916; " A Successful Calamity," 1917; " The Rescuing Angel," 1917; " Be Calm, Camilla," 1918; " Rollo's Wild Oat," 1920; " Bridges," 1921; " The Choir Rehearsal," 1921; " The Robbery," 1921; " Chinese Love," 1921; " Roxie," 1921; " The Light of Duxbury," 1921; " The Mountain Man," 1921; " Banco " (from the French), 1922; " One Kiss " (from the French), 1923; " Annie Dear " (on " Good Gracious, Annabelle ! "), 1924; " Madame Pompadour " (American version), 1924; " Pomeroy's Past," 1926; "Amourette," " Her Master's Voice," 1933; "Three Waltzes" (with Rowland Leigh), 1937; " Spring Thaw," 1938; " Many Happy Returns," 1944. *Address :* Carmel-by-the-Sea, P.O. Box 3201, California, U.S.A.
(Died 22 Apr., 1958; age 85)

KUMMER, Frederic Arnold, dramatic author ; *b.* Catonsville, Maryland, U.S.A., 5 Aug., 1873 ; *s.* of Arnold Kummer and his wife Mary Morris (Pancoast) ; *e.* Troy ; *m.* (1) Clare Rodman Beecher (mar. dis.) ; (2) Marion McLean ; is the author of " Are You a Suffragette ? " 1909 ; " Mr. Buttles," 1910 ; " The Other Woman," 1910 ; " The Brute," 1912 ; " The Diamond Necklace," 1912 ; "The Painted Woman," 1913 ; " The Magic Melody," 1919 ; " My Golden Girl," 1919 ; " The Bonehead," 1920 ; " The Voice," 1923 ; " Julie," 1934 ; " Song

of Omar," 1935 ; " Fatal Lady," 1936 ; "The Captive," 1938 ; has also written many novels, short stories, cinema plays, etc. *Address :* 224 West Lafayette Avenue, Baltimore, Maryland, U.S.A. *(Died 20 Nov., 1943; age 70)*

KUN, Magda, actress ; *b.* Szaszregen, Hungary, 7 Feb., 1912 ; *d.* of Armin Kun and his wife Maria (Grunfeld) ; *e.* Budapest ; *m.* Steve Geray ; made her first appearance on the stage at the King's Theatre, Budapest, 1929, as Babe O'Day in "Good News"; has played comedy parts in straight plays, musical comedy and *revue* at the King's and Town Theatres, Budapest, and at the Komödie and Moulin Rouge, Vienna; at the Summer Theater, Budapest, June, 1933, scored a big success in "Dancing for Happiness"; made her first appearance in London at the Duke of York's, 30 May, 1934, as Mitzi Prisky in "Happy Week-end !"; in Sept., 1934, toured in the same part; at the Embassy, Mar., 1935, and Shaftesbury, May, 1935, appeared in "Let's Go Gay"; Palace, Feb., 1936, Katja in "At the Silver Swan"; Ambassadors', Feb., 1938, Madeleine in "Nuts in May"; St. James's, Dec., 1938, Blinch in "Let's Pretend"; Richmond, May, 1939, Yvonne in "Progress in Paradise"; has appeared in films for several continental companies, and in England, since 1935, in "Dance Band" and "Old Mother Reilly in Paris." *Address :* 54 Northway, London, N.W.11. *Telephone No. :* Speedwell 0291.
(Died 7 Nov., 1945; age 33)

KUNNEKE, Eduard, composer; *b.* 1885; has composed the scores of the following musical plays: " Love's Awakening," 1922; " The Cousin from Nowhere," 1923; " Caroline " (part-composer), 1923; " Mayflowers," 1925; " The Love Song," 1925; " Riki-Tiki," 1926; " The Song of the Sea," 1928.

KURTON, Peggy (Gladys), actress and vocalist ; made her first appearance on the stage at the Adelphi Theatre, 19 Oct., 1912, in the chorus of "The Dancing Mistress," and in May, 1913, she played the part of Genie in the same piece; in Oct., 1913, played the Waitress in "The Girl from Utah," and June, 1914, appeared in "The Belle of Bond Street"; she then went to America, and made her first appearance in New York, at the Shubert Theatre, 24 Dec., 1914, as Lady Kitty Preston in "To-Night's the Night"; returning to London she appeared at the Gaiety, Apr., 1915, as Lady Pussy Preston in "To-Night's the Night"; at the Prince of Wales's, Mar., 1916, played Evelyn Amery in "Mr. Manhattan," and returning to the Gaiety, Sept., 1916, appeared as Fudge Robinson in "Theodore and Co."; at the New Theatre, Apr., 1917, played Violet Crawshaw in "Wurzel-Flummery," and June, 1917, Ethel Carlton in "His Excellency the Governor"; she reappeared at the Gaiety, Dec., 1917, as Bunny Chester in "The Beauty Spot"; at the St. Martin's Theatre, Nov., 1918, played Kitty Cavanagh in "The Officer's Mess"; at the Alhambra, Sept., 1919, appeared as Aurora Smart in "Eastward Ho!"; at the Globe, New York, Nov., 1921, played Ruby Manners in "Good Morning, Dearie"; on returning to London, appeared at the New Oxford, Dec., 1922, as Marigold in "Battling Butler"; in Sept., 1925, toured as Cassy in a musical version of "Uncle Tom's Cabin."

KURTY, Hella, actress and vocalist; *b.* Vienna; studied for the stage under Professor Arnau of Vienna; has appeared in straight plays and musical comedies for several years both in Berlin and Vienna; played "Liebelei" in Vienna, with great success; appeared at the Tribune Theater, Berlin, and at the Admiralspalast, Berlin; at the Metropol Theater, Berlin, 1929, appeared as the Princess Mi in "Das Land des Lächelns" ("The Land of Smiles"), on its first production; made her first appearance in Vienna at the Theater an der Wien, Sept., 1930, in the same part; first appeared in London, 8 May, 1931, at Drury Lane Theatre, in the same part, and again played the part at the Dominion, May,

1932; at the Adelphi, Oct. 1933, played Bertha in "Nymph Errant"; Duke of York's, May, 1935, Lisl Harford in "Roulette"; Lyric, Mar., 1942, Mitzi Keller in "Blossom Time"; Apollo, May, 1944, Lotta Schulberg in "How Are They at Home?"; King's, Hammersmith, Oct., 1945, Lolita in "Public Nuisance"; she also appeared in the film of "The Land of Smiles." *Recreations:* Mountaineering, sunbathing and swimming. *Address:* 50 Sloane Street, London, S.W.1. *Telephone No.:* Sloane 9042. (*Died 7 Nov., 1954; age 48*)

KYASHT, Lydia, *danseuse*; *b.* Petrograd, Russia, 25 Mar., 1886; *d.* of George Kyasht and his wife Agaffia (Poubiloff); *e.* at the School of the Imperial Theatres, Petrograd; *m.* Colonel Alexis A. Ragosin; was specially trained for the ballet by her brother, Paul Gerdt, Enrico Ceccetti, Mdme. Sokoloff, and Mdme. Joganson; made her first appearance on the stage at the Opera House, Petrograd, 23 Mar., 1902, dancing a *pas de deux* in "The Magic Flute"; she remained at the Imperial Opera House for some time; she came to England in 1908, and made her first appearance in London, at the Empire, Leicester Square, 10 Aug., 1908, when she appeared in a *divertissement* with Adolf Bolm; she was subsequently selected to succeed Adeline Genée as *première danseuse* at that house, making her first appearance in that capacity, 19 Oct., 1908, in "A Day in Paris"; she subsequently appeared there from 1909–13, in "Round the World," "The Fawn," "Ship, Ahoy!" "Sylvia," "New York," "The Water Nymph," "First Love," "Titania"; appeared in New York, for the first time, at the Winter Garden Theatre, in Jan., 1914, in "The Whirl of the World"; appeared at the Coliseum, London, 1914, in "The Encnanted Isle"; in 1915 in "Javotte," "Cythera," etc.; in 1916 in "Somewhere in France"; in 1917, in "La Fille Mal Gardée," and "Cupid's Conspiracy"; in Nov., 1924, appeared in "The 7.30 Cabaret," on tour; during 1925–6 toured with her own entertainment

" A la Russe "; during 1926-9 toured with her own company in cabaret entertainment "Gala Nights"; during 1930-1, toured in "The Piccadilly Cabaret"; during 1932, toured in "The Springtime Cabaret"; Gaiety, Oct., 1933, appeared as the Retiring Ballerina in "Ballerina"; in Nov., 1941, directed a short season of ballet at the Garrick Theatre; published her reminiscences, under the title of "Romantic Recollections," 1929; has also appeared at the Opera House, Vienna: Opera House, Berlin; Casino, Monte Carlo, etc.; in 1935 opened the Lydia Kyasht Dancing Academy; founder of the "Ballet de la Jeunesse Anglaise," of which the first performance was given at the Cambridge Theatre, London, May, 1939.

LABLACHE, Luigi, actor; is a grandson of the celebrated basso, Signor Lablache; s. of Frederick Lablache and his wife (Fanny Wyndham); m., 1874, Jane Breadon (Miss Emmerson); made his first appearance on the London stage at the Gaiety, 13 June, 1874, as Master Wilford in " The Hunchback "; at the Adelphi, Sept., 1877, played in " After Dark "; in Oct., 1877, appeared in " The Deal Boatman "; at the Park Theatre, Mar., 1878, played in " The Shaughraun "; at the Adelphi, Apr., 1878, appeared as Raoul in " Proof "; at the Olympic, 1879, played Maurice Dodd in " Sweet Bells Jangled," Jack Waverly in " The Worship of Bacchus "; Neil Crampton in " Davy Crockett," Paul Merrydash in " Cut and Come Again "; at the Princess's, Feb., 1880, played Paul Fairweather in " The Streets of London "; during 1880, toured in America with Mrs. Scott Siddons, playing Romeo, Charles Surface, Benedick, Orlando, Claude Melnotte, etc.; at the Haymarket, Oct., 1881, appeared as King Henry VIII in " Queen and Cardinal "; Nov., 1881, as Orlando in " As You Like It "; during 1882, toured as " The Romany Rye "; subsequently toured as " The Silver King "; he then toured with his own company in " Blind Justice," " The Galley Slave," " The Old Love and the New "; appeared at Drury Lane, Sept., 1888, as Don Alvarez da Silva in " The Armada "; at the Globe, Mar., 1889, supported the late Richard Mansfield as Richmond in " King Richard III "; at Drury Lane, Sept., 1889, played Colonel Anketelle in " The Royal Oak "; appeared at the Avenue, Feb., 1891, as Danglars in " Monte Cristo "; in 1892, toured as Harry Dunstable in " A Million of Money "; in 1893, toured as Mark Denzil in " Sunlight and Shadow," and with Miss Fortescue (1893-5) in " Moths," " Comedy and Tragedy," " Pygmalion and Galatea," etc.; in 1895 joined Miss Olga Nethersole for English and American tours, and played in " Denise," " Camille," " Carmen," " Romeo and Juliet," etc.; appeared at the Gaiety, June, 1896, as Lucas Mendes in " Carmen "; next

joined the Adelphi company and played in " Boys Together," " Black Eyed Susan," " Charlotte Corday," " The Lady of Lyons," etc.; toured with Olga Nethersole in America, 1898-9; at Kennington, Sept., 1899, played General Burgoyne in the original production of " The Devil's Disciple "; has since appeared at the Adelphi (1900) in " The Better Life "; Shaftesbury (1900), in " Society's Verdict "; Coronet (1900), in " Benvenuto Cellini "; Comedy (1901), in " The Revolted Daughter "; Garrick (1901), in " The Queen's Double "; Her Majesty's (1901), in " Robert Macaire "; Prince of Wales's (1901), in " Katawampus "; Lyric (1902), " Mice and Men "; Drury Lane (1905), in " The Prodigal Son "; Court (1907), in " The Philanderer "; Queen's (1907), in " The Devil's Disciple "; Duke of York's (1909), in " Strife "; Vaudeville (1909), in " The Brass Bottle." Club: Green Room. (Died 18 Dec., 1914; age 64)

LACKAYE, Wilton, actor; b. Loudoun County, Virginia, U.S.A., 30 Sept., 1862; s. of James Lackaye and his wife Margaret (Bagnam); e. Ottawa and Georgetown University; m. (1) Alice Evans; (2) Katherine Alberta Riley; made his first appearance on the stage, at the Star Theatre, New York, 27 Aug., 1883, as Lucentio in " Francesca da Rimini," with the late Lawrence Barrett; subsequently toured in " May Blossom "; and later he played with the late Fanny Davenport, and at Union Square Theatre, in Oct., 1886, he appeared with her as Claudio in " Much Ado About Nothing "; also appeared with her in " Fédora," " As You Like It," etc.; during 1887 he played Robert le Diable in " Allan Dare," and the Marquis de Vaux in " Paul Kauvar," and in 1888 he played the title-rôle of the same play; during the same year he toured as " The Spider " in " The Silver King "; during 1889 he appeared in a number of " original " parts, among them being the following: Prince Saviani in " Jocelyn," Don Stephano in " Featherbrain," Arthur Morton in " The American Countess," Captain Gilchrist in

"Bootles' Baby," General Haverill in "Shenandoah," Raymonde de Noirville in "Roger La Honte" ("A Man's Shadow"), the O'Donnell Don in "The Great Unknown," and Sir Edward Vanberg in "My Jack"; the year 1890 was likewise a very busy one, and he appeared in the following fresh "creations" during the twelve months: Jack Adams in "Money Mad," Antonio in "A Mighty Power," Jim Hogan in "The Canuck," Pierre Clemenceau in "The Clemenceau Case," Dr. William Brown in "Dr. Bill," Claudius Nero in "Nero," and Captain Walsh in "The Haunted Room"; he next played in "The Two Orphans" and "The Power of the Press"; in 1891 came to England and joined George Alexander on tour, playing Simeon Strong in "The Idler"; made his first appearance on London stage at the St. James's, 30 Sept., 1891, in same part; then returned to America, and during 1892 played in "Pompadour" and "Mr. Wilkinson's Widows," followed by Dick Brennan in "Imagination" and Jefferson Stockton in "Aristocracy"; he was at Palmer's Theatre in 1894, where he played Van Buren Crandall in "New Blood," Eric Langley in "The Transgressor," and Gerald Cazenove in "The New Woman"; at the American Theatre, 21 Jan., 1895, he appeared as John Stratton in "The District Attorney"; and at the Garden Theatre, 15 Apr., 1895, he was the "original" Svengali in "Trilby"; he played this part until 1897; at the Garden Theatre, 19 Apr., 1897, he played the part of Dr. Belgraff in a play of that name; in 1898 he was touring with Nance O'Neill in "East Lynne"; at the Broadway Theatre, 13 Mar., 1899, he played in "The Musketeers"; and at Herald Square, in Oct., 1899, appeared as "Reb" Shemuel in "The Children of the Ghetto"; he made his reappearance on the London stage, at the Adelphi Theatre, 11 Dec., 1899, in the same part; at Wallack's Theatre, in 1900 he played Geoffrey Townsend in "The Greatest thing in the World"; and at the Academy of Music, as Petronius in "Quo Vadis?"; at the Broadway, 21 Mar., 1901, he appeared as the Earl of Derwent in "The Price of Peace"; later in the same year, at Wallack's, he appeared in "Colorado" and "Don Caesar's Return"; while he also played Uncle Tom in "Uncle Tom's Cabin" at the Academy of Music; at the Bijou in Mar., 1902, he played in "A Modern Magdalen"; and in 1903 he toured as Richard Sterling in "The Climbers" and Jim Morley in "The Frisky Mrs. Johnson"; subsequently he played Curtis Jadwin in "The Pit," and appeared in that part, at the Lyric, New York, 10 Feb., 1904; on 15 Apr., 1904, at the same theatre, he played Consul Bernick in "The Pillars of Society"; at the New Amsterdam Theatre, in May, 1905, he played Svengali in a revival of "Trilby"; and at Waterbury, Conn., 14 May, 1906, he played Jean Valjean and M. Madeline in "Law and the Man," the play being an adaptation, by himself, from Hugo's "Les Misérables"; during the autumn of 1906 he was touring in the same play, appearing in New York, at the Manhattan Theatre, 20 Dec., 1906; during 1907, at Washington, he appeared in "Diplomacy," "Featherbrain," "Bruvver Jim's Baby," "Aristocracy," and "Trilby" at St. Louis, 16 Sept., 1907, appeared as Jason in "The Bondman"; at the Savoy, New York, Dec., 1908, played John Haggleton in "The Battle"; at St. Louis, July, 1909, played Manasse in "New Lamps for Old"; at the Lyric, New York, 10 May, 1910, played James Ralston in "Jim the Penman"; at Washington, 6 Feb., 1911, appeared as John Marshall in "The Stranger," playing the same part at the Bijou Theatre, New York, 21 Dec., 1911; same theatre, 11 Jan., 1912, played François Desclos in "The Right to Happiness"; in Apr., 1912, played in "vaudeville" in "Quits"; at the Cort Theatre, Chicago, Aug., 1912, appeared as John Brand in "Fine Feathers"; at Pittsburg, Sept., 1912, as Fagin in "Oliver Twist"; at the Astor, New York, 7 Jan., 1913, played John Brand in "Fine Feathers"; at the Fulton Theatre,

14 Mar., 1913, The Doctor in "Damaged Goods"; at the Shubert Theatre, 3 Apr., 1915 reappeared as Svengali in "Trilby"; subsequently appeared in "vaudeville" in "The Bomb"; at the Cort Theatre, Chicago, Mar., 1916, played Dr. John Calvert in "Everyman's Castle"; at the National, Washington, Feb., 1917, appeared in "Eleven p.m."; at the Tremont, Boston, Apr., 1917, played Archibald Carlyle in "East Lynne"; at the Lyric, New York, Aug., 1917, Dick Bolger in "The Inner Man"; during 1917-18 toured in "vaudeville" in "Quits"; at the Criterion, New York, Oct., 1918, played Prince Alexis in "The Awakening"; at the Princess, Chicago, Nov., 1918, Lord Goring in "An Ideal Husband"; at the Harris Theatre, Apr., 1919, Dr. John Calvert in "A Good Bad Woman" ("Everyman's Castle"); at the Playhouse, New York, Oct., 1919, Kaintuck in "Palmy Days"; at the National, Dec., 1921, Svengali in a revival of "Trilby"; at the Maxine Elliott, Apr., 1922, Count Stanislaus Nevski in "The Goldfish"; at the Thirty-ninth Street Theatre, Aug., 1922, Dr. Gustav Ziska in "The Monster"; at the Hudson, Sept., 1924, Richard Lennon in "High Stakes"; Sam H. Harris Theatre, Dec., 1925, Lorenzo in "The Monkey Talks"; Cosmopolitan, Apr., 1926, Count de Linières in "The Two Orphans"; New Amsterdam, Jan., 1927, James Telfer in "Trelawney of the Wells"; with Harry Wagstaffe Gribble, adapted "Oh, Mama," from the French, 1925; is an M.A. of Georgetown University. *Club*: Lambs', New York City.
(Died 22 Aug., 1932; age 69)

LACY, **Frank,** actor; *b.* Penge, 9 July, 1867; *s.* of John Stocken; *m.* Nita Alexander; *e.* King's College; made his first appearance on the stage at St. James's Theatre, 17 Oct., 1888, as a Servant in "A Patron Saint," subsequently playing in "Brantinghame Hall"; subsequently played Sir Charles Grandison in "A Pantomime Rehearsal," and Cavendish Howley in "A Highland Legacy," at the Shaftesbury, Toole's, and Court, 1891-2; Bro den in "First

Mate," Gaiety, 1891; played Beaujour in "A Broken Melody," Prince of Wales's, 1892; John Tuppit in "Dorothy," Trafalgar Square, 1892; Captain John Rattlebrain in "The Little Widow," with Miss Minnie Palmer, Royalty, 1894; De Pons in "Robespierre," with Sir Henry Irving, Lyceum; at the Princess's played in "Alone in London"; and "In Old Kentucky"; was for three years with Arthur Bourchier at the Garrick; toured during 1910 as Recklaw Poole in "The Little Damozel"; subsequently crossed to America, and at the Comedy Theatre, New York, Sept., 1910, played Captain Neil Partington in the same piece; afterwards played the part of Flattery in "Everywoman"; supported Forbes-Robertson on his farewell tour of the English provinces, Sept., 1912, and during his farewell season at Drury Lane, Mar.-June, 1913; accompanied him on his American tours, 1913-15; at the Chelsea Palace, Aug., 1915, played Raymond Vereker in "The Mannikin"; at the Criterion Theatre, Sept., 1915, William in "The Stormy Petrel"; at the New, Oct., 1915, the Sergeant of Police in "Stop Thief!" and the Bridegroom in "The Best Man"; from 1916-19, toured as Cornelius Van Tuyl in "Romance"; during 1919-21, toured as Lucius Welwyn in "Tilly of Bloomsbury"; during 1922-3 again toured as Van Tuyl in "Romance"; in the spring of 1923 toured in South Africa with Percy Hutchison in "Bull-Dog Drummond," "The Bat" "Nightie-Night" and "Brewster's Millions"; on returning to London appeared at Savoy, Apr., 1924, as Joseph McCloud in "Brewster's Millions"; at the Playhouse, May, 1924, played the Missionary in "White Cargo"; in Sept., 1924, left for a tour in Canada with Percy Hutchison; at the Comedy, Jan., 1927, played Mellish in "The Desperate Lovers"; Lyceum, Mar., 1927, Valmorin in "Madame X"; in 1928, toured in Canada with Seymour Hicks; on returning to London, appeared at the Court, July, 1928, in a revival of "The Farmer's Wife"; Globe, Apr., 1929, Inspector Hawkins in "The Stag"; Strand (for the Stage Society),

Apr., 1929, Von Stuermer in "Rasputin"; subsequently toured as Sir Charles Haywood in "Diversion"; in Aug., 1929, went to South Africa with John Deverell, to play in "The Whole Town's Talking," "Good Morning, Bill", "Thark", and "He Walked In Her Sleep"; on his return to London, appeared at the Royalty, June, 1930, as Sir Charles Freeman in "The Beaux' Stratagem"; in Aug., 1930, toured as George Bottle in "Art and Mrs. Bottle"; Prince of Wales's, June, 1931, played William Whiteman in "Lovers' Meeting"; Savoy, July, 1931, Sir Danvers Carew in "Dr. Jekyll and Mr. Hyde"; has also appeared in films, in "Service for Ladies," "Women Who Play," "Wedding Rehearsal," etc. *Recreations :* Golf, walking, and fishing. *Club :* The Players'. *(Died 10 Aug., 1937; age 70)*

LACY, George, actor; *b.* London, 27 Jan., 1904; *s.* of Edward Lacy and his wife Alice (Rawlings); *e.* privately in London; *m.* Daphne de Wit; made his first appearance in public at the Promenade Pavilion, Colwyn Bay, 1917, as a boy comedian in a concert-party, "The Zig-Zags"; subsequently appeared in variety, *revue,* and pantomime, in a double-act with his father, under the name of Peter and Potts; was also known in *revue,* as Georgie Potts; first appeared under his own name, at the Grand Theatre, Croydon, Christmas, 1921, when he appeared as the Mate in "Dick Whittington"; toured, Aug., 1926, as Octave in "The Blue Kitten," and 1927, as Charles Crawford in "Just a Kiss"; first appeared in London, at the Queen's Theatre, 3 Dec., 1928, as Scotty in "Burlesque," also understudying Nelson Keys as Skid; at the Theatre Royal, Leeds, Christmas, 1929, played the part of Mother Goose in the pantomime of that name, for the first time; he made such a great success in this part, that he played the same part at Christmas for the next eleven years, including Daly's, London, 1933, and London Hippodrome, 1936; during 1930, appeared in variety at the London Coliseum, Alhambra, and Palladium; during 1936, toured as Dr. Moon ("Moonface") in "Anything Goes," and during 1937, as Jimmy Smith in "No, No, Nanette," and also for a few weeks in "Flood-Light"; later in the same year, toured in South Africa, in *revue;* Opera House, Blackpool, summer 1938, appeared in the *revue,* "All the Best"; toured, 1940, as James Skippit in "It's a Boy"; at the Stoll Theatre, July, 1942, played Hard-Boiled Herman in "Rose-Marie"; at Colwyn Bay, Aug., 1943, appeared with the repertory company as Lord Fancourt Babberley in "Charley's Aunt"; Streatham Hill, Dec., 1943, played Muddles in "The Sleeping Beauty"; toured, 1944, as Simplicitas in "The Arcadians"; Adelphi, Nov., 1944, appeared in "Merry-Go-Round"; Grand, Leeds, Christmas, 1944, in "Jack and the Beanstalk"; toured, Apr., 1945, in "Happy Birthday," and 1946, in "Black Scandals," and "Love's a Luxury"; first appeared in films, 1933, in "Oh, What a Duchess." *Favourite part:* Lord "Babs" in "Charley's Aunt." *Hobbies:* Collecting old theatrical prints and toy theatre prints, designing theatrical scenery and modelling stage settings. *Address:* "White House," 18A Cotsford Avenue, New Malden, Surrey. *Telephone No.:* Malden 1045.

LAFFAN, Patricia, actress; *b.* London, 19 Mar., 1919; *d.* of Arthur Charles Laffan and his wife Elvira Alice (Vitali); *e.* Folkestone and the Institut Français, London; studied for the stage at the Webber-Douglas Dramatic School, and also studied dancing at the De Vos Ballet School; made her first appearance on the stage at the Playhouse, Oxford, Jan., 1937, as Jenny Diver in "The Beggar's Opera"; played repertory at Oxford and Worthing, 1937; at the "Q," Sept., 1937, played Nurse Gertrude in "Sweet Adversity"; first appeared in London, at the Ambassadors', 25 Feb., 1938, as the Young Girl in "Surprise Item"; "Q," May, 1938, played The Nurse in "One Way Street"; Aldwych, Jan., 1939, for a time, played Stephanie in "Number Six"; Richmond, May, 1939, Marjorie Saunders in "Honeymoon for

Three"; at the Open Air, Regent's Park, June, 1939, Diana in "Pericles"; at "Q," 1941, in "The Women," and later played Mabel in "The First Mrs. Fraser," on Marie Tempest's last tour; toured, 1942, as Myra in "Hay Fever" and Anne in "Other People's Houses"; Arts Theatre, Feb., 1943, played Lavinia in "Androcles and the Lion"; toured, 1943, as Isabella in "Wuthering Heights," and as Viola and Olivia in "Twelfth Night," for C.E.M.A.; Apollo, May, 1944, Eileen Stokes in "How Are They at Home?"; Wimbledon, Apr., 1945, Kay Mostyn in "Hidden Horizon"; New Lindsey, May, 1948, Madge Donnythorpe in "Corinth House"; Boltons, Nov., 1948, Miss Vulliamy in "Frolic Wind"; Playhouse, Mar., 1949, played Primrose Mallet in "Primrose and the Peanuts"; New Lindsey, Jan., 1950, Helen Wetherell in "New England Night"; Strand, Nov., 1951, played the Princess in "Mary Had a Little . . ."; Piccadilly, May, 1960, Comtesse de St. Marigny-Marbeaux in "The Golden Touch"; Lyric, Hammersmith, June, 1960, Lady Parsley in "Innocent As Hell"; first appeared in films, 1936, in "One Good Turn," and has since appeared in "Quo Vadis," and "23 Paces to Baker Street"; has also broadcast and appeared on television, where her appearances include "Anna Karenina," "The Aspern Papers," "Rembrandt" and "Call My Bluff"; now engaged in production and choreography. *Favourite parts:* Viola in "Twelfth Night," Saint Joan, and Rosalind. *Recreations:* Show jumping and riding. *Address:* 21 Gilray House, Gloucester Terrace, London, W.2. and 18 Marine Square, Brighton. *Telephone No.:* 01-262 9793.

LAHR, Bert (*né* Irving Lahrheim), actor; *b.* Yorkville, N.Y., 13 Aug., 1895; *m.* (1) Mercides Delpino (mar. dis.); (2) Mildred Schroeder; spent many years on the "vaudeville" stage and in burlesque; appeared at the Shubert Theatre, 28 Nov., 1927, in "Delmar's Revels"; Broadhurst, Oct., 1928, played Gink Schiner in "Hold Everything"; Apollo, Mar., 1930, Rusty Krause in "Flying High";

Ziegfeld, Mar., 1932, Alky Schmidt in "Hot-Cha"; Casino, Nov., 1932, appeared in "George White's Music Hall Varieties"; Winter Garden, Aug., 1934, in "Life Begins at 8.40"; New Amsterdam, Dec., 1935, in "George White's Scandals"; Winter Garden, Dec., 1936, in "The Show Is On"; 46th Street, Dec., 1939, Louis Blore and King Louis in "Du Barry Was a Lady"; Ziegfeld, Dec., 1944, appeared in "Seven Lively Arts"; Belasco, Dec., 1946, played Skid in "Burlesque"; at the Mark Hellinger, July, 1951, appeared in the *revue* "Two on the Aisle"; John Golden, Apr., 1956, played Estragon (Gogo) in "Waiting for Godot"; Henry Miller, Apr., 1957, Boniface in "Hotel Paradiso"; during the tour of "Romanoff and Juliet," Jan., 1959, took over the part of The General; Alvin, N.Y., Nov., 1959, appeared in the *revue* "The Girls Against the Boys"; U.S. tour, Sept., 1960–Feb., 1961, Bottom in "A Midsummer Night's Dream"; Bucks County Playhouse, Pa., Sept., 1961, Milo Weatherwax, Judge Rinderbrust, Hyacinth, and Harry Hubris in "The Beauty Part"; Dawson City, Canada, summer, 1962, the title-*rôle* in "Foxy"; Music Box, Dec., 1962, again played in "The Beauty Part" and also played Nelson Smedley; Ziegfeld, Feb., 1964, again played "Foxy," for which he received the Antoinette Perry (Tony) Award; Grand Ballroom, Waldorf-Astoria, May, 1964, starred in "The Milliken Breakfast Show"; first appeared in films, 1931, in "Faint Heart"; also appeared in "The Wizard of Oz," etc.; has appeared on television, notably as the Father in "The Fantasticks," Oct., 1964. *(Died 4 Dec., 1967; age 72)*

LAIDLER, Francis, manager; *b.* Yorkshire, 7 Jan., 1870; *s.* of Joseph Laidler, M.R.C.S.; *e.* Wharfedale College, Boston Spa; *m.* Gwladys Stanley; from the age of sixteen, for four years, was engaged in clerical work in National Provincial Bank of England; first entered management, 1901, when he became partner with Walter J. Piper in the management of the Prince's, Bradford; for many years has toured *revues* and pantomimes in the provinces; is the governing director of the Alhambra and Prince's Theatres at Bradford, Theatre Royal, Leeds, and the Hippodrome, Keighley; up to Christmas, 1950, had produced over 220 pantomimes, including 42 at Leeds and 43 at Bradford; has also produced pantomimes at Covent Garden, Daly's, and Victoria Palace, London, at London suburban theatres, and at many of the principal provincial theatres; also four pantomimes during the late War, for the late Sir Oswald Stoll, at the London Coliseum; is a member of the Theatrical Managers' Association, and of the Independent Theatres Association. (*Died 6 Jan., 1955; age 84*)

LAING, Peggie, theatrical press-representative; *b.* Balsall Common, Warwickshire, 14 May, 1899; *d.* of William Gabriel Blatch and his wife Jessie Mary (Bentley); *e.* Warwick High School, Clewer, Windsor and at the Royal College of Music; *m.* Hilary Laing-Oldham; was formerly engaged as a professional pianist; was first appointed press representative for the Windmill Theatre, 1934, which she still represents; Gate Theatre, 1935 to date; has publicised the Theatrical Garden Party (Actors' Orphanage Fund) since 1937; press representative of the Perranporth Summer Theatre from 1937. *Address:* 17–18 Great Windmill Street, W.1, and Strawbridge, Hatherleigh, Devon. *Telephone No.:* Gerrard 6294.

LAKE, Lew, comedian and sketch artist; among his successful productions may be noted "The Bloomsbury Burglars"; "My Pal Jerry"; "Old China's in China"; "King Nobbler"; "Cohen and Son"; "Daylight Robbery," etc. *Address:* 24 Kinglake Street, Old Kent Road, S.E. *Telephone No.:* Hop 3242.

LALLY, Gwen, actress, producer and pageant master; *b.* London, *d.* of the late Canon J. H. Lally Speck, M.A. and his wife Rosalie Hew (Dalrymple); *e.* privately; studied for the stage

under Rosina Filippi; made her first appearance on the stage at His Majesty's Theatre, 25 Jan., 1906, walking-on in "Nero"; was engaged at the Old Vic. 1914–16, where she played several male parts in Shakespearean repertory; during 1917–18, toured in variety theatres in her own sketch, "Reggie's Double," and 1919, in "The Great Moment"; in 1923, produced "Henry VIII" as a pageant play at Westerham, Kent; in 1931, ran her own repertory company at the Little Theatre, Leeds, producing all the plays presented; in 1933, was producer at the Palace Theatre, Southend-on-Sea; has produced most of Shakespeare's plays for various amateur societies; at various times has appeared as Hamlet, Romeo, Bassanio, Lorenzo, Charles Surface, etc.; has produced pageants since 1924, including Warwick, 1930; Tewkesbury, 1931; Battle Abbey, 1932; Runnymede, 1934; The Pageant of England, at Slough, 1935; has lectured on the Drama and Pageantry at Malvern and Tewkesbury Festivals. *Recreations:* Writing poetry and all outdoor sports. (*Died 14 Apr., 1963; age 81*)

LALOR, Frank, actor; *b.* Washington, D.C., U.S.A., 20 Aug., 1869; *s.* of Frank Lalor and his wife Annie (Rainbow); *e.* Massachusetts Institute; *m.* Vernie Conard; studied for the stage under Tom Carl of the Bostonian Opera Company; made his first appearance on the stage as a boy soprano at Austin and Stone's Variety Theatre, Boston, 1888, and his first appearance in New York, at Tony Pastor's, in 1892; has since been prominently associated with the musical-comedy stage, and has appeared successfully in "The Show Girl"; "Mr. Wix of Wickham"; "The Athletic Girl"; "The Filibusters"; at the Casino, New York, 1904, played Bliffkins in "An English Daisy"; at the Herald Square, Jan., 1906, played Nott in "Coming Thro' the Rye"; at the Knickerbocker, Apr., 1909, Saul Wright in "The Candy Shop"; at the Globe, New York, Nov., 1910, Tim Jones in "The Bachelor Belles"; at the New

Amsterdam, Mar., 1911, Philippe Dondidier in " The Pink Lady " ; made his first appearance in London, in the same part at the Globe Theatre, 11 Apr., 1912 ; at the Longacre Theatre, Dec., 1913, appeared as Clarence Guildford in " Iole " ; at the New Amsterdam, Nov., 1914, Achille Petipas in " Papa's Darling " ; at the Fulton, Aug., 1915, Dr. Josiah Smythe in " Some Baby " ; at the Globe, Dec., 1915, Gideon Gay in " Stop ! Look ! Listen ! " ; Sept., 1916, Percival Hopkins in " The Amber Empress " ; at the Astor, Apr., 1917, Abijah Smith in " His Little Widows " ; at the Hudson, Sept., 1917, Frank Foster in " Good-Night, Paul " ; at the Empire, London, Feb., 1918, played Prosper Woodhouse in " The Lilac Domino " ; at the Garrick, London, July, 1919, Colonel Bunting in " Nobody's Boy " ; returned to New York, 1919 ; appeared in " The Cameo Girl," May, 1921 ; at the Princess Theatre, New York, Nov., 1921, played Tony in " Suzette " ; at His Majesty's, London, Mar., 1925, Oliver J. Oosenberry in " The Bamboula " ; Casino, New York, Sept., 1928, Pontaves in " Luckee Girl " ; at Long Branch, July, 1929, Prefect of Police in " The Street Singer." *Recreations:* Golf, tennis, and motoring. *(Died 15 Oct., 1932; age 63)*

LAMB, Beatrice, actress ; *b.* 15 July, 1866 ; made her first appearance on the stage at the Comedy Theatre, 20 Apr., 1887, as a guest in " The Red Lamp " ; she accompanied Beerbohm Tree to the Haymarket Theatre, where she played in " The Ballad Monger " and " Cupid's Messenger " ; at the St. James's, May, 1888, played in " In the Old Times " ; at the Garrick, Apr., 1889, played Irene Stonehay in " The Profligate " ; at the St. James's, Feb., 1890, appeared as Phœbe in " As You Like It " ; at the Shaftesbury, Aug., 1891, played in " A Commission " and " A Pantomime Rehearsal " ; at the Strand, 1891, played Mrs. Webb in " The Late Lamented " ; she also played here as Hester Singleside in " The New Wing " in Jan., 1892, and in Apr., 1892, achieved a great

success, when she appeared as Niobe in the play of that name ; at Toole's Theatre, Mar., 1894, appeared as Mrs. Montaubyn in " The Best Man " ; at Drury Lane, Sept., 1894, played Lady Desborough in " The Derby Winner " ; at Stratford-on-Avon, Apr., 1895, played Hermione in " The Winter's Tale," and Rosalind in " As You Like It " ; subsequently toured in " Niobe " ; in 1898 went to Australia with Charles Cartwright, playing in " The Tree of Knowledge," " The Middleman," " The Idler," " Moths," " The Squire of Dames," [etc. ; reappeared in London, at the Garrick, Mar., 1899, when she played the Queen in " The Three Musketeers " ; since then her appearances in London have been very few ; she has, however, appeared in " Boy Bob," 1899 ; " Jim Belmont," 1900 ; and " The Ring Mistress," 1900.

LAMBELET, Napoleon, composer and musical director ; *b.* Corfu, 27 Feb., 1864 ; *s.* of Eduardo Lambelet and his wife Aspasia (Caruso) ; *e.* Naples Conservatoire ; *m.* Emily Ada Buckton ; for many years musical director at several West End theatres ; composed the scores of " M. Pardarmenos," Athens, 1890 ; " The Yashmak," at the Shaftesbury, London, Mar., 1897 ; " The Transit of Venus," 1898 ; " Pot-Pourri," Avenue, 1899 ; " The Shadow Dance," Princess's, 1901 ; " Fenella," Coliseum, 1905 ; " Valentine," St. James's, 1918. *Recreation :* Gardening. *(Died 25 Sept., 1932; age 68)*

LAMBERT, Constant, composer, conductor and critic; *b.* London, 23 Aug., 1905; *s.* of the late George Washington Lambert, A.R.A., and his wife Amelia Beatrice (Absell) ; *e.* Christ's Hospital and Royal College of Music; *m.* Florence Kaye; his first ballet, " Romeo and Juliet," was composed for the late Serge Diaghileff, and produced by him at Monte Carlo in 1926 ; has since composed " Pomona," 1927 ; " The Rio Grande," 1929 ; " Summer's Last Will and Testament," 1935 ; has also composed orchestral music, songs, pianoforte sonatas, etc. ; as musical director conducted ballet and opera at the Old Vic and Sadler's Wells, from 1932, until he resigned from this position in 1947; has also conducted at the Royal Opera House, Covent Garden; conductor for the Camargo Society; conducted the Sadler's Wells Ballet Season at Covent Garden, May, 1946; has contributed criticism to *Figaro, New Statesman*, etc.; was music critic to the *Sunday Referee* for some years from 1932. *Recreations:* Walking and talking. *Address:* 197 Albany Street, London, N.W.1. *Telephone No.:* Euston 1743. (*Died* 21 Aug., 1951.)

LAMBERT, Lawson, business manager; *b.* Bombay, 29 Aug., 1870; *s.* of Henry Wise Lawson and his wife Adelaide (Beadle); *e.* Dover College; *m.* Ella York; was an actor for several years, and appeared with the late Edward Terry, Willie Edouin, etc.; was also business manager at Terry's and the Garrick Theatres, London; was appointed assistant manager of the Brixton Theatre, at its opening, 1896; manager in 1899, and remained there until 1903; acting manager, King's, Hammersmith, 1903-4; general manager Grand Theatre, Croydon, 1904-8; manager, Theatre Royal, Brighton, 1908-35. *Recreations:* Reading and golf. *Club:* Savage.
(*Died 8 Mar., 1944; age 70*)

LA MILO (Pansy Montague), living statuary artiste; *b.* in Australia; made her first appearance on the stage at the Tivoli, Sydney, New South Wales, under the late Harry Rickards; made her first appearance in London, at the London Pavilion, 23 Apr., 1906, scoring an immediate success, and creating something of a sensation; for many years was a prominent attraction at the leading variety theatres in London and the provinces.

LANCASTER, Nora, actress; *b.* in London, 20 Oct., 1882; *d.* of the well-known actress Miss Ellen Lancaster Wallis and the late John Lancaster, a well-known merchant of Manchester, who built the Shaftesbury Theatre; *m.* Leonard Shoetensack; she received her early dramatic training from her mother, and first walked on at the St. James's, under George Alexander, in "The Wilderness," 11 Apr., 1901; at the Garrick, Sept., 1901, played Aurea Vyse in "Iris"; at the Comedy, Feb., 1902, played Jessie Ferbridge in "Memory's Garden"; toured as Little Britain in "Mice and Men," 1902; in 1903 joined Sir Henry Irving, playing the part of the Spirit of Beatrice in "Dante," at Drury Lane; she remained with Irving two years, touring with him in England, America, and Canada; returning to England she appeared at the Strand and Comedy, playing leading parts under Frank Curzon in "Off the Rank," etc.; she then went to the Queen's, Manchester, as Imogen in "Cymbeline," 1906; she also starred as Galatea in "Pygmalion and Galatea," and played leading parts with F. R. Benson at Stratford-on-Avon; in 1906 she was engaged by Beerbohm Tree as leading lady for his provincial tour of "The Ballad Monger" and "Business is Business"; at the Scala, in Apr., 1907, appeared as Miriam in "The Judgment of Pharaoh"; accompanied Mr. Lewis Waller on his autumn tour of 1907, playing Lady Marian in "Robin Hood" and Lady Mary in "Monsieur Beaucaire"; at the Lyric, Dec., 1907, played Adela in "Robin Hood"; Jan., 1908, played the Countess of Kerhill in "A White Man"; rejoined Benson in 1909, playing Juliet, Portia, Rosalind, etc.; appeared with him at His Majesty's, Apr., 1910, playing Bianca in "The Taming of the Shrew," and Virgilia in "Coriolanus"; at Stratford-on-Avon, Apr., 1910, played Sylvia in "The Two Gentlemen of Verona"; at the Queen's, Manchester, Jan., 1911, appeared as Hermione in "The Winter's Tale"; at the Strand Theatre, Mar., 1913, played Margaret Rolfe in "A Woman in the Case." *Address:* New Century Club, London, W.

LANCHESTER, Elsa, actress; *b.* Lewisham, 28 Oct., 1902; *d.* of James Sullivan and his wife, Edith (Lanchester); *e.* privately; *m.* Charles Laughton;

in 1918, she started the Children's Theatre, Charlotte Street, Soho; subsequently she started the Cave of Harmony, Gower Street; at the Cave of Harmony, presented several plays, including Pirandello's " The Man with a Flower in his Mouth," Housman's " The Queen, God Bless Her," Anatole France's " The King of the Jews," etc.; made her first appearance on the professional stage at the Kingsway, Apr., 1922, as the Second Shop Girl in " Thirty Minutes in a Street"; she next appeared at the Regent Theatre, May, 1923, as Larva in " The Insect Play "; since that date has played at Lyric, Hammersmith, Feb., 1924, Peggy in " The Way of the World "; Oct., 1924, Sancho in " The Duenna "; Garrick, Sept., 1925, Sophie Binner in " Cobra "; Lyric, Hammersmith, Apr., 1926, in " Riverside Nights "; " Q," Nov., 1926, and Royalty, July, 1927, the Kid in " Cautious Campbell "; Everyman, Feb., 1927, Rosie Betts in " The Pool "; Court, Nov., 1927, Mimi Winstock in " Mr. Prohack "; was associated with Harold Scott in the management of " The Cave of Harmony " Cabaret, 1927-8; at the Court, May, 1929, played Anna in " The Outskirts"; Gate, Jan., 1930, Mary Morgan in " Ten Nights in a Bar-Room"; Jan., 1931, Cedric in " Little Lord Fauntleroy "; St. James's, May, 1931, Winnie Marble in " Payment Deferred "; went to New York, and made her first appearance there, at the Lyceum Theatre, 24 Sept., 1931, in the last-mentioned part; joined the Old Vic-Sadler's Wells company, Oct., 1933, and during the season played Charlotta Ivanovna in "The Cherry Orchard," the Singer in "Henry VIII," Juliet in "Measure for Measure," Ariel in "The Tempest," Miss Prism in "The Importance of Being Earnest," Miss Prue in "Love for Love"; Palladium, Dec., 1936, played Peter Pan and toured in the same part, 1937; Golden Theatre, New York, Mar., 1941, played Emmy Baudine in "They Walk Alone"; of late years has appeared only in films, and as a *diseuse* at various night clubs; author of "Charles Laughton and I," published in 1938.

LANDAU, David, actor; *m.* Frances Newhall; has had over thirty years' experience on the stage, and in 1900 was appearing at Lakewood, Maine, in "The Private Secretary"; in 1903, was a member of the Imperial "stock" company, New York; appeared at the Casino, New York, 2 Apr., 1918, as Colonel Dodd Beane in "An American Ace"; Selwyn, Aug., 1919, played John Hayes in "The Challenge"; Cort, Dec., 1919, Stanton in "Abraham Lincoln"; Ritz, Nov., 1923, General Stonewall Jackson in "Robert E. Lee"; Belmont, May, 1924, Shauny Fronce in "Catskill Dutch"; Provincetown, Apr., 1925, Amos Horton in "Ruint"; Bijou, Aug., 1925, Tustine in "The Mud Turtle"; Maxine Elliott, Mar., 1926, Joel Givens in "Devils"; Greenwich Village, Oct., 1926, Gromoff in "The Humble"; Nov., 1926, Absolon in "The Witch"; Forrest, Sept., 1927, Daly in "Women Go on Forever"; Longacre, Apr., 1928, Clifford Barnes in "The Golden Age"; Maxine Elliott, Mar., 1929, Jacob McClosky in "The Octoroon"; Playhouse, May, 1929, succeeded Robert Kelly as Frank Maurrant in "Street Scene"; appeared at the Globe Theatre, London, 9 Sept., 1930, in the same part; commenced film career 1931, and has appeared in "Taxi," "Gentlemen for a Day" ("Union Depot"), "Street Scene," "The Reckless Age," "Arrowsmith," "Polly of the Circus," "Amateur Daddy," "The Roadhouse Murder," "The Purchase Price," "Horse Feathers," "70,000 Witnesses," "I am A Fugitive," "Air Mail," "False Faces," "Under-Cover Man," "Lawyer Man," etc. *(Died 20 Sept., 1935; age 57)*

LANDEAU, Cecil, director and manager; *b.* 1906; *m.* Janina Bregman; was formerly an actor; at the Prince's, 20 July, 1926, appeared as Lieutenant Maxwell in "Secret Service"; Scala, July, 1926, the Interned Soldier in "The Coward"; Apollo, Jan., 1927, played the Clerk of the Court in "An American Tragedy"; Everyman, Feb., 1928, Tom Hardcastle in "The Third Finger"; at the Court Theatre, with the Birmingham Repertory Company, Mar.–Apr., 1928, played Acis in "As Far As

Thought Can Reach" ("Back to Methuselah"), and Osgood in "Harold"; Apollo, June, 1929, Normie de Wit in "This Thing Called Love!"; Royalty, Dec., 1929, Brian Selwyn in "The Amorists"; Prince of Wales's, Feb., 1930, Sir Eamon O'Donoghue in "Forty-Seven"; Strand, May, 1930, Ted Morris in "Moloch"; during the War, served with the R.A.F.; at the Cambridge Theatre, May, 1949, directed "Sauce Tartare," of which he was the author; Dec., 1949, directed "Christmas Party" of which he was also the author; Apr., 1950, directed "Sauce Piquante"; at the Saville, May, 1954, directed "Cockles and Champagne."

LANDECK, Ben, dramatic author; *b.* London, 24 Oct., 1864; *s.* of Samuel B. Landeck and his wife Sophia (Sampson); *e.* Bristol; *m.* Valerie Crespin; was formerly engaged in the antique silver trade; his first play, " At Mammon's Shrine," was produced at Leicester, in May, 1887; since that date has written very many successful dramas; among his more prominent plays may be mentioned " My Jack," 1889; " The King of Crime " (with Arthur Shirley), 1892; " A Lion's Heart " (with Shirley), 1892; " A Guilty Mother," 1893; " Saved from the Sea " (with Shirley), 1895; " Tommy Atkins " (with Shirley), 1895; " Jack Tar " (with Shirley, 1896; " Woman and Wine " (with Shirley), 1897; " The Hue and Cry " (with Shirley), 1897; " A Soldier and a Man," 1898; " Going the Pace " (with Shirley), 1898; " The Shadow Dance " 1901; " Nick Carter," (with Shirley), 1910; " The Three Musketeers " (with Shirley), 1911; " The Women of France " (with Shirley), 1912; " The Open Door " (with Shirley), 1912; " The Wild Widow " (with Shirley), 1919; " The Savage and the Woman " (with Shirley), 1921; " What Money Can Buy " (with Shirley), 1923; etc. *Recreation :* Novel reading. *(Died 6 Jan., 1928; age 63)*

LANDI, Elissa, actress; *b.* Venice, 6 Dec.,1904; *d.* of the Countess Zanardi-Landi; *e.* privately in London; *m.* (1) John Cecil Lawrence (mar. dis.); (2) Curtiss Kinney Thomas; made her first appearance on the stage at the Playhouse, Oxford, 28 Apr., 1924, as Sheba in "Dandy Dick"; made her first appearance in London, at the Ambassadors' Theatre, 13 Aug., 1924, as Storm in the play of that name; has since played at the Everyman, Mar., 1925, Selina in "The Painted Swan"; New Oxford, Apr., 1925, Marsinah in "Kismet"; Comedy, July, 1925, April Clear in "Lavender Ladies"; Playhouse, Jan., 1926, Gloria Corsellis in "Blind Alley"; Everyman, Apr., 1926, the Rev. Mother and Ursula Aylmer in "Benediction"; New, Sept., 1926, Antonia Sanger in "The Constant Nymph"; Apollo (for the Lyceum Club Stage Society), Apr., 1927, Desdemona in "Othello"; Arts, Nov., 1927, Giulia in "The Glimpse of Reality"; Globe, Apr., 1929, Marion Temple in "The Stag"; Apollo (for the 300 Club), May, 1929, Greta in "After All"; Arts, Mar., 1930, Phyl in "After All"; went to New York, and made her first appearance there, at the National Theatre, 22 Sept., 1930, as Catherine Barkley in "A Farewell to Arms"; reappeared on the regular stage, after a five years absence, at the Shubert Theatre, Dec., 1935, as Iris Nordgren in "Tapestry in Gray"; Longacre, Sept., 1937, Countess Katinka in "The Lady Has a Heart"; St. James, Mar., 1938, Catherine in "Empress of Destiny"; at summer theatres, 1938, played lead in "The Warrior's Husband," "Veronica," "Tovarich," etc., and 1939, in "The Lady Has a Heart," "Tovarich," +c.; at Kansas City, Apr., 1941, played Cavallini in "Romance"; Montreal, Sept., 1941, in "The Lady Has a Heart"; Alexandra, Toronto, Aug., 1942, Mary in "Mary of Scotland"; Mansfield, New York, Mar., 1943, The Lecturer in "Apology"; at Chicago, 1943, played Leona Richards in "To-Morrow the World"; subsequently toured in "Theatre," and as Candida; Forrest, New York, Dec., 1944, played Florence McDavid in "Dark Hammock"; again toured, 1945, in "To-Morrow the World"; commenced film career, 1928, in "Underground"; published a novel in 1925, entitled "Neilson," and has since written "The Helmers," "House for Sale," "The Ancestor," and "Women and Peter." *Recreations:* Motoring, dancing, and tennis. *(Died 22 Oct., 1948; age 43)*

LANDIS, Jessie Royce, actress; *b.* Chicago, Ill., U.S.A.; *d.* of Paul Royce Medbury and his wife Ella (Gill); *m.* (1) Rex Smith (mar. dis.); (2) Major General J. F. R. Seitz; made her first appearance on the stage at the Playhouse, Chicago, 25th Dec., 1924, as the Young Countess in "The Highwayman"; subsequently played in "stock," at Detroit, Mich.; made her first appearance in New York, at the Booth Theatre, 25 Dec., 1926, as Flora Brazier in a revival of "The Honor of the Family," subsequently touring in the same part; at the Shubert, Apr., 1928, succeeded Estelle Winwood as Fern Andrews in "The Furies"; at the Klaw, Oct., 1928, played Princess Katerine in "The Command Performance"; Biltmore, Mar., 1929, Statira in "Young Alexander"; Ambassador, Oct., 1929, Caroline Goodwin in "Stripped"; Cosmopolitan, Dec., 1929, Cydalise Waring in "Damn Your Honor"; Lyceum, Oct., 1930, Leila Mae in "Solid South"; Fulton, Jan., 1931, La Baronne de Bannalac in "Colonel Satan"; Shubert, Apr., 1931, Mary, Duchess of Towers, in a revival of "Peter Ibbetson"; Bijou, Nov., 1931, Grace Trainor in "Marriage for Three"; Playhouse, Dec., 1931, Jo in a revival of "Little Women"; Playhouse, Aug., 1932, Lorette in "Domino"; in Detroit, Dec., 1932, the Duchess of Towers in "Peter Ibbetson"; Ritz, New York, Feb., 1933, Elsie Manning in "Before Morning"; in May, 1933, toured as Laura Roland in "Hard Boiled Angel"; at the Broad Street, Philadelphia, Mar., 1934, appeared in "The Dark Tower"; Music Box, New York, Sept., 1934, played Althoa Royce in "Merrily We Roll Along"; Empire, Sept., 1935, succeeded Judith Anderson as Delia Lovell in "The Old Maid"; Ethel Barrymore, Oct., 1935, played Audrey in "Substitute for Murder"; Lyceum, Apr., 1936, Vir-

ginia Barnard in "Pre-Honeymoon"; Fulton, Sept., 1936, Cecily Harrington in "Love from a Stranger"; Henry Miller, Apr., 1937, Christine Lathrup in "Miss Quis"; toured, 1937–8, in "To-Night at 8.30"; Westport, Conn., summer, 1938, Epiphania in "The Millionairess" and Madame Brisac in "Dame Nature," and repeated this last part at the Booth, Sept., 1938; Golden, New York, Jan., 1939, Lucie in "Where There's a Will"; toured, Mar., 1939, as Susan in "Susan and God"; Lyceum, New York, May, 1939, Erika in "Brown Danube"; Plymouth, May, 1940, Ann Hamilton in "Love's Old Sweet Song"; Little, Apr., 1941, Dorcas Winslow in "Your Loving Son"; at Woodstock, N.Y., Aug., 1941, Mildred Brent in "Dr. "Brent's Household"; Guild, New York, Jan., 1942, Mama in "Papa Is All"; Biltmore, Mar., 1943, Janet Archer in "Kiss and Tell," which she played for over two years; New York City Center, Dec., 1944, directed "Little Women"; Cort, Jan., 1946, Hermione in "The Winter's Tale"; Adelphi, New York, Dec., 1946, staged "Lovely Me"; Henry Miller Theatre, Jan., 1947, played Lucinda Storm in "Little A"; toured, 1947, from New York to San Francisco, for the Theatre Guild, as Hermione in "The Winter's Tale," and Mistress Ford in "The Merry Wives of Windsor"; Belasco, New York, Jan., 1948, Alice in "The Last Dance"; Mansfield, Apr., 1949, Laura Beaumont in "Magnolia Alley"; made her first appearance on the London stage at the Duke of York's, 7 Feb., 1950, as Julia Lambert in "Larger Than Life"; Savoy, Nov., 1950, played Maria Jones in "Mrs. Inspector Jones"; Vaudeville, June, 1951, played Maria Kazarez in "Come Live with Me"; New, Oct., 1951, appeared as Mistress Knight in the musical version of "And So to Bed"; at the New York City Center, Dec., 1953, played Queen Elizabeth in "Richard III"; at the Phoenix, Oct., 1954, played Fanny Collinger in "Sing Me No Lullaby"; toured, 1955, in "The International Set"; John Golden, Feb., 1956, Vera Nedlow in "Someone Waiting"; Booth, May, 1964, Muriel Chadwick in "Roar

Like a Dove"; Theatre de Lys, Nov., 1964, appeared in the concert reading "I Knock at the Door"; Goodspeed Opera House, East Haddam, Conn., Aug., 1966, played in "Maggie"; toured, 1967, in "Double Image"; Théâtre de Lys, Dec., 1967, Mrs. Ruggles in "The Club Bedroom"; toured, 1968, as Mrs. Fisher in "The Show-Off"; has also appeared in films, including "To Catch a Thief," "Tonight at 8:30" in London, "The Swan," "North by Northwest," "Airport," 1970, etc.; has made frequent appearances on television; published an autobiography, "You Won't Be So Pretty," 1954. *Recreations:* Bridge, swimming, walking, and flying. *Address:* Governor's Island, New York, U.S.A.

LANDSTONE, Charles, O.B.E., business manager, theatre administrator and dramatic author; *b.* Vienna, Austria, 30 Mar., 1891; *s.* of Adolph Landstone and his wife Rosalia (Squarenina); *e.* Haberdashers' School, Hampstead; formerly engaged as novelist and writer; was manager for J. T. Grein's Cosmopolitan Theatre, 1928–31; Embassy Theatre, 1929; Everyman Theatre Guild, 1929–30; was first business manager for People's Theatre at the Fortune, Oct. 1930–Aug., 1931; appointed business manager for Leon M. Lion, at the Royalty, Garrick, and Strand Theatres, 1931–3; subsequently business manager at various other London Theatres, including Duke of York's, Cambridge, Comedy, Little, Aldwych, etc.; business manager of the Open Air Theatre, 1938, and licensee and manager, 1939; business manager of the Neighbourhood Theatre and Vaudeville Theatre, 1940, when they were the only theatres open playing "straight" plays, during the London Blitz; was booking-manager for the Old Vic, 1941–2; deputy Drama Director for C.E.M.A., from 1942–5; General Manager for the Theatre Royal, Bristol (the first State-aided theatre in the country), 1942–59; Associate Drama Director of the Arts Council, 1945–52; General Manager, Bristol Old Vic Company, 1946–59; Chairman of the Repertory Committee of the Theatrical

Managers' Association 1952–65; is President, Council of Repertory Theatres; drama critic for the *Jewish Chronicle* to 1970; is the author of the following plays: "Front of House," 1936, re-produced as "Behind Your Back," 1937; "Ruby Morn," "On a Summer's Day," 1939; "The Best Triangles," 1939; is author of the book "Off Stage," 1953; and (with Audrey Williamson) "Ten Years with the Bristol Old Vic," 1957; was awarded the O.B.E., in the Birthday Honours, 1947. *Address:* 15 Springcroft Avenue, East Finchley, London, N2 9JH. *Telephone No.:* 01-883 1004.

LANE, Dorothy, actress; *b.* London, 26 Dec., 1890; *d.* of Pierrepont G. Lane and his wife Rosina Grace (Lilley); is a sister of Grace Lane; made her first appearance on the stage at the Lyric, 2 Dec., 1907, in "Monsieur Beaucaire"; at the Playhouse, Dec., 1910, appeared in "Our Little Cinderella"; made her first appearance on the New York stage, at Daly's Theatre, 11 Mar., 1912, as Miss Paitelot in "Monsieur Beaucaire"; at the Empire, New York, Apr., 1913, played Lady Wilhelmina in a revival of "The Amazons"; later, during 1913, toured in the United States as Peggy, in "A Butterfly on the Wheel"; on returning to England, toured, 1915, with Lewis Waller as Gabrielle in "The Three Musketeers"; at the Empire, Mar., 1917, appeared in "Hanky-Panky," and at Drury Lane, Dec., 1917, played Aladdin in the pantomime; at the Garrick, Mar., 1918, made a great success as Margot Latour in "By Pigeon Post"; at the New Theatre, Apr., 1919, appeared as Violet in "Time to Wake Up," and subsequently toured as Roxana in the play of that name; at the Little Theatre, Feb., 1920, appeared as Louise in "Mumsee"; at the Kennington Theatre, Oct., 1920, played Irene Gale in "Columbine"; at the Aldwych, July, 1921, Diana Quest in "James the Less"; at the New Scala, Dec., 1923, Ho-Yeh in "Almond Eye"; at the Globe, Mar., 1923, for a time played Monna in "Bluebeard's Eighth Wife"; Adelphi, Feb., 1925,

Susan in "Love's Prisoner"; in Aug., 1925, toured as Fanchette in "The Folly of Youth"; Little, Apr., 1926, played Beryl Carden in "The Nineteenth Hole"; during 1927–8, toured with Tod Slaughter's company, playing lead; at the St. Martin's, Sept., 1929, played Emma Blake in "Sorry You've Been Troubled"; during 1930, toured as Phoebe Selsey in the same play; Duke of York's, June, 1930, played Miss Masterton in "The Way to Treat a Woman"; Whitehall, Feb., 1931, Dolly Marsh in "Good Losers"; July, 1931, Mrs. Warrender in "Take a Chance"; Savoy, Dec., 1939, played Grace Torrens in "Design for Living"; Queen's, Apr., 1940, Mrs. Coleman Fortescue in "Rebecca," and again at the Queen's, May, 1942; Haymarket, Oct., 1944, Mrs. Shenstone in "The Circle," and Apr., 1945, The Old Lady in "The Duchess of Malfi"; Lyric, Hammersmith, Mar., 1946, Helen Jardine in "To-Morrow's Child"; New, June, 1946, the Very Old Lady in "Crime and Punishment."

LANE, Grace, actress; *b.* 13 Jan., 1876; *d.* of Pierrepont G. Lane and his wife, Rosina Grace (Lilley); *m.* Kenneth Douglas (Savory); prior to her appearance on the professional stage, appeared with great success in a number of Gilbert and Sullivan operas; made her first appearance on the professional stage 16 April, 1894, at T.R. Wolverhampton, in the late Willie Edouin's company, in "Turned Up"; subsequently played in "The Jerry Builder," etc.; made her first appearance on the London stage, at the Grand Theatre, Islington, 11 June, 1894, as Violet Fullerton in "Parallel Attacks"; first appeared in the West End, at the Strand Theatre, 2 July, 1894, as Elsie in "Our Flat," subsequently playing Lucy, and Margery in the same piece; at the Lyceum, Christmas, 1894, played Alan-A-Dale in "Santa Claus"; at Terry's, Apr., 1895, appeared as Violet Tracey in "The Passport," and then for a time appeared at Daly's in "An Artist's Model"; at the Lyceum, Christmas, 1895, appeared as Polly

Hopkins in "Robinson Crusoe"; understudied Ellaline Terriss at the Gaiety in "The Shop Girl"; subsequently toured, playing a wide range of parts; at the Theatre Royal, Manchester, Christmas, 1897, played the Princess in "Aladdin"; in 1898 toured as Evelyn in "The Happy Life"; toured for eighteen months as Lady Babbie in "The Little Minister," in which she scored a great success all over the United Kingdom; at Wyndham's, Feb., 1900, played Sheeba in revival of "Dandy Dick"; toured as Stella de Gex in "His Excellency the Governor"; next toured with Mr. and Mrs. Kendal, playing Sophia in "The Elder Miss Blossom," and Joy in "The Secret Orchard," her success in the latter mentioned part bringing her offers of engagement from nearly every important London Theatre; appeared as Sophia in "The Elder Miss Blossom," at the St. James's, Sept., 1901, and as Amy in "The Likeness of the Night," Oct., 1901; at the Haymarket, Jan., 1902, played Olive in "Frocks and Frills"; at the Shaftesbury, June, 1902, played Dora in "Jedbury, Junior"; then joined Lewis Waller at the Comedy, and in Oct., 1902, scored a great success when she appeared as Lady Mary Carlyle in "Monsieur Beaucaire," which she played throughout the long run of that play; accompanied Lewis Waller to the Imperial, where she appeared as the Comtesse de Candale in "A Marriage of Convenience," Elizabeth Philipse in "Miss Elizabeth's Prisoner"; at the Comedy, Nov., 1905, played Alice in "The Mountain Climber"; at the Court, Feb., 1906, appeared as Aglaë in "Pan and the Young Shepherd"; at the Comedy, Apr., 1906, played Fair in "Josephine"; appeared at Court in "You Never Can Tell," 1906; at the Comedy, in Apr., 1907, played Eve Lindon in "The Truth"; and at the St. James's, July, 1907, Stacey Trevor Coke and Anastasia in "The Eighteenth Century"; at the Criterion, Oct., 1908, appeared as Mrs. Paul Hughes in "Lady Epping's Lawsuit"; at the Garrick, June, 1909, played

Margaret Rolfe in " The Woman in the Case " ; at the Globe, Dec., 1910, appeared as Lady Patience Gascoyne in " Beau Brocade " ; at the Little, July, 1911, as Ariadne in " Ariadne in Naxos " ; at the Court, Sept., 1911, played in " The Admiral Speaks " ; went to New York, Mar., 1912, to appear with Lewis Waller, at Daly's, as Lady Mary in " Monsieur Beaucaire," and in May, 1912, as Mrs. Crowley in " The Explorer " ; at the Kingsway, Sept., 1912, played Mrs. Hugh Voysey in " The Voysey Inheritance " ; at the Comedy, June, 1913, played Mrs. Ralston in " Jim the Penman " ; at the Vaudeville, Oct. 1913, played Susan Digby in " Collision"; at the Queen's, Mar., 1914, appeared as Vera Revendal in " The Melting Pot " ; at the Comedy, May, 1914, as Hannah Vaughan in " Plaster Saints " ; at Wyndham's, Sept., 1914, as Valentine in " Outcast " ; at the St. James's, May, 1915, as Victoria Buckingham in " The Day Before the Day " ; at the New Theatre, July, 1915, as Grace Tyler in " Ready Money " ; at Drury Lane, Apr., 1916, appeared as An English Queen in " Shakespeare's Legacy " ; at the Apollo, May, 1917, played Lady Crandall in " Inside the Lines " ; at Devonshire Park, Eastbourne, Nov., 1917, Mrs. Phipps in " His Royal Happiness " ; at the Gaiety, Manchester, Dec., 1918, Glodagh Dymley in " Sixes and Sevens " ; same theatre, Dec., 1919, Lady Chantmass in " Homespun " ; at the Grand, Croydon, Jan., 1920, Lady De la Haye in " The Chinese Puzzle " ; at the Ambassadors', Apr., 1920, Emily Corbett in " A Grain of Mustard Seed " ; at the Criterion, Dec., 1920, Sylvia Gayford in " Lord Richard in the Pantry " ; at the Royalty, Jan., 1922, Lady Barchester in " The Eleventh Commandment " ; at the Lyric, Feb., 1922, Persis Lapham in " The Rise of Silas Lapham " ; at the Royalty, June, 1922, Emma Talbot in " The Green Cord " ; in Aug., 1922, toured as Mrs. Sabre in " If Winter Comes," and played the same part at the St. James's, Jan., 1923 ; at the Haymarket, June, 1923, Lady Jane Mannock in " Success " ; at Wyndham's, Apr., 1924, Mrs. Faithfull in " To Have the

Honour"; at the St. James's, Dec. 1924, Polly Harrington in " Pollyanna "; Garrick, Mar., 1925, Lady Jesmond in " Possessions "; New, Sept., 1925, Amy Strickland in " The Moon and Sixpence "; Globe, Apr., 1926, Elinor Bathurst in " By-Ways "; Shaftesbury, Apr., 1926, Bianca Sonino in " The Great Lover "; " Q," Sept., 1926, Lady Mary in " Miss Black's Son "; during 1927, toured as Mrs. Anstruther in " Dawn "; His Majesty's (for the Sunday Play Society), Jan., 1928, played Ella Jordan in " Icebound "; Vaudeville, Nov., 1928, Countess of Drumoor in " Clara Gibbings"; Garrick, Feb., 1930, Margaret Brent in "Almost a Honeymoon"; Savoy, Aug., 1931, Mrs. Rhombard in "Midnight Love"; Ambassadors', Oct., 1931, Queen Martha in "The Queen's Husband"; toured in Canada, Feb., 1932, in the same part, which she also played at the New, Mar., 1932, when the play was revived; Duchess, May, 1932, played Mrs. Silcox in "A Cold June"; " Q," Aug., 1932, Elizabeth Field in "Time's Fool"; again went to Canada, Sept., 1932, playing the Elderly Lady in "Too True to be Good," and Orinthia in "The Apple Cart"; Fortune, Sept., 1933, Mrs. Bromley in "What Happened Then?"; Daly's, Oct., 1933, Madame Bernin in "Maternité"; St. Martin's (for the Shop Window), Jan., 1934, Lady Harkness in "Nemesis"; went to Australia, 1934, and appeared as Lady Lilian in "Fresh Fields," Stella Tabret in "The Sacred Flame," and Lady Jane Kingdom in "The Old Folks at Home," also acting as producer; on her return to London, appeared at the Playhouse, May, 1935, as Amy in "The Skin Game"; Ambassadors', Sept., 1935, played the Duchess of Reculver in "As Bad as I Am"; Drury Lane, May, 1936, The Queen in "Rise and Shine"; Streatham Hill, Nov., 1936, The Queen in "Business with Royalty"; Wimbledon, May, 1937, Lady Somerton in "The Five Ways"; Embassy, Apr., 1938, Mabel Sterne in "Good and Proper"; Arts, Jan., 1944, Donna Antonia Pacheco in "Don Abel Wrote a Tragedy"; Scala, Mar., 1944, Gertrude in "Hamlet"; Prince's, Mar., 1945, the Duchess of Dorney in

"Three Waltzes"; Wimbledon, June, 1946, Anna Pavlovna in "Redemption." *(Died 14 Jan., 1956; age 80)*

LANE, Horace, comedian; *b.* in Surrey, July, 1880; *s.* of Pierrepont Greaves and his wife Rosina Grace (Lilley); *e.* Westminster School; *m.* Violet Lloyd; was intended for the law; made his first appearance on the stage at the Empire, Portsmouth, 1897; appeared at the Shakespeare, Clapham, 1897; appeared at the Lyceum with Sir Henry Irving, 1899, in "Robespierre"; toured for three years with Messrs. Cyril Maude and Frederick Harrison's company; appeared with Marie Tempest in "The Marriage of Kitty"; appeared at the Apollo, 1906, in "The Dairymaids"; made his first appearance on the London variety stage, at the Canterbury Music Hall; for some years has been associated with his wife, in musical sketches, the best known of which is "The Merry Buskers"; has appeared at most of the leading halls in London and the provinces; has fulfilled many pantomime engagements; is a brother of the well-known actress Grace Lane. *Rcereations :* Golf and motoring. *Club:* Vaudeville. *Address :* Vaudeville Club, 98 Charing Cross Road, W.C.

LANE, Lupino, actor and manager; *b.* London, 16 June, 1892; *s.* of Harry Lupino and his wife, Charlotte (Robinson); *e.* Brighton; *m.* Violet Blythe; made his first appearance on the stage at the age of four, at the Prince of Wales's Theatre, Birmingham, 1896, at a complimentary benefit performance to Vesta Tilley; made his first appearance in London, at the London Pavilion, in 1903; has since appeared at the Hippodrome, Palace, Empire, etc., he has toured the Moss and Stoll halls all over the kingdom, and has appeared in Paris, and the principal cities in the United States and Canada; appeared at the Empire, May, 1915, in "Watch Your Step"; Feb., 1916, in "Follow the Crowd"; July, 1916 in "We're All in It"; at the Kingsway, Oct., 1916, in "Extra Special"; at the Duke of York's Theatre, July,

1917, played Andrew Janaway in "What a Catch!"; during 1918 toured as Clarence in "Any Lady"; at the London Pavilion, Sept., 1919, appeared as Coucourli in "Afgar"; at the Palace, Manchester, Dec., 1919, played Pekoe in "Aladdin"; went to the United States, in 1920, and appeared at the Century Theatre, New York, Nov., 1920, as Coucourli in "Afgar"; returned to London in Dec., 1920; appeared at the London Hippodrome, Dec., 1920, as Pekoe in "Aladdin"; at the New Oxford, May, 1921, appeared in "The League of Notions"; at the London Hippodrome, Mar., 1923, played in "Brighter London"; at the New Amsterdam Theatre, New York, June, 1924, appeared in "The Ziegfeld Follies"; 44th Street Theatre, Apr., 1925, played Ko-Ko in "The Mikado"; returned to London, 1926; New Oxford, Jan., 1926, played George Medway in "Turned Up"; Strand, June, 1926, Jefferson in "Hearts and Diamonds"; subsequently again returned to America; reappeared on the London stage, at the Dominion, Feb., 1930, as Jerry Wimpole in "Silver Wings"; at the same theatre, Dec., 1930, played Pekoe in "Aladdin"; Streatham Hill, Dec., 1932, appeared as Freddy Stone in "The One Girl," playing the same part at the London Hippodrome, Feb., 1933; Savoy, Nov., 1933, appeared in "Please"; Coliseum, Feb., 1934, the Barber in "The Golden Toy"; in Apr., 1935, toured as Snibson in "Twenty to One," appearing in the same part at the London Coliseum, Nov., 1935, when he presented the play, in conjunction with Sir Oswald Stoll; in 1936 toured in the same play and eventually played Bill Snibson in that play 1025 times; Coliseum, Dec., 1936, played Buttons in "Cinderella"; Victoria Palace, Dec., 1937, produced and presented "Me and My Girl," in which he again played Bill Snibson, and appeared for 1550 consecutive performances; in this piece he created the celebrated dance, "The Lambeth Walk," and the piece ran for 1646 performances on its first run, and has since been revived on several occasions; Victoria Palace, Feb., 1942, again played Snibson in a revival of "Twenty to One"; Dec., 1942, Tim Pippin in "Babes in the Wood"; Mar., 1943, Bill Stub in "La-di-da-di-Da"; Apr., 1944, Bill Fish in "Meet Me Victoria"; Victoria Palace, Aug., 1946, played Harry Hawkins in "Sweetheart Mine," of which he was part-author; Wimbledon, July, 1949, Albert Kneebone in "Wanted on Voyage"; Winter Garden, Dec., 1949, again played Bill Snibson in "Me and My Girl"; Kingston Empire, Dec., 1950, appeared in "Humpty Dumpty"; at Bournemouth, Mar., 1952, produced "Nuts in May," in which he played Edward Rugg; Comedy, London, Sept., 1952, appeared as Henry Pugh in "Wishing Well"; King's, Hammersmith, Dec., 1952, played Buttons in "Cinderella"; purchased the Gaiety Theatre, 1948, but disposed of the property, without re-opening it, 1950; commenced film career, 1913, in "Nipper's Bank Holiday," and appeared in numerous silent and talking films, notably "Lady of the Rose," "The Love Parade," The Lambeth Walk," etc.; has also directed the production of several films, including "Love Lies," "The Love Race," "The Maid of the Mountains," etc.; is a member of the famous Lupino family of dancers and acrobats, whose connection with the stage dates back for over two centuries. *Recreations:* Music, swimming, boating and motoring. *Clubs:* Savage, and Stage Golfing Society. *(Died 10 Nov., 1959; age 67)*

LANG, Howard, actor; *m.* Gwen Heller; an actor of many years experience; appeared at the Thalia Theatre, New York, 5 Aug., 1907, as Adolphe Bleck in "Convict 999"; at the Third Avenue Theatre, Aug., 1908, played Topaz Carson in "The Sheriff of Angel Gulch"; he was for many years leading man with the Cecil Spooner "stock" company, in which he played hundreds of parts; during 1916–17, appeared with the Poli Players, Washington, D.C.; at the Republic, Dec., 1917, played Henri in "Blind Youth"; appeared at the Haymarket Theatre, London, 30 Aug., 1919, as Karl Pfeiffer in "Uncle Sam"; Bijou, New York, Mar., 1920, played Gabriel Mogador in "The Ouija Board"; Astor, Oct., 1920, David

Franks in "The Unwritten Chapter"; Henry Miller, Jan., 1921, Adam West in "Wake Up, Jonathan"; Knickerbocker, Oct., 1921, Issacher and Juan de Texeda in "The Wandering Jew"; Fulton, May, 1922, Dr. Jacob Samuels in "Abie's Irish Rose"; Eltinge, Sept., 1922, Lee Tai Cheng in "East of Suez"; 49th Street, Aug., 1923, Emmett Sheridan in "Thumbs Down"; Sam H. Harris, Nov., 1924, Matthew Slayton in "Dawn"; 49th Street, May, 1925, Barry Trevelyan in "Lady of the Rose"; Fulton, Sept., 1925, Cantor Rabinowitz in "The Jazz Singer"; Ambassador, Sept., 1929, Sam Hammerman in "A Strong Man's House"; Hudson, Feb., 1931, Dr. Xavier in "Doctor X"; Biltmore, Mar., 1932, Dr. Wolf Luckner in "Border Land." *(Died 26 Jan., 1941; age 65)*

LANG, Matheson, actor, manager, and dramatic author; *b.* Montreal, Canada, 15 May, 1879; *s.* of Rev. Gavin Lang, cousin of the late Archbishop of Canterbury; *m.* Hutin Britton; *e.* at Inverness College and St. Andrew's University; made his first appearance on the stage at Wolverhampton, 1897, in Louis Calvert's company, in "Proof," playing small parts in "Richelieu," "Othello," "The Hunchback," "The Lyons Mail," "A Royal Divorce," "The Three Musketeers," etc.; subsequently joined F. R. Benson's company, in which he played a number of parts; made his first appearance on the London stage at the Lyceum, 15 Feb., 1900, with Benson's company, as Montjoy in "King Henry V"; subsequently played Philostrate in "A Midsummer Night's Dream," Bushey in "Richard II," etc., ultimately playing such parts as Macduff, Laertes, Richmond, Bassanio, Joseph Surface, Paolo in "Paolo and Francesca," etc.; appeared with Mrs. Langtry, at Imperal, Dec., 1902, as Sir Charles Croffte in "The Cross-Ways," subsequently touring with her in the United States, 1902–3; reappeared in London, at the Imperial Theatre, 1903, when he succeeded Oscar Asche as Benedick in "Much Ado About Nothing," with Ellen

Terry; toured with Ellen Terry, 1903, as Benedick in "Much Ado About Nothing," also in "The Merchant of Venice" and "The Good Hope"; played leading parts on West Indian tour with F. R. Benson's company; at the Court, Oct., 1905, played Dr. Relling in "The Wild Duck"; at the Shaftesbury, Jan., 1906, appeared as David Martine in "The Jury of Fate"; at the Comedy, Apr., 1906, played Captain Hector MacGregor in "The Drums of Oude," and Bunting in "Josephine"; at the Adelphi, Sept., 1906, appeared as Tristram in "Tristram and Iseult"; Garrick, Dec., 1906, played Macduff in "Macbeth"; at Manchester, Jan., 1907, appeared very successfully as Othello; at the St. James's, Mar., 1907, played Trevor Lerode in "John Glayde's Honour"; at the Lyceum, Aug., 1907, played John Storm in "The Christian," and at the Savoy, Oct., 1907, he appeared as Dick Dudgeon in "The Devil's Disciple"; at the Lyceum, Mar., 1908, played Romeo in "Romeo and Juliet," scoring a great success; same theatre, Aug., 1908, played Pete in Hall Caine and Louis N. Parker's drama of that name; in Mar., 1909, appeared as Hamlet; in May, 1909, as Louis XIV and Philippe Marchiali in "The Man in the Iron Mask," and Sept., 1909, as King Robert of Sicily in "The Proud Prince"; he then went to New York, and appeared at the New Theatre, Dec., 1909, as Charles Surface in "The School for Scandal," and Stephen Bonnington in "Don"; in Jan., 1910, played Orsino in "Twelfth Night"; in Apr., 1910, went to Australia, under Clarke Meynell and Gunn, playing Pete, and the Stranger in "The Passing of the Third Floor Back"; in 1911 played Macbeth at Stratford-on-Avon; in 1911 toured in South Africa, playing among other parts, Petruchio in "The Taming of the Shrew," Bardelys in "Bardelys the Magnificent," King Charles in "Sweet Nell of Old Drury," Macbeth, Hamlet, Shylock, Romeo, Benedick, the Stranger in "The Passing of the Third Floor Back"; Othello and Don Caesar in "A Royal Rival"; at Cape Town, Oct. 1911, played the title-*rôle* in "Jack o'

Jingles"; the tour was highly successful; subsequently he sailed for India and the Far East, where he was equally successful; reappeared in London, at the Palladium, Feb., 1913, as Amyas Leigh in "Westward Ho!"; at His Majesty's, Apr., 1913, played Charles Surface in "The School for Scandal"; at the Strand, July, 1913, appeared as 'Poleon Doret in "The Barrier"; Nov., 1913, scored a great success when he appeared as Wu Li Chang in "Mr. Wu"; at His Majesty's, Nov., 1914, played Henry Percy (Hotspur) in "King Henry IV" (Part I); subsequently, in 1915, toured as Mr. Wu and as Gringoire in "The Ballad Monger"; at the Aldwych, July, 1915, reappeared as Pete in the play of that name; he then toured with his own company, and at Wimbledon, Sept., 1915, played Shylock in "The Merchant of Venice,' appearing at the St. James's, under his own management, Dec., 1915, in the same part; at the Gaiety, Hastings, Apr., 1916, played Henry Harford in "The Mystery of John Wake"; he then appeared at the Strand, Nov., 1916, as Henri Buxell in "Buxell," and Jan., 1917, as Stephen Denby in "Under Cover"; entered on the management of the Lyric Theatre, July, 1918, when he played the Comte de Trevières in his own adaptation "The Purple Mask"; entered on the management of the New Theatre, Feb., 1920, when he played Silvio Steno in "Carnival," of which he was also part-author with H. C. M. Hardinge; in the same month, for a series of *matinées*, also appeared as Othello; at the New, Sept., 1920, appeared as Matathias in "The Wandering Jew," which ran twelve months; Aug., 1921, played Christopher in "Christopher Sly"; Dec., 1921, El Gallardo in "Blood and Sand"; Dec., 1922, Peter Starling in "The Great Well"; Mar., 1923, Pancho Lopez in "The Bad Man"; June, 1923, Silvio Steno in a revival of "Carnival"; Oct., 1924, Julian Wear in "The Hour and the Man"; Nov., 1924, Matathias in a revival of "The Wandering Jew"; Mar., 1925, Cesare Borgia in "The Tyrant"; subsequently toured as Huan Sing in "The Chinese Bungalow," appearing in the same part at the King's, Hammersmith, Nov., 1925; appeared at the Cosmopolitan Theatre, New York, Feb., 1927, in " The Wandering Jew "; subsequently toured in America and Canada; reappeared in London, Drury Lane, May, 1927, when he played " The Wandering Jew," (for King George's Pension Fund); again toured 1927-8; appeared at the Duke of York's, Sept., 1928, as Count Pahlen in " Such Men Are Dangerous "; Jan., 1929, Yuan Sing in " The Chinese Bungalow"; Sept., 1929, Joseph Süss Oppenheimer in " Jew Süss"; in Feb., 1931, toured as General Crack in a play of that name; at the Cambridge, Sept., 1931, played Philip of Spain in "Elizabeth of England"; during 1932, toured in "Mr. Wu," and "The Wandering Jew"; during 1933, toured as the Duke of Wellington in "Wellington"; Prince's, Aug., 1933, again played Matathias in "The Wandering Jew"; during 1934, toured in "The Wandering Jew" and "For the Defence"; at the Duke of York's, Feb., 1935, played Sir Philip Holbrooke, K.C., in "For the Defence" ("There Go All of Us"); in the autumn of 1935, toured in the same play; Sept., 1936, again toured in "The Wandering Jew"; King's, Edinburgh, Mar., 1937, played Don José in "Matador," of which he was part-author with Marguerite Steen; in 1937, again toured in "The Chinese Bungalow"; subsequently, in 1941, went to South Africa; from 1916, was prominently identified with the cinema stage, and appeared in innumerable films; published a volume of reminiscences, "Mr. Wu Looks Back," 1940. *Favourite part:* Count Pahlen. *Hobbies:* Art and literature, and sailing. *(Died 11 Apr., 1948; age 68)*

LANGLEY, Noel, dramatic author; *b.* Durban, Natal, South Africa, 25 Dec., 1911; *s.* of Aubrey Samuel Langley and his wife Dora (Allison); *e.* Durban High School and Natal University College; *m.* (1) Naomi Legate (mar. dis.); (2) Pamela Deeming; author of the following plays: "Queer Cargo," 1934; "For Ever," 1934; "Farm of Three Echoes," 1935; "Cage Me a Peacock," 1946; "Edward,

My Son" (with Robert Morley), 1947; "Little Lambs Eat Ivy," 1947; "The Burning Bush" (adaptation), 1948; "The Gentle Rain," "Married Alive," 1952; "An Elegance of Rebels," 1962; "The Land of Green Ginger," 1966; in Hollywood, 1936-9, where he wrote a number of film scripts, including "The Wizard of Oz"; returned to England, 1946, where he wrote and directed many films, including: "Trio," 1950; "Prisoner of Zenda," 1952; "The Pickwick Papers," 1953; "Svengali," 1955; "The Search for Bridey Murphy," 1956.

LANGNER, Lawrence, dramatic author and producer; *b.* Swansea, S. Wales, 30 May, 1890; *s.* of Braham Langner and his wife Cecile; *m.* Armina Marshall; commenced his career as a junior clerk in the offices of the Ben Greet Co.; in New York was one of the founders of the Washington Square Players, where his first play, "License," was produced in 1914; is the author of the following, among other plays: "Another Way Out," 1916; "The Family Exit," 1917; "Matinata," 1920; "Don Juan"(adapted from the French), 1921; "Henry Behave," 1926; "These Modern Women," 1928; "Moses" (published), "The Pursuit of Happiness" (with his wife), adapted "Champagne Sec" ("Die Fledermaus"), "The School for Husbands" (with Arthur Guiterman), 1933; "For Love or Money" (with his wife), 1934; "On to Fortune" (with his wife), "Snowed Under," 1935; "Suzanna and the Elders" (with his wife), 1938; is probably better known as the founder, and a director of The Theatre Guild of New York since its inception in May, 1919; founder and director of the New York Repertory Company, 1931-3, and produced "The Streets of New York," and "The Pillars of Society," at the 48th Street Theatre, Oct., 1931; at the Fulton, Dec., 1931, produced "The Bride the Sun Shines On"; in 1931, built the Country Playhouse, Westport, Conn., where his New York Repertory Company appeared, 1931-2; has supervised with Theresa Helburn, over two hundred plays for Theatre Guild, including "Strange Interlude," "Mourning Becomes Elec-

tra," "Porgy and Bess," "Garrick Gaieties," "Oklahoma," "Carousel," "Biography," "Reunion in Vienna," "Mary of Scotland," "They Knew What They Wanted," "Come Back, Little Sheba," "Picnic," "Bells Are Ringing," "The Tunnel of Love," "Saint Joan," "Lo and Behold!" "Legend of Lovers," "Jane," "The Love of Four Colonels," and other works by major dramatists; for nine years was associated with the production of the radio programme known as "Theatre Guild on the Air"; in association with Armina Marshall and Theresa Helburn produced television plays and programmes 1947–53; with Miss Marshall and H. William Fitelson has produced television plays since 1953; is Founder of the American Shakespeare Festival Theatre and Academy, Stratford, Connecticut, the theatre opening 12 July, 1955; published his autobiography, "The Magic Curtain," 1952; is also author of "The Importance of Wearing Clothes," and "The Play's the Thing"; Fellow of the British Chartered Institute of Patent Agents, and founded the international patent specialists firm of Langner, Parry, Card and Langner; founder of the National Investors Council, Department of Commerce; with his wife and their son, Philip, is currently co-producer of Theatre Guild.
(Died 26 Dec., 1962; age 72)

LANGTON, Basil C., actor, manager, and producer; *b.* Clifton, Bristol, 9 Jan., 1912; *s.* of Samuel Calvert-Langton and his wife Esther (Shandel); *e.* in Canada; *m.* Louise Soelberg; was formerly engaged in a bank; made his first appearance on the stage at the Little Theatre, Vancouver, B.C., 30 Jan., 1930, in a *revue*, "Let's Go"; on returning to England, in 1933, studied at the School of Dance-Mime, and the Jooss-Leeder School of Dance, Dartington Hall; during the 1935 season, appeared at Stratford-on-Avon, with the Shakespeare Festival company; Duke of York's, Oct., 1935, appeared in "The Hangman"; again appeared with the Festival company at Stratford-on-Avon, 1936; New Theatre, Oct., 1936, played

Dolabella in "Antony and Cleopatra"; His Majesty's, Dec., 1936, Eliab in "The Boy David"; Embassy, May, 1937, and Strand, June, 1937, played Marek in "Judgment Day"; Westminster, July, 1937, Marcellus in "Hamlet"; Old Vic., Nov., and New Theatre, Dec., 1937, Lennox in "Macbeth"; Vaudeville (for the Stage Society), Feb., 1938, Ralph Berger in "Awake and Sing"; from Jan.–Apr., 1938, appeared in several productions at the "Q" and Embassy Theatres; Phoenix, Oct., 1938, played Nikolka Turbin in "The White Guard," and Dec., 1938, Sebastian in "Twelfth Night"; same theatre, Nov., 1939, played Conrad Noli in "Judgment Day"; subsequently, from Apr.–Sept., 1940, appeared with the Festival company, Stratford-on-Avon, playing Angelo in "Measure for Measure," Dr. Caius in "The Merry Wives of Windsor," the Dauphin in "King John," Arragon in "The Merchant of Venice," Tranio in "The Taming of the Shrew," and Hamlet; joined the Birmingham Repertory Theatre, Sept., 1940, playing leading parts; in Feb., 1941, formed the Travelling Repertory Theatre, which he has operated ever since; inaugurated the Open Air Theatre, Birmingham, 1941, and again ran seasons there in 1942 and 1944; Dec., 1941, to Nov., 1942, produced more than a dozen plays at the Birmingham Repertory Theatre; has also toured for E.N.S.A. and C.E.M.A., visiting hostels, all over the country; Whitehall Theatre, June, 1943, in conjunction with George Wood, presented "The Moon is Down"; in 1944, toured as John Tanner in "Man and Superman," Professor Higgins in "Pygmalion" and de Poulengey in "Saint Joan"; in 1945, toured as Martin Ladvenu and Robert de Beaudricourt in "Saint Joan," appearing in these parts at the King's, Hammersmith, Feb., 1945; formed T.R.T. Productions, Ltd., 1945, of which he was Administrator, and was responsible for a four months season, Mar.–June, 1946, at the King's, Hammersmith, presenting "Romeo and Juliet," "Saint Joan," "The Wise Have Not Spoken," "Man and Superman," "In Time to Come," and "Electra"; at the Arts,

Feb., 1947, played Francis in "The Wise Have Not Spoken," which he also produced, and Cain in "Back to Methuselah." *Hobby:* The theatre. *Address:* c/o Cliftons, 7 New Square, Lincoln's Inn, W.C.2. *Telephone No.:* Chancery 8991.

LANGTRY, Lillie, actress; *b.* Jersey, 13 Oct., 1852; *d.* of Very Rev. W. C. E. le Breton, Dean of Jersey; *m.* (1) Edward Langtry (died 1897); (2) Sir (then Mr.) Hugo de Bathe, Bart.; made her first appearance on the stage, at the Haymarket Theatre, 15 Dec., 1881, under Mr. and Mrs. Bancroft, as Kate Hardcastle in " She Stoops to Conquer "; subsequently appeared at the same theatre, as Blanche Haye in " Ours "; organised her own company and played a season at the Imperial, Sept., 1882, playing Hester Grazebrook in " An Unequal Match," and Rosalind in " As You Like It "; toured in America with great success; on returning to London, became manageress of the Prince's Theatre, opening in Jan., 1885, as Séverine in " Princess George "; in Feb., 1885, played there as Lady Teazle in " The School for Scandal "; and Apr., 1885, as Lady Ormond in a revival of " Peril "; at the same theatre, Jan., 1886, appeared as Margaret Glenn in " Enemies," subsequently playing Pauline in " The Lady of Lyons "; returned to America, and played there until 1889 : returning to England, she toured the English provinces; assumed the management of the St. James's, Feb., 1890, reviving " As You Like It "; in May, 1890, appeared as Esther Sandraz in the play of that name; assumed the management of the Princess's Theatre, Nov., 1890, opening as Cleopatra in a revival of " Antony and Cleopatra "; in Feb., 1891, produced " Lady Barter," and in Apr., 1891, " Linda Grey "; she then undertook a season at the Haymarket, opening in Sept., 1892, as Lady Violet Malvern in " The Queen of Manoa," followed in Oct., 1892, by her performance of Agatha Tylden in " Agatha Tylden, Merchant and Shipowner "; in Aug., 1894, became manageress of the Opéra Co-

mique, where she appeared as Mrs. Dudley in " A Society Butterfly "; subsequently made further American and provincial tours; reappeared in London, at the Grand, Islington, June, 1895, as Mrs. Barry in " Gossip," appearing in the same part at the Comedy, in the following year; produced " The Degenerates " at the Haymarket, Aug., 1899, playing the part of Mrs. Trevelyan with great success; opened the rebuilt Imperial Theatre, Apr., 1901, of which she took a long lease, with the production of " A Royal Necklace "; Jan., 1902, produced " Mademoiselle Mars," in which she appeared in the title-*rôle*; at the same theatre, Dec., 1902, played Virginia, Duchess of Keensbury in " The Cross-Ways," of which she was also part author; again toured in America, but returned to London in 1904; appeared at the Camden Theatre, Nov., 1904, as Mrs. Dering in " Mrs. Dering's Divorce," playing the same part at Terry's, Jan., 1905; toured in South Africa, 1905-6, playing " As You Like It," " The Degenerates," " The Walls of Jericho," and " The Second Mrs. Tanqueray "; toured in America in " vaudeville," 1906; appeared at the Haymarket, Apr., 1908, as Mrs. Arundel in " A Fearful Joy "; during 1910-11 appeared in sketch, " The Right Sort " (" The Degenerates "); at the Hippodrome, Mar., 1911, played in " Between the Nightfall and the Light "; at Drury Lane, Mar., 1911, appeared as Lady Marion Beaumont in " The Sins of Society "; at the Gala performance at His Majesty's, 27 June, 1911, appeared as Wonder in " The Vision of Delight "; during 1912-13, toured in music-hall sketch, " Helping the Cause "; appearing in the United States, Sept., 1912, in the same piece; at the Hippodrome, Manchester, Mar., 1914, played Lady Lambert in " Ashes "; at the Lyceum, Sheffield, Feb., 1915, appeared as Mrs. Thompson in a play of that name; in Oct., 1915, again went to America, where she toured in the same play; at the Colonial, New York, Nov., 1915, played in " Ashes "; at the Bandbox, New York, Nov., 1915, Harriet in " Overtones "; appeared at the Coliseum, London, Nov., 1917,

in the same part; at the Coliseum, Feb., 1918, the Lady in "Blame the Cinema"; had a large stable of racehorses, and was probably the best known lady owner on the turf; has won most of the important handicaps and the Gold Cup at Ascot; has written her reminiscences, under the title of "The Days I Knew."
(Died 12 Feb., 1929; age 75)

LANGTRY, Lillie, comédienne; *b.* in Wiltshire, 15 Sept., 1877; *d.* of Michael Edwards and his wife Millie; *e.* Brixton; formerly known as Baby Langtry; made her first appearance on the stage at the Elephant and Castle Theatre, at the age of five, giving an imitation of the late Charles Godfrey; appeared at the Pavilion Theatre, Mile End, Christmas, 1885, in "Jack and the Giant Killer," with Ada Reeve, Ida Heath, etc.; same theatre, Christmas, 1886, appeared in "The Babes in the Wood"; appeared at Drury Lane Theatre, Christmas, 1891, in "Humpty Dumpty"; has appeared at most of the principal variety theatres in the United Kingdom, and has played most of the leading tours; toured in America, 1900; South Africa, 1909; Australia, 1909, 1913-4; her earliest success in the halls was with a song entitled "Romping in the Playground"; other songs connected with her name are "The Cheap Excursion Train"; "On the Margate Boat"; "A Night Out," etc. *Recreations:* Photography and motoring. *Address:* West Hill Lodge, Hastings.

LAPARCERIE, Cora, French actress; *b.* at Bordeaux; *m.* Jacques Richepin; studied for the stage under Coquelin Aîné, Antoine, and Madame Favart; made her first appearance on the stage at Bordeaux; joined the Paris Odéon Company in 1896, making her first appearance there as Chiquita in "Capitaine Fracasse"; subsequently she played in "Plutus," "Mariannes," "La Marechale d'Ancre," etc.; next played François in "Richelieu,"; la Mignote in "Les Truands'; Eriphile in "Iphigénie," etc.; also appearing in "Don Juan," "La Double Méprise," "Chênecœur," "France d'Abord," "Le Chien de Garde," "Le Lion Amoureux," "Andromaque," "Athalie," "Cinna," "Le Cid," "Horace," etc.; she appeared at the Théâtre Antoine, 1900, in "Sur la foi des Etoiles"; at the Théâtre Sarah Bernhardt, 1901, in "La Cavalière"; and at the Porte-St.-Martin, 1901, appeared as Lygia in "Quo Vadis?"; at the Théâtre L'Œuvre, played in "Fausta," "Aert," "Dans la Nuit"; at the Vaudeville, in "Les Petites Jourdeuil"; at the Athénée, in "Ninon de L'Enclos"; at the Gaîte, 1904, played Roxane in "Cyrano de Bergerac"; at Porte-St.-Martin, Marjolaine in "La Marjolaine," 1907; at the Bouffes-Parisiens, 1909, played "Lysistrata," and in 1910, Gaby in the play of that name; assumed the management of the Bouffes-Parisiens, 1910, and appeared there in "Xantho chez les Courtisanes," and in 1911, in "Madame L'Amirale" and "La Revue des X"; in 1912, played Lysistrata, Léontine in "Les Maris de Léontine," Agnés in "Agnés, dame galante," Solange in "La Cote d'amour"; in 1913 assumed the management of the Renaissance Theatre, where she has played in "Le Minaret," "L'Autre Danger," "Les Deux Hommes," "L'Eventail," "La Chance du Mari," "Le Chemineau," "Les Deux Madame Delanges," "L'Instinct," "Le Demi-Monde," "La Bonne Intention," "Les Deux Courtisanes," "Bohémos," "La Poulailer," "Ce Vieux Gélier," "Aphrodite," "Les Roses Rouges," "L'Amour Buissonnier," "La Grève des Femmes," "Chouquette et son as," "La Passarelle," "Revivre," "La Matrone d'Ephèse," "La Guerre et L'Amour," "Mon Homme," "Zaza," "Le Divan Noir," "La Danseuse Rouge"; since the death of Madame Réjane, has played a number of parts associated with that actress; is an Officer of Public Instruction, etc.; at the New Royalty, Theatre London, 1906, appeared in "Le Paon," "Cabotins," "Les Affaires sont les Affaires," "Brichauteau," "Notre Jeunesse," and "Le Barbier de Seville"; at the Adelphi, 1909, with M. Guitry, as Virginie in "L'Assommoir," and

Grace Ritherford in "Samson." *Address :* 4 Avenue Elisée-Reclus, Paris.

LA PLANTE, Laura, actress; *b.* St. Louis, Missouri, U.S.A., 1 Nov., 1904; *d.* of William Alfred La Plante and his wife Elizabeth Elzira (Turk); *e.* St. Louis and San Diego, Cal.; *m.* (1) William A. Seiter (mar. dis.); (2) Irving Asher; made her first appearance, in films, 1919; made her first appearance on the regular stage at the Playhouse, Hollywood, 1931, as Sybil in "Private Lives"; subsequently played Miss Smith in "Springtime for Henry," Moya in "Conn, the Shaughraun," Dorothy Atwater in "The Unexpected Husband"; made her first appearance in London at the Shaftesbury, 6 Aug., 1934, as Gloria Gunn in "Admirals All"; first appeared in films, 1919, and has appeared in "The Old Swimming Hole," "Beware of Widows," "The Cat and the Canary," "The Last Warning," "King of Jazz," "Show Boat," "Hold Your Man," "Too Many Women," "Lonely Wives," "Meet the Wife," "The Captain of the Guard," "Scandal," "Arizona," "Her Imaginary Lover," "The Girl in Possession," "The Church Mouse," "Widow's Might," "Man of the Moment," etc. *Address :* 30 Montpelier Place, London, S.W.7. *Telephone No.:* Kensington 8420.

LARA, Madame, French actress; *b.* Chateau-Thierry 22 July, 1876; *d.* M. Delisle; *e.* Paris; *m.* Monti Autant; made her first appearance on the stage in 1889, at the Galerie Vivien; she studied at the Conservatoire, under M. Worms, Mdme. Sylvain, etc., and made her first appearance at the Comédie Française, 22 Sept., 1896, as Suzanne in "Le Monde ou l'on s'enniue"; she has played there during the past few years, such parts as Chrysothémie in Sophocles' "Electre," Sophie Bernier in "L'amour veille," Adèle in "Boubouroche," Elektra in "Les Erinnyes," Ismène in "Antigone," Germaine in "Les Affaires sont les Affaires," Henriette Ducrest in "Cher Maître," Irene Fergan in "Les Tenailles,"

Hortense in "Le Testament de César Girodot," Ophelia in "Hamlet," Loyse in "Gringoire," Charlotte in "Les Demoiselles de Saint-Cyr," Mdlle. de Brie in "Le Ménage de Molière," Princesse Rose in "Riquet à la Houppe," Henriette in "L'Envolée," "La Nouvelle Idole," etc.; elected a a *sociétaire* of the Comédie Française, 1898; is an Officer of Public Instruction; has also appeared at the Gaîte, Porte-St.-Martin, Renaissance, and Odéon Theatres. *Address :* 2 Rue Emile Menier, Paris.

LARIMORE, Earle, actor; *b.* Portland, Oregon, U.S.A., 2 Aug., 1899; *s.* of Eugene Elton Larimore and his wife Margaret Grace (Hughes); *e.* Oregon State College, Portland; *m.* Selena Royle; studied for the stage under Jessie Bonstelle and Samuel Kayzer; made his first appearance on the stage at Portland, in 1906, as one of the child pages in "The French Fête"; made his first appearance on the New York stage at the Cort Theatre, 14 Oct., 1925, as Bill Pickering in "Made In America"; at the Little Theatre, Jan., 1926, played Richard Cavendish in "The Love City"; Greenwich Village, Mar., 1926, Bill Weed in "Nirvana"; at Baltimore, Mar., 1926, played in "The Stranger in the House"; he then joined the company of the Theatre Guild, with which he was identified for many years; appeared at the Guild Theatre, Oct., 1926, as State Councillor Herzfield in "Juarez and Macmilian"; Nov., 1926, George Callahan in "Ned McCobb's Daughter"; John Golden Theatre, Dec., 1926, Robert in "The Silver Cord"; Guild, Apr., 1927, Alistin Lowe in "The Second Man"; Nov., 1927, Cutler Walpole in "The Doctor's Dilemma"; John Golden Theatre, Jan., 1928, Sam Evans in "Strange Interlude," Biltmore, Apr., 1929, Jerry Jordan in "Man's Estate"; Liberty, Mar., 1930, Marco Polo in "Marco Millions," and Mosca in "Volpone"; Martin Beck Theatre, Apr., 1930, Norman Ross in "Hotel Universe"; Ethel Barrymore Theatre, Apr., 1931, Pierre Belcroix in "Melo"; Guild, Oct., 1931, Orin Mannon in "The Hunted," and "The

Haunted" ("Mourning Becomes Electra"); at Philadelphia, Sept., 1932, Wang Lung in "The Good Earth"; Guild, Dec., 1932, Richard Kurt in "Biography"; Henry Miller (for the Guild), Jan., 1934, John in "Days Without End"; Philadelphia (for the Guild), Mar., 1934, Karlanner in "Races"; Playhouse, New York, Sept., 1934, Captain Cork Coates in "Too Many Boats"; Plymouth, Nov., 1934, Dr. Frederick Steele in "Dark Victory"; Cort, Feb., 1935, Sheridan Delaney in "It's You I Want"; Ethel Barrymore, Apr., 1935, Michael Dennison in "To See Ourselves"; at Cohasset, Mass., July, 1935, Prince Michael in "Meet the Prince"; Ritz, New York, Nov., 1935, Henry Marsden in "Abide ith Me"; at Washington, Dec., 1936, Geoffrey Carroll in "The Two Mrs. Carrolls"; at Cincinnati, June, 1937, Brent Chipley in "The Hill Between"; during 1937–8, was engaged in television drama series, with the N.B.C.; in 1939–40, went on a Trans-Continental tour of the United States, playing Solness in "The Master Builder," and Lovborg in "Hedda Gabler"; since that date has devoted himself to various Radio programmes; he has also appeared for the Guild, outside New York, in "At Mrs. Beam's," "R.U.R.," and "A Month in the Country"; has also appeared in pictures, in "The Kick-off" and "Inspiration"; is a Councillor of the Actors' Equity Association. *Recreations:* Travel, the Arts, swimming, and tennis. *Clubs:* The Lambs and The Players, New York. *Address:* The Lambs, 130 West 44th Street, New York City, 18, U.S.A.

LARRA, Mariano, Spanish actor; has appeared successfully at the Teatro Lara, Madrid, in "Los Conejos," "Casa de Banos," "Venta de Banos," "El Ultimo Drama," "Monja descalza," "El Petrolero," "El Marido de la Tellez," etc. *Address:* Teatro Lara, Madrid, Spain.

LARRIMORE, Francine; *b.* Verdun, France, 22 Aug., 1898; *d.* of J. Louis La Remée and his wife Sarah (Adler); is a niece of the late Jacob P. Adler, the famous Yiddish actor; *e.* Hunter High School, New York; *m.* Conrad Conrad (mar. dis.); made her first appearance on the stage as a small child at the Grand Opera House, New York, in "A Fool There Was"; at Weber's Theatre, New York, Feb., 1910, played Miss Wilson in "Where There's a Will," subsequently playing Elsie Darling in "Over Night"; appeared at the Princess Theatre, New York; Mar., 1913, as the Young Girl in "Any Night"; at Boston, July, 1914, appeared with Edmund Breese, as Mrs. Blount in "The Master Mind"; Harris Theatre, Oct., 1914, played Ida Summers in "The Salamander"; at Indianapolis, Mar., 1915, played in "The Lady We Love"; she next played a "stock" engagement at Union Hill, N.J., appearing in such parts as Wilhelmina in "The Rosary," Aggie Lynch in "Within the Law," Margery Seaton in "The Yellow Ticket," Gertrude Robinson in "Nearly Married," Loretty in "The Trail of the Lonesome Pine," Florence Cole in "A Pair of Sixes," etc.; at the Fulton Theatre, Aug., 1915, appeared as Sylvia Smythe in "Some Baby"; Jan., 1916, as Helen Vincent in "Moonlight Mary"; at the Cort Theatre, Chicago, later in the same year, played Blanche Wheeler in "Fair and Warmer," nearly 300 times; at the Cohan Theatre, Sept., 1917, played Ethel Sinclair in "Here Comes the Bride"; at the Republic, Dec., 1917, Nita Leslie in "Parlour, Bedroom, and Bath"; at the Bijou, Aug., 1918, Leckey Campbell in "Double Exposure"; at the Shubert, Oct., 1918, Enid Vaughan in "Sometime"; at the Thirty-ninth Street, Sept., 1919, Beatrix Vanderdyke in "Scandal"; at the Klaw Theatre, Mar., 1921, Theodora Gloucester in "Nice People"; at the Klaw Theatre, Oct., 1923, Marjorie Benton in "Nobody's Business" · at the Forty-ninth Street Theatre, Mar., 1924, Nancy Angeline Farr in "Nancy Ann"; at the Thirty-ninth Street Theatre, Nov., 1924, Joan Millett in "Parasites"; Hudson, May, 1925, Maria Avilon in "His Queen"; Klaw, Nov., 1926, played Carol Churt in "This Was a Man"; Music Box, Dec., 1926, Roxie Hart in "Chicago";

Little, Feb., 1929, Kitty Brown in "Let Us Be Gay"; Belasco, Nov., 1931, Abby Fane in "Brief Moment"; Selwyn, June, 1933, Julie Leander in "Shooting Star"; Morosco, Oct., 1934, Florrie Solomon in "Spring Song"; at the Shubert, New Haven, Jan., 1939, played Kate Colman in "What Every Woman Wants"; re-appeared on the stage, after seven years absence, at Wilmington, Del., Sept., 1946, as Natasha Smith in "The Temporary Mrs. Smith"; appeared in films, 1937, in "John Meade's Woman." *Address:* 912 Fifth Avenue, New York City, U.S.A. *Telephone No.:* Butterfield 8–5226.

LA RUE, Grace, actress and vocalist; *b.* Kansas City, Mo., U.S.A., 1882; *m.* (1) Byron Chandler (mar. dis.); (2) Hale Hamilton; made her first appearance on the stage at the age of eleven, when she appeared in Julia Marlowe's Company; subsequently she drifted into "vaudeville," and, with a partner, appeared as Burke and La Rue; later she appeared in musical comedy and extravaganza; at the Casino, New York, 3 Nov., 1906, appeared as Evelyn Ormsby in "The Blue Moon"; at the Jardin de Paris, July, 1907, played Pocahontas in "The Follies of 1907," and June, 1908, Miss Manhattan in "The Follies of 1908"; at the Hackett Theatre, Apr., 1910, played Molly May in a play of that name; at the Lyric, New York, Oct., 1910, Henriette in "The Troubadour"; at the Herald Square, Dec., 1911, appeared as Mrs. Elizabeth Killigrew in "Betsy"; in 1913 she came to London, and made her first appearance at the Palace Theatre, 4 Aug., 1913, where she created something of a sensation by her singing of a song, "You made me Love you—I didn't want to do it"; she then appeared at the Lyric Theatre, London, Dec., 1913, as Hella Bruckner in "The Girl who Didn't"; on her return to America in 1914 appeared in "vaudeville"; at the Geo. M. Cohen Theatre, 1917, appeared in "Hitchy-Koo"; at the Lyric, New York, Oct., 1919, played Gracie in "Nothing But Love"; at the Cort Theatre, Chicago, Feb., 1920, appeared as April Blair in "Dear Me," and played the same part at the Republic Theatre, New York, Jan., 1921; at the Music Box, Oct., 1922, appeared in "The Music Box Revue," in which she played for a year; opened in "vaudeville," Oct., 1923, at Palace, Chicago; reappeared in London, at the Coliseum, July, 1924, appearing in a singing act, and also in a sketch, with her husband, entitled "Dangerous Advice"; subsequently toured the English provinces; appeared at Los Angeles, Jan., 1926, in "The Love Call"; at the Winter Garden, New York, Apr., 1928, appeared in "The Greenwich Village Follies"; at the Fulton, May, 1929, played Eve Martin in "Stepping Out."
(Died 12 Mar., 1956; age 74)

LASHWOOD, George, comedian and descriptive vocalist; *m.* Lottie Williams; made his first appearance on the stage in the provinces in 1883; made his first appearance in London, 5 Aug., 1889, at the Middlesex, Gatti's, Charing Cross, and Gatti's, Westminster, singing "The Last Bullet"; "The Tipster"; and "My Poll"; has since appeared at all the leading London and provincial halls; has introduced a number of popular songs, among which may be mentioned "The Death or Glory Boys"; "Fol-de-rol-lol"; "The only girl I ever loved"; "The Gallant Twenty-first"; "Motherland"; "In the twi-twi-twilight"; "There's a girl wanted there"; "Three women to every man"; "Where are the lads of the village, to-night?" etc.

LATHAM, Frederick G., producer; *b.* England; *m.* Cynthia Brooke; was for many years engaged as stage-manager and producer at Drury Lane, for Sir Augustus Harris, Adelphi and Vaudeville for A. and S. Gatti, and other London theatres, and was responsible for the staging of many successful plays at those theatres for several years up to 1897; in that year he went to America to become manager for the Maurice Grau Opera company, at the Metropolitan Opera House; after leaving that company he staged many musical plays in New York, including "Mdlle. Modiste," 1905; "The Red Mill," 1906; "The Fair Co-Ed," 1908; "The Old Town," 1910; "The Slim Princess, 1910; "The Red Widow," 1911; "The Enchantress," 1911: "The Rose Maid," "The Fire-Fly," "Sybil," "The Madcap Princess," "Sweethearts," "Princess Pat," "The Only Girl," "The Century Girl," " Eileen," "The Echo," "The Canary," "Apple Blossoms," "The Night Boat," "The Half-Moon," "The Love Song," "The Candy Shop," etc.; of late years has directed motion pictures with great success; commenced film career 1929, and has directed such pictures as "Bull-Dog Drummond," "Three Wise Fools," "The Wandering Jew," "The Great Pursuit," etc.

(Died 31 Jan., 1943; age 90)

LATHBURY, Stanley, actor; *b.* Alderley Edge, Cheshire, 22 Apr., 1873; *s.* of Henry Lathbury and his wife Elizabeth Agnes (Ross); *e.* privately; *m.* Rita Rothwell; spent one year in his father's office before joining Miss Sarah Thorne at Margate, where he made his first appearance on the stage at the Theatre Royal, 10 June, 1895, as Harold in " An Ideal Husband "; he remained at Margate until 1897, playing nearly one hundred parts; made his first appearance in London, at the Haymarket, 17 Sept., 1898, as Andrew Mealmaker in " The Little Minister," as understudy to Holman Clark; he remained at the Haymarket until 1900; in 1903, visited Australia and New Zealand; at the Court, 1909, played a Shakespearean season with Gerald Lawrence and Fay Davis; and in the same year, accompanied them to Berlin; from 1910 to 1914, paid three visits to the United States; at the Criterion, Oct., 1915, played Nixon Trippett in " A Little Bit of Fluff," which he played throughout the long run of over 1200 performances, except for the short time he appeared in the same part at the 39th Street Theatre, New York, Aug., 1916; at the Strand, Dec., 1918, appeared as Lord Wickham in " Scandal "; Oct., 1920, as Fluellen in " Henry V "; Jan., 1921, as Tom Winch in " The Safety Match "; at the St. Martin's. Mar 1921, played Dr. Alliot in " A Bill of

Divorcement "; at the Strand, Dec., 1922, Abe Gray in " Treasure Island "; at the Everyman, Sept., 1923, and Garrick, Oct., 1923, Scrubby in " Outward Bound "; at the Little, Nov., 1924, Hammerway in " Falling Leaves "; Kingsway, Apr., 1925, Pothinus in " Caesar and Cleopatra "; Everyman, July, 1925, Dr. Genoni in Pirandello's " Henry IV "; Barnes, Sept., 1925, John D'Urbeyfield in " Tess of the D'Urbervilles "; Everyman, Jan., 1926, Friday in " The Man Who Was Thursday "; Apr., 1926, John in " Benediction "; Royalty, Oct., 1926, Judge Atherton in " Children of the Moon "; appeared with the New Shakespearean Company at Stratford-on-Avon, July-Sept., 1927; from Oct.-Dec., 1927, toured in Egypt with Robert Atkins in Shakespearean repertory; Prince of Wales's, Jan., 1928, again played Scrubby in " Outward Bound "; Lyric, Hammersmith, Apr., 1928, Justice Woodcock in " Love in a Village "; Comedy, Aug., 1928, Peters in " The Devil's Host "; Court, Feb., 1929, Ned and Sir Robert Mortimer in " The Rumour "; Strand, Apr., 1929, Si Gidali in " The Shadow of the East "; Haymarket, Apr., 1929, Pompey in " Measure for Measure "; Arts, June, 1929, Roderic Laverton in " Sybarites "; Lyric, June, 1929, Mr. Armitage in " Murder on the Second Floor"; Kingsway, Nov., 1929, Crabtree in " The School for Scandal"; King's, Hammersmith, Aug., 1930, Ramsey in " The Scorpion"; St. James's, Feb., 1931, Uncle Emile in " Etienne"; London Coliseum, Apr., 1931, Professor Hinzelmann in " White Horse Inn"; Phoenix (for G. Club), May, 1932, Mr. Marsh in " Rings on Her Fingers"; " Q," Oct., 1932, The Coroner in " Crime on the Hill"; Embassy, Nov., 1932, Alquist in " R.U.R."; Westminster, Feb., 1933 (for the Stage Society), The Guv'nor in " Oh, Hang!"; Apr.–Sept., 1933, appeared at the Stratford Memorial Theatre; Westminster, Sept., 1933, the Innkeeper in " The Man With a Load of Mischief"; Ambassadors', Nov., 1933, the Doctor in " Cabbages and Kings"; Royalty, Mar., 1934, Arthur Robertson in " Jane and Genius"; Open Air Theatre, May,

1934, Adam in "As You Like It"; appeared at the Malvern Festival, July, 1934; New, Sept., 1934, Barnabas in "A Man's House"; Kingsway, Nov., 1934, Isaac Disraeli in "Young Mr. Disraeli"; Royalty, Mar., 1935, Mr. Roxborough in "Frolic Wind"; May, 1935, Count Maurice in "The King of Rome"; Westminster, Oct., 1935, Dean Lesley in "Lady Patricia"; Ambassadors', Nov., 1935, Henry Lambeth in "Our Own Lives"; Daly's, Feb., 1936, Rev. Arthur Shapham in "Petticoat Fever"; Embassy, Apr., 1936, Perillard in "Return to Yesterday"; Imperial, New York, Nov., 1936, First Gravedigger in "Hamlet," with Leslie Howard and subsequently toured in the same part; Daly's, London, July, 1937, Rev. Charles Keene in "The First Legion"; Duke of York's, Oct., 1937, Latazaka in "Susannah and the Elders"; Westminster, Jan., 1938, Corbaccio in "Volpone" and May, 1938, William in "You Never Can Tell"; Haymarket, Oct., 1938, Mr. Podmore in "On Borrowed Time"; St. Martin's, June, 1939, Peter the Great in "Bridge of Sighs"; toured in Canada, 1939, with Maurice Colbourne and Barry Jones's company, in "Charles the King" and "Tobias and the Angel"; after returning to England, appeared at the New, Aug., 1940, as Scrubby in a revival of "Outward Bound"; next toured, for E.N.S.A., 1940, as Dr. Haggett in "The Late Christopher Bean"; was with the B.B.C. repertory company, 1941, and in 1942, at the Repertory Theatre, Birmingham, played Churdles Ash in "The Farmer's Wife"; again appeared with B.B.C., 1943; Prince of Wales's, Apr., 1944, played the Lord Justice-Clerk in "The Rest is Silence"; Lyric, Oct., 1944, Mr. Harding in "Scandal at Barchester"; Embassy, Apr., 1948, Marsden in "Portrait of Hickory"; Boltons, Aug., 1948, Mr. Justice Wills in "Oscar Wilde"; has also appeared in films. *Favourite parts:* Dogberry in "Much Ado About Nothing," and Scrubby in "Outward Bound." *Club:* Green Room.

LATHOM, Earl of (*see* Wilbraham, Edward).

LATIMER, Edyth, actress; *b.* Leadville, N.S.W., *e.* St. Vincent's College, Pott's Point, N.S.W.; *m.* William Haviland; studied violin under Kerr Kretchmann, and gained gold medal at the age of fourteen; when the late Wilson Barrett visited Australia in 1898, ran away from school and succeeded in persuading that gentleman to give her an engagement; she came to England in 1898 with Barrett, and remained a member of his company until his death in 1904; made her first appearance in London at the Lyceum, 14 Oct., 1899, as Maude Pevensey in "Man and His Makers"; from 1899-1904, played the following among other parts: Berenice in "The Sign of the Cross," Emilia in "Othello," Sylvia in "Man and His Makers," Elswitha in "The Christian King," etc., and was the last Mercia to play with him in "The Sign of the Cross"; joined William Haviland in 1905, for South African tour, as leading lady, and played Katusha in "Resurrection," Leah Kleschna, Ada Ingot in "David Garrick," and Olivia in the play of that name; during a second tour in South Africa in 1906 played Lady Macbeth, Portia, Nancy Sykes in "Oliver Twist," Miranda in "The Tempest," and other leading parts; at the Garrick, Feb., 1908, appeared as Princess Mary in "The Woman of Kronstadt"; Sept., 1908, played Minna Hart in "Idols," and Feb., 1909, Elsie Vernette in "Samson"; at the Comedy, Sept., 1909, appeared as Emily Chapman in "Smith"; at the Criterion, Jan., 1911, appeared as Fanny Perry in "Is Matrimony a Failure?"; at Bournemouth, July, 1911, played Margaret in "In the Clouds"; at the Court, July, 1912, played Mrs. Bodman in "The Hanging Outlook"; at the Apollo, Aug., 1912, appeared as Lucienne Bogard in "The Glad Eye"; at the Comedy, Aug., 1913, played Juanita in "The Scarlet Band"; at Wallack's, New York, Oct., 1914, Agnes Wickfield in "The Highway of Life" ("David Copperfield"); in 1915 toured as Domini Enfilden in "The Garden of Allah"; at the Fulton Theatre, New York, May, 1916, succeeded Margaret Anglin as Mrs.

Arbuthnot in "A Woman of No Importance"; Dec., 1916, played Katherine in "The Master"; during 1917-18 toured in "The Man who Stayed at Home"; at the Belmont New York, Nov., 1918, played Marie Breschofska in "The Little Brother." *Hobbies :* Riding and driving.

LATIMER, Sally, actress, director, and manager; *b.* London, 17 Dec., 1910; *d.* of Richard Latimer and his wife Fanny (Hornblow); *e.* privately; *m.* Wilfred Bodsworth; studied for the stage at the Royal Academy of Dramatic Art, and the Guildhall School of Music; made her first appearance on the stage at the Westminster Theatre, 17 Dec., 1934, as Ono in "The Faithful"; during 1936, toured Wales in "Taffy"; founded the Amersham Repertory Company, Dec., 1936, where nearly five hundred plays were produced; she played leading parts in many of these, including "Ghosts," "A Doll's House," "Hedda Gabler," "Candida," "Arms and the Man," "Pygmalion," "Amphitryon 38," "Private Lives," "Blithe Spirit," "Gaslight," "A Bill of Divorcement," "The Circle," "Young Woodley," "Uncle Vanya," "Watch on the Rhine," "The Importance of Being Earnest," "The Guardsman," "Autumn Crocus," "The Merchant of Venice," "Much Ado About Nothing," "Twelfth Night," "The Cherry Orchard," "The Flashing Stream," "The Linden Tree," "Love in Idleness," "Life With Father," etc., and also appeared in many new plays produced there; founded the Mobile Theatre, 1947, of which she is Director; she relinquished her management of the Amersham Playhouse, Mar., 1949; with the Liverpool Repertory Theatre, May, 1951, appeared as the Princess of Eboli in "That Lady"; Playhouse, Nottingham, Nov., 1956, played Pauline Viardot in "The End of Summer"; toured, May, 1960, as Ilse Richter in "A Piece of Silver"; television programmes in which she has appeared include the "Inspector Maigret" series. *Favourite parts:* Nora in "A Doll's House," Hilda in "The Master Builder," and Karen in "The Flashing Stream." *Recreations:* Reading and cooking.

Address: The Manor House, Guiting Power, Nr. Cheltenham, Glos. *Telephone No.:* Guiting Power 355.

LATONA, Jen, comedienne and entertainer at the piano; *b.* Birmingham, 15 Dec., 1881; *d.* of Henry William Carter and his wife Jane (Slade); *e.* Edgbaston; *m.* Frank Latona; made her first appearance as a child of eight as a solo pianist, at the Town Hall, Birmingham; made her first appearance on the music-hall stage at the Alhambra, Brighton, in 1894, as a vocalist and trick pianist, as Jenny Gabrielle; first appeared in London, at the Middlesex, 1894; for ten years, from 1900, appeared, in conjunction with her husband, as Frank and Jen Latona; since 1910, has appeared by herself; has appeared at almost every hall of note in the United Kingdom, has been twice round the world, and has appeared all over the United States, Australia, New Zealand and South Africa; has introduced several popular songs to the public, notably " In my airship "; " Rum-tum-tiddle "; " R-R-Rip that Melody "; " I've got rings on my fingers "; " Why do you keep laughing at me ? "; " I'm glad my boy grew up to be a soldier "; " Because I'm married now "; " Hush, here comes the dream-man "; " Keep on swinging me, Charlie "; " Maggie McLaren "; " When the wedding bells go ding-dong "; is the author and composer of most of her songs. *Recreations :* Sewing, poultry farming, and anything domestic. *Address :* Titus Lodge, Middleton Hall Road, King's Norton, Worcestershire.

LA TROBE, Charles, stage director and producer; *b.* London, 23 Apr., 1879; *s.* of Charles Albert La Trobe and his wife Carlotta (Addison); *e.* Bradfield College; *m.* Evelyn Dane; made his first appearance on the stage at the Grand Theatre, Derby, Nov., 1898, in "The Liars"; toured the provinces for seven years with Ellen Terry, George Alexander, Edward Compton, etc., as actor and stage-manager; accompanied the Benson company to the West Indies, 1903, and Marie

Tempest to the United States, 1904; was stage-manager for the Gaston Mayer French seasons, at the Royalty Theatre, 1906, followed by a matinée tour with Madame Sarah Bernhardt in the provinces; subsequently with Otho Stuart at Wyndham's, Adelphi, and Apollo, 1906, and Court Theatre, 1907, and with Lewis Waller at Lyric, 1907; stage-manager at the Haymarket, 1908–15; served in France, as Captain and Adjutant of the 2/7th Warwicks, 1916–18; won the Military Cross, 1917, and was mentioned in dispatches, 1918; staff-captain, 1918–19; at the Lyric, 1919, was stage-director for the production of "Romeo and Juliet"; subsequently at the Comedy, Alhambra, and Duke of York's; returned to the Haymarket, Apr., 1920, as stage-director for "Mary Rose," and has remained there, having been responsible for over 100 productions to 1946; appointed a Director of the Frederick Harrison Trust Ltd., Sept., 1934; acted as manager and stage-director for Tennent Plays Ltd., for John Gielgud's repertory season on tour and at the Haymarket, 1943–5; has represented the Haymarket Theatre as stage director and manager for the following plays: "Lady Windermere's Fan," "The Importance of Being Earnest" (Command Performance), 1945; "The Eagle Has Two Heads," "Present Laughter," "The Glass Menagerie," Ruth Draper Season, 1948; "The Heiress," 1949; "The Second Mrs. Tanqueray," 1950; "A Penny For a Song," "Waters of the Moon," 1951; "The Apple Cart," "Aren't We All?" "A Day By the Sea," 1953; "The Matchmaker," 1954; "Nina," "The Queen and the Rebels," 1955; "The Strong Are Lonely," "The Chalk Garden," 1956; "Flowering Cherry," 1957; "Two For the Seesaw," "The Pleasure of His Company," 1959, "Ross," 1960; retired, 1960. *Recreations:* Gardening and motoring. *Club:* Garrick. *(Died 10 Sept., 1967; age 88)*

LAUDER, Sir Harry (cr. 1919), Scotch comedian, author, and composer; *b.* Portobello, 4 Aug., 1870; *s.* of John Lauder and his wife Isabella (MacLennan;) *e.* Arbroath; *m.* Annie Vallance; as a lad worked in a flax mill; for ten years worked in a coal mine; made his first appearance on a public stage at Arbroath, 24 Aug., 1882, in a travelling show competition, when he sang "I'm a Gentleman Still"; had had some experience as an amateur before making his first professional appearance in Scotland; made his first appearance in London, at Gatti's, Westminster, 19 Mar., 1900, scoring an instantaneous success, when he sang "Tobermory," "Callaghan-Call Again," and "The Lass of Killiecrankie";

he opened at the Royal, Holborn, 24 Dec., 1900, and was subsequently engaged at the Oxford and London Pavilion, where he established his reputation; from that date his success was phenomenal and for years he earned the highest salary of any music-hall artist; has appeared at all the leading London and provincial halls, has toured through the United States, Africa, and Australia; was Commanded to appear before the late King Edward in 1908, at Rufford Abbey; during the Great War, 1914–18, he organised many concerts and entertainments for charitable purposes, raising very large sums of money; he also gave concerts on the French front, and was knighted in 1919 for his services; at the Shaftesbury Theatre, Dec., 1916, appeared in the *revue* " Three Cheers ! "; toured South Africa and Australia, 1920, returning in Dec., 1920; appeared at the Palace Theatre, Jan., 1921; has since toured all over the British Dominions; in 1929 was in New Zealand and Australia; reappeared in London, after a three years' absence, at the London Palladium, and Finsbury Park Empire, Dec., 1930; appeared at the Victoria Palace, Oct., 1931; during 1931–32, was still touring in provincial variety theatres; in Sept., 1932, sailed again for Canada and the United States, for his twenty-fifth tour; reappeared in London, at the Alhambra, Oct., 1934; again toured the provinces, 1934–35; is the author of "The Night Before," produced at Boston, Mass., 1915, and at Edinburgh, 1916; "Harry Lauder: At Home and On Tour," a small volume of reminiscences, 1907; "Roamin' in the

Gloamin'," further reminiscences, also of the book, "A Minstrel in France," a book of the war; "Wee Drappies," 1931; among numerous popular songs which he has introduced may be mentioned the following, "Hey, Donal'"; "I love a lassie"; "Killiecrankie"; "Mr. John Mackie"; "The Saftest of the Family"; "She is ma Daisy"; "Stop yer tickling, Jock"; "Tobermory"; "We parted on the Shore"; "The Weddin' of Sandy McNab"; "When I get back again tae Bonnie Scotland"; "Just a wee Deoch-an-Doris"; "Queen amang the Heather"; "Fou the nou"; "I've loved her ever since she was a baby"; "Roamin' in the Gloamin'"; "It's nice to get up in the morning"; "The Last of the Sandies"; "That's the reason noo I wear a Kilt"; "The Laddies who Fought and Won"; "The Waggle of the Kilt"; "My Bonnie, Bonnie Jean"; "The Kilty Lads"; "She is my Rosie"; "Bonnie Wee Annie"; "The Same as his Faither did before him"; "The End of the Road"; has also appeared in film versions of his songs, and in "Huntingtower," "Auld Lang Syne," and "The End of the Road."
(Died 26 Feb., 1950; age 79)

LAUGHTON, Charles, actor; *b.* Scarborough, 1 July, 1899; *s.* of Robert Laughton and his wife Elizabeth (Conlon); *e.* Stonyhurst College; *m.* Elsa Lanchester; studied for the stage at the Royal Academy of Dramatic Art, where he gained the Gold Medal; made his first appearance on the stage at the Barnes Theatre, 28 Apr., 1926, as Osip in "The Government Inspector," in which he also appeared at the Gaiety in May; since that date has played the following parts: Everyman, July, 1926, Rummel in "The Pillars of Society"; Barnes, Sept., 1926, Ephikhôdof in "The Cherry Orchard"; Oct., 1926, Vassily Solyony in "The Three Sisters"; Duke of York's, Dec., 1926, Ficsur in "Liliom"; Prince's, Feb., 1927, General Markeloff in "The Greater Love"; Royalty, Mar., 1927, Cantavalle in "Naked"; Prince's, Mar., 1927, Sir James Hartley in "Angela"; Apr., 1927, Creon in

"Medea"; made a great success when he appeared at the Criterion, June, 1927, as Frank K. Pratt in "The Happy Husband"; at the Court, Oct., 1927, played Count Pahlen in "Paul I"; made a further great impression when he appeared at the Court, Nov., 1927, as Mr. Prohack in a play of that name; he next appeared at the Little, Feb., 1928, as Mr. Crispin in "A Man with Red Hair"; at the Arts, Apr., 1928, played Ben Jonson in George Moore's "The Making of an Immortal"; scored another great success at the Prince of Wales's, May, 1928, when he played Hercule Poirot in "Alibi"; at the Haymarket, Dec., 1928, appeared as Mr. Pickwick in the play of that name; at the Strand, July, 1929, played Jacques Blaise in "Beauty; Apollo, Oct., 1929, Harry Heegan and the First Soldier in "The Silver Tassie"; Vaudeville, Jan., 1930, Brigadier-General Archibald Root in "French Leave"; Wyndham's, Apr., 1930, Tony Perelli in "On the Spot"; St. James's, May, 1931, William Marble in "Payment Deferred"; then went to New York, where he made his first appearance, at the Lyceum, 24 Sept., 1931, in the last-mentioned part; at the Booth Theatre, Feb., 1932, played Hercule Poirot in "The Fatal Alibi" ("Alibi"); on returning to London, joined the Old Vic.-Sadler's Wells Company Oct., 1933, and during the season played Lopahin in "The Cherry Orchard," King Henry in "Henry VIII," Angelo in "Measure for Measure," Prospero in "The Tempest," Rev. Canon Chasuble in "The Importance of Being Earnest," Tattle in "Love for Love," and Macbeth; in 1936, he went to Paris, and on 9 May, 1936, appeared at the Comédie Française, as Sganarelle in the second act of Molière's "Le Médecin malgré lui," the first English actor to appear at that theatre; he acted the part in French and received an ovation; at the London Palladium, Dec., 1936, played Captain Hook in "Peter Pan"; commenced film career in England, 1929, appearing in "Piccadilly"; went to Hollywood 1932, and appeared in several pictures; returned to England and appeared in "The Private Life of Henry

VIII"; returned to Hollywood and appeared in "White Woman," "The Barretts of Wimpole Street," "Ruggles of Red Gap," "Les Misérables," "Mutiny on the Bounty"; in 1937, with Erich Pommer, founded the Mayflower Picture Corporation, in England; returned to America, and subsequently became a naturalized American subject; continued to appear in films, then at the Coronet, Los Angeles, July, 1947, played the title-*rôle* in "Galileo," which he also adapted; Maxine Elliott, New York, Dec., 1947, again appeared as Galileo; since that date has frequently given readings from the Bible, and Standard Works, all over the United States; at Hollywood, June, 1950, appeared in "The Cherry Orchard"; at the New Century, New York, Nov., 1951, appeared as the Devil in "Don Juan in Hell," which he also directed; at the same theatre, Feb., 1953, directed the production of "John Brown's Body," which he adapted from Stephen Vincent Benet's poem; at the Plymouth, Jan., 1954, directed the production of "The Caine Mutiny Court Martial," which ran for a year; Martin Beck, Oct., 1956, played Andrew Undershaft, and also directed "Major Barbara"; returned to London, and at the New Theatre, May, 1958, played Richard Brough, and also directed "The Party"; Shakespeare Memorial Theatre, Stratford-on Avon, 1959 season, played Bottom in "A Midsummer Night's Dream," and the title-*rôle* in "King Lear"; his adaptation of "The Life of Galileo" was produced at the Mermaid, London, June, 1960; his biography, "Charles Laughton and I," was written by his wife and published in 1938. *Recreation:* Gardening.

(Died 15 Dec., 1962; age 63)

LAURIER, Jay, actor; *b.* Birmingham, 31 May, 1879; *s.* of Charles Chapman and his wife Jane (Sargent); *e.* Birmingham; *m.* (1) Sybil Viney, (2) Mollie Griffin; made his first appearance on the stage at the Public Hall, Abertillery, 1896, in "The Arabian Nights"; for many years was a very popular artist in variety, appearing in the principal music-halls all over the country and the West-End halls in

London; among his more popular songs may be mentioned "I'm always doing Something Silly," "Ring O'Roses," "S'what's S'nicer Than a S'nice S'ice S'ice," etc.; also played pantomime engagements at the leading provincial theatres; made his first appearance on the London stage proper, at the Queen's Theatre, 17 Apr., 1907, when he appeared as Gregory in "Tom Jones"; at the London Hippodrome, Dec., 1921, played Miffins in "Jack and the Beanstalk"; London Pavilion, Aug., 1922, Meander in "Phi-Phi"; Daly's, June, 1925, Pamphylosin "Cleopatra"; King's, Glasgow, Dec., 1925, Picasse in "Riquette"; toured in 1928, as Shortie McGee in "Oh, Kay!"; in 1929, as Tommy Robins in "Change Over"; at Drury Lane, Dec., 1929, played Rudolph the Reckless in "The Sleeping Beauty"; Prince Edward, Mar., 1931, the Baillee in "Les Cloches de Corneville"; Prince's, Manchester, Dec., 1931, Horace in "Goody Two-shoes"; London Hippodrome, Sept., 1932, Nisch in "The Merry Widow"; at the Theatre Royal, Birmingham, Dec., 1933, played Buttons in "Cinderella," and played the same part at the Empire, Liverpool, Dec., 1934; London Coliseum, Apr., 1935, Prohaska in "Dancing City"; Alhambra, Glasgow, Dec., 1935, again played Buttons in "Cinderella"; during 1936, toured as Popoff in "The Merry Widow"; joined the Old Vic. company, 1937, and appeared there from Sept.–Nov., as Alfred Doolittle in "Pygmalion" and Pompey in "Measure for Measure"; Stratford-on-Avon, 1938 season, the Porter in "Macbeth," Sir Toby Belch in "Twelfth Night," Launce in "The Two Gentlemen of Verona," Bottom in "A Midsummer Night's Dream," Stephano in "The Tempest"; Adelphi (for English School Theatre Society), Nov., 1938, Touchstone in "As You Like It"; Stratford-on-Avon, 1939 season, Christopher Sly in "The Taming of the Shrew," Touchstone, and Dogberry in "Much Ado About Nothing"; Kingsway, Feb., 1940, again played Sir Toby Belch, Dogberry, and the First Gravedigger in "Hamlet," and Mar., 1940, Christopher Sly; Stoll, Dec., 1941, played Simple Simon in "Babes in the Wood";

toured, 1943, in "Night of the Garter"; toured, 1944, as Tweedlepunch in "Florodora"; Palace, Mar., 1945, played Frosch in "Gay Rosalinda"; Aldwych, Oct., 1946, Dogberry in "Much Ado About Nothing"; Savoy, May, 1947, Sir Toby Belch in "Twelfth Night"; has also appeared in numerous films. *Recreations:* Golf and gardening. *(Died Apr., 1969; age 89)*

LAURILLARD, Edward, manager; *b.* 20 April 1870; Rotterdam, Holland, *s.* of John Laurillard and his wife Marie (Chastel); *e.* Osnabrück and Paris; *m.* (1) Priscilla O'Dowd (mar. dis.); (2) Adrah Fair (mar. dis.); was first engaged in a managerial capacity, at Terry's Theatre, 1894, for the production of "King Kodak"; subsequently responsible for the productions of "The Gay Parisienne," "The Lady Slavey," "The Dandy Fifth," etc.; at the Royalty, 1897, presented Louie Freear in "Oh! Susannah!"; also toured in the United States; at the Savoy, 1904, was responsible for the production of "The Love Birds"; subsequently became manager of the New Gallery Cinema, Regent Street, and at one time controlled no fewer than twenty-five cinema theatres; entered into partnership with George Grossmith, 1914, and under their joint management the following plays were produced: "Potash and Perlmutter," Queen's, 1914; "To-Night's the Night," Gaiety, 1915; "On Trial," Lyric, 1915; "Theodore and Co.," Gaiety, 1916; "The Only Girl," Apollo, 1916; "Mr. Manhattan," Prince of Wales's, 1916; "Yes, Uncle," Shaftesbury, 1917; "Tilly of Bloomsbury," Apollo, 1919; "Kissing Time," The Winter Garden, 1919; "Baby Bunting," Shaftesbury, 1919; "The Little Whopper," Shaftesbury, 1920; "The Naughty Princess," Adelphi, 1920; "The Great Lover," Shaftesbury, 1920; "A Night Out," The Winter Garden, 1920; "The Betrothal," Gaiety, 1921; "Faust-on-Toast," Gaiety, 1921; he retired from the joint-directorship of the firm in June, 1921; subsequently became lessee and manager of the Apollo Theatre; in April, 1922, he produced "Love's

Awakening" at the Empire, and in conjunction with Sir Alfred Butt, in Sept., 1922, "The Smith Family"; in Feb., 1923, produced "The Cousin from Nowhere" at the Prince's, and in Oct. 1923, at the Little Theatre, "Little Revue Starts at Nine o'Clock"; went to America, 1924, and produced "A Night Out," etc.; returned to London, 1927, and produced "The Butter and Egg Man," at the Garrick; in Apr., 1928, opened the new Piccadilly Theatre, with "Blue Eyes." *Clubs:* Eccentric and Stage Golfing Society. *(Died 7 May, 1936; age 66)*

LAVALLIÈRE, Eve, French actress; *b.* at Naples; made her first appearance on the stage at the Théâtre des Variétés, Paris, 1892, as Orestes in "La Belle Hélène" at the same theatre has appeared very successfully as Jacqueline in "Le Carnet du Diable," 1895; Mimile, in "Le Pompier de Service"; Lucie in "Les Petites Barnett," 1898; in "Le Nouveau Jeu," 1898; as Marie Avoine, in "Le Vieux Marcheur," 1899; Chochotte, in "Education de Prince," 1900; Joséphine in "La Veine," 1901; also in "Les Deux Écoles," 1902; "Le Sire de Vergy," 1903; "Le Beau Jeune Homme," 1903; "La Revue de Centenaire," 1906; Miquette in "Miquette et sa Mère," 1907; Marguerite Talloire in "Le Faux Pas," 1907; Yvonne Janson in "L'Oiseau Blessé," 1908; "Ange," 1909; Adrienne in "Le bois Sacré," 1910; Geo. Burdan in "Les Petits," 1912 (at the Antoine); at the Variétés, 1912, Marthe in "Le Roi," Brigitte Touchard in "L'Habit Vert"; at the Variétés, 1913, played Crevette in "La Dame de Chez Maxim"; Apr., 1914, played in "Ma Tante d'Honfleur"; appeared at the Garrick, London, 1902, with Jeanne Granier in "La Veine," etc.; at the Ambassadors', London, May, 1915, appeared as Suzanne in "Dieu! Que Les Hommes Sont Bêtes"; has now retired. *(Died 10 July, 1929; age 61)*

LAVEDAN, Henri, French dramatic author; *b.* Orleans, 9 Apr., 1859; *m.* Mathilde Aguez; has written the

following plays : " Une famille," 1890 ; " Le Prince d'Aurec," 1892 ; " Les deux Noblesses," 1894 ; " Viveurs," " Catherine," " Le Nouveau Jeu," 1898 ; " Le Vieux Marcheur," 1899 ; " Le Marquis de Priola," " Varennes " (with G. Lenôtre), 1904 ; " Le Duel " (" The Duel "), 1905 ; " Sire," 1909 ; " Le Goût de Vice," 1911 ; " La Chienne du Roi," 1913 : "Servir," 1913; " Pétard," 1914 ; is a prolific writer, and has over fifty published works to his credit ; is a Commander of the Legion of Honour, Member of the French Academy.
(Died Aug., 1940; age 81)

LAVER, James, C.B.E., Hon. R.E., F.R.S.A., F.R.S.L., dramatic author, novelist, etc.; *b.* Liverpool, 14 Mar. 1899; *s.* of Arthur James Laver and his wife Florence Mary (Barker); *e.* Liverpool Institute and New College, Oxford (B.A.); *m.* Veronica Turleigh; in 1918, served as Second Lieut. in the King's Own (Royal Lancaster) Regiment; appointed assistant-keeper at the Victoria and Albert Museum, 1922; was keeper of the Departments of Engraving, Paintings, Illustrations and Design, 1938–59, and was in charge of the theatrical collections; author of the following plays: "The Circle of Chalk" (from the German), 1928 ; "La Marquise d'Arcis" (with Frank Herz, from the German), 1929 ; "The House that Went to Sea," 1936 ; "The Heart Was Not Burned," 1938 ; "The Swiss Family Robinson" (lyrics), 1938; "Monsieur Trouhadec" (from the French), 1939 ; his novel "Nymph Errant," was dramatized by Romney Brent, 1933 ; gained the Newdigate prize at Oxford, 1921, with his poem "Cervantes"; with George Sheringham, collaborated in "Design in the Theatre," 1927, and contributed "Design for Ballet" to "Robes of Thespis," 1928 ; edited "English Costume of the 19th Century," 1929, and "English Costume of the 18th Century," 1930; author of "Whistler" (biography), 1930; "Nymph Errant," 1932; "Stage Designs by Oliver Messel," 1933; "Taste and Fashion" (French Revolution until To-day), 1938; "Drama: Décor and Costume," 1950; "Oscar Wilde," 1954; "Edwar-

dian Promenade," 1958; "Museum Piece," "Costume in the Theatre," 1963; in addition to his works relating to the theatre, has written several novels, collections of short stories, many essays, and numerous books on period costume and fashions, etc.; has lectured on the Theatre, at the Museum, Royal Academy of Dramatic Art, Drama League and Malvern Festival; sometime examiner in history of Drama for London University; received the honour of C.B.E., 1951. *Address:* 4/10 The Glebe, London, S.E.3. *Telephone No.:* Lee Green 3905.

LAVERICK, Beryl, actress; *b.* New Malden, Surrey, 12 June, 1919; *d.* of Eli Laverick and his wife Florence (Ridge); *e.* privately; made her first appearance on the stage at the Little Theatre, 21 Dec., 1932, as Alice in "Alice in Wonderland"; appeared at the London Coliseum, Feb., 1933, as soloist in season of ballet; Little Theatre, Mar., 1933, played Marjorie Fleming in "Scott of Abbotsford"; Apr., 1933, Youth in "Overture"; Duke of York's, Dec., 1933, again played Alice; Strand, Mar., 1934, Verna in "The Bride"; Duke of York's, Dec., 1934, "Alice in Wonderland"; Lyric, Hammersmith, Dec., 1935, Tiny in "The Magic Marble"; Westminster, June, 1936, Jonna in "The Emperor of Make Believe"; "Q," June, 1936, Sofya in "Uncle Vanya"; Garrick, May, 1937, Alftruda Bendish in "Sarah Simple"; at Oxford, for the O.U.D.S., Feb., 1938, Hero in "Much Ado About Nothing"; Playhouse, Apr., 1938, the Chrysalis in "The Insect Play"; Adelphi (for the English Schools Theatre Society), Nov., 1938, Audrey in "As You Like It"; Savoy (for Repertory Players), Dec., 1938, Lottie in "Two Roses"; in June, 1939, appeared with "stock" company at the Alexandra, Stoke Newington; has appeared in films in "The Constant Nymph," "The Unfinished Symphony," "A Girl Must Live," etc. *Hobby:* Animals. *Recreations:* Drawing and riding. *Address:* Highland Mansions, Tranquil Vale, Blackheath, S.E.3. *Telephone No.:* Lee Green 2546.

LA VERNE, Lucille, actress; *b.* near Memphis, Tenn., U.S.A., 8 Nov., 1872; made her first appearance on the stage as a child, and at the age of fourteen played Juliet and Lady Macbeth; made her first appearance in New York, at the Broadway Theatre, 3 Mar., 1888, in a small part in "La Tosca," with Fanny Davenport; next played May in "May Blossom"; in 1889, joined Fanny Ellsler's company; at the People's Theatre, 7 Apr., 1890, played Chrissy Rogers in "The Governess"; she also toured as Ethel in "Judge Not," and "The Egyptian"; in 1890–91, was with Margaret Mather in "Notre Dame"; made her first success in New York, when she appeared at the Garden Theatre, Jan., 1894, and played the part of Corin in "As You Like It," in an "all-woman" cast, in a performance given by the Professional Women's League; at the Herald Square Theatre, New York, 15 Apr., 1895, played Patsy in "Pudd'nhead Wilson," with the late Frank Mayo, in which she made a substantial success; Manhattan Opera House, Feb., 1898, played Betsy in "Way Down East"; she specialized in character parts and has many successes to her credit; played lead at the Grand, Baldwin, and Columbia Theatres, San Francisco, playing such widely diversified parts as Drusilla in "The Dancing Girl," La Frochard in "The Two Orphans," Camille, Frou-Frou, etc.; made a great success when she toured in the leading part in "Lady Windermere's Fan"; for fifteen years took her own company to Richmond, Va., where the La Verne Empire was built and named after her; appeared at the Duke of York's, London, 13 Sept., 1905, as Clancy, the old negress, in "Clarice," making an instantaneous success, which was repeated when she appeared in the same part at the Garrick, New York, Oct., 1906; at the Garrick, New York, Mar., 1908, played Minerva Ringler in "The Easterner"; at the Astor Theatre, Nov., 1909, played in "Seven Days"; subsequently starred as Aunt Mary Watkins in "The Rejuvenation of Aunt Mary," and as Katherine Wetherill in "Mother"; in 1911, appeared as Ann Boyd in her own adaptation of a play of that name,

from the novel; during 1913, toured in "The Rejuvenation of Aunt Mary"; Longacre, Jan., 1914, played Mrs. Owen Denbigh in "The House of Bondage"; at the Hudson, Jan., 1916, played the Great She-Bear in "The Cinderella Man"; subsequently toured in "Bonnie"; at the Broadhurst, July, 1920, Elzevir Nesbit in "Come Seven"; at the Eltinge, Aug., 1921, Lottie in "Back Pay"; at the Maxine Elliott, Apr., 1922, Magnolia in "The Goldfish"; subsequently played in "On the Stairs"; in 1923, played the Ayah in "East of Suez"; made another big success when she appeared at the Provincetown Theatre, New York, May, 1923, as the Widow Cagle in "Sun-Up," which ran on until 1924 at the Lenox Hill and Princess Theatres; appeared at the Vaudeville, London, May, 1925, in the same part; continued to play in "Sun-Up" in America until 1927; at Los Angeles, 1927, played "Salt Chunk Mary"; at the Lucille La Verne Theatre, New York, Oct., 1928, played in a revival of "Sun-Up," and Jan., 1929, Jessica Dale in "Hot Water"; again visited London, Aug., 1929, and appeared at the Little Theatre in a revival of "Sun-Up"; Sept., 1929, played Shylock in "The Merchant of Venice"; at the Mason Theatre, Los Angeles, Feb., 1932, played Aunt Mallie in "Shining Blackness"; Mansfield, New York, Feb., 1936, Dr. Emma Koloich in "Black Widow"; Suffield, Conn., Sept., 1938, Ma in "Jail for Sale"; has appeared in numerous films, silent and talking. *(Died 4 Mar., 1945; age 72)*

LAW, Arthur, dramatic author; *b.* 22 Mar., 1844; *s.* of Rev. Patrick Comerford Law, of Killaloe and Northrepps; *m.* Fanny Holland, actress and entertainer, for many years a member of the German-Reed company; entered the Army as Ensign, and served eight years with 21st Royal Scots Fusiliers, retiring in 1872 with the rank of Lieutenant; became an actor in 1872, and for some years followed this profession; was intimately associated with Mr. and Mrs. German-Reed's Entertainment, for which he

wrote a number of short plays; adopted play writing as his profession in 1882, since which date he has written a number of successful pieces, notably "Hope," 1882; "The Mystery of a Hansom Cab," 1888; "The Judge," 1890; "The Magic Opal," 1893; "The New Boy," 1894; "The Ladies' Idol," 1895; "The Sea Flower," 1898; "A Country Mouse," 1902; "Artful Miss Dearing," 1909, etc.
(Died 2 Apr., 1913; age 69)

LAW, Mary, violinist; *b.* London, 1 Apr., 1891; *d.* of Edward Gibbon Law and his wife Jane (Margerison); *e.* Royal College of Music, Royal Academy of Music and Chicago Musical College; *m.* H. S. Kingdom; made her first appearance, at the Tivoli, in 1909, since which date she has appeared at all the leading London and provincial halls; has toured in South Africa and Australia. *Recreations :* Tennis and gardening. *Club :* Three Arts. *Address :* 32 Streatham Hill, S.W. *Telephone No. :* Streatham 1100.

LAWFORD, Betty, actress; *b.* London, 1910; *d.* of Ernest Lawford; made her first appearance on the stage in New York, at the Knickerbocker Theatre, 31 May, 1926, as a Page in "King Henry IV"; at the Little Theatre, Nov., 1928, played Florence Rossiter in "The Lady Lies"; Fulton, Feb., 1931, Irene March in "Heat Wave"; Cort, Oct., 1935, Cecilia Wendover in "There's Wisdom in Women"; Ethel Barrymore, Dec., 1936, Chrystal Allen in "The Women"; Ethel Barrymore, June, 1940, played Carrie Gibson in "Walk with Music"; Booth, Nov., 1940, Lady Bonita Towyn in "Glamour Preferred"; at Chicago, Oct., 1944, Olive Lashbrooke in "The Voice of the Turtle."
(Died 20 Nov., 1960; age 50)

LAWFORD, Ernest, actor; made his first appearance on the London stage at the St. James's Theatre, 24 Feb., 1890, as Le Beau in "As You Like It"; was subsequently in "Charley's Aunt," "A Woman of No Importance," etc.; appeared at Drury Lane, Sept., 1894, as the Hon. Guy

Bagot in "The Derby Winner"; Drury Lane, Sept., 1897, Horace Saxonby in "The White Heather"; Shaftesbury, Jan., 1898, Sir Charles Braybourne in "Sporting Life"; toured with George Alexander, 1899, in "The Prisoner of Zenda," "Rupert of Hentzau," etc.; St. James's, Feb., 1900, played Bauer in "Rupert of Hentzau"; Comedy, Sept., 1901, Hughie Helmont in "When We Were Twenty-One"; Royalty, Oct., 1902, Eric Ward in "Sporting Simpson"; Royalty, Nov., 1902, Bertie Pilliner in "Lyre and Lancet"; went to America in 1903, and appeared in "The Man of Destiny," "Major André," etc., with Arnold Daly; at the Garrick, New York, 1904, appeared in "The Coronet of the Duchess," and then for fourteen years appeared under the management of Charles Frohman, playing all sorts of characters from Valentine Brown in "Quality Street," to Metternich in "L'Aiglon" and Captain Hook in "Peter Pan"; appeared at the Globe, London, Nov., 1910, as Fargette in "Decorating Clementine"; since 1925, has appeared at the Knickerbocker, New York, June, 1925, as Captain de Foenix in "Trelawney of the Wells"; Booth, Nov., 1925, Polonius in "Hamlet" (in modern dress); Plymouth, 1926, Lord Chancellor in "Iolanthe" and Major-General Stanley in "The Pirates of Penzance"; Charles Hopkins', Oct., 1927, the Chancellor in "The Ivory Door"; Shubert, Sept., 1928, Heinrich Heine in "White Lilacs"; Martin Beck (for the Theatre Guild), Dec., 1928, Walter Grantley in "Wings Over Europe"; Charles Hopkins, Feb., 1932, John in "They Don't Mean any Harm"; Belasco, Apr., 1932, William Blayds-Conway in "The Truth About Blayds"; Royale, May, 1932, Don Alfonso in "Christopher Comes Across"; Henry Miller, Oct., 1932, Davenport in "The Late Christopher Bean"; Alvin (for the Guild), Nov., 1933, Maitland of Lethington in "Mary of Scotland"; Plymouth, Dec., 1934, Frank Galloway in "Accent on Youth"; reappeared in London, at the Globe Theatre, Sept., 1935, in the last-mentioned part; Henry Miller, New York, Dec., 1935,

played Sir Wilfred Kelling in "Libel"; Plymouth, Oct., 1936, Chauffourier-Dubieff in "Tovarich"; Broadhurst, Oct., 1938, Bill in "The Fabulous Invalid"; Lyceum, May, 1939, Prince Otto in "The Brown Danube." *Clubs:* Lambs and Players, New York.
(Died 27 Dec., 1940; age 70)

LAWLOR, Mary, actress and vocalist; *b.* Utica, New York, U.S.A.; *m.* Lynford H. Lary; first attracted attention in New York, when she appeared at the Liberty Theatre, Dec., 1923, as Polly in "The Rise of Rosie O'Reilly"; at Chicago, June, 1924, played Winnie in the original production of "No, No, Nanette"; at Times Square, New York, Nov., 1924, played Gwen Morley in "Annie Dear"; Globe, Sept., 1925, Winnie in "No, No, Nanette"; Ambassador, Sept., 1926, Polly Nettleton in "Queen High"; Forty-sixth Street, Sept., 1927, Constance Lane in "Good News"; Knickerbocker, Sept., 1928, Sally Blake in "Cross My Heart"; Mansfield, Dec., 1928, Connie Block in "Hello, Daddy!"; at Atlantic City, July, 1929, played in "Great Day"; Forty-sixth Street, Jan., 1931, played Helen Holloway in "You Said It"; at the Maryland, Baltimore, Sept., 1932, Betty Harper in "Budget"; commenced film career, 1930, and has appeared in "Good News," "Shooting Straight," etc.

LAWRENCE, Boyle, dramatic author and lyrist; *b.* London, 1869; *m.* Verita Vivian, *d.* of Countess Farina; in 1890, was on London edition of the *New York Herald,* of which he was for some time sub-editor; was sub-editor of *The Sun* for some time, and was engaged on the staffs of *The Weekly Sun* and *The Daily Mail;* also filled the position of dramatic critic on the latter; joined *The Daily Express* in 1905, and was, for some years, assistant editor and dramatic critic of that paper; author of "A Man and His Word," produced at Imperial, 1901; part author with Louis N. Parker of "The Heel of Achilles," produced at Globe, 1901, and (with the late Frederick Mouillot) of "The Popinjay," produced at New-castle-on-Tyne, 1907, and at the New Theatre, 1911; adapted "Decameron Nights," Drury Lane, 1922, and "The First Kiss" (from the Spanish), New Oxford, 1924; lyrist to Sir Thomas Beecham Opera Book; also author of "A Promise" and "Her Own Rival." *Recreation:* Work. *Club:* Savage.
(Died 30 Dec., 1951; age 82)

LAWRENCE, Charles, actor; *b.* Worcester, Mass., U.S.A., 21 Apr., 1896; *s.* of Charles Edward Lawrence, and his wife Minnie M. (Boyd); *e.* Boston; *m.* Pauline van Camp; made his first appearance on the stage at the Academy of Music, Baltimore, 10 Nov., 1919, in "Elsie Janis and her Gang"; made his first appearance in New York, at the George M. Cohan Theatre; 1 Dec., 1919, in the same piece; during 1920–21, toured with Joseph Cawthorne in "The Half-Moon"; at the Globe, New York, Oct., 1921, played the Head Waiter in "The Love Letter"; at the Gaiety, New York, Jan., 1922, appeared in a different version of "Elsie Janis and her Gang"; at the Sam H. Harris Theatre, Sept., 1922, played William O'Toole in "It's a Boy!"; at the Longacre, Jan., 1923, Larry Payton in "Extra"; at the Selwyn Theatre, June, 1923, Theodore Mince in "Helen of Troy, New York"; Mar., 1924, toured with Julia Sanderson in "Moonlight"; made his first appearance on the London stage at the St. James's, 17 Sept., 1924, as Henry Williams in "The Nervous Wreck"; at the National, New York, Mar., 1926, played Johnny Martin in "The Half-Caste"; at the Winter Garden, London, Oct., 1926, succeeded Allan Kearns as Steve Burton in "Tip-Toes"; Lyric, New York, July, 1927, played Eugene Moreaux in "Kiss Me"; Majestic, Oct., 1927, Doctor Fenlon in "The Love Call"; Casino, Apr., 1929, Popkin in "Music in May"; George M. Cohan Theatre, Feb., 1930, appeared in "Nine-Fifteen Revue"; Little, Oct., 1930, played Willie Craft in "London Calling"; at the Fourty-fourth Street Theatre, Jan., 1933, Martin in "Face the Music"; Masque, Feb., 1934, Willie Parker in "No Questions

Asked"; Ambassador, July, 1934, Harry Van Etten in "Are You Decent?"; Longacre, Dec., 1934, Murphy in "Portrait of Gilbert"; Ritz, Feb., 1935, the Second Photographer in "The Eldest." *Favourite parts*: Henry in "The Nervous Wreck," and Theodore in "Helen of Troy, New York." *Recreations*: Motoring, golfing, and drawing. *Address*: 7 Florence Street, Worcester, Mass., U.S.A., or c/o Actors' Equity Association, 45 West 47th Street, New York City, U.S.A.

LAWRENCE, D. H., author, poet, painter, and dramatist; *b.* Eastwood, Nottingham, 11 Sept., 1885; *e.* Nottingham High School and Nottingham University; *m.* Frieda Von Richthofen; has written the following plays: " The Widowing of Mrs. Holroyd," " Touch and Go," " David "; among his books may be mentioned " The White Peacock," " Sons and Lovers," " The Rainbow," " Women in Love," " England, My England," " The Ladybird," " Lady Chatterley's Lover," etc.; an exhibition of his paintings was given in London, June, 1929.
(Died 3 Mar., 1930; age 44)

LAWRENCE, Gerald, actor; *b.* London, 23 Mar., 1873, originally intended for an engineer; *m.* Fay Davis; made his first appearance on the stage with F. R. Benson's company in 1893, at Stratford-on-Avon, in " Coriolanus "; in 1895, toured with A. B. Tapping's company in " The Idler," " Jim the Penman," and " The Importance of Being Earnest "; toured in South Africa with William Haviland, 1895, and again in 1897-8; made his first appearance in London at the Lyceum Theatre, 17 Sept., 1898, as Young Siward in " Macbeth," with Forbes-Robertson, subsequently succeeding Martin Harvey as Malcolm; he also appeared there as Fortinbras in " Hamlet "; at the Comedy Theatre, Mar., 1899, played the Duke of Osmonde in " A Lady of Quality "; subsequently touring in the same part; appeared at Her Majesty's, Sept., 1899, as the Dauphin in " King John," under Beerbohm Tree, ; also

appeared there in Jan., 1900, as Demetrius in " A Midsummer Night's Dream "; appeared at same theatre in " Rip Van Winkle," " Julius Caesar," " Herod," " Twelfth Night," " The Last of the Dandies," " Ulysses," " The Merry Wives of Windsor," " Trilby," etc., 1900-2; appeared at Drury Lane, Apr., 1903, as Bernardino in " Dante," with Sir Henry Irving; remained with Irving until his death in 1905, playing Nemours in " Louis XI," Henry II in " Becket," Bassanio in " The Merchant of Venice," playing those parts at Drury Lane, 1905; engaged by Klaw and Erlanger for their production of " A Prince of India " at the Amsterdam Theatre, New York, Jan., 1906, and next toured the States as leading man; reappeared in London, Mar., 1907, at the King's, Hammersmith, as Steerforth in " Dan'l Peggotty "; subsequently toured in " The Coping Stone," and as David Garrick, and at Manchester, in Aug., 1907, appeared as Orlando in a revival of " As You Like It "; produced " Romeo and Juliet," " Hamlet," " Twelfth Night," and " The Merchant of Venice " at the Court Theatre, Apr. and May, 1909; at Kroll's Theater, Berlin, Oct., 1909, produced "Hamlet," "Romeo and Juliet," and "As You Like It," playing Hamlet, Romeo, and Orlando; at the Duke of York's, Apr., 1910, played Ferdinand Gadd in " Trelawny of the Wells "; at His Majesty's, 1910-11, played the Earl of Surrey in " King Henry VIII," Theseus in " A Midsummer Night's Dream," Lorenzo in " The Merchant of Venice," Karl Blum in " The War God," etc.; at the Little Theatre, Oct., 1912, played Captain Brassbound in " Captain Brassbound's Conversion"; at the Globe, Sept., 1913, played Amos Thomas in "Years of Discretion"; Oct., 1913, Senor Don Fernando Laguera in "People Like Ourselves"; at the St. James's, May, 1915, Führman Max Von Ardel in " The Day Before the Day "; at His Majesty's, Oct., 1915, the Duke of Buckingham in " Mavourneen "; at Drury Lane, May, 1916, played in " Ollaya "; after the war, appeared at the Garrick, Mar., 1919, as the Comte de Guiche in " Cyrano de Ber-

gerac "; at Drury Lane, Sept., 1919, played Wenceslas Kolar in "The Great Day "; at the Duke of York's, Dec., 1919, played Alexis in "Arms and the Man "; in 1920, toured with Ethel Irving as Cavaradossi in "La Tosca," and appeared in the same part at the Aldwych Theatre, Oct., 1920 ; in May, 1922, toured as Mr. Garrick in a play of that name, and produced it at the Court Theatre, Sept., 1922, when he played the same part ; at Drury Lane, Mar., 1923, played Cipriano, Ignazio and the Lord Chamberlain in "Angelo "; in 1923 revived "Monsieur Beaucaire " in the provinces, playing the title-*rôle*, and produced it at the Strand, Feb., 1924 ; subsequently toured in the same part ; during 1925 toured in "Richard Lovelace " and "David Garrick "; at the Prince's, May, 1926, played Captain Thorne in a revival of "Secret Service "; "Q," Mar., 1927, Hon. Charles Cranley and Barney Rushton in Who's Who? "; during 1927, toured with The Bensonians, playing Hamlet, Charles Surface, etc.; at the Theatre Royal, Birmingham, Nov., 1928, played Beau Brummel in a play of that name; in Mar., 1929, went to South Africa, playing "Monsieur Beaucaire," "David Garrick," "The School for Scandal," "Beau Brummel," etc.; after returning to London, appeared at the Embassy, May–June, 1930, as Shylock and Hamlet; at the New, Sept., 1930, played Buckingham in "Richard III "; Court, Mar., 1931, Juggins in "Fanny's First Play "; subsequently toured as Sir Reginald Belsize in "The Marriage of Kitty "; "Q," Mar., 1932, played Charles Surface in "The School for Scandal"; Apr., 1932, David Garrick in the play of that name; Dec., 1932, Beaucaire in "Monsieur Beaucaire"; Oct., 1933, The King in "The Shadow Princess"; Nov., 1936, Commander Bailey in "Storm Over Europe"; Winter Garden, Oct., 1938, Richard Dawson in "Behind the Blinds"; during the War, served in the R.N.V.R. 1914–18; Lieutenant, 1917. *Clubs :* Green Room, Garrick, and Stage Golfing Society, London. *Address :* 21 Lyndhurst Road, Hampstead, N.W.3. *Telephone No. :* Hampstead 5961.
(Died 16 May, 1957; age 84)

LAWRENCE, Gertrude, actress ; *b.* London, 4 July, 1898 ; *d.* of Arthur Lawrence Klasen, and his wife Alice Louise (Banks) ; *e.* Convent of the Sacré Cœur, Streatham ; *m.* (1) Francis Gordon-Howley (mar. dis.) ; (2) Richard S. Aldrich ; studied dancing under Mdme. Espinosa and elocution and acting under Italia Conti ; made her first appearance on the stage at the Brixton Theatre, 26 Dec., 1910, as a child dancer in the pantomime of "The Babes in the Wood"; at Olympia, Dec., 1911, she appeared as one of the child choristers in "The Miracle "; she then toured in sketches in variety theatres ; at the Repertory Theatre, Liverpool, Dec., 1912, appeared as the principal dancer in "Fifinella," and Mar., 1913, as an Angel in "Hannele"; during 1913–14 toured in "All Aboard," "Miss Lamb of Canterbury," and "Miss Plaster of Paris"; during 1915–16 toured as Blanche-Marie in "The Little Michus"; at the Hippodrome, Dover, Mar., 1916, appeared in "Money for Nothing," in which she toured; while appearing in this piece, was seen by Lee White and Clay Smith, who brought her to town to the Vaudeville Theatre, where she was engaged, June, 1916, as principal dancer, and understudy to Billie Carleton in "Some "; subsequently she toured in the leading part in the same *revue*; returned to London, and was engaged at the Vaudeville, Apr., 1917, as general understudy in "Cheep," and appeared in all the leading parts on occasions; May, 1918, appeared in "Tabs," and subsequently played Beatrice Lillie's part in this for two months; Dec., 1918, appeared in "Buzz-Buzz"; during 1920 was engaged as leading lady at Murray's Club, in London's first cabaret entertainment; toured in "The Midnight Frolics," and at Christmas, 1920, was engaged at the London Hippodrome, understudying Phyllis Dare as the Princess in "Aladdin," and playing the part at *matinées*; during 1921, toured in variety theatres with Walter Williams ; at the Prince of Wales's, Oct., 1921, appeared as leading lady in "A to Z "; at the Garrick, Oct., 1922, played Denise in

" Dédé " ; at Christmas, 1922, appeared as leading lady at the Hotel Metropole, in " The Midnight Follies " ; at the Vaudeville, Feb., 1923, played lead in " Rats ! " ; at the Duke of York's, Sept., 1923, lead in " London Calling ! " ; she then went to America, and at the Times Square, New York, Jan., 1924, played joint lead with Beatrice Lillie in " André Charlot's Revue of 1924," and continued in this throughout the year ; reappeared in London at the Prince of Wales's Theatre, Mar., 1925, in " Charlot's Revue " ; returned to New York, and at the Selwyn Theatre, Nov., 1925, played in " The Charlot Revue, 1926 " ; Imperial, New York, Nov., 1926, played Kay in " Oh, Kay ! " ; returned to London, and appeared at His Majesty's, Sept.,1927, in the same part ; at the same theatre (for the Sunday Play Society), Jan., 1928, played Jane Crosby in " Icebound " ; again returned to New York, and appeared at the Alvin Theatre, Nov., 1928, as Ann Wainwright in " Treasure Girl " ; again returned to England, and at Southampton, Aug., 1929, played Marie in " Candle-Light," subsequently returning to New York, to play the same part, at the Empire, Sept., 1929 ; at the Majestic, Feb., 1930, appeared in " The International Review " ; returned to London, and appeared at the Phoenix, Sept., 1930, as Amanda Prynne in " Private Lives," and played the same part at the Times Square, New York, Jan., 1931 ; on her return to London, appeared at the Haymarket, Sept., 1931, as Diana in " Take Two from One" ; Dec., 1931, Harriet Noble in " Can the Leopard . . . ? " ; St. James's, Aug., 1932, played Sarah Cazenove in " Behold, We Live" ; at Wyndham's, Mar., 1933, played Jill in " This Inconstancy " ; Adelphi, Oct., 1933, Evangeline in " Nymph Errant " ; Opera House, Manchester, May, 1934, Deirdre Brummel in " The Winding Journey" ; Queen's, London, Sept., 1934, Josephine in " Moonlight is Silver" ; His Majesty's, May, 1935, Sophy Gerould in " Hervey House" ; in Oct, 1935, toured with Noel Coward in " To-Night at 7.30," appearing in the nine one-act plays, which made up three programmes ; the group of plays

was brought to the Phoenix Theatre, London, Jan., 1936, when the programme was re-named " To-Night at 8.30," and she appeared in the leading parts in " Family Album," " The Astonished Heart," " Red Peppers," " Hands Across the Sea," " Fumed Oak," " Shadow Play" ; in May, 1936, " Ways and Means" and " Still Life" were added ; she appeared at the National Theatre, New York, Nov., 1936, in these eight plays also in " We Were Dancing" ; at the Plymouth, New York, Oct., 1937, played Susan Trexel in " Susan and God" and toured in the same part, 1938–9 ; Mar., 1939, toured in the United States, as Lydia Kenyon in " Skylark" ; appearing in the same part at the Morosco, New York, Oct., 1939 ; Alvin, Jan., 1941, played Liza Elliott in " Lady in the Dark" ; Dennis, Mass., Aug., 1941, Sarah in " Behold, We Live," and Aug., 1942, Julia Sterroll in " Fallen Angels " ; Broadway, Feb., 1943, again played in " Lady in the Dark" ; toured in England, 1944, entertaining troops, and subsequently in France and Belgium ; Buffalo, Nov., 1944, played Bernice Forbes in " Errand for Bernice" ; toured the Pacific Ocean Area, for U.S.O., Apr., 1945, with her own company, and at Hawaii, July, 1945, appeared as Elvira in " Blithe Spirit" ; Ethel Barrymore, New York, Dec., 1945, played Eliza Doolittle in " Pygmalion" ; she played Eliza in New York, and on tour in U.S.A. and Canada, until 1947 ; toured from Nov., 1947, in a revival of " To-Night at 8.30," and appeared in this at the National, New York, Feb., 1948 ; returned to London, 1948, and appeared at the Aldwych, Dec., 1948, as Stella Martyn in " September Tide" ; in addition she has appeared at Dennis, Mass., as Crystal in " The Man in Possession," 1946 ; Lady Maria Fitzherbert in " The Lady Maria," 1947 ; Olivia Brown in " O Mistress Mine," 1948 ; Stella in " September Tide," 1949 ; Beatrice in " Travellers' Joy," 1950 ; commenced film career, 1929, and appeared in several pictures ; was Vice-president of the American Theatre Wing War Service ; President of the American branch of E.N.S.A. ; Director of British Actors' Orphanage ;

published her reminiscences, "A Star Danced," 1945. *Recreations:* Swimming and gardening. *Clubs:* Tavern, Chicago; Cosmopolitan, New York; Press, San Francisco; Rolling Rock, Ligonier, Pa.
(Died 7 Sept., 1952; age 54)

LAWRENCE, Margaret, actress; *b.* Trenton, New Jersey, U.S.A., 2 Aug., 1889; *m.* (1) Lt.-Commander Orson D. Nunn (mar. dis.); (2) Wallace Eddinger; made her first appearance on the stage, at Chicago, Aug., 1910, in " Her Son "; at the Hackett Theatre, New York, Jan., 1911, made a great success when she appeared as Elsie Darling in " Over Night "; at the end of that engagement she married and was absent from the stage for seven years; reappeared, at the Belasco Theatre, Washington, June, 1918, as the Wife in " Tea for Three," and played the same part at Maxine Elliott's Theatre, New York, Sept., 1918; at the Harris Theatre, Nov., 1919, played Rosalie in " Wedding Bells "; in the autumn of 1920 toured as Naima Duval in " Transplanting Jean," appearing in the same part at the Cort Theatre, New York, Jan., 1921; at the Republic, Jan., 1922, played Marion Dorsey and Marion Sylvester in " Lawful Larceny "; at the Cohan Theatre, Sept., 1922, Amy Reeves in " The Endless Chain "; at the Fulton Theatre, Dec., 1922, Mary and Lady Carlton in " Secrets "; Oct , 1924, Elise Clarendon in " In His Arms "
(Died 8 June, 1929; age 39)

LAWRENCE, Vincent, theatre press representative; *b.* London, 14 Jan., 1896; *s.* of Arthur Hamilton Lawrence and his wife Cora (Fisher); *e.* Ongar Grammar School; from 1911-14 was engaged as reporter, sub-editor, and contributor to the Hulton publications; served in the Royal West Kent Regiment on the outbreak of War; obtained a commission, 1915, in the Loyal North Lancs, retiring 1918, with the rank of captain and adjutant; awarded the M.C., and was twice mentioned in dispatches; was appointed sub-editor *Sunday Chronicle,* 1919; dramatic critic to *The Evening News,* 1920, and contributed to several other publications; has since acted as press representative for André Charlot, Benrimo, Archibald de Bear, "The Co-Optimists" (four years), William Gaunt and associated managers at the Gaiety, Adelphi, Apollo, Winter Garden, and His Majesty's, Edgar Wallace, S. W. Carroll, etc. *Favourite play:* "Cyrano de Bergerac." *Address:* Carlton Mansions, W.C.2. *Telephone No. :* Temple Bar 2288.

LAWRENCE, Vincent S., dramatic author; *b.* Roxbury, Mass., U.S.A., 1890; *e.* public schools, Andover, and Yale University; is the author of the following plays: " Fate Decides " (with Geo. Scarborough), 1916; " Weary Wives," 1917; " In Love With Love," " When He Comes Back," 1919; " The Ghost Between," " Love and Learn " (with Edgar Selwyn), 1920; " Two Fellows and a Girl," " The Twist," 1923; " Kelly's Vacation," 1924; " Two Married Men," " Spring Fever," 1925; " Sour Grapes," 1926; " Among the Married," " Happy " (with McElbert Moore), 1927; " A Distant Drum," " Treasure Girl " (with Fred Thompson), 1928; "Washington Heights," 1931; "The Overtons," 1945; has written for the films for many years. *(Died 25 Nov., 1946; age 56)*

LAWRENCE William John, theatrical historian and dramatic critic; *b.* Belfast, 29 Oct, 1862; *e.* Belfast Methodist College; began life as a commercial traveller, and while so engaged, in 1892, published his " Life of Gustavus Vaughan Brooke, Tragedian "; since then he has been a prolific contributor to periodical literature on theatrical and artistic subjects; author of two volumes of reprinted essays, " The Elizabethan Playhouse and Other Studies," 1912-13; collaborated with William Archer on the section " The Playhouse " in " Shakespeare's England," 1916; spent two years in the United States, and lectured on the Drama at Harvard, Columbia and Princetown Universities, and elsewhere; when America entered the war, worked as a common labourer in a Philadelphia munition factory; returned to Ireland, 1919, and resumed his position as chief Dublin correspondent of *The Stage*; in 1922, was granted a Civil List Pension, for services to the history and literature of the drama; in 1925, lectured on the English Drama in the United States; on his return, became, for a time, dramatic critic of *The Irish Sketch*; elected a Fellow of the Royal Society of Literature, May, 1930; received the Honorary degree of D.Litt., Queen's University, Belfast, July, 1931; since that date, besides other activities, has published several books, notably "Those Nut-cracking Elizabethans," "Speeding Up Shakespeare," and "Old Theatre Days and Ways." *Address:* Malvern House, 176 The Rye, Dulwich, S.E.22.

LAWSON, John, sketch artist and manager; *b.* Hollingwood, near Manchester, 9 Jan., 1865; *e.* Cheetham Hill, Manchester; *m.* Cissie Skinner; is the son of the proprietor of the old Theatre Royal, Bishop Auckland, Barrow-in-Furness, and Her Majesty's Theatre, Carlisle; was formerly engaged in business as an architect; made his first appearance on the dramatic stage at the St. James's, Theatre, Manchester, 1885, with the late Tom Sennett, in " Redemption "; subsequently toured in " The Trump Card," and as Dicey Morris in " After Dark "; toured for some time as Jacob Silvani in " Humanity," also " The Ruling Passion "; " Siberia," etc.; spent five years in the United States; on his return, reproduced " Humanity," which he subsequently turned into a sketch for the variety theatres, introduced into it the song, entitled " Only a Jew," and presented it for the first time at the Empire, Brighton, on 7 Sept., 1896; its success was instantaneous, and it was produced for the first time in London at the Middlesex, 21 Sept., 1896; probably no production in the music halls has secured such enduring success; has played in it at all the principal London and provincial halls, including the Moss and Stoll theatres, Barrasford Circuit, De Frece Circuit, London Theatre of Varieties Circuit,

in the United States and South Africa; other notable productions which he has made are " The Shield of David "; " Sally in our Alley "; " Man against Motor "; " Mr. Todd of London "; " A Bride for a Living "; " The Monkey's Paw "; " The King's Minister "; " The Miracle "; " The Open Door "; " The Mormon's Wife "; " Men must work and women must weep "; " The Baker Street Mystery "; " Disraeli "; " The Call to Arms," etc.; is the proprietor of the Camberwell Empire, and also of the Revue Theatre, Kingston. *Address:* Cappoquin House, Anglesea Road, Surbiton. *Telephone No.:* Kingston 1632.

LAWSON, John Howard, dramatic author; *b.* New York City, U.S.A., 25 Sept., 1895; *s.* of Simeon Levy Lawson and his wife Belle (Hart); *e.* Williams College; *m.* (1) Katharine Drain (mar. dis.); (2) Susan Edmond; formerly engaged in Reuter's Telegraph company, in Italy; during the War, 1917–19, served with the Volunteer Ambulance Corps; has written the following plays, "Standards," 1914; " Roger Bloomer," 1923; "Processional," 1925; "Nirvana," 1926; "Loud Speaker," 1927; "The International," 1928; "Success Story," 1932; "The Pure in Heart," "Gentlewoman," 1934; is the author of "Theory and Technique of Playwriting." *Address:* Moriches, Long Island, N.Y., U.S.A.

LAWSON, Mary, actress and vocalist; *b.* Darlington, 30 Aug., 1910; *d.* of Thomas Edward Lawson and his wife Jane (Walker); *e.* Arthur Pease School, Darlington; *m.* Francis W. L. C. Beaumont; made her first appearance on the stage, at the Theatre Royal, Darlington, 1918, at a charity *matinée*; was subsequently engaged on the variety stage at all the Moss Empire halls; made her first appearance on the regular stage at the Lyceum Theatre, 2 Sept., 1925, in "The London Revue"; was engaged as a concert artist during 1927; during 1928 was engaged with Archie Pitt's "Lido Follies"; was next engaged in cabaret at the Mayfair Hotel, London; Carlton Theatre, Nov., 1928, succeeded Zelma

O'Neal as Flo in "Good News"; subsequently toured in the same part; in May, 1929, was engaged by Sir George Tallis for his Australian company; and appeared there in "Follow Through," "Hold Everything," "The Belle of New York," "A Country Girl," "Turned Up"; on returning to England, appeared at the London Coliseum, Apr., 1931, as Gretel in "White Horse Inn"; May, 1932, played Annuschka in "Casanova"; at the Theatre Royal, Birmingham, Dec., 1933, played Dandini in "Cinderella"; at the Empire, Liverpool, Dec., 1934, again played Dandini in "Cinderella," and played the same part at the Alhambra, Glasgow, Dec., 1935; Adelphi, Feb., 1937, the Hon. Nigel Flower in "Home and Beauty"; Gaiety, Sept., 1937, Pomona in "Going Greek" and Aug., 1938, Lola in "Running Riot"; entered films 1933, and since 1936, has appeared in "A Fire Has Been Arranged," "House Broken," "To Catch a Thief," "Cotton Queen,"."Can You Hear Me, Mother?" "Toilers of the Sea," "Oh, Boy," etc. *Recreations :* Motoring, gardening, golf, and swimming. *(Died 4 May, 1941; age 30)*

LAWSON, Wilfrid, actor; *b.* Bradford, Yorks., 14 Jan., 1900; *s.* of John Mitchell Dowling Worsnop and his wife Isabella (McCubbin); *e.* Hanson School and Technical College, Bradford; *m.* Lillian Fenn; made his first appearance on the stage at the Pier Theatre, Brighton, 1916, as Gecko in "Trilby"; during 1918, served as a pilot in the Royal Air Force; during 1919–29 played over four hundred different parts in repertory companies; made his first appearance in London at the Elephant and Castle Theatre, 6 Feb., 1928, as Mark Ingestre in "Sweeney Todd"; at the Court Theatre, Dec., 1929, to Mar., 1930, with Charles Macdona's company, played Major Petkoff in "Arms and the Man," Alfred Doolittle in "Pygmalion," Roebuck Ramsden in "Man and Superman," Sir Patrick Cullen in "The Doctor's Dilemma," Colonel Craven in "The Philanderer," First Gravedigger in "Hamlet," and John Tarleton in "Misalliance"; at the same theatre, Mar., 1931, played Mr. Gilbey in "Fanny's First Play," and Sir George Crofts in "Mrs. Warren's Profession"; Lyric, Hammersmith, Dec., 1931, appeared as Salmon, the comic policeman in "Aladdin"; was then engaged by Sir Barry Jackson, and at the Queen's, Apr., 1932, played Membel in "Caravan," and Mangan in "Heartbreak House"; June, 1932, Arthur Kober in "Evensong"; Shaftesbury, May, 1933, John Brown in "Gallows Glorious"; Lyric, Aug., 1933, Unter-Offizer Keller in "The Ace"; Coliseum, Feb., 1934, Prince Samsthanaka in "The Golden Toy"; Old Vic., Sept., 1934, Mark Antony in "Antony and Cleopatra"; Playhouse, Nov., 1934, George Morel in "Hurricane"; Piccadilly, Jan., 1935, Edward Moulton-Barrett in a revival of "The Barretts of Wimpole Street"; Playhouse, May, 1935, John Builder in "A Family Man"; Malvern Festival, July-Aug., 1935, Volpone, Mr. Gilbey in "Fanny's First Play," Mr. Tarleton in "Misalliance"; in Nov, 1935, went to America, and made his first appearance in New York, at the Henry Miller Theatre, 20 Dec., 1935, as Thomas Foxley, K.C., in "Libel"; Guild, New York, Nov., 1936, played Richard Wagner in "Prelude to Exile"; Fulton, Feb., 1937, Benedict Arnold in "A Point of Honour"; St. Martin's, London, June, 1937, King James in "The King's Pirate"; Royalty, Sept., 1937, Walter Ormund in "I Have Been Here Before" and played the same part at the Guild, New York, Oct., 1938; Garrick, London, Jan., 1939, Bill Cooper in "Hundreds and Thousands"; Westminster, May, 1939, Stephen Moore in "Bridge Head"; rejoined the R.A.F., 1939; reappeared at the Duchess, July, 1942, as Captain McGrath in "Lifeline"; Cambridge Theatre, Jan., 1943, Gideon Bloodgood in "The Streets of London"; Opera House, Manchester, Mar., 1943, André Legrand in "Devil's Own"; Mercury, Feb., 1947, Dan Hillboy in "The Beautiful People"; toured in the United States, Apr., 1947, as Edward Moulton-Barrett in "The Barretts of Wimpole Street"; at the Arts, London, Feb., 1953, appeared as the Captain in "The Father"; Savoy, Sept., 1953,

played Korrianke in "The Devil's General"; Globe, Apr., 1954, played the Cell Warder in "The Prisoner", Phoenix, July, 1954, appeared as Lon Dennison in "The Wooden Dish"; at the same theatre, Oct., 1954, played Sidney Redlitch in "Bell, Book and Candle"; St. Martin's, May, 1956, played H. C. Curry in "The Rainmaker"; Arts, Sept., 1957, Thomas Johnson in "All Kinds of Men"; Royal Court, Sept., 1958, Sailor Sawnay in "Live Like Pigs"; at the same theatre, Sept., 1959, played Sailor Mahan in "Cock-a-Doodle-Dandy"; Arts, May, 1962, played Luka in "The Lower Depths"; Old Vic, Sept., 1962, played the Button-Moulder in "Peer Gynt"; entered films, 1935, and has since appeared in numerous pictures and television productions.
(Died 10 Oct., 1966; age 66)

LAWSON, Winifred, actress and vocalist; *b.* London, 15 Nov., 1894; *d.* of Alexander Lawson, artist, and his wife Florence (Thistlewood); *e.* Wolverhampton and Vevey, Switzerland; was formerly engaged on the concert platform, and appeared in concerts at the A bert Hall, Queen's Hall, and leading provincial halls; in 1920 appeared at the Glastonbury Festival, where she played Queen Guenevere in Rutland Boughton's " Round Table "; made her first appearance on the regular stage at the Old Vic, 17 Feb., 1921, as the Countess in " The Marriage of Figaro "; she also appeared there in May, 1921, as the Princess in " Prince Ferelon," and Oct., 1921, as Marguerite in " Faust "; she was then engaged for the D'Oyly Carte Opera Company, and made her first appearance with that company, at the Prince's Theatre, 23 Jan., 1922, playing Princess Ida in the opera of that name; has remained with the company ever since, playing Phyllis in " Iolanthe," Casilda in " The Gondoliers," Patience, Yum-Yum in " The Mikado," and Elsie Maynard in " The Yeomen of the Guard " ; appeared in all these parts during the seasons at the Prince's, Feb.-July, 1924, and Oct., 1926; continued with the company until 1929, when she toured as Lili in " Lilac

Time"; subsequently rejoined the D'Oyly Carte Opera Co., and appeared at the Savoy Theatre, 1929-30, in all her old parts; Old Vic.-Sadler's Wells, 1934-5; visited Australia, 1935, playing the soprano *rôles* in Gilbert and Sullivan repertory, under the management of J. C. Williamson, Ltd.; Open Air Theatre, Regent's Park, May, 1938, played the Countess in "The Marriage of Figaro"; during the War, sang at many concerts for C.E.M.A., and also toured in the Middle East, for E.N.S.A., in a classical music party. *Recreation:* Gardening.
(Died 30 Nov., 1961; age 67)

LAWTON, Frank, actor; *b.* London, 30 Sept., 1904; *s.* of the late Frank Mokeley Lawton and his wife Daisy May (Collier); *e.* Langley Hall; *m.* Evelyn Laye; made his first appearance on the stage at the Vaudeville Theatre, 29 Sep., 1923, in " Yes!"; and appeared at the same theatre, Jan., 1924, in "Puppets," and July, 1924, in "The Odd Spot"; at the Shaftesbury, June, 1925, played Flipeur in " Clo-Clo "; then went to the St. James's, Sept., 1925, where he appeared as George in " The Last of Mrs. Cheyney," and in Jan., 1927, as Fred in " Interference "; at the Prince's (for the Venturers), May, 1927, played the Second Ghost in "Might-Have-Beens"; Strand (for the Repertory Players), Dec., 1927, Littler in "Sadie Dupont"; New Theatre (for the 300 Club), Feb., 1928, and Savoy, Mar., 1928, appeared as Woodley in " Young Woodley," in which he made a great success; he appeared in this part throughout 1928, and toured in it during 1929; at the Strand (for the Repertory Players), June, 1928, played Freddie Coulson in "Chance Acquaintance"; Vaudeville Nov., 1929, Hon. Reggie Fanning in "The Roof"; Fortune, Dec., 1929, Harry Graham in "The Last Enemy"; St. James's, Feb., 1930, David in "Michael and Mary"; Comedy, Oct., 1930, Oliver Boulton in "Lucky Dip"; Duke of York's, May, 1931, Hec Hammond in "London Wall"; St. Martin's, May, 1932, Lance Perkins in "Somebody Knows"; Savoy, Nov., 1933, appeared in "Please"; made his first appearance on the New York stage, at the Ritz, 1 Feb., 1934, as Charles Tritton in "The Wind and the Rain"; St. James's, London, Mar., 1935, Ronald Vaughan in "Worse Things Happen at Sea"; Little, New York, Dec., 1936, Thierry Keller in "Promise"; Henry Miller, Sept., 1937, Hon. Alan Howard in "French Without Tears"; Playhouse, New York, Mar., 1938, Percy Bysshe Shelley in "I Am My Youth"; Wyndham's, London, Oct., 1938, Dallas Chaytor in "Quiet Wedding"; served in the Army, 1939–45; was awarded the U.S. Legion of Merit; reappeared on the stage, Sept., 1945, when he toured as Richard in "Three Waltzes"; toured, from Apr., 1946, as Gregg Grantley in "Elusive Lady," and appeared in this part at Wimbledon, July, 1946; Playhouse, Apr., 1947, Tom Collier in "The Animal Kingdom"; "Q," Dec., 1947, Leonard Ferris in "Mid Channel"; Comedy, Mar., 1949, Nigel Wainwright in "Summer in December"; Arts, Aug., 1949, played the Apparition in "The Romantic Young Lady"; toured, 1950, as Evan Davies in "September Tide"; at Wyndham's, Nov., 1952, for the Repertory Players, produced "The Woman With Red Hair"; Phoenix (Rep. Players), May, 1953, played Sam in "We Have Company"; Phoenix, Sept., 1953, appeared as Edward Forrest in "Four Winds"; St. James's, Apr., 1954, the Hon. Wm. Stephen Fitzharding Blue in "Waiting For Gillian"; Garrick, Feb., 1955, Mr. Grainger in "Serious Charge"; Cambridge, July, 1957, played Sir Robert Marlowe in "Silver Wedding"; toured, Feb., 1959, as Comte Raoul de Vriaac in "The Marquise" (which he also directed); Duke of York's, Nov., 1959, played Harry Markham in "And Suddenly It's Spring"; toured, Jan., 1961, as Commander "Midge" Metcalfe in "The Angry Deep"; Princes, Feb., 1962, played Charles Burcher in "The Big Killing"; Richmond, Oct., 1962, Hugo in "Angels on Horseback"; Ashcroft, Croydon, Apr., 1965, played Clive Champion-Cheney in "The Circle," subsequently appearing at the Savoy, June, 1965, in the same production; commenced film career, 1930, in "Young Woodley," and subsequently

appeared in numerous pictures. *Recreations:* Tennis, cricket and golf. *Clubs:* Green Room and Garrick.

(Died 28 July, 1969; age 64)

LAWTON, Thais, actress ; *b.* Louisville, Kentucky, U.S.A., 18 · June, 1881 ; *d.* of George Lawton and his wife Carrie (Thais) ; *m.* Thos. McDermott ; made her first appearance on the professional stage, at New Haven, Conn., 25 Sept., 1900, as Gladys Middleton in " Lost River " ; made her first appearance in New York, at the Fourteenth street Theatre, 3 Oct., 1900, in the same part ; she then joined James O'Neill's company, to play Mercedes in " Monte Cristo," and in 1902 went to San Francisco, where she remained with " stock " companies for over two years, playing nearly one hundred different parts ; during 1904-5 toured as Margaret Nevelle in " Heartsease," Muriel Mannering in " The Second in Command," etc. ; from 1905-9 was continuously engaged with various " stock " companies ; at Maxine Elliott's Theatre, New York, Sept., 1909, appeared as Florence Knight in " The Revellers " ; in Nov., 1909, was engaged for the New Theatre, New York, and here she appeared with the greatest success as Madge Thomas in " Strife," Lady Sneerwell in " The School for Scandal," Abigail Hawthorne in " The Witch," the Gipsy Girl in " Brand," Elizabeth Thompsett in " Don," Phyllis Mortimore in " The Thunderbolt," Night in " The Blue Bird," etc. ; also played in " Vanity Fair," " The Piper," etc. ; in Sept., 1911, she joined John Drew at the Empire Theatre, New York, to play Louise Parker in " A Single Man " ; in 1913 toured with Arnold Daly ; subsequently toured with Robert Mantell, playing Constance in " King John," Lady Macbeth, Portia in " The Merchant of Venice," etc. ; at Pittsburgh, Jan., 1914, played in " The Family Cupboard " ; at Cleveland, June, 1914, played in " Fine Feathers " and " Years of Discretion " ; at the Garrick, New York, Apr., 1915, appeared as Mrs. Fanny Wilton in " John Gabriel Borkman " ; at the Empire, New York, Nov., 1915, played Emily Bargus in " The Chief," with John

Drew; at the Astor, Aug., 1916, Heloise Lescuyer in " The Guilty Man " ; at the Lyric, New York, Sept., 1917, Eve Chilcote in " The Masquerader " (" John Chilcote, M.P.") ; in 1918 toured in Australia in the same play, with Guy Bates Post ; at the Broadhurst, New York, July, 1919, played Mrs. Dean in " The Crimson Alibi " ; at the Shubert Theatre, Mar., 1920, Clarissa Archibald in " The Blue Flame " ; at the Knickerbocker, Oct., 1921, Rachel in " The Wandering Jew " ; at the Times Square, Sept., 1922, Mrs. Hilary Rand in " The Exciters " ; at the Comedy, New York, Jan., 1923, Agnes Haldenstedt in " Jitta's Atonement " ; at the Forty-ninth Street Theatre, Aug., 1923, Fairy Berylune and Neighbour Berlingot in " The Blue Bird " ; at the Punch and Judy, Apr., 1924, Aunt Martha in " Two Strangers from Nowhere " ; at the Broadhurst, Oct., 1924, the Mother Superior and Contessa Felicia in " The Red Falcon " ; at the Lenox Little Theatre, Apr., 1925, Adah in Byron's " Cain " ; Selwyn, Sept., 1926, the Queen Regent in "Castles in the Air " ; Wallack's, Sept., 1927, Ethel Trundle in " Mister Romeo " ; Empire, Mar., 1928, Letizia in " Napoleon " ; Assembly, Dec., 1929, Francisca and Mistress Overdone in " The Novice and the Duke " (" Measure for Measure "); Booth, Mar., 1930, Queen Elizabeth in " The Royal Virgin " ; Eltinge, Aug., 1930, Margaret Chisholm in " The Ninth Guest "; Biltmore, Jan., 1931, Mrs. Randolph in " Philip Goes Forth " ; during 1932, produced a series of thirty-two plays for the Radio ; Morosco, Aug., 1933, Mrs. Smith in " Going Gay " ; 49th Street Theatre, Nov., 1933, Minna in " Birthright "; National, Feb., 1935, Hester Pentland in " Times Have Changed "; Ritz, Dec., 1937, Mrs. Robert Andrews in " Love in My Fashion "; Playhouse, Dec., 1940, played the Baroness Burdett-Coutts in " Romantic Mr. Dickens."
(Died 26 Dec., 1956; age 78)

LEADLAY, Edward O., theatrical press representative ; *b.* Stratford, Ont., Canada ; *s.* of Edward Leadlay ; *e.* Canada ; was engaged as press representative and journalist in New York, Chicago, Winnipeg and Toronto prior to 1914 ; served with the Canadian Forces in France until 1918, gaining the Military Cross at Vimy Ridge, 1917 ; has been engaged as press representative by Charles B. Cochran since 1922 ; has been press representative at one time or another for most of the leading theatres in London ; also for the Rodeo at Wembley, Olympia Circuses and Horse Shows; Exposition Coloniale Internationale, Paris, for Great Britain and the Irish Free State ; Sundry Political and Commercial activities ; has publicised over 500 theatrical productions ; is Chairman of the Leadlay News Service. *Clubs :* City Carlton, Junior Naval and Military, International Sportsmen, and Press.
(Died 7 Feb., 1951)

LEAHY, Eugene, actor ; *b.* Newcastle West, Co. Limerick, Ireland, 14 Mar., 1883 ; *s.* of Maurice Patrick Leahy and his wife Helena (O'Callaghan) ; *e.* at Clongowes Wood College, Co. Kildare, and Trinity College, Dublin (B.A. and B.A.I.) ; was formerly an engineer and practised in England and India until 1914 ; studied singing at the Royal Irish Academy of Music, where he gained a scholarship and bronze medal ; served in the 1914–18 War in Italy with the Royal Artillery ; studied for the stage at the Royal Academy of Dramatic Art ; made his first appearance on the stage at the Court Theatre, Feb., 1919, as the second officer in " Twelfth Night," appearing at the same theatre as Sir Harry Bumper in " The School for Scandal," Frank Ormsby in " The Lost Leader," and Salanio in " The Merchant of Venice "; at the Duke of York's, July, 1920, played Mr. Edmondson in " Brown Sugar " ; Court, Dec., 1920, Theseus in " A Midsummer Night's Dream," followed by Lord Chief Justice in " Henry IV " (Part II), and Montano in " Othello "; Comedy, June, 1921, P.C. Moon in " A Family Man "; Sept., 1921, the Gaoler in " The Love Thief "; Haymarket, June, 1923, Digby in " Success "; Aug., 1923, Detchard in

" The Prisoner of Zenda "; Apollo, Feb., 1924, Lord Landor in " The Fairy Tale "; New, Mar., 1924, the Bishop of Beauvais in " Saint Joan," and appeared in the same part at the Regent, Jan., 1925; Queen's, June, 1925, played Low in " Salomy Jane "; Empire, Dec., 1925, Norfolk in " Henry VIII "; Mar., 1926, Savella in " The Cenci "; Garrick, July, 1926, Blowers in " None But the Brave "; Prince's, Dec., 1926, Ross in " Macbeth "; 1927–28 played leads in South Africa with Phyllis Neilson-Terry's Company; at the Strand, Nov., 1928, played Ernest Stratton in " High Treason "; Haymarket, Dec., 1928, Mr. Skimpin in " Mr. Pickwick "; Strand, Feb., 1929, the Earl of Moray in " The Borderer "; Arts, June, 1929, Purishkevitch in " Red Sunday "; July, 1929, Dr. Crofts in " Gentlemen of the Jury "; New, Sept., 1929, Captain Trowbridge in "Emma Hamilton"; St. James's, Oct., 1929, James Weysmith in "Heat Wave"; Duke of York's, Dec., 1929, succeeded Frank Harvey as Duke Karl Alexander in " Jew Süss "; Arts, May, 1930, Konrad in " The Ugly Duchess "; Apollo, Oct., 1930, Sir Montague Tollemache in "The Outsider"; Globe, Jan., 1931, Baron Kamp in "The Improper Duchess"; Arts, Mar., 1931, Poing in "Lui" (in French); Westminster, June–Oct., 1932, Enrique in "The Kingdom of God," Don Adriano in "Love's Labour's Lost," and Mr. Gladstone in "Dizzy"; Palace, Jan., 1933, Mr. Fitch in "Dinner at Eight"; Playhouse, Feb., 1934, Atkins in "The Big House"; Arts, Oct., 1934, Charles Ducroix in "No Greater Crime"; Fulham, Nov., 1934, the Prince of Wales in "Court Cards"; Piccadilly, July, 1935, Otto Krantz in "Public Saviour No. 1"; Arts, Jan., 1936, Inspector Moll in "Repayment"; Duke of York's, Dec., 1936, Andrew MacTavish in "Eskimos, Ahoy"; "Q," Feb., 1938, James Mayo in "Beyond the Horizon"; Arts, Apr., 1938, Sir Nathan Grimmett in "Murder Without Tears"; Drury Lane, Sept., 1938, Mac Morris and Burgundy in "Henry V"; during the late War, toured camps in England for E.N.S.A., and played various repertory seasons at Brighton, Southport, Leicester, Bristol, etc.; Apollo, Aug., 1940, played Captain Mulrooney in "Margin for Error"; during 1943, toured with the Old Vic company in "Shirley," "The Confederacy," "The Seagull," "Abraham Lincoln," etc.; Scala, Dec., 1943, played The Lion in "Alice Through the Looking Glass"; during 1944, toured for C.E.M.A. in "A Bill of Divorcement," and "Dr. Knock"; toured, 1945, as Peter Cauchon in "Saint Joan," in England, Belgium, Germany and France; at the Old Vic, Sept., 1951, played the King of Morocco and the First Physician in "Tamburlaine the Great"; Old Vic, Feb., 1953, played Popilius Lena in "Julius Caesar"; has also appeared in films, since 1928; also played numerous leading parts for the Phoenix and Renaissance Societies, and for the Fellowship of Players.
(Died 1967; age 80)

LEAMORE, Tom, comedian; *b.* 1865; made his first appearance on the stage in 1880, at the old Rodney Music Hall; his first engagement of any note was at the Star, Bermondsey, in 1882; he then appeared at the Middlesex; his first appearance in a West End hall was made at the Trocadero, under the late Sam Adams, and subsequently he was engaged at the London Pavilion, Oxford, etc.; has since appeared at every principal hall in London and the provinces, and has played all the leading tours and circuits; among many popular songs which he has introduced may be noted " Serving 'em all alike "; " My Intended "; " Last Night "; " The Shipwrecked Captain "; " Percy from Pimlico "; " The Fireman," etc.

LEAN, Cecil, actor; *b.* London, Ontario, Canada, 7 July, 1878; *m.* (1) Florence Holbrook (mar. dis.); (2) Cleo Mayfield; first came into prominence in 1903, when he toured with Frank Daniels in " Miss Simplicity"; in 1903 went to the La Salle Theatre, Chicago, where he appeared in " The Time, the Place, and the Girl," and he was connected with this piece for some years; subsequently appeared there in " The Honeymoon Trail," and " The Soul Kiss " ; he appeared at the New York Theatre, Jan., 1908, as Ketcham Short in " The Soul Kiss " ; Feb., 1910, played Tom Genowin in " Bright Eyes " and toured in the same part 1911-12 ; at the Ziegfeld Theatre, Chicago, Aug., 1912, played Slim Henderson in his own play, " The Military Girl " ; at Weber and Fields' Theatre, Jan., 1913, he played Hans Zifler in " The Man with Three Wives " ; the following year he went to England, and made his first appearance in London, at the Victoria Palace, July, 1914 ; at the Casino, New York, Aug., 1915, appeared as Rudolph Stoeger in " The Blue Paradise," and during 1916-17 toured in the same play ; at the Century Theatre, Nov., 1917, played in " Miss 1917 " ; during 1919-20 toured as Robert Holmes in " Look Who's Here ! " and played the same part when the play was produced at the Forty-fourth Street Theatre, New York, Mar., 1920 ; at the Astor, Feb., 1922, played Coley Collins in " The Blushing Bride " ; at the Winter Garden, New York, May, 1924, appeared in "Innocent Eyes" ; at the Grand Opera House, Chicago, Sept., 1932, played Matthew Arnold Fulton in "Of Thee I Sing." *Club :* Lambs'. (*Died 18 July, 1935; age 57*)

LEAVER, Philip, actor and dramatic author ; *b.* London, 1904 ; *e.* St. Paul's School; studied for the stage at the Royal Academy of Dramatic Art; made his first appearance on the stage in 1924, and acted under the name of Philip Brandon ; appeared at the New, Sept., 1926, in "The Constant Nymph"; the Royalty, Mar., 1931, as Hubert Capes in "The World of Light"; Adelphi, Sept., 1931, Schweimann in "Grand Hotel"; Wyndham's, Jan., 1934, played Omichand in "Clive of India"; Old Vic., Nov., 1934, Archbishop of Rheims in "Saint Joan"; Embassy, Apr., 1936, Decourtray in "Return to Yesterday"; Savoy, Nov., 1936, Otto Farenthold in "Young Madame Conti," and played the same part at the Music Box, New York, Mar., 1937 ; Embassy, London, May, and Strand, June, 1937, Kurt Schneider in " Judgment Day"; West-

minster, Dec., 1937, Sir Sholto Spielman in "Out of the Picture"; Vaudeville, Feb., 1938, François in "Mirabelle"; Arts, Sept., 1938, Henry Harrican in "Blind Man's Buff"; Apollo, Dec., 1938, Rowland Westmore in "Windfall"; Phoenix, Nov., 1939, General Rakovsky in "Judgment Day"; from 1941–3, was engaged with the B.B.C. as propaganda and script writer; Theatre Royal, Glasgow, Feb., 1944, played the Hotel Manager in "The Fifth Column"; Adelphi, July, 1945, M. de Vigny in "Sweet Yesterday"; Embassy, Dec., 1946, Don Mendoza in "Drake's Drum"; Lyric, Hammersmith, July, 1947, Landrieu in "Men Without Shadows," and subsequently, at the "Q," 1947, Maldonado in "Iris"; Arts, Feb., 1948, Mr. Gas Jones in "A Comedy of Good and Evil"; Lyric, Hammersmith, Apr., 1949, played Prince Philip of Coburg in "Royal Highness"; Prince's, May, 1950, Col. Paul Dobrieda in "His Excellency"; Westminster, May, 1952, played Mr. Tupman in "The Trial of Mr. Pickwick"; at the "Q," May, 1954, played Count Fosco in "The Lovers"; has also appeared in films, and television plays in England, France, and the United States; author of the following plays: "Ships in Sargasso," 1924 ; "Tomorrow will be Friday," Haymarket, 1932 ; "The Way to the Stars," Wyndham's, 1932; "The Winding Journey," 1934; "Three Set Out," 1936; "Causes Unknown," 1936; "Sweet Yesterday," Adelphi, 1945, "More Things in Heaven," Wyndham's, 1956. *Address:* c/o Barclays Bank, 52 Regent Street, London, W.1.

LE BARGY, Charles Gustave Auguste, French actor ; *b.* La Chapelle, Seine, France, 1858 ; prepared for the stage at the Conservatoire, under M. Gôt, where he took the first prize for comedy in 1879 ; made his first appearance on the stage at the Comédie Française, 27 Nov., 1880, as Clitandre in " Les Femmes Savantes " ; admitted as *sociétaire,* 1887 ; was a professor at the Conservatoire, from 1896-1912 ; appeared at the Comédie Française with great success in the following, among other plays : " Hern-

ani," " L'Etrangère," " Les Tenailles,"
" Le Fils de l'Aretin," " Le Gendre de
M. Poirier," " Patrie," " Raymonde,"
" La Premier Baiser," " Les Fossiles,"
" Struensée," " Margot," " L'autre
danger," " Une Famille," " L'Ami de
la Maison," " Les Romanesques,"
" L'Enigme," " Marion de Lorme,"
" Le Duel," " Les deux Hommes,"
" Le Dédale," " Le Marquis de Priola,"
" Le Demi-Monde," " Connais-toi,"
" Aprés Moi," " Le Respect de L'Am-
our," " Le Père Prodigue," " L'Ami
des Femmes," " On ne badine pas
avec l'Amour," " Il ne fait jurer de
rien," " Les Caprices de Marianne,"
" Frou-Frou," " Le Fils de Giboyer,"
etc. ; in 1912, he quitted the Comédie
Française, and was absent for eight
years ; at the Porte-St.-Martin, 1912,
played Laurent Bouquet in " Les
Flambeaux," and subsequently
Cyrano in " Cyrano de Bergerac " ;
Apr., 1914, played Séverin in " Le
Destin est Maître " ; he re-entered the
Comédie Française in 1920, as a
pensionnaire ; at Brussels, Feb., 1921,
appeared in his own play, " Une
danseuse est morte " ; at the Comédie
Française, June, 1921, again played
Abbé Daniel in " Le Duel " ; appeared
at the Royalty Theatre, London, 1907,
in a number of plays ; is a Chevalier
of the Legion of Honour. *Address :*
5 Rue du Cirque, Paris.

LE BARON, William, dramatic
author ; *b.* Elgin, Ill., U.S.A., 16 Feb.,
1883 ; *s.* of John K. Le Baron and his
wife Mary (Bundy) ; *e.* Chicago University and New York University ;
m. Mabel H. Hollins ; has written the
following plays : " The Echo," 1909 ;
" A la Broadway," 1911 ; " The
Antique Girl " (with C. B. de Mille),
1912 ; " The Trained Nurses," 1912 ;
" The Earl and the Girls," 1913 ; " The
Red Canary " (with Alex. Johnstone),
1913 ; " Her Regiment," 1917 ; " The
Very Idea," 1917 ; " Back to Earth,"
1918 ; " I Love You," 1919 ; " Apple
Blossoms," 1919 ; " The Half-Moon,"
1920 ; " The Scarlet Man," 1921 ;
" Nobody's Money," 1921 ; " The
Love Letter " (from the Hungarian),
1921 ; " The Yankee Princess " (from
the Hungarian), 1922 ; " Moonlight "

(founded on " I Love You "), 1924 ;
" Oh! Baby," 1924 ; " Something to
Brag About " (with Edgar Selwyn),
1925 ; was editor of *Collier's Weekly,*
1918-19 ; director of the Cosmopolitan
Film Productions, 1919-24 ; Supervisor
of Famous Players-Lasky Corporation,
Long Island Studios, 1924-7 ; vice-
president Film Booking Office Studios,
1927-8 ; vice-president of R.K.O.
Productions, 1929-31 ; director of
all Paramount Pictures Inc., productions, 1931-40 ; producer for 20th
Century-Fox Film Corporation since
1941 ; has written and collaborated
in many films. *Clubs :* Lotos, Players',
Coffee House, and Dutch Treat.
(Died 9 Feb., 1958; age 76)

LEBLANC, Georgette, French actress
and vocalist ; *b.* Rouen, 1876 ; *d.*
of Emile Bianchini (Leblanc) and
his wife, formerly Mdlle. de Brohy ;
e. at home ; *m.* Maurice Maeterlinck (mar. dis.) ; made her first
appearance on the stage at the Opéra
Comique, Paris, 1893, as Françoise
in " L'Attaque du Moulin " ; subsequently at the same theatre appeared
as Carmen, and Sapho ; at the
Théâtre de la Monnaie, Brussels, appeared in the leading *rôles* in " La
Navarraise, " Fidelio," " Thaïs " ; has
since founded the Théâtre Maeterlinck
and played " Monna Vanna," " Joy-
zelle," " La Mort de Tintagiles,"
Charlotte Corday ; between times, she
has appeared at the Opéra Comique
and played Ariane, Barbe-Bleu, Marguerite in " Faust " ; at Saint-Wan-
drille, she has played Lady Macbeth,
and Mélisande in " Pelléas et Méli-
ande " ; appeared in London, June,
1902, as Monna Vanna, at a private
performance ; has also frequently presented M. Maeterlinck's works at
artistic conferences.
(Died 26 Oct., 1941; age 66)

LE BRETON, Flora, actress ; *b.*
Croydon, 1898 ; studied for the stage
at the Academy of Dramatic Art,
where she gained the Silver Medal ;
made her first appearance on the stage
at Wyndham's Theatre, 1917, succeeding Mab l Russell as Cherry Walters
in " London Pride " ; at the St.

Martin's, Nov., 1918, played Martha in "The Officers' Mess"; subsequently toured in "The Maid of the Mountains" and "Eliza Comes to Stay"; at the Prince of Wales's, Aug., 1919, appeared in "Bran Pie"; she then turned her attention to the cinema stage, making her first appearance in "La Poupée"; other films in which she played a prominent part were "Through Fire and Water," "Little Miss Nobody," "Tons of Money," "I Will Repay"; went to the United States in Oct., 1923, appearing in several film productions; made her first appearance on the regular stage in New York, at the Comedy, 8 Jan., 1925, when she played Lass in "Lass o' Laughter"; at Chicago, in 1926, played in "Betsy Nobody"; reappeared in London, at the Palace, Sept., 1927, when she played Miss Wendell in "The Girl Friend"; returned to New York, and appeared at the Casino de Paris, Jan., 1928, with "The Optimists"; at the Mansfield, Apr., 1928, played Lady Delphine in "Present Arms"; appeared at the London Coliseum, Jan., 1930, in "The Photophone Girl"; at the Selwyn Theatre, New York, Sept., 1931, played Regina in "The Singing Rabbi"; Globe, Oct., 1931, Maisie Gripps in "The Cat and the Fiddle"; Empire, New York (for Theatre Guild), Oct., 1933, Lisette in "The School for Husbands"; at Toronto, Dec., 1934, played Cinderella; returned to Europe, 1935, and at the Folies Bergère, Paris, Nov., 1935, appeared in "La Folie d'Amour." *Recreations:* Dancing and motoring.

LECONTE, Marie (Lacombe), French actress; *b.* in Paris; made her first appearance on the stage at the Château d'Eau Théâtre, 1891, in "Sainte Russie"; subsequently appeared at the Ambigu Théâtre in "Les Deux Orphelines"; appeared at the Gymnase Théâtre, where she played Jeanne, in "Les Demi-Vierges," Yvonne in "La Carrière," etc.; made her first appearance at the Comédie Française as Mimi, in "La Vie de Bohême," 9 Sept., 1897; has made many successes at that theatre in "Les Femmes Savantes," "Le

Médecin Malgré Lui," "Adrienne Lecouvreur," "Cabotins," "Patrie," "Frou frou," "L'Ami des Femmes," "Les Demoiselles de Saint Cyr," "Le Monde où l'on s'ennuie," "La Chance de Françoise," "Molière et Scaramouche," "La Plus Faible," "Claudie," "Le Paon," "Le Dieu Terme," "L'Amour Veille," "Amoureuse," "Le Bon Roi Dagobert," "Le Masque et le Bandeau," "L'Imprévu," "La Fleur Merveilleuse," "Le Respect de l'amour," "Connais-toi," "Sire," "Primerose," "Le Ménage de Molière," "Poil de Carotte," "Bagatelle," "Les Ombres," "Le Prince Charmant," "D'Un jour a l'autre," "Turcaret," "L'Ami Fritz," "Paraître," "Le Mariage de Figaro," "Les Deux Ecoles," "Le Filibustier," "Barberine," etc.; elected a *sociétaire* of the Comédie Française, 1903; is an Officer of the Academy. *Address:* 36 Avenue d'Iéna, Paris.

LEDERER, Francis, actor; *b.* Karlin, Prague, 6 Nov., 1906; *s.* of Joseph Lederer and his wife Rosa (Ornstein); *e.* Prague Conservatorium; *m.* (1) Ada Mejedly (mar. dis.); (2) Marguerita Bolado (mar. dis.); (3) Marion Irvine; was formerly engaged in business; studied for the stage at Prague and in Berlin; made his first appearance on the stage at Prague, Apr., 1926, as an extra in "Das Heisse Herz"; subsequently appeared at Brünn and Breslau, playing juvenile leads in "Hay Fever," "Outward Bound," "Volpone," etc.; in Berlin, in 1928, played Prince Henry in "King Henry IV" (Part I), Octavius in "Man and Superman," etc.; at the Renaissance Theatre, Berlin, in 1929, he appeared in "Cœur Bube"; next appeared in "The Wonderful Lie of Nina Petrowa," and was then engaged by Max Reinhardt to play Romeo, with Elizabeth Bergner; subsequently appeared in "Wonder Bar"; made his first appearance in London, at Streatham Hill, 9 Feb., 1931, as Fleuriot in "My Sister and I," and appeared in the same part at the Shaftesbury, 23 Feb., 1931; at the Lyric, Apr., 1931, played Andreas Steiner in "Autumn Crocus"; Garrick,

Jan., 1932, Mosca in "Volpone"; Palace, Mar., 1932, Victor Florescu in "The Cat and the Fiddle"; he then went to America and made his first appearance on the New York Stage, at the Morosco Theatre, 19 Nov., 1932, as Andreas in "Autumn Crocus"; at the El Capitan, Hollywood, Jan., 1934, again played in "Autumn Crocus"; San Francisco, Sept., 1937, and on tour, 1938, played Joe Buonaparte in "Golden Boy"; at the Civic Theatre, Chicago, 1939, played Chico in "Seventh Heaven"; Ethel Barrymore, New York, July, 1939, succeeded Laurence Olivier as Gaylord Easterbrook in "No Time for Comedy"; toured, 1941, in "Pursuit of Happiness," and 1942, in "The Play's the Thing"; at the Playhouse, Wilmington, Nov., 1942, played General Bonaparte in "The Man of Destiny," Kenneth Dovey in "The Old Lady Shows Her Medals," and The Master in "Playgoers"; toured, Oct., 1944, as Oswald in "Ghosts," as well as in "A Doll's House"; Fulton, July, 1950, played Lafont in "Parisienne"; in summer theatres, 1950, appeared in "The Silver Whistle"; at the Arena (Hotel Edison), Oct., 1950, played Capt. Bluntschli in "Arms and the Man"; re-appeared on the English stage at the Palace, Manchester, Apr., 1951, as Adrian Van Dyck in "Collector's Item"; at the London Hippodrome, Feb., 1955, succeeded Anton Walbrook as Jacques Devallée in "Wedding in Paris"; toured America, 1956, as the Prince Regent in "The Sleeping Prince"; toured America, 1957, as Jaques Balard in "The Dazzling Hour"; again toured America, 1958, as Mr. Frank in "The Diary of Anne Frank"; since 1929, has also appeared in innumerable films on the Continent and in Hollywood; directed films in Hollywood, 1961. *Hobby:* Acting. *Address:* Box 32, Canoga Park, California.

LEDERER, George W., manager; *b.* Wilkesbarre, Pa., U.S.A., 1861; *m.* (1) Reine Davies (mar. dis.); (2) Adele Burt; his first theatrical venture dates back as far as 1878, when, in conjunction with Sydney Rosenfeld, he was responsible for a tour of "Florizel," prior to which he had been actor, reporter, and dramatist; in partnership with A. H. Canby, became lessee of the Casino Theatre, New York, in Oct., 1893, opening with the production of "The Princess of Nicotine," also producing "Prince Kam," "About Town," "The Passing Show," and "The Little Trooper"; in Nov., 1894, with Canby, became manager of the Bijou Theatre, which they opened with "Miss Dynamite"; resuming the management of the Casino in 1895, in conjunction with Canby, they produced "The Merry World," "The Sphinx," "In Gay New York," "An American Beauty," "The Whirl of the Town," "The Belle of New York," and "The Telephone Girl"; he became sole lessee in 1898, and made the following productions: "In Gay Paree," "The Jolly Musketeer," "The Singing Girl," "Princess Chic," "The Casino Girl," "The Belle of Bohemia," and "Florodora"; in Apr., 1899, he became manager of the New York Theatre, opening with "The Man in the Moon"; in 1903 he produced "The Blonde in Black" at the Knickerbocker Theatre and "The Jersey Girl" at the Victoria; and in 1904 was manager of the production of "The Southerners," which had an extended tour; subsequent productions were "Madame Sherry," "Mama's Baby Boy," "The Charity Girl" etc.; later in partnership with H. H. Frazee, as Frazee and Lederer, producing musical plays; produced "Angel Face," 1920; "The Girl in the Spotlight" 1920; "Peaches" 1923; in July, 1928, was appointed General Manager for Sam H. Harris productions; in 1931 produced "The Joy of Living" (with G. F. Womrath); in London he has been responsible for the production of many musical comedies, the most notable having been "The Belle of New York," at the Shaftesbury, in 1898.
(*Died 8 Oct., 1938; age 77*)

LEE, Auriol, actress and producer; *b.* London, 13 Sept., 1880; *d.* of Dr. Robert Lee, physician; is related to General Robert Lee, who served with distinction in the American Civil War; *e.* England and on the Continent; prepared for the stage by M. Vermandèle, *directeur de la mise-en-scene* at the Théâtre Monnaie, Brussels; *m.* Frederick W. Lloyd (mar. dis); made her first appearance on the stage at Drury Lane Theatre, 14 Nov., 1900, as the Hon. Mrs. Sydney in " The Price of Peace "; she was next seen in London, at the Strand Theatre, 10 Aug., 1901, as Lady Golightly in " Newspaper Nuptials," also understudying Hilda Trevelyan in " The Talk of the Town "; she then appeared at the Haymarket Theatre, 2 Jan., 1902, as Victorine in " Frocks and Frills "; at the St. James's, Aug., 1902, played Jehanneton in "If I were King"; at the Avenue, Feb., 1903, appeared as Flora Beasley in " The Adoption of Archibald "; in 1903, accompanied Forbes-Robertson to America, and appeared as Bessie Broke in " The Light that Failed "; subsequently toured the English provinces with Forbes-Robertson for some time ; at the Criterion, July, 1905, played Vicky Ventry in " The Axis "; at the St. James's, 1907, appeared as Nina in " His House in Order," for some time, subsequently touring in the same part ; also appeared as Muriel Glayde in " John Glayde's Honour "; at the Savoy, 30 Dec., 1907, appeared as Louka in " Arms and the Man "; at His Majesty's, Apr.,1908, appeared as Jessica in " The Merchant of Venice "; at the Haymarket, May, 1908, played Edith Bridgenorth in " Getting Married "; subsequently toured as Raina in " Arms and the Man,' and Violet in " Man and Superman "; during 1909, appeared at the Lyric, as Engracia in " The Chief of Staff," Miladi in " The Three Musketeers," Lady Percy in " King Henry IV " (part I), Mrs. Belmont and Sadie Adams in " Fires of Fate "; at the Playhouse, Aug., 1909, played Mrs. Hay in " A Sense of Humour "; at His Majesty's, Feb., 1910, appeared as Fancy Free in " The O'Flynn "; at the Lyceum, Sept., 1910, played Gertie Coleman in " The Sins of London "; at the Aldwych, Dec., 1910, appeared as Sophie Coventry in " The Girl Who Took the Wrong

Turning "; at the Royalty, Apr., 1911, played Elizabeth Spender in " The Master of Mrs. Chilvers "; at the Kingsway, May, 1911, played Madame Vestris in " The First Actress "; at the Globe, Nov., 1911, played Lucienne Bocard in " The Glad Eye "; at the Savoy, Nov., 1911, played Mariette Vrend in " Pains and Penalties "; in Sept., 1912, appeared at the King's, Hammersmith, as Gertrude Rhead in " Milestones," subsequently crossed to the United States, and appeared at the Liberty Theatre, 17 Sept., 1912, in the same part ; on her return to England, appeared at the Theatre Royal, Brighton, June, 1914, as Madeleine in " The Nut "; in Aug., 1914, toured as Gobette in " Who's the Lady ? "; at the Strand, Oct., 1914, reappeared as Lucienne Bocard in " The Glad Eye "; at the New Theatre, Mar., 1915, played Bella Wilson in " Seven Days "; at the Little Theatre, May, 1915, Lèchy Elbernon in " Exchange "; at the Kingsway, Oct., 1915, played Mrs. Gus Weedlemay in " Iris Intervenes " : at Devonshire Park, Eastbourne, Nov., 1915, Vera Ormonde in " Whose Wife ? "; in 1916 went to America ; at the New Amsterdam Theatre, New York, May, 1916, played Jessica in " The Merchant of Venice," with Sir Herbert Tree ; at the Park Theatre, Jan., 1917, Mistress Quickly in " The Merry Wives of Windsor "; at the Fulton Theatre, Feb., 1917, Aunt Alicia in " Pals First "; during 1917-18 toured in " The Man who Stayed at Home "; at the Fulton Theatre, New York, May, 1918, played Miss Miller in " Her Honor the Mayor "; at the Belasco Theatre, Nov., 1918, Lizzie in " Tiger ! Tiger ! "; returned to England, 1920 : appeared at the Garrick, Sept., 1920, as Margot Allfrey in " Her Dancing Man "; at the Playhouse, Mar., 1921, Jeannette Asnière in " Love ? ! "; at the Comedy, Apr., 1921, Mrs. Barter in " A Matter of Fact "; June, 1921, Camille in " A Family Man "; at the Court, Mar., 1922, the Unknown Lady in " The Silver Box "; at the Little Theatre, May, 1922, played in a series of " Grand Guignol " plays ; Aug., 1922, played Zozo in a play of that

name ; at the Shaftesbury, Oct., 1922, Susan Sillsby in " The Cat and the Canary " ; at the Garrick, Sept., 1923, Harriet Nichols in " Ambush " ; at the Comedy, May, 1924, Nan Court- field in " This Marriage " ; at the Everyman, July, 1924, Lesbia Gran- tham in " Getting Married " ; Long- acre, New York, Feb., 1925, Vi Beau- mont in " The Dark Angel " ; Henry Miller, Sept., 1925, Helen Saville in " The Vortex " ; Klaw, Nov., 1926, Zoe St. Mervin in " This Was a Man " ; returned to London and appeared at the Garrick (for the Play Actors), Feb., 1928, as Madame Amour in "A Wise Child " ; with Noel Scott, adapted " The Fairway " (from the French), 1925 ; of late years has developed into one of the most successful pro- ducers ; produced "Diversion," "The Clandestine Marriage," 1928 ; "After All," 1929 ; "Nine Till Six," "How to be Healthy Though Married," "Jeal- ousy," "Dance with No Music," 1930 ; "London Wall," "Sea Fever," "There's Always Juliet," 1931 ; "I Lived with You," "Pleasure Cruise," "Some- body Knows," "Behold, We Live," "Another Language," 1932 ; "Mother of Pearl," "The Distaff Side," "The Wind and the Rain," 1933 ; "The Dark Tower," "Line Engaged," "Family Affairs," "Flowers of the Forest," 1934 ; "Grief Goes Over," 1935 ; "The Lady of La Paz," 1936 ; "Gertie Maude," "People at Sea," 1937 ; "Peace and Goodwill," "On Borrowed Time," 1938 ; in New York, has produced "Oliver Oliver," 1934 ; "Times Have Changed," "Most of the Game," "Eden End," 1935 ; at Bos- ton, Mass., 1939, produced "West of Broadway" ; with John Van Druten adapted "Sea Fever," 1931 ; has acted in French and Greek plays.
(Died 2 July, 1941; age 60)

LEE, Bert, author and composer ; *b.* Ravensthorpe, Yorks., 11 June, 1880 ; *s.* of Thomas Lee and his wife Sarah (Swire) ; *e.* Wheelwright Gram- mar School, Dewsbury ; *m.* Marlie Longmire ; began writing in 1909, and has written over 2,000 songs ; among the more popular of these may be mentioned " Joshu-ah," " Hello! Hello! Who's Your Lady Friend," " Fancy You Fancying Me," " Somebody would shout out, 'Shop'!", "The Gypsy Warned Me," "Could Lloyd George do It?", "How Time Flies," "A Couple o' Ducks," "The Body in the Bag," "Don't Let 'em Scrap the British Navy," "The Rich Man Rides by in his Carriage and Pair," "Good by-ee," "Samoa," etc., mostly in collabora- tion with R. P. Weston ; also in collab- oration with Weston contributed songs to "Cheep," 1916 ; "U.S.," 1918 ; "Back Again," 1919 ; "Cinderella," 1920 ; "Puss-Puss," 1921 ; "Pot Luck," 1921 ; "A to Z," 1922 ; contributed scenes to "Round in Fifty," 1922 ; "Brighter London," 1923 ; "Leap Year," 1924 ; part-author with Weston, of "Rations," "Any Lady," "Ciro's Frolics," "Crystals," 1918 ; "Black- Hand George," "The Follies of 1919," "The Whirl of To-day," 1919 ; "The Follies of 1920"; "The Scrap Book," 1921 ; "Listening In," "Sunshine and Laughter," "The Virgin Queen," 1922; "Better than Ever," "Carte Blanche," "Lightning," "Stars of 1923," "Yes, We Have," 1923 ; "Tilly," "You'd Be Surprised," "22 Carat," 1924 ; "Reve- lations," "Running Riot," "Mr. Tickle, M.P.," "Better Days," "Flyaway Peter," "Playtime Treasures," 1925 ; "Turned-Up," "Hullo, George," "The Merry-Go-Round," "Tom Arnold's Follies," "King Rags," "Merely Play- ers," 1926 ; "Hit the Deck," "Love and Money," "The Girl Friend," 1927 ; "Virginia," "Lucky Girl," 1928 ; "Merry, Merry," "Hold Everything," 1929 ; "Here Comes the Bride," "Little Tommy Tucker," "The Sleeping Beauty," 1930 ; "The Song of the Drum," 1931 ; "Tell Her the Truth," 1932 ; "He Wanted Adventure," "Give Me a Ring," 1933 ; "Yes, Madam ? " 1934 ; "Please, Teacher !" 1935 ; "O.K. for Sound," "Certainly, Sir !" 1936 ; since the death of R. P. Weston, has collaborated in "Big Business," "London Rhapsody," "Oh ! You Letty," 1937 ; "The Fleet's Lit Up," "Bobby, Get Your Gun," "These Foolish Things," 1938 ; "Black and Blue," 1939. *Recreation :* Golf. *Clubs :* Savage and Stage Golfing Society.
(Died 23 Jan., 1946; age 65)

LEE, Canada (*né* Leonard Lionel Cornelius Canegata), actor; *b.* New York City, 3 Mar., 1907; *s.* of James Cornelius Canegata and his wife Lydia (Whaley); *e.* public schools, New York; was formerly a pugilist, jockey, and violinist; made his first appearance on the stage at the Princess Theatre, New York, 6 Feb., 1928, in "Meek Mose"; first came into prominence at the Civic Repertory Theatre, 1 Oct., 1934, when he appeared as Blacksnake in a revival of "Stevedore"; with the Negro People's Theatre, 1936, played Banquo in "Macbeth"; Biltmore, Dec., 1937, appeared as Henry in "Brown Sugar"; with the Federal Theatre, 1938, appeared as Christopher in "Haiti" and in "The Front Page"; Empire, Jan., 1939, played Drayton in "Mamba's Daughter," and again at the Broadway, Mar., 1940; Lincoln, Oct., 1940, Victor Mason in "Big White Fog"; at the St. James's, Mar., 1941, made a great success when he played Bigger Thomas in "Native Son"; Belasco, Aug., 1942, played Thomas Piper in "Across the Board on To-Morrow Morning," and Blackstone Boulevard in "Talking to You"; Majestic, Oct., 1942, again played Bigger Thomas in "Native Son"; Cort, Dec., 1943, Sam Johnson in "South Pacific"; Mansfield, Aug., 1944, played Danny in "Anna Lucasta"; Alvin, Jan., 1945, scored another great success, when he played Caliban in "The Tempest"; Cort, May, 1946, played David Bennett in "On Whitman Avenue"; Ethel Barrymore, Oct., 1946, Daniel de Bosola in "The Duchess of Malfi"; Hudson, Nov., 1948, played George in "Set My People Free"; first appeared in films, 1943, in "Lifeboat." *Recreation:* Horse-riding.
(Died 9 May, 1952; age 45)

LEE, Gypsy Rose (*née* Rose Louise Hovick), actress, dancer, dramatic author, and novelist; *b.* Seattle, Washington, U.S.A., 9 Feb., 1913; *d.* of John Olav Hovick and his wife Anna; *m.* (1) Arnold Mizzy (mar. dis.), (2) Alexander Kirkland (mar. dis.); (3) Julio de Diego; has been on the stage since early childhood, having appeared at the age of six, in vaudeville, with her sister, June Havoc, as a member of a juvenile troupe of singers and dancers; first appeared in New York, at Minsky's, 14th Street; appeared in her mother's company, 1930, in an act, "Madam Rose's Dancing Daughters"; first attracted attention when she appeared in burlesque, at the Irving Place Theatre, New York; at the Ziegfeld Theatre, 8 Mar., 1932, under the name of Rose Louise, appeared as the Girl in the Compartment in "Hot-Cha!"; Majestic, Mar., 1933, played in "Strike Me Pink"; Ziegfeld, Sept., 1936, appeared in "Ziegfeld Follies"; first appeared in "straight" comedy, at the Vanderbilt, July, 1939, when she succeeded Nancy Carroll as Birdie Carr in "I Must Love Someone"; subsequently toured as Bonnie in "Burlesque"; appeared at the New York World's Fair, 1939, in "The Streets of Paris" and "Gay New Orleans," and became noted for her "strip-tease" act; subsequently, at the 46th Street Theatre, Sept., 1940, played May Daly in "Du Barry Was a Lady"; Music Box, June, 1942, appeared in "Star and Garter"; first appeared in films, 1937, in "You Can't Have Everything"; is the author of the play, "The Naked Genius," 1943; is also the author of the novels: "The G. String Murders" and "Mother Finds a Body."
(Died 26 Apr., 1970; age 56)

LEE, Jennie, actress; *b.* London; *d.* of Edwin George Lee, artist; *m.* J. P. Burnett, dramatic author and actor; made her first appearance on the stage at the Lyceum, 22 Jan., 1870, as Henry in "Chilperic"; at the same theatre, she appeared in "Le Petit Faust," and in July, 1870, joined Mrs. Swanborough at the Strand, playing in "The Pilgrim of Love," "Orpheus and Eurydice," "Eily O'Connor," "Richard Cœur de Lion," and "The Idle 'Prentice"; accompanied the late E. A. Sothern to America, to play Mary Meredith in "Our American Cousin"; was a member of the Union Square Theatre company, New York, where she played in 1872, in "Agnes," "Frou-

Frou," "Caste," etc.; subsequently played for two years in San Francisco, where she appeared for the first time, in 1875, in her famous part of Jo in "Bleak House"; reappeared in London, at the Surrey Theatre, Christmas, 1875 as Jack in "Jack the Giant Killer"; appeared at the Globe Theatre, 21 Feb., 1876, as Jo, scoring an immense success; twenty years of her career were associated almost entirely with this play, in which she has appeared all over the world; she appeared at the Imperial, July, 1876, as Andy Blake in the play of that name; at the Globe, Feb., 1877, played Don Leander in "The Invisible Prince"; at the Royalty Theatre, Jan., 1880, played Midge in a play of that name; subsequently went to Australia, where she remained until 1885; reappeared in London, at the Strand Theatre, 1885, in "Jo"; in Apr., 1885, played there in "Good Luck"; at the Olympic, Sept., 1888, played Sam Willoughby in "The Ticket-of-Leave Man"; at the Royalty, Aug., 1904, played Mrs. James Blackwood in "The Chetwynd Affair"; at His Majesty's, July, 1905, played Mrs. Bedwin in "Oliver Twist"; Apr., 1906, Mistress Quickly in "The Merry Wives of Windsor"; at the Oxford Music Hall, Dec., 1910, played in "The Fourth Time of Asking"; at the Lyric Theatre, 7 Feb., 1921, appeared at a *matinée* in aid of the Charles Dickens Memorial House, as Jo in a scene from "Bleak House"; is one of the pensioners of King George's Pension Fund for Actors. *(Died 3 May, 1930; age 84)*

LEFEAUX, Charles, actor and director; *b.* London, 14 Jan., 1909; *s.* of Charles Ernest Lefeaux and his wife Louisa Stevenson (Clark); *m.* (1) Pauline Sheridan Whitehead (mar. dis.); (2) Isobel Filkin; studied for the stage at the Royal Academy of Dramatic Art, where he gained the Silver Medal; made his first appearance on the stage at the Arts Theatre, 1 July, 1928, as the Attendant in "The Tragic Muse"; during 1929–30, played repertory seasons at Huddersfield and Hull; appeared at the Embassy, Sept., 1930; at the London Hippodrome, Mar., 1931, played Henry Clyde-Burkin in "Stand Up and Sing"; Embassy, Sept., 1932, Baillard in "Miracle at Verdun"; Duchess, June, 1933, the Steward in "Eight Bells"; Globe, Mar., 1934, Edward Mortimer in "Double Door"; at Fulham, Nov., 1934, played the Bishop in "Court Cards" and Fred in "Anthony and Anna"; Little, Jan., 1935, General Su in "Lady Precious Stream"; Duke of York's, Oct., 1935, the Cooper in "The Hangman"; Playhouse, Dec., 1935, The Physician in "Mary Tudor"; His Majesty's, Apr., 1936, Beau Brummell in "The Happy Hypocrite"; St. James's, Dec., 1936, Soper in "O Mistress Mine"; Gate, Mar. 1937, James Porter in "Out of Sight"; Strand, May, and New, June, 1937, Dupont in "The Great Romancer," also producing the play; Apollo, Feb., 1938, William Heather in "Black Swans"; Garrick, Jan., 1939, Mr. Bleat in "Hundreds of Thousands"; Aldwych, Mar., 1940, Mr. Joll in "Nap Hand"; served in the R.A.F., Sept., 1940–Oct., 1945; reappeared in London, at the Embassy, May, 1946, when he played Sir Reginald Barbee in "Guest in the House"; Comedy, Aug., 1946, played Col. Maulnier in "The Other Side"; Dec., 1946, appeared as D.D.A.2. (Mr. Vincent) in "The Man From the Ministry"; has appeared on numerous occasions for the Repertory Players, (for whom he has also directed several plays), and in several productions at the Embassy, Gate, and "Q" Theatres; entered films, 1933, and has appeared in innumerable pictures; joined B.B.C. Repertory Company, Aug., 1946; was in charge of the B.B.C. Drama Script Unit, 1951–3; has since been a director in the Drama Department winning the Italia Prize in 1968, for his radio production of "Albert's Bridge"; has also been responsible for the series "Style in Acting" and "Our Changing Theatre"; directed his first television production, 1956, and subsequently a number of plays and modern operas; has taught at the R.A.D.A., and the Central School of Speech and Drama. *Recreations:* Walking and working. *Address:* Flat 7, 104 Fitzjohns Avenue, London, N.W.3. *Telephone No.:* 01-794 4519.

LE FEUVRE, Guy, actor, vocalist, and composer; *b.* Ottawa, Canada, 17 Oct., 1883; *s.* of Le Feuvre Anstruther-Mainguy and his wife Ann Maria (Layton); *e.* Collegiate Institute, and privately, in Canada; studied music and composition under Dr. Hugo Felix, and at the Guildhall School of Music, London; *m.* Evelyn Bruce Graham Stamper; made his first appearance on the stage at Opera House, Leicester, 1905, in the chorus of "The Officers' Mess"; first appeared in London, at the Garrick Theatre, 2 Oct., 1905, walking-on in "The Walls of Jericho"; following a two-years illness, went to America, and made his first appearance in New York, at the Knickerbocker Theatre, 2 Sept., 1908, in "The Girls of Gottenburg," for which he was also chorusmaster; from 1910–12, studied singing in Florence, under Enrico Gorelli; reappeared in London, at the Tivoli, Jan., 1912, playing Julien in "The Daring of Diane"; engaged by George Edwardes in 1912, he understudied Robert Michaelis in "Gypsy Love," at Daly's, and toured as Baron Montalba in "The Dancing Mistress"; Gaiety, Feb., 1914, played Baron Cleves in "After the Girl"; during the first World War, served in the 18th Royal Fusiliers, invalided out, 1915; then toured in "The Pearl Girl"; next appeared at the Vaudeville, 1916–8, under André Charlot in "Some," "Cheep," and "Tabs"; Ambassadors', Aug., 1919, appeared in "Back Again," subsequently appearing at the Prince of Wales's, in "Bran Pie"; from 1920–2, studied composition in Vienna; Garrick, Oct., 1922, played Robert le Bas in "Dédé"; toured, 1923, as Crosby in "The Thirteenth Chair"; Lyric, Hammersmith, 1924–5, played Don Carlos in "The Duenna," Sir Lucius O'Trigger in "The Rivals," and Agazzi in "And That's the Truth"; Scala, Oct., 1925 (for Phoenix Society), played Malvolio in "Twelfth Night"; Everyman, Jan.–Dec., 1926, Wednesday in "The Man Who Was Thursday," Mr. Pembleton in "Mr Pepys," and Sparkish in "The Country Wife"; spent the next seven years in Austria, giving operatic song recitals and concerts; returned to London, and at the Saville, Dec., 1933, played George IV in "Beau Brummell"; Vaudeville, Mar.,1934, Philippe Baucq in "Nurse Cavell"; Embassy in Apr.–May, 1934, appeared in "The City of Ships" and "The Roof"; Playhouse, May, 1934, succeeded Nigel Playfair as Counsel for the Defence in "Libel"; St. Martin's, Apr., 1936, the Editor in "The Great Experiment"; Savoy, Nov., 1936, Dr. Schönberg in "Young Madame Conti"; appeared at the Embassy and "Q," in various plays, 1937; Duke of York's, Jan., 1938, Anthony Laszlo in "Gentleman's Agreement"; again retired through illness, 1938–9; was engaged in Postal Censorship, 1939–41; Whitehall, Apr., 1940, played the Rev. Simon Peters in "Without the Prince"; "Q," 1941, appeared in "Nurse Cavell," "Love All," and "School for Slavery"; during 1942, toured as Captain Joshua in "Thunder Rock," and then joined the Oxford Repertory company; during 1942–3, again appeared in several plays at the "Q" Theatre; toured, 1943, as the Dean in "Kiss the Girls," and 1944, as Laroque in "Madame X"; Prince of Wales's, Apr., 1944, the Lord Advocate in "The Rest is Silence"; Arts Theatre, Cambridge, Nov.–Dec., 1944, the Doctor in "The Father" and Roebuck Ramsden in "Man and Superman"; New, July, 1945, the Bishop of Salisbury and Sir Richard Croft in "The First Gentleman"; composed the score of "Arlette," 1917; and contributed numbers to the Charlot *revues* at the Vaudeville, "The Kiss Call," "Yes, Uncle," etc.; has also composed songs and various pieces of Church music. *Favourite parts:* Malvolio and Captain Joshua in "Thunder Rock"; first appeared in films, 1943, in "Thunder Rock." *Recreations:* Reading and gardening. *(Died 15 Feb., 1950; age 66)*

LEFEVRE, Maurice, French dramatic author; has written the following plays: "Scaramouche" (with Henry Vuagneux, music by Messager and Georges Street), 1890; "Conte de Printemps" (with Felix Régamey), 1892; "Nuit de Noël" (with M. de Roddaz), 1893; "Le Discobole" (with P. Bilhaud), 1895; "Horribles Détails" (with Louis Decori),1903; "Le Crime d'un fils,'* 1905 ; " De l'Amour aux Larmes," 1906 ; "La Bonne Entente," 1907 ; "L'Homine de Proie " (with. C. de la Porte), 1908.

LE FRE, Albert, comedian and entertainer ; *b.* London, 3 Mar., 1870 ; *s.* of the late James Albert De Voy and his wife Sarah (Lefevre) ; made his first appearance on the stage as a child, at the Criterion, Sheerness, 1876, in pantomime, appearing as a dancer and skater ; for many years appeared with the Le Fre Trio ; made his first appearance in London, at the Surrey Theatre, at Christmas, 1879, under the late William Holland, playing in the pantomime " Aladdin " ; toured in the United States, with the Hanlon-Lees ; among the sketches in which he has achieved popularity may be mentioned " The Gentleman Scamp " ; " The Professor " ; " The Dancing Family," in which he appeared with his brothers ; as a single turn has introduced " That's what you see in the halls " ; " The Tip-top Topper " ; has also appeared on the theatrical stage in musical comedy, etc. ; is a prominent Freemason ; his son and daughter have both adopted their father's profession. *Recreations : * Golf, motoring, photography, and sports. *Address : * " St. Asaph," Upper Tulse Hill, S.W. *Telephone No. : * Brixton 1411.

LEFTWICH, Alexander, producer; in 1913 was stage director for the Academy Players, Halifax, N.S., and subsequently directed many other " stock " companies: in New York he has staged the following, among other, plays: " Dame Fashion's Demands," 1916; " Fashions of 1924," 1923; " The Melody Man," 1924; " Sky High," 1925; " Set a Thief ——," " Hit the Deck," " A Connecticut Yankee," " Take the Air," 1927 ; " Rain or Shine," " Present Arms," " The Song Writer," " Chee-Chee," " Hello, Daddy !," 1928; " Spring Is Here," 1929; " Strike up the Band," " Nine-Fifteen Revue." " Girl Crazy," " Sweet

and Low," 1930; "The Third Little Show," 1931 ; "Hey, Nonny, Nonny," 1932; "Orchids Preferred," 1937 ; in Mar., 1939, was appointed State-Director, for California, of the Federal Theatre Project.
(Died 13 Jan., 1947; age 63)

LEGARDE, Millie, actress and vocalist ; made her first appearance on the stage as a child, at the Theatre Royal, Birmingham, as Little Willie Carlyle in " East Lynne " ; subsequently, with her sister, appeared at the Royal Music Hall, Holborn, as the Sisters Gould ; after leaving school, toured in South Africa for some time, playing leading parts in " Maritana," " Paul Jones," " The Grand Duchess," etc. ; returning to England, toured under George Edwardes and Milton Bode ; made her reappearance on the London stage, at the Grand Theatre, Fulham, Christmas, 1897, as Pekoe in " Aladdin " ; next appeared at the Lyric, 21 May, 1898, as Maud in " Don Quixote," with Arthur Roberts ; played at the Adelphi, Dec., 1898, as Captain Spanker in " Dick Whittington " ; subsequently appeared at the Vaudeville in " On and Off " ; at the last named theatre, Sept., 1899, appeared as Mena in " The Elixir of Youth " ; subsequently toured as Dudley in " San Toy " ; appeared at the Apollo, May, 1902, as Lady Rosemary Beaulieu in " Three Little Maids " ; she was next seen at the Gaiety, 1902, where she played Dora Selby in " The Toreador," also taking part in " The Linkman," Feb., 1903 ; at the Apollo Theatre, during 1903, appeared as Winnie Harborough in " The Girl from Kay's " ; at the Strand, May, 1905, played Sonia Wingrove in " Miss Wingrove " ; at the Criterion, Aug., 1905, appeared as Betty Kenyon in " The White Chrysanthemum " ; at the Haymarket, May, 1907, played Miriam Hawthorne in " My Wife," and at the Adelphi, Christmas, 1907, appeared as Aladdin ; at the Queen's Theatre, Dec., 1908, succeeded Lily Iris as Denise de la Vire in " The Belle of Brittany " ; during 1910 appeared at the Empire, Leicester Square, in the *revue* " Hullo,

London ! " and as Mrs. Lewson in " Widow's Weeds."

LE GRAND, Phyllis, actress and vocalist ; *m.* Robert Michaelis ; made her first appearance on the st^ge at Daly's Theatre, 8 June, 1907, as Clo-Clo in " The Merry Widow " ; same theatre, Sept., 1909, played Lady Augusta in " The Dollar Princess " ; toured as Sonia in " The Merr v Widow " ; at the Adelphi, Nov., 1910, appeared as Diane in " The Quaker Girl " ; at the Prince's, Manchester, Dec., 1911, played Angèle Didier in " The Count of Lu ,embourg " ; at the Adelphi, Aug., 1912, played Alix Luttrell in " Autumn Manoeuvres " ; subsequently toured in " The Count of Luxembourg " ; in 1913 toured as Lady Rosabelle in " The Sunshine Girl " ; at Daly's, Oct., 1914, played Mrs. Quinton Raikes in " A Country Girl " ; in Aug., 1916, toured as the Countess of Frayle and Vivien Ingoldsby in " My Lady Frayle " ; in 1917 toured as Madame Rabelais in " High Jinks " ; in 1918-19 as Diana Fairlie in " The Boy " ; at the Fulton Theatre, New York, Sept., 1922, played Helene de Vasquez in " Orange Blossoms " ; in Sept., 1914, toured the English provinces as Louise in " Our Nell " ; at the Duke of York's, Nov., 1925, played Nicolette in the play of that name. *Address :* 8 Eton Villas, South Hampstead, N.W.3. *Telephone :* Primrose 3448

LEHÁR, Franz, composer ; *b.* Komarom, Hungary, 30 Apr., 1870 ; *s.* of Franz Lehár and his wife Christine (Neubrandt) ; *e.* Sternberg and Prague Conservatoire ; studied violin under Herr Bennewitz ; in 1888, was first violin, and later concert-master at the combined city theatres in Barmen-Elberfeld ; in 1889, entered the regimental band ; subsequently appointed military musical director at Losoncz, where he composed songs and his first opera " Der Kürassier " ; in 1894, appointed musical director of the Austrian Navy Band ; is the composer of " Kukuscha," 1896, subsequently renamed " Tatjana " ; forsook the writing of opera for operetta, and has since composed " Der Rastelbinder," " Wie-

ner Frauen," 1902 ; " Der Klavierstimmer," " Der Göttergatte," 1903 ; " Die Juxheirat," 1905 ; " Mitislaw der Moderne," " Peter und Paul im Schlaraffenland," 1906 ; " Die Lustige Witwe" (" The Merry Widow"), " Der Mann mit den 3 Frauen," 1907 ; " Das Fürstenkind," " Der Graf von Luxemburg" (" The Count of Luxembourg "), 1909 ; " Ziegeunerliebe" (" Gipsy Love "), 1910, " Eva," 1911 ; " Der Sterngucker," 1916 ; " Die Blaŭe Mazur " (" The Blue Mazurka "), 1920 ; " Frühling," 1922 ; " Die Ideale Gattin," " Endlich Allein," " Frasquita," " Clo-Clo," " Die Gelbe Jacke," 1923 ; " Libellentanz " (" The Three Graces "), 1924 ; " Paganini," 1925 ; " Czarevitch," 1927 ; " Das Land des Lächelns " (" The Land of Smiles "), 1928 ; " Frederica," 1929 ; " Schön ist die Welt," 1932 ; " Giuditta," 1934 ; in 1940, composed a new overture to " The Merry Widow," performed for the first time in May, 1940. *(Died 24 Oct., 1948; age 78)*

LE HAY, Daisy, actress and vocalist ; *b.* 1883 ; *m.* J. T. H. Sample ; made her first appearance on the stage at Daly's Theatre in the chorus of " A Greek Slave," 8 June, 1898 ; in Oct., 1899, she appeared in " San Toy," which ran for two years ; in Sept., 1902, appeared as Miss Ecroyd in " A Country Girl," remaining in this piece, for a perod of two years, playing at different times, Mrs. St. Quinten and Nan ; at the Comedy, Feb., 1904, played Leobia in " Amorelle " ; subsequently toured for two years in " Kitty Grey " ; she was then absent from the stage for two years, during which period she was studying music ; made her reappearance on the stage, at the Savoy Theatre, Mar., 1910, as Princess Cynthia i.1 " Two Merry Monarchs " ; at the Apollo, Sept., 1912, appeared as Princess Athanasia in " The Grass Widows " ; at the Tivoli, July, 1913, played Daphne Manners in " What Ho ! Daphne " ; subsequently toured in the same part ; in Aug., 1915, toured as Kitty Grey in the musical comedy of that name, and during 1916, toured in the same part, also in " A Little Bit of Fluff."

LE HAY, John (Healy), actor ; *b.* in Ireland, 25 Mar., 1854 ; made his first appearance on the London stage in 1879 in chorus of " The Zoo," at Royalty Theatre ; at the Opéra Comique, 1879, appeared in the chorus of " H.M.S. Pinafore " ; subsequently appeared at the Savoy in small parts, and remained there for some years ; in 1884, toured in " Vice-Versâ," and " Silver Guilt " ; subsequently played an extended engagement with Edward Terry ; at the Gaiety, Sept., 1886, played Tom Strutt in " Dorothy," and played the part throughout the " run " of that opera, extending to 1889 ; at the Lyric, Apr., 1889, played Crook in " Doris," and Nov., 1889, Private Smith in " The Red Hussar " ; in 1890, at the Globe, played Jacob in " The Black Rover " ; at the Prince of Wales's, Dec., 1890, appeared as Prince Bulbo in " The Rose and the Ring," and Mar., 1891, Sir Guy of Gisborne in " Maid Marian " ; at Lyric, Oct., 1894, played Mat in " His Excellency " ; appeared at the Adelphi, 1893, in " The Black Domino," and in " La Périchole " at Garrick, 1897 ; in 1898 played at the Comedy in " The Topsy-Turvy Hotel " ; appeared as Alexander McGregor in " My Girl " at Gaiety, 1896 ; in 1903 appeared as Coquenard in " Véronique " at Apollo ; toured the United States three times with comic opera ; also toured in South Africa for eighteen months, after the war ; is also an excellent ventriloquist and *raconteur*, having appeared on several occasions before King Edward, at Buckingham Palace and Sandringham, and has appeared at several London halls ; has toured with his own sketch company, playing " Poor Beggar " ; appeared at the Hippodrome, Dec., 1909, in " Mitislaw, or the Love Match " ; during 1914 toured in variety theatres, playing " Just My Luck " ; during 1915 toured as Abe Potash in " Potash and Perlmutter ; toured in 1917 as Caesar Montague, J.P., in " My Uncle the J.P." ; during 1918 toured as Baron Pepsicorn in " Violette " ; during 1919-20 as Henry Block in " Uncle Sam " ; during 1921 as General Root in " French Leave " ; during 1921–22 as the Pawnbroker in

" Skittles." *Address :* 12 Lancaster Road, N.W.3, or A.A.
(Died 2 Nov., 1926; age 72)

LEHMANN Carla, actress ; *b.* Winnipeg, Canada, 26 Feb., 1917 ; *d.* of Julius Edward Lehmann and his wife Elsa Ida Louisa (Hillerns) ; *e.* Riverbend Girls' School, Winnipeg ; *m.* (1) George Anderson McDowell Elliott (mar. dis.) ; (2) John R. C. Townsend ; studied for the stage at Royal Academy of Dramatic Art ; made her first appearance on the stage, at the Repertory Theatre, Croydon, Sept., 1936, as Lynda Kent in " Dusty Ermine " ; first appeared in London, at the Apollo, 24 Nov., 1937, as Nona Stockton in " People at Sea " ; Haymarket, Feb., 1938, played Shirley Davis in " Mary Goes to See " ; Strand, Apr., 1938, Cora Pound in " Banana Ridge," and Aug., 1939, Patricia in " Spotted Dick," in which she subsequently toured, and again played in it at the Strand, Dec., 1939 ; toured, June, 1941, as Esmé in " The Nutmeg Tree " ; at the " Q " and Arts Theatres, Mar., 1943, played Cherry in " The Young and Lovely " ; Whitehall, June, 1943, Molly Morden in " The Moon is Down " ; Piccadilly, Mar., 1945, Sarah King in " Appointment with Death " ; " Q," Oct., 1948, Joan Karlill in " The Annex " ; Jan., 1950, played Louise in a play of that name ; first appeared in films, 1938, in " So This is London." *Address :* 25 Hartington Road, London, W.4. *Telephone No. :* Chiswick 1929.

LEIBER, Fritz, actor ; *b.* Chicago, Ill., U.S.A., 31 Jan., 1883 ; *s.* of Albrecht Leiber and his wife Meta (Klet) ; *e.* Lake View High School, Chicago ; *m.* Virginia Bronson ; made his first appearance on the stage at the old Dearborn Theatre, Chicago, in the " stock " company, 1902, as Private Jones in " The Girl I Left Behind Me " ; remained with that company until 1905 ; joined Ben Greet's company, 1905, and made his first appearance on the New York stage, at the Garden Theatre, 1905, as Macduff in " Macbeth " ; with this company until 1907, playing Prospero in " The Tempest,"

Brutus in "Julius Caesar," etc.; toured with Olga Petrova and Julia Marlowe, 1908; joined Robert B. Mantell's company, Aug., 1908, and remained until 1915, playing Brutus, Macduff, Laertes, Bassanio, Jacques, Iago, Othello, Faulconbridge, Mark Antony, Mercutio, Edgar, etc.; in 1915, toured with David Warfield in "Vanderdecken"; returned to Mantell's company, 1916–18, playing leads, alternating Othello and Iago, also playing Hamlet and Romeo; started his own Shakespearean company in 1920; appeared in repertory of Shakespearean plays at the 48th Street Theatre, Jan., 1922; at the Punch and Judy, Apr., 1924, played Angelo in "Two Strangers from Nowhere"; 48th Street, May, 1924, Eilert Lovborg in "Hedda Gabler"; Greenwich Village, Apr., 1927, Hardy Gilchrist in "The Field God"; in 1929, was engaged to direct and play leading parts with the Chicago Civic Shakespeare Society, and continued in that company to 1932; appeared in repertory of plays with this company at the Shubert, New York, Mar., 1930; Ambassadors' Dec., 1930, and Royale, Nov., 1931; National, Dec., 1933, played Reb Melech in "Yoshe Kalb"; during 1934–35, toured with his own company, from Newark to the Pacific Coast; at Hollywood Bowl, 1937, played Death in "Everyman"; has played over one hundred Shakespearean parts, including Macbeth, King Lear, Shylock, Richard III, and Petruchio; first entered films, 1917, and has appeared in innumerable pictures, silent and talking. *Recreations:* Golf, tennis, reading (has a library of 8000 volumes), and carpentering. *(Died 14 Oct., 1949; age 67)*

LEICESTER, Ernest, actor; *b.* 11 June, 1866; made his first appearance on the stage in 1881, at the New Cross Public Hall, as Captain Smooth in "Money"; subsequently toured in "Called Back," "Dark Days," etc.; at the Princess's, Dec., 1887, played Ivan in "Siberia"; toured as Wilfred Denver in "The Silver King," David Kingsley in "The Harbour Lights," also in "Chispa," "Bootles' Baby," and "Hands Across the Sea"; from 1891 to 1894 was

leading man at the Surrey Theatre, under the late George Conquest; at the Comedy, in 1893, played in "The Ordeal"; at the Adelphi, May, 1894, played Armand in "The Two Orphans"; at Terry's, May, 1895, appeared as Ted Morris in "The Prude's Progress"; in July, 1895, joined Olga Nethersole to play lead in "Denise," "Romeo and Juliet," "Frou-Frou," "Camille," "Carmen," etc.; accompanied Miss Nethersole to the United States; on his return appeared at the Princess's, Aug., 1896, as Tom Chichester in "In Sight of St. Paul's"; in Sept., 1896, played George Thornton in "Two Little Vagabonds"; July, 1897, played Harold Wilson in "Tommy Atkins"; Aug., 1899, played Richard Mervyn in "Going the Pace"; at the Adelphi, Feb., 1900, appeared as the Rev. Mark Verner in "The Better Life"; at the Surrey, in Oct., 1900, played Captain Fraser in "The Fighting Fifth"; in 1901, toured with Fanny Brough as Triplet in "Masks and Faces"; subsequently toured as Tom Birch in "The Rake's Wife"; at the St. James's, Mar., 1903, appeared as Von Asterberg in "Old Heidelberg," subsequently touring with George Alexander, as Thibaut D'Aussigny in "If I were King," etc.; at the St. James's, Mar., 1904, played Harold Hoffmann in "Love's Carnival"; during 1905, toured as Tom Logan in "Human Hearts"; at the Lyric, Aug., 1906, played William Jackson in "The Sin of William Jackson"; in 1907, went to Australia, and appeared in a round of popular plays; on his return to England in 1909, toured in music-hall sketch, "The Loyal Traitor"; at the Adelphi, Nov., 1909, succeeded Henry Miller, as Robert Smith in "The Servant in the House"; at the Garrick, Jan., 1910, played Robert Bertram in "Dame Nature"; subsequently toured in "The Ticket of Leave Man"; at the Garrick, Sept., 1910, played Thorkell Mytrea in "The Bishop's Son"; subsequently toured in "Tracked by Wireless," and "East Lynne"; during 1911 appeared in music halls in a sketch by W. W. Jacobs, entitled "In the Library";

at the Aldwych, Sept., 1912 appeared as Delaney in " The Great John Ganton " ; at the Prince's Theatre, 1914, played Colonel Hildebrand in " The Story of the Rosary " ; subsequently went to the United States, and at the Manhattan Opera House, New York, Sept., 1914, appeared in the same part ; during 1915 toured in the same part in the United States ; returned to England, Apr., 1915 ; at the Prince of Wales's, Feb., 1916, played Raymond du Barry in " The Silver Crucifix " ; during 1916-17 toured in South Africa, with A. E. Anson's Company in " Romance," " The Barton Mystery," " The Hawk," and " Children of Earth " ; on returning to England, 1917, went on tour playing Colonel Sharrow in " Seven Days' Leave," in which he continued to play until 1919. *(Died 5 Oct., 1939; age 73)*

LEIGH, Andrew George, actor and producer; *b.* Brighton, 30 Nov., 1887; *s.* of Thomas Leigh, F.R.C.S., L.R.C.P., and his wife Georgina (Geere); *e.* Brighton; was for three years engaged as secretary to the late T. H. S. Escott, author and journalist; made his first appearance on the stage at the Theatre Royal, Worthing, Sept., 1908, as Rugby in " The Merry Wives of Windsor," with the Benson company, with which he remained for five years, playing a great number of parts, including most of the Shakespearean clowns, and also acting as stage-manager ; made his first appearance in London, at the Coronet Theatre, June, 1913, as Dromio of Ephesus in " The Comedy of Errors " ; during 1913-14 toured in South Africa with Henry Herbert's company ; in Sept., 1914, became a member of the first Shakespearean Company at the Old Vic., first appearing there 5 Oct., 1914, as Biondello in " The Taming of the Shrew," also acting as stage-manager, and produced " The Merry Wives of Windsor," " Twelfth Night," and (in co-operation with Estelle Stead) "As You Like It " ; at the St. James's, Dec., 1915, played Launcelot Gobbo and the Prince of Aragon in " The Merchant of Venice " ; at the Strand, 1916, appeared in " Pete," and

" Mr. Wu " ; after two years' military service, was transferred to the N.A.C.B., and toured the camps, playing in modern repertory ; during 1919 appeared with the Benson company, and with the original New Shakespeare Company ; at the St. Martin's, Jan., 1920, played the Ship Boy in " Pompey the Great," and Osric in " Hamlet " ; in Sept., 1920, rejoined the Old Vic. Company, and remained two years as leading comedian ; in the summer of 1922, toured with Mrs. Patrick Campbell as Tesman in " Hedda Gabler," and Charles Gaylord in " Voodoo " ; at the Duke of York's, Nov., 1922, appeared as Launcelot Gobbo and Aragon in the operatic version of " The Merchant of Venice " ; during 1923, appeared with the Lena Ashwell Players ; at the Regent (for the Phoenix), Mar., 1923, played Abel Drugger in " The Alchemist " ; Apr., 1923, played Mr. Cricket in " The Insect Play " ; at His Majesty's, Sept., 1923, Abdu in " Hassan " ; at the Regent (for the Fellowship of Players), July, 1924, played Touchstone in " As You Like It " ; rejoined the Old Vic. Company, Oct., 1924 ; appointed producer at the Old Vic., Sept., 1925, and acted in this capacity to May, 1929 ; during this period made thirty-eight productions of Shakespearean and other plays ; exclusive of the Shakespearean productions, produced " The Shoemaker's Holiday," " St. Patrick's Day," " A Child in Flanders," " Christmas Eve," " Everyman," " The Vikings," "Adam's Opera," " Caste," " Mary Magdalene," " The School for Scandal," " She Stoops to Conquer," " The Two Noble Kinsmen"; Little Theatre, Sept., 1929, played Launcelot Gobbo in "The Merchant of Venice"; Everyman and Globe, Feb., 1930, George Dyer in "Charles and Mary"; Mar., 1930, played Mr. Hardy in "B.J. One"; went to New York, and at the Maxine Elliott Theatre, Sept., 1930, staged "Twelfth Night," for Jane Cowl, and at Times Square, Dec., 1930, produced "The Merchant of Venice," for Moscovitch; on returning to London, appeared at the Fortune, Dec., 1930–Jan., 1931, as Bob Cratchit in "A Christmas Carol," and Roper in "The

Silver Box"; Arts, Apr., 1931, played Henry Vanner in "To-Morrow"; July, 1931, Demos in "Demos, King and Slave"; 1931-2, toured in Canada, in Sir Barry Jackson's company; Little, Oct., 1932, again played Roper in "The Silver Box"; Arts, Nov., 1932, Lavache in "All's Well that Ends Well"; Ambassadors', Dec., 1932, Puffy in "The Streets of London"; Little, May, 1933, Frost in "Strife"; Embassy, July, 1933, George Porter in "Beauty and the Barge"; Open Air Theatre, Sept., 1933, Trinculo in "The Tempest"; June, 1934, Dromio of Ephesus in "The Comedy of Errors"; at the Little, June, 1934, The Little Man in the play of that name; Open Air, July, 1934, Androcles in "Androcles and the Lion"; and Sept., 1934, Quince in "A Midsummer Night's Dream"; Little, Nov., 1934, Dragon General Su and Mu in "Lady Precious Stream"; Sadler's Wells, Jan., 1935, Christopher Sly in "The Taming of the Shrew"; Whitehall, Jan., 1935, George Harrys in "Paganini"; Ambassadors', Mar., 1935, Goods in "Everyman"; Westminster, May, 1935, Roderigo in "Othello"; July, 1935, Tony Lumpkin in "She Stoops to Conquer"; Ambassadors', Sept., 1935, Dr. Melliflower in "As Bad as I Am"; Grafton, Sept., 1935, Dromio of Syracuse in "In Such a World"; Old Vic., Nov., 1935, Fyodor Ḳuligin in "The Three Sisters" and Mar., 1936, the Clown in "The Winter's Tale"; Little, Nov., 1936, Wang Yun in "Lady Precious Stream"; Ring, Blackfriars, Nov., 1936, Fluellen in "Henry V"; Little, Dec., 1936, Tweedledum in "Alice Through the Looking Glass" and Dick Tipple in "Curse It, Foiled Again!"; Embassy, Jan., 1937, Alfred Baker in "Climbing"; appeared at the Memorial Theatre, Stratford-on-Avon, during the seasons 1937-41, and produced "A Midsummer Night's Dream" there, in 1938; Kingsway, Dec., 1939, played Su and Mu in "Lady Precious Stream"; produced "King John" at Stratford-on-Avon, 1940, and "Julius Caesar," 1941; Mercury, Aug., 1942, played the Innkeeper in "The Man With a Load of Mischief"; Court, Liverpool, Dec., 1942, for the Old Vic,

again played Androcles, also Cuffney in "Abraham Lincoln"; New, Feb., 1943, Launcelot Gobbo in "The Merchant of Venice"; Winter Garden, July, 1943, the Professor in "It's Time to Dance"; Lyric, Hammersmith, May, 1944, Firk in "The Shoemaker's Holiday"; Arts, July, 1944, Mr. Blanquet in "Bird in Hand"; toured in the autumn of 1944, as William in "You Never Can Tell," Burgess in "Candida," etc.; toured, 1945, as the Steward and the Inquisitor in "Saint Joan," in England and North-West Europe, for E.N.S.A.; St. James's, Sept., 1946, Alfred in "But for the Grace of God"; Palace, May, 1947, Franz in "The Red Mill"; Boltons, June, 1947, Amil in "Mary of Magdala"; Nov., 1947, George in "The Patched Cloak"; "Q," Dec., 1947, Tweedledum in "Alice Through the Looking-Glass"; Arts, Mar., 1948, Heble Tyson in "The Lady's Not For Burning"; Lyric, Hammersmith, Sept., 1948, played L.A/C. Brightside in "An English Summer"; at the Pitlochry Festival Theatre, May, 1951, produced "Mary of Scotland"; Pitlochry, May–June, 1952, produced "The Doom of Devorgoil," and played Andreas Nero in "Double Redoubled"; Her Majesty's, Brighton, Mar., 1953, played Merstisen in "Westward Journey"; Duchess, London, Jan., 1954, played Dr. Anderson in "No Other Verdict"; toured Australia, 1955, with the Old Vic Company, appearing as Escalus in "Measure for Measure," Gremio in "The Taming of the Shrew," and Old Gobbo in "The Merchant of Venice"; has frequently broadcast for the B.B.C., and in Canada; author of a pantomime, "Harlequin Jack Horner," Old Vic., 1925, several of the Old Vic Birthday revels; "The Empress Maud," comedy, 1944, and a series of verses, "Kings and Queens of London," which appeared in *Punch*. *Favourite parts:* The Fool in "King Lear," and Puck. *Recreations:* Walking, reading, writing, and drawing.
(*Died 21 Apr., 1957; age 69*)

LEIGH, Dorma, actress and dancer; *b.* London, 11 Nov., 1893; *d.* of Ernest Woodleigh and his wife Fannie Wellesley (Hack) ; *e.* London ; *m.* Captain Southouse-Cheyney (mar. dis.) ; made her first appearance on the stage at Daly's Theatre, May, 1911, in "The Count of Luxembourg"; has also appeared at Gaiety, and toured in America as Linda in "The Girl on the Film"; made her first appearance on the variety stage at the Coliseum, and has also played the Stoll and Moss tours; at the Lyceum, Edinburgh, Dec., 1916, appeared as Princess Caesar and Empress Poppoea in " Great Caesar !", subsequently touring in the same parts ; during 1917–18 toured in " Hanky-Panky " ; during 1919 toured as Susan in " Petticoat Fair " ; at the Palace Theatre, Dec., 1919, appeared in " The Whirligig "; at the Garrick, Feb., 1923, appeared in " Via Crucis "; at the Lyric, June, 1924, danced in " The Street Singer." *Recreations :* Reading, riding, dancing, and outdoor sports. *Address :* 61 West Cromwell Road, S.W.5. *Telephone No. :* Frobisher 3965.

LEIGH, Charlotte, actress and singer; *b.* London, 3 Nov., 1907; *d.* of Ernest Leigh and his wife Charlotte Emmeline (Lindemann) ; *e.* Woodlands School, Hampstead, and South Hampstead High School; studied for the stage at the Royal Academy of Dramatic Art and voice training under Alice Prowse Mallison; made her first appearance on the stage at Playroom Six, 11 Oct., 1927, as a Reveller in "Miss Julie"; at the New Theatre, in the autumn of 1928, succeeded Joan Hickson as Miss Mould in "A Damsel in Distress"; in 1930, was stage-manager for J. T. Grein's Cosmopolitan Theatre; during 1932, appeared at the Festival Theatre, Cambridge, in a number of parts; St. Martin's, July, 1932, played Miss Adelaide in "The Pride of the Regiment"; Savoy, Mar., 1933, Prudence Wary in "Jolly Roger"; during 1934, toured the West Indies in a repertory of twelve plays; at the Gate Theatre, Oct., 1934–Feb., 1935, appeared in "Miracle in America," "Nichevo," "The Seven Deadly Virtues," and was the *Commère* in "The Gate Revue"; Embassy, Mar., and Shaftesbury, Apr., 1935, appeared

in the *revue* "Let's Go Gay"; Gate, Dec., 1935, was the *Commère* in "This World of Ours"; Embassy, May, 1936, played Phaedra in "Chastity, My Brother"; London Hippodrome, July, 1936, Pauline in "No! No! Nanette", Vaudeville, Dec., 1936, for a time played the Fairy Carabosse in "The Sleeping Beauty"; Little, Jan., 1938, appeared in "Nine Sharp," which ran until Jan., 1939, and same theatre, Apr., 1939, in "The Little Revue"; entered films, 1935.

LEIGH, Gracie, actress ; *d.* of Edwin Ellis, R.B.A., and Lilith Ellis, actress ; *m.* Lionel Mackinder (killed in action, in France, Jan., 1915) ; made her first notable success at the Lyric, 1898, when she appeared in " Little Miss Nobody " ; was then seen at Daly's, Oct., 1899, as Rhoda in " San Toy " ; appeared in a front piece at the Vaudeville, " You and I " ; appeared at Daly's, as Madame Sophie in " A Country Girl," during 1902 ; then with Edward Terry in " My Pretty Maid " at Terry's Theatre ; at the Strand, as Mrs. Pineapple in " A Chinese Honeymoon," 1903 ; joined E. S. Willard at the St. James's in 1903, playing Lucy White in " The Professor's Love Story " ; at Daly's appeared as Peggy Sabine in " The Cingalee," 1904 ; appeared in " The Gay Lord Vergy," Apollo, 1905, and in Apr., 1906, played Eliza in " The Dairymaids "; at the Prince of Wales's, Jan., 1907, played Mina in " Miss Hook of Holland " ; same theatre, Apr., 1908, played Popotte in " My Mimosa Maid " ; Sept., 1908, appeared as Militza in " King of Cadonia " ; Sept., 1909, played Ophelia in " Dear Little Denmark "; at the Adelphi, Nov., 1910, appeared as Phoebe in " The Quaker Girl " ; May, 1912, played Lady Larkins in " Autumn Manoeuvres "; Oct., 1912, Jeanie McTavish in " The Dancing Mistress "; Oct., 1913, Clancy in " The Girl from Utah "; at the Prince of Wales's, Oct., 1914, reappeared as Mina in " Miss Hook of Holland "; at the Palace, June, 1917, played in " Airs and Graces " ; after a lengthy absence reappeared on the stage

1455

at His Majesty's Theatre, Oct., 1921, as Wei Wa Shi in " Cairo " ; at the New Scala, Dec., 1923, played Cha-Ku in " Almond Eye " ; at the Regent (for the Phoenix Society), June, 1924, Lucy in " The Old Bachelor " ; at the New, Oct., 1924, Lucille in " The Hour and the Man " ; Palace, Mar., 1925, Pauline in " No, No, Nanette " ; Vaudeville, May, 1928, Gertrude in " Who's Who? " ; Court, Oct., 1928, Adoracion in " The Lady from Alfaqueque" ; broadcast for the B.B.C., Sept., 1937.
(Died 24 June, 1950; age 75)

LEIGH, Mary, actress and vocalist ; *b.* London, 11 Feb., 1904 ; *d.* of W. H. Eveleigh and his wife Josephine (Brown) ; *e.* Holt Hill Convent (F.C.J.), Cheshire ; *m.* Sir William Gray, Bart. ; made her first appearance on the stage, as a child, at the Theatre Royal, Dundee, 1907 ; made her grown-up *début* at the Alhambra, Glasgow, 1919, followed by a tour in " The Better 'Ole " ; made her first appearance in London, at the Winter Garden Theatre, 18 Sept., 1920, as Flora in " A Night Out " ; at the Gaiety, Apr., 1921, played Elsa in " Faust on Toast," and May, 1921, Madeline in the revised version of the same piece ; at the Vaudeville, Dec., 1921, played in " Pot-Luck " ; Aug., 1922, in " Snap ! " ; during 1922-3, appeared at the " Bal Cabarin " at the Grafton Galleries, and also with the Queen's Hall Roof Follies ; at the Globe, July, 1923, played Margot Beaufort in " Reckless Reggie " ; she then toured as Marilynn Morgan in " The Cabaret Girl " ; at the Kingsway, June, 1924, appeared in " Yoicks ! " ; at His Majesty's, Oct., 1924, played Elizabeth in " Patricia " ; at the King's, Glasgow, Dec., 1924, Daisy in " The Dollar Princess," playing the same part at Daly's, Feb., 1925 ; Adelphi, Nov., 1925, played Kitty in " Betty in Mayfair " ; appeared at His Majesty's, Aug., 1926, with " The Co-Optimists " ; during 1927 toured as Tip-Toes in the play of that name ; His Majesty's, Jan., 1928 (for the Sunday Play Society), Jan., 1928, played Nettie in " Icebound " ; in Mar., 1928, toured as Kitty Carleton in " So

This is Love " ; His Majesty's, Sept., 1928, played Kitty in " Song of the Sea," and in 1929 toured in the same part. *Favourite part:* Marilynn in " The Cabaret Girl." *Recreations:* Motoring, golf, reading and walking.
(Died 19 Mar.. 1943; age 38)

LEIGH, Rowland, dramatic author and lyric writer ; *b.* 16 May, 1902 ; *s.* of the Hon. Rowland Charles Frederick Leigh and his wife Mabel (Gordon) ; his first play was an adaptation, "The Monkey Talks" (from the French), 1925 ; author of " Oh Patsy," 1926 ; lyrics for " Jumbles," 1927 ; adapted " Might-Have-Beens" (from the French), 1927 ; contributed lyrics to "Charlot 1928" ; "Charlot's Masquerade," 1930 ; adapted "Wonder Bar" (from the German), 1930 ; with Desmond Carter, adapted "The Dubarry" (from the German), 1932 ; collaborated with Clare Kammer in "Three Waltzes," 1937 ; produced "The Jack-Pot" at the Prince of Wales's, 1932 ; contributed to "After Dinner," 1932 ; "Music Hath Charms," 1934 ; "You Never Know," 1938 ; "A Gift for the Bride" (adaptation), 1945 ; wrote the book and lyrics of "My Romance," which he staged at the Shubert Theatre, New York, 1948 ; has also written several film scenarios.
(Died 8 Oct., 1963; age 61)

LEIGH, Vivien (*née* Vivian Mary Hartley), actress ; *b.* Darjeeling, India, 5 Nov., 1913 ; *d.* of Ernest Richard Hartley and his wife Gertrude ; *e.* Convent of the Sacred Heart, Roehampton, and in France, Germany, and Italy ; *m.* (1) Herbert Leigh Holman (mar. dis.) ; (2) (Sir) Laurence Olivier (mar. dis.) ; studied for a time under Mdlle. Antoine at the Comédie Française, and also, for a short time, at the Royal Academy of Dramatic Art ; made her first appearance in films, 1934, as one of the schoolgirls in "Things Are Looking Up" ; subsequently played in "The Village Squire," "Gentleman's Agreement" and "Look Up and Laugh" ; made her first appearance on the regular stage at the "Q" Theatre, 25 Feb., 1935, as Giusta in "The Green Sash" ; appeared at the Ambassadors'

Theatre, May, 1935, as Henriette in "The Mask of Virtue"; at Oxford, for the O.U.D.S., Feb., 1936, played the Queen in "Richard II"; His Majesty's, Apr., 1936, Jenny Mere in "The Happy Hypocrite"; Open Air Theatre, June, 1936, Anne Boleyn in "Henry VIII"; Wyndham's, Feb., 1937, Pamela in "Because We Must"; Ambassadors', Mar., 1937, Jessica Morton in "Bats in the Belfry"; Kronborg Castle, Elsinore, with the Old Vic. company, June, 1937, played Ophelia in "Hamlet"; Old Vic., Dec., 1937, Titania in "A Midsummer Night's Dream"; Gate, Sept., 1938, Serena Blandish in the play of that name; subsequently went to Hollywood; made her first appearance on the New York stage, at the 51st Street Theatre, May, 1940, as Juliet in "Romeo and Juliet"; after returning to London, appeared at the Haymarket, Mar., 1942, as Jennifer Dubedat in a revival of "The Doctor's Dilemma," which ran for a year; toured for three months, 1943, in the Middle East, entertaining H.M. Forces; Phoenix, May, 1945, played Sabina in "The Skin of Our Teeth"; Piccadilly, Sept., 1946, again played Sabina in "The Skin of Our Teeth"; toured in Australia and New Zealand for the Old Vic, 1948, in "Richard III," "The School for Scandal," and "The Skin of Our Teeth"; on her return, at the New Theatre, for the Old Vic Company, Jan.–Feb., 1949, played Lady Teazle in "The School for Scandal," Lady Anne in "Richard III," and Antigone; Aldwych, Oct., 1949, appeared as Blanche du Bois in "A Streetcar Named Desire"; went to Hollywood, 1950, to appear in the same part in the film; at the St. James's, London, May, 1951, appeared as Cleopatra in Sir Laurence Olivier's productions of "Caesar and Cleopatra" and "Antony and Cleopatra"; again appeared in these productions at the Ziegfeld, New York, Dec., 1951; Phoenix, London, Nov., 1953, played Miss Mary Morgan in "The Sleeping Prince"; joined the Shakespeare Memorial Theatre Company, at Stratford-on-Avon, 1955, and during the season appeared as Viola in "Twelfth Night," Lady Macbeth, and as Lavinia in "Titus Andronicus"; Lyric, Apr., 1956, played Lady Alexandra Shotter in "South Sea Bubble"; with the Shakespeare Memorial Theatre Company appeared in Paris, Vienna, Belgrade, Zagreb, etc., May–June, 1957, as Lavinia in "Titus Andronicus," subsequently playing the same part at the Stoll Theatre, London, July, 1957; Apollo, Apr., 1958, played Paola in "Duel of Angels"; Royal Court, July, 1959, Lulu d'Arville in "Look After Lulu," subsequently transferring with the production to the New, Sept., 1959; Helen Hayes, N.Y., Apr., 1960, again played Paola in "Duel of Angels," and also toured with the play; toured Australia, New Zealand, and South America, 1961–2, with the Old Vic Company, appearing as Viola in "Twelfth Night," Paola in "Duel of Angels," and as Marguerite in "The Lady of the Camelias"; Broadway, New York, Mar., 1963, made her début in a musical as Tatiana in "Tovarich," for which she received the Antoinette Perry Award, 1963; on returning to England, toured, Apr., 1965, as Contessa Sanziani in "La Contessa"; notable films in which she has appeared include "Gone With the Wind" (Oscar Award), 1939; "Lady Hamilton," "Caesar and Cleopatra," "A Streetcar Named Desire" (Oscar Award), 1951; "The Roman Spring of Mrs. Stone," etc.; television appearances include Sabina in "The Skin of Our Teeth," 1959; "The Valiant Years," 1961; received the Knight's Cross of the Légion d'Honneur, 1957. *Recreations:* Serendipity and arranging flowers. *(Died 8 July, 1967; age 53)*

LEIGH, Walter, composer; *b.* London, 22 June, 1905; *s.* of Ernest Leigh and his wife Charlotte Emmeline (Lindemann); *e.* University College School and Christ's College, Cambridge; *m.* Marion Blandford; studied composition in Berlin under Paul Hindemith; his first work for the theatre was the music for the pantomime "Aladdin" at the Festival Theatre, Cambridge, 1931, and he composed incidental music for several productions at that theatre, 1931–3; composed the music for "The Pride of the Regiment" (comic opera), 1932; "Jolly Roger" (comic opera), 1933; and for the *revues*," Yours Sincerely," 1934; "Nine Sharp," 1938; "Little Revue," 1939; composed the incidental music for "The Silent Knight," 1937, and has composed various orchestral and chamber works, songs, etc. *Recreations:* Fencing, tennis, and golf. *Club:* Savage. *Address:* 19 Ladbroke Road, W.11. *Telephone No.:* Park 6040.

LEIGHEB, Claudio, Italian actor; *b.* Fano, 20 Aug., 1848; *s.* of Giovanni Leigheb, actor; *m.* Teresa Migliotti; made his first appearance on the stage in "Œdipus Rex," as a child; fulfilled engagements with most of the leading Italian managers, including Lambertini, Enrico Capelli; from 1868-70, was with Luigi Bellotti-Bon; in 1871, joined Fanny Sadowski, under the management of Cesare Rossi, remaining till 1873; 1874-6, with Bellotti-Bon; 1877-81, at Turin; 1883-7, at National Theatre, Rome; 1888-90, with Marini; 1891-3, with Novelli; 1894-6, with Flavio Andó; 1897, with Virginia Reiter, with whom he toured for some time, playing in "Le Controleur des Wagons-lits," "Jalouse," "Zaza," "Le demimonde," "Frou-Frou," "Fernande," "Fédora," etc.

LEIGHTON, Frank (Athelstone), actor; *b.* Sydney N.S.W., Australia, 16 July, 1908; *s.* of Frank Scott Leighton and his wife Ethel Nottingham (Doughty); *e.* Cleveland High School and St. John's, Sydney; *m.* (1) Helen Barnes (mar. dis.); (2) Pamela Mary Steward; was formerly in the Royal Australian Navy; made his first appearance on the stage, at the Criterion Theatre, Sydney, 24 June, 1926, as Vogl in "Lilac Time"; for the next ten years appeared in "The Girl Friend," "Hit the Deck," "The Five O'Clock Girl," "The Merry Widow," "The Maid of the Mountains," "The Love Race," "Follow Through," "Mr. Cinders," "Sons O'-Guns," "Yes, Madam !", "Gay Divorce," "Blue Roses," "Hold My Hand," "Roberta," and "Jill, Dar-

ling"; came to England in 1937; first appeared in London, at the "Q," 27 Dec., 1937, as Charles II in "Sweet Nell of Old Drury"; Arts, Jan., 1938, played Pierre Cellier in "Beloved"; "Q," Mar.–May, 1938, John Tilyard in "Blind Corners" and Tony Forrester in "Youth and Mrs. Meredith"; London Hippodrome, Aug., 1938, Cliff Reeves in "The Fleet's Lit Up"; Golders Green, Oct., and Prince's, Dec., 1939, appeared in "Shephard's Pie"; toured in this, 1940–1, and reappeared in it at the Prince's, May, 1941; at the same theatre, Aug.,1941, appeared in" Fun and Games," and Aug., 1942, played Tom Blair in "Wild Rose"; Saville, Mar., 1943, played Willis Reynolds in "Junior Miss"; His Majesty's, Mar., 1945, Donald Marshall in "Irene"; Savoy, June, 1945, Jim Blachman in "Chicken Every Sunday"; Aldwych, Aug., 1945, Digger in "The Hasty Heart"; Prince's, Oct., 1947, Louis XV in "The Dubarry"; toured, 1949, as Prince Danilo in "The Merry Widow"; "Q," Mar., 1950, played Peter Perry in "The Prodigal Father," and appeared in the same part at the Whitehall, June,1950, when the play was renamed "The Dish Ran Away"; Aldwych, Sept., 1951, played Major Michael Turner in "Ten Men and a Miss"; Fortune, May, 1952, Det.-Insp. Marshall in a revival of "Murder in Motley"; in Aug., 1952, again appeared as Prince Danilo in "The Merry Widow"; toured, Dec., 1952, as Cosmo Constantine in "Call Me Madam"; Vaudeville, Mar., 1954, played David Slater in a revival of "The Moon Is Blue"; toured, 1955, as Marcus Saintsbury in "Breakfast in Salisbury" (subsequently renamed "Postman's Knock"); Adelphi, Dec., 1959, played Henry Persichetti in "When In Rome . . ."; first appeared in films, 1932, in Australia; has appeared in films in England since 1938 his most recent production being "The Stateless Man." *Favourite part:* Danilo in "The Merry Widow." *Recreations:* Surf-riding and tennis. *Clubs:* N.S.W Tennis (ex) and Green Room, London *(Died 17 Oct., 1962; age 54)*

LEIGHTON, Queenie, actress and vocalist; *b.* 18 July, 1872; *d.* o

Dorothy Gerard; *m.* Lieut. Frederick Cockerill, 1st Northants Regt.; made her first appearance on the stage as a child of eight years of age, at the Oxford Music Hall, as a mimic; subsequently returned to school, and made her grown-up *debût* as Lillie Leighton, at the Opera House, Northampton, Christmas, 1889, as the " first mate " in the pantomime, " Dick Whittington "; after playing lead in pantomime in several provincial cities, was engaged as principal boy at Drury Lane, 1904, and played several seasons there; she has toured as Nora Honeycombe in " The Gay Parisienne "; as Marcelle in " A Night Out," for twelve months; as Flo Honeydew in " The Lady Slavey," for two years; twelve months' tour in " Ma Mie Rosette "; twelve months as Victoria Chaffers in " H.M.S. Irresponsible," which part she originated, with Arthur Roberts, 1900; she also appeared at the Gaiety, June, 1901, as Donna Theresa in " The Toreador," and played the part over a year; subsequently toured in the title-*rôle* of " Kitty Grey," in George Edwardes's company; in 1906 toured in " The Girl on the Stage "; subsequently appeared at several of the leading variety theatres in London and the provinces, and, later, appeared on the cinema stage; in 1929 appeared with Monty Banks in " The Compulsory Husband."
(Died 19 Nov., 1943; age 71)

LEISTER, Frederick, actor; *b.* London, 1 Dec., 1885; *s.* of George Leister and his wife Marie (Le Capelain); *e.* Dulwich and at Worthing Grammar School; *m.* Dora Luther, a direct descendant of Martin Luther; was originally intended for the Law, and served his time as an articled clerk; made his first appearance on the stage at the Crown Theatre, Peckham, in 1906, in the chorus of " A Country Girl "; spent six years touring in various musical comedies; also toured in leading parts in " The Whip," " The Hope," " The Flag Lieutenant," etc.; at the Prince's, Feb., 1913, played Captain Manley in " The Indian Mutiny "; at the Lyceum, Oct., 1913, played the Marquis of Rockingham in

" Under Two Flags," subsequently appearing there in other plays; appeared at the Duke of York's, Sept., 1914, as Sergeant Davidson in " The Little Minister "; Dec., 1914, Great Big Little Panther in " Peter Pan "; Mar., 1915, Crashay in " Rosy Rapture "; then joined the Army, and served in the Royal Artillery in France for three years; after the War, appeared at the St. Martin's, July, 1919, in " The Very Idea "; subsequently joined Miss Lena Ashwell's Players, as producer and actor, playing Falstaff in " The Merry Wives of Windsor," Faulconbridge in " King John," etc.; at the Globe, Sept., 1922, played Sernoise in " The Return "; Lyceum Apr., 1923, Prince Rudolph in " A Night of Temptation "; Everyman, Sept., 1923, Rev. Mr. Duke in " Outward Bound "; Savoy, Feb., 1924, Frederick Mathison in " Lord o' Creation "; Royalty, May, 1925, Lord Nevern in " Jacob's Ladder "; Barnes, July, 1925, and at Wyndham's, Alfred Stapleton in " The Offence "; Adelphi, Sept., 1925, Dr. Masters in " The Green Hat "; Comedy, Dec., 1925, Doane in " 9.45 "; Criterion, Sept., 1926, Rev. John Pryce in " The Scarlet Lady "; Everyman, Dec., 1926, Uncle Remus in " Brer Rabbit "; St. Martin's, June, 1927, Harvey Lennox in " Meet the Wife "; Wyndham's, Sept., 1927, Edmond Bolbec in " The Lady in Law "; Arts, Dec., 1927, Montcel in " La Prisonnière "; Lyceum, Mar., 1928, John MacDonald in " Lumber Love "; St. Martin's, Aug., 1928, Ephraim Tucker in " Knight Errant "; Wyndham's, Oct., 1928, Thomas Fairfield in " To What Red Hell "; Arts, Feb., 1929, Mr. Harper in " Black Velvet "; Queen's, Mar., 1929, Inspector Dawford in " The Man at Six "; Lyric, June, 1929, Joseph Reynolds in " Murder on the Second Floor "; Royalty, May, 1930, Brother Peter in " Our Ostriches "; Savoy (for Repertory Players), Sept., 1930, and Prince of Wales's, Dec., 1930, the Husband in " The Queen Bee "; London Coliseum, Apr., 1931, The Emperor in " White Horse Inn "; Queen's, June, 1932, the Archduke Theodore in " Evensong "; went to America, and made his first appearance in New

York, at the Selwyn, 31 Jan., 1933, in the same part; on returning to London, appeared at the Vaudeville, Apr., 1933, as Doctor Roberts in "The Soldier and the Gentlewoman"; St. James's, May, 1933, Davenport in "The Late Christopher Bean," which ran over a year; Arts, May, 1934, the Duke of Marlborough in "Viceroy Sarah"; at the Plymouth, New York, Nov., 1934, Dr. Parsons in "Dark Victory"; Embassy, London, May, 1935, and Criterion, July, 1935, Mr. Penshott in "This Desirable Residence"; Henry Miller Theatre, New York, Dec., 1935, Sir Arthur Tuttington in "Libel"; Lyric, Sept., 1936, Dr. Kada in "Farewell Performance"; Apollo, Nov., 1936, Charles Donkin in "Housemaster," which ran for a year, and the same part at the Morosco, New York, Jan., 1938, when the play was renamed "Bachelor Born"; on returning to London, appeared at the Haymarket, Oct., 1938, as Captain Quilliam (Gramps) in "On Borrowed Time"; Duke of York's, Mar., 1939, Martin Bennett in "Lady Fanny"; Globe, Mar., 1940, Sir Hubert Sylvester in "Cousin Muriel"; New, Aug., 1940, Rev. Frank Thomson in "Outward Bound"; Lyric, Oct., 1941, Sir William Warring in "The Nutmeg Tree"; Apollo, Jan., 1944, the Doctor in "The Cradle Song"; Vaudeville, Oct., 1944, Captain Geoffrey Radcliffe in "No Medals," which ran until July, 1946; Lyric, Apr., 1947, succeeded Walter Fitzgerald as Arthur Winslow in "The Winslow Boy"; Arts, Apr., 1950, played Pavel Lebedyev in "Ivanov"; Lyric, Hammersmith, Jan., 1951, played John Barthwick in "The Silver Box"; Vaudeville, May, 1951, Dr. West in "The Thistle and the Rose"; Arts, Apr., 1953, Peter Nikoleyavitch in "The Seagull"; Savoy, Sept., 1953, Sigbert von Mohrungen in "The Devil's General"; Saville, Dec., 1954, Count d'Eguzon in "Accounting for Love"; Comedy, Dec., 1955, played Theodore Swanson in "Morning's At Seven," subsequently transferring to the Westminster, Feb., 1956; St. James's, Sept., 1956, played Mathew Treves in "Towards Zero"; Winter Garden, Dec., 1958, Professor Christie

in "The Bright One"; has appeared in innumerable films. *Recreations:* Walking and painting. *Club:* Green Room. *(Died 1970)*

LÉLY, Madeleine, French Actress; appeared at the Odéon, 1907, as Geneviève in "La Française," and Claire in "Monsieur de Prévan"; at the Antoine, 1907, as Jeannine in "La Sacrifiée"; at the Vaudeville, 1908, in "La Lys"; at the Variétés, 1910, as Germaine in "La Rubicon"; at the Gymnase, 1911, in "L'Amour Défendu"; at the Antoine, 1912, as Lady Falkland in "L'Homme qui assassina"; at the Gymnase, 1912, as Jacqueline in a revival of "Le Détour," and also as Renée de Rould in "L'Assaut"; at the Bouffes-Parisiens, 1913, as Henriette Hoxleur in "Le Secret"; at the Vaudeville, 1913, as Hélène de Trevillac in "La Belle Aventure"; at the Théâtre du Sarah Bernhardt, 1916, as Camille; at the Gymnase, 1919, played in "La Veille d'Armes"; at the Theatre de Paris, Mar., 1921, Lilas in "Le Coeur de Lilas"; appeared at the Prince's, London, Apr., 1921, with André Brulé in "Le Coeur dispose," "L'Epervier," and "Coeur de Moineau"; at the Nouvel-Ambigu, Nov., 1921, played Marina de Dasetta in "L'Epervier." *Address:* 7 Boulevard de Montparnasse, Paris.

LEMAITRE, Jules, French dramatic critic, dramatic author, poet and novelist, member of French Academy; *b.* at Vennecy. Loiret, 27 Aug., 1853; *e.* at Orléans, Paris and Charlemagne; is a doctor of letters, and was professor of rhetoric at Havre, 1875-9; professor at Algiers, 1879-81; professor of letters at Besançon, 1881-3; professor at Grenoble, 1883-4; appointed dramatic critic to the *Journal des Débats,* the *Révue des Deux-Mondes,* 1885; author of a book of collected criticism, "Impressions de Théâtre"; has written the following, among other plays: "Révoltée," 1889; "Le Député Leveau," 1891; "Mariage Blanc," 1891; "Flipote," 1893; "Les Rois," 1893; "L'Âge Difficile," 1895; "Le

Pardon," 1895 ; " La Bonne Hélène," 1896 ; " L'Amie," 1898 ; " La Massière," 1905 ; " Bertrade," 1905 ; " Le Mariage de Télémaque " (with Maurice Donnay), 1910.
(Died 7 Aug., 1914; age 60)

LE MOYNE, Sarah Cowell, actress ; *o.* New York City, 22 July, 1859 ; *d.* of Emma (Paul) and Lewis Cowell ; *m.* W. J. Le Moyne ; made her first appearance on the stage at the Union Square Theatre, 1878, as Madeline in " A Celebrated Case " ; at the same theatre, also played Lizette in " The Banker's Daughter," Sister Cecilia in " The Lost Children," Bianca in " French Flats," Mrs. Chauncey in " A False Friend," etc. ; she then gave dramatic recitals for some years, and visited England in 1884 ; returned to the stage in 1898, and played Mrs. Lorrimer in " The Moth and the Candle," at the Lyceum, New York ; subsequently appearing as the Duchess de Coutras in " Catherine " ; commenced her career as a " star," at Wallack's, New York, Oct., 1900, as Mrs. Virginia Bryant in " The Greatest Thing in the World," and the Duchess in " The Moment of Death " ; at Wallack's, 1901, played the Queen in Browning's play, " In a Balcony " ; during 1902-3, appeared in " Among Those Present " ; at the Majestic, New York, 1906, played in Browning's " Pippa Passes " ; at Maxine Elliott's Theatre, Sept., 1910, appeared as the Marquise de Rio-Zares in " Diplomacy " ; at the Herald Square Theatre, Feb., 1911, played Truth in " Everywoman " ; at Poughkeepsie, Oct., 1912, played Frau Naomi in " The Five Frankforters."
(Died 17 July, 1915; age 56)

LENA, Lily, comedienne ; *b.* London, 17 July, 1879 ; *d.* of John Charles Archer and his wife Mary Ann ; *m.* (1) William Newhouse ; (2) Flight Sub-Lieut. S. A. Turpin ; made her first appearance on the stage in 1893, at the old Falstaff Theatre of Varieties, with a partner, as the Sisters Lena ; subsequently appeared singly and met with great success ; has appeared at most of the leading halls, and has toured the Moss, Stoll, Syndicate, London Variety Theatres, and Controlling Theatres of Varieties' halls ; has played many successful pantomime engagements ; first visited the United States in 1905, and again in 1907, and since that date has been more or less identified with the American "vaudeville" stage ; re-appeared in London, 1915 ; has several successful songs to her credit, among which may be mentioned " Swing me higher, Obadiah " ; " Have you another little girl at home like Mary ? " *Recreations :* Golf, motoring, and fishing. *Address :* 29 Oakhill Court, S.W. *Telephone No. :* Putney 2391.

LENDER, Marcelle (*née* Marie Bastien), French actress ; has appeared at the Gymnase, 1907, as Gisèle Vaudreuil in " L'Eventail " ; at the Variétés, 1908, as Thérèse in " Le Roi," and 1912, as Suzy Barsac in " Le Bonheur sous la main " ; at the Comédie-Marigny, Feb., 1914, played Mdme, Gréhart in " Le Mannequin " ; at the Porte-St,-Martin, 1917, appeared in " Grand-Père " ; at the Nouvel-Ambigu, 1919, played Cléonne de Citry in " Les Baisers de Minuit," Léontine in " Le Vieux Marcheur " ; at the Vaudeville, 1921, Madame Walton in " Peg de Mon Cœur " (" Peg o' My Heart ") ; at the Théâtre de Paris, 1921, Madame Bianca Cordier in " La Possession." *Address :* 1 Rue de Courcelles, Paris.

LENIHAN, Winifred, actress ; *b.* New York City, U.S.A., 6 Dec., 1898 ; *d.* of Peter Lenihan and his wife Martha (Howell) ; *e.* New York public schools ; *m.* Frank Wheeler ; studied for the stage at the American Academy of Dramatic Arts ; made her first appearance on the stage at the Shubert Theatre, New York, 18 Nov., 1918, as Belline in " The Betrothal " ; at the Playhouse, New York, Dec., 1919, played Anne Woodstock in " For the Defense " ; at the Greenwich Village, Mar., 1921, Betty Lyons in " The Survival of the Fittest " ; subsequently toured as Kate in " The Detour " ; at the Bijou, New York, Dec., 1921, played Anne in

"The Dover Road"; at the National, Jan., 1923, Anne Hathaway in "Will Shakespeare"; at the Garrick, New York, Nov., 1923, Juliet in "The Failures"; Dec., 1923, Joan in the first performance of Bernard Shaw's "Saint Joan"; at the Comedy, New York, Sept., 1924, played Peggy Thatch in "Nerves"; Booth Theatre, Oct., 1926, Mary Todd in "White Wings"; Guild Theatre, Nov., 1928, Barbara Undershaft in "Major Barbara"; 48th Street, Feb., 1930, Margaret Larson in "The Boundary Line"; at Kingston, R.I., July, 1935, played Isobel in "The Truth About Blayds," Fanny in "Autumn Crocus," Leonora in "There's Always Juliet"; at Nantucket, Aug., 1935, Carrie in "Ned McCobb's Daughter"; Westport, Conn., June, 1936, Suzy de Coudray in "The Difficulty of Getting Married"; Mansfield, New York, Nov., 1936, Naomi Charrington in "Black Limelight"; at the Longacre, Dec., 1924, was responsible for the stage-production of "The Mongrel"; "Blind Mice" (of which she was also part-author), 1930; "The Pillars of Society," 1931; founded the Theatre Guild's School of Acting, 1925, which she conducted 1925-6. *Favourite parts:* Anne in "Will Shakespeare," and Juliet in "The Failures."
(Died 27 July, 1964; age 65)

LENNARD, Arthur, comedian and character vocalist; *b.* Woolwich, 8 Mar., 1867; commenced life as a barrister's clerk; made his first appearance on the variety stage at Lovejoy's, Peckham, Boxing Day, 1887, and then appeared at the old Trevor Music Hall, Knightsbridge, 13 Feb., 1888; was next engaged at the Royal, Holborn, 1888, under the late Sam Adams; eventually appeared at the Tivoli, Oxford, and London Pavilion; has since appeared at all the leading halls in London and the provinces, and has played all the leading tours and circuits in the kingdom; among many popular songs which he has introduced, may be noted "All through the Motor-car"; "At Waterloo"; "Baby"; "Big Ben struck one"; "Clementina

Brown"; "The Collier's Child"; "It's hard to say good-bye"; "The Old Toll-gate"; "One of the brave old Guards"; "Our Johnny"; "Pardners"; "Skylark, Skylark"; "So was I"; "That's what I'm weeping for"; "Three makes jolly fine company," etc. *Address:* "Homeleigh," Prentis Road, Streatham, S.W. *Telephone No.:* Streatham 1056.

LENNOX, Vera, actress and vocalist; *b.* Thornton Heath, 25 Nov., 1904; *m.* (1) Arthur Margetson (mar. dis.); (2) William Berkeley; first appeared on the stage at the Court Theatre, 18 May, 1914, in "The Swineherd and the Princess"; next appeared at the Little Theatre, Dec., 1914, in "The Cockyolly Bird"; subsequently appeared in several children's Christmas plays; appeared at the Vaudeville, May, 1918, in "Tabs"; Dec., 1918, in "Buzz-Buzz"; at the Scala, Dec., 1919, played Fifinella in the musical fantasy of that name; at the Apollo, in 1920, took up the part of Amelia in "Tilly of Bloomsbury," subsequently touring in the same part; at the Gaiety, Jan., 1921, played Milette in "The Betrothal"; subsequently toured as Mary Howells in "Mary"; at the Winter Garden Theatre, Sept., 1922, played Effie Dix in "The Cabaret Girl"; Sept., 1923, Kitty Wren in "The Beauty Prize"; in 1924 appeared in "To-Night's the Night"; Sept., 1924, May Rooker in "Primrose"; May, 1925, Bonnie Reeves in "Tell Me More"; Feb., 1926, Jane Martin in "Kid Boots"; Shaftesbury, Sept., 1926, Rita Reynolds in "Just a Kiss"; Everyman, Jan.-Mar., 1927, Peggy Travers in "The Square Peg," and Judy Donaldson in "Jazz-Patterns"; "Q," Mar., 1927, and Savoy, May, 1927, Anne Briston in "Anne, One Hundred"; Duke of York's, Nov., 1927, Sally Smith, M.D., in "Good Morning, Bill"; Gaiety, Jan., 1930, Peggy Sylvester in "Darling, I Love You"; Palace, Sept., 1930, Salomea in "Frederica"; Comedy, Jan., 1931, Sally Rogers in "Hawk Island"; Garrick, June, 1931, Iris Thorpe in "The Bandits"; went to New York and made her first appearance there, at the 44th Street Theatre, 1 Oct., 1931, as Susie Dean in "The Good Companions"; after returning to London, appeared at "Q," Oct., 1932, as Sylvia Kennett in "Crime on the Hill"; Arts, Nov., 1932, played Meg in "Other People's Lives"; Royal Opera House, Leicester, Christmas, 1932, appeared as Aladdin in the pantomime; Stage Guild, Apr., 1933, Margaret Apsley in "My Lady Crook"; Fulham, Nov., 1933, Schatze in "The Greeks Had a Word for It"; Dec., 1933, toured as Aladdin in pantomime; King's, Hammersmith, Feb., 1934, Peg Drummond in "The Happy Hostage"; Royalty (for "G" Club), Apr., 1934, Miss Diver in "Murder in Motley"; at the Saville, May, 1934, played Sally Smith in "Good Morning, Bill"; Westminster, July, 1934, Robina Hutt in "French Salad"; Nov., 1934, Dorothy Wilson in "Youth at the Helm"; Little, Nov., 1934, Silver Stream in "Lady Precious Stream"; at the Theatre Royal, Leeds, Dec., 1934, played Colin in "Mother Goose"; Palace, May, 1935, appeared with "The Co-Optimists"; Piccadilly, July, 1935, Delena in "Public Saviour No. 1"; in Aug., 1935, toured as Schatze in "The Greeks Had a Word for It"; St. Martin's, Jan., 1936, Babs Delaney in "Sauce for the Goose"; Cambridge, May, 1936, Lucie in "Sonata"; Little, Nov., 1936, Silver Stream in "Lady Precious Stream"; Wimbledon, Dec., 1936, Jack in "Jack and Jill"; Coventry, Dec., 1937, Aladdin; Garrick, Apr., 1938, Daphne Baines in "As Husbands Go"; "Q." Sept., 1938, Rose Waller in "They Fly by Twilight"; Playhouse, Nov., 1938, Sybil in "The Shoemaker's Holiday"; Southport, Dec., 1938, Dick in "Dick Whittington"; Richmond, Jan., 1939, Ellen Hamble in "I Done a Murder"; then, for some years, appeared in various B.B.C. programmes; at the Cambridge Theatre, Feb., 1944, appeared in "The Gay Follies"; Open Air Theatre, Regent's Park, June, 1944, played the Princess of the Western Regions in "Lady Precious Stream"; subsequently again with the B.B.C.; has also appeared on several occasions for the Phoenix and Renaissance Societies; was a prominent member of the Midnight Follies at the Hotel Metropole. *Recreations:* Dancing and motoring. *Address:* 24 Decoy Avenue, London, N.W.11. *Telephone No.:* Speedwell 8617.

LENORMAND, Henri-René, dramatic author; *b.* Paris, 3 May, 1882; is the author of the following among other plays, "Les Possédés," 1909; "L'Esprit Souterrain," 1912; "Terres Chaudes," 1913; "Poussière," "Le Temps et un Songe," 1919; "Les Ratés," "Le Simoun," 1920; "Le Mangeur de Rêves," "La Dent Rouge," 1922; "L'Ombre du Mal," "L'Homme et ses Fantômes," 1924; "Le Lâche," 1925; "L'Amour Magicien," 1926; "Mixture," 1927; "Une Vie Secrète," 1929; "Les Trois Chambres," 1931; "Asie," "Sortilèges," 1932; "Crépuscule du Théâtre," 1934; "La folle du ciel," 1936; "Pacifique," 1937; his collected plays have been published in nine volumes; is also the author of "A l'écart" and "L'armée secrète," volumes of tales; is an Officier de la Légion d'Honneur and Vice-President de la Société Universelle du Théâtre. *(Died 17 Feb., 1951; age 68)*

LEO, Frank, lyrist, composer and entertainer; *b.* Chatham, 10 Sept., 1874; *s.* of Vincent Gregory Peers and his wife Cordelia (Holmes); *m.* Sable Fern; was formerly engaged as a Fine Art Decorator; for many years was popularly known as the writer and composer of hundreds of songs, and especially of those sung by Wilkie Bard, which helped to form that artist's peculiar style; among the songs which he composed for that artist may be mentioned: "I fell off the 'bus"; "Do you know any more funny stories?"; "I wish I'd bought ducks"; "That's where she sits all day"; "There's a peculiar thing"; "Is there anything else you'd like?"; "I'd like to go halves in that"; "I think we shall have some rain"; "Has anyone seen our cat?"; "I'm not such a goose as I look"; "You, You, You!"; "One and a penny a day"; "The Night Watchman"; "The Cowslip and the Cow";

" My little Deitcher Girl " ; " Let me sing " ; " When the Bugle calls," etc. ; is also the writer and composer of " What is the use of loving a girl ? " ; " She ain't a bit like the other girls " ; " My Lily of the Valley," etc. ; after twenty years of writing for others, decided to appear on the stage himself, and made his first appearance on the music-hall stage at the Palace, Bath, Mar., 1915, singing his own songs ; first appeared in London, at the Bedford, Camden Town, 3 May, 1915. *Address :* 8 Clifden Road, Twickenham. *Telephone No. :* Richmond 486.

LEON, Anne, actress ; *b.* London, 8 Dec., 1925 ; *d.* of Sir Ronald George Leon, Bart., and his wife Rosemary (Armstrong) ; *e.* Wychwood School, Oxford ; *m.* Michael Gough (mar. dis.) ; studied for the stage at the Royal Academy of Dramatic Art ; while still at the R.A.D.A., made her first appearance on the stage at the Intimate Theatre, Palmer's Green, Sept., 1943, as Adèle in "Jane Eyre"; from Jan., 1944 to Dec., 1945, served in the W.R.N.S. ; after demobilization, joined the Worthing Repertory company ; made her first appearance in London, at the Piccadilly Theatre, 30 May, 1946, as Winifred Talbot in "Portrait in Black"; Lyric, Hammersmith, Mar., 1947, played Alice in "The Rossiters"; Strand, June, 1947, Maude Neve in "Angel"; Strand, July, 1947, Veronica Bellamy in "My Wives and I"; Lyric, Hammersmith, Jan., 1948, Doris Gow in "Bred in the Bone"; subsequently joined repertory company, at the Lyceum, Sheffield, remaining until Sept., 1948; Aldwych, Dec., 1948, appeared as Cherry Davies in "September Tide"; Apollo, Sept., 1949, Veronica Howard in "Treasure Hunt"; Saville, July, 1955, appeared as Liz in "The Shadow of Doubt"; Duchess, Mar., 1956, Mary Trellington in "Tabitha"; Saville, Dec., 1956, Foible in "The Way of the World"; Cambridge, Mar., 1957, Jean in "The Iron Duchess"; Aldwych, Aug., 1958, Pamela in "Brouhaha"; toured, May, 1960, as Millie Foster in "The Birds and the Bees"; has also appeared in films, including "Reach for the Sky,"

"Appointment in London", "The Horse's Mouth," etc. *Address:* c/o Eric Goodhead (Management) Ltd., 27 Old Bond Street, London, W.1. *Telephone No.:* Hyde Park 9016.

LEONARD, Billy, actor ; *b.* Dublin, 15 Dec., 1892 ; *s.* of William Leonard and his wife Annie (Lowry) ; brother of Alf. and Cressie Leonard ; *e.* by the Christian Brothers, Kingstown, Dublin ; *m.* Esmé Scott Harston ; has been on the stage since childhood, making his first appearance at the Empire, Belfast, in 1901, as Buttons in a sketch entitled " At a Moment's Notice," with the Norman and Leonard trio ; made his first appearance in London, at the Granville Theatre of Varieties, Waltham Green, 1902, in the same part ; has appeared at all the principal theatres in the provinces, and in the leading music halls all over the United Kingdom ; during 1916 toured as the Hon. Billy Baxter in " A la Carte " ; in 1917 toured in the *revue* " Smile " ; at the Hippodrome, Dec., 1917, appeared in " Zig-Zag " ; in 1918 toured in " Ocean Waves " ; at the Apollo Theatre, June, 1918, played Monty Mainwaring in " Soldier Boy " ; at the Prince's, Manchester, Dec., 1918, played Jim Marvin in " Oh ! Joy ! " and the same part at the Kingsway Theatre, Jan., 1919 ; at the Shaftesbury, Sept., 1919, played the Bailiff in " Baby Bunting " ; at the Palace, Dec., 1919, played in " The Whirligig " ; at the Prince of Wales's, May, 1921, played Lord Boniface in " The Gipsy Princess " ; at the Gaiety, Dec., 1921, Salimac de Flavigny in " The Little Girl in Red " ; at the Empire, Feb., 1922, William Rowan in " Jenny " ; Apr., 1922, Dr. Pedantius in " Love's Awakening " ; at the Gaiety, Oct., 1922, Baron Ippolith Mekchwitch in " The Last Waltz " ; Sept., 1923, Count Wasili Bronin in " Catherine " ; at the Duke of York's, May, 1924, appeared in " The Punch Bowl " ; at His Majesty's, Oct., 1924, played Ogden Scales in " Patricia ; Mar., 1925, Larry Wyndham in " The Bamboula " ; Shaftesbury, June, 1925, William in "Clo-Clo"; 1925–6, toured in variety theatres ; July, 1926, toured as Leander in "Katja the Dancer"; during 1926–7 toured as Billy Early in "No, No, Nanette"; at the Gaiety, Nov., 1927, played Baron Anatole Lavoux in "The Girl from Cook's"; Vaudeville, Oct., 1928, appeared in "Charlot, 1928"; went to Australia, and at the St. James's, Sydney, N.S.W. Feb., 1929, appeared in "Lido Lady"; after returning to London, toured 1929, as Tony in "The Girl in the Limousine," and 1930, as George Black-Fox in "Open Your Eyes"; Savoy, Mar., 1930, played Jan in "The Damask Rose"; Piccadilly, Sept., 1930, in "Open Your Eyes"; Cambridge, June, 1931, in "The Sign of the Seven Dials"; Arts, Oct., 1931, played the Major in "Vile Bodies"; Gaiety, May, 1932, succeeded Sonnie Hale as Pop Curry in "Hold My Hand"; toured Nov., 1932, as the Marquis de la Marche in "The Dubarry"; Whitehall, July, 1934, played Worthington Smythe in "Elizabeth Sleeps Out"; London Hippodrome, Sept., 1934, Tony Tolliver in "Yes, Madam?"; toured, 1936, as Sir Evelyn Oakleigh in "Anything Goes" and 1937 as Ladislaus Kohanyi in "Venus in Silk"; Open Air Theatre, Aug., 1938, played Touchstone in "As You Like It"; toured, 1938, as Bones in "The Sun Never Sets"; in 1939, was touring in variety theatres; Adelphi, Feb., 1940, appeared in "Fig Leaves"; toured 1940–1, for E.N.S.A.; toured, 1943, as Jimmy Blake in "Lady Behave," and 1944, as Officer O'Hara in "Arsenic and Old Lace," appearing in the latter part, at the Strand, Mar., 1945, until the end of the run, in 1946; Duchess, Mar., 1946, appeared in "Make It a Date"; toured, Apr., 1947, as the Common Man in "1066 and All That"; toured, 1947–8, as Sir George Basingstoke in "She Wanted a Cream Front Door"; he has recently appeared in films and on television. *Recreations:* Golf, swimming, tennis, and motoring. *Club:* Savage. *Address:* 69 Montagu Mansions, London, W.1. *Telephone No.:* Welbeck 1945.

LEONARD, Patricia, actress and vocalist; *b.* London, 9 Nov., 1916; *d.* of Theodore Leonard and his wife Elena Livingstone (Cadden); *e.* Sydney, N.S.W.; *m.* Captain Francis Francis; studied for the stage and singing under her father and mother, and at the Joan Davis School of Dancing; spent her infancy in South Africa before being educated in Australia; made her first appearance on the stage at the Comedy Theatre, London, 25 Apr., 1933, in the chorus of "How d'you Do?", under André Charlot; remained with Charlot three years, playing small parts and understudying in various *revues* at the Comedy and Vaudeville; Vaudeville, Jan., 1936, played Queen Arabella in "The Sleeping Beauty," and at the same theatre, Sept., 1936, played Joan in "Gentle Rain," and Ethel Paske in "Do You Remember . . ."; during 1937, appeared there in "non-stop" *revues*; Palace, Dec., 1937, played Louise in "Oh! You Letty," and July, 1938, Countess Lisa in "Maritza"; Palladium, Oct., 1939, appeared in "The Little Dog Laughed"; Victoria Palace, Apr., 1941, in "Black Vanities"; Vaudeville, Apr., 1942, in "Scoop"; Hippodrome, Nov., 1942, Jean Blanchard in "Let's Face It"; Adelphi, Nov., 1944, appeared in "Merry-Go-Round." *Recreations:* Riding, tennis, and reading. *Address:* 39 Albion Gate, Hyde Park, W.2. *Telephone No.:* Paddington 9656.

LEONARD, Robert, actor; during early career on the American stage was mainly engaged on "vaudeville" stage; made his first appearance on the London stage, at the Queen's Theatre, 14 Apr., 1914, as Mawruss Perlmutter in "Potash and Perlmutter," making an instantaneous success; in Apr., 1915, appeared there as Abraham Jacobsen in "Cheap at Half the Price," of which he was the author; at the Coliseum, Dec., 1915, played Marcus Greenbaum in "In Lingerie"; at the Queen's Theatre, Sept., 1916, played Mawruss Perlmutter in "Potash and Perlmutter in Society"; at the London Opera House, Mar., 1917, played Issy Bing in "The Other Bing Boys"; at the Savoy, London, Apr., 1919, appeared as Mawruss Perlmutter in "Business Before

Pleasure "; at the Coliseum, Jan., 1920, played in " In Hosiery "; at Brooklyn, N.Y., May, 1921, appeared in " The Red Trail "; at the Garrick, London, Feb., 1923, played Mawruss Perlmutter in " Partners Again "; at the Broadhurst, New York, Sept., 1924, Isaac Iskovitch in " Izzy "; Times Square, June, 1925, Moses Ginsburg in " Kosher Kitty Kelly "; Ritz, Aug., 1926, Mawruss Perlmutter in " Potash and Perlmutter, Detectives "; George M. Cohan, Sept., 1927, Rudolf Schwartz in "Ten Per Cent"; Lyric, Nov., 1929, Ira Rosen in "Fifty Million Frenchmen"; Biltmore, June, 1931, Moses Kaufman in "The Wooden Soldier"; Alvin, Oct., 1931, Sam Benfeld in "Wonder Boy"; reappeared in London, at Streatham Hill, Oct., 1932 as Perlmutter in a revival of "Potash and Perlmutter"; playing the same part at the Gaiety, Nov., 1932; Longacre, Oct., 1934, Weinstein in "Geraniums in My Window"; Park, Apr., 1935, again played Maurus Perlmutter in "Potash and Perlmutter"; White Plains, N.Y., July, 1935, played Abe Rothberg in "Menagerie"; Bijou, New York, Feb., 1936, Goldfarb in "The Sap Runs High"; Brighton Beach, Aug., 1936, Uncle Morty in "Awake and Sing"; Alvin, New York, Oct., 1936, Senator Malvinsky in "Red, Hot and Blue"; St. James's, London, Aug., 1938, Mr. Buonaparte in "Golden Boy"; Cort, Jan., 1942, Lipsky in "Café Crown"; Carnegie Hall, Sept., 1942, in "The New Moon"; toured, 1943-4, as Solomon Levy in "Abie's Irish Rose"; Ambassador, Sept., 1944, Morris Mandel in "Down to Miami." *(Died 5 Jan., 1948; age 59)*

LEONARD-BOYNE, Eva, actress; *b.* 1885; *d.* of Leonard Boyne and his wife Mary (Everington); *m.* (1) Thomas Pauncefort (mar. dis.); (2) Gordon Ash; toured in the English provinces, 1906-11, in "Charley's Aunt," "The Lady of Ostend," "When Knights Were Bold," "Irene Wycherley," and as Diana in "Diana of Dobson's," and Miss Heseltine in "A Single Man"; appeared at the Coronet Theatre, 25 Apr., 1911, as Dennis in "As You Like It"; appeared at Newport, Mon., May, 1911, as Miss Baines in

"The Bells of Lin-Lan-Lone"; at the Kingsway Theatre, 1912, succeeded Dorothy Minto as Dora Delaney in "Fanny's First Play"; she then went to America, and at the Comedy, New York, Sept., 1912, played the same part, and toured through the United States, 1913-14, in the same part; returned to London, and appeared at the Ambassadors' Theatre, July, 1914, as Effie Pemberton in "The Blindness of Virtue"; again went to America, and at Wallack's Theatre, New York, Jan., 1915, played Alison in "The Man who Married a Dumb Wife"; Feb., 1915, Hermia in "A Midsummer Night's Dream"; Mar., 1915, Minnie Tinwell in "The Doctor's Dilemma"; at the Booth Theatre, Sept., 1915 appeared as Molly Thornhill in "A Pair of Silk Stockings," and toured in this part, 1916; returning to London, appeared at the Garrick Theatre, July, 1916, as Estelle Clugston in "The Rotters"; at the Haymarket, Feb., 1917, played Ninetta Monday in "Felix Gets a Month"; at the Prince of Wales's, Birmingham, June, 1918, Marion Barchester in "Sinners"; subsequently again returned to New York, and at the Playhouse, in that city, Feb., 1920, played Dulcie Fosdick in "The Wonderful Thing"; at the Punch and Judy Theatre, Oct., 1921, played Germaine de Landeve in "The Fan"; at the Longacre, Feb., 1923, Rose in "The Laughing Lady"; at the Lyceum, New York, Aug., 1923, Lulu in "Little Miss Bluebeard"; Martin Beck, Feb., 1926, Lady Blessington in "The Shanghai Gesture"; Morosco, Sept., 1927, Mrs. Joyce in "The Letter"; Henry Miller, Nov., 1928, Alice in "The Sacred Flame"; Maxine Elliott, Mar., 1929, Lacey in "Security"; Martin Beck (for the Theatre Guild), Feb., 1930, Amanda in "The Apple Cart"; has since appeared in "The Modern Virgin," "A Kiss for Cinderella," "Experience Unnecessary," "Late One Evening"; at the Plymouth, New York, Jan., 1933, played the Nurse in "Late One Evening"; Martin Beck, Dec., 1933, Mrs. Hemingway in "The Lake"; in the autumn of 1935, toured in repertory with Eva Le Gallienne, in "Camille," "Women Have Their Way," etc., and appeared in the same plays at the Shubert, New York, Dec., 1935; Broadhurst, Sept., 1936, played the Second Princess in "Victoria Regina" and at the Martin Beck, Oct., 1938, the Duchess of Sutherland in the same play; subsequently toured in the same play, from coast to coast; Booth Theatre (for Theatre Guild), Oct., 1939, played the Society Lady in "The Time of Your Life"; National Theatre, July, 1941, Mrs. Watty in "The Corn is Green," which she played in all for three years, in New York and on tour; Playhouse, Feb., 1945, Mrs. Gregory in "The Stranger"; toured, 1945–7, as Mrs. Latham in "The Two Mrs. Carrolls"; Plymouth, New York, Sept., 1946, Miss ffoliot-ffoulkes in "Hidden Horizon"; toured, 1947–9, as Paulton in "O Mistress Mine"; for A.N.T.A., Dec., 1950, played Sadie in "Twentieth Century," and appeared in this at the Fulton, Jan., 1951; at the National, Dec., 1951, played Barbara Fawcett in "The Constant Wife"; Playhouse, Sept., 1953, Mrs. Almond in "A Pin to See the Peepshow"; at Boston, Washington and Baltimore, 1954, appeared in "Portrait of a Lady"; Ethel Barrymore, New York, Oct., 1955, played the Third Applicant in "The Chalk Garden." *(Died 12 Apr., 1960; age 74)*

LE ROUX, Hugues, French dramatic author, novelist and explorer; *b.* Havre, 23 Nov., 1860; *e.* Havre and Paris; *m.* Maria-Corona Colonna di Arbruzzesi; has written the following plays: "Crime et Châtiment" (with Paul Ginisty), 1888; "Tout pour l'Honneur," 1893; "L'Autre France" (with Pierre Decourcelle), 1900; "L'Instantané" (with De Caillavet), 1901; has also written many novels and works on travel. *Recreations :* Music and riding. *Address :* 58 Rue de Vaugirard, Paris.

LE ROY, Servais, conjuror and illusionist; *b.* Spa, Belgium; *m.* Mdlle. Talma; made his first appearance on the stage in 1874, at the Alcazar, Brussels, as a conjuror; made his first appearance in England in 1882, at the London Pavilion; subsequently

toured in Spain; on his return, appeared at the Royal Aquarium, Jan., 1889, remaining there for several months; he then spent three months at the Crystal Palace, and made his re-appearance on the regular music-hall stage, 20 Oct., 1890, at the Tivoli, and Royal, presenting "The Three Graces," and "The Birth of Love"; worked "single-handed" for many years, subsequently joining forces with Leon Bosco and Mdlle. Talma; some of the most startling illusions are credited to Le Roy, and the entertainment furnished by Le Roy, Talma and Bosco is one of the most finished and artistic "mystery" turns on the variety stage; they have appeared at all the leading London and provincial halls, and have toured all over the world. *Address :* 52 Spenser Road, Herne Hill, S.E.

LE SAGE, Stanley, business manager; *b.* Brighton, 19 Mar., 1880; *s.* of Sir John Merry Le Sage, managing editor of *The Daily Telegraph* and his wife Elizabeth (Lord); *e.* King's College, London, and Heidelberg; *m.* Ella M. Stonhouse (mar. dis.); was formerly engaged as a tea-planter in Ceylon, in fruit farming in Canada, and was for some time engaged with the famous firm of caterers, J. Lyons & Co., Ltd., was first engaged as business manager for provincial tours of "The Sign of the Cross," 1904, and "The Earl and the Girl," 1905, with William Greet; has fulfilled engagements in a similar capacity with Arthur Collins, 1906, and Ethel Irving, 1908-10; J. E. Vedrenne, at the Queen's, 1910; Vedrenne and Eadie, at Royalty, 1911; Vedrenne and Vernon, at Little Theatre, 1920; Sir Oswald Stoll, Stoll Picture Theatre, London Opera House, 1920. *Favourite play :* "Milestones." *Recreations :* Shooting, fishing, rowing, and photography. *(Died 27 Feb., 1932; age 51)*

LESLIE, Enid, actress; *b.* London, 4 Jan., 1888; *e.* privately; made her first appearance on the stage, at the Lyric Theatre, 5 Jan., 1905, in the chorus of "The Talk of the Town"; appeared at the Aldwych

Theatre, Dec., 1905, as Night-Belle in " Blue Bell " ; Mar., 1906, as Currant Bun in "The Beauty of Bath"; at the Gaiety, Feb., 1908, played Hana in " The Girls of Gottenburg "; Apr., 1908, played in " Havana "; Jan., 1909, Lady Trixie in " Our Miss Gibbs," and Mar., 1911, Diamond in " Peggy "; was next engaged by Charles Hawtrey and appeared at the Prince of Wales's, Apr., 1911, as Estelle in " Better Not Enquire " ; Sept., 1911, played Senta Brand in " The Great Name " ; Oct., 1911, Berthe Gonthier in " The Uninvited Guest " ; and Feb., 1912, Agnes in " Dear Old Charlie "; accompanied Charles Hawtrey to New York to play the last-mentioned part ; at the Globe, Oct., 1912, appeared as Sadie Small in " Officer 666." *Favourite part :* Senta in " The Great Name." *Hobby :* Antiques. *Recreations :* Tennis, golf, swimming, and dancing.

LESLIE, Fred (Hobson), actor ; *b.* London, 19 May, 1881 ; *s.* of the late Fred Leslie, the famous comedian, and his wife Louie (Agate) ; made his first appearance on the London stage, at the Savoy Theatre, 10 Feb., 1904, as the Maharajah of Moohooch in " The Love Birds " ; next toured in the United States with Miss Edna May in " The School Girl," appearing at Daly's, New York, in Sept., 1904 ; remained with this company some months, and returning to London, appeared at the Prince of Wales's Theatre, Oct., 1905, as Bill Stratford in " Lady Madcap "; next toured with Mr. George Edwardes's companies ; in 1907, accompanied the Seymour Hicks Musical Comedy Company to South America ; appeared at Theatre Royal, Birmingham, Christmas, 1907, in " Cinderella "; at the Queen's Theatre, May, 1908, played Lieutenant Frank Meredith in a revival of " The Dairymaids " ; understudied Mr. Joseph Coyne at Daly's, in " The Merry Widow," subsequently touring in that piece and in " The Dollar Princess " ; at the Adelphi, Dec., 1909, played Dandini in " Cinderella "; at the

Shaftesbury Theatre, May, 1912, played Nicola in " Princess Caprice "; at the Comedy, New York, Sept., 1913, played the same part, when the production was re-named, "Lieber Augustin " ; at the Winter Garden, New York, Oct., 1914, played Lord Graham in " Dancing Around " ; on returning to England, toured in the autumn of 1915, in " Made in England " ; at the London Opera House, May, 1916, played Jack Charlton in " The Miller's Daughters " ; at the Gaiety, Sept., 1916, the Rt. Hon. George Wye in " Theodore and Co."; at the Prince of Wales's, Dec., 1917, George Bellamy Stark in " Yes, Uncle "; at the Winter Garden, Oct., 1919, played Max Touquet in " Kissing Time "; Sept., 1920, Paillard in " A Night Out"; during 1921 toured in " Mary "; at the New Oxford, Dec., 1922, played Hugh Bryant in " Battling Butler "; at the Times Square, New York, Jan., 1924, appeared in " André Charlot's Revue of 1924." *Club :* Green Room. *Address :* Green Room Club, 46 Leicester Square, W.C.2.

LESLIE, Lew, author, composer and producer; *b.* 1886; *m.* Irene Wales; first appeared, on the "vaudeville" stage, in America, 1909, in a singing and talking act; subsequently managed cabaret at the Café de Paris, New York, when he conceived the idea of "The Plantation Revue," which was produced at the 48th Street Theatre, New York, July, 1922; this was included in the *revue* "Dover Street to Dixie," at the London Pavilion, May, 1923; Broadhurst, New York, Oct., 1924, produced "Dixie to Broadway"; London Pavilion, Sept., 1926, "Black-Birds"; His Majesty's, May, 1927, "Whitebirds"; Liberty, New York, May, 1928, "Blackbirds of 1928"; Majestic, Feb., 1930, "The International Review"; Royale, Oct., 1930, "Lew Leslie's Blackbirds"; Sam H. Harris, May, 1931, "Rhapsody in Black"; Apollo, New York, Dec., 1933 "Blackbirds of 1933"; London Coliseum, Aug., 1934, "Blackbirds of 1934"; Dec., 1934, "Blackbirds of 1935"; Gaiety, London, July, 1936, "Blackbirds of 1936"; Adelphi, London, Nov., 1936, a second edition of the same production; 44th Street, New York, Dec., 1938, "Blackbirds of 1939." *(Died 10 Mar., 1963; age 76)*

LESLIE, Marguerite, actress; *b.* in Sweden 3 Apr., 1884; *m.* Marquis de Santa Rosa; made her first appearance on the stage at the Manhattan Theatre, New York City, 5 Jan., 1904, as Mrs. Ogden in "The Virginian"; made her first appearance in London at His Majesty's Theatre, Jan., 1906, as Viola in "Nero"; at the Aldwych, Mar., 1906, played Lady Delbeck in "The Beauty of Bath"; subsequently toured as Sylvaine in "My Darling"; at the Criterion, July, 1907, played Marcelle in "A Night Out"; Oct., 1907, Isabella in "Concerning a Countess," and in "A Scotch Marriage"; at the New Theatre, Oct., 1908, played the Duchess of Havant in "Bellamy the Magnificent"; at the Duke of York's, Aug., 1909, appeared as Germaine in "Arséne Lupin"; at the Comedy, Sept., 1910, played Mrs. Verney in "A Woman's Way"; Jan., 1911, played Dulcie Anstice in "Preserving Mr. Panmure"; at the Duke of York's, Aug., 1911, played Eva Wharton in "The Concert"; at the Whitney (now Strand) Theatre, Feb., 1912, played Mrs. Craven in "A Member of Tattersall's"; at the Prince of Wales's, Apr., 1912, Linda Moore in "At the Barn"; then went to America, and joined the "stock" company at the Burbank Theatre, Los Angeles, Sept., 1912, playing leading parts in "The Gamblers," "The Money Moon" and "The Witching Hour"; at the Belasco Theatre, New York, Dec., 1913, played Henriette Durand in "The Secret"; at the Lyceum, New York, Nov., 1914, appeared as Valentine in "Outcast"; at the Empire, New York, Oct., 1916, played Mrs. Radford in "The Basker"; at the Globe, New York, Jan., 1917, succeeded Miss Gail Kain as Zeila Vorona in "The Harp of Life"; is a sister of Martha Hedman. *Recreations:* Shooting, riding, and golfing. *(Died 1958; age 73)*

LESLIE, Sylvia, actress and vocalist; *b.* London, 1 Sept., 1900; *d.* of the late Sir Leslie Ward ("Spy") and his wife Judith (Topham-Watney); *e.* in a London convent, and privately; *m.* Evan Thomas (mar. dis.); studied for the stage under Kate Rorke at the Florence Etlinger Dramatic School; made her first appearance on the stage at the Shaftesbury Theatre, 1918, in the chorus of "Yes, Uncle!"; at the same theatre, Sept., 1919, played Miss Raymond in "Baby Bunting"; Apr., 1920, Maud in "The Little Whopper"; June, 1920, Vinette in "Oh! Julie," also on occasions playing the part of Julie; at the Adelphi, Oct., 1920, played Seraphine in "The Naughty Princess"; Oct., 1921, Zozo in "The Golden Moth"; at the New Oxford, Dec., 1922, Mrs. Battling Butler in "Battling Butler"; during 1923 toured in "Toni"; at the Empire, Jan., 1924, played Charlotte in "The Three Graces"; at the Lyric, June, 1924, Marie in "The Street Singer"; during 1925 toured in "Stop Press"; at the Lyric, Dec., 1925, played Marini in "Lilac Time";

Empire, Apr., 1926, Josephine Vanderwater in "Lady, Be Good"; Apollo (for the Venturers), Dec., 1926, and Prince of Wales's, Jan., 1927, Maud Kendicott in "Tuppence Coloured"; Savoy, May, 1927, Heloise in "Double Dan"; Daly's, July, 1927, Dolores Barnes in "Peggy-Ann"; Winter Garden, Apr., 1928, Kitty Carleton in "So This is Love"; during 1929, toured in "Lilac Time"; went to New York, and made her first appearance there, at the Ziegfeld Theatre, 5 Nov., 1929, as Gussi in "Bitter Sweet"; after returning to London, appeared at the London Hippodrome, Mar., 1931, as Rowena Clyde-Burkin in "Stand Up and Sing"; Little, June, 1932, played Jane Gommery in "Intimate Relations"; Vaudeville, July, 1933, appeared in "After Dark"; at the 44th Street Theatre, New York, Oct., 1934, played Sophie Otford in "Conversation Piece"; Palace, London, Sept., 1936, Laura Buxton in "This'll Make You Whistle"; Saville, Apr., 1940, and again in May, 1941, appeared in "Up and Doing," and in Apr., 1942, in "Fine and Dandy"; Lyric, Aug., 1943, in "Flying Colours";

Palace, Manchester, Dec., 1944, in "Queen of Hearts"; Saville, Mar., 1947, succeeded Ellen Pollock as Wilma in "The Wizard of Oz"; Cambridge, Aug., 1948, played Mrs. Woodhouse-Jones, M.P., in "Trouble in the House." *Recreations:* Motoring and swimming. *Address:* 34 Redcliffe Road, Old Brompton Road, London, S.W.5. *Telephone No.:* Flaxman 0221.

LESLIE-STUART, May, actress; *b.* Manchester; *d.* of Leslie Stuart, the famous composer; *m.* (1) Cecil Cameron (mar. dis.); (2) Lieut. Ball; (3) James Mayhew; made her first appearance on the stage at His Majesty's Theatre, 16 Dec., 1909, as Beauty in the revival of "Pinkie and the Fairies"; appeared at Daly's, May, 1911, as Jacqueline in "The Count of Luxembourg"; at Drury Lane, Sept., 1911, appeared in "The Hope"; at the Coliseum, Mar., 1912, played Delhi in "The Crown of India"; at the Queen's, Jan., 1913, appeared as Dorothy in "Get-Rich-Quick Wallingford"; at the Lyric, Feb., 1915, played Lady Holyrood in "Florodora"; subsequently appeared at the Palladium, Coliseum, etc., in songs, accompanied by her father; in Aug., 1915, appeared at the Alhambra in "5064 Gerrard"; at the Savoy, Oct., 1915, played Lady Camber in "The Case of Lady Camber"; from 1922–24, appeared in variety theatres with her father, singing many of his well-known popular songs to his accompaniment. *Address:* 14 Thurlow Road, N.W.3.

LESSING, Madge, actress and vocalist; *b.* London; made one of her earliest appearances on the stage in New York, at the Casino Theatre, 12 May, 1894, as Lady Tom-a-Line in "The Passing Show"; at the same theatre, 29 June, 1896, she played in "In Gay New York," and 2 Nov., 1896, appeared as Jack Hubbard in "Jack and the Beanstalk"; on 25 May, 1897, she played Dimples in "The Whirl of the Town"; 12 Nov., 1898, Ilona in "A Dangerous Maid"; and 25 July, 1900, appeared in "The Rounders"; she made her first appearance on the London stage at

Drury Lane, 26 Dec., 1900, as the principal girl in "The Sleeping Beauty and the Beast"; when the New Adelphi was opened under the tentative title of the New Century Theatre, on 11 Sept., 1901, she appeared as Dimples in "The Whirl of the Town," and 27 Nov., 1901, played Violet in a revival of "The Belle of New York"; at the Shaftesbury Theatre, 3 Apr., 1902, she appeared as Eliza Carter in "All on Account of Eliza," and at Drury Lane, 26 Dec., 1902, she played in "Mother Goose"; at the Adelphi, 1 Aug., 1903, she appeared as Little Em'ly in "Em'ly"; she then returned to America, and in 1903 toured with Francis Wilson in "Erminie"; she appeared at the Casino, New York, 19 Oct., 1903, as Javotte in "Erminie"; in 1904 she toured with De Wolf Hopper as Mataya in "Wang," and played the same part at the Lyric Theatre, New York, on 18 Apr., 1904; returning to London in 1904 she appeared at the Prince of Wales's Theatre as Aurora Brue in "Sergeant Brue," and in various song scenas at the Coliseum; at the Waldorf Theatre, 1 Jan., 1906, was seen as Elsie in "Noah's Ark"; played in Paris, 1907-8, in "The Prince of Pilsen"; at the Metropol, Berlin, 1909, played in "Halloh!"; and in May, 1911, appeared there in "His Majesty Amuses Himself"; at La Cigale, Paris, 1912, played in "Pourvu qu'on rigole"; reappeared in London, at the Criterion, May, 1914, as Kitty Vernon in "The Blue Mouse"; at the Knickerbocker Theatre, New York, Mar., 1915, played Mrs. Hunter-Rumpuss in "Fads and Fancies"; subsequently toured in "vaudeville," in "The Oriole"; on returning to England, appeared at the Garrick, Sept., 1916, as Mdlle. Cecile in "The Girl from Ciro's"; at the St. Martin's, Dec., 1917, as She in "Sleeping Partners"; at the Park Theatre, New York, Jan., 1921, played Captain Delauney in "Erminie."

LESTER, Alfred (Leslie), actor; *b.* Nottingham, 25 Oct., 1874; *s.* of Annie (Ross) and Alfred Leslie; *e.*

Nottingham and London; both his father and mother were members of the theatrical profession, his father being a well-known comedian some thirty years ago, and figured in that capacity at the Royal Opera House, Covent Garden; made his first appearance on the stage, when quite a child, at the Theatre Royal, Nottingham, as Little Willie Carlyle in " East Lynne "; toured the provinces for many years, playing such parts as Charles Middlewick in " Our Boys," Captain MacManus in " Betsy," Philosopher Jack and Seth Preene in " The Lights o' London," Conn in " The Shaughraun," Myles in " The Colleen Bawn," Shaun the Post in " Arragh-Na-Pogue," etc.; while playing at Terry's, in 1905, in " The Officers' Mess," was engaged by Alfred Butt for the Palace Theatre, where he made an instantaneous success in his monologue as a " Scene-shifter," and subsequent successes in a similar line were scored with " A Restaurant Episode," " A Labour Candidate," " The Broker's Man," and other sketches, etc.; appeared at the Gaiety Theatre, Sept., 1906, as the Lost Constable in " The New Aladdin," with great success; at the same theatre, Apr., 1908, played Nix, the Bo'sun, in " Havana "; at the Shaftesbury, Apr., 1909, made a further hit, when he played Peter Doody in " The Arcadians," and he appeared in this part for a greater portion of two years; at the Gala performance, at His Majesty's, 27 June, 1911, appeared as the Constable in " The Critic "; subsequently appeared at various music halls in " The Amateur Hairdresser "; " The Village Fire Brigade "; at the Apollo, Sept., 1912, played Vodka in " The Grass Widows "; returned to the music halls, 1912-13, appearing in " Longshoreman Bill "; at the Shaftesbury, Sept., 1913, played Byles in " The Pearl Girl "; May, 1915, played his old part of Peter Doody in " The Arcadians "; at the Coliseum, Dec., 1915, played in " Simpson's Stores "; at the Alhambra, Apr., 1916, played Oliver Bing in " The Bing Boys are Here "; July, 1917, Umpicof in " Round the Map "; at Drury Lane, Aug., 1918, Hu-Du in

" Shanghai "; at the Garrick, Nov., 1919, George in " The Eclipse "; at the Gaiety, Mar., 1920, Miggles in " The Shop Girl "; at the Royalty, May, 1921, appeared in " Pins and Needles "; at the London Pavilion, Oct., 1921, played lead in " Fun of the Fayre "; at the Vaudeville, Feb., 1923, in " Rats "; at the Duke of York's, May, 1924, in " The Punch Bowl "; between these performances has appeared at the Coliseum and Alhambra in various playlets; has the unique distinction of being the only person who has been selected to appear at both the Royal Command Theatrical and Music Hall performances. (*Died* 6 May, 1925; *age 50*)

LESTER, Mark, actor; *b.* Wiltshire, 12 Oct., 1876; *e.* privately; *m.* Nora Morra; first appeared in 1900, and with Maurice E. Bandmann's company, toured through the West Indies, South America, Canada, India, China, Japan, Java, etc., for five years; in 1908 was touring in England, as Joseph in " The Gay Deceivers," of which he was also part-author and producer; then toured the provinces in George Dance's Company in " Havana"; first appeared in London, at the Kennington Theatre, 5 June, 1911, as Rob Robinson in " The Algerian Girl," and appeared at the same theatre 19 June, 1911, as Maximilian IX in " The King's Bride "; at the Queen's Theatre, Sept., 1911, played Pedro in " Bonita "; he was then engaged by the late George Edwardes, and during the next four years toured continuously in his companies, playing in " The Count of Luxembourg," " Gipsy Love," " The Marriage Market," and " Betty "; at the Oxford, June, 1914, played Johnny Bull in " Mam'selle Champagne "; at the Prince's, Manchester, Dec., 1915, played Cupid in " The Miller's Daughters "; he then appeared at Daly's Theatre, May, 1916, as M. Drinkavinck in " The Happy Day "; Feb., 1917, as General Malona in " The Maid of the Mountains," which he played for over three years; May, 1920, Walter Wex in " A Southern Maid "; at the Prince of Wales's Theatre, May, 1921, played

Count Feri in "The Gipsy Princess"; at the Gaiety, Dec., 1921, Hyacinth Borel in "The Little Girl in Red"; Sept., 1923, General Stepanovitch in "Catherine"; at the Kingsway, June, 1924, appeared in "Yoicks!"; at the Vaudeville, Oct., 1924, in "The Looking Glass," after which he returned to the Kingsway in "Yoicks!"; appeared at the Alhambra, Apr., 1925; Daly's, May, 1926, played Professor Savigny in "Yvonne"; Winter Garden, Apr., 1927, Guy Tabarie in "The Vagabond King"; Piccadilly, July, 1928, succeeded W. H. Berry as Henry Pilbeam in "Blue Eyes"; Dominion, Oct.,1929, played Bickersley Blewitt in "Follow Through," and in 1930, toured in the same part; London Hippodrome, Dec., 1930, played General Malona in "The Maid of the Mountains"; Daly's, Dec., 1931, Hilarius in "La Poupée"; Mar., 1932, Mr. Hook in "Miss Hook of Holland"; in Sept., 1932, toured in "La Poupée"; during 1933, toured as Ben Blister in "Jolly Roger"; His Majesty's, Dec., 1935, played Hilarius in "La Poupée"; toured, 1936, as Guy Tabarie in "The Vagabond King"; Garrick, Southport, Dec., 1938, played Selina, the Cook, in "Dick Whittington"; toured, 1939, as Sir John in "Me and My Girl"; first appeared in films, 1935. *Clubs:* Stage Golfing Society and Green Room. *Address:* The Spinney, Horsebridge, Hailsham, Sussex.

LESTOCQ, William (Lestocq Boileau Wooldridge), actor, dramatic author, and manager; made his first appearance on the stage at the old Cremorne Gardens, 1869; was for many years a member of the company at the Vaudeville Theatre, under David James and Thomas Thorne, 1873-1885, where he appeared in "Petticoat Government," "Green Old Age," "Romulus and Remus," "Our Boys," "Divorce," "Tom Pinch," "Punch," "The Half-Way House," "The Girl He Left Behind Him," "The School for Scandal," "Money," "A Bad Penny," "Saints and Sinners," etc.; is the author of several successful plays, notably, "A Bad Penny," 1882; "The Sultan of Mocha," 1887; "Uncles and Aunts" (with Walter Everard),

1888; "In Danger" (with H. Cresswell), 1889; "Jane" (with Harry Nicholls), 1890; "The Sportsman" (from the French), 1893; "The Foundling" (with E. M. Robson), 1894; London representative of Charles Frohman, 1893-1915; on the formation of the Company, Charles Frohman, Incorporated, July, 1915, was appointed London representative; is a life member of the A.A.
(Died 16 Oct., 1920; age 69)

L'ESTRANGE, Julian, actor; *b.* 6 Aug., 1878; *m.* Constance Collier; appeared at His Majesty's Theatre, Oct., 1900, as the Cupbearer in "Herod"; Feb., 1901, appeared as Curio in "Twelfth Night"; Feb., 1902, as Hermes in "Ulysses," and in June, 1902, as Pistol in "The Merry Wives of Windsor"; at the Imperial Theatre, Apr., 1903, played Mees in "The Good Hope," and in May played Don Pedro in "Much Ado About Nothing"; at the Botanic Gardens, July, 1903, played the First Brother in "Comus," and Perigot in "The Faithful Shepherdess"; he then toured with Miss Ellen Terry, and at Liverpool, Nov., 1903, appeared as Rudolph II in "The Mistress of the Robes"; at His Majesty's, Sept., 1904, played Sebastian in "The Tempest"; Jan., 1905, Borachio in "Much Ado About Nothing," and Mar., 1905, Teddy Meyrick in "Agatha"; at the St. James's, June, 1905, appeared as Langlade in "The Man of the Moment"; at the Royalty, June, 1905, played Harry Hagberd in "One Day More"; appeared at the Garrick, Oct., 1905, as Bassanio in "The Merchant of Venice"; July, 1906, as Lambert Lane in "Down Our Alley," and Aug., 1906, as Sebastian Pasquale in "The Morals of Marcus"; at His Majesty's Theatre, Dec., 1906, played Sextus Pompeius in "Antony and Cleopatra," and at Drury Lane, Sept., 1907, appeared as Sir Dorian March in "The Sins of Society"; at the Court, June, 1908, played in "On the Right Road"; subsequently went to America as leading man with Maxine Elliott, and appeared at Philadelphia, Sept., 1908, as John Marshall in "Myself, Bettina," playing the same part at Daly's, New York, Oct., 1908; at the Maxine Elliott Theatre, Dec., 1908, played Jim Ogden in "The Chaperon"; at the Haymarket, London, May, 1909, played Count André in "Love Watches"; at the Coliseum, July to Aug., 1909, appeared in "Companions of the Road," and "The Robber"; at the Lyceum, New York, Jan., 1910, played Gerald Halstane in "Mrs. Dot"; in Sept., 1910, toured in the same part; at the Lyceum, New York, Dec., 1910, played Albert Delpierre in "Suzanne"; in Sept., 1911, toured in America in "Thaïs"; at the Criterion, New York, Jan., 1912, appeared as Roger Wade in "White Magic"; at the Hudson, Feb., 1912, as Bertram of Allamanon in "The Lady of Dreams"; and Mar., 1912, as Paul de Valreas in "Frou-Frou," with Madame Simone; at Chicago, in Sept., 1912, and at Wallack's, New York, Oct., 1912, played Jim Benziger in "The New Sin"; at Wallack's, Nov., 1912, the Marquis of Belange in "The Paper Chase"; at the Empire, New York, Jan., 1913, Marcel Beaucourt in "The Spy" ("The Turning Point"); Mar., 1913, the Hon. Gerald Tanqueray in "Liberty Hall"; at Syracuse, Apr., 1913, Mr. Willmott in "Her First Divorce"; at the Empire, New York, Sept., 1913, George Gunning in "The Tyranny of Tears"; at Springfield, Nov., 1913, played Baron von Hanau in "Miss Jenny O'Jones"; at the Eltinge Theatre, Jan., 1914, Count Nikolai Rostov in "The Yellow Ticket"; Sept., 1914, Horace Irving in "Innocent." (*Died 22 Oct., 1918; age 40*)

LETHBRIDGE, J. W., acting manager, etc.; *b.* Wellingborough, Northamptonshire; *s.* of the Rev. J. Watts Lethbridge (compiler of the first Shakespeare Almanac); after spending some years in journalism in the country, he came to London and became the late Wilson Barrett's private secretary while the "Sign of the Cross" was being played at the Lyric (1896); on Mr. Barrett leaving England he became associated with Mr. Henry Arthur Jones in a similar capacity, remaining with the well-known author some years, and afterwards joining Sir Charles (then Mr.) Wyndham, at Wyndham's Theatre, where he was acting manager; his services were retained when Frank Curzon took over the theatre, and he afterwards managed the Criterion and Comedy Theatres for the same gentleman; severing his connection with Mr. Curzon, he was the first business manager of the Scala Theatre, when Mr. Forbes-Robertson opened there with the Duchess of Sutherland's play, "The Conqueror," but he has since returned to Sir Charles Wyndham at the Criterion Theatre. *Address:* Criterion Theatre; or 85 Regent Street, W. *Club:* Eccentric.

LEVEAUX, Montagu V., theatrical manager; *b.* Teddington, 28 Dec., 1875; *e.* St. Paul's School, and St. John's College, Cambridge; has officiated as business manager at the Garrick Theatre, with Arthur Bourchier; at the New, with Sir Charles Wyndham; was for some time at the Empire, and is now joint director of the Alhambra Theatre. *Recreations:* Yachting and rowing. *Clubs:* Royal Corinthian Yacht, and Cambridge University Cruising. *Address:* 82 Shaftesbury Avenue, W.C. *Telephone No.:* 818 Gerrard. *Telegraphic Address:* "Uvelexa, London."

LEVEY, Adèle, "story-teller"; one of the Three Sisters Levey; made her first appearance on the stage with her sisters, 19 Sept., 1887, at the old Trocadero; after the marriage of her sister May, continued to appear with Carlotta, for some time; they appeared in all the leading halls in London, the provinces, Continent, and United States; commenced her turn as a "story-teller" at Dublin, Apr., 1910; in June, 1915, she appeared at the Queen's Hall, as entertainer and "story-teller," in monologues entitled "Cheer, O!"; "Criticise"; and "Don't Worry." *Address:* 63 Rosebery Square, E.C.

LEVEY, Carlotta, vocalist and instrumentalist; one of the Three Sisters Levey; made her first appearance on the stage with her sisters, 19 Sept., 1887, at the Trocadero; after the marriage of her sister May, continued to appear with Adéle, for some time; appeared at all the leading halls in London, the provinces, Continent, and United States; of late years has appeared as a single turn, and among some of her popular songs may be mentioned " Do a good turn when you are able "; " Put a little bit away for a rainy day "; " Honolulu Lulu "; " The Gambling Man "; " British Boys "; " My Boy," etc.

LEVEY, Ethel, actress and vocalist; *b.* San Francisco, 22 Nov., 1881; *e.* San Francisco; *m.* (1) George M. Cohan (mar. dis. 1907); (2) Claude Grahame-White (mar. dis.); made her first appearance on the stage at the Columbia Theatre, San Francisco, 31 Dec., 1897, in "A Milk White Flag"; she was first seen in New York, at Weber and Fields' Music Hall, and was subsequently engaged at Koster and Bial's; for several years she appeared with Weber and Fields, and with Hyde and Behman; it was while with this latter company that she became associated with George M. Cohan, and from 1901-7, she appeared in all of the productions made by him; she played Emerald Green in " The Governor's Son," 1901; Gertie Gayland in " Running for Office," 1903; Goldie Gates in " Little Johnny Jones," 1904; Dolly Johnson in " George Washington, Jun.," 1906; during 1903-4 she also played the title-*rôle* in " My Lady Molly," under Charles Frohman; since 1908 has principally appeared in leading music halls in the United States, England, and the Continent; has played frequent engagements at the London Alhambra, and taken part in several *revues* in Paris; made her first appearance on the London stage at the Tivoli, on " Mafeking " Night, 18 May, 1900, for one night only; her next appearance in London was at the Alhambra, 20 Sept., 1909; appeared at the Apollo Theatre, Vienna, in *revue*; after returning to London appeared at the Hippodrome, Dec., 1912, in the *revue* " Hullo, Ragtime ! "; Dec., 1913, in " Hullo, Tango ! "; at Wyndham's Theatre, Sept., 1914, made a great success, when she played Miriam in " Outcast "; at the Empire, May, 1915, played in " Watch Your Step "; Feb., 1916, appeared as Sheila Ryve in " Follow the Crowd "; at the London Opera House, July, 1916, in " Look Who's Here "; at the Shaftesbury, Dec., 1916, in " Three Cheers "; at the Empire, Nov., 1917, in " Here and There "; at the Shaftesbury, June, 1920, played Julie in " Oh ! Julie "; at the Longacre Theatre, New York, May, 1922, played Mabel Montmorency in " Go Easy, Mabel ! "; at the Vaudeville, London, Nov., 1923, appeared in " Yes "; has since fulfilled several engagements in variety theatres; at the Gaiety, Dec., 1925, played Totoche in " The Blue Kitten "; reappeared on the variety stage, in the provinces, 1932; subsequently again returned to America; reappeared on the New York stage, St. James, Dec., 1941, as Lolita in "Sunny River"; Winter Garden, July, 1945, played Madame Sacher in " Marinka "; at the Selwyn, Chicago, Oct., 1950, appeared as Lillian in "Springboard to Nowhere"; appeared in the film, "Call Me Mame."
(Died 27 Feb., 1955; age 72)

LEVY, Benn W., M.B.E., dramatic author; *b.* London, 7 Mar., 1900; *s.* of Octave Levy and his wife Nannie (Joseph); *e.* Repton and University College, Oxford; *m.* Constance Cummings; formerly managing director of Jarrolds, the publishers; author of the following plays: "This Woman Business," 1925; "A Man with Red Hair" (adaptation), "Mud and Treacle," "Mrs. Moonlight," 1928; "Art and Mrs. Bottle," 1929; "The Devil," "Topaze" (adaptation), "Ever Green," 1930; "Springtime for Henry," "The Church Mouse" (adaptation), "Hollywood Holiday (with John Van Druten), 1931; "The Devil Passes" ("The Devil"), 1932; "Young Madame Conti" (adaptation with Hubert Griffith, from Bruno Frank), 1936; "The

Poet's Heart," "Madame Bovary" (adaptation), 1937; "If I Were You" (with Paul Hervey Fox), 1938; "The Jealous God," 1939; "Clutterbuck," 1946; "Return to Tyassi," 1950; "Cupid and Psyche," 1953; "The Rape of the Belt," 1957; "The Tumbler," 1960; "Public and Confidential, 1966; in addition to his own plays, he also staged "Wild Decembers," 1933; "Sour Grapes," "Accent on Youth," 1934; "Skylark," 1942; "Before the Party," 1949; "Legend of Sarah" (New York), 1950; during the late War, joined the Royal Navy as an ordinary seaman, subsequently took a commission as Lieutenant; was wounded and decorated, Adriatic, 1944; elected Socialist Member of Parliament for Eton and Slough, 1945–50; an Executive of the Arts Council, 1953–60. *Clubs:* Garrick. *Address:* Cote House, Cote, Aston, Oxfordshire. *Telephone No.:* Bampton Castle 249.

LEVY, José G., manager and dramatic author; *b.* Portsmouth, 29 June, 1884; *s.* of Samuel Levy and his wife, Jeanette (Neumann); *e.* Portsmouth Grammar School, and L'École de Commerce, Lausanne, Switzerland; *m.* Mary Teesdale; has adapted several plays from the French, including " The Glad Eye," 1911; " Who's the Lady ? " 1913; " The Double Mystery," 1914; " A Daughter of England," 1915 ; "The Girl from Ciro's," 1916 ; " Arlette," 1917 ; " Yes, Uncle," 1917 ; " Sleeping Partners," 1917; " The Risk," 1922 ; " Zozo," 1922; " The Padre," 1926; "Maica," 1928; "The Queen Bee," 1930; "Beginner's Luck" (with Reginald Arkell), 1932; "Once Upon a Time" (from the French), 1934; also several one-act pieces produced at variety theatres, including "Striking Home," "The Medium," "Seven Blind Men," "Cupid, Unlimited," etc.; is proprietor of the Strand Theatre, and is lessee and manager of the Little Theatre, where from Sept., 1920, to 1922 he was responsible for the "Grand Guignol" plays; has since made several productions at this theatre; in Mar., 1934, received the order of Chevalier of the Legion of Honour, from the French Government, in recognition of his services to French Dramatic Art in England. *Recreations:* Golf and swimming. *Club:* Savage.
(Died 8 Oct., 1936; age 52)

LEWES, Miriam, actress; *b.* Starie, in Russia, of English parentage; coming to this country when she was five years old, she displayed considerable aptitude for dancing, in which she commenced her professional career, but cherished a desire to become an actress, and secured an engagement in a " stock " company to play a small part in " Driven from Home," 1898 ; toured for some time in old comedy, with Lancelot Loader's Old English Comedy Company, playing Kate Hardcastle in " She Stoops to Conquer," Kitty Clive in " Masks and Faces," Lady Sneerwell in " The School for Scandal," etc.; toured as Mrs. Fleeter in "My Sweetheart"; made her first appearance in London, at the Lyric, Hammersmith, 26 May, 1902, as the Duchesse de Verviers in "The Broken Melody"; later in 1902, toured as Belle Langrish in " One of the Right Sort " and in 1903 as Mrs. Devenish in " The Golden Luck "; other stock seasons and tours followed ; later she filled engagements with Miss Fortescue in old English comedy; with Walter Melville, at the Lyric, Hammersmith, Feb.–Mar., 1903, in "With Flying Colours," "Cheer! Boys, Cheer!" Martha in "Little Em'ly," Lina Nelson in "The Harbour Lights," etc.; toured as Donna Clotilda in "Captain Kettle," and "starred" with Ida Molesworth in " Under Two Flags," also with Louis Calvert as Princess Eleanor in " The Garden of Lies "; engaged to support and understudy Miss Julia Neilson in " The Scarlet Pimpernel " and " Dorothy o' the Hall "; during 1907 played Sephora Lewis in " The Popinjay "; at the New Theatre, Feb., 1908, played Red Jill in " Matt of Merrymount," and again played Lady Blakeney in " The Scarlet Pimpernel "; at the Tyne Theatre, Newcastle-on-Tyne, Nov., 1908, played Marguerite de Valois in " Henry of Navarre "; appeared at the New Theatre, July, 1909, in the same part; at the Haymarket, Sept.,

1909, played Miss Cunningham in "Gentlemen of the Road"; at the Duke of York's, Feb., 1910, played Hypathia Tarleton in "Misalliance"; at the New Theatre, Feb., 1911, played Sephora Lewis in "The Popinjay"; May, 1911, appeared as Celia in "As You Like It," and Dec., 1911, Lady Castlemaine in "Sweet Nell of Old Drury"; at the Duke of York's, Oct., 1912, played Mrs. Juno in "Overruled"; at the Aldwych, Feb., 1913, Agrafena in "The Brothers Karamazov"; at the Haymarket, June, 1913, the Countess von Hoenstadt in "Elizabeth Cooper"; at the Royalty, Sept., 1913, played Iris Mahoney in "Interlopers"; at the Vaudeville, Nov., 1913, Varinka in "Great Catherine"; at the Savoy, Jan., 1914, Thais in "Paphnutius"; at the Coronet, June, 1914, Stephanie de Mohrivart in "Forget-Me-Not"; at the Savoy, July, 1914, Miriam in "The Sin of David"; at the Little, Sept., 1914, Stephanie in "Forget-Me-Not"; at the King's, Hammersmith, Nov., 1914, Mercy Merrick in "The New Magdalen"; at the Devonshire Park Theatre, Eastbourne, Nov., 1914, Mary Latimer in "The Bargain"; at the King's, Hammersmith, Mar., 1915, Catherine Jadot in "The Kommandatur"; at the Queen's, Mar., 1916, Mary Martin in "The Love Thief"; at His Majesty's, Mar., 1916, Orange Moll in "Stand and Deliver"; at His Majesty's, May, 1916, played Chorus in "Henry V"; Dec., 1916, appeared as Zahrat-al-Kulub in "Chu-Chin-Chow"; at the St. James's, Jan., 1917, as Toinon Chépy in "The Aristocrat"; at the Coliseum, Mar., 1918, Baroness de Beaumont in "The Trap"; at Covent Garden, Dec., 1919, played Gertrude in "Hamlet"; at the Strand, July, 1920, Adele Tacé in "At the Village Rose"; subsequently went to America, and at Chicago, Jan., 1921, appeared in the same part; at the Knickerbocker Theatre, New York, Oct., 1921, played Joanne de Beaudricourt in "The Wandering Jew"; at the Ambassadors', London, Sept., 1922, Queen Henrietta Maria in "Charles I"; Nov., 1922, Winnie Verloc in "The Secret Agent"; in Oct., 1923, toured in United States and Canada with Sir

John Martin-Harvey, playing Jocasta in "Œdipus Rex," and Everyman's Mother in "Via Crucis"; at the Queen's, June, 1925, played Lize Heath in "Salomy Jane"; Lyceum, July, 1925, Mrs. Stanton in "The Fake"; Little, Oct., 1925, Irina Arkadin in "The Sea Gull"; Scala (for the Renaissance Society), Dec., 1925, Alice in "Arden of Feversham"; "Q," and Royalty, Oct., 1926, Laura Atherton in "Children of the Moon"; Lyric, Hammersmith, June, 1927, Mrs. Vincent Crummles in "When Crummles Played"; Arts, Oct., 1927, Elisa in "The Duchess of Elba"; Apollo, Jan., 1928, Alice in "The Dance of Death"; Court, Oct., 1928, Amaranta in "Fortunato"; Fortune, Sept., 1929, Irina Arkadin in "The Sea-Gull"; Court, Feb., 1930, Gertrude in "Hamlet"; Prince of Wales's (for Stage Society), Dec., 1930, Pauline Maligé in "The Borrowed Life"; Royalty, Jan., 1931, Lady Kite in "The Limping Man"; Court, Mar., 1931, Mrs. Warren in "Mrs. Warren's Profession"; Duchess, Dec., 1931, Mistress Ford in "The Merry Wives of Windsor"; "Q," Jan., 1932, Portia in "Julius Caesar"; Feb., 1932, Gertrude in "Hamlet"; Little, Nov., 1932, Mrs. George in "Getting Married"; Arts, May, 1933, Madame Delphine in "The Sowers"; His Majesty's, May, 1935, Mrs. Landis in "Hervey House"; Covent Garden, Sept., 1936, again played Jocasta in "Œdipus Rex." *Address:* 64D Fairholme Road, W.14. *Telephone No.:* Fulham 3953.

LEWIS, Ada, actress; *b.* New York City; *e.* San Francisco; *m.* John Parr; made her first appearance on the stage in San Francisco, at the Alcazar Theatre, 1883, in "Siberia"; she played with various "stock" companies for the next seven years; made her first appearance on the New York stage, at Harrigan's Theatre, 29 Dec. 1890, as Kittie Lynch in "Reilly and the Four Hundred"; Dec., 1891, she played Mary Ann Brennan in "The Last of the Hogans"; at the Bijou, Dec., 1893, Maggie McIntyre in "A Country Sport"; Sept., 1895, Felicity Jones in "The Widow Jones"; Dec.,

1896, Mdlle. Nocodi in " Courted into Court " ; at the Victoria, Mar., 1899, Clementine Clapper in " A Reign of Error " ; at the Grand Opera House, Feb., 1900, Lotta Hintz in " The Rogers Brothers in Wall Street " ; at the Belasco, Dec., 1902, appeared as Setsu in " The Darling of the Gods " ; during 1905 appeared in " Fritz of Tammany Hall " ; at the Casino, Apr., 1906, as Kittie La Verne in " The Social Whirl " ; May, 1907, as Winnie Wiggles in " Fascinating Flora " ; Feb., 1908, as Gwendolyn Doolittle in " Nearly a Hero " ; in Mar., 1909, she went on tour, starring in " The Head of the House " ; at the Herald Square Theatre, Nov., 1909, played Alma Villianyi in " Old Dutch " ; at the Broadway, June, 1910, Mrs. McGuirk in " The Summer Widowers" ; at the Folies Bergères, New York, Apr., 1911, played the Royal Governess in " Gaby," and also played in the burlesque " Hell " ; at the Broadway, Feb., 1912, Susie Slimson in " Bunty Bulls and Strings " ; at the Winter Garden, Feb., 1913, Mdme. de Bressie in " The Honeymoon Express " ; at the Casino, Aug., 1914, played Tilly in " The Dancing Duchess " ; at the Gaiety, New York, May, 1915, Ann Rayner in " She's in Again " ; at the Princess, Dec., 1915, Mdme. Matroppo in " Very Good, Eddie " ; at the Winter Garden, Oct., 1917, played Annabelle Lee in " Doing Our Bit " ; at the Plymouth, Aug., 1918, Mrs. Mandelharper in " A Very Good Young Man " ; at the Knickerbocker, Dec., 1918, Mrs. Tillie Mumm in " Listen, Lester " ; at the Liberty, Feb., 1920, Mrs. Maxim in " The Night Boat " ; at the Globe, New York, Nov., 1921, Madame Bompard in " Good Morning, Dearie " ; at the Fulton, Nov., 1923, Madame Doremi in " One Kiss " ; at the Bijou, Sept., 1924, Mrs. Cornelia Culpepper in " The Busybody."
(Died 24 Sept., 1925; age 50)

LEWIS, Arthur, actor ; *b.* Hampstead, 19 Aug., 1846 ; *m.* Essex Dane ; made his first appearance on the stage in Paris, in 1872 ; made his first appearance in London, at the old King's Cross Theatre, 1874 ; from 1876-8, was a member of the old Dublin Theatre " stock " company ; toured the provinces 1879-81 ; went to the United States, 1882, and though long identified with the American stage, has appeared in London on numerous occasions ; he was a member of Mary Anderson's company at the Lyceum and elsewhere, 1883-9, and appeared with her at the Lyceum, Dec., 1883, as Mimos in " Pygmalion and Galatea," and Jan., 1884, as De la Festé in " Comedy and Tragedy " ; the following Nov., he played Benvolio in " Romeo and Juliet," and Feb., 1885, appeared as Lord Tinsel in " The Hunchback " ; appeared at the Strand, 1887, in " Jack in the Box " ; rejoined Mary Anderson and accompanied her to the United States, and reappeared with her at the Lyceum, Sept., 1887, as Cleomenes in " The Winter's Tale " ; again toured with her in America, and played throughout her farewell tour ; played at the Adelphi, Feb., 1898, in " The Lady of Lyons " ; at the Comedy, Oct., 1902, as M. de Mirepoix in " Monsieur Beaucaire " ; on tour, 1904, as Montague Brent in " Winnie Brooke, Widow " ; at the Imperial, Apr., 1904, as John Edwards in " Miss Elizabeth's Prisoner " ; Oct., 1904, as Tom Fielding in " His Majesty's Servant " ; Apr., 1905, as Peter in " Romeo and Juliet " ; May, 1905, Count Ivan Pavlovic in " Hawthorne, U.S.A." ; Oct., 1905, John Collis in " The Perfect Lover " ; at the Hicks Theatre, Aug., 1907, as Mr. Viveash in " The Hypocrites " ; at the Queen's, Sept., 1910, The Dean in " The Man from the Sea " ; Oct., 1910, General Sir Gresham Thurlow in " Mrs. Skeffington " ; Dec., 1910, the Rt. Hon. Thomas Ashland, M.P., in " The House Divided," and at the Kingsway, Feb., 1911, Huzar in " The Lily " ; at the Century Theatre, New York, Oct., 1911, played Father Roubier in " The Garden of Allah " ; at the Lyceum, New York, Dec., 1911, appeared as M. de Ferney in " The Marionettes " ; during 1912 toured in the same play ; at Atlantic City, Dec., 1912, played the Cardinal in " Primrose " ; at the Little Theatre, Philadelphia, Oct., 1913, played in " The Elder

1477

Brother"; at the Empire, New York, Jan., 1914, appeared as Mr. Justice Grimdyke in "The Legend of Leonora"; at the Eltinge Theatre, Sept., 1914, played His Excellency in "Innocent"; at the Longacre Theatre, Nov., 1915, Dr. Stetson in "The Great Lover," and the following year, Mr. Stapleton in the same piece; during 1917 toured with Blanche Bates in "The Witness for the Defence"; during 1918 toured as the Bishop in "Maggie; at the Bijou Theatre, New York, Oct., 1918, played the Servant in "Sleeping Partners"; on returning to England. appeared at the Comedy Theatre, July, 1919, as the Hon. James Turnbull in "Three Wise Fools"; at Drury Lane, June, 1920, appeared as Father Roubier in "The Garden of Allah"; Apr., 1922, as Bessano and the King of Algarve in "Decameron Nights"; at the Vanderbilt Theatre, New York, Nov., 1923, Dr. Dickinson in "The Camel's Back"; at the Princess, Dec., 1924, Mr. Archer in "Tame Cats"; Selwyn, Feb., 1925, Father Hollister in "Two by Two"; 48th Street Theatre, Apr., 1925, Rev. James Makeshyfte in "The Servant in the House"; Princess, June, 1925, Mr. Montressor in "The Family Failing"; Knickerbocker, Dec., 1925, Crabtree in "The School for Scandal"; Empire, Sept., 1926, Georges in "The Captive"; Mar., 1927, Charly in "Her Cardboard Lover"; Oct., 1927, Childers in "Interference"; Craig, Dec., 1928, Mr. Justice Henry in "Potiphar's Wife"; during 1929 toured as Manuel in "One Hundred Years Old"; managed Madame Réjane, Madame Sarah Bernhardt, M. Coquelin, and M. Antoine in London, for six years, *(Died 13 June, 1930; age 83)*

LEWIS, Bertha, actress and vocalist; *b.* London, 12 May, 1887; *d.* William Thomas Lewis and his wife Emily Eleanor (Bacon); *e.* Ursuline Convent, Upton, and at Royal Academy of Music, of which she is an Associate; *m.* Captain Herbert Heyner; made her first appearance on the stage at the Grand Theatre, Southampton, 30 June, 1906, as Kate in "The Pirates of Penzance"; made her first appear-

ance in London at the Savoy, 15 July, 1908, as Gwenny Davis in "A Welsh Sunset"; has been associated with the D'Oyly Carte Opera Company for some years, and has sung all the leading contralto parts in the repertory; has also appeared in grand opera, as Carmen, Dalila in "Samson and Dalila," Amneris in "Aïda," etc.; has also toured the United Kingdom on concert tours; during the season at the Prince's Theatre, Sept., 1919, to Jan., 1920, appeared as the Duchess of Plaza-Toro in "The Gondoliers," the Fairy Queen in "Iolanthe," Katisha in "The Mikado," the Lady Jane in "Patience," Dame Carruthers in "The Yeomen of the Guard," Lady Blanche in "Princess Ida," Lady Sangazure in "The Sorcerer," Buttercup in "H.M.S. Pinafore"; during 1920 also played Dame Hannah in "Ruddigore"; appeared in the same parts at the Prince's Theatre, 1921-22, 1924, and 1926. *(Died 8 May, 1931; age 43)*

LEWIS, Curigwen, actress; *b.* Llandrindod Wells, Wales; *d.* of Maurice Jones-Lewis and his wife Martha Elizabeth (Evans); *e.* Llandrindod Wells; *m.* Andrew Cruickshank; made her first appearance on the stage at the Festival Theatre, Cambridge, 13 Oct., 1928, as the Shy Young Girl in "Thirty Minutes in the Street"; remained at the Festival Theatre, Cambridge, until 1929; played at the Opera House, Northampton, with the repertory company, until 1931; during 1930 toured with Billy Merson in "Playmaker"; played repertory at the Leas Pavilion, Folkestone, 1931; played with the Rusholme Repertory Theatre, Manchester, 1931-3; during 1933, toured as Alice in "Alice in Wonderland"; played with the Birmingham Repertory Theatre company, 1933-6; during these eight years in repertory played over two hundred parts; appeared at the Malvern Festivals 1934-6, playing among other parts Blanaid in "The Moon in the Yellow River," Dolly Clandon in "You Never Can Tell," Maya in "The Simpleton of the Unexpected Isles," Celia in "Volpone," Fanny in "Fanny's First Play," Rose

1478

Trelawny in "Trelawny of the Wells," Blanche, Seymour, and Nell Gwyn in "1066 and All That," Fanny Sterling in "The Clandestine Marriage," Jane Eyre in the play of that name, Clara in "Pygmalion" and Precious Stream in "Lady Precious Stream"; made her first appearance in London at the Queen's Theatre, 13 Oct., 1936, in the title-*rôle* of "Jane Eyre"; "Q," Nov., 1937, played Jenny in "Jenny Frensham"; Embassy, Dec., 1937, Pat Allington in "Portrait of a Lady"; Old Vic., Feb., 1938, Desdemona in "Othello"; at Oxford, for the O.U.D.S. June, 1938, Bianca in "The Taming of the Shrew"; New, Nov., 1938, Lyndall in "The Story of an African Farm"; Jan.–Apr., 1939, toured with the Old Vic. company on the Continent and Egypt, playing Rose in "Trelawny of the Wells," Ann Whitefield in "Man and Superman," Julia in "The Rivals," etc.; "Q," July, 1939, played Ninian in "Printer's Devil"; Canterbury, Aug., 1939, for the Old Stagers, played Anne in "The Dover Road"; Chanticleer, Feb., 1940, Helen Waring in "September Rain." *Recreations:* Mountaineering, riding, and walking. *Address:* 56 Chester Square, London, S.W.1. *Telephone No.:* Sloane 3573.

LEWIS, Eric (Fred Eric Lewis Tuffley); *b.* Northampton, 23 Oct., 1855; made his first appearance in public as an entertainer at the St. James's Hall, Brighton, Oct., 1879; made his first appearance in London, at the Polytechnic, Christmas, 1880; made his first appearance on the stage, at the Haymarket Theatre, 5 Sept., 1881, as Pilate Pump in "Blue and Buff"; at the Court Theatre, Sept., 1881, played Lord Glenmuir in "Honour"; in 1882, toured with the Alice Barth Opera Company; in the same year was engaged at the Savoy, as understudy to George Grossmith, and he continued in that capacity until 1887; in Apr., 1887, he appeared at the Royalty, with Willie Edouin, in "Ivy," and "A Tragedy"; at the Strand, July, 1887, played in "Devil Caresfoot"; joined Beerbohm Tree, Jan., 1888, at Haymarket Theatre, to play in "Partners"; after touring as Caleb Deecie in "Two Roses," and Doctor Dossemoffen in "Dr. D.," appeared at the Court, Sept., 1888, as Tom Shadbolt in "Mamma"; also appeared there in "Aunt Jack," "The Weaker Sex," and "The Queen's Shilling"; at the Lyric, Oct., 1890, appeared as the Duke of Fayensburg in "La Cigale"; at the Comedy, Apr., 1892, played in "The Widow"; at the Prince of Wales's, Oct., 1892, appeared as the Duke of Duffshire in "In Town"; Oct., 1893, played Sir Alfred Grey in "A Gaiety Girl"; at Daly's, Feb., 1895, played Sir George St. Alban in "An Artist's Model"; at the Court, Feb., 1896, played Mervyn Thorp in "Mrs. Ponderbury's Past"; at the Avenue, Aug., 1896, appeared as General Boomerang in "Monte Carlo"; at the Comedy, Nov., 1896, played the Earl of Bawcombe in "A White Elephant"; at Terry's, Apr., 1897, appeared as M. Camembert in "The French Maid"; at the Comedy, Apr., 1898, played the Marquis of Quarmby in "Lord and Lady Algy"; at the Garrick, Apr., 1899, played Sir Barely Standing in "Change Alley"; at the Criterion, Feb., 1900, played the Rt. Hon. Henry Carlton in "His Excellency the Governor"; Apr., 1900, the Rev. Audley Pillenger in "Lady Huntworth's Experiment"; Sept., 1901, Gresham Banthorpe in "The Undercurrent"; at the Haymarket, Mar., 1903, appeared as Canton in "The Clandestine Marriage"; at Wyndham's, Sept., 1903, played Sir Jennings Pyke in "Little Mary"; at the Duke of York's, Apr., 1904, played Bryce Kempshaw in "The Rich Mrs. Repton"; at the Criterion, Sept., 1904, appeared as Montague Brent in "Winnie Brooke, Widow"; at the Comedy, Oct., 1904, played the ex-King of Ingra in "His Highness My Husband"; at the St. James's, Jan., 1905, appeared as Lord Augustus Lorton in "Lady Windermere's Fan," and Feb., 1905, played Mollentrave in "Mollentrave on Women"; at the Haymarket, June, 1905, appeared as the Rt. Hon. Julian Twombley in "The Cabinet Minister"; in Sept., 1905, played John Gripleigh in "On the Love Path"; at the Duke of

York's, Feb., 1906, played Lord Crackenthorpe in "All-of-a-Sudden Peggy"; June, 1906, John Travers in "The Marriage of Kitty"; appeared as Sir Hubert Pennefeather in "The Amateur Socialist," at Criterion, Oct., 1906; Sir Ralph Bloomfield Bonnington in "The Doctor's Dilemma," Court, Nov., 1906; Samuel Jackson in "The Return of the Prodigal," Court, Apr., 1907; Dormer in "The Eighteenth Century," and Sir Peter Teazle in "The School for Scandal," St. James's, July to Sept., 1907; the Duke of St. Edmunds in "The Barrier," Comedy, Oct., 1907; and Christopher Keswick in "Angela," Comedy, Dec., 1907; at the Duke of York's, Mar., 1908, played the Earl of Loam in the revival of "The Admirable Crichton"; at the Criterion, Oct., 1908, appeared as Mr. Justice Wray in "Lady Epping's Lawsuit"; at the Comedy, Jan., 1909, played Mr. Davenport Barlow in "Penelope"; at the Duke of York's, Aug., 1909, played Gournay-Martin in "Arsène Lupin"; at Wyndham's, Apr., 1910, appeared as Mr. Hayter in "The Naked Truth"; at the Haymarket, Nov., 1910, as Humphrey Wharton in "The Kiss"; same theatre, Mar., 1911, Dean Lesley in "Lady Patricia"; at the St. James's, Oct., 1911, played Lord Augustus Lorton in "Lady Windermere's Fan"; at the Prince of Wales's, Feb., 1912, played Gab·iel Peploe in "Dear Old Charlie"; went to New York, to play the same part; at the New Theatre, May, 1912, played Canon Bonsey in "Mrs. Dane's Defence"; at the Criterion, Feb., 1913, Montague Jordan in "Eliza Comes to Stay"; at the Duke of York's, Sept., 1913, played Sir Robert Backus in "The Adored One"; at the Royalty, Nov., 1913, Peter Dodder in "The Pursuit of Pamela"; at the Criterion, May, 1914, Sir Henry Dowse in "The Blue Mouse"; at His Majesty's, 22 May, 1914, Brownson in the "all-star" revival of "The Silver King," given in aid of King George's Actors' Pension Fund; at the Criterion, Oct., 1914, Sir James Aplin, M.D., in "Sir Richard's Biography"; at the Duke of York's, Mar., 1915, Cholmondeley in

"Rosy Rapture"; at the Playhouse, Jan., 1916, George Delmar in "Please Help Emily"; at the Coliseum and at the London Opera House, June, 1916, appeared as the Earl of Loam in "The Admirable Crichton," for charitable purposes; at the Royalty, Sept., 1916, played Sir Joseph Stanley in "The Hawk"; at the Queen's, Feb., 1917, the Rev. Hubert Swizel in "The Double Event"; at the London Pavilion, Oct., 1917, Sir John Goyder in "A Kiss or Two"; at the New Theatre, Apr., 1918, appeared as Mr. Miffle in "Monica's Blue Boy"; at the Royalty, May, 1918, as Mr. Priestly in "The Man from Toronto"; at the Haymarket, Sept., 1919, as Parker in "Daddies"; at the Shaftesbury, Apr., 1920, played Sir Willoughby Gregor, K.C., in "The Little Whopper"; at the Duke of York's, July, 1920, the Earl of Knightsbridge in "Brown Sugar"; at the Strand, Aug., 1921, Sir Temple Chambers in "The Trump Card"; at the Aldwych, Jan., 1922, Lord Belton in "Money Doesn't Matter"; Sept., 1922 Dorking in "Double or Quit"; at the Apollo, Dec., 1922, Colonel Stumper in "Through the Crack"; at the Court, Jan., 1923, Philip Kent in "Three's a Crowd"; at the Globe, Apr., 1923, the Rev. Ernest Lynton in "Aren't We All?"; at the Kingsway, Feb., 1924, The Constable in "Kate"; author of "A Lesson in Shakespeare," a play in one act. *Club:* Garrick.
(Died 1 Apr., 1935; age 79)

LEWIS, Fred, actor; *b.* Kingston-on-Thames, 23 Dec., 1860; *s.* of Louisa (Trimbey) and Fred. J. Till, solicitor; *e.* Beaumont College, Old Windsor; was originally intended for the law, but made his first appearance on the stage at the Alexandra Theatre, Liverpool, Dec., 1880, under the management of the late Edward Saker; made his first appearance on the London stage, at the old Philharmonic Theatre, Islington, Sept., 1882, as Archibald Carlyle in "East Lynne"; spent many years touring, and appeared in such plays as "The Private Secretary," "Called Back," "Our Boys," "The Magistrate," "The

Parvenu," etc. ; was manager to the late Helen Barry for two years, and was also connected with the late Wybert Rousby at Jersey ; appeared at the Strand, June, 1904, as Sir Fergus Treherne in " Sergeant Brue " ; he made his first notable success in London, at the Haymarket, 12 Jan., 1907, when he appeared as the Rev. Audley Pillenger in a revival of " Lady Huntworth's Experiment " ; in Apr., 1907, at His Majesty's, Shakespearean Festival, he played Sir Toby Belch in " Twelfth Night," and the Host of the Garter in " The Merry Wives of Windsor," and accompanied Sir Herbert Tree to Berlin, to play the same parts ; he appeared at the Haymarket, May, 1907, as M. Dupré in " My Wife " ; at the Comedy, Dec., 1907, played William Bithers in "Angela" ; again appeared at the Shakespearean Festival at His Majesty's, Apr., 1908 ; at the Court, July, 1908, played Mortimer Wilberley in " The Boys " ; at the Coronet, Nov., 1908, played Von Bulow Bismarck Schmidt in " The Man from Mexico " ; at the Criterion, Jan., 1909, played Colonel Jardine in " Mrs. Gorringe's Necklace," and Apr., 1909, John Bounsall in " Mr. Preedy and the Countess " ; at Terry's, July 1909, played the Hon. Thomas Burmester in " The Price " ; at Wyndham's, Jan., 1910, appeared as Duffy in " Captain Kidd "; at the Playhouse, Feb., 1910, appeared as Thomas H. Pepper in " Tantalising Tommy," and Mar., 1910, as the Old Actor in " The Toymaker of Nuremberg " ; at the St. James's, Nov., 1910, played Brook Farlowe, M.P., in " Eccentric Lord Comberdene " ; at the Royalty, May, 1911, played Henry Cawthorne in " Half-a-Crown " ; at the Prince of Wales's, Oct., 1911, appeared as M. Gonthier in " The Uninvited Guest " ; at the Court, Dec., 1911, played Backus in " The Great Gay Road " ; at the Comedy, Feb., 1912, played Mr. Felgate in " The Bear Leaders " ; at Drury Lane, Sept., 1912, Wealth in " Everywoman " ; at the St. James's, Jan., 1913, Brigella in " Turandot, Princess of China " ; at the Shaftesbury, Feb., 1913, Uncle Noel Jollibeau in " Oh ! Oh !! Delphine !!! " ;

at the Prince of Wales's, June, 1913, appeared as Sir Ernest Craddock, K.C., in " The Faun " ; at the Little Theatre, Nov., 1913, played The Duke in " Magic " ; at the Court, Mar., 1914, the Earl of Bornsham in " Rags " ; at the Little, Apr., 1914, the Rt. Hon. Roger Paxton, M.P., in " Account Rendered " ; at the Court, June, 1914, the Hon. Thomas Burmester, M.P., in " Compensation " ; at the Scala, June, 1914, Saint-Gaudens in " La Dame Aux Camelias " ; at the Globe, Sept., 1914, Umbezi in " Mameena " ; at the Victoria Palace, Feb., 1915, William Oldbright in " You're What ? " ; at the Prince of Wales's, Mar., 1915, Major Drinkwater in " He Didn't Want to Do It " ; at the Apollo, May, 1915, Donald Macrae in " Striking " ; at the Prince of Wales's, Birmingham, Sept., 1915, Sir Oliver Petrie in " The Light Blues " ; at the Empire, Finsbury Park, July, 1916, the Duke of Droneborough in " Lord and Lady Algy " ; at the Shaftesbury, Sept., 1916, Sir Oliver in " The Light Blues " ; at the Haymarket, Feb., 1917, Matthew Janson in " Felix Gets a Month " ; at the Queen's, Apr., 1918, Lemuel Bush in " Lot 79 " ; at the London Pavilion, June, 1918, Horace Parkyns in " The Profiteers " ; at the Strand, Dec., 1918, Major Alex Thatcher in " Scandal " ; at the Apollo, July, 1919, Abel Mainwaring in " Tilly of Bloomsbury " ; at the Aldwych, Dec., 1920, Cattermole in " The Private Secretary " ; at the Shaftesbury, June, 1921, Bolt in " Out to Win " ; at the New, Oct., 1921, succeeded Arthur Whitby as John Plake in " Christopher Sly " ; at the Royalty, Nov., 1921, played Joseph Grimes in " Two Jacks and a Jill " ; at the St. James's, Nov., 1922, Count Svirin in " The Beating on the Door " ; at His Majesty's, Sept., 1924, the Marquis de Chamarande in " The Royal Visitor " ; at the Strand, Dec., 1924, Squire Trelawney in " Treasure Island." *Favourite part :* The Vicar in " Lady Huntworth's Experiment." *Club :* Green Room.
(Died 25 Dec., 1927; age 67)

LEWIS, Frederick G., American actor ; *b.* Oswego, New York, 14 Feb.,

1873 ; *s.* of Jeannette and James L. Lewis ; *m.* Charlotte Kauffman ; made his first appearance on the stage at Savannah, Georgia, as Armand Duval in " Camille," 18 Aug., 1891 ; gained a large and varied experience for the next six years; in Jan., 1897, appeared at the Lyceum, New York, in " When a Man's Married," subsequently touring with the Lyceum " stock " company ; next played in " The Prisoner of Zenda," " My Friend from India," " The Heart of Maryland," etc. ; at the Carnegie Lyceum, New York, 17 Jan., 1900, played Ragnar Brovik in " The Master Builder " ; during 1903 toured as Oswald Alving in " Ghosts," also appearing in the same part at the Manhattan Theatre, New York ; at the same theatre, Sept., 1903, played Orlando in " As You Like It," with Henrietta Crosman ; subsequently toured in " The Raven " ; at the Knickerbocker Theatre, 7 Mar., 1905, played Professor Arnold Rubek in Ibsen's play, " When We Dead Awaken," and this was followed by a " stock " engagement at Rochester, New York ; in the autumn of 1905 joined the Sothern-Marlowe Company, playing Mercutio in " Romeo and Juliet," Don Pedro in " Much Ado About Nothing," Horatio in " Hamlet," etc. ; at the Knickerbocker Theatre, New York, Oct. and Nov., 1905, played Lucentio in " The Taming of the Shrew," Bassanio in " The Merchant of Venice," and Orsino in " Twelfth Night " ; at the Lyric, New York, Jan. and Feb., 1907, appeared as Manasseh in " John the Baptist," Charles VII in " Jeanne D'Arc," Mercutio in " Romeo and Juliet," and Horatio in " Hamlet," etc. ; made his first appearance in London at the Waldorf Theatre, 24 Apr., 1907, as Charles VII in " Jeanne D'Arc," and also playing his old parts in the repertory presented during the Sothern-Marlowe season, in addition, appeared as Orlando in " As You Like It," and as Sir Edwin Caskoden in " When Knighthood was in Flower " ; engaged by Julia Marlowe for " lead " for season 1907-8 ; at Washington, June, 1908, played Stephen Boyd in " That Little Affair

at Boyd's " ; at the Savoy, New York, Sept., 1908, appeared as Michael Dean in " Mater " ; subsequently toured with Wilton Lackaye as Phillip Ames in " The Battle " ; rejoined E. H. Sothern in 1909, and in Mar. appeared at Daly's, New York, as De Mauprat in " Richelieu " ; at the Hudson Theatre, Oct., 1909, played Vassili in " On the Eve " ; at the Berkeley Lyceum, Dec., 1909, played Pavail in " Know Thyself " ; with the Sothern-Marlowe company, at the Broadway Theatre, Dec., 1910, played Macduff in " Macbeth " ; remained with the same company, 1911-15; at the Garrick, Chicago, Apr., 1914, appeared in " Charlemagne " ; during 1916 toured in " The Other Wife " ; at the Manhattan Opera House, New York, Feb., 1917, appeared as Haggai in " The Wanderer " ; again returned to the Sothern-Marlowe company, and appeared with them during 1919-21, in his old parts ; at the Sam H. Harris Theatre, Nov., 1922, played Horatio in " Hamlet," with John Barrymore ; at the Empire, New York, Mar., 1923, Dalimier in " Pasteur " ; at the Jolson Theatre, Oct., 1923, Iachimo in " Cymbeline " ; at the Martin Beck Theatre, Nov., 1924, King Louis XV in " Madame Pompadour "; Little, Oct., 1925, Joseph Surface in " The School for Scandal "; has since toured in the leading parts in " The Dice of God," " Frail Emma," and since 1928, at the head of his own Shakespearean Company ; at the Longacre Theatre, Nov., 1931, played Hamilton Hart in " In Times Square"; Masque, June, 1933, A. H. McGee in " The Ghost Writer"; Maxine Elliott, Jan., 1934, the Shadow of Death in " Come of Age." *(Died 19 Mar., 1946; age 73)*

LEWIS, Mabel Terry—(*see* TERRY-LEWIS, MABEL).

LEWIS, Martin, actor ; *b.* Blackheath, 8 Sept., 1888 ; *s.* of Joshua Lewis and his wife Jessie Logan (Martin) ; *e.* privately ; *m.* Edna Arnold ; was formerly engaged as a clerk in his father's business ; made his first appearance on the stage, at the

St. James's Theatre, 24 May, 1909, as one of the students in a revival of " Old Heidelberg " ; in Nov., 1909, played the Rev. Everard Bayne in " Lorrimer Sabiston, Dramatist " : for the next three years toured the provinces in George Alexander's provincial company, and in Oct., 1912, went to Australia, where he remained two years and a half, playing a number of juvenile parts ; returned to England in 1915, and in Oct., 1915, was engaged by Dion Boucicault to play in " Half-an-Hour," at the Coliseum, etc. ; appeared at the New Theatre, Dec., 1915, as Mr. Darling in " Peter Pan," subsequently appearing at the same theatre, 1916–18, as Rex Cunningham in " Caroline," Cecil Orme in " The Riddle," Richard Belden in " Her Husband's Wife," Reginald Hornby in " The Land of Promise," Richard Meriton in " Wurzel-Flummery," Captain Charles Carew in " His Excellency the Governor," Arthur Gower in " Trelawny of the Wells," and Private Lance Lovejoy in " Monica's Blue Boy " ; at the Royalty, July, 1918, played Tranto in " The Title " ; at the Victoria Palace, Dec., 1918, Flash Harvey in " The Harbury Pearls " ; at the St. Martin's, July, 1919, Bill Farrimond in " The Bantam V.C. " ; he then went to America, and at Springfield, Mass., Nov., 1919, played Neil Whitway in Pinero's " Quick Work " ; at the Belasco, New York, Sept., 1920, appeared as Michael Jaffray in " One " ; at the Garrick, London, Aug., 1921, played Beauty in " The Edge o' Beyond " ; at the Savoy, Apr., 1922, Harry Cockburn in " The Card Players "·; at the Royalty, Oct., 1922, Leonard Ferris in " Mid-Channel " ; at the Globe, Apr., 1923, John Willocks in " Aren't We All ? " ; at the Duke of York's, July, 1923, Billy Arkwright in " Civilian Clothes " ; at the Savoy, May, 1924, in conjunction with Evan Thomas, directed "The Lure," in which he appeared as Henry Dane ; subsequently toured as Captain Angus Stewart in " The Lonely House " and Corfedrop in " The Sixth Man " ; at the Fortune, Feb., 1925, played Frank Perry in " Are You a Mason ? " ; Strand, May, 1925, Jim Baxter in " The Signal " ; subsequently toured in " Stop

Press " ; Jan., 1926, toured with Zena Dare as Lord Arthur Dilling in " The Last of Mrs. Cheyney " ; during 1927 toured as Beccles in " Ask Beccles " ; appeared at the " Q," Jan.-Feb., 1928, as Campbell Edwards in " The Man at Six," and Lord Dasent in " The Last Guest " ; during 1928-9 toured in South Africa, with Zena Dare, in " The High Road," " The Trial of Mary Dugan," " The Squeaker," " Aren't We All ? " " Other Men's Wives " ; on returning to London, appeared at the Duke of York's, July, 1929, as Alec D'Urberville in " Tess of the D'Urbervilles" ; Fortune, Sept., 1929, played Trigorin in " The Seagull" ; Criterion, Nov., 1929, Sebastien in "Candle Light" ; Arts, Mar., 1930, played Duff Wilson in "After All" ; Royalty, May, 1930, Dr. Hodges in " Our Ostriches" ; in the autumn of 1930, toured as Antony Peel in "Other Men's Wives" ; Criterion, Feb., 1931, Duff Wilson in " After All" ; subsequently toured as Jim Warlock in "Cynara" ; Strand, May, 1932, Lord Ellerton in "Party" ; Cambridge (for G. Club), Oct., 1932, Mr. Barwick in " Well Gentlemen ——? " ; New Theatre, Dec., 1932, Frank Lockwood in "The Cathedral" ; Palace, Jan., 1933, Dr. Wayne Talbot in "Dinner at Eight" ; Fortune, Sept., 1933, Robert Bromley in "What Happened Then ?" ; St. Martin's, Jan., 1934, Philip Harkness in "Nemesis" ; Piccadilly, Apr., 1934, Roy Darwin in "Counsellor-at-Law" ; "Q," Aug., 1934, and Vaudeville, Sept., 1934, Dr. Perry Colt in "Night Hawk" ; Fulham, Oct., 1934, Ralph Dexter in "The Shadow" ; King's, Hammersmith, Feb., 1935, George Turney in "All Rights Reserved" ; Arts, June, 1935, John Allingham in "The Benefit of the Doubt" ; Savoy, Mar., 1936, Hubert Pargiter in "Wisdom Teeth" ; Comedy, Dec., 1936, Rev. Simon Goodacre in "Busman's Honeymoon" ; "Q," May, 1938, George Morrison in "Vantage Point" ; Richmond, Feb., 1939, Professor Manson in "Africa Flight" ; Piccadilly, July, 1941, Dr. Bradman in "Blithe Spirit," which he played for nearly five years; in 1947 joined the B.B.C. Repertory Company, acting in plays for over five years; since 1952 has broadcast in various radio programmes as a free-lance; has also appeared in films. *Recreation:* Gardening. *Club:* Green Room.

(Died Apr., 1970; age 81)

LEWISOHN, Victor Max, actor; *b.* London, 21 Apr., 1897; *s.* Bernhardt Lewisohn and his wife Lydia (Moses); *e.* Parmiter's; *m.* Ruth Miriam Trenner; studied for the stage at Stedman's Academy, Guildhall School of Music, and the Royal Academy of Dramatic Art; made his first appearance on the stage at His Majesty's, Apr., 1913, as the Second Officer in " Twelfth Night," and remained a member of Tree's company until 1915, playing numerous small parts; joined the Old Vic Company in Sept., 1915; served in the Army from 1915-19; in 1921 toured with Shakespearean Company; at the New Theatre, Nov., 1922, played Marzio in " The Cenci "; Sept., 1923, Caius Lucius in " Cymbeline "; Mar., 1924, De Poulengy and The Executioner in " Saint Joan "; Holborn Empire, Nov., 1924, Nicetas and Mahomet in " Heraclius "; at the Regent, Jan., 1925, played his old parts in " Saint Joan "; at the Lyric, July, 1925, General Malakoff in " The Czarina "; at the Lyceum, Mar., 1926, again appeared in " Saint Joan "; at the Globe, July, 1926, Inspector Daniel in " Ask Beccles "; Strand, Feb., 1928, the Herald in " Judith of Israel "; Queen's, Mar., 1929, George Wolmer in 'The Man at Six"; Duchess, Nov.– Dec., 1929, The German Private in "Tunnel Trench," and Wolmer in " The Man at Six"; Comedy, Apr., 1930, Arthur Dinton in "The Silent Witness"; Duchess, Nov., 1931, Solness in "The Master Builder"; Regent, Oct., 1932, Mr. Moses in "Cohen and Son"; has also appeared in nearly sixty different parts at the " Q " Theatre, including Golaud in "Pelleas and Melisande," Halvard Solness in " The Master Builder," Mark Antony, Hamlet, Sir Peter Teazle, etc., and has played many parts for the Stage Society, etc. *Recreations:* Swimming and gardening. *Address:* 8 Elms Lane, Sudbury Town, Middlesex. *Telephone No.:* Wembley 2823.

(Died 13 Nov., 1934; age 36)

LEXY, Edward, actor; *b.* London, 18 Feb., 1897; *s.* of William Little and his wife Catherine (Currie); *e.* St. Andrews College, Dublin, and Royal Military College, Sandhurst; obtained a Commission in the Royal Dublin Fusiliers, 1915, served in the War and was awarded the Military Cross; subsequently joined the Indian Army; after a short period in the Civil Service, read law and was called to Irish Bar, 1929; made his first appearance on the stage at the Gate Theatre, Dublin, and subsequently appeared at the Abbey Theatre; made his first appearance in London with the Dublin Gate company at the Westminster Theatre, 3 June, 1935, as Dr. Berkeley in "Yahoo," subsequently appearing there as the First Redcoat in "The Old Lady Says 'No'" and Polonius in "Hamlet"; at the same theatre, May, 1936, made a notable success as Uncle Sid in "Ah, Wilderness" and July, 1936, played Albert in "A Bride for the Unicorn"; Mercury, Feb., 1937, and Little, Apr. 1937, Lord Stagmantle in "The Ascent of F.6"; Duchess, Jan., 1940, Mr. Pull in "The Golden Cuckoo"; rejoined the Army in 1940, and served for five years, mainly abroad; demobilized, Dec., 1945; broadcast for B.B.C., 1946, in "A Man of Property"; first appeared in films, 1937. *Recreations:* Golf, tennis, riding, and yachting. *Club:* Arts Theatre. *Address:* c/o Derek Glynne, 115 Shaftesbury Avenue, London, W.C.2.

LEYEL, Carl F., manager; *b.* Co. Durham, 30 Dec., 1875; *s.* of Carl Fredrik Leijel and his wife Emma (Swan); *e.* Gateshead School and University College, London; *m.* (1) Hilda Winifred Ivy Wauton (mar. dis.), (2) Nancy M. Manfield; was formerly engaged as an analytical chemist; was originally secretary and subsequently manager for F. R. Benson's Company from Sept., 1897, joining the company at Kettering; business manager for his Lyceum season, 1900, Comedy, 1901, etc.; manager for Otho Stuart and Oscar Asche at Adelphi, 1904–7; fulfilled similar engagements with Otho Stuart at Wyndham's and the Apollo; also manager for him at the Court, 1907–8 ; manager for Herbert Trench at Haymarket, 1909–10 ; manager for Oscar Asche and Lily Brayton, at New Theatre, 1910, Garrick 1911 ; in 1912 produced " Kipps " at the Vaudeville on his own account, and " A Young Man's Fancy " at the Criterion ; in partnership with Kenneth Douglas at the Comedy, 1913 ; manager for Oscar Asche and Lily Brayton at Globe, 1914 ; His Majesty's, for " Chu-Chin-Chow " (1916–21), and " Cairo " (1921–22) ; subsequently appointed manager for Grossmith and Malone at His Majesty's ; is the business representative for Oscar Asche and Lily Brayton. *Recreation :* Riding. *Clubs :* Savage and Devonshire.

(Died 1 Oct., 1925; age 50)

LEYTON, George, descriptive and character vocalist ; *b.* New Orleans, U.S.A., 28 Apr., 1864 ; made his first appearance on the stage at the Princess's Theatre, London, 3 June, 1889, in " True Heart," singing the song from which the play took its title ; remained on the dramatic stage for a year, and then made his first appearance on the variety stage at the Royal Music Hall, 17 Mar., 1890 ; he next appeared at the Trocadero, under the late Sam Adams, singing " The Emigrant Ship " ; he then appeared at a *matinée* at the Oxford, and immediately obtained an engagement ; has since appeared at every leading hall in London and the provinces ; among numerous successful songs with which his name is associated may be mentioned " All for a Lady " ; " All hands on Deck " ; " Always Ready " ; " Boys of the Chelsea School " ; " Different styles of singing " ; " Wellington," etc. *Address :* 27 Hilldrop Road, Kentish Town, N.W. *Telephone No. :* North 3175.

LIAGRE, Jun., Alfred de, producer and manager; *b.* New York City, U.S.A., 6 Oct., 1904; *s.* of Alfred de Liagre and his wife Frida (Unger); *e.* Riverdale School and Yale University; *m.* Mary Howard; commenced his career at the Woodstock Playhouse, 1930; in 1931 was assistant stage-manager to Jane Cowl; in conjunction with Richard Aldrich produced the following plays in New York : " Three Cornered Moon," 1933; " By Your Leave," 1934; " Pure in Heart," 1934; " Petticoat Fever," 1935; " Fresh Fields," 1936; has since produced " Yes, My Darling Daughter," 1937; " I Am My Youth," 1938; " No Code to Guide Her," 1939; " Mr. and Mrs. North," " The Walrus and the Carpenter," 1941; " Ask My Friend Sandy," " The Voice of the Turtle," 1943; " The Mermaids Singing," 1945; " The Druid Circle," 1947; " The Madwoman of Chaillot," 1948; " Second Threshold," 1950; " The Deep Blue Sea," 1952; " Escapade," 1953; " The Golden Apple," 1954; " The Caine Mutiny Court Martial" (tour), and "Janus" (New York), 1955, (London), 1957; "Nature's Way," 1957; "The Girls in 509," and "J.B.," 1958; "The Tumbler" (with Roger L. Stevens), 1960; "Kwamina," 1961; "Photo Finish," 1963; "The Irregular Verb to Love," 1964; at the Paper Mill Playhouse, Millburn, N.J., Jan., 1965, directed a revival of "Janus"; member of the Board of Directors of the Actors Fund of America, A.N.T.A., League of New York Theatres, National Repertory Theatre, Shakespeare Festival and Academy, John F. Kennedy Cultural Center, Committee of Theatrical Producers, Yale Drama School; President of the American Theatre Wing. *Recreations:* Tennis and golf. *Clubs:* Yale, Century, River, Maidstone. *Address:* 322 East 57th Street, or 55 West 42nd Street, New York City, U.S.A. *Telephone No.:* PE. 6–6678.

LICHINE, David, dancer and choreographist; *b.* Rostov, Russia, 25 Dec., 1909; *s.* of Michael Lichtenstein, well known as a composer under the name of Michael Olshansky; *m.* Tatiana Riabouchinska; left Russia with his parents at the age of nine and went to Constantinople; educated at the Russian High School, Paris; studied dancing under Egorova, former *prima ballerina* of the Imperial Ballet, and, later, with Bronislava Nijinska; subsequently joined Anna Pavlova's company, and later, joined that of Ida

Rubinstein; was in Massine's production of "La Reine de Sabat" at Milan; joined Colonel de Basil's company, 1932, first in opera and then with the Ballet Russe, making notable successes in "Les Présages," "Cotillon," "Plage," "Choreartium," "L'Après-Midi d'un Faune," etc.; was responsible for the choreography of "Nocturne," 1933; "Les Imaginaires," 1934; "Protée," 1938; "Le Fils Prodigue," "Perpetuum Mobile," 1939; appeared at the St. James, New York, Jan., 1934, in "Petrouchka," etc., subsequently appearing at the Metropolitan Opera House; also responsible for "Le Pavillon," 1936; "Francesca de Rimini," 1937; "The Gods Go a-Begging," "Le Lion Amoreux," etc.; at the Century, Nov., 1944, the dances in "Rhapsody"; Alvin, Oct., 1945, arranged the choreography for "Polonaise"; at Covent Garden, July, 1947, appeared with Col. de Basil's Ballet Russe, subsequently touring the Continent with the Company; Prince's, 1948, appeared with Les Ballets des Champs-Elysées; is an American citizen. *Address:* c/o Michael Riabouchinsky, 75 Troy Court, London, W.8.

LIEVEN, Albert (*né* Albert Fritz Liéven-Lieven), actor; *b.* Hohenstein, East Germany, 23 June, 1906; *s.* of Dr. Walther Liéven-Lieven, M.D., and his wife Elfride (Schultze); *e.* Koenigsberg, and Berlin University; *m.* (1) Tatiana Lieven (mar. dis.); (2) Valerie White (mar. dis.); (3) Susan Shaw; made his first appearance on the stage at the Court Theatre, Gera-Thuringia, 1 Aug., 1927, as Orlando in "As You Like It"; between this date and 1936, played nearly one hundred parts in various Continental centres; made his first appearance on the London stage, at the Lyric, 21 June, 1937, as Prince Ernest in "Victoria Regina," subsequently touring as Prince Albert in the same play; was subsequently engaged for New York and London, as play-reader for Gilbert Miller; at the Torch, Feb., and Wyndham's, Apr., 1940, played the Count in "Jeannie"; London Hippodrome, Nov., 1941, Ravener in "Get a Load of This," which ran until 1943; same the-

atre, June, 1943, appeared as Carl von Schriner in "The Lisbon Story"; from 1940-5, was engaged on the staff of the B.B.C., in the European Overseas Propaganda service; "Q," Sept., 1946, played Oles Walewski in "The Rocking Horse"; Oct., 1948, Dr. Edward Karlill in "The Annex"; Bedford, Camden Town, Feb., 1950, Peer Halvorsen in "The Leopard"; People's Palace, May, 1950, Paul Tabor in "Birdcage"; first appeared in films, 1932, and has appeared in over fifty pictures on the Continent and in England. *Hobbies:* Stamp collecting, old glasses, gardening, and hydro-biology. *Club:* Green Room. *Address:* c/o Lloyd's Bank, Ltd., 16 St. James's Street, London, S.W.1.; and Pine Tree Cottage, Tilford, near Farnham, Surrey. *Telephone No.:* Frensham 386.

LIEVEN, Tatiana, actress; *b.* Leningrad, U.S.S.R., 1910; *m.* (1) Albert Lieven (mar. dis.); (2) Miles Malleson; studied for the stage at the Reinhardt School, Berlin; made her first appearance on the stage at the Volksbuehne Theater, Berlin, Sept., 1929, as Julie in "Danton," and remained there until July, 1930; subsequent engagements were at the Altes Theater, Leipzig, 1930-1; Schauspielhaus, Koenigsberg, 1931-3; Volkstheater, Vienna, 1936; first appeared in London, at the Apollo Theatre, June, 1938, as Irene in "Idiot's Delight," as understudy for Tamara Geva, and played the same part when the play was revived at His Majesty's, Oct., 1938; at the Shaftesbury Theatre, May, 1939, was engaged understudying Luise Rainer, as Françoise in "Behold the Bride"; at the Torch, Feb., and Wyndham's, Apr., 1940 played The Blonde in "Jeannie" "Q," Sept., 1942, Gretl in "London W.1"; was engaged in War work 1942-5; at the Embassy, Mar., 1945 played Sally Carroll in "The Two Mrs Carrolls"; Granville, Walham Green May, 1946, Nada in "The Nineteenth Hole of Europe"; New Lindsey, Apr. 1947, Elsa in "Waifs that Stray" Playhouse, Feb., 1948, Anna in "Cock pit"; first appeared in films, 1930, i "The Two Worlds." *Address:* 6

Wigmore Street, W.1. *Telephone No.:* Welbeck 3021.

LIFAR, Serge, dancer and choreographist; *b.* Kieff, South Russia, 2 April, 1905; in 1920 was a pupil of Bronislava Nijinska, in his native town; joined the Diaghileff company in Paris in 1923, and after a time studied under Cecchetti; made his *début* in "Cimarosiana" and subsequently appeared in all the favourite ballets, including "Le Lac des Cygnes," "Les Fâcheux," "Romeo and Juliet," "La Pastorale," "Les Matelots," "Barubau," "Zephyr and Flora," "Petrouchka," "The Triumph of Neptune," "La Chatte," "Le Fils Prodigue," etc.; his first work as choreographer was the production of Stravinsky's "Renard," 1929, and in the same year he produced "Prométhée" at the Opera House, Paris; first appeared in London, 1924, at the Coliseum in "Cimarosiana" and "Les Fâcheux"; appeared at the London Pavilion, Mar., 1930, in "Cochran's 1930 Revue"; returned to Paris, where he danced in and produced "Prélude Dominical," "L'Orchestre en Liberté," "Bacchus and Ariadne," "Le Spectre de la Rose" and "Giselle," 1931; "Après-midi d'un Faune," 1932; "Icare," "David Triomphant," "Le Roi Nu," 1936; "Alexandre le Grand," 1937; arranged a season of ballet at the Cambridge Theatre, London, June, 1946, and reappeared as a dancer, in "L'Après-midi d'un Faune"; at the Paris Opéra, Mar., 1953, danced in a new ballet, "Cinéma," for which he devised the choreography; another new ballet, "Variations," was also presented in this programme; as director of the Paris Opéra Ballet, appeared with the company at Covent Garden, Sept., 1954; was appointed choreographer at the Scala, Milan, for the season of 1954–5; author of a book on ballet, "Traditional to Modern," 1938, and "Diaghilev," a biography, 1940; author of "History of the Russian Ballet," 1954.

LIGHTNER, Winnie (*née* Hanson), actress and vocalist; *b.* Greenport. Long Island, U.S.A., 17 Sept., 1901; *e.* public schools, Buffalo, N.Y.; *m.* George Holtrey; made her first appearance on the stage in "vaudeville," in Buffalo 1919, as one of the Lightner Sisters and Alexander; remained in "vaudeville" for four years; appeared at the Globe Theatre, New York, 18 June, 1923, in "George White's Scandals," and appeared at the Apollo, June, 1924, in the 1924 version of "Scandals"; at the Shubert, Aug., 1925, appeared in "Gay Paree"; Winter Garden, Nov., 1926, in "Gay Paree"; Shubert, Nov., 1927, in "Delmar's Revels"; commenced film career 1929, and has appeared in "The Gold Diggers of Broadway," "Song of Songs," "Hold Everything," "She Couldn't Say No," "The Life of the Party," "Top Speed," "Sit Tight," "Why Change Your Husband?" ("Gold-Dust Gertie") "Side Show," "Manhattan Parade," "Playgirl," "She Had to Say Yes," "Dancing Lady," "I'll Fix It," etc.

(Died 5 Mar., 1971; age 71)

LILLIES, Leonard, business manager; *b.* Chudleigh, Devonshire, 18 Sept., 1860; *s.* of Charlotte Welch (Collyns) and George William Lillies, M.D.; brother of Arthur Chudleigh; *e.* Honiton Grammar School and Epsom College; previously engaged in insurance business; has always been associated with his brother's theatrical enterprises; was business manager at the Court Theatre, 1888; since then has officiated in a similar capacity at the Criterion, Wyndham's, and since 1905 at the Comedy. *Club :* Motor.

(Died 2 Aug., 1923; age 63)

LIMBERT, Roy, theatre and producing manager; *b.* Surbiton, Surrey, 26 Dec., 1893; *s.* of Charles Alberic William Limbert and his wife Florence Isabel Strahan (Campbell); *e.* Nelson College, Blackheath, and Bedford School; commenced his managerial career, 1911, touring "The Girl in the Picture"; in 1912–13, was general manager for touring production of "The Girl in the Train"; early in 1914, toured his own concert parties; served during the War, Sept., 1914, to Oct., 1919; on being demobilized, engaged in commercial business until 1923; in 1923, founded Ad-Visers, Ltd., of which he is Chairman and Governing Director; is lessee of the Festival Theatre, Malvern, Worcs., where in association with Sir Barry Jackson he has been responsible for the Malvern Festivals, 1929 to 1937; 1929, saw the first production of Bernard Shaw's "The Apple Cart," and notable productions there since that date were "The Barretts of Wimpole Street" (Besier), 1930; plays typifying "Five Centuries of British Drama," 1931; "Too True to Be Good" (Bernard Shaw), 1932; "A Sleeping Clergyman" (James Bridie), 1933; "A Man's House" (Drinkwater) and "The Moon in the Yellow River" (Denis Johnston), 1934; "The Simpleton of the Unexpected Isles" (Shaw), 1935; in 1938, undertook the entire direction of the Malvern Festival and produced five new plays: "Geneva," by G. Bernard Shaw; "Music at Night," by J. B. Priestley; "Coronationtime at Mrs. Beam's," by C. K. Munro; "Alexander," by Lord Dunsany and "The Last Trump," by James Bridie; he also revived "Saint Joan," with Elizabeth Bergner as Joan; in 1939, at the eleventh Malvern Festival, produced six new plays, including Shaw's "In Good King Charles's Golden Days," and Bridie's "What Say They?"; during 1931, toured "Private Lives," in conjunction with Barry O'Brien; produced "The School for Husbands," at the Court Theatre (with Herbert Jay), 1932; in Mar., 1932, founded the Malvern Company, which has played continuously since that date, not only at Malvern, but at many other prominent centres, and has produced several new plays, including "Barnet's Folly"; at the Saville, London, presented "She Shall Have Music," 1934; with Sir Barry Jackson, at the Haymarket, presented "Barnet's Folly," 1935, and toured this piece subsequently; produced "The Last Trump," Duke of York's, 1938; "Geneva," Saville, 1938; "Worth a Million," Saville, 1939; "In Good King Charles's Golden Days," New, 1940; "Rookery Nook," (with Barry O'Brien), St. Martin's, 1942; "Mr. Bolfry" (with

Linnit and Dunfee Ltd., and Alastair Sim), Westminster, 1943; "It Depends What You Mean" (with Robert Donat and Alastair Sim), Westminster, 1944; "The Forrigan Reel," Sadler's Wells, 1945; with ReandcO: "Dr. Angelus," Phoenix, 1947; "School for Spinsters," Criterion, 1947; "The Anatomist," Westminster, 1948; "Miss Mabel," Duchess, 1948; "Two Dozen Red Roses," Lyric, 1949; "Black Chiffon," Westminster, 1949; "Background," "Beauty and the Beast," Westminster, 1950; "Lace on Her Petticoat," Ambassadors', 1950; with Jack Hylton, "Buoyant Billions," and "Lady Audley's Secret," Prince's, 1949; has also played seasons at the Arts Theatre, Cambridge, 1940–50, in conjunction with the Cambridge Arts Theatre Trust, and at the Memorial Theatre, Stratford-on-Avon, 1944–6; is a member of the Theatrical Managers' Association. *Hobbies:* Books and the theatre. *Recreations:* Motor-boating, car-driving, table tennis, lawn tennis. *Clubs:* Royal Automobile, Savage, Green Room, Town and County, Bedford, Malvern, and Stage Golfing Society. *Address:* Panton House, 25 Haymarket, S.W.1. *Telephone No.:* Whitehall 3332; and Festival Theatre, Malvern, Worcester. *Telephone No.:* Malvern 777 and 888.

LIMERICK, Mona, actress; *b.* South America; *m.* Ben Iden Payne; at Bristol, May, 1902, played Cynthia Doone in "A Touch of Nature"; prominently associated with Miss Horniman's Repertory scheme both at the Midland Theatre and at the Gaiety, Manchester, where she played, among other parts during 1907-9, Mrs. Ormond in "His Helpmate," Margaret Martin in "The Street," Hortense Harvey in "Lucifer"; Anna in "The Three Barrows," Helga in "The Feud," Christophera in "Trespassers will be Prosecuted," Nan in the play of that name, Blanche in "Widowers' Houses," Beatrice in "Much Ado About Nothing," etc.; appeared at the Coronet, June, 1909, in the two first-mentioned plays, and as Isopel in "When the Devil was Ill"; Blanche in "Widowers'

Houses "; at His Majesty's (Afternoon) Theatre, 11 Nov., 1909, played Sarah Casey in "The Tinker's Wedding "; at the Gaiety, Manchester, Feb., 1910, played Anna in "Before the Dawn "; at the Haymarket, Nov., 1910, appeared as Mary Fitton in "The Dark Lady of the Sonnets "; in Feb., 1911, toured as Ann Whitefield in "Man and Superman," Nora in "A Doll's House," etc.; in the autumn of 1911, in partnership with Ben Iden Payne, toured with a repertory of plays; subsequently appeared at the Gaiety, Manchester, Nov.-Dec., 1911, as Delia in "Fancy Free," and Princess Eldreda in "Snow White "; at the Little Theatre, May, 1912, appeared as Melibea in "The Spanish Lovers "; in Mar., 1913, toured as Phyllis Chester in "Phyl," and Nan in the play of that name. Subsequently proceeded to the United States; in Nov., 1913, joined the company of the Fine Arts Theatre, Chicago, with her husband, appearing in a round of parts; in May, 1914, appeared at the Lyceum, Edinburgh, with Esmé Percy, playing in "The Silver Box," "Man and Superman," "The Awakening," "The Notorious Mrs. Ebbsmith," "Candida," and "The Philanderer "; at the Gaiety, Manchester, Aug., 1914, played Brenda Tremayne in "Brenda," and Ruth Butterworth in "The Northerners "; subsequently returned to America; at Boston, Mass., Feb., 1915, played in "Chitra," "The Bear," "Lonesome Like," etc.; during 1916, toured with Esmé Percy and Kirsten Graeme's company, in "Overruled," "Man and Superman," etc.; at the Queen's, Feb., 1917, appeared as Enriqueta in "The Cleansing Stain "; at the Strand, June, 1917, played Mara in "The Tidings Brought to Mary "; at the Lyric, Jan., 1929, played Augusta Leigh in "Byron."

LIMPUS, Alban Brownlow, producing manager; *b.* Twickenham, 2 Feb., 1878; *s.* of Canon Henry Francis Limpus and his wife Agnes (Layard); *e.* H.M.S. Worcester; *m.* Leonice Corinne Sturmdorf; from 1892-99 served in sailing ships, tramp steamers, and finally in the P. & O. service; in 1899

served in the South African War, with Paget's Horse; joined F. R. Benson's company in 1905 in a managerial capacity, and remained until 1909; started management on his own account in 1910, with a tour of "The Thief," and during the next five years successfully toured "Tantalizing Tommy," "The Witness for the Defence," "Bella Donna," "The Turning Point," and "The Land of Promise "; served in the War as Lieut-Commander, R.N.V.R., with the Dover Patrol and 10th Cruiser Squadron; resumed management in Feb., 1920, when, in conjunction with the late Dion Boucicault, he produced "Mr. Pim Passes By "; since that date he has produced "Miss Nell o' New Orleans " (with Boucicault), 1921; "If Four Walls Told," 1922; "Trespassers," 1923; "Collusion " (with the late T. C. Dagnall), 1924; "The Blue Peter " (with Charles Kenyon), 1924; "The Vortex," 1924; "Hay Fever," 1925; "The Cat's Cradle," 1926; "The Scarlet Lady," 1926; "The Marquise," 1927; "The Spot on the Sun," 1927; "The Masque of Venice," 1928; "Passing Brompton Road," 1928; "Her Shop," 1929; "The First Mrs. Fraser," 1929; "Once a Husband," 1932; "Double Harness," 1933; "Sheppey," 1933; "Sixteen," 1934; "This Desirable Residence," "Wise Woman," "Zero," 1935; "Ladies and Gentlemen," "The Last Straw," 1937; "Little Stranger," 1938; "Tony Draws a Horse," 1939. *Recreations:* Sailing and golf. (*Died 21 Mar., 1941; age 63*)

LINARES-RIVAS, Manuel, Spanish playwright; has written the following, among other plays: "Bodas de Plata," "Añoranzas," "Aires de Fuera," etc.

LIND, Letty, actress and dancer,; *b.* 21 Dec., 1862; *d.* of H. Rudge; sister of Lydia Flopp, Millie Hylton, Fanny Dango, and Adelaide Astor (Mrs. George Grossmith, jnr.); made her first appearance on the stage at the Theatre Royal, Birmingham, in 1867, as the child Eva in "Uncle Tom's Cabin "; appeared in the provinces with the late Howard Paul in 1879, making her first appearance in London with that gentleman, at the Princess's Theatre, 27 Oct., 1879, as Lillie Lee in "Locked Out"; subsequently played in "A Nine Days' Queen" at the Gaiety, 1880, and in "The Exiles of Erin" at the Olympic, 1881; at the Criterion, Sept., 1882, played Mary in "Little Miss Muffet"; at the Gaiety, Nov., 1882, played in "A Madcap Prince," with Harriet Jay; engaged by Charles Wyndham at Criterion, as understudy to Nellie Bromley in "Betsy"; subsequently toured in "Truth"; at Her Majesty's Theatre, Mar., 1883, played Phoebe in "A Trip to the Moon"; then toured in "Stormbeaten"; at Christmas, 1883, played Milly in "Queen of Hearts," at Birmingham; next toured as Tina in "My Sweetheart"; toured in "The Corsican Sisters," at the Avenue, Mar., 1885, played Winifred Lawson in "Tact," and in Apr., Madge Primrose in "The Fashionable Beauty"; in May, 1885, same theatre, appeared in the revival of "Les Manteaux Noirs"; at Christmas, 1885, played Cinderella at the Alexandra, Liverpool; in 1886, toured as Dora in "Fun on the Bristol"; at Christmas, 1886, played the Princess in "Aladdin," at the Prince of Wales's, Birmingham; in Apr., 1887, joined the Gaiety company, to play in "Monte Cristo, Jr.," and she remained with George Edwardes until 1892, playing in "Miss Esmeralda," "Ruy Blas," "Carmen Up-to-Data," and "Cinder-Ellen," and touring in America and Australia; subsequently appeared at the Shaftesbury, 1893, in "Morocco Bound"; at Trafalgar Square, 1894, in "Go-Bang"; then rejoined George Edwardes at Daly's, 22 Sept., 1894, to play Alma Somerset in "A Gaiety Girl"; she remained at Daly's to play Daisy Vane in "An Artist's Model," Feb., 1895; Molly Seamore in "The Geisha," Apr., 1896; Iris in "A Greek Slave," June, 1898; at the Globe, Nov., 1900, played Clotilde in "The Gay Pretenders"; at the Lyric, Nov., 1902, appeared as Ellen in "The Girl from Kay's"; she appeared at Drury Lane, at Christmas, 1887, as Princess Sweetarte in "Puss in Boots." *Address* : Brookside,

Salt Hill, Slough, near Windsor. *Telephone No.* : Slough 13. (*Died* 27 *Aug., 1923; age* 60)

LINDBERG, August, Swedish actor and stage director; *b.* Hedemora, Delarue, 3 Sept., 1846; *s.* of Stina (Yansdotter) and Karl Lindberg; *e.* Stockholm; *m.* Augusta Blomstedt, actress, was formerly engaged as a waiter in the well-known Stockholm restaurant, "Laporte Bleu"; studied for the stage at the dramatic school of the Theatre Royal, Stockholm; made his first appearance on the stage in 1866; he made his first appearance in London, Oct., 1866, giving a dramatic recital of "The Tempest"; in 1870, appeared in Stockholm; from 1871-4, was engaged in Finland; in 1875, went to Paris to continue his studies; re-appeared in Stockholm, 1877, as Hamlet, which he played all over Scandinavia, 1877-9; 1880-1, at Stockholm; appointed director of the provinces 1882-4; became Intendant of the Theatre Royal, 1885, has played all the principal *rôles* in the plays of Shakespeare and Ibsen, including "Hamlet," "Othello," "Richard II," "King Lear," etc., "Rosmersholm," "Brand," "Peer Gynt," "The Master Builder," "John Gabriel Borkman," "Ghosts," "Lady Inger of Ostrat," "The Pillars of Society," "Little Eyolf," "The Wild Duck," "Gustaf Vasa," "Kung Midas," "Monna Vanna," etc.; has also appeared in Denmark, Norway, Finland, and Russia; was director of the two theatres in Gottenburg 1891-3; manager at Helsingfors, 1894; engaged at Stockholm, 1897-9; gave dramatic recitals from 1900-2; instructor at the Royal Opera, Stockholm, 1903-5; stage director of the National Theatre, Stockholm, 1906-13 where he still plays leading parts. *Favourite part* : Hamlet, which he has played over five hundred times. *Recreation* : Gardening, in the summer on his estate at Dalaro. *Address* National Theatre, Stockholm, Sweden.

LINDEN, Eric, actor; *b.* New York City, 15 Sept., 1909; *e.* De Witt

Clinton High School and Columbia University; made his first appearance on the stage at the Guild Theatre, New York, 9 Jan., 1928, as a slave in "Marco Millions"; Oct., 1928, played the He-Ape in "Faust"; he also played in "Buckaroo," "One Way Street" and "You Never Can Tell"; appeared at the Théâtre Femina, Paris, for three months; from 1931–34, was in Hollywood, in films; at the Ethel Barrymore Theatre, New York, Nov., 1934, played Eddie in "Ladies' Money"; made his first appearance on the London stage at the St. James's Theatre, 22 Aug., 1938, when he succeeded Luther Adler as Joe Buonaparte in "Golden Boy"; entered films 1931, in "Are These Our Children?", and has since appeared in innumerable pictures. *Address:* c/o Berg-Allenberg Inc., 9484 Wilshire Boulevard, Beverly Hills, Cal., U.S.A.

LINDEN, Marie, actress; *b.* Devonshire, 8 Nov., 1862; made her first appearance on the stage at the Theatre Royal, Oxford, Christmas, 1876, as a Fairy in "Dick Whittington"; in 1879-80, toured with the Majiltons as Berte Kelvin in "Round the Clock" and as Polly Grub in "Gabriel Grub"; made her first appearance on the London stage at Sadler's Wells Theatre, 18 Apr., 1881, as Rose Magenta in "The Census"; subsequently fulfilled an engagement at the Philharmonic Theatre, Islington, where she played a round of melodrama; in July, 1881, appeared at the Royalty, in "Perfection" and "Ixion"; then returned to the Philharmonic, where she played Meenie in "Rip Van Winkle," Aladdin, Phoebe in "London Pride," Leicester in "Kenilworth," etc.; at Her Majesty's, Dec., 1882, played King Aureole in "The Yellow Dwarf," and was then engaged by the late John L. Toole for Toole's Theatre, where she played from Feb., 1883, until the autumn of 1888; during this period, she appeared as Lucy Garner in "Dearer than Life," Countess Asteriski in "Artful Cards," Fédora in "Stage-Dora," Kate Vandeleur in "A Fool and his Money," Mrs. Bunny in "Auntie," Mary Belton in "Uncle

Dick's Darling," Almi-i-da in "Paw Clawdian," Alice Marshall in "The Butler," Rosy in "Ruddy-George," and Dora in "The Don"; at the Strand, 1888, played the title-*rôle* in "Atalanta"; during 1889, played in "The Bookmaker," "Young Mrs. Winthrop," "In Danger," "Caprice," and "The Field of the Cloth of Gold"; at the Avenue, 1890, appeared as Ellen in "Dr. Bill"; at Terry's, 1890, Minnie in "Sweet Lavender"; at the Garrick, 1891, played Margaret Veale in "Lady Bountiful"; appeared at the Haymarket, Sept. to Oct., 1892, with Mrs. Langtry, as Dorothy in "The Queen of Manoa," and as Winifred March in "Agatha Tylden"; at the Comedy, 1894, played Louise in "Frou-Frou," and at the Adelphi, in the same year, appeared as Cecile Austin in "The Fatal Card"; in 1899 she played Anne Williams in "A Lady of Quality" at the Comedy, and at the Haymarket, appeared as the Hon. Mrs. Denbigh in "The Bugle Call"; in 1901 toured in America with E. S. Willard, playing Claricia in "The Cardinal," etc.; in 1905 she again toured in America with E. S. Willard, playing in "Lucky Durham," "David Garrick," etc.; at the Playhouse, June, 1908, played Lady Dugdale in "The Flag Lieutenant"; at His Majesty's (Afternoon) Theatre, Dec., 1908, appeared as Sister Martha and Hannele's mother in "Hannele"; at the Globe, May, 1910, played Madame Brideau in "Parasites"; at the Court, Oct., 1910, played Lady Paygrave in "The Career of Henry Jones," and Nov., 1910, Lady Hale in "False Dawn"; accompanied Mr. H. B. Irving on his South African tour 1912–13; after her return to London appeared at the Coronet, Dec., 1913, as Mdlle. de Meuriot in "Woman on Her Own"; at the Savoy, July, 1914, played Martha in "The Sin of David"; during 1914-15 toured with Martin Harvey in "The Breed of the Treshams," "The Only Way," etc.; at the New Theatre, May, 1915, played Mrs. Bagshaw in "The Breed of the Treshams"; at His Majesty's, May, 1916, with Martin Harvey, played Gertrude in "Hamlet," and the Widow in "The Taming of the Shrew"; has since toured, 1916-39, in Martin Harvey's Company, in previously mentioned parts, and as Mrs. Cruickshank in "Rosemary," Mrs. Smith in "David Garrick," Akulina in "A Cigarette Maker's Romance," Lady Honoria in "The Raparee Trooper" ("Boy O'Carroll"), Belief in "Via Crucis," Comtesse de Plougastel in "Scaramouche," Catherine in "The Bells," etc.; at the Savoy, Sept., 1933, played Lady Huland in "If Only Father ———."

LINDLEY, Audra, actress; b. Los Angeles, Calif., U.S.A., 24 Sept., 1918; d. of Bert Lindley and his wife Bessie (Fisher); m. Dr. Aaron Hardy Ulm; studied for the stage under Max Reinhardt; made her first appearance on the stage under Reinhardt's direction, at Los Angeles, 1940, as Mother in "Six Characters in Search of an Author," and subsequently played Mrs. Levi in "The Merchant of Yonkers"; first appeared in New York, at the Jolson Theatre, 26 May, 1942, as Judy Garrett in "Comes the Revelation"; subsequently toured, 1942, for the Theatre Guild, as Emma in "Papa is All"; Playhouse, New York, Oct., 1946, played Erica Marlowe in "Hear That Trumpet"; Cort, May, 1947, Helen Sheldon in "Heads or Tails"; Fulton, Nov., 1948, Frances Morritt in "The Young and Fair"; first appeared in films, 1941, in "Manpower." *Address:* 524, East 20th Street (Apart. 7.F.), New York City, 9, U.S.A. *Telephone No.:* Gr. 3–5560.

LINDO, Olga, actress; b. London, 13 July, 1898; d. of Frank Lindo and his wife Winnie Louise (Marion Wakeford); e. Gloucester House School, Kew Gardens; made her first appearance on the stage at Drury Lane Theatre, 26 Dec., 1913, in "The Sleeping Beauty Re-Awakened"; also appeared there Dec., 1914, as Lili in "The Sleeping Beauty Beautified," and Apr., 1915, as the Flower Girl in "Sealed Orders"; at the same theatre, Sept., 1916, played Jane Smith in "The Best of Luck," and Dec., 1916, as the Tweenie Maid in "Puss in New Boots"; subsequently toured in her father's company; from 1919–21 toured the

provinces as Blanny Wheeler in "Fair and Warmer," Leila Calthorpe in "The Man from Toronto," and Judy Abbott in "Daddy Long-Legs"; at the Royalty Theatre, in 1922, succeeded Moyna MacGill as Hope Tregoning in "If Four Walls Told"; at the Apollo, Sept., 1922, played Suzanne Winkelried in "The Torch"; at the Strand, Feb., 1923 (for the Repertory Players), played April Clear in "Lavender Ladies"; she then appeared at the Coliseum, with Godfrey Tearle, as Loyse in "The Ballad Monger"; was then engaged by Reandean, and appeared at the St. Martin's Theatre, April, 1923, as Helena II in "R.U.R."; July, 1923, Myrtle West in "Melloney Holtspur"; Aug., 1923, Mrs. Kemp in "The Likes of Her," and Mrs. Ross in "The Will"; Jan., 1924, Marget in "Gruach"; at the Ambassadors', Feb., 1924, Muriel Hanbury in "The Way Things Happen"; at the Apollo, Sept., 1924, Pearl Hennig in "The Fool"; Vaudeville, Mar., 1925, Nettie Dark in "Tarnish"; Garrick, May, 1925, Sadie Thompson in "Rain"; Comedy, Nov., 1925, Gillian Hobbs in "The Ring o' Bells"; Lyric, Mar., 1926, Millie in "The Best People"; Apollo, Feb., 1927, Grace Livingstone in "The First Year"; Garrick, Mar., 1927, Pamela in "All the Men and Women"; Apollo (for the Lyceum Club Stage Society), Apr., 1927, Bianca in "Othello"; same theatre (for Fellowship of Players), June, 1927, Portia in "The Merchant of Venice"; Globe, July, 1927, Nell Smith in "The Village"; New, Aug., 1927, Kitty Macdonald in "The Wolves"; "Q," Dec., 1927, Elsie in "Enchantment"; Little, May, 1928, played in "Something More Important," "A Private Room," and "The Wedding Day," as part of the "Grand Guignol" programme; June, 1928, played Dagmar Krumback in "Samson and the Philistines"; subsequently directed "The Monster" at Cardiff, and toured as Queenie Brett in "Gossip," and Maisie in "The Night-Hawk"; appeared at the Coliseum, Jan., 1929, as Hilary in "The Perfect Marriage"; Garrick, June, 1929, Molly in "The Stranger Within," subsequently touring in the same part; went to South Africa, Jan., 1930, and played in "Her Past," "The Stranger Within," "The Patsy," "The Constant Nymph," "A Private Room," "Peg O' My Heart," etc.; on returning to London, appeared at the Comedy, Mar., 1931, as Germaine Leverrier in "Naughty Cinderella"; Saville, Oct., 1931, Stella Rees in "For the Love of Mike"; Phoenix (for the G. Club), Apr., 1932, Cherry Grey in "Rings on Her Fingers"; Globe, June, 1932, Tanya Varda in "Men About the House"; in Aug., 1932, toured as Miranda Clayfoot in "Party"; Arts, Sept., 1932, Natasha Lyvof in "Many Women"; Garrick, Oct., 1932, Eliza-veta Orlov in "The Bear Dances"; in Dec., 1932, went on tour playing Alice in "The Cat and the Fiddle"; Shaftesbury (for Overture Players), July, 1933, Hilda Benson in "Laying the Devil"; in Jan., 1934, again visited South Africa, playing in "The Barretts of Wimpole Street," "While Parents Sleep," etc.; after returning to England, appeared at Birmingham, Aug., 1934, as Poppy Jacques in "Headline"; Playhouse, London, Oct., 1934, played Nita Romand in "C.I.D."; Whitehall, Feb., 1935, Abigail Hill in "Viceroy Sarah"; Playhouse, May, 1935, Chloe in "The Skin Game"; Cambridge, Nov., 1935, Tondeleyo in "White Cargo"; "Q," Apr., and Duke of York's, June, 1936, Miss Smith in the play of that name; Lyric, Feb., 1937, Colley in "Wise To-Morrow"; "Q," Aug., 1937, Paula Tanqueray in "The Second Mrs. Tanqueray"; Embassy, Nov., 1937, the Queen in "Cymbeline"; "Q," Feb., 1938, Ruth Atkins in "Beyond the Horizon"; Strand, Apr., 1938, Susan Long in "Banana Ridge"; "Q," May, 1939, Jitta in "Jitta's Atone-ment," and Dec., 1939, Mrs. Gill in "The Two Bouquets"; Shaftesbury, Apr., 1940, Mrs. Warburton in "Good Men Sleep at Home"; "Q," Nov., 1941, the Princess in "School for Slavery," and Jan., 1942, Josephine in "The Devil Within"; St. Martin's, Feb., 1942, Laura Amberley in "Jam To-day"; Whitehall, May, 1942, Vera Sheldon in "Other People's Houses"; "Q," Sept., 1942, Pauline in "London, W.1"; Ambassadors', Feb., 1943, Pamela in "A Little Bit

of Fluff"; Playhouse, June, 1943, Marya in "The Russians"; St. Mar-tin's, July, 1943, Mrs. Brown in "Claudia"; Lyric, Oct., 1944, Mrs. Crawley in "Scandal at Barchester"; Playhouse, Mar., 1945, Mrs. Mumford in "Great Day"; Arts, Sept.–Oct., 1945, Mrs. George in "Getting Mar-ried," Rose in "The Thunderbolt," and Gertrude in "Hamlet"; toured, from Apr., 1946, as Hilda Prescott in "The Poltergeist," and played the same part at the Vaudeville, July, 1946; "Q," Sept., 1947, Essie in "Little Lambs Eat Ivy"; Wyndham's, July, 1948, Mrs. Bateson in "People Like Us"; Embassy, Apr., 1949, played Maud Barren in "On Monday Next . . .," and appeared in this part at the Comedy, June, 1949; Phoenix, Oct., 1950, Susan Throssel in "Dear Miss Phoebe"; Westminster, Jan., 1952, played Lady Archer in "Sunset in Knightsbridge"; Royal, Brighton, Oct., 1952, played Alicia Hockforth-Barnes in "A Fiddle at the Wedding"; St. Martin's, Apr., 1953, Doris Delaney in "The Teddy Bear"; at Westminster, Abbey, June, 1953, appeared as Ellen Daye in "Out of the Whirlwind"; Strand, Dec., 1953, for the Repertory Players, appeared as Mrs. Morrell in "Tranquil House"; Royal, Windsor, Oct., 1954, Anna in "Kind Cousin"; Garrick, Feb., 1955, Mrs. Phillips in "Serious Charge"; Duchess, May, 1956, played Mrs. Hanmer in "The Silver Whistle"; Westminster, Apr., 1960, played Miss Slee in "A Lodging For The Bride"; at the Connaught, Worthing, Oct., 1960, played Iris Floria in "The Warm Peninsula"; Dublin Festival, Sept., 1963, played Mother Agnes in "Inquiry at Lisieux"; has also appeared in several productions for the Repertory Players and in numerous films, including "Sapphire," etc.; has also appeared in many tele-vision productions, and broadcast with the B.B.C. Drama Repertory Com-pany. *(Died 7 May, 1968; age 69)*

LINDON, Millie, mimic and vocalist; *b.* 24 Sept., 1878; *m.* T. E. Dunville (mar. dis.); made her first appearance on the stage, as a mimic, at the Metro-politan Music Hall, 23 July, 1894, meeting with immediate success; she was then engaged at the London Pavilion, Oxford, Tivoli, and South London, and appeared at nearly all the leading halls in London and the provinces; after a time she relinquished her mimetic entertainment and appeared with great success as a vocalist; among several successes which she introduced were " For old time's sake "; " If only your heart could speak "; " Sometimes "; " Pussy had another sardine "; " For my lady's bright blue eyes "; " The Angel of my dreams "; " The rain came pitter-patter down," etc.; is a cousin of Letty Lind, Millie Hylton, Adelaide Astor, Lydia Flopp, and Fanny Dango.

LINDSAY, Howard, actor, dramatic author and director,; *b.* Waterford, N.Y., U.S.A., 29 Mar., 1889; *e.* Boston Latin School, and Harvard University; *m.* Dorothy Stickney; made his first appearance on the stage, 1909, touring in " Polly of the Circus "; subsequently appeared in silent pictures; appeared in "vaudeville," tent-shows, burlesque, and toured with McKee Rankin; joined Margaret Anglin, 1913, as stage-manager, and played in her repertory, remaining with her five years; during the War, 1918, served in U.S. infantry regiment; at the Playhouse, New York, Oct., 1919, played Laramy in "A Young Man's Fancy"; Frazee, Aug., 1921, Vincent Leach in "Dulcy"; Punch and Judy, Nov., 1922, in "The '49 ers"; 48th Street, May, 1923, Rollins in "Sweet Nell of Old Drury"; Selwyn, Feb., 1925, Richard Graham in "Two by Two"; Morosco, Jan., 1934, Henry Smith in "By Your Leave"; Empire, Nov., 1939, Father in "Life with Father"; Empire, Oct., 1948, Father in "Life With Mother"; Morosco, Oct., 1951, Benjamin Goodman in "Remains To Be Seen"; Royale, Mar., 1952, Julian Prescott in "One Bright Day"; has written the following plays in collaboration with Bertrand Robinson: "Tommy," 1927; "Your Uncle Dudley," 1929; "Oh, Promise Me," 1930; dramatized "She Loves Me Not," 1933; with Russel Crouse revised the book of

"Anything Goes," 1934; with Damon Runyon, co-author of "A Slight Case of Murder," 1935; has written the following plays in collaboration with Russel Crouse: "Red, Hot and Blue!" 1936; "Hooray for What!" 1937; "Life With Father," 1939, which ran over seven years without a break; "Strip for Action," 1942; "State of the Union," 1945, which gained the Pulitzer prize, 1945–6; "Life With Mother," 1948; "Call Me Madam," 1950; "Remains To Be Seen," 1951; "The Prescott Proposals," 1953; "The Great Sebastians," 1955; "Happy Hunting," 1956; "Tall Story," 1958; "The Sound of Music," 1959; "Mr. President," 1962; as director was responsible for "Dulcy," 1921; "To the Ladies," 1922; "The Good Old Days," 1923; "The Poor Nut," 1925; "Tommy," 1927; "This Thing Called Love," "The Beaux' Stratagem," 1928; "Your Uncle Dudley," 1929; "Oh, Promise Me," "The Up and Up," 1930; "Gay Divorce," "Child of Manhattan," 1932; "She Loves Me Not," "The Party's Over," 1933; "By Your Leave," "Anything Goes," 1934; "A Slight Case of Murder," 1935; "Red, Hot and Blue!" 1936; "Hooray for What!" 1937; "The Prescott Proposals," 1953; "A Lovely Light," (New York and London), 1960; "A Lovely Light," revival, Jan., 1964; presented "Arsenic and Old Lace," with Russel Crouse, 1941, which ran over three years; "Strip for Action," with Crouse and Oscar Serlin, 1942; "The Hasty Heart," with Crouse, 1945; "Detective Story," with Crouse, 1949; "One Bright Day," with Crouse, 1952; "The Great Sebastians," with Crouse, 1956. *Club:* The Players (President, 1955–65). *(Died 11 Feb., 1968; age 78)*

LINDSAY, James, actor; *b.* Devonshire, 26 Feb., 1869; *s.* of Major Charles Douglas Lindsay and his wife Elizabeth (Lindsay); *e.* Rugby; was formerly in the Army; made his first appearance on the stage at the Theatre Royal, Norwich, 1894, as Sir George Orreyd in " The Second Mrs. Tanqueray "; made his first appearance in London at the Opéra Comique, 13 June, 1895, as the Hon. Bertie Thoytes in " An Average Man " ; at the Adelphi Theatre, 26 Aug., 1896, appeared as the Hon. Fred Cholmondely in " Boys Together " ; subsequently appeared in " The Prisoner of Zenda " and " Rupert of Hentzau " ; in 1899 was in the United States, and appeared with John Drew in " The Liars " ; subsequently played with Henry Miller, in his first repertory season at San Francisco ; toured in Australia, 1904-6, in " Sweet Nell of Old Drury," " Old Heidelberg," " 'Op o' me Thumb," " Pretty Peggy," etc., with Nellie Stewart ; from 1906-10 was engaged with Meynel and Gunn, playing in " The Hypocrites," " Lucky Durham," " The Midnight Wedding," " Love Against the World," " Jim the Penman," etc. ; returned to England in 1910 ; appeared at the Globe with Arthur Bourchier, and in 1911 at Drury Lane, played Captain Sartoris in " The Whip," also touring in the same part ; at the Globe, Apr., 1913, played Lord Cazalet in " Vanity " ; at the St. James's, June, 1913, Sir George Orreyd in " The Second Mrs. Tanqueray " ; at the Criterion, Feb., 1914, Mr. Macintyre in " A Pair of Silk Stockings " ; at the Strand, Sept., 1914, Sam Baxter in " The Silver King " ; was engaged at the Savoy, with H. B. Irving, 1915-17, playing Dr. Firmin in " Searchlights," Buckle in " The Case of Lady Camber," Dennis O'Meara in " The Barton Mystery," Sir George Gilding in " The Professor's Love Story," Marcellus in " Hamlet," Viscount Loosehanger in " Humpty Dumpty " ; at the London Pavilion, Oct., 1917, played the Duke of Mallorie in " A Kiss or Two " ; at the St. James's, Sept., 1918, appeared as Robert Goring in " The Eyes of Youth " ; at the Strand, Nov., 1919, as Robert Dorrington in " The Crimson Alibi " ; at the Playhouse, Nov., 1920, appeared as Henry Knowle in " The Romantic Age " ; at the Comedy, Mar., 1921, as Alfred Sexton in " The Ninth Earl " ; at the Garrick, Aug., 1921, played Major Egerton in " The Edge o' Beyond " ; Jan., 1922, Captain Hatch in " The Bird of Paradise " ; at the Duke of York's, June, 1922, Seymour Revelsent in " Pomp and Circumstance " ; at the St.

James's, Nov., 1922, Anton in " The Beating on the Door " ; then toured with Iris Hoey in " Just a Girl " ; at the Ambassadors', May, 1923, played Lord Batte in "The Piccadilly Puritan"; then toured with Harry Welchman, as the Earl of Sidthorpe in " Sir Jackanapes " ; at the Shaftesbury, Apr., 1924, played Mr. Kettering in " A Perfect Fit " ; at the Prince of Wales's, June, 1924, Detective-Inspector Caillard in " The Rat " ; at the Garrick, Dec., 1924, Mr. Stapleton in " Six Cylinder Love." *Club :* Savage. *(Died 9 June, 1928; age 59)*

LINDSAY, Vera *(née* Vera Poliakoff) ; *b.* St. Petersburgh, Russia, 27 Nov., 1911 ; *d.* of Vladimir Poliakoff and his wife Xenia (Leon) ; *e.* Kensington High School, London ; *m.* Basil Burton ; studied for the stage at the Royal Academy of Dramatic Art; made her first appearance on the stage at the Theatre Royal, Ryde, Isle of Wight, 1929, as the Countess von Baltin in " By Candle Light"; subsequently appeared at the Festival Theatre, Cambridge; made her first appearance in London, at the Royalty, 23 June, 1931, as Mary Magdalen in " Judas"; Duchess, Feb., 1932, played Margery Morton in "The Rose Without a Thorn"; Westminster, July, 1932, Princess of France in "Love's Labour's Lost"; Oct., 1932, Renée de Montesson in "Dizzy"; Kingsway, Nov., 1932, Camille in "The Werewolf"; Embassy, Apr.–May, 1933, Valentina in "Bargains in Brides," and Joan Hartigan in "Sometimes Even Now"; Daly's, Apr., 1934, Ruth Serle in "Dark Horizon"; then joined the Compagnie de Quinze, and remained 1934–35; during 1935, played Lucréce in "Le Viol de Lucréce," with that company; Westminster (for the Group Theatre), Oct., 1935, Catherine in "Sowers of the Hills"; New, Oct., 1936, Octavia in "Antony and Cleopatra"; Old Vic., Nov., 1937, Lady Macduff in "Macbeth," which she again played at the New, Dec., 1937; Phoenix, Dec., 1938, Olivia in "Twelfth Night"; Rudolf Steiner Hall, Dec., 1939, Estella in "Great Expectations"; Old Vic., May, 1940, Ceres in "The

Tempest." *Address:* 2 Russell Avenue, St. Albans, Herts. *Telephone No.:* St. Albans 4563.

LINLEY, Betty, actress; *b.* England; *m.* Maurice G. Roux; made her first appearance on the stage at the Garrick Theatre, London, 4 Sept., 1914, as Mistress Barbara in "Bluff King Hal," and in Oct., 1914, played Elsie in "The Double Mystery"; subsequently went to America and understudied Lenore Ulric in "Tiger Rose," at the Lyceum, New York, Oct., 1917; at the Belasco, 1918, understudied Ina Claire in "Polly with a Past"; subsequently played the part of Myrtle Davis in that play and also toured in it; Booth, Nov., 1920, played Ursula Ballard in "Not So Long Ago"; at the Sam H. Harris, Aug., 1921, played Phyllis Burton in "Six-Cylinder Love"; Punch and Judy, Nov., 1921, Iris Tenterden in "The Great Broxopp"; Fulton, 1922, Elizabeth in "The Circle"; Bijou, Oct., 1922, played Mildred Dunham in "That Day"; toured, Jan., 1923, as "The Nurse" in "Her Temporary Husband"; at Stamford, Conn., May, 1924, played Jo Costello in "The Baronet and the Butterfly"; toured, Sept., 1924, as Lorna Webster in "In the Next Room"; at Salem, Mass., July, 1925, played Mary Rose, and Eliza Doolittle in "Pygmalion"; Greenwich Village, Nov., 1925, Denise in "The Pilgrimage"; at the Guild Theatre, Dec., 1925, Yvonne in "Merchants of Glory"; Daly's, Feb., 1926, Kitty Pook in "Port o' London"; Lyceum, May, 1926, Dulcie Primrose in "The Sport of Kings"; Neighbourhood Playhouse, Nov.-Dec., 1926, Vasantasena in "The Little Clay Cart," and Leah in "The Dybbuk"; Belmont, Apr., 1927, Nell Tuttle in "Fog-Bound"; Garrick, Oct., 1927, Bianca in "The Taming of the Shrew" (in modern dress); Comedy, Jan., 1928, Elena and Francesca in "So Am I"; toured, Nov., 1928, as Hero in "Much Ado About Nothing," with Mrs. Fiske; Erlanger's, Mar., 1930, Julia Melville in "The Rivals"; at Chicago, Aug., 1930, Seela Clannish in "Love Technique"; Booth, Sept., 1931, Judy in "The Bread-

winner"; Avon, Dec., 1931, Sorel Bliss in "Hay Fever"; Playhouse, New York, Aug., 1933, Lily, and subsequently, Miranda in "A Party"; Morosco, Sept., 1934, Diana in "No More Ladies"; Masque, May, 1936, Laura Hamilton in "A Private Affair"; after an absence of eight years, reappeared on the stage, Aug., 1944, when she commenced touring as Vinnie in "Life With Father," and continued in this until July, 1946; Biltmore, Sept., 1947, played Mrs. Montgomery in "The Heiress"; Aug., 1948, succeeded Patricia Collings as Lavinia Penniman in the same play. *(Died 9 May, 1951; age 61)*

LINN, Bambi, actress and dancer; *b.* Brooklyn, N.Y., U.S.A., 26 Apr., 1926; *d.* of Henry William Linnemeier and his wife Mimi (Tweer); *e.* Children's Professional School, New York City; *m.* (1) Rod Alexander Burke (mar. dis.); (2) Joseph de Jesus; studied dancing with Michael Mordkin, Agnes de Mille and others; made her first appearance on the stage at the St. James Theatre, 31 Mar., 1943, as Aggie in "Oklahoma!"; Majestic, Apr., 1945, played Louise in "Carousel"; International, Apr., 1947, Alice in "Alice in Wonderland"; Martin Beck, May, 1948, Sally in "Sally"; Winter Garden, Mar., 1950, Bonnie in "Great to Be Alive!"; first appeared in London, at Drury Lane Theatre, 7 June, 1950, when she again appeared as Louise in "Carousel"; Opera House, San Francisco, July, 1951, played Daisy in "Bloomer Girl"; at New York City Center, June, 1954, appeared as Louise in a revival of "Carousel"; City Center, Sept., 1957, again played Louise in "Carousel"; in 1958 toured the Eastern U.S.A. in "Dance Jubilee"; Spoleto Festival, Italy, 1959, danced as a soloist with the American Ballet Company; Shubert, New York, Mar., 1962, Blanche Bushkin in "I Can Get It for You Wholesale"; director of dance school in Westport, Conn., where she teaches ballet and modern dancing. *Favourite parts:* Alice in "Alice in Wonderland," and Louise in "Carousel." *Recreations:* Walking and reading. *Address:* 45 South Compo Road,

Westport, Conn., U.S.A. *Telephone No.:* 227–0977.

LINNIT, S. E., manager; President of the Society of West End Theatre Managers; *m.* Mrs. Hope Astley; for some years was general manager for Edgar Wallace; is a director in the firm of Linnit and Dunfee, Ltd., which has presented the following plays in the West End: "Aren't Men Beasts!" 1936; "A Spot of Bother," "The Phantom Light," 1937; "Elizabeth, La Femme Sans Homme," "Banana Ridge," "Golden Boy," "Good-bye Mr. Chips," 1938; "Gaslight," "The Jealous God," "Saloon Bar," 1939; "Women Aren't Angels," "Once a Crook," "Cottage to Let," 1940; "Quiet Week-end," "Love in a Mist," "Warn that Man," 1941; "Lifeline," "Men in Shadow," "The Duke in Darkness," 1942; "Brighton Rock," "Mr. Bolfry," "Acacia Avenue," 1943; "A Soldier for Christmas," "The Banbury Nose," "No Medals," 1944; "Lady from Edinburgh," "Madame Louise," "Young Mrs. Barrington," 1945; "The Poltergeist," 1946; "Ill Met By Moonlight," "Now Barabbas . . .," "The Chiltern Hundreds," "Outrageous Fortune," "The Blind Goddess," "Fools Rush In," 1947; "Dark Eyes," "Little Lambs Eat Ivy," "Cage Me a Peacock," "Ambassador Extraordinary," "One Wild Oat," "The Wild Duck," "Slings and Arrows," "The Paragon," 1948; "A Woman's Place," "Love's a Funny Thing," "Master of Arts," "The Non-Resident," "Bonaventure," 1949; "Cry Liberty," "Will Any Gentleman?" "Ardèle," 1950; "The Thistle and the Rose," "The Love of Four Colonels," "The Moment of Truth," "Fortune Came Smiling," 1951; "Lords of Creation," "The Young Elizabeth," "Wild Horses," 1952; "The Bad Samaritan," "As Long As They're Happy," "Trial and Error," "The Devil's General," "No Sign of the Dove," 1953; "The Fifth Season," "Intimacy at 8.30," "Salad Days," 1954; "Uncertain Joy," "Small Hotel," 1955; the firm was also associated with the production of "French Without Tears," 1936; "George and Margaret," "Judgment Day," 1937;

"Death on the Table," "Can We Tell?," "Quiet Wedding," 1938; "The Women," 1940; "Flare Path," 1942; "While the Sun Shines," 1943; "Another Love Story," "Uncle Harry," 1944; "The Winslow Boy," "A Play for Ronnie," "Strange as it may Seem," 1946; "I Capture the Castle," 1954. *Address:* 139 Piccadilly, London, W.1. *Telephone No.:* Mayfair 7211. *(Died,* 11 *August,* 1956*; age 58)*

LION, Leon M., actor-manager, and dramatic author; *b.* London, 12 Mar., 1879; *e.* London; *m.* Kathleen Creighton (mar. dis.); studied elocution with Henry Neville; made his first appearance on the stage as Midshipman Easy in "True Blue," at Olympic, 19 Mar., 1896; in 1897 appeared in "The Three Musketeers" at Globe; in "Sweet Nell of Old Drury" at Haymarket, Aug., 1900; in "The Three Musketeers," at Lyceum, Nov., 1900; in "Lion Hunters" at Terry's, 1901; toured with Forbes-Robertson in "Hamlet," "Othello," etc.; toured with George Edwardes's Co. in "The Toreador" and "The Messenger Boy," 1905; at New Theatre played in "The Scarlet Pimpernel," 1905-6; appeared at the New Theatre, Nov., 1907, in the title-*rôle* of "The New Boy"; at His Majesty's, Feb., 1908, played Asticot in "The Beloved Vagabond," and in Apr., Tubal in "The Merchant of Venice," and Simple in "The Merry Wives of Windsor"; at the Royalty, 1909, appeared as the Count de Moret in "The Noble Spaniard," and as Simon Macquoid in "What the Public Wants"; at His Majesty's, Sept. to Dec., 1909, played in "False Gods," "Trilby," "Beethoven" and "The Lethal Chamber"; during 1910, toured as Jakes in "The House of Temperley"; at the Little Theatre, Mar., 1911, appeared as Knut Brovik in "The Master Builder"; at the Queen's Theatre, Mar., 1912, played Veerland in "The Chalk Line"; at the Haymarket, Nov., 1912, played Aristide Pujol in "An Adventure of Aristide Pujol," Apr., 1913, Hironari in "Typhoon"; May, 1913, Henry Cassidy in "Within the Law"; at the

Apollo, May, 1914, played Albert Vichey in "The Little Lamb"; at the Gaiety, Leo Schutzmacher in "The Doctor's Dilemma"; at the Kingsway, Apr., 1915, Adolf in "Advertisement"; at His Majesty's, July, 1915, Achille Grigoux in "Peter Ibbetson"; at the Adelphi, Nov., 1915, played Alfonse in "Tina"; Aug., 1916, the Maitre d'Hotel in "High Jinks"; at the Globe, Oct., 1917, Kimura in "The Willow Tree"; he then entered on the management of the New Theatre, and on 11 July, 1918, opened with "The Chinese Puzzle," in which he appeared as the Marquis Chi-Lung; at the Gaiety, Manchester, Dec., 1919, played Jacques Mindot in "Homespun"; at the Duke of York's, July, 1920, produced "Brown Sugar," but did not take part in the play; at the Garrick, Sept., 1920, in conjunction with Charles Kenyon, produced "The Right to Strike," in which he appeared as Gordon Montague; in Jan., 1921, revived "The Three Daughters of M. Dupont," in which he played M. Dupont; Feb., 1921, produced "The Fulfilling of the Law"; Apr., 1921, produced "Count X," in which he played Paul Tchertkoff; at the Comedy, Oct., 1921, produced "Araminta Arrives," Nov., 1921, "The Faithful Heart," and Mar., 1922, "Other People's Worries"; at the Court, Feb., 1922, he commenced the revival of a "Galsworthy Cycle" of plays; he opened with "Justice," in which he played William Falder, followed by "The Pigeon," in which he appeared as Christopher Wellwyn; he then revived "The Silver Box," followed by the production of "Windows," Apr., 1922; at the Royalty, Oct., 1922, revived "Mid-Channel," in which he played the Hon. Peter Mottram; in Dec., 1922, revived "Sweet Lavender" at the Ambassadors'; at the St. James's, May, 1923, produced "The Outsider"; and July, 1923, "The Coming of Gabrielle"; at the Savoy, Feb., 1924, produced "Lord o' Creation," in which he played Lord Leithling; in Mar., 1924, produced "Blinkers"; in June, 1924, produced "Tiger Cats," and July, 1924, produced "In the Snare"; in Oct., 1924, sailed for South Africa,

where he toured in "A Chinese Puzzle," "Tiger Cats," "Outward Bound," and "The Mask and the Face"; returning to London, appeared at the New, Aug., 1925, as Ben in "No. 17"; Wyndham's, Dec., 1925, played Edmond Vernier in "The Godless"; Garrick, Apr., 1926, the Old Dealer in "Enchantress"; "Q," June, 1926, Bill Waters in "A Dog's Chance"; Ambassadors', Aug., 1926, the Fellow Convict and the Old Gentleman in "Escape"; Grand, Croydon, Sept., 1926, Joe Puccini in "Queer Fish"; Ambassadors', Nov.1926, Henry Earlnforward in "Riceyman Steps"; Wyndham's, Feb., 1928, Sir Richard Norton in "Listeners"; Palace (for King George's Pension Fund), May, 1928, the Viscomte de Tournai in "The Scarlet Pimpernel"; Ambassadors', June, 1928, "The Elephant" in "The Man They Buried"; Wyndham's, July, 1928, William Falder in a revival of "Justice"; Aug., 1928, Ferdinand de Levis in a revival of "Loyalties"; Daly's, Jan., 1930, Maurice Spandrell in "This Way to Paradise"; Royalty, Feb., 1931, Scaramanzia in "Money, Money"; Garrick, May, 1932, the Man from the Sea in "Man Overboard"; July, 1932, again played in "Escape"; Sept., 1932, Mr. Justice Floyd in "Justice"; Royalty, Dec., 1932, Tobias Gigg in "A Cup of Happiness"; Garrick, Apr., 1933, Jaggat Singh in "Beggars in Hell"; Playhouse, Apr., 1934, Thomas Foxley, K.C. in "Libel"; Oct., 1934, Bob Skipley in "C.I.D."; Apr., 1935, Hector Frome in "Justice"; May, 1935, the Auctioneer in "The Skin Game"; at the Little Theatre, Sept., 1935, played Wang Yun in a revival of "Lady Precious Stream"; King's, Southsea, Apr., 1938, Achmed Rotha in "Lady With Designs"; Garrick, June, 1938, Count Nikolaus von Ahlenfeld in "Trumpeter, Play!"; "Q.," Nov., 1938, Charles Petrie in "Strange Family"; Garrick, Jan., 1939, Skimpy in "Hundreds and Thousands"; toured, Apr., 1939, as Ben in "No. 17"; "Q," Aug., 1939, Mr. Freeman in "The Fanatics"; Golder's Green, June, 1941, Lord Muckleton in "No Name in the Visitors' Book"; Grand, Blackpool, Apr., 1942, Chief-Inspector Silence in "Inspector Silence Takes the Air"; Lyric, Hammersmith, Sept., 1944, Mr. Munce in "Jane Clegg"; Theatre Royal, Brighton, Sept., 1945,. Sir Henry Bryce in "Thirteen to the Gallows"; lessee and manager of Wyndham's Theatre from 1927–29; Royalty, 1930–32; Garrick, 1932–33; Playhouse, 1933–35; in addition to producing the plays in which he has appeared since 1918, has also produced since 1925, "Cristilinda," 1925; "The Fanatics," "The One-Eye'd Herring," "Meet the Wife," "The Lady-in-Law," 1927; "Two White Arms," "The Stranger in the House," "Many Waters," "Napoleon's Josephine," "To What Red Hell," "The Love-Lorn Lady," 1928; "Living Together," "Mariners" (with Lewis Casson), "Exiled," "The Skin Game," 1929; "Bandits," "Street Scene," 1930; "The World of Light," "Black Magic," 1931; "While Parents Sleep," "Hocus-Pocus," "The Bear Dances," 1932; produced "The Holmses of Baker Street," "Beggars in Hell," "So Good! So Kind!!" "Night Club Queen," 1933; "The Big House," "Libel," 1934; "C.I.D.," "Hurricane," series of Galsworthy plays, 1935; "My Son's My Son," 1936; "Awake and Sing," "Trumpeter, Play!" 1938; "Hundreds and Thousands," 1939; "It Happened in September," 1942; went to America, 1929, to produce "Many Waters"; from 1918–39, had presented seventy plays at various theatres; in 1928, was invited by the French Government to represent Great Britain at the International Festival in Paris, and produced "Justice" and "Loyalties," at the Odéon Theatre; was made a Chevalier of the Legion of Honour, 1928; has appeared in films, in "The Chinese Puzzle," "No. 17," etc.; author and adaptor (in collaboration with Tom Gallon) of "The Man Who Stole the Castle" and "The Touch of the Child"; of "Love's Comedy" (with Frederick Sargent), "Filby the Fakir," "The Crook," and (with Malcolm Cherry) of "Mr. Jarvis," and "Jack o' Jingles"; "Playing the Game" (with Austin Phillips); "The Creole," "The King Who Had Nothing to Learn," "The Hanging Judge," "Felix

Gets a Month" (with Tom Gallon); "Pistols for Two" (with Gallon), "The Chinese Puzzle" (with Marian Bower), "The Altar of Liberty" (with Marian Bower), "The Balance" (with Frank Dix); "Blinkers" (with H. A. Vachell); "In the Snare" (with Rafael Sabatini), "The Capital Crime" (with Basil Mitchell), "Hundreds and Thousands" (with Sarah Benedict Tapping), "No Name in the Visitors' Book" (with L. E. Jones), etc. Clubs: Authors' and Savage.
(Died 28 Mar., 1947; age 68)

LIPMAN, Clara, actress and dramatic author; b. Chicago, 6 Dec., 1869; d. of Abraham Lipman and his wife Josephine; made her first appearance on the stage at Niblo's Gardens, New York, 30 Nov., 1885, as Nettie in "The Rat-catcher," subsequently played in "Odette" in Madame Modjeska's company; at the Bijou, New York, 22 Feb., 1892, appeared as Molly Somers in "Incog."; at Hermann's Theatre, New York, 3 Dec., 1892, played Madge in "Little Tippett"; and at Palmer's, May, 1895, appeared as Saffa in "The Viking"; at the Standard, New York, 2 Dec., 1895, played Clara Loveridge in "The Strange Adventures of Miss Brown," subsequently succeeding to the leading part of Angela Brightwell; at Herald Square, Dec., 1896, played Julie Bon-Bon in "The Girl from Paris"; "The Telephone Girl," at the Casino, in 1897; "The Girl in the Barracks," at the Garrick, New York, 1899; "All on Account of Eliza," same theatre, 1900; "The Red Kloof," at the Savoy, 1901, and "Julie Bon-Bon," at Field's, 1906; made her first appearance in London at the Waldorf Theatre, 26 Nov., 1906, in the title-rôle of "Julie Bon-Bon;" after a three years absence, reappeared on the stage at Atlantic City, Dec., 1909, in "Marjorie's Mother"; at the Hackett Theatre, New York, Aug., 1910, played Simone La Fee in "The Marriage of a Star"; after many years absence from the stage, reappeared at the Ritz, Mar., 1927, as Nina de Poulet in "That French Lady"; is the author of "Pepi," and "Julie Bon-

Bon"; of "The Italian Girl," in collaboration with Edward Freiberger; and, with Samuel Shipman, of "Elevating a Husband," 1911; "Children of To-Day," 1913; "Two Sweethearts," "Over Here," "Work for Uncle Sam," "Nature's Nobleman," etc. *Address :* Montrose-on-the-Hudson, N.Y., U.S.A.

LIPSCOMB, William Percy, dramatic author; *b.* Merton, Surrey, 1887; *m.* Florence Taub; has written the following plays; "Three," "Persecuting Peter," "The Synthetic Virgin" (with L. du Garde Peach), 1933; "Clive of India" (with R. J. Minney), 1934; "Thank You, Mr. Pepys" (adaptation), 1937; "The Gay Pavilion," 1945; at the Shaftesbury, Jan., 1938, played King Charles II in "Thank You, Mr. Pepys"; wrote the scenarios for the following films: "Jack's the Boy," "The Faithful Heart," "The Man from Toronto," "Good Companions," "I Was a Spy," "Clive of India," "Richelieu," "Les Miserables," "A Tale of Two Cities," "A Message to Garcia," "Under Two Flags," "Lloyd's of London," "The Garden of Allah," etc.; author of the film "Channel Crossing"; wrote and directed the production of the films, "Captain Blood," "Under Two Flags," etc. *Recreation :* Tennis. *Club :* Savage. *(Died 24 July, 1958; age 70)*

LIPTON, Celia, actress and vocalist; *b.* Edinburgh, Scotland, 25 Dec., 1923; *d.* of Sydney John Lipton and his wife Marion Johnston (Parker); *e.* St. Joseph's Convent, Hendon, and Park Lodge, Surbiton; *m.* Victor Farris; studied for the stage at the Royal Academy of Dramatic Art, and singing under Professor Cunelli; made her first appearance on the stage at the Palladium, 1939, singing with her father's orchestra, and she continued to do so, 1939–40; next appeared as a single turn in variety, June, 1941; Palladium, July, 1941, appeared in "Apple Sauce"; London Hippodrome, Nov., 1941, played Celia in "Get a Load of This," which she played for fifteen months; toured for E.N.S.A., entertaining troops, 1942; toured, May, 1943, in "The Old Town Hall," and July, 1943, in "Skylarks";

King's, Hammersmith, Dec., 1943, played Jack in "Jack and Jill"; toured, Feb., 1944, as Peter in "Peter Pan"; London Coliseum, May, 1944, scored a big success when she appeared as Prudence in the revival of "The Quaker Girl," and again played the part at the Stoll, Feb., 1945; at the Scala, Dec., 1945, appeared as Peter in "Peter Pan"; Casino, Dec., 1946, played Colin in "Mother Goose"; His Majesty's, Feb., 1949, Lili in "Lilac Time"; made her first appearance in New York at the National, 18 Feb., 1953, as Sybil Tenterdon in "Maggie"; at the Imperial, Dec., 1953, appeared in the *revue* "Almanac"; first appeared in films, 1939, in "Old Mother Riley in Society." *Recreations :* Dancing, swimming, tennis, skating, reading. *Address :* 57 Bryanston Court, George St., W.1. *Telephone No.:* Paddington 3543.

LISLE, Lucille, actress; *b.* Melbourne, Victoria, Australia; *e.* St. Vincent's College, Sydney, N.S.W.; *m.* Nicholas Harris; made her first appearance on the stage, as a child, at the Princess Theatre, Melbourne, 1916, as a dancer in the pantomime of "Dick Whittington"; after she had grown up, appeared in several productions under the management of J. C. Williamson, Ltd., notably as Phyllis in "Old English," Anne Hall in "Cradle Snatchers," in which she toured for a year; for nearly twelve months, 1928–9, toured with Maurice Moscovitch, with whom she appeared as T'Mala in "The Silent House"; she also played in "Saturday's Children" and "Baby Cyclone," under Sir Benjamin Fuller, and went to the United States in 1930, and made her first appearance in New York, at the Empire Theatre, 6 Oct., 1930, as Bertina Farmer in "Stepdaughters of War"; Times Square, Dec., 1930, played Stephano in "The Merchant of Venice"; subsequently toured for six months as Sonia in "Art and Mrs. Bottle," with Jane Cowl; Cort Theatre, Nov., 1931, played the Harkness Girl in "A Widow in Green"; Playhouse, New York, Mar., 1932, Leonora Dunbar in "Alice Sit-by-the-Fire"; went to London at the end of 1932,

1500

and made her first appearance, at the Lyric, Jan., 1933, succeeding Edna Best as Stella Hallam in "Another Language," which she also subsequently played at the Playhouse, Liverpool; at the St. James's, May, 1933, played Susan Haggett in "The Late Christopher Bean," which ran for fifteen months, subsequently touring in the same part; on returning to London, appeared at the Little Theatre, Dec., 1934, as Silver Stream in "Lady Precious Stream," which she played throughout 1935; Arts, May, 1936, Janetta Smith in "An Apple a Day"; Whitehall, July, 1936, succeeded Jessica Tandy as Anna in "Anthony and Anna," which she played until 1938; Aldwych (for Repertory Players), Mar.,1938, Daphne in "Marcia Gets Her Own Back"; Vaudeville, June, 1938, Vera Brender in "Sexes and Sevens"; Phoenix, Dec., 1938, Maria in "Twelfth Night"; Aldwych (for Repertory Players), Jan., 1939, Theresa in "Juggernaut"; "Q," Feb., 1939, Ann Mortimer in "Stolen Time"; Richmond, Apr., 1939, Margot Grey in "Behind the Curtain"; subsequently, during July–Aug., 1939, at Birmingham and Glasgow, played lead in a repertory of Shaw's plays; toured, 1940, in "Find the Lady"; joined the B.B.C. repertory company, Oct., 1940, with which she continued for five years; at the Garrison Theatre, Salisbury, Oct., 1945, played Lydia Languish in "The Rivals"; was engaged with the B.B.C. Repertory Company from Jan., 1946 to Nov., 1949; has since broadcast in various programmes. *Recreations:* Books and motoring. *Club:* Arts Theatre. *Address:* Flat 15, De Walden Court, 85 New Cavendish Street, London, W.1. *Telephone No.:* Museum 9271.

LISTER, Eve, actress and singer; *b.* Brighton, 12 Dec., 1918; *d.* of Philip George Watson and his wife Lillian (Terry); *e.* Girton House School and Clarence House School, Hove; *m.* (1) Hugh French (mar. dis.); (2) Bernard Hunter; studied for the stage under Dorothy Kennard and Gladys Toye; made her first appearance on the stage, as a child dancer, at the Grand Theatre, Brighton, in panto-

mime; first appeared on the London stage, at the Adelphi Theatre, 16 Sept., 1932, as one of C. B. Cochran's young ladies, in "Words and Music"; His Majesty's, May, 1933, played Sieglinde Lessing in "Music in the Air"; appeared in films, 1934–8, also playing principal girl in pantomimes at the New Theatre, Oxford, 1935, and Streatham Hill, 1937; appeared in South Africa, 1938–9, as Morgiana in the pantomime, "Aladdin"; played four summer seasons in "Half-Past Eight," at the Lyceum, Edinburgh, and the King's, Glasgow, 1941–4, under the management of Howard and Wyndham; toured, 1944, as Nan in "A Country Girl," and 1945, in "Happy Birthday"; at the Stoll, Aug., 1945, appeared in the *revue,* "For Crying Out Loud"; toured, 1946, as Gabrielle Girard in "The Lisbon Story"; Prince's Theatre, July, 1947, played Mai Cha in "The Nightingale"; Casino, Dec., 1947, Prince Charming in "Cinderella"; toured, 1948, as Sonia in "The Merry Widow," and 1949, as Sari Linden in "Bitter Sweet"; His Majesty's, Nov., 1950, played Anita Gunn in "Blue for a Boy," which ran for over eighteen months; Princes, May, 1953, played Yolande in "Happy As a King"; Drury Lane, May, 1955, succeeded Valerie Hobson as Anna in "The King and I"; Bournemouth Pavilion, Aug., 1956, again played this last part; toured, 1960, as Katherine in "The Pleasure of His Company"; has played Principal Boy in pantomimes, since 1941, at Sheffield, Coventry, Bournemouth, Manchester, Birmingham, Oxford, Golder's Green, and Streatham Hill. *Recreations:* Decorating, sewing and travel. *Hobby:* Collecting antiques. *Address:* 2 Blithfield Street, Kensington, London, W.8. *Telephone No.:* Western 2891.

LISTER, Francis, actor; *b.* London, 2 Apr., 1899; *s.* of the late Frank Lister, actor, and his wife Clara (Cissy Farrell): *m.* (1) Nora Swinburne (mar. dis.); (2) Margot Grahame (mar. dis.); was a pupil at the Academy of Dramatic Art; made his first appearance on the stage at the Haymarket; 28 Nov., 1914, in a revival of "The Flag Lieutenant"; next appeared at the

Court, Mar., 1916, as Lieut. Delmann in "Kultur at Home"; at the Empire, Finsbury Park, July, 1916, played Lieut. Standidge in "Lord and Lady Algy"; Apollo, Dec., 1916, Harry Marsland in "The Private Secretary"; he then served two years in the R.H. and R.F.A.; after demobilization, in 1919, toured with Louis Calvert, as Winfield Gribble in "Bo'sun 'Enry," and Thomas Craigie in "Daddalums"; at Wyndham's, June, 1920, appeared as Thomas in "Daddalums"; at the Garrick, Nov., 1920, played Valentine in "You Never Can Tell"; at the Aldwych, Jan., 1921, Ferdinand in "The Tempest"; at the Comedy, Apr., 1921, Egerton Chilton, in "A Matter of Fact"; June, 1921, Guy Herringhame in "A Family Man"; at the Strand, Jan., 1922, Geoffrey Cranford in "Old Jig"; at the Royalty, Apr., 1922, Ned Mason in "If Four Walls Told"; at the Duke of York's, Aug., 1922, Philip Marvin in "The Broken Wing"; at the Apollo, Dec., 1922, Dennis, Viscount Roxton, in "Hawley's of the High Street"; at the Ambassadors', Apr., 1923, Quintin Coombes in "Trespasses"; at the Belasco Theatre, New York, Sept., 1923, Geoffrey in "Mary, Mary, Quite Contrary"; on returning to London, appeared at the Apollo, Mar., 1924, as Clifford Hope in "The Fake"; at the Shaftesbury, Apr., 1924, as Robert Bassett in "A Perfect Fit"; at the St. Martin's, June, 1924, played James Godfrey in "In the Next Room"; at the Queen's, Dec., 1924, Raymond de Mericourt in "Orange Blossom"; Vaudeville, Mar., 1925, Emmett Carr in "Tarnish"; Globe, Sept., 1925, Nigel Gerrard in "Beginner's Luck"; Nov., 1925, Freddie Maynard in "Lullaby"; Mar., 1926, Stephen Meynell in "By-Ways"; Adelphi, May, 1926, Bob Holden in "Aloma"; St. Martin's, Aug., 1926, Sabien in "The Queen Was In the Parlour"; Apollo, Nov., 1927, Christian in "Cyrano de Bergerac"; during 1928 appeared with Margaret Bannerman in Australia, in "Our Betters," "Diplomacy," "Other Men's Wives," etc.; reappeared in London, Wyndham's, Dec., 1928, as Larry Tindall in "The Love-Lorn Lady"; Haymarket, Feb.,

1929, played Valentine Brown in "Quality Street"; Apr., 1929, King Perivale in "The Ivory Door"; May, 1929, Harry and Simon Blake in "Mary Rose"; Globe, Sept., 1929, John Ashley in "The Bachelor Father"; went to New York, and appeared at the Empire, Feb., 1930, as the Marquess of Farnborough in "Dishonored Lady"; on returning to London, at the Lyric, Aug., 1930, played Townley Town in "Let Us Be Gay"; Whitehall, Feb., 1931, Major Cunningham in "Good Losers"; July, 1931, the Hon. Archibald Burton in "Take a Chance"; St. Martin's, Dec., 1931, Richard Fayre in "The Nelson Touch"; Wyndham's, Sept., 1932, Peter Destinn in "The Way to the Stars"; New, Feb., 1933, Robert de Vere in "Richard of Bordeaux"; went to America, 1934, and at the Empire, New York, Feb., 1934, appeared in the same part; at the Strand, London, Apr., 1934, succeeded Owen Nares as Robert Van Bret in "Double Door"; returned to New York, and at the Broadhurst, Sept., 1934, played Baron Fernand Cassini and Eugéne Charlier in "The Red Cat"; Ethel Barrymore, Oct., 1935, John in "Substitute for Murder"; Queen's, Sept., 1936, Charles Hastings in "Follow Your Saint"; rejoined Royal Artillery, 1939, with rank of Captain; invalided out of Army, Apr., 1942; reappeared on the stage, at the Piccadilly, July, 1942, as Macduff in "Macbeth"; at the Cambridge, Mar., 1943, played Randall Utterwood in "Heartbreak House"; joined John Gielgud's repertory company at the Haymarket, Oct., 1944, and played Horatio in "Hamlet," and Jan., 1945, Demetrius in "A Midsummer Night's Dream"; toured in Germany, 1945, as Cassius in "Julius Caesar"; Torch, Nov., 1946, James VI of Scotland in "The Wisest Fool"; New Lindsey, Dec., 1946, George Buchanan in "High Horse"; "Q," Apr., 1947, Nevil Kingsley in "Quiet in the Forest"; Criterion, June, 1947, Dr. Marshall in "A Sleeping Clergyman"; Wyndham's, Oct., 1947, Fergus Crampton in "You Never Can Tell"; Criterion, Feb., 1948, Henry Aspen in "The Indifferent Shepherd"; St. James's,

Sept., 1948, Daniel Bachelet in "Don't Listen, Ladies!"; Phoenix, Jan., 1950, Major Sanderson in "The Non-Resident"; Vaudeville, May, 1950, Jan Daubek in "The Ivory Tower"; commenced film career, 1929, and has appeared in numerous pictures. *Clubs:* Savage, Green Room, and Garrick. *(Died 28 Oct., 1951: age 52)*

LISTER, Frank, actor; *b.* Calverley, Yorks., 26 July, 1868; *s.* of John Lister; *m.* Cissy Farrell; *e.* privately; was originally engaged in commerce in the City, but made his first appearance on the stage at the Victoria Opera House, Burnley, 1890, as Tiny Spurts and a Chinaman in "The New Babylon," with the late Clarence Holt; made his first appearance on the London stage at the Surrey Theatre, in 1891, in "The English Rose," and remained a member of the "stock" company at that house for several years; for five years was a member of the Pavilion Theatre company, and played many leading parts at several suburban theatres, including Cyrus Blenkarn in "The Middleman," Bob Brierley in "The Ticket of Leave Man," Job Armroyd in "Lost in London," etc.; at the Scala Theatre, 1906, played Napoleon in "A Royal Divorce"; other West End engagements have been with George Grossmith at the old Globe; with the late Isaac Cohen at the Princess's; with Murray Carson at the Apollo and Avenue, etc.; re-appeared as Napoleon in "A Royal Divorce," at the Lyceum, July, 1911; at the Duke of York's, June, 1913, played the Chorus in "The Yellow Jacket"; at the Lyceum, Sept., 1914, played Private Mason in a revival of "Tommy Atkins"; Nov., 1914, Colonel Graham in "The Soldier's Wedding"; Mar., 1915, Napoleon in a revival of "A Royal Divorce"; has played in the principal music halls since 1907, with his own sketch company, in "No. 99," and "The Sundowner"; has played in many pantomimes, both in London and the provinces. *Favourite part:* Cyrus Blenkarn in "The Middleman." *Recreations:* Cricket and golf. *Clubs:* Honor Oak Park Golf Club and Surrey County Cricket Club. *(Died 29 July, 1917; age 49)*

LISTER, Lance (*né* Solomon Lancelot Inglis Watson), actor; *b.* 1901; first appeared on the stage in 1916, when he toured as David Playne in "Betty"; at the St. James's, 7 June, 1917, played Geoffrey Holdsworth in "Sheila"; at the Strand, Oct., 1917, Leicester Boyd in "Wild Heather"; from 1917–19 toured the provinces as Hughie Cavanagh in "The Boy"; at the Comedy, June, 1920, appeared as Dallis Mortimer in "The 'Ruined' Lady," subsequently touring in the same part; in 1920 went to Australia and again played Hughie in "The Boy," subsequently, in 1921, toured there with Joseph Coyne, playing in "Nightie Night," "Wedding Bells," "His Lady Friends"; at the Duke of York's, London, Feb., 1924, played in "London Calling"; London Pavilion, Apr., 1925, in "On With the Dance"; Nov., 1925, "Still Dancing"; Apr., 1926, "Cochran's Revue (1926)"; May, 1927, "One Dam Thing After Another"; May, 1928, "This Year of Grace"; Mar., 1929, "Wake Up and Dream"; went to New York, and at the Selwyn Theatre, Dec., 1929, played in "Wake Up and Dream"; London Hippodrome, Mar., 1931, played the Ship's Officer and Mr. Whitelaw in "Stand Up and Sing"; Gaiety, Oct., 1932, appeared in "After Dinner," which he also produced; Palace, June, 1935, played the Purser in "Anything Goes"; in 1937, directed Collins Music Hall, Islington, as a repertory theatre and for a time directed a repertory season at Margate; toured, 1939, as the Burglar and the Guide in "I can Take It"; toured, 1946, in "Big Ben." *Address:* 3 Coburg Mansions, Handel Street, London, W.C.2.

LITTELL, Robert, dramatic critic; *b.* Milwaukee, Wis., U.S.A., 15 May, 1896; *s.* of Philip Littell and his wife Fanny (Whittemore); *e.* Groton School and Harvard University; *m.* Anita Blaine Damrosch; formerly on the editorial staff of the *New York*

Evening Post; appointed dramatic critic, 1928; acted as dramatic critic of the *New York World*, 1929–31; formerly associate-editor of *The New Republic* and *Readers Digest*; author of "Read America First," "Candles in the Storm" and a play, "Gather Ye Rosebuds" (with Sidney Howard). *Clubs:* Coffee House, Century, Hardware and Harvard. *Address:* 158 East 71st Street, New York City, U.S.A. *Telephone No.:* Butterfield 8–2135.

LITTLEFIELD, Catherine, *première danseuse* and choreographer; *b.* Philadelphia, Pa., U.S.A., 16 Sept., 1904; *d.* of Caroline Littlefield, dancer; *m.* Sterling Noel; studied under her mother and also received tuition from Luigi Albertieri, Staats, and Lubov Egorova; made her first appearance on the stage at the New Amsterdam Theatre, New York, 22 Dec., 1920, in Florenz Ziegfeld's production of "Sally"; subsequently danced at the Earl Carroll, Dec., 1923, in "Kid Boots"; Times Square, Nov., 1924, in "Annie Dear"; Cosmopolitan, Mar., 1925, in "Louie the XIV"; in 1925, joined the Philadelphia Civic Opera company, as *première danseuse*, and was with the Philadelphia Grand Opera company, 1926–33, in a similar capacity; also produced the ballets in many of the operas presented; founded the Littlefield Ballet, in Oct., 1935, which, in 1936, became the Philadelphia Ballet company; made her first appearance in London, at the London Hippodrome, with her company, 15 June, 1937, in "Barn Dance," "Moment Romantique," and "Terminal"; subsequently she appeared there in "Bolero," "Fête Champêtre," "Fairy Doll," etc.; has devised the choreography for more than 20 ballets; in 1940, appeared at the New York World's Fair in "American Jubilee"; devised many numbers for "It Happens on Ice," 1940; "Hats Off to Ice," 1944; "Follow the Girls," 1944; "The Firebrand of Florence," 1945. (*Died 19 Nov., 1951; age 47*)|

LITTLER, Blanche, manager; *b.* Ramsgate, Kent, 26 Dec., 1899; *d.* of F. R. Littler and his wife Agnes; *m.* (Sir) George Robey (dec.); from the age of sixteen was engaged in business management, at the Royal Artillery Theatre, Woolwich, of which her parents were the Lessees; managing director of Blanche Littler Productions, Ltd.; with her brother, was joint managing director of Prince Littler Theatres and Tours, Ltd.; their first production was the tour of "The Best People," 1927, from which date they were responsible for tours of "The Silent House," "Oh, Kay!," "Lido Lady," "The Farmer's Wife," "Yellow Sands," "Bird in Hand," "Evensong," "Jolly Roger," "White Horse Inn," etc.; at the Alhambra, 1934, revived "The Bing Boys Are Here"; toured "Glamorous Night," 1935; presented the pantomime "Jack and the Beanstalk," Drury Lane, 1935 and "Cinderella" at the London Coliseum, 1937; toured in Australia, 1939, with her husband; on returning to England, assisted at concerts for the troops, and in war-savings campaign; has toured various plays and *revues*, also presented many suburban and provincial pantomimes; in association with Star Theatricals, Ltd., presented "She Wanted a Cream Front Door," Apollo, 1947. *Recreations:* Cooking, and collecting miniatures. *Address:* 3 King's Gardens, Hove, Sussex.

LITTLER, Prince, C.B.E., theatre proprietor and producing manager; *b.* Ramsgate, Kent, 25 July, 1901; *s.* of F. R. Littler and his wife Agnes; *e.* Stratford-on-Avon; *m.* Nora Delany; for some years resident manager of the Royal Artillery Theatre, Woolwich, of which his parents were the lessees; joined the board of New Theatre, Cambridge, 1927, and was appointed Managing-Director, 1930; Aug., 1931, purchased Opera House, Leicester, and Theatre Royal, Leicester, and appointed Managing-Director, Oct., 1931; purchased the New Theatre, Cardiff, 1935, and Prince of Wales's, Cardiff, 1936; acquired the lease of the Prince's, Manchester, 1937; was the lessee of the New Theatre Royal, Norwich, 1939; with his sister Blanche, revived "The Bing Boys Are Here," Alhambra, 1934; has been responsible for provincial tours of numerous well-known plays, including "The Best People," "Lido Lady," "Baby Cyclone," "The Farmer's Wife," "Yellow Sands," "Bird in Hand," "Oh! Kay," "The Barretts of Wimpole Street," "White Horse Inn," "Glamorous Night," "Music in the Air," "The Frog," "Careless Rapture," "George and Margaret," "Banana Ridge," "Quiet Wedding," "Goodbye, Mr. Chips," "Number Six," etc.; has presented over 200 pantomimes in the provinces, and presented "Jack and the Beanstalk" at Drury Lane, 1935, and "Cinderella" at the London Coliseum, 1936, and at the Princes, 1937; also at the Coliseum, June, 1936, presented "Glamorous Night"; has since presented "White Horse Inn" (revival), Coliseum, 1940; "It's Foolish But It's Fun," Coliseum, 1943; "Show Boat" (revival), Stoll, 1943; "Pacific 1860," Drury Lane, 1946; "The Farmer's Wife" (revival), Apollo, 1947; "Brigadoon," His Majesty's, 1949; "Wild Violets" (revival), Stoll, 1950; "Carousel," Drury Lane, 1950; "Rainbow Square," Stoll, 1951; he has since presented or co-presented the following: "Guys and Dolls," Coliseum, 1953; "Teahouse of the August Moon," Her Majesty's, 1954; "Can-Can," Coliseum, 1954; "The Pajama Game," Coliseum, 1955; "Plain and Fancy," Drury Lane, 1956; "No time for sergeants," Her Majesty's, 1956; joined Board of Stoll Theatres Corporation, Ltd., in Mar., 1942, and appointed Chairman and Managing Director of that company and its subsidiaries in May, 1942; appointed Chairman and Managing Director of Associated Theatre Properties (London), Ltd., and subsidiaries, Jan., 1943; became Chairman and Managing Director of Theatre Royal, Drury Lane, Ltd., 1944;

Director of Moss Empires Ltd., 1945, and Director of Howard & Wyndham, Ltd., 1945; in 1947 became Chairman of Moss Empires, Ltd.; is a member of the Council of the Theatrical Managers' Association; Vice-President of the Society of West End Theatre Managers; Past President of the Denville Home for Aged Actors and Actresses; and Vice-President of the Variety Artistes' Benevolent Fund; Member of the South Bank Theatre and Opera House Board; received the honour of Commander of the British Empire in the New Year Honours, 1957. *Hobbies:* Farming: breeding pedigree Guernsey dairy cattle and Sussex cattle. *Address:* Cranbourn Mansions, Cranbourn Street, London, W.C.2. *Telephone No.:* 01-437 2274.

LITTLEWOOD, Samuel Robinson, dramatic critic; *b.* Bath, 27 Feb., 1875; *y. s.* of Rev. W. E. Littlewood and his wife Lætitia (Thornton); *e.* Merchant Taylors', Dover College, and St. Paul's School, London; *m.* Phœbe Stella, *d.* of Edwin Cooper Hayes, solicitor, of Dublin; dramatic critic of *Morning Leader*, 1897–1903; *Daily Chronicle*, 1904–14; *The Referee*, 1915; *Lady's Pictorial*, 1915–21; *Pall Mall Gazette*, 1915–22; *Pioneer*, 1919–30; *Morning Post*, 1927–37; was also dramatic critic for the B.B.C. during 1935; film critic, *Referee*, 1928–32; editor of *The Stage*, 1943–52; contributor of articles on theatrical matters to *The Fortnightly Review*, *The Bookman, Drama*, and also to other papers; is the author of " The Story of Pierrot," " Perrault's Fairy Tales," " The Story of Santa Claus," " The Fairies—Here and Now," " The Child of the Sea," " Valentine and Orson," " Elizabeth Inchbald and Her Circle," "Dramatic Criticism," etc.; was Honorary Secretary of the Critics' Circle, 1913–22, and President, 1923; is a Fellow of the Institute of Journalists, the was Chairman of the London District, 1920 ; is a well-known authority on Shakespeare, and has frequently lectured on the poet and his works. *Clubs:* Savage, and Green Room. *(Died 10 Aug., 1963; age 88)*

LIVERIGHT, Horace B., producing manager and publisher; *b.* Osceola Mills, Pa., U.S.A., 10 Dec., 1886; *s.* of Henry Liveright and his wife Henrietta (Fleisher); *e.* Philadelphia; *m.* (1) Lucile Elsas; (2) Elise Bartlett (mar. dis.); has produced the following plays: " The Firebrand " (with Schwab and Mandel), 1924; " Hamlet " (in modern dress), 1925; " Black Boy," and " An American Tragedy," 1926;

" Rapid Transit," " Dracula," and " The Dagger and the Rose," 1927; is president of the firm of Horace Liveright, publishers, and has published many notable books and plays. *Address :* 31 West 47th Street, New York City, U.S.A. *Telephcne No. :* Bryant 9–5860.

(Died 24 Sept., 1933; age 49)

LIVESEY, Barrie, actor; *b.* 16 Oct., 1904; *s.* of Sam Livesey and his wife Mary Catherine (Edwards); *e.* Westminster City School; *m.* Blanche Locke; appeared at the Apollo. 21 Sept., 1921, as Cuthbert in "Crooked Usage"; Royalty, Nov., 1921, played Herbert in "The Resurrection of David Grant"; Duke of York's, Mar., 1926, Theodore Kirton in "Life Goes On"; Piccadilly, Apr., 1928, Captain Pickering in "Blue Eyes"; Drury Lane, Apr., 1929, Fouchet in "The New Moon"; Sept., 1929, Emil La Flamme in "Rose Marie"; Criterion, Dec., 1929, Douglas Cattermole in "The Private Secretary," playing the same part at the Apollo, Dec., 1930; Phoenix, Jan., 1931, Michael in "Frailties"; 49th Street, New York, Nojd in "The Father" and Dering in "Barbara's Wedding"; Queen's, Apr., 1932, Fritz Kling in "Caravan"; Westminster, Nov., 1932, Graham Anderson in "Follow Me"; Old Vic., Mar., 1934, Valentine Legend in "Love for Love"; Piccadilly, Aug., 1934, Captain Alan Harley in "Queer Cargo"; Phoenix, Mar., 1935, Josh Blain in "Glory Be ——"; His Majesty's, Dec., 1935, Count Battly in "A Royal Exchange"; Comedy, Dec., 1936, Frank Crutchley in "Busman's Honeymoon"; Fortune, June, 1938, Jackson in "White Secrets"; Winter Garden, Oct., 1938, Peter Derrick in "Behind the Blinds"; toured, 1940, as Archie Leadenhall in "Full House," and subsequently, as Appius in "Family Portrait"; Stoll, Oct., 1944, Michael O'Rourke in "The Lisbon Story"; Granville, Dec., 1945, Black Dog and George Merry in "Treasure Island," and Jan., 1946, Jack Kurton in "The Third Visitor"; Aldwych, July, 1946, played Jimmy Martin in "Dear Murderer"; Whitehall, Dec.,

1946, Black Dog and George Merry in "Treasure Island,"and again appeared in these parts at the Fortune, Dec., 1948.

LIVESEY, E. Carter, actor and sketch artist; *b.* Wolverhampton; had nearly fifteen years' experience on the dramatic stage before making his first appearance on the variety stage, in July, 1905, when, in conjunction with Lilian Rosebery, he appeared in the sketch, " The Would-be Actors "; appeared in this sketch in many of the leading London and provincial halls, and has since appeared in " An Amateur Anarchist," etc.

LIVESEY, Jack, actor; *b.* Barry, South Wales, 11 June, 1901; *s.* of Sam Livesey and his wife Mary Catherine (Edwards); *e.* London, and Barry County School; *m.* Eileen Lovett-Janison; made his first appearance on the stage at Tottenham, Sept., 1916, as a miner in "Tiger's Cub"; in 1917, toured in Sir George Alexander's company in "The Aristocrat"; first appeared in the West End, at the Savoy, 22 Oct., 1917, as Harry Marsland in "The Private Secretary"; several minor engagements followed; at the Duke of York's, May, 1921, played Geoffrey Hudson in "The Tartan Peril"; next toured in "The Knave of Diamonds"; toured in India with the Maurice Bandmann repertory company; played a season at the Old Vic., and toured in "Kissing Time"; Dec., 1922, toured in South Africa in "Partners Again" and " Welcome Stranger "; on returning to England, Aug., 1923, toured in "Partners Again," for forty weeks; Aug., 1924, toured as the Detective in " Katja the Dancer," and appeared in the same part at the Gaiety, Feb., 1925; during the eighteen months run of this play he also appeared at different times as Prince Carl and Leander; during 1926, toured as Det.-Inspector Wembury in "The Ringer"; went to America, and made his first appearance in New York, at the Fulton Theatre, 10 Sept., 1927, as Arthur Varwell in "Yellow Sands"; Oct., 1927–May, 1928, toured in America, as Robert

Phelps in "The Silver Cord"; returned to London, and appeared at the Strand, July, 1928, as Carl Behrend in "The Enemy"; at Shaftesbury, Dec., 1928 played Lord Arthur Madderley in "The Lad"; Drury Lane, Feb., 1929, Steve in "Show-Boat"; Apr., 1929, Captain Georges Duval in "The New Moon"; Sept., 1929, Edward Hawley in the revival of "Rose-Marie"; Mar., 1930, Athos in "The Three Musketeers," and in Sept., 1930, succeeded Dennis King as D'Artagnan; Haymarket, Jan., 1931, played Vandenberg in "Colonel Satan"; Fortune, June, 1931, George Norwood in "The Ship"; Lyceum, Aug., 1931, Wembury in "The Ringer"; "Q," Dec., 1931, Robin Hood in the play of that name; Arts, Jan., 1932, Paul Tanner in "Avalanche"; Criterion, Apr., 1932, Geoffrey Preston in "Musical Chairs"; Arts, Apr., 1932, Bill Grube in "The Mews"; Phoenix (for Repertory Players), Dec., 1932, Malcolm Praed in "Earthquake in Surrey"; Little, Feb., 1933, Richard Lane in "Cock Robin"; Alhambra, Mar., 1934, Bassanio in "The Merchant of Venice"; Ambassadors', Aug, 1934, Harvey in "Family Affairs"; Strand, Apr., 1936, Oxley Pugh-Jones in "Baby Austin"; Savoy, Apr., 1936, Hseih-Ping-Kuei in "Lady Precious Stream"; Little, Oct., 1936, the Parasite and Commander of the Ants in "The Insect Play"; Little, Nov., 1936, again played in "Lady Precious Stream"; Prince's, July, 1937, Jack Rendall in "The Gusher"; "Q," Jan., 1938, Edward Bell in "The Prodigal Mother"; toured, Feb., 1939, in "The Bowery Touch"; Kingsway, Dec., 1939, played Hseih-Ping-Kuei in "Lady Precious Stream"; Duke of York's, July, 1940, Dr. Jimmie Galen in "High Temperature"; London Hippodrome, June, 1943, and Stoll, Oct., 1944, David Warren in "The Lisbon Story"; "Q," May, 1946, and toured from June, 1946, as Rawdon Crawley in "Vanity Fair," appearing in this part at the Comedy, Oct., 1946; Torch, Oct., 1948, played Dr. Erasmus Baring in "Breach of Marriage"; Plymouth, N.Y., Oct., 1956, played Nicobar in "The Apple Cart"; Lyceum, Oct., 1957, played Colonel Redfern in "Look Back in

Anger"; has also played in numerous films; American citizen, since 1958. *Favourite part:* D'Artagnan. *Recreations:* Cricket and golf.
(Died 12 Oct., 1961; age 60)

LIVESEY, Sam, actor; *b.* Flintshire, 14 Oct.. 1873; *s.* of Thomas Carter Livesey and his wife Mary; *m.* Cassie Edwards; made his first appearance on the stage as an infant of nine months, being carried on by his father in an old play entitled "The Sea" on 17 July, 1874; has spent all his life on the stage; at the age of sixteen toured in such parts as Hamlet, Othello, Richard III, Ingomar, etc.; for many years toured the provinces in melodrama, playing leading parts in "The Shaughraun," "The Black Flag," "The Still Alarm," "The Span of Life," "The King of Crime," etc.; for ten years, with his own company, he toured "The Village Blacksmith"; made his first appearance on the London stage at the Elephant and Castle Theatre, Apr., 1895; first appeared in the West End, at the Court Theatre, 26 Dec., 1912, as Amos Larpent in "Written in Red"; at the Lyceum, Mar., 1913, played Flash Howard in "Nell Gwynne"; at the Aldwych, June, 1914, appeared as Rath Rayne in his own production of "A Heritage of Hate," which he toured for two years; at the Garrick, Jan., 1916, played Hank Bloss ("The Tiger") in "Tiger's Cub"; at the St. James's, Sept., 1917, played Fergusson in "The Pacifists," Gilbert Nepean in "The Liars," and Nov., 1917, John Brown in "Loyalty"; at the Strand, Feb., 1918, Steve Wilson in "Cheating Cheaters"; at the Comedy, Apr., 1918, James Bristol in "The Knife"; at the Lyceum, Oct., 1918; General Grant in "The Female Hun"; at the Globe, Mar., 1919, appeared as Martin Ricardo in "Victory"; at the Haymarket, Sept., 1919, Henry Allen in "Daddies"; at the Apollo, June, 1920, Captain Perkins in "Such a Nice Young Man"; at the Queen's, Sept., 1920, George B. Nettleton in "A Pair of Sixes"; subsequently toured as Ellis Dooley in "Teddy Wants a Wife"; at the Duke of York's, May, 1921, played

James L. Hudson in " The Tartan Peril," and June, 1921, Ritchie in " The Wrong Number " ; at Wyndham's Sept., 1921, played Carl Peterson in " Bull-Dog Drummond," and went to New York in Dec., 1921, to play the same part at the Knickerbocker Theatre ; at the Kingsway, London, Sept., 1922, played Tom Whiteley in " I Serve " ; at the Lyceum, Feb., 1923, Jacques in " The Orphans " ; at Wyndham's, Jan., 1924, Victor Boussat in " The Flame " ; at the Comedy, July, 1924, Oliver Hart in " The Creaking Chair " ; Vaudeville, Jan., 1925, Sir William Jesmond in " Possessions " ; New Oxford, Apr., 1925, Hajj in " Kismet " ; Wyndham's, July, 1925, Cady in " Beggar on Horseback " ; Little, Dec., 1925, Sir Francis Drake in " Gloriana " ; Playhouse, Jan., 1926, Canon Corsellis in " Blind Alley " ; Duke of York's, Mar., 1926, Latimer Newlock in " Life Goes On " ; St. Martin's, May, 1926, Tony in " They Knew What They Wanted " ; Garrick, Sept., 1926, Jim Bailey in " Easy Come, Easy Go " ; Winter Garden, Dec., 1926, Bottom in " A Midsummer Night's Dream " ; Everyman and Duke of York's, Jan., 1927, Sol Cohen in " Lost Property " ; His Majesty's, Feb., 1927, Bud Hildreth in " The Wicked Earl " ; Duke of York's, July, 1927, Dr. Van Helsing in " Dracula " ; New, Aug., 1927, Job in " The Wolves "; Golder's Green, Dec., 1927, Long John Silver in " Treasure Island " ; Winter Garden, Mar., 1928, Inspector Reilly in " The Spider " ; Strand, July, 1928, August Behrend in " The Enemy " ; Garrick, Nov., 1928, Matthew Borlase in " The Runaways " ; Haymarket, Apr., 1929, Bruno in " The Ivory Door " ; Daly's, Oct., 1929, Arthur Pendragon and King Arthur in "A Yankee at the Court of King Arthur"; Playhouse, Feb., 1930, Elias Widecombe in "Devonshire Cream"; Fortune, Nov. 1930, Gabriel Gilwattle in "The Man from Blankley's"; Little, Sept., 1931, the Old Bird-Watcher in "Off the Map"; Lyceum, Oct., 1931; Sir George Grainger in "Sensation", Feb., 1932, toured as the King of Poldavia, in "The Improper Duchess"; New, June, 1932, Duke of Gloucester in " Richard of Bordeaux"; Kingsway,

Oct., 1932, Clemenceau in "Versailles "; " Q," Nov., 1932, Chief Inspector Stanton in "Third Degree"; Ambassadors', Dec., 1932, Gideon Bloodgood in "The Streets of London"; in Sept., 1933, toured as Dan Packard in "Dinner at Eight"; Old Vic., Mar., 1934, Sir Sampson Legend in "Love for Love"; Globe, Apr., 1934, Orrin Kinnicott in "Biography"; "Q," July, 1934, Sam Morley in "Line Engaged"; His Majesty's, Sept., 1934, Barras in "Josephine"; Royalty, Jan., 1935, the Stranger in "Father of Lies"; has appeared in numerous films, including "Zero," "Raise the Roof," "Young Woodley," "The Girl in the Night," "The Hound of the Baskervilles," "The Wickham Mystery," "Dreyfus," "Mr. Bill the Conqueror," "Up for the Cup," "Jealousy," "Many Waters," "The Wonderful Story," "The Shadow," "The Private Life of Henry VIII," "Commissionaire," "Tangled Evidence," "The Great Defender," "Jew Süss," "Drake of England," "Where's George ?," "For the Defence," "Variety," "The Turn of the Tide," etc. *Clubs :* Savage and Stage Golfing Society. *(Died 7 Nov., 1936; age 63)*

LLEWELLYN, Fewlass, actor, producer, and dramatic author; *b.* Hull, 5 Mar., 1866 ; *s.* of Robert Drinkall Jones, builder, and his wife, Isabella (Fewlass) ; *m.* Caroline Sarah Lewis, L.R.A.M., 1898 ; *e.* at Hull ; made his first appearance on the stage at Theatre Royal, Eastbourne, in " The Harbour Lights," Mar., 1890 ; made his first appearance in London, at the Parkhurst Theatre, Holloway, 1891 ; in 1891 toured in " Theodora," and subsequently toured in many plays ; appeared at the Princess's, 1897, in " How London Lives " ; at Wyndham's, 1900, in " Cyrano de Bergerac," " David Garrick," etc. ; appeared at the Garrick, 1900, in " The Wedding Guest," and at Drury Lane, 1902, in " Ben Hur " ; at the Criterion, 1903, played in " The Altar of Friendship " ; subsequent engagements have been, at the Waldorf, 1905, in " Lights Out " ; at the Shaftesbury, 1907, in " The Christian " ; at the Kingsway, 1910, in " Company for

George "; at the Little Theatre, 1911, in " Fanny's First Play," and " Nan "; at the Kingsway, May, 1912, in " The Double Game "; at the Playhouse, July, 1912, played Sir Timothy Farrar in " Hindle Wakes "; at the Savoy, June, 1913, played Signor Tito Castelli in " A Cardinal's Romance "; at the Coronet, Dec., 1913, M. Mafflon in " Woman on Her Own "; at the New, Dec., 1913, Plumber in " The Poor Little Rich Girl "; at the Court, Mar., 1914, Bang in " A King," and the Bishop of Glossop in " The One Thing Needful "; at Wyndham's Theatre, July, 1914, Richard Carstairs in " From 9 to 11 "; Sept., 1914, toured as Alfred Doolittle in " Pygmalion "; at the Kingsway, Feb., 1915, played Robin Gilroy in " Fanny's First Play "; at the New, Apr., 1915, Biedenkopf in " The Joker "; July, 1915, Mr. George Tyler in " Ready Money "; appeared in France, during the war, 1915, in Lena Ashwell's concert party; at the Kingsway, May, 1916, played Colonel Blodwell in " Ye Gods "; at the Haymarket, Mar., 1917, Albert Smith in " General Post "; May, 1918, Mr. Petter in " Uncle Anyhow "; at the Kingsway, Sept., 1918, Professor Carino in " A Week End "; Apr., 1919, Charmis in " Judith "; June, 1919, Farmer John Copplestone in " St. George and the Dragons "; at the St. Martin's, Dec., 1919, played in " Once Upon a Time "; at the Ambassadors', Apr., 1920, John Garforth, M.P., in " The Grain of Mustard Seed "; at the Comedy, Dec., 1920, Homer Johns in " The Charm School "; at the St. Martin's, Feb., 1921, Doctor Crump in " The Wonderful Visit "; Mar., 1921, the Rev. Christopher Pumphrey in " A Bill of Divorcement "; at the St. James's, Nov., 1922, Masrak in " The Beating on the Door "; at the Kingsway Mar., 1923, the Rev. Henry Luttrell in " Love in Pawn "; at the Criterion, Feb., 1924, John Howard in " The Audacious Mr. Squire '; at the Queen's, Sept., 1924, David Cleghorne in " The Claimant "; at the Everyman, Nov., 1924, William Simister in " Clogs to Clogs "; Ambassadors', Mar., 1925, Simon Blaize in " Anyhouse "; Strand, May, 1925, Herbert Bronson in " The

Signal "; " Q " and Royalty, Sept., 1925, Rev. Ben Watkin in " Taffy "; Kingsway, Nov., 1925, Mr. Shadlock in " The Old Adam "; Prince of Wales's, Jan., 1926, Mr. McClellan in " The House of Glass "; at " Q," June-Oct., 1926, played in " For None Can Tell," " The Curate of St. Chad's," and " Children of the Moon "; Apollo, Nov., 1926, Gabriel Bearse in " Shavings "; Comedy, Jan., 1927, Mr. Seed in " The Desperate Lovers "; Globe, July, 1927, Andrew Sparks in " The Village "; Everyman, Sept.-Nov., 1927, played in " A Family Man " and " He Who Gets Slapped "; Wyndham's, Mar., 1928, Pastor Manders in " Ghosts "; Arts, May, 1928, in " For Better, For Worse," and " Six Characters in Search of an Author "; Court, Oct., 1928, Don Victorio in " Fortunato "; Royalty, Mar., 1929, Stephen Alden in ".Afraid of the Dark "; Globe, Sept., 1929, Larkin in " The Bachelor Father "; Criterion, Dec., 1929, Mr. Cattermole in " The Private Secretary "; Ambassadors', Oct., 1930, John Garforth in " The Grain of Mustard Seed "; Arts, May, 1931, Jean Massieu in " The Trial of Jeanne D'Arc "; Savoy, Aug., 1931, Rev. Reginald Rhombard in " Midnight Love "; Duchess, Dec., 1931, Sir Hugh Evans in " The Merry Wives of Windsor "; Kingsway, May, 1932, Mr. Hardcastle in " She Stoops to Conquer "; Lyric, Hammersmith, June, 1932, Dr. Delaney in " Sweet Lavender "; " Q," July, 1932, General Cope-Davis in " Action "; Oct., 1932, Dr. Moody in " Crime on the Hill "; Royalty, Nov., 1932, the Bishop of Annandale in " Playground "; Shaftesbury, Apr., 1933, Dr. Moody in " Crime on the Hill "; Grafton (for the Stage Society), Apr., 1934, The Mayor in " Intermezzo "; Duke of York's, Nov., 1934, Justin Emery in " The Greeks Had a Word for It "; Open Air, Sept., 1935, Holofernes in " Love's Labour's Lost "; His Majesty's, Apr., 1936, the Bishop of St. Aldred's in " The Happy Hypocrite "; Daly's, July, 1937, Rev. Edward Quarterman, S.J., in " The First Legion "; appeared at several London Churches at Easter and Christmas, 1938, in mystery plays; is part-author of " The Coal King,"

"A Gentleman of England," "At Evensong," and other plays; has done considerable work in pastorals, playing among other parts Sir Toby Belch and Bottom; was, for six years, Chairman of The Play Actors' Society; has played in numerous films and since 1936 has appeared in "Jack of All Trades," "On Top of the World," "Good Morning, Boys," "Second Bureau," "A Spot of Bother," "Special Edition," "Brief Ecstasy," "Stormy Weather," "It's a Grand Old World," "Crackerjack," etc., and has done a good deal of work for the British Broadcasting Company. *Club:* Green Room. *(Died 16 June, 1941; age 75)*

LLOYD, Alice, comedienne; *b.* London, 20 Oct., 1873; *d.* of John Wood and his wife, Matilda Mary Caroline (Archer); *e.* London; *m.* Tom MacNaughton; younger sister of Marie Lloyd; made her first appearance on the stage. with her sister, Grace, as the Sisters Lloyd, at the Foresters' Music Hall, 20 Feb., 1888, as duettist and dancer; at Christmas, 1889, appeared at Portsmouth, in pantomime, at Christmas, 1890, appeared at the Grand Theatre, Islington, with her sister, as the Babes in "The Babes in the Wood"; and the following year appeared at the Pavilion Theatre, as Little Robin Hood; continued to appear with her sister for several years, at all the leading London and provincial halls; after the marriage of her sister, appeared as a single turn at most of the leading halls; it was not until after she appeared in the United States, that she attracted considerable notice, and during the past seven or eight years has been identified with the American "vaudeville" stage; for some time she sang songs associated with her more famous sister Marie, but she also introduced several popular successes on her own account.

LLOYD, Doris, actress; *b.* Liverpool; *e.* Liverpool; first attracted attention as a member of the Liverpool Repertory Theatre Company, in 1914; appeared with this company at the Kingsway, London, May, 1915, when she played Miss St. Aubyn in "Nobody Loves Me," and Connie Trustaford in "A Bit of Love"; at the Ambassadors', July, 1919, played in "The Latest Craze"; at the Garrick, Aug., 1921, played Joyce in "The Edge o' Beyond"; at the Kingsway, Mar., 1922, Chee Moo in "The Yellow Jacket"; June, 1922, Maria del Carmen in "Spanish Lovers"; at the St. James's, Nov., 1922, Princess Tatiana Rosanova in "The Beating on the Door"; at the Everyman, Jan., 1923, Mrs. Tranfield in "The Philanderer"; at the Kingsway, Mar., 1923, Lilian Luttrell in "Love in Pawn"; Apr., 1923, Mrs. Cornish in "South Wind"; Sept., 1923, Mitza in "The Harwood Blood"; during 1930, toured in California, as Orinthia in "The Apple Cart"; has since devoted herself to the cinema stage, and has played in innumerable pictures; since 1936 has appeared in "Peter Ibbetson," "Kind Lady," "Too Many Parents," "Mary of Scotland," "The Plough and the Stars," "Tovarich," "Alcatraz Island," "The Black Doll," "I'm From Missouri," "Murder is News," "Brilliant Marriage," etc. *Address:* c/o Max Shagrin Agency, 6253 Hollywood Boulevard, Beverly Hills, Cal., U.S.A.

LLOYD, Florence, actress and vocalist; *b.* Swansea, 25 Mar., 1876; *d.* of Samuel Lloyd, sister of Violet Lloyd, second cousin of Lydia Thompson, cousin of Violet Cameron, Zeffie Tilbury; *m.* Captain A. H. C. Walker-Leigh; made her first appearance on the stage in the provinces, when only four years of age, as Tiny Tim in "The Christmas Carol"; made her first appearance in London at the Avenue Theatre, Christmas, 1882, in a children's pantomime, "Dick Whittington"; her first speaking part was Isabel in the children's production of "The Pirates of Penzance," at the Savoy, Dec., 1884; appeared at the Strand, 1887, in "The Sultan of Mocha"; at the Avenue, 1887-9, appeared in "The Old Guard," "Nadgy," "Lancelot the Lovely"; at the Globe, 1890, played in "The Black Rover"; was engaged by Mr. George Edwardes for the Gaiety in 1891, and succeeded

Maud Hobson in " Carmen Up-to-Data " ; at the Gaiety also appeared in " Cinder-Ellen," " In Town," " A Gaiety Girl," etc. ; in 1894 went to America with the Gaiety Girl Company, subsequently visiting Australia ; on returning to England appeared at the Gaiety, 1895, in " The Shop Girl," and later in " My Girl " ; subsequently succeeded Miriam Clements, at the Garrick Theatre, in " My Friend the Prince " ; again visited America in 1897 ; at the Strand, 1898, appeared as Flo in " The J.P. " ; at the Adelphi, played in " With Flying Colours," 1899 ; at the Garrick, 1899, played Colin in the pantomime, " Puss in Boots " ; at the Prince of Wales's, 1901, played Mrs. Winkworth in " Becky Sharp " ; at the Vaudeville, appeared in " Self and Lady," " Alice in Wonderland," " Scrooge," " Bluebell in Fairyland," etc. ; at the Adelphi 1903-4, played Liza in " The Earl and the Girl " ; in 1905 toured in Australia in " The J.P." ; subsequently appeared at Aldwych and Hicks Theatres n musical comedies ; at the Apollo, 1907, played in " The Education of Elizabeth " ; at the Queen's, 1908, in " The Dairymaids " and " The Old Firm " ; at the Waldorf, Nov., 1908, appeared in " The Antelope " ; during 1909 again toured as Flo Neville in " The J.P." ; during 1910-11 toured s Claire Forster and subsequently as Margaret Rolfe in " The Woman in he Case " ; at the Royalty, May, 1912, played Kitty Roman in " Peter's Chance " ; at the Garrick, Aug., 1912, appeared as Mrs. Howard Jefferies, un., in " Find the Woman " ; appeared t the London Pavilion, in " The Girl in Possession " ; at the Palace, Sept., 1913, played Uraine in " A La Carte " ; at the Globe, Nov., 1913, Martine in " The Blue Stockings " ; at the New, Dec., 1913, Jane in " The Poor Little Rich Girl " ; t the Haymarket, May, 1914, Mrs. Parrott in " The Silver Lining " ; at the Aldwych, Nov., 1914, reappeared as Liza in " The Earl and the Girl " ; in 1914-15 toured in the same part ; at the New Theatre, Feb., 1916, played Cooper in " Caroline."

LLOYD, Frederick William, actor ; London, 15 Jan., 1880 ; s. of the Rev.

Frederick Charles Lloyd and his wife Mary Florence ; e. Bradfield College ; m. (1) Auriol Lee (mar. dis.) ; (2) Yvette Juliette Eva Plancon (mar. dis.) ; was formerly engaged in farming in New Zealand ; studied for the stage at the Academy of Dramatic Art ; made his first appearance on the stage at the Comedy Theatre, 28 Mar., 1905, as the Butler in " Lady Ben " ; appeared at the Court and Savoy, 1905-7, with the Vedrenne-Barker Company ; toured in the United States, 1907, with Ellen Terry, playing Redbrook in " Captain Brassbound's Conversion " ; spent one year at the Lyric, 1908-9, with Lewis Waller, appearing in " The Explorer," " The Fires of Fate," " The Three Musketeers," etc. ; appeared at the Duke of York's, from Feb., 1910, with Charles Frohman's repertory company ; toured in America, 1912-13, in " Milestones " ; enlisted in the Army 5 Aug., 1914, and served four years ; in 1918 returned to America and played successively with Maxine Elliott in " Lord and Lady Algy," with Henry Miller in " A Marriage of Convenience," with George Arliss in " The Green Goddess," etc.; toured in Australia, 1924, with Seymour Hicks in " The Man in Dress Clothes," " Scrooge," " Old Bill, M.P.," etc.; reappeared in London at the Aldwych (for the Stage Society), Feb., 1925, as James Maddox in " The Bright Island " ; Queen's, May, 1925, played Dr. Rice in " Beggar on Horseback " ; Playhouse, Nov., 1925, Nils Krogstad in " A Doll's House "; Little, Feb., 1926, Col. Molp in " The Forcing House " ; Comedy, Apr., 1926, Rev. Jeremiah Tulkhart in " The Rescue Party " ; Shaftesbury (for the Stage Society), May, 1926, General Zelikin in " The Mountain "; Everyman, Aug., 1926, Rev. William Duke in " Outward Bound "; Strand, Apr., 1927, Mortimer Durham in " The Constant Wife " ; Duke of York's, June, 1927, Mr. Jarvis in " Nearly Divorced " ; Wyndham's, Feb., 1928, Lord Marlow in " Listeners " ; Mar., 1928, Jacob Engstrand in " Ghosts "; Criterion, May, 1928, George Merridew in " Skin Deep " ; Prince of Wales's, Sept., 1928, Count Von Baltin in " By Candle Light "; Mar., 1929 (for the Sunday Players),

Prosper in "Hunter's Moon"; Apollo, (for the 300 Club), May, 1929, Mr. Thomas in "After All"; New, Sept., 1929, Sir Henry Featherstonhaugh in "Emma Hamilton"; Criterion, Nov., 1929, George Bottle in "Art and Mrs. Bottle"; Arts, Mar., 1930, Nils Krogstad in "A Doll's House"; New, Oct., 1930, Muche in "Topaze"; Fortune, Nov., 1930, Bodfish in "The Man from Blankley's"; New, Apr., 1932, General Count Carnot in "Napoleon"; Kingsway, Oct., 1932, Lloyd George in "Versailles"; New, Feb., 1933, Earl of Arundel in "Richard of Bordeaux"; June, 1934, the Earl of Morton in "Queen of Scots"; Wyndham's, July, 1934, Major Luddington in "The Maitlands"; Saville, Dec., 1934, Colonel Crawford in "Jill Darling!"; New, Oct., 1935, Capulet in "Romeo and Juliet"; New, May, 1936, Peter Sorin in "The Seagull," and Sept., 1936, Count Armaila in "Girl Unknown"; St. James's, Dec., 1936, Matterby in "O Mistress Mine"; New, Feb., 1937, Touchstone in "As You Like It," and Mar., 1937, Gremio in "The Taming of the Shrew"; Queen's, Sept., 1937–June, 1938, Earl of Northumberland in "Richard II," Sir Oliver Surface in "The School for Scandal," Tchebutykin in "Three Sisters," and Prince of Morocco in "The Merchant of Venice"; Duchess, Sept., 1938, The Squire in "The Corn is Green"; Globe, Dec., 1941, Dr. Datcher in "The Morning Star"; Phoenix, Aug., 1943, Count Rostov in "War and Peace"; Aldwych, Dec., 1943, Uncle Leonidas, in "There Shall Be No Night"; Apollo, June, 1946, Philip Balfour in "Grand National Night"; has also played in numerous films. *Favourite parts:* Sir Oliver Surface, and Sorin in "The Seagull." *(Died 25 Nov., 1949; age 69)*

LLOYD, Marie (Matilda Alice Victoria Lloyd), comedienne; *b.* London 12 Feb., 1870; *d.* of John Wood and his wife, Matilda Mary Caroline (Archer); *e.* London; *m.* (1) Percy Courtney (mar. dis.); (2) Alec Hurley (*d.* 1913); (3) Bernard Dillon; made her first appearance on the stage at the Royal Eagle Music Hall, under the name of Bella Delmere, 9 May, 1885,

under the management of Thomas Broom, singing "My Soldier Laddie" and "Time is Flying"; her own name figured in the bills for the first time, at the same hall, on 22 June, 1885; next appeared at the old Falstaff Music Hall, Old Street; she was then engaged at Belmont's Sebright Music Hall, Feb., 1886, and subsequently she appeared at the Star Music Hall, Bermondsey; her songs at this period were: "And the leaves begin to fall," "Sure to fetch them," "Harry's a Soldier," "She has a sailor for a lover," etc.; engagements followed at the Bedford and the Middlesex, and it was at the last-mentioned hall that she scored her first substantial success with "The Boy that I love sits up in the gallery"; was then engaged at the Oxford, where she appeared for twelve months consecutively; has since appeared at every leading hall in the United Kingdom, United States of America, South Africa, and Australia; appeared at Drury Lane Theatre for three years, 1891-3, as principal girl in the pantomimes "Humpty Dumpty," "Little Bo-Peep," and "Robinson Crusoe," and has also appeared in pantomime at other London and provincial theatres; in 1898, made a theatrical tour in a musical play, specially written for her by H. Chance Newton, entitled "The A.B.C.; or Flossie the Frivolous"; has retained her position at the head of her profession for the past twenty-five years, and is, if possible, more popular than ever, at the present time; among a very great number of popular songs which she has introduced may be mentioned the following: "Oh! Jeremiah, don't you go to sea"; "Madam Duvan"; "Never let a chance go by"; "That was before my time"; "Don't laugh!" "How dare you come to London"; "Poor Thing"; "What do you take me for?"; "Actions speak louder than words"; "Then you wink the other eye"; "Oh! Mr. Porter"; "The Naughty Continong" ("You should go to France"); "Whacky, Whacky, Whack"; "Keep off the Grass"; "Twiggy Voo?"; "Among my Nic-Nacs"; "Johnny Jones"; "There they are, the two of them on their own " ; " Salute my bicycle " ; " Hulloa ! Hulloa ! ! Hulloa ! ! ! " ; " Everybody wondered how he knew " ; " As if she didn't know " ; " Clever, ain't you ? " " The Coster's Christening " ; " Everything in the garden's lovely " ; " Folkestone for the Day " ; " Garn away " ; " It's a jolly fine game played slow " ; "Rum-tiddley-um-tum-tay " ; " Silly Fool " ; " Tiddley-om-pom " ; " Tricky Little Trilby " ; " The Wedding March " (" The wedding bells were ringing ") ; " You can't stop a girl from thinking "; " You're a thing of the past, old dear "; " Customs of the Country " ; " Maid of London, ere we part " ; " She'd never had a ticket punched before " ; " Millie " ; " The Bond Street Cake Walk " ; " I'd love to live in Paris all the time " ; " A little of what you fancy does you good," etc. *Recreations :* Racing and motoring. (*Died 7 Oct., 1922; age 52*)

LLOYD, Rosie, comedienne ; *b.* London, 5 June, 1879 ; *d.* of John Wood and his wife, Matilda Mary Caroline (Archer) ; *e.* London ; younger sister of Marie Lloyd ; has appeared successfully at several London halls, and most of the leading provincial halls ; has also appeared successfully in pantomime in London and the provinces.

LLOYD, Violet, actress ; *b.* London, 25 Nov., 1879 ; sister of Florence Lloyd ; second cousin of Lydia Thompson and cousin of Violet Cameron and Zeffie Tilbury ; *m.* Horace Lane ; made her first appearance on the stage at the Theatre Royal, Nottingham, 8 Feb., 1889, as Daisy Desmond in " A White Lie," with Mr. and Mrs. Kendal ; made her first appearance on the London stage, 18 Nov., 1889, at the Avenue Theatre, in " The Belles of the Village " ; she then returned to school ; on leaving she made her reappearance, on tour, playing in " Morocco Bound," " Don Juan," and " A Pantomime Rehearsal"; in 1894-5 was understudying at the Gaiety, in " The Shop Girl " ; in 1895, went to New York, to play in this piece ; on her return appeared for a

time at Daly's, London, Sept., 1895, as Maud Cripps in " An Artist's Model," and in 1896 in " The Geisha," and returning to New York, appeared at Daly's, in Sept., 1896, as Molly Seamore in the same musical play ; on returning to England, appeared in 1898, as Stella in " Bilberry of Tilbury," and as Flora in " The Topsy-Turvey Hotel," and returning to the Gaiety, again understudied Ellaline Terriss ; she appeared at the Gaiety in " A Runaway Girl," 1898 ; at Daly's, 1898, in " A Greek Slave " ; in 1900 toured in " The Messenger Boy," and returning to the Gaiety, Sept., 1900, played Nora in the same piece, and in 1901 appeared there in " The Toreador " ; has toured in many of George Edwardes's com-panies ; at the Lyric, 1905, played Millicent in " The Blue Moon," subse-quently touring in the same part ; at the Coronet, Christmas, 1907, played Humpty Dumpty in pantomime : during 1909 toured in various music halls in " Trixie," and " Visitors " ; at Christmas, 1909, at the Court, Liverpool, played Boy Blue in " Red Riding Hood " ; during 1910 toured in " The Merry Buskers " ; at Christ-mas, 1910, at Theatre Royal, Man-chester, played Jack in " Jack and the Beanstalk " ; at Christmas, 1911, appeared at the King's, Hammersmith, as Aladdin ; and at Christmas, 1912, at the Opera House, Belfast, as Jack in " Jack and the Beanstalk " ; during 1914 toured in " Bubbles " ; at the Oxford, Jan., 1917, played in " Seeing Life." *Address :* 5 Trebovir Road, S.W.5.

LOADER, A. McLeod, manager and dramatic author ; *b.* London, 3 May, 1869 ; *s.* of Alfred Loader and his wife Sarah (Smith) ; *e.* St. Mark's Collegiate School, Camberwell ; *m.* Louise Wild ; in his youth was apprenticed to an optical and mathematical instrument maker ; was subsequently an actor, and made his first appearance on the stage, at Astley's Theatre, 1887, in G. H. Macdermott's sporting drama " Racing," in which Cyril Maude appeared ; has written, played in, and produced many dramas, comedies, and pantomimes ; was acting manager at the Princess's, the old Strand, Garrick, and Duke of York's theatres; now general manager of the St. Helens and Warrington theatres; was for some time licensee and manager of the Aldwych Theatre for Sir Joseph Beecham. *Recreations :* Motoring and country rambles. *Address :* Edale, Latchford, Warrington, Lancs. *Telephone No. :* Gerrard 2231.

LOADER, Rosa, entertainer; *b.* London; *d.* of James John Loader and his wife Rosa (Smythe) ; *e.* London ; made her first appearance at the early age of seven, at the Polytechnic, Regent Street, as a reciter and comedy vocalist; made her first appearance on the variety stage, in London, at the Euston Theatre of Varieties, as Rosa Rosetti, 10 Sept., 1906, in a musical sketch ; has appeared at many London halls ; has toured the Moss and Stoll halls, the London Variety Theatre Circuit, and has also toured in South Africa, Australia, and New Zealand ; among her more popular sketches may be mentioned " My Missus's Party " ; " Stage-struck Jane " ; " At the Opera " ; " Vocal Impressions " ; " Miscellaneous Musicalities " ; " A Concert Revue," etc. ; is an Associate of the London College of Music, and writes all her own sketches. *Address :* 25 Rochester Square, N.W. *Telephone No. :* North 3127.

LOCKE, Edward, dramatic author ; *b.* Stourbridge, Worcestershire, 18 Oct., 1869 ; *s.* of Joseph Locke and his wife, Louisa (Drewry) ; *e.* Worcester ; settled in America, 1884 ; formerly an actor, and spent several years in various " stock " companies in America ; has written " A Mad Love," " The Climax," " The Case of Becky," " The Silver Wedding," " The Revolt," " The Bubble," " The Land of the Free," " Dangerous Years," " The Dancer " (with Louis K. Anspacher and Max Marcin), " The Dream Song," " Dorothy Dixie Lee," " The Woman Who Laughed," " Mike Angelo," " Swanee River," " The Love Call," " 57 Bowery," " In This Room " ; also several " vaudeville " sketches. *Club :* Players', New York. *(Died 1 Apr., 1945; age 75)*

LOCKE, Katherine, actress; *b.* Boston, Mass., U.S.A., 24 June, 1910 ; *d.* of Maurice Locke and his wife Jenny (Zcheliznak) ; *e.* Madison High School and New York University; *m.* (1) Morris A. Helprin (mar. dis.) ; (2) Norman Corwin ; was formerly a pianist, and studied at the Damrosch Academy ; made her first appearance on the stage, 1928–9 at the Province-town Theatre, New York, in " The Joy of the Serpents " ; at the Theatre Mart, Hollywood, May, 1931, played Paras Velca in " Balloon " ; at the Empire, New York, Nov., 1932, one of the Girl Tenants in " Firebird," and subsequently toured in this; in 1933, toured with Pauline Lord, as Ada Haggett in " The Late Christopher Bean " ; Fulton, New York, Jan., 1934, played Ruth Allen in " Halfway to Hell " ; Biltmore, Jan., 1934, the Second Girl in " Crime and Punishment" ; Biltmore, Apr., 1935, Helen Rainsford in " If A Body " ; Lyceum, Feb., 1937, scored a decided hit when she played Teddy Stern in " Having Wonderful Time " ; Martin Beck, Feb., 1938, Kitty in " How To Get Tough About It" ; St. James, Oct., 1938, played Ophelia in " Hamlet," in its entirety, with Maurice Evans, and at the St. James, Dec., 1939, the same part; Henry Miller, Dec., 1939, Julia in " Christmas Eve " ; Alvin (for Theatre Guild), Mar., 1940, Dorothy Bridges in " The Fifth Column " ; Belasco, Dec., 1941, Peggy Coffey in " Clash by Night" ; Morosco, Dec., 1942, Connie in " Proof Thro' the Night" ; entered films, 1936, and appeared in " Straight From the Shoulder." *Favourite parts :* Teddy Stern, Kitty and Ophelia. *Recreations :* Ping-pong, attending country auctions, and hiking. *Hobby :* Collecting cooking recipes. *Address :* Ringals, New Jersey, U.S.A. *Telephone No. :* Hopewell 206 R.2.

LOCKE, William John, novelist and dramatist; *b.* 20 Mar., 1863 ; *e. s.* of John Locke, of Barbadoes ; *e.* Queen's Royal College, Trinidad, and St. John's College, Cambridge, graduating Mathematical Tripos, 1884 ; *m.* Aimée, *d.* of the late T. Maxwell

Meath; author of the plays, "Mr. Cynic," produced at the Royalty, 1899; "The Lost Legion," Great Queen Street Theatre, 1900; "The Morals of Marcus" (founded on his own novel, "The Morals of Marcus Ordeyne"), Garrick Theatre, 1906; "The Palace of Puck," at the Haymarket, 1907; "The Beloved Vagabond," produced by H. Beerbohm Tree at His Majesty's, Feb., 1908; "Butterflies," a musical version of "The Palace of Puck," at Apollo, May, 1908; "A Blank Cheque," Empire, Dec., 1908; "The Man from the Sea," Queen's, 1910; "An Adventure of Aristide Pujol," Haymarket, 1912; "The Mountebank" (with Ernest Denny), Lyceum, New York, 1923; "The Light on the Mountain," Regent, 1926; his publications include over forty novels. *Club:* Garrick. *(Died 15 May, 1930; age 67)*

LOCKHART, Gene (Eugene), actor; *b.* London, Ontario, Canada, 18 July, 1891; *s.* of John Coates Lockhart and his wife Ellen Mary (Delaney); *e.* St. Michael's School, Toronto, and at Brompton Oratory, London, England; *m.* Kathleen Arthur; is a descendant of John Gibson Lockhart, the biographer of Sir Walter Scott; as a child of seven appeared as a Scottish dancer, in Toronto, with the 48th Highlanders "Kilties" Band; subsequently appeared on the "vaudeville" stage; made his first appearance on the New York stage at the New Amsterdam Theatre, 24 Sept., 1917, as Gustav in "The Riviera Girl"; joined the Boston Opera Company, 1922, and played Robin Oakapple in "Ruddigore"; at the Provincetown, New York, May, 1923, played Bud in "Sun Up"; 39th Street, Mar., 1925, Charlie in "The Handy Man"; Waldorf, Oct., 1926, Herby Brewster in "Sure Fire"; from 1927–31, toured all over the United States with his wife in "Recital-Revue" programmes; during this period he also appeared at the Edyth Totten Theatre, Jan., 1927, as Mephisto in "Faust"; at the Empire Theatre, New York, June, 1930, as Gregoire in "The Little Father of the Wilderness," and Guild Theatre, June, 1931, as

Waitwell in "The Way of the World," both the latter in a series of performances for the Players' Club; during 1932, toured in his own *revue*, "How's Your Code?"; at the Alvin Theatre, New York, (for the Players'), May, 1933, played Gumption Cute in "Uncle Tom's Cabin"; Guild Theatre, Oct., 1933, Sid Davis in "Ah, Wilderness!"; at the Hollywood Bowl, 1935, staged the revival of "Sumurun"; Shubert, New York, Oct., 1935, played Samuel Blanker in "Sweet Mystery of Life"; Center, Sept., 1937, Fortesque in "Virginia"; Morosco, Nov., 1949, succeeded Lee J. Cobb as Willy Loman in "Death of a Salesman"; at the Shubert, Boston, Jan., 1952, played Obadiah Rich in "A Month of Sundays"; is the author of "Heigh-Ho," 1921; "The Bunk of 1926"; "How's Your Code?" 1932; also the author of a number of songs, and has directed the production of several plays; entered films, 1934, and has appeared in innumerable pictures since that date, having devoted himself almost exclusively to that medium; in recent years has appeared in television programmes. *Recreations:* Golf, tennis and swimming. *Clubs:* Players', Dutch Treat, and Writers', New York, and Masquers', Hollywood. *(Died 31 Mar., 1957; age 64)*

LOCKRIDGE, Richard, dramatic critic and author; *b.* St. Joseph, Mo., U.S.A., 26 Sept., 1898; *s.* of Ralph David Lockridge and his wife Mary Olive (Notson); *e.* Kansas City; *m.* Frances Louise Davis; was a reporter on the Kansas City *Kansan*, 1921, Kansas City *Star*, 1922, and New York *Sun*, 1923–8; appointed dramatic critic N.Y. *Sun*, 1928, in succession to Gilbert Gabriel; author of the novels: "The Darling of Misfortune," "Mr. and Mrs. North" (with Frances Lockridge), "The Norths Meet Murder," "Murder Out of Turn," "A Pinch of Poison," "Death on the Aisle," "Hanged for a Sheep"; author, with his wife, of the play, "Mr. and Mrs. North," 1942. *Address:* 74 Washington Place, New York City, U.S.A.

LOCKTON, Joan, actress and vocalist; *b.* London, 1901; *e.* London; *m.*

Harry Levy; made her first appearance on the stage at the London Pavilion, June, 1918, as Genevieve Middleton in " The Profiteers "; in 1919, appeared in " Kissing Time "; subsequently appeared on the cinema stage, playing in " No More Servants for Me," " The Disappearance of the Judge," " The Hour of Trial," " Pillars of Society," etc.; appeared at Daly's Theatre, Apr., 1923, as Rosina in " The Lady of the Rose "; again returned to the cinema stage, appearing in " White Slippers," " A Woman Redeemed," " The King's Highway," etc.; subsequently appeared on the variety stage; at the Lyceum, Mar., 1928, appeared as Jean MacDonald in " Lumber Love." *Address :* 115 Chadwick Road, S.E.15. *Telephone No. :* New Cross 4616.

LODER, Basil, actor; *b.* Lillingston-Daryll, Bucks, 14 July, 1885; *s.* of Colonel Alfred Basil Loder and his wife Anne Kathleen (Crosse); *e.* Eton; *m.* Kate Blanche Davies; formerly in the Army; Brevet-Major, in the Scots Guards, 1905; Beds. Regt., 1914-20; made his first appearance on the stage, at Wyndham's Theatre, 5 Feb., 1924, as the Governor of the Prison in " Not in Our Stars "; Apr., 1924, played Captain Holt in " To Have the Honour "; Oct., 1924, Marston Gurney in " The Ware Case "; at the Everyman, May, 1925, John Shattering in " The Swallow "; St. James's, Sept., 1925, the Hon. Willie Wynton in " The Last of Mrs. Cheyney "; Jan., 1927, Douglas Helder in " Interference "; Winter Garden, Mar., 1928, The Man in " The Spider "; Prince of Wales's, May, 1928, Major Blunt in " Alibi "; Globe, Apr., 1930, the First Lord of the Admiralty in " B. J. One "; St. James's, June, 1930, Colonel Wunderlich in " The Swan "; Adelphi, Sept., 1931, the Reception Clerk in " Grand Hotel "; Globe, Apr., 1932, Lord Vivian Vere in " Wings Over Europe "; Kingsway, Oct., 1932, Earl Balfour in " Versailles." *Favourite part :* Captain Holt in " To Have the Honour." *Recreations :* Shooting, golf, and astronomy. *Club :* M.C.C. *Address :* c/o National Provincial Bank, Prescott's Office, 50 Cornhill, E.C.3.

LODGE, Ruth, actress; *b.* Iver, Bucks, 13 Aug., 1914; *d.* of Thomas Lodge, C.B., and his wife Isobel (Scott), *e.* Beech Grove, Ascot, Berks; *m.* Douglas Dickson; studied for the stage at the Central School of Speech Training and Dramatic Art; made her first appearance on the stage at the Lyric Theatre, 19 Oct., 1933, walking on in "This Side Idolatry"; appeared at the Croydon Repertory Theatre, 1933-4; Theatre Royal, Margate, in repertory, 1935; Arts Theatre, London, Nov., 1935, Evelyn in "Wholly Matrimony"; Embassy, June 1936, Deirdre Dobbs in "Storm Song"; joined the Liverpool Repertory company at the Playhouse, Liverpool, 1936, and remained two seasons, playing leading parts; joined the Mask Theatre company at the Westminster Theatre, Sept., 1938, and played Cressida in "Troilus and Cressida" (in modern dress), Freda Caplan in "Dangerous Corner," Miss Julie in the play of that name, Jennifer Dubedat in "The Doctor's Dilemma," Mary in "The Family Reunion," Cecily Barrington in "Bridge Head"; from 1940-5, was engaged in Administrative War work, as a temporary Civil Servant; reappeared on the stage, Nov., 1945, when she played leads with The Dundee Repertory company;

Comedy, London, (for the Reunion Theatre), Mar., 1946, played Dr. Elizabeth Payling in "And No Birds Sing"; Stratford-on-Avon, from Apr., 1946, appeared at the Memorial Theatre, as Rosalind in "As You Like It," with great success, as Princess Katharine in "Henry V," Rosaline in "Love's Labour's Lost," etc.; King's, Hammersmith, Nov., 1946, Jane Hilary in "The Robber"; New Lindsey, Jan., 1947, Miss Margaret Allison in "Caviar to the General," playing the same part at the Whitehall, Mar., 1947; Arts, Sept., 1947, Mary Bannister in "Child's Play"; New Lindsey, Nov., 1947, Jane Sullivan in "Gingerbread House"; Boltons, May, 1949, Ann in "No. 10, Downing Street"; at the Open Air Theatre, from May, 1950, appeared as Hermione in "The Winter's Tale," Portia in "The Merchant of Venice," Katherine in "The Taming of the Shrew"; following this season,

1516

toured Australia as Adelyn in "Message for Margaret"; after returning to England, toured, Feb., 1952, as Yvonne Trout in "Treasure on Pelican"; at the Irving, May, 1953, played Dr. Clare Ryder in "The Ryders"; then Bromley, Sept., 1953, played Bunty Nelson in "La Plume de ma Tante," and Oct., 1953, Joan Erskine in "A Question of Time"; at the "Q," Nov., 1953, Alma Proudfoot in "The Summerhouse"; Lyric, Hammersmith, Sept., 1954, understudied Peggy Ashcroft in "Hedda Gabler," and subsequently appeared in the production on tour in Holland, Denmark and Norway; Haymarket, Apr., 1956, played Second Applicant and understudied Dame Edith Evans as Mrs. St-Maugham, (sometimes playing the part) in "The Chalk Garden"; Edinburgh Festival, Aug., 1960, played Queen Margaret in "The Wallace"; Flora Robson Playhouse, Newcastle, Nov., 1962, played Nora in "A Squib in the Henhouse"; has also played leading parts in television productions. *Favourite parts:* Portia and Lady Macbeth. *Recreations:* Cooking and window-box gardening. *Address:* Flat 5, King's House, 396 King's Road, London, S.W.10. *Telephone No.:* Flaxman 9054.

LOEB, Philip, actor and producer; *b.* Philadelphia, Pa., U.S.A., 1894; *s.* of Leopold Loeb and his wife Hannah (Rosenberg); *e.* High School, Philadelphia and University of Pennsylvania; *m.* Jeanne La Gue; studied for the stage at the American Academy of Dramatic Arts; was formerly a newspaper reporter; made his first appearance on the stage at the Lyric Theatre, New York, 29 Apr., 1916, as Colin de Cayeux in "If I Were King," with E. H. Sothern; served in the Great War from 1917; returned to the theatre at the Playhouse, New York, Jan., 1920, as stage-manager for "The 'Ruined' Lady"; joined the Theatre Guild, Nov., 1921, and remained with that organization over five years as actor, stage-manager and casting director; during that period he appeared in "The Wife With a Smile," "He Who Gets Slapped," "The Failures," "Processional," "The

Guardsman," "Merchants of Glory," "Garrick Gaieties," "The Goat Song," "The Brothers Karamazov," "Juarez and Maximilian," "Ned McCobb's Daughter," "Right You Are If You Think You Are," etc.; also staged and acted in "Garrick Gaieties," 1925, 1926, 1930; after quitting the Guild, he appeared at the Klaw, May, 1927, in "Merry-Go-Round"; Lew Fields', Sept., 1928, in "Chee-Chee"; Broadhurst, Oct., 1929, Benny Fox in "June Moon"; Guild, June and Oct., 1930, in "Garrick Gaieties"; New Amsterdam, June, 1931, in "The Band Wagon"; Imperial, Sept., 1932, in "Flying Colors"; Oct., 1933, Kruger in "Let 'Em Eat Cake"; Cort, May, 1937, Harry Binion in "Room Service"; Music Box, Sept., 1938, in "Sing Out the News"; Guild, Apr., 1939, Ben Alexander in "My Heart's in the Highlands"; Broadhurst (for the Group Theatre), Feb., 1940, Al in "Night Music"; National, Apr., 1940, Rocky Mountain Red in "Heavenly Express"; Mansfield, Dec., 1942, Harry Trott in "Sweet Charity"; Music Box, Jan., 1944, Joel Nixon in "Over Twenty-one"; Fulton, Apr., 1945, Buzz Bernard in "Common Ground"; Coronet, Dec., 1946, played Max Levene in "Wonderful Journey"; Belasco, Feb., 1948, Jake Goldberg in "Me and Molly"; staged sketches in "Life Begins at 8.40," "1934" and "Parade," 1935; a member of the Council of Actors' Equity since 1934, and of the Executive Committee since 1937; member of the Faculty of American Academy of Dramatic Arts; entered films, 1938, and appeared in "Room Service." *(Died 1 Sept., 1955)*

LOESSER, Frank, composer; *b.* New York City, 29 June, 1910; *s.* of Henry Loesser and his wife Julia (Ehrlich); *e.* City College of New York; *m.* (1) Lynn Garland (mar. dis.); (2) Jo Sullivan; staged his first production at the 48th Street Theatre, 1936, with "Illustrator's Revue"; has since composed the music and written the lyrics for the following productions: "Where's Charley?" 1948; "Guys and Dolls," 1950; "The Most Happy Fella" (also book), 1956; "Greenwillow," 1960;

"How to Succeed in Business Without Really Trying" (Pulitzer Prize), 1961; "Pleasures and Palaces" (with Sam Spewack), 1965; since 1936 has composed numerous scores for films including: "Three Smart Girls," "Neptune's Daughters" (Academy Award), "Hans Christian Andersen," etc.; received the New York Drama Critics' Award for the Best Musical Score, on three occasions; Hon. member of the Consular Law Society. *Recreation:* Cabinet-making. *Club:* Dutch Treat.

(Died 10 June, 1969; age 64)

LOFTUS, Kitty; *b.* Kenilworth, 16 June, 1867; *m.* P. Warren-Smith; made her first appearance on the stage in 1879 as Puck in " A Midsummer Night's Dream "; subsequently played several juvenile *rôles* in Shakespearean plays; toured as Polly Eccles in " Caste," and with the Milton-Rays; toured as Jack in " Little Jack Sheppard "; was with Auguste Van Biene's company at the Gaiety, in 1889, in " Faust Up-to-Date "; in 1893 toured in " Cinder-Ellen "; subsequently toured in " The Lady Slavey "; at the Lyceum, Christmas, 1894, played in " Santa Claus "; at the Prince of Wales's played in " Gentleman Joe," 1895; " Biarritz," 1896, " The White Silk Dress," 1896; appeared at the Vaudeville, 1897, in " The French Maid " and " Her Royal Highness," 1898; in 1899 crossed to the United States and at the New York Theatre, 6 Nov., 1899, made her American *début* as Denise in " In Gay Paree "; played a season at the Lyceum with F. R. Benson, 1900, playing Puck, Ariel, Maria in " Twelfth Night," etc.; at the Comedy, Dec., 1901, played the Hon. Maude Sportington in a revival of " Morocco Bound "; toured in " English Nell " and " Bébé "; engaged to play title-*rôle* in revival of " Betsy," at Criterion; she took the Savoy, 1902, and produced " Naughty Nancy "; toured subsequently in " A Maid from School, " appearing in the same piece at Terry's, Mar., 1904; appeared in music halls, Dec., 1905, followed by an engagement at Coliseum, subsequently touring in the provinces; after an absence of many years from the stage, made a single reappearance, at the Apollo Theatre, 27 May, 1921, as Betty Venn in " The Reappearance of Betty." *(Died 17 Mar., 1927; age 59)*

LOFTUS, Marie, comedienne; *b.* Glasgow, 24 Nov., 1857; made her first appearance on the stage at Brown's Music Hall, Glasgow, Mar., 1874; subsequently appearing at various provincial music halls, making an early success with " Kilkenny Kate," and was known as " The Hibernian Hebe "; she appeared at the Grafton, Dublin, in Apr., 1876; appeared at the Lyceum, Sunderland, Christmas, 1876, as Boy Blue in " Little Bo-Peep "; made her first appearance in London, on 2 Apr., 1877, at the Oxford, Lusby's and the Star, Bermondsey; one of her earliest successes in London, was " I'm so Shy "; subsequently she fulfilled engagements at all the leading London and provincial halls, and for many years was one of the most popular artistes on the variety stage; has fulfilled innumerable successful pantomime engagements in London and the provinces, and has toured in the United States and South Africa; first visited America in Aug., 1884, with Moore and Holmes's burlesque company; among many popular songs identified with her name may be mentioned " Don't you believe it, dear boys "; " Sister Mary "; " And she lisped when she said ' Yes ' "; " That is love ! "; " One touch of nature makes the whole world kin "; " She wore a little safety pin behind "; " To err is human, to forgive, divine "; " A thing you can't buy with gold," etc. *(Died 7 Dec., 1940; age 83)*

LOFTUS, (Marie) Cecilia (Cissie), actress; *b.* Glasgow, 22 Oct., 1876; *d.* of Ben Brown and Marie Loftus, variety artists; *e.* at Convent of the Holy Child, Blackpool; *m.* (1) Justin Huntly McCarthy (marriage dissolved in America); (2) Dr. A. H. Waterman; made her first appearance on the stage at the Alhambra, Belfast, Oct., 1892, singing a ballad entitled "Molly Darling"; first appeared in London at the Oxford Music Hall, 15 July, 1893, making an immediate success; appeared at the Gaiety Theatre, 31 July, 1893, giving her impersonations in "In Town"; made her first appearance on the regular stage at the Gaiety, 28 Oct., 1893, when she played the part of Haidee in "Don Juan"; in 1895 she crossed to America, making her first appearance in "vaudeville" at Koster and Bial's, New York, 21 Jan., 1895; at the Lyceum, New York, 1 Apr., 1895, she played in "The Highwayman"; she went back to the music halls for a while on her return to London, giving her admirable imitations at the Empire, but abandoned them in 1897; at the Court Theatre, 13 Oct., 1897, she appeared as the Goose girl in "The Children of the King," with Martin Harvey, and then again appeared at various music halls; she finally abandoned the halls in 1900 and, crossing to America, she made her *début* in comic opera, at the American Theatre, 19 Feb., 1900, when she appeared as Bettina in "The Mascot"; she then joined Madame Modjeska's company, and appeared at Miner's Fifth Avenue Theatre, 3 Mar., 1900, as Leonie in "The Ladies' Battle"; on 6 Mar., she played Viola in "Twelfth Night," and, 10 Mar., Hero in "Much Ado About Nothing"; she was next engaged by Daniel Frohman for Daly's Theatre, and 26 Nov., 1900, she appeared there as Elsie in "The Man of Forty," and followed this on 21 Dec., 1900, by playing Lucy in "Lady Huntworth's Experiment"; at the Broadway Theatre, 1 Mar., 1901, she appeared as Lady Mildred Yester in "The Shades of Night," and she then joined E. H. Sothern as leading lady; she appeared with him at the Garden Theatre, 9 Sept., 1901, as Lucy Sacheverell in "Richard Lovelace," and 14 Oct., 1901, as Katherine in "If I were King"; she was next engaged by the late Sir Henry Irving, and, returning to England, appeared with him at the Lyceum Theatre, 26 Apr., 1902, as Margaret in a revival of "Faust," and also played

Nerissa and Jessica in "The Merchant of Venice" with him; she then again returned to America and rejoined E. H. Sothern, playing Katherine in "If I were King," Ophelia in "Hamlet," etc.; at Boston, 23 Apr., 1903, she played Sally in "A Luncheon at Nicks," and after touring with Sothern as Perpetua in "The Proud Prince," played that part at the Herald Square Theatre, New York, 12 Oct., 1903; she commenced her career as a "star" at the Lyceum Theatre, New York, 13 Sept., 1904, when she played Eileen O'Keefe, *alias* Nelly O'Neill, in Zangwill's comedy, "The Serio-Comic Governess"; she reappeared in London at the Duke of York's Theatre, 19 Dec., 1905, as Peter Pan in a revival of Barrie's play of that name; she again returned to New York in 1906 and went on a "vaudeville" tour, playing Cecil Raleigh's miniature drama, "The Diamond Express"; she returned to New York in Dec. to appear at Weber's Theatre in the new burlesque," Dream City"; she next played an eight weeks engagement in "vaudeville" Theatres, and in July, 1907, proceeding to St. Louis, Mo., appeared most successfully as Miss Hobbs in Jerome's play of that name, and as Mrs. Dane in "Mrs. Dane's Defence"; at Hartford, Conn., Sept., 1907, appeared as Marcia Tremaine in "The Lancers," subsequently touring in the same play, and appeared at Daly's, New York, 2 Dec., 1907, in the same part; at Washington, 15 June, 1908, played Kittie Cameron in "That Little Affair at Boyd's"; subsequently returned to England, made her reappearance, at the Coliseum, Nov., 1908, giving a series of imitations with great success; again toured in the United States, Sept., 1909; at the Duke of York's Theatre, 7 June, 1910, played Frederika in "A Slice of Life"; at the Lyceum, Oct., 1911, played Nora in scenes from "A Doll's House"; during 1912-13, continued to appear in the principal variety theatres, in England and America; during 1913-14, toured with William Faversham in the United States, playing Juliet in "Romeo and Juliet," and Desdemona in "Othello"; at the Lyric, New York, 9 Feb., 1914,

played Desdemona; after returning to England, appeared at the Grand Theatre, Croydon, Apr., 1915, as Mrs. Dane in " Mrs. Dane's Defence," and at the Theatre Royal, Brighton, 7 June, 1915, as Helen Grant in " Enterprising Helen "; subsequently restricted her performances to occasional appearances at the Coliseum and other leading variety houses in her imitations of popular actors and actresses; returned to the United States in 1923, and appeared at the Palace, New York, Sept., 1923; at the Masque Theatre, New York, Dec., 1927, played Virgie Gibbs in " Venus "; Erlanger's, May, 1928, the Marquis de Rio-Zares in " Diplomacy "; Knickerbocker, June, 1929, Miss Crawley in " Becky Sharp "; 49th Street, Nov., 1929, Sarah Gaunt in "The Patriarch"; Eltinge, Jan., 1930, Mrs. Stuart Romney in " Recapture"; Selwyn, May, 1930, Mrs. Wampus in " Lost Sheep "; Cort, Nov., 1931, Angelica in " A Widow in Green "; Selwyn, Jan., 1932, Beatrice Messiter in " The Devil Passes "; Cort, Mar., 1933, Mrs. Rimplegar in " Three-cornered Moon "; Alvin (for Players' Club), May, 1933, Aunt Chloe in "Uncle Tom's Cabin"; Playhouse, Aug., 1933, appeared in " A Party," giving imitations; Nov., 1933, Vera Lyndon in "Strange Orchestra"; Ritz, Jan., 1934, Adèle Zigurny in "The Wooden Slipper"; Apr., 1934, toured as Frau Lucher in "Reunion in Vienna"; Music Box, Sept., 1934, Mrs. Riley in "Merrily We Roll Along"; National, Feb., 1935, Mrs. Pentland in " Times Have Changed"; Ritz, Nov., 1935, Mrs. Marsden in " Abide With Me "; Masque, Dec., 1936, Mrs. Watson in "The Holmeses of Baker Street"; Erlanger, Philadelphia, Feb., 1937, "Ma" Morgan in "Glory for All"; in summer theatres, 1937, played in "Storm Over Patsy," "The Palace of Truth," and "As Husbands Go"; Windsor, New York, Mar., 1938, Mrs. Weatherby in "There's Always a Breeze"; Little, New York, Mar., 1938, gave impersonations in a series of Sunday night performances; in summer theatres, 1938, appeared in "To-Night at 8.30"; Vanderbilt, New York, Oct., 1938, gave a further series of Sunday night performances; has appeared in films, in "East Lynne," "Doctors' Wives," "Young Sinners," etc.
(Died 12 July, 1943; age 66)

LOGAN, Ella, actress and vocalist; *b.* Glasgow, Scotland, 6 Mar., 1910; made her first appearance on the stage as a child vocalist, at the Grand Theatre, Paisley, 1916, and continued to appear in music-halls for ten years; first appeared in the United States, as a vocalist, with Abe Lyman's band; subsequently appeared in films, in Hollywood; made her first appearance on the New York stage, at the Hollywood Theatre, 13 Dec., 1934, in " Calling All Stars"; at the Alvin Theatre, Aug., 1939, appeared in "George White's Scandals"; Winter Garden, Dec., 1941, in "Sons o'Fun"; Broadhurst, Sept., 1942, in "Show Time"; during the War, from 1943–6, was with the E.T.O., entertaining troops in Africa and Italy; reappeared in New York, 46th Street Theatre, Jan., 1947, as Sharon McLonergan in "Finian's Rainbow"; during 1950, appeared in various night clubs.
(Died 1 May, 1969; age 56)

LOGAN, Stanley, actor and producer; *b.* Earlsfield, 12 June, 1885; *s.* of Thomas Logan and his wife Dora (Bassett); *e.* Dulwich College and Brussels; *m.* Alice Ellen Hirst (mar. dis.); was a pupil of the late Henry Neville; made his first appearance on the stage at the Theatre Royal, Middlesbro', Feb., 1903, as Squire Armytage in " Lights o' London "; during 1904 toured with Martin Harvey in " The Only Way," etc.; in 1907 toured as Peter in " Merely Mary Ann," Rev. Edward Ellice in " The Stormy Petrel," and Durham in " The Knave of Hearts "; made his first appearance in London at the New Theatre, 28 Nov., 1907, as Arthur Wakefield in " The Fairy Uncle," and Bullock Major in "The New Boy"; at the Royalty, Jan., 1908, played Frederick in " Susannah, and Some Others "; appeared at the Vaudeville Theatre, Paris, 1909, as Mr. Darling in " Peter Pan "; subsequently toured in Germany with Meta Illing in repertory; during 1910 toured with Lewis Waller in " Sir Walter Ralegh," " The Fires of Fate," etc.; appeared at the Globe, Feb., 1911, in " Bardelys the Magnificent "; appeared at the Royalty, 1911-15, as Mr. Hopper in " The Master of Mrs. Chilvers," George Mallins in " Half-a-Crown," Rory Megan in " The Pigeon," Ned Pym and Lord Monkhurst in " Milestones," Laurence Enderby in " The Odd Man Out," Percival Pennicuik in " The Man Who Stayed at Home," also playing Christopher Brent in the last-mentioned play, at the Apollo, Mar., 1916; at the Queen's, May, 1916, played Dr. Gerald Sumner in " The Boomerang "; at the Shaftesbury, Sept., 1916, the Duke of Dorchester in " The Light Blues "; at the Palace, Nov., 1916, played in " Vanity Fair "; at the Alhambra, July, 1917, in " Round the Map "; at the Playhouse, Apr., 1918, played Darrell McKnight in " The Naughty Wife "; at Drury Lane, Sept., 1919, Frank Beresford in " The Great Day "; at the Haymarket, Feb., 1920, played the Friend in " Tea for Three "; at the Gaiety, Manchester, Nov., 1920, appeared as John in " Hanky-Panky John," appearing in the same part at the Playhouse, Jan., 1921; at the same theatre, Mar., 1921, played Frank Layham in " Love "; at the Garrick, Mar., 1922, played Henri de la Tour in " The Man in Dress Clothes "; in 1923 went to New York and at the Lyceum, New York, Aug., 1923, played Bob Talmadge in " Little Miss Bluebeard "; at the Cort Theatre, New York, Dec., 1924, Rudolf in "Carnival"; Longacre, Feb., 1925, Sir Evelyn Fahnestock in " The Dark Angel "; Ritz, Nov., 1925, Ralph Carteret in " Loose Ends "; Greenwich Village, Nov., 1925, Don Juan in " The Last Night of Don Juan "; Ritz, Dec., 1926, Count Pierre in " The Padre "; Lyceum, Feb., 1927, Nicholas Trask in " The Dark "; Empire, Mar., 1927, Tony Lagorce in " Her Cardboard Lover "; Bayes, Aug., 1927, Carey Maxon in " Her First Affaire "; 48th Street Theatre, Nov., 1927, Ted Converse in " People Don't Do Such Things "; Cosmopolitan, Feb.-Mar., 1928, James Risby in " Mrs. Dane's Defence," Dr. Watson in " Sherlock Holmes," and Eddie Griggs in " Within the Law "; Henry Miller, Nov., 1928, Dr. Harvester in " The Sacred Flame "; in addition, he staged " The Red Robe," 1928; "Security," "Broadway Nights." "Young Sinners," 1929; "Topaze," "His Majesty's Car," "As Good as New," 1930; "Colonel Satan," "A Modern Virgin," "Society Girl," 1931; " Alice Sit-by-the-Fire," 1932; "Dinner for Three," "Marriage is for Single People," 1945; since 1933, has directed films, in Hollywood; is the author of "De Mortuis," Little, 1922; part-author of " The Smith Family," Empire, 1922; adapted "The Padre," 1926. *Clubs:* Savage, London; and Players, New York, U.S.A. *Address:* 1837 North La Brea Avenue, Hollywood, Cal., U.S.A. *Telephone No.:* Gladstone 1406.

LÖHR, Marie, actress; *b.* Sydney, N.S.W., 28 July, 1890; *d.* of Lewis J. Löhr, formerly treasurer of the Opera House, Melbourne, and his wife Kate (Bishop); *m.* Anthony Leyland Val Prinsep (mar. dis.); made her first appearance on the stage at Sydney, N.S.W., 1894, in " The World Against Her," and subsequently appeared with Charles Arnold in " Captain Fritz " and " Hans the Boatman "; made her first appearance on the London stage at the Garrick, 14 Dec., 1901, in " Shock-Headed Peter " and " The Man Who Stole the Castle "; during 1902 toured with the Kendals, as Barbara Trecarre in " St. Martin's Summer "; at the West Pier, Brighton, Dec., 1903, played Ellie Harthover in " Water Babies "; during 1904 toured as Trixie Blenkinsopp in " Whitewashing Julia "; at the St. James's, Jan., 1905, played The Princess in " White Magic "; at the Comedy, Aug., 1905, appeared as Miss Petherton in " The Duffer "; at Daly's, Jan., 1906, as Ernestine in " The Little Michus "; toured with the Kendals in 1906, appearing as Clara in " A Tight Corner," etc.; at His Majesty's, May, 1906, played Rosey Mackenzie in " Colonel Newcome "; at the Shakespeare, Aug., 1906, appeared as Lillian Nugent in " The

Adventurer "; with the Kendals, 1907, played Muriel Lestrange in " The Melcombe Marriage," etc. ; at the Haymarket, May, 1907,; played Beatrix Dupré in " My Wife " on rejoining the Kendals appeared as Joy Marrable in " The Other Side "; reappeared at the Haymarket, Jan., 1908, as Irene Forster in " Her Father "; May, 1908, played Mrs. Reginald Bridgenorth in " Getting Married "; was next engaged by Beerbohm Tree to play Margaret in " Faust " at His Majesty's, Sept., 1908; appeared at the same theatre, in Dec., 1908, as Hannele in the play of that name, and as Cinderella in " Pinkie and the Fairies "; during 1909 appeared at His Majesty's as Lydia Bashville in " The Admirable Bashville," 26 Jan., Sybil Crake in " The Dancing Girl," 16 Feb., Lady Teazle in the famous revival of " The School for Scandal," 7 Apr., and Ophelia in " Hamlet," 29 June ; she was next seen at the Comedy Theatre, 30 Sept., 1909, as Smith in the comedy of that name; at the Playhouse appeared on 1 Dec., 1909, as Juliet in " Little Mrs. Cummin," and 15 Feb., 1910, as Tommy in " Tantalizing Tommy "; at the Comedy, 19 Jan., 1911, played Josepha Quarendon in " Preserving Mr. Panmure "; at the Prince of Wales, 20 Apr., 1911, appeared as Alix Maubrun in " Better Not Enquire "; at the Gala performance at His Majesty's, 27 June, 1911, appeared as Spring in " The Vision of Delight "; Comedy, 23 Sept., 1911, appeared with Sir John Hare as Fernande de Monclars in " The Marionettes "; Duke of York's, 17 Feb., 1912, appeared as Lily Paradell in "The 'Mind-the-Paint' Girl"; 14 June, 1912, Lady Thomasin Belturbet in a revival of "The Amazons"; at Wyndham's, 3 Oct., 1912, Leila in "Doormats"; Savoy, 4 Oct., 1913, played Adèle Vernet in "The Grand Seigneur"; at His Majesty's, 17 Jan., 1914, Yo-San in "The Darling of the Gods"; at Wyndham's, 23 Apr., 1914, Rose Effick in "The Clever Ones"; at His Majesty's, 22 May, 1914, Olive Skinner in the "all-star" revival of "The Silver King," given in aid of King George's Actors' Pension Fund; Duke of York's, 3

Sept., 1914, appeared as Lady Babbie in "The Little Minister"; St. James's, 16 Jan., 1915, H.M. Queen Charlotte in "Kings and Queens"; Haymarket, 19 Mar., 1915, Nelly in "Five Birds in a Cage"; at His Majesty's, 8 June, 1915, Marie-Odile in the play of that name; at Wyndham's, Sept., 1915, played Lady Ware in "The Ware Case"; Coliseum, Mar., 1916, appeared in Sir J. M. Barrie's skit, "The Real Thing at Last"; Globe, Apr., 1916, played Bettina Dean in "The Show Shop"; New, Sept., 1916, Irene Randolph in "Her Husband's Wife"; at the Royalty, Oct., 1916, appeared as Constance Luscombe in "Home on Leave"; Mar., 1917, as Remnant in the play of that name; Haymarket, June, 1917, as Joan Rochford in "The Mirror"; she then entered on the management of the Globe Theatre, opening on 26 Jan., 1918, as Sybil Bruce in "Love in a Cottage"; May, 1918, played Lady Anthony Fitzurse in "Press the Button"; June, 1918, Lady Gillian Dunsmore in "Nurse Benson"; in Nov., 1918, in aid of a war charity, she produced "L'Aiglon," for a single performance, with an "all-star" cast and played the part of Francis Charles; Mar., 1919, appeared as Lena in "Victory"; June, 1919, revived "L'Aiglon," appearing in her old part; Aug., 1919, played Lady Caryll in " The Voice from the Minaret "; Apr., 1920, Constance in " Birds of a Feather "; May, 1920, the Comtesse de Candale in " A Marriage of Convenience "; Sept., 1920, Dahlia Lavory in " Every Woman's Privilege "; Oct., 1920, Princess Fédora Romazova in a revival of " Fédora "; Feb., 1921. Lady Aline Draper in " The Hour and the Man "; Mar., 1921, Irene Randolph in a revival of " Her Husband's Wife "; later in the year, proceeded to Canada, where she toured in a repertory of plays ; she then went to New York, where she made her first appearance, at the Hudson Theatre, 30 Jan., 1922, as Lady Caryll in " A Voice from the Minaret," followed in Feb., 1922, by a revival of " Fédora "; on returning to London appeared at the Globe Theatre, Sept., 1922, as Colette Vandières in " The Return "; Nov., 1922, played Lady Marjorie

Colladine in " The Laughing Lady " ; Apr., 1923, the Hon. Margot Tatham in " Aren't We All ? " ; at the Comedy, Mar., 1924, Ruth Tedcastle in " Far Above Rubies " ; at the Adelphi, June, 1924, in aid of King George's Pension Fund for Actors, played Lady Ware in a revival of " The Ware Case," and played the same part, Oct., 1924, when the play was revived at Wyndham's Theatre; at the latter theatre, Mar., 1925, played Nancy Last in " A Man With a Heart " ; in Apr., 1926, toured with Oscar Asche as Dorothy Travers in " Big Business " ; Playhouse, June, 1926, played Isabella Trench in " Caroline " ; in Aug., 1926, toured as Margaret Armstrong in " The Love Game"; Apollo (for the Venturers), Dec., 1926, and Prince of Wales, Jan., 1927, played Susan Marvill in " Tuppence Coloured " ; Coliseum, Dec., 1927, Valerie Ashton in " Richmond Park " ; Gaiety, Dec., 1927, Mrs. Darling in " Peter Pan " ; Jan., 1928, toured as Lady Lancaster in " The Temptation of Eve " ; at the Old Vic., Dec., 1928, played Mother Earth in " Adam's Opera " ; Garrick, Dec., 1928, May Smythe in " These Pretty Things " ; Dec., 1928, again played Mrs. Darling in " Peter Pan"; His Majesty's, Jan., 1929, Lady Patricia in " Beau Geste " ; Lyric, Mar., 1929, the Duchess of Devonshire in " Berkeley Square " ; Arts, July, 1929, and Garrick, Aug., 1929, again played May Smythe in " These Pretty Things"; Apollo, Sept., 1929, Lady Lavinia Quinton in " Yesterday's Harvest"; Ambassador's, Oct., 1929, Joan Trevor in " A Girl's Best Friend " ; St. James's, Dec., 1929, again played Mrs. Darling in " Peter Pan"; Lyric, Hammersmith, Jan., 1930, Georgina Tidman in " Dandy Dick"; Comedy, Apr., 1930, Mary Howard in " The Silent Witness"; Vaudeville, Sept., 1930, Margery Battle in " The Breadwinner"; Shaftesbury, Apr., 1931, Mary in "Mr. Faintheart"; Prince of Wales's, July, 1931, Margaret Armstrong in " The Love Game"; went to New York, and at the Booth, Sept., 1931, played Margery in " The Breadwinner " ; on returning to London, appeared at the Vaudeville, Feb., 1932, as Margaret Westcott in "Important People"; London Coliseum, May,

1932, played the Empress Marie Thérèse of Austria in " Casanova"; Embassy, May, 1933, Mrs. Grey in "Sometimes Even Now"; Playhouse, Oct., 1933, Lady L'Estrange in "So Good! So Kind!!"; Palladium, Dec., 1933, Mrs. Darling in "Peter Pan"; Cambridge, Feb., 1934, Mary in "Birthday"; Palladium, Dec., 1934, again played Mrs. Darling in "Peter Pan"; Court, Mar., 1935, Lady Frinton in "Aren't We All?"; Daly's, May, 1935, Mrs. Sydney Rankin in "Chase the Ace"; Arts, June, 1935, Mrs. Cloys in "The Benefit of the Doubt"; Globe, Oct., 1935, Muriel Weston in "Call It a Day" which ran over a year; Aldwych (for Repertory Players) Dec., 1936, Mabel in "Family Hold Back"; Savoy, Apr., 1937, appeared in the revue, "And On We Go"; Drury Lane, Sept., 1937, Duchess of Cheviot in "Crest of the Wave"; Wyndham's, Oct., 1938, Mary Jarrow in "Quiet Wedding"; Lyric, Dec., 1939, Pansy Bird in "Somewhere in England"; Ambassadors' Oct., 1941, Vera Sheldon in "Other People's Houses"; Embassy, Apr., 1946, Mrs. Brown in "National Velvet"; Aug., 1946, Mrs. Jennings in "Sense and Sensibility"; Duke of York's, Jan., 1947, Marquise de St. Maur in "Caste"; Strand, July, 1947, Gertrude Paradine in "My Wives and I"; Phoenix, Sept., 1948, appeared as Dame Maud Gosport in " A Harlequinade"; Apollo, Sept., 1949, Consuelo Howard in "Treasure Hunt"; Haymarket, Mar., 1951, played Hester Bellboys in "A Penny For a Song"; toured, Apr., 1952, as Phillippa Bennington in "Adam's Apple"; St. James's, Dec., 1952, Mrs. Jevons in "Sweet Peril"; Haymarket, Aug., 1953, appeared as Lady Frinton in a revival of "Aren't We All?"; Duchess, Apr., 1954, the Countess of Lister in "The Manor of Northstead"; Streatham Hill, Mar., 1956, played Lady Graine in "Jubilee Girl"; Fortune, Nov., 1956, played Matilda "Hope" in "The Devil Was Sick"; Cambridge, July, 1957, Lady Charlton in "Silver Wedding"; at the Belgrade, Coventry, Mar., 1958, played Lady Bracknell in "Half in Earnest"; Grand, Leeds, Sept., 1958, played Winifred Wing in

"These People, Those Books"; Palace, May, 1959, Lady Mortlake in "The World of Paul Slickey"; Duke of York's, Sept., 1960, May Davenport in "Waiting in the Wings"; Ashcroft, Croydon, Mar., 1963, played Aunt Fluffy in "The West Lodge"; Haymarket, Aug., 1963, Lady Julia Marcia in "The Ides of March"; New Arts, Aug., 1964, Mrs. Grisley-Williams in "Mr. Whatnot"; New Arts, Nov., 1965, Mrs. Whitefield in "Man and Superman," transferring to the Vaudeville, Jan., 1966, and to the Garrick, Feb., 1966; entered films, 1932, in "Aren't We All?" and has appeared in numerous pictures since that date. *Address:* 199 Sussex Gardens, London, W.2.

LOM, Herbert, actor; *b.* Prague, 11 Sept., 1917; *s.* of Charles Lom and his wife Olga (Gottlieb); *e.* Prague; *m.* Dina Scheu; studied for the stage at the Prague School of Acting, and in London at the Vic.-Wells School, Embassy School, etc.; spent a number of years in this country in repertory and touring companies, and in films; first appeared on the West End stage at the Prince's, 14 Mar., 1951, as Dr. Larsen in "The Seventh Veil"; Duke of York's, July, 1952, played Pless in "The Trap"; at Drury Lane, Oct., 1953, made a notable success when he appeared as The King in "The King and I." *Recreations:* Playing the piano, composing, and reading. *Address:* c/o John Redway, 31 Davies Street, London, W.1. *Telephone No.:* Hyde Park 5581.

LOMAS, Herbert, actor; *b.* Burnley, Lancs, 1887; was a pupil at the Academy of Dramatic Art, 1905-6; made his first appearance on the stage at His Majesty's Theatre, 1 Sept., 1906, walking on in "The Winter's Tale"; subsequently toured in "The Bondman," "His House in Order," and with Ellen Terry in "Captain Brassbound's Conversion"; he was also associated with Miss Horniman's Repertory Company at the Gaiety, Manchester, from 1909, when he played small parts in "Much Ado About Nothing," etc., and played a

varied round of characters in the numerous productions made there; was the original Nathaniel Jeffcote in "Hindle Wakes"; also played a "stock" season at the Theatre Royal, Leeds, Nov., 1913, when he played the Rev. James Morrell in "Candida," John Anthony in "Strife," Stuart Manners in "The Whip Hand," and Sir Charles Worgan in "What the Public Wants"; after the War and during 1919–20 toured as Abraham Lincoln in the play of that name; subsequently went to America and at the Bijou Theatre, New York, Oct., 1920, played Hornblower in "The Skin Game"; at the Vanderbilt Theatre, May, 1922, played Nat Jeffcote in "Fanny Hawthorn" ("Hindle Wakes"); from 1924-7 was a member of the repertory company at the Playhouse, Liverpool; at the Everyman, Sept., 1927, to Feb., 1928, appeared in "A Family Man," "Israel," "The Soul of Nicholas Snyders," "The Eldest Son," "Comrades"; at the Royalty, Apr., 1928, played Thomas Greenleaf in "Bird in Hand"; went to New York, and at the Booth, Apr., 1929, played the same part; Everyman, Oct., 1930, played Werle in "The Wild Duck"; Fortune, Jan., 1931, Snow in "The Silver Box"; Arts and New, Mar., 1931, the Hon. Josiah Pringle in "O.H.M.S."; Windmill, June, 1931, The Coroner in "Inquest"; Embassy, Oct.-Dec., 1931, played in "Well Caught," "Britannia of Billingsgate," "Rutherford and Son," and "Mary Broome"; St. Martin's, Dec., 1931, played Lord Granton in "The Nelson Touch"; Garrick, June, 1932, Muggins in "Hocus-Pocus"; St. Martin's, Jan., 1933, Mr. Owen in "The Green Bay Tree"; Embassy, Oct., 1933, and Alhambra, Nov., 1933, Wickham in "The Tudor Wench"; Fulham, Nov., 1934, George in "Anthony and Anna"; Haymarket, Feb., 1935, Mark Lannacott in "Barnet's Folly"; Embassy, June, 1935, Peter Renshaw in "Harvest in the North"; Duke of York's, Oct., 1935, the Carpenter in "The Hangman"; Prince's, Apr., 1936, John Bennett in "The Frog"; Haymarket, Sept., 1937, Wal Treherne in "The Phantom Light"; Duchess, May, 1939, Anton Veerkind in "Glorious

Morning"; Duke of York's, May, 1939, again played the Coroner in "Inquest"; at the Malvern Festival, Aug., 1939, appeared in "Good King Charles's Golden Days," and "Big Ben"; New, May, 1940, played George Fox in "Good King Charles's Golden Days"; Apollo, June, 1941, Thaddeus Arnold in "Actresses will Happen"; Arts, Dec., 1942, Friar Innocence in "Holy Isle"; Playhouse, Apr., 1943, again played the title-*rôle* in "Abraham Lincoln," and at the Lyric, May, 1944, played Abraham Lincoln in "Crisis in Heaven"; Arts, July, 1944, again played Greenleaf in "Bird in Hand"; St. Martin's, Apr., 1945, Evan Howell in "The Wind of Heaven"; Lyric, Apr., 1949, Peter Ignatych in "The Power of Darkness"; St. Martin's, Sept., 1949, Stephen Dawlish in "Summer Day's Dream"; Arts, Nov., 1949, Nathaniel Jeffcote in "Hindle Wakes"; at the Lyric, Hammersmith, Mar., 1950, appeared as the Rev. Martin Gregory in "The Holly and the Ivy," and played the same part at the Duchess, May, 1950; Lyric, Hammersmith, Dec., 1952, played John of Gaunt in "Richard II"; at the same theatre, May, 1953, appeared as Priuli in "Venice Preserv'd"; has also played in numerous films. *Clubs:* Green Room and Stage Golfing Society. *(Died 11 Apr., 1961; age 74)*

LONG, John Luther, dramatic author; *b.* Philadelphia, 1861; has written the following plays: "The Darling of the Gods" (with David Belasco), "Madame Butterfly" (with David Belasco), "Dolce," and "Adrea" (with David Belasco), "The Dragon Fly" (with E. C. Carpenter), "Kassa," "Lady Betty Martingale" (with Frank Stayton), "Crowns."

(Died 31 Oct., 1927; age 66)

LONGDEN, John, actor; *b.* West Indies, 11 Nov., 1900; *s.* of the Rev. John Birchenhall Longden and his wife Lily (Culmer); *e.* Kingswood School, Bath; *m.* Charlotte Frances Jay; for some time was apprenticed to a colliery engineer; made his first appearance on the stage at the Lyceum, 12 July, 1922, in "Old Bill, M.P."; in 1923 toured in the provinces, and subsequently joined the Liverpool repertory company; appeared at the Court Theatre, London, for some time in "The Farmer's Wife," produced by Sir Barry Jackson, in 1924; subsequently entered pictures; appeared at the Prince of Wales's, Sept., 1930, as Samson in "Samson and Delilah," with Edith Evans, and Feb., 1931, as Costigan in "The Ninth Man"; Arts, July, 1937, played Michael in "But Not Your Heart"; Richmond, Sept., 1937, Kenneth Rayne in "False Horizon" and Nov., 1937, Howard Marsh in "Spangled Hemp"; "Q," Feb., 1939, Doughty in "Stolen Time" and May, 1939, Mark Proust in "Independence," which was renamed "To Kill a Cat," when it was transferred to the Aldwych, June, 1939; commenced film career 1925, and since 1936 has appeared in "Little Miss Somebody," "French Leave," "Jennifer Hale," "Thoroughbred," "Dial 999," "Young and Innocent," "The Gaunt Stranger," "Q Planes," "Jamaica Inn," etc. *Address:* 5 Hyde Park Place, W.2.

LONGFORD, Earl of (Edward Arthur Henry Pakenham, 6th Earl), dramatic author and manager; *b.* 29 Dec., 1902; *s.* of Thomas, 5th Earl of Longford and his wife Lady Mary Julia Child (Villiers); *e.* Eton and Christ Church, Oxford (M.A.); *m.* Christine Patti Trew, M.A.; a director of the Dublin Gate Theatre from 1931; chairman of Dublin Gate Theatre Co., Ltd., from 1931; proprietor of Longford Productions; is the author of the following plays: "The Melians," 1931; "Yahoo," 1933; "Ascendancy," 1935; "Armlet of Jade," 1936; "Carmilla" (adaptation), 1937; "The Vineyard," 1943; "Tartuffe" (adaptation), 1948; the Gate company appeared at the Westminster Theatre, 1935, 1936, and 1937, producing "Yahoo," "Hamlet," "The Old Lady Says 'No'," "The Armlet of Jade," "Ah, Wilderness," "Carmilla," etc.; with his wife he has translated the "Oresteia" of Aeschylus, produced at the Gate, Dublin, 1933. *Address:* 123 Leinster Road, Dublin, Ireland. *Telephone No.:* Dublin 92118. *(Died 4 Feb., 1961; age 58)*

LONNEN, Jessie (Beatrice Helen Lonnen), actress; *b.* Bristol, 6 Feb., 1886; *d.* of the late Edwin Jesse Lonnen, actor, and his wife, Emily Inman, *première danseuse*; *e.* privately; was afterwards a student at the Guildhall School of Music and Crompton's Dancing Academy; *m.* Albert Edward Goodwin; first appeared at the Court, 23 Sept., 1901, as a Schoolgirl in revival of "The Strange Adventures of Miss Brown"; was afterwards at the Vaudeville in "Bluebell in Fairy Land," "Quality Street," and "The Cherry Girl"; toured with her sister on the Moss and Stoll Circuit as duettist and dancer, also appearing at London Pavilion, 1905; appeared in "The Spring Chicken," Gaiety, and on tour, 1906; appeared as "The Charm of Paris" in "The New Aladdin," on tour, 1906-7; toured in "The Beauty of Bath," 1907-8; at the Apollo, May, 1908, played Myra in "Butterflies"; subsequently for a time played Rhodanthe in the same piece; in 1909 toured as Mary Gibbs in "Our Miss Gibbs"; in 1910-11 toured as Phœbe in "The Quaker Girl"; at Kennington, June, 1911, played Airs in "The King's Bride"; in 1912 went to Australia where she toured successfully as Prudence in "The Quaker Girl," and Delia Dale in "The Sunshine Girl"; at Melbourne, 1913, played Ganem in "The Forty Thieves"; on her return to England toured during 1914 as Nan in "A Country Girl"; during 1916 toured as Tina in the play of that name; during 1917 toured as Vittoria in "The Maid of the Mountains"; at Prince's, Manchester, Dec., 1917, played Chiquita in "A Southern Maid"; at the Hippodrome, Newcastle-on-Tyne, Dec., 1918, Frances Talbot in "Petticoat Fair," and toured in this during 1919; at the Prince's, Manchester, Dec., 1919, played Kitty Clive in "Our Peg"; during 1920 toured as Peg Woffington in the same piece. *Recreations:* Golfing, punting, and swimming.

LONNEN, Nellie (Ellen Farren Lonnen), actress; *b.* London, 25 Sept., 1887; second *d.* of the late Edwin Jesse Lonnen, actor and his wife, Emily Inman, god-daughter of the late Nellie Farren; *e.* privately; received stage training at Crompton's Dancing Academy; first appeared at Vaudeville in "Bluebell in Fairyland," 18 Dec., 1901, afterwards playing at the same theatre in "Quality Street" and "The Cherry Girl"; has appeared on the Moss and Stoll tour and at the London Pavilion with her sister as duettist and dancer; under George Edwardes at Gaiety in "The Spring Chicken," 1906; toured in 1906-7 as Laolah in "The New Aladdin"; at Aldwych Theatre, Sept., 1907, played Lady Millicent Graeme in "The Gay Gordons"; subsequently toured as Victoria Siddons in the same piece; during 1910 toured as the Duc de Richelieu in "The Dashing Little Duke," and as Tommy in "Tantalising Tommy."

LONNON, Alice, actress; *b.* Oakland, California, 28 Dec., 1872; *d.* of Charlotte (Pilkington) and Joseph Perkins; *e.* San Francisco public schools, and the Cogswell Polytechnic College; studied for the stage under Mrs. Louise Humphrey-Smith in San Francisco; *m.* H. G. Lonsdale; after several engagements walking on, she appeared with Madame Modjeska as Teresa in "Magda," 1897; from 1897 to 1900, assumed a variety of *rôles*, supporting Madame Modjeska, Joseph Haworth, L. R. Stockwell, Frank Bacon, Clay Clement, and others; in Nov., 1900, she joined Mr. E. S. Willard, with whom she played for seven seasons, gradually advancing until in 1902-4 she played the leading *rôles* in "The Rogue's Comedy," "All for Her," "Tom Pinch," and "The Cardinal"; made her first appearance on the London stage at the St. James's, 31 Aug., 1903, as Benedetta in "The Cardinal"; during 1905-7 played entire "lead" in Mr. Willard's *répertoire*; was then engaged by Klaw and Erlanger for the part of Kathleen in "The Right of Way," at Wallack's Theatre, New York, 4 Nov., 1907; at the Garrick Theatre, London, Sept., 1914, played Anne Askew in "Bluff King Hal."

LONSDALE, Frederick (*né* Frederick Leonard), dramatic author; *b.* Jersey, Channel Islands, 5 Feb., 1881; *m.* Leslie Brooke Hogan; formerly a private in the South Lancs. Regiment, and an A.B. seaman; has written the following plays; "The Early Worm," 1908; "King of Cadonia," 1908; "The Best People," 1908; "The Balkan Princess" (with Frank Curzon), 1910; "Betty" (with Gladys Unger), Daly's, 1915; "High Jinks" (adaptation), 1916; "Waiting at the Church," 1916; "The Maid of the Mountains," 1916; "Monsieur Beaucaire" (adaptation), 1919; "The Lady of the Rose" (from the Austrian), 1922; "Aren't We All?" 1923; "Spring Cleaning," 1923; "Madame Pompadour" (with Harry Graham), 1923; "The Fake," 1924; "The Street Singer," 1924; "Katja the Dancer" (with Harry Graham, from the German), 1925; "The Last of Mrs. Cheyney," 1925; "On Approval," 1927; "The High Road," 1927; "Lady Mary" (with J. Hastings Turner), 1928; "Canaries Sometimes Sing," 1929; "Never Come Back," 1932; "The Foreigners," 1932; "Once is Enough," 1938; "Another Love Story," 1943; "But for the Grace of God," 1946; "The Way Things Go," 1950; wrote the film, "Lovers Courageous," and collaborated in "The Private Life of Don Juan." *Recreations:* Golf, tennis, and motoring.
(Died 4 Apr., 1954; age 73)

LOPOKOVA, Lydia, dancer and actress; *b.* Russia, 21 Oct., 1892; *d.* of Vassili Lopokoff and his wife Constanzia (Douglas); *m.* (1) Randolfo Barocchi (mar. ann.); (2) J. M. (later, Baron) Keynes; studied at the Imperial Ballet School, St. Petersburg, and first appeared at the Marinsky Theatre, St. Petersburg, 1901; appeared in 1901, as the Page in "The Sleeping Beauty"; subsequently played Mamilius in "The Winter's Tale," Peasblossom in "A Midsummer Night's Dream," and many other plays and operas; for several years danced solo-parts in the Imperial Russian Ballet; appeared at the Opera House, Paris, June, 1910, as Columbine in "Carnaval"; Paysanne in "Giselle," also in "Scheherazade," "Le Festin," etc.; at the Winter Garden Theatre, New York, 14 June, 1911, as the Favourite Slave in "Cleopatra," and in "Scheherazade"; at the Globe, New York, Oct., 1912, appeared as *première danseuse* in "The Lady of the Slipper"; at the Empire, Syracuse, Oct., 1914, made her first appearance as an actress, when she played the part of Euphemia Kendal in "The Young Idea," which was re-named "Just Herself," when the play was produced in New York, at the Playhouse, 23 Dec., 1914; at the Knickerbocker Theatre, Mar., 1915, played the Spirit of Pleasure in "Fads and Fancies"; at the Bandbox Theatre, Oct., 1915, Julie Bonheur in "The Antick"; Nov., 1915, the Comtesse de Chavigny in "Whims"; rejoined Diaghileff, 1916, in the United States; made her first appearance in London with Diaghileff's Russian Ballet, at the Coliseum, 5 Sept., 1918, as the Favourite Slave in "Cleopatra"; subsequently appeared in "The Good-Humoured Ladies," "Carnival," "The Midnight Sun," "Children's Tales," etc.; in Apr., 1919, appeared in a further series of ballets at the Alhambra, including "La Boutique Fantasque," "The Fire-Bird," etc.; at the Ambassador Theatre, New York, Feb., 1921, appeared in "The Rose Girl"; reappeared in London, at the Prince's Theatre, May, 1921, with Diaghileff's company, in her old repertory; at the Alhambra, Sept., 1921, appeared in "The Sleep-ing Princess"; at Covent Garden, Jan., 1923, appeared in "You'd be Surprised"; has since fulfilled engagements at the Alhambra, Coliseum, Covent Garden, etc.; appeared at the Coliseum, Apr., 1925; at the Coliseum, 1926, again appeared in "La Boutique Fantasque"; Arts Theatre, July, 1927, played the Princess in "The Tale of a Soldier"; at the A.D.C. Theatre, Cambridge, 1929, played Rosanna in Calderon's "Life's a Dream"; at the Arts, Dec., 1930, appeared as the Lady in "Comus"; subsequently to 1930, appeared in several performances for the Camargo Society in "Façade," "Rio Grande," "The Origin of Design," and with the Vic.-Wells Ballet, 1932, in "Coppelia"; at the Old Vic., Sept., 1933, played the Countess Olivia in "Twelfth Night"; Arts, Mar., 1934, Nora Helmer in "A Doll's House," a performance she repeated at the Criterion, Mar., 1936, when she also played Hilda Wangel in "The Master Builder"; Ambassadors', Feb., 1937, Célimène in "The Misanthrope"; Globe, Feb., 1939, Anna Vrodny in "On the Frontier"; appointed a member of the Arts Council of Great Britain, Aug., 1946. *Address:* 46 Gordon Square, W.C.1. *Telephone No.:* Euston 3875.

LORAINE, Robert, actor-manager; *b.* New Brighton, Liskard, Cheshire, 14 Jan., 1876; *s.* of the late Henry Loraine; *m.* Winifred Lydia Strangman, *d.* of Sir Thomas Strangman; made his first appearance on the stage in 1889, in the English provinces, in "The Armada"; made his first apappearance in London at the Strand Theatre, 22 May, 1894, as Alfred Dunscombe in "The Ne'er-do-Well"; appeared at the Standard Theatre, Bishopsgate, 24 Sept., 1894, as Arthur Tredgold in "The Lights of Home"; appeared at the Criterion, July, 18 5, as De Mauprat in the first act of "Richelieu," on the occasion of his father's benefit; subsequently toured as Georges Bernay in "The City of Pleasure"; appeared at the St. James's Theatre, 7 Jan., 1896, as Toni in "The Prisoner of Zenda"; also appeared at the St James's, Dec., 189 , as Jaques du

Bois in "As You Like It," and July, 1897, as Captain Hentzau in "The Prisoner of Zenda"; subsequent performances in London were Dick Beach in "The White Heather," at Drury Lane, 1897; Kit French in "Admiral Guinea," at the Avenue, 1897; Claudio in "Much Ado About Nothing," at the St. James's, 1898; Prince Kassim Wadia in "The Great Ruby," 1898, at Drury Lane; Dudley Keppel in "One of the Best," at the Princess's, 1899, and D'Artagnan in "The Three Musketeers," at the Garrick, 1899; also appeared at the Garrick, 1899, in "Change Alley"; at the Metropole, Sept., 1899, played Hervey Blake in "The Rebels"; in 1899 he went to South Africa, and served with distinction in the Boer War; he made his first appearance on the New York stage at the Knickerbocker Theatre, 4 Mar., 1901, as Ralph Percy in "To Have and To Hold"; at Daly's Theatre, New York, 7 Jan., 1902, he appeared as Noel, Viscount Doughton, in "Frocks and Frills"; returning to England in the same year, he played Henry V in a revival of that play at the Metropole, Camberwell, 23 Apr., 1902; at the Prince of Wales's, Apr., 1902, played Enrico Carbaval in "The President"; July, 1902, William in "There and Back"; at Wyndham's, June, 1903, played in "The Queen of the Roses," and at the Avenue, June, 1903, Tom Faggus in "Lorna Doone"; again returned to America, and in 1903 was touring with Grace George as David Garrick in "Pretty Peggy"; subsequently played Ah Chang in a "vaudeville" sketch, entitled "A Little Tragedy at Tientsin"; at Rochester, New York, in 1904, he played in "The Liars," "Americans Abroad," "The Mysterious Mr. Bugle," and "Diplomacy"; at the Lyric, New York, 17 Sept., 1904, he appeared as Lieutenant Von Lauffen in "Taps" ("Lights Out"); at the Garrick, Philadélphia, 26 Dec., 1904, he appeared as King Edward IV in "The Lady Shore," and at the Criterion, New York, 15 Mar., 1905, he played the part of Danvers Macgregor in "Nancy Stair"; he appeared at the Hudson Theatre, New York, 27 Mar., 1905, in "The Lady Shore," and at the Manhattan Theatre, 24 Apr., 1905, appeared as The Invermorach in "The Proud Laird"; at the Hudson Theatre, 5 Sept., 1905, he played John Tanner in "Man and Superman" with great success; appeared in no fresh part for two years; reappeared in London at the Court Theatre, 27 May, 1907, in the same part of John Tanner; same theatre, 4 June, 1907, he played Don Juan in "Don Juan in Hell"; at the Savoy, 30 Dec., 1907, appeared as Bluntschli in "Arms and the Man"; at the Haymarket, May, 1908, played St. John Hotchkiss in "Getting Married"; at the Aldwych, Sept., 1908, played Joseph Brooks in "Paid in Full"; at Wyndham's, Oct., 1908, appeared as Stephens in "Bellamy the Magnificent"; at the Haymarket, Nov., 1908, played Harry Telfer in "Dolly Reforming Herself"; at the Haymarket, 20 Feb., 1909, played Young Marlow in "She Stoops to Conquer"; at His Majesty's, 7 Apr., 1909, appeared as Charles Surface in "The School for Scandal"; at the Lyric, 11 May, 1909, appeared as Prince Henry in "King Henry IV" (part I); at the Comedy, 30 Sept., 1909, appeared as Thomas Freeman in "Smith"; at the Lyric, 4 Apr., 1910, played Bob Acres in "The Rivals"; at Stratford-on-Avon, 30 Apr., 1910, appeared as Benedick in "Much Ado About Nothing"; at the Queen's, 20 Sept., 1910, played Jan Redlander in "The Man from the Sea"; at the Duke of York's, 24 Feb., 1911, the Rev. Canon Theodore Spratte in "Loaves and Fishes"; at the Comedy, 27 Apr., 1911, Henry Longton in "Playing with Fire"; he then secured a lease of the Criterion Theatre, and opened his managerial campaign on 28 Sept., 1911, with a revival of "Man and Superman," in which he again played John Tanner, with the greatest success; Feb., 1912, appeared as Stanley Miles in "98.9"; afte another revival of "Man and Superman" returned to America, where he played "Man and Superman," Jimmie Shannon in "Not for Sale," and in "The Cradle Snatcher"; returned to England, and reappeared in London, at the Comedy, 3 Nov., 1913, as Dick Blair in " A Place in the Sun " ; 5 Feb., 1914, played Mr. Parbury in " The Tyranny of Tears " ; on the outbreak of war, Aug., 1914, joined the Royal Flying Corps, and was wounded in action ; subsequently promoted to a Captaincy, and was awarded the Military Cross " for con- "spicuous gallantry and skill, on 26 " Oct., 1915, when he attacked a German " Albatross biplane, getting within "fifteen yards of it. When the hostile " machine dived, he dived after it and " followed it from a height of 9,000 ft. to " 600 ft. The enemy pilot was hit, and "his camera and wireless transmitter " were subsequently found to have bullet "holes through them. The Albatross "fell in our lines"; had formerly created a great reputation as an aviator, having accomplished many notable feats and journeys in the air ; was awarded the D.S.O. in the Birthday honours of 1917 ; retired from the Army after the end of the war, with the rank of Lieut.-Colonel ; made his re- appearance on the stage at the King's Theatre, Edinburgh, 3 Mar., 1919, as Cyrano de Bergerac in the play of that name ; and appeared in the same part at the Garrick Theatre, 28 Mar., 1919 ; subsequently entered on the management of Drury Lane Theatre, and transferred the play ;

entered on tne management of the Duke of York's Theatre, to continue the run of the play ; at the Duke of York's, Dec , 1919, again appeared as Bluntschli in " Arms and the Man " ; at the Haymarket Theatre, Apr., 1920, appeared as Harry and Simon Blake in " Mary Rose "; at the Ambassadors', Nov., 1921, played Deburau in the play of that name ; at the Duke of York's, Jan., 1922, Robert Andrew in " The Nightcap "; June, 1922, Angelo Pageant in " Pomp and Circumstance " ; at the St. James's, Nov., 1922, Dale Conway in " The Happy Ending " ; at the Haymarket, Aug., 1923, Rudolf Rassendyl and King Rudolf in a revival of " The Prisoner of Zenda " ; at the Lyric, Hammersmith, Feb., 1924, Mirabell in a revival of " The Way of the World " ; at the Savoy, June, 1924, André Chaumont in " Tiger Cats " ; in the autumn went to America, and played the same part at the Belasco Theatre, New York, Oct., 1924 ; subsequently returned to London ; again went to New York and at the Ritz, Oct., 1925, played the Nobleman in " The Man With a Load of Mischief "; Little, Dec., 1925, Geoffrey David Thorne in " The Master of the Inn "; Cosmo- politan, Apr., 1926, De Vaudrey in " The Two Orphans "; after returning to London, appeared at the Everyman, Sept., 1926, as Bluntschli in a revival of " Arms and the Man "; Apollo (for the Fellowship of Players), Sept., 1926, played Petruchio in " The Taming of the Shrew "; Strand (for the same), Dec., 1926, Mercutio in " Romeo and Juliet " ; Apollo (for Lyceum Club Stage Society), Apr., 1927, Othello; Everyman and Savoy, Aug., 1927, Adolph in " The Father "; Savoy, Aug., 1927, the Colonel in " Barbara's Wedding "; Apollo, Nov., 1927, again played Cyrano de Bergerac; Jan., 1928, Edgar in " The Dance of Death "; Mar., 1928, Selby Clive in " The Man Who Changed His Name "; June, 1929, Tice Collins in " This Thing Called Love "; Aug., 1929, again played " The Father " and " Barbara's Wedding"; Criterion, Nov., 1929, Max Lightly in " Art and Mrs.Bottle"; Strand, Dec., 1929, Long John Silver and Pew in "Treasure Island"; Streatham, Apr., 1930, Oskar von Holderlin in "The Man I Killed"; went to New York, and at the Fulton, Oct., 1930, played Geoffrey Lymes in "Canaries Sometimes Sing"; Royalty, London, May, 1931, André Chaumont in a revival of "Tiger Cats"; 49th Street, New York, Oct., 1931, the Colonel in "Barbara's Wedding" and Adolph in "The Father"; Selwyn, Jan., 1932, the Rev. Herbert Messiter in "The Devil Passes"; Playhouse, Aug., 1932, Heller in "Domino"; has appeared in films, in "S.O.S.", "Birds of Prey," etc.; lessee of the Apollo Theatre, 1927–30. *Clubs :* Green Room and Stage Golfing Society. *(Died 23 Dec., 1935; age 59)*

LORAINE, Violet, actress and vocalist; *b.* London, 26 July, 1886; *e.* Trevelyan House, Brighton; *m.* Edward Raylton Joicey, M.C.; made her first appearance on the stage at Drury Lane Theatre, Boxing Day, 1902, in the chorus of the pantomime, " Mother Goose "; she next appeared at the Lyric Theatre, Apr., 1903, as Tita in "The Medal and the Maid," and in Oct., 1903, appeared in " The Duchess of Dantzic "; at the Strand, June, 1904, played in " Sergeant Brue "; at the Comedy, Feb., 1905, played Madame Volant in " Our Flat," and at the Strand, Mar., 1905, Cynthia Ponjab in " Off the Rank "; made her first appearance on the variety stage, at the Palace Theatre, 21 Aug., 1905, in " The New Régime," subsequently, in Sept., 1905, taking part in " The Palace Review "; was then engaged by George Edwardes to tour in " The Spring Chicken," followed by a tour as Mitzi in " The Girls of Gottenburg ";

made her first appearance on the music-hall stage as a single turn at the Oxford; subsequently appeared at most of the leading London and provincial halls; was a popular " principal boy " in pantomime; appeared at Drury Lane, 1911, in the leading part of " Hop o' my Thumb "; has also played at several of the leading provincial theatres, and has toured in pantomime in Australia and New Zealand; in 1914 she appeared at the London Hippodrome, in " Hullo, Tango ! "; same theatre, Nov., 1914,

appeared in " Business as Usual," and May, 1915, in " Push and Go "; she next went to the Alhambra, where she appeared, Apr., 1916, as Emma in " The Bing Boys are Here "; Feb., 1917, as Emma in " The Bing Girls are There "; July, 1917, as Tootsie in " Round the Map "; Feb., 1918, as The Duchess in " The Bing Boys on Broadway," and Sept., 1919, as Busta Neath in " Eastward Ho ! "; at the Palace, May, 1920, appeared in " The Whirligig "; at the London Pavilion, Mar., 1921, appeared in " London, Paris, and New York "; at the conclusion of the run of this play, retired from the stage on the occasion of her marriage; at the Palace (for King George's Pension Fund), May, 1928, played Sally Jellyband in " The Scarlet Pimpernel "; reappeared, professionally, at the King's, Edinburgh, 5 Nov., 1928, as Clara Gibbings in " The Broken Line "; and appeared in the same part, at the Vaudeville, 19 Nov., 1928, when the play was renamed " Clara Gibbings "; Prince Edward, June, 1932, played in " Fanfare "; Alhambra, Aug., 1932, played in " Over the Page "; at the Alhambra, Dec., 1934, reappeared as Emma in a revival of " The Bing Boys Are Here "; her latest appearance was at the Royal Albert Hall, Sept., 1945, for the *Daily Telegraph* R.A.F. pageant, when she sang several of her old successful songs; appeared in films, 1934. *Recreations:* Golf and music. *Address.* Blenkinsopp Castle, Haltwhistle, Northumberland.

(Died 18 July, 1956; age 69)

LORD, Pauline, actress; *b.* Hanford, California, U.S.A., 8 Aug., 1890; *d.* of Edward Lord and his wife Sarah (Foster); *m.* O. B. Winter; studied for the stage under Jennie Morrow Long; made her first appearance on the stage at the Alcazar Theatre, San Francisco, 1903, in the Belasco Stock Company, as the Maid in " Are You a Mason? "; in 1905 was engaged by Nat Goodwin and toured with him in his repertory, also appearing with him in New York; subsequently she fulfilled many "stock" engagements, notably in Milwaukee and at Springfield, Mass.; made a hit when she appeared at the Harris Theatre, Jan., 1912, as Ruth Lenox in "The Talker"; during 1915 appeared in "vaudeville," and then at the Candler Theatre, New York, succeeded Mary Ryan as Mrs. Strickland in "On Trial"; at Atlantic City, Apr., 1917, played in "Under Pressure"; subsequently toured as 'Aunted Annie in "Out There"; at the Hudson Theatre, Aug., 1917, made a further success when she played Sadie in "The Deluge," and then toured in "The Harvest"; at the Punch and Judy Theatre, Apr., 1918, played Nancy Bowers in "April"; at the Belmont Theatre, Apr., 1919, appeared in "Our Pleasant Sins"; at the Olympic, Chicago, Sept., 1919, played in "Midnight"; at the Plymouth Theatre, New York, Dec., 1919, Nastia in "Night Lodging"; at the Fulton, Jan., 1920, Marie Smith in "Big Game"; at the Greenwich Village, Nov., 1920, Dagmar Krumback in "Samson and Delilah"; at the Vanderbilt Theatre, Nov., 1921, made a great success when she played Anna Christopherson in O'Neill's "Anna Christie"; she toured in this during 1922–23 and then came to London, making her first appearance at the Strand Theatre, 10 Apr., 1923, in the same part, and scoring an immediate success; returning to New York appeared at the Plymouth Theatre, Oct., 1923, as Launzi in a play of that name; at the Garrick, New York, Nov., 1924, played Amy in "They Knew What They Wanted"; at the Knickerbocker, July, 1925, succeeded Gladys Hanson as Imogen Parrott in "Trelawney of the Wells"; Gaiety, Sept., 1926, played Lucy Carpenter in "Sandalwood"; New Amsterdam, Jan., 1927, again played Imogen in "Trelawney of the Wells"; Plymouth, Mar., 1927, Lily Cobb in "Mariners"; Earl Carroll, Nov., 1927, Ethel in "Spellbound"; Empire, Jan., 1928, Bethany Jones in "Salvation"; John Golden (for the Guild), 1928, succeeded to the part of Nina Leeds in "Strange Interlude," and toured in the same part, 1928–9; Belasco, Jan., 1932, played Eunice Wolfhill in "Distant Drums"; Apr., 1932, Isobel in "The Truth About Blayds"; Henry Miller, Oct., 1932, Abby in "The Late Christopher Bean"; National, Jan., 1936, Zenobia in "Ethan Frome"; went to Australia, May, 1939, to play Ann Murray in "Yes, My Darling Daughter" and Sanchia Carson in "Robert's Wife"; Playhouse, New York, Apr., 1940, played Mrs. Smith in "Suspect"; Henry Miller, Jan., 1941, Beatrice Godden in "Eight o'clock Tuesday"; toured, 1941, as Janet Cannot in "The Great Adventure"; Cort, Nov., 1941, Essie Stuyvesant in "The Walrus and the Carpenter"; toured, 1943, as Gwenny in "The Late Christopher Bean"; Playhouse, New York, Nov., 1944, played Alicia Sturdevant in "Sleep, My Pretty One"; appeared in films, 1934, in "Mrs. Wiggs of the Cabbage Patch."
(Died 10 Oct., 1950; age 60)

LORDE, André de, French dramatic author; *b.* Toulouse, 11 July, 1871; stepson of the late Jean Mounet-Sully, the *doyen* of the Comédie Française; has written the following, among other plays: "Dans le nuit" (with E. Morel), 1897; "Madame Blanchard," 1898; "Hermance a de-la vertu," 1901; "La Dormeuse," 1901;

" Au Télèphone " (with Chas Foley), 1901 ; " Le système du docteur Goudron et du professeur Plume," 1903 ; " L'Attaque Nocturne," 1903 ; " Miss Chipp," 1903; " Dernière torture," 1904 ; " Sur la dalle," 1904 ; " La nuit rouge," 1905 ; " Baraterie," 1906 ; " Petite Bourgeoise," 1906 ; " Terre d'Epouvante " (with E. Morel), 1907 ; " Une leçon à la Salpétrière," 1908 ; " Cochon d'Enfant " (with J. N. Raphael), 1909 ; " L'Horrible Experience," 1909 ; " Un concert chez les Fous " (with Foley), 1909 ; " Figures de Cire " (with G. Montignac), 1910 ; " Bagnes d'Enfants," 1910 ; " L'Homme Mystérieux " (with A. Binet), 1910 ; " L'Obsession," 1910 ; " Le Coeur de Floria " (with Madame Maraquita), 1911 ; " L'amour en cage," 1911 ; " La petite Roque " (with P. Chaine), 1911 ; " La Bête " (with M. Marsèle), 1912 ; in collaboration with M. Bauche, wrote " Le Mystère de la Maison Noire," 1915 ; " Le Château de la Mort Lente," 1916 ; " Le Baiser Mortel," 1916 ; " Le Laboratoire des Hallucinations," 1917 ; " La Grande Épouvante," 1917 ; author of " Napoléonette " (with Jean Marséle, from Gyp's novel), 1918 ; " La Dernière Torture " (with E. Morel), 1919 ; " La Maffia " (with Marséle), 1919 ; " Le Systeme Goudron et du Professeur Plume," 1919 ; " Les Pervertis " (with P. Chaine), 1920 ; " La Main du Mort " (with A. Binet), 1921 ; " Forfaiture " (with Paul Milliet), 1921 ; " Au Petit Jour " (with Jean Bernac), 1921 ; has published several volumes including " Le Théâtre de la Folie " ; " Le Théâtre d'Epouvante," " Le Théâtre de la Peur," " Le Théâtre de la Mort," " Les Drames Mystérieux," and which contain all his plays ; has also written several novels ; was formerly critic of the *Petit Parisien* ; is a Chevalier of the Legion of Honour. *Address :* 5 Rue de l'Abbé-de-l'Epée, Paris.

LORENZO, Tina di, Italian actress ; *b.* Turin, 4 Dec., 1872 ; *d.* of Amelia (Colonnello) and Corrado di Lorenzo dei Marchesi di Castellaccio ; *e.* Noto and Naples ; *m.* Armando Falconi ; her mother was a famous actress, who appeared with Salvini ; made her first appearance on the stage at Naples in 1887 ; in 1890, was engaged by Francesco Pasta at Florence, and in a short time established a brilliant reputation, both in modern and classical plays ; has appeared most successfully as Magda, Paula in " The Second Mrs. Tanqueray," Margherita in " La Dame aux Camélias," Mirandolina in " La Locandiera," Denise, Dora in Sardou's play of that name, Leonore in " Onore " (" Die Ehre "), Adrienne Lecouvreur, " Amants," Suzanne in " Le monde ou l'on s'ennuie," Marcelle, Evelina Paoli in " Infidele," also in " Le Feu de Couvent," " La Bataille des dames," " Le Remplaçant," " La Sœur aînée," " Frou-Frou," " La guerre en temps de paix," " La Fine d'un idéale," " La Moglie d'Arturo," " Andréa," " I Disertori," " Fedora," " Romeo and Juliet," " Faust," " Magda," " Zaza," " Maria Antonetta," " La Rafale," " Théodora," " Odette," etc.; has toured under the management of Flavio Ando for some years ; has appeared in Turin, Milan, Venice, Florence, and Rome ; has the reputation of being second only to Eleonora Duse among Italian actresses. *(Died 1 Apr., 1930; age 57)*

LORIMER, Jack, Scotch comedian and dancer ; *b.* Forres, N.B., 26 Jan., 1883 ; *s.* of Alexander W. Lorimer ; *e.* Aberdeen and Glasgow ; *m.* Maud Mitcham ; formerly engaged as a painter and sign-writer ; made his first appearance on the stage at the Scotia Music Hall, Glasgow, 1894 ; appeared at the Palace, Shaftesbury Avenue, 1905 ; has appeared at most of the leading London and provincial halls, including the principal tours and circuits ; has written most of his own songs. *Address :* 13 Endymion Road, Brixton Hill, S.W.

LORING, Norman, producing manager, actor, and producer; *b.* London, 8 May, 1888; *s.* of Marie Tempest; *e.* Harrow and Trinity College, Cambridge (B.A.); *m.* Lilian Cavanagh; was formerly in the Indian Army, 1911-13; appeared at the Playhouse, 6 May,

1914, as Matthews in " The Wynmartens "; June, 1914, played Ambrose Hicks in " The Duke of Killiecrankie "; he first appeared in New York, at the Comedy Theatre, 2 Nov., 1914, as Pollard in " Mary Goes First "; served in the Army during the War, 1915–19, and after; retired from the Canadian General Staff, 1922; at the Duke of York's Theatre, Mar., 1923, played Norbury in "The Marriage of Kitty"; at the Globe, Feb., 1925, Count Basoulin in "The Grand Duchess"; Ambassadors', Apr., 1925, Ralph Twiller in "The Torchbearers"; Arts, May, 1928, Henry Wentworth in " Let's All Talk About Gerald"; Arts, Feb., 1930, Prince Munterra in "The Command to Love"; he produced "Potiphar's Wife," 1927; " Old Mrs. Wiley," 1927; " Let's All Talk About Gerald," " The Lord of the Manor," 1928; " Two Women," " Keepers of Youth," 1929; "The Command to Love," "The Bond," "The Honeymoon," "The Man from Blankley's," 1930; "Crime on the Hill," 1932; stage-director for Gilbert Miller for "The Vinegar Tree," 1932; "The Late Christopher Bean," 1933; "This Side Idolatry," 1933; "Reunion in Vienna," 1934; general manager for C. B. Cochran, 1933–7; produced "Strange Family," 1938; Garrick, Jan., 1939, played Colonel Kingswood in "Hundreds and Thousands"; produced "Third Party Risk," St. Martin's, 1939; also staged "Mozart" in New York. *Favourite play:* "Reunion in Vienna." *Recreation:* Farming. *Club:* Savage.
(Died 9 Mar., 1967; age 78)

LORNE, Marion, actress; *b.* Pennsylvania, U.S.A., 12 Aug., 1888; *d.* of Dr. William Lorne MacDougall; *e.* Wyoming Seminary, Kingston, Pa.; *m.* Walter Hackett (dec.); was a pupil of the American Academy of Dramatic Arts, prior to making her first appearance on the stage at Madison Square Theatre, New York, 1 Feb., 1905, as Dorothy in " Mrs. Temple's Telegram "; at the Garden Theatre, Aug., 1908, played Mimi in " The Devil "; at the Liberty Theatre, Aug., 1909, Angelica Perkins in " The Florist Shop," from 1909 to 1914 was a member of the

Hunter-Bradford Stock Company, Hartford, where she played over one hundred parts, including Dora in " Diplomacy," Angela in " The Royal Family," Mary Ann in " Merely Mary Ann," Katherine in " If I were King," Lady Babbie in " The Little Minister," Kitty in " Sweet Kitty Bellairs," Mary Tudor in " When Knighthood was in Flower," etc.; at Maxine Elliott's Theatre, Jan., 1914, appeared as Mrs. Kent in " Don't Weaken " ; she made her first appearance on the London stage at the Prince of Wales's Theatre, 6 Mar., 1915, as Marjorie Thompson in " He Didn't Want to Do It "; at the Comedy, June, 1915, played Mrs. Ponsonby in " Mr. and Mrs. Ponsonby "; at the Savoy, Aug., 1917, Angela Hilary in " The Invisible Foe "; at the Haymarket, Aug., 1918, Jenny Weathersbee in " The Freedom of the Seas " ; at the Queen's, Jan., 1920, Fancy Phipps in " Mr. Todd's Experiment " ; at the Criterion, July, 1921, Poppy Faire in " Ambrose Applejohn's Adventure " : at the Queen's, Aug., 1924, Pansy Forde in " Pansy's Arabian Night "; His Majesty's, Feb., 1927, Sally Lunn and Sally Perkins in " The Wicked Earl "; St. Martin's, Apr., 1928, Angela Worthing in " Other Men's Wives " ; Oct., 1928, Sophie Rye in " 77 Park Lane"; Sept., 1929, Phoebe Selsey in "Sorry You've been Troubled"; Duke of York's, June, 1930, Linda Leigh in ' The Way to Treat a Woman"; Whitehall, Feb., 1931, Lady Frances Heather in "Good Losers"; July, 1931, Wilhelmina Ryde in "Take a Chance"; Dec., 1931, July Romney in "The Gay Adventure"; Oct., 1932, Kitty Hamble and Bella Tout in "Road House"; Whitehall, Nov., 1933, Tilly Whim in "Afterwards"; Apollo, Oct., 1934, Sophie Wittering in "Hyde Park Corner"; Oct., 1935, Mrs. Lancing in "Espionage"; May, 1936, Phoebe and the Woman in "The Fugitives"; Apr., 1937, Ambrosia Seabrook in "London After Dark"; Vaudeville, Mar., 1938, Dollie in "Toss of a Coin"; after returning to America, toured, 1946–7, as Veta Louise Simmons in "Harvey," and played the part for a time at the 48th Street Theatre, New York, Oct., 1948; Royale, Jan., 1950, appeared in

the *revue*, "Dance Me a Song."
(Died 9 May, 1968; age 79)

LORRAINE, Irma (*née* Maria Berényi), living statuary and tableau impersonator, and dancer ; *b.* Paris, 28 July, 1885 ; *d.* of Henri Berényi and his wife Karoline ; *e.* Notre Dame Convent, Pozsony ; made her first appearance on the stage at Fövarosi, Orpheum, Budapest, in *tableaux vivants ;* made her first appearance in London, at the Holborn Empire, 21 May, 1906, remaining there for ten weeks ; subsequently, for a time, appeared under the name of "Klio " ; has appeared in most of the leading music halls in London and the provinces, on the Continent, throughout the United States, and South Africa. *Recreations :* Motoring, swimming, and dancing. *Address :* 34 Flanchford Road, Shepherd's Bush, W. *Telephone No. :* Hammersmith 1255.

LORRAINE, Lilian, actress (*née* Eulallean de Jacques) ; *b.* San Francisco, Cal., U.S.A., 1 Jan., 1892 ; *d.* of M. Jacques and his wife, Mary (Brennan) ; *m.* Frederick Gresheimer (mar. dis.) ; made her first appearance on the stage as a small child, in 1896, as Little Eva in " Uncle Tom's Cabin " ; she continued to play children's parts for some time in various " stock " companies ; in 1908 she appeared in " The Gay White Way," with Blanche Ring ; at the New York Theatre, Nov., 1908, played Angèle in " Miss Innocence " ; appeared at the Jardin de Paris, 1909–11, in " The Follies of 1909–10–11 " ; at the Globe, Jan., 1912, played Myrtle Billtopper in " Over the River " ; at the Moulin Rouge, Oct., 1912, in " The Follies of 1912 " : at the Winter Garden, Jan., 1914, Fifi in " The Whirl of the World " ; at the Bijou, Nov., 1917, in " Odds and Ends " ; at the New Amsterdam, June, 1918, in " The Ziegfeld Follies of 1918 " ; at the Central, Nov., 1919, played Paulette Divine in " The Little Blue Devil " ; at the New Amsterdam, Mar., 1920, played in " The Nine o'Clock Revue " ; and " The Midnight Frolic " ; at

Washington, Nov., 1920, appeared in " Sonny " ; at the Selwyn Theatre, New York, Jan., 1922, played Totoche in " The Blue Kitten."
(Died 17 Apr., 1955; age 63)

LOSCH, Tilly (*née* Ottilie Ethel Losch), *danseuse; b.* Vienna, 15 Nov., 1907; *d.* of Otto Emil Losch and his wife Eugenie (Dreucker), *e.* Vienna; *m.* (1) Edward Francis Willis James (mar. dis.); (2) The Earl of Carnarvon (mar. dis.); made her first appearance on the stage at the Stadt Opera House, Vienna, 1912, as a child dancer in "Wiener Wältzer" ("Waltzes from Vienna"); subsequently appeared in Korngold's ballet "Das Schneemädchen" ("The Snow Maiden"); subsequently became *première danseuse* of the Opera House; associated with Max Reinhardt in Vienna and Berlin, and went with his company to America in 1927 ; made her first appearance on the New York stage at the Century Theatre, 17 Nov., 1927, as the First Fairy in Reinhardt's production of " A Midsummer Night's Dream "; appeared at the same theatre, Dec., 1927, as principal dancer in " Everyman," and "Danton's Tod "; she staged and supervised the dances in all these productions; she then came to London, and made her first appearance at the London Pavilion, 22 Mar., 1928, in "This Year of Grace"; later in the year she danced at the Salzburg Festival, for Reinhardt; returned to London, and appeared at the London Pavilion, Mar., 1929, in "Wake Up and Dream"; again went to America and appeared at the Selwyn, New York, Dec., 1929, in the same production ; at the Imperial Theatre, New York, Feb., 1931, produced the ballet in "The Gang's All Here"; New Amsterdam Theatre, June, 1931, appeared in "The Band Wagon"; returned to London, and at the Lyceum Theatre, Apr., 1932, appeared as the Nun in the revival of "The Miracle"; formed her own ballet company, 1933, under the title of "Les Ballets 1933" and appeared at the Savoy Theatre; Palace, Sept., 1934, appeared in "Streamline"; Ambassadors', Mar., 1935, played the Angel in "Everyman"; at Ridgeway,

Conn., U.S.A., July, 1938, played in "Till Ulenspiegel"; Morosco, Dec., 1947, played Suzanne Courtoise in "Topaze"; also appeared in films in 1936; is also an artist of some note, and has held exhibitions of her work in New York, Philadelphia, San Francisco, and London.

LOTINGA, Ernest, actor; *b.* Sunderland, 1876; *e.* Merton House College, Sunderland; *m.* (1) Hetty King (mar. dis.); (2) Kathleen Susie Barbor; commenced his career as a comic vocalist at smoking concerts; made his first appearance on the variety stage at the Tivoli, Dover, under the name of Dan Roy, 1898; from 1899, appeared as one of the Brothers Luck; toured their own pantomime "Sinbad the Sailor," 1900; made his first appearance in London at Sadler's Wells, 15 Nov., 1901, in "The Demon of the Cellar"; continued to appear on the variety stage in sketches for many years; went to America, 1909, making his first appearance at the Broadway, in "Her Husband"; at the Queen's Theatre, London, 27 Dec., 1915, appeared in the *revue,* "Oh! La! La!"; toured continuously in *revues,* 1916–25, including "Bluebottles," "Jimmy Josser K.C.," "Capital Levy," "Number Nine," etc.; at the Palladium, Sept., 1925, appeared in "Folies Bergère"; Garrick, Mar., 1931, played Jimmie Gay in "My Wife's Family"; Garrick, June, 1933, Jimmie Josser in "Mrs. Bluebeard"; for many years has familiarized variety audiences with the character of "Jimmie Josser" in numerous *revues* and sketches; among these may be mentioned "House Full," "Khaki," "Sailors Don't Care," "The Police Force," "August 1914," "Ernie's End," "Stop Me and Buy One," "The Gas Inspector," "The Means Test," "Rates and Taxes," etc.; has toured all over the world; since 1935, has toured in "Up She Goes," "Love Up the Pole," "Sanctions," "The Chestnut Tree"; has appeared in numerous films exploiting adventures of Jimmie Josser, in "The Raw Recruit," "Dr. Josser, K.C.," "Josser Joins the Army,"

"P.C. Josser," "Josser on the River," "Stop Me," "House Full," "Josser Goes to Sea," "Josser on the Farm," "Smith's Wives," "Love Up the Pole," "The Air Force," "Barnacle Bill the Sailor," "The Atom Bomb," "Open the Door, Richard," "Adam and Eve," "Spivs and Drones," etc.; played in the first talking pictures made in England. *Recreations:* Photography, motoring, tennis, swimming, and cricket. *Club:* Radnor Hall County Club.
(Died 28 Oct., 1951; age 75)

LOTTA (Charlotte Crabtree), actress (retired); *b.* New York, 7 Nov., 1847; made her first appearance on the stage in 1858, at Petaluma, Cal., as Gertrude in "The Loan of a Lover"; made her first appearance in New York at Niblo's Gardens, 1864; subsequently appeared at Tripler Hall; in July, 1867, appeared at Wallack's Theatre as Paul in "The Pet of the Petticoats" and Liddy Larrigan in "Family Jars"; in Aug., played Little Nell and the Marchioness; her acting in this created a sensation; the following year she appeared at the Broadway Theatre; at Niblo's Gardens, Nov., 1869, she appeared as Fanchon in "Firefly," Andy Blake in "The Little Detective," and Fanny Gribbles in "An Object of Interest"; during 1872, played an engagement at Booth's Theatre; in Nov., 1876, appeared at Abbey's Park Theatre, in "Musette," and the following Jan. in "Zip"; at the same theatre, in 1879, she played in "La Cigale"; made her first appearance in London at the Opéra Comique Theatre, 22 Dec., 1883, as Musette; the following month made a great success by her performance of Little Nell and The Marchioness in "The Old Curiosity Shop"; subsequently appeared with great success as Mam'selle Nitouche; on her return to America played a number of successful engagements all over the country; practically retired from the stage after the season of 1890.
(Died 25 Sept., 1924; age 77)

LOU-TELLEGEN, actor (Isidor Louis Bernard van Dammeler); *b.* 26 Nov.,

1881; *e.* Holland and France; *m.* (1) Comtesse de Broncken (mar. dis.); (2) Geraldine Farrar (mar. dis.); (3) Isabel Craven (Nina Romano) (mar. dis.); (4) Eva Casanova; made his first appearance on the stage in 1903, as Romeo, subsequently playing Oswald Alving in "Ghosts"; on removing to Paris, studied for a time under Paul Mounet, and appeared at the Odéon; he then left the stage for a time and travelled in South America; on returning to France was engaged by Sarah Bernhardt, and with her played the Duc D'Esta in "Lucrezia Borgia," Hippolytus in "Phèdre," Armand Duval in "La Dame aux Camelias," Justinian in "Théodora," Baron Scarpia in "La Tosca," Earl of Essex in "La Reine Elizabeth," etc.; toured with her in the United States, 1910-11, first appearing as Raymond in "Madame X," at Chicago; made his first appearance in London, at the Coliseum, Oct., 1912, with Sarah Bernhardt; took the Vaudeville Theatre, London, for a short season, opening on 28 Aug., 1913, as Dorian Grey in "The Picture of Dorian Grey"; subsequently went to America again, and at the Thirty-ninth Street Theatre, Jan., 1914, appeared as Ramon in "Maria Rosa"; at the Longacre Theatre, Dec., 1914, played René Marquenne in "Secret Strings"; at the Thirty-ninth Street Theatre, Mar., 1915, played the Count de Lastra in "Taking Chances"; at the Maxine Elliott Theatre, Nov., 1915, played Sir Herbert Ware in "The Ware Case"; Mar., 1916, Godfred in "A King from Nowhere"; at the Republic Theatre, Dec., 1917, appeared as Maurice Monnier in "Blind Youth," of which he was part-author, with Willard Mack; at Binghampton, N.Y., Nov., 1919, produced "The Lust of Gold," of which he was part-author, with Andor Garvay; at Wilkes Barre, May, 1920, played John Pont Pierre in "Underneath the Bough"; at the Garrick, New York, Sept., 1921, played Don Juan in a play of that name; then spent many years acting for the cinema stage, appearing in such film plays as "Greater Than Marriage," "The Outsider," "Siberia," "Three Bad Men," "Silver Treasure," etc.; reappeared in New York on regular stage at the Lyceum, May, 1928, as Peter Torrelli in "Anna"; at Syracuse, New York, June, 1929, played in "Cortez," and appeared in the same part at the Mansfield, New York, Nov., 1929; at Chicago, Aug., 1930, played Gail Montaign in "Love Technique"; Waldorf, Oct., 1932, appeared as Jean Paurel in "The Great Lover"; wrote his reminiscences under the title of "Women Have Been Kind," 1931. *(Died 29 Oct., 1934; age 53)*

LOVAT, Nancie, actress and vocalist; *b.* 7 July, 1900; *m.* Cecil W. Langlands (mar. dis.); is a niece of Walter Passmore; made her first appearance on the stage in 1915, in her uncle's company, with whom she made her earlier appearances in such productions as "Sweet Williams," "Queer Fish," "The Soldier's Mess," "Ducks and Quacks," etc.; appeared at the Shaftesbury Theatre, Sept., 1916; played Mildred Petrie in "The Light Blues"; during 1916–17 toured as Virginia Desborough in "My Lady Frayle"; during 1918 toured as Eileen Cavanagh in "The Arcadians," and Mrs. Calthorpe in "The Man from Toronto"; at the Gaiety, Mar., 1920, appeared as Lady Dodo Hazlemere in "The Shop Girl"; at the Adelphi, Feb., 1921, appeared as Princess Sophia in "The Naughty Princess"; at the Gaiety, Apr., 1921, as Siebel in "Faust-on-Toast," and May, 1921, Elsa in the revised version of the same piece; at the Adelphi, Oct., 1921, played Aline in "The Golden Moth"; Oct., 1922, Mary Baynham in "The Island King"; at Daly's, May, 1923, Natalie in "The Merry Widow"; at the Lyceum, May, 1924, Sonia in the same musical comedy; New Oxford, Jan., 1926, played Mary Baltic in "Turned Up"; His Majesty's, Apr., 1926, played in "The Student Prince"; London Hippodrome, Oct., 1926, played Marcia Manners in "Sunny"; during 1927-8 toured as Rose Marie in the play of that name. *Recreations:* Travelling and reading. *(Died 16 Aug., 1946; age 46)*

LOVE, Mabel, actress; *b.* 16 Oct., 1874; *d.* of Lewis Grant Watson and his

wife Kate (Love); niece of the late Robert Grant Watson, of the Diplomatic Service (first Secretary of the Embassy in Washington, and Chargé d'Affaires in Japan); *g.-d.* of William Edward Love, a popular entertainer in his day; made her first appearance on the stage at the Prince of Wales's Theatre, Christmas, 1886-7, as the Rose in the first production of " Alice in Wonderland "; next appeared at the Opéra Comique, Mar., 1887, as Roxalana in " Masks and Faces," with the late Kate Vaughan; appeared at the Gaiety, Oct., 1888, as Totchen the little Vivandière, in " Faust Up-to-Date "; at the Grand Theatre, Islington, Apr., 1890, played Polly in " The Harbour Lights," with William Terriss; at the Lyric, Oct., 1890, appeared as Françoise in " La Cigale," subsequently playing La Frivolini in the same piece; it was here that her graceful dancing first attracted attention, and the following May she appeared at Covent Garden as *première ballerina* in "The Light of Asia" and "Orféo"; at Christmas, 1891, she appeared at Drury Lane, also as principal dancer, in "Humpty Dumpty"; in 1892 appeared at the Strand and Vaudeville in " Vote for Giggs "; toured with Arthur Bourchier; appeared at the Trafalgar Square Theatre, in " The Wedding Eve " and " Dorothy," and at Drury Lane, in pantomime, "Little Red Riding Hood"; in Jan., 1893, was transferred to the Tyne Theatre, Newcastle-on-Tyne, to play Princess Allfair in the pantomime "Humpty-Dumpty"; subsequently returned to Drury Lane, Feb., 1893, and later appeared at the Prince of Wales's, in " The Magic Ring "; at the Criterion, in "La Mascotte"; at the Strand, in " Don Quixote " and " The Other Fellow," and at Christmas, appeared in " Red Riding Hood," at Leeds; in 1894, appeared at Terry's, in " King Kodak," and at the Lyric, succeeded Eva Moore, and Alice Lethbridge in "Little Christopher Columbus," doubling both parts; Prince of Wales's, Liverpool, Christmas, 1894, played Maid Marian in "The Babes in the Wood"; in 1895 appeared at the Folies Bergères in Paris, and went to America to play in "His Excellency," at the Broadway Theatre, New York, where she made a big "hit"; appeared at the Garrick, Mar., 1896, as Nurse Phœbe in "Lord Tom Noddy"; at the Shaftesbury, 1897, in " The Yashmak," subsequently touring as the Comtesse de Condale in "A Marriage of Convenience," with Lewis Waller; appeared at Her Majesty's, Nov., 1898, as Constance in "The Musketeers," with Beerbohm Tree; at the Strand, May, 1900, played the leading part in " Miss Cinderella," and in June played Petunia Perkins in " The Brixton Burglary"; in 1901 toured as Joan in " Sweet and Twenty "; since that date has practically devoted her whole time to touring in " star " parts, and she has been seen as Bluebell in " Bluebell in Fairyland," Suzanne in " The Freedom of Suzanne," Lady Frederick Berolles in " Lady Frederick," Effie Waldron in " A Woman's Way," etc.; in Jan., 1904, at Drury Lane, succeeded Marie George as Blossom in "Humpty Dumpty"; during 1911 she again "starred" in " A Woman's Way," and she was also seen at various music halls, as Mrs. St. George in her own sketch, "Quick Work "; at the Criterion, Feb., 1912, played Grace Challismore in " 98.9 "; subsequently accompanied Robert Loraine to New York, and at the Hudson Theatre, Sept., 1912, played Violet Robinson in "Man and Superman"; was later a teacher of dancing and elocution; reappeared on the stage at the Embassy, May, 1938, when she played Mary Goss in "Profit and Loss."
(Died 15 May, 1953; age 78)

LOVE, Montagu, actor; *b.* Portsmouth, Hants, 1877; *s.* of Henry Love; *e.* Portsmouth Grammar School, and at Cambridge; *m.* Marjorie Hollis; started life as an artist with David Allen and Sons, theatrical printers; was engaged for some years as a newspaper artist; served in the Boer War, South Africa, 1900–1902; as an amateur, had played over 100 parts in six years; made his first appearance, professionally, as an entertainer, in sketches at the piano; he then toured, 1904, in "A Snug Little Kingdom" and 1905, in "David Garrick," "Mrs. Dane's Defence," etc.; toured, 1906, in "The Lion and the Mouse," and was subsequently engaged as stage-manager with Leonard Boyne, on tour, in "Raffles"; he also toured in "Merely Mary Anne," "The Flag Lieutenant," "Smith," etc.; in 1911, he went to South Africa with Matheson Lang's company, playing in "The Taming of the Shrew," "Bardelys the Magnificent," "Sweet Nell of Old Drury," "Macbeth," "Hamlet," etc., subsequently toured with him in India and the Far East; on returning to London, appeared at the Haymarket Theatre, 13 Feb., 1913, as Dagfinn Bonde in "The Pretenders"; in Mar., 1913, rejoined Matheson Lang's company, and toured as Don Guzman in "Westward Ho!"; he then joined Cyril Maude's company and appeared at the Theatre Royal, Glasgow, Sept., 1913, as Mr. Jarvis in the original production of "Grumpy"; went to America with Cyril Maude, and first appeared in New York, at Wallack's Theatre, 3 Nov., 1913, as Lieut.-Colonel Miles Anstruther in "The Second in Command," subsequently appearing there as Malcolm in "The Ghost of Jerry Bundler," Major Smedley in "Beauty and the Barge," and Jarvis in "Grumpy"; returning to England, appeared at the New Theatre, May, 1914, as Jarvis in "Grumpy"; returned to America, and after finishing his engagement with Cyril Maude, appeared at Maxine Elliott Theatre, Mar., 1915, as Sir George Sylvester in "The Adventure of Lady Ursula"; next appeared at the Garrick, New York, Apr.-May, 1915, as Bohun in "You Never Can Tell"; Sergius Saranoff in "Arms and the Man," Rev. James Morell in "Candida"; Gaiety, New York, Aug., 1915, played Ganley in "Search Me"; 48th Street, Sept., 1915, Patrick Alliston in "Husband and Wife"; Maxine Elliott Theatre, Nov., 1915, Michael Adye, K.C., M.P., in "The Ware Case"; Shubert, Mar., 1916, Sir John Harding in "The Great Pursuit"; he then entered pictures; reappeared on the stage in New York, at the Greenwich Village Theatre, Mar., 1921, as John

Webster in "The Survival of the Fittest," and then returned to picture work; at the Fulton, New York, Dec., 1930, played Gilbert Courcel in "A Kiss of Importance"; at Pasadena, Cal., Aug., 1932, played in "Captain Brassbound's Conversion"; at the Empire, New York, Nov., 1932, Szentesi in "Firebird"; St. James, New York, Feb., 1933, Prin in "Hangman's Whip"; 49th Street Theatre, Nov., 1933, Jakob Eisner in "Birthright"; Ritz, Jan., 1934, Otto in "The Wooden Slipper"; Empire, Feb., 1934, the Earl of Arundel in "Richard of Bordeaux"; commenced film career 1916, and has appeared in innumerable films; since 1936 has appeared in "The Country Doctor," "Sutter's Gold," "Champagne Charlie," "The White Angel," "Sing, Baby, Sing," "Lloyd's of London," "Reunion," "One in a Million," "The Prince and the Pauper," "Parnell," "The Life of Emile Zola," "The Prisoner of Zenda," "A Damsel in Distress," "Tovarich," "The Buccaneer," "The Adventures of Robin Hood," "Kidnapped," "Professor, Beware," "If I Were King," "Gunga Din," "Juarez," "The Man in the Iron Mask," etc. *Club:* Players, New York. *(Died 17 May, 1943; age 66)*

LOVELL, Raymond, actor; *b.* Montreal, Canada, 13 Apr., 1900; *s.* of Herbert James Lovell-Robinson and his wife May (Fisher); *e.* Cheltenham and Pembroke College, Cambridge; *m.* (1) Margot Collis (mar. dis.); (2) Tamara Desni; he made his first appearance on the stage at the Town Hall, Dundalk, Ireland, Dec., 1924, as Lord Mountsevern in "East Lynne"; subsequently toured in "Charley's Aunt," and also toured as Matt Burke in "Anna Christie," the Rajah in "The Green Goddess," Hilary in "A Bill of Divorcement," etc.; made his first appearance in London, at the "Q" Theatre, 17 Nov., 1930, as Major Verney in "Gossip"; subsequently ran his own company at the Little Theatre, Leeds, and was producer, and leading man at Bradford, 1932-3; in 1933, took over the leases of the Theatre Royal, Bournemouth, and Grand Theatre, Southampton, which he ran as repertory theatres, and played leading parts at both theatres alternately; made his first appearance in the West End, at Daly's, Oct., 1933, playing the Counsel for the Defence in "Maternité"; Grand, Fulham, Nov., 1933, played Van Heuval in "The Colour Bar"; Kingsway, Feb., 1934, made a success when he played Henry VIII in "The Queen Who Kept her Head"; Piccadilly, Aug., 1934, played Dan O'Mara in "Queer Cargo"; Shaftesbury, Nov., 1934, Geri del Bello in "For Ever"; Winter Garden, Feb., 1935, Det.-Inspector Marshall in "Murder in Motley"; Embassy, Sept., 1936, General Boulanger in "The Tiger"; St. Martin's, July, 1937, King James in "The King's Pirate"; subsequently toured in South Africa as Isopod in "Late Night Final"; Westminster, Jan., 1938, played Corvino in "Volpone"; Playhouse, Apr., 1938, Nicholas in "Whiteoaks"; New, Sept., 1938, Dr. MacFarlane in "Can We Tell?"; Gate, Oct., 1938, Mr. Maxton in "Private History"; Royalty, Nov., 1938, Professor Stüpdich in "So English"; "Q," Dec., 1938, Broadbent in "John Bull's Other Island"; Garrick, Mar., 1939, the Father in "The Mother"; Tavistock Little Theatre, Feb., 1940, King Henry VIII in "The Rose Without a Thorn"; "Q," Apr., 1940, Sir Francis Farquharson in "Temporary Residence"; New, Oct., 1941, Richard Drewitt in "Jupiter Laughs"; Comedy, July, 1942, Matthew in "Murder Without Crime," which ran for a year; Westminster, Aug., 1943, Mr. Bolfry in the play of that name; Phoenix, Nov., 1943, Adhemer de Janze in "Arc de Triomphe"; "Q," May, 1944, Adrian Blenderbland in "The Millionairess"; St. Martin's, Feb., 1945, Waldo Lydecker in "Laura"; toured, June, 1945, as Francis in "Four Days"; Embassy, Sept., and Whitehall, Dec., 1945, Lord Wimpole in "Fit for Heroes"; Embassy, Oct., 1946, Hugo Bastin in "Away From It All"; Winter Garden, Dec., 1946, the Wizard in "The Wizard of Oz"; Aldwych, June, 1948, Sir Hartley Harris in "Ambassador Extraordinary"; Embassy, July, 1949, again played Lord Wimpole in "Fit for Heroes"; Jan., 1950,

George in "Party Manners"; made his first appearance on the New York stage at the Mansfield, 11 Apr., 1950, as the General in "Cry of the Peacock"; St. Martin's, London, May, 1950, played the Visitor in "A Lady Mislaid"; Prince's, Oct. 1950, again appeared as George in "Party Manners"; has also appeared in numerous productions for the Repertory Players, Stage Society, etc., and at the "Q" and Richmond Theatres; commenced film career in "Love, Life, and Laughter," and has since appeared successfully in numerous pictures; was elected a Fellow of the Royal Society of Arts, Oct., 1949. *Favourite part*: Sylvanus Heythorpe in "Old English." *Hobbies*: Rare books and first editions. *Club*: Green Room. *(Died 1 Oct., 1953; age 53)*

LOVELL, W. T., actor; made his first appearance on the stage at the St. James's Theatre, 17 Apr., 1884, as a servant in "The Ironmaster," under Hare and Kendal; subsequently toured in the "Caste" company; went to America in 1888, making his first appearance at Wallack's, New York, Jan., 1888, in "L'Abbé Constantin"; toured for two years, 1888-9, in "Sweet Lavender"; toured in "On 'Change"; at Terry's, Oct., 1891, played in "The Times"; at the Haymarket, 1892, appeared in "Agatha Tylden"; returned to Terry's, Dec., 1892, and played in "Uncle Mike," "Kerry," "The Churchwarden," "Flight," etc.; at the Opéra Comique, 1893, played in "Men and Women"; at Terry's 1893, appeared in "Gudgeons"; at the Comedy, 1894, played in "The Middleman"; subsequently toured in the United States with Mrs. Langtry in "Peril," "Agatha Tylden," "Gossip," etc.; at the Comedy, May, 1895, played in "The Prude's Progress"; at the Garrick, 1895-6, played in "Alabama," "The Rise of Dick Halward," "The Rogue's Comedy," etc.; at the Comedy, 1896-7, in "The White Elephant," "The Saucy Sally"; subsequently toured in "My Friend the Prince"; appeared at the Adelphi, 1898, in "Charlotte Corday" and "The Lady of Lyons "; at the Comedy, 1898, appeared in " The Sea Flower "; at the Avenue, 1898, in " The Club Baby "; in Sept., 1898, started on a tour round the world, under the management of Robert Brough, and appeared in Australia, New Zealand, China, India, etc.; on his return to England, appeared at the Avenue, 1901, in " The Night of the Party," and at the Criterion, 1902, in " The Sequel "; during 1903 toured in the United States with Julia Marlowe in " Fools of Nature "; at Wyndham's, 1904, played in " When a Man Marries "; at Terry's, 1904, appeared in " The House of Burnside " and " Cyrus Q. Blake "; at the Shaftesbury, 1904, played in " The Flute of Pan," subsequently proceeding to the United States with Edward Terry; on his return, appeared at His Majesty's, 1905, in " Business is Business "; at the Comedy, 1905, played in " The Duffer "; at the Lyric, 1906, in " Mauricette "; during 1907 toured with Weedon Grossmith in " Among the Brigands "; and at the Apollo, 1907, appeared in " The Night of the Party "; at His Majesty's, Feb., 1908, played in " The Beloved Vagabond "; subsequently toured with Weedon Grossmith and, later with Sir John Hare; after that date he devoted himself to stage-management; in 1909 was engaged by Frank Curzon as stage-manager at Wyndham's Theatre, commencing with " An Englishman's Home," and remained there in the same capacity with Frank Curzon and Sir Gerald du Maurier for nineteen years; has since fulfilled similar engagements with Leon M. Lion, Cyril Campion, and B. A. Meyer. *Address:* Green Room Club, 46 Leicester Square, W.C.2.

LOWE, Douglas, business manager; *b.* Worthing, 12 May, 1882; *s.* of Frederick Lowe and his wife Florence (Fenton); *e.* Worthing College; was formerly engaged as a sugar-planter; has been associated as business manager with Mr. J. E. Vedrenne since 1904; his first experience was at the Court Theatre, 1904–7, and Savoy, 1907, with Vedrenne and Barker;

Royalty, 1911–19, Vedrenne and Eadie; Little, 1920, Vedrenne and Vernon. *Address:* 34 Gordon Mansions, Francis Street, W.C.1. *Telephone No.:* Museum 977.

LOWE, Edmund, actor; *b.* San José, Cal., U.S.A., 3 Mar., 1892; *s.* of Edward Lowe; *e.* San José High School and Santa Clara University, Cal. (B.A.); *m.* (2) Lilyan Tashman (dec.); (3) Rita Kaufman (mar. dis.); he taught at the University for one year, while studying for the Bar; made his first appearance on the stage in 1911, at San Francisco, under Oliver Morosco; played "stock" at San Francisco and Los Angeles under Morosco for six years; made his first appearance on the New York stage at the Harris Theatre, 1 Mar., 1917, as Steven Forrester in "The Brat"; Morosco, Sept., 1918, played Robert Winston in "The Walk-Offs"; Republic Nov., 1918, David Marsh in "Roads of Destiny"; Belasco, Nov., 1919, Tom Lee in "The Son-Daughter"; Century, Jan., 1921, Lieut. D'Artelle in "In the Night Watch"; Comedy, Oct., 1921, Dr. Wrigley in "The Right to Strike"; National, Dec., 1921, Little Billee in "Trilby"; Princess, Feb., 1922, Pickering in "Desert Sands"; reappeared on the New York stage, after over twenty years' absence, at the Plymouth Theatre, Sept., 1945, when he played Miley Gaylon in "The Ryan Girl"; toured, July, 1946, as Thomas Cranton in "Mary Had a Little"; commenced film career 1921, and has played in innumerable pictures. *Address:* c/o Schulberg-Jaffe Inc., 8555 Sunset Boulevard, Hollywood, Cal., U.S.A.

LOWE, Enid, actress and singer; *b.* Taunton, Somerset, 9 Feb., 1908; *d.* of Tom Lowe and his wife Amy Florence (Southcott); *e.* Bishop Fox's School, Taunton; studied for the stage under Flossie Freedman, and at the Durelle School of Dancing; made her first appearance on the stage at His Majesty's Theatre, Nov., 1927, in the chorus of "Oh, Kay!" also understudying Gertrude Lawrence; at the Lyric, May, 1930, played Fiametta Marini in "Lilac Time," and toured in the same part, also as Juliska in "The Gipsy Princess," Polly in "Tell Her the Truth," and Diane in "The Quaker Girl," appearing in the last-mentioned at the Garrick, May, 1934; Gaiety, May, 1935, played Enid in "Gay Deceivers"; subsequently toured as Juliana in "The Red Mill"; London Palladium, Mar., 1936, appeared in "All Alight at Oxford Circus," and Sept., 1936, in "Okay for Sound"; played a repertory season at Newcastle-on-Tyne, 1936-7; London Palladium, Sept., 1937, played lead in "London Rhapsody," and Nov., 1937, appeared there at the Royal Variety Performance; London Coliseum, May, 1938 played the Journalist in "The Engadine Express"; London Hippodrome, Aug., 1938, Tilly in "The Fleet's Lit Up," and Mar., 1939, appeared there in the revue, "Black and Blue"; Saville, Apr., 1940, in "Up and Doing"; in May, 1941, went to the Middle East, with Sir Seymour Hicks in "London Varieties," the first company to tour Syria, Iraq, Iran, Palestine, etc.; toured with this until Sept., 1942, when she toured in South Africa as Lucille in "No, No, Nanette," Charlotte in "Hit the Deck," the Prince in "The Sleeping Beauty," and Dick in "Dick Whittington"; returned to the Middle East and Egypt, in "No, No, Nanette"; at the Opera House, Cairo, Mar., 1945, played Mabel Crum in "While the Sun Shines"; Winter Garden, Nov., 1947, played Esther Turner in "Outrageous Fortune"; His Majesty's, Feb., 1949, again appeared as Marini in "Lilac Time"; Strand (for Repertory Players), Sept., 1950, Delia in "I Married Two Men"; at the "Q," July, 1951, played Eve in "Who On Earth!"; London Casino, Mar., 1952, appeared in the revue "Excitement"; 1953-4, toured as Madame Blum in "The Quaker Girl"; Nov., 1956, toured as Miss Mallet in "Small Hotel"; Coliseum, Dec., 1958, appeared as the Queen in "Cinderella"; Wimbledon, Aug., 1960, played Marion Medwin in "Happy the Bride"; Cambridge, Nov., 1964, played Lady Eggleston in "Little Me"; has also played repertory seasons, and principal boy in various provincial pantomimes. *Favourite parts:* Lucille in "No, No,

Nanette," and Marini in "Lilac Time." *Recreations:* Walking, reading, and going to the theatre. *Address:* 61 Queen Anne Street, London, W.1. *Telephone No.:* 01-486 2401.

LOWE, Rachel, comedienne; *b.* London, 1 Mar., 1876; *d.* of Thomas Lowe and his wife Sarah Emmeline (Phillips); *e.* Liverpool and Calcutta; *m.* Chas. Warren; made her first appearance on the stage at the Shakespeare Theatre, Liverpool, as the child in "The Barricade"; made her first appearance on the variety stage when quite a small child, at Liverpool; subsequently she toured as Cissie Denver in "The Silver King," and also appeared in Shakespearean plays with Osmond Tearle and F. R. Benson; at the age of thirteen went to India and the Straits Settlements, where she remained for four years; on her return appeared in various musical comedies, and then re-appeared on the music-hall stage in a sketch with the Collins trio in "A Private Séance"; subsequently she appeared as a single turn, at Moss and Thornton's Edinburgh, and played at all the leading London and provincial halls; among her songs may be noted "Any Rags!"; "The Lucky Duck"; "My Boy Bill"; "Take me down to Blackpool"; "Up with woman and down with man"; "They all go to Church on Sunday," etc.; is a popular "principal boy" in pantomime; appeared at the Empire, 1913, in "All the Winners"; in 1915, went on tour playing Fi-Fi in "A Chinese Honeymoon." *Recreations:* Riding, gardening, and motoring. *Address:* 7a Soho Square, W. *Telephone No.:* Central 12887.

LOWELL, Helen (*née* Helen Lowell Robb), actress; *b.* New York City, U.S.A., 2 June, 1866; made her first appearance on the stage at the Academy of Music, New York, 8 May, 1884, as Iolanthe in the comic opera of that name; subsequently played Mrs. Errol in "Little Lord Fauntleroy"; attracted attention in New York, when she appeared at the Herald Square Theatre 25 Mar., 1895, as Simonne Everard in

"Charlotte Corday," with Mrs. Brown-Potter; at the Manhattan Theatre, Sept., 1895, played Mrs. Dale in "The Capitol"; at the Garden, Nov., 1900, played Polly Love in "The Christian"; Knickerbocker, Nov., 1901, Susan Throssell in "Quality Street"; Empire, Nov., 1902, Miss Perrott in "Imprudence"; made a great success when she appeared at Louisville, Ky., Oct., 1903, as Miss Hazy in "Mrs. Wiggs of the Cabbage Patch," repeating her success when the play was produced in New York, at the Savoy Theatre, Sept., 1904; continued in this play till 1906; Savoy, Nov., 1906, played Mrs. Chope in "Sir Anthony"; at the Astor, Jan., 1907, played Mrs. Finnerty in "The Straight Road"; at the Bijou, Dec., 1909, scored another great success when she played Lizzie Roberts in "The Lottery Man"; Daly's, Sept., 1911 Sophie Brush in "Next"; Nov., 1912, Sophie in "The Red Petticoat" (musical version of the same play); 48th Street, Aug., 1913, Gladiola Huntley in "Kiss Me Quick"; Maxine Elliott, July, 1914, Mrs. Gordon Newhouse in "Apartment 12K."; Gaiety, May, 1915, Matilda Martingale in "She's In Again"; Maxine Elliott, Aug., 1916, Mary Denby in "Broadway and Buttermilk"; Lyceum, Nov., 1916, Amelia in "Mile-a-Minute Kendall"; Liberty, Apr., 1917, Mrs. Hofmeir in "Bosom Friends"; Booth, Aug., 1917, Ruth Grellet in "Friend Martha"; Liberty. Dec., 1917, Annette in "The Grass Widow"; Morosco, Jan., 1919, Aunt Lucy Bartlett in "Cappy Ricks"; Princess, Aug., 1920, Sallie Jenkins in "Blue Bonnet"; Longacre, Aug., 1921, Mrs. Judson in "Nobody's Money"; Apollo, Nov., 1921, Belle Brand in "Nature's Nobleman"; Belmont, Feb., 1922, Camille and the Duchesse de Grival in "Montmartre"; Frazee, Apr., 1922, Martha Stuart-Scott in "The Night Call"; 48th Street, Aug., 1922, Nelly Fell in "The Torchbearers"; Playhouse, Feb., 1924, Mrs. Fisher in "The Show-Off"; Maxine Elliott, Oct., 1926, Mrs. Midge in "God Loves Us"; Cort, Jan., 1927, Caroline Twiggam in "Arabian Nightmare"; Martin Beck, Aug., 1927, played in "A La Carte"; Mansfield, Feb., 1928, Ma Nebblepedder in "Atlas

and Eva"; 49th Street, Apr., 1928, Miss Wimpole in "A Lady for a Night"; Belasco, Aug., 1929, Mrs. Stanton in "It's a Wise Child"; Biltmore, Oct., 1931, Charlotte Powers in "The Guest Room"; 48th Street, Apr., 1932, Mrs. Henry Merrill in "Take My Tip"; Belasco, Aug., 1933, Mrs. Ward in "Come Easy"; entered films 1934, and has appeared in "The Happy Family" ("The Merry Frinks"), "Madame Du Barry," "A Woman in Her Thirties" ("Side Streets"), "Midnight Alibi," "The Dragon Murder Case," "Big Hearted Herbert," "The Case of the Howling Dog," "Maybe It's Love," "Devil Dogs of the Air," "Living on Velvet," "Party Wire," "The Goose and the Gander," "Dr. Socrates." *(Died 28 June, 1937; age 71)*

LOWELL, Mollie, actress; *b.* in Newcastle, of Irish parentage; *m.* Benjamin Robson; made her first appearance on the stage with the Carl Rosa Opera Company in the provinces; made her first appearance in London, at the Gaiety Theatre, where she walked on; next appeared at the Vaudeville Theatre, Sept., 1898, in "Her Royal Highness"; at Liverpool, 1898, played Principal Girl in pantomime; at the Vaudeville, 1899, played in "The Elixir of Youth," and at Drury Lane, 1899, played in "Jack and the Beanstalk"; on the first night of the pantomime she played the leading part owing to the sudden illness of Nellie Stewart who was to appear as Jack, and made an immediate success; at Daly's, Sept., 1900, appeared as Mrs. Harley Streeter in "San Toy"; at the Lyric, in 1901, played Gillian in "The Silver Slipper," and at the Savoy, Sept., 1902, Lady Barbara Dawn in "Naughty Nancy"; at the Vaudeville, Sept., 1904, played Lady Crystal in "The Catch of the Season"; at the Aldwych Theatre, Dec., 1905, played in revival of "Bluebell in Fairyland"; Mar., 1906, played Lady Bunn in "The Beauty of Bath"; at the Hicks Theatre, May, 1907, appeared as Mrs. Dan de Mille in "Brewsters' Millions"; at the Playhouse, Apr., 1908, appeared as Madame

Tasselin in " Pro Tem." ; at Wyndham's, Jan., 1910, played Madame Ducrot in " Captain Kidd " ; she then went to America and appeared at the Knickerbocker Theatre, Aug., 1910, as Mrs. Farquhar in " Our Miss Gibbs " ; at the Whitney Theatre, London, Apr., 1911, played Cornelia in " Baron Trenck " ; at the Vaudeville, Aug., 1914, played Mrs. Tarbolton in " My Aunt " ; at the Comedy, Apr., 1915, Jeantire in " Wild Thyme " : at the Prince's Theatre, Dec., 1916, played Mrs. Hearty and the Reigning Queen in " Bluebell in Fairyland."

LOWNE, Charles Macready, actor ; *m.* Mrs. Stevenson ; made his first appearance on the professional stage in Aug., 1884, as a member of the late John L. Toole's Company, at Blackpool ; made his first appearance in London at Toole's Theatre, 4 Apr., 1885, in a farce, and subsequently played Doubledot in " Paul Pry " ; for many years after he continued with Toole, appearing as Claud in " Uncle Dick's Darling," Charley Garner in " Dearer than Life," Harry in " Paul Pry," Percival Ransome in " Chawles," etc. ; also took part in " The Shuttlecock," " The Great Taykin," " The O'Dora," " Going It," " Faust and Loose," " The Don," " The Butler," " Walker, London," " The Best Man," " Thoroughbred," etc. ; accompanied Toole on his Australian tour in 1890-1 ; his engagement with that comedian lasted in all eleven years, and was only terminated by the illness which removed Toole from the stage in 1896 ; since that date he has fulfilled engagements at a number of West End theatres, notably at Drury Lane, where he played in the autumn dramas for some years from 1896, appearing in " The Duchess of Coolgardie," " The White Heather," " The Great Ruby," " The Best of Friends," etc. ; appeared at Wyndham's as Haynes Webbmarsh in " A Wife Without a Smile," Oct., 1904 ; and also played very successfully at the St. James's, as Pryce Ridgely in " His House in Order," 1906 ; at the Court, Sept., 1907, appeared as Cotter in " Barry Doyle's Rest Cure," and

in Oct., as Mr. Paradine Fouldes in " Lady Frederick " ; he played this last-mentioned part for over a year, and at five different theatres ; at the Haymarket, Nov., 1908, played Matthew Barron in " Dolly Reforming Herself " ; Apr., 1909, played Lord Herbert Penrose in " Bevis " ; at the St. James's, Sept., 1909, appeared as the Hon. Peter Mottram in " Mid-Channel " ; in Nov., 1909, appeared there as Richard Kelham in " Lorrimer Sabiston, Dramatist " ; at the Duke of York's, Feb., 1910, played John Tarleton in " Misalliance " ; at the Comedy, Nov., 1910, was Marmaduke Paradine in " Vice-Versâ " ; at the Duke of York's, Feb., 1911, played Earl Spratte in " Loaves and Fishes " ; at the Comedy, Sept., 1911, played Raymond Nizerolles in " The Marionettes " ; at the Lyric, May, 1912, played Samuel in " The Five Frankforters " ; at the Criterion, Sept., 1912, Lord Porth in " A Young Man's Fancy " ; at the Queen's, Nov., 1912, Colonel Greer in " Sylvia Greer " ; at the Globe, Apr., 1913, reappeared as Paradine Fouldes in " Lady Frederick " ; at His Majesty's, 22 May, 1914, played Cripps in the " all-star " revival of " The Silver King," given in aid of King George's Actors' Pension Fund ; at the St. James's, Oct., 1914, resumed his original part of Pryce Ridgeley in " His House in Order " ; at Daly's, Apr., 1915, appeared as the Duke of Crowborough in " Betty " ; at the Royalty, Mar., 1917, played Jules in " Remnant " ; at the Queen's, July, 1917, Sir Granville Pomeroy in " Mrs. Pomeroy's Reputation " ; at the New Theatre, July, 1917, during " Navy week," Charles in " Trelawney of the Wells " ; at the Adelphi, Sept., 1917, Colonel Bagot in " The Boy " ; at the Coliseum, Mar., 1920, the Hon. Bill in " The Truth About the Russian Dancers " ; at the St. James's, Aug., 1921, Colonel Septimus Packinder in " Threads " ; at the Comedy, Mar., 1922, the Hon. Rigby Rawes in " Other People's Worries " ; at the Adelphi, Oct., 1922, Admiral Lord John Fairchilde in " The Island King " ; at the Criterion, Feb., 1924, Henry Smallwood in " The Audacious Mr. Squire " ; at the New, Oct., 1924, Lord Severn in " The Hour and the Man " ; Globe, Jan., 1925, Major-General Leighton in " Camilla States Her Case " ; Wyndham's, Apr., 1925, Sir John Barstow in " Little Miss Bluebeard " ; Savoy, Sept., 1925, Sir Henry Hasketh in " The Unfair Sex " ; His Majesty's, Feb., 1927, Sir Francis Mordaunt in " The Wicked Earl " ; Prince's, Sept., 1927, John Bannerton in " Compromising Daphne " ; Little, May, 1928, Sir George Darenth in " A Private Room " ; Apollo, Sept., 1928, General Sir George Fleeter in " The Lord of the Manor " ; Haymarket, Apr., 1929, the Chancellor in " The Ivory Door " ; St. Martin's, July, 1929, Rev. Christopher Pumphrey in " A Bill of Divorcement " ; Embassy, Nov., 1930, and New, Mar., 1931, played Mr. Postlethwaite in " A Seat in the Park ; at the Duchess, May, 1932, produced " A Cold June " ; from Sept., 1915, to the end of 1919 was Administrator of the Academy of Dramatic Art. *Club:* Garrick. *(Died 30 July, 1941; age 78)*

LOXLEY, Violet, actress; *b.* Southport, Lancs., 3 Mar., 1914; *d.* of William Eason Humphreys and his wife Adeline (Aukland); *e.* Havergal College, Toronto, Canada; made her first appearance on the stage at the Empire, Toronto, Sept., 1930, as Angela in "To Have the Honour"; played repertory in Canada for three years; came to England, 1933; studied singing with Gwynn Davies and dancing with Buddy Bradley; appeared in cabaret at Grosvenor House; made her first appearance on the London stage at "Q" Theatre, 25 June, 1934, in "Triumph"; King's, Hammersmith, Aug., 1934, played Molly and Mary Rivers in "The Master of Thornfield" and Dulcie in "Almighty Dolla"; Gate, Nov., 1934, Sasha in "Nichevo"; St. James's, 1935, for a time played Sally in "The Two Mrs. Carrolls"; Palladium, Dec., 1935, Wendy in "Peter Pan"; during 1936–7, appeared in various productions at the "Q" and Embassy; toured, May, 1937, as Patricia in "The Five Ways"; Haymarket, Sept., 1937, played Sylvia Fern in "The Phantom Light"; at the "Q," 1938–9, appeared

in "The Old Master," "Crime," "The Outsider," "I Have Been Here Before," etc.; has appeared on several occasions for the Repertory Players, etc.; entered films, 1933, and has appeared in numerous pictures. *Recreations:* Riding, swimming, and music. *Address:* 6 Green Tiles, Denham, Uxbridge, Middlesex. *Telephone No.:* Denham 2160.

LUCE, Polly (*née* Pauline Marion Luce), actress; *b.* Indiana, U.S.A., 29 Mar., 1905; *d.* of Frederick Luce and his wife Maude (Heinz); *e.* New York; *m.* Wilfred H. Troutbeck; made her first appearance on the stage at the Gaiety Theatre, New York, 13 Apr., 1925, in the chorus of "Tell Me More"; at the Earl Carroll Theatre, July, 1925, appeared in "Earl Carroll Vanities"; at the Globe, June, 1926, appeared in " No Foolin'" (Ziegfeld's Revue), New Amsterdam, Aug., 1927, in "Ziegfeld Follies of 1927"; went to England in 1928, and made her first apppearance on the London stage, at the Queen's Theatre, Jan., 1929, when she deputized for her sister, Claire, in the part of Bonny in "Burlesque"; Apr., 1929, toured in the same part; at the Phoenix June, 1931, played Pearl in "Late Night Final"; Lyceum, Aug., 1931, Cora Ann Milton in a revival of "The Ringer"; New, Oct., 1931, Jacqueline Kisse in "Hollywood Holiday"; Saville June, 1932, Polly in "Tell Her the Truth"; Piccadilly, Apr., 1933 (for Repertory Players), Dolly Winslow in "Clear All Wires"; Queen's, May, 1933, Adrienne Dietmar in "Spendlove Hall"; Palace, Apr., 1934, appeared in "Why Not To-Night?"; in Oct., 1934, toured as Helen in "Saturday to Monday"; appeared in films "Send 'Em Back Half Dead," "Maid Happy," etc. *Favourite parts:* Cora Ann in "The Ringer," and Bonny in "Burlesque." *Recreations:* Riding and literature.

LUDERS, Gustav, composer ; has composed the music for the following among other musical pieces : " The Burgomaster," 1900 ; " King Dodo," 1902 ; " The Prince of Pilsen," 1903 ; " Ma'm'selle Napoleon," 1903 ; " The

Sho-Gun," 1904 ; " Woodland," 1905 ; " The Grand Mogul," 1906 ; " Marcelle," 1908 ; " The Fair Co-Ed," 1908 ; " The Old Town," 1909 ; *Address :* The Lambs' Club, 130 West 44th Street, New York City, U.S.A.
(Died 24 Jan., 1913; age 47)

LUGG, Alfred, secretary of the Actors' Association ; *b.* London, 4 Feb., 1889 ; *s.* of William Lugg and his wife Ellen Florence (Smith) ; *e.* Malines, Belgium ; *m.* Beatrice Lyons ; was originally intended to follow the scholastic profession ; studied for the stage under his father ; made his first appearance on the stage at the Theatre Royal, Yarmouth, Sept., 1907, walking on in " John Glayde's Honour," with Sir George Alexander ; made his first appearance in London, at the Aldwych Theatre, 22 June, 1909, as Dallel in " On Jhelum River " ; has fulfilled engagements at the Strand, Garrick, New, Wyndham's, Lyric, Lyceum, etc. ; has played in over two hundred dramas ; in 1917, started propaganda for converting the Actors' Association into a trade union ; in 1918, was elected to the Council, and in 1919 the Association was reorganised as a trade union, and he was appointed general secretary. *Recreations :* Most games, and walking. *Hobby :* Politics. *Address :* 79 St. Martin's Lane, W.C.2. *Telephone No. :* Gerrard 1753.

LUGG, William, actor ; *b.* Portsea, Portsmouth, 4 June, 1852 ; made his first appearance on the stage at the Savoy Theatre, 5 Jan., 1884, as Synthius in Gilbert and Sullivan's opera, " Princess Ida " ; he next appeared at the Court Theatre in small parts in " The Magistrate," " The Schoolmistress," and " Dandy Dick," subsequently appearing at the Olympic, 1888, in " Christina," and at the Strand in " Run Wild," " Kleptomania," and " Aladdin " ; at the Comedy Theatre, 1889, he played in " Æsop's Fables," " The Pink Dominos," " Queen's Counsel," and " Domestic Economy " ; returning to the Strand, for some time he appeared as Nathaniel Glover in " Our Flat " ; in 1891 he appeared at Drury Lane

in " A Sailor's Knot," subsequently joining the company of Mr. and Mrs. Kendal ; remained with them for some years, playing such parts as Colonel Daunt in " The Queen's Shilling," The Earl of Portland in " Clancarty," Sir John Ingram in " A Scrap of Paper," etc. ; with Forbes-Robertson at the Lyceum, appeared as Polonius in " Hamlet " and Duncan in " Macbeth " ; in 1899 joined Sir Henry Irving's company, playing such parts as Benjamin Vaughan in " Robespierre," Titus Lartius in " Coriolanus," Lambert in " The Lyons Mail," Ireton in " King Charles I," François de Paule in " Louis XI," Salanio in " The Merchant of Venice," The Witch of the Kitchen in " Faust," Ruggieri in " Dante," Roger in " Becket," etc. ; at the Shaftesbury, 2 Jan., 1906, played the Stranger in " The Jury of Fate " ; at the Aldwych, 19 Mar., appeared as Viscount Bellingham in " The Beauty of Bath," and same theatre, 10 Sept., 1907, as Andrew Quainton in " The Gay Gordons " ; in Apr., 1908, toured with Ellaline Terriss, in " Sweet and Twenty " ; at the Prince of Wales's, Feb., 1910, played Count Boethy in " The Balkan Princess " ; subsequently toured with Olga Nethersole ; toured in " The Quaker Girl," 1910-11 ; appeared at the Lyceum, 1912, in " The Monk and the Woman," and at the Prince's, in " Ben-My-Chree" ; in 1913 toured with Olga Nethersole ; at the Prince of Wales's, Feb., 1914, played Peter Pembroke in " Broadway Jones " ; at the Comedy, Apr., 1915, Edouard de Fontaine in " Wild Thyme " ; at the Comedy, Apr., 1915, appeared as The Judge in " On Trial " ; at the Lyceum, Sept., 1915, appeared in " Between Two Women " ; at Wyndham's, Mar., 1 16, played the King in " A Kiss for Cinderella " ; at the St. James's, Jan., 1917, the Bishop of Carcassone in " The Aristocrat " ; at the Lyceum, July, 1918, Colonel Hildebrand in " The Story of the Rosary " ; at the Apollo, Nov., 1918, the Comte de Belleville in " Soldier Boy " ; at the Lyric, Sept., 1919, Mr. Sysonby in " The Bird of Paradise " ; at the Savoy, Oct., 1919, Father Thibaut in " Tiger Rose " ; at the Coliseum, Mar., 1920, appeared as the Clergyman in "The Truth About the Russian Dancers"; at the Aldwych, Nov., 1920, played Duncan in "Macbeth"; at the Aldwych Theatre, Aug., 1921, the Comte de Courson in "The Legion of Honour"; at the Royalty, Oct., 1922, Simeon Rititch in "Mr. Budd (of Kennington)"; at the Lyceum, Mar., 1924, Father Pius in "Under His Protection"; at the Gaiety, Sept., 1924, Judge Delafield, J.P., in "Poppy"; Lyric, Hammersmith, June, 1927, Mr. Snevellicci in "When Crummles Played"; since 1920 has been principally engaged in acting for the cinema. *(Died 1940; age 88)*

LUGNÉ-POË, A. F., French actor; founder and manager of the Théâtre de L'Oeuvre, Paris; *b.* San Francisco, Cal., 20 Jan., 1870; *e.* Condorcet; prepared for the stage, under M. Worms, at the Paris Conservatoire, which he entered 1889; was awarded second prize for comedy in 1891; *m.* Mdme. Suzanne-Després; founded the Théâtre de L'Oeuvre, 1892, which has been subsidized by the French Government, since 1903; introduced to the French public Maeterlinck's "Pelleas and Mélisande," 1892; "L'Intruse," 1893; "Intérieur," 1895; "Monna Vanna," 1901; Ibsen's "Rosmersholm," 1893; "L'Ennemi du Peuple," "Brand," "Solness le Constructeur," 1894; "Peer Gynt," 1896; "John Gabriel Borkmann," 1897; "Maison de Poupée," 1903; Oscar Wilde's "Salomé," 1895; D'Annunzio's "Gioconda," and "La Fille de Jorio," 1903; also works by Georges Brand, Tolstoy, Synge, Gorki, Strindberg, Claudel, Gommelynck, and José Échegaray; has also managed seasons of Eleonora Duse and the Sicilians; appeared at the Shaftesbury Theatre, May, 1908, in "Poil du Carotte"; has also produced plays by Henry Bataille, Romain Coolus, Edmond Sée, Tristan Bernard, etc.; author of "Claudine à Paris" (with MM. Willy and Weyre), produced at Bouffes Parisiens, 1902; is an Officer of Public Instruction, and an Officer of the Legion of Honour; has made more than twenty tours round the world, from Norway to Bolivia; has

also conducted tours for Eleonora Dusé, M. de Féraudy, Giovanni Grasso, Ermete Zacconi, Isadora Duncan, etc.; is the dramatic cirtic of *L'Eclair*; is chief of the foreign service of *Comoedia*; during 1920-21, he gave more than 250 performances at the Salon de Théâtre de la Maison de L'Oeuvre; in May, 1920, revived "Maison de Poupée," and "Solness le Constructeur"; Oct., 1920, appeared as Gustave in "Créanciers," and also revived "L'Intruse"; in Dec., 1920, revived "La Couronne de Carton," and "Cocu Magnifique," in the latter of which he appeared as Bruco; Apr., 1921, played Monseigneur de Lescure in "Le Pécehur d'Ombres"; in Oct., 1921, produced Strindberg's play "La Danse de Mort." *Hobby:* Collecting autographs.

(Died 9 June, 1940; age 70)

LUGOSI, Bela, actor; *b.* Lugos, Hungary, 20 Oct., 1888; *s.* of Stephan Blasko and his wife Paula (von Vojnics); *e.* Lugos and at the Academy of Theatrical Art, Budapest; *m.* Lilian Arch; made his first appearance on the stage in 1900; by 1911 he was the leading actor at the Magyar Szinhaz, Budapest, and in 1913 became leading actor of the Royal National Theatre in that city; he played leading parts here from Hamlet, Manfred and Cyrano de Bergerac to Liliom; left Hungary after the War and revolution, and after appearing in films in Berlin, went to the United States; after playing and producing various Hungarian plays he made his first appearance on the English speaking stage at Greenwich Village Theatre, New York, 20 Dec., 1922, as Fernando in "The Red Poppy"; National, Oct., 1925, the Sheik of Hammam in "Arabesque"; Daly's, Dec., 1925, Sergius Chernoff in "Open House"; Charles Hopkins, Dec., 1926, Father Petros in "The Devil in the Cheese"; Fulton, Oct., 1927, Count Dracula in "Dracula," which ran throughout the season and in which he toured for two years; New Amsterdam, Sept., 1933, Siebenkase in "Murder at the Vanities"; returned to the stage, 1944,

after an absence of ten years, when he toured in the United States, as Jonathan Brewster in "Arsenic and Old Lace"; originally entered films, 1915, and played in several notable Continental films; re-entered films in the United States, 1924, in "The Silent Command"; has since appeared in innumerable pictures. *Hobbies :* Sculpturing and hunting.
(Died 16 Aug., 1956; age 73)

LUGUET, André, actor; *b.* Fonteney-sous-Bois, France, 15 May, 1892; was formerly engaged in commerce in London; made his first appearance on the stage, at the Royalty Theatre, London, 1909, in the company of Felix Galipaux; returned to Paris, 1910, and entered the *Conservatoire,* under Jules Leitner; appeared at the Théâtre des Arts, 1910, in "L'Eveil du Printemps"; was engaged at the Capucines, 1911–3; served in the Army, 1914–9; re-appeared on the stage at the Théâtre Michel, 1919, and subsequently appeared at the Capucines and the Casino de Paris; at the Femina, 1919, appeared in "Souris d'Hotel," and 1920, in "Une Faible Femme"; Marigny, 1921, in "L' Atlantide"; Vaudeville, 1921, in "La Tendresse"; Potinière, 1921, in "Alain, sa mère et sa maitresse"; Capucines, 1922, in "Simone est comme ça"; Variétés, 1922, in "Le Belle Angevine"; Potinière, 1922, in "Un jeune ménage"; has appeared at most of the Boulevard theatres.

LUKAS, Paul, actor; *b.* Budapest, Hungary, 26 May, 1895; *s.* of Janos Lukas and his wife Maria (Zilahy); *e.* Budapest and Vienna; *m.* Gizella Benes; served in the first World War, 1914–15, and was discharged, wounded; studied for the stage at the Hungarian Academy of Acting, Budapest; made his first appearance at the National Theatre, Kassa, 1916, and remained two years, playing nearly fifty parts; he then went to the Comedy Theatre, Budapest, 1918, making his *début* there as Liliom in the play of that name; he remained there nearly nine years, appearing in leading parts in classic repertory and modern plays, including "Ivanov," "Spring Cleaning," "The Importance of Being Earnest," "Six Characters in Search of an Author," "Captain Brassbound's Conversion," "Great Catherine," "The Cherry Orchard," and many plays by Eugene O'Neill, Henry Bernstein, August Strindberg, Ferenc Molnar, etc.; went to Hollywood, 1927, and appeared in films for nearly ten years, making many notable pictures; made his first appearance on the New York stage, at the Morosco Theatre, 27 Dec., 1937, as Dr. Rank in "A Doll's House"; made an outstanding success, when he appeared at the Martin Beck Theatre, Apr., 1941, as Kurt Müller in "Watch on the Rhine," and appeared in the film of the play, 1943, for which he received the Motion Picture Award, 1943; in summer theatres, 1949, appeared in "Accent on Youth," "The Play's the Thing," and "The Heiress"; at the Imperial, New York, Oct., 1950, played Cosmo Constantine in "Call Me Madam"; Music Box, Mar., 1952, Franz Engel in "Flight Into Egypt"; re-appeared in Great Britain at the Edinburgh Festival, 1953, when he played Dr. Bartok in "Night of the Fourth"; at the Cort, New York, Feb., 1955, appeared as Baron Nicholas de Balbus in "The Wayward Saint"; first appeared in films in Budapest, 1918, and in England, 1938, in "The Lady Vanishes"; first appeared on television in Dec., 1931, and has since played numerous parts. *Recreation :* Tennis. *Clubs :* Racquet Club of Palm Springs, California, and River Club of New York. *Address :* c/o Actors' Equity Association, 226 West 47th Street, New York City, U.S.A.

LUKYANOV, Sergei Vladimiro-vich, actor; *b.* Nizhnee, Voroshilovgrad region, Ukraine, 27 Sept., 1910; *s.* of Vladimir Grigoriev Lukyanov and his wife Raisa Viktorovna Romova; secondary education; *m.* Klara Stepanovna Luchko; studied for the theatre at the Kharkov Studio, Shevchenko Theatre, Kiev; made his first appearance on the stage at the All-Donbass Theatre, Stalino, in 1929, as a sailor in "Captive of the

Apple Tree"; between 1930–1942, he appeared at the Red Army Theatre, Kiev, Grand Drama Theatre, Archangel, and the Chkalov Russian Drama Theatre, Nikolaev, playing such parts as Filka in "Intervention" by L. Slavin, Laertes in "Hamlet," Lopakhin in "The Cherry Orchard," Goretsky in Ostrovsky's "Wolves and Sheep," and Rybakov in "Kremlin Chimes" by N. Pogodin; in 1942, he joined the Vakhtangov Theatre Company, Moscow, playing in classic and contemporary repertory until 1957, when he joined the Moscow Art Theatre Company, of which he is still a member; principal parts he has played include Pastor Anders in "The Devil's Disciple," Kleshch in Gorky's "Lower Depths," Serdyuk in "The Irkutsk Story," by A. Arbuzov, Florindo in Goldoni's "Servant of Two Masters," Kudryash in "Storm" by Ostrovsky, Insarov in "On the Eve" by Turgenev, and Egor Bulychov in "Egor Bulychov and Others" by M. Gorky; made his first appearance in London, Sadler's Wells, May, 1958, when he appeared as Lopakhin in the Moscow Art Theatre production of "The Cherry Orchard"; made his first appearance in films, 1944, and has since appeared in twenty films; was one of the first actors to appear on Russian television, and has played in many televised theatre productions. *Favourite parts:* Egor Bulychov, and Lopakhin in "The Cherry Orchard." *Recreation:* Carving wooden figures. *Club:* All-Russian Theatrical Society. *Address:* Flat 25, Block B., 1/15 Kotelniki Embankment, Moscow, U.S.S.R.

LUPINO, Barry, actor, pantomimist, and dancer; *b.* London, 7 Jan., 1882; *s.* of George Lupino and his wife Florence (Webster); *e.* Blackheath; *m.* (1) May Anstruther; (2) Gertrude Letchford; (3) Doriel Myrtle Phillips; studied dancing under Espinosa, and was trained as pantomimist by his father; made his first appearance on the stage as a baby in arms at Drury Lane Theatre, Mar., 1884, being carried on in the pantomime of "Cinderella"; played for several years as "stock" comedian at the Britannia Theatre, Hoxton, under Mrs. Sara Lane; toured the con-

tinent of Europe, and subsequently went to America, where he appeared in "A Barnyard Romeo"; appeared in Drury Lane pantomimes 1910–12, in "Aladdin," "Jack and the Beanstalk," "Hop o' My Thumb," and "The Sleeping Beauty"; in 1913, went to Australia; subsequently toured in South Africa and the Far East; again went to America, and appeared at the Winter Garden, New York, Feb., 1916, as Howell Louder in "Robinson Crusoe Jr."; went to Australia, and appeared there, 1917, as Eddie Kettle in "Very Good Eddie," and also played in "The White Chrysanthemum"; returned to America, where he remained for five years; appeared at the London Hippodrome, Mar., 1922, as Tippett in "Round in Fifty"; again toured, and in 1927 again appeared in America; at the Majestic, New York, Oct., 1927, played Reginald Pargester in "The Love Call"; Shubert, Dec., 1928, Hercule in "The Red Robe"; Jolson, Dec., 1929, Gonzorgo in the revival of "Babes in Toyland"; returned to England, 1930; in Jan., 1931, toured the provinces as Reggie Powley in "The Love Race"; at the Gaiety, May, 1931, played Charlie Bang in "The Millionaire Kid"; Phoenix, Feb., 1932, Arthur Tilbury in "Lovely Lady"; in May, 1932, toured in "Between Ourselves," of which he was part-author; Aug., 1932, toured as Wun-Hi in "The Geisha"; in Sept., 1933, toured as Archibald in "Frivolity"; at the Grand, Leeds, Dec., 1933, played Mrs. Crusoe in "Robinson Crusoe"; during 1934, toured as Blake in "That's a Pretty Thing"; Wimbledon, Dec., 1934, played Dame Durden in "Jack and the Beanstalk"; in Apr., 1935, toured as Timothy Quaintance in "Twenty to One"; in the autumn of 1935, toured in "Pleasure Bound"; King's, Hammersmith, Dec., 1935, again played the Dame in "Jack and the Beanstalk"; again toured, 1936, in "Twenty to One"; Alexandra, Birmingham, Dec., 1936, played Mother Goose; toured, 1937, as Peter Fenton in "Married in Haste" and Maxie Mumm in "Swing Along"; Alexandra, Birmingham, Dec., 1937, Widow Twankey in "Aladdin"; toured, 1938, as Bertie Barnes in "Crazy Days";

Prince's, Manchester, Dec., 1938, Martha in "Humpty-Dumpty"; again toured, 1939, in "Crazy Days"; Saville, Nov., 1939, played Trott in "Runaway Love," of which he was part-author; Streatham Hill, Dec., 1939, in "Aladdin"; toured, 1940, as Amos Burge in "Happy Birthday," of which he was part-author; London Coliseum, June, 1941, played Sir John in "Me and My Girl"; Golders Green, Dec., 1943, played Mother Goose in the pantomime of that name; Brighton, Dec., 1944, Sarah, the Cook, in "Dick Whittington"; again toured, 1945, in "Happy Birthday"; Golders Green, Dec., 1945, again played the Widow Twankey in "Aladdin"; Victoria Palace, Aug., 1946, Mr. Sam in "Sweetheart Mine"; Grand, Croydon, Dec., 1946, Dame Durden in "Jack and the Beanstalk"; Granville, Walham Green, May, 1949, Alf Huggins in "Blonde for Danger"; Prince's, Dec., 1949, Sarah in "Dick Whittington"; Empire, Portsmouth, Dec., 1950, Widow Twankey in "Aladdin"; Coliseum, Harrow, Dec., 1954, Dame Sarah in "Dick Whittington"; is the author or part-author of more than fifty pantomimes; has also appeared in several films. *Hobby:* Collecting theatrical literature. *Club:* Savage. *(Died 25 Sept., 1962; age 80)*

LUPINO, Stanley, actor and dancer; *b.* London, 15 May, 1894; *s.* of George Lupino and his wife Florence (Webster); *e.* London; *m.* Connie Emerald; was trained by his father; made his first appearance on the stage at the Britannia Theatre, Hoxton, at Christmas, 1900, as a Monkey in the pantomime "King Klondyke"; subsequently he appeared on the variety stage as a member of the Albert and Edmunds troupe of acrobats, also with the Brothers Luck; in 1908 toured in "Viviana's Toy Shop" and "The American Heiress"; made his first appearance in the West End of London, at the Lyceum, Christmas, 1910, as the Cat in "Dick Whittington"; appeared at the Empire, Apr., 1913, in "All the Winners"; at Drury Lane, Christmas, 1914, played in "The Sleeping Beauty"; at the

Oxford, 1915, played in "Go to Jericho," and "This is the Life," and at Christmas again played at Drury Lane in "The Sleeping Beauty"; during 1916 toured in "Girl Wanted," and at Christmas appeared at Drury Lane as Puss in "Puss-in-Boots"; at the Globe, Mar., 1917, played Tibbs in "Suzette"; at the Shaftesbury, Sept., 1917, Rono in "Arlette,"; at Drury Lane, Christmas, 1917, Widow Twankey in "Aladdin"; at the Palace, Sept., 1918, appeared in "Hullo! America"; at Drury Lane, Christmas, 1918, Horace in "The Babes in the Wood"; at the Gaiety, Oct., 1919, played Dr. Thomas Pym in "The Kiss Call"; at Drury Lane, Christmas, 1919, Pipchin in "Cinderella"; at the London Hippodrome, June, 1920, appeared in "Jig-Saw"; at the Shaftesbury, Sept., 1920, in "Oh! Julie!"; at the Queen's, Dec., 1920, in "It's All Wrong"; at the London Hippodrome, Apr., 1921, in "The Peep-Show"; at the Gaiety, Apr., 1922, played James Hicks in "His Girl"; at the London Pavilion, Aug., 1922, Mercury in "Phi-Phi"; May, 1923, played in "Dover Street to Dixie"; at the Vaudeville, Jan., 1924, in "Puppets"; subsequently toured as George Medway in "Who's My Father?" London Hippodrome, Mar., 1925, played in "Better Days"; went to New York, and appeared at the Cosmopolitan, Sept., 1926 as Theophile Michu in "Naughty Riquette"; Jolson, Jan., 1927, Mr. Carp in "The Nightingale"; after returning to England, 1927, toured in "Up With the Lark"; appeared at the Winter Garden, London, Apr., 1928, as Potiphar Griggs in "So This is Love"; Gaiety, Mar., 1929, played Jerry Walker in "Love Lies"; June, 1930, Reggie Powley in "The Love Race"; Dec., 1931, Eddy Marston in "Hold My Hand"; Mar., 1934, Percy Brace in "Sporting Love"; Saville, Sept., 1936, Tommy Teacher in "Over She Goes"; Shaftesbury, Sept., 1937, Bertie Barnes in "Crazy Days"; Prince's, Dec., 1937, Buttons in "Cinderella"; London Hippodrome, Aug., 1938, Horatio Roper in "The Fleet's Lit Up"; commenced film career, 1931, in "Love Lies," and since 1936 has appeared in "Honeymoon for Three," "Sporting Love," "Over She Goes," "Hold My Hand," etc.; part-author of "Turned Up" (musical version), 1926; "So This is Love" (with Arthur Rigby), 1928; "Room for Two" (with Rigby), 1932; adapted "Oh, Letty" (from "So Long, Letty"), 1928; "Love Lies" (with Rigby), 1929; author of "Change Over," 1929; "The Love Race," 1930; "Hold My Hand," 1931; "That's a Pretty Thing," 1933; "Sporting Love," 1934; "Over She Goes," 1936; "Crazy Days," 1937; published a novel, "Crazy Days," 1932, and a book of reminiscences "From the Stocks to the Stars," 1934. *Recreations:* Painting and writing. *(Died 10 June, 1942; age 48)*

LUPINO, Wallace, actor; b. Edinburgh, Scotland, 23 Jan., 1897; s. of Henry Charles Lupino and his wife Charlotte (Robinson); e. London; m. (1) Rose Jones (mar. dis.); (2) Iris Webb; is a brother of Lupino Lane; studied for the stage under his father; made his first appearance on the stage at the Theatre Royal, Edinburgh, Christmas, 1906, as the Boy Babe in "The Babes in the Wood"; made his first appearance in London, as a dancer, at the Standard Music Hall, Pimlico, 1907; remained in variety theatres until 1914, playing in pantomime annually, under Howard and Wyndham; during 1915, toured in "To-Night's the Night"; in the same year joined the Royal Air Force, and served until 1918; reappeared on the stage, Mar., 1919, when he toured in "The Follies of 1919," under Wylie and Tate, with whom he remained until 1924; he played in "The Follies" of 1920 and 1921, and played in five "Aladdin" pantomimes; then spent nearly five years in pictures; appeared at the Dominion, Dec., 1930, as the Grand Vizier in "Aladdin"; at Streatham Hill, May, 1931, and toured as Skid Kennedy in "Speed"; in Sept., 1933, toured as Professor Moutarde in "Frivolity"; at the Theatre Royal, Birmingham, Dec., 1934, played the King in "Jack and the Beanstalk"; London Coliseum, Dec., 1936, the

Baron in "Cinderella"; Victoria Palace, Dec., 1937, Parchester in "Me and My Girl," which ran over sixteen hundred times, and played the same part at the Coliseum, June, 1941; at the Victoria Palace, Feb., 1942, played General Wallington in "Twenty to One"; Dec., 1942, Baron Stoney in "Babes in the Wood"; Mar., 1943, Mr. Digbat in "La-di-da-di-Da"; Apr., 1944, Dad in "Meet Me Victoria"; Aug., 1945, again played in "Me and My Girl"; Victoria Palace, Aug., 1946, Jock McStrapp in "Sweetheart Mine"; Streatham Hill, Dec., 1952, the Prime Minister in "Humpty Dumpty"; commenced film career 1925, and appeared in over seventy "shorts" at the Educational Studios, Hollywood. *Recreations:* Swimming, fishing, and motoring. *(Died 11 Oct., 1961; age 64)*

LYEL, Viola, actress; b. Hull, Yorks., 9 Dec., 1900; d. of Frederick Watson and his wife Elizabeth (Lyel); e. Hull High School, and Kilburn High School, London; m. John Anthony Edwards; studied for the stage at the Guildhall School of Music, and was a student at the Old Vic; made her first appearance at the Old Vic, 1918, where she played small parts and understudied; toured in the Ben Greet company, and in 1922, went to the Liverpool Repertory Theatre; in 1925, joined the company of the Birmingham Repertory Company; at the Court, 1926, played in "The Farmer's Wife"; Haymarket, Nov., 1926, played Emma Major in "Yellow Sands"; Lyric, Hammersmith, Apr., 1928, Margery in "Love in a Village"; Gate, Jan., 1929, and Kingsway, Feb., 1929, Gertrude in "Fashion"; Everyman, May, 1929, in "Morning, Noon, and Night"; then went to America, and made her first appearance in New York, at the Eltinge Theatre, 11 Sept., 1929, as Lucy Timson in "Murder on the Second Floor"; on her return, appeared at the Gate, Jan., 1930, as Mrs. Slade in "Ten Nights in a Bar Room"; Criterion, Jan., 1930, Nancy Sibley in "Milestones"; Everyman, July, 1930, Prim in "Prunella"; again went to New York, and appeared at the Ritz, Sept., 1930, as Clare Pembroke in "Nine Till Six"; on her return, appeared at the Duchess, Dec., 1930, as Ivy in "Jane's Legacy"; Arts, May, 1931, Mary Regan in "The Mantle"; at the Gate, 1931, appeared in "The Heir," "Reign," and "The Red Rover's Revenge"; at the Little, Nov., 1932, played Edith in "Getting Married"; May, 1933, Enid Underwood in "Strife"; Gate, Nov., 1933, Prudence in "The Lady of the Camellias"; Dec., 1933, Eliza in "Uncle Tom's Cabin"; in Aug., 1934, toured as Gwen in "The Late Christopher Bean"; Royalty, Dec., 1934, played Bluebell Blade in "The Red Rover's Revenge"; Phoenix (for Repertory Players), Apr., 1935, Alice Peabody in "It's a Wise Child"; Apollo, June, 1935, Dolly Kelvin in "Duet in Floodlight"; toured, 1935, as Gwenny in "The Late Christopher Bean"; Little, Nov., 1935, the Princess of the Western Regions in "Lady Precious Stream"; St. James's, Feb., 1936, Miss Bingley in "Pride and Prejudice," which ran for nearly a year; Garrick, Sept., 1937, Marianne Bell-Mason in "Sarah Simple"; Old Vic, Apr., 1938, Valeria in "Coriolanus"; Whitehall, June, 1938, Judith in "Lot's Wife," and toured in the same part, 1939; St. James's, June, 1939, Julia Browne in "After the Dance"; Aldwych, Nov., 1939, Miss Leeper in "Married for Money"; Comedy, Jan., 1941, Anna Portal in "The Blue Goose"; St. Martin's, Aug., 1941, Emily Creed in "Ladies in Retirement"; Savoy, Dec., 1941, Miss Preen in "The Man Who Came to Dinner," which ran two years, and in 1944, played the same part on a tour for E.N.S.A.; Stratford-on-Avon Memorial Theatre, Apr.–Sept., 1944, played the Queen in "Hamlet," Helena in "A Midsummer Night's Dream," and Lady Politick Would-Be in "Volpone"; toured, Nov.–Dec., 1944, in France and Belgium, for E.N.S.A., in "Lady from Edinburgh"; Stratford-on-Avon Memorial Theatre, Apr.–Sept., 1945, Mistress Page, Octavia in "Antony and Cleopatra," Mrs. Hardcastle in "She Stoops to Conquer," Queen Katharine in "Henry VIII," the Nurse in "Romeo and Juliet," and Emilia in "Othello"; St. Martin's, Jan., 1946, succeeded Cathleen Nesbitt as Mathilde Heiss in

"The Shop at Sly Corner"; Open Air Theatre, June, 1947, played the Princess of the Western Regions in "Lady Precious Stream"; Arts, Oct., 1947, Mabel Simcox in "Cupid and Mars"; Apollo, Mar., 1948, Miss Gosssage in "The Happiest Days of Your Life," which ran over six hundred performances; Embassy, Mar., 1950, Miss Irma Thackeray in "The Lady Purrs"; Wyndham's, Mar., 1951, played Thelma Cressingdon in "Count Your Blessings"; at the "Q," June, 1951, Mrs. Chester-Glossop in "Navy at Sea"; Aldwych, Oct., 1951, Aunt Louise in "Figure of Fun"; Westminster, May, 1952, Miss Rachel Wardle in "The Trial of Mr. Pickwick"; toured, Oct., 1952, as April Lane in "All Cats Are Grey"; "Q," Feb., 1953, Helen Holmes in "The Full Treatment"; joined the Old Vic Company for the 1953–4 season, and appeared as the Widow of Florence in "All's Well That Ends Well," Queen Elinor in "King John"; at the Arts, Feb., 1954, played Miss Ashford in a revival of "The Private Secretary"; Duchess, Apr., 1954, Lady Cleghorn in "The Manor of Northstead"; joined the Bristol Old Vic Company, 1955, and among other parts appeared as Mrs. Laughton-Moore in "The Mulberry Bush," and Eugenie in "Ondine"; Duchess, Dec., 1956, played Blodwen Morgan-Jones in "The Bride and the Bachelor"; Edinburgh Festival, Aug., 1958, played Mother Marie Therese Vauzon in "Bernadette"; Strand, Mar., 1959, Lady Blore in "Wolf's Clothing"; Winter Garden, May, 1959, Gwen Garroway in "The Prodigal Wife"; Bristol Old Vic, May, 1960, played Mrs. Hardcastle in "She Stoops to Conquer," subsequently appearing in Lebanon with the same company, summer, 1960, as the Abbess in "The Comedy of Errors," and as the Nurse in "Romeo and Juliet"; Vaudeville, London, Dec., 1960, Mrs. Gow in "The Bride Comes Back"; Duke of York's, Sept., 1962, played Hilda Rose in "Big Fish, Little Fish"; Duchess, Jan., 1964, Lady Cleghorn in "The Reluctant Peer"; Chichester Festival, June–Aug., 1966, Trusty in "The Clandestine Marriage," Witch and Gentlewoman in "Macbeth," Bise in "The Fighting

Cock," re-opening in the latter production at the Duke of York's, Oct., 1966; Comedy, May, 1967, Miss Phipps in "Horizontal Hold"; Jeanetta Cochrane, Dec., 1967, Aunt March in "Little Women"; Chichester Festival, July, 1969, Old Lady Squeamish in "The Country Wife"; has also appeared for the Fellowship of Players, Repertory Players, etc.; commenced film career, 1928, and has appeared in numerous pictures. *Recreation:* Swimming. *Address:* c/o Plunket Greene Ltd., 110 Jermyn Street, St. James's Square, London, S.W.1.

LYLE, Lyston (Edward Gibson), actor ; *e.* at Cheltenham and Oscott ; made his first appearance on the stage at Adelphi, 10 Mar., 1894, as Dr. Gilbert in " The Cotton King " ; in May, 1894, played Marquis de Presles in " The Two Orphans " at same theatre ; appeared as Percival Lumley in " Delia Harding " at Comedy, Apr., 1895 ; Mr. Blackstone, Q.C., in " Her Advocate," Sept., 1895 ; Stephen Raymond in " Tommy Atkins," Dec., 1895, and Martin in " The Fool of the Family," Jan., 1896 ; at Duke of York's, played Sir Roland Stanmore in " The Star of India," Apr., 1896 ; Gillie Fletcher in " In Sight of St. Paul's," Aug., 1896 ; and Captain Darville in " Two Little Vagabonds," at Princess's, Sept., 1896 ; then joined Charles Hawtrey and appeared as Percival Chudleigh in " The Saucy Sally," Mar., 1897 ; and Seth in " One Summer's Day," Sept., 1897 ; Hon. Crosby Jethro in " Lord and Lady Algy," Apr., 1898 ; at the Avenue, played Colonel Gower in " The Cuckoo," Mar., 1899, and at the Comedy, the Policeman in " A Message from Mars," Nov., 1899 ; at the Prince of Wales's, played Nathaniel Bodfish in " The Man from Blankley's," Apr., 1901 ; General Tufto in " Becky Sharp," Aug., 1901 ; Sir Henry Fox in " The President," Apr., 1902 ; and Guy Grimling in " There and Back," May, 1902 ; he then became general manager for Lewis Waller at Imperial and Lyric Theatres, and remained in this capacity from 1902 to 1908 ; resumed acting in 1909, appearing

at Wyndham's, with Charles Hawtrey, Oct., 1909, as Captain Neil Partington in " The Little Damozel " ; at the Comedy, Mar., 1910, played Handler in " Alias Jimmy Valentine " ; at Wyndham's, Apr., 1910, appeared as Dr. Masters in " The Naked Truth " ; then went to the St. James's, where in Nov., 1910, he played Joseph Radburn in " Eccentric Lord Comberdene," and Feb., 1911, Stephen Ballantyne in " The Witness for the Defence " ; at Drury Lane, Sept., 1911, played Major Hector Grant in " The Hope " ; at Wyndham's, Feb., 1912, played General Sir John Manning in " The Dust of Egypt " ; subsequently toured as Willard Brockton in " The Easiest Way " ; at the Comedy, Feb., 1913, Lord Orrington in " Lady Noggs " ; at the Comedy, Nov., 1913, appeared as Sir John Capel in " A Place in the Sun " ; at the Apollo, Mar., 1914, played Colonel Apthorp in " Things We'd Like to Know " ; at the Royalty, May, 1914, Mynheer Cornelis, and Sir Charles in " My Lady's Dress " ; at the Lyric, Oct., 1914, Louis Scribner in " The New Shylock " ; at Wyndham's, Dec., 1914, the Earl of Amersteth in " Raffles " ; June, 1915, Major Stocks in " Gamblers All." *Hobbies :* Cricket, tennis, motoring. *(Died 19 Feb., 1920; age 64)*

LYND, Rosa, actress ; *b.* New York City, U.S.A., 23 July, 1884 ; *d.* of William Holt Secor and his wife Augusta (Nolan) ; *e.* Flushing, Long Island, U.S.A. ; *m.* Guy Chetwynd ; studied for the stage under Kate Rorke and at the Guildhall School of Music ; made her first appearance on the stage at the Empire Music Hall, Penge, Aug., 1914, as Estelle in " Guardian Angel " ; first appeared in London at the Victoria Palace, 12 July, 1915, as Isabel Farrington in " How to Get On " ; at the Oxford, Sept., 1915, appeared as Fanny in " The Dandy " ; at Wyndham's Theatre, Dec., 1916, played Miss Topleigh-Trevor in " London Pride " ; at the Strand, May, 1917, The Duchess in " Pierrot Philanders " ; subsequently went to New York, and at the Punch and Judy Theatre, 21 Feb., 1918, played Margaret Tinworth in "Her Country"; returning to England appeared at the Lyric, Hammersmith Dec., 1918, as the Queen, Aunt Jane and Mrs. Hubbard in "Make Believe"; during 1919 toured in Holland in "Mid-Channel" and "Candida"; took the Comedy Theatre for a short season in May, 1920, opening as Helen in "Why Marry?"; June, 1920, appeared as Ann Mortimer in "The 'Ruined' Lady," and Aug., 1920, as Aunt Sneyd in "A Nice Thing." *Club:* Ladies' Athenaeum.

(Died 8 Oct., 1922; age 38)

LYNDON, Barré, dramatic author; *b.* London, 12 Aug., 1896; *m.* Grace Travellor; was formerly a journalist, specialising in motor-racing, and contributing short stories to English and American magazines; is the author of the following plays: "Speed," 1931; "The Amazing Dr. Clitterhouse," 1936; "Hell-for-Leather," 1936; "They Came By Night," 1937; "The Man in Half-Moon Street," 1939; also author of the following books, "Grand Prix," "Combat," "Circuit Dust," "Sundown." *Recreation:* Golf.

LYNN, Ralph, actor; *b.* Manchester, 18 Mar., 1882; is a grand-nephew of Eliza Lynn Linton, the novelist; *m.* Gladys Miles; made his first appearance on the stage at Wigan, in "The King of Terrors," in 1900; spent many years in the provinces and in the United States; appeared at the Colonial Theatre, New York, May, 1913, as Algy Slowman in "The Purple Lady"; made his first appearance on the London stage, at the Empire, 19 Oct., 1914, when he played Montague Mayfair in "By Jingo, if We Do—"; during 1915, he toured in "Peaches"; at the Theatre Royal, Brighton, Oct., 1916, played Paul Dartignac in "The Spring Song"; at the Empire, Mar., 1917, appeared in "Hanky-Panky"; Aug., 1917, in "Topsy-Turvey"; at the Prince of Wales's, Mar., 1918, appeared as the Earl of Knowse in "Flora"; at the Palace, May, 1918, as Al Cleveland in "Very Good, Eddie"; at the St. Martin's

Theatre, Nov., 1918, played Lieutenant Turnbull in "The Officer's Mess"; at the Alhambra, Sept., 1919, Marmalade Ball in "Eastward Ho!"; at the Vaudeville, Mar., 1920, played in "Just Fancy"; at the Court, Liverpool, Dec., 1920, played Will Atkins in "Robinson Crusoe"; at the Queen's Theatre, Apr., 1921, Gaston Marceau in "Mary," and Aug., 1921, the Hon. Percival Todhunter in "My Nieces"; at the Shaftesbury, Apr., 1922, made a great hit, when he played Aubrey Henry Maitland Allington in "Tons of Money," which ran nearly two years; at the Aldwych, Feb., 1924, made another success, as Rodney Martin in "It Pays to Advertise"; has since appeared at the same theatre, July, 1925, as Peter Wykeham in "A Cuckoo in the Nest"; June, 1926, Gerald Popkiss in "Rookery Nook"; July, 1927, Ronald Gamble in "Thark"; June, 1928, D'Arcy Tuck in "Plunder"; May, 1929, Charlie Tutt in "A Cup of Kindness"; Feb., 1930, Clifford Tope in "A Night Like This"; Nov., 1930, Walford Gibbs in "Marry the Girl"; May, 1931, David Winterton in "Turkey Time"; Mar., 1932, James Milligan in "Dirty Work"; Sept., 1932, David Blake in "Fifty-Fifty"; Jan., 1933, "Dandy" Stratton in "A Bit of a Test"; Shaftesbury, June, 1934, Kenneth Bixby in "Hello, Again!"; Saville, Nov., 1935, Freddie Widgeon in "The Inside Stand"; toured, 1937, as P.C. Reginald Sinclair in "London After Dark"; Aldwych, Mar., 1940, played Freddie Quibble in "Nap Hand"; St. Martin's, May, 1942, again played Gerald Popkiss in "Rookery Nook"; Duke of York's, Aug., 1944, Lawrence Vining in "Is Your Honeymoon Really Necessary?," which he also produced; the play ran for over two years; Winter Garden, Nov., 1947, played Wilkinson King in "Outrageous Fortune"; King's, Hammersmith, Mar., 1951, played Hubert St. Michael in "Daddy Wore Velvet Gloves"; Royal, Huddersfield, Feb., 1952, Arthur Fishel in "Mixed Grill"; Aldwych, London, Nov., 1952, Trumper Norton in "Wild Horses"; toured, Feb., 1954, as Leonard Bilker, M.P., in "Liberty Bill," and played the same part at the

Piccadilly, Sept., 1954, when a revised version of the play was presented as "The Party Spirit"; Grand, Leeds, June, 1955, appeared as Chesney Van Velt in "Three Times a Day"; toured, Mar., 1956, as Harry Harper in "Universal Uncles"; Bromley, Jan., 1958, played the leading part in "Mixed Grill"; commenced film career, 1929, in "Rookery Nook," and subsequently appeared in "Tons of Money," "Plunder," "Mischief," "Thark," "A Cuckoo in the Nest," "Turkey Time," "A Cup of Kindness," "Dirty Work," and numerous other pictures; was responsible for the staging of "Mr. Abdulla," 1926; "Happy-Go-Lucky," 1926; "Dirty Work," "Fifty-Fifty," 1932; "Spotted Dick," 1939. *Clubs:* Green Room and Stage Golfing Society. *(Died 8 Aug., 1962; age 80)*

LYNNE, Carole (*née* Helen Violet Carolyn Haymen), actress and vocalist; *b.* Rochester, Kent, 16 Sept., 1918; *d.* of Victor Cecil Haymen and his wife Helen Debroy Somers; *e.* "St. Hilary's" private school, Cliftonville, Margate; *m.* (1) Derek Capel Farr (mar. dis.); (2) Bernard Delfont; made her first appearance on the stage at the Canterbury Repertory Theatre, 1937, as Miss Thing in "A Kiss for Cinderella"; made her first appearance in London, at His Majesty's, 15 Sept., 1938, as Susan Townsend in "Paprika"; Apollo, Nov., 1938, played Angelica in "The Robust Invalid"; Gate, Dec., 1938, and Ambassadors', 1939, appeared in "The Gate Revue"; London Hippodrome, Mar., 1939, in "Black and Blue," and Nov., 1939, in "Black Velvet"; Comedy, June, 1941, in "Rise Above It," and June, 1942, in "It's About Time"; Prince's, Feb., 1943, played Mary Fenton in "Old Chelsea," and subsequently toured as Kathie in "The Student Prince"; His Majesty's, Dec., 1943, appeared as Cinderella; Winter Garden, Apr., **1944**, appeared as Jill Sonning in "Jill, Darling"; Hippodrome, Oct., 1944, Dilys in "Jenny Jones"; toured, 1946, as Grace Green in "Big Ben," and played this part at the Adelphi, July, 1946; Casino, Dec., 1947, ap-

peared as Cinderella; at the same theatre, Dec., 1949, played Little Miss Muffet; Prince of Wales's, May, 1950, appeared in the *revue* "Touch and Go"; London Palladium, Dec., 1950, played Maid Marion in "The Babes in the Wood"; first appeared in films, 1940, in "The Ghost Train." *Favourite part:* Mary Fenton in "Old Chelsea." *Recreations:* Painting (water-colours), riding, and tennis. *Address:* c/o Foster's Agency, 33 Regent Street, London, S.W.1.

LYNTON, Mayne, actor; *b.* Bowness, Cumberland, 4 May, 1885; *m.* (1) Annie Hughes (mar. dis.), (2) Nancye Stewart; made his first appearance on the stage in 1907, with F. R. Benson's company; subsequently gained experience in comedy and drama, and appeared at the Standard Theatre, Shoreditch, in several melodramas; went to America in 1911, with the Ben Greet Pastoral Players; at Wallack's, New York, Sept., 1911, played Flooks in "Disraeli," with George Arliss; subsequently played with the Sothern-Marlowe company, and in Nov., 1912, appeared at the Astor Theatre, in "Hawthorne of the U.S.A.," and at the 39th Street, in "Much Ado About Nothing" and "The Rivals"; toured with Blanche Bates in "Half-an-Hour"; at the Lyceum, New York, Feb., 1915, played Sergeant Crosby in "Inside the Lines"; Shubert, Aug., 1916, King Carlos in "The Happy Ending"; subsequently toured in "A Lady's Name"; during the latter part of the War, was attached, first to the Toronto Mobilization Centre, and later, to British Military Mission to the U.S.A.; at the Century, New York, Nov., 1919, played Horatius in "Aphrodite"; went to Australia, 1922, under J. C. Williamson, Ltd., and appeared in "The Bat," in the leading *rôle*; subsequently appeared there in support of Emilie Polini, Gertrude Elliott, Pauline Frederick, etc.; later played "lead" with Muriel Starr; has appeared in "The Flaw," "Eyes of Youth," "If Winter Comes," "Bluebeard's Eighth Wife," "The Pelican," "Spring Cleaning," "The Ghost Train," "Our Betters," "Seventh Heaven," "Monsieur Beaucaire," "The Flying Squad," "The Squeaker," "It Pays to Advertise," "In the Next Room," "The Enemy," "My Old Dutch," "Why Smith Left Home," "The Last Warning," "The Donovan Affair," "Dearest Enemy," etc.

LYON, Ben, actor; *b.* Atlanta, Georgia, U.S.A., 6 Feb., 1901; *s.* of Benjamin Lyon and his wife Alvine; *e.* Baltimore; *m.* Bebe Daniels; made his first appearance on the stage in New York, Booth Theatre, Jan., 1918, in "Seventeen"; played in "stock" companies at Providence and Buffalo, N.Y.; in 1920, toured with Jeanne Eagels in "The Wonderful Thing"; 39th Street Theatre, New York, Feb., 1923, played William, Robert, and Lynn in "Mary the 3rd"; after eleven years in Hollywood, in 1934, toured as Jeffry Crane in "Hollywood Holiday"; made his first appearance in England, at the London Palladium, 29 June, 1936, with his wife, in a programme of songs; toured in variety theatres all over Great Britain, 1936–9; Holborn Empire, Dec., 1939, appeared in "Haw-Haw!"; London Palladium, Dec., 1941, in "Gangway"; from 1939–41, broadcast "Hi-Gang," for B.B.C. and from 1941–3, "Stars and Stripes in Great Britain," for B.B.C. North American programme; 1940–42, toured for the entertainment of troops all over England, also in Normandy and Italy; volunteered 1942, and served in the U.S. Army Air Force, with rank of Lieut.-Colonel; was decorated with the Legion of Merit, 1946; commenced film career 1923, and appeared in innumerable pictures, including "Hell's Angels," and "I Cover the Waterfront"; was engaged as Talent Executive with 20th Century Fox Film Company, in London and Beverly Hills, 1945–6; Assistant Chief of Productions, London, 1948–51; since 1950 has broadcast with particular success in the radio and television series "Life With the Lyons," and has also appeared in many other television shows; reappeared on the stage at the Hippodrome, Blackpool, June, 1952, in a dramatized version of "Life With the Lyons"; Senior Executive Producer of Light Entertainment for Associated-Rediffusion Television Ltd. *Recreations:* Golf, tennis, bridge, and Canasta. *Hobby:* Aviation, for which he holds a Government's pilot's licence. *Clubs:* Water Rats, Queen's Tennis, and Coombe Hill Golf (Great Britain), Beverly Hills Tennis (Calif., U.S.A.).

LYON, Wanda, actress; *b.* Salt Lake City, Utah, U.S.A., 14 May, 1897; *d.* of Mathew Thompson Lyon and his wife Adele (Mangum); *e.* Salt Lake City; *m.* James Lyman Pratt; appeared in Salt Lake City as an amateur, prior to making her first appearance on the professional stage at the Garrick Theatre, in that city, 31 Dec., 1913, as Mdlle. Floriette in "Lover's Isle"; joined Al Jolson's company, in 1915, and appeared with it on tour as Susie in "Dancing Around"; made her first appearance on the New York stage, at the Winter Garden Theatre, 17 Feb., 1916, as Gladys Brookville in "Robinson Crusoe Jun."; in Apr., 1917, played there, in "The Passing Show of 1917"; at the Plymouth Theatre, Nov., 1917, played Martha Hornblower in "The Star Gazer"; Cort, Dec., 1917, Angelina Stokes in "Flo-Flo"; at the Tremont, Boston, Oct., 1918, played in "She Took a Chance"; subsequently went to Europe in War Relief work; made her first appearance on the London stage at the London Hippodrome, July, 1919, in "Joy-Bells," and also appeared at the Palace, Dec., 1919, in "The Whirligig"; she also appeared in Paris, in pictures with Max Linder in "The Best One," "The Little Café," and "Broadway to Piccadilly"; on returning to New York, at the Republic Theatre, Sept., 1921, succeeded Hazel Dawn as Gertie in "Getting Gertie's Garter"; at the Eltinge Theatre, 1922, succeeded Florence Reed as Daisy in "East of Suez"; at the Morosco, Jan., 1923, played Annabelle Carlton in "Mike Angelo"; Ritz, Aug., 1923, Marion Sears in "In Love With Love"; subsequently played Elise in "Cobra," at its first performance, and at the Longacre Theatre, Mar., 1924, played Georgia in "Moonlight"; Martin Beck, Nov., 1924, Belotte in "Madame Pompadour"; Gaiety, Dec., 1924,

Belle Sheridan in "Close Harmony"; Cort, Jan., 1925, Margot in "The Stork"; National, Dec., 1925, Marjorie in "Just Beyond"; during 1926, toured in "The Lady Next Door" ("Close Harmony"); Royale, New York, Jan., 1927, played Suzanne Fair in "Piggy"; Feb., 1927, went to the Princess's, Chicago (for the Chicago Theatre Guild), and played in "The Ragged Edge"; subsequently rejoined the cast of "Piggy"; in April, 1929, went on tour, playing Mary Dugan in "The Trial of Mary Dugan"; at the Royale, New York, Feb., 1931, played Mrs. Archer Satterlee in "Rock Me, Julie"; Bayes Theatre, Mar., 1931, Liane Duval in "Wonder Bar"; at Los Angeles, July, 1931, played Jean in "The Greeks Had a Word for It"; has also appeared in pictures. *Recreations:* Reading and travel. *Address:* 2 East 70th Street, New York City, U.S.A. *Telephone No.:* Rhinelander 4–9789.

LYONS, A. Neil, dramatic author and novelist; *b.* Kimberley, Cape Colony, 1880; *s.* of Henry Lyons and his wife, Elizabeth; *e.* Bedford Grammar School and in Hanover; *m.* Dorothy Worrall; originally intended for the Law, and subsequently studied accountancy; in 1899 was on the staff of *The Critic,* and in 1900 on *The Topical Times,* and for many years a regular contributor to the periodical press; is the author of the following plays: "The Gentleman Who Was Sorry" (with P. E. Hubbard), 1912; "A Penny Bunch" (with Vera Beringer), 1912; "London Pride" (with Gladys Unger), 1916; "A Bit of a Lad," 1917; "The Ring o' Bells," 1925; has written over twenty works of fiction, including "Hookey," "Matilda's Mabel," "Arthurs," "Cottage Pie," "Clara," "Kitchener Chaps," "Moby Lane," "A London Lot," etc. *Club :* Savage.

(Died 4 Jan., 1940; age 60)

LYTELL, Bert, actor; *b.* New York City, 24 Feb., 1885; *s.* of William H. Lytell and his wife Blanche (Mortimer); *e.* Upper Canada College, Toronto; *m.* (1) Evelyn Vaughan (mar. dis.), (2) Claire Windsor (mar. dis.), (3) Grace

Menken; has been on the stage since early childhood, making his first appearance in the Columbia "stock" company in Newark, New Jersey; toured with own company in 1907; in 1911, played leading parts at the Alcazar Theatre, San Francisco; in 1912, managed the "stock" company, at Albany, N.Y.; at the 39th Street Theatre, New York, 28 Dec., 1914, played Robert Hickman in "A Mix-Up"; Fulton, Feb., 1917, Walter Brand in "If"; Bijou, Aug., 1917, Doctor Hampton in "Mary's Ankle"; during 1919–20, toured in vaudeville, in "The Valiant"; from 1920–8, engaged in pictures; at the 48th Street Theatre, Dec., 1928, played Robert Naughton and Eddie Connelly in "Brothers"; in May, 1931, toured as Sandor Turai in "The Play's the Thing," and Prince Sirki in "Death Takes a Holiday"; Playhouse, Oct., 1931, Baron Von Ullrich in "A Church Mouse"; at the Playhouse. New York, Jan., 1933, Craig Baldwin in "Bad Manners"; at the Masque, June, 1933, succeeded Osgood Perkins as Kenneth Bixby in "Good-Bye Again"; at Dennis, Mass., Aug., 1933, appeared as Gilbert Wilding in "Survival"; toured, Dec., 1933, as Colin Derwent in "Ten Minute Alibi"; Erlanger Theatre, Boston, Apr., 1934, played Clark Storey in "The Second Man"; 46th Street, New York, Oct., 1934, Rev. Mark Ahern in "The First Legion," which he also presented; Princeton, N.J., Apr., 1937, Barrie Trexel in "Susan and God"; Washington, D.C., Aug., 1938, Doctor Clitterhouse in "The Amazing Doctor Clitterhouse"; Plymouth Theatre, New York, Nov., 1939, played Dr. Jennings in "Margin for Error"; Golden, Nov., 1940, Geoffrey Armstrong in "Return Engagement"; Alvin, Jan., 1941, Kendall Nesbitt in "Lady in the Dark"; Booth, June, 1945, Doc Ritchie in "The Wind is Ninety"; Golden, Mar., 1946, Sebastian Merryweather in "I Like it Here"; in summer theatres, 1947, played in "The Apple of His Eye," and "Ah! Wilderness"; commenced film career 1917, and has appeared in numerous pictures, notably "The Lone Wolf" series; has also directed films; was President of Actors' Equity Association of America,

1943–5. *Clubs :* Masquers and Hollywood Athletic, Hollywood; Lambs, New York.
(Died 28 Oct., 1954; age 59)

LYTTELTON, Edith, D.B.E., dramatic author ; *d.* of Archibald Balfour ; *m.* the late Hon. Alfred Lyttelton, M.P. ; has written the following plays : " Warp and Woof," 1904 ; " The Macleans of Bairness," 1906 ; " The Thumbscrew," 1912 ; " Peter's Chance," 1912.
(Died 2 Sept., 1948; age 83)

LYTTON, Doris, actress ; *b.* Manchester, 23 Jan., 1893 ; *d.* of Reuben Partington and his wife Jean (Lytton) ; *e.* at Upton Ursuline Convent; *m.* Geoffrey Toye (mar. dis.) ; made her first appearance on the stage, at the opening of the Scala Theatre, 23 Sept., 1905, when she appeared as the child Amaranza in "The Conqueror"; appeared at the Kingsway Theatre, Oct., 1907, as Muriel Wycherley in "Irene Wycherley," and Feb., 1908, as Miss Morton in "Diana of Dobson's " ; at the Haymarket, Nov., 1909, played Miss Delafield in " Might is Right " ; and Dec., 1909, Milk in " The Blue Bird " ; at His Majesty's, July, 1910, appeared with the Beecham Opera Company, as Madame Pfeil in " Der Schauspieldictor " ; at the Prince of Wales's, Oct., 1910, played Micheline in " Inconstant George " ; at the Criterion, Sept., 1911, appeared as Violet Robinson in " Man and Superman " ; at the Playhouse, Feb., 1912, played Muriel Mannering in " The Second in Command " ; in Oct., 1912, went to New York, and at the Thirty-ninth Street Theatre, 28 Oct., 1912, played Effie Pemberton in " The Blindness of Virtue " ; subsequently toured in the same part ; at the Apollo, Sept., 1913, played Violet Stevenson in " Never Say Die " ; at the Coliseum, July, 1914, Patience in " The Compleat Angler " ; at the Apollo, Sept., 1914, Mary Norton in " Seven Keys to Baldpate " ; Jan., 1915, Adela Goadby in " A Busy Day " ; at the New, Apr., 1915, Kitty Hildebrand in " The Joker " ; at Wyndham's, June, 1915, Ruth Long-

worthy in " Gamblers All " ; at the Haymarket, Feb., 1916, Irene Harding in " Who is He ? " ; at Bournemouth, Apr., 1916, Diana Terlbot in " The Basker " ; at the Queen's, May, 1916, Marion Sumner in " The Boomerang " ; at the Haymarket, May, 1916, Prudence Rockley in " Fishpingle " ; Sept., 1916, Bianca Bright in " Mr. Jubilee Drax " ; at the Apollo, Nov., 1916, Lady Clara Teviot in " Poached Eggs and Pearls " ; in Dec., 1916, toured as Margaret Potts in " Oh ! Caesar " ; at the Haymarket, Feb., 1917, played Joy Twentyman in " Felix Gets a Month " ; at the Playhouse, May, 1917, Maud Bray in " Wanted, a Husband " ; at Wyndham's, Oct., 1917, Joanna Trout in " Dear Brutus " ; at His Majesty's, Dec., 1917, Jane in the " all-star " performance of " The Man from Blankley's," given in aid of King George's Pension Fund for Actors ; at Wyndham's, Aug., 1918, Claudia Meriton in " The Law Divine " ; at the Globe, Nov., 1918, for a charity performance, the Countess Napoleone Camerata in the " all-star " cast of " L'Aiglon " ; at the Little Theatre, May, 1920, Mrs. Eastwood in " Husbands for All " ; at the Globe, Sept., 1920, Mdlle. Juliette in " French Leave " ; at the Garrick, Feb., 1921, Barbara Lumley in " The Fulfilling of the Law " ; at the Comedy, Apr., 1921, Beatrice Sinclair in " A Matter of Fact " ; at the Apollo, Nov., 1921, Vera Hawley in " Thank You, Phillips ! " ; at the Aldwych, Jan., 1922, the Hon. Pansy Berkely in " Money Doesn't Matter " ; at the Ambassadors', Apr., 1923, Dora Grayling in " Trespasses " ; at the Duke of York's, May, 1923, succeeded Edna Best as Blanche Ingram in " Her Temporary Husband " ; at Wyndham's, Oct., 1924, Celia Wilson in " The Ware Case " ; Ambassadors', Nov., 1925, Marion Yates in " The Madras House"; Arts, Sept., 1931, Constance Peyton in " Behold the Bridegroom"; Playhouse, Feb., 1932, Kitty Egmont in " King, Queen, Knave " ; at the Playhouse, Aug., 1934, succeeded Frances Doble as Lady Loddon in " Libel"; King's, Glasgow, Apr., 1935, played Mavis in " Love from a Stranger"; St. Martin's, Feb.,

1937, Lady Const in "Suspect"; Apollo, Dec., 1938, Alice Amory in "Windfall"; from 1940–5, was mainly engaged in broadcasting with the Drama section of the B.B.C. *Recreations:* Lawn-tennis, golf, swimming, and dancing.

(Died 3 Dec., 1953; age 60)

LYTTON, Henry, Jun. (Lord Alva Lytton), actor and vocalist; *b.* London, 1904; *s.* of Henry A. Lytton and his wife Louie (Henri); *e.* Brighton College; *m.* (1) Jessie Matthews (mar. dis.); (2) Joan Barbara Weale; made his first appearance on the stage at Glasgow in 1921, when he played the Hon. Dud Wellington in "The Beauty Spot"; during 1924 toured as Toby Kerwin in "Archie," appearing in that part at the King's Theatre, Hammersmith, Dec., 1924; at the Little Theatre, July, 1925, played in "Nine to Eleven Revue"; at the Prince of Wales's, Oct., 1926, in "The Charlot Show of 1926"; during 1927-28 toured as Robert Mason in "The Girl Friend"; during 1929 toured as Lord Compton in "Virginia"; during 1930-31, toured as Frederick Tile in "Here Comes the Bride"; during 1931, also toured in "Folly to be Wise"; during 1932, toured in "The Spice of Paris"; Garrick, Aug., 1934, appeared in "West-End Scandals"; in 1935 toured in "West-End Scandals," "Out of Town To-Night," and in "Stop Press!" *(Died 16 Sept., 1965; age 61)*

LYTTON, Sir Henry A. (cr. 1930), actor; *b.* London, 3 Jan., 1867; *e.* St. Mark's Schools, Chelsea; *m.* Louie Henri; made his first appearance on the stage at the Royalty Theatre, Glasgow, 4 Feb., 1884, in the chorus of "Princess Ida," and understudied David Fisher, Jun., as King Gama; during 1885–86, toured in "All for Her," "Tom Tug," and "Masters and Servants"; subsequently toured for several years with the D'Oyly Carte Opera Company; in 1887, was engaged at the Savoy, understudying George Grossmith as Robin Oakapple in "Ruddigore," and occasion-

ally played the part; he went to New York, in 1890, and appeared at Palmer's Theatre, Feb., 1890, as the Duke of Plaza-Toro in "The Gondoliers"; subsequently toured the English provinces with the D'Oyly Carte Company, for several years; appeared at the Savoy, Apr., 1897, as Ferdinand the Fifth in "His Majesty"; and May, 1897, as Wilfred Shadbolt in "The Yeomen of the Guard"; Dec., 1897, Prince Paul in "The Grand Duchess"; Mar., 1898, Guiseppe in "The Gondoliers"; May, 1898, Simon Lemal in "The Beauty Stone"; Sept., 1898, Dr. Daly in "The Sorcerer" and the Judge in "Trial by Jury"; Jan., 1899, Baron Tabasco in "The Lucky Star"; June, 1899, Captain Corcoran in "H.M.S. Pinafore"; in July, 1899, became manager of the Criterion for a short season, producing "The Wild Rabbit"; Nov., 1899, the Sultan Mahmoud in "The Rose of Persia"; June, 1900, Major-General Stanley in "The Pirates of Penzance"; Nov., 1900, Archibald Grosvenor in "Patience"; Apr., 1901, Pat Murphy in "The Emerald Isle"; Dec., 1901, Strephon in "Iolanthe"; Apr., 1902, the Earl of Essex in "Merrie England"; Jan., 1903, Jelf in "A Princess of Kensington"; next appeared at Adelphi, Dec., 1903, as Dick Wargrave in 'The Earl and the Girl"; at the Lyric, Jan., 1905, played Lieutenant Reggie Drummond in "The Talk of the Town"; at the Criterion, Aug., 1905, played Lieutenant Reginald Armitage in "The White Chrysanthemum"; at the Gaiety, 1906, succeeded Lionel Mackinder as Boniface in "The Spring Chicken,' and subsequently, at Daly's, succeeded Louis Bradfield as Aristide Vert in "The Little Michus"; he then appeared in variety theatres in "The Amateur Raffles" and "United Services"; at the Hicks (now Globe) Theatre, Mar., 1907, played Jack Hylton in "My Darling"; rejoined the Savoy Company, June, 1907, playing Strephon in "Iolanthe"; Apr., 1908, played the title-*rôle* in "The Mikado"; July, 1908, Dick Deadeye in "H.M.S. Pinafore"; Oct., 1908, Strephon in "Iolanthe"; Dec., 1908, the Pirate King in "The Pirates of Penzance"; 1909–19, toured in the provinces with the D'Oyly Carte Opera Company; appeared at the Prince's Theatre, Sept., 1919–Feb., 1920, as the Duke of Plaza-Toro in "The Gondoliers," the Lord Chancellor in "Iolanthe," Ko-Ko in "The Mikado," Reginald Bunthorne in "Patience," Jack Point in "The Yeoman of the Guard," John Wellington Wells in "The Sorcerer," Sir Joseph Porter in "H.M.S. Pinafore"; while touring during 1920 again appeared as Robin Oakapple in "Ruddigore"; during the season at the Prince's Theatre, Oct., 1921, played Major-General Stanley in "The Pirates of Penzance," and Sir Ruthven Murgatroyd in "Ruddigore"; Jan., 1922, King Gama in "Princess Ida"; played the above-mentioned parts again, at the Prince's, 1924, and in 1926; toured in Canada in 1927 and 1929, and in the United States, 1929; appeared in all his old parts at the Savoy, 1929–30 and 1932–33; announced his intention to retire after the season which commenced at the Savoy, Oct., 1932, when he again appeared in "The Gondoliers," and subsequently in most of his old parts; after the Savoy season, again toured until 30 June, 1934, on which date, at the Gaiety, Dublin, he appeared with the company for the last time, playing Jack Point in "The Yeoman of the Guard"; at the Prince of Wales's, Birmingham, Dec., 1934, appeared as the Emperor of China in the pantomime, "Aladdin," his first appearance in pantomime; was created a Chief of the tribe of Sarcee Indians, with the name of "Burning Wolf," 1927. *Club:* Stage Golfing Society. *(Died 15 Aug., 1936; age 69)*

LYTTON, Ruth, comedienne; is a niece of the late Ada Lundberg; appeared at the old Gaiety Theatre in 1903, in "The Linkman," and subsequently toured for some time as Mrs. Pineapple in "A Chinese Honeymoon"; for three years appeared at the London Hippodrome as principal boy in spectacular productions; appeared at Drury Lane, two seasons as second boy; toured in South Africa in "La Poupée"; "The Shop Girl," etc.; appeared at the Palace, 1906, as Dolly de Grey in "The Palace Review"; has since appeared at many of the principal halls in London and the provinces; is a favourite "boy" in pantomime.

MACARTHUR, Charles, dramatic author; *b.* Scranton, Pa., U.S.A., 5 Nov., 1895; *m.* (1) Carol Frink (mar. dis.); (2) Helen Hayes; originally a journalist; is the author of "Lulu Belle" (with Edward Sheldon), 1926; "Salvation" (with Sidney Howard), 1928; "The Front Page" (with Ben Hecht), 1928; "Twentieth Century" (with Hecht), 1932; "Jumbo" (with Hecht), 1935; "Ladies and Gentlemen" (with Hecht), 1939; "Johnny On a Spot," 1941; "Swan Song" (with Hecht), 1946; has also written notable films, including "Crime Without Passion," "Twentieth Century," "The Scoundrel," etc.; acted as co-director for the production of "Crime Without Passion" and "The Scoundrel." *Clubs:* River, and Coffee House, New York.
(Died 21 Apr., 1956; age 60)

MACAULAY, Joseph, actor and singer; *b.* San Francisco, Cal., U.S.A.; *e.* San Francisco; studied Law at the University of California; made his first appearance on the stage at the Alcazar Theatre, San Francisco, and subsequently played in "stock" companies in various cities; made his first appearance on the New York stage at Greenwich Village, 11 Nov., 1919, as Thomas Houlihan in "The Lost Leader," and also appeared there in "Ile," "Efficiency," "Pan and the Young Shepherd," etc., and in Jan., 1920, played Norbert in "The Passion Flower"; 48th Street, Aug., 1921, played King Stefan in "Sonya"; National, Apr., 1923, Dr. Arnold in "The Dice of the Gods"; Liberty, Oct., 1923, the Vizier in "The Magic Ring"; Garrick (for Theatre Guild), Dec., 1923, the Inquisitor in "Saint Joan"; Music Box, Dec., 1924, in "The Music Box Revue"; Little, Feb., 1925, Angelo in "Don't Bother Mother"; 48th Street, May, 1925, Freman in "A Bit of Love"; Martin Beck, Oct., 1926, Baron Frederick in "The Wild Rose"; Provincetown, Apr., 1927, Imre Szabo in "Rapid Transit"; Masque, May, 1927, Archibald Grosvenor in "Patience"; Lyric, July, 1927, Prince Hussein in "Kiss Me"; Majestic, Oct., 1927, Tony Mus-

tano in "The Love Call"; Lyric, Mar., 1928, Aramis in "The Three Musketeers"; Ziegfeld, July, 1929, in "Show Girl"; Hammerstein's, Sept., 1930, Paul Wilson in "Luana"; Erlanger's, May–Aug., 1931, with the Civic Light Opera Co., Captain Corcoran in "H.M.S. Pinafore," Giuseppe in "The Gondoliers," Grosvenor in "Patience," Strephon in "Iolanthe," Counsel in "Trial by Jury"; New Amsterdam, Feb., 1932, Rodney St. Clair in "Face the Music"; Morosco, Oct., 1933, Falke in "Champagne Sec"; New Amsterdam, Nov., 1934, Alonzo in "Revenge with Music"; Lyceum, Oct., 1936, General Gourgaud in "St. Helena"; Manhattan Opera House, Jan., 1937, Judah, The Angel of Death and the Dark Angel in "The Eternal Road"; Alvin, New York, Nov., 1937, played the Federal Theatre Director in "I'd Rather Be Right"; Majestic, New York, Dec., 1938, Captain Jacques in "Great Lady"; Maxine Elliott, Nov., 1939, Captain Wickford in "Sea Dogs"; 44th Street, Mar., 1940, the Policeman in "Liliom"; Imperial, Oct., 1941, Julian Watson in "Let's Face It"; Broadhurst, Apr., 1944, El Magnifico in "Early to Bed"; toured, Sept., 1945, as Colonel Roland Peoples in "Spring in Brazil"; Century, New York, Sept., 1946, played Stephan, Duke of Roncevalle in "Gypsy Lady"; Music Box, New York, May, 1952, appeared as the Friar in "Much Ado About Nothing"; at the Mark Hellinger, Oct.–Nov., 1952, appeared in a season of Gilbert and Sullivan comic opera, when he played the title-rôle in "The Mikado," Richard in "The Pirates of Penzance," Dick Deadeye in "H.M.S. Pinafore," and the Earl of Mount Ararat in "Iolanthe"; Cherry Lane, Apr., 1961, Lawyer Manson in 'Smiling the Boy Fell Dead"; Jan Hus Playhouse, Apr., 1962, Maloney in "King of the Whole Damn World"; Winter Garden, Mar., 1964, Tom Keeney in "Funny Girl"; has also played in stock seasons at Denver, Skowhegan and Dayton, and during the summers of 1933–42, appeared in "musical" stock seasons at the Municipal Theatre, St. Louis; at the Bucks County Playhouse, New Hope, Pa., played in "The

Solid Gold Cadillac," "The Seven Year Itch," "The Lady's Not for Burning," 1945–50; played a ten week summer season at the Dallas State Fair, 1950; in 1951, appeared in a season of musicals at Overton Park, Memphis, Tennessee; between 1953–63, played 86 rôles at the Starlight Theatre, Kansas City; appeared at the Masonic Temple with the Detroit Civic Light Opera Company during seven winter seasons; television appearances include the series "From These Roots." *(Died 6 Oct., 1967; age 76)*

MACBETH, Helen, actress; *b.* Galesburg, Michigan, U.S.A.; *d.* of William Macbeth, of Galesburg; *m.* Frank Mills, actor; made her first appearance on the stage at Harrisburg, Pennsylvania, with Mrs. Fiske; appeared at the Lyceum Theatre, New York, in 1897, as Blanche Oriel in "The Princess and the Butterfly"; made her first appearance on the London stage, at the Adelphi, 8 Apr., 1898, in "The Heart of Maryland"; subsequently appeared at various London Theatres; at Lyric, New York, Sept., 1908, played in "Glorious Betsy," and later, toured with Mary Mannering, in "The Struggle"; during 1909, toured with Mary Mannering in "Step by Step," and "The Independent Miss Gower"; with Edmund Breeze in "The Earth," and with Robert Edeson, 1910, in "A Man's Man"; at the Star, Buffalo, Feb., 1914, appeared in "The Plant."

MacCAFFREY, George, dramatic and music critic; *b.* Galway, Ireland, 15 Sept., 1870; *s.* of Robert MacCaffrey and his wife Marie (Burke); *e.* Downside, near Bath; engaged for some time on *The Spectator*; formerly proprietor of *The Universe*; has been dramatic and music critic to the *Sheffield Daily Telegraph*, since Apr., 1915; music critic to *The Scotsman* since 1918; dramatic and music critic to *The Central Press*, since 1925; is a member of the Council and Executive Committee of The Critics' Circle. *Clubs:* Savage and Press. *(Died 12 Mar., 1939; age 68)*

MacCARTHY, Sir Desmond, LL.D., F.R.S.L.; (cr. 1951); *b.* Plymouth, 1877; *s.* of Charles Desmond MacCarthy, agent of the Bank of England; *e.* Eton; entered Trinity College, Cambridge, 1894; took degree in history, 1897; in 1904 became dramatic critic for *The Speaker*; author of "The Court Theatre," 1904–7, published by A. H. Bullen, 1907; Editor of *The New Quarterly*, 1907–10; wrote the Memoirs of Lady John Russell, 1910; dramatic critic for *The New Statesman* (subsequently *New Statesman and Nation*), from 1913; editor of *Life and Letters* till 1932; literary critic to *The Sunday Times*; also the author of five works, "Portraits," "Criticism," "Experience," "Drama," and "Shaw"; received the honour of Knighthood in the New Years Honours, 1951. *(Died 7 June, 1952; age 75)*

MAC DERMOT, Robert (*né* Robert MacDermot Barbour) dramatic author; *b.* Poona, India, 19 Mar., 1910; *s.* of Major John Humphrey Barbour, R.A.M.C., and his wife Eileen Margaret (Morrison); *e.* Stowe School and Balliol College, Oxford; *m.* Diana Morgan; was formerly an actor; is part-author of the following *revues*: "This Year, Next Year," 1934; "Spread it Abroad," 1936; "Members Only," 1937; "Black and Blue," 1939; with his wife, has collaborated in "This World of Ours," 1935; "Your Number's Up," 1936; "Bats in the Belfry," 1937; "The Gate Revue," 1938; "All Clear," "Let's Face It," 1939; "Swinging the Gate," 1940; "The New Ambassadors' Revue," 1941; lyrics for "Three Waltzes," 1945; again with his wife collaborated in "Swing Back the Gate," 1952; "Set to Music," 1953; "Love Is News" (adapted from "L'Amour en Papier"); engaged at the B.B.C. in various administrative capacities, 1934–46; was Story Editor for the J. Arthur Rank Film Organization, 1946–8; Head of B.B.C. Television Drama, 1948–9; now a radio and television free-lance. *Recreations:* Fencing and fishing. *Hobby:* Heraldry. *Clubs:* O.U.D.S., Garrick. *(Died 22 Nov., 1964; age 54)*

MACDERMOTT, Norman, producer and theatre director; *b.* Edinburgh, 15 Oct., 1889; *e.* Edinburgh and Liverpool College; *m.* (1) Elvie Hutchinson Blackburn; (2) Beatrice Cuthbert (mar. dis.); (3) Mary Nielson Robertson; Founder of the Everyman Theatre, Hampstead, the experimental Arts Theatre, of which he was the director and producer; opened on 15 Sept., 1920, with Benavente's "Bonds of Interest"; re-introduced Bernard Shaw's plays to the London stage after years of neglect, producing eight in a series of "Shaw Seasons"; his productions at this theatre resulted in official invitations to represent Great Britain at several International Festivals in Switzerland, Holland, Germany, etc.; made first British productions of many previously unknown authors and transferred successes to West End Theatres, including "The Mask and the Face," by C. B. Fernald from Chiarelli; "The Vortex," by Noel Coward; "At Mrs. Beam's," by C. K. Munro; "Outward Bound," by Sutton Vane; "The Man Who Was Thursday," by G. K. Chesterton; "T' Marsdens," by J. R. Gregson; first productions in England also included Eugene O'Neill's, "In the Zone," "Different," etc.; "Beyond Human Power," by Björnsen; "Suppressed Desires," by Susan Glaspell; translated and first presented numerous plays from the French, German, and Hungarian; revivals included Shakespeare's "Romeo and Juliet" and "Twelfth Night"; Galsworthy's "The Foundations"; Masefield's "Tragedy of Nan"; Zangwill's "The Melting Pot"; Arnold Bennett's "Honeymoon"; Ibsen's "The Wild Duck," "John Gabriel Borkman," "The Doll's House," "Hedda Gabler" (with Mrs. Patrick Campbell); presented Ellen Terry in her last two performances; subsequently, from 1927–37, produced at the "Q" Theatre, at the Arts Theatre, and at the Royalty Theatre (where he presented Sean O'Casey's "Within the Gates," Alasdair Rhind's "Marriage Settlement," and revivals); many prominent actors and actresses were given their first London engagements by him at the Everyman; much important experimental work was also carried on at the Everyman and notable results achieved in settings and lighting where he installed the modern "Phoebus" remote-control system of lighting; retired from direction of the Everyman, 1926; appointed Director of Entertainments at the Empire Exhibition, Glasgow, 1938; during the second world war was Controller for Scotland for E.N.S.A.; in 1949–51 General Manager of the South Bank Exhibition for the Festival of Britain; in 1952 appointed National Organizer of the Braille Centenary Fund and later for the United Appeal for the Blind and the Greater London Funds. *Clubs:* National Liberal and International Music Club. *Address:* 24 Fitzjohn's Avenue, London, N.W.3.

MACDONA, Charles, manager; *b.* Dublin; *s.* of William Macdona; *m.* Nellie Hodson; was formerly an actor and studied for the stage at the Neville Dramatic Studio; made his first appearance as an actor at Edinburgh, Apr., 1884, as Novio in " Ingomar "; made his first appearance in London, at the old Olympic Theatre, in 1887, in " The Pointsman "; toured the provinces for many years, and played leading parts with Marie de Grey; for three years toured with " The Private Secretary," and for several years played Henry Beauclerc in " Diplomacy," on tour; he also toured in " Mr. Popple," " The Gay Parisienne," " Niobe," " The Captain of the School," etc.; sent out touring companies of many West-End successes; in 1921, organized The Macdona Players, in plays by Bernard Shaw; his companies have toured all over Great Britain and Ireland, South Africa, India, and the Far East, also to the Continent; presented repertory of Shaw plays at the Court, 1929–30, and 1931; at the Prince's, 1933–34, produced " Diplomacy," " The Wandering Jew," " Sweet Nell of Old Drury "; Winter Garden, 1933, " On the Rocks "; Cambridge, 1934, " Queer Cargo " and revivals of Shaw plays; also associated with Kathleen Robinson productions; reappeared on the stage after twenty years, at the Court, Feb., 1930, as

Polonius in "Hamlet"; Mar., 1931, played Mr. Knox in "Fanny's First Play," and in Sept., 1939, was playing in the Bernard Shaw plays at the Alhambra, Glasgow. *Recreations:* Motoring and golfing. *Clubs:* Green Room and Stage Golfing Society. *(Died 16 Nov., 1946; age 86)*

MACDONALD, Donald, actor; *b.* Denison, Texas, U.S.A., 13 Mar., 1898; *s.* of Robert Don Macdonald and his wife Minnie Mary (Hughes); *e.* Lima, Ohio; *m.* Ruth Hammond; studied for the stage at the American Academy of Dramatic Arts; made his first appearance on the stage in "stock," at Ottawa, Canada, 1913, in "The Witching Hour"; made his first appearance in New York, at the Lyric Theatre, 18 Aug., 1913, as Denny in "When Dreams Come True"; Globe, Sept., 1916, played Tom Brenner in "The Amber Empress"; Liberty, Jan., 1917, Ted Sheldon in "Have A Heart"; George M. Cohan, Mar., 1918, Lieut. Harry Mallory in "Toot-Toot!"; Republic, Aug., 1921, Ken Walrick in "Getting Gertie's Garter"; Globe, Mar., 1923, Jack Andrews in "Jack and Jill"; Guild, Jan., 1925, Phillpotts in "Processional"; Maxine Elliott, Dec., 1925, Bill Bradford in "Beware of Widows"; Sam H. Harris, Feb., 1926, Billingsley in "Love 'Em and Leave 'Em"; Booth, Oct., 1926, Kit Canari in "White Wings"; Guild, July, 1927, succeeded Earle Larimore as Austin Lowe in "The Second Man"; Music Box, Dec., 1927, Richard Parrish in "Paris Bound"; during 1928–9, toured with Pauline Lord as Sam Evans in "Strange Interlude"; Biltmore, New York, Sept., 1930, Duggie in "The Up and Up"; made his first appearance on the London stage, 3 Feb., 1931, as Sam Evans in "Strange Interlude"; on returning to New York, appeared at the Little Theatre, Oct., 1931, as Waldo Lynde in "The Left Bank"; Ethel Barrymore, Sept., 1932, Philip Graves in "Here To-Day"; Morosco, Oct., 1932, Thompson Porter in "Black Sheep"; Times Square, Mar., 1933, Shepherd Perry in "Forsaking All Others"; Fulton, Feb., 1934, Hugo Dickens in

"Sing and Whistle"; Playhouse, Jan., 1935, Clyde Middleton in "Little Shot"; Mansfield, Oct., 1935, Edward Gilson in "On Stage"; Shaftesbury, London, May, 1936, J. Carlyle Benson in "Boy Meets Girl," and toured in the United States, in the same part, 1936–7; American Music Hall, New York, Oct., 1938, played Alkali in "The Girl from Wyoming"; Empire, July, 1940, Dr. Humphreys in "Life With Father"; Fulton, May, 1942, Officer O'Hara in "Arsenic and Old Lace," subsequently touring with the play until May, 1944; Fulton, Feb., 1946, played Roy Maxwell in "Deep Are the Roots"; subsequently engaged in radio and television; toured, 1950, as Mr. Lundie in "Brigadoon." *Club:* Lambs, New York. *(Died 9 Dec., 1959; age 61)*

MacDONALD, Jeanette, actress and vocalist; *b.* Philadelphia, Pa., U.S.A., 18 June, 1907; *d.* of Daniel MacDonald and his wife Anna M. (Wright); *e.* West Philadelphia Girls' High School, and private school in New York; *m.* Gene Raymond; made her first appearance on the stage at the Capital Theatre, New York, Jan., 1920, in the chorus of "The Demi-Tasse Revue," produced by Ned Wayburn; at the Liberty Theatre, Apr., 1920, appeared in "The Night Boat," and subsequently played Eleanor in "Irene," for the Chicago run; appeared at the Casino, Oct., 1921, as Kate Allen in "Tangerine"; at Greenwich Village Theatre, Sept., 1922, appeared in "A Fantastic Fricasee"; at the Liberty Theatre, Oct., 1923, made a hit when she played Iris Bellamy in "The Magic Ring"; same theatre, Dec., 1925, played Sylvia Metcalf in "Tip-Toes"; at the Garrick, Philadelphia, Aug., 1926, appeared in "Bubbling Over"; Sam H. Harris Theatre, Oct., 1927, played Yvette Ralston in "Yes, Yes, Yvette"; Imperial, Feb., 1928, Ginette Bertin in "Sunny Days"; Ambassador, Dec., 1928, Princess Angela in "Angela"; Casino, Jan., 1929, Jean in "Boom-Boom"; subsequently appeared in pictures; went to Europe, 1931, and appeared at the Empire, Paris, 4 Sept.,

1564

1931, in a repertory of songs, and made her first appearance in London, at the Dominion Theatre, 21 Sept., 1931; toured the concert platforms of France, Holland, Belgium and Switzerland, 1933; made her American debut as a concert artist, 1939, and subsequently undertook a series of annual tours; made her first appearance in grand opera at Montreal, 1943, in "Romeo and Juliet"; with the Chicago Civic Opera Company, 1944, appeared in "Faust" and "Romeo and Juliet"; appeared with the same company, 1945–46; appeared with the Cincinatti Civic Opera, 1945; made concert appearances at the Hollywood Bowl, 1945 and 1948; gave recitals at Carnegie Hall, New York, Oct., 1950, and Jan., 1953; toured, 1951, as the Actress in "The Guardsman"; made concert appearances at Lewisohn Stadium, New York, 1951, and at Red Rocks, Denver, in 1952, 1953, and 1954; toured summer theatres, 1954–55, in "Bittersweet"; appeared at the First Annual American Composers' Festival, Sacramento, California, 1955; first appeared in films, 1929, in "The Love Parade," and subsequently appeared in many notable productions, including "Monte Carlo," "The Vagabond King," "One Hour With You," "Love Me Tonight," "The Merry Widow," "Naughty Marietta," "Rose Marie," "Maytime," "The Firefly," "Sweethearts," "New Moon," "Bittersweet," "Smilin' Through," "I Married An Angel," etc.; awarded Hon. Degree of Doctor of Music, Ithaca College, N.Y., 1953. *(Died 14 Jan., 1965; age 57)*

MacDONELL, Kathlene, actress; *b.* Toronto, 7 May, 1890; *e.* Toronto; *m.* George D. Parker; made her first appearance on the stage in a "stock" company in Philadelphia, 1909, and remained there for two and a half seasons; made her first appearance in New York, at the Lyceum Theatre, 3 Apr., 1911, as Violet de Salle in "Mrs. Bumpstead-Leigh," with Mrs. Fiske; subsequently, 1911–12, toured with her in "The New Marriage," and "Julia France"; from 1912–14, toured continuously as Virginia Blane in "Bought and Paid For"; at the Manhattan

Opera House, New York, Oct., 1914, played Ruth in "Life"; Gaiety, Aug., 1915, Madge Davis in "Just Outside the Door"; Maxine Elliott Theatre, Jan., 1916, Louise Calhoun in "The Pride of Race"; Hartford, Conn., Apr., 1916, Margery Hamilton in "The Dawn," and Princess, New York, Dec., 1916, the same part, when the play was renamed "Margery Daw"; in 1917, she went to Australia to play Judy Abbott in "Daddy Long-Legs," and also appeared in "Cheating Cheaters" and "L'Aiglon"; during 1918, appeared there in "Peter Pan," "The Rainbow," "Outcast," and "The Willow-Tree"; reappeared in New York, at the 48th Street Theatre, Feb., 1919, as Allayne in "The Net"; Longacre, Mar., 1921, p'ayed Hester Lane in "The Hero"; 39th Street Theatre, Dec., 1921, Mary Hubbard in "Danger"; Plymouth, Jan., 1922, Sadie in "The Deluge"; Garrick (for the Theatre Guild), Oct., 1922, Helena Glory in "R.U.R."; Bijou, Feb., 1925, Evelyn Ryesdale in "Episode"; Gaiety, Oct., 1926, Helen Hayle in "On Approval"; Empire, Oct., 1927, Deborah Kane in "Interference."

MACDONNELL, Leslie A., C.B.E., manager and producer; *b.* Llanelly, Carmarthenshire, 10 Aug., 1903; *s.* of Arthur Macdonnell and his wife Catherine; *e.* Seaford College; *m.* Doris Manson; began his career at the Palace Theatre, London, Mar., 1925, as manager of Percival Mackey and his Orchestra in "No, No, Nanette"; between 1929–33 worked with Keith Prowse Music Publishing Company; in 1936, opened his own office of Personal Management; served in the Royal Air Force, 1940–5, retiring as Wing Commander; 1946–58, engaged in Personal Management; appointed Joint Managing Director of Moss' Empires, Ltd., Jan., 1959; appointed Managing Director, Jan., 1960, taking over the direction of the London Palladium; has been responsible for over ninety productions, including pantomimes, revues, variety presentations, etc.; President of the Society of West End Theatre Managers Association, 1962–3; President of Agents Association, 1951–8; was a director of Winter

Gardens, Morecambe, Ltd., Potteries Theatres, Ltd., Coombe Roads Association, Ltd., Keith Prowse Music Publishing, Ltd., West End Theatre Managers (1953), Ltd., Moss' Empires Properties, Ltd., General Building and Theatre Equipment, Ltd., Associated Catering Company, Ltd., Stoll Theatres Corporation, Ltd., Stoll Properties, Ltd., Associated Theatre Properties (London), Ltd.; Theatre Royal, Drury Lane; was a member of the London Theatre Council; Variety and Allied Entertainment Council, National Theatres' Committee; was Vice-Chairman of the Combined Services Entertainment Advisory Committee; retired, 31st Dec., 1969; received the Honour of the O.B.E. in the Birthday Honours, 1957, and the C.B.E. in the Birthday Honours, 1970. *Recreation:* Horse racing and golf. *Clubs:* Royal Air Force, Eccentric, Royal Wimbledon, Saints and Sinners, Variety Club of Great Britain. *Address:* Beverley Wood, Beverley Lane, Coombe Hill, Kingston-on-Thames, Surrey. *Telephone No.:* 01-949 4948.

MACDONOUGH, Glen, librettist and playwright; has written the following, either alone or in collaboration : " The Gold Bug," " The Marquis of Michigan," " Kate Kip," " Buyer," " Sister Mary," " Chris and the Wonderful Lamp," " Vienna Life," " The Algerian," " Among Those Present," " Babes in Toyland," " Bird Center," " It Happened in Nordland," " Wonderland," " Too Near Home," " Algeria," " The Jolly Bachelors " (" The Midnight Sons "), " The Rose of Algeria," " The Golden Widow," " The Summer Widowers," " The Henpecks," " The Never Homes " ; the American version of " The Count of Luxembourg," " Eva," " Fads and Fancies," " Hitchy-Koo," " The Kiss Burglar," " Snapshots of 1921 " (with Frances Nordstrom), " The Elusive Lady," 1922 ; " Within Four Walls," 1923. *(Died 30 Mar., 1924; age 57)*

MACFARLANE, Bruce, actor; first appeared on the stage on the Pacific Coast, in "The Front Page"; made

his first appearance on the New York stage at the John Golden Theatre, 22 Oct., 1929, as Arthur in "Week End"; Sam Harris, Feb., 1930, played Frost in "The Last Mile"; Cort, Dec., 1930, Rooney in "Five Star Final"; Alvin, Oct., 1931, Sol Griffith in "Wonder Boy"; Times Square, Feb., 1932, Roy Denny in "Wild Waves"; Ambassador, Mar., 1932, Hoyte Proctor in "Intimate Relations"; Martin Beck, Mar., 1933, Patrick in "Far Away Horses"; Waldorf, June, 1933, Walter Hallam in "Another Language"; Lyceum, Sept., 1933, "Dynamite" Jones in "Sailor Beware"; Longacre, Oct., 1934, Slater Jones in "Geraniums ln My Window"; Mansfield, Nov.,1934, Bingo Nelson in "Page Miss Glory"; Cort, May, 1935, Christian Hugo in "Knock on Wood"; 48th Street, Nov., 1935, Adrian Reed in "Stick-in-the-Mud"; Lyceum, July, 1936, Ken Arnold in "Pre-Honeymoon"; at summer theatres, July–Aug., 1936, Ralph Miller in "Timber House" and Tommy in "Happy Valley Ltd"; Mansfield, New York, Jan., 1937, Joe Burke in "Behind Red Lights"; Little, St. Louis, Mar., 1937, the King in "The Celestial Holiday"; Guild, Nov., 1940, Bill Brady in "Quiet Please"; Biltmore, Dec., 1940, Chic Clark in "My Sister Eileen," which ran two years; Cort, Oct., 1944, Howard Stickney in "The Odds on Mrs. Oakley," and Nov., 1944, Captain Purvis in "A Bell for Adano"; Detroit, Dec., 1945, McGuire in "Of All People"; Royale, New York, Sept., 1946, Murphy in "The Front Page." *(Died 25 Nov., 1967)*

MACFARLANE, Elsa, actress and vocalist ; *b.* London, 23 May, 1899 ; *d.* of Joseph Macfarlane and his wife Beatrice (Odgers) ; *e.* at Eastbourne and in Switzerland ; *m.* Clifford Whitley ; studied singing at the Royal Academy of Music · made her first appearance on the stage at the Winter Garden Theatre, 20 May, 1919, in the chorus of " Kissing Time " ; at the Shaftesbury, Apr., 1920, played Vivienne Rogers in " The Little Whopper " ; at the Winter Garden,

Sept., 1920, played Kiki in "A Night Out"; at the Royalty, June, 1921, was one of "The Co-Optimists"; she also appeared at the Hotel Metropole, in "The Midnight Follies"; at the Lyric, Hammersmith, Oct., 1924, played Donna Louisa in the revival of "The Duenna"; Winter Garden, Apr., 1925, Peggy Van de Leur in "Tell Me More"; Vaudeville, June, 1927, played in "Blue Skies"; Shaftesbury, Apr., 1928, in "Will o' the Whispers"; Vaudeville, July, 1929, again appeared with "The Co-Optimists; London Hippodrome, Apr., 1930, appeared with "The Co-Optimists of 1930"; in 1932, appeared at the Royal Albert Hall, as Minnehaha in "Hiawatha"; St. Martin's, July, 1932, succeeded Kathlyn Hilliard as Millicent Blazes in "The Pride of the Regiment." *Recreations:* Tennis and motoring. *Address:* 4 Avenue Close, London, N.W.8. *Telephone No.:* Primrose 0573.

MACGILL, Moyna (*née* Chattie McIldowie); actress; *b.* Belfast; *d.* of William McIldowie and his wife Cissie (Mageean); *e.* Belfast and Scarborough; *m.* (1) Reginald Denham (mar. dis.); (2) Edgar Lansbury; had had some amateur experience before making her first appearance on the London stage at the Globe Theatre, 26 Jan., 1918, as Hortense in "Love in a Cottage"; was next seen at Wyndham's Theatre, June, 1918, as Joanna in "Dear Brutus," which part she understudied; she also understudied the part of Daphne Grey in "The Law Divine," at the same theatre, Sept., 1918, and appeared, on occasions, in this part also; in June, 1919, understudied the part of Marjorie Caner in "The Cinderella Man," at the Queen's Theatre, also playing the part in the absence of Renée Kelly; at the Gaiety Theatre, Manchester, Dec., 1919, played Comfort Tuke in "Homespun"; at the Lyric, Hammersmith, Feb., 1920, appeared as Hannah Ferguson in "John Ferguson"; Apr., 1920, as Phoebe in "As You Like It"; at the Prince of Wales's, May, 1920, played the title-*rôle* in "Chitra"; at the St. Martin's Theatre, Feb., 1921,

appeared as Delia in "The Wonderful Visit"; at the Ambassadors', Mar., 1921, played Rhoda Fleming in an adaptation of Meredith's novel, at the Garrick, Apr., 1921, appeared as Cathleen Rossiter in "Count X"; at the Court, May, 1921, succeeded Madge Titheradge as Desdemona in "Othello"; at the Shaftesbury, Nov., 1921, played Ann Hathaway in "Will Shakespeare"; at the Everyman, Mar., 1922, Leo in "Getting Married"; at the Royalty, Apr., 1922, Hope Tregoning in "If Four Walls Told"; at Wyndham's, May, 1922, Mrs. Purdie in "Dear Brutus"; at the Empire, etc., 1922, Michaela in "Arlequin"; at Drury Lane, Mar., 1923, Undine, Giulia and Eufemia in "Angelo"; at the Haymarket, June, 1923, Sally in "Success"; at the St. Martin's, Jan., 1924, Joan Potten in "A Magdalen's Husband"; at the Apollo, Feb., 1924, Lesley Stanley in "The Fairy Tale"; Wyndham's, June, 1925, played Fame in "Raleigh"; Barnes, Sept., 1926, Elizabeth Jane in "The Mayor of Casterbridge"; Criterion, Dec., 1926, Delia in "The White-Headed Boy"; St. James's, Jan., 1927, Faith Marlay in "Interference"; Strand (for Stage Society), June, 1927, Margaret in "The Great God Brown"; Arts, Mar., 1928, Rosaleen Moore in "The Way"; Gate, Apr., 1928, Eurydice in "Orphée"; Arts, Oct., 1928, Norah Burke in "The Shadow of the Glen"; Everyman, Dec., 1928, Asta Allmers in "Little Eyolf"; Court, Jan., 1929, The Woman in "The Eternal Flame"; Apollo (for Stage Society), Feb., 1929, Princess Helena in "The Princess"; Everyman, Apr., 1929, Hara Deren in "Requital"; Everyman, Aug., 1930, Jacqueline Heron in "The Bond." *Recreations:* Painting, golf, and swimming. *Address:* 7 Weymouth Avenue, N.W.7. *Telephone No.:* Mill Hill 2240.

MAC GINNIS, Niall, actor; *b.* Dublin, Ireland, 29 Mar., 1913; *s.* of Patrick Mac Ginnis and his wife Mary (Kelly); *e.* Stonyhurst College and Trinity College, Dublin; served as Surgeon-Lieut. in R.N.; made his first appearance on the stage at the Peacock

Theatre, Dublin, 1931; during the season 1932–3, appeared with the Sheffield Repertory company; in the summer of 1933, toured in Ireland in a "fit-up" company with Dorothy Grafton; joined the company of the Gate Theatre, Dublin, in the autumn of 1933, and remained until the spring of 1934; next played "stock" with Terence Byron's company at Wolverhampton, 1934; made his first appearance in London, at the New Theatre, 12 Sept., 1934, as the First Servant in "A Man's House"; then played with the repertory company at the Playhouse, Oxford, 1934–5; Westminster, June, 1935, played the Ghost in "Hamlet," with the Dublin Gate company; then spent nearly two years in films; Westminster, Apr.–Oct., 1937, played Matt Burke in "Anna Christie," Aleksiei in "A Month in the Country" and Terence Killigrew in "Youth's the Season?"; Old Vic., Nov. and New, Dec., 1937, Malcolm in "Macbeth"; Westminster, Jan., 1938, Bonaria in "Volpone"; Ambassadors', Mar., 1938, Michael Griffin in "Moonshine," and May, 1938, Michael Byrne in "Spring Meeting"; Gate, Apr., 1939, Lennie in "Of Mice and Men," playing the same part at the Apollo Theatre, May, 1939; Playhouse, Apr., 1947, Richard Regan in "The Animal Kingdom"; Lyric, Hammersmith, Aug., 1949, Bartley Dowd in "The King of Friday's Men"; St. James's, May, 1951, in Sir Laurence Olivier's season, played Rufio in "Caesar and Cleopatra" and Pompey in "Antony and Cleopatra"; appeared in the two last-mentioned parts at the Ziegfeld, New York, Dec., 1951; entered films, 1935, and has appeared in numerous pictures. *Address:* c/o Connie's Ltd., 92 Regent Street, London, W.1.

MACGOWAN, Kenneth, dramatic critic and author and producing manager; *b.* Winthrop, Mass., U.S.A., 30 Nov., 1888; *s.* of Peter Stainforth Macgowan and his wife Susan Arletta (Hall); *m.* Edna Behre; was assistant dramatic critic to the *Boston Transcript*, 1910-13; dramatic and literary editor *Philadelphia Evening Ledger*, 1914-17; on staff of *New York*

Tribune, 1918; dramatic critic of *New York Globe*, 1919-23; dramatic critic of *Vogue*, 1920-4; dramatic critic and associate-editor of the *Theatre Arts Magazine*, 1919-25; also officiated as publicity director to the Goldwyn Pictures Corporation; was director of the Provincetown Players, 1924-5; associated with Eugene O'Neill and Robert Edmond Jones in the direction of the Greenwich Village Theatre, 1925-7; producer for The Actors' Theatre, 1927; he has produced the following, among other plays: "Fashion," "All God's Chillun Got Wings," "Desire Under the Elms," "The Great God Brown," "Outside Looking In," "Bride of the Lamb," "Young Love," "These Modern Women," "Children of Darkness," "Twelfth Night"; with J. Verner Read, he presented "Art and Mrs. Bottle," 1930; "Lean Harvest," "The Lady With a Lamp," "Springtime for Henry," 1931; author of "The Theatre of To-morrow," 1921; "Continental Stagecraft" (with Robert Edmond Jones), 1922; "Masks and Demons" (with Rosse), 1923; "What is Wrong with Marriage?" (with Dr. G. B. Hamilton), 1929; "Footlights Across America," 1929; successively editor, editor-in-chief, and associate producer for R.K.O. Pictures, 1932. *Clubs:* Players', Harvard, and Coffee House. *(Died 27 Apr., 1963; age 74)*

MacGOWRAN, Jack, actor; *b.* Dublin, Ireland, 13 Oct., 1918; *s.* of Matthew Joseph MacGowran and his wife Gertrude (Shanahan); *e.* Christian Brothers School, Dublin; *m.* Gloria Nugent; formerly an insurance drafter; trained at the Abbey and Gate Theatres, Dublin, and appeared with both theatre companies between 1944–50; studied mime in Paris, 1949; made his first London appearance at the New Lindsey, May, 1954, as the Young Covey in a revival of "The Plough and the Stars"; Lyric, Hammersmith, Jan., 1957, played Seumas Shields in a revival of "The Shadow of a Gunman"; Arts, Cambridge, June, 1957, title-part in "Amédée," by Ionesco; Arts, Jan., 1958, Harry Hope in "The Iceman Cometh," transferring with the production to the Winter Garden, Mar.,

1958; Royal Court, Oct., 1958, played Clov in "End-Game"; made his first appearance in New York, at the Winter Garden, Mar., 1959, when he played "Joxer" Daly in the musical "Juno"; on returning to London, at the Lyric, Hammersmith, June, 1959, played Captain Kelly in "The Rough and Ready Lot"; Cambridge, Sept., 1959, Jug Ears in "The Crooked Mile"; joined the Shakespeare Memorial Theatre Company, Stratford-on-Avon, for the season, 1960, and played the following parts: Speed in "The Two Gentlemen of Verona," Old Gobbo in "The Merchant of Venice," Christopher Sly in "The Taming of the Shrew," and Autolycus in "The Winter's Tale"; Bristol Old Vic, 1963, played Berenger in "The Killer"; Dublin Theatre Festival, and subsequently, New Arts, London, Oct., 1962, devised and appeared in a solo programme "End of Day," based on the works of Samuel Beckett; Duchess, June, 1963, Davis in "In the Zone," and A Night Clerk in "Hughie," in the triple bill "Hughie"; Aldwych, July, 1964, again played Clov in "End-Game"; Royal Court, Dec., 1964, Lucky in "Waiting for Godot"; Lantern, Dublin, Sept., 1965, devised and appeared in a new solo programme from the works of Beckett, "Beginning to End"; Gaiety, Dublin, Aug., 1966, played Joxer Daly in "Juno and the Paycock"; Mermaid, Apr., 1967, Sammy in "A Pound on Demand," and Seumas Shields in "The Shadow of a Gunman," which he also directed; Playhouse, New York, Oct., 1970, played the title part in "Gandhi"; Estelle R. Newman, Nov., 1970, gave his solo programme under the title "Jack MacGowran in the works of Samuel Beckett"; since 1950, he has also appeared in the following films: "No Resting Place," "The Quiet Man," "The Titfield Thunderbolt," "Rooney," "Cyrano et D'Artagnan" (France), "Tom Jones," "Lord Jim," "Young Cassidy," "Dr. Zhivago," "Cul de Sac," "The Ceremony," "Mix Me a Person," "Darby O'Gill and the Little People of Hollywood"; first appeared on television in 1955, in "Sailor of Fortune," subsequent appearances include: Fluther Good

in "The Plough and the Stars," Huish in "Ebb Tide," Vladimir in "Waiting for Godot," and the Father in "Point of Departure," "Acte sans Paroles" (Ireland), and in the Monitor of Samuel Beckett's Works; has broadcast regularly; he has also directed plays for the Abbey Experimental Theatre, and the Irish provincial theatre; has given many readings and lectures on the works of Samuel Beckett and Sean O'Casey; member of Advisory Board of Theatre Workshop, London. *Recreations:* Literature, athletics, horse racing, wiring. *Address:* c/o Al Parker, 50 Mount Street, London, W.1.

MAC HUGH, Augustin, dramatic author ; was formerly an actor, and while playing in Keith and Proctor's "stock " company in New York, wrote his first play, " Officer 666," in 1912 ; he has since written " Value Received," 1913 ; " What Would You Do ? " 1914 ; " Search Me," 1915 ; " It's up to You " (with A. D. Leavitt), 1920 ; " The Meanest Man in the World," 1920 ; at Los Angeles, Apr., 1921, appeared as Frank Melton in his own play " True to Form."

MACK, Andrew (Andrew McAloon), actor and vocalist ; *b.* Boston, 25 July, 1863 ; *e.* Public Schools, Boston ; made his first appearance on the stage as a variety artist in 1876, under the name of Williams; subsequently played Bruce Ashton in " Aunt Bridget's Baby," and appeared with Pete Dailey in " A Country Sport " ; made his first " hit " in " Ivy Leaf " ; in 1895, made his first appearance as a " star " in " Myles Aroon " ; since that date has appeared with unvarying success as Jack Shannon in " An Irish Gentleman," 1897 ; Gerald Fitzgerald in " The Ragged Earl," 1899 ; Clifford in " The Last of the Rohans," 1899 ; Jack Blake in " The Rebel," 1900 ; Tom Moore in a play of that name, 1901 ; the title-*rôle* in " The Bold Soger Boy," 1903 ; Shaun the Post in " Arrah-Na-Pogue," 1903 ; Mickey O'Dowd in " My Lady Molly," 1903 ; Dan Maguire in " The Way to Ken-mare," 1904 ; has paid two visits to Australia, in 1905 and 1907 ; during 1896 played Sir Lucius O'Trigger in the " all-star " cast of " The Rivals " ; in 1906 completed ten years' engagement with Rich and Harris ; on his return from Australia toured throughout the United States as Victor O'Brien in " Sergeant Devil-May-Care " (" The Royal Mounted ") ; at the Hackett Theatre, New York, Jan., 1910, appeared as Dick Conyers in " The Prince of Bohemia " ; at the Casino Theatre, May, 1910, played Nanki-Poo in an " all-star " revival of " The Mikado " ; in 1912 toured in a revival of " Tom Moore " ; at Buffalo, Feb., 1913, appeared as Captain Holbrook in " At Bay " ; appeared in " vaudeville," 1913-15 ; in Oct., 1915, toured as Charles O'Malley in " The Irish Dragoon " ; in 1918 toured in " Molly Dear " ; at the Ritz Theatre, New York, Jan., 1923, played Brutus J. Finn in " The Humming Bird " ; in 1924 appeared at the Republic Theatre, as Patrick Murphy in "Abie's Irish Rose," which he continued to play throughout the record run of the piece.

MACK, Willard, actor and dramatic author; *b.* Morrisburg, Ontario, Canada, 17 Sept., 1878; his real name is Charles W. McLaughlin; *e.* Brooklyn, N.Y., and Georgetown University; *m.* (1) Maude Leone; (2) Marjorie Rambeau; (3) Pauline Frederick; (4) Beatrice Banyard; was well known on the "vaudeville" stage for some years, where he appeared in his own sketches; for several years was leading man of the Alcazar "Stock" Company, San Francisco; made his first appearance in New York, at Proctor's Fifth Avenue, 10 Mar., 1913, as Chick Hewes in " Kick-In," which he subsequently extended to a three-act play; during a "stock" engagement at Salt Lake City, 1913, he produced "Their Market Value," and "So Much for So Much," the last-mentioned being produced at the Longacre Theatre, New York, Dec., 1914, when he played the leading part of Tom Hughes; at the Lyceum, New York, Oct., 1917, played Constable Michael Devlin in his

own play of "Tiger Rose"; at the Forty-eighth Street Theatre, Oct., 1918, Bertie Thorndyke in "The Big Chance," of which he was part-author, with Grant Morris; and at Morristown, N.J., Dec., 1920, played in his own play "Her Man"; at Greenwich Village Theatre, New York, Jan., 1921, played Bill Travers in his own play "Near Santa Barbara"; at the Lexington Theatre, Feb., 1921, played in his own play "Smooth as Silk"; at the Frazee Theatre, June, 1921, played Captain Isaiah Bartlett in "Gold"; Lyceum, Sept., 1925, Herman Strauss in his play " Canary Dutch "; Nov., 1926, Joe Holly in his play " Lily Sue "; Morosco, Jan., 1927, John Connell in his play, " Honor Be Damned "; Masque, Mar., 1928, Michael Devlin in his play " The Scarlet Fox " ; in addition to the above-mentioned plays, he is also the author of " God's Country," " Men of Steel," " My Friend Judas," " Miracle Mary," "A Double Exposure," 1916 ; " Broadway and Buttermilk," 1916 ; " King, Queen, Jack," 1916 ; "Alias," 1917 ; " Every Day in the Year," 1917 ; " The Deserter " (with Thomas Fallon), 1917 ; " Blind Youth " (with Lou Tellegen), 1917 ; " I.O.U." (with Hector Turnbull), 1918 ; "A Voice in the Dark" (with R. E. Dyar), 1919 ; " Breakfast in Bed " (with Hilliard Booth), 1919 ; " The Unknown Woman " (with Marjorie Blaine), 1919 ; " Sunrise," 1919 " Poker Ranch " (" Near Santa Barbara "), 1920 ; " The Ziegfeld Follies of 1921 " (with Channing Pollock), 1921 ; " That Casey Girl " (with G. V. Hobart), 1923 ; " Blackmail " (subsequently " High Stakes "), 1924 ; " The Dove " (from a story), 1925 ; " Fanny " (with David Belasco), " The Noose " (from a story), " Hangman's House " (from a novel), 1926 ; " Weather Clear Track Fast," 1927 ; "A Free Soul " (from a novel), " The Common Sin," "Gang War," 1928; appeared in films 1913, and has played in "The Conqueror," "The Corner," "The Devil Decides," "The Barbarian," "The Woman in the Index," "Your Friend and Mine," "The Voice of the City," "Beauty and Bullets," "The Girl Said No," etc. ; has also written and directed many notable films.
(Died 18 Nov., 1934; age 61)

MACKAY, Barry, actor; *b.* London, 8 Jan., 1906; *s.* of the late Leonard Mackay, actor, and his wife Octavia (Barry); *e.* London; made his first appearance on the stage in 1922; appeared at Drury Lane Theatre, Feb., 1926, in "Rose-Marie"; and at the same theatre, Apr., 1927, played Captain Paul Fontaine in "The Desert Song"; in 1928, toured as King Alexis in "The White Camellia," and appeared in the same part at Daly's, Feb., 1929; Palace, June, 1929, played Flash in "Hold Everything," subsequently touring as Jim Brookes in the same play; during 1930–1, toured as Fontaine in "The Desert Song," and appeared at the Alhambra, June, 1931, in the same part; Daly's July, 1931, succeeded Donald Mather as Reginald Fairfax in "The Geisha"; Drury Lane, Sept., 1933, played Celestin Fromant in "Ball at the Savoy"; during the war, served with the Grenadier Guards, from 1940; Devonshire Park, Eastbourne, May, 1946, played Sextus in "Cage Me a Peacock"; Palace, May, 1947, played Franz Joseph in "The Bird Seller"; Prince's, Oct., 1947, Comte Dubarry in "The Dubarry"; toured, 1948–50, as Anthony Allen in "Glamorous Night"; toured, 1950–51, as Major Lord Wamstead in "A Guardsman's Cup of Tea"; first appeared in films, 1933. *Address:* 72 Roland House, Roland Gardens, London, S.W.7.

MACKAY, Elsie, actress; *b.* Australia, 1894; *e.* Switzerland; *m.* Lionel Atwill (mar. dis.); made her first appearance in London, at His Majesty's, 11 Apr., 1914, walking on in "Pygmalion"; first attracted attention, at the New Theatre, in 1914, when she succeeded Margery Maude as Virginia in "Grumpy"; was a member of Mr. Cyril Maude's Company in the United States in 1914–15, when she played such parts as Virginia Bullivant in "Grumpy," Muriel Mannering in "The Second in Command," etc.; in 1916 joined Sir Herbert Tree's Company on tour in the United States, and played Anne Bullen in "King Henry VIII," Jessica in "The Merchant of Venice," etc.; at the New Amsterdam Theatre, New York, Apr., 1917, appeared as Ethel Newcome in "Colonel Newcome"; at the Thirty-ninth Street Theatre, Sept., 1918, played Dora in "Another Man's Shoes"; at the Hudson, Sept., 1919, Violet Pinney in "Clarence"; at the Park, Sept., 1920, Maria in "Poldekin"; at the Belasco, Dec., 1920, Marie Duplessis in "Deburau"; at the Lyceum, New York, Mar., 1923, Jacqueline in "The Comedian"; Longacre, Feb., 1925, Madge Wilmerding in "The Dark Angel"; Cort, Sept., 1925, Veronica Valiant in "The New Gallantry."

MACKAY, J. L., character and juvenile actor; *b.* Scarborough, 1 May, 1867; *m.* 4 July, 1895, to Lina Humphreys; *e.* Bedford, King's College, and St. George's Hospital for the medical profession; first appeared with German Reed, Jan., 1891, in "The Verger," by Walter Frith, followed by "In a Carnival Time," by Malcolm Watson; in 1892 he joined the Kendals for an American tour, playing Archie in "A Scrap of Paper," etc.; on his return he toured under Charles Hawtrey in "The Private Secretary"; next toured with "Captain Swift"; in 1895 he went to Terry's for "The Passport," playing Schmirkoff, and next appeared in "Mrs. Ponderbury's Past" at the Avenue; "Jedbury, Jnr.," at Terry's; "Under the Red Robe," at Haymarket; "Sporting Life," Shaftesbury; "On and Off," Vaudeville; "My Daughter-in-Law," at the Criterion; "The Adventure of Lady Ursula," at the Duke of York's, "Raffles," at the Comedy; "Brewster's Millions" at the Hicks, 1907; "Lady Frederick," at the Garrick, 1908; "The Adventure of Lady Ursula," at the Garrick, 1909; "Eunice," at the Hicks Theatre, 1909; "The King's Cup," at the Adelphi, 1909; in Oct., 1910, went to America, and at Atlantic City, Oct., 1910, appeared as Valtier in "A Thief in the Night"; at Montreal, Jan., 1911, appeared as Hugh Meyers in "Disraeli"; at Brighton, Mar., 1913, played Morris Blindon in "Margery Marries"; during 1905 toured through South Africa with the late Robert Brough. *Favourite*

parts : Schmirkoff in " The Passport "
and Sweeting in " My Daughter-in-
Law." *Recreations :* Golf, shooting,
and cycling. *Clubs :* Beefsteak, Green
Room, and Northwood Golf. *Address :*
Green Room Club, 46 Leicester Square,
W.C.2.

MACKAY, Ruth, actress ; *b.* London ; *m.* Eille Norwood ; made her
first appearance on the stage in the
provinces ; appeared at the Metropole
Theatre, 20 Sept., 1897, as Madame
Hanotaux in " Toto and Tata " ; at
the Royalty, Apr., 1898, played Bessie
Broke in " The Light That Failed " ;
May, 1898, played in " The Cat and the
Cherub " ; in 1902 was touring in Australia in " Ben Hur," etc. ; appeared at
His Majesty's Theatre, Feb., 1903, as
Carrots in " Resurrection " ; May,
1903, as the Comtesse de Florentin
in " The Gordian Knot " ; in 1904
went to America to play lead with
Nat Goodwin, appearing with him
in " A Gilded Fool," " The Usurper,"
etc. ; on her return to London, 1905,
appeared at the Coliseum in " Joseph
and his Brethren," " The Spy," etc. ;
appeared in " The Sin of William
Jackson," Lyric, 1906, and at the
Haymarket in Oct., 1907, succeeded
Miss Maud Hoffman as Lady Bab
in " Sweet Kitty Bellairs " ; at
Terry's, Dec., 1907, played Mrs.
Caudell in " Is Marriage a Failure ? " ; at Eastbourne, May, 1908,
appeared as Lady Patience Gascoyne
in " Beau Brocade " ; during 1909,
toured as Mrs. Vidal in " Raffles,"
and Heléne Vaillant in " The Devil " ;
in 1910, toured as Joanna, Countess
of Rushmere, in " Mr. Preedy and the
Countess " ; appeared at the Palladium, June, 1911, in " The King's
Ransom " ; subsequently toured as
the Duchess of Quenton in " The
Bishop's Move " ; at the Duke of
York's, Feb., 1912, played the Hon.
Mrs. Arthur Stidulph in " The ' Mind-
the-Paint ' Girl " ; June, 1912,
" Sergeant " Shuter in " The
Amazons " ; in Mar., 1913, joined the
Glasgow Repertory Theatre Company,
where she appeared in several parts,
notably Mrs. Warren in " Mrs. War-
ren's Profession," and Lady Corisande

in " The Bill " ; at the Little Theatre,
Feb., 1914, played Madame Dupont
in " Damaged Goods " ; at the Haymarket, May, 1914, the Princess in
" The Great Gamble " ; June, 1914,
Barbara Cullen in " Driven " ; Sept.,
1914, Mrs. Forrester in " The Impossible Woman " ; at the Royalty, Dec.,
1914, Miriam Leigh in " The Man
Who Stayed at Home " ; at the Playhouse, May, 1915, played Yolande in
" Godefroi and Yolande " ; at the
Globe, Oct., 1916, Muriel Sarbitter
in " The Clock Goes Round " ; at
the New Theatre, July, 1918, Mrs.
Melsham in " The Chinese Puzzle " ;
at the New Theatre, Aug., 1918,
Mrs. Gordon Peel in " The Luck of
the Navy " ; at the Shaftesbury, 1921,
played Bianca in " The Great Lover " ;
Fortune, Apr., 1925, Lady Symonds in
" Yetta Polowski." *Address :* " Top
o' the Hill," Pine Ridge, Farnham,
Surrey. *Telephone No. :* Frensham
144.

MACKAYE, Percy, author and dramatist ; *b.* New York, 16 Mar., 1875 ;
s. of Steele Mackaye and his wife Mary
(Medbery) ; *e.* Harvard University
(B.A., 1897), and Leipzig University ;
m. Marion Homer Morse, 8 Oct., 1898 ;
the first of his plays to be produced was
his " Jeanne d'Arc," presented by the
Sothern-Marlowe Company at Philadel-
phia, 15 Oct., 1906 ; the following com-
prise his chief works : " The Canterbury
Pilgrims," " Fenris, the Wolf,"
" Jeanne d'Arc," 1906 ; " Sappho and
Phaon," produced at the Lyric Theatre,
New York, by Harrison Grey Fiske,
1907 ; " Mater," produced at the Sa-
voy, New York, Sept., 1908 ; adapted
" Hannele," with Mary Safford, pro-
duced at Lyceum, New York, 1910 ;
" Anti-Matrimony," 1910 ; " The
Scarecrow," 1910 ; " A Thousand Years
Ago " (" Turandot "), 1913 ; " The
Antick," 1915 ; " Caliban " (a Masque)
1917 ; " Washington ; The Man Who
Made Us," 1919, subsequently re-
vised and produced as " George
Washington," 1920 ; " This Fine-
Pretty World," 1923 ; " Napoleon
Crossing the Rockies," 1924 ; " Kinfolk
of Robin Hood," 1924 ; " The Sphinx,"
1929 ; " Wakefield," a Folk-Masque of

1572

America, produced by the U.S. Government, 1932; in 1949, the Pasadena Playhouse, California, produced his tetralogy, "The Mystery of Hamlet, King of Denmark," which received the 1948 Fellowship Award of the Academy of American Poets; author of the libretti of the following operas: "The Immigrants," 1915; "Sinbad the Sailor," 1917; "Rip Van Winkle," 1920; also of numerous essays on the theatre and the drama, folk-plays, masques, etc.; author of "The Life of Steele Mackaye," 1927; he has also delivered a number of lectures on the Drama; in Mar., 1955, the Harvard College Library established the Marion and Percy MacKaye Collection. *Clubs:* The Players', Harvard, and MacDowell (New York), Cosmos (Washington), Everglades (Palm Beach).
(Died 31 Aug., 1956; age 81)

MACKELLAR, Helen, actress; *b.* Detroit, Michigan, U.S.A., 13 Feb., 1895; *d.* of Donald B. MacKellar and his wife Mary Ellen (Alexander); *e.* Spokane and Chicago; *m.* George D. MacQuarrie; had had some amateur experience before making her first professional appearance, at the Hotel Plaza, New York, 16 May, 1916, as Thérèse in " Woman on Her Own "; she next appeared at the Cohan Theatre, Aug., 1916, as Georgiana Garrison in " Seven Chances "; was then engaged to support John Drew, at the Criterion, New York, Oct., 1916, as Laura Bell in " Major Pendennis "; at the Cohan and Harris Theatre, Aug., 1917, played Tanya Huber in " A Tailor-Made Man "; at the Lyric, New York, Sept., 1918, Mrs. James Dawson in " The Unknown Purple "; at the Forty-eighth Street Theatre, Oct., 1919, Manette Fachard in " The Storm "; at the Morosco Theatre, Feb., 1920, Ruth Atkins in " Beyond the Horizon "; subsequently toured in " The Storm "; at the Eltinge Theatre, New York, Aug., 1921, played Hester Bevins in " Back Pay "; at the Playhouse, New York, Dec., 1921, Virginia Blaine in " Bought and Paid For "; at the Klaw, Apr., 1922, Hester Dunnybrig in " The Shadow "; at the Eltinge, Dec., 1922, Diane Dela-

tour in " The Masked Woman "; at the Longacre, Nov., 1924, Maggie Fortune in " The Desert Flower "; Comedy, Feb., 1925, Eileen Donovan in " A Good Bad Woman "; Bijou, Aug., 1925, Kate in " The Mud Turtle "; Daly's, Dec., 1925, Eugenie Bellamy in " Open House "; Little, Oct., 1927, Neena Dobson in " Romancin' Round "; Masque, Aug., 1930, Inez Talbot in "Through the Night"; Republic, Oct., 1930, succeeded Anne Forrest as Frankie in "Frankie and Johnnie"; 49th Street, Dec., 1931, played Greta in "Bloody Laughter"; San Francisco, Feb., 1937, Imilcea in "The Return of Hannibal"; Fulton, during 1943, played Abby Brewster in "Arsenic and Old Lace"; toured, 1944–5, as Mame Phillips in "Ramshackle Inn"; Henry Miller, New York, July, 1945, Edith Wilkins in "Dear Ruth"; toured, 1946–7–8, and 1949, as Amanda Wingfield in "The Glass Menagerie"; has appeared each year as guest star in summer stock; first appeared in films, 1932. *Address:* 11 East 32nd Street, New York City, 16, U.S.A.

MACKENNA, Kenneth, actor; *b.* Canterbury, New Hampshire, U.S.A., 19 Aug., 1899; *s.* of Leo Mielziner and his wife Ella MacKenna (Friend); *e.* Paris, New York, Hatfield (England), and Columbia University; *m.* (1) Kay Francis (mar. dis.); (2) Mary Philips; formerly a bank clerk and, for a time, served in the U.S. Army; made his first appearance on the stage at the Playhouse, New York, 28 June, 1919, as Jim Everett in "At 9.45"; 48th Street, Aug., 1920, played Arthur Bodkin in "Immodest Violet"; same theatre, Jan., 1922, Max Hamelin in "The Nest"; Cohan, Sept., 1922, Kenneth Reeves in "The Endless Chain"; Jolson, Oct., 1922, Felix and the Commander of the Ants in "The World We Live In" ("The Insect Play"); Belmont, 1923, Roderick White in "You and I"; Playhouse, Aug., 1923, Wally Spencer in "The Mad Honeymoon"; Hudson, Sept., 1923, Robert Colby in "The Crooked Square"; Garrick (for the Theatre Guild), Oct., 1923, Johnny March in "Windows"; Belmont, Nov., 1923, Ted

Stone in "Dumb-Bell"; Gaiety, Mar., 1924, Richard in "We Moderns"; Belmont, May, 1924, Peetcha in "Catskill Dutch"; Comedy, Sept., 1924, Jack Coates in "Nerves"; Cort, Sept., 1924, Dick Clayton in "The Far Cry"; Selwyn, Apr., 1925, Dr. Erno Memeth in "The Sapphire Ring"; Playhouse, Aug., 1925, Georges La Garde in "Oh, Mama!"; Mansfield, Mar., 1926, Jack Cazenove in "The Masque of Venice"; Bijou, Apr., 1926, John Shand in "What Every Woman Knows"; same theatre, Aug., 1928, Pierre de Mirande in "The Big Pond"; Booth, Nov., 1928, John Russell in a play without a name; at the Belasco, Los Angeles, Sept., 1932, played in "The Bride the Sun Shines On"; Morosco, Jan., 1934, David Mackenzie in "By Your Leave"; Ethel Barrymore, Apr., 1934, Gregory Langdon in "Wife Insurance"; Central City, Denver, July, 1934, Iago in "Othello"; Music Box, New York, Sept., 1934, Richard Niles in "Merrily We Roll Along"; at the Plymouth, New York, Apr., 1935, succeeded Nicholas Hannen as Steven Gaye in "Accent on Youth"; Ethel Barrymore, Sept.–Oct., 1935, Iago in "Othello," and Macduff in "Macbeth"; at the Maryland, Baltimore, Nov., 1935, played Alan Squier in "The Petrified Forest" and Steven Gaye in "Accent on Youth"; Ritz, Feb., 1936, staged "Co-Respondent Unknown"; Elitch's Gardens, Denver, 1936, played in "Sweet Aloes," "Libel," etc.; Lyceum, New York, Dec., 1936, played Charles Armitage Brown in "Aged 26"; Morosco, Apr., 1937, Gordon in "Penny Wise"; at Elitch's Gardens, summer season, 1937, played a repertory season of several weeks; is a Freeman of the Governor and Company of the Massachusetts Bay Colony, also of the Sons of the Revolution, New York, and a member of Actors' Equity Association; commenced film career, 1925, and has appeared in innumerable pictures; from 1937–42, was head of Scenario and Story departments, Metro-Goldwyn Mayer Studios, Culver City; from 1942–6, served as a Major in Signal Corps, as Director of the Morale Films Division, and was awarded the Legion of Merit, also combat star on Asiatic Theatre Ribbon;

returned to M.G.M., 1946, as executive in charge of Story and Scenario Departments. *Hobby:* Book collecting. *Recreation:* Yachting. *Clubs:* Players' and Coffee House, New York. *(Died 15 Jan., 1962; age 62)*

MACKENZIE, Mary, actress; *b.* Burnley, Lancs., 3 May, 1922; *d.* of Basil Mackenzie and his wife Rose Tegwedd (Rich); *e.* St. Stephen's College, Folkestone, Kent; made her first appearance on the stage at His Majesty's Theatre, Carlisle, 1937, with the repertory company, playing Dora in "Night Must Fall"; played in repertory companies for some years, at Bexhill, Dundee, etc.; first appeared in London, 1942, at the Comedy Theatre, when she took over the part of Grena in "Murder Without Crime"; same theatre, 1944, appeared as Effie in "This Was a Woman"; Embassy, Sept., 1946, played Jane Eyre in a play of that name; St. Martin's, Feb., 1948, Myrtle Gray in "Gathering Storm"; Embassy, May–Dec., 1948, played in "Symphony in Violence," "That Mighty Heart," "A Lady Mislaid," etc.; Embassy, Apr., and Comedy, June, 1949, appeared as Sandra Layton in "On Monday Next"; toured, 1950, in "Damascus Blade"; Comedy, Nov., 1952, played Ann Selley in "Tomorrow's Too Late"; at the "Q," Feb., 1953, played Carol Bestwood in "Birthday Honours"; New, Bromley, Apr., 1953, Celia Clive in "Foreign Field"; Strand, Oct., 1953, for the Repertory Players, appeared as Ruth Martyn in "The Secret Tent"; Wyndham's (Rep. Players), Feb., 1954, Janet Forbes in "Shadow of the Vine"; toured, 1954, as Ruth Martyn in "The Secret Tent"; Lyric, Feb., 1956, played Nurse Catty in "Ring For Catty"; Arts, Cambridge, Feb., 1957, played Olga in "The Cardinal"; Richmond, Apr., 1963, played Jan Dellasandro in "All About Love"; first appeared in films, 1944, in "Wanted for Murder"; has since played in many pictures; has broadcast extensively and recent television appearances include: *Z Cars, No Hiding Place, Ghost Squad, Probation Officer,* and the "Gilbert and Sullivan" serial. *Recreations:* Swimming, sun-bathing and dog-breeding. *(Died 20 Sept., 1966; age 44)*

MACKINDER, Lionel, actor ; *m.* Gracie Leigh ; in 1893, was playing in pantomime at the Theatre Royal, Brighton, and the following year he toured with his own company in " The Water Babies " ; first attracted attention in London when for a time he replaced Mr. Seymour Hicks as Charlie Appleby in " The Shop Girl," at the old Gaiety in 1895 ; since that date he has been almost continuously under the management of Mr. George Edwardes, either in London or on tour, and has appeared in " The Circus Girl," " A Runaway Girl," " The Messenger Boy," " The Toreador," " The Orchid," " The Girls of Gottenberg," " The Captain of the School," " Our Miss Gibbs," etc. ; he has also appeared at the Empire in *révues*, etc. ; at the Queen's, Sept., 1911, played Frederico in " Bonita," and at His Majesty's, Dec., 1911, Pluto in " Orpheus in the Underground."

(Died 10 Jan., 1915; age 46)

MACKINLAY, Jean Sterling, actress, *b.* London ; *d.* of Antoinette Sterling and John Mackinlay ; *e.* at Roedean School, Brighton ; studied for the stage with Geneviève Ward ; *m.* E. Harcourt Williams ; made her first appearance on the stage, 13 Feb., 1901, in " Coriolanus," with F. R. Benson at Comedy ; at the St. James's, Mar., 1902, played Cristina in " Paolo and Francesca," and Aug., 1902, Isabeau in " If I were King " ; at Wyndham's, Mar., 1903, played Peggy Macrae in " When a Man Marries " ; at the Apollo, Apr., 1904, appeared as Page Dearborn in " The Wheat King " ; at the Avenue, June, 1904, played Mathurine in " A Gentleman of France " ; subsequently toured in " Mice and Men," " Sunday," and " His House in Order " ; in the autumn of 1907 joined Sir John Hare's company, and in Nov. had the honour of appearing at Windsor Castle as Mrs. Goldfinch in " A Pair of Spectacles " ; at the Garrick, Apr., 1908, played Muriel Eden in " The Gay Lord Quex " ; June, 1908, played Mrs. Goldfinch in " A Pair of Spectacles " ; subsequently toured with Mr. George

Alexander in " The Thief " ; at the Court, Jan., 1909, played Sally in " John Malone's Love Story " ; subsequently appeared at the Playhouse, Feb., 1909, in " Her Proper Mate " ; Nov., 1909, played in " The Nursery Governess " ; at the Criterion, May, 1911, played Louka in " Arms and the Man " ; at the Kingsway, Sept., 1912, played Alice Maitland in " The Voysey Inheritance " ; at the Shaftesbury, Dec., 1914, played Katherine in " King Henry V," with F. R. Benson ; May, 1915, The Marquise in " Romance " ; of late years has achieved much success with a series of dramatic and folk-song recitals ; was the originator of the Children's Theatre movement in this country ; gives an annual season of her Children's Theatre *matinées* in London, each Christmas. *Hobbies :* Music and reading.

(Died 15 Dec., 1958; age 76)

MACKINTOSH, William, actor ; *b.* Melbourne, 23 July, 1855 ; made his first appearance on the stage, at the Theatre Royal, Elgin, 24 Dec., 1872, in " Christmas Eve " ; after playing various " stock " engagements in 1875 he joined Mrs. John Wood at Dublin, playing Crabtree in " The School for Scandal " ; he remained in the provinces until the end of 1878 ; he made his first appearance on the London stage, at the Court Theatre, under John Hare, 4 Jan., 1879, when he played Dr. Penguin in " A Scrap of Paper " ; subsequently played Sam Pilcher in " The Queen's Shilling," and at the St. James's under Hare and Kendal, played in " Old Cronies," " William and Susan," " Good Fortune," " The Money Spinner," " The Cape Mail," and " The Squire " ; appeared at the Court, Dec., 1882, as Tom Stirrup in " Comrades " ; appeared at the same theatre, 1883, in " The Rector," and " The Millionaire " ; in 1884 in " Margery's Lovers," " Dan'l Druce, Blacksmith," " Play " ; appeared at the Criterion, 1884, in " Featherbrain " ; at the Vaudeville, 1884, appeared as Samuel Hoggard in " Saints and Sinners " ; at the Haymarket, 1886, played in " Nadjesda," and " Engaged " ; at the St.

James's, 1886, in " The Hobby Horse," and in 1887, he made a great " hit " when he played King William III in " Lady Clancarty "; in 1888, he appeared there as Jabez Sneed in " The Wife's Secret," Moulinet in " The Ironmaster " and his original part of Gunnion in " The Squire "; at the Shaftesbury, Oct., 1888, played Touchstone in " As You Like It "; and in Nov., Colonel Damas in " The Lady of Lyons " ; in 1889, he appeared there as Baron Hartfeld in " Jim the Penman," and as Joseph Chandler in " The Middleman " ; in Sept., 1890, appeared at the Lyceum, making a great impression by his performance of Caleb Balderstone in " Ravenswood " ; in Jan., 1891, he played Dogberry in " Much Ado About Nothing," and at the Garrick, Sept., 1891, appeared as Beau Farintosh in " School "; at Terry's, Apr., 1892, played Colonel Lukyn in " The Magistrate "; at the Comedy, Apr., 1895, played Stanley French in " Delia Harding "; subsequently toured as Sir Richard Kato in " The Case of Rebellious Susan "; at the Lyceum, Jan., 1896, played Andrew Gibbard in " Michael and his Lost Angel " ; in Feb., 1896, appeared as Ibrahim in " For the Crown "; at the Adelphi, Aug., 1896, played Rudolph Klein in " Boys Together "; at the Lyceum, Apr., 1897, played Fouché in " Madam Sans-Gêne " ; Jan., 1898, Peter Tolstoi in " Peter the Great "; May, 1898, Bill Burge in " The Medicine Man " ; June, 1898, Nathan Oldworthy in " Nance Oldfield "; at the Adelphi, Mar., 1900, played King James II in " Bonnie Dundee " ; at the Garrick, Apr., 1901, played Cardinal de Rohan in " The Queen's Double "; at the Comedy, Feb., 1902, played the Rev. Mr. Cartwright in " Memory's Garden "; at the Criterion, Feb., 1903, played Farmer Tullidge in " A Clean Slate "; and in Mar., 1903, appeared as Joseph Pinner in " The Altar of Friendship "; his appearances since that date have been but few, but he toured during 1905 as Fagin, in Beerbohm Tree's company, in " Oliver Twist "; at the Lyric, Apr., 1907, repeated his former success of King William III in " Clancarty "; at the Royalty, Glasgow,

May, 1909, played Sir Pertinax Macsycophant in " Sir Pertinax " (an adaptation of " The Man of the World ") ; at His Majesty's, Feb., 1910, played Beggles in " The O'Flynn."
(Died 5 Jan., 1929; age 73)

MACLAREN, Ian, actor; *b.* Lynmouth, North Devon, 1 May, 1879 ; *e.* Queen Mary's School, Basingstoke, Hants.; made his first appearance on the stage at Shakespeare Theatre, Liverpool, 26 Apr., 1896, as Captain Chisholm in "The Derby Winner"; subsequently became a member of F. R. Benson's company, with which he remained some time, and then toured for some years in melodrama; after touring with his own company, made his first appearance on the London stage, at the Garrick Theatre, 27 Oct., 1902, as George in "My Lady Virtue"; appeared at the same theatre in "The Water Babies" and "Whitewashing Julia"; at the Criterion, Sept., 1905, played in "Billie's Little Love Affair"; subsequently again toured with his own company, in Shakespearean and modern repertory; played Macbeth, Othello, Brutus, Marc Antony, Malvolio, Romeo, Hamlet, Shylock, etc.; appeared at the Gaiety, Manchester, with Miss Horniman's Repertory Company; went to America in 1911, and made his first appearance in New York at Wallack's, 18 Sept., 1911, as Viscount Deeford in "Disraeli," with George Arliss; same theatre, Apr.,1912, played Hamlet; in the same year, toured as Hilary Cutts in "The New Sin"; Century Theatre, Dec., 1912, succeeded Basil Gill as the Emperor of China in "The Daughter of Heaven"; New Amsterdam, June, 1913, played Hawkeye in "The Follies of 1913"; subsequently toured with Margaret Anglin as Orlando, Marc Antony in "Antony and Cleopatra," Orestes, etc.; at Wallack's, New York, Jan.-Mar., 1915, appeared with Granville Barker's company in "Androcles and the Lion," "The Doctor's Dilemma," "A Midsummer Night's Dream," etc.; in 1916, toured in Australia, under J. C. Williamson, Ltd.; at the Punch and Judy, New York, Oct., 1921, played

François in "The Fan"; Comedy, Mar., 1922, Denton Morgan in "The Hindu"; from 1922–27, was leading man at the Neighborhood Playhouse, sustaining a variety of *rôles*; during this period he also appeared at the Lyceum, Dec., 1922, as Antonio in "The Merchant of Venice"; at the Garrick (for the Theatre Guild), Dec., 1923, Bishop of Beauvais in "Saint Joan"; Klaw, Sept., 1924, Chang Hong in "The Green Beetle"; at the Gallo Theatre, Dec., 1927, played Aegisthos in "Electra" of Sophocles; Shubert, Mar., 1928, Dr. Hemmingway in "The Furies"; subsequently toured with Mrs. Fiske, as Benedick in "Much Ado About Nothing"; at Los Angeles, Oct., 1931, John Tanner in "Man and Superman"; at Provincetown Theatre, New York, Apr., 1932, played The Chief in "Merry Go Round"; Shakespeare Theatre, Nov., 1932, played Shylock, Hamlet, Macbeth, Benedick, Marc Antony, etc.; in July, 1934, toured in "Mary of Scotland"; 58th Street, New York, Dec., 1935, played Francesco Cenci in "This Our House"; Vanderbilt, Feb., 1936, Arnold in "Hallowe'en"; from 1928–32, appeared annually at Hollywood, as Christus in "The Pilgrimage Play" ("The Life of Christ"); Mansfield, Nov., 1941, played Father Bede in "The Seventh Trumpet"; Blackfriars, N.Y., Apr., 1944, The Narrator in "Earth Journey"; commenced film career 1923. *Address:* c/o Actors' Equity Association, 45 West 47th Street, New York City, U.S.A.

MacLEAN, R. D. (Shepherd), actor; *b.* New Orleans, 7 Mar., 1859; *e.* Washington and University of Virginia; *m.* Odette Tyler; made his first appearance on the stage in 1886, with his own company, playing Pygmalion in "Pygmalion and Galatea" at Kingston, N.Y., and subsequently played Ingomar, Malvolio in "Twelfth Night," Romeo, etc.; subsequently appeared as Richard III, Brutus in "Julius Caesar," Petruchio in "The Taming of the Shrew"; he then joined Marie Prescott, playing Shylock and Spartacus in "The Gladiator"; appeared in the last-mentioned part at the Union Square Theatre, New York,

21 Nov., 1891; at the same theatre he also played Mark Antony, Shylock, and Othello; subsequently quitted the stage for seven years, reappearing in 1898, in a company headed by Odette Tyler, C. B. Hanford, and himself, playing Othello, Romeo, Brutus, and Shylock; next toured as Lord Wheatley in "Phroso," and then joined Madame Modjeska as leading man, playing King John, Macbeth, Othello, and Leicester in "Marie Stuart"; in 1903, toured as Coriolanus and King John; in 1905, he played lead with Mrs. Leslie Carter in "Adrea," and "The Heart of Maryland"; once again he quitted the stage for seven years, and did not reappear until 1912, when he played at the Manhattan Opera House, New York, Sept., 1912, as Korihor in "An Aztec Romance"; during 1912-13 with Odette Tyler, C. B. Hanford, and Marie Drofnah, toured in Shakespearean repertory; in 1913-14 toured with William Faversham, playing Othello, Brutus, and Mercutio; appeared at the Lyric, New York, in these parts, Feb., 1914; during 1915 appeared at Boston with Henry Jewett's company, playing Brutus, Shylock etc.; in 1923 at San Gabriel, California, played Fray Junipero Serra in "The Mission Play." *(Died 27 June, 1948; age 89)*

MACLEOD, W. Angus, manager; *b.* Kingston-on-Thames, 20 Mar., 1874; *m.* Blanche Latimer; was formerly an actor and appeared in small parts with F. R. Benson's Company in 1896; was business manager for William Haviland, 1899; F. R. Benson, 1902; next, assistant-manager for Sir Herbert Tree, at His Majesty's Theatre, 1903–5; in partnership with William Haviland, in South Africa, 1905–7; manager for Miss Ellen Terry, 1907–8; manager for Miss Evelyn Millard at the Garrick and Criterion Theatres, 1908–9; toured his own company in the provinces with "Pinkie and the Fairies," 1909–11; manager on tour for Anna Pavlova, 1911–12; took "The Blue Bird" company to Australia for Frederick Harrison, 1912; toured in India, Far East, and Australasia, 1913–15; since 1915, a director of the firm of Daniel Mayer Co., Ltd.,

which has produced in London, amongst many other plays—"Damaged Goods," 1917; "The Way of an Eagle," 1922; "Havoc," "The Street Singer," 1924; "Rose Marie" (with Sir Alfred Butt), 1925; "Betty in Mayfair," 1925; "Aloma," "Merely Molly," 1926; "The Squall," 1927; "The Silver Cord" (with Alec Rea), 1927; "The Second Man," 1928; "The Song of the Sea," 1928; "Beau Geste," 1929; "Bitter Sweet" (with C. B. Cochran), 1929; "St. Joan" (revival), 1931; "The Good Companions" (with Julian Wylie), 1931; "Pleasure Cruise," 1932; "Double Harness," 1933; "First Episode," 1934; "The Golden Arrow," 1935; "Youth at the Helm," 1935; "Black Limelight," 1937; Comedie Française Season at Savoy, 1939; "Off the Record," 1947; "Mountain Air," 1948; "The Silver Curlew," 1950; "MacAdam and Eve," "The White Sheep of the Family," 1951; "Sweet Peril," 1952; "Anastasia," 1953; "Angels in Love," 1954; for many years from 1930, presented "Peter Pan." *Recreations:* Reading and motoring. *Club:* R.A.C.
(Died 2 Feb., 1962; age 87)

MAC MANUS, Clive, dramatic critic and journalist; *b.* Highgate; *s.* of Joseph Edward Mac Manus and his wife Delia (Lees); *e.* privately; was engaged on the editorial staff of the *Daily Mail*, and on the Continental *Daily Mail*, in Paris and Nice; during the Great War, served in France and Flanders, with the 1/7 Royal Warwickshire Regiment; was Civil Administration Officer, Rhine Army, 1919; subsequently on the *Daily Graphic*, and was film critic of the *Evening Standard*, 1927-30; from 1930-36, engaged in the film industry; was dramatic critic of the *Daily Mail*, 1936-8; is a member of the Critics' Circle. *Recreations:* The Theatre, reading, talking, lawn-tennis. *Club:* Savage. *(Died 3 May. 1953)*

MAC OWAN, Norman, actor and dramatic author; *b.* St. Andrews, 2 Jan., 1877; *s.* of the Rev. James M. MacOwan and his wife Grace (Pullar);

e. Edinburgh; *m.* Violet Stephenson; made his first appearance on the stage at the Grand Theatre, Douglas, Isle of Man, July, 1900, as Jacob in "The Road to Ruin"; was with the Compton Comedy Company, 1900-2; from 1902-4 toured in "The Night of the Party," "Monsieur Beaucaire," etc.; played the title-*rôle* in "Monsieur Beaucaire," 750 times in provinces; made his first appearance in London at the Lyceum, 1 Mar., 1911, as the Earl of Rassendyll in "The Prisoner of Zenda"; at the Duke of York's, Oct., 1911, played David Wylie in "What Every Woman Knows"; at the Savoy, Dec., 1911, The Genie of the Carpet and Captain Carey in "Where the Rainbow Ends"; at the Comedy, Sept., 1912, Alec Inglis in "A Scrape o' the Pen"; at the Duke of York's, Sept., 1914, Rob Dow in "The Little Minister"; Mar., 1915, the Junker in "Rosy Rapture"; from 1915-19 served in the Army in Gallipoli, Egypt and Palestine; during 1919-20 was acting-manager at the Adelphi Theatre; at the Apollo, May, 1923, again played David Wylie in "What Every Woman Knows"; during 1926-7 toured in Australia with Dion Boucicault in a repertory of Barrie's plays; "Q," Feb., 1927, played Thomas in "Priscilla the Rake"; Duke of York's, Sept., 1927, Comte de Vernet in "The Beloved Vagabond"; Garrick (for Jewish Drama League), Dec., 1927, De Silva in "Uriel Acosta"; Arts, Nov., 1928, Fyodor Ivanich in "The Fruits of Enlightenment"; Jan., 1929, the Father in "The Age of Unreason"; Arts and Comedy, Apr., 1929, Dr. Ralstan in "The Infinite Shoeblack"; New, Sept., 1929, played Sir William Hamilton in "Emma Hamilton"; went to New York, and at the Maxine Elliott Theatre, Feb., 1930, played Dr. Ralstan in "The Infinite Shoeblack"; after returning to London, appeared at the Arts, Jan., 1932, as Captain Draper in "The Judgment of Dr. Johnson," and John Morley in "The Comforter"; "Q" and Royalty, Mar., 1933, Mr. Carruthers in "Francis Thompson"; Garrick, Apr., 1933, Frank Marriott in "Beggars in Hell"; Winter Garden, Nov., 1933, Mr. Glen-

morison in "On the Rocks"; New, June, 1934, Ruthven in "Queen of Scots"; Royalty, Feb., 1936, Horace Skirving in "Storm in a Teacup"; Daly's, July, 1937, Father Fraser in "The First Legion"; toured, Nov., 1942, for E.N.S.A., as the Doctor in "Hobson's Choice"; Lyric, Mar., 1943, played Alec Wylie in "What Every Woman Knows"; Cambridge, May, 1944, Barbaruccio in "A Night in Venice"; toured, 1948-9, as Professor Linden in "The Linden Tree," and Douglas Sheldon in "Random Harvest"; since 1950, has appeared mainly in films; is the author of the following plays: "The Demagogue," 1912; "The Chalk Line" (with Fabrian Ware), 1912; "The Blue Lagoon" (with Charlton Mann), 1920; "Lord o' Creation," 1924; "Jacob's Ladder," 1925; "The New Tenant," 1928; "The Infinite Shoeblack," 1929; "Glorious Morning," 1938; author of the novels "The Infinite Shoeblack," 1924; "Glorious Morning," 1939. *Club*: Green Room.
(Died 29 Dec., 1961; age 84)

MACQUEEN-POPE, W. J., theatre press-representative and historian; *b.* Devonshire, 11 Apr., 1888; after a short period as a shipping-clerk, entered the theatrical profession and became secretary to the late Sir George Dance, for several years; subsequently business manager for Sir Alfred Butt at the Queen's, St. James's, Globe, Palace, Covent Garden, and Lyric Theatres; subsequently manager of the Alexandra Palace, 1922-5; press manager at Palladium, 1925-6; manager for Billy Merson, Shaftesbury, 1926; general manager of the Duke of York's Theatre, 1927-9; manager for Walter Hackett at Whitehall Theatre, 1929-32; director, Duke of York's, 1932; with R. Lowris Pearson, founded the Famous Players' Guild; was associated with the Tom Walls-Ralph Lynn management at the Aldwych and Fortune Theatres; was then press representative for Drury Lane and many other London theatres and managements, including H. M. Tennent Ltd., Julian Wylie, O'Brien, Linnit and Dunfee, Alec Rea, Basil

Dean, Tom Arnold, Sir Seymour Hicks, London Coliseum, Harold Holt, Jack Hylton, etc.; at the outbreak of War, 1939, joined E.N.S.A., as Public Relations Officer, remaining in that position until 1943, when he resigned, to join Tom Arnold; is the author of "The Punctual Sex," 1914; "The Burning Forest," 1915; "Train 68," 1915; "Cold Mutton," 1918; is an expert on pantomime and theatrical history; contributes articles to the Press on theatrical and general subjects, and is a well-known broadcaster and lecturer on the Theatre, Music Hall, Old London and Pleasure resorts; President of the Association of London Press Representatives, 1950; author of the history "Theatre Royal, Drury Lane," published 1946; "Indiscreet Guide to Theatreland," 1946; "Carriages at Eleven," 1947; "Haymarket: Theatre of Perfection," 1947; "Twenty Shillings in the Pound," 1948; "Gaiety: Theatre of Enchantment," 1949; "The Melodies Linger On," 1950; since 1950 has written "Ivor" (a biography of Ivor Novello), "Ladies First," "Ghosts and Greasepaint," "Shirtfronts and Sables," "Fortune's Favourite" (with D. L. Murray—A biography of Franz Lehar), "Back Numbers," "Pillars of Drury Lane"; at the Metropolitan, Edgware Road, Sept., 1955, he devised and produced a programme of old-time variety entitled "Music Hall at the Met"; also Oct., 1955, commenced a series of television talks on theatrical matters, entitled "Popie." *Recreations*: Motoring, ornithology, and gardening.
(Died 27 June, 1960; age 72)

MACQUOID, Percy, R.I., J.P., artist, designer and decorator; *b.* 1852; *s.* of the late Thomas Robert Macquoid, R.I., and his wife Katherine Sarah (Gadsdon), the well-known authoress; *e.* Marlborough and R. A. Schools; *m.* Theresa Dent; designed costumes and decorations for many of the productions made by Sir Herbert Tree at His Majesty's Theatre, including "King Henry VIII," "Othello," "Joseph and his Brethren," "The School for Scandal," "Romeo and Juliet," "King Henry IV" (part I), "David Copperfield," "The Perfect Gentleman," "Ariadne in Naxos," etc.; also for "Mary Rose" at the Haymarket; "A Marriage of Convenience" at the Globe; "La Tosca" at the Aldwych, etc. *Recreation:* Shooting. *Club:* Arts. *Address:* 8 Palace Street, Bayswater, W.2. *Telephone No.:* Park 2400.

MACRAE, Arthur, actor and dramatic author; *b.* London, 17 Mar., 1908; *s.* of Paul Arthur Schroepfer and his wife Margaret (Don); was a pupil of Italia Conti, and made his first appearance on the stage at the St. James's Theatre, 15 Dec., 1921, as the third Wolf in "Peter Pan"; at the Holborn Empire, Xmas, 1922 and 1923, played William in "Where the Rainbow Ends"; studied at the Royal Academy of Dramatic Art, 1925–7; at the Court Theatre, Oct.–Nov., 1927, appeared in "Paul I," and "Mr. Prohack"; appeared in repertory, 1928–9, at Bristol, Glasgow, and Edinburgh; at Daly's, Dec., 1929, played Charles Wykeham in "Charley's Aunt"; Arts, Feb., 1930, Emile Ardillot in "The Command to Love"; New, May, 1930, Vaughan Carter in "The Last Chapter"; Arts, July, 1930, George in "Dance With No Music"; Prince Edward, Sept., 1930, Leslie Waring in "Sexton Blake"; Drury Lane, Jan., 1931, Babe in "Song of the Drum"; New, June, 1931, The Quartermaster in "Sea Fever"; Embassy, July, 1931, and St. Martin's, Aug., 1931, Sholto in "The Young Idea"; Drury Lane, Oct., 1931, Edward Marryot in "Cavalcade"; Comedy, 1933, appeared in "Ballyhoo"; Apr., 1933, in "How D'You Do?"; Westminster, Nov., 1934, played Kenneth Rimplegar in "Three Cornered Moon"; Arts, Sept., 1935, Gilbert Kent in "Dusty Ermine"; Shaftesbury, Dec., 1936, Tony Willis in "Heart's Content"; Embassy, Apr., 1937, Amyas Florin in "Festival Time"; Morosco, New York, Sept., 1937, Dudley in "George and Margaret"; King's, Glasgow, Mar., 1938, Hon. Peter Lambert in "A Thing Apart"; Criterion, Mar., 1939, Ned Eccles in "Sugar Plum"; Old Vic., June, 1939, David Gunn in "The Ascent of F.6."; Piccadilly, Nov.,

1939, Dudley in "George and Margaret"; Haymarket, Mar., 1941, Makepeace Lovell in "No Time for Comedy"; served in the R.A.F., Apr., 1941–Feb., 1946; reappeared on the stage at the Criterion, June, 1948, as Tom Wright in "Traveller's Joy"; Aldwych, Oct., 1951, played Edgar in "Figure of Fun"; Globe, June, 1953, played Eteoneus in "The Private Life of Helen," which he also directed; Apollo, June, 1954, Tom Davenport in "Both Ends Meet"; Lyric, Apr., 1956, played John Blair Kennedy in "South Sea Bubble"; he is the author of "Flat to Let," 1931; "Indoor Fireworks," 1934; "Shall We Reverse?" 1935; "Tavern in the Town," 1937; "Sugar Plum," 1939; "Under the Counter," 1945; "Traveller's Joy," 1948; "Both Ends Meet," 1954; part-author of "How D'You Do?", 1933; "Charlot's Chara-a-Bang," 1935; "The Town Talks," 1936; "Under Your Hat," 1938; "All Clear," 1939; "Full Swing," 1942; "Something in the Air," 1943; "Tuppence Coloured," 1947; "Slings and Arrows," 1948; "The Lyric Revue," 1951; "The Globe Revue," 1952; "Airs On a Shoestring," 1953; "Living For Pleasure," 1958; he adapted the following plays from the French of André Roussin: "Figure of Fun," 1951; "The Private Life of Helen," 1953; "Nina," 1955. *(Died 25 Feb., 1962; age 53)*

MACRAE, Duncan, actor; *b.* Glasgow, Scotland, 20 Aug., 1905; *s.* of James Macrae and his wife Kate (Graham); *e.* Allan Glen's School, and Glasgow University; *m.* Peggy Scott; formerly a teacher; studied for the stage with Anne McAllister, L.L.D., and R. F. Pollok; made his first appearance in London at Sadler's Wells Theatre, Oct., 1945, as Donald Macalpin in "The Forrigan Reel"; at the Citizens', Glasgow, 1947, played Jamie in "Jamie the Saxt"; Edinburgh Festival, Assembly Hall, Aug., 1948, played Flatterie in "The Thrie Estates"; Embassy, London, June, 1949, played Mr. Oliphant in "Let Wives Tak Tent"; subsequently appeared at the Citizens', Glasgow, where he played the following leading parts: Dame in "The Tintock Cup," 1950; King Dod III in "Right

Royal," George Triple in "Meeting at Night," 1954; Palladium, Edinburgh, Aug., 1954, Harry MacGog in "Gog and MacGog"; Palladium, Edinburgh, Aug., 1955, played Michael Scott in "The World's a Wonder"; at the Lyceum, Edinburgh, Apr.–June, 1956, played the following parts: Mr. Oliphant in "Let Wives Tak Tent," Judas in "A Man Named Judas"; Aggie Mac-Luckie in "Rabbie Burns Slept Here," and Wullie Speedie in "Tullycairn"; Aldwych, London, July, 1956, played Mr. McCrimmon in the revival of "Mr. Bolfry"; Gateway, Edinburgh, Aug., 1957, played Thomas Aucterlecki in "The Flowers o' Edinburgh"; made his first appearance in New York at the Manhattan Center, Nov., 1959, in Concert Party; Royal Court, London, Apr., 1960, played John in "Rhinoceros," subsequently transferring with the production to the Strand, June, 1960; Grand, Blackpool, summer 1964, appeared in "What a Joy Ride"; Metropole, Glasgow, Oct., 1964, played Gilbert Dalgleish in "Bachelors Are Bold"; Arts, Cambridge, Feb., 1965, McLeavy in "Loot"; King's, Glasgow, summer season, played the Rev. Lionel Toop in "See How They Run"; in 1952, formed a partnership with Tim Watson under the name of "Scottishows," and presented plays on tour in Scotland, and at the Edinburgh Festival, 1952–55; has also appeared in many pantomimes in Glasgow, 1950–61; films in which he has appeared include: "Whisky Galore," "The Kidnappers," "Tunes of Glory," "Our Man in Havana," etc.; principal television appearances include: "Better Late," "Para Handy," "White Heather," "Conscientious Gauger"; author of the pamphlet "Be Not Too Tame Neither" (Federation of Theatre Unions in Scotland), 1965. Chairman of Actors' Equity Association in Scotland. *Favourite parts:* Dignified Fools. *Recreations:* Yoga and walking. *(Died 23 Mar., 1967; age 61)*

MADDEN, Cecil (Charles), M.B.E., dramatic author; *b.* H.B.M. Consulate, Mogador, Morocco, 29 Nov., 1902; *s.* of Archibald Maclean Madden, C.M.G., and his wife Cecilia Catherine (Moor); *e.* French Lycées, Morocco, Spanish Schools, Aldeburgh Lodge Preparatory School and Dover College; *m.* Muriel Emily Cochrane; is the author of the following plays: "Little Angel," 1927; "The Hero," 1928; "The Equator" (from the French of H. R. Lenormand), 1928; "Through the Veil" (with X. Y. Stone), 1930; "Max and Mr. Max" (from Eduardo Ugarte and José Lopez Rubio), 1931; "Prestige" (with Theodora Benson), 1932; "To-Night We'll Dream," 1933; "Saturday's Children" (adapted from Maxwell Anderson), 1934; "All's Well," 1936; "The President's Double" (from J. I. Luca de Tena), 1939; "Chatterbox" (with George Beardmore), 1948; "Loophole" (with Macgregor Urquhart), "Chelsea Reach" (with Vincent McConnor), 1950; "Silent Witness" (with Macgregor Urquhart), 1952; "A Touch of Magic" (U.S.A.), 1955; "Investigation" (with Max Hart), 1958; has also written *revues* in Spain (in Spanish), in Paris (in French) and New York; is the author of numerous original features, sketches, *revues*, stories and talks for broadcasting; also adaptor of many radio plays; author of articles on the technical side of the theatre and foreign drama; author of the following books: "Anywhere for a News Story," "Meet the Detective," "My Grimmest Nightmare," "Living Dangerously," "Not Long for this World"; joined the B.B.C. in the Talks Department, subsequently in Outside Broadcasting, then senior producer to the Empire Service, subsequently first producer for Television at Alexandra Palace, Aug., 1936; creator of weekly feature, "Picture Page," and programmes organizer of Television; in 1940, was Head of Overseas Entertainments Unit, and created all Radio programmes to British, Dominion, and Colonial Forces serving abroad, notably "Variety Band Box," the British Command Performance, "Merry Go Round," and the "American Eagle in Britain" series, for U.S.A. forces in the United Kingdom, which ran weekly, continuously, for five years; in 1944–5, was in charge of Production of Allied Expeditionary Forces Radio programmes; in 1946, resumed his position as Programmes Organizer of Television; Head of Television Children's Programmes, 1950; Assistant to the Controller of Television Programmes, 1951–64. *Recreation:* Television photomontage. *Address:* 16 St. Loo Mansions, Chelsea, London, S.W.3. *Telephone No.:* Flaxman 8297.

MAETERLINCK, Maurice, dramatic author and poet; *b.* Ghent, Belgium; 29 Aug., 1862; *m.* (1) Georgette Leblanc, actress and vocalist (mar. dis.); (2) Renée Dahou; is the author of the following plays: "La Princesse Maleine," 1890; "L'Intruse" ("The Intruder"), 1890; "Pelléas et Mélisande," 1892; "La Mort de Tintagiles" ("The Death of Tintagiles"), 1894; "Aglavaine et Sélysette," 1896; "Ariane et Barbe-Bleu," 1899; "Souer Beatrice" ("Sister Beatrice"), 1899; "Monna Vanna," 1902; "Joyselle," 1903; "L'Oiseau Bleu" ("The Blue Bird"), 1909; "Mary Magdalene," 1910; "Fiancée" ("The Betrothal"), 1918; "Le Bourgmestre de Stilemonde" ("The Burgomaster of Stilemonde"), 1918; "L'Abbot du Setubal," 1940; all of these, with the exception of "Ariane," "Joyselle," and "L'Abbot du Setubal," have been produced in London, and several in New York; has also written numerous books and poems, and made many translations of other authors; among his other works, the most famous is, perhaps, "La Vie des Abeilles" ("The Life of the Bees"), translated into English, 1901.

MAGNIER, Pierre, French actor; *b.* 22 Feb., 1869; studied at the Conservatoîre, and gained first prize for Tragedy, under M. Gôt, 1894; made his first appearance on the stage at the Odéon, 25 Sept., 1894, in "Barynia"; has appeared at most of the principal Parisian theatres, and has played the following among other parts : Roux in "Le mannequin d'Osier," at Renaissance; at the Odéon, played in "Pour la Couronne," "Le Modéle," "Le Crise Conjugale," "La Vie de Bohéme," "Le Roman d'un jeuue homme pauvre," etc. ; appeared as De Fersen in "Varennes," Armand Duval in "La Dame aux

Camélias," Flambeau in "L'Aiglon," also the leading parts in "Francesca de Rimini," "Theroigne de Méricourt," "Werther," "La Tosca," "Dalila," "Théodora," etc., at the Théâtre Sarah Bernhardt ; Gaston in "Ma Cousine," Mario Albert in "La Fille de Jephte," Harry Belroë in "Paris—New York," Dufresne in "Zaza," Marco Fiore in "Après le Pardon," De Neipperg in "Madame Sans-Gêne," also in "La Souris," "Suzeraine," "Qui peur Gagne," "La Vierge Folle," etc., at the Théâtre Réjane; Artanezzo in "Le Scandale" and Christian in "Le Juif Polonais," at the Renaissance ; "L'Age s'aimer," "Tour de Main," etc., at the Gymnase ; Bertrand in "Le Poulailer," at the Théâtre Michel ; Leclercq in "La Griffe," Chantecler in the play of that name, L'Abbé Constantin in the play of that name, André Varèze in "L'Aventurier," Colonel Boncour in "La Flambée," Coupeau in "L'Assommoir," Christian, and subsequently Cyrano in "Cyrano de Bergerac," Napoleon in "Madame Sans-Gêne," also leading parts in "La Voile du Bonheur," "Les Demi-Vierges," "L'Appassionata," at the Porte-St.-Martin ; L'abbé Thibault in "Ces Messieurs," at the Ambigu ; Georges Charmier in "L'Ange Gardien"; of late years has devoted much time to the Cinema stage. *Address :* 86 Rue Cardinet, Paris.

MAHONEY, Will, actor; *b.* Helena, Montana, 5 Feb., 1896; *s.* of William Jas. Mahoney; *m.* (1) Sue Wilson (mar. dis.); (2) Evie Hayes; made his first appearance on the stage at Spokane, Washington, at the age of eight, as a dancer; was then employed as an electrician; then went into "vaudeville," as a singer, and became one of the best-known on the American variety stage; appeared at the Apollo Theatre, New York, 30 June, 1924, in "George White's Scandals"; appeared at the London Palladium, 1926; at the Waldorf Theatre, New York, Nov., 1927, played Happy Hokum in "Take the Air"; again appeared in London 1928, at the Victoria Palace; at the

Earl Carroll Theatre, July, 1929, appeared in "Earl Carroll's Sketch Book"; again appeared at the London Palladium, June, 1931; at the Earl Carroll Theatre, Aug., 1931, played in "Earl Carroll Vanities"; he then returned to "vaudeville"; again appeared in London, at the Palladium, Aug., 1934, subsequently touring the provinces; at the Palace, Manchester, Dec., 1934, made his first appearance in pantomime, playing the Cat in "Puss in Boots"; during 1935, toured in variety theatres in "Radio New York"; appeared at the Palladium, 1935, in the Royal Command Performance; toured, and appeared in London variety theatres, 1935–6, in "Why Be Serious?"; 1936, in "Bats in the Belfry"; Victoria Palace, May, 1937, in "Wonderful World"; toured, 1937–38, in "Ride 'Em Cowboy"; toured in Australia, 1938–49; reappeared at London Palladium, 1950; at the New York City Center, May, 1955, appeared as Finian McLonergan in a revival of "Finian's Rainbow"; Jan Hus Playhouse, New York, Nov., 1958, Reverend Bernard White and Adam Steele in "The Man Who Never Died."
(Died 9 Feb., 1967; age 73)

MAINWARING, Ernest, actor; *b.* East Grinstead, 22 May, 1876; *s.* of Ellen (Saulez) and General William George Mainwaring; *e.* Charterhouse; *m.* Carrie L. Keeler; made his first appearance on the stage, at the Theatre Royal, Richmond, Jan., 1895, as Hubbard in "The Romance of a Shopwalker"; made his first appearance in London, at the Olympic Theatre, 9 Mar., 1897, as Lieutenant Portland in "The Mariners of England"; made his first "hit" when he succeeded Herbert Sleath in "What Happened to Jones," at the old Strand Theatre, 1898; toured with Marie Tempest in England and America; toured in "Charley's Aunt," "Miss Francis of Yale," "The Second in Command," etc.; appeared at the Playhouse, 1907, in "French as he is Spoke"; subsequently appeared at the same theatre, in "The Drums of Oude," "The Earl of Pawtucket"; Jan., 1908, played Clive Grainger in "The O'Grindles"; Mar.,

1908, Parson Cranch in "Marjory Strode"; June, 1909, Walter Crutchley in "The Flag Lieutenant"; Dec., 1909, Colonel Macmichel in "The Visit"; Nov., 1910, Henry Worthington in "A Single Man"; at the Criterion, Sept., 1911, played Roebuck Ramsden in "Man and Superman"; at Wyndham's, Feb., 1912, played Dan Smith in "The Dust of Egypt"; at the Prince of Wales's, Apr., 1912, William Lewis in "At the Barn"; subsequently appeared at the same theatre in "Art and Opportunity," and "Esther Castways"; at the Savoy, June, 1913, played Frank Lester in "A Cardinal's Romance"; at the Globe, Oct., 1913, played Sir George Rawley in "People Like Ourselves"; at the Criterion, Feb., 1914, Sir John Gower in "A Pair of Silk Stockings"; after an absence of eight years reappeared on the stage in Aug., 1922, when he toured as Major Millet in "If Winter Comes," and played the same part at the St. James's, Jan., 1923; at the Shaftesbury, Apr., 1924, played Mr. Cattestock in "A Perfect Fit"; at the Ambassadors', Aug., 1924, Lord Early in "Storm"; Vaudeville, Jan., 1925, the Earl of Northallerton in "Possessions"; Criterion, June, 1925, Rev. Arthur Escott in "Mixed Doubles"; Playhouse, Jan., 1926, Marquis of Olde in "Blind Alley"; Globe, Mar., 1926, Lord Snowdon in "By-Ways"; Savoy, Oct., 1926, Geoffrey Kennion in "Love's a Terrible Thing"; May, 1927, Robert Hanbury in "Double Dan"; Arts, May, 1927, Jim Mordaunt in "The Bridge"; St. James's, Feb., 1928, Martin in "S.O.S."; Lyric, June, 1929, the Inspector in "Murder on the Second Floor"; Apr., 1930, Tom Reed in "Debonair"; Prince Edward, Oct., 1930, Sir William Dering in "Nippy"; Arts, May, 1931, Albert Page in "Make Up Your Mind"; "Q," May, 1932, Lewis Marshall in "An Average Man"; Shaftesbury, Dec., 1933, General Maynard in "A Present from Margate"; Globe, Feb., 1935, Roberts in "Youth at the Helm"; Prince's, July, 1937, John Forrester and the Captain in "The Gusher." *Favourite parts:* Binks in "The Second in Command" and

Billy in "At the Barn." *Hobby :* Gardening. *Club :* Green Room.
(Died 22 Oct., 1941; age 65)

MAIR, George Herbert, C.M.G. ; dramatic critic and journalist ; *b.* 8 May, 1887 ; *e. s.* of the late Fleet-Surgeon G. Mair, R.N. ; *e.* Aberdeen University (M.A.), and Christ Church College, Oxford (B.A., 1st class) ; *m.* Maire O'Neill ; was engaged on the editorial staff of the *Manchester Guardian,* 1909 ; was literary-editor and political correspondent in London for the same paper, 1911-14 ; assistant-editor *Daily Chronicle,* 1914 ; dramatic critic of *The Evening Standard,* 1923 ; received the decoration of a Chevalier of the Legion of Honour, Paris, 1919 ; created C.M.G., 1920.
(Died 2 Jan., 1926; age 39)

MAIS, Stuart Petre Brodie, author and dramatic critic ; *b.* 4 July, 1885 ; *s.* of John Stuart Brodie Mais and his wife Horden (Tamlyn) ; *e.* Christ Church, Oxford ; *m.* Doris Lilian Frances Snow ; formerly a schoolmaster ; appointed dramatic critic to *The Daily Graphic,* Jan., 1924 ; is the author of over twenty books, including " A Public School in War Time," " April's Lonely Soldier," " Interlude," " Rebellion," " From Shakespeare to O. Henry," " A Schoolmaster's Diary," " Prunello," " Perissa," " Eclipse," " Orange Street," etc. *Recreation :* Beagling. *Address :* 22A First Avenue, Hove, Sussex.

MAITLAND, Lauderdale, actor ; *b.* London ; *s.* of Adela Louisa (Wollams) and William Lauderdale Maitland, better known as " Bill " Mansell, actor and manager ; *e.* Margate ; originally studied medicine, but never qualified ; *m.* Janet Alexander ; made his first appearance on the stage, at the Queen's Theatre, Longton. 20 Aug., 1901, in " Women of London " ; toured for several years in leading parts in " The Silver King," " One of the Best," " Two Little Vagabonds," " Rob Roy," etc. ; also played in several Shakespearean productions, " Hamlet," " Romeo

and Juliet," " Twelfth Night," " Julius Cæsar," etc. ; made his first appearance in London, at the Lyceum Theatre, 14 Mar., 1908, as Benvolio in " Romeo and Juliet " ; subsequently appeared at the same theatre, as Prince Olof in " The Prince and the Beggar Maid," June, 1908 ; Laertes in " Hamlet," Mar., 1909 ; toured in 1909 as the Marquis de Sabran in " An Unpardonable Sin " ; at the Lyceum, Nov., 1911, played Athos in " The Three Musketeers " ; Feb., 1912, John in " The Monk and the Woman " ; at the New Prince's, July, 1912, Dan Mylrea in " Ben-My-Chree " ; Oct., 1912, Edmond Dantes in " Monte Cristo " ; at the Lyceum, Feb., 1913, King Charles II in " Nell Gwynne " ; May, 1913, Ivanhoe in the play of that name ; July, 1913, Harry Maylie in " Oliver Twist " ; Aug., 1913, Jack Cunningham in " The Beggar Girl's Wedding " ; Oct., 1913, Bertie Cecil and Louis Victor in " Under Two Flags " ; at the Aldwych Theatre, Apr., 1914, played Harold Armytage in " The Lights o' London " ; at the King's, Hammersmith, Nov., 1914, Julian Grey in " The New Magdalen " ; during 1915 toured in variety theatres in " The Contemptible Little Army " ; at the Lyceum, May, 1915, played Captain Russell Squires in " In Time of War " ; July, 1915, George Madison in " Her Forbidden Marriage " ; Sept., 1915, Philip Carton in " Between Two Women " ; at the Kingsway, May, 1916, Silas P. Raymond in " Ye Gods " ; in 1918 toured as Joseph Marks in " The Bubble " ; at the Lyceum, Feb., 1919, played General Grant in " The Female Hun " ; at the Garrick, Sept., 1920, Ben Ormerod in " The Right to Strike " ; at the Duke of York's, Jan., 1921, Samuel Dennison Jun. in " Lonely Lady " ; in Mar., 1921, joined the " Grand Guignol " Company at the Little Theatre, playing in " The Seven Blind Men," " The Kill," and " The Chemist " ; at the Apollo, May, 1922, played Talbot Wynne (" Taffy ") in " Trilby " ; Jan., 1923, Mr. Moody in " A Roof and Four Walls " ; at the Prince's, Oct., 1923, Col. Sebastian Moran in " The Return of Sherlock Holmes " ; at the Lyceum, Apr., 1924,

Vere Hamilton in " Her Market Price."
Recreations : Golf and rowing. *Club :*
Savage. *(Died 28 Feb., 1929; age 52)*

MAITLAND, Ruth, actress ; *b.*
London, 3 Feb., 1880 ; *d.* of Charles
Erskine and his wife, the Comtesse
Marie Lucie de Chastelain ; *e.* Church
of England High School ; *m.* Major
James Seafield-Grant, M.C. (dec.) ;
made her first appearance on the stage
at the Garrick Theatre, Mar., 1898, as
Dulcie Meredith in " The Nettle " ; at
the Globe, Feb., 1901, played Lady
Olivia Vernon in " Sweet Nell of Old
Drury " ; at the Princess's, Oct., 1901,
played Barbara Scarth in " Two Little
Vagabonds " ; at Her Majesty's, Feb.,
1902, played Clyti in " Ulysses " ; at
the Garrick, Apr., 1908, played Mrs.
Jack Eden in " The Gay Lord Quex " ;
at the Hippodrome, Aug., 1908, played
in " The Sands o' Dee " ; appeared at
the St. James's, 1908–10, in " John
Glayde's Honour," " The Thief,"
" Mid-Channel," " Eccentric Lord
Comberdene " ; appeared at the
Queen's, with H. B. Irving ; at the
Haymarket, 1913, played in " Within
the Law " ; at the Kingsway, Dec.,
1915, played Mother in " The Starlight Express " ; she then left the
stage for four years ; reappeared at
the Lyceum, Mar., 1920, when she
played Lady Ethel Wendover in
" Boy of My Heart " ; at the Comedy,
Nov., 1921, Miss Gatterscombe in
"The Faithful Heart" ; Mar., 1922, Mrs.
Ormandy Browne in " Other People's
Worries " ; at the Aldwych, Sept.,
1922, Blanche Bacton in " Double
or Quit " ; at the St. James's, May,
1923, Pritchard in " The Outsider " ;
July, 1923, Martin in " The Coming
of Gabrielle " ; at the Kingsway, June,
1924, played in " Yoicks ! " ; at the
Comedy, Dec., 1924, played Mrs. U.
Makepeace Witter in " Just Married " ;
New Oxford, Jan., 1926, Mrs. Medway
in " Turned-Up " ; Duke of York's,
Apr., 1926, Sarah Britt in " Loose
Ends " ; Strand, Sept., 1926, Mrs.
Harriet Simmons in " The Whole
Town's Talking " ; King's, Hammer-
smith, May, 1927, Adela in " A Warm
Corner " ; Wyndham's, Nov., 1927,
Lady Wishfort in " The Way of the

World " ; Criterion, May, 1928, Blanche
Cory in " Skin Deep " ; Adelphi, Feb.,
1929, Lady Lancaster in "Mr.Cinders";
Phoenix, Jan., 1931, the Comtesse de
Brémonteuil in " Frailties " ; Savoy,
July, 1931, Rebecca Moor in "Dr.
Jekyll and Mr. Hyde" ; Comedy, Dec.,
1931, Miss Gatterscombe in " The
Faithful Heart" ; Vaudeville, Apr.,
1932, Lottie Crump in "Vile Bodies" ;
London Hippodrome, Feb., 1933, Mrs.
Hastings in " The One Girl" ; Old Vic.,
Mar., 1935, Lady Undershaft in
"Major Barbara" ; Strand, May, 1936,
Zelina Potter in "Aren't Men Beasts!",
and July, 1937, Mrs. Watney in "A
Spot of Bother" ; toured, 1938–9, as
the Duchess of Cheviot in "Crest of the
Wave" ; St. Martin's, Dec., 1939,
played Mrs. Palfrey in "Giving the
Bride Away" ; Strand, July, 1940,
and again in Apr., 1941, Thelma
Bandle in "Women Aren't Angels" ;
toured, 1941–2, as Frau Stomp in
"Blossom Time" ; Garrick, Nov.,
1942, played Zelina Potter in "Aren't
Men Beasts" ; Saville, June, 1944,
Queen Anita in "The Gipsy Princess" ;
Garrick, Feb., 1945, Mrs. Trout in
"Madame Louise" ; Nov., 1946, Mrs.
Schofield in "Treble Trouble" ; Dec.,
1948, Lydia Gilbey in "One Wild
Oat" ; Strand, Sept., 1950, Mrs.
Whittle in "Will Any Gentleman?" ;
Grand, Blackpool, Nov., 1951, played
Sister Ruby in "Something In the
Cellar" ; Aldwych, Nov., 1952, Mrs.
Beebee in "Wild Horses" ; toured,
Oct., 1954, as Flora Ransom in "It's
Different for Men" ; Grand, Leeds,
June, 1955, played Fleurette in "Three
Times a Day" ; has also appeared in
films. *Recreation :* Motoring.
(Died 12 Mar., 1961; age 82)

MAJOR, Bessie, actress ; has had a
long and varied experience ; in the
early nineties of the last century was
engaged with Robert Brough and Dion
Boucicault at the Gaiety Theatre,
Sydney, where she played for several
years ; coming to England, she
appeared at the Theatre Royal,
Margate, Oct., 1903, as Caroline in
" The New Housemaid " ; during
1904, toured as Martha in " Who's
Brown ? " ; subsequently returned to
Australia ; in 1909 became a member

of Oscar Asche's Company, then touring in Australia, and returning with the company to England, appeared at the New Theatre, 20 Oct., 1910, as Madame Caffat in "Count Hannibal"; at the Garrick, 25 Feb., 1911, played Mistress Quickly in "The Merry Wives of Windsor"; at the Garrick Theatre, 19 Apr., 1911, Narjis in "Kismet"; accompanied Oscar Asche on his second Australian tour, and also to South Africa; reappeared in London, at the Globe Theatre, 10 Mar., 1914, as Narjis in "Kismet"; same theatre, 30 Sept., 1914, played Unkomazi in "Mameena; at the Strand Theatre, 22 Apr., 1915, played Mrs. Beauregard in "The Argyle Case"; at the Devonshire Park Theatre, Eastbourne, Oct., 1915, Martha in "Willie Goes West"; at the Prince of Wales's, Birmingham, Dec., 1915, Martha Callender in "The Division Bell"; rejoined Oscar Asche's company at His Majesty's Theatre, Aug., 1916, when she played Zanim in "Chu-Chin-Chow," which she played almost continuously throughout the long run of the play, of nearly five years; at the same theatre, Oct., 1921, played Zarka in "Cairo." *Address :* 38 Vincent Square, Westminster, S.W.1.

MAKEHAM, Eliot, actor; *b.* London, 22 Dec., 1882; *s.* of Thomas Reed Makeham and his wife Alice Rosa (Elliott); *e.* private schools; *m.* (1) Anne de Vries; (2) Rose Elizabeth Kerr; was formerly an accountant; studied for the stage under Rosina Filippi; made his first appearance on the stage at the Corporation Theatre, Chesterfield, 26 Mar., 1910, as Norman Popple in "Mr. Popple"; first appeared in London, at the Vaudeville Theatre, 26 Oct., 1910, as Pierrot in "The Maker of Dreams"; subsequently appeared at the Alhambra, Dec., 1910, in "Pelissier's Revue"; appeared with the Glasgow Repertory Company 1911-12; at the Vaudeville, Aug., 1912, in "Little Miss Llewellyn"; was engaged with Miss Horniman's Company at Manchester, 1912-13; on the outbreak of War, joined the Sportsman's Battalion; in Apr., 1915, was granted a commission and served in France; in Oct., 1917, organized the

famous "Rouges et Noirs" Concert Party; after the War continued to manage this organization, which was renamed "Splinters," and which was produced at the Queen's, Savoy, and the Coliseum; remained with "Splinters" until Nov., 1924; at the Everyman, Dec., 1924, appeared as Major Elphingham in "The Tyranny of Home"; at the "Q" and Little, Mar, 1925, played Andrew Gordon in "Adam and Eva"; Wyndham's, May, 1925, Philip Flahive in "The Round Table"; St. Martin's, July, 1925, in "The Show"; Sept., 1925, Abraham Lombard in "Easy Money"; at Wyndham's, Oct., 1925, for a time, played Ben in "No. 17"; Court, Feb., 1927, James Parsons in "The Blue Comet"; appeared in several productions at the Everyman; at Golders' Green, Dec., 1927, played Billy Bones and Ben Gunn in "Treasure Island"; Garrick, Feb., 1928, Lane in "Tin Gods"; New, Apr., 1928, Sam Blott in "Come With Me"; Playhouse, June, 1928, Mr. Grey in "The Return of the Soldier"; Prince's, July, 1928, Sanders in "Contraband"; Strand, Nov., 1928, Timbury in "Out of the Sea"; Haymarket, Dec., 1928, Sam Weller in "Mr. Pickwick"; Comedy, June, 1929, Chubbock in "The Devil in the Cheese"; at the Masque Theatre, New York, Dec., 1929, played Mr. Blanquet in "Bird in Hand," in which he continued until Mar., 1931; after returning to London, appeared at the Phoenix, June, 1931, as Mr. Townsend in "Late Night Final"; New, Dec., 1931, played Black Dog and Ben Gunn in "Treasure Island"; Prince of Wales's, Mar., 1932, Mr. Wallace in "I Lived With You"; in the autumn of 1932, toured in the same part; Piccadilly (for Repertory Players), June, 1933, Rev. John Mallaby in "Clean Hands"; Lyric, Nov., 1933, Anaxagoras in "Acropolis"; Comedy, Dec., 1933, Billy Bones and Ben Gunn in "Treasure Island"; Drury Lane, Apr., 1934, Will Barbour in "Three Sisters"; Aldwych, Dec., 1934, Herbert in "Half-a-Crown"; Playhouse, May, 1935, Topping in "A Family Man"; Adelphi, Feb., 1936, in "Follow the Sun"; St. Martin's, May, 1937, James McNiven in "A Ship Comes

Home"; Garrick, Dec., 1937, Tobias Marks in "Bedtime Story"; Lyceum, May, 1938, Henri Floque in "Money Talks"; Open Air Theatre, Aug., and St. Martin's, Sept., 1938, Tobit in "Tobias and the Angel"; Garrick, Mar., 1939, the Old Man in "The Mother"; Open Air, Aug., 1939, again played in "Tobias and the Angel"; Aldwych, Nov., 1939, Percy Fish in "Married for Money"; Richmond, Apr., 1940, Hubert Briggs in "Blue Goose"; "Q," May, 1940, Joseph Summers in "Wise Guys"; Cambridge, Sept., 1942, the Professor and Igñaz in "Waltz Without End"; Open Air, June, 1943, again in "Tobias and the Angel"; toured, 1944, as Charles Robinson in "Acacia Avenue"; "Q," Jan., 1945, played Rev. Mr. Bartlett in "Not so Fast, My Pretty"; Mar., 1947, Alan Marlowe in "The Tightrope Walkers"; Globe, May, 1949, the Chaplain in "The Lady's Not For Burning"; Wyndham's (for Repertory Players), June, 1950, Sid Gullet in "Taking Things Quietly"; Dunfermline Abbey, Aug., 1950, Turgol in "The Saxon Saint"; Royale, New York, Nov., 1950, again played the Chaplain in "The Lady's Not For Burning"; first appeared in films, 1932, in "Rome Express," and has since played in innumerable pictures. *Recreation:* Motoring.
(Died 8 Feb., 1956; age 73)

MALDEN, Herbert John, business manager; *b.* London, 9 June, 1882; *s.* of B. J. Malden; *e.* privately; *m.* Dinkie Jeune; assisted his father, from an early age, in the preparation and presentation of his dioramic entertainment; from 1898–1910, engaged in the mechanical engineer's department of the old L.B.S.C. Railway; 1910–13, was engaged as stage-manager with J. Bannister Howard at the Crystal Palace, and during the same period was also engaged with George Dance's touring companies; engaged as business or stage manager at numerous West-End theatres, including the London Palladium, Strand, Criterion, Queen's, etc.; was manager at Hammersmith and Wimbledon, for two seasons, with the late J. B. Mulholland;

has also had much managerial experience with various film companies; was director of special publicity for "Murder in the Cathedral," at the Duchess and Old Vic.; in 1938, general manager for J. W. Pemberton, at the Ambassadors' and Shaftesbury Theatres, also for various seasons at the St. Martin's, Adelphi, Vaudeville, and Palace; succeeded the late J. W. Pemberton as Managing Director of J. W. Pemberton & Co., Ltd., Lessees of the Ambassadors' Theatre. Aug., 1947. *(Died 5 June, 1966; age 83)*

MALLALIEU, Aubrey, actor; *b.* Liverpool, 8 June, 1873; *s.* of William Mallalieu and his wife Nelly (Smith); *e.* Blue School, Wells, Somerset; *m.* Winifred Anne Chadwick; made his first appearance on the stage as a child of eight, and played children's parts for some years; after leaving school, studied Art for eight years; reappeared on the stage in 1895, at the Theatre Royal, Leicester, in "Across the Continent"; made his first appearance in London at the Adelphi Theatre, 19 Aug., 1899, as Lieutenant Derrick in "With Flying Colours"; has played innumerable parts in all sorts of plays, and played with Mrs. Bandmann-Palmer's old English and Shakespearean Repertory Co.; W. S. Penley's company in "Charley's Aunt," Weedon Grossmith in "The Night of the Party," etc.; at the old Avenue Theatre, 1903, played Watts in "The Adoption of Archibald" and Valdemar in "The Prophecy"; visited Australia, 1905, and again in 1907; returned to England, 1913, and toured; served during the War, in France with the London Rifle Brigade; after the War, toured in "Diplomacy," "By Pigeon Post," and for three years in "Daddy Long-Legs"; Comedy, Jan., 1927, played Bulger in "The Desperate Lovers"; toured in Canada, 1928; in 1929, with Sir Barry Jackson at Birmingham and Malvern; Queen's, Sept., 1929, Pliny in "The Apple Cart"; Sept., 1930, Dr. Chambers in "The Barretts of Wimpole Street"; toured in Australia, 1932, as the elder Strauss in "Waltzes from Vienna"; Ambassadors', London, Nov., 1933,

General Miollis in "Cabbages and Kings"; Kingsway, Feb., 1934, Roger Harley in "The Queen Who Kept Her Head"; Shaftesbury, Apr., 1934, Luke Carlingford in "There's Always To-Morrow"; Playhouse, Oct., 1935, Sir John Burroughs in "A Butterfly on the Wheel"; Royalty, Apr., 1936, Mr. Crowther in "Glass Houses"; Garrick, Oct., 1943, Admiral Hardy-Hardy in "She Follows Me About"; Saville, Sept., 1944, the Doctor in "Three's a Family"; has appeared in nearly 150 films. *Recreation:* Gardening. *Hobby:* Collecting autographs.

(Died 28 May, 1948; age 74)

MALLESON, Miles, actor and dramatic author; *b.* Croydon, 25 May, 1888; *s.* of Edmund Taylor Malleson and his wife Myrrha Bithynia (Borrell); *e.* Brighton College and Emmanuel College, Cambridge; B.A. Hist. Tripos, and Mus. Bach. (Pt. 1); *m.* (1) Colette O'Neil (mar. dis.); (2) Joan Graeme Billson (mar. dis.); (3) Tatiana Lieven; was a pupil at the Academy of Dramatic Art; made his first appearance on the professional stage at the Repertory Theatre, Liverpool, Nov., 1911, as Clipton in "Justice"; he had previously appeared at the Kingsway Theatre, Sept., 1911, in two burlesques, "The Girl with the Cash," and "Sherbert Jones," produced by amateurs; made his first professional appearance in London, at the Royalty, 15 Sept., 1913, as Amos Thorpe in "Interlopers"; at the Little Theatre, Nov., 1913, played Joseph Somers in "The Three Wayfarers"; Apr., 1914, Percy Davison, M.P., in "Account Rendered"; July, 1914, Midhurst in "Woman Alone"; at the Kingsway Theatre, Mar., 1915, appeared as Trotter in "Fanny's First Play"; at the Haymarket, Apr., 1916, as Mr. Lomax in "The Mayor of Troy"; at the Court, Oct., 1918, played Sir Andrew Aguecheek in "Twelfth Night"; Mar., 1919, Sir Benjamin Backbite in "The School for Scandal"; June, 1919, Augustus Smith in "The Lost Leader"; Oct., 1919, Launcelot Gobbo in "The Merchant of Venice"; at the Lyric, Hammersmith, Feb., 1920, appeared as "Clutie" John

Magrath in "John Ferguson"; Apr., 1920, as Le Beau and William in "As You Like It"; at the Court, Dec., 1920, as Quince in "A Midsummer Night's Dream"; at the Aldwych, Feb., 1921, Trinculo in "The Tempest"; at the Vaudeville, Sept., 1921, played William Shakespeare in "Now and Then"; at the Court, Dec., 1921, Diggory in "She Stoops to Conquer"; at the Queen's, Mar., 1922, Chivy in the opera of "David Garrick"; at the Strand, Oct., 1922, Professor Barlow in "Angel Face"; at the St. James's, Nov., 1922, Harold Bagby in "The Happy Ending"; at Wyndham's, Dec., 1923, Prince Bulbo in "The Rose and the Ring"; at the Queen's, Mar., 1924, Lorenzo in "Conchita"; at the Gaiety, Apr., 1924, Timothy in "Our Nell"; at Drury Lane, Dec., 1924, Snout in "A Midsummer Night's Dream"; Lyric, Hammersmith, Mar., 1925, David in "The Rivals"; June, 1925, Filch in "The Beggar's Opera"; Apr., 1926, appeared in "Riverside Nights"; Nov., 1926, played the Dancing Master and the Mufti in "The Would-Be Gentleman"; Jan., 1927, Scrub in "The Beaux' Stratagem"; Daly's, Jan., 1930, Sydney Quarles in "This Way to Paradise"; Royalty, June, 1930, again played Scrub in "The Beaux' Stratagem"; Lyric, Hammersmith, Sept., 1931, Sir Joseph Wittol in "The Old Bachelor"; Phoenix, Apr., 1943, Foresight in "Love for Love," which then ran for a year; Haymarket, Oct., 1944–Apr., 1945, with the John Gielgud repertory company, played Foresight in "Love for Love," Polonius in "Hamlet," Quince in "A Midsummer Night's Dream," and Castruccio in "The Duchess of Malfi"; joined the Old Vic company, at the New Theatre, and from Sept., 1945–Apr., 1946, appeared as Northumberland in "Henry IV" (Part I), Northumberland and Justice Silence in "Henry IV" (Part II), the first Messenger in "Œdipus," and Sir Fitful Plagiary in "The Critic"; went with the company to New York, May, 1946, and appeared in these parts, at the Century Theatre, May–June, 1946; Wyndham's, July, 1948, played Mr. Underwood in "People Like Us";

St. Martin's, Nov., 1948, Old Ekdal in "The Wild Duck"; at the New, for the Old Vic Company, during the 1949–50 Season, appeared as Sir Nathaniel in "Love's Labour's Lost," Mr. Hardcastle in "She Stoops to Conquer," Harpagon in "The Miser"; St. James's, Oct., 1950, Mr. Pitt in "Top of the Ladder"; with the Bristol Old Vic Company, Sept., 1951, appeared as M. Jourdain in "The Prodigious Snob"; Royal, Glasgow, Apr., 1953, played Cyril Poges in "Purple Dust"; Savoy, Dec., 1953, played Matthew D'Urt in "No Sign of the Dove"; Apollo, June, 1954, Lord Minster in "Both Ends Meet"; Old Vic., Feb., 1959, played the title part and directed "Sganarelle," in his own adaptation of the play by Molière; at the same theatre, June, 1959, played Trinculo in "The Tempest, or the Enchanted Island"; Edinburgh Festival, Aug., 1959, played Sir Paul Plyant in "The Double Dealer," subsequently appearing in the same production at the Old Vic., Sept., 1959; also at the Old Vic., Oct., 1959, played the Rev. Canon Chasuble in "The Importance of Being Earnest"; Royal Court, Apr., 1960, played Mr. Butterfly in "Rhinoceros," transferring to the Strand, June, 1960; Glyndebourne, Sussex, July, 1962, played Monsieur Jourdain and directed the actors in his own adaptation of "Le Bourgeois Gentilhomme"; Drury Lane, Aug., 1964, played Merlyn in "Camelot"; is the author of "Hide and Seek," 1913; "A Man of Ideas," 1914; "Paddly Pools," 1916; "D. Co.," 1917; "The Artist" (from the Russian), 1919; "Conflict," 1925; "Merrileon Wise," 1926; "A Night in Montmartre" (with Walter Peacock), 1926; "The Bargain" (from a novel), 1926; "The Fanatics," 1927; "Love at Second Sight," 1927; "Four People," 1927; "The Ace" (adaptation), 1933; "Before Sunset" (adaptation), 1933; "April Clouds" (with Peggy Barwell), 1938; "Six Men of Dorset" (with H. Brooks), 1938; "The Mother" (adaptation, with Paul Selver) 1939; "The Miser" (adaptation), 1950; "Tartuffe" (adaptation), 1950; "The Prodigious Snob" (adaptation), 1951; "School For Wives" (adaptation),

1954; "Sganarelle" (adaptation), 1959; also of "The Slave of Truth" (adapted from "Le Misanthrope"), "The Imaginary Invalid" (adaptation); author of "The Little White Thought," "Maurice's Own Idea," "Black 'Ell," "Young Heaven," "Youth," etc.; has acted as director of several of his own plays and others; has also appeared in films *(Died 15 Mar., 1969; age 80)*

MALO, Gina, actress and vocalist; *b.* Cincinnati, Ohio, U.S.A., 1 June, 1909; *d.* of Michael Joseph Flynn and his wife Amélie (Schildmeyer); *e.* Ursuline Convent and the Schuster Martin School, Cincinnati; *m.* Romney Brent; made her first appearance on the stage in 1921, at the Little Playhouse, Cincinnati, as Becky in "The Little Princess"; made her first appearance on the New York stage, at the Apollo Theatre, 14 June, 1926, in the chorus of "George White's Scandals"; at the Ziegfeld, Feb., 1927, appeared with the Albertina Rasch Girls in "Rio Rita"; subsequently went to Paris, and appeared in the French version of the same piece; subsequently appeared in the French version of "Broadway," and played Julie in "New Moon"; she then returned to New York, and at the Imperial Theatre, June, 1930, succeeded Lily Damita as Yvonne in "Sons o' Guns"; at the same theatre, Mar., 1931, played Julie Winterbottom in "The Gang's All Here"; she made her first appearance on the London stage at the Palace Theatre, 17 Sept., 1931, as Riquette in "Viktoria and Her Hussar"; same theatre, Mar., 1932, played Angie Sheridan in "The Cat and the Fiddle"; London Hippodrome, June, 1933, Tony in "Give Me a Ring"; Palace, Apr., 1934, appeared in "Why Not To-Night?"; Gaiety, May, 1935, Vivienne in "Gay Deceivers"; Playhouse, Oxford, Nov.–Dec., 1936, played a season of repertory and appeared in "East Lynne," "Private Lives," "Love from a Stranger," "Heartbreak House," etc.; Palace, Feb., 1937, played Frankie Frayne in 'On Your Toes"; Embassy, June, 1937, Anne Sawyer in "Lovers' Meeting"; Ambassadors', Apr., 1938, April Larcombe in "Lady With Designs"; "Q," July, 1938, Rayetta in "Diversion"; Playhouse, Oxford, June, 1939, again played a repertory season; Strand, July, 1939, played Stella Goodman in "The Gentle People"; subsequently returned to America; first appeared in films, 1932, in "Good Night, Vienna." *Favourite part:* Yvonne in "Sons o' Guns." *Recreations:* Bowls and dogs. *(Died 30 Nov., 1963; age 54)*

MALONE, J. A. E., Theatrical manager and producer; *b.* Mhow, India; *s.* Captain J. Malone, V.C., 6th Inniskilling Dragoons; *e.* at R.H.S., Edinburgh, and at Edinburgh University; studied medicine at Edinburgh University, and at St. Mary's Hospital, Paddington; began his theatrical career as an actor, and subsequently took to stage management; became stage manager at the Prince of Wales's, Liverpool, Oct., 1887, under Fanny Josephs, where his first production was Walter Parke and Bond Andrews's comic opera, "Herne's Oak"; his first London production was "Our Flat," at the Opéra Comique, June, 1889, under Willie Edouin; joined the management of George Edwardes in 1893, and remained with him until the latter's death in 1915; in 1894, managed "A Gaiety Girl," on its tour round the world, playing across America to Australia, and in addition produced "In Town," "The Shop Girl," and "Gentleman Joe," with that Company; since that date he produced the following plays for George Edwardes in London: "A Gaiety Girl," Prince of Wales's, 1893; "The Geisha," Daly's, 1896; "The Circus Girl," Gaiety, 1896; "A Runaway Girl," Gaiety, 1898; "A Greek Slave," Daly's, 1898; "San Toy," Daly's, 1899; "The Messenger Boy," Gaiety, 1900; "Kitty Grey," Apollo, 1900; "The Toreador," Gaiety, 1901; "A Country Girl," Daly's, 1902; "Three Little Maids," Apollo, 1902; "The School Girl," Prince of Wales's, 1903; "The Cingalee," Daly's, 1904; "Lady Madcap," Prince of Wales's, 1904; "The Girls of Gottenburg," Gaiety, 1907; "The Merry Widow,"

Daly's, 1907; "A Waltz Dream," Hicks, 1908; "The Quaker Girl," Adelphi, 1910; "The Sunshine Girl," Gaiety, 1912; "The Dancing Mistress," Adelphi, 1912; "The Girl from Utah," 1913; produced "High Jinks," Adelphi, 1916; "Vanity Fair," Palace, 1917; "Who's Hooper"? 1919; "Monsieur Beaucaire," Prince's, 1919; "The Naughty Princess," Adelphi, 1920; in New York, he has produced among other plays, "In Town," "The Circus Girl," "A Gaiety Girl," "The Geisha," "The School Girl," "The Dairymaids," "The Girls of Gottenburg," "The Dollar Princess," "The Quaker Girl," and "The Sunshine Girl"; was licensee of the Adelphi Theatre; appointed Director of the Victoria Palace, 1910; was appointed a Director of the Gaiety Theatre (Ltd.), 1914; Director of Musical Plays, Ltd., controlling the Adelphi Theatre, 1914; in Nov., 1920, appointed a Director of the firm of Grossmith and Laurillard, Ltd.; in 1921, on the retirement from the firm of Mr. Edward Laurillard, the firm was reconstructed as Grossmith and Malone, Ltd., and now controls the Winter Garden, Shaftesbury, and His Majesty's Theatres; for some years has been the London Representative of J. C. Williamson, Ltd., Australia, and the South African Theatres Trust; on the outbreak of war, Aug., 1914, appointed Captain in the Westminster Dragoons. *Favourite play:* "The Merry Widow." *Recreation:* Racing. *(Died 3 Feb., 1929; age 69)*

MALONE, Patricia, actress and vocalist; *b.* London, 17 Nov., 1899; *d.* of George John Marsden-Clark and his wife Georgina (Malone); *e.* Ursuline Convent, Ilford, Essex; *m.* Bobbie Howes; made her first appearance on the stage at Daly's Theatre, 1917, in the chorus of "The Maid of the Mountains"; at the Gaiety, Mar., 1920, played in "The Shop Girl"; during 1921 toured as Eleanor Worth in "Irene," and subsequently appeared in "The Knots" Concert Party; at the Gaiety, Apr., 1922, played Lady Diana Mellowes in "His Girl"; Sept.,

1922, toured with Jack Hulbert in "Pot Luck"; in 1924 was with "The Five o'Clock Follies," at the Prince's Restaurant; in 1925 toured in "Tricks"; Prince's, Dec., 1925, played Alice Barker in "When Knights Were Bold"; at the Garrick, May, 1926, played Pierrette Pêche in "Ourselves"; appeared at the Gaiety, Aug, 1926, in "By-the-Way"; appeared at the Hotel Metropole, 1926, in "The Midnight Follies"; at the Prince of Wales's, June, 1927, played Mollie Drew in "The Blue Train"; subsequently toured as Lady Jane Grey and Kittle in "The Yellow Mask"; Carlton, 1928, occasionally appeared as Mary Bannister in the same piece; Apollo, Apr., 1929, played Doris Beckwith in "Little Accident." *Favourite parts :* Lady Diana in "His Girl," and parts in "Pot Luck." *Recreations :* Motoring and tennis. *Address:* 46 Grove End Road, St. John's Wood, N.W.8. *Telephone No.:* Primrose 4235.

MALTBY, Henry Francis, actor and dramatic author; *b.* Ceres, Cape Colony, 25 Nov., 1880; *s.* of Henry Edward Maltby and his wife Johannah Henrietta (Beck); *e.* Bedford; was formerly a bank clerk; *m.* Norah May Pickering; made his first appearance on the stage at the Pier Pavilion, Aberystwith, 21 Aug., 1899, in "The Sign of the Cross," in Ben Greet's Company; had many years experience in "stock" companies, and with Ben Greet, Charles Sugden, Mrs. Bandmann-Palmer, Robert Arthur, Miss Horniman, and Osmond Tearle's Companies; is the author of "The Youngest of Three," 1905; "The Miser's Legacy," 1907; "Sir George of Almack's," 1907; "Ernestine," 1908; "The Laughter of Fools," 1909; "Haunted," 1911; "What Some Men Don't Know," 1911; "Profit and the Loss," 1914; "The Rotters," 1916; "Rapid Promotion" (with Louis Hillier, from the French), 1916; "Petticoats," 1917; "A Temporary Gentleman," 1919; "Maggie" (with Fred Thompson), 1919; "Such a Nice Young Man," 1920; "What did her Husband Say?" 1920; "The Person Unknown," 1921; "Mr. Budd (of Ken-nington, S.E.)," 1922; "Three Birds," 1923; "The Right Age to Marry," revised "On 'Change," "Old Roses," 1925; "The Shingled Honeymoon," "The New Religion," "What Might Happen," 1926; "Our Countess," "Something More Important," 1928; "Bees and Honey," "The Age of Youth" (with Fredi Wynne), 1928; "Azaïs" (adaptation), 1929; "All for the Love of a Lady"; revised "Bed Rock," 1930; "For the Love of Mike," "The Red Light" (with John Trevor), 1931; "Rings on Her Fingers," "When Churchyards Yawn," "Fifty-Fifty" (adapted from "Azaïs"), 1932; "Learning to Love" (with Charles Windermere), 1933; "The Shadow," 1934; "Off the Gold Coast" (with Clifford Grey), 1934; "Jack O' Diamonds" (with Grey), 1935; "Love Hunger," 1938; "From Dusk to Dawn," 1941; "Susie" (from "Jack o' Diamonds"), 1942; "The Compleat Wangler," 1943 (subsequently renamed "The Wanglers," 1944); "Nightingale House" (operetta), 1943; "Meet Me Victoria," 1944; "Have a Heart," 1945; revised the book and lyrics of "The Lilac Domino," 1948; wrote "Wet Week in Westbourne," 1954; author (with Vera Gray) of "May I Borrow Your Wife?" 1956; at the Kingsway, June, 1931, played Robert Hartley-Merrick in "The Age of Youth"; Gaiety, Oct, 1933, Kessel in "Ballerina"; Playhouse, Apr., 1936, Ronald Austin in his own play, "The Shadow"; has appeared in innumerable films, and has contributed to the writing of over thirty; published his reminiscences, "Ring Up the Curtain," 1950. *Recreations:* Swimming and reading. *Clubs:* Dramatists' and Savage. *(Died 25 Oct., 1963; age 82)*

MAMOULIAN, Rouben, director; *b.* Tiflis, Caucasus, Russia, 8 Oct., 1898; *s.* of Zacchary Mamoulian and his wife Virginia (Kalantarian); *e.* Lycée Montaigne, Paris; Tiflis Gymnasium, and Moscow University; *m.* Azadia Newman; studied for the Law, but never practised; his first production was "The Beating on the Door" at the St. James's Theatre, London, Nov., 1922; he then went to the United States, and became producer at the Eastman Theatre,

Rochester, N.Y., where he presented, 1924-6, "Carmen," "Faust," "Boris Goudonoff," Gilbert and Sullivan opera, and "Sister Beatrice"; then became director to the Theatre Guild in New York, his first production being "Porgy," at the Guild Theatre, Oct., 1927; between that date and 1931, he staged "Marco Millions," "These Modern Women," "Wings Over Europe," "Congai," "R.U.R.," "The Game of Love and Death," "Farewell to Arms," "Solid South," and "A Month in the Country"; he also directed "The Hand of Fate," opera, at the Metropolitan Opera House, New York, 1931; "Porgy and Bess," 1935; directed the production of "Oklahoma!" for Theatre Guild, 1943, which ran for 2,248 performances; directed "Sadie Thompson" (of which he was part-author), 1944; "Carousel," 1945; "St. Louis Woman," 1946; "Leaf and Bough," "Lost in the Stars," "Arms and the Girl," 1950; "Oklahoma!" (for Berlin Art Festival), 1951; "Carousel" (Los Angeles and San Francisco), 1954; "Oklahoma" for the "Salute to France" programme sponsored by A.N.T.A. and the American State Dept., 1955; author (with Maxwell Anderson), of "The Devil's Hornpipe"; is also the author of short stories and verse, and articles on the stage and screen, and of the books "Abigayil," 1964, and "Hamlet, A New Version," 1965; is a fluent linguist, speaking eight languages; directed the production of the film "Applause," 1928; directed innumerable films from 1931 to 1943, and has since divided his time between stage and films. *Recreations:* Reading detective stories, swimming, and riding. *Address:* 1112 Schuyler Road, Beverly Hills, California.

MANDEL, Frank, dramatic author and librettist and producing manager; *b.* San Francisco, Cal., U.S.A., 31 May, 1884; *s.* of Emmanuel Mandel and his wife Carrie (Hirschfelder); *e.* University of California; *m.* (1) Alice Solis; (2) Isolde Illian; is the author of the following plays: "Our Wives" (with Helen Craft), 1912; "Miss Princess," 1913; "Trifling With To-morrow," 1914; "The High Cost of Living" (from the German), 1914; "The Lady We Love," 1914; "Sherman was Right," 1915; "The Sky Pilot" (with G. H. Brennan), 1918; "Bosom Friends," 1918; "Look Who's Here," 1919; "Luck," 1919; "The Five Million," 1919; "My Lady Friends," 1919; "Jimmie" (with Oscar Hammerstein 2nd and Otto Harbach), 1920; "Mary" (with Harbach), 1920; "Tickle Me" (with Hammerstein and Harbach), 1920; "The O'Brien Girl" (with Harbach), 1921; "Queen o' Hearts" (with Hammerstein), 1922; "Paradise Alley" (part-author), 1922; "Nobody's Business" (with Guy Bolton), 1923; "Sweet Little Devil" (with Lawrence Schwab), 1924; "The Lady Killer" (with Alice Mandel), 1923; "No, No, Nanette" (with Harbach), 1924; "Captain Jinks" (with Schwab), 1925; "The Desert Song" (with Hammerstein), 1926; "The New Moon" (with Schwab and Hammerstein), 1927; "East Wind" (with Hammerstein), 1931; with Lawrence Schwab, has produced "The Firebrand," 1924; "The Desert Song," 1926; "The New Moon," "Good News," 1927; "Follow Thru," 1929; "America's Sweetheart," "Free for All," "East Wind," 1931; "May Wine," 1935; dissolved partnership with Schwab, June, 1932; producer for Warner Bros. Picture Corporation, 1937-8; presented and produced "Vickie," 1942. *Recreations:* Bridge, vegetable gardening, and stock exchange speculation. *Clubs:* Lambs and Authors' League.

(Died 20 Apr., 1958; age 74)

MANN, Charlton, manager and dramatic author; *b.* London, 2 July, 1876; commenced his career as an actor in 1896 in "fit-ups," with W. Payne Seddon, and has learned his business in every department, as actor, manager, stage-manager, producer and author; held his appointment as business manager at the Adelphi Theatre from 1909-23, under the management of George Edwardes, Sir Alfred Butt, and Grossmith and Laurillard; was subsequently co-licensee of the Adelphi and Apollo Theatres; resigned 1924; has been associated with Herbert Jay in several provincial tours; also associ-

ated in management with Mrs. T. C. Dagnall; as an author, adapted " The Blue Lagoon," 1920; " The Knave of Diamonds," 1921; " Beau Geste" (with Basil Dean, from the novel), 1929. *Hobby:* The theatre.
(Died 27 Mar., 1958; age 81)

MANN, Christopher, theatrical artistes' and authors' representative; *b.* Hull, 23 July, 1903; *s.* of John Christopher Mann and his wife Emily Marian (Stevens) *e.* King Edward's High School, Birmingham, and Birmingham University; *m.* Eileen Joyce; reconstituted and became first President of the Birmingham University Dramatic Society; was originally a civil engineer; joined Dennis Eadie as press representative at the Royalty Theatre, 1926; established his own firm, 1928; became representative for stage and screen artistes, authors and directors, 1932, subsequently being joined by Alan Grogan and Aubrey Blackburn. *Address:* 140 Park Lane, London, W.1. *Telephone No.:* Mayfair 8444.

MANN, Louis, actor and dramatic author; *b.* New York, 20 Apr., 1865; *s.* of Daniel Mann and his wife Carolina; *e.* N.Y. public schools and University of California; *m.* Clara Lipman; made his first appearance on the stage in 1868, at the New Stadt Theatre, New York City, in " Snow Flake," a German pantomime; when quite a youth joined the late Lawrence Barrett and John McCullough's " stock " company in San Francisco; in 1882 was playing with Signor Tomasso Salvini, Lewis Morrison, and Marie Prescott, in " Othello," " The Gladiator," etc.; at the Union Square Theatre, 20 Aug., 1883, he played Page in the late Oscar Wilde's first play, " Vera, the Nihilist "; subsequently toured in " Called Back," " Lost," etc., and in this company played with E. H. Sothern, Cyril Maude, etc.; played with the late D. E. Bandmann in " Dr. Jekyll and Mr. Hyde "; toured with his own company as Robert Audley in " Lady Audley's Secret," and other plays; made a " hit " at the Bijou, New York, 22 Feb., 1892,

when he played Dick Winters in " Incog."; subsequently toured with G. W. Lederer's company in " Nothing but Money," etc.; with his own company toured with " The Laughing Girl " and " Hannah "; at the Casino, New York, 8 June, 1895, he appeared as Svengali in " The Merry World "; at the Standard, New York, 2 Dec., 1895, he scored a great hit by his performance of Herr Von Moser in " The Strange Adventures of Miss Brown "; subsequently played Hans in " The Girl from Paris " (" The Gay Parisienne "); Hans Nix in " The Telephone Girl "; Le Bardy in " The Girl in the Barracks "; at the Garrick, 3 Sept., 1900, he was the original exponent of the part of Franz Hochstuhl in " All on Account of Eliza "; his subsequent appearances include: " The Red Kloof," " Hoch the Consul," a series of burlesques at Weber and Field's; Baron Von Walden in " The Second Fiddle "; and at Field's Theatre, 1 Jan., 1906, " Julie Bon-Bon "; he made his first appearance in London at the Waldorf Theatre, 26 Nov., 1906, as Jean Poujol in the last-mentioned play, but the play failed to attract in London, and had but a short run; returning to America, appeared at the Casino, New York, in Feb., 1907, as Hensie Blindner in " The White Hen," subsequently touring in the same piece; at Chicago, Sept., 1908, appeared as John Krauss in " The New Generation," and at the Circle Theatre, New York, Oct., 1908, played the same part, when the piece was re-named " The Man Who Stood Still "; at the Lyric Theatre, New York, June, 1910, played Godfried Plittersdorf in " The Cheater "; in 1911 toured as Charles Sample in " Elevating a Husband," of which his wife was part-author; at the Liberty Theatre, New York, Jan., 1912, played the same part; at the Harris Theatre, Dec., 1913, played George Raimund in " Children of To-Day "; at the Booth Theatre, Apr., 1915, Gustave Muller in " The Bubble"; at the Palace, New York, Jan., 1917, appeared in " The Warriors "; at the Hudson Theatre, July, 1918, played Karl Pfeiffer in " Friendly Enemies " (" Uncle Sam "); toured in this during 1919-20; at the Astor Theatre, Oct., 1920, played Hyam Salomon in " The Unwritten Chapter "; at the Winter Garden, June, 1921, played Karl Bauer in " The Whirl of New York "; at the Apollo, New York, Nov., 1921, Carl Schnitzler in " Nature's Nobleman "; during 1922 toured in " In the Mountains "; at the Forty-ninth Street Theatre, Jan., 1923, John Bauer in " Give and Take "; at Wallack's, Dec., 1924, David Milgrim in " Milgrim's Progress "; Ritz, Mar., 1927, Karl Kraft in " That French Lady "; subsequently toured in " The Thieves' Paradise "; is Vice-President of the Actors' Fidelity League; he is the author of a one-act play, " Hannah "; in conjunction with Mrs. D. F. Verdenal was responsible for " The Laughing Girl "; part-author of " The Bubble " and " The Thieves' Paradise "; sole author of " The Cheater." *Club:* The Friars.

(Died 15 Feb., 1931; age 65)

MANNERING, Doré Lewin, actor; *b.* Poland, 19 Jan. 1879; *s.* of James Lewin and his wife Augusta (Kriss); *e.* London; *m.* Elizabeth Wellbourn; came to England when eighteen months old; made his first appearance on the stage in 1896, when he toured as Tigellinus in " The Sign of the Cross "; made his first appearance on the London stage, at the Court Theatre, 4 Nov., 1897, as Benito in " The Vagabond King "; his early experience was gained in provincial " stock " and Shakespearean companies; from 1903-06 toured as Baron Bonelli in " The Eternal City," Zakkuri in " The Darling of the Gods "; Fagin in " Oliver Twist," and Svengali in " Trilby "; from 1910-14 was associated with the Glasgow, Liverpool, and Manchester Repertory Theatres; in 1914 toured as Mr. Wu in the play of that name; 1915-16 as Mawruss Perlmutter in " Potash and Perlmutter "; at the Apollo Theatre, May, 1917, appeared as Yucca Len in " Inside the Lines "; at the Strand, July, 1918, as Sir Charles Rosenbaum in " The Hidden Hand "; at the Scala, May, 1919, as Baron Von Arnheim in " The Black Feather "; subsequently

toured as the Marquis Chi Lung in " The Chinese Puzzle "; at the Aldwych, Nov., 1920, appeared as Wang Fu Chang in " The Dragon "; at Wyndham's, 1922, played Dr. Henry Lakington in " Bull-Dog Drummond "; subsequently touring in the same part; in the autumn of 1922 toured as De Levis in " Loyalties," subsequently touring as Jean Paurel in " The Great Lover," Pancho Lopez in " The Bad Man "; at the Strand, Dec., 1923, played Israel Hands in " Treasure Island " at the Haymarket, June, 1924, Ebag in " The Great Adventure "; subsequently toured in a repertory of plays by Sir A. W. Pinero; Kingsway, Apr., 1925, The Great God Ra in " Caesar and Cleopatra "; St. James's, June, 1925, Theodore Messell in " The River "; Scala (for the Renaissance Society), Dec., 1925, Mosbie in " Arden of Feversham "; Garrick, Dec., 1925, Bread in " The Blue Bird "; Little, Feb., 1926, Professor Salaret in " The Forcing House "; Globe, July, 1926, Matthew Blaze in " Ask Beccles "; Royalty, Jan., 1927, Hemming in " The Joker "; " O," and Royalty, June to July, 1927, Dr. Morris Morton in " The Man Responsible "; Criterion, Sept., 1927, Garcia Alvarez in " When Blue Hills Laughed "; Apollo, May, 1928, Friedman in " The Squeaker "; Opera House, Blackpool, July, 1929, Rabbi Gabriel in " Jew Süss "; has played in thirty of the thirty-six plays of Shakespeare, has produced many plays, and has appeared in several productions of the Stage Society, Phoenix Society, Play Actors, and Elizabethan Stage Society. *Hobby:* Book-collecting. *Recreation:* Driving.

(Died 8 June, 1932; age 53)

MANNERING, Mary, actress; *b.* in England, 29 Apr., 1876; *d.* of Richard and Florence Friend; *e.* privately; studied for the stage under Hermann Vezin; *m.* (1) James K. Hackett (mar. dis.); (2) Frederick E. Wadsworth; made her first appearance on the stage in England, under her own name of Florence Friend, at the Prince's, Manchester, 9 May, 1892, as Zela in " Hero and Leander," with H. Kyrle Bellew and Mrs. Brown-Potter; she made her first appearance on the London stage, in the same part, at the Shaftesbury Theatre, 2 June, 1892; then she played a number of parts in the provinces; other parts in which she appeared in London were Beatrice in " A Night in Town," at the Royalty, 28 June, 1894, and as the heroine in " Villon, Poet and Cut-throat," on the same evening, she made a pronounced hit; at the Opéra Comique, 26 Nov., 1894, she played Cecily Allardyce in " The Wife of Dives," and subsequently undertook many leading parts in the English provinces; in 1895 toured as Pauline in " Called Back "; while playing Mrs. Castello in " The Late Mr. Castello," at the Grand, Islington, in 1896, she was seen by Daniel Frohman, who immediately engaged her for the Lyceum Theatre, New York; she made her first appearance in America at Hartford, Conn., on 20 Nov., 1896, as Leonie in " The Courtship of Leonie," playing for the first time as Mary Mannering; she made her New York début at the Lyceum Theatre, 1 Dec., 1896, in the same part; she remained at the Lyceum until 1900, playing the following parts : Sadie in " The Late Mr. Castello," Daphne in " The First Gentleman of Europe," Joan in " The Mayflower," Fay Zuliani in " The Princess and the Butterfly," Monica in " The Tree of Knowledge," Rose Trelawney in " Trelawney of the Wells," Mildred in " Americans at Home," and Ann Singleton in " John Ingerfield "; she was also seen at Daly's, under Daniel Frohman, as Juliet Gainsborough in " The Ambassador," and as Violet Babington in " The Interrupted Honeymoon "; she commenced her career as a " star " at the Star Theatre, Buffalo, New York, 1 Oct., 1900, when she played Janice Meredith in a play of that name; she appeared in the same part for the first time in New York at Wallack's Theatre, 10 Dec., 1900; at the Broadway, 1 Mar., 1901, she appeared in " White Roses," and since that date has " starred " in the following parts : Pauline in " The Lady of Lyons,"

Geraldine in " The Stubbornness of Geraldine," Harriet Baird in " Harriet's Honeymoon," Judith in " Judith," Nancy Stair in the play of that name, Lady Alethea Frobisher in " The Walls of Jericho," Beatrice in " The House of Silence," Betsy in " Glorious Betsy," Helen Medfield in " The Struggle," and " A House of Cards "; during 1909, toured as Rose Marvin in " Step by Step "; at the Belasco Theatre, Washington, Apr., 1909, played Freda Saville in " The Truants "; at the Garrick, Chicago, May, 1909, appeared as Miss Gower in " The Independent Miss Gower "; subsequently toured in " Kiddie "; at the Comedy, New York, Feb., 1910, played Frank Ware in " A Man's World "; at the Century Theatre, New York, Oct., 1910, appeared as Dominie Enfilden in "The Garden of Allah."

(Died 21 Jan., 1953; age 76)

MANNERING, Moya (*née* Doyle); actress and vocalist; *b*. 22 Nov., 1888; made her first appearance on the stage as a child; made her grown-up *début* in 1904, when she was engaged by George Dance, playing Jantz in " A Soldier and a Man "; she appeared in several musical comedies, in the chorus, and in 1908 was understudying at the Gaiety, in " Havana," and in Sept., 1908, appeared as Lola in that play : at Christmas, 1908, appeared at Cardiff in pantomime; at the Queen's Theatre, London, 27 Apr., 1909, appeared as Mai-i in " The Persian Princess "; at the Gaiety, Aug., 1909, played Lady Gwen in " Our Miss Gibbs "; at Daly's, Sept., 1909, was engaged as understudy in " The Dollar Princess "; appeared at Leeds, Dec., 1909, in " Cinderella "; at the Shaftesbury, June, 1910, succeeded to the part of Chrysea in " The Arcadians," subsequently proceeding to America, to play the same part opening at the New York Theatre, New York, Sept., 1910; she toured in " The Arcadians " throughout the United States, until Apr., 1911; at the Knickerbocker Theatre, New York, 28 Aug., 1911, played Suzanne in " The Siren "; at the

Criterion, New York, 25 Aug., 1912, Clementine in " The Girl from Montmartre " ; at the Knickerbocker, New York, 22 Sept., 1913, Emma in " The Marriage Market " ; at the Princess, Montreal, 23 Feb., 1914, Honora May in " Nobody's Daughter " ; on her return to England, appeared at the Prince's Theatre, Bristol, Christmas, 1914, as Princess Joy in " Humpty Dumpty " ; appeared at the Gaiety, 28 Apr., 1915, as Victoria, in " To-Night's the Night " ; at the Globe Theatre, 9 Aug., 1915, played Peg in " Peg o' My Heart " ; at the Palace, Nov., 1916, played in " Vanity Fair " ; at the Globe, July, 1917, appeared as Julyann Dempsey in " Julyann " ; at the Gaiety, Dec., 1917, played Leonie Bramble in " The Beauty Spot " ; after several years' absence from the stage, reappeared at the Prince of Wales's, Sept., 1928, as Lulu Keck in " By Candle Light " ; at the Prince's, Dec., 1931, played Peg in " Peg O' My Heart " ; Playhouse, Mar., 1932, Mrs. Lyall in " Doctor Pygmalion " ; Theatre Royal, Brighton, Dec., 1932, Mildred Grayson Brown in " Happy Easter."

MANNERS, David, actor; *b.* Halifax, Nova Scotia, Canada, 30 Apr., 1905; *s.* of George Moreby Acklom and his wife Lilian (Manners); *e.* Trinity School, New York, and University of Toronto; studied for the stage under the late Bertram Forsyth, at the Hart House Theatre, Toronto; made his first appearance on the stage, at the Hart House Theatre, Toronto, 1924, as Hippolytus in " Hippolytus," of Euripides; made his first appearance in New York, at the Booth Theatre, 11 Aug., 1924, as Kenneth in " Dancing Mothers"; at Chicago, 1924, played Bezano in " He Who Gets Slapped "; subsequently went to Hollywood, and from 1929–40, appeared exclusively in pictures; after the War reappeared in New York, at the Belasco Theatre, Feb., 1946, as Wing-Commander Hern in " Truckline Cafe " ; Plymouth, Sept., 1946, played Smith in " Hidden Horizon"; Cort Theatre, Dec., 1946, succeeded Henry Daniell as Lord Windermere in " Lady Windermere's Fan " ;

first appeared in films, 1929, as Raleigh in " Journey's End " ; has written several novels; is a member of the Authors League of America. *Address:* Rancho Yucca Loma, Victorville, Calif., U.S.A. *Telephone No.:* Victorville 4946.

MANNERS, John Hartley, dramatic author and novelist; *b.* London, 10 Aug., 1870 ; *e.* privately ; *m.* Laurette Taylor ; was formerly an actor, and acted from Feb., 1898, to Apr., 1905 ; made his first appearance on the stage, at the Bijou Theatre, Melbourne, with Charles Cartwright, 19 Feb., 1898, as Lord Chetland in " The Squire of Dames " ; on returning to England, joined George Alexander's company at the St. James's Theatre, making his first appearance on the London stage, 26 Apr., 1899, in " In Days of Old " ; subsequently played Laertes in " Hamlet " with Forbes-Robertson, and at the Imperial, Dec., 1902, played Lord Scarlett in his own play, " The Crossways," with Mrs. Langtry, subsequently proceeding with her to America, to play the same part; has written the following plays : " A Queen's Messenger," 1899 ; " Just as Well," 1902 ; " As Once in May," 1902 ; " Virginia," subsequently entitled " The Crossways," 1902 ; " Lady Clivebrook's Mission," 1904 ; " Zira," 1905 ; " The Indiscretion of Truth," 1906 ; " A Marriage of Reason," 1907 ; " The Patriot " (with William Collier), 1908 ; " Ganton and Co " (" The Great John Ganton "), 1909 ; " The Majesty of Birth " (" The House Next Door "), 1909 ; " The Girl and the Wizard," 1910 ; " The Prince of Bohemia," 1910 ; " The Girl in Waiting," 1910 ; " Peg o' My Heart," 1912 ; " The Woman Intervenes," 1912 ; " The Money Moon," 1912 ; " Barbaraza," 1912 ; " The Wooing of Eve," 1912 ; " Happiness," 1914 ; " The Day of Dupes," 1914 ; " The Panorama of Youth," 1915 ; " The Harp of Life," 1916 ; " Out There," 1917 ; " Happiness " (extended to a four-act play), 1917 ; " Getting Together " (with Ian Hay and Percival Knight), 1918 ; " One Night in Rome," 1919 ; " The National Anthem," 1922 ; " Peg o' My Dreams " (musical version of " Peg o' My Heart "), 1924 ; in addition, he was responsible for almost all the dialogue of " Sweet Nell of Old Drury," 1900, the last act being entirely his, and the whole of Paul Kester's play was adapted by him ; he was also associated with the authorship of " Count Tezma," 1901 ; also the author of " The Fool's Comedy," " Feroza," " Devil Montague," " The Tree of Life," " Barbaraza," " Gauntlett's Pride," " Lady Clivebrook's Mission " ; has also written several plays which have been published but not yet acted, entitled " Wreckage," " God's Outcast," " All Clear," and " God of My Faith." *Clubs :* Lotos, Players', and Whist, New York ; Devonshire, London

(Died 19 Dec., 1928; age 58)

MANNHEIM, Lucie, actress; *b.* near Berlin, Germany, 30 April, 1905; *m.* Marius Goring ; while still attending school made her first appearance on the stage, 1920, as Käthie in "Old Heidelberg," subsequently playing Ännchen in "Jugend" and Christine in "Liebelei"; she then studied for the stage at the Reichersche Hochschule; was then engaged at Hanover and subsequently for a season at Libau, where she played Lulu in "Erdgeist," with Conrad Veidt; was next engaged at Königsberg, under Leopold Jessner, playing Hedwig in "The Wild Duck," Lulu in "Erdgeist," etc.; was then seen at the Volksbühne, Berlin, under Friedrich Kayssler, playing Cordelia in "King Lear," Amal in Tagore's "Postamt," Agafia in "Heirat," also in Hauptmann's "Armselige Besenbinder," etc.; she then appeared at the Staatstheater, Berlin, 1924–30, playing Nora in "A Doll's House," Puck in "A Midsummer Night's Dream," Juliet in "Romeo and Juliet," Irina in "The Three Sisters," Annchen in "Jugend," Hannele in the play of that name, "Käthchen von Heilbronn." and numerous other plays, appearing with Fritz Kortner, Werner Krauss, Albert Bassermann, Oscar Homolka, etc.; she also played here in the musical plays "Die Göttliche Jette," "Hunderttausend Taler," etc., and in farces, comedies, etc., while still under engagement at the Staats-

theater, appeared under other managements, at Berlin theatres, playing Mary Dugan in "The Trial of Mary Dugan," Raina in "Arms and the Man," and at the Lessing Theater, played with Albert Bassermann in "Monsieur Lamberthier" ("Jealousy"); at the Nollendorf Theater, played Gonda in "Die Geschiedene Frau" ("The Girl in the Train"); under Erik Charrell, appeared in "Wie einst im Mai"; the last part she played at the Staatstheater, was Katherina in Wedekind's "Liebestrank"; made her first appearance in London, at the Criterion Theatre, 17 Sept., 1935, as Nina Gallas and Trude Mielitz in "Nina," scoring an immediate success; at the New, Sept., 1936, played Anna in "Girl Unknown"; Comedy, Sept., 1937, Sonia Duveen in "The Last Straw"; Theatre Royal, Birmingham, Apr., 1938, Maritza in "The Countess Maritza"; Duke of York's, Feb., 1939, Nora in "A Doll's House"; Mar., 1939, Fanny Wetherell and Polly in "Lady Fanny"; Apr., 1939, appeared in a revival of "Nina"; toured, 1947, in Germany, playing in English and German, in "Monsieur Lamberthier"; Arts, July, 1948, played Rebecca West in "Rosmersholm," and the Nurse in "Too True to Be Good"; Oct., 1948, Madame Popov in "The Bear"; Nov., 1948, Germaine in "The Third Man" ("Jealousy"); during 1949, translated and directed in Berlin, "Daphne Laureola," in which she played Lady Pitts; during 1950, appeared at the Volksbühne, Berlin, as Miss Moffatt in "The Corn is Green"; made further appearances in Germany, 1951, in musical comedy; 1952, in "The Rose Tattoo"; 1953, in "Relative Values"; 1954, in Hauptmann's play, "Rats"; Berlin Festival, 1956, appeared in Tolstoy's "Power of Darkness"; Berlin Festival, 1958, in the European *première* of "Look Homeward, Angel"; Cologne, 1959, in Hauptmann's "Biberpelz"; Berliner Theater, 1960, appeared in "Tonight at 8.30," and in "La Voix Humaine"; Volkesbühne, Berlin, 1961, appeared in "La Grotte"); Phalia, Hamburg, 1965, appeared in "Die Rätten"; has appeared in several films in Berlin, Paris, and London;

during the War, broadcast frequently to Germany, in the B.B.C. European service; appeared as Emily Pankhurst on television (Bremen), 1965; received the Order of Merit, 1953, and Grand Cross of the Order (Bonn, Germany), 1959; nominated Berlin State Actress for services to the theatre, 1963. *Address:* "Middle Court," Hampton Court, Surrey. *Telephone No.:* Teddington Lock 4030.

MANNING, Ambrose, actor ; *s.* of the late John Manning, actor, at one time low comedian at the old Grecian Theatre ; made his first appearance on the stage, at the age of seven, at the Old Grecian Theatre, in pantomime ; at the age of eighteen, he was engaged at the Haymarket Theatre, under the late E. A. Sothern ; subsequently appeared at the old Greenwich Theatre in 1880 ; at the Princess's 10 Sept., 1881, he played Waters in "Lights o' London," and for over twenty years was associated with Wilson Barrett's company ; spent many years playing in the provinces in Barrett's companies ; reappeared in London, at the New Olympic Theatre, 4 Dec., 1890, when he appeared with the late Wilson Barrett, as Mr. Hackett in " The People's Idol " ; remained a member of Barrett's company until 1904, during which time he played numerous parts in " The Acrobat," " The Silver King," " The Lights o' London," " Pharaoh," " Othello," " The Sign of the Cross," " The Daughters of Babylon," " The Manxman," " Man and his Makers," etc. ; after the death of Wilson Barrett, appeared at Daly's, Apr., 1905, as Pierre Michu in " The Little Michus " ; at the Apollo, Apr., 1906, played Dr. O'Byrne in " The Dairymaids " ; appeared in the same part at the Queen's, May, 1908 ; at the Apollo, Apr., 1907, played Squire Western in " Tom Jones " ; during 1910, toured as Uncle Gregory in " Pinkie and the Fairies " ; in 1910, went to Australia, playing the part of Tom Lambert in " The Whip " ; appeared in the same part at the Manhattan Opera House, New York, Nov., 1912 ; at His Majesty's, 22 May, 1914, appeared as Eliah Coombe in

the " all-star " revival of " The Silver King," given in aid of King George's Actors' Pension Fund, also assisting Mr. E. S. Willard in the production ; at the Shaftesbury, June, 1914, played the Constable in " The Cinema Star " ; at the Strand, Sept., 1914, again played Eliah Coombe in " The Silver King " ; at the Shaftesbury, May, 1915, Sir George Paddock in " The Arcadians"; at the Prince of Wales's, Sept., 1915, played Babbing in " The Dummy " ; at the Garrick, Jan., 1916, Sheriff Carson in " Tiger's Cub " ; at Daly's, Dec., 1916, Sam Best in " Young England " ; during 1917, toured as Old Bill in " The Better 'Ole " ; at the Prince's, Nov., 1918, played Ben Bartimus in " Jolly Jack Tar "; at the Alhambra, Sept., 1919, Sir Porter Blogg-Blogg in " Eastward Ho ! " ; at the Ambassadors', Mar., 1920, Captain John Ball in " Grierson's Way " ; subsequently toured as Stillbottle in " Tilly of Bloomsbury " ; at the Aldwych, Feb., 1921, played Stephano in " The Tempest " ; at the Queen's, Apr., 1921, Mr. Goddard in " Mary " ; at the Apollo, Sept., 1921, Bruce Jennings in " Crooked Usage " ; at the Royalty, Apr., 1922, Toby Crouch in " If Four Walls Told " ; at the Savoy, Jan., 1923, Hiram J. Walkin in " The Young Idea " ; at His Majesty's, Oct., 1924, Peter Rumble in " Patricia "; during 1927-28 toured as Siegfried Peters in " Sunny "; Palace (for King George's Pension Fund), May, 1928, played Jellyband in " The Scarlet Pimpernel " ; Haymarket, Dec., 1928, Mr. Wardle in "Mr. Pickwick"; Playhouse, Sept., 1929, Matey in "Dear Brutus" ; Comedy, Mar., 1930, Simson in "Odd Numbers"; Alhambra, Aug., 1931, Karl Hirsch in "Waltzes from Vienna"; in Aug., 1932, toured in the same part ; went to America, 1934, and at the Center Theatre, New York, Sept., 1934, again played the same part, when the play was entitled "The Great Waltz"; toured, Oct., 1937, as the Priest in "Venus in Silk." *Club:* Stage Golfing Society. *(Died 22 Mar., 1940; age 79)*

MANNING, Irene (*née* Inez Harvuot), actress and singer; *b.* Cincinnati,

Ohio, U.S.A., 17 July, 1917; *d.* of Shirley Errett Harvuot and his wife Inez (Odella); *e.* Los Angeles High School, and Eastman School of Music, Rochester, N.Y.; *m.* Clinton H. Green; studied for the stage at the Eastman School where she trained for opera; later studied voice with various teachers in U.S.A., and in London studied with Mrs. Davis-Reynolds; made her first appearance on the stage at the Eastman Theatre, Rochester, Dec., 1935, as Margot in "The Desert Song"; subsequently appeared with the St. Louis Municipal Opera company; with the Los Angeles Light Opera company, sang the leading *rôles* in "The Gypsy Baron," 1939; "H.M.S. Pinafore," 1940; "The Chocolate Soldier," "The Merry Widow," and "Show Boat," 1941, under the name of Hope Manning; toured, 1944–5, for U.S.O. overseas; in 1945, while in London, played in the film, "I Lived in Grosvenor Square"; made her first appearance on the New York stage, at the National Theatre, 22 Nov., 1945, as Katherine Townsend in "The Day Before Spring"; with the Los Angeles Light Opera company, 1946, appeared as Rose Marie; Jan.–Mar., 1947, was engaged on a Concert tour, and in May, 1947, played the title-*rôle* in "Rosalinda," with the Los Angeles Light Opera company; she then went to England, and made her first appearance in London, at the Prince's Theatre, 8 Oct., 1947, as Jeanne in a revival of "The Dubarry"; Empire, Edinburgh, Aug., 1948, played Eleanor Barrett in "Serenade"; Adelphi, London, Dec., 1949, played her first straight part as Mrs. Dunne in "Castle in the Air"; at the Alcazar, San Francisco, Nov., 1952, appeared in "The Second Man"; Barbizon-Plaza, New York, Apr., 1961, Ella, Countess Mattatorini in "The Tattooed Countess"; first appeared in films, 1941, in "The Big Shot," subsequently appearing in "Yankee-Doodle Dandy," "The Desert Song," "Shine On Harvest Moon," and also in "The Doughgirls," etc. *Favourite parts:* Marie in "The Gypsy Baron," Rosalinda, and Mrs. Dunne in "Castle in the Air." *Hobbies:* Photography and collecting gramophone records, candlesticks, and decanters. *Recreation:* Swimming.

MANNOCK, Patrick L., dramatic and film critic; *b.* London, 24 Dec., 1887; *s.* of J. P. Mannock; *e.* Latymer Foundation School, Hammersmith; *m.* Laura Whetter; formerly engaged as scenario editor and author of films; started his career as film critic for the *Kinematograph Weekly*, 1923; was editor of the *Picturegoer*, monthly, Apr., 1927–Mar., 1930; joined *The Daily Herald*, Jan., 1930, as film critic, and dramatic critic, in addition, Jan., 1931–53; President of The Critics' Circle, 1943–5, and is a member of the Council; as "Playfellow," wrote for *Truth*, 1947–53; is the author of radio scripts on theatrical subjects. *Address:* c/o The Savage Club, 1 Carlton House Terrace, London, S.W.1.

MANSFIELD, Alice, actress; *m.* C. J. Hope; has had over fifty years' experience, having made her first appearance on the stage, as a child, at Sadler's Wells Theatre, under the management of Alice Marriott (Mrs. Richard Edgar), playing such parts as the Prince of Wales in "Richard III," Fleance and the Apparition in "Macbeth," etc.; she then spent many years in provincial "stock" companies, at Liverpool Manchester, Edinburgh, etc., and also in the United States, where she supported E. A. Sothern as Mary Meredith in "Our American Cousin," etc.; for some years she was also engaged at the Chestnut Street Theatre, Philadelphia, and she has appeared in all the principal cities in the United States; subsequently toured in the West Indies and Jamaica; she returned to England in 1891 and toured as Mrs. Birkett in "Betsy," Helen Griffin in "Niobe," etc.; reappeared in the West End of London at the Comedy, May, 1895, as Mrs. Wheedles in "The Prude's Progress," and the following year as Mrs. Jones in "Gaffer Jarge"; at the Strand, Feb., 1896, played Miss Peck in "On 'Change"; at the Royalty, Apr., 1896, Drusilla Walker in "The New Baby"; at the Lyceum, June, 1896, with Forbes-Robertson, played Francisca in "Magda"; returning to the Comedy, July, 1896, played Alvina Garsop in "The Mummy," and Nov., 1896, Letitia Ogden in "A White

Elephant"; at the Royalty, Oct., 1897, appeared as Susannah Sheppard in "Oh! Susannah!"; at the Prince of Wales's, Apr., 1901, played Mrs. Gilwattle in "The Man from Blankley's," playing the same part in the Command performance, at Sandringham, before the late King Edward; she has played at most of the leading London theatres, and in 1909 was engaged at His Majesty's Theatre, under Sir Herbert Tree; during 1910-11 was a member of the Glasgow Repertory Company at the Royalty, Glasgow; at the Queen's, Nov., 1912, played Mrs. Harte in "Sylvia Greer"; at the Criterion, Jan., 1913, Aunt Fanny in "Billy's Fortune"; at the Vaudeville, Oct., 1913, Mrs. Higgins in "Between Sunset and Dawn"; at the Kingsway, May, 1915, with the Liverpool Repertory Company, played Mrs. Ferrard in "Nobody Loves Me," and Mrs. Burlacombe in "A Bit o' Love"; at the Shaftesbury, Sept., 1916, Mrs. Budd in "The Light Blues"; at the Queen's, Sept., 1917, Mrs. Meecher in "The Off-Chance"; at the Oxford, June, 1919, Mrs. Hope in "A Temporary Gentleman"; at the Kingsway, Sept., 1920, Mrs. Hunter in "The Daisy"; at the Garrick, Dec., 1920, Martha in "The Shepherdess Without a Heart"; during 1922 toured in "Mrs. Winterbotham's Woes"; at the Garrick, Apr., 1926, played Mrs. Gault in "The Unseemly Adventure"; Globe, June, 1927, The Fiancée in "The Spook Sonata"; Kingsway, June, 1931, the Visitor in "The Age of Youth."
(Died 17 Feb., 1938; age 80)

MANTELL, Robert Bruce, actor and manager; *b.* Irvine, Scotland, 7 Feb., 1854; *e.* at Belfast, Ireland; *m.* Geneviève Hamper; made his first appearance on the stage at the Theatre Royal, Rochdale, Lancs, 21 Oct., 1876, as the Sergeant in "Arrah-Na-Pogue," under the name of Robert Hudson; made his first appearance in America, under his own name, at the Leyland Opera House, Albany, New York, in Nov., 1878, as Tybalt in "Romeo and Juliet," with Madame Modjeska; first appeared in New York, at the Grand Opera House, 5 May, 1879,

as Old Dill in "East Lynne," also with Modjeska, with whom he remained some time; he returned to England in 1880 and played lead with Miss Wallis; at the Windsor Theatre, New York, 23 Oct., 1882, he played in "The World"; and at Booth's, 30 Oct., 1882, he appeared as Jack Herne in "The Romany Rye"; he next played leading parts with the late Fanny Davenport, appearing as Loris Ipanoff in "Fédora"; at Stetson's Fifth Avenue, 1 Sept., 1884, he played Gilbert Vaughan in "Called Back"; and at the Lyceum, New York, 6 Apr., 1885, he appeared as Dakolar in the play of that name; he made his *début* as a "star" at Stetson's, Fifth Avenue, 13 Dec., 1886, in "Tangled Lives," since which date he has appeared in the leading parts of the following plays: "Monbars," 1888; "The Corsican Brothers," 1890; "The Marble Heart," 1891; "The Louisianian," 1892; "The Face in the Moonlight," 1892; also in "The Veiled Picture," "A Lesson in Acting," "Hamlet," "The Dagger and the Cross," "Othello," both as Othello and Iago, "The Lady of Lyons," "Romeo and Juliet," "The Light of Other Days," "Richard III," "King Lear," "Macbeth," "The Merchant of Venice," "Julius Caesar," "King John," "The O'Flynn," "Louis XI," "Richelieu." *Recreation :* Golf.
(Died 27 June, 1928; age 74)

MANTLE, Burns, dramatic critic and author; *b.* Watertown, New York, U.S.A., 23 Dec., 1873; *s.* of Robert Burns Mantle and his wife Susan (Lawrence); *e.* public schools and normal college; *m.* Lydia Holmes Sears; dramatic editor of *Denver Times*, 1898-1900; *Denver Republican*, 1901; *Chicago Inter-Ocean*, 1901-7; *Chicago Tribune*, 1907-8; Sunday-editor, 1908-11; dramatic critic *Evening Mail*, New York, 1911-22; *Daily News*, New York, 1922-44; dramatic correspondent *Chicago Tribune*, since 1911; editor of Best Plays and Year Book of the Drama in America, 1899-1945; author of "American Playwrights of To-day," 1929; "Con-

temporary American Playwrights,"
1938; co-editor (with John Gassner)
of "A Treasury of the Theatre," 1935.
Clubs: Dutch Treat and Pomonock
Country Club.
(Died 9 Feb., 1948; age 74)

MAPES, Victor, author, journalist,
dramatic author, and manager; *b.*
New York, 10 Mar., 1870; *s.* of
Charles V. Mapes and his wife Martha
Meeker (Halsted); graduate of Columbia College (1st Class), 1891; *e.* also in
Paris; from 1892, to 1896, was Paris
correspondent of the *New York Sun*;
in 1897, was appointed stage-manager
of the New York Lyceum Theatre,
under Daniel Frohman; during
1898-9 officiated as dramatic critic
for the *New York World* under the
pseudonym of Sidney Sharp; during 1900-1 was general stage director
of Daly's Theatre, New York, subsequently fulfilling a similar capacity
at the Garrick, New York; author
of the following plays: "La Comtesse
de Lisne" (in French, produced at
Théâtre Mondain, Paris, 1895), "A
Flower of Yeddo" (Empire, 1899),
"The Tory's Guest" (Empire, 1900),
"Don Caesar's Return" (Wallack's,
1901), "Captain Barrington" (Manhattan, 1903), "The Undercurrent"
(Chicago, 1907); "The Curious Conduct of Judge Le Garde" (with
Louis Faust), 1902; "No. 6 Washington Square" (with Winchell Smith),
1913; "The New Henrietta" (with
Smith), 1913; "The Boomerang"
(with Smith), 1915; "The Lassoo,"
1917; "The Liberty Gun" (with
R. Mears Mackay), subsequently re-
named "The Long Dash," 1918; "The
Hottentot" (with William Collier),
1920; "The Kangaroo," 1921; "The
Lame Duck," 1921; author of the
novel "The Gilded Way," 1910; during 1904-5 was manager of the Globe
Theatre, Boston, and during 1906 was
director of the New Theatre, Chicago.
Clubs: University, Lambs, Players,
Strollers', and Psi Upsilon, New York.
(Died 27 Sept., 1943; age 73)

MARAVAN, Lila, actress; *d.* of
Percival Muschamp and his wife Alice
(Bayne-Foulds); *m.* Ronald Simpson;

studied for the stage at the Royal
Academy of Dramatic Art; made her
first appearance on the stage at the
St. James's Theatre, 19 Oct., 1916, as
Lady Simeta Parsons in "Lucky
Jim"; at the Strand, Oct., 1917,
played Trixie in "Wild Heather";
at the Haymarket, May, 1918, Christine
Farndon in "Uncle Anyhow"; Dec.,
1919, toured as Peter Pan; Jan., 1921,
toured as Mary Rose; at the Adelphi,
June, 1922, played Olga Ratcliffe in
"The Way of an Eagle"; at the
Strand, Oct., 1922, Esther Morrison in
"The Balance"; at the Playhouse,
Mar., 1923, Marie in "Magda"; at
the Adelphi, Dec., 1923, Wendy in
"Peter Pan"; at the New Theatre,
Oxford (with the O.U.D.S.), Mar.,
1924, Ophelia in "Hamlet"; in the
autumn of 1924 again toured as Mary
Rose; 1925-28, appeared in several
productions at the "Q" Theatre,
notably in "Uncle Ned," "A Pair of
Silk Stockings," "The Man from
Toronto," "The Lonely Road," "Con-
traband," "The Intruder," "Secret
Egypt," etc.; at the Fortune Theatre,
Sept., 1928, played Angélique in
"Napoleon's Josephine"; Everyman,
Oct., 1931, Aurea in "The Fountain
of Youth"; Gate, Apr., 1932, played
in "The Pleasure Garden." *Favourite
parts*: Peter Pan, Wendy, and Mary
Rose. *Recreations*: Swimming and
diving, golf and tennis.
(Died 29 Aug., 1950; age 54)

MARCH, Fredric, actor; (*né* Frederick McIntyre Bickel); *b.* Racine,
Wisconsin, U.S.A., 31 Aug., 1897; *e.*
Racine High School and University of
Wisconsin; *m.* Florence Eldridge;
formerly a bank clerk; made his first
appearance on the stage at Ford's
Theatre, Baltimore, 7 Dec., 1920,
under his own name of Fred Bickel, as
the Prompter in "Deburau," and made
his first appearance in New York, in
the same part, at the Belasco Theatre,
23 Dec., 1920; at the Booth, Feb.
1922, played Tom Fowler in "The Law
Breaker"; next played "stock" at
Dayton, Ohio, followed by a tour as
Emmett Carr in "Tarnish"; at the
Ritz, New York, May, 1924, played
Donald Clemens in "The Melody Man";
Selwyn, Mar., 1925, Bruno Monte in

"Puppets"; Belmont, Sept., 1925, Richard Knight in "Harvest"; National, Mar., 1926, Dick Chester in "The Half-Caste"; Charles Hopkins Theatre, Dec., 1926, Jimmie Chard in "The Devil in the Cheese"; after a summer season at Elitch's Gardens, Denver, toured for the Theatre Guild, playing lead in "Arms and the Man," "The Silver Cord," "Mr. Pim Passes By" and "The Guardsman"; subsequently, in San Francisco and Los Angeles, played Anthony Cavendish in "The Royal Family"; spent the next ten years in films; reappeared on the New York stage at the Broadhurst, Jan., 1938, as Richard Steele in "Yr Obedient Husband"; Center Theatre, New York, Jan., 1939, played Martin Gunther in "The American Way"; Guild, Nov., 1941, Elliott Martin in "Hope for a Harvest"; Plymouth, Nov., 1942, Mr. Antrobus in "The Skin of Our Teeth"; Cort, Nov., 1944, Major Victor Joppolo in "A Bell for Adano"; Mansfield, Dec., 1946, Clinton Jones in "Years Ago"; Broadhurst, Mar., 1950, Gen. Leonidas Erosa in "Now I Lay Me Down to Sleep"; Dec., 1950, Dr. Stockmann in "An Enemy of the People"; Coronet, Mar., 1951, appeared as Nicholas Denery in "The Autumn Garden"; Helen Hayes, Nov., 1956, played James Tyrone in "Long Day's Journey into Night," (for which performance he received the N.Y. Drama Critics Award for the Best Actor in a Straight Play, and the Antoinette Perry "Tony" Award, 1956–7); during the seasonal lay-off on Broadway, July, 1957, he appeared in the same production at the Sarah Bernhardt Theatre, Paris, during the Theatre of Nations Season; Plymouth, Nov., 1961, Angel in "Gideon"; toured Greece, Egypt, Italy, and the Near East with his wife for the U.S. State Department, spring, 1965, in readings and scenes from plays; commenced film career 1928, in "The Dummy," subsequent films include: "Smilin' Through," "Dr. Jekyll and Mr. Hyde" (for which he received the Academy Award Oscar), "The Barretts of Wimpole Street," "Les Miserables," "Anna Karenina," "A Star Is Born," "Bedtime Story," "The Best Years of Our Lives" (Academy Award), "Death of a Salesman," "The Desperate Hours," "The Middle of the Night," "Inherit the Wind," etc. *Recreations:* Tennis, swimming, and riding. *Club:* Players.

MARCH, Nadine, actress; *b.* London, 30 July, 1898; *d.* of Reginald Charles March and his wife Clare (Streatfield); *e.* Parson's Mead, Ashstead, Surrey; *m.* (1) Douglas Stephenson (mar. dis.); (2) Stephen Thomas; studied for the stage at the Royal Academy of Dramatic Art; made her first appearance on the stage at the Theatre Royal, Portsmouth, Nov., 1917, as Planchette in "The Girl from Upstairs"; in 1918 toured as Miss Dorton in "Cook," and Faith in "The Dancing Girl"; during 1919 as Posy in "Quinney's"; during 1920, Blanny Wheeler in "Fair and Warmer"; made her first appearance in London, at the Prince's Theatre, 3 Nov., 1920, as Elsie Cranford in "Columbine"; appeared at the Garrick Theatre, Nov., 1920, as Dolly Clandon in "You Never Can Tell"; at the Aldwych, Dec., 1920, played Eva Webster in "The Private Secretary"; at the Garrick, Mar., 1921, played Esme in "The Muddler"; at the Strand, Mar., 1922, Anne in "The Love Match"; at the Everyman, May, 1922, Dolly in "You Never Can Tell," followed by a tour on the Continent in the same part; at the Everyman, Dec., 1922, played Brer Rabbit in a play of that name; Jan., 1923, Sylvia Craven in "The Philanderer,"; at the Ambassadors', Mar., 1923, Babs in "Marriage by Instalments"; at the Everyman, Apr., 1923, Olive in "T'Marsdens"; at the Criterion, Oct., 1923, Gwen Lupton in "Trust Emily"; at the Everyman, Mar., 1924, Bella Buckley in "Young Imeson"; at the Savoy, June, 1924, Yvonne in "Tiger Cats"; at the Everyman, Dec., 1924, again played Sylvia in "The Philanderer"; Everyman, Jan., 1925, played Margot Latreux in "Home Affairs"; "Q," Mar., 1925, Eva King in "Adam and Eva"; St. Martin's, Apr., 1925, succeeded Edna Best as Fay Collen in

"Spring Cleaning"; Lyric, Hammersmith, Oct., 1925, Jenny in "Lionel and Clarissa"; Golder's Green, Apr., 1926, Margaret in "Big Business"; Everyman, Aug., 1926, Gleddis in "A Balcony"; Little, Oct., 1926, played in "The Potinière Revue"; Everyman, Dec., 1926, Brer Rabbit in a play of that name; Court, Mar., 1927, Iris in "Bert's Girl"; Lyric, Hammersmith, June, 1927, Miss Snevellicci in "When Crummles Played"; Garrick, May, 1928, Veronica in "Call Me Georges"; Prince of Wales's (for Sunday Play Society), Oct., 1928, Maica in the play of that name; Embassy, Nov., 1928, Erica Ridley in "The Perfect Wife"; Arts, Jan., 1929, Dagny in "The Age of Unreason"; Little, Feb., 1929, Mania in "Red Rust"; June, 1929, Flora Dickson in "Water"; in the autumn of 1929, toured as Lady Herbert in "The Lady With a Lamp"; Strand, May, 1930, played Lily Greaves in "Moloch"; New, July, 1930, Madeleine in "Désiré"; Duke of York's, May, 1931, Miss Hooper in "London Wall"; Arts, Oct., 1931, Chastity in "Vile Bodies"; Lyric, Hammersmith, Dec., 1931, Fairy Dewdrop in "Aladdin"; Vaudeville, Apr., 1932, again played in "Vile Bodies"; Duke of York's, June, 1932, in continuous "Grand Guignol"; St. Martin's (for Sunday Playgoers), July, 1932, the Countess of Slough in "Mutual Benefit"; Little, Sept., 1932, played in "The Oxford Blazers"; St. Martin's, Sept., 1932, played Freda in "Strange Orchestra"; Arts, Jan., 1933, Phoebe Marks in "Lady Audley's Secret"; St. James's, May, 1933, Ada Haggett in "The Late Christopher Bean," which ran over a year; Embassy, May, 1935, Mrs. Dester in "This Desirable Residence"; Arts, Jan., and St. Martin's, May, 1936, Lady Caroline Lamb in "Bitter Harvest"; Daly's, July, 1936, Dorothy in "The Visitor"; Duke of York's, Sept., 1936, Ursula in "No Ordinary Lady"; Arts, Feb., 1937, Sally Armstrong in "First Night"; Gate, Dec., 1937, appeared in the *revue*, "Members Only"; Phoenix, Mar., 1938, Mrs. Viola Fayne in "Flood Tide"; "Q," Feb., 1939, Mary Wilson in "Stolen Time"; St.

James's, May, 1939, Collette Ardis in "Sixth Floor"; entered films 1932, and since 1936 has appeared in "The Rat," "Dangerous Fingers," etc. *Recreations*: Riding, swimming, and dogs. *(Died 10 Oct., 1944; age 54)*

MARCIN, Max, dramatic author and producing manager; *b.* Posen, Germany, 6 May, 1879; *s.* of Herman Marcin and his wife Johanna (Feibel); *e.* New York; *m.* Clara May Mings; went to New York in early childhood, and was formerly a journalist; has written the following plays: "Are You My Wife?" (with Roy Atwell), 1910; "The House of Glass," 1915; "See My Lawyer," 1915; "Cheating Cheaters," 1916; "The Eyes of Youth" (with Charles Guernon), 1917; "Here Comes the Bride" (with Atwell), 1917; "The Rape of Belgium" (with Louis K. Anspacher), 1918; the American version of "Seven Days Leave," 1918; "The Dancer" (with Anspacher and Edward Locke), 1919; "The Woman in Room 13" (with Samuel Shipman), 1919; "Three Live Ghosts," 1920; "The Night Cap" (with Guy Bolton), 1921; "Silence," 1924; "Badges" (with Edward Hammond), 1924; "Los Angeles" (with Donald Ogden Stewart), 1927; "Trapped" (with Samuel Shipman), "The Big Fight" (with Milton Herbert Gropper), 1928; "The Humbug," 1929; as a producing manager has presented "Three Live Ghosts," 1920; "The Nightcap," 1921; "The Faithful Heart," 1922; "Give and Take," 1923; "Trapped," 1928; "The Humbug," 1929; "Censored" (with Conrad Seiler), 1938.
(Died 30 Mar., 1948; age 68)

MARGETSON, Arthur, actor and vocalist; *b.* London, 27 Apr., 1897; *s.* of Edward John Margetson, and his wife Marion (Wardroper); *e.* Royal Masonic Schools, Bushey, Herts; *m.* (1) Vera Lennox (mar. dis.); (2) Shirley Grey; (3) Barbara Wood; was formerly an insurance clerk at Lloyd's; made his first appearance on the stage at the Prince's Theatre, Edinburgh, Dec., 1917, as the Footman in

" Theodore and Co."; made his first appearance in London, at the Ambassadors' Theatre, 31 Aug., 1918, as Captain Laverdet in " Telling the Tale "; appeared at the Strand and Criterion, 1919, in the revival of the " H. G. Pelissier Follies "; at the Palace, Dec., 1919, played in " The Whirligig "; at the Queen's, Dec., 1920, appeared with Elsie Janis in " It's All Wrong "; at the Gaiety, Dec., 1921, played Hubert Faverolles in " The Little Girl in Red "; Apr., 1922, the Hon. Geoffrey Custance in " His Girl "; he then went to America and made his first appearance in New York, at the Winter Garden, 20 Sept., 1922, in " The Passing-Show of 1922 " ; at the same theatre, Jan., 1923, played in " The Dancing Girl"; at the Lyceum, New York, 1923, succeeded Bruce McRae as Larry Charters in " Little Miss Bluebeard," and remained in this in New York, and on tour, throughout 1924; appeared in the same part at Wyndham's, London, Apr., 1925; at the Winter Garden, London, May, 1925, played Kenneth Dennison in " Tell Me More "; Adelphi, Nov., 1925, Barnaby Haddon in " Betty in Mayfair"; Winter Garden, Feb., 1926, Tom Sterling in " Kid Boots "; Shaftesbury, Sept., 1926, Kenneth Courtney in " Just a Kiss"; Prince of Wales's, May, 1927, Lord Antony Stowe in " The Blue Train "; Criterion, Sept., 1927, succeeded A. E. Matthews as Harvey Townsend in " The Happy Husband "; Duke of York's, Oct., 1927, Peter Chelsworth in " Home Chat "; went to America, 1928, and at the Music Box, New York, Oct., 1928, played Guy Pennel in " Paris "; on returning to London, appeared at the Palace, July, 1929, when he succeeded Owen Nares as Jim Brooks in "Hold Everything"; "Q," Feb., 1930, played Victor Beverly in "Watch Beverly"; Palace, May, 1930, Jack Mason in "Heads Up"; Lyric, Aug., 1930, Bob Brown in "Let Us Be Gay"; Comedy, Mar., 1931, Gerald Gray in "Naughty Cinderella"; Playhouse, Sept., 1931, Charles Townsend in "The Painted Veil"; Phoenix, Feb., 1932, George Letts in "Lovely Lady"; Globe, June, 1932, Count Anthony Darro in "Men

About the House"; went to New York, and at the Avon Theatre, Oct., 1932, played Henry Cade in "Nona"; at the Avon, New York, Jan., 1933, Bill Smith in "A Good Woman, Poor Thing"; Playhouse, New York, Feb., 1933, Dick Carrington in "A Saturday Night"; His Majesty's, London, May, 1933, Bruno Mahler in "Music in the Air"; Wyndham's, Sept., 1934, Edward Warren in "No More Ladies"; 46th Street, New York, Feb., 1936, Roger Storer in "Mainly for Lovers"; Adelphi, London, Oct., 1937, The Laughing Cavalier in the play of that name; toured, Feb., 1938, as Richard Sheldon in "Back Your Fancy"; His Majesty's, Jan., 1939, Count Ferenc in "Magyar Melody"; went to America again, 1939; Playhouse, New York, Dec., 1939, played Dr. Howard Fleming in "Billy Draws a Horse"; toured with Jane Cowl, as Captain Brassbound in "Captain Brassbound's Conversion"; National, Mar., 1940, Mr. Mayflower in "A Case of Youth"; Cort, Oct., 1940, Sir Francis Chesney in "Charley's Aunt"; Booth, June, 1941, Jerry Sycamore in "Claudia"; Hudson, Nov., 1941, Michael Gosselyn in "Theatre"; Henry Miller, Dec., 1942, Peter Kyle in "Flare Path"; Fulton, Oct., 1943, John Asprey in "Another Love Story"; 48th Street, Feb., 1944, Harold Burton in "Mrs. Kimball Presents"; Plymouth, Mar., 1944, succeeded Henry Daniell as Edmund Alexander in "Lovers and Friends"; Empire, June, 1944, appeared as Father in "Life With Father," which he played for a year; Martin Beck, Mar., 1946, played Norman Barlow in "Little Brown Jug"; Adelphi, May, 1946, Phileas Fogg in "Around the World"; Shubert, Nov., 1946, Ogden Bennett in "Park Avenue"; Booth, Apr., 1948, Almady in "The Play's the Thing"; Biltmore, Dec., 1949, Arthur Pomfret in "Clutterbuck"; has appeared in numerous films. *Recreations:* Painting, music, and lyric writing. *Clubs:* Savage, London; Players, N.Y. Athletic and Lambs, New York. (*Died 13 Aug., 1951; age 54*)

MARGO (*née* Maria Margarita Bolado), actress and dancer; *b.* Mexico

City, 10 May, 1918; *d.* of Dr. Emilio Bolado; *m.* (1) Francis Lederer (mar. dis.); (2) Edward Albert; made her first appearance at the age of six as a juvenile dancer in Mexico City; first appeared in New York as a dancer in cabaret at the Waldorf-Astoria and was subsequently, for a time, dancing partner with George Raft, at the Paramount Theatre; entered films 1934, making her first appearance in "Crime Without Passion," subsequently appearing in "Rumba" and "Robin Hood of Eldorado"; made her first appearance on the regular stage at the Martin Beck Theatre, New York, 25 Sept., 1935, making an immediate success, in the part of Miriamne in "Winterset," and the following year appeared in the film of the same name; at the Shubert Theatre (for Theatre Guild), Feb., 1937, played the Baroness Mary Vetsera in "The Masque of Kings" and subsequently appeared in the film, "The Lost Horizon"; at the Pilgrimage, Hollywood, and at San Francisco, Sept., 1938, played Margharita in Prof. Max Reinhardt's production of "Faust"; Broadhurst, June, 1939, appeared in "The Streets of Paris"; at the Civic Theatre, Chicago, July, 1939, played Diane in "Seventh Heaven," also danced in the ballet, "El Amor Brujo," with the National Symphony Orchestra, in Mexico; Guild, Nov., 1939, played Virginia McKay in "The World We Make"; Little, Jan., 1941, Hessy McMorna in "Tanyard Street"; Cort, Nov., 1944, Tina in "A Bell for Adano"; in summer theatres, 1950, played in "The Respectful Prostitute," and "Red Peppers." *Recreations:* Walking and swimming. *Address:* 1410½ North Havenhurst, Los Angeles, Calif., U.S.A.

MARGUERITTE, Victor, French dramatic author; *b.* Blidah, Algeria, 1 Dec., 1866; *e.* Lycée Henri IV; *m.* Mdlle. Bernet; was formerly a soldier; is the author of the following plays: "Le Coeur et la Loi" (with Paul Margueritte), 1905; "L'Autre" (with Paul Margueritte), 1908; "La Double Méprise," "L'Imprévu," 1910; "La Maison de L'Homme", either in

collaboration with his brother, or alone, has also written numerous novels and historical works; his novel "Prostituée," was dramatised by Desfontaines, and produced at the Ambigu, 1910; is a Commander of the Legion of Honour, and Hon. President of the Société des Gens de Lettres. *(Died 23 Mar., 1942; age 75)*

MARIANI-ZAMPIERI, Teresina, Italian actress; *b.* Florence, 1871; *m.* Vittorio Zampieri; made her first appearance on the stage, as a child, with Mdme. Ristori, in 1878, playing in "Medea." "Marie Antoinette," etc.; was for some years, leading lady with Cesare Rossi; has appeared successfully in the following, among other plays: "Il Segreto," "Niobe," "Spiritisme," "Magda," "La Maison paternelle," "Fernande," "Dante," "Cavalleria Rusticana," "La Dame aux Camelias," etc.; has been one of the leading actresses on the Italian stage for some years.

MARINOFF, Fania, actress; *b.* Odessa, Russia, 20 Mar., 1890; *d.* of Morris Marinoff and his wife Leah (Tuerkenitch); *e.* New York; *m.* Carl Van Vechten; made her first appearance on the stage at the age of eight, in a "stock" company at Denver, 1898, as one of the children in "Cyrano de Bergerac"; in 1900, appeared as Orange Moll in "Mistress Nell," with Henrietta Crosman; made her first appearance in New York, at Daly's Theatre, 19 Nov., 1903, as O Haru San in "A Japanese Nightingale," at Daly's Theatre; at the Lyceum, New York, Sept., 1904, played in "The Serio-Comic Governess"; she next played with Mrs. Patrick Campbell in "The Sorceress"; was then engaged by Henry W. Savage to play Miss Daros in "The Stolen Story," in Boston; during 1906–7 toured with Arnold Daly as Dolly in "You Never Can Tell"; subsequently played "stock" at Keith and Proctor's, New York; during 1907-8 was with Max Figman in "The Man on the Box"; at the Gaiety, New York, 12 Apr., 1909, played Esther Jacobson in "The House Next Door"; continued in this 1909-10 ; at the Fifth Avenue, Mar., 1911, played Dago Annie in " A Romance of the Underworld "; during 1912 played in " The Rainbow "; during 1913-14 appeared in various cinema plays; at Boston, Dec., 1913, played Zelima in " A Thousand Years Ago "; Comedy, New York, Oct., 1914, Gladys Lipski in " Consequences "; at the Park, May, 1915, Louka in " Arms and the Man "; at the Century, Apr., 1916, Ariel in " The Tempest "; during 1917-18, played leading parts with the Greenwich Village Players, among which were Karen in a play of that name, Columbine in " Behind a Watteau Picture," and Aglaë in " Pan and the Young Shepherd "; at the Morosco, Sept., 1918, played Sonia Orloff in " The Walk-Offs "; at the Empire, New York, Aug., 1920, Balog-Mari in " Call the Doctor "; at the Belmont, Sept., 1921, Marthe Roche in " The Hero "; at the Park, Feb., 1922, appeared in "Frank Fay's Fables "; at the Times Square, Apr., 1922, Dhima in " The Charlatan "; at the Bijou, Mar., 1923, Rosette Pompom in " The Love Habit "; at the Belmont, Oct., 1923, Nettie Dark in " Tarnish," and continued with this during 1924; reappeared after seven years absence, at the Country Playhouse, Westport, July, 1931, as Luella in "The Comic Artist," and in Aug., 1931, played Phoebe in "As You Like It "; reappeared in New York, at the 49th Street Theatre, Oct., 1931, as Alida Bloodgood in a revival of "The Streets of New York," and Martha Bernick in a revival of "The Pillars of Society"; Fulton, Dec., 1931, played Mrs. Lane in "The Bride the Sun Shines On"; Royale, May, 1932, the Marchioness in "Christopher Comes Across"; Belasco, Sept., 1934, Giulia Crevelli in "Judgment Day"; National, Feb., 1935, Suzanne Pentland in "Times Have Changed"; Westport, Conn., June, 1936, Mrs. Frail in "Love for Love"; Mansfield, New York, Nov., 1937, Charmian in "Antony and Cleopatra"; during the War, was engaged with the American Theatre War Wing Service, at the Merchant Seaman's Club, New York, 1943–5; at Westport Playhouse, 1948,

appeared as the Fortune Teller in " The Skin of Our Teeth," with Thornton Wilder. *Address :* 101 Central Park West, New York City, U.S.A. *Telephone No. :* Endicott 2-8748.

MARIO, Emilio, Spanish actor and manager ; has been associated with the Teatro de la Comedia, Madrid, since 1875 ; has produced successfully, and acted in the following, among other plays : " L'Abbé Constantin," " El Cura de Longueval," " L'Amigo Fritz," " Bébé, ou El Chiquitin le la Casa," " Dona Perfecta," " Muerete, si veras," "La Zarzuela," etc. *Address :* Teatro de la Comedia, Madrid, Spain.

MARION, George, Jr., librettist; *s.* of the late George Marion, actor; collaborated in the writing of many film scenarios from 1930, including "Along Came Youth," "Love Me To-night," "The Big Broadcast," etc.; author of new adaptation of "The Gypsy Baron" (with Ann Rowell), 1938; "Too Many Girls," 1939; "Beat the Band" (with George Abbott), 1942; "Early to Bed," 1943; "Allah Be Praised," 1944; "Marinka," 1945; "Toplitzky of Notre Dame," 1946. *(Died 25 Feb., 1968; age 68)*

MARION, Joan, actress; *b.* Launceston, Tasmania, 28 Sept., 1908; *d.* of Harry Ernest Nicholls and his wife Marion (Huston); *e.* London; *m.* L. E. de Rouet; studied for the stage at the Royal Academy of Dramatic Art; made her first appearance on the stage, 1927, touring as Kitty in "Charley's Aunt" in England and Canada; during 1928, toured as T'Mala in "The Silent House"; made her first appearance in London, at St. Martin's, 1929, during the run of "77 Park Lane"; St. Martin's, Sept., 1929, played Erminia in "Sorry You've Been Troubled"; Duke of York's, June, 1930, Ethel Grayson in "The Way to Treat a Woman"; Whitehall Feb., 1931, Mary Gray in "Good Losers"; in the summer of 1931, appeared at the Comédie Caumartin, Paris, as Mary in "The Well of Loneliness"; spent one year in films; during 1932, played leading parts at the Oxford Repertory Theatre; at the Garrick, June, 1933, played Kate Nelson in "Clear All Wires"; Drury Lane, Sept., 1933, Nina in "Ball at the Savoy"; Wyndham's, Nov., 1933, Nonie Watson in "Man Proposes"; Duke of York's, Mar., 1934, Phyllis Treyford in "Without Witness"; Lyric, June, 1934, Barbara Denny in "Men in White"; Wyndham's, July, 1934, Mrs. Roger Maitland in "The Maitlands"; Comedy, Mar., 1935, Anna in "Delusion"; Embassy, July, 1935, Raina in "Arms and the Man"; Royalty, Sept., 1935, Joan in "Closing at Sunrise"; then went to America, and made her first appearance in New York, at the Henry Miller Theatre, 20 Dec., 1935, as Lady Enid Loddon in "Libel"; Haymarket, London, Aug., 1936, played Nurse Ann in "The Amazing Doctor Clitterhouse," which ran over a year; Globe, Oct., 1937, Rita Warren in "Blondie White"; Garrick, Nov., 1937, Joyce Stanton in "It's a Wise Child"; Richmond, Mar., 1938, Gina Desti in "The Delano Case"; "Q," Sept., 1938, Jane in "The Judge"; Richmond, Nov., 1938, Frieda Renstone in "Chain Male"; "Q," Feb., 1939, Mavis Fulton in "Rovina"; reappeared on the stage, June, 1946, when she toured as Florence Lane in "Soldier's Wife," and appeared in this play at the Duchess Theatre, Aug., 1946; "Q," Dec., 1949, played Caroline Moore in "If This Be Error"; New, Hull, Oct., 1951, appeared as Romana in "Double Alibi"; has appeared frequently for the Repertory Players; television performances include "The Last Reunion" and "Sanitorium"; she has also appeared in films.

(Died 30 Nov., 1945; age 85)

MARKOVA, Alicia (*née* Lilian Alicia Marks), *prima ballerina*; *b.* London, 1 Dec., 1910; *d.* of Arthur Marks and his wife Eileen (Barry); *e.* London; studied dancing under Seraphine Astafieva; joined the Diaghileff Ballet in 1924, and appeared in "Le Lac de Cygnes," "Aurora's Wedding," "Cimarosiana," "The Cat," "The Story of the Nightingale";

at the Lyric, Hammersmith, Oct., 1930, appeared in "Marriage à la Mode"; appeared for the Ballet Club and for the Camargo Society; appeared at the New Theatre, Sept., 1931, in "Façade"; London Coliseum, Feb., 1933, in "The Nightingale and the Rose"; appeared at the Old Vic.-Sadler's Wells, from Feb., 1932, also during seasons of 1933–5; with Anton Dolin appeared in a special season of ballet, Sadler's Wells, May, 1935, and at the Shaftesbury Theatre, June, 1935; subsequently toured with Dolin; at Drury Lane, May, 1935, at the Marie Tempest *matinée*, danced "The Blue Bird," with Harold Turner, before their Majesties the King and Queen; Duke of York's, Jan., 1936, again appeared with Dolin in a season of ballet, subsequently touring; London Hippodrome, Dec., 1936, danced in "Mother Goose"; again toured, 1937, with Dolin; Drury Lane, July, 1938, appeared with the Ballet Russe de Monte Carlo; subsequently went to the United States; from 1941–5, appeared at the Metropolitan Opera House, New York, with the Opera Ballet; toured, Nov., 1945, with Anton Dolin, in their own company; Metropolitan Opera House, Apr.–May, 1946, appeared with Ballet Theatre, in "Giselle," "Firebird," "Swan Lake," "Aurora," "Les Sylphides," "Romeo and Juliet," "Nutcracker Suite," etc.; toured in the United States, 1947, with the original Ballet Russe; toured the Far East with Anton Dolin, 1948, and, with Dolin, appeared as Guest Star in the Sadler's Wells Ballet, at Covent Garden; toured, 1949, with Dolin, in South Africa; appeared at the Empress Hall, London, 1950; danced with Anton Dolin and the Festival Ballet at the Stoll, May, 1951; danced as guest artiste with the Sadler's Wells Ballet at Covent Garden, Mar., 1953; appeared for a special performance at Royal Albert Hall, Apr., 1954; in the same month gave a ballet concert at the Palais de Chaillot, Paris; at the Royal Festival Hall, Dec., 1954, appeared as the Spirit of the Lake in "Where the Rainbow Ends"; in Copenhagen, Sept., 1955, danced with the Royal Danish Ballet; has appeared in television programmes; a book,

"Study of Alicia Markova" was published in 1935, and a collection of photographic studies, collected by Gordon Anthony, was issued in 1935.

MARLOWE, Charles. *See* JAY, HARRIETT.

MARLOWE, Julia, actress; *b.* Caldbeck, eight miles from Keswick, in Cumberland, 17 Aug., 1866; *d.* of John Frost and his wife Sarah (Hodgson); she went to America in 1870; *e.* at the public schools, Cincinnati, Ohio, and Kansas City, Kansas; *m.* (1) Robert Taber (mar. dis.); (2) E. H. Sothern; she made her first appearance on the stage at Vincennes, Indiana, Oct., 1878, under the name of Fanny Brough, as a sailor in a juvenile " H.M.S. Pinafore " company; subsequently she played the part of Sir Joseph Porter in the same opera; she also appeared in the parts of Suzanne in " The Chimes of Normandy," and the Page in " The Little Duke "; in 1882-83 she played the part of Heinrich in " Rip Van Winkle," with Robert McWade; under the management of R. E. J. Miles, 1883-4, she toured as Balthazar in " Romeo and Juliet," Stephen in " The Hunchback," Maria in " Twelfth Night," and Myrine in " Pygmalion and Galatea "; she then studied for three years under the tuition of Ada Dow, a well-known American actress; her first appearance as a " star " took place at New London, Conn., 25 Apr., 1887, when she played Parthenia in " Ingomar "; subsequently she toured in this part under the direction of R. E. J. Miles, also playing Pauline in " The Lady of Lyons," she made her first appearance in New York, at the Bijou Theatre, 20 Oct., 1887, as Parthenia in " Ingomar," at a *matinée* performance specially organised for the occasion; she made an instantaneous success, and commenced her regular career as a " star," at the Star Theatre, New York, 12 Dec., 1887, when she appeared as Juliet for the first time; on 14 Dec., 1887, she also appeared for the first time as Viola in " Twelfth Night "; on tour, in Feb., 1888, she appeared as Julia in " The Hunch-back," followed in Jan., 1889, by Rosalind in " As You Like It "; at Tompkins' Fifth Avenue, 27 Jan., 1890, appeared as Rosalind in " As You Like It," for the first time in New York; 10 Feb., 1890, Julia in " The Hunchback "; 15 Feb., 1890, Galatea in " Pygmalion and Galatea "; during 1891 she played Charles Hart in " Rogues and Vagabonds "; Constance in " The Love Chase," 1892; Imogen in " Cymbeline," 1893, followed by Letitia Hardy in " The Belle's Stratagem," Thomas Chatterton in " Chatterton," Colombe in " Colombe's Birthday " (Nov., 1894), Lady Teazle in " The School for Scandal " (Dec., 1894), Prince Hal in " Henry IV " (Part I), Sept., 1895; she appeared at Palmer's Theatre, during the month of Mar., 1896, in the following parts: Juliet, Kate Hardcastle in " She Stoops to Conquer," Julia in " The Hunchback," Prince Hal, and Rosalind; she then toured for four weeks as Lydia Languish in an " all-star " revival of " The Rivals," when the cast included Joseph Jefferson, W. H. Crane, Robert Taber, Francis Wilson, Nat Goodwin, and Mrs. John Drew; she appeared in this part at the American Theatre, 7 May, 1896; at Milwaukee, Sept., 1896, played Romola in a play of that name, and at Buffalo, Jan., 1897, Mary in " For Bonnie Prince Charlie "; appeared at Palmer's, Feb., 1897, in the last-mentioned part; at the Broadway, Mar., 1897, appeared in " Chatterton "; at the Knickerbocker Theatre, 10 Jan., 1898, she played the part of the Countess in " Countess Valeska," and 3 Apr., 1899, she appeared as Colinette de ·Bouvray in " Colinette "; at the Criterion, New York, 23 Oct., 1899, she appeared in the title-*rôle* of " Barbara Frietchie "; 14 Jan., 1901, she played Mary Tudor in " When Knighthood was in Flower "; at Boston, 5 Oct., 1902, the Queen in " Queen Fiametta "; at the Criterion, New York, 8 Dec., 1902, Charlotte Oliver in " The Cavalier "; at the Hyperion Theatre, New Haven, Conn., 21 Sept., 1903, she was seen as Lady Branchester in H. V. Esmond's play, " Fools of Nature "; at the Alvin Theatre, Pittsburg, Pa., 25 Mar., 1904, she again revived "Ingomar," and was seen as Parthenia in the same play at the Empire, New York, 16 May, 1904; in the autumn of the same year she became co-star with E. H. Sothern, under the management of Charles Frohman, and at the Illinois Theatre, Chicago, 19 Sept., 1904, they appeared for the first time together in "Romeo and Juliet"; on 26 Sept. she played Beatrice in "Much Ado About Nothing," and 3 Oct. Ophelia in "Hamlet"; she was subsequently seen in the same parts, at the Knickerbocker Theatre, New York, in Oct. and Nov. of the same year; at Cleveland, Ohio, 18 Sept., 1905, she appeared as Katherine in "The Taming of the Shrew," and 21 Sept. as Portia in "The Merchant of Venice," subsequently appearing in the same parts at the Knickerbocker Theatre, New York, on 16 and 30 Oct., respectively; at the Knickerbocker, on 6 Nov., 1905, she played Viola in "Twelfth Night"; at the Lyric Theatre, Philadelphia, 15 Oct., 1906, under the management of Messrs. Shubert she appeared as Jeanne D'Arc in a play of that name, and 30th Oct., appeared as Salome in "John the Baptist"; at Washington, 15 Nov., 1906, played Rautendelein in "The Sunken Bell"; at the Lyric Theatre, New York, 21 Jan., 1907, appeared in the last-mentioned part, subsequently appearing at the same theatre as Jeanne D'Arc, Rautendelein, Juliet, Ophelia, Portia, and Viola; made her first appearance on the London stage at the Waldorf Theatre, 22 Apr., 1907, as Rautendelein in "The Sunken Bell"; during her five weeks engagement she earned considerable praise for her performances, scoring notable successes as Jeanne D'Arc, Viola, Juliet, Ophelia, and Rosalind in "As You Like It"; "When Knighthood was in Flower," produced on 13 May, was not successful; returning to America, she played a short engagement at the Academy of Music, New York, and at Philadelphia; the artistic partnership was temporarily dissolved in June, 1907 at Philadelphia, Dec., 1907, appeared in a new play, entitled "Gloria," at the head of her own company; at the

Majestic, Boston, 21 Dec., 1908, played Yvette in "The Goddess of Reason," and appeared in the same part at Daly's, New York, 15th Feb., 1909; at the opening of the New Theatre, New York, 8 Nov., 1909, appeared as Cleopatra in "Antony and Cleopatra" to the Antony of E. H. Sothern; during 1910 toured in Shakespearean repertory with E. H. Sothern; at New Haven, Conn., 4 Nov., 1910, appeared for the first time as Lady Macbeth in "Macbeth," playing the part for the first time in New York, at the Broadway, 5 Dec., 1910; toured in Shakespearean repertory, 1911-13; her retirement from the stage, due to ill-health, was announced in Aug., 1915, but subsequently she reappeared with her husband, and in 1921 was still playing in Shakespearean repertory, appearing at the Century, New York, Oct, to Dec., 1921, and at the Jolson Theatre, New York, Oct. to Dec., 1923; while fulfilling an engagement at Pittsburg in 1924, she met with an accident, and has since retired from the stage; in Apr., 1926, with her husband, presented the entire productions of ten Shakespearean plays to the Memorial Theatre, Stratford-on-Avon; received the Hon. Degree of LL.D., George Washington University, 1921, and Hon. Doctor of Letters, Columbia University, New York, June, 1943.

(Died 12 Nov., 1950; age 84)

MARMONT, Percy, actor; *b.* Gunnersbury, London, 25 Nov., 1883; *s.* Cecil Joseph Marmont and his wife Emily Charlotte (Wyatt); *e.* St. Ann's School, Redhill; *m.* Dorothy Stewart-Dawson; made his first appearance on the stage at the New Theatre, Cambridge, 14 May, 1900, as M. de Maury in "The Only Way"; first appeared in London, at the Haymarket Theatre, 23 Aug., 1902, as the servant in "There's Many a Slip"; spent many years touring in comedy and drama; visited South Africa in 1913, where he also appeared in his first film; subsequently toured in Australia; in 1916, was engaged with the Liverpool Repertory Theatre company; subsequently went to America, and made his first appearance in New York, at the Empire Theatre, Nov., 1917, as Dr.

Forsyth in "The Three Bears"; and in Dec., 1917, played de Varville in "The Lady of the Camellias"; at the Harris Theatre, Dec., 1919, Stephen Pryde in "The Invisible Foe"; he also appeared in America, in "The Laughter of Fools" and "The Silver Fox"; during the next ten years devoted himself to films; after returning to England, he appeared on tour as King Charles II in "Gentlemen! The King," 1929; Anthony Brenton in "The Scorpion," 1930; Ferdinand Wragg in "Lucky in Love," 1931; at the Arts Theatre, Apr., 1931, appeared as "Ducky" Mallard in "The Years Between"; Embassy, Nov., 1932, played Domain in "R.U.R."; in Mar., 1933, toured as Gabriel in "Service"; Gate, Nov., 1933, the Man in "Murder"; in Aug., 1934, toured as Robin Herriot in "Touch Wood"; Royalty, Sept., 1935, played Stanley in "Closing at Sunrise"; toured, 1937, as Roger Hilton in "Call It a Day"; "Q," June, 1938, Stephen in "Calling Bellamy"; Haymarket, Oct., 1938 Robert Firbanks in "A Party for Christmas"; "Q," Feb., 1939, Mr. Mortimer in "Stolen Time"; toured, Mar., 1939, as Julian Philips in "Drawing Room"; toured, Apr., 1940, as Lord Hannington in "Full House"; Piccadilly, Oct., 1942, played William Marshall in "The Little Foxes"; toured, 1944, as Harry Archer in "Kiss and Tell," and played the same part at the Phoenix, Aug., 1945; Fortune, June, 1949 Sir William Bligh in "My Mother Said . . ."; "Q," Sept., 1949, Guy Maitland in "Marriage Playground"; Duchess, Dec., 1949, Seth Lord in "The Philadelphia Story"; Winter Garden, Oct., 1953, played Mr. Justice Wainwright in "Witness For the Prosecution"; toured Australia, 1956–7, in his original part in "Witness For the Prosecution"; Pembroke, Croydon, Oct., 1961, played Judge Samuel Addison in "The Winner"; toured, Apr., 1965, as Count Sanziani in "La Contessa"; commenced film career, 1913, and has appeared in innumerable films. *Clubs:* Devonshire and Green Room, London; Lambs, New York. *Address:* 20 Carlyle Square, London, S.W.3. *Telephone No.:* Flaxman 4376.

MARNAC, Jane, French actress and vocalist; first came into prominence when she appeared at La Cigale, June, 1910, in " T'en as du Vice ! "; at the Fémina, Apr., 1912, played Anna in " Les Fils Touffe sont à Paris "; made a great success when she appeared in the title *rôle* of " La Reine Joyeuse " (" The Naughty Princess "), 1918; she then appeared at the Apollo, as Vénus in " Vénus à Paris "; was next seen in " L'Ecole des Cocottes," and at the Variétés, Dec., 1919, played Simone in " La Chasse à l'Homme "; at the Porte-St.-Martin, Oct., 1920, played Bianca Banella in " L'Appassionata "; at the Michel, 1921, Francine in " La Femme de Luxe "; in Apr., 1921, toured in France, Switzerland, Tunis, and Algeria, as Hélène Ardan in " La Douloureuse," Sazy in " Les Amants de Sazy," Bianca in " L'Appassionata," Gilberte in " Frou-Frou "; at the Potinière, Dec., 1921, played Gaby Desanges in " L'Enfant Gâtée." *Address :* 17 Quai Voltaire, Paris.

MAROT, Gaston, French dramatic author; has written the following, among other plays: " La Bande June " (with F. Oswald), " Desaix " (with L. Pericaud), 1889; " La Petite Mionne," 1890; " Les Héritiers Guichard," 1891; " La Mère la Victoire " (with Pericaud), 1893; " Le Train No. 6," " Les Aventures de Thomas Plumepatte," 1895; " Le Voyage de Mistress Robinson," 1896; "La Fille du Gardien de la Paix," " La Goualeuse " (with M. Alévy), 1900; " Le Drame de la Rue Murillo " (with Alévy), 1902; " Les Grandes Manœuvres," 1903; " Le Rabiot," " Madame X—" (with Ernest Depré), 1904; " Les Aventures de Gavroche " (with Victor Darlay), 1909. *Address :* 7 and 9 Rue des Acacias, Montmorency, Paris. *(Died 1916)*

MARQUET, Mary, actress; *b.* Paris, 1895; made her first appearance on the stage, 1912, touring with Paul Porel; entered the Conservatoire, 1913; appeared at the Théâtre Sarah-Bernhardt, 1914, in "Les Trois Mousquetaires,"and 1915, in "Les Cathédrales"; subsequently played the

Duc de Reichstadt in "L'Aiglon," also appeared in a revival of "La Tour de Nesles," and a further revival of "L'Aiglon"; she then retired for four years; reappeared, 1920, on tour with Edouard de Max; at the Théâtre de Paris, 1921, appeared in "L'Homme à la Rose," at the Théâtre Antoine, in "La Bataille"; Theatre Antoine, 1921, in "La Dolorès"; subsequently entered the Comédie Française in 1923, and has appeared in most of the classical revivals and original plays at that house, notably "Le Maître de son Cœur," 1931; "Christine," 1932; "Madame Quinze," 1935;"Andromaque," 1936;"Bajazet," 1937; "Athalie," 1939; "Polyeucte," 1942; "Phèdre," 1943; "Le Soulier de Satin," 1944; since 1947, has appeared in many comedies, and in dramatic *rôles* on the Boulevards, including "Pour Lucrèce," and "Le Château."

MARQUIS, Don, dramatic author and novelist; *b.* Walnut, Illinois, U.S.A., 29 July, 1878; *s.* of James Stewart Marquis and his wife Virginia Elizabeth (Whitmore); *m.* (1) Reina Melcher; (2) Marjorie Vonnegut; was for some years on the staff of the *Evening Sun,* New York, and subsequently on the *New York Tribune;* is the author of "The Old Soak" (adapted from his own novel), 1922; "Out of the Sea," 1927; "Everything's Jake," 1930; is the author of the following novels: "Danny's Own Story," "Dreams and Dust," "The Cruise of the Old Jasper B.," "Carter, and Other People," "Noah an' Jonah an' Cap'n John Smith," "The Dark Hours," "Archie and Mehitabel." *Club :* Players'. *(Died 29 Dec., 1937; age 59)*

MARR, Paula, actress ; *b.* Washington ; *m.* William Collier ; has appeared in William Collier's company, as Violet in "The Patriot"; Miranda in "The Man from Mexico," 1909 ; Nell Van Buren in "A Lucky Star," 1910 ; Bonny in "I'll be Hanged If I Do," 1910 ; Lucy Sheridan in "The Dictator," 1911 ; Paula Brooks in "Take My Advice," 1911 ; Violet

Stevenson in "Never Say Die," 1912 ; Aline Ford in "Who's Who," 1913 ; Madge Fleming in "A Little Water on the Side," 1913.

MARRIOTT-WATSON, Nan. actress and dramatic author ; *b.* 30 December, 1899 ; *d.* of F. Marriott Watson, manager and dramatic author, and his wife Florence (Edwin), actress made her first appearance on the stage in her father's company, and continued to act in the provinces, until 1922 ; she made a great success when she appeared at the Queen's Theatre, Apr., 1922, as Jean Sterling in "Lass o' Laughter," of which she was part-author, with Edith Carter ; at the Savoy, June, 1922, she played Lizzie Dewhirst in "Concerning Mary Dewhirst"; at the Regent, Sept., 1922, Blanche Nixon in "Body and Soul"; at Wimbledon, Dec., 1922, Oenone Pontifex in "Archibald's Afternoon"; at the Ambassadors, Feb., 1923, Pamela Ayers in "A Little Bit of Fluff"; at the Everyman, Nov., 1923, Barbara Hatteras in "The Second Round"; at the Aldwych, May, 1924, Chloris Morgan and Chloris Grey in "Before Sunset," of which she was also the author; she then went to America, and played three seasons with the Copley Repertory Company, at Boston; at the Little, New York, Oct., 1927, played A Lady of Fashion in "If"; 49th Street Theatre, Jan., 1928, Mabs Kellet in "Diversion"; returned to England, 1928; during 1929 toured as Patricia Harrington in "The Patsy"; "Q," Nov., 1929, played Ruth Croft in "The Devil's Pulpit," and at the Player's Theatre, Aug., 1930, played the same part.

MARS, Marjorie, actress; *b.* Hampstead, 31 Jan., 1903; *d.* of Ivon Brown and his wife Maud (Evans); *e.* Convent of the Sacred Heart; *m.* Graeme Muir; made her first appearance on the stage at the Winter Garden Theatre, 18 Sept., 1920, as a Student in "A Night Out"; at the Adelphi, Oct., 1921, played Marie in "The Golden Moth"; Shaftesbury, May, 1923, appeared in "Stop Flirting "; at the Little, Sept., 1924, played Grace Mowbray in " Morals "; in Mar., 1925, toured as Sally Morgan in " The Nervous Wreck "; at the Scala, Sept., 1925, played Lavinda in " Fires Divine "; New Oxford, Dec., 1925, Liz Walker in " Alf's Button "; Queen's, June, 1926, Edna in " Down Hill "; Haymarket, Oct., 1926, succeeded Fay Compton as Jenny Bell in " The White Witch "; Royalty, Oct., 1926, played Mavis Haughton in " The Lash "; Duke of York's, Dec., 1926, Louise in " Liliom "; Lyceum, Mar., 1927, Hélène in " Madame X "; at the King's, Southsea, May, 1927, Honor in " The Zoo "; at the St. Martin's, Sept., 1927, made a distinct success when she played Hester in " The Silver Cord "; May, 1928, played Jill Chitterden in " Four People "; Garrick, Aug., 1928, Mary Frampton in " The Moving Finger "; Arts, Nov., 1928, Fanny in " The Clandestine Marriage "; Duke of York's, Jan., 1929, Sadie Sing in " The Chinese Bungalow "; Apollo, June, 1929, Ann Marvin in " This Thing Called Love"; Fortune, Dec., 1929, Cynthia Perry in "The Last Enemy"; Little, Apr., 1930, Jolanthe in "In-sult"; Queen's, Sept., 1930, Henrietta Moulton-Barrett in "The Barretts of Wimpole Street"; Prince of Wales's (for the Stage Society), Mar., 1931, Blanche in "Widowers' Houses"; Globe, June, 1932, Maureen Elliott in "Ourselves Alone"; "Q," Sept., 1932, Lucy Fane in "All She Wants"; Globe, Nov., 1932, Lois in "For Services Rendered"; Fortune, Sept., 1933, Alicia Deverton in "What Happened Then?"; at the King's, Edinburgh, Oct., 1933, played Marilyn in "No Surrender"; Royalty, Feb., 1934, the Young Whore in "Within the Gates"; Lyceum, May, 1934, Anna Courvin in "King of the Damned"; Criterion, Dec., 1934, Julia Price in "The Ghost Train"; Piccadilly, Jan., 1935, Henrietta in a revival of "The Barretts of Wimpole Street"; Ambassadors', Mar., 1936, Audrey in "Children to Bless You"; Savoy, July, 1936, Precious Stream in "Lady Precious Stream"; Strand, Jan., 1937, Gwen Bingham in "Behind Your Back"; "Q," Oct., 1937, Joey in "Square Pegs"; Shaftesbury, Nov., 1937, Nell

Gwyn in "Thank You, Mr. Pepys"; Saville, Feb., 1938, Mary Clarke in "Welcome Stranger"; "Q," May, 1938, Poppy Watson in "One Way Street"; Saville, June, 1939, Thérèse in "Juggernaut"; Garrick, May, 1940, Dr. Marie Latour in "By Pigeon Post"; "Q," June, 1940, Jill in "House Party"; Vaudeville, Aug., 1941, Ludmilla in "Squaring the Circle," and July, 1942, Yvonne Laroche in "Salt of the Earth"; Granville, Jan., 1946, Vera Kurton in "The Third Visitor"; Prince's, Apr., 1949, Madam Popov in "The Bear"; Drury Lane, June, 1950, Mrs. Mullin in "Carousel"; Her Majesty's, Brighton, Mar., 1953, played Sensuhet in "Westward Journey"; has also appeared in numerous films, and broadcast on radio. *Recreations:* Gardening, tennis, and golf.
(Died 17 Feb., 1915; age 53)

MARSH, Garry, actor; b. St. Margaret's, Richmond, Surrey, 21 May, 1902; s. of George Marsh Gerahty and his wife Laura (Fagg); e. Richmond, Surrey; m. (1) Adèle Lawson (mar. dis.); (2) Muriel Martin-Harvey (mar. dis.); made his first appearance on the stage at the King's Theatre, Southsea, Sept., 1917, in "The Dowry" (a music-hall sketch) with the late John Lawson, with whose company he remained two years, appearing in "Humanity," "The Monkey's Paw," "Disraeli" and "The Little Brother"; subsequently toured in "Belinda" and "Nurse Benson"; made his first appearance in London, at the Duke of York's Theatre, Sept., 1920, succeeding Charles Kenyon as George Edmonston in "Brown Sugar"; at the Ambassadors', Mar., 1921, played Algernon Blancove in "Rhoda Fleming"; at the Lyceum, Oct.–Dec., 1921, played Charles Darnay and St. Evremonde in "The Only Way," and Francis Tresham in "The Breed of the Treshams"; Duke of York's, Jan., 1922, Fred Hammond in "The Nightcap"; Comedy, Mar., 1922, appeared in "The Faithful Heart"; Aldwych, May, 1922, Arthur in "A Prodigal Daughter"; Kingsway, May, 1922, Dickie Cleeve in "Life's a Game"; Apollo, Sept., 1922, Peter Gabel in "The Torch"; went to

Australia, Feb., 1923, and toured there, and in New Zealand, as Mark Sabre in "If Winter Comes," and Paul Jones in "The Cat and the Canary"; reappeared in London, at the Savoy, May, 1924, as Philip Cresswell in "The Lure"; during 1925, toured as Sir Francis Levison in "East Lynne," and Philip Wortley in "Educating a Husband"; toured as Charles in "The Last of Mrs. Cheyney," 1926–7; at the Arts, Dec., 1927, played Don Juan in "Nathaniel Bendersnap"; in 1928, toured in "The High Road"; in 1929, toured as Captain Leslie in "The Squeaker," and 1930 as Garry Anson in "The Calendar"; appeared at the Lyceum, Apr., 1930, in the last-mentioned part; at the Duke of York's, Oct., 1932, played Freddy Petworth in "Cold Blood"; Royalty, May, 1937, President Konrad in "The Good Fairy"; toured, 1938, as George Cave in "Plan for a Hostess"; during the War, served with the R.A.F. from Sept., 1939 to June, 1944; St. Martin's, July, 1952, played Sgt. "Nobby" Clark in "Lion's Corner"; New, Dec., 1952, Sir Michael Anstruther in "Dear Charles"; Duke of York's, May, 1954, Eric Stanford in "The Facts of Life"; Criterion, Dec., 1959, played Mr. Senior in "A Clean Kill"; toured, Jan., 1961, as Admiral Sir Humphrey Lumsden in "The Angry Deep"; Streatham Hill, Sept., 1961, directed "Another Man's Playground"; St. Martin's, Sept., 1962, William Blore in a revival of "Ten Little Niggers"; Richmond, Oct., 1962, played Mike in "Angels on Horseback"; Lyric, July, 1963, Sir Henry Lamphrey in "Windfall"; commenced film career 1929, and has appeared in innumerable films, and on television. *Recreations:* Athletics. *Clubs:* Stage Golfing Society and Brighton Sailing. *Address:* c/o Connie's Ltd., 92 Regent Street, London, W.1.

MARSHALL, Everett, actor and vocalist; *b.* Lawrence, Mass., U.S.A., 31 Dec., 1901; *s.* of Robert Arthur Marshall and his wife Harriet (Benoit); *e.* Grammar School, Cincinatti Conservatory of Music, London, and Milan; *m.* Agnes Cecilia Cassidy; formerly engaged, for some years, in the office of a large engineering firm;

made his first appearance on the stage at Palermo, Italy, Oct., 1926, as the Conte di Luna in "Il Trovatore"; made his first appearance on the New York stage, at the Metropolitan Opera House, 12 Nov., 1927, as the Herald in "Löhengrin," and remained a member of the company until 1931; at the Apollo Theatre, New York, Sept., 1931, appeared in "George White's Scandals"; Casino, Feb., 1933, played Tristan Robillard in "Melody"; Winter Garden, Jan., 1934, appeared in "The Ziegfeld Follies"; at the Hollywood Theatre, Dec., 1934, appeared in "Calling All Stars"; appeared at Fort Worth, Texas, 1936–7, in "Casa Manana"; 46th Street, Dec., 1938, played Schubert in "Blossom Time"; at the New York World's Fair, 1939, played in "Acquacade"; then toured for three years, all over the United States, playing Count Rudolph, Otto, and Max in "Three Waltzes," Schubert in "Blossom Time," and Dr. Engell in "The Student Prince"; at the Broadway Theatre, June, 1943, appeared in the last-mentioned part. *Favourite parts:* Germont in "La Traviata," Scarpia in "La Tosca," and Schubert in "Blossom Time." *Recreations:* Golf, farming, and sailing. *Address:* 1614 York Avenue, New York City, U.S.A. *Telephone No.:* Re 4–6842; or Rockville, Rhode Island, U.S.A.

MARSHALL, Herbert, actor; *b.* London, 23 May, 1890; *s.* of Percy F. Marshall and his wife, Ethel (Turner); *e.* St. Mary's College, Harlow; *m.* (1) Mollie Maitland (mar. dis.); (2) Edna Best (mar. dis.); (3) Lee Russell (mar. dis.); (4) Boots Mallory; was formerly engaged as an articled clerk to a firm of chartered accountants in the City; made his first appearance on the stage in 1911, at the Opera House, Buxton, as a Servant in "The Adventure of Lady Ursula"; made his first appearance on the London stage at the Prince's Theatre, 12 May, 1913, as Tommy in "Brewster's Millions"; subsequently accompanied Cyril Maude on tour in the United States and Canada, playing Ernest Heron in "Grumpy"; served in the Army until 1918; on being demobilized joined the company of the Lyric Opera House, Hammersmith, Dec., 1918, playing the Red Prince, Pirate Bill, etc., in "Make Believe"; Feb., 1919, played Arthur in "The Younger Generation," and Johnson White and Edward Stanton in "Abraham Lincoln"; in Jan., 1920, appeared at the Duke of York's, as Antonio in "The Merchant of Venice"; at the Lyric, Hammersmith, Feb., 1920, played Andrew Ferguson in "John Ferguson"; Apr., 1920, Jaques in "As You Like It"; at the Duke of York's, July, 1920, appeared as Lord Sloane in "Brown Sugar"; at the Comedy, Sept., 1920, as Antony Grimshaw in "The Crossing"; at the Strand, Jan., 1921, as Jim Carthew in "A Safety Match"; at the Garrick, Apr., 1921, as Colin Rossiter in "Count X"; in Aug., 1921, accompanied Marie Löhr on her Canadian and American tour, playing Andrew Fabian in "The Voice from the Minaret," Loris Ipanoff in "Fédora," and Saville in "Her Destiny"; at the Hudson, New York, Jan., 1922, played in "The Voice from the Minaret," and Feb., 1922, in "Fédora"; on his return to London appeared at the Court, Apr., 1922, as Geoffrey March in "Windows"; at the Globe, July, 1922, played John Tremayne in "Belinda"; at the Savoy, Feb., 1923, George Brent in "The Young Idea"; at the Globe, Apr., 1923, the Hon. Willie Tatham in "Aren't We All?"; at the Savoy, Dec., 1923, Laurence Blake in "Paddy the Next Best Thing"; at the Comedy, Jan., 1924, Steve Rolls in "Alice Sit-by-the-Fire"; Mar., 1924, Constantine Tedcastle in "Far Above Rubies"; May, 1924, Christopher Maitland in "This Marriage"; at the Little, Oct., 1924, Dick in "Morals"; at the Ambassadors', Oct., 1924, Marcus Heriot in "The Pelican"; at the Scala (for the Play Actors), Nov., 1924, George Crawford in "Dear Father"; Aldwych, June, 1925, Sir John Verney in "The Verdict"; Comedy, July, 1925, Hayward Clear in "The Lavender Ladies"; then went to New York, and appeared at the Gaiety, Oct., 1925, as Geoffrey Allen in "These Charming People"; returned to London, and at the Globe,

Mar., 1926, played Jim Bathurst in "By-Ways"; June, 1926, Tom Harraway in "Engaged"; St. Martin's, Aug., 1926, Prince Keri in "The Queen Was In The Parlour"; St. James's, Jan., 1927, Philip Voaze in "Interference"; Feb., 1928, Sir Julian Weir in "S.O.S."; New, Apr., 1928, Ronald Luckin in "Come With Me"; again went to New York, and at the Fulton, Sept., 1928, played the Duke of Warrington in "The High Road"; returned to London, and at Golder's Green and Lyric, Apr., 1929, played Jim Hulton in "Paris Bound"; St. Martin's, July, 1929, Hilary Fairfield in a revival of "A Bill of Divorcement"; he then went to the St. James's, where he appeared, Oct., 1929, as Hugh Dawltry in "Heat Wave"; Feb., 1930, as Michael in "Michael and Mary"; and June, 1930, as Prince Albert in "The Swan"; then went to New York, and at the Henry Miller Theatre, Jan., 1931, played Nicholas Hay in "To-Morrow and To-Morrow"; returned to London, and at the Apollo, Oct., 1931, played Dwight Houston in "There's Always Juliet"; again went to New York, and appeared at the Empire, Feb., 1932, in the same part; returned to London, and appeared at the Lyric, Dec., 1932, as Victor Hallam in "Another Language"; then spent six years in films in Hollywood; re-appeared on the regular stage, at Santa Barbara, Cal., July, 1939, when he played Campbell in "Ladies and Gentlemen," with Helen Hayes; commenced film career, 1927, in "Mumsie," and has appeared in the leading parts in innumerable pictures. *Clubs:* Green Room and Garrick, London; Players, New York. *(Died 22 Jan., 1966; age 75)*

MARSHALL, Tully, actor and stage director; *b.* Nevada City, Cal., 13 Apr., 1864; *s.* of William L. Phillips and his wife Julia Mattie (Tully); *e.* Nevada and Santa Rosa; *m.* Marion Fairfax; made his first appearance on the stage, when a child, in 1869; made his grown-up *début*, in San Francisco, at the Winter Garden, as Fred Carter in "Saratoga," 12 Mar., 1883; fulfilled engagements with Dion Boucicault,

Mdme. Modjeska, E. H. Sothern, etc. ; has figured successfully in America in " Held by the Enemy," " Because She Loved Him So," " Hearts are Trumps," " To Have and to Hold," " The Best of Friends," " The Other Girl," " The Little Princess," " Just Out of College," " The Stolen Story," " Paid in Full " (as Joe Brooks), " The Builders " (as Herbert Grant), " The City " (as George Frederick Hannock) ; and " The Talker," written by his wife, Marion Fairfax ; " The Trap " (as Martin), " The Girl and the Pennant " (as John Bohannan) ; in 1914 succeeded Robert Edeson on tour as Bob Reynolds in " Fine Feathers " ; since 1915 has confined his activities to the cinema stage, and has appeared in innumerable films ; since 1936, has appeared in " A Tale of Two Cities," "A Yank at Oxford," "Souls at Sea," "Stand-In," "Arséne Lupin Returns," "College Swing," "The Kid from Texas," etc. *Club:* Writers.
(Died 9 Mar., 1943; age 78)

MARSON, Aileen, actress ; *b.* Alexandria, Egypt, 13 Sept., 1912 ; *d.* of the Rev. Arthur Pitt-Marson and his wife Amélie Schroëder ; *e.* privately in Egypt and Roumania, and three years at North London Collegiate School ; studied for the stage at the Royal Academy of Dramatic Art ; made her first appearance on the stage at the "Q" Theatre, Kew, Dec., 1932, as Mary in " The Third Degree " ; in Feb., 1933, played a season of repertory at the Theatre Royal, Bournemouth ; toured in South Africa, May-Sept., 1933, as Manuela in " Children in Uniform," and Gracie Abbott in "From Nine Till Six," with Leontine Sagan ; made her first appearance in the West-End, at the Ambassadors' Theatre, 21 Nov., 1933, as Mattea in "Cabbages and Kings "; Haymarket Jan., 1934, succeeded Jessica Tandy as Betty Findon in "Ten Minute Alibi "; St. Martin's, Dec., 1934, for a time, succeeded Celia Johnson as Anne Hargraves in " The Wind and the Rain "; Westminster, Feb., 1935, played Polly in " They Do These Things in France "; Garrick, Nov., 1935, Vicky in " Vicky," produced

under her own management ; has appeared in films since 1934, in " Lucky Loser," " Passing Shadows," " My Song for You," " The Green Pack," " The Way of Youth," " Road House," "Ten Minute Alibi," " Honeymoon for Three," " Black Mask," " Living Dangerously," etc. *Address:* 36 Charles Square, London, W.10. *Telephone No.:* Park 5986.

MARTHOLD, Jules de, French dramatic author ; *b.* Paris, 1842 ; has written the following plays : " Les Amants de Ferrara," 1880 ; " Pascal Fargean," 1881 ; " Henry VIII," 1883 ; " Cain," 1885 ; " Le Juge d'Instruction," 1888 ; " Esther à Saint-Cyr," 1889 ; " L'Ogre," 1890 ; " Neiges d'Antan," 1894 ; " La Grande Blonde," 1894 ; " Camille Fauvel," 1896 ; " Pierrot Municipal," 1896 ; " Les Faux Dieux," 1898 ; " Le Coupable," 1899 ; " Eline de Rouen," 1905. *(Died May, 1927; age 80)*

MARTIN, Edie, actress ; *b.* London, 1 Jan., 1880 ; *d.* of David Rubans Martin and his wife Laura Susannah (Robinson) ; *e.* London ; *m.* Felix William Pitt (dec.) ; made her first appearance on the stage at the Prince of Wales's Theatre, 26 Dec., 1886, as a Glow-worm and an Oyster in " Alice in Wonderland "; Royalty, Apr. 1887, played in "Ivy," and at the Court, Dec., 1888, Cupid in "Little Goody Two-shoes "; continued as a child-actress for many years, touring, playing in "stock" companies and in pantomime; continued touring almost continuously until 1904 ; played "stock" seasons at the Elephant and Castle Theatre, 1905 ; in 1906, toured as Dick in "Two Little Vagabonds"; from 1909-13, toured in Robert Macdonald's musical-comedy companies; Aldwych, May, 1915, played Eliza in "The Dairymaids"; Criterion, July, 1920, Gladys in "Lord Richard in the Pantry," subsequently touring in the same part; from 1924-7, played in repertory; during 1929, toured as Mrs. Hackett in "The Ringer"; Drury Lane, Oct., 1931, Mrs. Snapper in "Cavalcade"; Palace, Jan., 1933, Miss Copeland in "Dinner at Eight";

Embassy, Nov., 1933, Aunt Branwell in "The Brontës of Haworth Parsonage"; Piccadilly, Apr., 1934, Lena Simon in "Counsellor-at-Law"; Duke of York's, Apr., 1935, Mrs. Read in ". . . And a Woman Passed By"; St. Martin's, Feb., 1936, Bunty in "No Exit"; Strand, July, 1937, Mrs. Cake in "A Spot of Bother"; Richmond, May, 1938, Ada Tinkler in "Time Gentlemen, Please!"; Saville, Feb., 1939, Mrs. Medlock in "Worth a Million"; toured, Sept., 1940, as Flo in "Divorce for Chrystabel"; Savoy, Dec., 1941, played Harriet Stanley in "The Man Who Came to Dinner," which she continued to play until Aug., 1943, subsequently touring in the same part; "Q," Nov., 1948, Mrs. Doyle in "For Better, for Worse"; Lyric, Hammersmith, Mar., 1949, Mrs. Bergen in "Dark of the Moon," appearing in the same part at the Ambassadors', Apr., 1949; Embassy, and Playhouse, Aug., 1949, Grandma Lester in "Tobacco Road"; Embassy, Oct., 1950, played Mrs. Burnaby in "Surfeit of Lampreys"; Royal, Brighton, Oct., 1951, played Mme. Georges in "Colombe"; at the "Q," Oct., 1953, Miss Pearce in "One Fair Daughter"; entered films, 1932, and has appeared in innumerable pictures: has also appeared on television, and broadcast on radio. (*Died 23 Feb., 1964; age 84*)

MARTIN, Vivian (Louise), actress; *b.* near Grand Rapids, Mich., U.S.A., 22 July, 1893; *m.* (1) William Jefferson; (2) Arthur Samuels; made her first appearance on the stage, as a child; subsequently she appeared in children's parts with Andrew Mack, and later she toured as " Peter Pan "; subsequently appeared as Frances in " The Spendthrift "; at the Gaiety, New York, Oct., 1911, played Gertrude Brainerd in " The Only Son "; Jan., 1912, Sadie Small in " Officer 666 "; Dec., 1912, Joan Carr in " Stop Thief "; Comedy, Oct., 1913, Racie Updegraff in " The Marriage Game "; Republic, Aug., 1914, Cora in " The High Cost of Living "; subsequently turned her attention to the cinema stage, and during 1916-17 was seen in " The Girl from Home," " Giving Becky a Chance," " Little Miss Optimist," " The Sunset Trail," " The Trouble Buster," "Molly Entangled," "The Fair Barbarian," "Miss Nancy," "Her Father's Son," "The Right Direction," "The Stronger Love," etc.; for a time managed her own company, "Vivian Martin Productions"; during the past few years she has been seen on the regular stage, at the Comedy, New York, Apr., 1921, as Roberta Adams in " Just Married," in which she played over two years; at the Frazee, Dec., 1923, played Agatha Westcott in " The Wild Westcotts "; made her first appearance on the London stage, at the Comedy Theatre, 15 Dec., 1924, as Roberta Adams in " Just Married "; on returning to America, toured Keith vaudeville circuit, 1925, in " Just Married," with Donald Brian; at the Forty-eighth Street Theatre, New York, Jan., 1926, played Jean Brent in " Puppy Love "; Morosco, Apr., 1927, Arlette Millois in " Hearts Are Trumps "; Waldorf, Sept., 1927, Antoinette in " Half-a-Widow "; Mansfield, Dec., 1927, Jean Farquhar in " Caste "; Cosmopolitan, Feb., 1928, Janet Colquhoun in " Mrs. Dane's Defence," and Alice Faulkner in " Sherlock Holmes "; Fulton, Apr., 1929, Mollie Jefferies in " Marry the Man ! "

MARTIN-HARVEY, Sir John (*see* Harvey, Sir John Martin-).

MARTIN-HARVEY, Muriel, actress; *b.* London, 6 Oct., 1891; *d.* of Sir John Martin-Harvey and his wife Nina (de Silva); *m.* Ronald Squire (mar. dis.); (2) Garry Marsh (mar. dis.); (3) Anthony Gordon; made her first appearance on the stage at the Lyceum Theatre, 11 July, 1911, as a Servant in " Pelleas and Melisande "; was then seen at the Comedy Theatre, 1 Feb., 1912, as Lady Majorie Hillborn in " The Bear Leaders "; at the Queen's Theatre, Dec., 1912, played Maisie Bretherton in " The Tide "; at the Vaudeville, Feb., 1913, played Dinah in " The Schoolmistress "; at the Prince of Wales's, June, 1913, played Vivian in " The Faun," in her father's company; at the Duke of York's, Sept., 1913, played Henrietta

Turnbull, in " Quality Street " ; at the Prince of Wales's, Dec., 1914, Kitty Verdun in " Charley's Aunt " ; at the Duke of York's, Oct., 1915, Suzette in " Romance " ; in 1916 went to America with Mr. Cyril Maude, and at the Empire, Syracuse, Oct., 1916, played in " Jeff " ; at the Empire, New York, Oct., 1916, played Diana Terlbot in " The Basker," and subsequently played Virginia Bullivant in " Grumpy " ; after returning to England appeared at the St. Martin's Theatre, Feb., 1919, as Just Susan in " A Certain Liveliness " ; at the Palace, Westcliff-on-Sea, May, 1919, played Skittles in the play of that name ; subsequently accompanied Mr. Percy Hutchison to America, and at the Manhattan Opera House, New York, Oct., 1919, played Cynthia in " The Luck of the Navy " ; also touring in Canada, in the same part ; at the Harris Theatre, New York, May, 1920, played Clara Warrington in " The Respect for Riches " ; at the Booth Theatre, Aug., 1920, Tilly in " Happy-Go-Lucky " (" Tilly of Bloomsbury ") ; at the Playhouse, London, Sept., 1921, played Helen Regan in " The Sign on the Door " ; in 1923 toured in Australia as Lady Tybar in " If Winter Comes " ; during 1924 toured in England in " When My Ship Comes Home " ; during 1925 toured as Suzanne in " East Lynne," and Rosemary in " Educating a Husband " ; Ambassadors', Dec., 1927, played Ruth Jordon in " 9.45 " ; during 1928 toured as Elsie Hilary in " The High Road " ; Embassy, Nov., 1928, played Lydia in " The Perfect Wife " ; Shaftesbury, Dec., 1928, Pauline Grant in " The Lad " ; Embassy, Apr., 1929, Belinda Treherne in " Engaged " ; subsequently toured as Alice Jarvis in " Blackmail " ; in July, 1930, toured as Hetty in Wild-Cat Hetty" ; Savoy, Oct., 1930, played Julie in " The Lyons Mail" ; Phoenix, Nov., 1931, The Maid in " Little Catherine" ; during 1933, toured as Leonora Yale in " The Green Bay Tree" ; Feb., 1934, toured as Mrs. Stuyvesant in " The Man Who Was Fed Up" ; in Aug., 1934, toured as Sybil Kingdom in " The Old Folks at Home," and Nov., 1934, as Maureen in " Man in Hiding" ; in Mar., 1935,

played a season of repertory at the Pleasure Gardens, Folkestone ; " Q," June, 1935, Norah Hamilton in " Parody for Living" ; in Aug., 1935, toured as Helena Warwick in " Family Affairs" ; Arts, Oct., 1936, Violet Ballantyne in " The Champblays" ; toured, 1938, as Mrs. Ruddle in " Busman's Honeymoon" ; in Jan., 1939, appeared with the Brighton Repertory Company.

MARTINETTI, Paul, pantomimist ; *b*. 22 June, 1851 ; is descended from a famous family of mimes, his father, grandfather, and great-grandfather having been prominently engaged in the same profession ; made his first appearance on the stage in America, when only six years of age ; made his first appearance in England, at the Princess's Theatre, under the management of F. B. Chatterton, 30 Sept., 1876, when he appeared in " The Magic Flute," subsequently appearing there in " Jocko " ; in Feb., 1877, at the same theatre, appeared for the first time in his famous impersonation of Jacques Strop in " Robert Macaire" ; made his first appearance on the music-hall stage, at Lusby's Music Hall, Mile End, 2 Apr., 1877, in " The Magic Flute " ; then appeared at the South London and other halls, in various comic ballets ; for many years his troupe of pantomimists was one of the greatest attractions on the variety stage, and they appeared at all the leading halls all over the kingdom ; other productions with which they secured enormous success were " A Terrible Night " ; " The Duel in the Snow " ; " The Remorse " ; " After the Ball " ; " Paris Night by Night " ; " The Village Schoolmaster," etc. *Address :* 1 King Edward's Mansions, Shaftesbury Avenue, W.C.

MARTINOT, Sadie, actress and vocalist ; *b*. New York, 19 Dec., 1861 ; *d*. of Mary Lydia (Randall) and William Alexander Martinot ; *e*. at Ursuline Convent, Westchester, Co. New York ; *m*. Louis F. Nethersole ; made her first appearance on the stage at the Eagle Theatre, New York, 21 Aug., 1876, when she appeared as Cupid in a revival of " Ixion " ; same theatre, 23 Jan., 1877, she appeared as Benika in " Across the Continent " ; and 26 Jan., 1877, played in " Ben McCullough " ; she then went to the Boston Museum, where she remained some years ; at this theatre, on 25 Nov., 1878, she was the " original " American Hebe in " H.M.S. Pinafore "; and in 1879 played Emma Willner in " My Son " ; subsequently she played leading " soubrette " parts at this theatre ; she made her first appearance on the London stage, at the Alhambra, 26 Dec., 1880, as the Spirit of the Brocken in " Mefistofele II " ; same theatre, 28 Mar., 1881, she appeared as Celine in the opera of " Jeanne, Jeannette, and Jeanneton " ; at the Comedy Theatre, 14 Oct., 1882, first performance of the opera of " Rip Van Winkle," she appeared as Katrina ; on her return to America she was engaged by the late Dion Boucicault, and at the opening of the Star Theatre, New York, 26 Mar., 1883, appeared as Mrs. Clingstone Peach in " Vice-Versâ " ; during Apr. and May of the same year appeared there as Moya in " The Shaughraun," Dora in " The Omadhaun," and Eily O'Connor in " The Colleen Bawn " ; at Stetson's Fifth Avenue Theatre, in 1884, appeared as Portia in " Distinguished Foreigners," Pauline in " Delicate Ground," and Rose Mumpleford in " Confusion " ; at the Union Square Theatre, 18 Aug., 1884, she played Florence in " Queena," and at the Lyceum Theatre, 7 Apr., 1885, appeared as Sophie in " Dakolar " ; at the Casino Theatre, 29 June, 1885, played Nanon Patin in the opera of " Nanon," and shortly afterwards temporarily disappeared from the stage ; she made her re-appearance at the Garden Theatre, New York, 27 Sept., 1890, as Lois in " Sunset " and Mrs. Horton in " Dr. Bill " ; during 1892 she played " Camille," " Frou-Frou," and " Madame Pompadour " ; at the Star Theatre, 24 Oct., 1892, appeared as Dora in " Diplomacy," and at the American Theatre, 2 Dec., 1893, played Suzette in " The Voyage of Suzette " ; at the Bijou Theatre,

13 May, 1895, appeared as Mrs. D'Arcy in " My Official Wife " (" The Passport "), and at Herald Square, 13 July, 1896, as Lady Angela in " Patience " ; at the Garrick, 13 Sept., 1897, played Hattie in " A Stranger in New York," and at the Manhattan, 3 Sept., 1898, Leonie in " The Turtle " ; at the Victoria, Dec., 1901, played in " The Marriage Game," and in 1903 was touring as Paula in " The Second Mrs. Tanqueray " and Stella de Gex in " His Excellency the Governor " ; in 1904 played in " Winning a Widow " at various " vaudeville " houses ; at Boston, 13 Mar., 1905, appeared in " Piff-Paff-Pouf," and at the Manhattan, New York, 11 Sept., 1905, was Mary Erwin in " Mary and John " ; during 1906 was touring as Mrs. Temple in " Mrs. Temple's Telegram " ; at the Savoy, Mar., 1908, played Lady Dover in " Toddles."

(Died 7 May, 1923; age 61)

MARTLEW, Mary, actress ; *b.* Atherton, Manchester, 8 Aug., 1919; *d.* of Richard Sydney Greenhalgh and his wife Edna (Garnett-Pickles) ; *e.* Brentwood, Southport, and La Casita, Lausanne ; studied for the stage under Elsie Leivesley, of Southport, Royal Academy of Dramatic Art, and London Academy of Music ; made her first appearance on the stage at the "Q" Theatre, 19 Apr., 1937, as Diana Morley in "The Second Shot"; Arts, June, 1937, played Sylvia Warner in "In the Best Families," and July, 1938, Sylvia in " . . . and Life Burns On"; Arts and Haymarket, Oct., 1938, Pamela Sutton in "A Party for Christmas"; Adelphi, Nov., 1938, Celia in "As You Like It"; "Q," Aug., 1939, Frances Sewell in "The Fanatics"; Tavistock Little, Jan., 1940, Lady Flora in "The Widow of Windsor"; she then joined the Altrincham, Manchester, Repertory company and played leading parts there, 1940–1; "Q," Nov., 1941, and Westminster, Mar., 1942, appeared as Kathrin Corvin in "School for Slavery"; at the Open Air Theatre, July-Aug., 1942, played Viola in "Twelfth Night," Helena in "A Midsummer

Night's Dream," and Katherine in "The Taming of the Shrew"; St. Martin's, Sept., 1942, Julia Naughton in "Claudia," which ran over a year; Palace, Oct., 1944, played Roberta Chase in "Something in the Air"; toured, 1945, in Gibraltar, Malta, North Africa, and Italy, in a *revue* company, with Cicely Courtneidge; St. Martin's, Nov., 1945, Stella Tabret in "The Sacred Flame," subsequently transferred to the Westminster; "Q," June, 1946, played Joyce Gunning in "Through the Door"; appeared in various plays at the "Q" and Embassy, 1946–7; St. James's, Oct., 1947, played Lady Harkalong in "The Man in the Street"; Comedy, Jan., 1948, Noel in "Mountain Air"; at the New, with the Old Vic Company, Oct.–Nov., 1948, appeared as Mrs. Fainall in "The Way of the World," Varya in "The Cherry Orchard." *Favourite parts :* Viola, Millamant in "The Way of the World," and Charlotte Brontë. *Recreations :* Reading and riding. *Hobbies :* Collecting unusual antique jewellery and furniture, and visiting old churches. *Address :* Green Hall, Atherton, Manchester. *Telephone No. :* Atherton 92.

MARVENGA, Ilse (*née* Marling); actress and vocalist; *b.* Bremen, Germany; studied music at Bremen and made her first appearance on the stage there, at the Municipal Opera House; subsequently toured in Germany, Austria, and France; made her first appearance in America in 1922 ; first appeared on the New York stage, at the Jolson Theatre, 2 Dec., 1924, when she played Kathie in "The Student Prince"; made her first appearance in London, at His Majesty's Theatre, 3 Feb., 1926, in the same part; played Kathie nearly 1,300 times; in 1928, toured with her own company in "Nobody's Girl"; at the Jolson Theatre, New York, Oct., 1929, played Marietta in "Naughty Marietta"; during 1930, toured in "vaudeville," on the Radio-Keith-Orpheum Circuit; at Erlanger's Theatre, New York, Nov., 1931, again played Marietta, and also appeared as Nina in "The Firefly"; George M. Cohan Theatre, May, 1932, played Carolita Rodriguez in "There You

Are"; Waldorf, Oct., 1932, Ethel Warren in the revival of "The Great Lover"; toured, 1936, as Marietta in "Naughty Marietta"; toured, 1936–7, as Marie in "May Wine."

MARY, Jules, French dramatic author and novelist; *b.* Launois-sur-Vence, Ardennes, 20 Mar., 1851 ; *e.* Charleville ; *m.* Gabrielle Mesnier ; has written the following plays : "Les Dernières Cartouches," "Roger La Honte " (" A Man's Shadow," with Georges Grisier), 1888 ; "Le Régiment " (with Grisier), 1890 ; "Maître d'Armes " (" The Swordsman's Daughter," with Grisier), "Fée Printemps," 1894 ; " Sabre au Clair ! " 1896 ; "La Pocharde," 1898 ; " La Mioche," 1899 ; " Le Chanson du Pays," 1901 ; " Roule-Ta-Bosse " (with E. Rochard), 1906 ; " Le Beauté du diable " (with E. Rochard), 1908 ; " La Bête féroce," 1908 ; " L'Enfant de fortifs," 1911 ; " La Gueuse," 1911 ; is also the author of nearly fifty novels ; is an Officer of the Legion of Honour and a member of the Societies of Men of Letters and Dramatic Authors. *Recreations :* Hunting, tennis, fencing, and canoeing. (*Died July, 1922; age 71*)

MASCHWITZ, Eric, O.B.E., dramatic author; *b.* Birmingham, 10 June, 1901 ; *s.* of Albert Arthur Maschwitz and his wife Leontine Hilda (Boekmann); *e.* Repton School, Gonville, and Caius College, Cambridge; *m.* (1) Hermione Gingold (mar. dis.); (2) Phyllis Gordon; was formerly editor of *The Radio Times,* 1927–33 ; Variety Director of the B.B.C., 1933–7 ; during the War, served with the Intelligence Corps, 1940–5 (Lt.-Colonel); intelligence mission to N. and S. America, 1941–2 ; story-editor of "The True Glory," the official D-day film, 1944 ; Chief Broadcasting Officer, 21 Army Group, 1945 ; Head of Light Entertainment, B.B.C. Television, 1958 ; appointed Executive Producer of Rediffusion Television, 1963 ; is the author of the following plays and musical productions: "The Double Man" (with Val Gielgud), 1930 ; "The Gay Hussar," 1933 ; "Spread It Abroad" (with Herbert Farjeon), "Balalaika," 1936 ;

"Paprika," 1938; rewritten with Fred Thompson and Guy Bolton as "Magyar Melody," 1939; "New Faces," 1940; "Waltz Without End," 1942; "Flying Colours" (with Ronald Jeans), 1943; contributed to the *revue* "Between Ourselves," 1946; lyrics for "Starlight Roof," 1947; author of "Carissima," 1948; "Belinda Fair" (with Gilbert Lennox), 1949; "Zip Goes a Million," 1951; "Love From Judy" (adaptation), 1952; "Thirteen for Dinner" (adaptation), 1953; "Pink Champagne," "Happy Holiday" (with Arnold Ridley), 1954; "Romance in Candlelight," "Summer Song" (with Hy Kraft), 1955; author of many screen plays; has written several well-known songs for films; author of the novels "A Taste of Honey," "Angry Dust," "Husks in May," "The Passionate Clowns," "Death at Broadcasting House," "Death as an Extra," "Death in Budapest," "Under London" (with Val Gielgud); "The First Television Murder" (with Gielgud); received O.B.E., 1936. *Club:* Savile.
(Died 27 Oct., 1969; age 68)

MASEFIELD, John, O.M., C.Lit., Poet Laureate, dramatic author; *b.* Ledbury, Herefordshire, 1 June, 1878; *m.* Constance de la Cherois-Crommelin (dec.); at the age of 13 joined the, training ship "Conway"; subsequently joined the Merchant Navy, in which he remained until 1895; returned to England, 1897, and for a time, was engaged as a journalist on *The Manchester Guardian*, and other papers; has written the following plays: "The Campden Wonder," 1907; "Nan," 1908; "Pompey the Great," 1910; "Philip the King," 1914; "The Faithful," 1915; "The Locked Chest," "The Sweeps of '98," 1916; "Good Friday," 1917; "Melloney Holtspur," 1923; "The Trial of Jesus," 1926; "Tristan and Isolt," 1927; "The Coming of Christ," "A King's Daughter," 1928; "The Empress of Rome," an adaptation of a French Miracle play, 1937; President of the Incorporated Society of Authors, Playwrights and Composers, since 1937; was awarded the Hanseatic Shakespeare Prize, Ham-

burg University, Oct., 1938; is an Honorary Doctor of various universities; created Poet Laureate, 1930; received the Order of Merit, in the Birthday Honours, 1935; created Companion of the Royal Society of Literature, 1961.
(Died 12 May, 1967; age 88)

MASKELYNE, John Nevil, entertainer and illusionist; *b.* Cheltenham, 22 Dec., 1839; *s.* of John Nevil Maskelyne; as an amateur gave frequent conjuring entertainments; made his first professional appearance, in conjunction with his late colleague, George Cooke, at Cheltenham in 1865, with an exposition of the tricks and illusions of the famous Davenport Brothers; subsequently appeared at the Crystal Palace; opened their famous entertainment at the old St. James's Hall, Apr., 1873; in May, 1873, appeared at the Egyptian Hall, which subsequently became known as " The Home of Mystery "; remained there until the end of 1904; on the death of Mr. Cooke he was joined in the management of the entertainment by David Devant, and in Jan., 1905, they opened at the St. George's Hall; this partnership lasted until 1915; has produced an enormous number of illusions, mostly introduced through the media of sketches written round them. *Address :* St. George's Hall, Langham Place, W. *Telephone No.:* Mayfair 2482.

MASON, Alfred Edward Woodley, dramatic author and novelist; *b.* 7 May, 1865; *s.* of the late William Woodley Mason, Dulwich; *e.* Dulwich College and Trinity College, Oxford; was formerly an actor 1888-94; has written the following plays : " Blanche de Maletroit " (on Stevenson's Story), 1894; " The Courtship of Morrice Buckler " (with Miss Isabel Bateman), 1897; " Marjory Strode," 1908; " Colonel Smith," 1909; " The Princess Clementina " (with George Pleydell), 1910; " The Witness for the Defence," 1911; " Open Windows," 1913; " At the Villa Rose," 1920; " Running Water," 1922; " The House of the Arrow," 1928: " No

Other Tiger," 1929; "A Present from Margate" (with Ian Hay), 1933; is also the author of the following, among other books: "A Romance of Wastdale," "The Courtship of Morrice Buckler," "The Philanderers," "Lawrence Clavering," "Parson Kelly" (with Andrew Lang), "Miranda of the Balcony," "The Watchers," "Clementina," "The Four Feathers," "The Broken Road," "The Summons," "At the Villa Rose," "The Truants," "Running Water," "Ensign Knightley," "From the Four Corners of the World," "The Turnstile," "The Winding Stair," "The House of the Arrow," etc.; wrote the biography of "Sir George Alexander," 1935; was Member of Parliament for Coventry (1906); served in the Intelligence Department of the Admiralty, abroad, from 1914–18; was gazetted Captain, 1914; Major, 1916; Naval Attaché to Mexico, 1918. *Clubs:* Garrick, Alpine, and Royal Highland Yacht.
(Died 22 Nov., 1948; age 83)

MASON, Elliot C., actress; *b.* Glasgow, Scotland; *d.* of George Mason and his wife Mary (Cranston); *e.* Glasgow, Paris, and in Germany; commenced her career as a student with the Scottish National Players at Glasgow, 1919; made her first appearance professionally, with this company, at the Alhambra, Glasgow, 1922, as Mrs. Haggerty in "The Old Lady Shows her Medals"; appeared at Balmoral Castle, with this company, by Royal Command, Oct., 1922, as Maggie Jamieson in "A Valuable Rival"; made her first appearance in London at the Coliseum, 1 Jan., 1923, in the same part; remained with the Scottish Players for ten years; at the Westminster Theatre, Nov., 1932, played Kate Anderson in "Follow Me"; Arts, Feb., and Westminster, Mar., 1933, Lady Kerton in "The Lake," and made her first appearance in New York at the Martin Beck Theatre, 26 Dec., 1933, in the same part; Haymarket, London, May, 1934, played Annie McCrossan in "Touch Wood"; Comedy, Feb., 1935, Elizabeth Kemp-Walton in "Mrs. Nobby

Clark"; Globe, June, 1935, Nanny in "Grief Goes Over"; Embassy, Jan., 1936, Bunty in "No Exit"; Booth, New York, Mar. 1936, Esther Warren in "Sweet Aloes"; Queen's, London, May, 1937, Georgina Dell in "He Was Born Gay"; Globe, Oct., 1937, Miss Plumby in "Blondie White"; Phoenix Dec., 1937, the Queen in "A Kiss for Cinderella"; Embassy, Apr. 1938, Lucy Baggot in "Good and Proper"; Strand, Feb., 1939, Miss Philpott in "Little Ladyship"; Aldwych, Jan., 1940, Emma Pearson in "As You Are"; Apollo, Feb., 1940, and Globe, June, 1941, Mrs. Lothian in "The Light of Heart"; Globe, Dec., 1941, Mrs. Parrilow in "The Morning Star"; toured in the Middle East, 1944, with Emlyn Williams, in "Night Must Fall," "Flare Path," "Blithe Spirit," and "The Druid's Rest"; St. James's, Dec., 1944, played the Stepmother in "The Glass Slipper"; toured, May, 1945, and at the Winter Garden, Sept., 1945, as the elder Mrs. Barrington in "Young Mrs. Barrington"; Embassy, May, 1946, played Janet Proctor in "Guest in the House"; entered films, 1935, and has appeared in numerous pictures. *Recreations:* Golf and swimming.
(Died 20 June, 1949; age 52)

MASON, Gladys, actress; *b.* London, 9 Mar., 1886; *d.* of H. W. Mason; *e.* South Hampstead High School and Düsseldorf; *m.* Cecil Humphreys; made her first appearance on the stage at the Haymarket Theatre, 1 June, 1905, as Miss Munkittrick in "The Cabinet Minister"; played in "The Duffer" and "My Cousin Marco" with Weedon Grossmith, 1905; "The Lady Burglar" and "The New Clown," at Terry's, with James Welch, 1906; toured as Lady Clarice Howland in "The Fascinating Mr. Vanderveldt" and Lady Alethea in "The Walls of Jericho"; at the Playhouse, 1908, appeared as Madame de Chambry in "Toddles"; took part in the Chelsea Pageant, 1908, as Nell Gwyn; at the Queen's, Sept., 1908, played Lila Hake in "The Old Firm"; at the New Theatre Oct., 1908, played Pamela Gray in "Bellamy the Magnificent"; at the

Adelphi, Apr., 1909, appeared as Yvonne de Nerval in "The Devil"; at Wyndham's, Oct., 1909, played Sybil Craven in "The Little Damozel"; at the Coronet, Nov., 1910, appeared as Blanche Giberne and Gabrielle in "Behind the Veil"; at the Haymarket, Dec., 1910, played Light in "The Blue Bird"; at the Queen's, Mar., 1911, played the Princess Clementina in the play of that name; subsequently toured in the title-*rôle* of "Princess Clementina," Ophelia in "Hamlet," and Mrs. Jekyll in "Dr. Jekyll and Mr. Hyde," with H. B. Irving; at the Court, Nov., 1911, played Jessie in "The Hartley Family"; at the Whitney (now Strand) Theatre, Feb., 1912, played Lady Flashington in "A Member of Tattersall's"; at the King's, Hammersmith, Sept., 1912, appeared as Emily Rhead in "Milestones," and crossing to the United States, appeared at the Liberty Theatre, New York, Sept., 1912, in the same part; at the Criterion, Jan., 1913, played Mrs. Benjamin Gameboys in "Billy's Fortune"; in May, 1913, went to South Africa, where she played Peggy Admaston in "The Butterfly on the Wheel"; Emily Rhead in "Milestones"; Fanny Jasper in "Get-Rich-Quick Wallingford"; and Grace Tyler in "Ready Money"; in Oct., 1914, toured in the United States as Margaret Knox in "Fanny's First Play"; at Drury Lane, Apr., 1915, played Lady Felicia Gaveston in "Sealed Orders"; at the Vaudeville, July, 1915, Lady Margery in "Enterprising Helen"; at the Lyceum, Feb., 1917, appeared as Constance Morel in "Seven Days' Leave"; Oct., 1918, as Grace Pearson in "The Female Hun"; at the Playhouse, Mar., 1921, as Grace Merrion in "Love?!"; at the Royalty, Feb., 1922, played Mrs. Flora Preston in "Enter Madame!"; in July, 1922, went to Australia with Oscar Asche as leading lady, playing Zahrat-al-Kulub in "Chu-Chin-Chow," Shatazad in "Cairo," and Portia in "Julius Caesar"; the tour lasted until Sept., 1923; at the Royalty, London, June, 1924, played Betty Lonimer in "Bachelor Husbands"; in the spring of 1926, toured in the United States with

Frances Starr in "The Best of Us"; at the Little, June, 1932, played Maggie in "Intimate Relations"; has also appeared in numerous films. *Address:* Mapleton House, W.1. *Telephone No.:* Whitehall 4033.

MASON, Herbert, producer; is a nephew of the late Edward Terry; *m.* Daisy Fisher; was formerly an actor and was a member of the Compton Comedy company and F. R. Benson's Company; was subsequently stage-manager for Pélissier's "Follies," at the Palace Theatre, 1913–14; served in the Army, in the Machine Gun Corps, 1914–18; decorated with the M.C., 1916; demobilized with the permanent rank of Major; was stage-manager of the Gaiety Theatre, 1919–20; London Pavilion, 1921–22; produced "Snap!" 1922; "Rats!" 1922; "Yes!" 1923; "The Punch Bowl," 1924; "The Cave Man," 1927; of late years has been engaged in the production of films; since 1936, has directed the production of "East Meets West"; "His Lordship," "First Offence," "The Silent Battle," "Take My Tip," "Strange Boarders," etc. *Address:* 45 Hodford Road, N.W.11. *Telephone No.:* Speedwell 5232.

MASON, James, actor; *b.* Huddersfield, Yorks., 15 May, 1909; *s.* of John Mason and his wife Mabel Hattersley (Gaunt); *e.* Marlborough College and Peterhouse College, Cambridge; *m.* Pamela Kellino (mar. dis.); was intended to follow the profession of an architect; made his first appearance on the stage at the Theatre Royal, Aldershot, 23 Nov., 1931, as Prince Ivan in "The Rascal"; made his first appearance in London at the Arts Theatre, 30 Apr., 1933, as Oliver Brown in "Gallows Glorious," playing the same part at the Shaftesbury, May 1933; joined the company of the Old Vic.-Sadler's Wells, Sept. 1933, and during the season played Valentine in "Twelfth Night," Yash in "The Cherry Orchard," Cromwell in "Henry VIII," Claudio in "Measure for Measure," Jeremy in "Love for Love," etc.; New Theatre, June 1934 played the Earl of Arran and Paris in "Queen of Scots"; played with the Dublin Gate Theatre company 1934–7; Gate, London, Apr. 1936, Captain O'Shea in "Parnell"; Embassy and Savoy, Mar. 1937, Hannibal in "The Road to Rome"; "Q," June 1937, Antoine in "A Man Who Has Nothing"; New, Sept. 1937, Christopher Carson in "Bonnet Over The Windmill"; Gate, Nov. 1938, Byron in "The Heart Was Not Burned"; St. James's, May, 1939, Henri Jouval in "Sixth Floor"; toured, Sept., 1940, as John Garside in "Divorce for Chrystabel"; New Theatre, Oct., 1941, played Paul Venner in "Jupiter Laughs"; first appeared on the New York stage at the Ethel Barrymore, 26 Mar., 1947, as David in "Bathsheba"; at the Shakespearean Festival, Stratford, Ontario, 1954, appeared as Angelo in "Measure for Measure," and Œdipus in "Œdipus Rex"; Playhouse, La Jolla, California, July, 1957, Constantine Chase in "Paul and Constantine"; Playhouse, Ivoryton, Connecticut, July, 1958, starred in "Mid-Summer"; author, with his wife, of a book "The Cats in Our Lives," for which he also supplied the drawings, 1949, and "Favourite Cat Stories of James and Pamela Mason," 1957; entered films, 1935, in "Late Extra," and notable films in which he has appeared include: "Fanny By Gaslight," "The Seventh Veil," "The Wicked Lady," "East Side, West Side," "Botany Bay," "The Desert Rats," "Julius Caesar," "The Trials of Oscar Wilde," "The Fall of the Roman Empire," and "The Pumpkin Eater"; was the winner of *The Daily Mail* award for the most popular male film-artist, 1946 and 1947. *Address:* c/o Al. Parker, 50 Mount Street, Park Lane, London, W.1. *Telephone No.:* Grosvenor 3080.

MASON, John B., actor; *b.* Orange, New Jersey, 28 Oct., 1857; *s.* of Daniel and Susan (Becher) Mason; made his first appearance on the stage at the Standard Theatre, New York, 18 Mar., 1878, in "Mignon"; subsequently played at the Walnut Street Theatre, Philadelphia, in 1878; in Aug., 1879, joined the company of the Boston Museum, and he remained at this theatre, playing leading parts, for seven years; his first appearance with the company was on 1 Sept., 1879, when he played De Taldé in "The Danischeffs"; at Union Square Theatre, 6 Oct., 1884, he appeared as the Count of Louvois in "The Artist's Daughter"; 25 Oct., 1884, as Billardo in "French Flats"; and 8 Dec., 1884, as Andrew Dobbs in "Three Wives to One Husband"; at the Lyceum, Apr., 1885, he appeared in "Dakolar"; and at Stetson's Fifth Avenue, Feb., 1886, he played Laertes in "Hamlet," with the late Edwin Booth; at the Lyceum, Sept., 1886, he played in "The Main Line of Rawson's Y"; he made his first appearance on the London stage at the St. James's Theatre, 26 Feb., 1891, when he made a hit as Simeon Strong in "The Idler"; returning to America in 1892, he appeared at Hermann's Theatre, New York, in Dec., as Jack Charteris in "If I were You"; he again appeared at the St. James's, London, 4 July, 1895, in his old part in "The Idler," and at the Garrick, London, 2 Sept., 1895, he appeared with E. S. Willard as Colonel Moberley in "Alabama"; he then organised the "Mason-Manola" company and toured for some time in "Caste," "Friend Fritz," etc.; at the Knickerbocker Theatre, in 1898, he played Horatio Drake in "The Christian"; and in Dec., 1899, at Hoyt's Theatre, he played Lord Eric Chantrell in "Wheels Within Wheels"; he joined Daniel Frohman's company at Daly's Theatre, in 1900, and appeared in "The Ambassador," "The Interrupted Honeymoon," "The Man of Forty," and "Lady Huntworth's Experiment"; at the Garrick Theatre, New York, in 1903, he played Mark Embury in "Mice and Men"; and at Boston, in Nov., 1903, he played in "The Younger Mrs. Parling"; during 1904 he appeared in "vaudeville" in "Another Story"; he was next engaged as leading man with Mrs. Fiske, at the Manhattan Theatre, and appeared with her as Lovborg in "Hedda Gabler," Paul Sylvaine in "Leah Kleschna," and Michael

Kerouac in "A Light from St. Agnes"; subsequently he played John Erwin in "Mary and John"; during 1906, at the Columbia Theatre, Washington, he played in "The Indiscretion of Truth," "The Liars," "Jane," and "The Tyranny of Tears"; at Milwaukee, 9 Oct., 1906, he appeared with Mrs. Fiske in "The New York Idea," as John Karslake, subsequently playing the same part when the piece was produced at the Lyric, New York, on 19 Nov.; at New Haven, Conn., 30 Aug., 1907, played Alexis Karenin in "Anna Karenina," with Virginia Harned, subsequently appearing at the Herald Square Theatre, in the same play, on 2 Sept., 1907; at the Hackett Theatre, 18 Nov., 1907, scored a great success as Jack Brookfield in "The Witching Hour"; toured with this play throughout 1908; at the Hackett Theatre, Feb., 1910, played John Hare in "None So Blind"; at the New Theatre, New York, Feb., 1910, appeared as Marc Arron in "A Son of the People"; at the Lyric, New York, May, 1910, appeared as Captain Redwood in "Jim the Penman"; at the Thirty-Ninth Street Theatre, Mar., 1911, played Doctor Seelig in "Fritz," etc.; at the Knickerbocker "As a Man Thinks"; subsequently toured in the same part; at the Garrick, New York, Sept., 1912, appeared as Alexander Merital in "The Attack"; at the Empire, New York, Mar., 1913, played Mr. Owen in a revival of "Liberty Hall," at the Criterion, New York, Oct., 1913, played Frank Whitney in "Indian Summer"; at the Eltinge Theatre, Jan., 1914, Baron Stepen Andrey in "The Yellow Ticket"; at the New York Theatre, Oct., 1914, John Dexter in "Big Jim Garrity"; at the Eltinge Theatre, Dec., 1914, Senator Daniel E. Collins in "The Song of Songs"; at Atlantic City, Aug., 1915, played Judge Samuel Filson in "Common Clay."

(Died 12 Jan., 1919; age 60)

MASON, Kitty, dancer; *b.* Stamford Bridge, Yorks., 1882; *d.* of William Augustus Mason; *m.* Algernon Aspinall; made her first appearance on the stage at Christmas, 1896, at the Theatre Royal, Brighton, as a dancer in "The Babes in the Wood" and "Robin Hood"; at Christmas, 1897, made her first appearance in London, at the Grand, Fulham, in the pantomime of "Aladdin"; she next appeared at the Gaiety Theatre, May, 1898, as a dancer in "A Runaway Girl," since which date she has appeared in "San Toy," 1899; "The Messenger Boy," 1900; "The Toreador," 1901; "The Orchid," 1903; "The Spring Chicken," 1905; "The New Aladdin," 1906; "The Girls of Gottenburg," 1907; "Havana," 1908; "Our Miss Gibbs," 1909; appeared at Knickerbocker Theatre, New York, Aug., 1910, in the last-mentioned production. *Address:* 3 Ashley Gardens, S.W. *Telephone No.:* 2176 Victoria.

MASON, Reginald, actor; *b.* San Francisco, Cal., U.S.A., 27 June, 1882; *s.* of Charles Mason, H.B.M. Consul and his wife Fanny (Philpot); *e.* Bedford, England; *m.* Phyllis Young; was formerly engaged in Insurance; made his first appearance on the stage at the Alcazar Theatre, San Francisco, Oct., 1903, in "The Club Baby"; during 1905, toured with Digby Bell in "The Education of Mr. Pipp"; made his first appearance in New York, at the Garrick Theatre, early in 1907, in "Caught in the Rain," and toured in this play 1907-8; at the Garrick, Nov., 1908, played Gainsford in "The Patriot"; May, 1909, Willie Loveall in "The Man from Mexico"; Hudson, Jan., 1910, Rudolph Brederode in "A Lucky Star"; Garrick, Feb., 1911, Count de la Beauv in "The Zebra"; Lyceum, Mar., 1911, George Osborne in "Becky Sharp"; Harris, Aug., 1912, Clarence Van Amberg in "The Model"; Cort, Dec., 1912, Chris Brent in "Peg O' My Heart"; Mar., 1914, the Financier in "The Day of Dupes"; Princess, Oct., 1915, Jas. Ridgeway Carroll in "The Mark of the Beast"; Hudson, Feb., 1916, Walter Nicolls in "The Cinderella Man"; Harris, Aug., 1917, Herbert Rankin in "Daybreak"; Hudson, Nov., 1917, Max Benson in "The Pipes of Pan"; Princess, Feb.,

1918, Cyril Twombley in "Oh! Lady, Lady"; Longacre, Sept., 1919, Clinton de Witt in "Adam and Eva"; Times Square, Sept., 1920, Wally Stuart in "The Mirage"; Bijou, Dec., 1921, Leonard in "The Dover Road"; Cort, June, 1924, Frank Gabbington in "The Locked Door"; Belasco, Oct., 1924, Count de Vauzelle in "Tiger Cats"; Henry Miller, Dec., 1924, D'Allouville in "The Man in Evening Clothes"; Longacre, Feb., 1925, Hilary Trent in "The Dark Angel"; Booth, Aug., 1925, Larry Webb in "The Fall of Eve"; next appeared at the Guild Theatre, 1926, when he succeeded Alfred Lunt as Mr. Dermott in "At Mrs. Beam's"; Nov., 1926, played Professor Henry Higgins in "Pygmalion"; Feb., 1927, Lamberto Laudisi in "Right You Are if you Think You Are"; at the Bijou, Oct., 1927, the King of Aragon in "Immoral Isabella"; Empire, Sept., 1928, Malcolm West in "Heavy Traffic"; in 1929, toured as Lieutenant Osborne in "Journey's End"; Henry Miller, Sept., 1930, the Count von Dubois-Schottenburg in "One, Two, Three," and the Composer in "The Violet"; Lyceum, Feb., 1931, succeeded Reginald Owen as Reggie Melcombe in "Petticoat Influence"; Guild Theatre, Mar., 1931, played The Bishop in "Getting Married"; Avon, Oct., 1931, Peter Vare in "Divorce Me, Dear"; Longacre, Nov., 1931, J. Wilbur Craig in "In Times Square"; Belasco, Los Angeles, Mar., 1932, James Fraser in "The First Mrs. Fraser"; El Capitan, Hollywood, Oct., 1933, played Dr. Haggett in "The Late Christopher Bean"; Plymouth, New York, Sept., 1934, Professor Charles Kingdom in "Lady Jane"; Guild, Dec., 1934, Sir William Howe in "Valley Forge"; Ethel Barrymore, Apr., 1935, Freddie Allerton in "To See Ourselves"; 48th Street, Oct., 1935, succeeded Lawrence Grossmith as Theodore Whitelaw in "A Slight Case of Murder"; Lyceum, Oct., 1936, General Count Bertrand in "St. Helena"; Chicago and Boston, 1937, Mr. Kirby in "You Can't Take It With You"; Broadhurst, New York, Jan., 1939, Charles Randolph in "Dear Octopus"; Empire, Sept., 1939, Lieut. Osborne in "Journey's

End"; Belasco, May, 1940, Thomas Fairfield in "At the Stroke of Eight"; Biltmore, Sept., 1940, Dr. Drewett in "Jupiter Laughs"; St. James's, Oct., 1941, Lord Godolphin in "Anne of England"; Ethel Barrymore, Dec., 1942, Consul Busman in "R.U.R."; Lyceum, Apr., 1944, Waiter in "The Doughgirls," in which he also toured; Ethel Barrymore, Jan., 1945, Colonel Julyan in "Rebecca"; at Detroit, Dec., 1945, Joseph in "Of All People"; Shubert, New York, Nov., 1947, Philip Logan in "The First Mrs. Fraser"; Booth, Jan., 1949, John Elliot in "The Shop at Sly Corner"; at the Playhouse, Albany, Jan., 1951, played Mr. Fiske in "Alexander"; Westport Country Playhouse, July, 1951, played Pulano Alani in "Island Fling"; Shubert, New York, Jan., 1953, appeared as the Mayor of Herzogenberg in "The Love of Four Colonels"; entered films 1932, and has appeared in numerous pictures. *Recreations:* All outdoor sports. *Club:* The Lambs. *(Died 10 July, 1962; age 80)*

MASSARY, Fritzi (*née* Friederike Massarik), actress and vocalist; *b.* Vienna, Austria, 21 Mar., 1882; *d.* of Leopold Massarik and his wife Hermine (Herzfeld); *e.* Vienna; *m.* Max Pallenberg (dec.); made her first appearance on the stage in her native town at a very early age, appearing in a *revue*; established her reputation when she appeared in the title-*rôle* of Leo Fall's operetta "The Empress"; subsequently appeared in the leading parts in "Madame Pompadour," "The Gypsy Princess," "The Rose of Stamboul," "The Spanish Nightingale"; between 1914 and 1931 she appeared in "Cleopatra," "The Carnival Fairy," "The Merry Widow," "The Last Waltz," "Your Highness's Mistress," "Sybil," etc.; in comedy she has played lead in "One Wife," "Nina," "The First Mrs. Fraser," etc.; made her first appearance on the London stage at His Majesty's Theatre, 16 Mar., 1938, as Liesl Haren in "Operette." *Favourite parts:* Pompadour, Countess Vera in "The Last Waltz" and the First Mrs. Fraser. *Recreation:* Reading. *(Died Feb., 1969; age 86)*

MASSINE, Léonide, dancer, *maître de ballet* and choreographer; *b.* Moscow, 9 Aug., 1896; *s.* of Teodor Affanasievitch and his wife Eugenia (Nikolaevna; *e.* Moscow Imperial School of Ballet; *m.* Tatiana Vladimorovna Milisnikova; was a pupil of Domashoff, Checchetti, and Nicolas Legat; made his first appearance in 1912, and subsequently studied dancing under Michel Fokine; he went to Germany with the Diaghileff Ballet, and made his first appearance with them, as one of the policemen in "Petrouchka," subsequently undertaking the leading *rôle* in "La Légende de Joseph," at the National Opera House, Paris, 23 May, 1914; first appeared in London, at Drury Lane Theatre, 23 June, 1914, in the same part; became chief choreographer to Diaghileff in succession to Michel Fokine, 1915, his first production being "The Midnight Sun" ("Soleil de Nuit"); made his first appearance in New York, at the Century Theatre, 1916, in "La Légende de Joseph"; subsequently appeared in "Boutique Fantasque," "The Three Cornered Hat," "Coq d'Or," "Parade," "Good Humoured Ladies," "Pulcinella," "Chout," "Cimarosiana"; other ballets which he conceived, are "Las Meninas," "Contes Russes," "Le Chant du Rossignol," etc.; leaving Diaghileff in 1921, he studied for some time in Rome but returned in 1924, to produce "Zephyre and Flora," "Les Matelots," "Le Pas d'Acier," "Les Fâcheux," "Ode," etc.; subsequently toured his own company in Buenos Aires, and founded a ballet school in London; was associated with several of C. B. Cochran's productions, and at the London Pavilion, Apr., 1925, appeared in "On With the Dance"; Nov., 1925, in "Still Dancing"; Apr., 1926, "Cochran's Revue, 1926"; then for three years, was producer of ballet at the Roxy, New York, and among his productions here was Stravinsky's "Sacre de Printemps"; subsequently produced ballet at the Opera House, Paris, and at La Scala, Milan; produced "Belkis," and "Reine de Sabat," for Ida Rubinstein; Adelphi, London, Jan., 1932, produced the dances in "Helen!," and at the Lyceum, Apr., 1932, in "The Miracle," under Reinhardt, for C. B. Cochran, in which he appeared as the Spielmann; he then joined Col. de Basil's Ballets Russes de Monte Carlo, in Monte Carlo, Dec., 1932, producing "Jeux d'Enfants" and remaining as director until 1942; he produced over forty productions for this organization, besides taking part in many of them; among the ballets which he created for this company are "Le Beau Danube," "Beach," "Les Présages," "Scuola di Ballo," "Union Pacific," "Le Bal," "Jardin Public," "La Symphonie Fantastique," "Choreartium," "Rouge et Noir" ("L'Etrange Farandole"), "Bogatyri," "Salade," "Gigue," "Mercuro," "Les Enchantments d' Alcine," "Le Roi David," "Vecchia Milano," "Gaieté Parisienne," "Seventh Symphony," "St. Francis," "Cappriccio Espagnol," "Bacchanal," "Wiena," "New Yorker," "Labyrinth," "Saratoga," "Aleko," "Don Domingo," "Mdlle. Angot," "Daphnis and Chloe," "The Unfortunate Painter," "Antar," "Fantaisie Poétique," "Moonlight Sonata," "Mad Tristan," etc.; appeared with the company at the St. James, New York, Apr., 1934, and at Covent Garden, 1934–7; Drury Lane, 1938; subsequently Director of the Ballet Theatre, New York City; arranged the dances for "Helen Goes to Troy," Alvin, New York, Apr., 1944; returned to England, 1946, and toured in "A Bullet in the Ballet." *Address:* 28 Forester Avenue, Long Beach, N.Y., U.S.A.

MASSINGHAM, Dorothy, actress and dramatic author; *b.* Highgate, London, 12 Dec., 1889; *d.* of the late Henry William Massingham and his wife, Emma (Snowdon); *e.* Graham High Street School; studied for the stage under Rosina Filippi and at the Academy of Dramatic Art; made her first appearance on the stage at the Liverpool Repertory Theatre, Feb., 1912, as Kalleia in "The Perplexed Husband," followed by Mrs. Perrin in "The Situation at Newbury"; made her first appearance in London at the Vaudeville Theatre, 18 Nov., 1913, as Claire in "Great Catherine"; from 1917–19 was a member of Repertory

Theatre Company, Birmingham, where she played, among other parts, Lady Windermere in " Lady Windermere's Fan," Flora Lloyd in " The Honeymoon," Viola in " Twelfth Night," Hero in " Much Ado About Nothing," Gwendoline in " The Importance of Being Earnest," Everyman in the play of that name, the Hon. Monica Somerset in " St. George and the Dragons," the Second Chronicler in " Abraham Lincoln," etc. ; at the Lyric, Hammersmith, Feb., 1919, again played the last-mentioned part ; during 1921–22 was at the Everyman Theatre, where she played Margaret Knox in " Fanny's First Play," etc. ; at the St. Martin's, Mar., 1922, played Lady Adela in " Loyalties " ; at Daly's (for the Phoenix Society), May, 1922, Alcmena in " Amphytrion " ; at the R.A.D.A. (Three Hundred Club), May, 1924, Lady Medway in " The Discovery " ; at the Everyman, Dec., 1924, Julia Craven in " The Philanderer "; Aldwych (for the Phoenix Society), Jan., 1925, Lucretia in " The Assignation "; Kingsway, Aug., 1925, Gertrude in " Hamlet " (in modern dress) ; Barnes, Jan., 1926, Hèlena in " Uncle Vanya "; joined the Old Vic Company, Sept., 1926, and played Constance in " King John," Helena in " A Midsummer Night's Dream," Lady Macbeth, Viola, Hermione, Emilia in " Othello," Adriana in " The Comedy of Errors," etc.; Strand, Oct., 1927, Maria Gabel in " The Kingdom of God "; Everyman, Jan., 1928, Norah in " A Night in June "; joined the New Shakespeare Company at Stratford-on-Avon, Apr., 1928, and remained with the company until 1932, touring in the United States and Canada, 1928–9, and again in 1931-32, and playing Cleopatra, Hermione, Doll Tearsheet in " Henry IV " (Part II), etc. ; is the author of the following plays: " Glass Houses," 1918; " The Goat," 1921 ; " Washed Ashore," 1922; " Not in Our Stars," 1924; " The Haven," 1930. *Favourite parts :* Viola in " Twelfth Night," Everyman, and Major Barbara.

(Died 30 Mar., 1933; age 42)

MATHER, Aubrey, actor; *b.* Minchinhampton, Glos., 17 Dec., 1885; *s.* of the Rev. Frank Mather, Prebendary of Wells Cathedral, and his wife, Jessie Caroline (Clay); *e.* Charterhouse, and Trinity College, Cambridge; made his first appearance on the stage at the Theatre Royal, Ilkeston, June, 1905, as Bernardo in " Hamlet "; toured with various Shakespearean repertory companies until 1908; made his first appearance on the London stage, June, 1909, at Wyndham's Theatre, as Joseph McCloud in " Brewster's Millions "; from 1908-14 almost continuously engaged with Percy Hutchison; also toured in South Africa, 1912, as Pine in " Passers-By " and Dr. Blundell in " Peter's Mother "; in 1914 toured as Travers Gladwyn in " Officer 666 "; appeared at the Criterion, May, 1914, as Gingold in " The Blue Mouse "; served in the War from 1915-19, with the R.A.M.C., during which time he ran a Pierrot troupe, " The Tanks "; in 1919 went to America, and made his first appearance in New York, at the Manhattan Opera House, Oct., 1919, as Sub-Lieut. Louis Peel in " The Luck of the Navy," and then toured in Canada as Sir Dennys Broughton in " General Post "; on returning to London, appeared at the Queen's, Sept., 1920, as Daniel Fox in " A Pair of Sixes "; Mar., 1921, Dr. Bentley in " Nightie Night "; Shaftesbury, Jan., 1922, William Moultrie in " The Rattlesnake "; from 1922-24 toured in South Africa and Australasia with Gertrude Elliott, in " Woman to Woman," " Smilin' Through," " Bluebeard's Eighth Wife," " Paddy the Next Best Thing," etc.; returning to England, 1924, appeared at the Everyman in a variety of parts; at the Criterion, Oct., 1924, succeeded Ion Swinley as Gabriel Fay in " Fata Morgana "; has since appeared at the Vaudeville, Mar., 1925, as Adolph Lee Tevis in " Tarnish "; St. Martin's, July, 1925, The Editor in " The Show"; Ambassadors', Nov., 1925, Henry Huxtable in " The Madras House "; Savoy, Mar., 1926, Henri Ramel in " The Snow Man "; Regent, Mar., 1926, and Comedy, Apr., 1926, Rev. Timothy Bray in " The Rescue Party "; Royalty, July, 1926, Daniel Leeson in " The Awful Truth "; New, Sept., 1926, Kiril Trigorin and Sir Bartlemy

Pugh in " The Constant Nymph "; Daly's, Nov., 1927, Rev. Sampson Crutch in " Sirocco "; Prince of Wales's, Jan., 1928, Rev. Frank Thomson in " Outward Bound "; New (for the 300 Club), Feb., 1928, Mr. Woodley in " Young Woodley "; Royalty, Mar., 1928, Louis Harcourt in " Tinker, Tailor ——"; New, Apr., 1928, Sir William Zaidner in " Come With Me "; Playhouse, June, 1928, Dr. Gilbert Anderson in " The Return of the Soldier "; New, Aug., 1928, Albert Keggs in " A Damsel in Distress "; Apr., 1929, the Rev., Aubrey Wyndrum in " Baa, Baa, Black Sheep "; Shaftesbury, Aug., 1929, Marine Ogg in " The Middle Watch"; Sept., 1930, Eddie Cootes in "Leave It to Psmith"; Criterion, Feb., 1931, Mr. Thomas in "After All"; Royalty, Mar., 1931, Mr. Wenham in "The World of Light"; St. Martin's, Nov., 1931, Ernest Dengler in "Lady-in-Waiting"; at the Little, Nov., 1932, Collins in "Getting Married"; Gaiety, Jan., 1933, Maurice Veal in "Mother of Pearl"; Playhouse, Oct., 1933, Marcus Fenwick in "So Good! So Kind!!"; Nov., 1933, Leslie Hale in "Night Club Queen"; Dec., 1933, Mr. Wenham in "The World of Light"; Playhouse, Feb., 1934, Rev. Henry Brown in "The Big House"; Apr., 1934, Sir Arthur Tuttington in "Libel"; Shaftesbury, Aug., 1934, Chief P.O. Dingle in "Admirals All"; Savoy, June, 1935, the President in "A Kingdom for a Cow"; Strand, Apr., 1936, George Phelps in "Baby Austin"; Imperial, New York, Nov., 1936, Polonius in "Hamlet," with Leslie Howard, subsequently touring in the same part; Morosco, New York, Jan., 1938, played Frank Hastings in "Bachelor Born"("Housemaster"); Hudson, Nov., 1938, Brigadier-General Hargreaves in "Good Hunting"; Strand, London, Feb., 1939, Mr. Jessup in "Little Ladyship"; toured, Aug., 1939, as the Bishop of Winterbury in "Robert's Wife"; subsequently went to Hollywood, where he remained five years; at the Playhouse, New York, Dec., 1944, played the Man from London in "Hand in Glove"; Martin Beck (for the Guild), Mar., 1945, Horatio Wing in "Foolish Notion"; at Stamford,

Conn., Aug., 1945, played Burgess in "Candida"; toured, Sept., 1945–Mar., 1946, in "Foolish Notion"; Coronet Theatre, Los Angeles, Mar., 1948, Professor Thaddeus in "The Vigil"; Cort, New York, Jan., 1950, the Banished Duke in "As You Like It," and subsequently toured in the same part until 1951, when he returned to England; at the Watergate, Mar., 1952, played Professor Burton in "Damaris"; Theatre Royal, Bath, Sept., 1952, appeared as Maitland in "Pagan In the Parlour," and subsequently toured in this part; Savoy, Feb., 1953, played the Ven. Archdeacon Daubeny in a revised version of Oscar Wilde's "A Woman of No Importance"; for the Repertory Players appeared at the Strand, Dec., 1953, as Mr. Petter in "Tranquil House," and at Wyndham's, Apr., 1954, as the Bishop of Cinnabar in "The Sultan's Turret"; St. James's, Sept., 1954, appeared as Mr. Fowler in "Separate Tables" ("The Window Table" and "Table Number Seven"); commenced film career, 1930, in "Young Woodley," and has since appeared in innumerable pictures; has frequently broadcast and appeared in television; he has also appeared in numerous plays for various play-producing societies, for which he acted as producer. *Favourite parts:* Huxtable in "The Madras House," and Rev. Timothy Bray in "The Rescue Party." *Recreations:* Foreign travel, and care of his garden.
(Died 15 Jan., 1958; age 72)

MATHER, Donald, actor and vocalist; *b.* Wallasey, Cheshire, 24 June, 1900; *s.* of Harold Mather and his wife Edwina May (Belcham); *e.* Sedbergh, Yorks.; *m.* (1) Freda Pettitt; (2) Sylvia Phipps; studied singing at the Royal College of Music, for three years; made his first appearance on the stage, at the Shaftesbury Theatre, Dec., 1921, in minor parts in "Will Shakespeare"; at the Kingsway, Dec., 1922, understudied lead in "Polly"; Daly's, Dec., 1923, played the Lieutenant in "Madame Pompadour"; Lyceum, Sept., 1925, appeared in "The London Revue"; in 1925–6, toured in "The First Kiss," and "The

Gipsy Princess,"; Winter Garden, Apr., 1927, played René de Montigny in "The Vagabond King"; during 1928–9, toured as François Villon in the same piece; Piccadilly, Nov., 1929, played Prince Karl in the revival of "The Student Prince"; Dominion, Feb., 1930, Philip Marvin in "Silver Wings"; Daly's, Sept., 1930, José de Barros in "Eldorado"; Prince Edward, Mar., 1931, the Marquis de Corneville in "Les Cloches de Corneville"; Daly's June, 1931, Reginald Fairfax in "The Geisha"; July, 1931, toured with Evelyn Laye, as René in "Madame Pompadour"; Daly's, Feb., 1932, played Lieut. Bobbie Preston in "San Toy"; during 1932–3, toured as Young Strauss in "Waltzes from Vienna"; in 1934, toured as Hoffman in "Wild Violets"; went to South Africa, 1934, and toured in "Wild Violets" and "Waltzes from Vienna"; Streatham Hill, Dec., 1934, the Emperor of Morocco in "Dick Whittington"; in 1935–6, again toured in "Waltzes from Vienna "; in 1936, toured as François Villon in "The Vagabond King"; during 1937–8, toured as Rochester in "Jane Eyre"; toured, Sept., 1938, as Robert Holden in "Aloma and Nuitane"; toured, 1939, with the Macdona Players, in a repertory of Bernard Shaw's plays. *Recreation :* Golf. *Club :* Green Room. *Address :* 145 Sutton Court, Chiswick, W.4.

MATHEWS, Frances Aymar, author and playwright; *b.* New York; *d.* of Sarah E. (Webb) and Daniel A. Mathews ; *e.* New York ; has written the following novels : " My Lady Peggy Goes to Town," " The Coming of the King," " Billy Duane," " The Marquise's Millions," " The Staircase of Surprise " ; among her plays may be noted, " A Little Tragedy at Teintsin," " Pretty Peggy," " Joan D'Arc," " A Dakota Divorce," " Renunciation," " A Soldier of France " (" Joan D'Arc "), etc. *Address :* Hotel Kenesaw, West 103rd Street, New York City, U.S.A.

MATHEWS, James W., business manager ; *b.* Dunedin, New Zealand, is the son of the famous *prima donna,* Julia Mathews, the original Grand Duchess in England of Offenbach's comic opera of that name ; was formerly an actor, and made his first appearance on the stage at the Princess's Theatre, under the management of the late Wilson Barrett, on 6 Dec., 1883, when he played the part of Captain of the Scythians in " Claudian " ; he acted in various companies for ten years, and then became business manager for William Lestocq and Harry Nicholl's " Jane " company ; subsequently toured with his own companies, playing " The Real Little Lord Fauntleroy," " Gloriana," etc. ; from the year 1897 to 1915 officiated as business manager at the Duke of York's Theatre for the late Charles Frohman ; after the death of Mr. Frohman, was engaged by Charles B. Dillingham for the Hippodrome, New York, and in July, 1915, left England to take up his position there ; is a prominent Freemason, having served as Master of the Asaph and Chelsea Lodges, also holds office in many other London lodges ; was appointed an officer of the Grand Lodge of England, 1909. *Clubs :* Sketch, Savage, Genesius.
(Died 14 Dec., 1920; age 56)

MATTESON, Ruth, actress; *b.* San José, Calif., 8 Dec., 1909; *d.* of Frederick Matteson and his wife Ethel (Lee); *e.* San José, California, and Columbia University; *m.* Curt Peterson; made her first appearance on the stage in Henry Duffy's stock company, in 1929, at the Alcazar, San Francisco, in "Daddies"; subsequently played in stock companies, at Southampton and elsewhere; first appeared in New York, at the Longacre Theatre, 26 Oct., 1934, as Kathie Starr in "Geraniums in My Window"; Cort, Oct., 1935, played Marylou Dayton in "Symphony"; Fulton, Oct., 1935, Gloria Kendall in "Triumph"; Ethel Barrymore, Nov., 1935, Mrs. Steele in "Parnell"; Ambassador, Feb., 1936, Karen Andre in "The Night of January 16th"; Empire, Aug., 1936, Kate McKim in "Spring Dance," and Dec., 1936, Faith Ingalls in "The Wingless Victory"; Martin Beck, Nov., 1937, Eleanor Bold in "Barchester Towers"; Biltmore, Apr., 1938, Miss Shea in "What a Life!"; Booth, Feb., 1939, appeared in the *revue*, "One for the Money"; Cort, Jan., 1940, Ellen Turner in "The Male Animal"; Majestic, Aug., 1943, Natalie in "The Merry Widow"; Ethel Barrymore, 1943, succeeded Shirley Booth, as Leona Richards in "To-morrow the World"; Belasco, Nov., 1944, Jennie Moore in "In Bed We Cry"; Century, Sept., 1945, Hetty Strauss in "Mr. Strauss Goes to Boston"; Cort, Feb., 1946, Ismene in "Antigone"; Shubert, Nov., 1946, Myra Fox in "Park Avenue"; Biltmore, Dec., 1949, Jane Pugh in "Clutterbuck"; Morosco, Nov., 1950, Amanda in "The Relapse"; toured, 1954–5, as Claire Martin in "Sailor's Delight"; Cherry Lane, Nov., 1955, Harriet in "The Dragon's Mouth"; Lyceum, Nov., 1956, Mrs. Anthony J. Drexel Biddle in "The Happiest Millionaire"; Cort, Feb., 1960, Mrs. Newton in "There Was a Little Girl"; Biltmore, July, 1965, took over as Mrs. Banks in "Barefoot in the Park"; has appeared on variety and dramatic programs in television. *Address:* c/o Actors Equity Association, 165 West 46th Street, New York, N.Y. 10036, U.S.A.

MATTHEWS, A. E., O.B.E. (Alfred Edward Matthews), actor; *b.* Bridlington, Yorks, 22 Nov., 1869; *s.* of William Matthews; *e.* Stamford, Lincs; *m.* (1) May Blayney; (2) Pat Desmond; his father was one of the Matthews Brothers of the original Christy Minstrels; is a great-nephew of the famous clown, Tom Matthews, who was a pupil of Joe Grimaldi; commenced his career as call-boy, at the Princess's Theatre, under Rowley Cathcart, Dec., 1886, with "The Noble Vagabond"; subsequently succeeded Cathcart as stage-manager; he was assistant stage-manager at the Princess's, when "Held by the Enemy" was produced, Apr., 1887, and at one time or another, played every male part in the play with the exception of Colonel Prescott: when the play was transferred to the Vaudeville, he transferred with it, and was assistant

stage-manager there for eighteen months; subsequently toured with Charles Warner in "Held by the Enemy" and "In the Ranks"; then toured with "Dandy Dick" and "The Magistrate," with Richard Edgar, and was also stage-manager; in 1889, accompanied Lionel Brough to South Africa, and played forty-three parts in twelve months; from 1891-93, toured in "The Private Secretary," "Dr. Bill," etc.; in Aug., 1893, went to Australia, where he remained until 1896, playing Jack Chesney in "Charley's Aunt," Douglas Cattermole in "The Private Secretary," and he also appeared with Charles Arnold in "Hans the Boatman," etc.; on his return, reappeared at the Princess's Theatre, Apr., 1896, as Mr. Wentworth in "The Star of India"; at the Comedy, Oct., 1896, played Algy Pakenham in "Mr. Martin"; at Terry's, Dec., 1896, appeared as Dick in "The Eider Down Quilt"; was in the original cast of "Lord and Lady Algy," Comedy, Apr., 1898; "Lady Huntworth's Experiment," Criterion, Apr., 1900; "The Wisdom of the Wise," St. James's, Nov., 1900; "The Awakening," St. James's, Feb., 1901; "The Undercurrent," Criterion, Sept., 1901; at the Criterion, Jan., 1902, played Dick in "A Pair of Spectacles"; at Wyndham's, Apr., 1902, appeared as the Hon. Peter O'Hagan in "The End of a Story"; in July, 1902, played Adolphus Birkett in "Betsy"; at the Haymarket, Dec., 1902, played Robert Fielding in "The Unforeseen"; Mar., 1903, Brush in "The Clandestine Marriage"; at Wyndham's, Sept., 1903, was the Earl of Plumleigh in "Little Mary"; at the Duke of York's, Apr., 1904, played Lord Charles Dorchester in "The Rich Mrs. Repton"; at the Garrick, Aug., 1904, appeared as Charlie Inskip in "The Chevaleer"; at the Criterion, Nov., 1904, as Tommy Keston in "The Freedom of Suzanne"; at the Duke of York's, Apr. 1905, as Cosmo Grey in "Alice Sit-by-the-Fire"; at the Haymarket, Sept., 1905, as Gerald Marvel in "On the Love Path"; at the Court, Sept., 1905, appeared as Eustace Jackson in "The Return of the Prodigal"; at the

Comedy, during 1906, played the Duke of Ranelagh in " The Alabaster Staircase," Dick in " A Pair of Spectacles," and Andrew in " Josephine "; at Wyndham's, Sept., 1906, played Peter Crewys in " Peter's Mother "; at the Court, Sept., 1906, appeared as Jack Barthwick in " The Silver Box "; at the Haymarket, May, 1907, played the Hon. Gibson Gore in " My Wife "; at the Comedy, in Oct., appeared as Lord Roland Dumaray in " The Barrier "; at the Playhouse, in Nov., as Lord Ronald Corfe in " A Lesson in Shakespeare "; and at the Duke of York's, in Dec., as Mr. Darling in " Peter Pan "; at Wyndham's, Sept., 1908, played the Duke of Tadcaster in " The Early Worm "; at the Haymarket, Apr., 1909, appeared as the Marquis of Bewdley in " Bevis "; at the Comedy, Sept., 1909, played Algernon Peppercorn in " Smith "; the following year went to America, and in Aug., 1910, appeared at the Garrick, New York, as Theodore Saunders in " Love Amongst the Lions "; at the Lyceum, New York, Nov., 1910, played Algernon Moncrieffe in " The Importance of Being Earnest "; on returning to London appeared at the St. James's, June, 1911, in the same part; same theatre, Sept., 1911, appeared as Bertie Fawsitt in " The Ogre "; at the Playhouse, Feb., 1912, played the Hon. Hildebrand Carstairs in " The Second in Command "; Apr., 1912, Billy Hargrave in " Billy "; at the Garrick, June, 1912, Howard Jefferies junior in " Find the Woman "; Nov., 1912, Gerald in " Phipps "; at the Globe, Dec., 1912, succeeded Wallace Eddinger as Travers Gladwin in " Officer 666 "; at Wyndham's, June, 1913, played Algy Fairfax in " Diplomacy "; in 1914 toured in " Find the Woman "; at the Comedy, Oct., 1914, played Jerry in " Peg o' My Heart "; at the Empire, Nov., 1914, appeared in " The Woman Intervenes "; continued to play Jerry in " Peg o' My Heart," 1915-16; at the Globe Theatre, Apr., 1916, played Jerome Belden in " The Show Shop "; Oct., 1917, Geoffrey Fuller in " The Willow Tree "; at the Savoy, Feb., 1918, Robert Bennett in " Nothing But the

Truth "; at the Haymarket, Sept., 1919, Robert Audrey in " Daddies "; Feb., 1920, The Husband in " Tea for Three "; subsequently went to America, and at the Cort Theatre, New York, Feb., 1921, again played Jerry in " Peg o' My Heart "; returned to London, and at Wyndham's Theatre, July, 1921, succeeded Gerald Du Maurier as Captain Hugh Drummond in " Bulldog Drummond," prior to leaving for America, to play the same part; at the Knickerbocker, New York, Dec., 1921, appeared as Captain Hugh Drummond in " Bulldog Drummond "; at the Comedy, London, Aug., 1922, succeeded Owen Nares as Tony Blunt in " Quarantine "; at the Duke of York's, May, 1923, played Clarence Topping in " Her Temporary Husband "; at the Eltinge Theatre, New York, Nov., 1923, played Ernest Steele in " Spring Cleaning," and continued in this part, 1924; returned to London, and at the Queen's, May, 1925, played Neil McRae in " Beggar on Horseback," which he revived at Wyndham's, July, 1925; at the Playhouse, Aug., 1925, succeeded Ronald Squire as Ernest Steele in " Spring Cleaning "; returned to New York, and at the Fulton, Nov., 1925, played Charles in " The Last of Mrs. Cheyney "; Klaw, Nov., 1926, Edward Churt in " This Was a Man "; returned to London, and appeared at the Criterion, June, 1927, as Harvey Townsend in " The Happy Husband "; again returned to New York, and appeared at the Empire, Oct., 1927, as Philip Voaze in " Interference "; May, 1928, again played Harvey Townsend in " The Happy Husband "; Sept., 1928, Ralph Corbin in " Heavy Traffic "; Morosco, Jan., 1929, Martin in " Serena Blandish "; Playhouse, Dec., 1929, James Fraser in " The First Mrs. Fraser," and continued in this, 1930-1; Booth, Sept., 1931, Charles Battle in " The Breadwinner "; Playhouse, Oct., 1932, Lucien Galvosier in "Mademoiselle"; Selwyn, Jan., 1934, the Man in " A Hat, A Coat, A Glove "; Henry Miller, May, 1934, Tom Rowlands in " These Two "; Cort, Apr., 1935 Joe Clayton in " The Dominant Sex "; reappeared in London, at the Queen's Theatre, Nov., 1935, when he

played Simon Leigh in "Short Story"; Playhouse, New York, Nov., 1936, Victor Martineau in "Matrimony Pfd."; Shaftesbury, London, June, 1937, Dr. Richard Mackenzie in "Satyr"; Whitehall, Apr., 1938, Martin Tracey in "Ghost for Sale"; Morosco, New York, Dec., 1938, Sir Richard Furze in "Spring Meeting"; after returning to England, toured, June, 1942, as Mr. Hampden in "To Dream Again"; Globe, London, Apr., 1943, played Sir George Gedney in "They Came to a City"; Phoenix, Dec., 1944, John Asprey in "Another Love Story"; toured, Oct., 1945, as Sir Tristram Mardon in "Dandy Dick"; toured, Jan., 1946, as Dr. Thornton in "A Play for Ronnie," and July, 1946, as Charles in "But for the Grace of God," playing the last named part at the St. James's, Sept., 1946; Vaudeville, Aug., 1947, appeared as the Earl of Lister in "The Chiltern Hundreds," which ran until 1949; Strand, Aug., 1949, again played the same part; Booth, New York, Oct., 1949, played the same part, when the play was renamed "Yes, M'Lord"; after returning to England, toured, Nov., 1950, as Crank in "The Gay Invalid," and played this part at the Garrick, Jan., 1951; at the Duchess, Apr., 1954, appeared as the Earl of Lister in "The Manor of Northstead"; has also appeared in films; was the managing-director of the British Actors' Film Company, 1917–18; "Matty," his autobiography, was published in 1953; received the O.B.E. in the Birthday Honours, 1951. *Clubs:* Garrick and Green Room.
(Died 25 July, 1960; age 90)

MATTHEWS, Adelaide, dramatic author; *b.* 1886; formerly an actress; is the author of the following, among other plays: " Nightie Night " (with Martha Stanley), 1919; " Just Married " (with Anne Nicholls), 1921; " Puppy Love " (with Martha Stanley), 1925; " The Wasp's Nest " (with Martha Stanley), 1927; " Scrambled Wives " (with Martha Stanley), 1920; " The Teaser " (with Martha Stanley), 1921; " Heart's Desire " (with Anne Nicholls).

MATTHEWS, Bache, Literary adviser to the Birmingham Repertory Theatre; *b.* Birmingham, 23 Mar., 1876; *s.* of Arthur Bache Matthews and his wife, Mary (Marsh); *e.* privately; formerly an elementary school teacher, and subsequently held several minor offices under the Birmingham Corporation; he was a member of the Pilgrim Players, which afterwards developed into the Birmingham Repertory Theatre, and which commenced operations, Dec., 1907, with the production of " Eager Heart "; he played a number of minor parts with the Pilgrims, and was appointed treasurer in 1911; in 1913, became business manager of the Birmingham Repertory Theatre; general manager, 1922; assistant director, 1923–31; is the author of " A History of the Birmingham Repertory Theatre," 1924; was Chairman of Midland Entertainments Managers' Association. *Recreations :* Books and the study of stage history.
(Died 12 Oct., 1948; age 72)

MATTHEWS, Brander, Litt.D., D.C.L., author and playwright; *b.* New Orleans, 21 Feb., 1852; *e.* Columbia College ; Professor Emeritus of Dramatic Literature, Columbia University ; studied law, and was admitted to the Bar ; has written numerous works on dramatic subjects, among them " The Theatres of Paris," " French Dramatists of the Nineteenth Century," Studies of the Stage," " Development of the Drama," " Actors and Actresses of Great Britain and the United States " (with Laurence Hutton), " A Study of the Drama," a life of Molière, " Shakespeare as a Playwright," " The Principles of Playmaking," " A Book about the Theatre," etc. ; his plays include " The Picture," " A Gold Mine," and " On Probation " (in collaboration with Geo. H. Jessop), " Margery's Lovers," " The Decision of the Court," " Peter Stuyvesant " ; was one of the founders of the Authors' and Players' Clubs, New York ; one of the founders of the American Copyright League and of the Dunlap Society ; received the decoration of the Legion of Honour from the French Government, 1907 ; promoted Officier

in 1922. *Recreation :* Book-collecting.
Clubs : Athenaeum, London ; Century and the Players' New York.
(Died 31 Mar., 1929; age 77)

MATTHEWS, Ethel, actress ; *b.*
12 Oct., 1870 ; *d.* of the late Colonel
Garland Matthews, 44th and Manchester Regiments ; made her first
appearance on the stage, Dec., 1888,
walking on at the Lyceum in " Macbeth " ; next appeared at the Court,
Mar., 1889, as Lady Struddock in
" The Weaker Sex," with Mr. and
Mrs. Kendal ; appeared at the
Gaiety, Apr., 1890, as Lady Jane
Grey in " The Prince and the Pauper " ; then joined Charles Hawtrey
at the Comedy, appearing in
" Nerves," " Jane," " Husband and
Wife," " Godpapa," etc. ; at Terry's,
Dec., 1896, played Lucy Pemberton
in " The Eider Down Quilt " ; at the
Court, Jan., 1899, played in " A Court
Scandal " ; at the Criterion, Mar.,
1901, appeared as Diana Pontifex in
" Mamma " ; in June, 1901, played
Iris Waverley in " A Short Exposure " ;
at the Shaftesbury, Sept., 1901, appeared as Eva in "Are You a Mason ? "
at the Princess Theatre, New York,
Oct., 1903, appeared as Mrs. Vidal
in " Raffles " ; at Wyndham's, June,
1904, played Lady Rose in " The
Finishing School " ; at the Vaudeville,
Sept., 1904, played the Hon. Sophia
Bedford in " The Catch of the Season";
appeared in " All-of-a-Sudden Peggy,"
Duke of York's, 1906 ; played in
" The Amateur Socialist," Criterion,
1906 ; in Jan., 1907, appeared at
Haymarket in " Her Grace the Reformer," one-act play by Mrs. de la
Pasture, also understudying Miss
Compton in " Lady Huntworth's
Experiment " ; at the Apollo Theatre,
Nov., 1907, played Mrs. Vida Pennington in " The New York Idea " ;
at the Garrick, Feb., 1908, appeared
as Mdme. de Bellegarde in " The
Woman of Kronstadt " ; at the Haymarket, Mar., 1908, played Mrs.
Ridgeley-Fane in " Her Father " ;
in Oct., 1909, appeared at the Hippodrome in a sketch with Mr. Allan
Aynesworth. *Recreations :* Motoring
and shooting. *Address :* 38 High
Street, Reigate. *Telephone No. :*
Reigate 498.

MATTHEWS, Lester, actor ; *b.*
Nottingham, 3 Dec., 1900 ; *s.* of Percy
Lester Matthews and his wife Mary
Elizabeth Alice (Davison) ; *e.* Waverley,
Nottingham, and Paston, North Walsham ; *m.* (1) Frances Elizabeth Walper (mar. dis.) ; (2) Anne Grey ; made
his first appearance on the stage at
the Theatre Royal, Nottingham, June,
1916, walking on in Armitage and
Leigh's Repertory Company ; from
1916-19 toured with Repertory Company ; 1920-23, engaged with the
Compton Comedy Company at Nottingham and on tour, playing a variety of
parts in Shakespeare, costume, and
modern plays ; in 1923 toured under
Robert Courtneidge, as Lawrence
Blake in " Paddy the Next Best
Thing," followed by tours as Algy
Spriggs in " The Sport of Kings," and
Geoffrey in " The Unfair Sex " ; made
his first appearance in the West End,
at Daly's, 19 Feb., 1927, as Von
Freyhoff in " The Blue Mazurka " ;
went to New York, Aug., 1927, making
his first appearance there at the Fulton
Theatre, Sept., 1927, as Joe Varwell in
" Yellow Sands " ; returned to London,
to play the same part at the Haymarket Theatre ; at the Court (for
Lyceum Club Stage Society), Nov.,
1927, played David Renny in " Boomerang " ; at Daly's, Feb., 1928,
played James Wayne in " Lady Mary,"
and in Oct., 1928, toured as Richard
Howe in the same piece ; at the Fortune,
Mar., 1929, played John Willcocks in
" Aren't We All ? " ; at the Scala (for
the Venturers), May, 1929, Prince
Oshima in " The Shanghai Gesture";
Strand (for Repertory Players), May,
1929, Anthony in " Black St. Anthony" ; Garrick, Oct., 1929, Michael
Carthew in "Happy Families"; "Q,"
Nov., 1929, Walter Holt in "The
Devil's Pulpit"; Royalty, Mar., 1930,
Fred Kellard in "Appearances"; in
July, 1930, toured as Baldasarre in
"The Maid of the Mountains"; "Q,"
Jan., 1933, Larry Moreton in "The
Scoop," and Henry Walcote in "The
Silent Menace" ; "Q," Feb., 1933, and
Lyric, Mar., 1933, Mr. Murray in "Gay
Love"; Daly's, Apr., 1934, Dick
Hammond in "Dark Horizon"; in
the autumn of 1934, toured as Ned
Marshall in "Cut for Partners"; then

1633

went to the United States to appear in films; at the Curran Theatre, San Francisco, Aug., 1937, played Doc Davidson in "Story to be Whispered"; commenced film career, 1930, and has appeared in innumerable pictures in England and Hollywood; since 1936, has appeared in "Professional Soldier," "Song and Dance Man," "Too Many Parents," "Thank You, Jeeves," "Lloyd's of London," "Mysterious Mr. Moto," "15 Maiden Lane," "Crack-Up," "Tugboat Princess," "The Prince and the Pauper," "Lancer Spy," "There's Always a Woman," "The Adventures of Robin Hood," "Three Loves has Nancy," "I Am a Criminal," "If I Were King," "Time Out for Murder," "Three Musketeers," "Susannah of the Mounties," "Enemy Agent," "Girl from Nowhere," "Ruler of the Seas," "Conspiracy," etc. *Favourite part:* Prince Hal in "Henry IV" (Part I). *Recreation:* Motoring. *Address:* 420 Beviewil Drive, Beverly Hills, Cal., U.S.A.

MATTHISON, Edith Wynne, actress; *b.* Birmingham, 23 Nov., 1875; *d.* of Henry Matthison and his wife Kate (Wynne); *m.* Charles Rann Kennedy; made her first appearance on the stage at Blackpool, Dec., 1896, in "The School Girl," with Miss Minnie Palmer; in 1897, toured in "The New Magdalen," "The Sorrows of Satan," etc.; joined Ben Greet's Company, playing Miladi in "The Three Musketeers," Queen Catherine in "Henry VIII," Portia in "The Merchant of Venice," Peg Woffington in "Masks and Faces," Clara Douglas in "Money," etc.; appeared at the Court Theatre, Oct., 1899, as the Princess Angela in "A Royal Family"; at the Comedy Theatre, 1900, with Ben Greet's company, played Lady Teazle in "The School for Scandal," Rosalind in "As You Like It," and Hilary Unett in "In Spite of All"; first came prominently before the public, when at short notice, she played the part of Violet Oglander in "The Lackey's Carnival," at the Duke of York's Sept., 1900; rejoined Ben Greet's company, and played lead in Shakespearean repertory; appeared at Regent's Park, July, 1901, as Iolanthe in "King René's Daughter"; Imperial, in June, 1902, played in "Everyman," in which she was highly successful; appeared in the same play at Mendelssohn Hall, New York, later in the same year; at the Knickerbocker Theatre, New York, Feb., 1904, played Viola in "Twelfth Night"; at Daly's, New York, Mar. 1904, played Kate Hardcastle in "She Stoops to Conquer"; at the New Lyceum, New York, May, 1904, played Portia in "The Merchant of Venice"; on her return to England was engaged by the late Sir Henry Irving, and toured with him as Portia in "The Merchant of Venice," and Rosamund in "Becket"; appeared at the Court, Apr., 1905, as Andromache in "The Trojan Women," of Euripides; Drury Lane, May, 1905, as Portia to Sir Henry Irving's Shylock; at the Court, Nov., 1905, played Mrs. Baines in "Major Barbara"; Jan. 1906, played Electra in Gilbert Murray's translation of Euripides' tragedy; in May, 1906, played Emilia in Mr. Lewis Waller's "all-star" production of "Othello" at the Lyric, and Brangwaine in Comyns Carr's "Tristram and Iseult," at the Adelphi, Sept., 1906; was next seen as Greeba in "The Bondman," Adelphi, Jan., 1907; at the Court, Jan. 1907, played in "The Philanderer"; at the Playhouse, in Mar., was seen as Crystal Wride in "Her Son"; at the Court, in Apr., as Vida Levering in "Votes for Women"; at the Imperial, in May, as Robina Fleming in "Clothes and the Woman"; at the Bijou, Bayswater, in June, she played in "The Servant in the House" and in "The Winterfeast"; at the Savoy, in Sept., she played Mrs. Gwyn in "Joy," and in Oct., Judith Anderson in "The Devil's Disciple"; engaged to appear in America under the management of Mr. Henry Miller, 1908, in "The Great Divide" and in her husband's two plays, "The Servant in the House" and "The Winterfeast"; at the Adelphi, London, Sept., 1909, played Ruth Jordan in "The Great Divide," and Oct., 1909, Auntie in "The Servant in the House"; at the New Theatre,

New York, 1910-11, played Sister Beatrice in Maeterlinck's play of that name, Hermione in "The Winter's Tale," Mistress Ford in "The Merry Wives of Windsor," The Piper in the play of that name, Light in "The Blue Bird," and the Chisera in "The Arrow Maker"; in Oct., 1911, toured in "The Piper," under the management of Winthrop Ames; at the Little Theatre, New York, Mar., 1912, played Tchan-Kiun in "The Flower of the Palace of Han," and the Peasant Woman in "The Terrible Meek"; then toured with Richard Bennett in "The Stronger Claim"; at the Empire, New York, Jan., 1913, appeared as Monique Felt in "The Spy"; at the Children's Theatre, New York, Mar., 1913, again played Everyman; at Chicago, May, 1913, played the Woman in "The Necessary Evil"; at Maxine Elliott's Theatre, New York, Jan., 1914, played Madame Norma in "The Deadlock"; during 1915 toured with her husband in "The Servant in the House"; at the Adolf Lewisohn Stadium, New York, May, 1915, played Andromache in "The Trojan Women"; at Bar Harbour, Aug., 1915, played Iolanthe in "King René's Daughter"; at the New Amsterdam Theatre, New York, Mar., 1916, Queen Katherine in "King Henry VIII," with Sir Herbert Tree; at the Stadium, New York College, May, 1916, at the Shakespeare Tercentenary celebration, played Miranda in "Caliban by the Yellow Sands"; at Hollis Street, Boston, Oct., 1916, Mistress Ford in "The Merry Wives of Windsor," with Sir Herbert Tree; at the Cort Theatre, Jan., 1918, again played Everyman; Feb., 1918, Rosalind in "As You Like It"; at the Vieux Colombier Theatre, New York, Apr., 1918, Mary Bliss in "The Army with Banners"; at the Shubert Theatre, Nov., 1918, Light in "The Betrothal"; during 1919 appeared as Ferda in "The Fool from the Hills," and since then in the annual Greek plays at Millbrook, N.Y.; she has also toured in Shakespearean repertory, and in her husband's repertory of plays for three players, "The Chastening," "The Admiral," and "The Salutation"; at the Forty-eighth Street Theatre, New York, Feb., 1923, played the Carpenter's Wife in "The Chastening," and Apr., 1924, the Queen in "The Admiral"; appeared in these two last-mentioned plays at St. Paul's Church, and the Mary Ward Settlement, London, June–July, 1924; returned to America, Aug., 1924; again appeared in London, July, 1926, when she appeared at the St. Pancras People's Theatre, as Francesca da Rimini in "The Salutation"; returned to America, and in 1930, made a great success when she appeared as Hamlet; tours with her husband's company, and has lately appeared in "Old Nobody," "Crumbs," "Flaming Ministers," "Everyman," "As You Like it" (as Rosalind), etc.; trustee and Head of Drama Department, Bennett Junior College, Millbrook, New York, U.S.A.; awarded gold medal for diction by the American Academy of Arts and Letters, 1927; hon. M.A., Mount Holyoke College, U.S.A., 1927; hon. Litt.D., New Jersey College for Women, and Oberlin College, U.S.A., 1933, and Russell Sage College, U.S.A., 1934. (Died 23 Sept., 1955; age 79)

MATURIN, Eric, actor; b. in India, 30 May, 1883; s. of Colonel F. H. Maturin and his wife Edith (Money); e. Tonbridge School; prior to making his appearance on the stage was engaged in the City; made his first appearance on the stage at the Haymarket Theatre, in the summer of 1901, as a Sergeant in "The Second in Command"; then went on tour playing Lieutenant Barker in "The Second in Command"; at the Imperial Theatre, Jan., 1902, played Felix in 'Mdlle. Mars"; played four tours with Mr. and Mrs. Kendal, appearing as Archie Hamilton in "A Scrap of Paper"; Gilbert in "Dick Hope," etc.; toured as the Earl of Plumbleigh in "Little Mary," with Sir John Hare; also toured in "Beauty and the Barge," and "The Mountain Climber"; toured in the United States and Canada with Forbes-Robertson, and Olga Nethersole, and also appeared in Paris with Miss Nethersole; at the Lyric Theatre, Sept., 1907, played Sir Kenneth

Friarly in "Under the Greenwood Tree," and appeared in the same part, at the Garrick Theatre, New York; at the St. James's, Sept., 1909, appeared as Leonard Ferris in "Mid-Channel," and also played the same part in the New York production; at the Playhouse, 1910, appeared in "The Flag Lieutenant"; at the Comedy, Sept., 1910, played Otho Dundas in "A Woman's Way"; at the Royalty, June, 1911, played in "The Parisienne"; at the Shaftesbury, Sept., 1911, played Captain Yamaki in "The Mousmé"; at the Playhouse, May, 1912, played Lieutenant Frank Ettridge in "Love—and What Then?"; at the Aldwych, Sept., 1912, Will Ganton in "The Great John Ganton"; at the Little, Dec., 1912, Reggie Moody in "If We Had Only Known"; at His Majesty's, Mar., 1913, Gilbert Hall in "The Happy Island"; at the Little, Apr., 1913, the Duke of Dartford in "The Cap and Bells"; at the Globe, June, 1913, appeared as Lionel Seaton Glastonbury in "The Gilded Pill"; at the Playhouse, New York, Sept., 1914, played Hubert Willoughby in "The Elder Son"; at the Lyric, New York, Oct., 1914, Major Pollock in "Evidence"; after returning to England, was granted a commission as Lieutenant in the Royal Field Artillery; served 1914–18 (Mesopotamia); he reappeared on the London stage, at the Kennington Theatre, Mar., 1919, as Robert Hayes in "The Governor's Lady"; during 1920 toured with Miss Gertrude Elliott as Randolph Weeks in "Come Out of the Kitchen," Paolo Salvo in "The Eyes of Youth," and Peter Dawson in "Lonely Lady"; at the Shaftesbury, June, 1921, played Oliver Lawrence in "Out to Win"; at the Court, Oct., 1921, Randall Utterwood in "Heartbreak House"; at the St. Martin's, Mar., 1922, Captain Ronald Dancy in "Loyalties"; at the Haymarket, Aug., 1923, Rupert of Hentzau in "The Prisoner of Zenda"; at Wyndham's, Feb., 1924, Thorpe Savile in "Not in Our Stars"; at the Comedy, July, 1924, John Cutting in "The Creaking Chair"; Queen's, May, 1925, Homer Cady in "Beggar on Horseback"; Adelphi, Sept., 1925, Gerald March in "The Green Hat"; Prince of Wales's, Mar., 1926, Hon. Victor Anton in "Ashes"; Globe, July, 1926, Sir Frederick Boyne in "Ask Beccles"; Everyman, Mar., 1927, Dawson in "Flotsam"; Lyric, May, 1927, Henri Glessing in "The Garden of Eden"; Court, Feb., 1928, Macbeth (in modern dress); Globe, May, 1928, Hector Wilson in "Mud and Treacle"; Wyndham's, Aug., 1928, Captain Ronald Dancy in a revival of "Loyalties," which he also played at the Odéon, Paris; Globe, Mar., 1929, Keith Staines in "The Stag"; Strand, July, 1929, Paul de Severac in "Beauty"; Vaudeville, Nov., 1929, Mr. Brice in "The Roof"; Everyman, July, 1930, Lord Darlington in "Lady Windermere's Fan"; Comedy, Dec., 1930, Harry West in "Twelve Hours"; Whitehall, Feb., 1931, Chief-Inspector Preston in "Good Losers"; Dec., 1931, George Aram in "The Gay Adventure"; Vaudeville, Apr., 1933, Major Stansbury in "The Soldier and the Gentlewoman"; Piccadilly, June, 1933 (for Repertory Players), Gerald Martyn in "Clean Hands"; Shaftesbury, Dec., 1933, Major Chepstow in "A Present from Margate"; Fortune, May, 1935, Owen Willis in "Double Error"; Apollo, Oct., 1935, Stelling in "Espionage"; Ambassadors', Mar., 1937, Sir Charles Carnworthy in "Bats in the Belfry"; Whitehall, Dec., 1937, Count Victor Mattoni in "I Killed the Count"; New, Mar., 1940, Adrian de Brune in "The Silver Patrol"; toured, Apr., 1942, as Lanyon Kelsey in "Inspector Silence Takes the Air"; Richmond, Sept., 1942, Mark Lewis in "All This and To-Morrow"; Wyndham's, Sept., 1944, Colonel Algernon Hume-Banbury in "The Banbury Nose"; toured, 1946, as Sir Gervase Tulse in "Day After To-Morrow," and played this part at the Fortune, Aug., 1946; Boltons, Mar., 1948, Major Macaw in "Hog's Blood and Hellebore"; Covent Garden, July, 1948, appeared as the Interpreter and the Master of Ceremonies in "The Pilgrim's Progress"; New Lindsey, Sept., 1950, Sir Gerald Corbett in "Lovely, Lovely, Money"; has appeared in numerous films.

Favourite part: Leonard in "Mid-Channel." *Recreations:* Cricket, golf, squash racquets, riding, motoring, and tennis. *Club:* Junior Carlton.
(Died 17 Oct., 1957; age 74)

MAUDE, Charles Raymond, actor; *s.* of R. W. de L. Maude and Jenny Maria Catherine Goldschmidt (Maude); *e.* at Brasenose College, Oxford University; *m.* Nancy Price; while at Oxford, in 1904, appeared with the O.U.D.S. as Orlando in "As You Like It," Claudio in "Much Ado About Nothing," and Duke Orsino in "Twelfth Night"; was a pupil at the Academy of Dramatic Art, 1905; made his first professional appearance at the Garrick Theatre, under the management of Arthur Bourchier, when he walked on during the run of "The Walls of Jericho," 1905; then appeared at His Majesty's, Mar., 1905, as Maurice Fancourt in "Agatha"; appeared at the Comedy, 28 Mar., 1905, as Harry Ballantyne in "Lady Ben"; at His Majesty's, Apr., 1905, played Little Billee in "Trilby"; at Terry's, Sept., 1905, appeared as Algernon Wood in "An Angel Unawares"; at the Comedy, Feb., 1906, played Sir Harold Airlie in "The Alabaster Staircase"; at the Waldorf, Mar., 1906, appeared as Henry Morland in "The Heir-at-Law," and in Apr., as Lieutenant Peter Barker in "The Second in Command"; at the Duke of York's, 3 Sept., 1906, played Freddy Gunner in "Toddles," and Charlie in "The Scapegrace" ("Good for Nothing" in dumb show); at the Playhouse, Jan., 1907, played Lieutenant Alan Hartley in "The Drums of Oude"; at the Duke of York's, Mar., 1908, played Rev. John Treherne in the revival of "The Admirable Crichton"; at the Garrick, June, 1908, Percy in "A Pair of Spectacles"; at the Haymarket, Nov., 1908, Captain Wentworth in "Dolly Reforming Herself"; at the Lyric, June, 1909, played Captain Jack Archer in "Fires of Fate"; at the Adelphi, Dec., 1909, appeared as Captain Jack Temperley in "The House of Temperley"; then joined the Duke of York's company for repertory season, and from Feb.

to May, 1910, appeared in "Justice," "The Sentimentalists," "The Madras House," "Trelawney of the Wells," "Prunella," and "Helena's Path"; appeared at the Haymarket, June, 1910, as Henry, Prince of Lucerne, in "Priscilla Runs Away"; Feb., 1911, played Kenneth Mason in "All that Matters"; at the Royalty, Feb., 1911, played Nablotsky in "The Career of Nablotsky"; at the Haymarket, Mar., 1911, played William O'Farrell in "Lady Patricia"; June, 1911, played Slag in "The Gods of the Mountains," and Gerard de Mayran in "Above Suspicion"; at the Queen's, Sept., 1911, made a fresh departure when he appeared as Joachim in the comic opera "Bonita"; while still playing in this piece, appeared at the Palace Theatre, Oct., 1911, as Walter Cozens in "The Man in the Stalls"; at His Majesty's, Nov., 1911, appeared as the King of Gothia in "The War God"; at the St. James's, Dec., 1911, played the Hon. Nigel Armine in "Bella Donna"; at the Haymarket, Apr., 1912, appeared as Geronimus in "Pitch and Soap"; at the Criterion, Sept., 1912, as the Hon. Gerald Porth in "A Young Man's Fancy"; Oct., 1912, as Charlton Vansittart in "Tantrums"; at the Gaiety, Apr., 1913, played Valentine Twiss in "The Girl on the Film"; at the Little Theatre, New York, Dec., 1913, played Leonard Charteris in "The Philanderer"; at the Belasco Theatre, Washington, Apr., 1914, played in "Ambition"; after the outbreak of war, 1914, applied for a commission in the Army, subsequently promoted to the rank of Lieut.-Colonel; has now retired from the stage; is an accomplished composer of music; part author with Lady Mary Cholmondeley, of "The Hand on the Latch," produced at the Playhouse, Mar., 1911.
(Died 14 Nov., 1943; age 61)

MAUDE, Cyril, actor-manager; *b.* London, 24 Apr., 1862; *s.* of Captain Chas. H. Maude and the Hon. Mrs. Maude; *e.* at Charterhouse; *m.* (1) Winifred Emery (*d.* 1924); (2) Mrs. P. H. Trew; studied for the stage under Charles Cartwright and the late Roma Le Thiere, but was forced to quit the country owing to ill-health, and went to Canada, subsequently going down to America; it was at Denver, Colorado, that he made his first appearance on the stage, as a member of the late Daniel Bandmann's Company, as the servant in " East Lynne," Apr., 1884; made his first appearance in New York, at Stetson's Fifth Avenue Theatre, 27 Oct., 1884, as Basil Giorgione in " The Colonel "; subsequently appeared at the People's Theatre, Dec., 1884, in " Called Back "; he also played in " Lost " and " Impulse "; he returned to England in 1885, and made his first appearance on the London stage, at the Criterion Theatre, 18 Feb., 1886, as Mr. Pilkie in " The Great Divorce Case "; he then went on tour, playing Alaric Baffin in " The Candidate," Penryn in " Truth," and Jack Howard in " The Man with Three Wives "; he appeared at the Strand, 2 Aug., 1886, as Sir Charles Harwood in " The Rubber of Life "; at the Grand Theatre, Islington, 5 Sept., 1887, he appeared as the Duke of Courtland in " Racing," in which he made quite a hit; he was next engaged at the Gaiety, and appeared there on 8 Oct., 1887, as Christopher Larkings in " Woodcock's Little Game "; at the Prince of Wales's, 13 Dec., 1887, made another notable success as Austin Woodville in " Handfast "; at the Gaiety, he also played Mondelico in " Frankenstein," and Horace Newlove in " Lot 49 "; he was then engaged for the Vaudeville Theatre, and appeared there, 8 Mar., 1888, as Lord Fellamar in " Joseph's Sweetheart "; he also played there the parts of Charles Farlow in " That Doctor Cupid," 1889; Charles Spangle in " Angelina," 1889; John Hackabout in " The Old Home," 1889; Joseph Surface in " The School for Scandal," 1890; Mr. Solmes in " Clarissa," 1890, and Lory in " Miss Tomboy," 1890; he then joined Charles Wyndham at the Criterion, appearing there 27 Nov., 1890, as Cool in " London Assurance," and he also appeared there as Sir Benjamin Backbite in " The School for Scandal," Sir Richard

Steele in " Richard Savage," subsequently touring as Squire Chivey in " David Garrick "; he then joined Henry Arthur Jones's company at the Avenue, and appeared there, Jan., 1892, as Palsom in " The Crusaders " and Juxon Prall in " Judah "; returned to the Criterion, 1892, to play the Duke of Mayfair in " The Fringe of Society "; and also appeared there as Desmarets in " Plot and Passion "; after appearing at the Strand, July, 1892, as Woodcock in " A Lucky Dog," he joined Mrs. Langtry at the Haymarket, and played, in Sept., 1892, Baron Finot in " The Queen of Manoa," in Oct., Grahame M'Farlane in " Agatha Tylden," and in Nov., Justice Gyves in " The Burglar and the Judge "; at the Trafalgar Square Theatre, Feb., 1893, played Cripps in " The County Councillor," and the Duke of Salop in " The Babble Shop "; at the St. James's, 27 May, 1893, he was Cayley Drummle in " The Second Mrs. Tanqueray "; in Sept., 1893, he joined Comyns Carr at the Comedy, and remained there until 1896, playing Mr. Watkin in " Sowing the Wind," Lord Dazzleton in " Dick Sheridan," Brigard in " Frou-Frou," Colonel Cazenove in " The New Woman," Sir Arthur Studley in " Delia Harding," Ben Dixon in " The Prude's Progress," Sir Fletcher Portwood in " The Benefit of the Doubt," Sir Pinto Wanklyn in " The Late Mr. Castello," Gaffer Jarge, and Sir Wellington Port in " A Mother of Three "; he then played Sir Benjamin Backbite in " The School for Scandal," at the Lyceum, June, 1896, with Forbes-Robertson, and then entered into partnership with Frederick Harrison at the Haymarket Theatre, the association lasting from 17 Oct., 1896, until July, 1905; during this period he produced and played in the following plays : " Under the Red Robe " as Captain Larolle, 17 Oct., 1896; " A Marriage of Convenience," as the Chevalier de Valclos, 5 June, 1897; " The Little Minister," as the Rev. Gavin Dishart, 6 Nov., 1897; " The Manoeuvres of Jane," as Lord Bapchild, 20 Oct., 1898; " A Golden Wedding," as Professor Horace Courtley, 30 Nov., 1898; " The Black Tulip," as Dr. Cornelis

Van Baerle, 28 Oct., 1899; "She Stoops to Conquer," as old Hardcastle, 9 Jan., 1900; "The Rivals," as Bob Acres, 27 Mar., 1900; "The School for Scandal," as Sir Peter Teazle, 19 June, 1900; "The Second in Command," as Major Christopher Bingham, 27 Nov., 1900; "Frocks and Frills," as Sir Richard Kettle, 2 Jan., 1902; "Caste," as Eccles, 26 Apr., 1902; "There's Many a Slip," as Gustave de Grignon, 23 Aug., 1902; "The Unforeseen," as the Rev. Walter Maxwell, 2 Dec., 1902; "The Clandestine Marriage," as Lord Ogleby, 17 Mar., 1903; "Cousin Kate," as Heath Desmond, 18 June, 1903; "The Monkey's Paw," as Mr. White, 6 Oct., 1903; "Joseph Entangled," as Sir Joseph Lacy, 19 Jan., 1904; "Lady Flirt," as the Comte de la Roche, 25 May, 1904; at the New Theatre, while the Haymarket was undergoing alterations, "Beauty and the Barge," as Captain James Barley 30 Aug., 1904; and transferred to the Haymarket in Jan., 1905; "Everybody's Secret," as Sir Michael Parkes, 14 Mar., 1905; "The Creole," as Napoleon Buonaparte, 6 May, 1905; and "The Cabinet Minister," as Joseph Lebanon, 1 June, 1905; after quitting the Haymarket, he acquired the Avenue Theatre, which he was having demolished and rebuilt, when, on 5 Dec., 1905, the roof of Charing Cross Station adjoining collapsed and wrecked the building; in the autumn of 1905, he toured as Sir Julian Twombley in "The Cabinet Minister"; pending the reconstruction of the Avenue (re-named The Playhouse, on completion), he took over the management of the Waldorf (now Strand) Theatre, and opened there on 17 Jan., 1906, as Albert Edward Tutt in "The Partik'ler Pet," and Mr. Tister in "The Superior Miss Pellender"; from Feb. to Apr., 1906, gave revivals of "She Stoops to Conquer," and "The Second in Command"; on 20 Mar., 1906, played Dr. Pangloss in "The Heir-at-Law," and 21 May, 1906, appeared as Nathaniel Barron in "Shore Acres"; he next entered into an arrangement with Charles Frohman, and at the Duke of York's, on 3 Sept., 1906, appeared as Lord

Meadows in "Toddles"; this was subsequently transferred to Wyndham's, and thence to the rebuilt Playhouse, which he opened on 28 Jan., 1907; he has since appeared there as Richard Gasgoyne in "Her Son," 12 Mar., 1907; The Earl of Cardington in "The Earl of Pawtucket," 25 June, 1907; Peter in "French as he is Spoke," 15 Aug., 1907; James Entwhistle in "Fido," 26 Nov., 1907; Jim O'Grindle in "The O'Grindles," 21 Jan., 1908; Christopher Strode in "Marjory Strode," 19 Mar., 1908; Dodo Brezard in "Pro Tem.," 29 Apr., 1908; Richard Lascelles in "The Flag Lieutenant," 16 June, 1908; Captain Bambazone in "A Merry Devil," 3 June, 1909; James Cottenham in "Tantalising Tommy," 15 Feb., 1910; The Toymaker in "The Toymaker of Nuremberg," 15 Mar., 1910; Robin Worthington in "A Single Man," 8 Nov., 1910; Lord Punterfield in "Our Little Cinderella," 20 Dec., 1910; the Duke of Rye in "One of the Dukes," 18 Mar., 1911; Admiral Sir Peter Antrobus in "Pomander Walk," 29 June, 1911; Rip Van Winkle in the play of that name, 21 Sept., 1911; Sir Joseph Lorrimer, Bart., in "Dad," 4 Nov., 1911; Major Christopher Bingham in "The Second in Command," 8 Feb., 1912; the Bishop of Munbridge in "Love—and What Then?" 2 May, 1912; Albert Loriflan in "The Little Café," 28 Sept., 1912; Rev. Cuthbert Sanctuary, D.D., in "The Headmaster," 22 Jan., 1913; at the Theatre Royal, Glasgow, 19 Sept., 1913, appeared as Andrew Bullivant in "Grumpy"; in the same month sailed for Canada, and opened at Toronto, 6 Oct., 1913, in "Toddles"; made his first appearance in New York, at Wallack's Theatre, 3 Nov., 1913, as Major Bingham in "The Second in Command"; subsequently revived "Beauty and the Barge," "The Ghost of Jerry Bundler," "Grumpy"; the last-mentioned piece proved a great success; reappeared in London, at the New Theatre, 13 May, 1914, as Andrew Bullivant in "Grumpy," repeating the New York success; again toured in America, 1914, and again in 1915; in Sept., 1915, terminated his lease of the Playhouse, London; again returned to America, and at the Empire, Syracuse, Oct., 1916, appeared as Jeff in a play of that name; at the Empire, New York, Oct., 1916, played the part of George de Lacorfe in " The Basker "; then visited Australia, 1917-18, playing " Grumpy," Dr. Lucius O'Grady in " General John Regan," " Caste," etc.; at the Empire, New York, Sept., 1918, appeared as Blinn Corbett in " The Saving Grace "; returned to London, 1919, and made his reappearance, at the Criterion, Nov., 1919, as Lord Richard Sandridge in " Lord Richard in the Pantry," which ran over twelve months; in Mar., 1921, appeared as Andrew Bullivant in a revival of " Grumpy "; at the Shaftesbury, Oct., 1921, played Timothy O'Flyn in " Timothy "; at the Criterion, Aug., 1922, Henry Talboyes in " The Dippers "; at the Gaiety, New York, Apr., 1923, Mark Sabre in " If Winter Comes "; May, 1923, Lord Grenham in " Aren't We All ? "; in Sept., 1924, appeared in the same part at the Hollis Street Theatre, Boston, subsequently touring in the same part, and appeared at the Globe, New York, Apr., 1925, in a revival of the same piece; at the Gaiety, New York, Oct., 1925, played Sir George Crawford in " These Charming People "; at His Majesty's, London, Feb., 1927, Ronald Tremayne in " The Wicked Earl "; after over five years' absence, reappeared on the London stage, at the Haymarket, Oct., 1932, as Admiral Sir Rupert Ellis in " Once a Husband "; Ambassadors', Nov., 1933, played Don Geronimo in "Cabbages and Kings"; he appeared at the Coliseum in Jan., 1910, as Mr. Jellicoe in " Jellicoe and the Fairies "; and Jan., 1912, in aid of the *Daily Telegraph* Dickens Fund, as Mrs. Sairey Gamp in a sketch of that name; appeared by Command of the late King Edward at Sandringham, 9 Nov., 1907, in " French as he is Spoke," and the dressing room scene from " The Clandestine Marriage "; 13 Nov., 1908, in " The Flag Lieutenant "; at Balmoral Castle, by Command of King George, 13 Sept., 1913, in " The Headmaster "; at the Command performance at Drury Lane, 17 May, 1911,

he played Sir Frederick Blount in " Money," and at the Gala performance at His Majesty's, 27 June, 1911, played Don Ferolo Whiskerandos in " The Critic "; author of " The Haymarket Theatre," 1903; " The Actor in Room 931 " (novel), 1925; " Behind the Scenes with Cyril Maude," 1927; "Strange Cousins," a play (with Peter Garlard), 1934; was elected President of the Council of the Royal Academy of Dramatic Art, July, 1936; on his 80th birthday, 24 Apr., 1942, at the Haymarket Theatre, in aid of the R.A.F. Benevolent Fund and the Actors' Orphanage, played Sir Peter in the quarrel scene from "The School for Scandal," and in the one-act play, "A Seat in the Park"; has appeared in films, having made his first picture, "Beauty and the Barge," in 1913; subsequently he appeared in "Peer Gynt," "The Antique Dealer," "Grumpy," "These Charming People," "Counsel's Opinion," "Orders is Orders," "Girls Will Be Boys," "Heat Wave." *Recreations:* Fishing and shooting. *Club:* Garrick. *(Died 20 Feb., 1951; age 88)*

MAUDE, Elizabeth (Betty), actress; *b.* 3 Sept., 1912; *d.* of Charles Raymond Maude and his wife Nancy (Price); made her first appearance on the stage at the Everyman Theatre, 11 Apr., 1925, as Youth in "Overture"; Apr., 1926, played David in "Benediction"; Queen's, Sept., 1926, Lettice in "And So to Bed"; at the "Q," Sept., 1927, Helen in "Old Mrs. Wiley"; "Q," and Little, Oct., 1927, Rosie in "The Red Umbrella"; "Q," Dec., 1928, played in "Helen With the High Hand"; Court, Feb., 1929, Suzanne in "Thérèse Raquin"; Queen's, Feb., 1929, Laura in "Mafro Darling"; Fortune, Dec., 1930, Hon. Lily Belgrave in "A Pantomime Rehearsal"; June, 1931, Hester in "The Ship"; Duchess, Dec., 1931, Anne Page in "The Merry Wives of Windsor"; June, 1932, Barbara Westaway in "The Secret Woman"; Little, Oct., 1932, the Unknown Lady in "The Silver Box"; Little, Dec., 1932, the Queen of Hearts in "Alice in Wonderland"; Feb., 1933, Jorund in "The Witch,"

and Maria Scott in "Cock Robin";
Mar., 1933, Wilhelmina Belches in
"Scott of Abbotsford"; Apr., 1933,
Lady Jasmine in "Overture"; Ful-
ham, Oct., 1933, Camamilla in "Fin-
ished Abroad," and the same part at
the Savoy, Mar., 1934; Little, Oct.,
1934, Nell Gwyn in "Royal Baggage";
Arts, May, 1935, Fanny Cornforth in
"Rossetti"; Little, July, 1935, Regina
in "Ghosts"; Playhouse, Dec., 1935,
the White Queen and Sheep in "Alice
Through the Looking Glass," which
she also played, 1936 and 1937; Little,
Apr., 1936, Meg in "Whiteoaks,"
which she played until 1938; Little,
June, 1936, Iris in "The Insect Play";
Arts, Nov., 1936, Ashton in "The
King's Pleasure"; Playhouse, Nov.,
1938, Rose in "The Shoemaker's Holiday"; St. James's, Dec., 1938, Claire
in "Let's Pretend"; toured, May,
1939, as Meg in "Whiteoaks"; at the
Tavistock Little Theatre, Jan., 1940,
played Fraulein Lehzen in "The Child
of Kensington," and Belle Collins in
"Down Our Street."

MAUDE, Gillian, actress; *d.* of
Ralph Alexander Maude; studied
for the stage at the Royal Academy of
Dramatic Art, 1931-2; made her first
appearance in London at Daly's The-
atre, 19 Oct., 1933, as Annette in
"Maternité"; at "Q," Dec., 1933,
played Romaine Denby in "Stormy
Passage"; Royalty, Jan., 1935, June
Bedford in "Father of Lies"; Grand,
Blackpool, Aug., 1936, Rosemary Jor-
dan in "Laughter in Court"; Little,
Feb., 1937, Joan Saunders in "Strange
Barrier"; Duchess, Apr., 1937, Ann
Chilgrove in "Mile Away Murder";
New, Sept., 1937, Dinah Tilney in
"Bonnet Over The Windmill"; Vaude-
ville, June, 1938, Susie Brent in "Sexes
and Sevens"; Richmond, July, 1939,
Lucy Barton in "Lucy, Bless Her";
"Q," Apr., 1940, Claire Stuart in
"Passing-By"; Citizen's Theatre, Glas-
gow, Sept., 1944, played in "The
Comedy of Good and Evil"; Gateway,
June, 1946, Eve Marsden in "As Good
as a Feast."

MAUDE, Joan, actress; *b.* Rickmans-
worth, 16 Jan., 1908; *d.* of Charles
Maude and his wife Nancy (Price);

m. Frank Waters; made her first
appearance on the stage at His
Majesty's Theatre, 15 Oct., 1921, as
a solo dancer in "Cairo"; subse-
quently at Huddersfield, played Puck
in "A Midsummer Night's Dream,"
and at Worthing, Puck, and Ariel in
"The Tempest"; at the Adelphi,
Sept., 1922, succeeded Lila Maravan
as Olga Ratcliffe in "The Way of an
Eagle"; at the New. Oct., 1922,
Chorus in "Medea"; at the St.
James's, Dec., 1922, Tootles in "Peter
Pan"; at the Regent, Apr., 1923, the
Chrysalis in "The Insect Play";
at Drury Lane, Sept., 1923, the Hon.
Mary Carstairs in "Good Luck";
at the Adelphi, Dec., 1923, again played
Tootles in "Peter Pan"; at the
Haymarket, Oct., 1924, Phyllis in
"Old English"; Adelphi, Mar., 1925,
Aurea Vyse in "Iris"; Aldwych, June,
1925, Lady June in "The Verdict";
"Q," Aug., 1925, Adela Frampton in
"The Odd Man"; "Q" and Royalty,
Sept., 1925, Marged in "Taffy";
Comedy, Nov., 1925, Margery in "The
Ring o' Bells"; Ambassadors', Mar.,
1926, Jill Lambert in "The Widow's
Cruise"; Fortune, Dec., 1926, Norah
Hennessey in "Biddy"; "Q," Apr.,
1927, Nan Sparks in "The Village";
Aug., 1927, Betty Grapt in "Mr.
Faithful"; King's, Hammersmith,
May, 1927, Peggy in "A Warm
Corner"; "Q," Mar., 1929, Anna in
"The Far-Off Hills"; May, 1929,
Mary Bowing in "Bachelors' Wives";
Duke of York's, Sept., 1929, Magdalen
Weissensee in "Jew Süss"; Kingsway,
Apr., 1930, Ethel Carlton in "His
Excellency the Governor"; May, 1930,
Blanche Chilworth in "Liberty Hall";
in Feb., 1931, toured as Maria Luisa
in "General Crack"; Fortune, May,
1931, Lady Henrietta in "The Duke of
Killicrankie"; Criterion, Aug., 1931,
Maud Wilder in "Those Naughty
'Nineties"; Savoy, Oct., 1931, Salome
in Wilde's play of that name; Wynd-
ham's, Feb., 1932, Jacqueline Thurston
in "The Green Pack"; Gate, Oct.,
1932, Solveig in "Peer Gynt"; during
1933, toured with Matheson Lang, as
Harriett Arbuthnot in "Wellington";
Little, May, 1933, played Madge
Thomas in "Strife"; at Oxford, June,
1933, for the O.U.D.S., played Helena

in "A Midsummer Night's Dream"; Duke of York's, Nov., 1933, played Katheryn Howard in "The Rose Without a Thorn"; "Q," Aug., 1934, Lady Marjorie in "Strangers in Paradise"; St. Martin's, June, 1935, Cecily in "The Two Mrs. Carrolls"; Little, Nov., 1936, Jane Shore in "The King and Mistress Shore"; she then left the stage and appeared only in films and television, until 1950; reappeared on the stage at the New Lindsey, June, 1950, as Honor Burklynch in "The Family Honour"; "Q," Nov., 1950, played Sheila Arnold in "Celestial Fires." *Address:* 1 Robert Street, Adelphi, London, W.C.2. *Telephone No.:* Trafalgar 3874.

MAUGHAM, William Somerset, C.H., M.R.C.S., L.R.C.P., author and dramatist; *b.* Paris, 25 Jan., 1874; *y.s.* of the late Robert Ormond Maugham; *g.-s.* of Robert Maugham, a founder of the Incorporated Law Society; *e.* King's School, Canterbury, Heidelberg University, and St. Thomas's Hospital; *m.* Gwendolen Maude Syrie Wellcome, *o. d.* of Dr. Barnardo (mar. dis.); author of the plays, " Schiffbrüchig," produced at Berlin, in German, 1901; " A Man of Honour," produced at the Avenue, 1904; " Mdlle. Zampa," Avenue, 1904; " Lady Frederick," Court, 1907; " Jack Straw," Vaudeville, Mar., 1908; " Mrs. Dot," Comedy, 1908; " The Explorer," Lyric, 1908; " Penelope," Comedy, 1909; " The Noble Spaniard " (from the French), Royalty, 1909; " Smith," Comedy, 1909; " Grace," Duke of York's, 1910; " Loaves and Fishes," Duke of York's, 1911; " The Perfect Gentleman " (from Molière's Comedy " Le Bourgeois Gentilhomme "), His Majesty's, 1913; " The Land of Promise," Duke of York's, 1914; " Caroline," New, 1916; " Our Betters," Hudson, New York, 1917, and Globe, London, 1923; " Love in a Cottage," Globe, London, 1918; " Caesar's Wife," Royalty, 1919; " Home and Beauty," Playhouse, 1919; " The Unknown," Aldwych, 1920; " The Circle," Haymarket, 1921; " East of Suez," His Majesty's, 1922; " The Camel's Back," Playhouse, 1924; " The Letter," Playhouse, 1927;

" The Constant Wife," Strand, 1927; " The Sacred Flame," New York, 1928, and Playhouse, London, 1929; "The Breadwinner," Vaudeville, 1930; "For Services Rendered," Globe, 1932; "Sheppy," 1933; "Theatre" (with Guy Bolton), 1941; created a theatrical "record" in 1908, by having four original plays performed in London concurrently; his published works include " Liza of Lambeth," 1897; " The Hero," 1901; " Mrs. Craddock," 1902; " The Merry Go Round," 1904; " The Land of the Blessed Virgin," 1905; " The Magician," 1909; "Cakes and Ale," "First Person Singular," "The Narrow Corner," "Ah King," "Don Fernando," "Theatre," "The Summing Up" (a survey of his life and work to 1938), "Christmas Holiday," "The Mixture as Before," "Up at the Villa," "The Razor's Edge," "Then and Now," "A Writer's Notebook," "The Partial View," "Ten Novels and their Authors," "The Magician," etc.; after the outbreak of war, 1914, served as a doctor in France; was created a Chevalier of the Legion of Honour, 1929, and a Commander in 1939; created a Companion of Honour, 1954; Companion of the Royal Society of Literature, 1961; Hon. D.Litt., Oxford and Toulouse Universities; Hon. Senator of Heidelberg University, 1961; Hon. Fellow of the Library of Congress, Washington; Hon. Fellow of Arts and Letters, New York. *Clubs:* Bath and Garrick. *(Died 16 Dec., 1965; age 91)*

MAULE, Robin, actor; *b.* London, 23 Nov., 1924; *s.* of Donovan Maule and his wife Mollie (Shiells); *e.* in France and London; made his first appearance on the stage at the Cambridge Theatre, 22 Dec., 1936, as Keith in "The Boy Who Lost His Temper"; Gate, Feb., 1937, played Gerard in "Invitation to a Voyage"; St. James's, Aug., 1937, Nicholas Decker in "Old Music"; Garrick, Dec., 1937, again played Keith in "The Boy Who Lost His Temper"; Duke of York's (for London International Theatre Club), Dec., 1937, the Boy in "Identity Unknown"; Shaftesbury, Sept., 1938, Linford in "Good-bye, Mr.

Chips"; Drury Lane, Mar., 1939, Carl in "The Dancing Years"; during 1938, appeared in the film "Good-bye, Mr. Chips," *Recreations*: Reading, cycling, skating, and riding. *(Died 2 Mar., 1942; age 17)*

MAUREY, Max, French dramatic author and manager; *b.* Paris; *e.* College Rollin, Janson, and Paris; has written the following plays: "Rosalie," "Pochard," "Sardanapale," "La Fétiche," "La Glissade," "La Recommandation," "La Fiole," "Un début dans le Monde," "L'Aventure," "Les Cigarettes," "M. Lambert," "Marchand de tableaux," "Au Rez-de Chaussée" (with A. Thierry, *fils*), 1895; "Le Camelot" (with MM. Andry and Jubin), 1897; "Asile de Nuit" (" The Pertik'ler Pet "), 1906; "Depuis Six Mois," "La Savelli," 1906; "Le Chauffeur," 1908; "Stra-divarius," 1909; "Entre Eux," 1910; "Le Pharmacien," 1910; "La délais-sée," 1911; "David Copperfield," 1911 (from Dickens's work); "Michel," "M. Bixion " (with Robert Chauvelot), "Un beau Rôle " (with H. Duvernois); is a Chevalier of the Legion of Honour; was director of the famous Grand Guignol, and is now Director of the Variétés, Paris. *Recreation :* Sword-fighting. *(Died 27 Feb., 1947; age 76)*

MAURICE, Edmund (Edmund Fitz-Maurice Lenon), actor; *s.* of the late Major Lenon, V.C.; made his first appearance on the stage in 1880; in 1882, was at the Surrey Theatre, where he played in " Law, not Justice," " Men and Women," etc. ; appeared at the Court, Mar., 1883, in " The Rector " ; at the Gaiety, May, 1883, played in " After Darkness, Dawn " ; and at the Court, Sept., 1883, in " The Millionaire " ; in 1884, played there in " Margery's Lovers," " Dan'l Druce, Blacksmith," " Devotion," etc. ; appeared at the Haymarket, 1884, in " Evergreen " ; at the Lyceum, Nov., 1884, played Paris in " Romeo and Juliet," with Mary Anderson ; joined the Bancrofts at the Haymarket, 1885, and played Quin in " Masks and Faces," Sergeant Jones in " Ours " ; at the same theatre played in " Dark

Days," " Nadjesda," " Jim the Pen-man " ; at the Court, 1887, played Sir Tristram Mardon in " Dandy Dick " ; at the Globe, May, 1887, played Sir Alger-non Ferrers (" Bootles ") in " Bootles' Baby " ; at the Gaiety, Sept., 1888, played Kallikrates and Leo Vincey in " She " ; at the Haymarket, Apr., 1889, played the Hon. Clive Dashwood in " Wealth " ; at the Criterion, Aug., 1890, appeared as Darrtell Roe in " Welcome Little Stranger " ; at the Haymarket, Nov., 1890, played Anthony Musgrave in " Beau Austin " ; at the Princess's, Apr., 1891, played in " Linda Grey " ; at the Haymarket, Sept., 1892, played in " The Queen of Manoa," and in Oct., in " Agatha Tylden " ; at Terry's, June, 1893, played in " Foreign Policy " and " Becky Sharp " ; at the Comedy, 1893-4, played in " Sowing the Wind " and " Dick Sheridan " ; at the Hay-market, Nov., 1894, played in " John-a-Dreams " and in May, 1895, in " Fédora " ; in Oct., 1895, played Taffy in " Trilby " ; at the Criterion, Dec., 1896, appeared in " Sweet Nancy " ; in 1897, toured in " The Fortune Hunter " ; at the Comedy, 1899, in " Matches " ; at the Haymarket, 1899, played Sir William Saumarez in " The Degenerates " ; at the Comedy, 1900, in " Kenyon's Widow," " Pygmalion and Galatea " ; at the Metropole, 1900, in " Jim Bel-mont " ; at the Prince of Wales's, Feb., 1901, played Quin in " Peg Woffington " ; at the Imperial, Apr., 1901, was the Cardinal Rohan in " A Royal Necklace " ; at Her Majesty's, Oct., 1901, played Lord Ascot in " The Last of the Dandies " ; at the Apollo, 1903, in " The Londoners " ; at the Haymarket, Jan., 1904, played Professor Tofield in " Joseph En-tangled " ; May, 1904, Lord Mel-borough in " Lady Flirt " ; at the New, Aug., 1904, Major Smedley in " Beauty and the Barge " ; at the Haymarket, Mar., 1905, Sergeant Morris in " The Monkey's Paw " ; and Captain Pierre-point in " Everybody's Secret " ; Sept., 1905, Denbigh Thrayle in " On the Love Path " ; at the New Theatre, Jan., 1906, Mr. Moxon in " Captain Drew on Leave " ; at Wyndham's, Mar., 1906, Amos Martlett in " The

Candidate " ; at the Waldorf, May, 1906, Martin Barron in " Shore Acres " ; at His Majesty's, May, 1907, played the Ven. James Daubeny in " A Woman of No Importance " ; at the Apollo, Nov., 1907, he appeared as Sir Wilfred Cates-Darby in " The New York Idea " ; at the Haymarket, Apr., 1908, played Rossiter in " A Fearful Joy " ; at Wyndham's, Oct., 1908, succeeded Robert Loraine as Stephens in " Bellamy the Magnificent " ; at Wyndham's, Nov., 1908, played Percy Bulgar in " Sir Anthony," Jan., 1909, appeared as Prince Yoland in " An Englishman's Home " ; at the Garrick, Sept., 1909, played Lord Parkhurst in " Making a Gentleman" ; at the Globe, Feb., 1910, Lord Francis Etchingham in " The Tenth Man " ; at the Comedy, Sept., 1910, appeared as General Sir Harry Dundas in " A Woman's Way " ; Jan., 1911, as Alfred Hebblethwaite in " Preserving Mr. Panmure " ; at Drury Lane, Command performance, 17 May, 1911, appeared as Toke in " Money " ; at the Little Theatre, Nov., 1911, played Sir Harry Sims in " The Twelve Pound Look " ; at the Kingsway, Sept., 1912, played Mr. Voysey in " The Voysey Inheritance " ; Nov., 1912, Sir William Cheshire, Bart., in " The Eldest Son " ; at the Strand, Feb., 1913, Sir Everard Titsy Chilworth in " The Son and man " in the Savoy, May, 1913, Baron Radviany in " The Seven Sisters " ; at the Royalty, Apr., 1914, Mynheer Cornelis and Sir Charles in " My Lady's Dress " ; at the Haymarket, May, 1914, Colonel Herrick in " The Great Gamble " ; at His Majesty's, May, 1915, Sir Archibald Falkland in " The Right to Kill " ; at the Prince of Wales's, Feb., 1917, Herbert Clatterby, K.C., in " Anthony in Wonderland " ; at the Coliseum, Mar., 1917, played Major Tompkins in " The Passing of the Third-Floor-Back " ; at the Playhouse, Jan., 1918, M. Zoubatoff in " The Yellow Ticket " ; is a Fellow of the Royal Microscopical Society. *Recreations :* Painting, sailing, microscopy, shooting, and fishing. *Clubs :* Savage, National Sporting and Quickett.

(Died 6 Apr., 1928; age 65)

MAX, Edouard Alexandre de, French actor ; *b.* Jassy, Roumania, 14 Feb., 1869 ; studied at the Paris Conservatoire under M. Worms, and took first prize for comedy and tragedy in 1891 ; made his first appearance on the stage at the Odéon as Neron in " Britannicus," 1891 ; appeared at the Renaissance in 1893, in " Izeyl," " Gismonda," " La Princesse Lointaine " ; subsequently appeared at the Odéon in " Don Carlos," " Don Juan en Flandre " ; at the Théâtre Antoine, 1897, where he appeared successfully in " Le Repas du Lion," " Joseph d'Arimathie," " La Gitane," etc. ; at the Nouveau Théâtre, appeared in leading parts in " Le Roi de Rome " and " Salomé " ; at the Odéon, played in " Guerre en Dentelles," 1900, " Pour l'Amour," 1901 ; at the Porte-St.-Martin, played Peter in " Quo Vadis ? " Claude Frollo in " Notre Dame de Paris," Le Roi Christian in " Le Manteau du Roi," and De Pantoya in " Electra " ; at the Théâtre Sarah Bernhardt played in " Francesca da Rimini," " Theroigne de Méricourt," " Werther," " Polyeucte " and " La Sorcière " ; at the Odéon, 1907, played in " L'Otage " ; at Théâtre Antoine, 1907, " Timon d'Athènes " ; at Théâtre Réjane, 1908, " Israel " ; at Théâtre Michel, 1908, " Après " ; at the Théâtre des Arts, 1909, in " Le Tour de Silence " ; at the Théâtre de l'Oeuvre, 1909, in " Pierce Neige et Les Sept Gnomes " ; at the Théâtre Sarah Bernhardt, 1909-11, in " La Conquête d'Athènes," " Le Procès de Jeanne d'Arc," " Le Typhon," etc. ; at the Châtelet, 1912, in " Hélène de Sparte," and 1913, in " Pisanelle " ; at the Renaissance, 1914, played the Prince de Bergue in " L'Homme Riche " ; entered the Comédie Française, and was elected a *sociétaire* in 1917 ; has appeared there as Nero in " Britannicus," Esope, The Monk in " La Cloître," Baron de Horn in " Le Prince d'Aurec," Jules de Miremmont in " Le Repas du Lion," Bazile in " Le Barbier de Seville," Oreste in " Andromaque," Sisyphe in " La Morte Enchaînée," Xerxes in " Les Perses," etc.; appeared at the Opéra, June, 1920, as Antony in " Antoine et Cléopatre " ; has appeared on many occasions in London, playing lead with Madame Bernhardt. *Address :* 66 Rue Caumartin, Paris.

MAXWELL, Gerald, F.R.G.S., author, former dramatic critic ; *b.* London, 19 Mar., 1862 ; was formerly an actor, making his first appearance as far back as 1885, in Wilson Barrett's company, playing in " The Silver King " ; appeared with Barrett at the Princess's in 1886, and in the United States ; played lead with Mrs. Bernard-Beere and Miss Fortescue, also fulfilling an engagement with Augustin Day ; has written novels, edited a weekly paper and produced his own plays ; appointed Dramatic Critic to *The Daily Mail,* 1912, a position he occupied for several years ; published " The Military Map," in two volumes, 1916–18. *(Died 14 Jan., 1930; age 67)*

MAXWELL, Walter, business manager ; *b.* Worthing, 4 Sept., 1877 ; *s.* of Augusta (Doveton) and General William Maxwell, R.A. ; *e.* Blundell's School, Tiverton, N. Devon ; *m.* Christine Silver (mar. dis.) ; originally educated for the Army ; made his first appearance as an actor in 1897 ; entering management, his first production was made at Blackpool in 1901, when he commenced touring " The Sportsman " ; has since successfully toured " The Little Minister," " Quality Street," " Little Mary," " Merely Mary Ann," " The Lion and the Mouse," " When it was Dark," " Kipps," etc.; also toured J. M. Barrie's plays in conjunction with the late Addison Bright ; engaged as business manager by Lena Ashwell for the Kingsway Theatre, Oct., 1907 ; for Evelyn Millard at Criterion, 1909, and at New Theatre, 1910 ; in July, 1910, assumed the management of the Pier, Hastings, which he retained until 1912 ; in 1913, toured " Mr. Preedy and the Countess " ; 1913-14, " Charley's Aunt " ; enlisted as a private in H.M. Forces, Aug., 1914 ; received his commission, 1915 ; wounded in France, 1916 ; served in East Africa, 1917, and West Africa, 1919 ; toured

a concert party through the Far East, 1920 ; toured " The Ninth Earl," 1921. *Favourite play :* " The Little Minister." *Recreations :* Golf and Cricket.

MAY, Ada, actress and dancer ; *b.* 8 Mar., 1900 ; *m.* Colonel Wilson Potter (mar. dis.) ; formerly known as Ada Mae Weeks ; studied dancing under Madame Cavalazzi-Mapleson ; made her first appearance on the New York stage, at the Metropolitan Opera House New York, 28 Nov., 1912, as a dancer in the opera of "Parsifal," subsequently appearing also in "Hansel und Gretel," and in Dec., 1912, in "Aida," with Caruso; in 1915, appeared in "vaudeville," with Fred Nice in "Come to Bohemia"; at the New Amsterdam Theatre, New York, Nov., 1915, danced in "Round the Map"; June, 1916, in "Ziegfeld's Midnight Frolic"; Sept., 1916, appeared as *première danseuse* in "Miss Springtime"; Astor Theatre, May, 1918, joined the cast of "Fancy Free"; at the Knickerbocker Theatre, Dec., 1918, played Mary Dodge in "Listen Lester"; Cort, Oct., 1920, June Ward in "Jim Jam Jems"; Liberty, Oct., 1921, Eloise Drexel in "The O'Brien Girl"; Knickerbocker, Jan., 1924, Laura Lamb in "Lollipop"; she then married and left the stage; reappeared at the Ziegfeld Theatre, Feb., 1927, as Dolly in "Rio Rita"; made her first appearance in London, at the Dominion Theatre, 3 Oct., 1929, as Angy Howard in "Follow Through," scoring an immediate success; at the London Pavilion, Mar., 1930, played in "Cochran's 1930 Revue," and in Mar., 1931, in "Cochran's 1931 Revue"; appeared at the London Palladium, Apr., 1931, in certain numbers from the last-mentioned *revue*; subsequently returned to America; at the Shubert Theatre, New Jersey, Aug., 1932, appeared in "Follies Bergère"; appeared for the first time in a legitimate play, at the Forrest Theatre, New York, Nov., 1932, as Lu in "The Good Fairy"; at Los Angeles, June, 1933, appeared as Frieda Hatzfeld in "Music in the Air," and Apr., 1934, as Minnie in "Biography"; in summer theatres, 1936, played Karen André in "The

Night of January 16"; at Cleveland, July, 1938, played Mimi in "Gay Divorce"; has appeared in films in "Dance, Girl, Dance," etc.

MAY, Akerman, actor ; *b*. London, 12 Nov., 1869 ; *s*. of William Henry May, dental surgeon, and his wife, Jane Mary (Akerman); *e*. Harrow; after some amateur experiences, first engaged professionally at the Strand with Willie Edouin in June, 1891, as utility and understudy, making his first appearance on the stage, at that theatre, 1 Aug., 1891, as the Porter in " The Late Lamented " ; subsequently played a variety of parts with Charles Wyndham, Beerbohm Tree, George Edwardes (with whom he remained for six years), George Alexander, Frank Curzon, Arthur Collins, Charles Frohman, and Robert Courtneidge, playing at nearly all the London theatres ; he has played in leading variety halls as a pantomimist in the wordless plays, " La Main " and " Le Reve"; was on the committee of the Actors' Benevolent Fund, and established the Ackerman May Theatrical Agency ; retired Dec., 1925. *(Died 21 Mar., 1933; age 65)*

MAY, Edna (Pettie), actress and vocalist ; *b*. Syracuse, New York, 2 Sept., 1878 ; *m*. Oscar Lewisohn ; made her first appearance on any stage at her native town of Syracuse, in the spring of 1883, as Little Willie Allen in " Dora "; in 1885 appeared at Syracuse in children's opera company in " H.M.S. Pinafore " and as Mabel in " The Pirates of Penzance "; studied music at the New York Conservatoire; made her first appearance on the professional stage at Syracuse, N.Y., 21 Feb., 1895, in " Si Stebbings," under the management of Dan Darleigh ; made her first appearance on the New York stage at Hammerstein's, 14 Sept., 1896, as Clairette in "Santa Maria," under her own name of Edna May Pettie; at Hoyt's Theatre, 4 Jan., 1897, she appeared as Calliope Ayre in "A Contented Woman," and was then engaged at the New York Casino by George W. Lederer to play the part

of Violet Gray in "The Belle of New York," first produced on 28 Sept., 1897; she made her first appearance on the London stage, at the Shaftesbury Theatre, 12 Apr., 1898, in the same part ; at the Shaftesbury Theatre, 25 Apr., 1900, she played Gabrielle Dalmonte in "An American Beauty": she then returned to the United States; at the Herald Square Theatre, New York, 7 Jan., 1901, she played Olga in "The Girl from Up There," and reappeared in London, at the Duke of York's, 23 Apr., 1901, in the same part ; in Sept., 1901, she joined George Edwardes at the Apollo, playing the Baroness de Trégue in "Kitty Grey," and afterwards Edna Branscombe in "Three Little Maids"; she was next seen at the Prince of Wales's, 9 May, 1903, as Lillian Leigh in "The School Girl," and appeared in the same part at Daly's Theatre, New York, 1 Sept., 1904, afterwards touring in the piece ; at the Prince of Wales's, during 1904, she played Alesia in a revival of " La Poupée " ; at Daly's, New York, 28 Aug., 1905, she played Angela Crystal in " The Catch of the Season "; she reappeared in London, at the Vaudeville Theatre, 11 Apr., 1906, as Julia Chaldicott in " The Belle of Mayfair " ; her sudden resignation of the part, in Sept., caused a newspaper sensation ; at the Aldwych Theatre, 10 Jan., 1907, appeared as Nelly Neil in the play of that name ; this proved to be her last professional engagement, as shortly afterwards she was married and quitted the stage ; she appeared at the Savoy Theatre, in Feb., 1911, for one week, in her old part in " The Belle of New York," in a series of performances given in aid of the Prince Francis of Teck Memorial Fund. *(Died 1 Jan., 1948; age 69)*

MAY, Hans, composer and musical director; *b*. Vienna, 1891; studied music at the Academy of Music, Vienna; composed incidental music to innumerable silent films in Berlin and Paris; came to England, 1930 where he continued to compose music and conduct for innumerable films; composed the score of "Carissima," Palace,

1948; "Waltz Time," 1949; composed additional music for "Music at Midnight," His Majesty's, 1950; composed the score of "Wedding in Paris," Hippodrome, 1954.
(Died 1 Jan., 1959; age 67)

MAY, Jane, French actress and vocalist; *b.* Paris; studied for the stage at the Conservatoire, under M. Gôt; made her first appearance on the stage at the Gymnase Théâtre, Paris, as Geneviève in Pailleron's "L'Age Ingrat"; at the same theatre she also appeared in "Le Fils de Coralie," "Jonathan," "Nos bons villageois," "Le demi-monde"; at the Vaudeville, she played in "Le Conseil judiciaire"; at the Ambigu, in "Martyre"; subsequently appeared at the Vaudeville and Variétés, in "Mdlle. Nitouche," "Niniche," etc.; at the Palais Royal, in "Divorçons," "La brebis égarée"; has lately turned her attention to the Cinema stage; is an Officer of the Academy; is well-known in Paris as a Professor of Elocution; made her first appearance in London, at the Royalty, 1884, as Suzanne in "Le Monde ou l'on s'ennuie"; has frequently appeared in London since; made a great success at the Prince of Wales's, 1891, when she played Pierrot in "L'Enfant Prodigue." *Favourite part :* Pierrot. *Recreation :* Writing. *Address :* 7 Avenue des Ternes, Paris.

MAY, Pamela, *première danseuse*; *b.* San Fernando, Trinidad, B.W.I., 30 May, 1917; *d.* of Reginald Henry May and his wife Hilda May (Curtis); *e.* Babington House School, Eltham; *m.* (1) Lieut. Painton Sidney Cowen, R.M., Fleet Air Arm (dec.); (2) Charles Howard Gordon I.C.S.; trained for ballet by Freda Grant and the Sadler's Wells Ballet School; originally appeared under the name of Doris May; made her first appearance on the stage at the Savoy Theatre, 23 Dec., 1930, in the ballet in "Alice in Wonderland"; in 1931, appeared at the Royal Opera House, Copenhagen, with English Ballet company; at Sadler's Wells, and at the New Theatre and Covent Garden (with the Sadler's Wells company) has appeared successfully in "Orpheus and Eurydice," "The Gods Go a'Begging," "Les Patineurs," "Checkmate," "The Prospect Before Us," "Horoscope," "Carnaval," "Dante Sonata," "The Sleeping Princess," "Les Sylphides," "Le Lac des Cygnes," "Coppelia," "Symphonic Variations," etc.; appeared in the ballet, in the film "Escape Me Never." *Favourite parts :* "Le Lac des Cygnes," "The Sleeping Beauty," "Sylphides," "Coppelia." *Address :* c/o Sadler's Wells Ballet, Covent Garden, W.C.2.

MAYER, Daniel, J.P., dramatic and musical agent; *b.* 1856; originally intended for a civil engineer; started his famous concert direction agency in 1891; has piloted and introduced many famous artists to the London public, including Paderewski, Jean Gerardy, Ada Crossley, Mark Hambourg, Harold Bauer, Arthur Nikisch, Anna Pavlova, etc.; he also arranged the first concerts in this country for Madame Melba, Van Dyck, Plancon and Mischa Elman; has been three times Mayor of Bexhill; is a prominent Freemason; during the past few years his firm have made many notable productions at London theatres.
(Died 20 Aug., 1928; age 72)

MAYER, Edwin Justus, dramatic author; *b.* New York, 1896; was formerly engaged in a commercial career; subsequently engaged as a reporter on New York newspapers, *The Call* and *The Globe*; next engaged as a press-agent to a film company, and subsequently as caption-writer; then went on the stage, and appeared at the Sam H. Harris Theatre, New York, Nov., 1922, in a minor part in "Hamlet," with John Barrymore; author of "The Firebrand," 1924; "Children of Darkness," 1930; "I am Laughing," 1935; has also written a book "A Preface to Life."
(Died 11 Sept., 1960; age 63)

MAYER, Gaston, manager and journalist; *b.* London, 1869; *e.* Paris

and London ; *m*. Mdlle. Maud Thécla ; is the son of the late M. L. Mayer, the famous theatrical manager, under whose direction many French companies appeared in London ; was for some years engaged in journalistic work ; Paris correspondent to several English and American papers ; founded and edited *The International Theatre Magazine*, in Paris ; was lessee of the Avenue Theatre, 1891, where he produced " Yvette " ; rebuilt and opened the New Royalty Theatre, Jan., 1906, where he presented several seasons of French plays, with many of the leading artistes of Paris, including Mdme. Sarah Bernhardt, Mdme. Réjane, Mdlle. Jeanne Granier, Mdme. Simone, MM. Le Bargy, de Feraudy, Coquelin, etc. ; in Apr., 1907, he secured a lease of Terry's Theatre, and produced " Mrs. Wiggs of the Cabbage Patch," with Mrs. Madge Carr-Cook and an American company ; the play was so successful that he subsequently transferred it to the Adelphi Theatre, where it ran until Dec. ; was responsible for the production of " The Brass Bottle," at the Vaudeville, Sept., 1909 ; " The Yellow Jacket," at the Duke of York's, Mar., 1913, and the season of French plays at the New Theatre, June, 1913 ; adapted the one-act play " The Chauffeur " and " English as She is Spoke," both produced at the Playhouse by Cyril Maude, and " In the Clouds," produced at Bournemouth, 1911.
(Died 18 Jan., 1923; age 53)

MAYER, Henry, French actor ; *b.* Paris ; was originally a musician, but entered the Conservatoire to study under M. Gôt ; made his first appearance at the Vaudeville, Paris, where he appeared in " Le Prince d'Aurec," " Hedda Gabler," " La Maison de Poupée," " Viveurs," 1895 ; " Le Partage," 1896 ; at the Gymnase, played in " Les Demi-Vierges," " L'Age Difficile," 1895 ; " Les Trois filles de M. Dupont," 1897 ; " L' Aimé," 1898 ; " L'Engrenage " etc. ; appeared at the Odéon, in " Château Historique " ; made his first appearance at the Comédie Française, 21

May, 1901, as Paul in " Le Bonheur qui Passe " ; has since appeared there in the following, among other plays : " L'Ami des Femmes," " La Plus Faible," " L'Enigme," " L'Irrésolu," " Le Marquis de Villemer," " Le Misanthrope," " La Parisienne," " Les Erynnes," " Sapho," " La Brebis Perdue," " Vouloir " ; was elected a *sociétaire* of the Comédie Francaise in 1905.
(Died Oct., 1941; age 80)

MAYER, Renée, actress and dancer ; *b.* Chiswick, 9 Dec., 1900 ; *d.* of William and Mary Mayer ; *e.* privately ; was taught dancing by Madame Sismondi ; made her first appearance on the stage, at the Playhouse, 3 Mar., 1910, as the Pearl Fairy in " The Goldfish " ; same theatre, Dec., 1910, played the Fairy Teenie Wee in " Our Litle Cinderella " ; at Wydham's, Mar., 1911, played Little Peter in " Passers-By " ; at the Playhouse, Sept., 1911, Lucy in " Rip Van Winkle " ; at Drury Lane, Dec., 1911, appeared as Hop o' my Thumb in the pantomime of that name, and Dec., 1912, as Puck in " The Sleeping Beauty " ; reappeared at Drury Lane, Dec., 1913, as Puck in " The Sleeping Beauty Re-awakened " ; at His Majesty's, 22 May, 1914, played Cissie Denver in the " all-star " revival of " The Silver King," given in aid of King George's Actors' Pension Fund ; at the Strand, Sept., 1914, played the same part ; at the Lyric, Oct., 1914, played the Little Girl in " The New Shylock " ; at Drury Lane, Dec., 1914, reappeared as Puck in " The Sleeping Beauty Beautified " ; and Dec., 1915, as Puss in Boots in the pantomime of that name ; at the same theatre, Sept., 1916, played Kitty in " The Best of Luck " ; at the Midland, Manchester, Dec., 1917, Pinkie in " Pinkie and the Fairies " ; at the New Theatre, Dec., 1919, Wendy in " Peter Pan " ; at the Kingsway, June, 1920, Hélène in " The Children's Carnival " ; at the Everyman Theatre, Dec., 1920, Nixie in " Through the Crack " ; at the Kingsway Theatre, Nov., 1924, appeared in " Yoicks! " *Recreations :* Outdoor sports of all kinds. *Address :* 9 Stuart Avenue, W.5. *Telephone No. :* Acorn 3076

MAYERL, Billy (*né* Joseph W. Mayerl), conductor and composer; *b.* London, 31 May, 1902; *s.* of Joseph Mayerl and his wife Elise (Umbach); *e.* Trinity College, London; *m.* Jill Bernini; his first engagement was in variety, 1920; his first London engagement was at Covent Garden Theatre, 27 Jan., 1923, in "You'd Be Surprised"; composed music for "The Punch Bowl," 1924; "The London Revue," 1925; appeared in "Shake Your Feet," and "White Birds," 1927; composed "Nippy," 1930; appeared with "The Co-Optimists," 1930–2; composed "Between Ourselves," 1932; "Sporting Love," 1934; "Love Laughs," 1935; "Twenty to One," 1935; "Over She Goes," 1936; "Crazy Days," 1937; "So Long Letty," 1937; "Runaway Love," 1939; "Happy Birthday," 1940; has also composed numerous successful piano numbers, including "Marigold," "The Four Aces Suite," "Aquarium Suite," "Legends of King Arthur," "Sennen Cove," etc.; is director of the Billy Mayerl School of Pianoforte Tuition. *Hobby :* Aquaria (is a Fellow of the Zoological Society). *Recreations :* Golf and motoring. *Clubs :* Savage and Junior Constitutional. *(Died 27 Mar., 1959; age 56)*

MAYEUR, E. F., actor; *b.* London, 1866; *e.* St. Paul's School and Trinity College, Cambridge; *m.* Helen Ferrers; prepared for the stage under the late Carlotta Leclerq, who was a friend of his; first appeared in 1888 at Devonshire Park Theatre, Eastbourne, as Leucippe in "Pygmalion and Galatea," with Miss Fortescue; engaged at the Princess's Theatre, 1888, in "Hands Across the Sea"; appeared under Sir John Hare in England and America; with Sir Charles Wyndham at Criterion; also played at Drury Lane, and has toured in leading *rôles* in America, Australia, and South Africa, and appeared at the Haymarket in "Sweet Kitty Bellairs," 1907; at the Playhouse, June, 1908, played Colonel McLeod in "The Flag Lieutenant"; at the Gaiety,

Dec., 1910, played Martin Leonard in "The Captain of the School" at the Comedy, Feb., 1912, played Byles in "The Bear Leaders"; at the Kingsway, Sept., 1912, Trenchard Voysey, K.C., in "The Voysey Inheritance"; at the Comedy, June, 1913, played Mr. Netherby in "Jim the Penman"; at the Vaudeville, Oct., 1913, played Rai Sahib Badri Nath in "Collision"; the Marquis de Lansac in "The Green Cockatoo"; Nov., 1913, Naryshkin in "Great Catherine"; at the Coronet, June, 1914, Prince Maleotti in "Forget-Me-Not." *Clubs :* New Oxford and Cambridge, and Green Room. *Address :* 4 Greville Place, St. John's Wood, N.W. *Telephone :* 1680 Hampstead.

MAYFIELD, Cleo, actress (*née* Empy); *m.* Cecil Lean; first attracted attention when she appeared at the Ziegfeld Theatre, Chicago, Aug., 1912, as Miss Understood in "The Military Girl"; she next appeared at Weber and Fields', New York, Jan., 1913, as Alice in "The Man with Three Wives"; made her first appearance in London at the Victoria Palace, July, 1914; on her return to America appeared at the Casino, New York, Aug 1915, as Hazel Jones in "The Blue Paradise," subsequently touring for two years in the same piece; at the Century, New York, Nov., 1917, appeared in "Miss 1917," continuing in this 1918–19; during 1919–20 toured as Rosamund Purcell in "Look Who's Here !" and played the same part at the Forty-fourth Street Theatre, Mar., 1920; at the Astor Theatre, Feb., 1922, played Lulu Love in "The Blushing Bride"; at the Winter Garden, New York, May, 1924, played in "Innocent Eyes"; at the Cort, Chicago, May, 1934, appeared in "Big-Hearted Herbert"; at the Erlanger, Philadelphia, Nov., 1934, played in "The Milky Way"; at the Broad, Philadelphia, May, 1935, played Hester Grantham in "The Bishop Misbehaves." *(Died 8 Nov., 1954; age 59)*

MAYHEW, Charles, actor and vocalist; *b.* London, 18 Dec., 1908; *s.* of

John Edward Smith and his wife Cecily Osborn (Mayhew); *e.* privately and at Christ's College, Finchley; studied singing at the Guildhall School of Music, where he gained a scholarship and seven prizes, including the Gold Medal for vocalists; while at the School, took part in several light operas; made his first appearance on the stage at the London Coliseum, 11 June, 1932, in the title-*rôle* of "Casanova"; at Scarborough, July, 1933, played Tom Jones in the opera of that name; in Aug., 1934, toured as Baron Schober in "Lilac Time"; New, Oct., 1934, played the Prince of Wales in, "By Appointment"; Criterion, Mar. 1935, Captain Macheath in "The Beggar's Opera"; Coliseum, July, 1936, again played Schober in "Lilac Time," and toured in the same part, 1936-7; from 1937-9, studied opera and lieder singing in Germany; at the Odeon, Munich, May, 1938, sang the title-*rôle* in Schumann's "Faust," in German; in 1939, was studying singing at the Royal Conservatoire, Naples; appeared in films, 1934, in "Catherine the Great"; has sung in oratorios and concerts in provincial cities and in London. *Recreations:* Fencing, riding, swimming, and skating. *Address:* "Oaktrees," Belmont Lane, Stanmore, Middlesex. *Telephone No.:* Stanmore 506.

MAYNE, Clarice, actress and vocalist; *b.* London, 6 Feb., 1886; *d.* of the late Henry Purser Dulley and his wife Esther (Burdis); *e.* London; *m.* (1) the late Jas. W. Tate; (2) Albert Edward Cromwell Knox; made her first appearance on the variety stage at the Oxford Music Hall, 4 June, 1906; the following month was engaged for the Palace Theatre, where she opened on 27 Aug., 1906, and made an immediate success; subsequently appeared at the leading variety theatres in London, the provinces, and America; for some years appeared in conjunction with her late husband ("That"), their entertainment being exceedingly popular; among some of her more popular songs may be mentioned: "Every Little While," "Give Me a Little Cosy Corner," "A Broken Doll," "I'm in Love," "Put on your tat-ta,

little girlie," "Joshua," "Nursie, Nursie," "I was a good little girl, till I met you," "In the Days of Good Queen Bess," "Over the Garden Wall," "I'm longing for someone to love me," etc.; was also a clever mimic; appeared at the Comedy, Sept., 1916, in "This and That"; Palace, Manchester, Dec., 1916, the Prince in "Cinderella"; Theatre Royal, Birmingham, Dec., 1919, Dick in "Dick Whittington"; at the London Hippodrome, Dec., 1921, played Jack in "Jack and the Beanstalk"; at the Vaudeville, Aug., 1922, played in "Snap"; at the Hippodrome, Dec., 1922, the Prince in "Cinderella"; at the Palladium, Dec., 1923, Dick in "Dick Whittington"; at the Vaudeville, May, 1924, played in "Puppets"; at the Theatre Royal, Birmingham, Dec., 1924, Jack in "Jack and the Beanstalk"; Palladium, Aug., 1926, played in "Life"; Dec., 1926, Aladdin in the pantomime; Dec., 1927, Prince Charming in "Cinderella"; during 1929 toured as Clara Gibbings in the play of that name; appeared at the first four variety command performances

(Died 16 Jan., 1966; age 79)

MAYNE, Ernie, comedian; made his first appearance on the stage with a partner, as the Maynes (Fred and Ernie), in 1892, in the provinces; subsequently appeared as a single turn, making his first appearance in London in 1899; among some of his more popular songs may be mentioned "She pushed me into the parlour"; "Ten little fingers, ten little toes"; "Goosey, goosey, gander," etc. *Address:* "Derwent," Clarence Road, Clapham Park, S.W. *Telephone No.:* Brixton 1408.

MAYO, Margaret (*née* Lilian Clatten), dramatic author; *b.* Illinois, U.S.A., 19 Nov., 1882; *e.* Salem, Ore., Fox Lake, Wis., and Stanford University, Cal.; *m.* Edgar Selwyn (mar. dis.); was formerly an actress, and made her first appearance on the stage at the Garrick Theatre, New York, 20 Apr., 1896, in "Thoroughbred"; subsequently toured in

"Charley's Aunt" and "Secret Service"; at Hoyt's Madison Square Theatre, Jan., 1899, played Susan in "Because She Loved Him So"; she toured for some time as Lena in "Arizona," and after playing Polly in "Pretty Peggy," with Grace George, in 1903, at the Herald Square Theatre, she retired from the stage to devote herself to playwriting; has written the following plays: "Under Two Flags," "The Jungle," and "The Marriage of William Ashe," adapted from the books of the same name; "The Winding Way," "The Austrian Dancer," "Nip and Tuck," "Polly of the Circus," "The Debtors," "Baby Mine," "Behind the Scenes," "The Flirt," "The Wall Street Girl" (with Edgar Selwyn); "Twin Beds" (with Salisbury Field); "His Bridal Night" (with Lawrence Rising); "Heads Up" (with Zellah Covington), "Being Fitted," "Prisoner of the World," "Seeing Things" (with Aubrey Kennedy), "The White Way," 1923; "Pettie Darling," 1924, and "Loving Ladies," 1926, all with Aubrey Kennedy. *(Died 25 Feb., 1951; age 68)*

MAYO, Sam (Samuel Cowan), comedian; *b.* London, 31 July, 1881; *e.* London; *m.* Stella Stanley; made his first appearance on the variety stage, at the Alhambra, Sandgate, 1898; has introduced many popular songs to the public, among which may be mentioned "At a minute to seven last night"; "Doh, ray, me, fah, soh, lah, te, doh"; "Kind Friends"; "When I woke up in the morning"; "I went to sleep again"; "The Chinaman"; "I never stopped running till I got home"; "The old tin can"; "Didn't I? Wasn't I?"; "I played my concertina"; "The Fireman"; "I'm going to sing a song to you this evening"; "She cost me seven-and-sixpence"; "I feel very, very bad"; "I've only come down for the day"; "Futurist Pictures"; "The Widow"; "The Trumpet," etc. *Address:* "Laleham," Finchley Road, Golder's Green, N.W. *Telephone No.:* Finchley 1253.

McARDLE, J. F., actor; *b.* Philadelphia, U.S.A.; *s.* of the late Arthur McArdle; in 1897, toured as McIntyre in "Skipped by the Light of the Moon," and appeared in that part at the Metropole, Camberwell, 5 Apr., 1897; in 1898, toured as Herr Pumpernickle in "The Transit of Venus"; in 1899 toured as Major Fossdyke in "The Gay Parisienne"; appeared at the Court Theatre, Liverpool, Christmas, 1899, as the Baron in "The Babes in the Wood"; in 1901 toured as the King of Illyria in "Kitty Grey"; attracted the attention of London audiences at Wyndham's Theatre, Apr., 1906, by his performance of the part of Sir Wilkie Willoughby in "The Girl Behind the Counter"; at the Hicks Theatre, Mar., 1907, he played Sir Henry Heldon in "My Darling"; in 1908 succeeded to the part of Baron Popoff in "The Merry Widow" at Daly's; in Aug., 1909, toured as Joachim XIII in "A Waltz Dream"; at the Empire, Feb., 1910, appeared in the *revue* "Hullo, London!"; appeared at Daly's Oct., 1910, as Harry Q. Conder in "The Dollar Princess," and Jan., 1911, as Joachim XIII in a revival of "A Waltz Dream"; in June, 1911, appeared at the Empire, in the *revue,* "By George!"; in 1912, played in music-hall sketch, "The Last of the Dukes"; appeared at the Alhambra, Oct., 1912, in the *revue,* "Kill that Fly"; appeared at the London Opera House, May, 1913, in the *revue* "Come Over Here"; at the Shubert Theatre, New York, Dec., 1913, played Cornelius Clutterbuck in "The Girl on the Film"; in 1914 went to Australia; reappeared in London at the Alhambra, Jan., 1916, in "Now's the Time"; at the Prince's, Bristol, Christmas, 1916, and at the Grand, Leeds, 1917, played the Baron in "Cinderella"; at the Duke of York's, Sept., 1919, played Sir John Porter in "The Girl for the Boy."

McARTHUR, Molly, artist and designer; *b.* London, 1900; her first work for the theatre was executed for the Playhouse, Oxford, 1923-4; designed the production of "The Cradle Song," at the Fortune Theatre. Nov. 1926; subsequently studied abroad; on her return designed dresses, etc.,

for "The Anatomist," "Six Charac-
ters in Search of an Author," "The
Kingdom of God" and "Love's
Labour's Lost," at the Westminster
Theatre, 1931–2; has since designed
for "Napoleon," "Twelfth Night,"
"Philomel," 1932; "Is Life Worth
Living?," "The Green Bay Tree,"
"The Cherry Orchard," 1933; "The
Importance of Being Earnest," "Mary
Read," 1934; "Hervey House," "Two
Share a Dwelling," "The Black Eye,"
"Call it a Day," 1935; "Bitter Har-
vest," "Winter Sunshine," "Love's
Labour's Lost," "As You Like It,"
"Busman's Honeymoon," 1936;
"Twelfth Night," "Black Limelight,"
"Bonnet Over the Windmill," "Pyg-
malion," 1937; "Black Swans," "The
King of Nowhere," "People of Our
Class," "She, Too, Was Young," "Can
We Tell?" "Quiet Wedding," 1938;
"Georgian Springtime," 1939; "The
Venetian," "Jeannie," "Full House,"
1940; "A Doll's House," 1946;
"Fotheringhay," 1953. *Address:* 95
Westbourne Terrace, London, W.2.
Telephone No.: Paddington 5895.

M'CARTHY, Justin Huntly, dramatic
author, novelist, etc.; *b.* 30 Sept.,
1860; *s.* of Justin M'Carthy; *m.* Cissie
Loftus (mar. dis.); author of the following among other plays; "The Candidate," 1884; "The Wife of Socrates,"
1888; "The Highwayman," 1891;
"My Friend the Prince," 1897; "If I
were King," 1901; "The Proud Prince,"
1903; "Caesar Borgia," 1907; new version of "The Duke's Motto," 1908;
"The O'Flynn," 1910; "The Madcap
Duchess" (with David Stevens), 1913;
"Charlemagne," 1914; "Sir Roger de
Coverley," 1914; "Stand and Deliver,"
1916; "Nurse Benson" (with R. C.
Carton), 1918; has written many
histories and novels, also books of
travel. *Recreations:* Fencing and
walking. (*Died 20 Mar., 1936; age 75)*

McCARTHY, Daniel, actor; *b.* Cheltenham, 3 May, 1869; *s.* of J. Mc-
Carthy, F.R.A.S., brother of Lillah
McCarthy; first B.A. of London University; was originally a schoolmaster and private tutor; before
adopting the stage as a profession,
appeared as an amateur and studied
under William Poel; first appeared
on the stage, Dec., 1893, at the
Theatre Royal, York, as Clayton
in "Two Christmas Eves"; first
appeared in London at the Lyric
Theatre, 4 Jan., 1896, as Siguinus
in "The Sign of the Cross," under
the late Wilson Barrett; visited
Australia in 1897 with Barrett, with
whom he remained until 1900; has
since fulfilled engagements with Mrs.
Patrick Campbell, 1901, and again
in 1905; Vedrenne and Barker at
Court Theatre, 1905; H. B. Irving,
1906; joined Cyril Maude in Sept.,
1906, and appeared under that gentleman's management in "Toddles,"
"The Earl of Pawtucket," "The
O'Grindles," "Marjory Strode,"
"French as he is Spoke," "Pro Tem.,"
"The Flag Lieutenant"; "A Merry
Devil" and "The Visit"; at Wyndham's, Feb., 1911, played Captain
Drummond in "Mr. Jarvis"; at the
Savoy, July, 1911, played Mr. Wardle
in "Two Peeps at Pickwick"; at
the Playhouse, Sept., 1911, appeared
as Dominie John Hutchinson in
"Rip Van Winkle," Nov., 1911, Mr.
Vivian in "Dad"; Feb., 1912, Mr.
Fenwick in "The Second in Command"; at the Apollo, Sept., 1913,
played Verchesi in "Never Say Die";
during 1918 toured as Fishpingle in
the play of that name. *Favourite
part:* The Frenchman in "French
as he is Spoke." *Recreation:* Fishing.
Club: Green Room.

McCARTHY, Lillah, O.B.E.; *b.* Cheltenham, 22 Sept., 1875; *d.* of J.
McCarthy, F.R.A.S.; sister of Daniel
McCarthy; *e.* at Cheltenham; studied
elocution with Hermann Vezin, and
voice production with Emil Behnke;
m. (1) H. Granville Barker, whom she
divorced in 1918; (2) Sir Frederick
Keeble, C.B.E., F.R.S., of Magdalen
College, Oxford; made her first appearance on the stage in 1895, in A. E.
Drinkwaters company; subsequently
joined Ben Greet's company in the
same year, playing Desdemona, Juliet,
Peg Woffington, Pauline, and Beatrice; appeared at the Lyric with
Wilson Barrett, 1896, as Berenice

in "The Sign of the Cross," and on occasions Mercia in the same play; toured as Mercia, subsequently proceeding to America under William Greet to play the same part; on returning to England in 1897 toured in "The Sorrows of Satan"; rejoined Wilson Barrett in 1897 and then toured in Australia; on her return appeared at the Garrick, Apr., 1899, in "Change Alley," at the Princess's, Sept., 1899, as Nan in "Alone in London," and in Nov., 1899, played Kathleen Ivor in "The Absent Minded Beggar"; again rejoined Wilson Barrett in 1900, this time as leading lady, and she then appeared with him as Lygia in "Quo Vadis?"; Mercia in "The Sign of the Cross," Almida in "Claudian," Virginia in "Virginius," Mona Mylrea in "Ben-My-Chree," Kate in "The Manxman," Nellie Denver in "The Silver King," Jane Humphries in "Man and His Maker," Ophelia in "Hamlet," Desdemona in "Othello," Princess Zebuda in "The Christian King," Ellula in "In the Middle of June"; accompanied Barrett to Australia and South Africa; appeared with him at the Adelphi, Dec., 1902, in "The Christian King"; remained with Barrett until 1904; on leaving him appeared at the Avenue, Oct., 1904, as Rosamund in "The Master of Kingsgift"; appeared at His Majesty's, with Beerbohm Tree, 1904, as Lady Fancourt in "Agatha," Henriette in "A Man's Shadow," Loyse in "The Ballad Monger," and Calpurnia in "Julius Cæsar"; at the Court Theatre, 1905, played Nora in "John Bull's Other Island," and Ann Whitefield in "Man and Superman"; appeared in "The Jury of Fate," Shaftesbury, 1906; at the Court, 1906, played in "Pan and the Young Shepherd," "The Youngest of the Angels," "You Never Can Tell" (Gloria), and "The Doctor's Dilemma" (Jennifer); at the Garrick, Aug., 1906, played Judith Mainwaring in "The Morals of Marcus"; at the Comedy, Oct., 1907, appeared as Lady Studland in "The Barrier," and in Nov., as Mary Pembridge in "Angela"; at the Savoy, in Dec., 1907, played Raina in "Arms and the Man"; at

the Royalty, May, 1908, played Nan Hardwick in "Nan"; at the Duke of York's, Sept., 1908, played Lady Sybil Lazenby in "What Every Woman Knows"; at the Court, Nov., 1908, played Dionysus in "The Bacchae" of Euripides; at the Duke of York's, Mar., 1909, played Madge Thomas in "Strife"; at same theatre, Oct., 1910, played Miss Vernon of Foley in "Grace"; at the Court, Jan., 1911, appeared as Anne Pedersdotter in "The Witch"; at the Palace, Feb., 1911, played Mimi in "A Farewell Supper"; at the Court, Feb., 1911, played Nan Hardwick in "The Tragedy of Nan"; she then assumed the management of the Little Theatre, opening on 11 Mar., 1911, with Schnitzler's "Anatol" episodes; on 28 Mar., 1911, appeared as Hilda Wangel in "The Master Builder"; on 19 Apr., 1911, played Margaret Knox in "Fanny's First Play"; at the Gala performance at His Majesty's, 27 June, 1911, appeared as Revel in "The Vision of Delight"; at the Little Theatre, 3 Oct., 1911, played Astrace in "The Sentimentalists," and Kate in "The Twelve Pound Look"; specially engaged by Sir Herbert Tree to appear at His Majesty's, Nov., 1911, as the Lady Norma in "The War God"; at Covent Garden, Jan., 1912, appeared as Jocasta in Martin Harvey's production of "Œdipus Rex"; at the Kingsway, Mar., 1912, as Iphigenia in "Iphigenia in Tauris"; then entered on the management of the Savoy Theatre, in conjunction with Granville Barker, Sept., 1912, opening as Hermione in "The Winter's Tale"; in Nov., 1912, played Viola in "Twelfth Night"; in conjunction with Granville Barker entered on a four months' lease of the St. James's, opening on 1 Sept., 1913, as Lavinia in "Androcles and the Lion"; Oct., 1913, reappeared as Anne in "The Witch"; Dec., 1913, played Nan Hardwick in a revival of "Nan"; Dec., 1913, Ygraine in "The Death of Tintagiles"; returning to the Savoy, appeared there in Feb., 1914, as Helena in "A Midsummer Night's Dream"; at His Majesty's, 22 May, 1914, played Nellie Denver in the "all-star" revival of "The Silver King," given in aid of

King George's Actors' Pension Fund; at the Haymarket, Sept., 1914, played Mercedes Okraska in "The Impossible Woman" ("Tante"); subsequently went to America, and appeared at Wallack's Theatre, New York, Jan.-Mar., 1915, in "Androcles and the Lion," "The Man Who Married a Dumb Wife," "A Midsummer Night's Dream," and "The Doctor's Dilemma"; at Yale Bowl, Conn., May, 1915, played the title-rôle in "Iphigenia in Tauris"; at the Adolph Lewisohn Stadium, New York, May, 1915, Hecuba in "The Trojan Women"; after returning to London, appeared at the Queen's Theatre, Jan., 1916, as Judith in a play of that name; at the New Theatre, Feb., 1916, played Maude Fulton in "Caroline"; at the Coliseum and at the London Opera House, June, 1916, at matinées in aid of the "Star and Garter" Fund, and King George's Pension Fund for Actors, played Lady Mary Lasenby in the "all-star" cast of "The Admirable Crichton"; at the Ambassadors', Mar., 1917, appeared in "The Man Who Married a Dumb Wife," and "Class"; at the Kingsway, Oct., 1917, played Lady Fenton in "One Hour of Life"; at the Ambassadors', Apr., 1918, Annabel Bradly in "Too Much Money"; took over the management of the Kingsway Theatre, and in Apr., 1919, reappeared as Judith in the play of that name; June, 1919, played the Hon. Monica Somerset in "St. George and the Dragons"; at the New Theatre, Sept., 1920, played Joanne in "The Wandering Jew," Dec., 1921, Doña Sol in "Blood and Sand"; at the Kemble Theatre, Hereford, June, 1931, in connection with the celebration of the Siddons Centenary, appeared in the chronicle play, "Sarah Siddons, the Greatest of the Kembles"; after ten years' absence from the London stage, reappeared for a single performance, Haymarket, Dec., 1932, as Iphigenia in "Iphigenia in Tauris"; at Playhouse, Oxford, July, 1935, appeared as Boadicea in a play of that name; published her autobiography, "My Life," 1930, and a further volume, "Myself and My Friends," 1933. *Hobbies*: Walking, sailing, and outdoor sports. *Clubs*: Ladies' Carlton, Lon-

don; Fowey Golf Club, Cornwall. *(Died 15 Apr., 1960; age 84)*

McCLINTIC, Guthrie, actor, producing manager, and stage director; *b.* Seattle, Washington, U.S.A., 6 Aug., 1893; *s.* of Edgar D. McClintic; *e.* University of Washington; *m.* Katharine Cornell; studied for the stage at the American Academy of Dramatic Arts; made his first appearance on the stage, 1913, in "Her Own Money"; made his first appearance on the New York stage at the Little Theatre, 14 Apr., 1914, as a Messenger in "The Truth"; in 1915–16 was engaged with Grace George at the Playhouse, New York, where he appeared as Nogam in "The New York Idea," George Nepean in "The Liars," Morrison in "Major Barbara," James Bent in "The Earth," and Marzo in "Captain Brassbound's Conversion"; he fulfilled several engagements in various "stock" companies, and in 1918 was with Jessie Bonstelle's "stock" company in Buffalo; was subsequently assistant stage director with Winthrop Ames at the Little Theatre, New York; he then became a producing manager on his own account, and has produced and staged the following plays: "The Dover Road," 1921; "Gringo," 1922; "A Square Peg," "In the Next Room," 1923; "The Way Things Happen," 1924; "Mrs. Partridge Presents," "All Dressed Up," "The Green Hat," 1925; "Glory Hallelujah," "The Shanghai Gesture," 1926; was appointed director of The Actors' Theatre, Inc., 1927, and staged "Saturday's Children"; has since directed "Mariners," "The Letter," "John," 1927; "Cock Robin," "The Age of Innocence," "Jealousy" (in which he also played Maurice), 1928; "The Skyrocket," "The Cross Roads," 1929; "Dishonored Lady," 1930; "The Barretts of Wimpole Street," "Brief Moment," 1931; "Distant Drums," "The Truth About Blayds," "Criminals at Large," 1932; "Lucrece," 1932; "Alien Corn," "Jezebel" 1933; "Yellow Jack," "Divided by Three," "Romeo and Juliet," 1934; "The Old Maid," "Winterset," "Parnell," 1935; "Ethan Frome,"

1654

"Hamlet," "The Wingless Victory," 1936; "High Tor," "Candida," "The Star Wagon," "Barchester Towers," 1937; "How to Get Tough About It," "Missouri Legend" (with Max Gordon), 1938; "Mamba's Daughters," "No Time for Comedy," "Key Largo," "Christmas Eve," 1939; "An International Incident," 1940; "The Lady Who Came to Stay," "The Doctor's Dilemma," "Spring Again," 1941; "The Morning Star," "The Three Sisters," 1942; "Lovers and Friends," 1943; "You Touched Me," 1945; "The Playboy of the Western World," "Antigone," 1946; "Antony and Cleopatra," 1947; "Life With Mother," 1948; "Medea," "That Lady," "The Velvet Glove," 1949; "Burning Bright," "Captain Carvallo," 1950; staged "The Constant Wife," 1951; "Come of Age," "To Be Continued" (which he presented), and "Bernadine," 1952; also during 1952 he presented the company of the National Theatre of Greece in the productions of "Electra" and "Œdipus Tyrannus"; presented "Mrs. Patterson," 1954; staged "The Dark Is Light Enough," "A Roomful of Roses" (which he presented in association with Stanley Gilkie), 1955; staged "Four Winds," 1957; presented (with Sol Hurok) "Dear Liar," 1959–60; staged "The Ante-Room," in London, 1936; has also directed films. *Clubs:* Coffee House and Players', New York. *(Died 29 Oct., 1961; age 68)*

McCORMICK, Myron, actor; *b.* Albany, Indiana, U.S.A., 8 Feb., 1907; *s.* of Walter Perlee McCormick and his wife Bess (Eviston); *e.* High School, Muncie, Ind., New Mexico Military Institute, and Princeton University; *m.* (1) Martha Hodge (mar. dis.); (2) Barbara MacKenzie; made his first appearance on the professional stage at West Falmouth, Mass., with the University Players, June, 1930, as the Butler in "Murray Hill"; made his first appearance on the New York stage, at the Biltmore Theatre, 29 Oct., 1932, as James Campbell in "Carry Nation"; Masque, Dec., 1932, played Bellboy in "Goodbye Again"; Booth, Nov., 1933, Gaston Marchezais in "I Was Waiting For You"; Martin Beck, Mar., 1934, Brinkerhoff in "Yellow Jack"; Golden, Sept., 1934, Eddie in "Small Miracle"; Fulton, Feb., 1935, Donald Sloane in "On to Fortune"; Plymouth, Sept., 1935, Private Langlois in "Paths of Glory"; Ethel Barrymore, Oct., 1935, Dick Hardy in "Substitute for Murder"; Booth, Nov., 1935, Humble Jewett in "How Beautiful With Shoes"; Ritz, Dec., 1935, Clark in "Hell Freezes Over"; Martin Beck, Feb., 1936, Trock in "Winterset"; Empire, Dec., 1936, Ruel McQuestion in "The Wingless Victory"; Vanderbilt, Oct., 1937, James Freeman in "In Clover"; Martin Beck, Feb., 1938, Dan Grimshaw in "How To Get Tough About It"; in summer theatres, July–Aug., 1938, played Charles in "Charles and Mary" and Van Van Dorn in "High Tor"; Mansfield (for the Group), Nov., 1939, Streeter in "Thunder Rock"; Booth, Jan., 1941, Gard Dunham in "The Cream in the Well"; Windsor, Jan., 1942, Shorty in "Lily of the Valley"; Playhouse, Oct., 1942, Jimmy Randall in "The Damask Cheek"; Belasco, Jan., 1944, Sergeant Peter Moldau in "Storm Operation"; Golden, Oct., 1944, John Rogers in "Soldier's Wife"; Hudson, Nov., 1945, Spike McManus in "State of the Union"; Plymouth, Mar., 1948, played J. Newton McKeon in "Joy to the World"; Majestic, Apr., 1949, Luther Billis in "South Pacific"; City Center, Jan., 1955, played Nick in "The Time of Your Life"; Alvin, Oct., 1955, played Sgt. King in "No Time for Sergeants"; Playhouse, April, 1955, Jake Meighan in "27 Wagons Full of Cotton"; toured summer, 1955, as Doc in "Come Back, Little Sheba"; California Civic Light Opera, Los Angeles and San Francisco, summer, 1957, repeated Luther Billis in "South Pacific"; again played Nick in "The Time of Your Life" at the Brussels World Fair, Oct., 1958; summer, 1959, toured as Willie in "Death of a Salesman"; Wilbur, Boston, Jan., 1960, played Wally in "Motel"; first entered films, 1936, in "Winterset," and has since appeared in many notable productions; has also made numerous appearances on television. *(Died 30 July, 1962; age 54)*

McCOMAS, Carroll, actress; *b.* 27 June, 1891; *d.* of Judge C. C. McComas and his wife Ellen (Moore); made her first appearance on the stage, 1909, in "The Pearl and the Pumpkin"; during 1910–11, appeared in "The Dollar Princess" and "Mrs. Dot," on tour; at the Empire, New York, Sept., 1911, played Maggie Cottrell in "A Single Man," with John Drew; at the Lyceum, Sept., 1912, Jimmie Birch in "The 'Mind-the-Paint' Girl"; subsequently toured, Dec., 1912, as Lolotte in "The Siren"; at the Knickerbocker, Sept., 1913, Kitty Kent in "The Marriage Market"; Harris, Aug., 1914, Louise Lloyd in "What Happened at 22"; Oct., 1914, Dodo Baxter in "The Salamander"; Longacre, Feb., 1915, Jane Gerson in "Inside the Lines"; Cohan, Aug., 1916, Anne Windsor in "Seven Chances"; Criterion, Sept., 1917, Kitty Rowland in "The Scrap of Paper"; Princess, Jan., 1918, May Barber in "Oh! Lady, Lady!'"; Morosco, Sept., 1918, Kathleen Rutherford in "The Walk-Offs"; Thirty-ninth Street, Oct., 1918, Amy Legrande in "Not With My Money"; Punch and Judy, Sept., 1920, Verna Cromwell in "Merchants of Venus"; Belmont, Dec., 1920, Lulu Bett in "Miss Lulu Bett"; Lyceum, June, 1923, Maria in the "all-star" revival of "The School for Scandal"; National, Aug., 1923, Hilda Barnes in "The Jolly Roger"; Nov., 1923, Roxane in "Cyrano de Bergerac"; Cort, Sept., 1925, Alice Conway in "The New Gallantry"; Klaw, Feb., 1926, Laura Dawson in "You Can't Win"; George M. Cohan, July, 1926, Joan Amory in "Pyramids"; Frolic, Dec., 1926, Maisie Buck in "Night Hawk"; Earl Carroll, June, 1927, Madame X in the play of that name; Cort, 1928, Margaret Newell in "The Ladder; appeared in films, 1915, in "At the Rainbow's End," and "Where Love is King."
(Died 9 Nov., 1962; age 76)

McCORD, Nancy, actress and vocalist; *b.* Long Island, N.Y., U.S.A.; studied music at the Juilliard School of Music; made her first appearance on the stage in the chorus of the American Opera company; at Chicago, 1930, and on tour played Beate-Marie in "Three Little Girls"; 1931–33, was prima-donna in the Muny Opera Company; 44th Street, New York, Jan., 1933, played Kit Baker in "Face the Music"; Shubert, Jan., 1934, Queen Erna in "All the King's Horses"; St. Louis, July, 1935, appeared in "The Beloved Rogue"; Pittsburgh, Oct., 1935, played Princess Stephanya in "Venus in Silk"; St. James, New York, Dec., 1935, Baroness von Schlewitz in "May Wine"; San Francisco, 1937, appeared in "Meet My Sister"; St. Louis, 1938, played Hedi Mahler in "The Lost Waltz"; Martin Beck, New York, May, 1939, Mary Stone in "The Devil and Daniel Webster"; St. Louis, June, 1939, Katinka in the operetta of that name; Dallas, June, 1941 layed in "Rio Rita," and St. Louis, Aug., 1941, in "Balalaika"; Louisville, July, 1942, in "Sweethearts," and "The Vagabond King"; St. Louis, Aug., 1942, played Stephanie in "Roberta"; has also appeared as soloist with the New York Philharmonic Orchestra.

McCORMICK, Arthur Langdon, dramatic author; *b.* Port Huron, Mich., U.S.A.; *e.* Albion College, Michigan; *m.* Sylvia Bidwell; was formerly an actor, and was for two seasons in Otis Skinner's company, subsequently touring in his own plays; is the author of the following plays: "The Western Girl," "Money and the Woman," "The Toll-Gate Inn," 1900; "Old Love Letters," 1902; "Hearts Adrift," 1903; "How Hearts are Broken," 1906; "The Burglar and the Lady," 1906; "Out of the Fold," "Wanted by the Police," 1907; "Our Friend Fritz," 1907; "The Women who Dare," 1907; "The Life of an Actress," 1907; "Jessie Left the Village," 1907; "When the World Sleeps," "The Storm," 1910, "The Pace," "The Gulf," "Shipwrecked," 1924. *Clubs:* American Dramatists, and Green Room, New York.
(Died 25 June, 1954; age 81)

McCRACKEN, Esther (Helen), dramatic author and actress; *b.* Newcastle-on-Tyne, 25 June, 1902; *d.* of

Henry Armstrong and his wife Maud (Clapham); *e.* Central Newcastle High School; *m.* (1) Lt.-Col. Angus Mc-Cracken, D.S.O., M.C., R.A. (*d.* 1943); (2) Mungo Campbell; formerly an actress, and spent eight years with the Newcastle Repertory company from 1929; author of the following plays: "The Willing Spirit," 1936; "Quiet Wedding," 1938; "Counter Attractions," 1938; "White Elephants," 1940; "Quiet Week-end," 1941, which ran over 1000 performances; "Living Room," 1943; "No Medals," 1944; "Cry Liberty," 1950; at Richmond, Apr., 1938, played Marcia Brent in "Quiet Wedding," and Feb., 1940, Meggie Pryce in "White Elephants"; Wyndham's, Aug., 1943, she played in succession the parts of Ella Spender, Marcia Brent, and Mary Jarrow in "Quiet Week-End." *Recreation:* Reading. *Address:* Rothley Lake House, Hartburn, Morpeth. *Telephone No.:* Scots Gap 255.

McCRACKEN, Joan, actress, vocalist, and dancer; *b.* Philadelphia, 31 Dec., 1922; *d.* of Frank McCracken; and Mary Weston (Humes); in 1934, at the age of eleven, became a member of Catherine Littlefield's ballet classes; first appeared in New York, at the Radio City Music Hall, as a solo dancer in ballet; appeared in numerous *rôles* in the Littlefield American Ballet company, 1934–5; made her first appearance in London, at the London Hippodrome, 15 June, 1937, with the Philadelphia Ballet Company in "Barn Dance," and scored an immediate success; remained with the Philadelphia Ballet for some years, during which time she toured Europe in various *rôles*, and subsequently toured with Eugene Loring's Dance Players; St. James Theatre, New York, Mar., 1943, appeared as Sylvie in "Oklahoma!"; Shubert, Oct., 1944, played Daisy in "Bloomer Girl"; Alvin, Dec., 1945, Maribelle Jones in "Billion Dollar Baby"; Maxine Elliott, Dec., 1947, Virginia in "Galileo"; Westport, Connecticut, July, 1948, Myrrhina in "Lysistrata"; National, Feb., 1949, Dixie Evans in "The Big Knife"; Royale, Jan., 1950, appeared as Nellie in "Dance

Me a Song"; in the summer of 1950, toured as Lizzie Shaw in "Angel in the Pawnshop"; Booth, New York, Jan., 1951, appeared as Lizzie Shaw in "Angel In the Pawnshop"; at the Civic Opera House, Chicago, Apr., 1951, played Peter Pan in Barrie's play; Majestic, New York, May, 1953, appeared as Betty in "Me and Juliet"; Ann Arbor, Michigan, May, 1957, appeared in "The Sleeping Prince"; Phoenix, New York, Feb., 1958, the Sphinx in "The Infernal Machine"; first appeared in films in 1944; first television appearance in Jan., 1952, in "Claudia." *Recreation:* Painting. (*Died 1 Nov., 1961; age 38*)

McCULLOUGH, Paul, actor; *b.* 1883; made his first appearance in 1900; joined forces with Bobby Clark as Clark and McCullough in 1905, in "vaudeville," and they have remained together ever since; appeared at the Madison Square Gardens, in the spring of 1907, in Barnum and Bailey's Circus; played all over the United States until 1922; appeared at the New Oxford Theatre, London, 19 June, 1922, with Clark, in "Chuckles of 1922"; at the Music Box, New York, 23 Oct., 1922, appeared in "The Music Box Revue," and Dec., 1924, in the second "Music Box Revue"; Lyric, Sept., 1926, played Sparrow in "The Ramblers"; Times Square, Jan., 1930, Gideon in "Strike Up the Band"; at the London Pavilion, Mar., 1931, appeared in "Cochran's 1931 Revue"; 46th Street Theatre, New York, Oct., 1931, played Blodgett in "Here Goes the Bride"; St. James, New York, Dec., 1932, appeared in "Walk a Little Faster"; same theatre, Dec., 1934, in "Thumbs Up." *Clubs:* The Lambs', and Friars, New York.
(*Died 25 Mar., 1936; age 52*)

McDERMOTT, Hugh (Patrick), actor; *b.* Edinburgh, 20 Mar., 1908; *s.* of Hugh Patrick McDermott and his wife Mary (McLuskey); his parents were Irish; *e.* Edinburgh; *m.* (1) Daphne Courtney (mar. dis.); (2) Angela June Laurillard; formerly a golf professional, and golf-course constructor; made his first appearance on the stage at the Richmond Theatre, 24 Jan., 1938, as Duggan in "Death on the Table," and played the same part at the Strand Theatre, Mar., 1938; toured, Sept., 1938, in "Bobby, Get Your Gun"; at Richmond, Nov., 1938, played Jergens in "Thieves Fall Out," and Apr., 1939, Bill Kelly in "Galleon Gold"; played this last-mentioned part, at the Criterion, May, 1939, when the play was re-named "Grouse in June"; Apollo, Aug., 1940, Thomas S. Denny in "Margin for Error"; "Q," Aug.–Oct., 1941, appeared in "Kick-In" and "The Best People"; Savoy, Dec., 1941, played Bert Jefferson in "The Man Who Came to Dinner," which he played throughout the run of the play, until Aug., 1943; Globe, Dec., 1943, Lieut. Wiseman in "While the Sun Shines," which ran until 1946; toured, July, 1946, as Geoffrey Wainwright in "But for the Grace of God," and played this part at the St. James's, Sept., 1946; Haymarket, July, 1948, played the Gentleman Caller in "The Glass Menagerie"; Arts, May, and New, June, 1949, appeared as Joe Ferguson in "The Male Animal"; Vaudeville, May, 1950, Harry Taylor in "The Ivory Tower"; Savoy, Nov., 1951, Don Lucas in "Relative Values"; New, Mar., 1954, Clive Mortimer in "I Am a Camera"; Duke of York's, July, 1958, played Kit Shaeffer in "The Joshua Tree"; Winter Garden, Dec., 1958, Curtis in "The Bright One"; Saville, Dec., 1959, Larry Hoffman in "The Amorous Prawn," which ran for over two years; first appeared in films, 1936, in "David Livingstone"; television appearances include Dwight Cooper in the series "The Flying Swan"; author of a book, "So You Want to be an Actor," 1946. *Recreations:* Golf, American bowls, shooting, riding, reading, and collecting antiques. *Club:* Wentworth Golf. *Address:* c/o Stanley Dubens Ltd., 58 Old Compton Street, London, W.1.

McDONALD, Christie, actress and vocalist; *b.* Picton, Nova Scotia, 28 Feb., 1875; *m.* Henry Lloyd Gillespie; made her first appearance on the professional stage as a member of Pauline Hall's company, in 1892, in

"Puritania"; was subsequently, in 1893, with Francis Wilson's company, appearing in "Erminie," "The Devil's Deputy," "The Chieftain," "Half-a King," etc.; during 1897-9 played Minutezza in "The Bride Elect"; she made her *début* as a star in Feb., 1899, when she appeared in the title-*rôle* in "Princess Chic"; in 1900-1 she played lead in "Hodge Podge and Co.," and "Champagne Charlie," and then rejoined Francis Wilson, to play Nancy Staunton in "The Toreador," 1901; at Wallack's, 1903, in "The Sho-Gun," at the Casino, 1904, she played in "An English Daisy"; and subsequently appeared in "2905," and "Mexicana"; during 1906-7 played Julia Caldicott in "The Belle of Mayfair," and the following season Sally Hook in "Miss Hook of Holland"; she played the latter part until the end of 1909; at the Hackett, Jan., 1910, played Angela Tritton in "The Prince of Bohemia"; at the Casino, May, 1910, Pitti-Sing in "The Mikado"; at the Liberty Theatre, Dec., 1910, played the Princess Bozena in "The Spring Maid," and continued in this part throughout 1911-12; at Baltimore, Mar., 1913, played Sylvia in "Sweethearts"; appearing in the same part, at the New Amsterdam Theatre, New York, Sept., 1913; in 1915, again toured in the same piece; she then retired for a time, and was not seen again in New York, until she appeared at the Palace, June, 1918, in "Cupid's Mirror"; at the Century Theatre, Apr., 1920, played Lady Holyrood in a revival of "Florodora."
(Died 25 July, 1962; age 87)

McEVOY, Charles, dramatic author; *b.* London, 30 June, 1879; *s.* of the late Captain Ambrose McEvoy, and *b.* of A. A. McEvoy, the distinguished painter; *m.* Margery Notley; his first play, entitled "David Ballard," was produced by the Stage Society, at the Imperial Theatre, June, 1907; since that date has written "His Helpmate," "Gentlemen of the Road," and "Lucifer," "When the Devil was Ill," "The Three Barrows," "The Village Wedding," "Anna Firth," "All that Matters," "The Situation at Newbury," "The Red Hen," "The Likes of Her " ; is a member of the Gipsy Lore Society ; is a frequent writer on stage matters, and a prolific contributor to contemporary magazines. *Hobby :* Idling in the open air.

(Died 17 Feb., 1929; age 49)

McEVOY, J.P., dramatic author and librettist; *b.* New York City, U.S.A., 10 Jan., 1894 ; *s.* of Patrick Griffin McEvoy and his wife Mary (McCabe) ; *e.* Notre Dame University; *m.* (1) Mary B. Crotty; (2) Eugenie Wehrle; (3) Margaret Santry; is the author of "The Potters," 1923; "The Comic Supplement," "The Ziegfeld Follies," 1925 ; "Americana," "God Loves Us," "No Foolin'," 1926; "Allez-Oop," "Americana," 1927 ; "Americana," 1932; "Stars In Your Eyes," 1939 ; has also written verse and novels, including "Show Girl," "Mr. Noodle," "Are You Listening?" "Father Meets Son." *(Died 8 Aug., 1958; age 64)*

McGLYNN, Frank, actor ; *b.* San Francisco, Cal., U.S.A., 26 Oct., 1866 ; *s.* of Frank McGlynn and his wife Mary (Buckley) ; *e.* Presentation Convent, and Hastings Law School ; *m.* Rose O'Byrne ; was originally intended to practice as an attorney and was admitted to the Bar, 1894 ; made his first appearance on the New York stage, at the Casino Theatre, 14 Sept., 1896, in " The Gold Bug " ; subsequently toured for several years as Richelieu in " Under the Red Robe," also playing many " stock " engagements ; subsequently again toured, with Charles Frohman's companies, playing such parts as Defarge, in " The Only Way," Rupert of Hentzau in " Rupert of Hentzau " ; in 1909, turned his attention to the cinema stage, to which he devoted some years ; first sprang into prominence when he appeared at the Cort Theatre, New York, Dec., 1919, as Abraham Lincoln in Drinkwater's play of that name, in which he achieved an instantaneous success ; he played this part almost continuously in New York and in other cities for over three years ; at the Ambassadors, New York, Oct., 1923, played Rabbi Nathan Judah in " Steadfast " ; at the Belmont

Theatre, May, 1924, Case Steenkoop in " Catskill Dutch " ; at the Morosco, Sept., 1924, Andrew Jackson in " That Awful Mrs. Eaton " ; during 1925-26 toured as Ephraim Cabot in " Desire Under the Elms " ; appeared in Vaudeville in a " Lincoln" playlet, 1927-28 ; at the Maxine Elliott Theatre, Feb., 1929, played Reb Velvele Slomner in " The Broken Chain"; Forrest, Oct., 1929, again played Abraham Lincoln. *Club :* The Friars.

(Died 17 May, 1951; age 84)

McGOOHAN, Patrick, actor; *b.* New York, 19 Mar., 1928 ; *s.* of Thomas McGoohan and his wife Rose (Fitzpatrick); *e.* Ratcliffe College ; *m.* Joan Drummond ; formerly a banker and poultry farmer ; studied for the stage under Geoffrey Ost, making his first appearance at the Playhouse, Sheffield, 1948, as the Rev. William Weightman in "The Brontës"; played the same part at the St. James's, London, 15 June, 1948; subsequently played in repertory; at the "Q," June, 1954, played Roy Mawson in "Spring Model," and July, 1954, Leonard White in "Time On Their Hands"; at the Garrick, Feb., 1955, appeared as the Rev. Howard Phillips in "Serious Charge," in which he made a marked success; Duke of York's, June, 1955, played the Serious Actor in "Moby Dick"; Lyric, Feb., 1956, played Leonard White in "Ring For Catty"; Lyric, Hammersmith, Jan., 1959, played St. Just in "Danton's Death"; at the same theatre, Apr., 1959, played the title part in "Brand"; first appeared in films, 1954, in "The Dam Busters"; television appearances include John Drake in the series "The Danger Man," 1964-5. *Address:* c/o Eric Glass, Ltd., 28 Berkeley Square, London, W.1.

McGOWAN, John W., dramatic author and librettist; *b.* Muskegon, Mich., U.S.A.; has written the following; "Mama Loves Papa" (with Mann Page), "Sweet Lady" (musical play based on "Mama Loves Papa"), 1926 ; "Tenth Avenue" (with Lloyd Griscon), "Excess Baggage," 1927 ; "Hold Everything" (with B. G. De Sylva), 1928 ; "True Colours,"

"Heads Up" (with Paul Gerard Smith), contributions to "Murray Anderson's Almanac," "Nigger Rich," 1929; "Girl Crazy" (with Guy Bolton), "Flying High" (with De Sylva and Brown), 1930; "Singin' the Blues," 1931; "Heigh-Ho Everybody" (with H. Polesie), 1932; "Earl Carroll Vanities," 1932; "Say When," 1934; has since devoted himself to the films, as author, director, and player. *Clubs:* Lambs and Players, New York. *Address:* c/o R. W. McGowan, F. and M. Stageshows, Inc., Paramount Building, 1501 Broadway, New York City, 18, U.S.A.

McGUIRE, William Anthony, dramatic author and producing manager; *b.* Chicago, 9 July, 1885; *e.* public schools, Chicago; *m.* Lulu Irene Cation; was formerly engaged in journalism on the *South Bend News,* Indiana; is the author of the following plays: "A Soldier of the Cardinal," 1902; "The Absinthe Fiend," 1903; "The Walls of Wall Street," 1908; "The Devil," 1909; "The Heights" (with Frank Keenan), 1910; "The Divorce Question," 1912; "The Cost of Living," 1913; "Everyman's Castle," "The Man Without a Country," 1916; "A Good Bad Woman," "In and Out of Bed," "Mary, Be Careful," 1919; "Frivolities of 1920," "Stand from Under," 1920; "Six Cylinder Love," 1921; "It's a Boy," 1922; "Kid Boots" (with Otto Harbach), 1923; "The Ziegfeld Follies" (with Will Rogers), 1924; "Tin Gods," "Twelve Miles Out," 1925; "If I Was Rich," 1926; "Trial Divorce" (with J. Sabath), "Rosalie" (with Guy Bolton), 1927; "The Three Musketeers" (on Dumas' romance), "Whoopee" (from "The Nervous Wreck"), 1928; "The Show Girl," 1929; "Ripples," "Smiles," 1930; "The Bad Penny," 1931; since 1926 has produced all his own plays; author of several notable films, including "Roman Scandals," "The Kid from Spain," "Little Man, What Now?" "The Great Ziegfeld," etc.
(Died 16 Sept., 1940; age 59)

McHUGH, Florence, A.R.C.M., actress and vocalist; *b.* Calgary, Alberta, Canada, 14 Oct., 1906; *d.* of Felix A. McHugh and his wife Florence (O'Doherty); *e.* Sacred Heart Convent, Calgary; *m.* J. E. Piercy, F.R.C.S.; studied singing in Calgary, but came to London in 1923 to continue her studies at the Royal College of Music; studied singing under Albert Garcia and Herman Grünebaum, and for the stage under Cairns James; became an Associate of R.C.M., 1924; made her first appearance on the stage at the Everyman Theatre, 10 Feb., 1926, as Deborah Willett in "Mr. Pepys," and appeared in the same part at the Royalty; at the Ambassadors', June, 1926, played Penny Holt in "Granite"; at the Lyric, Hammersmith, Aug., 1926, succeeded Kathlyn Hilliard in "Riverside Nights"; Nov., 1926, played Nicole in "The Would-Be Gentleman"; at the Arts Theatre, Apr., 1927, played in "The Picnic" *revue;* at the "Q," Nov., 1927, Enid in "The Lovely Liar"; Strand, Dec., 1927, Imogene in "Dr. Syn"; Everyman, Apr., 1928, Patty Skyblue in "The Dumb Man of Manchester," and in "The Sabine Women"; Oct., 1928, Hilda Wangel in "The Master Builder"; Nov., 1928, toured as Magnolia in "The Show Boat"; at Oxford, for the O.U.D.S., June, 1929, played Luce in "The Knight of the Burning Pestle"; Duchess, Mar., 1930, played in "The Intimate Revue"; Arts, Jan., 1931, played Chang-Hi-Tang in "The Circle of Chalk"; Little, Sept., 1932, played in "The Oxford Blazers"; King's, Hammersmith, and Piccadilly, Apr., 1935, Clare in "The Shadow Man"; has been frequently engaged in broadcasting for the B.B.C. *Favourite parts:* Deborah in "Mr. Pepys," and Penny in "Granite." *Recreations:* Ice-skating, swimming, and walking. *Club:* Arts Theatre. *Address:* 14 Daleham Gardens, London, N.W.3. *Telephone No.:* Hampstead 1532.

McHUGH, Therese, theatre press-representative; *b.* Sligo, Ireland; *d.* of Thomas McHugh and his wife

Elizabeth (Edwards); *e.* Marlborough; *m.* John Scott Barron; was first engaged with H. C. G. Stevens, and with the Lead-lay News Service; joined Firth Shephard in 1939 and remained with his organization exclusively until 1949; subsequently with John Clements; now a free-lance publicist. *Address:* 93 Woodcote Road, Caversham, Berks. *Telephone No.:* Reading 72061; or Suite 2, 26 Charing Cross Road, W.C.2. *Telephone No.:* Covent Garden 1611.

McINTOSH, Madge, actress and producer; *b.* Calcutta, 8 Apr., 1875; *e.* London; *m.* W. Graham Browne (mar. dis.); prepared for stage by Hermann Vezin and Emil Behnke; gained early experience with F. R. Benson and Ben Greet; made her first appearance in London at the St. George's Hall, 1893, as Peg Woffington in "Masks and Faces"; at the Court, Sept., 1893, played Adrienne in "The Other Fellow"; next toured in "The New Sub," and "Aunt Jack"; joined Edward Terry on tour, and also appeared at Terry's, 1895, in "An Innocent Abroad," "The Blue Boar," etc.; in 1897, toured as Nelly Denver in "The Silver King," and took an English company to Brussels, playing Shakespeare and Old Comedy; then toured in the United States with Olga Nethersole, as Maria in "The Termagant," Ellean in "The Second Mrs. Tanqueray," and in "Camille," "Sapho," etc.; at the Matinée Theatre, May, 1898, played Juliet and Portia with Ben Greet's company; next appeared at Comedy Theatre in "The Weather Hen," 1899; in 1900, joined Mr. and Mrs. Kendal, and appeared in "The Likeness of the Night"; appeared at the Lyric Club, Jan., 1902, as Vivie in "Mrs. Warren's Profession"; at the Imperial, Jan., 1902, as Mdlle. Leverd in "Mademoiselle Mars"; at the Comedy, May, 1902, Myra Beaumont in "The Silver Link"; at the St. James's, Oct., 1904, Lady Hudspeth in "The Decree Nisi"; toured in America with Forbes-Robertson, 1904-5, playing Miss Wagoneur in "Love and the Man," Gertrude in "Hamlet," etc.; in Feb., to Mar., 1906, at the

Court, played Aphrodite in "The Hippolytus" of Euripides; Miss Harcourt in "The Convict on the Hearth," Beatrice in "The Voysey Inheritance"; at the Adelphi, Oct., 1906, played the Virgin in "The Virgin Goddess"; at the Duke of York's, Mar., 1907, played Josephine in "The Great Conspiracy"; in 1907 went to Australia with Messrs. Meynell and Gunn to play leading parts; on her return appeared at the Globe, Nov., 1909, as Mrs. Scott-Gamble in "The Great Mrs. Alloway"; she went to the Royalty Theatre, Glasgow, in 1910 as producer, and played a number of parts with the repertory company established there; at the Haymarket, Dec., 1910, played Mummy Tyl in "The Blue Bird"; at the Queen's Theatre, Mar., 1911, appeared as Nell in "A Fool There Was"; subsequently toured in "The Prisoner of Zenda," and "Stephen Maquoid, M.P."; at the Queen's Theatre, Dec., 1911, played Night in "The Blue Bird"; at the New Prince's, Feb., 1912, appeared as Muriel Ruthven in "Travellers"; in Feb., 1912, visited Australia in "The Blue Bird"; at the Little Theatre, Feb., 1913, as Mary in "The Arbour of Refuge"; at the Haymarket, Feb., 1913, Ingeborg in "The Pretenders"; in Apr., 1913, appeared at the Grand, Croydon, in connection with the Repertory season, as Maggie Massey in "Chains," Miss Woodward in "The Tyranny of Tears," Mrs. Perrin in "The Situation at Newbury," Olive Jaggard in "Dropping the Pilot," and Candida; at the Queen's, Nov., 1913, played Mrs. Moody in "If We had only Known"; made her first appearance on the variety stage, at the Palace, Mar., 1914, as Strega in "The Music Cure"; at the Comedy, May, 1914, played Martha in "The Holy City"; entered on a short season at the Savoy, May, 1914, when she played Mrs. Patrick Beufre in "Break the Walls Down"; appointed Director of the Liverpool Repertory Theatre, Oct., 1914, and appeared there as Mrs. Arbuthnot in "A Woman of No Importance," Kate Spencer in "Cousin Kate," Candida, Jennifer in "The Doctor's Dilemma," Mrs. D'Arcy in "The Passport," Mrs.

Cassilis in "The Cassilis Engagement," and in "Hullo, Repertory!"; at the Kingsway Theatre, May, 1915, played Violet Sylvester in "Trelawny of the Wells," Beatrice Strangway in "A Bit of Love"; subsequently appeared at the Coliseum, in "Hullo, Repertory!"; during 1916 toured with her own company in "The Thief," etc.; during a "stock" engagement at Portsmouth, 1918, played Mrs. Erlynne in "Lady Windermere's Fan," Mrs. Arbuthnot in "A Woman of No Importance," Lady Huntworth in "Lady Huntworth's Experiment," Donna Roma in "The Eternal City," etc.; subsequently toured as Madame La Grange in "The Thirteenth Chair"; toured during 1919-20 as Zahrat-Al-Kulub in "Chu-Chin-Chow"; at Wyndham's, July, 1923, played Stella Trainor in "The Writing on the Wall"; subsequently toured as Mammy Pleasant in "The Cat and the Canary"; at the Aldwych, Dec., 1923, played Mrs. Hearty and the Reigning Queen in "Bluebell in Fairyland"; Court (for 300 Club), Feb., 1925, Lady Torrent in "Smaragda's Lover"; King's, Hammersmith, June-July, 1925, played eight week's repertory season, producing all the plays; subsequently toured as Sophie Dimsdale in "A Girl for Sale"; Regent, July, 1926, played Hon. Marjorie Hardress in "A House Divided," and Aug., 1926, Lady Adela Wynne in "The Light on the Mountain"; at the Strand (for the Play Actors'), Mar., 1927, produced "Two and Two"; subsequently toured in "The Queen Was In The Parlour"; later in the same year, went to Australia, playing Julia Price in "The Ghost Train"; appeared at the "Q," Nov., 1928, as Mary Howard in "The Man in the Dock"; St. Martin's (for the Shop Window), Dec., 1932, produced "Mona Lisa"; Pleasure Gardens, Folkestone, Apr., 1935, played Lady Madehurst in "Family Affairs"; Arts, Mar., 1936, Aunt Ada in "Cold Comfort Farm"; King's Hammersmith, Sept., 1938, Mrs. Westmoreland in "People at Sea"; is a teacher at the Royal Academy of Dramatic Art, and is well known as a stage-producer of great ability.

(Died 19 Feb., 1950; age 74)

McINTYRE, Frank, actor; *b.* Ann Arbor, Mich., U.S.A., 25 Feb., 1879; was formerly engaged as a newspaper reporter, before making his first appearance on the stage at Rome, N.Y., 27 Sept., 1901, in "The Hon. John Grigsby"; made his first appearance in New York, at the Manhattan Theatre, Jan., 1902, in the same play; Manhattan, Sept., 1902, appeared in "Captain Molly"; Savoy, 1903, Joseph Allen in "Major André," with Arnold Daly; Manhattan, Sept., 1903, appeared in "Becky Sharp," with Mrs. Fiske; at Madison Square, Sept., 1903, played Senator Metzoon in "My Wife's Husbands"; toured with Nat Goodwin 1903-4, in "My Wife's Husbands," and "A Gilded Fool"; at the Savoy, Theatre, Sept., 1905, played Billy Saunders in "Strongheart"; made his first appearance on the London stage, at the Aldwych Theatre, 8 May, 1907, in the same part; at the Hudson, Aug., 1907, played Bubby Dumble in "Classmates"; at the Gaiety, New York, Sept., 1908, Bob Blake in "The Travelling Salesman"; at the Hudson, Sept., 1911, Henry Disney in "Snobs"; at the Knickerbocker, Sept., 1912, Alphonse Bouchotte in "Oh! Oh!! Delphine!!!"; during 1913-14, played in "A Pair of Sixes," at Chicago, Boston and on tour; at Atlantic City, Aug., 1915, played in "Brother Masons"; at the Globe, New York, Sept., 1916, Montgommery Blainey in "Fast and Grow Fat" (subsequently re-named "Fate Decides"); during 1917, toured in "Miss Springtime"; at the Lyric, New York, Nov., 1919, Wilson Peters in "The Rose of China"; at the Playhouse, New York, June, 1920, James Moseley in "Seeing Things"; at Brooklyn, May, 1921, appeared in "The Red Trail"; at the Fulton, Apr., 1924, played Joe in "Sitting Pretty," and then toured for a season in the same part, with the Dolly Sisters; 46th Street Theatre, Dec., 1925, played in "The Greenwich Village Follies"; Ambassador, Sept., 1926, George Nettleton in "Queen High"; Imperial, Feb., 1928, Leon Dorsay in "Sunny Days"; Casino, Jan., 1929, Worthington Smith in "Boom Boom"; during 1930-1, toured in the same part; from 1934-6, engaged in Radio, as Captain Henry in "The Showboat"; has also composed music, written lyrics and short stories. *Clubs*: Lambs, New York; University, Barton Hills Country and The Elks, Ann Arbor, Mich.

(Died 8 June, 1949; age 70)

McKEE, Clive R., manager; *b.* Woodstock, Ont., Canada, 6 Oct., 1883; *s.* of A. O. McKee and his wife Ella (Sawtell); *m.* Grace Dove; has held the post of general manager for the various enterprises of C. B. Cochran, at the Apollo, Garrick, Oxford, London Pavilion, Ambassadors',etc., from 1914–24; subsequently business-manager at the new Fortune Theatre, 1924. *Recreation*: Motoring.

McKINNEL, Norman, actor; *b.* Maxwelltown, Kirkcudbrightshire, N.B., 10 Feb., 1870; *s.* of J. B. A. McKinnel, J.P.; *e.* Edinburgh and Leipzig; *m.* Gertrude Scott; originally intended to follow his father's profession of engineer; made his first appearance on the stage at Clacton-on-Sea, 19 July, 1894, when he played Mr. Joyce in "A Jonathan Without a David," in Otho Stuart's Company; played with Mrs. Bandmann-Palmer, and with Edward Compton; made his first appearance in London, at the Elephant and Castle Theatre, 21 Oct., 1895, as John in " Davy Garrick," and Harry Selbourne in " Hook and Eye "; was three years with H. Beerbohm Tree, appearing at Her Majesty's, 22 Jan., 1898, as Varro in " Julius Caesar "; Nov., 1898, as Rochefort in " The Musketeers "; Apr., 1899, as the Maharajah of Motiala in " Carnac Sahib "; Sept., 1899, as Lymoges in " King John "; Jan., 1900, as Philostrate in " A Midsummer Night's Dream "; May, 1900, as Seth in " Rip Van Winkle "; June, 1900, as Derrick Beekman in the same play; Sept., 1900, in " Julius Caesar "; Feb., 1901, in " Twelfth Night "; appeared as Poseidon (Neptune) in " Ulysses," Feb., 1902; at Wyndham's, Mar., 1902, played Laurent in " Caesar's Wife "; at same theatre, Nov., 1902, played Lord Carshalton in " The Vanity of Youth "; was

engaged by Sir Henry Irving to support him as Nello della Pietri in " Dante," at Drury Lane, Apr., 1903; at the same theatre, Sept., 1903, played Menotti Derago in " The Flood Tide "; at the New Theatre, Dec., 1903, appeared as Geoffrey Oakleigh in " Mrs. Oakleigh "; at the Royalty, Feb., 1904, played Martial in " Ferreol de Meyrac "; at the Imperial, Apr., 1904, appeared as Major John Colden in " Miss Elizabeth's Prisoner "; at the Court, Apr., 1904, appeared as the Rev. James Mavor Morell in " Candida "; at the Imperial, Oct., 1904, played General Lambert in " His Majesty's Servant "; Jan., 1905, played Williams in " King Henry the Fifth "; at the St. James's, Feb., 1905, appeared as Sir Joseph Balsted in " Mollentrave on Women "; at the Imperial, Oct., 1905, played William Tremblett in " The Perfect Lover "; Jan., 1906, played Tancred in " The Harlequin King "; at the Court, Feb., 1906, played Pan in " Pan and the Young Shepherd "; appeared as Simeon Krillett in " The Shulamite," Savoy, May, 1906; Sir Timothy Crewys, in " Peter's Mother," New, Sept., 1906, and created leading *rôle* in " On the Side of the Angels," produced by the Pioneers at the Royalty, Dec., 1906; at the Court, Jan., 1907, he played John Perry in " The Campden Wonder "; in June, 1907, appeared as the Devil in " Don Juan in Hell "; and at the Kingsway, Oct., 1907, as Philip Wycherley in " Irene Wycherley "; at the Kingsway, during 1908 appeared as P. C. Fellowes in " Diana of Dobson's," Harcourt Wilson in " The Latch," George Lomax, K.C., in " The Sway Boat," and Jim Barr in " Grit "; during 1909 he appeared at the Kingsway, Feb., as Lord Strelland in " The Truants," at the Duke of York's, Mar., as John Anthony in " Strife "; at the Kingsway, Apr., as Sir Felix Janion in " The Earth "; he was then engaged as stage director at the Haymarket Theatre, and Sept. appeared as King Lear; in Oct. he played Albert Thompsett in " Don "; at the New Theatre, Aug., 1910, played Adrien Serval in " The Crisis," and Sept., 1910, Derrick Lowne in " Young

Fernald " ; at the Little Theatre, Mar., 1911, played Halvard Solness in " The Master Builder " ; at the Globe, Apr., 1911, appeared as Sir Robert Fyffe in " A Butterfly on the Wheel " ; at the Royalty, May, 1911, played Wing Shee in " The Cat and the Cherub " ; in Sept., 1911, toured with Julia Neilson as King Christian in " The Popinjay " ; at the Coliseum, Jan., 1912, in aid of the *Daily Telegraph* Dickens Fund, he played Sergeant Buzfuz in " Bardell *v.* Pickwick " ; at the Court. Jan., 1912, and subsequently at the Little and Vaudeville Theatres, played John Rutherford in " Rutherford and Son " ; played the same part at the Little Theatre, New York, 24 Dec., 1912 ; appeared at His Majesty's, Mar., 1913, as Andrew Remmington in " The Happy Island " ; at the Comedy, May, 1913, reappeared as John Anthony in " Strife," and June, 1913, played James Ralston in a revival of " Jim the Penman " ; in conjunction with Frederick Whelen entered on the management of the Vaudeville Theatre, Oct., 1913, opening on 1 Oct., 1913, as George Digby in " Collision " ; Oct., 1913, also played Jim Harris in " Between Sunset and Dawn." and Henry in " The Green Cockatoo " ; in Nov., 1913, appeared as Prince Patiomkin in " Great Catherine " ; Jan., 1914, as Ezra Sheppard in " Mary Girl " ; Feb., 1914, James Ollerenshaw in " Helen with the High Hand " ; at the Queen's, July, 1914, played Guido Colonna in " Monna Vanna " ; at the Coliseum, Dec., 1914, The Emperor in " Der Tag " ; at the Victoria Palace, July, 1915 Bob Trotter in " How to Get on " ; at Wyndham's, Sept., 1915, played Michae Adye, K.C., in " The Ware Case " at the Apollo, June, 1916, Henry Horatio Hobson in " Hobson's Choice"; Nov., 1916, Pierrot in " Pierrot's Christmas " ; at the Haymarket, Mar., 1917, appeared as Sir Dennys Broughton in " General Post " ; at the Queen's, Mar., 1919, as Wachner in " The House of Peril " ; at the Court, June, 1919, as Lucius Leniham in " The Lost Leader " ; at the Globe, Aug., 1919, played Sir Leslie Caryll in " A Voice from the Minaret " ; at the Ambassadors', Apr., 1920,

Jerry Weston, M.P., in " The Grain of Mustard Seed " ; in Mar., 1921, entered on the management of the Comedy Theatre, and appeared there as Richard Ffellowes, Earl of Radenham in " The Ninth Earl " ; Apr., 1921, as Sir Phillip Marlow in " A Matter of Fact " ; June, 1921, as John Builder in " A Family Man " ; Sept., 1921, Neri in " The Love Thief "; he then appeared at the Globe, Dec., 1921, when he played Oliver Blayds in " The Truth About Blayds " ; at the Queen's, Aug., 1922, John Brown in " Bluebeard's Eighth Wife " ; at the Queen's, Nov., 1923, Thomas Whamond in " The Little Minister " ; at the Adelphi, June, 1924, in aid of King George's Pension Fund for Actors, reappeared as Michael Adye, K.C., M.P., in " The Ware Case " ; at the Comedy, June, 1924, Peter Weston in the play of that name ; at the Haymarket, Oct., 1924, Sylvanus Heythorp in " Old English " ; Dec., 1924, the Policeman in " A Kiss for Cinderella " ; Garrick, Mar., 1925, Sir William Jesmond in " Possessions " ; Adelphi (for King George's Pension Fund), May, 1925, Mynheer Cornelis in " My Lady's Dress " ; Adelphi, Sept., 1925, Sir Maurice Harpenden in " The Green Hat " ; Savoy, Dec., 1925, succeeded C. M. Lowne, as Sir Henry Hesketh in " The Unfair Sex " ; May, 1926, Sir Charles Middleton in " Intimate Enemies " ; " Q " and Criterion, Aug., 1926, Sir James Carruthers in " Thy Name is Woman " ; Apollo (for the Venturers), Dec., 1926, and Prince of Wales's, Jan., 1927, Sir Simon Marvill in " Tuppence Coloured " ; Globe, Mar., 1927, Captain McWhirter in " A Hen Upon a Steeple " ; Drury Lane (for King George's Pension Fund), May, 1927, Gonzales Ferara in " The Wandering Jew " ; later in the same year, went to South Africa and Australia with Irene Vanbrugh and Dion Boucicault, playing in " The High Road," " The Letter," " Caroline," " All the King's Horses," " On Approval," " The Truth About Blayds," " The Notorious Mrs. Ebbsmith " ; returned to London, 1929 ; reappeared at the Little, June, 1929, as Tom Scarsdale in " Water " ; succeeded the late Sydney Valentine as Chairman of the Actors' Association,

but subsequently resigned; author of "The Bishop's Candlesticks," founded on an incident in "Les Misérables," and produced at the Duke of York's Theatre, 1901; "Dick's Sister," 1905; and part-author of "Intimate Enemies," 1926. *Favourite part:* Heythorp in "Old English." *Recreation:* Reading. *Clubs:* Garrick, Beefsteak, and Green Room.
(Died 29 Mar., 1932; age 62)

McLELLAN, C. M. S., dramatic author; *b.* 1865; was editor of New York *Town Topics;* author of "The Belle of New York," "The Whirl of the Town," "In Gay New York," "An American Beauty," "The Telephone Girl," "Yankee Doodle Dandy," "The Wire Walker," "The Girl from Up There," "Glittering Gloria," produced at Wyndham's, 1903; "Leah Kleschna," produced at the New, 1905; "On the Love Path," Haymarket, 1905; "The Jury of Fate," Shaftesbury, 1906; "Nelly Neil," Aldwych, 1907; "The Shirkers," produced in New York, 1907; "The Pickpockets," Atlantic City, 1908; "The Strong People," Lyric, 1910; "Marriage à la Carte," Casino, New York, 1911; "The Pink Lady," New Amsterdam Theatre, New York, 1911; "The Affair in the Barracks," Chicago, 1911; "Oh! Oh!! Delphine!!!" 1912; "The Little Café," 1913; "The Fountain," 1914; wrote his earlier productions under the pen name of Hugh Morton. *(Died 22 Sept., 1916; age 51)*

McMASTER, Anew, actor; *b.* Co. Monaghan, Ireland, 24 Dec., 1894; *e.* Birkenhead; *m.* Marjorie Willmore; made his first appearance on the stage at the New Theatre, 2 Jan., 1911, as the Aristocrat in "The Scarlet Pimpernel," with Fred Terry, remaining under his management for three years, playing Rollins in "Sweet Nell of Old Drury," Armand St. Just in "The Scarlet Pimpernel," etc.; at the Savoy, Apr., 1920, played Jack O'Hara in "Paddy the Next Best Thing"; Kingsway (for Stage Society), Feb., 1921, Colin Langford in "At Mrs. Beams"; went to Australia, and from 1921–24,

was engaged with J. C. Williamson, Ltd., playing Baldasarre in "The Maid of the Mountains," and with Oscar Asche, Iago in "Othello," Laurence in "Iris," etc.; His Majesty's, Sept., 1924, played Rivelot in "The Royal Visitor"; at the Adelphi, London, Mar., 1925, played Laurence Trenwith in Gladys Cooper's revival of "Iris"; formed his own Shakespearean company, 1925, and has played most of the leading parts including Hamlet, Macbeth, Coriolanus, Petruchio, Othello, Richard III, Shylock, etc.; at the Winter Garden Theatre, Dec., 1932, played Ford in "The Merry Wives of Windsor"; at Stratford-on-Avon Memorial Theatre, 1933, Hamlet, Coriolanus, Petruchio, and Macduff; Chiswick Empire, Nov., 1933, played Othello, Macbeth, Shylock, Jaques, Petruchio and Richard III; in 1936–37, toured in the near East, Egypt, Malta, etc., playing Othello, Malvolio and Charles Surface in "The School for Scandal." *Recreations:* Grand opera and playgoing.
(Died 25 Aug., 1962; age 67)

McNAUGHTON, Gus, actor; *b.* London, 29 July, 1884; *s.* of Charles Howard and his wife Georgina (Wright); *e.* Royal Savoy Chapel School; *m.* Charlotta Poluski; made his first appearance on the stage at the Surrey Theatre, Christmas, 1899, as a Chinese Policeman in "Aladdin"; appeared in variety theatres with Fred Karno's company; appeared in variety all over Great Britain and Ireland; made his first appearance in the West-End, at the Alhambra Theatre, 1918, in "The Bing Boys on Broadway"; Duke of York's, Sept., 1919, appeared as Harry Kilmartin in "Girl for the Boy"; Aldwych, Oct., 1920, as Frank Lomax in "My Nieces"; Queen's, May, 1924, appeared in "Come In"; toured, in musical comedy, *revue*, and variety, all over India, Federated Malay States, China, Phillipines, and Australia; at the London Hippodrome, Mar., 1929, played Oswald in "The Five o'Clock Girl"; subsequently played in variety and films, and has regularly appeared in pantomime, in London and

leading provincial cities; at the
Piccadilly, Jan., 1943, played Roger
Tunbridge in "Sleeping Out"; at the
New, Feb., 1944, the First Gravedigger
in "Hamlet"; Wimbledon, Feb.,
1945, Smythe Wallop in "Gather No
Moss"; toured, in the autumn of
1945, as Blore in "Dandy Dick";
"Q," Nov., 1947, Smythe-Wallop in
"Gather No Moss"; Cambridge, Aug.,
1948, Joe Hawkins in "Trouble in the
House"; Playhouse, Apr., 1949,
L/Cpl. Murphy in "Maiden's Prayer";
first appeared in films, 1930, in
"Murder," and has played in in-
numerable pictures. *Recreations:* Box-
ing, golf, cricket, and football (rugger).
Club: Stage Golfing Society.

(Died Nov., 1969; age 85)

McNAUGHTON, Tom, actor; b.
1 July, 1867; m. Alice Lloyd; formerly
engaged with his brother Fred in
music halls for many years, appearing
as the McNaughtons; after a varied
experience in the provinces, appeared at
Sebright's Music Hall, Hackney, where
they attracted the attention of the
late George Ware; shortly after, on 14
Oct., 1889, they appeared at the Middlesex, followed by engagements at
several of the West End halls, first
as " knockabout comedians," subsequently as boxers and finally in their
famous " cross-talk " act; fulfilled
engagements at most of the leading
West End and provincial halls, also
in South Africa and the United States;
since 1909 has appeared principally in
the United States; in 1910 he appeared
on the musical comedy stage for the
first time, appearing at the Liberty
Theatre, New York, 26 Dec., 1910, as
Roland in " The Spring Maid "; he
toured in this, 1911–13; at the New
Amsterdam, Sept., 1913, played Mikel
Mikeloviz in " Sweethearts "; at the
Casino, Nov., 1914, Dr. Herring in
" Suzi "; at the Knickerbocker, Mar.,
1915, Chase Clews in " Fads and
Fancies "; at the Cohan Theatre, Feb.,
1916, Policeman No. 13 in " Pom-
Pom "; reappeared in London, at the
London Hippodrome, Mar., 1918, in
" A Box o' Tricks "; at the Shubert,
New York, Nov., 1919, played Sir
Reggie Chester in " The Magic Me-
lody," and toured in this 1920–21.

(Died 28 Nov., 1923; age 57)

McNAUGHTONS, The (Fred and
Gus), comedians; Fred McNaughton
was born in 1869; m. Georgina
Preston; appeared with his brother
Tom for several years, making his
first appearance in London, at
Sebright's Music Hall, Hackney; subsequently, 14 Oct., 1889, appeared at the
Middlesex, and other West End halls;
toured with Tom, in the United States
and South Africa; when his brother
Tom went to the United States, in
1909, was joined by Gus McNaughton,
and they have appeared together at
most of the leading London and
provincial halls, in their comedy act.
Address: 43 Lansdowne Gardens,
South Lambeth, S.W.

McPHERSON, Mervyn, theatrical
press representative; b. Bristol, 19
July, 1892; s. of Duncan Matheson
McPherson and his wife Alice (Iles);
e. Clifton College; for some years was
engaged as a political organizer for
the Conservative Party, and was
subsequently engaged in journalism;
was press representative for Grossmith
and Laurillard, throughout the existence of that firm, 1914–20; press representative for Clayton and Waller,
until the firm was dissolved (1924–30);
he represented Leslie Henson and
Firth Shephard, among other theatrical managers; has acted as publicity
director for the Empire Theatre, since
1929. *Favourite play:* "Hassan."
Recreations: Golf and tennis. *Address:*
Empire Theatre Chambers, Leicester
Square, W.C.2. *Telephone No.:* Gerrard 7178 and 1234; or 74 Antrim
Mansions, Antrim Road, London,
N.W.3. *Telephone No.:* Primrose
3548.

McRAE, Bruce, actor; b. in India,
of English parents, 15 Jan., 1867;
e. Boulogne-sur-Mer, France; is a
nephew of Sir Charles Wyndham;
made his first appearance on the
stage at Proctor's Twenty-third Street
Theatre, New York, in " Thermi-
dor," 5 Oct., 1891; next played
the Earl of Crayston-Leigh in " Aristocracy," 1892; on tour as Marquis of Normandale in " Aristocracy," 1893; next appeared on

tour as Captain Heartsease in
" Shenandoah," 1894 ; with Marie
Burroughs in *répertoire*, 1895 ; Harry
Burgess in " The Fatal Card," 1895 ;
with Olga Nethersole in *répertoire*,
playing Gaston Rieux in " Camille,"
1896 ; with Herbert Kelcey and Effie
Shannon as Hamilton Walboys in
" A Coat of Many Colours," 1897 ; as
Douglas Rhodes in " The Moth and
the Flame," 1898 ; with William Gil-
lette as Dr. Watson in " Sherlock
Holmes," 1899 ; with Julia Marlowe
as Captain Trumbull in " Barbara
Frietchie," 1900 ; and as Charles
Brandon in " When Knighthood was
in Flower," 1901 ; with Ethel
Barrymore for several seasons as
leading man in " A Country Mouse "
and " Carrots," 1902 ; " Cousin
Kate," 1903 ; " Sunday " and Ib-
sen's " A Doll's House," 1904 ;
" Alice Sit-by-the-Fire," 1905 ; " Cap-
tain Jinks," " The Silver Box,"
" His Excellency the Governor," and
" The Step-Sister," 1907 ; has also
played Jean de Servigny in " Yvette "
(Knickerbocker, 1904) ; John Russell
in " The Embarrassment of Riches "
(Wallack's, 1906), and Lieutenant
Rafferty in " Told in the Hills "
(Chicago, 1906) ; also several " stock "
seasons at Denver, etc. ; at the Gar-
rick, New York, Nov., 1907, played
Dr. Forester Wake in " Dr. Wake's
Patient," and at the Lyric, Dec., 1907,
John Rosmer in " Rosmersholm " ;
at Poughkeepsie, Sept., 1908, played
Paradine Fouldes in " Lady Frederick," and the same part at the
Hudson, New York, Nov., 1908 ;
at the Criterion, New York, Aug.,
1909, played Richard Lascelles in
" The Flag Lieutenant " ; at Baltimore, Oct., 1909, played in " The
Commanding Officer " ; at the Stuyvesant Theatre, New York, Dec., 1909,
appeared as Huzar in " The Lily " ;
at the Hudson Theatre, New York,
Nov., 1910, played the Duke of Moreland in " Nobody's Widow " ; during
June, 1911, played a " stock " engagement at Denver, Colorado ; during
1911-12 toured in " The Right to
be Happy " ; subsequently played
" stock " at Elitch's Gardens, Denver ;
at the Belasco Theatre, New York,
Dec., 1912, appeared as Michael

Doyle in " Years of Discretion " ;
in June, 1913, at Atlantic City, played
Harry Lindsay in " Nearly a Husband " ;
appeared in the same part at the
Gaiety, New York, Sept., 1913, when
the play was re-named " Nearly
Married " ; in 1914 toured in the same
part ; at Washington, Dec., 1914,
played in " The Fallen Idol " ; at the
Empire, New York, Jan., 1915, appeared
as Gerard Tregnier in " The Shadow";
at the Shubert Theatre, Mar., 1916,
as Simeon Strong in " The Great
Pursuit " (" The Idler ") ; at the
Cohan Theatre, Oct., 1916, as Burton
Crane in " Come Out of the Kitchen " ;
at the Belasco Theatre, Sept., 1918,
played Robert Audrey in " Daddies " ;
at the Lyceum, New York, Sept., 1919,
Stephen Lee in " The Gold Diggers,"
which ran nearly two years ; at the
Henry Miller Theatre, Sept., 1922,
Norman Satterly in " The Awful
Truth " ; at the Lyceum, New York,
Aug., 1923, Larry Charters in " Little
Miss Bluebeard " ; at the Thirty-ninth
Street Theatre, Dec., 1923, Bobby
Brandon in " The Alarm Clock " ; at
the Princess, Nov., 1924, William
Trimble in " The Steam Roller." *Rec-
reation :* Boat sailing. *Clubs :* The
Players', The Lambs', The Actors' Fund.
Business address : The Players',
16 Gramercy Park, New York.
(Died 7 May, 1927; age 60)

McWADE, Robert, actor ; *b.* Buffalo,
N.Y., U.S.A., *s.* of Robert McWade,
actor ; was for three seasons, 1902–5,
a member of the Murray Hill " stock "
company, and for a further three years
toured as Simonides in " Ben Hur " ;
appeared with great success at the
Majestic Theatre, New York, 9 Nov.,
1908, as Colonel Taylor in " Blue
Grass " ; Wallack's, Oct., 1909, played
Ross McHenry in " The Fourth Estate ";
Liberty, Aug., 1910, Fred Merkle in
" The Country Boy"; Astor, Feb.,
1912, McSherry in " The Greyhound ";
Republic, Sept., 1912, Wesley Merritt
in " The Governor's Lady"; Belasco,
Dec., 1912, Amos Thomas in " Years
of Discretion " ; Republic, Aug., 1915,
W. P. Yates in " Common Clay " ;
Empire, Apr., 1916, Major Lane in
" Rio Grande"; Eltinge, Aug., 1916,

Steve Wilson in "Cheating Cheaters"; Hudson, Aug., 1917, Frazer in "The Deluge"; Cohan, Nov., 1917, Bourdier in "The King"; Hudson, Oct., 1917, Major Kelinsky in "The Rescuing Angel"; Vanderbilt, Oct., 1918, Sam McNaughton in "The Matinée Hero"; Lyric, July, 1919, Otis Weaver in "The Five Million"; Hudson, July, 1920, Fred Robinson in "Crooked Gamblers"; Plymouth, Jan., 1922, Fraser in a revival of "The Deluge"; Aug., 1922, Webster Parsons in "The Old Soak"; Playhouse, Aug., 1923, Richard Walcott in "We've Got to Have Money"; Frazee, Nov., 1923, Harvey Wallick in "The Deep Tangled Wildwood"; Fulton, Feb., 1924, George Clark in "New Toys"; Nov., 1924, Thomas Bates in "New Brooms"; Hudson, Aug., 1926, P. H. Bancroft in "The Home Towners"; Charles Hopkins Theatre, Dec., 1926, Mr. Quigley in "The Devil in the Cheese"; since that date has mostly been engaged with Henry Duffy's companies at Los Angeles, Hollywood, and San Francisco; has appeared in innumerable pictures. *Address:* Players' Club, 16 Gramercy Park, New York City, U.S.A.

House for ten years, and sang in all the Wagner operas; made his first appearance outside grand opera at the Globe, New York, 15 Oct., 1931, as Pompineau in "The Cat and the Fiddle"; Morosco, Oct., 1933, played Von Eisenstein in "Champagne Sec" ("Die Fledermaus"); 44th Street, May, 1934, Saunders in "The Only Girl"; at the Nixon, Pittsburgh (for the Theatre Guild), Apr., 1935, played Biondello in "The Taming of the Shrew," playing the same part at the Guild Theatre, New York, Sept., 1935; Shubert (for the Guild), Mar., 1936, Dumpsty in "Idiot's Delight"; St. Louis, Aug., 1937, appeared in "The Pink Lady," "Robin Hood" and "Wild Violets"; Shubert, New York (for the Guild), Nov., 1937, played Sosie in "Amphitryon 38"; made his first appearance in London, at the Lyric, 17 May, 1938, in the same part; returned to America and toured, 1938–39, in "Idiot's Delight" and "Amphitryon 38"; Ziegfeld, Oct., 1945, played Franz in "The Red Mill"; *Address:* c/o Actors' Equity Association, 45 West 47th Street, New York City, U.S.A.

MEADER, George, actor and vocalist; *b.* Minneapolis, Minn., U.S.A., 6 July, 1888; *s.* of William Francis Meader and his wife Jane Birdsal (Stephens); *e.* University of Minnesota (LL.B., 1908); *m.* Maria Karrer; studied singing in Germany, under Madame Schoen-René; from the age of eight sang in choirs as a boy soprano, and was soloist at the Grace Church, Chicago, and at St. George's, New York; originally intended for the Law; made his first appearance on the professional stage on the Keith and Proctor "vaudeville" circuit; made his first appearance in Opera, at the Civic Opera House, Leipzig, 1910, as Lionel in "Martha"; joined the Metropolitan Opera Company, New York, 1920; has appeared as Almaviva in "The Barber of Seville," Ferrando in "Cosi Fan Tutte," David in "Die Meistersinger," Max in "Der Freyschutz," Mime in "Siegfried," also in "Boccaccio," "The Bartered Bride," etc.; he appeared at the Metropolitan Opera

MEASOR, Adela, actress; *b.* Ireland, 2 Sept., 1860; *d.* of Charles Pennell Measor, author and member of the Civil Service; *m.* the late J. C. Buckstone, actor; made her first appearance on the stage in the provinces, 1 79; made her first appearance on the London stage, at the Gaiety Theatre, 22 Nov., 1879, as Ethel Lyster in "Just Like a Woman"; she then appeared at the Court Theatre, 24 Sept., 1881, as Leonie de Latour in 'Honour," subsequently playing there in "Engaged," "The Manager," and "My Little Girl"; then at Haymarket under the Bancrofts in "Odette," 1882; from 1882 to 1885 appeared in principal theatres in America as juvenile leading lady; in 1886 appeared at the Prince's Theatre in "The Jilt," with the late Dion Boucicault; subsequently toured with Geneviève Ward and Miss Fortescue; from 1890 to 1895 was again in America, playing with the late Richard Mansfield; returned to England in

1895, and appeared at the Vaudeville in " Between the Posts," " The Strange Adventures of Miss Brown," etc. ; since then has appeared at the Haymarket, Vaudeville, New, Wyndham's, Court, and other theatres in " A Golden Wedding," "The Manoeuvres of Jane," " Lady Flirt," " Quality Street," " A Cabinet Minister," " Beauty and the Barge " ; " Fanny and the Servant Problem," etc., and on provincial tours ; has lately appeared in the music halls in sketches, " Scrooge," " The Postman's Knock," etc. ; at the Prince of Wales's, Feb., 1914, played Mrs. Spotswood in " Broadway Jones " ; at the Comedy, Apr., 1915, Mdme. Dupré in " Wild Thyme " ; subsequently toured in " Broadway Jones " ; at the Kingsway, Aug., 1917, played Mrs. Meadows in " Cook " ; subsequently toured in the provinces ; at the Garrick, Mar., 1922, played Jeannette in " The Man in Dress Clothes " ; at the Playhouse, Mar., 1923, Augusta Schwartz in " Magda " ; St. James's, June, 1925, played the Usher in " The Guardsman " ; Lyceum, Nov., 1925, Jeannette in " The Man in Dress Clothes " ; Fortune, July, 1928, Mrs. Krabbe in " Mischief."

(Died 9 June, 1933; age 72)

MEASOR, Beryl, actress ; *b.* Shanghai, China, 22 Apr., 1908 ; *d.* of Ernest Anthony Measor and his wife Mary (Humphreys) ; *e.* St. Margaret's School, Bushey, Herts ; *m.* Terence de Marney ; studied for the stage at the Royal Academy of Dramatic Art ; made her first appearance on the stage at the Whitehall Theatre, 28 July, 1931, walking-on in " Take a Chance" ; during 1931-2, toured as Luella Carmody in " Late Night Final" ; from 1932-4, played in repertory at Worthing, Croydon, and Hull ; appeared at the Kingsway, Jan., 1934, as Sophie Elsner in "Hemlock" ; Westminster, Oct., 1934, played Ilse in "Children in Uniform" ; Old Vic., Nov., 1934, Margaret in "Much Ado About Nothing" ; Embassy, Nov., 1935, in "Murder Gang" ; Embassy, Feb., 1937, and Daly's, Mar., 1937, Vi Hanway in "Night Alone" ; Ambassadors', Apr., 1937, Polly in "Miserable

Sinners" ; New, May, 1938, Geraldine Morley in "People of Our Class" ; New, Sept., 1938, Miss Hill in "Can We Tell?" ; Rudolf Steiner Hall, Dec., 1939, Mrs. Joe Gargery in "Great Expectations" ; Haymarket, Apr., 1943, Monica Reed in "Present Laughter," and Edie in "This Happy Breed" ; Duchess, Aug., 1943, Madame Arcati in "Blithe Spirit" ; King's, Edinburgh, Oct., 1945, and Embassy, Jan., 1946, Mrs. Willis in "Now the Day is Over" ; Playhouse, Dec., 1946, appeared in the *revue* "Between Ourselves" ; St. James's, Oct., 1947, played Laura Henekin in "The Man in the Street" ; Embassy, Oct., 1948, Gertrude Seagar in "That Mighty Heart" ; Duke of York's, Mar., 1949, Esta Muirhead in "The Queen Came By" ; Winter Garden, Oct., 1949, Lady Constance Winter in "Top Secret" ; Wimbledon, Nov., 1950, played Judith in "Mantrap" ; Embassy, Apr., 1951, appeared as Mrs. Elsie Walsh in "Cosh Boy," and played the same part at the Comedy, Dec., 1951, when the play was renamed "Master Crook" ; at the Civic Theatre, Chesterfield, Sept., 1952, played Laura in "It's Never Too Late" ; St. James's, London, Sept., 1954, appeared as Miss Cooper in "Separate Tables" ("The Window Table" and "Table Number Seven"), gaining the Clarence Derwent Award for her performance in this production ; made her first appearance on Broadway at the Music Box, N.Y., Oct., 1956, in the same part and plays ; at the Arts, London, Sept., 1958, played Cornelia Scott in "Something Unspoken," and Mrs. Holly in "Suddenly Last Summer," in the double bill "Garden District" ; Edinburgh Festival, Gateway, Aug., 1959, played Lady Saill in "Breakspear in Gascony" ; first appeared in films, 1938. *Recreations:* Golf and ski-ing.

(Died 8 Feb., 1965; age 58)

MEEK, Donald, actor ; *b.* Glasgow, Scotland, 1880 ; made his first appearance on the stage, as a child of eight years, at the Palace Theatre, Glasgow ; subsequently toured in "Voyage en Suisse," and then went to Australia, to play Cedric in "Little Lord Fauntleroy"; appeared at the Castle Square Theatre, Boston, U.S.A., under John Craig, 1912–13; in Apr., 1914, was at the Hollis Street Theatre, Boston, as Archibald Wayne in "The Reformers"; first appeared in New York, at the Liberty Theatre, 25 Dec., 1917, as F. H. Douglas in "Going-Up"; at the Lyric, Oct., 1919, played Doctor Tibbetts in "Nothing But Love"; George M. Cohan, Mar., 1920, Swift in "The Hottentot"; Plymouth, Sept., 1920, Bunny Waters in "Little Old New York"; Sam H. Harris, Aug., 1921, Richard Burton in "Six-Cylinder Love"; Frazee, Aug., 1923, Philemon in "Tweedles"; Plymouth, Dec., 1923, Pa Potter in "The Potters"; National Sept., 1925, Ed in "Easy Terms"; Criterion, Dec., 1925, Mr Gillicuddy in "Fool's Bells"; Sam H. Harris, Feb., 1926, Lem Woodruff in "Love 'Em and Leave 'Em"; Morosco, Sept., 1926, Rev. Herbert Chetswold in "The Shelf"; Martin Beck, Apr., 1927, Mike Riordan in "Spread Eagle"; Shubert, Oct., 1927, Darwin P. Johnson in "My Princess"; Charles Hopkins Theatre, Oct., 1927, Old Beppo in "The Ivory Door"; Liberty, Oct., 1928, John Jones in "Mr. Moneypenny"; Bijou, Apr., 1929, Henry Jones in "Jonesy"; Ritz, Nov., 1929, Cyrus Bumpsted in "Broken Dishes"; Morosco, Nov., 1930, Luther Bowen in "Oh, Promise Me"; John Golden Theatre, Aug., 1931, Willie Taylor in "After To-Morrow"; 48th Street, Apr., 1932, Henry Merrill in "Take My Tip"; Grand Opera House, Chicago, Sept., 1932, played in "Of Thee I Sing"; has played 800 parts since his first appearance; has also appeared in innumerable films.

(Died 18 Nov., 1946; age 66)

MÉGARD, Andrée, French actress *(née* Marie Chamonal); *b.* Saint-Amour, Jura, 1869; *m.* Firmin Gémier; was engaged at the Palais-Royal in 1895; subsequently appeared at the Renaissance, Gymnase, Variétés, and Odéon; appeared successfully in " Le Paradis," "L'Education de Prince," " Les Amants de Sazy," etc.; has appeared at the Théâtre Antoine, 1907, as Anna in " Anna Karénina ";

Flore Brazier in " La Rabouilleuse "; Lucienne Helloin in " Coeur à Coeur"; in 1910, as Thérèse Duvigneau in "L'Ange Gardien"; Lucienne in " La Bête "; in 1912, as Germaine Lesage in " Une Affaire d'Or "; at the Renaissance, 1912, played Madeleine in " Le Feu de St. Jean "; at the Porte-St.-Martin, 1913, appeared as Roxane in a revival of " Cyrano de Bergerac "; at the Antoine, played Portia, Cléopatre, etc.; at the Théâtre des Champs-Élysées, Shéhérazade in " Les Mille et une Nuits "; at the Antoine, the Grande Duchesse Aurore in " Koenigsmark," Etiennette in " La Maison de l'Homme," etc. *Address :* 54 Rue Blanche, Paris.

MEGRUE, Roi Cooper, dramatic author; *b.* New York City, 12 June, 1883; *s.* of Frank Newton Megrue and his wife Stella Georgiana Haile (Cooper); *e.* Trinity School, N.Y., and Columbia University; was formerly a partner with Elisabeth Marbury, as a play-broker; has written the following plays : " Her Only Way," 1911 ; " White Magic," 1912 ; " To Kill a Man," 1912 ; " An Unlucky Star," " Interviewed "; " The Neglected Lady " (from the French), 1914 ; " Under Cover," 1914 ; " It Pays to Advertise " (with Walter Hackett), 1914 ; " Under Fire," 1915 ; " Potash and Perlmutter in Society " (with Montague Glass), 1915 ; " Seven Chances " (formerly entitled " Not for Sale," and " The Cradle Snatcher "), 1916 ; " Under Sentence " (with Irvin S. Cobb), 1916 ; " Where Poppies Bloom " (from the French), 1918 ; " Tea for Three," 1918 ; " Among the Girls," 1919 ; " Honours are Even," 1921. *Recreation :* Roulette. *Clubs :* Players', Dutch Treat, American Dramatists, Lambs', etc.

(Died 27 Feb., 1927; age 43)

MEIGHAN, Thomas, actor; *b.* Pittsburgh, Pa., 9 Apr., 1879; *m.* Frances Ring; originally intended for a doctor; made his first appearance on the stage with Henrietta Crosman in " Mistress Nell "; he then played for one season with Grace George, appearing at the Manhattan Theatre, Oct., 1900, as Colonel Gorda in "Her Majesty the Girl Queen of Nordenmark," followed by two seasons in "stock," at Pittsburg; subsequently appeared with William Collier in "The Dictator"; in 1904 appeared in the "all-star" cast of "The Two Orphans," and next appeared with Grace George, Elsie de Wolfe and John Mason; in 1907 appeared as Billy Bolton in "The College Widow"; made his first appearance in London, at the Adelphi Theatre, 20 Apr., 1908, in the same part; at the Comedy, New York, Oct., 1910, played Paul Churchill in "The Family"; at the Belasco Theatre, Oct., 1911, played James Hartmann in "The Return of Peter Grimm," a part he played for three seasons; reappeared in London, at the Prince of Wales's Theatre, Feb., 1914, as Robert Wallace in "Broadway Jones"; on returning to America, appeared as the Defendant in "On Trial"; since 1916 has devoted himself to the cinema stage and has appeared with great success in "The Fighting Hope," "M'liss," "The Heart of Wetona," "The Miracle Man," "The Prince Chap," "The Easy Road," "The City of Silent Men," "A Prince There Was," "The Bachelor Daddy," "Homeward Bound," etc. *Address:* Athletic Club, Los Angeles, Cal., U.S.A.

MELFORD, Austin, actor, dramatic author, and director; *b.* Alverstoke, 24 Aug., 1884; *s.* of the late Austin Melford and his wife Alice (Batey); *e.* Portsmouth Grammar School; *m.* Jessie Winter; made his first appearance on the stage as a baby at the Theatre Royal, Portsmouth, in "In Camp"; next appeared with the late Wilson Barrett, as Ned in "The Silver King," at the Theatre Royal, Manchester, in 1889; rejoined Wilson Barrett in 1900, and remained with him two years; other engagements included eighteen months with G. M. Polini and his father's company, as Henry Corkett in "The Silver King," two years with William Greet in drama and musical comedy, and a year with Walter Melville; next in 1904, he was

touring as Brudds in "The Never Never Land," and made his first appearance on the London stage, in this part, at the King's Theatre, Hammersmith, 21 Mar., 1904; subsequently toured in "Lucky Durham," "The Talk of the Town," and "Faust Up-to-Date"; in 1907 toured in "A Soldier's Wedding"; appeared at Drury Lane, Sept., 1908, in "The Marriages of Mayfair"; toured with Albert Chevalier, 1909, followed by tour in "The Flag Lieutenant," 1909-10; at Drury Lane, Mar., 1910, played Tom Foster in "The Whip"; Dec., 1910, Uncle Tom Cobbley in "Jack and the Beanstalk"; Mar., 1911, Captain Carruthers in "The Sins of Society"; Sept., 1911, Lord Eardley in "The Hope"; Dec., 1911, John, the Woodcutter in "Hop o' My Thumb"; Apr., 1912, Drusus in "Ben Hur"; at the Prince's Theatre, July, 1912, appeared as Davy Fayle in "Ben-My-Chree"; at Drury Lane, Sept., 1912, Flattery in "Everywoman"; Dec., 1912, Jacques in "The Sleeping Beauty"; appeared at the Alhambra, May, 1913, as Compère in the *revue* "Eightpence a Mile"; at the Duke of York's, Nov., 1913, played Ensign Blades in "Quality Street"; subsequently, 1915, toured in *revue* "Sugar and Spice"; at the Prince of Wales, Mar., 1916, played Bobby Washington in "Mr. Manhattan"; at the Gaiety, Oct., 1916, succeeded Mr. George Grossmith as Lord Theodore Wragge in "Theodore and Co."; May, 1918, Hopkinson Brown in "Going-Up"; Oct., 1919, Christopher Deare in "The Kiss Call"; at the Winter Garden Theatre, Sept., 1920, Maxime Paillard in "A Night Out"; he then joined the Co-Optimists, but left to appear at the Winter Garden later in the year as Otis Hooper in "Sally"; at the Lyric, May, 1922, played Horace Wiggs in "Whirled Into Happiness"; at the New Oxford, Dec., 1922, Algernon Hosier in "Battling Butler"; at the Globe, July, 1923, Gerald Beaufort in "Reckless Reggie"; during 1923-4 rejoined the Co-Optimists and remained a member until the company disbanded in 1927; he then appeared at the Adelphi, Aug., 1927, as Jack Murray in "Up With the Lark"; subsequently appeared at the Criterion, Dec., 1928, as Samuel Stanton in " Out Goes She "; at the London Pavilion, Mar., 1929, succeeded Gene Gerrard as Hudson Greener in " Lucky Girl," which he directed when the play was originally performed at the Shaftesbury, Nov., 1928; at the Everyman, June, 1929, played Fred Fairburn in " Speed Limit"; Garrick, Nov., 1929, Andy Lewis in "The Woman in Room 13"; Prince's, Dec., 1929, Peter Price in "A Warm Corner"; Strand, Oct., 1930, Dudley Leake in "It's a Boy"; Dec., 1931, Rodney Smith in "It's a Girl"; Aug., 1932, Bunthorp Phipps in "Night of the Garter"; Aldwych, Nov., 1933, Fred Bonner-Bonner in "Ladies' Night"; from 1934–48 was engaged in writing and directing films; reappeared on the stage at the Saville, May, 1948, as Mandeville in "Bob's Your Uncle"; Winter Garden, Dec., 1949, played Sir John in "Me and My Girl"; His Majesty's, Nov., 1950, Dudley Leake in "Blue for a Boy"; Princes, May, 1953, played Baron Klopp in "Happy As a King"; toured, 1954, as Philip Russell in "Affairs of State"; Palace, Dec., 1954, played Admiral Dallas–Buckingham in "Happy Holiday"; Cambridge, May, 1959, played Morton in "Let Them Eat Cake"; is author of "It's a Girl," and part-author of "Ring Up," "Battling Butler," "Patricia," "Nippy"; adapted "It's a Boy," "Oh, Daddy!" "Night of the Garter," "Ladies' Night" (with Douglas Furber), "Here's How!"; "Magic Carpet" (part author); wrote the libretto of "Gay Rosalinda" (with Rudolph Bernauer); author of "Bob's Your Uncle"; adapted "Blue for a Boy"; has staged, among other plays, "Odd Numbers," "Oh, Daddy!," "Naughty Cinderella," "It's a Girl" (with Leslie Henson), "Night of the Garter" (with Henson), "It's a Boy" (with Henson), "She Wanted a Cream Front Door," "Bob's Your Uncle," "Blue for a Boy"; has appeared in films, in "A Warm Corner," "Night of the Garter," etc. *Recreation:* Golf. *Clubs:* Green Room. *Address:* Green Room Club, 8/9 Adam Street, London, W.C.2.

MELFORD, Jack, actor ; *b.* London, 5 Sept., 1899 ; *s.* of the late Austin

Melford and his wife Alice (Gambier-Batey) ; *e.* Cranleigh ; *m.* (1) Leila Marguerite Tufnell (mar. dis.); (2) Dorothy Irene Mallory-Corbett (dec.); (3) Cynthia Hathaway Teal (mar. dis.); (4) Roberta Huby; he first appeared on the stage at the Prince of Wales Theatre, Birmingham, 1912, as Ned Denver in " The Silver King "; in 1916 toured in " Brides," " The Private Secretary," and " The Kiss Cure "; made his first appearance in London, at the King's, Hammersmith, in 1917, as Harry Leyton in " The Thief "; subsequently played with John Lawson in " Humanity " and " The Dowry "; from 1917-19 served with the Artists Rifles O.T.C.; in 1919 toured in " Fair and Warmer "; appeared in variety theatres, 1920, in " Misery and Co."; during 1921 toured in " A Family Affair " and " Marriage by Instalments "; at the Apollo, July, 1921, understudied Geoffrey Kerr in " Skittles "; at the Duke of York's, Dec., 1921, played Jack Chesney in " Charley's Aunt " ; at the Aldwych, 1922, understudied Donald Calthrop, and played for him in " Money Doesn't Matter " and " A Prodigal Daughter "; at the Vaudeville, 1922, appeared in " Pot Luck " ; at the Little, Aug., 1922, played Maurice de Parvis in " Zozo " ; at the Shaftesbury, May, 1923, Perry Reynolds in " Stop Flirting " ; at the Comedy, Dec., 1924, Jack Stanley in " Just Married "; New Oxford, Jan., 1926, Frank Steadley in " Turned Up"; " Q," June, 1926, William Hemingway in " Virginia's Husband "; Strand, Sept., 1926, Roger Shields in " The Whole Town's Talking "; Little, Oct., 1926, played in " The Potinière Revue "; during 1927 toured as Jim Demming in " Sunny "; Lyric, Aug., 1928, played Tony Lagorce in " Her Cardboard Lover "; Adelphi, Feb., 1929, Lumley in "Mr. Cinders"; in Feb., 1931, toured as Stephen in "A Pair of Trousers"; Wyndham's, May, 1931, played Keith Keller in "The Old Man"; in Oct., 1931, toured as the Man in "Two's Company"; Embassy, Jan., 1932, played Miles Duckworth in " Rough to Moderate"; Feb., 1932, toured as Logan in "Counsel's Opinion"; Strand, Aug., 1932, played

Kenneth Warwick in "Night of the Garter"; Saville, Feb., 1934, Hon. Hugh Possett in "Here's How!"; Westminster, Nov., 1934, Randolph Warrender in "Youth at the Helm"; Criterion, Jan., 1935, Ronnie Long in "Between Us Two"; Winter Garden, Apr., 1935, played Jimmy O'Ryan in "Murder in Motley"; Garrick, Nov., 1935, Count Conrad in "Vicky"; Duke of York's, Sept., 1936, The Unknown in "No Ordinary Lady"; Streatham Hill, Nov., 1936, Prince Peter in "Business with Royalty"; Strand, Jan., 1937, Archie Bentley in "Behind Your Back"; Embassy, May, 1937, Charles Surface in "The New School for Scandal"; Vaudeville, Feb., 1938, Stephen Brinkway in "Mirabelle"; New, Mar., 1940, Lord Montague Rayson in "The Silver Patrol"; from Aug., 1940, until disbandment, served as part-time member of Civil Defence; from May, 1941–Aug., 1942, engaged with variety department and repertory company, B.B.C.; toured, Jan., 1942, as Bill Blake in "Skylark"; Strand, Sept., 1942, played Burthorpe Phipps in "Night of the Garter"; toured, 1943, as Hon. Dudley Mitten in "To-Night's the Night"; 1944, as Lance Corpl. Clive Widd in "It's That Moon Again"; 1945, as Bertie Hastings in "Happy Birthday"; Cambridge, May, 1949, appeared in the *revue* "Sauce Tartare"; Dec., 1949, appeared in Cecil Landeau's "Christmas Party"; Drury Lane, June, 1950, played the Heavenly Friend in "Carousel"; at the Ziegfeld, New York, Dec., 1951, with Sir Laurence Olivier's company, appeared as the Wounded Soldier in "Caesar and Cleopatra" and Maecenas in "Antony and Cleopatra"; New, London, Sept., 1952, played Miles Lamprey in "Hanging Judge"; at the "Q," Oct., 1953, Gilbert Archer in "Trouble at No. 13"; New Lindsey, Nov., 1953, Dr. Clive Esmond in "Angels Unaware"; Embassy, Nov., 1954, Michael Dean in "The Average Man"; toured 1955, as Tom Davenport in "Both Ends Meet"; Savoy, June, 1956, took over the part of Henry Hailsham-Brown in "Spider's Web"; Strand, Nov., 1956, directed "Tontine" for the Repertory Players;

toured 1959, as Inspector Findley in "One Upon a Crime"; St. Martin's, Sept., 1962, played Dr. Armstrong in a revival of "Ten Little Niggers"; has also directed and appeared in several productions at the "Q" and Richmond theatres; commenced film career, 1930, in "The Sport of Kings," and has played in numerous pictures since that date; has also appeared in the televisions series "Educated Evans," "Billy Bunter," "Z Cars," "Emergency Ward 10," and many other television plays. *Recreations:* Golf, swimming. *Clubs:* Green Room and Stage Golfing Society. *Address:* 6 York Court, The Albany, Kingston-on-Thames, Surrey. *Telephone No.:* Kingston 2617.

MELLISH, Fuller, actor; *b.* 3 Jan., 1865; *s.* of Charles Perry Fuller and his wife Rose (Leclercq); *m.* Eliza Archdekin Buckley; made his first appearance on the stage at the Park Theatre, 25 Apr., 1881, in "The Bonnie Fishwife"; for some years he was a member of his mother's company; he made his first "hit" at the Olympic Theatre, in Dec., 1883, when he played in "The Crimes of Paris"; subsequently he appeared there in "Cast Adrift," "The School for Scandal," etc.; while at the Olympic, he was engaged for the Lyceum by the late Sir Henry Irving, and appeared there, 8 July, 1884, as Curio in "Twelfth Night"; subsequently he played the Duc d'Orleans in "Richelieu"; he also accompanied the Lyceum company to America, playing Salanio in "The Merchant of Venice," Guildenstern in "Hamlet," Sebastian in "Twelfth Night," Toison d'Or in "Louis XI," etc.; on his return to England he toured with the late Ada Cavendish in "The New Magdalen"; and then went to the Novelty Theatre, where he appeared in "Money Bags," and "The Babes"; he then proceeded to the Vaudeville, where he remained some time; subsequently he appeared at the Lyceum with Mary Anderson in "The Winter's Tale"; joined Beerbohm Tree at Haymarket, 1888; rejoined Irving, remaining with him five years; in 1900 played at Prince of Wales's in " English Nell " ; he has played engagements at nearly every prominent theatre in London; since 1902 he has played exclusively in the United States ; in Sept., 1903, he played in " Ulysses " at the Garden Theatre, New York ; at Boston, 1904, he played in " The Dictator " ; then joined Mrs. Patrick Campbell, and appeared as Cleofas in " The Sorceress " ; at the Criterion, New York, Apr., 1905, he appeared as Gaffer Quarles in " Jinny the Carrier " ; then played with Richard Mansfield in " Don Carlos " ; during 1906 joined Viola Allen, and played Pisanio in " Cymbeline," Sir Toby Belch in " Twelfth Night," Touchstone in " As You Like It," etc. ; at the Lyric Theatre, New York, 15 Nov., 1906, played Canon Bonsey in " Mrs. Dane's Defence," with Lena Ashwell, Margaret Anglin, etc. ; in Feb., 1907, he toured with Viola Allen as Iachimo in " Cymbeline," and in the autumn, joined Robert Mantell, to play Gratiano, Polonius, Buckingham in " King Richard III," and Gloucester in " King Lear " ; next joined Mrs. Fiske, and at the Lyric, New York, Dec., 1907, played Rector Kroll in " Rosmersholm " ; at Philadelphia, Oct., 1908, played Roger Hagan in " The Panic " ; Dec., 1908, at Norfolk, Va., played Sir Oliver Holt in " The Dawn of a To-Morrow " ; appeared in the same part, at the Lyceum, New York, Jan., 1909 ; during July and Aug., 1909, played a " stock " season at Denver, Col. ; at the Lyceum, New York, Mar., 1910, appeared with Mrs. Fiske, as Rummel in " The Pillars of Society " ; in Apr., 1910, played Mattern in " Hannele " and the Marquis de Lansac in " The Green Cockatoo " ; Aug., 1910, appeared as Professor Anthony Futvoye in " The Brass Bottle " ; during the autumn toured in " The Dawn of a To-Morrow " ; at Kansas City, May, 1911, played Father Hervey in " Rebellion " ; at Washington, July, 1911, appeared as Corporal Brewster in " Waterloo," Sir Henry Irving's original part ; at the Maxine Elliott Theatre, Oct., 1911, played his old part in " Rebellion " ; at the New Amsterdam Theatre, Feb., 1912,

appeared as Mr. Grimwig in " Oliver Twist " ; at the Lyric, New York, Nov., 1912, played Julius Caesar in William Faversham's revival of that tragedy, subsequently touring in the same part ; in 1913-14 toured with Margaret Anglin as Jaques in " As You Like It," Malvolio in " Twelfth Night," in " The Taming of the Shrew," and " Antony and Cleopatra " ; appeared at the Hudson Theatre, Mar., 1914, in " As You Like It," " The Taming of the Shrew," " Twelfth Night " ; at the Empire, New York, May, 1914, played Brisemouche in " A Scrap of Paper " ; at the Playhouse, New York, Oct., 1914, Mynheer Cornelis and Sir Charles in " My Lady's Dress " ; at the Greek Theatre, Berkeley, Ca., Aug., 1915, played in ' Iphigenia " and " Medea " ; at the Forty-fourth Street Theatre, New York, Nov., 1915, played Friar Lawrence in " Romeo and Juliet " ; at the Criterion, New York, Mar., 1916, played Master Page in " The Merry Wives of Windsor " ; at the Booth Theatre, Jan., 1917, Mine Host of the Garter in " The Merry Wives of Windsor " ; at the Lyceum, Oct., 1917, Father Thibaut in " Tiger Rose " ; at the Carnegie Hall, Feb., 1918, the Guardian of Orestes in " Electra " ; at the Lyric, New York, Jan., 1920, Nathan in " The Light of the World " ; at the Cohan Theatre, Sept., 1920, Gaspardo Tagliani in " Genius and the Crowd " ; at the Lexington Opera House, Jan., 1922, Lord Ragdon in " Rosa Machree " ; at the Ritz, Feb., 1922, Bodier in " Madame Pierre " ; at the Playhouse, New York, Sept., 1922, Mr. Gregg in " On the Stairs " ; at the Lyceum, New York, Dec., 1922, Old Gobbo in " The Merchant of Venice " ; at the Forty-Fourth Street Theatre, Apr., 1923, Corin in " As You Like It " ; at the Jolson Theatre, Dec., 1924, Von Mark in " The Student Prince " ; Martin Beck, Oct., 1926, King Augustus III in " Wild Rose " ; Jolson, Sept., 1927, Mr. Frietchie in " My Maryland " ; Klaw, Apr., 1929, Justin Rawson in a revival of " Mrs. Bumpstead-Leigh " ; Little, May, 1930, Bernard Huddlestone in " The Traitor " ; Ethel Barrymore, Apr., 1931, the Priest in " Melo " ; Times Square,

Sept., 1931, the Doctor in "I Love an Actress"; Biltmore, Mar., 1932, Malachi in "Border Land"; Oct., 1932, Grandfather in "The Other One"; at the New Amsterdam, Nov., 1932, Annas in "The Dark Hours"; Morosco, Jan., 1935, Sir Guy Wells in "Living Dangerously"; Shubert, Apr., 1935, Fritz, in "A Journey by Night."

(Died 8 July, 1936; age 71)

MELNOTTE, Violet, manageress, former actress; *m.* the late Frank Wyatt; made her first appearance on the stage at Hull, under the management of the late Sefton Parry, in pantomime; made her first appearance in London at the Folly Theatre (subsequently Toole's), 16 Oct., 1876, when she played Fezz in "Blue Beard"; she next appeared at the Royalty, Dec., 1876, playing Ganymede in "Orphée aux Enfers" and Selina in "A Quiet Family," and at the Aquarium, Feb., 1877, played Gnatbrain in the burlesque, "Black-Eyed Susan";

(Died 17 Sept., 1935; age 79)

MELTZER, Charles Henry; *b.* London; was for some years Paris correspondent of the *Chicago Tribune,* and also of the *New York Herald,* went to New York in 1888, and acted as dramatic critic for the *New York Herald* until 1892; subsequently performed similar duties for the *New York World* from 1893 to 1896; was for some years also New York correspondent for the *Daily Chronicle*; has written or adapted the following among other plays: "The Story of Rodion the Student" (from the Russian), "Hannele" (Hauptmann), "Madame Sans-Gêne" (Sardou and Moreau), "The Woman of Arles" (Daudet's "L'Arlésienne"), "Manon Lescaut" (Prevost), "The Sunken Bell" (Hauptmann), "The Queen's Necklace" (Decourcelles), "More than Queen" (Bergerat, adapted in collaboration with C. F. Nirdlinger), "Salomé," "His Honor the Mayor" (in collaboration with A. E. Lancaster), "The First Duchess of Marlborough," and "Five

Hundred Years Ago"; adapted "The Big Scene" (from Schnitzler); for four years he acted as secretary to the late Heinrich Conried, operatic impresario, at the Metropolitan Opera House, New York, the engagement terminating at the end of Aug., 1907; resumed journalistic work as critic for the *New York American.*

(Died 14 Jan., 1936; age 83)

MELVILLE, Andrew, manager; *b.* Highgate, London, 6 June, 1912; *s.* of Andrew Melville and his wife Rose (Ralph); *e.* Highgate School; *m.* (1) Winifred Wright (dec.); (2) Joan Matheson; was formerly known as Andrew Emm Jun.; commenced his career at the Grand Theatre, Brighton, June, 1926, in "The Great World of London," also acting as callboy; subsequently became assistant stage-manager besides playing small parts; in 1931, joined the Brixton repertory company, first appearing in "Seven Days Leave," and remained there two years; appeared at the Lyceum, Mar., 1933, as Charley Bates in "Oliver Twist," and was also assistant stage-manager; May, 1934, played K. 138 in "King of the Damned"; Princes, Sept., 1934, played the Queen's Fool in "Merrie England," and from 1935-7, was stage-manager for "The Rose of Persia," "The Gay Masquerade," "The Alchemist," "The Frog," and "The Gusher"; was acting-manager at the Lyceum from Apr., 1938, to Feb., 1939; assumed the management of the Palace, Watford, Mar., 1939; during the War, served in the Royal Navy, 1943-6; resumed management of the Palace, Watford, after the war, presenting repertory throughout the year, and an annual pantomime; co-director of the Richmond Theatre, 1947-50; in 1949, joined Stanley French as Production Manager at the Savoy Theatre, subsequently becoming Joint Managing Director of Firth Shephard, Ltd., and Stanley French, Ltd., until May, 1951; in Feb., 1956, became assistant manager at the Princes Theatre; Aug., 1956, gave up management of the Palace Theatre, Watford; in Apr., 1957, succeeded Bert E. Hammond as General Manager and Licensee of the Princes Theatre. *Recreations:* Gardening and swimming. *Address:* 128 Kensington Park Road, London, W.11. *Telephone No.:* Park 7790.

MELVILLE, Frederick, dramatic author and manager; *b.* Swansea, 1876; *s.* of Andrew Melville, for many years manager of the Standard Theatre; *m.* Jane Eyre; at the age of ten was office-boy, with his father at the Queen's and Grand Theatres, Birmingham; in Jan., 1889, was engaged at the Grand, Birmingham, of which his father was then lessee; was an actor for several years, and played in a number of melodramas; is the author of " Her Forbidden Marriage," 1904; " The Ugliest Woman on Earth," 1905; " The Beast and the Beauty," 1905; " Married to the Wrong Man," 1908; " The Bad Girl of the Family," 1909; " The Monk and the Woman," 1912; " Monte Cristo " (with Walter Melville), 1912; co-lessee and manager, with his brother Walter, of the Lyceum, since 1909, and of the Prince's Theatre, since 1911.
(Died 5 Apr., 1938; age 62)

MELVILLE, June, actress and manager; *b.* Worthing, Sussex, 17 Sept., 1915; *d.* of Frederick Melville and his wife Jane (Eyre); *e.* Convent of St. Mary the Virgin, Wantage; *m.* John Elton Le Mesurier Halliley (mar. dis.); studied for the stage under her father; made her first appearance on the stage at Brixton Theatre, 26 Dec., 1931, as the Fairy Queen in " Puss in Boots "; subsequently played in repertory; at the Lyceum Theatre, Mar., 1933, played Mary in " Oliver Twist "; after a season with Charles Macdona, appeared at Brixton, Dec., 1934, as Cinderella; acted as stage-manager at Brixton, during repertory seasons since 1936, where she has also played numerous parts; played principal boy in pantomime at Brixton, 1935–6; subsequently played engagements with Gilbert Miller and Firth Shephard; Lyceum, Aug., 1937, played Florrie in " Wanted for Murder," and Dec., 1937, played Sunray in " Beauty and the Beast "; in Jan., 1938, for a time, played

the Prince in the same pantomime; proprietor and manager of the Brixton Theatre from Apr., 1938; Lyceum, Christmas, 1938, wrote additional scenes for the last pantomime produced there, " Queen of Hearts "; Malvern Festival, Aug., 1939, played Jessie Crofter in " Big Ben "; was, for some years, leading lady with the Repertory Company at the Palace Theatre, Watford; subsequently became director at this theatre, and associated in the management; at Bournemouth, Mar., 1952, directed "Devil's Highway "; at the Comedy, London, May, 1952, directed "Cold Turkey" (with Alwyn Fox); Richmond, Aug., 1953, appeared as Miss Stratton in "Wide Boy "; at Bournemouth, Feb., 1954, directed "Lovely Woman." *Recreation:* Reading.
(Died 15 Sept., 1970; age 54)

MELVILLE, Rose, actress; *b.* Terre Haute, Ind., U.S.A., 30 Jan., 1873; *e.* at St. Mary of the Woods Convent, and Franklin College, Ind.; *m.* Frank Minzey; made her first appearance on the stage in 1889, at Zanesville, Ohio, as Arthur Sidney in " Queen's Evidence "; during the next three years played, among other parts, Topsy in " Uncle Tom's Cabin," Louise in " The Two Orphans," Fanchon the Cricket in the play of that name, Ned in " The Black Flag," etc.; subsequently, in conjunction with her sister, Ida, formed a travelling " stock " company, and when a play entitled " Zeb " was produced, Miss Melville appeared in the part of Sis Hopkins; this part she so elaborated that it became the feature of the performance, and was so successful that, on going to New York in 1894, she was immediately engaged to introduce Sis Hopkins in " Little Christopher," at the Garden Theatre; she was seen in the same speciality when she played Dolly Bond in " The Prodigal Father," 1896-7, and also in " By the Sad Sea Waves," 1898-9; she appeared in a " vaudeville " sketch, " Sis Hopkins' Visit," in 1899, and then had a play written round the character which was produced for the first time at

Buffalo, 11 Sept., 1899, since which date she has appeared almost continuously in the same piece. *(Died 8 Oct., 1946; age 68)*

MELVILLE, Walter, author, actor, and theatrical manager; *b.* London, 1875; *s.* of Andrew Melville, for many years manager of the Standard Theatre; *m.* (1) Eva Dare (dec.); (2) Barbara Crosbie; in Jan., 1889, entered his father's office at the Grand Theatre, Birmingham; was subsequently business-manager of the same house; author of numerous well-known melodramas, including " The Worst Woman in London," "A Girl's Cross Roads," " The Girl Who Lost her Character," " The Girl Who Took the Wrong Turning," " The Girl Who Wrecked His Home," " The Female Swindler," "A Disgrace to Her Sex," " That Wretch of a Woman," "A World of Sin," " On His Majesty's Service," " The Great World of London," " The Beggar Girl's Wedding," " The Sins of London," " The Shop-Soiled Girl," " The Female Hun "; has managed the Aldwych Theatre, and from 1909, in conjunction with his brother Frederick, the Lyceum Theatre; in Dec., 1911, opened the New Prince's Theatre, which, in conjunction with his brother, he had built. *(Died 28 Feb., 1937; age 62)*

MELVILLE, Winnie, actress and vocalist; *m.* Derek Oldham; was formerly a concert singer; made her first appearance on the regular stage at the Comedy Theatre, Dec., 1916, in " See-Saw "; at the same theatre, May, 1917, in " Bubbly "; during 1918 appeared at the Folies-Bergères, Paris, in " Zig-Zag "; at the London Hippodrome, Mar., 1919, in " Joy-Bells "; June, 1920, in " Jig-Saw "; during 1921 toured in " Sybil "; subsequently appeared at His Majesty's, as Zummurud in " Cairo "; at the Lyric, Aug., 1922, succeeded Margaret Campbell as Florrie in " Whirled Into Happiness," and in 1923 toured in the same piece; left the stage for three years after her marriage; reappeared at His Majesty's, Apr., 1926, when she played Kathie in " The Student Prince "; Palace, Oct., 1926, Princess Elaine in " Princess Charming "; Winter Garden, Apr., 1927, Katherine de Vaucelles in " The Vagabond King," which ran over a year; at the Coliseum, Sept., 1928, appeared with a repertory of songs; Dec., 1928, toured as Winona in a play of that name; in 1929 joined the D'Oyly Carte Opera Company, and appeared at the Savoy, 1929–30, as Gianetta in "The Gondoliers," Rose Maybud in "Ruddigore," Elsie Maynard in "The Yeoman of the Guard," Josephine in "H.M.S. Pinafore," Yum-Yum in "The Mikado," Mabel in "The Pirates of Penzance"; subsequently, in 1930, toured as Nancy in " Blue Eyes "; since that date, has appeared at numerous variety theatres, and has toured in "For Ever After." *(Died 19 Sept., 1937; age 42)*

MELVIN, Duncan, theatre press-representative; *b.* Edinburgh, 11 July, 1913; *s.* of J. G. Melvin and his wife Elizabeth MacKimmie (Cowie); *e.* George Watson's College, Edinburgh, and Goudhurst, Kent; *m.* Olwen Vaughan; formerly a professional photographer; has acted as press-representative at various theatres, for Donald Albery, Wolf Mankowitz and Oscar Lewenstein, Leon Heppner, Peter Daubeny, Victor Hochhauser, Theatre Workshop, etc., and as personal representative for John Osborne, Alma Coogan, Willis Hall, etc. *Recreations:* Painting, sculpture, and photography. *Club:* Arts. *Address:* 27 Chester Street, London, S.W.1. *Telephone No.:* Belgravia 1033.

MENDEL, the blind pianist (James Samuel Smith); *b.* Fairfield, near Manchester, 11 Apr., 1875; *s.* of James Smith; *e.* Royal Normal College, Upper Norwood; was for some time engaged as an organist at Southport; made his first appearance on the stage at the Alhambra, Blackpool, 17 Feb., 1902; first appeared in London, at the London Hippodrome, 10 Mar., 1902, remaining there ten weeks; this engagement was followed by a tour of the Moss and Thornton halls, and has since appeared at all the principal halls in London and the provinces, playing all the leading tours.

MENGES, Herbert, O.B.E., composer and conductor; *b.* Hove, Sussex, 27 Aug., 1902; *s.* of Johanes Georg Menges and his wife Kate (Whitcher); *m.* Evelyn Stiebel (mar. dis.); was a musical "prodigy" as a small child, and appeared in public as a violinist at the age of four; later gave up this instrument for piano and composition; has a considerable reputation as a symphonic conductor; first associated with the theatre, 1927, when he was appointed musical director at the Royalty Theatre; has conducted at many other theatres; Musical Director to the Old Vic, from 1931 to 1950, and has also been associated as Conductor to the Sadler's Wells Opera company; has composed original scores for over 100 productions, and has been associated with Sir John Gielgud's and Sir Laurence Olivier's productions; appointed Musical Director to the Chichester Festival, 1962; received the O.B.E. in the New Year Honours, 1963. *Recreations:* Books, gardening. *Address:* 64 Belsize Park Gardens, London, N.W.3. *Telephone No.:* 01-722 1953.

MENKEN, Helen, actress; *b.* New York City, U.S.A., 12 Dec., 1901; *m.* (1) Humphrey Bogart (mar. dis.); (2) Dr. Henry T. Smith (mar. dis.); (3) George N. Richard; appeared at the opening of the Astor Theatre, New York 21 Sept., 1906, as one of the Fairies in "A Midsummer Night's Dream"; played continuously with De Wolf Hopper in "The Pied Piper of Hamelin," 1908; with Eddie Foy in "Mr. Hamlet of Broadway," 1909; with Adeline Genée in "The Silver Star," 1910; from 1911–15, played in "stock" companies at Cleveland, Salem, Lynn, Reading, Utica, and Denver; in 1915, toured in "Sinners"; she was next engaged to appear at the Criterion Theatre, New York, Oct., 1916, when she played Blanche Amory in "Major Pendennis," with John Drew; at the Republic, Dec., 1917, played Virginia Embry in "Parlour, Bedroom, and Bath"; at the Criterion, Oct., 1918,

scored a big hit when she played Miss Fairchild in "Three Wise Fools"; in the spring of 1921, toured in "Drifting"; at the Comedy, Aug., 1921, played Phyllis in "The Triumph of X," and Nov., 1921, Maria in "The Mad Dog"; at the Booth, Oct., 1922, made a further success when she appeared as Diane in "Seventh Heaven"; at the Charles Hopkins Theatre, Jan., 1926, played Emilia Marty in "The Makropoulos Secret"; at the Guild Theatre, Feb., 1926, The Rat Wife in "Little Eyolf"; Empire, Sept., 1926, Irene De Montcel in "The Captive"; made her first appearance on the London stage, at the Strand Theatre, 2 Sept., 1927, as Diane in "Seventh Heaven"; appeared at Hampden's, New York, June, 1928, as Dorinda in "The Beaux' Stratagem"; at the Sam H. Harris, Nov., 1928, Thi-Lingh in "Congai"; at the Mayan Theatre, Los Angeles, July, 1929, Gerba Carhart in "Top o' the Hill"; Maxine Elliott Theatre, New York, Feb., 1930, played Mary in "The Infinite Shoeblack"; Royale, Feb., 1931, Charlotte Satterlee in "Rock Me, Julie"; subsequently toured in "Petticoat Influence," and "Death Takes a Holiday"; later in the same year joined the Chicago Civic Shakespeare Society, and appeared with that Company at the Royale, New York, Nov., 1931, as Portia in "The Merchant of Venice," Calpurnia in "Julius Caesar," and Ophelia in "Hamlet"; at the Lyceum, New York, Jan., 1933, produced "Saint Wench," in which she appeared as Mara; Alvin (for the Theatre Guild), Nov., 1933, Elizabeth Tudor in "Mary of Scotland"; Empire, Jan., 1935, Charlotte Lovell in "The Old Maid," and subsequently toured in the same part; Golden, Oct., 1936, played Ingrid Rydman in "The Laughing Woman"; Maplewood, N. J., July, 1938, played Candida; Players', New York, Feb., 1961, produced "Three Modern Japanese Plays"; National, Washington, Feb., 1961, played the Fortune Teller in "The Skin of Our Teeth"; has starred in "Second Husband" radio programme, 1933–45, and produced the "Stage Door Canteen" series for the American Theatre Wing, 1942–6; Vice-President of the Institute for

Crippled and Disabled; Vice-President of the Society for the Facially Disfigured; Trustee of the American Shakespeare Festival Theatre and Academy; from the American Woman's Association, received the Award of the Woman of Achievement of the Year— 1958. *Favourite parts:* Marty in "The Makropoulos Secret," and Cassie Cook in "Drifting."

(Died 28 Mar., 1966; age 64)

MENZIES, Archie (*né* Archibald Norman Menzies), dramatic author; *b.* London, 10 Sept., 1904; *s.* of Norman Hay Menzies and his wife Gertrude (Mackenzie); *e.* Melbourne and Sydney Grammar Schools, Australia; *m.* M. H. Sparshott-Smith (Valerie Fraser); is the author of "Between Friends" (with "Major"), 1933; "A Knight in Vienna," 1935; "A Royal Exchange" (with Fred Herendeen), 1935; "The Astonished Ostrich," 1936; "No Sky So Blue" (with Henry C. James), 1938; "Under Your Hat" (with Jack Hulbert and Arthur Macrae), 1938; "Full Swing" (with Hulbert and Macrae), 1942; "Something in the Air" (with Hulbert and Macrae), 1943; new book and lyrics, "The Gipsy Princess," 1944; "Under the Gooseberry Bush," 1945; "Quartette in Discord," 1946; "Return Journey," 1947; "Her Excellency" (with Harold Purcell and Max Kester), 1949; "That Woman," 1952; "Hell's Lagoon," 1953; "Take Your Partners," 1954; "Universal Uncles," 1956. *Recreations:* Travel, shooting, and reading. *Hobbies:* Firearms and engineering. *Clubs:* Savage and Lord's Taverners. *Address:* Savage Club, 37 King Street, London, W.C.2.

MERANDE, Doro, actress; *b.* Columbia, Kansas; made her New York début at the Vanderbilt, 4 Feb., 1935, as Sophie Tutle in "Loose Moments"; Lyceum, Nov., 1935, Sarah in "One Good Year"; Morosco, Feb., 1937, Mildred in "Fulton of Oak Falls"; National, Mar., 1937, Belle Smith in "Red Harvest"; National, Oct., 1937, Bessie in "Angel Island"; Henry Miller's, Feb., 1938, Mrs. Soames in "Our Town"; Plymouth, May, 1940,

Leona Yearling in "Love's Old Sweet Song"; Fulton, Nov., 1940, Miss White in "Beverly Hills"; Cort, Sept., 1941, Miss Hogben in "The More the Merrier"; Guild, Nov., 1941, A Woman in "Hope for a Harvest"; Lyceum, 1942, took over as Hilda in "Junior Miss"; Longacre, May, 1943, Adelaide in "Three's a Family"; Plymouth, Oct., 1943, Myrtle McGuire in "The Naked Genius"; New York City Center, Jan., 1944, Mrs. Soames in "Our Town"; 48th Street, May, 1944, Miss Porter in "Pick-up Girl"; Belasco, Oct., 1944, Mrs. Elfie Tunison in "Violet"; Fulton, Feb., 1945, Mrs. Bassett in "Hope for the Best"; Biltmore, Feb., 1946, Stella Springer in "The Apple of His Eye"; Biltmore, Nov., 1948, Mrs. Hanmer in "The Silver Whistle"; Ethel Barrymore, Dec., 1949, Soda in "The Rat Race"; 48th Street, Jan., 1951, Jane Dupré in "Four Twelves Are Forty-Eight"; Booth, Dec., 1951, Minnetonka Smallflower in "Lo and Behold!"; Phoenix, Nov., 1956, Lubinka in "Diary of a Scoundrel"; McCarter, Princeton, New Jersey, Jan., 1958, Miss Kane in "This Is Goggle"; 41st Street, Dec., 1964, Mrs. Martin in "Her Master's Voice"; New York City Center, June, 1965, Eulalie Mackecknie Shinn in "The Music Man"; Ethel Barrymore, May, 1969, Jenny in "The Front Page"; has appeared in the film of "Our Town," 1940, and in "The Man with the Golden Arm," "The Seven Year Itch," "The Cardinal," etc.; has appeared frequently on television, notably on the series *Bringing Up Buddy* and *That Was the Week That Was. Address:* 115 East 39th Street, New York, N.Y., U.S.A. 10016.

MERCER, Beryl, actress; *b.* Seville, Spain, 13 Aug., 1882; *d.* of Effie (Martin) and Edward Sheppard Mercer; *e.* Jersey College; *m.* Maitland Sabrina Pasley; studied dancing under the tuition of Madame Katti Lanner; made her first appearance on the stage at Theatre Royal, Yarmouth, 14 Aug., 1886, as little Willie Carlyle in "East Lynne"; in 1892-3 toured in "Love's Battle," "Hand in Hand," and "The Shadow Hand"; after finally leaving school, toured as Shakespeare Jarvis in

" The Lights o' London," Micah Dow in " The Little Minister," etc. ; first appeared in London at the Princess's, 4 Oct., 1896, as Wally in " Two Little Vagabonds " ; toured in this part, 1897-9 ; understudied at His Majesty's and Adelphi, 1900-2 ; understudied Louie Freear, 1903 ; Lena Ashwell, 1904 ; appeared at Savoy, 1906, as Meinke, the black girl in " The Shulamite " ; made her first appearance in New York, in the same part, at the Lyric Theatre, Dec., 1906 ; at the Kingsway Theatre, Feb., 1908, played the Old Woman in " Diana of Dobson's " ; appeared at the Lyceum, July, 1909, in her old part in " Two Little Vagabonds " ; at the Lyric, May, 1910, played Pedro in " Don César de Bazan " ; at the Playhouse, Apr., 1912, played Mrs. Bartlet in " Her Point of View " ; Apr., 1914, La Grisa and Mrs. Moss in " My Lady's Dress " ; at the Maxine Elliott Theatre, New York, May, 1916, played Emily in " A Lady's Name " ; at the Forty-eighth Street Theatre, Aug., 1916, Susan in " Somebody's Luggage " ; at the Maxine Elliott Theatre, Jan., 1917, Mrs. Bunting in " The Lodger " (" Who is He ? ") ; at the Empire, New York, May, 1917, Mrs. Dowey in " The Old Lady Shows Her Medals " ; at the Century, New York, May, 1918, played in " Out There " ; at the Lyceum, Sept., 1918, played Mrs. Mott in " Humpty-Dumpty " ; at the Belasco Theatre, Apr., 1919, Katty McCabe in " Dark Rosaleen " ; at the Garrick, Washington, Apr., 1920, played Mrs. Gubbins in " Three Live Ghosts," and the same part at the Greenwich Village Theatre, New York, Sept., 1920 ; at the Punch and Judy Theatre, Oct., 1922, played Mdme. O'Halloran in " The Ever Green Lady " ; Nov., 1922, played in " The '49ers " ; at the Forty-eighth Street Theatre, Nov., 1923, played Alexandrina Victoria in " Queen Victoria " ; at the Ritz, Jan., 1924, Mrs. Midgett in " Outward Bound " ; at Washington, Oct., 1924, played in " The Steam Roller " ; at the Henry Miller Theatre, New York, Dec., 1924, Pinsent in " Quarantine " ; 48th Street Theatre, May, 1925, Mrs. Burlacombe

in "A Bit of Love " ; Criterion, Dec., 1925, Mrs. Carey in " Fools' Bells " ; Guild Theatre, Nov., 1926, Mrs. Pearce in " Pygmalion " ; Mar., 1927, Signora Frola in " Right You Are, If You Think You Are " ; Bijou, Dec., 1927, Mrs. Flynn in " Brass Buttons " ; since that date has devoted herself to the cinema stage, and has appeared in " Mother's Boy," " Three Live Ghosts," " All Quiet on the Western Front," " Seven Days' Leave," " In Gay Madrid," " The Matrimonial Bed," " Outward Bound," " Dumbells in Ermine," " Medals," " Common Clay," " Inspiration," " East Lynne," " Always Goodbye," " Merely Mary Anne," " The Man in Possession," " Forgotten Women," " The Devil's Lottery," " Are These Our Children ? " " Lovers Courageous," " We Humans " (" Young America "), " Lena Rivers," " Divine Love," " Unholy Love," " Smilin' Through," " Six Hours to Live," " Enemies of the Public," " Cavalcade," ' Supernatural," " Berkeley Square," " Her Splendid Folly," " Blind Adventure," " Broken Dreams," " Change of Heart," " Jane Eyre," " The Little Minister," " The Age of Indiscretion," etc. *(Died 28 July, 1939; age 56)*

MÉRÉ, Charles, dramatic author ; *b.* Marseilles, France, 1883 ; formerly a novelist, and his first work was a book, " Races de Soleil " ; is the author of the following among other plays : " L'Hydre," 1906 ; " Les Hommes de Proie," 1907 ; " Les Trois Masques," 1908 ; " Les Ruffians," 1909 ; " L'Ingenu," (with Régis Gignoux), 1913 ; " Scemo," " Le Captive," " Les Conquerants," 1920 ; " La Flamme," " La Vertige," 1922 ; " Le Prince Jean," 1923 ; " La Danse de Minuit," " La Tentation," 1924 ; " Une Nuit de Don Juan," " Par la Force " (with Henri de Weindel), 1925 ; " Le Lit Nuptiale," " Le Plaisir," 1926 ; " Berlioz," 1927 ; " Le Carnaval d'Amour," 1928 ; " Shanghai," 1929 ; " Le Chair," 1930 ; " Le Désir," " Un Homme du Nord," " Le Passage des Princes," 1933 ; " Zizippe," " Indiana," 1935 ; is President of the Society of Authors and Composers ; President of the International Confederation of the Society of Authors. *Address:* 11 *bis* Rue Ballu, Paris, IX, France.

MERIVALE, Bernard, dramatic author; *b.* Newcastle-on-Tyne, 15 July, 1882; *s.* of John Herman Merivale and his wife Blanche (Liddell); *e.* Sedbergh, and St. John's College, Cambridge; *m.* Cicely Stuckey; is the author of "The Night Hawk," 1913; "Fancy Dress," 1918; "Matrimonial Secrets," 1919; "Mr. Peter" (with Lechmere Worrall), 1920; "Marriage by Instalments" (with Richard Bird), 1923; "None But the Brave" (with Brandon Fleming), "A House Divided," 1926; "The Wrecker" (with Arnold Ridley), 1927; "The Flying Fool" (with Ridley), 1929; "The Command to Love" (adaptation), 1930; "Tattenham Corner" (with Fleming), 1934; "Death in Vienna" (with Margaret Masterman), 1935; "The Unguarded Hour" (from the Hungarian), 1935; "Vicky" (adaptation), 1935; also of the one-act plays "A Unique Opportunity" and "Are You Insured?" (both with Fleming). *Recreations:* Motoring and flying. *Clubs:* Savile and Savage.

(Died 10 May, 1939; age 56)

MERIVALE, Philip, actor; *b.* Rehutia near Manikpur, India, 2 Nov., 1886; *s.* of Walter Merivale, M.I.C.E.; *e* St. Edward's School, Oxford; *m.* (1) Viva Birkett (dec.); (2) Gladys Cooper; was formerly engaged in commerce in the City; made his first appearance on the stage, at the Coronet Theatre, 4 Mar., 1905, in Orestean Triology of Æschylus ("Agamemnon," "The Libation Bearers," and "The Furies"), in F. R. Benson's company; subsequently played a number of parts with F. R. Benson; in 1908 joined Fred Terry and Julia Neilson's company on tour; appeared at the New Theatre, Jan., 1909, as M. de Besme in "Henry of Navarre"; Jan., 1910, played the same part and the Duc de Guise in a revival of the same play; Mar., 1910, appeared as the Prince of Wales in "The Scarlet Pimpernel"; Feb.,

1911, the Marquis of Hezeta in "The Popinjay"; May, 1911, Frederick in "As You Like It"; at the Lyceum, Apr., 1911, Meleager in "Atalanta in Calydon"; was then engaged by Sir Herbert Tree for His Majesty's, where he has appeared as Ross in "Macbeth," Sept., 1911; Mars in "Orpheus in the Underground," Dec., 1911; Dodor in "Trilby," Feb., 1912; Cassio in "Othello," Apr., 1912; during the Shakespearean Festival, May-June, 1912, played Antonio in "The Merchant of Venice," Antonio in "Twelfth Night," Earl of Surrey in "King Henry VIII," Decius Brutus in "Julius Caesar," and Master Page in "The Merry Wives of Windsor"; June, 1912, Monks in "Oliver Twist"; Sept., 1912, Thomas Doughty in "Drake"; Apr., 1913, Joseph Surface in "The School for Scandal"; May, 1913, Dorante in "The Perfect Gentleman"; June, 1913, Cassius in "Julius Cæsar"; June, 1913, Romeo in "Romeo and Juliet"; Sept., 1913, Reuben in "Joseph and His Brethren"; Jan., 1914, Inu in "The Darling of the Gods"; Apr., 1914, Colonel Pickering in "Pygmalion"; Aug., 1914, Thomas Doughty in a revival of "Drake"; accompanied Mrs. Patrick Campbell to America, and appeared at the Park Theatre, New York, Oct., 1914, as Henry Higgins in "Pygmalion"; at Yale Bowl, Conn., May, 1915, played the Messenger in "Iphegenia in Tauris"; at the Adolf Lewisohn Stadium, New York, May, 1915, Menelaus in "The Trojan Women"; at Detroit Opera House, Aug., 1915, played in "Pollyanna"; at Rochester, N.Y., Mar., 1916, played in "The Wooing of Eve"; at the Hudson, New York, Sept., 1916, John Pendleton in "Pollyanna"; at the Globe, New York, Nov., 1916, Marshall Brooke in "The Harp of Life"; served in the Canadian Air Force, 1917-18; in 1919, toured with George Arliss as Mr. Baxter in "The Mollusc" and in "A Well Remembered Voice"; at the Playhouse, New York, Oct., 1919, appeared as Pickering in "A Young Man's Fancy"; at the Criterion, New York, Dec., 1919, as Richard Oak in "One Night in Rome";

at the Thirty-ninth Street Theatre, Feb., 1920, played Dick Gurvil in "The Tragedy of Nan"; at the Empire, New York, Aug., 1920, Dudley Townsend in "Call the Doctor"; toured in the same part, 1921; reappeared in London at the Shaftesbury Theatre, Nov., 1921, when he played Will Shakespeare in the play of that name; at the Apollo, Feb., 1922, played Captain Leslie Yeullat in "The Wheel"; at the Lyceum, New York, Dec., 1922, Bassanio in "The Merchant of Venice"; at the Cort Theatre, Oct., 1923, Prince Albert in "The Swan"; at the Empire, New York, Sept., 1924, Maurice Sorbier in "Grounds for Divorce"; Oct., 1925, Bela Kovacsy in "Antonia"; Sam H. Harris, Dec., 1925, Sam Wick in "The Monkey Talks"; Knickerbocker, May, 1926, Hotspur in "King Henry IV" (Part I); Klaw, Sept., 1926, David Campbell in "Scotch Mist"; Waldorf Nov., 1926, Andor Tamas in "Head or Tail"; Playhouse, Jan., 1927, Hannibal in "The Road to Rome"; Lyceum, Oct., 1927, Nick Faring in "Hidden"; reappeared in London, at the Strand, May, 1928, as Hannbail in "The Road to Rome"; returned to New York, and appeared at the Majestic, Nov., 1928, as Peter Parrot and Pierrot in "The Jealous Moon"; Forrest, Apr., 1929, played Paolo in "Paolo and Francesca"; Ethel Barrymore, Dec., 1929, H.S.H. Prince Sirki in "Death Takes a Holiday"; toured in this 1930–31; Morosco, Nov., 1931, Jim Warlock in "Cynara"; toured in this, July, 1932; at the Playhouse, Hollywood, July, 1933, played Sidney Carton in "A Tale of Two Cities"; Alvin, New York (for Theatre Guild), Nov., 1933, Bothwell in "Mary of Scotland"; Guild, Dec., 1934, General George Washington in "Valley Forge"; Ethel Barrymore, Sept.–Oct., 1935, in conjunction with Gladys Cooper, produced "Othello" and "Macbeth," in both of which he played the title-rôle; Morosco, New York, Jan., 1936, played Roger Hilton in "Call It a Day"; Locust Valley, L.I., July, 1936, Peter Brignall in "White Christmas"; Golden, New York, Feb., 1937, Rev. Howat Freemantle in "And Now Goodbye"; toured, Apr., 1937, as Gustav Bergemann in "Close Quarters"; returned to England, and at the Phoenix, London, Nov., 1937, played Brian Lorimer in "Goodbye to Yesterday"; Palace, Feb., 1938, Samuel Dodsworth in "Dodsworth"; Open Air Theatre, June–Sept., 1938, Prospero in "The Tempest," Malvolio in "Twelfth Night," Kinesias in "Lysistrata," Jaques in "As You Like It" and Theseus in "A Midsummer Night's Dream"; returned to New York, and at the Longacre, Nov., 1938, played Eric Rumpau in "Lorelei"; toured, Jan., 1939, in "Angela is 22"; at White Plains, N.Y., June, 1939, played Sir Reginald Furze in "Spring Meeting"; is the author of "The Wind over the Water," "The Cromwell of the Caribbees," stories and poems, and of the play "White Christmas," 1936. *Recreations*: Reading and walking. *Clubs*: Green Room, and Stage Golfing Society, London, and the Players', New York.

(Died 12 Mar., 1946; age 59)

MERKEL, Una, actress; *b.* Covington, Kentucky, 10 Dec., 1903; *d.* of Arno Merkel and his wife Bessie (Phares); *e.* Covington and Philadelphia; *m.* Ronald L. Burla (mar. dis.); at the Selwyn Theatre, Feb., 1925, was in the chorus of "Two by Two"; at the Henry Miller Theatre, May, 1925, appeared in "The Poor Nut"; at the Little, June, 1925, played Lenore Hastings in "Pigs," in which she remained twelve months; in Sept., 1926, toured as Mildred Cushing in the same play; at the Little Feb., 1927, played Sarah Miller in "Two Girls Wanted"; Mansfield, Apr., 1927, Anna Sterling in "The Gossipy Sex"; Maxine Elliott, Theatre, Nov., 1927, played Betty Lee Reynolds in "Coquette," which ran until Sept., 1928, and also toured in this, 1928-9; John Golden, Nov., 1929, played Marion Potter in "Salt Water"; commenced film career, 1930, in 'Abraham Lincoln," and appeared in over 80 films to 1943; reappeared on the New York stage, at the Longacre Theatre, Apr., 1944, when she succeeded Ethel Owen as Irma Dalrymple in "Three's a Family," subsequently touring in the same part; toured, 1950, in "Summer and Smoke"; Coronet, New York, Dec., 1953, played Aunt Jane Pennypacker in "The Remarkable Mr. Pennypacker," in which she appeared until July, 1955; Music Box, N.Y., Feb., 1956, played Edna Earle Ponder in "The Ponder Heart"; at the Colonial, Boston, Dec., 1958, appeared as Faith Borrow in "Listen To the Mocking Bird"; in summer theatre, July, 1959, starred in "Cradle and All"; Shubert, N.Y., Oct., 1959, played Essie Miller in "Take Me Along"; entered films, 1930, and recent pictures include: "The Mating Game," "Summer and Smoke," "A Tiger Walks," etc. *Favourite part:* Betty in "Coquette." *Recreations:* Reading, walking, and travelling.

MERRALL, Mary, actress; *b.* Liverpool; *d.* of William Edward Lloyd and his wife Emily (Tidswell); *e.* at convents at Tirlemont, Belgium, and London; *m.* (1) J. B. Hissey (mar. dis.); (2) Ion Swinley (mar. dis.); (3) Franklin Dyall (dec.); made her first appearance on the stage under the name of Queenie Merrall, at Christmas, 1907, as Columbine in harlequinade of "Cinderella," at the Marlborough Theatre, Holloway; at the Prince of Wales, Apr., 1908, appeared in the chorus of "My Mimosa Maid," and Sept., 1908, appeared as Natine in "King of Cadonia"; she then left the stage until Apr., 1912, when she appeared at the Hippodrome in "Arms and the Girl"; subsequently toured as the Hon. Muriel Pym in "Milestones" · at the Palace, Dec., 1912, appeared as Miss Wilcox in "Susan's Embellishments"; at the Royalty, Mar., 1913, succeeded Gladys Cooper as the Hon. Muriel Pym in "Milestones"; in the autumn of 1913 accompanied Cyril Maude to Canada and the United States; made her first appearance in New York, at Wallack's, 3 Nov., 1913, as Norah in "The Second in Command"; on returning to London, 1914, played in repertory season at Croydon, and subsequently toured as Pamela in "The Pursuit of Pamela"; in 1915 toured in "The Man who Stayed at Home," subsequently joining the Birmingham Repertory Company, where she played leads until the following spring; at the Kingsway, May, 1916, appeared as Kitty Roylance in "Ye Gods"; during 1917-18 toured as Judy Abbott in "Daddy Long-Legs"; subsequently assumed the management of the Abbey Theatre, Dublin, with Franklin Dyall, and produced several plays; at the Criterion, Apr., 1919, played the Hon. Jane Bagley in "Our Mr. Hepplewhite," and subsequently supported Dion Boucicault and Irene Vanbrugh in their repertory season at the Gaiety, Manchester; at the St. Martin's, Feb., 1920, played Beatrice Draycott in "Just Like Judy"; at the Little, Apr., 1920, Sylvia Maitland in "Other Times"; at the Kingsway, Sept., 1920, Julia in "The Daisy"; subsequently toured as Nellie Redfern in "By all Means, Darling"; at the Playhouse, Mar., 1921, played Barbara in "Love?"; at the St. James's, Sept., 1921, Enid Stonor in "The Speckled Band"; at the Court, Jan., 1922, Kate Hardcastle in "She Stoops to Conquer"; at the Kingsway, May, 1922, Lady Pamela Farres in "Life's a Game"; at the Royalty, June, 1922 Clementina in "The Green Cord"; at the Apollo, Nov., 1922, Lina in "Devil Dick"; at the Everyman, Jan., 1923, the Wife in "Medium"; at the Lyceum, Feb., 1923, Louise in "The Orphans"; Apr., 1923, Princess Viola in "A Night of Temptation"; at the Shaftesbury (for the Phoenix Society), June, 1923, Amoret in "The faithful Shepherdess"; at the New; Oct., 1923, Lucy Shale in "The Lie"; at the St. James's, June, 1924, succeeded Isobel Elsom as Lucilla Crespin in "The Green Goddess"; at the Apollo, Sept., 1924, Clare Jewett in "The Fool"; Scala (for Play Actors), May, 1925, played Irene Short in "By Right of Conquest"; Queen's, Aug., 1925, Vivien Carsdale in "The Man from Hong-Kong"; in Oct., 1925, went to South Africa to play in "Sacred and Profane Love," "At Mrs. Beam's," and "Smilin' Through"; reappeared in London at the Duke of York's, Apr., 1926, as Nina Grant in "Loose Ends"; "Q," Nov., 1926, played Gabby in "Cautious Campbell"; Wyndham's,

Apr., 1927, Juliette Corton in "Mr. What's His Name?"; Court, Feb., 1928, Lady Macbeth in "Macbeth" (in modern dress); Comedy, June, 1928, Lady Cynthia in "If We But Knew"; Everyman, Dec., 1928, Rita Allmers in "Little Eyolf"; "Q," Dec., 1928, Helen in "Helen With the High Hand"; Lyceum, Mar., 1929, again played in "Mr. What's His Name?"; Strand, Apr., 1929, Isabel in "The Shadow of the East"; Arts, June, 1929, Mrs. Ullsworth in "Sybarites"; Garrick, Nov., 1929, played Laura Bruce in "The Woman in Room 13"; during 1930, toured as Gloria in "The Limping Man," and Leonora in "Sentenced"; went to New York, and appeared at the Fulton, Oct., 1930, as Ann Lymes in "Canaries Sometimes Sing"; after returning to London, appeared at Prince of Wales, June, 1931, as Muriel Harding in "Lovers' Meeting"; Duchess, Nov., 1931, played Aline Solness in "The Master Builder"; Embassy, Jan., 1932, Caryll Anderton in "Full Fathom Five"; Kingsway, May, 1932, Kate Hardcastle in "She Stoops to Conquer"; from Sept., 1932, visited Manchester, Birmingham, etc. in "Grand Guignol" plays; Lyceum, Mar., 1933, Nancy in "Oliver Twist"; Kingsway, Apr., 1933, Riosama in "The Voice"; Fortune, Sept., 1933, Mrs. Caroline Coutts in "The House of Jealousy"; Lyric, Oct., 1934, Kitty le Moyne in "Theatre Royal"; Playhouse, Oct., 1935, Lady Atwill in "A Butterfly on the Wheel"; Gate, Nov., 1936, Amelia Tilford in "The Children's Hour"; Queen's, Apr., 1937, Mary Madison Preble in "Post Road"; toured, May, 1937, as the Comtesse Rochecourt in "The Lady of La Paz"; Duke of York's (for London International Theatre Club), Dec., 1937, Lady Inglestone in "Identity Unknown"; "Q," Feb., 1938, Mrs. Atkins in "Beyond the Horizon" and June, 1938, Charlotte Shaw in "Little Stranger"; Vaudeville, Oct., 1938, Mrs. Priskin in "Goodness, How Sad!" and toured in the same part, 1939; St. James's, Dec., 1939, Leonora Fiske in "Ladies in Retirement"; Richmond, June, 1940, Marie-Louise in "Between Five and Seven"; toured, 1940, as Amy in "French for

Love," and 1941, as Mathilde Hess in "Play With Fire" ("The Shop at Sly Corner"); Strand, May, 1942, Mrs. Danvers in "Rebecca"; Piccadilly, Oct., 1942, Birdie Hubbard in "The Little Foxes"; toured, 1943, as Mrs. Smith in "The Strange Case of Margaret Wishart" ("Suspect"); Phoenix, Sept., 1943, Mrs. McQuestion in "The Wingless Victory"; toured, Apr., 1944, as Abby Brewster in "Arsenic and Old Lace"; Embassy, Nov., 1945, the Princess in "The Gambler"; Savoy (for the Repertory Players), Jan., 1946, Margery in "The Quick and the Dead"; at the New, Aug., 1948, succeeded Marie Ney as Nurse Braddock in "The Gioconda Smile"; Duchess, Feb., 1949, played Tilly Cuff in "The Foolish Gentlewoman"; St. Martin's, Oct. 1949, Mrs. Skinner in "Before the Party"; New Boltons, Nov., 1950, Mrs. Amelia Tilford in "The Children's Hour"; at the King's, Glasgow, Nov., 1951, played Florence Cooksey in "A Multitude of Sins"; at the Plymouth, New York, Mar., 1952, played Helen Allistair in "Women of Twilight"; at the Prince's, London, Aug., 1953, appeared as Alice Nutting in "Age of Consent"; Westminster, June, 1954, played Grannie in "It's Never Too Late"; at the "Q" Theatre, Jan., 1956, played Mrs. Trout in "Start From Scratch"; Duchess, May, 1956, Mrs. Sampler in "The Silver Whistle"; Cambridge, Mar., 1958, Alice, Lady Miller in "Breath of Spring"; St. Martin's, July, 1962, played Sybil Walling in "Brush With a Body"; toured, June, 1964, as May Beringer in "The Old Ladies"; toured, Feb., 1965, as Laura Pocock in "Oh Dear! What Can the Matter Be"; Palace, Westcliff, May, 1965, Mrs. Ashley in "I Found April"; toured, Mar., 1967, as Aunt Abby in "Arsenic and Old Lace"; Arts, June, 1968, Old Mrs. Lemmy in "The Foundations"; Hampstead Theatre Club, Mar., 1971, played the name part in "Ellen." *Recreation:* Reading. *Club:* Three Arts. *Address:* 33 Sussex Square, Brighton, Sussex.

MERRICK, Leonard, novelist and dramatic author; *b.* Belsize Park, 21 Feb., 1864; *o.s.* of William Miller

(" Merrick " by deed-poll) ; *e.* Brighton College and privately ; *m.* 1894, Hope, *y.d.* of Thomas Butler-Wilkins, of Northampton ; author of the novels " Violet Moses," " The Man who was Good," " This Stage of Fools," " Cynthia," " One Man's View," " The Actor-Manager," " The Worldlings," " When Love Flies out o' the Window," " Conrad in Quest of his Youth," " The Quaint Companions," " A Chair on the Boulevard," " The House of Lynch," " The Man Who Understood Women," " All the World Wondered," " The Position of Peggy Harper," " While Paris Laughed," " To Tell You the Truth," " The Little Dog Laughed"; his plays include (with G. R. Sims), " When the Lamps are Lighted," " My Innocent Boy," " The Elixir of Youth," " A Woman in the Case"; " The Free Pardon" (With F. C. Philips); " The Impostor," subsequently " The Fraud " (with Michael Morton). *Recreations:* Music, reading other novels, and seeing other people's plays. *Club:* Savage.

(Died 7 Aug., 1939; age 75)

MERRILL, Beth, actress; during 1916 was engaged with the Oliver Stock Company at Lincoln, Nebraska; appeared at the National Theatre, New York, Dec., 1922, as Adele in "Fashions for Men"; at the Princess, Oct., 1923, played Mary Kane in "The White Desert"; Vanderbilt, Sept., 1924, Agnes Fanning in "Lazybones"; Lyceum, Dec., 1924, Kay Beatty in "Ladies of the Evening"; Nov., 1926, Lily Sue in a play of that name; Oct., 1927, Violet Cadence in "Hidden"; at Atlantic City, Aug., 1932, played in "Exit the Queen"; after some years' absence, reappeared in New York, at the Henry Miller Theatre, Dec., 1939, as Hanka in "Christmas Eve"; Maxine Elliott, Jan., 1941, played Katherine in "The Lady Who Came to Stay"; Booth, Apr., 1942, Gussie Rogers in "Autumn Hill"; toured, Aug., 1942, as Harriet Carroll in "The Two Mrs. Carrolls"; at the Great Northern, Chicago, Apr., 1944, Lettie in "Uncle Harry"; Coronet, New York, Jan., 1947, played Kate Keller in "All My Sons." *Address:* c/o Actors' Equity Association, 45 West 47th Street, New York City, U.S.A.

MERRITT, Grace, actress; *b.* 24 July, 1881 ; *m.* Henry Keble Merritt ; was a pupil of the American Academy of Dramatic Arts, under Franklin H. Sargent, and made her first appearance on the stage at the Empire Theatre, New York, 16 May, 1899, as the Strange Lady in " The Man of Destiny " ; subsequently she quitted the stage for some years, and was not seen again in New York until she appeared at the Princess Theatre, Apr., 1904, in " An African Millionaire " (" Colonel Clay "), and at the Madison Square Theatre, in " The Braisley Diamond " ; subsequently joined Arnold Daly, 1906, to play in " A Man of Destiny," and then toured in " Alice, Where Art Thou ? " ; for three years she toured as Mary Tudor in " When Knighthood Was in Flower " ; during 1909-10 toured in " The Master Key " ; in Aug., 1910, toured in " The Blue Mouse " ; in 1916 toured in " Some Baby."

MERSON, Billy (William Henry Thompson), actor and comic vocalist : *b.* Nottingham, 29 Mar., 1881; first appeared on the variety stage at Birmingham, 1900; for some years toured the provinces as an acrobat and clown, under the name of Ping-Pong; first appeared in London at the old Middlesex Music Hall, 1905; appeared in 1909, at the Oxford; was engaged for some time at the Hippodrome in the *revue* " Hullo, Tango! " 1913; at the London Opera House, July, 1916, appeared in " Look Who's Here "; at the Palace, Dec., 1918, appeared in " Hullo ! America "; May, 1920, in " The Whirligig "; at the Lyric, May, 1922, played Matthew Platt in " Whirled Into Happiness "; at the London Hippodrome, Mar., 1923, appeared in " Brighter London "; at the Palladium, Mar., 1924, in " The Whirl of the World "; at the Olympia, Liverpool, Dec., 1924, Puss in " Puss in

Boots"; at Drury Lane, Mar., 1925, played Hard-Boiled Herman in "Rose Marie"; Palladium, Feb., 1926, played in "Palladium Pleasures"; entered on the management of the Shaftesbury Theatre, Nov., 1926, and produced "My Son John," in which he played Benjamin Littlewood; London Hippodrome, July, 1927, appeared in "Shake Your Feet"; Vaudeville, Jan., 1928, played Basil in "Lord Babs"; Wimbledon, Sept., 1928, and Shaftesbury, Dec., 1928, The Lad in a play of that name; toured 1929, as Gene Curtalli in "Playmates"; 1930, in variety theatres; 1931, toured in "Whirled into Happiness," and "Happy Snaps"; 1932, toured in "Meet Mr. Merson"; at the Alhambra, Aug., 1932, played in "Over the Page"; Alexandra, Birmingham, Dec., 1933, appeared in "The Babes in the Wood"; toured, Oct., 1936, as Josiah Clutterbuck in "The Cinema Star"; Garrick, Southport, Dec., 1937, played Buttons in "Cinderella"; toured, 1939, as Hard-Boiled Herman in "Rose Marie"; Comedy, Jan., 1941, played Hubert Briggs in "The Blue Goose"; among his popular songs may be mentioned "I'm setting the village on fire"; "I'm going away"; "The Spaniard that blighted my life"; "The Gay Cavalier," etc; has appeared in films, in "The Show Goes On," "Scruffy," etc. *Recreations :* Golf and wireless.
(Died 25 June, 1947; age 66)

MÉRY, Andrée, French actress; appeared at the Théâtre des Arts, Apr., 1910, as Suzanne Daniloff in "Les Yeux qui Changent"; at the Sarah Bernhardt, 1919, played Marguerite Gauthier in "La Dame aux Camelias"; Apr., 1920, the Duc de Reichstadt in "L'Aiglon"; at the Nouvel-Ambigu, June, 1921, Comtesse Sarah in "Les Mystères de Paris." *Address :* 1 Villa la Terrasse, Paris.

MESSAGER, André, French composer; *b.* Montlucon, 30 Dec., 1853; *m.* Hope Temple; director of the Opera House, Paris; formerly director of music and conductor at the Opéra Comique, Paris, and Royal Opera, Covent Garden, London; has com-

posed the following operas : "François les Bas-Bleus," 1883; "La Fauvette du Temple," 1884; "Les Deux Pigeons," "La Béarnaise," 1886; "Le Bourgeois de Calais," 1887; "Isoline," 1888; "Le Mari de la Reine," 1889; "La Basoche," 1890; "Hélène," 1891; "Madame Chrysanthème," 1893; "Mirette," 1894; "La Fiancée en Loterie," "Le Chevalier d'Harmental," 1896; "Les P'tites Michus" ("The Little Michus"), "La Montagne Enchantée," 1897; "Véronique," 1898; "Une aventure de la Guimard," 1900; "Les Dragons de l'Impératrice," 1905; "Fortunio," 1907; "Monsieur Beaucaire," 1919; "La Petite Fonctionaire," 1921; is an Officer of the Legion of Honour. *Address :* 103 Rue Jouffroy, Paris.

METAXA, Georges, actor and vocalist; *b.* Bucharest, Rumania, 11 Sept., 1899; *s.* of Nicolas Metaxa and his wife Emilie (Theophilatos); *e.* Bucharest University; *m.* (1) Hélène Valoary (mar. dis.); (2) Peggy Stafford (dec.); (3) Byrenice McFadden Muckerman; was formerly engaged as the Chef de Cabinet of Agricultural Ministry, Rumania; made his first appearance on the stage at the Strand Theatre, London, 1 June, 1926, as Alexander Dorotchinsky in "Hearts and Diamonds"; in Dec., 1926, toured as the Count Olinski in "The Blue Mazurka," subsequently appearing at Daly's Theatre, 1927, in the same part; at the Prince of Wales's, Oct., 1927, appeared in "The Bow-Wows"; Shaftesbury, Apr., 1928, in "Will o' the Whispers"; at the London Pavilion, Mar., 1929, in "Wake Up and Dream"; at His Majesty's, July, 1929, played Carl Linden in "Bitter Sweet," in which he continued throughout 1930; went to New York, where he made his first appearance, at the Globe Theatre, 15 Oct., 1931, as Victor Florescu in "The Cat and the Fiddle"; at the Masque, New York, May, 1933, played Claude de Rozay in "$25 an Hour"; New Amsterdam, Dec., 1934, Carlos in "Revenge with Music"; appeared in the films, "The Secrets of a Secretary," "Swing Time," etc.
(Died 8 Dec., 1950; age 51)

METCALFE, James Stetson, journalist and critic ; *b.* Buffalo, New York, 27 June, 1858 ; *e.* Yale ; was editor and publisher of *The Modern Age,* 1883-4 ; editorial writer for *Buffalo Express,* 1884-5 ; editor of *People's Pictorial Press,* 1886 ; manager of American Newspapers Publishers' Association, 1886-9 ; dramatic editor of *Life,* 1889-1921 ; literary editor of *Life,* 1890-5 ; in 1895 was managing editor of *The Cosmopolitan Magazine* ; is the author of " Mythology for the Moderns," 1900 ; " The American Slave," 1900 ; " Another Three Weeks ; not by El-n-r Gl-n," 1908 ; in 1918 received the decoration of a Chevalier of the Legion of Honour ; since 1922 dramatic editor of *The Wall Street Journal* ; the action of the so-called Theatrical Syndicate to prevent him entering their various theatres caused much comment during 1905, and resulted in an action at law. *(Died 26 May, 1927; age 68)*

MÉTÉNIER, Oscar, French dramatic author and novelist ; *b.* Sancoins, Cher, 17 Jan., 1859 ; *e.* Jesuit College, Yseure, Allier ; has written, either alone or in collaboration, the following plays : " En Famille," 1887 ; " La Puissance des Ténèbres," 1888 ; " L'Orage," " La Casserole," 1889 ; " Les Frères Zemganno," " Monsieur Betsy " (with Paul Alexis), 1890 ; " Rabelais," " La Bonne à toute faire " (with Dubut de Laforest), 1892 ; " Charles Démailly " (with Paul Alexis), " Très Russe," 1893 ; " Mademoiselle Fifi," 1896 ; " Le Loupiot," " La Brème," " Lui," 1897 ; " Le Lezard," " Le Chien," " Une Manille," " La Revanche de Dupont l'Anguille," 1898 ; " Le Million," 1899 ; " Son Poteau," " Royal-Cambouis," 1901 ; " La Voix," " Boule-de-Suif," " L'Absinthe," 1902 ; " La Sonate du Clair de Lune," " La Consigne," 1905 ; has also written nearly thirty novels ; member of the Societies of Men of Letters and Dramatic Authors. *Recreations :* Hunting and riding. *(Died Feb., 1913; age 54)*

MEYER, Bertie Alexander, manager ; *b.* 17 June, 1877; *m.* (1) Dorothy Grimston (mar. dis.) ; (2) Rosemary Ames (mar. dis.) ; (3) Diana Hamilton (dec.) ; (4) Beryl Menzies ; his first theatrical experience was at the Garrick Theatre, under the direction of Arthur Lewis, who was presenting Madame Réjane in a series of plays, 1902 ; was next assistant manager at Wyndham's, 1903, and Madame Réjane's season at Terry's, 1904 ; was general manager of German theatre in London ; manager for Miss Tita Brand at the Shaftesbury, 1905; was next director of M. Coquelin's season at Shaftesbury Theatre, then business manager for Charles Frohman at the Aldwych, and in Oct., 1917, at the Queen's Theatre, Shaftesbury Avenue ; general manager for Oscar Asche and Miss Lily Brayton from May, 1908, and for both their Australian tours was appointed manager to Rupert Clarke and Clive Meynell's enterprises in Australia ; returned to England, 1913, and was appointed manager of the Globe Theatre, London; built St. Martin's Theatre, West Street, and became lessee in Nov., 1916; served four and a half years in the army as interpreter and in the R.A.O.D. ; at the end of the war became general manager Ambassadors' Theatre, for H. M. Harwood ; in conjunction with Owen Nares, produced " The Enchanted Cottage " and " If Winter Comes," 1922 ; was also manager of the Shaftesbury Theatre for Malone and Grossmith, 1922 ; in 1923 produced " The Return of Sherlock Holmes " at the Princes ; was temporary lessee of the Strand, 1924 ; subsequently in partnership with Dennis Neilson-Terry and Mary Glynne, and toured " The Terror," subsequently produced at Lyceum, May, 1927; made several productions at the Little Theatre, 1927-8, including "A Man With Red Hair," The Grand Guignol Season, etc. ; produced "Alibi" at Prince of Wales, 1928; " Lucky Girl," Shaftesbury, 1928; " Her Cardboard Lover" (with Gilbert Miller), Lyric, 1928 ; " The Flying Fool," Princes, 1929; opened the Cambridge Theatre, Sept., 1930, with "Charlot's Masquerade," and in 1931, produced "Elizabeth of England"; Lyric, 1933, "The Holmeses of Baker Street"; visited the U.S.A., 1936, and presented "The Two Mrs. Carrolls"; lived abroad 1936–9; produced "Ten Little Niggers," St. James's 1943; "Ten Little Niggers," Théâtre Antoine, Paris, 1946; "Appointment with Death," Piccadilly, 1945; "Murder at the Vicarage," Playhouse, 1950; "They Got What They Wanted," Phoenix, 1950; "Meet Mr. Callaghan," Garrick, 1952; "Noddy in Toyland," Stoll, 1954, and five subsequent productions at the Princes Theatre; "Ten Little Niggers," St. Martin's, "Noddy in Toyland," Scala, 1962; resumed administration and again became Licensee of the St. Martin's Theatre, 1960. *Club:* Savage. *(Died 16 Nov., 1967; age 90)*

MEYER, Louis, theatrical manager; *b.* Birmingham, 20 Oct., 1871; *s.* of Joel Meyer; *e.* King Edward VI Grammar School, Birmingham; *m.* Nina Wood; was formerly a "Black and White" artist, and editor; his first venture into theatrical management was with "The Woman in the Case," which he sent on tour in 1910; he next became manager of the Globe Theatre, where he produced "The Glad Eye," Nov., 1911; his next production was "The Great John Ganton," at the Aldwych, Sept., 1912, followed by "Where there's a Will—" at the Criterion, Nov., 1912; he then became lessee of the Strand, to which theatre," The Glad Eye" had been transferred, and his remaining productions at that house have been "The Son and Heir," Feb., 1913, and "The Chaperon," Apr., 1913; he is also the managing director of The Garrick Renters, Ltd. (Garrick Theatre), Art Editor and joint managing director of *London Opinion.* *Favourite play:* "His House in Order." *Recreations:* Drawing and racing. *Club:* Press.
(Died 1 Feb., 1915; age 43)

MEYNELL, Clyde, manager; *b.* Dover, 7 Apr., 1867; *s.* of Elizabeth (Crosse) and Colonel F. van Straubenzee; *e.* at Sherborne and Edinburgh University; *m.* Ethel Carlisle Kelly; was intended for the medical profession, and practised as a physician and surgeon; made his first appear-

ance on the stage in 1885, under the management of Victor Stevens; subsequently joined the Compton Comedy Company and the late Frank Harvey's company; made his first appearance on the London stage, at the Grand Theatre, Islington, 1 Aug., 1887, as Harold Vernon in "The World Against Her"; left the stage in 1889, and qualified as a doctor at Edinburgh; rejoined the theatrical profession in 1895, when in partnership with Horace Lingard he managed a tour of "A Man's Shadow" in the English provinces; was subsequently manager for Miss Fortescue, Mouillot and Morell, with whom he spent six years as manager of the Theatre Royal, Bournemouth, Grand, Southampton, and Grand, Boscombe; he was also interested in a tour of "My Friend the Prince," with Wilfred Cotton, and was for a time in partnership with Wentworth Croke; was engaged by Sir Herbert Tree in 1901, and was appointed general manager and stage director for the company which Sir Herbert Tree sent to Australia in 1902, under the management of J. C. Williamson; he remained in Australia to manage the company headed by Julius Knight and Maude Jefferies; then entered into partnership with the late John Gunn, their first venture being a tour of "The J.P.," with J. J. Dallas and Florence Lloyd in the leading parts; he produced "The Fatal Wedding," "The Midnight Wedding," "Her Love Against the World," etc.; Sir Rupert Clarke, Bart., then joined the firm, and in conjunction with another firm, they produced "Miss Hook of Holland," "The Belle of Mayfair," "The Girl Behind the Counter," and "Cinderella"; it was under their auspices that Oscar Asche, Lily Brayton and company, paid their first Australian visit, while others who appeared under their management were Matheson Lang, Hutin Britton and company, etc.; his firm subsequently amalgamated with J. C. Williamson, and he was appointed managing director of the firm of J. C. Williamson, Ltd., which controlled most of the leading theatres in Australia and New Zealand.
(Died 18 June, 1934; age 66)

MICHAEL, Gertrude, actress; *b.* Talladega, Alabama, U.S.A., 1 June, 1910; *d.* of Carl Henry Michael and his wife Gertrude (White); *e.* University of Alabama, Converse College, and Cincinnati Conservatory of Music; made her first appearance on the stage at the Taft Auditorium, Cincinnati, 1928, in Stuart Walker's stock company; made her first appearance in New York, at the Golden Theatre, 4 Nov., 1931, as Dolores Winthrop in "Caught Wet"; at the Majestic, Mar., 1932, played Echo Allen in "The Round-Up"; at Dennis, Mass., Aug., 1937 played Deborah Sampson in "Damn Deborah"; commenced film career, 1931, and has played in numerous pictures, notably the "Sophie Lang" series; since 1936, has appeared in " Just Like a Woman," "Star of the Circus," "The Woman Trap," "Till We Meet Again," "The Return of Sophie Lang," "Second Wife," "Make Way for a Lady," "Mr. Dodd Takes the Air," "Sophie Lang Goes West," etc. *Recreations:* Music, swimming, playing the violin and collecting first editions. *Association:* American Society of Penwomen.

(Died 1 Jan., 1965; age 53)

MICHAELIS, Robert, actor and vocalist; *b.* in Paris, 22 Dec., 1884; *s.* of Georges and Marie Michaëlis; *e.* Dulwich College and in Paris; studied singing in Vienna under Signor Bottelli, and in London under Franklin Clive; *m.* Phyllis Le Grand; made his first appearance on the stage, Dec., 1898, at the Opera House, Cork, in the pantomime " The Babes in the Wood "; made his first appearance in London, at the Palace Theatre, 12 Jan., 1903, as a vocalist; in June, 1903, appeared at Kennington Theatre, as François in " Amorelle "; toured in " The Gay Parisienne," " Three Little Maids," and " The Belle of New York "; at the Comedy, Dec., 1903, played Harry Gordon in " The Girl from Kay's "; made his first appearance in New York, at the Casino Theatre, Feb., 1907, as Paul in " The White Hen," and at the Knickerbocker Theatre, Sept., 1907, played René in " Mdlle. Modiste ";

appeared at Daly's, 10 Aug., 1908, as Prince Danilo in " The Merry Widow "; at the Prince's, Manchester, Dec., 1908, played Freddy Fairfax in " The Dollar Princess," and appeared in the same part at Daly's, 25 Sept., 1909; at Daly's, Jan., 1911, played Lieutenant Niki in " A Waltz Dream "; at the Prince's, Manchester, Dec., 1911, played Count René in " The Count of Luxembourg "; at Daly's, June, 1912, Joszi in " Gipsy Love "; May, 1913, Jack Fleetwood in " The Marriage Market "; Oct., 1914, Geoffrey Challoner in " A Country Girl "; at the Palace, June, 1915, appeared in " The Passing Show "; served four years in the British Expeditionary Force, 1915-19; reappeared on the stage at the Adelphi Theatre, Sept., 1919, as James in " Who's Hooper ? "; at the Empire, April, 1920, played J. P. Beaudon in " Irene"; at the Adelphi, Oct., 1921, Pierre Caravan in " The Golden Moth "; at the Fulton Theatre, New York, Sept., 1922, Baron Roger Belmont in " Orange Blossoms "; at the Gaiety, London, Sept., 1923, Field-Marshal Menshikoff in " Catherine"; April, 1924, Tom Miles in " Our Nell " ; in Sept., 1924, toured as King Charles II in the same play; at the Lyceum, Edinburgh, Dec., 1924, played Armand in " Frasquita "; Shaftesbury, Aug.,1925, played the Hon. Harry Somerset in " Dear Little Billie "; Adelphi, Aug., 1927, Baron Fretigny in " Up With the Lark." *Hobby:* Collecting Japanese and Chinese works of art. *Recreations:* Motoring, lawn tennis, swimming, and punting.

(Died 29 Aug., 1965; age 80)

MICHAELSON, Knut, Swedish Manager and dramatic author; *b.* Stockholm, 1 Apr., 1846; *s.* of Hilda (Strokirk) and August Michaelson; *e.* Stockholm; *m.* Kate Arfwedson; was formerly the head of large steel and ironworks in Sweden; his first production took place in 1878, in the shape of a drama entitled " Marguerite," which was produced at the Svenska Theatre, Stockholm, in the same year; his principal productions since, have been, " Marquis de la

Ferrière," 1884 ; " Ett Val," 1886 ;
" Ätergäng," 1887 ; " Moln," 1890 ;
" Skandalen i Natt," 1891 ; " Ett
Ungkarlshen," 1892 ; " Förr i Värl-
den," 1893 ; " Unge Grefven," 1894 ;
" En skugga," 1899 ; " I fru Karin-
sohus," 1900 ; " En Aftonstund på
Tre Liljor," 1910, etc. ; from 1908-
1911, was manager of the National
Theatre, Stockholm ; is now manager
of the Intimate Theatre, Stockholm.
Favourite play : " Ett Ungkarlshen."
Recreation : Painting. *Club :* Svenska
Theaterförbundet. *Address :* Kar-
lavägen 13, Stockholm, Ö.

MIDDLETON, Edgar, dramatic
author; *b.* London, 26 Nov., 1894; *m.*
Yevonde Cumbers; formerly engaged
as a journalist; is the author of scenes
in " Bits and Pieces," 1926; " Poti-
phar's Wife," 1927; " Tin Gods," 1928;
" Morning, Noon, and Night," 1929 ;
"England Expects," 1935; has pub-
lished a volume "Banned by the
Censor" (ten short plays), 1929.
Favourite play : " The Doctor's
Dilemma." *Hobby :* Politics. *Club :*
National Liberal.

(Died 10 Apr., 1939; age 44)

MIDDLETON, George, dramatic au-
thor ; *b.* Paterson, N.J., U.S.A., 27
Oct., 1880 ; *s.* of George Middleton and
his wife Ida (Blakeslee) ; *m.* Fola la
Follette ; has written the following
plays : " The Cavalier " (with Paul
Kester), 1902 ; " The Vital Issue,"
1904 ; " The Wife's Strategy," 1905 ;
" The Sinner " (with L. Westerveldt),
1907 ; " The House of a Thousand
Candles," 1908 ; " Rosalind at the
Red Gate," 1910 ; " The Enemy,"
1911 ; " The Prodigal Judge," 1913 ;
" Criminals," 1914 ; " Hit-the-Trail
Holliday " (with Geo. M. Cohan and
Guy Bolton), 1915 ; " A Happy
Thought " (with Guy Bolton), 1916 ;
" Polly with a Past " (with Bolton),
1917 ; " Adam and Eva " (with Bol-
ton), 1919 ; " The Cave Girl " (with
Bolton), 1920 ; " The Light of the
World," 1920 ; " Cercle," 1922 ; " The
Unknown Lady," 1923 ; " The Other
Rose " (from the French), 1923 ; " The
Road Together," 1924 ; " Accused "

(from the French), 1925; " Blood
Money " (from a story), 1927 ; " Polly "
(on " Polly With a Past "), 1929 ;
" The Big Pond " (with A. E. Thomas),
1929 ; "Madame Capet" (adaptation),
1938 ; has also written the following
volumes of published one-act plays :
"Embers," "Tradition," " Possession,"
"Masks," "Criminals," also "Hiss!
Boom!! Blah!!!" (1930) ; "That Was
Balzac," 1936; was President of the
Guild of Dramatists of the Authors'
League of America, 1927. *Club :*
Players'. *(Died 23 Dec., 1967; age 87)*

MIDDLETON, Guy, actor ; *b.* Hove,
Sussex, 14 Dec., 1907 ; *s.* of Eustace
Middleton-Powell and his wife Catherine (Hogg) ; *e.* Harrow ; *m.* Anita
Arden ; formerly on the Stock Ex-
change ; made his first appearance on
the stage at the Palace Theatre, Salis-
bury, Feb., 1928, as Richard Easton
in "The Crooked Billet" ; made his
first appearance in London at Daly's
Theatre, 26 Apr., 1929, as the Captain
of the Guard in "The Lady of the
Rose"; King's, Hammersmith, Nov.,
1930, played Charles Plunket in
"Daphne"; toured 1931, in "The
Outsider" and "Counsel's Opinion" ;
Players', May, 1931, played the Hon.
Bruce Seville in "The Gun Runner" ;
London Hippodrome, Feb., 1933, Pierre
in "The One Girl" ; at the same theatre,
June, 1933, Evan Maxwell in "Give
Me a Ring"; subsequently appeared
at the Caumartin Theatre, Paris, as
Jonathan Brockett in "The Well of
Loneliness"; King's, Hammersmith,
Feb., 1934, played Hubert Drummond
in "The Happy Hostage"; Lyceum,
May, 1934, Captain Roget in "The
King of the Damned"; Victoria
Palace, Sept., 1934, Jabez Hawk in
"Young England"; Duke of York's,
Apr., 1935, Jevan Adams in ". . . And
a Woman Passed By"; Royalty, May,
1936, Captain Chatteridge in "Marriage
Settlement"; Daly's, July, 1936,
Richard Armstrong in "The Visitor";
Criterion, Nov., 1936, Brian Curtis in
"French Without Tears"; made his
first appearance in New York at the
Henry Miller Theatre, Sept., 1937, in
the same part; on returning to Eng-
land, again appeared in "French With-
out Tears," 1938–9; Strand, Aug.,

1939, played Gurney in "Spotted Dick"; served in the King's Royal Rifle Corps, 1939–44; entered films, 1935, and has since appeared in numerous pictures, including "The Rake's Progress," "A Man About the House," "The Happiest Days of Your Life," "Conflict of Wings," "The Belles of St. Trinian's," "Doctor At Large," etc.; re-appeared on the stage at the Cambridge, May, 1959, when he played Lord Rayne in "Let Them Eat Cake"; Princes, Aug., 1962, played Sir Francis Beekman in "Gentleman Prefer Blondes"; has also appeared in many television plays and programmes. *Recreations:* Cricket, tennis, cooking. *Club:* M.C.C. *Address:* c/o Eric Glass, Ltd., 28 Berkeley Square, London, W.1.

MIDDLETON, Josephine, actress; *b.* Nashville, Tenn., U.S.A.; *d.* of Count Bernard J. Alcock, J.P., and his wife Helen (Devereux-Lane); *e.* London and Germany; studied for the stage under Miss Bateman (Mrs. Crowe); made her first appearance on the stage at the Kingsway Theatre, Mar., 1908, as Ada in "The Kleptomaniac"; then toured in "Charley's Aunt," "A Message from Mars," "What the Butler Saw," "The Mollusc," etc.; subsequently toured in music-hall sketches and played in repertory companies; toured, 1916, in "The Love Thief" and "Caroline"; Oxford, June, 1919, played Alice Hope in "A Temporary Gentleman," subsequently touring in the same play until 1922; during 1922, toured with the Irish Players; from 1923–6, played leading parts with the Southend Repertory company; Court, Mar., 1927, Mary Parsons in "The Blue Comet"; subsequently toured, 1927, as Mrs. Livingston in "The First Year"; at the Gate Theatre, Nov., 1928, played Mrs. Harris in "All God's Chillun Got Wings"; at the Haymarket, 1929, appeared in "Quality Street" and "The Ivory Door"; during 1929–30, appeared at the Gate Theatre, in "Martine," "Eater of Dreams," "Long Live Death," "Maya," "Obertag," etc.; Embassy, Sept., 1930–Mar., 1931, played Miss Furse in "The House of

Pretence," Lady Bagot in "Rich Man, Poor Man," Mrs. Pryce in "The Scarlet Lady," Caroline Amory in "Black Coffee," Julia Dengler in "Lady in Waiting," Mrs. Fell in "The Torch Bearers," Mrs. Hatherton in "The By-Pass"; St. Martin's, Apr., 1931, played Caroline in "Black Coffee"; appeared at the Embassy, 1931–2, in several further productions; Embassy, Sept., and Comedy, Oct., 1932, appeared in "Miracle at Verdun"; Duke of York's, Dec., 1932, played Mrs. Summers in "Recipe for Murder"; Croydon, Feb., 1933, Miss Branwell in "The Brontës"; Westminster, Mar., 1933, Lady Stanway in "The Lake"; Vaudeville, 1933, the Mother in "Sunshine House"; Vaudeville, Jan., 1934, Mrs. Pritchard in "The Man Who Was Fed Up"; Westminster, July, 1934, Hannah in "French Salad"; Royalty, Feb., 1937, Rebecca in "The Ripening Wheat"; Gate, Sept., 1937, Queen Victoria in "Mr. Gladstone"; Embassy, May, 1938, Lady Mary in "Open Verdict"; Whitehall, July, 1938, Mrs. Bell in "Lot's Wife"; Vaudeville, May, 1940, Ellen in "Peril at End House"; from 1940–1, played in repertory at Aberdeen, Perth, and Dundee; Arts, Oct., 1942, Mdme. Krohne in "The House of Regrets," and Feb., 1943, Magaera in "Androcles and the Lion"; joined the Old Vic company at the Liverpool Playhouse, Aug., 1943, playing Catherine Petkoff in "Arms and the Man," Essie in "Ah! Wilderness," the Nurse in "Romeo and Juliet," etc.; Lyric, May, 1944, Florence Nightingale in "Crisis in Heaven"; Fortune, Sept., 1946, Mrs. Mandrake in "Fools Rush In"; "Q," Apr., 1947, appeared in "Those Were the Days"; Duchess, Nov., 1948, played the Vicar's Wife in "Miss Mabel"; Arts, Aug., 1949, Jane in "The Schoolmistress"; New Boltons, Jan., 1951, Gertrude in "Rainbow"; at the Pitlochry Festival, 1952, appeared as Eleanor in "The Doom of Devorgoil," Anna in "Tobias and the Angel," and also played in "The Witch"; Arts, London, Sept., 1953, played Mrs. Watson in a revival of "Penelope"; Arts, Feb., 1954, Mrs. Stead in "The Private Secretary";

Golder's Green, July, 1956, played Mrs. Eichelbury in "Sight Unseen"; has also played many parts with the Repertory Players, Stage Society, etc.; first appeared in films, 1928, in "Houp La!"; and has since played regularly in many pictures; has also taken part in many radio and television productions, and television films. *Favourite part:* Queen Anne in "Viceroy Sarah." *Recreations:* Gardening and yachting. *Club:* Arts Theatre.
(Died 4 Apr., 1971; age 88)

MIGNOT, Flore, French actress; made her first appearance at the Ambigu, 21 Apr., 1907, as Claire Fleury in " Le P'tit Mitron "; appeared at the same theatre, 1907, as Louise in " Les Deux Orphelines," and as Le Dauphin and Petit Léninger in " L'Enfant du Temple "; also in " Sous l'Épaulette "; at the Châtelet, 1909, played Pervenche in " La Petite Caporale "; at the Ambigu, 1909, Julie Lesurques in " Le Courrier de Lyon "; at the Odéon, 1910, Marie in " Les Corbeaux "; appeared at the Shaftesbury Theatre, London, 1908, as Isabelle de Raguais in " La Loi de l'Homme " and paulette in " La Dédale," with Madame Bartet; at the Odéon, May, 1921, appeared as Vivette in " L'Arlésienne "; Dec., 1921, played Solange in " Les Bouffons.

MILLAR, Douglas, manager; *b.* Glasgow, 21 Sept., 1875; *s.* of James Millar and his wife Annie (Mushet); *e.* Glasgow; *m.* Ethel Callanan; was formerly an actor and made his first appearance on the stage in 1893, when he toured in a " fit-up " company; for some years he toured with Isabel Bateman, and with Louis Calvert, as low comedian; played several " stock " seasons; toured with William Greet's Company in " Dandy Dan "; subsequently toured as the Rev. Gavin Dishart in " The Little Minister," and for two years toured as Major Christopher Bingham in " The Second in Command "; in 1902 he retired from the stage and was touring manager for the late Charles Frohman; fulfilled similar position with the late George

Edwardes, and in 1906 joined Robert Courtneidge, and remained in association with him until 1931; was part-proprietor and resident manager of the Theatre Royal, Bristol, to 1931. *Address:* Southend Road, Westbury-on-Trym, Glos.

MILLAR, Gertie, actress; *b.* Bradford, Yorkshire, 21 Feb., 1879; *m.* (1) Lionel Monckton; (2) the 2nd Earl of Dudley (*d.* 1931); first appeared as the Girl Babe in " The Babes in the Wood," St. James's Theatre, Manchester, Dec., 1892; fulfilled many provincial engagements in pantomime and musical comedy; made her first appearance on the London stage, at the Grand Theatre, Fulham, 23 Dec., 1899, as Dandini in " Cinderella "; made her first appearance in the West End, 17 June, 1901, when she appeared as Cora Bellamy in " The Toreador " at the Gaiety; she remained there for seven years, playing in " The Orchid," 1903; " The Spring Chicken," 1905; " The New Aladdin," 1906; " The Girls of Gottenberg," 1907; at the Hicks Theatre, Mar., 1908, played Franzi in " A Waltz Dream "; subsequently proceeded to New York, and at the Knickerbocker Theatre, Sept., 1908, appeared there as Mitzi in " The Girls of Gottenberg "; returned to England in Dec., 1908; at the Gaiety, Jan., 1909, played Mary Gibbs in " Our Miss Gibbs "; at the Adelphi, Nov., 1910, appeared as Prudence in " The Quaker Girl "; at the Gala performance, at His Majesty's, 27 June, 1911, played Pollina in " The Critic "; at Daly's, June, 1912, played Lady Babby in " Gipsy Love "; at the Adelphi, Oct., 1912, Nancy Joyce in " The Dancing Mistress "; at Daly's, May, 1913, played Kitty Kent in " The Marriage Market "; made her first appearance on the variety stage at the Coliseum, 7 Sept., 1914, in a repertory of songs; at Daly's, Oct., 1914, played Nan in " A Country Girl "; at the Palace, Sept., 1915, appeared in " Bric-a-Brac "; at the St. Martin's Theatre, Nov., 1916, appeared as Tillie Runstead ın " Houp

La ! " ; at the Palace, June, 1917, played in " Airs and Graces " ; at the New Theatre, July, 1917, during " Navy Week," played Imogen Parrott in " Trelawny of the Wells " ; at the Prince of Wales's, Mar., 1918, Flora Brapwick in " Flora." *Recreations :* Driving, and the care of animals.

(Died 25 Apr., 1952; age 73)

MILLAR, Robins, dramatic author and journalist; *b.* Nanaimo, British Columbia, Canada, 28 Feb., 1889; *s.* of the Rev. James Millar and his wife Ann (Ferries); *e.* Queen's College, Georgetown, British Guiana, and Whitehill, Glasgow, Scotland; *m.* Edith Gordon; author of the following plays, "Let Greytown Flourish," 1921; "Thunder in the Air," 1928; "Colossus," 1928; "Dream Island," 1929; "Throwing the Dice," 1930; "Wellington," 1933; "Franz Liszt," 1935; "Studio Party," 1937; "Once a Lady," 1937; "Emergency Call," 1938; "There's Money in It," 1939; "Hot Water," 1945; is editorial writer on Scottish *Daily Express.* *Club :* Savage.

(Died 12 Aug., 1968; age 79)

MILLARD, Evelyn, actress and manageress ; *b.* Kensington, 18 Sept., 1869 ; *d.* of John Millard, teacher of elocution at R.A.M. and R.C.M. ; *m.* Robert Porter Coulter ; made her first appearance on the stage at the Haymarket Theatre, 25 Jan., 1891, when she walked on in the third act of " The Dancing Girl " ; she then went to Margate, where she studied under the late Miss Sarah Thorne at the Theatre Royal ; her first part was that of Emma Torrens in " The Serious Family," in June, 1891, and during her stay there she played, among other parts, Julia in " The Hunchback," Hero in " Much Ado About Nothing," Juliet in " Romeo and Juliet," etc. ; in Sept., 1891, she was engaged by Thomas Thorne for a provincial tour, during which she played Fanny Goodwill in " Joseph's Sweetheart " ; Clara Douglas in " Money " ; Fanny Hoyden in " Miss Tomboy " and Sophia in the play of

that name ; she appeared at the Grand, Islington, 19 Oct., 1891, as Fanny in " Joseph's Sweetheart," and was then engaged by the Gattis for the Adelphi, where she made her first appearance on 12 Dec., 1891, taking up the part of Constance Cuthbertson in " The Trumpet Call " ; she remained at the Adelphi nearly two years, and appeared there as Alice Lee in " The White Rose," Sybil Garfield in " The Lights of Home," Margaret Knowlton in " The Lost Paradise," and Mildred Vavasour in " The Black Domino " ; in 1894 she toured as Rosamund in " Sowing the Wind," and also as Dulcie Larondie in " The Masqueraders " and Paula in " The Second Mrs. Tanqueray " with George Alexander ; on returning to London, she appeared at the St. James's, 10 Nov., 1894, as Dulcie in "TheMasqueraders"; she also appeared at that theatre, as Mary Brasier in " Guy Domville," Maud Verner in " Too Happy by Half " and Cecily Cardew in " The Importance of Being Earnest " ; she appeared at the Comedy, Mar., 1895, as Rosamund in a revival of " Sowing the Wind," and then returned to the St. James's, 20 June, 1895, to play Paula in " The Second Mrs. Tanqueray," and July, 1895, played Lady Harding in " The Idler " ; she then toured with the St. James's company, and in Sept. appeared with George Alexander before the late Queen Victoria, at Balmoral, as Blanche Ferraby in " Liberty Hall " ; she appeared in this part at the St. James's, Nov., 1895, and in the same month played Löis in " The Divided Way " ; in Jan., 1896, she appeared as the Princess Flavia in " The Prisoner of Zenda," in which she made a great success ; the following year she was engaged by Beerbohm Tree for Her Majesty's Theatre, and appeared there in July, 1897, as Mdlle. de Belle-Isle in " The Silver Key " ; she then toured with the company playing Drusilla Ives in " The Dancing Girl," Olga Morakoff in " The Red Lamp," etc. ; at Her Majesty's, Jan., 1898, played Portia in "Julius Caesar," and in June, played Nanny in " Ragged Robin " ; was next engaged by Charles Frohman for the Duke of York's

Theatre, and remained there until 1901, playing Lady Ursula Barrington in " The Adventure of Lady Ursula," Oct., 1898 ; Glory Quayle in " The Christian," Oct., 1899 ; Miss Hobbs in the play of that name, Dec., 1899 ; Cho-Cho-San in " Madame Butterfly," Apr., 1900 ; Loretta in " The Swashbuckler," Nov., 1900 ; she returned to the St. James's, Mar , 1902, to play Francesca in " Paolo and Francesca," and appeared at the Haymarket, Dec., 1902, as Margaret Fielding in " The Unforeseen " ; with the exception of a single appearance at Drury Lane, July, 1903, when she played Jessica in the " all-star " revival of " The Merchant of Venice," given in aid of the Actors' Benevolent Fund, she was not seen again until she joined Lewis Waller at the Imperial, Oct., 1904, when she played Lady Lettice Pierrepoint in " His Majesty's Servant " ; on 19 Nov., 1904, with Lewis Waller, appeared at Windsor Castle as Lady Mary Carlyle in " Monsieur Beaucaire," in command performance before the late King Edward ; at the Imperial, Apr., 1905, played Juliet in " Romeo and Juliet " ; May, 1905, appeared as the Princess Irma in " Hawthorne, U.S.A." ; Oct., 1905, played Lilian Tremblett in " The Perfect Lover " ; Jan., 1906, played Colombina in " The Harlequin King " ; in Mar. appeared as the Comtesse de Roquelaure in " Brigadier Gerard " ; accompanied Lewis Waller to the Lyric, and in May played Desdemona in " Othello " ; in June played Lady Mary in " Monsieur Beaucaire " ; in Oct. Lady Marian de Vaux in " Robin Hood " ; appeared at Windsor Castle, 16 Nov., 1906, in the same part in command performance before King Edward ; at the Lyric, Mar., 1907, played Annie Churchill in " The Little Admiral " ; Apr., 1907, played Lady Clancarty in " Clancarty " ; next appeared at His Majesty's, Feb., 1908, playing Joanna Rushworth in " The Beloved Vagabond " ; returned to the Lyric, in June, to play Lucy Allerton in " The Explorer " ; she then entered into management on her own account, and opened at the Garrick Theatre, 2 Sept., 1908, when she played Irene Merriam in " Idols " ;

in Jan., 1909, she played Lady Ursula in a revival of " The Adventure of Lady Ursula " ; she next had a short season at the Criterion, appearing in Feb., 1909, as Lady Arden in " The Real Woman " ; appeared at His Majesty's, Apr., 1910, as Ophelia in " Hamlet " ; her next season she played at the New Theatre, opening in Aug., 1910, when she played Camille de Lancay in " The Crisis," followed in Sept. by her appearance as Carey Fernald in " Young Fernald" ; during 1911, she played Cho-Cho-San in " Madame Butterfly " at various music halls, appearing at the Palace in Mar. ; at the Savoy June, 1911, played Edith Dombey in " Dombey and Son " ; at the gala performance at His Majesty's, 27 June, 1911, appeared as Grace in " The Vision of Delight " ; in Aug., went on tour, playing " The Adventure of Lady Ursula " ; at the Savoy Theatre, Nov., 1912, played Olivia in " Twelfth Night " ; at His Majesty's, 8 Sept., 1914, appeared as Queen Elizabeth in " Drake " ; at the Coliseum, Dec., 1914, as Mavis Daverill in " My Friend Thomas Atkins " ; at His Majesty's, Dec., 1914, played Agnes Wickfield in " David Copperfield " ; at Drury Lane, May, 1916, on the occasion of the Shakespearean Tercentenary performance, appeared as Calpurnia in " Julius Caesar " ; she also appeared on the variety stage, Feb., 1912, at the Manchester Hippodrome, in " The Adventure of Lady Ursula."
(Died 9 Mar., 1941; age 70)

MILLARD, Ursula, actress ; *b.* London, 20 Sept., 1901 ; *d.* of the late R. P. Coulter and his wife Evelyn (Millard) ; *m.* A. Warburton ; made her first appearance on the stage at the Birkbeck College Theatre, 22 June, 1921, as the Moss Maiden in " The Pierrot of the Minute " ; at the Ambassadors', Dec., 1921, played Ethel Warrender in " Clothes and the Woman " ; at the Court, Feb., 1922, Ann in " The Pigeon " ; at the Duke of York's, June, 1922, Asphodel Forres in " Pomp and Circumstance " ; at His Majesty's, Sept., 1922, Sylvia Knox in " East of Suez."

MILLER, Agnes, actress ; *b.* London ; made her first appearance on the professional stage, at the Prince of Wales's Theatre, Liverpool, 7 Sept., 1885, as Matilda Collum in " The Tinted Venus," with the late Rosina Vokes ; accompanied Miss Vokes on her American tour ; made her first appearance in New York, at the Standard Theatre, 21 Dec., 1885, in " In Honour Bound " and " A Pantomime Rehearsal " ; after her return to England, appeared at the Globe Theatre, Oct., 1887, as a Patient in " The Doctor " ; Nov., 1887, as Daisy Maitland in " The Arabian Nights " ; at the Haymarket, under Beerbohm Tree, June, 1888, as Mabel Seabrook in " Captain Swift " ; toured with Mr. and Mrs. Kendal in " The Ironmaster," " A Scrap of Paper," and " The Weaker Sex " ; returned to America in 1889, and remained there for six years ; in 1889-90 toured in the United States with the late Joseph Jefferson and W. J. Florence, playing Lucy in " The Rivals," and Caroline Dormer in " The Heir-at-Law " ; next engaged by the late Richard Mansfield, and appeared with him at Madison Square Theatre, May, 1890, as Mariana Vincent in " Beau Brummell " ; at the Standard Theatre, Sept., 1890, played Belle Cameron in " The Whirlwind " ; at Madison Square, 1891, played Maud in " Sunlight and Shadow," Maud Landon in " The Pharisee," Carey Preston in " Alabama " ; appeared at Palmer's, Nov., 1891, as Nancy Blenkarn in " The Middleman," when E. S. Willard made his first appearance in America ; same theatre, Mar., 1892, played Light Barbour in " Colonel Carter of Cartersville " ; and at Miner's Fifth Avenue, Aug., 1892, Alice Plunkett in " Settled Out of Court " ; at the Standard, Apr., 1893, played Rose Columbier in " The Arabian Nights " ; then joined the Empire Theatre company, under Charles Frohman, and Aug., 1893, played Amy Chilworth in " Liberty Hall " ; subsequently, at the same theatre, appeared as Primrose Green in " The Councillor's Wife," Maud Fretwell in " Sowing the Wind," Gussie in " The Bauble Shop," and

Cecily Cardew in " The Importance of Being Earnest " ; returned to London, 1895, and appeared at the Garrick, Sept., 1895, as Carey Preston in " Alabama " ; again returned to America, and at the Garrick, New York, Mar., 1897, played Octavie in " Never Again " ; played the same part, at the Vaudeville, London, Oct., 1897 ; at the Duke of York's, Oct., 1898, played Dorothy Fenton in " The Adventure of Lady Ursula," and Dec., 1899, Mrs. Kingsearl in " Miss Hobbs " ; at the Shaftesbury, Sept., 1901, appeared as Annie in " Are You a Mason ? " ; she then toured in South Africa with Mrs. Lewis Waller, playing Nathalie in " Zaza," Rosalie in " The Marriage of Kitty," Leah in " A Woman's Reason," and Hester Worsley in " A Woman of No Importance " ; subsequently toured there with Robert Brough ; returned to England, Apr., 1905 ; Duke of York's, Oct., 1907, Mrs. Hunt in " Miquette " ; Comedy, Dec., 1907, Mrs. Smith-Newcome in " Angela " ; Duke of York's, Sept., 1910, Eugénie in " A Bolt from the Blue " ; at the Court, June, 1911, Nina Leblane Gaston in " A Good Sort " ; Comedy, Sept., 1912, Mrs. Blaikie in " A Scrape o' the Pen " ; at Atlantic City, N.Y., Feb., 1914, played Julia Pendleton in " Daddy Long-Legs."

MILLER, David, actor ; *b.* Glasgow, 31 Mar., 1871 ; *s.* of James Miller and his wife Mary Jane (Morrison) ; *e.* Hutchinson Grammar School, Glasgow ; *m.* Beatrice Guiver ; was formerly an assistant in a soft-goods warehouse ; commenced his career as an actor, on tour, in 1898, in " A Runaway Girl," with George Edwardes' company, with which he remained three years, during which time he was appointed assistant stage manager ; other provincial engagements followed, and in 1906 he went to South Africa with Frank Wheeler's comedy company, subsequently playing a round of parts with Wheeler's Musical comedy company ; on his return to England, produced several musical comedies for George Dance, besides acting in them ;

after a further engagement with George Edwardes' company in " The Quaker Girl " and " The Dancing Mistress," he toured " 5064 Gerrard " for André Charlot ; was subsequently appointed stage director for André Charlot's productions ; he made his first appearance in London, as an actor, at the Whitney (now Strand) Theatre, Mar., 1912, in " A Member of Tattersall's " ; appeared at the Globe, June, 1913, as Dr. Carmichael in " The Gilded Pill " ; at the Prince of Wales's, May, 1918, scored a great success as Billy Bartlett in " Fair and Warmer " ; during 1919-20 toured in Canada and the United States in " Keep Her Smiling " ; at the Comedy, London, Dec., 1920, played David Mackenzie in " The Charm School " ; at the Empire, July, 1921, Babbing in " ' Some ' Detective " ; at Drury Lane, Apr., 1922, Imliff in " Decameron Nights " ; Mar., 1923, Luigi Lamberti and Florio in " Angelo " ; at the Criterion, Apr., 1923, Mr. Parker-Jennings in " Jack Straw " ; staged the production of " My Son John," Shaftesbury, 1926 ; " A Yankee at the Court of King Arthur," Daly's, 1929 ; appeared at the Duke of York's, June, 1932, in continuous " Grand Guignol " plays.
(Died 1 Jan., 1933; age 61)

MILLER, Gilbert Heron, producing manager ; b. New York City, 3 July, 1884 ; s. of Henry Miller and his wife Bijou (Heron) ; e. New York, Paris, Dresden, and Bedford County School ; m. Kathryn Bache ; formerly an actor, and in that capacity appeared at the Waldorf (now Strand) Theatre, Nov., 1906, as Freddie in " Julie Bon-Bon " ; his first managerial venture in London was his production of " Daddy Long-Legs," at the Duke of York's, May, 1916 ; at the Garrick, Oct., 1917, was associated with Charles Hawtrey in the production of " The Saving Grace " ; at the Globe, Oct., 1917, produced " The Willow Tree " ; at the Savoy, Feb., 1918, " Nothing but the Truth " ; at the Princes, Apr., 1919, Messager's romantic operette, " Monsieur Beaucaire " ; at the St. James's, in association with Henry Ainley, Sept., 1919, " Reparation " ;

Jan., 1920, " Julius Caesar " ; Mar., 1920, " Uncle Ned " ; Dec., 1920, " Peter Pan " ; under his own management, at the St. James's, produced " Daniel," Jan., 1921 ; " Polly with a Past," Mar., 1921 ; " The Bat," 1922 ; " The Green Goddess," 1923-4 ; with Sir Gerald du Maurier produced "The Last of Mrs. Cheyney," 1925 ; "Interference,"1927 ; "S.O.S.," "The Return Journey," "The Play's the Thing," 1928 ; "Fame," 1929 ; under his own management produced "Heat Wave," 1929 ; "Michael and Mary," "The Swan," 1930 ; "Payment Deferred," 1931 ; "The Vinegar Tree," "Behold, We Live," 1932 "The Late Christopher Bean," 1933 ; acquired the lease of the Lyric, 1929, where he has presented "Her Cardboard Lover," "Berkeley Square," 1929 ; "Let Us Be Gay," 1930 ; "Strange Interlude," 1931 ; "Dangerous Corner," "Another Language," 1932 ; "This Side Idolatry," "Acropolis," 1933 ; "Reunion in Vienna," "Men in White," 1934 ; "Tovarich," 1935 ; Playhouse, in conjunction with Gladys Cooper, presented "Firebird," 1932 ; Apollo, with Jack Buchanan and Ronald Squire, "Springtime for Henry," 1932 ; has since produced "Pride and Prejudice," St. James's, 1936 ; "Boy Meets Girl," Shaftesbury, 1936 ; "Yes, My Darling Daughter," St. James's, 1937 ; "Victoria Regina," Lyric, 1937 ; "Old Music," "The Silent Knight," St. James's, 1937 ; "Sixth Floor," St. James's, 1939 ; Lyric, with Jack Buchanan, "The Women," 1939 ; "Dear Ruth," 1946 ; St. James's, with Sir Laurence Olivier, "The Happy Time," 1952 ; Hippodrome, "The Caine Mutiny Court Martial," with Henry Sherek, 1956 ; Strand, "Change of Tune," 1959 ; Lyric, "Write Me a Murder" (with H. M. Tennent), 1962 ; in June, 1921, was appointed manager of Charles Frohman (Inc.) ; in New York he has presented the following productions : "Casanova," 1923 ; "The Captive," "The Constant Wife," 1926 ; "Her Cardboard Lover," "Interference," and Max Reinhardt's Company, 1927 ; "The Patriot," "The Happy Husband," "Paris," "Olympia," "The Play's the Thing," "The

Sacred Flame," "The Age of Inno- cence," 1928; "The Skyrocket," "Journey's End," "One Hundred Years Old," "The Love Duel," "Candle Light," "Berkeley Square," 1929; "Dishonored Lady," "One, Two, Three," "Marseilles," "Petticoat In- fluence," 1930; "To-morrow and To- morrow," "The Sex Fable," "The Good Fairy," 1931; "The Animal Kingdom," "There's Always Juliet," "The Late Christopher Bean," 1932; "Firebird," 1933; "The Bride of Torozko," "Ode to Liberty," 1934; "The Petrified Forest" (with Leslie Howard), "Victoria Regina," "Li- bel," 1935; "Tovarich," "The Country Wife," 1936; "The Amazing Doctor Clitterhouse," "Promise," "French Without Tears," 1937; "Once is Enough," "I Have Been Here Before," 1938; "Ladies and Gentlemen," 1939; "Geneva," "Ladies in Retirement" (with Vinton Freedley), "Delicate Story" (which he adapted from Mol- nar), 1940; "Anne of England," 1941; "Lily of the Valley," "Heart of a City," "Lifeline," "Flare Path," 1942; "Harriet," 1943; "For Keeps," "The Rich Full Life," 1945; "Anti- gone," 1946; "The Play's the Thing," "Edward, My Son," 1948; "Montserrat," 1949; "The Cocktail Party," "Ring Round the Moon," 1950; "Gigi," Sir Laurence Olivier's productions of "Caesar and Cleopatra" and "Antony and Cleopatra," 1951; "Horses in Midstream," 1953; "The Living Room," "Witness For the Prosecution," 1954; "The Reluctant Debutante," "The Sleeping Prince," 1956; "Under Milk Wood" (with Henry Sherek and Roger L. Stevens), "The Rope Dancers" (with the Play- wrights Co.), 1957; "The Broken Date" (with Jules Borkon), "Patate," 1958; "Look After Lulu" (co-produced) and "Golden Fleecing" (with Courtney Burr), 1959; "The Caretaker," 1961; "The White House," 1964; "Diamond Orchid" (with Roger L. Stevens), 1965; on 13 June, 1965, received American Theatre Wing Antoinette Perry (Tony) Award for a distinguished career in the theatre. *Favourite play:* "Tovarich." *Recreations:* Travelling and aviation. *Clubs:* Players', New York; Buck's, and Green Room, London; English Speaking Union; Royal Thames Yacht Club; Cowdray Park Polo Club. *(Died 2 Jan., 1969; age 84)*

MILLER, Henry, actor and manager; *b.* London, England, 1 Feb., 1860; *s.* of John Miller and his wife Sophia (Newton); *e.* at Cowper Street Schools, London, and at Toronto, Canada; *m.* Bijou Heron; made his first appearance on the stage, at the Grand Opera House, Toronto, in "Amy Robsart"; first appeared on the New York stage, at Booth's Theatre, 26 Apr., 1880, as Arviragus in "Cymbeline," with the late Adelaide Neilson, 27 Apr., he played the Sea Captain in "Twelfth Night," 4 May he appeared as Oliver in "As You Like It," 12 May, he played in "The Hunchback," 14 May, in "The Lady of Lyons," and 24 May he appeared as Froth in "Measure for Measure," this was Adelaide Neil- son's last appearance in New York; at the Grand Opera House, in Sept., 1880, he played in "The Soul of an Actress" and "The New Magdalen"; at Daly's, in Apr., 1882, appeared in "Odette"; at Madison Square Theatre, 9 Oct., 1882, he played Herbert Winthrop in "Young Mrs. Winthrop"; same theatre, 7 Sept., 1885, he appeared as Count Marcelin in "Anselma"; and at the Star, 15 Mar., 1886, he played the part of Sir Budleigh Woodstock in "The Jilt"; he then joined the New York Lyceum company under Daniel Froh- man, and appeared on 15 Apr., 1887, in "This Picture and That"; 1 Nov., 1887, he played Robert Gray in "The Wife," and on 4 May, 1888, he appeared in "Ernestine"; 13 Nov., 1888, he played the part of Clement Hale in "Sweet Lavender"; and then, at Madison Square, 21 Dec., 1888, he played Mark Field in "Honour Bright"; at the Lyceum, 18 Mar., 1889, he played Rodolphe de Chamery in "The Marquis"; and at the Star, 9 Sept., 1889, he played Colonel Ker- chival West in "Shenandoah"; at Proctor's, 23rd Street, 19 Apr., 1890, he appeared as Claude Melnotte in "The Lady of Lyons"; and on 8 Sept., 1890, as Alfred Hastings in

" All the Comforts of a Home " ; at the Garden Theatre, 20 Apr., 1891, he played Henri, Marquis D'Alein, in " Betrothed," and at Madison Square, 4 May, 1891, played Carroll Cotton Vanderstyle in " The Merchant " ; at Palmer's, 7 Sept., 1891, he appeared as the Earl of Leicester in " Amy Robsart," and at Hermann's, on 27 Feb., 1892, he appeared as Frederic Lemaitre in a play of that name ; same theatre, 23 Mar., 1892, was Lieutenant Jack Bandle in " Chums " ; at the Garden, 3 Apr., 1893, played Dick Wellington in " His Wedding Day," and at the Empire, New York, 21 Aug., 1893, he appeared as Mr. Owen in " Liberty Hall " ; at the Garden, in Sept., 1893, he appeared as Oscar O'Flaherty Wilde in " The Poet and the Puppets " ; he then returned to the Empire, and remained there as leading man until 1896 ; during that period he played the following parts : Paul Kirkland in " The Younger Son," Ted Morris in " The Councillor's Wife," Mr. Brabazon in " Sowing the Wind," James Ffolliott in " Gudgeons," David Remon in " The Masqueraders," Harold Wynn in " John-a-Dreams," John Worthing in " The Importance of Being Earnest," Michael Faversham in " Michael and His Lost Angel," Stephen D'Acosta in " A Woman's Reason," and Rudolph in " Bohemia " ; he made his first " star " appearance in New York at the Garden Theatre, 11 Jan., 1897, as Eric Temple in " Heartsease " ; same theatre, 15 Feb., 1898, he played Thomas Faber in " The Master " ; at the Herald Square Theatre, 16 Sept., 1899, he played Sidney Carton in " The Only Way," and at the Lyceum, 4 Feb., 1901, Richard Savage in a play of that name ; at the Savoy, New York, Dec., 1901, he played D'Arcy in " D'Arcy of the Guards " : at the same theatre, 30 Mar., 1903, appeared in " The Taming of Helen " ; later in the same year joined forces with Margaret Anglin, and played Dick Dudgeon in " The Devil's Disciple," Armand in " Camille," also in " Aftermath " (" The Ironmaster ") ; at the Hudson Theatre, New York, 14 Mar., 1904, played

Lord Wykeham in " Man Proposes," and 18 Apr., 1904, Armand Duval in " Camille " ; at San Francisco, in July and Aug., 1904, played Mark Embury in " Mice and Men," and Sir Joseph Lacy in " Joseph Entangled " ; appeared in the latter part, at the Garrick Theatre, New York, on 11 Oct., 1904 ; assumed the management of the Princess Theatre in 1906, and appeared there on 18 Jan., 1906, as James Grierson in " Grierson's Way " ; at the Majestic Theatre, 23 Apr., played the Rev. Gordon Clavering in " Zira," of which he is part author with J. Hartley Manners ; at the Majestic Theatre, Boston, 28 May, appeared as David Lowne in " Young Fernald," and at Albany, 10 Sept., as Stephen Ghent in " The Great Divide " ; he opened his autumn season at the Princess Theatre, New York, on 3 Oct., with the same play, and this ran throughout the season ; he appeared in the same play, at Daly's, New York, Aug., 1907, when the play was again enthusiastically received ; at the Van Ness Theatre, San Francisco, Aug., 1908, played the Hon. Arthur Cullen in " Mater " ; at the Century Theatre, St. Louis, Mar., 1909, played Ulrich Michaelis in " The Faith Healer " ; made his first appearance on the London stage, 15 Sept., 1909, at the Adelphi Theatre, playing Stephen Ghent in " The Great Divide," and 25 Oct., 1909, played Robert Smith in " The Servant in the House " ; returning to New York, appeared at the Savoy, 19 Jan., 1910, in " The Faith Healer " ; at the Garrick, New York, 9 May, 1910, played John Belden in " Her Husband's Wife " ; at the Bijou Theatre, 9 Jan., 1911, appeared as Richard Craig in " The Havoc " ; subsequently toured in the same play ; at San Francisco, Aug., 1911, played in " The End of the Bridge " ; at the Liberty Theatre, New York, Mar., 1912, played Neil Summer in " The Rainbow," subsequently touring in the same part ; during 1915 played Jervis Pendleton in " Daddy Long-Legs " ; at Hollis Street, Boston, Mar., 1916, played Fréderic Lemaitre in a play of that name ; at the Criterion, New York, Oct., 1917, Anthony Silvertree in

"Anthony in Wonderland"; at the Henry Miller Theatre, Apr., 1918, Gerald Place in "The Fountain of Youth"; May, 1918, the Comte de Candale in "A Marriage of Convenience"; Oct., 1918, Fergus Wimbush in "Perkins" ("The Man from Toronto"); Nov., 1918, Jervis Pendleton in "Daddy Long-Legs". at the Liberty Theatre, Mar., 1919, appeared as Molière in a play of that name; at the Henry Miller Theatre, Dec., 1919, Jeffrey Fair in "The Famous Mrs. Fair"; at the Empire, New York, Sept., 1922, played Paul Barnac in "La Tendresse"; Mar., 1923, Louis Pasteur in "Pasteur"; at the Henry Miller Theatre, Sept., 1923, Wallace Aldcroft in "The Changelings"; Dec., 1924, Count de Laussange in "The Man in Evening Clothes"; is the proprietor of the Henry Miller Theatre; also controls several "stars" and touring companies. *(Died 9 Apr., 1926; age 66)*

MILLER, Hugh (Lorimer), actor and director; *b.* Berwick-on-Tweed, Northumberland, 22 May, 1889; *s.* of Alexander Lorimer Miller and his wife Jane Hartforth (Short); *e.* Berwick Grammar School, and Armstrong College, Durham University; *m.* Olga Katzin; formerly engaged as an engineer; made his first appearance on the stage at the Theatre Royal, Glasgow, 1911, walking on in "The Prisoner of Zenda"; made his first appearance in London, at the Shaftesbury Theatre (for the Phoenix Society), 19 Mar., 1922, as Dollabella in "All for Love"; Wyndham's, Oct., 1925, played the Mulatto in "Doctor Syn"; went to America in 1925, and at Chicago, Apr., 1926, played Rabbi Azrael in "The Dybbuk"; made his first appearance in New York, at the Empire, 5 Sept., 1927, as Alfred Jingle in "Pickwick"; Broadhurst, Jan., 1928, played Gratiano in "The Merchant of Venice"; Garrick, Oct., 1928, Master Crummles in "When Crummles Played"; Forrest, Feb., 1929, Martin and Robert Condell in "Whispering Gallery"; Assembly, Oct.–Dec., 1929, Daniel Gaylord in "Lolly," and Lucio in "The Novice and the Duke" ("Measure for Mea-

sure"); Belmont, Mar., 1930, Stanislaus in "Mayfair"; Ethel Barrymore, Oct., 1930, Peter in "His Majesty's Car"; Charles Hopkins, Mar., 1931, John Reader in "Give Me Yesterday"; Stockbridge, Mass., Aug., 1931, Prince Myshkin in "The Idiot"; subsequently toured as Boffi in "As You Desire Me"; 46th Street, New York, Mar., 1932, played Ivan Tarnoff in "Marching By"; New Amsterdam, Nov., 1932, Judas Iscariot in "The Dark Hours"; returned to England, 1933, and joined the Birmingham Repertory Company, Sept., 1933; reappeared in London, at the Ambassadors', Nov., 1933, as The Lawyer in "Cabbages and Kings," which he also directed; at the Piccadilly, Apr., 1934, George Simon in "Counsellor-at-Law"; Daly's, Dec., 1934, played Garrett Fielding in "The Moon is Red"; Embassy and Prince's, Mar., 1935, Subtle in "The Alchemist"; Croydon, May, 1935, the Abbé in "The Abbé Prévost"; Criterion, Sept., 1935, Schimmelmann in "Nina"; Garrick, Mar., 1936, succeeded Leslie Banks, as Geoffrey Carroll in "The Two Mrs. Carrolls"; New, Sept., 1936, Georgio Selvi in "Girl Unknown"; Malvern Festival, 1937, the Egyptian Doctor in "The Millionairess"; Apollo, Mar., 1938, Achille Weber in "Idiot's Delight"; Westminster, Feb., 1939, Cutler Walpole in "The Doctor's Dilemma"; Torch, 1939, directed "The Venetian," and 1940, "The House of Women"; Garrick, May, 1940, played Laeken in "By Pigeon Post"; Neighbourhood, Aug., 1940, Baron Lennox in "Take Back Your Freedom"; Strand, May, 1942, Jack Favell in "Rebecca"; Piccadilly, Oct., 1942, Oscar Hubbard in "The Little Foxes"; Prince of Wales's, Apr., 1944, M. de Mean in "The Rest is Silence"; Hippodrome, Oct., 1944, directed "Jenny Jones"; Granville, Walham Green, from May, 1945, appeared in a season of Grand Guignol; Adelphi, June, 1945, played M. de Vigny in "Sweet Yesterday"; New Lindsey, Apr., 1947, appeared as Lord Firth in "The 49th State"; Prince's, Oct., 1947, directed "The Dubarry"; St. Martin's, Mar., 1948, played Mr. Prince in "Rocket to the Moon"; Covent Garden, July, 1948, appeared as Lord Hate-Good in "The Pilgrim's Progress"; Booth Theatre, New York, Dec., 1948, played Baron de Characnay in "Don't Listen, Ladies"; Arts, London, Sept., 1950, Count Mario Grazia in "The Mask and the Face"; Dec., 1950, the Honourable Reader in "Lady Precious Stream"; Embassy, May, 1951, played David Cole in "Café Crown"; Arts, May, 1952, Mr. Voysey in "The Voysey Inheritance"; at Westminster Abbey, June, 1953, he directed "Out of the Whirlwind"; Arts, Feb., 1954, directed "The Private Secretary"; Scala, Dec., 1956, directed "Peter Pan," and subsequently at the same theatre, Dec., 1957; in 1925, was associated with the Hon. Ivor Montagu in founding the Film Society in London; in 1932, gave a series of Dickens Recitals at American Colleges, and at Columbia and Harvard Universities; commenced film career, 1931, and has played in numerous pictures; dialogue director for "Dr. Zhivago," 1965. *Club:* Savage. *Address:* 29 Brookfield, Highgate West Hill, London, N.6. *Telephone No.:* Mountview 2316.

MILLER, Marilynn, actress and dancer; *b.* Findlay, Ohio, U.S.A., 1898; *m.* Jack Pickford; has been on the stage since early childhood, having made her first appearance, with her parents, 20 Aug., 1903, at Lakeside Park, Dayton, Ohio, as one of "The Columbian Trio"; subsequently formed one of "The Five Columbians," and for some time appeared in "A Bit of Dresden China" for ten years she toured all over the world, and it was while appearing at the Lotus Club, London, in 1913, that she was seen by Lee Shubert, who immediately engaged her for the Winter Garden, New York; she made her first appearance there 10 June, 1914, as Miss Jerry in "The Passing Show of 1914"; she also appeared there, May, 1915, in "The Passing Show of 1915"; Oct., 1916, in "The Show of Wonders"; Apr., 1917, in "The Passing Show of 1917"; at the Astor, Apr., 1918, played Betty Pestlethwaite in "Fancy Free"; at the New Amsterdam, June, 1918,

appeared in "The Ziegfeld Follies of 1918"; same theatre, Dec., 1920, appeared as Sally in the musical play of that name; continued in that piece until 1923; at the Knickerbocker Theatre, Nov., 1924, played Peter Pan in the play of that name; New Amsterdam, Sept., 1925, "Sunny" Peters in "Sunny," in which she continued 1926-7; Jan., 1928, Princess Rosalie in "Rosalie."

(Died 7 Apr., 1936; age 37)

MILLER, Martin (Rudolf), actor; *b.* Kremsier, Czechoslovakia, 2 Sept., 1899; *s.* of Heinrich Muller and his wife Regina (Kulka); *e.* Vienna and Prague; *m.* Hannah Norbert; studied for the stage under Robin Robert; made his first appearance on the stage at the Raimund Theater, Vienna, 2 Sept., 1921, as Hippler in "Florian Geyer"; he remained in Vienna for two years; subsequently fulfilled engagements at Lodz, Poland, one year; Reichenberg, five seasons; Aussig, two seasons; Ostrau, two seasons; Strassbourg, one season, and then, 1936, returned to Vienna until 1938; he then filled an engagement at the Berlin Jewish Culture Theater, until Mar., 1939; he then came to London, where he founded the Little Viennese Theatre, June, 1939; made his first appearance on the London stage, at the Arts Theatre, 20 May, 1942, as Jacob in "Awake and Sing," and played the same part at the Cambridge, Aug., 1942; Strand, Dec., 1942, played Dr. Einstein in "Arsenic and Old Lace," which ran over three years; "Q," Apr., 1947, appeared as Herr Doktor Johann Hubermann in "Mountain Air," and played the same part at the Comedy, Jan., 1948; Wyndham's, Mar., 1949, George in "Daphne Laureola"; Winter Garden, Apr., 1950, the Inspector and Block in "The Trial"; made his first appearance on the New York stage at the Music Box, 18 Sept., 1950, when he again play George in "Daphne Laureola"; St. James's, Feb., 1951, appeared as the Prospector in "The Madwoman of Chaillot"; Palace, Manchester, Apr., 1951, played Papa Birka in "Collector's Item"; Embassy, Nov., 1951, Mr. Emmanuel in "Magnolia Street Story," and Dec., 1951, Melchior Stack in "The Merchant of Yonkers"; same theatre, Mar., 1952, David Gold in "Stately Homes"; Vaudeville, May, 1952, Hans Klein in "Sweet Madness"; Ambassadors', Nov., 1952, played Mr. Paravinci in "The Mousetrap," and appeared in this part for 1000 performances of the play's record-breaking run; Arts, May, 1956, played Dr. Czernik in "Off the Mainland"; New, Oxford, Sept., 1956, Cristos Papadiamantis in "The Gates of Summer"; Phoenix, Apr., 1957, Baron de Charlus in "Camino Real"; Royal Court, June, 1957, William the Pope in "The Making of Moo"; at the same theatre, July, 1957, the Director in "The Apollo de Bellac"; Edinburgh Festival, Aug., 1957, played Demidoff in "Nekrassov," appearing in the same part at the Royal Court, Sept., 1957; Saville, Jan., 1958, Sir Joseph Vandenhoven in "A Touch of the Sun"; Piccadilly, Oct., 1958, Matias Rakosi in "Shadow of Heroes"; New, July, 1959, Maxwell Archer in "Once More, With Feeling"; New, Dec., 1959, played Maurice Wendl in "Make Me an Offer"; Edinburgh Festival, Sept., 1960, Jason in "The Dream of Peter Mann"; Comedy, Apr., 1961, played Alper in "The Tenth Man"; Glasgow, Citizens, Apr., 1963, Goldberg in "The Birthday Party"; at the Theater am Dom, Cologne, Oct., 1964, played Sam Old in "Photo Finish" (in German); Vaudeville, Feb., 1966, played his original part of Dr. Einstein in "Arsenic and Old Lace"; directed plays in Europe from 1928; appeared in European films, and in London, 1942, in "Squadron Leader X." *Favourite parts:* Shylock and Caliban. *(Died 25 Aug., 1969; age 69)*

MILLER, Ruby, actress; *b.* London, 14 July, 1889; *d.* of Arthur Miller and his wife Augustine (Leon); *e.* London and at Convent in Amiens; *m.* (1) Lieut. Philip Samson (d. 1918); (2) Max Darewski (d. 1929); was a pupil at the Academy of Dramatic Art; made her first appearance on the stage at His Majesty's Theatre, 25 Jan., 1906, as a dancer in " Nero "; she remained at His Majesty's throughout 1906-7, dancing, understudying, and appearing

in various Shakespearean plays; accompanied Sir Herbert Tree on his tour to Berlin, Apr., 1907; at the Lyceum, Aug., 1907, played Betty Belmont in " The Christian "; she then toured in the leading parts in " Miss Elizabeth's Prisoner," " The Eternal City," etc.; at Wyndham's, 1909, understudied May Blayney in " The Little Damozel "; at Wyndham's, Jan., 1910, played Miss Williams in " The Parents' Progress "; she was next engaged as understudy at the St. James's; at the Criterion, Sept., 1911, played Violet Robinson in " Man and Superman "; appeared at the Court, Feb., 1912, as Jashodhara in " Buddha "; at the Tivoli Music Hall, Aug., 1912, played the Woman in " A Woman Intervenes "; Nov., 1912, Phyllis Grey in " Between Five and Seven "; and Jan., 1913, Phyllis Meriton in " The Wrong House," and toured with these pieces in leading music halls for some time; at the Criterion, May, 1913, appeared as Claudine in " Oh ! I say ! "; Oct., 1915, Maimie Scott in " A Little Bit of Fluff "; at the Comedy, Dec., 1916, played in " See-Saw "; at the Duke of York's, July, 1917, played Kitty in " What a Catch ! "; at the Gaiety, May, 1918, Miss Zonne in " Going Up "; subsequently appeared in various cinema plays; during 1921 appeared on tour in " The Edge o' Beyond," in which she had previously appeared in a cinema version; in Aug., 1921, entered on the management of the Garrick Theatre, producing " The Edge o' Beyond," in which she appeared as Dinah, and which she had adapted (with Roy Horniman) from the novel; at Golder's Green, July, 1925, played Julia Price in " The Ghost Train "; Strand, Oct., 1926, succeeded to the part of Norma Lythe in " The Whole Town's Talking "; Strand, Apr., 1928, succeeded Jane Welsh as Julie Cartier in " The Monster"; Savoy, Aug., 1931, played Desirée Le Fre in " Midnight Love"; Kingsway, May, 1932, Lady Diana Wyncott in " The Cheque-Mate"; Aldwych, July, 1934, Mary Lister in "That Certain Something"; Playhouse, Apr., 1936, Lady Schofield in "The Shadow"; Saville, Feb., 1939,

Diamond Dolly in "Worth a Million"; "Q," Nov., 1943, Carmen Del Monte in "Three Wives called Roland"; Arts Theatre, Cambridge, Apr., 1945, and "Q," June, 1946, Madam Barrymore in "Through the Door"; part-author (with Evadne Price) of the play "Big Ben," 1939; published her reminiscences, "Believe Me or Not!" 1934; commenced film career, 1933, and has appeared in several pictures. *Recreations*: Horse-riding swimming, travelling, reading, and music.

MILLETT, Maude, actress; *b.* Rajunpûr, India, 8 Nov., 1867; *d.* of late Colonel Hugh Ley Millett; *m.* Captain Henry Lancelot Tennant; made her first appearance on the stage, at the Novelty Theatre, 6 Mar., 1884, as Ruby in "The Barringtons," after which she was engaged by Charles Hawtrey for the Globe Theatre, where she appeared in May, as Eva Webster in "The Private Secretary"; at the Gaiety, in Aug., she played Herminie in "The Little Viscount"; at the Novelty, in Nov., played Maud Walsingherd in "Homespun"; at the Gaiety, Dec., played Anna Maria Poppytop in "The Wedding March," and Miss Vandelen in "Ethel's Test"; in Oct., 1886, she went to the Vaudeville Theatre, and played Fanny Walsingham in "Cupid's Messenger"; she appeared there also as Grace Wentworth in "Plebeians," as Violet in "Confusion," as Eveline Doo in "Doo, Brown & Co.," Ada Baltic in "Turned Up," Molly Seagrim in "Sophia," etc.; she also appeared at the Gaiety, 1886, with Kate Vaughan, as Isabinda in "The Busybody" and Julia in "The Rivals"; played at Comedy, 1886, in "Turned Up"; in 1887, she toured as Sophia in the play of that name, and as Gladys Farwell in "Hans the Boatman"; in Sept., 1887, at the Vaudeville, appeared as Sophia; at Terry's, Nov., 1887, she played Hester Lorrington in "The Favourite of Fortune"; at the Criterion, in Dec., made a hit when she played Ida in "Two Roses"; at the Vaudeville, played Lola Nepean in "Proposals," and at

the Criterion, made another success as Leonie Lamarque in "Wyllard's Weird"; in Mar., 1888, she appeared at Terry's, as Minnie Gillfillian in "Sweet Lavender"; at the Shaftesbury, Aug., 1889, played Mary Blenkarn in "The Middleman"; she was then seen at the Comedy, June, 1890, as Violet Armitage in "Nerves"; joined George Alexander at the Avenue, Nov., 1890, and played Maud in "Sunlight and Shadow"; accompanied him to the St. James's, and Feb., 1891, played Kate Merryweather in "The Idler"; at the Avenue, Nov., 1891, she succeeded Winifred Emery as Cynthia Greenslade in "The Crusaders"; at the Globe, Feb., 1892, played Sybil Bellairs in "A Bohemian"; in the same year, toured with Fred Kerr in "The Fancy Fair," "Leap Year," and "Our Greek Play"; returned to the St. James's, Dec., 1892, to play Blanche Ferraby in "Liberty Hall"; in May, 1893, played Ellean in "The Second Mrs. Tanqueray"; at the Haymarket, Jan., 1895, played Mabel Chiltern in "An Ideal Husband"; at the Criterion, May, 1895, appeared as Esmé Brammerton in "The Home Secretary"; at the Shaftesbury, Dec., 1895, as Agatha Pretious in "A Woman's Reason"; at Terry's, 1896, she played Dora Hedway in "Jedbury, Junior," and the Hon. Constance Crawley in "The Sunbury Scandal"; at the Strand, 1896, appeared as the Hon. Mrs. Miles in "Teddy's Wives"; she then quitted the stage temporarily, on the occasion of her marriage, but re-appeared, at Terry's, Feb., 1899, in a revival of "Sweet Lavender"; she was next seen at the Criterion, Apr., 1899, as Hyacinth Woodward in "The Tyranny of Tears"; played the same part at Wyndham's, Jan., 1902; made a popular re-appearance at the Apollo, Oct., 1907, when she played Lucy Middleton in "The Education of Elizabeth"; appeared during 1908, at several music halls, as Lady Peggy in "The Toast of the Town"; at the Criterion, Nov., 1908, played Celia White in "The Builders"; at the Court, Feb., 1909, played the Hon. Margaret Dallison in "Strangers Within the Gates"; Aug., 1909, toured as Mrs. Cameron in "The Flag Lieutenant," and played the same part at the Playhouse, Nov., 1909; her next appearance was at Wyndham's, Sept., 1911, when she played Agatha Margell in "The Perplexed Husband"; at the Little Theatre, Apr., 1913, played Lady Chislehurst in "The Cap and Bells"; and at the Apollo, June, 1913, Miss Scandrett in "The Perfect Cure." *Recreation:* Golf. *(Died 16 Feb., 1920; age 52)*

MILLICAN, Jane, actress; *b.* New York City, U.S.A., 3 Nov., 1902; *d.* of Dr. Kenneth William Millican and his wife Bertha Camille (Müeller); *e.* St. Paul's Girls' School, London; *m.* E. P. Clift; studied for the stage at the Royal Academy of Dramatic Art and with Kate Rorke and Kate Emil Behnke; made her first appearance on the stage in 1922, at the New Theatre, Cardiff, as Mabel in "Loyalties," with Dee Cee Tours; under the same management she remained on tour until 1924, playing Monica in "Lilies of the Field," 1923, Kitty in the same play, 1924; Lady Sybil in "What Every Woman Knows," and Mavis in "The Fake," 1924; made her first appearance in London, at the Globe theatre, June, 1925 (as understudy to Edna Best), in the part of Jane Banbury in "Fallen Angels"; at the St. Martin's, Oct., 1927, played the Maid in "Berkeley Square," also understudying; Mar., 1927, Mabel in "No Gentleman"; Sept., 1927, the Maid in "The Silver Cord," and subsequently played Christine, as understudy for Clare Eames; May, 1928, Rivers in "Four People"; New, June, 1928, Grace in "Spread Eagle"; she next played a season as leading lady in the London Repertory company, at the Regent Theatre; Arts, Feb., 1929, played Mrs. Kemp in "The Likes of 'Er"; in the same year, toured as Laura Simmons in "Young Woodley"; St. Martin's, Feb., 1930, scored a success when she played Kate Frost in "Honours Easy"; June, 1930, played the Countess of Darnaway in "Petticoat Influence," and in Dec., 1930, played Peggy Chalfont in the same piece; New, Jan., 1931, Laura

Wadham in "To Account Rendered"; St. Martin's, Apr., 1931, Lucia Amory in "Black Coffee"; Aug., 1931, Cicely in "The Young Idea"; Dec., 1931, Lady Duncaster in "The Nelson Touch"; in May, 1932, joined the Masque Theatre company, Edinburgh, and played Eve Redman in "To-Morrow and To-Morrow"; at the Lyceum, Edinburgh, Aug., 1932, played lead in a round of modern plays, including "The Painted Veil," "The Queen Was In The Parlour," "The High Road," etc.; at the same theatre, Oct., 1932, played Sybil Livingstone in "Double Harness"; St. Martin's, Mar., 1933 (for R.A.D.A. Players), Eve Redman in "To-Morrow and To-Morrow"; Fulham, May, 1934, Nell in "Forsaking All Others"; toured, 1936, as Belinda Warren in "Sweet Aloes"; Richmond, Apr., 1938, played Mary Jarrow in "Quiet Wedding"; Apollo, Oct., 1938, Dr. Smith in "Tree of Eden"; Richmond, Jan., 1940, Geraldine Strachan in "First Night"; has also appeared in films. *Favourite part:* Laura in "Young Woodley." *Recreations:* Riding, reading, and motoring. *Address:* 24 Smith Street, Chelsea, London, S.W.3. *Telephone No.:* Flaxman 4683.

MILLIET, Paul, French dramatic author, librettist, journalist, and historian; *b.* Rio de Janeiro, Brazil, 24 June, 1858; *e.* College Sainte-Barbe; *m.* Mdme. Adiny; has written the following plays and operas: "Esmeralda" (music by Goring Thomas), "Heriodate" (music by Massenet), "Kerim" (with Henri Lavedan, music by Alfred Bruneau); "Nadia" (music by Borlier), 1887; "Werther" (with Blau and Hartmann; music by Massenet), 1893; "Le Duc de Ferrare" (music by Georges Marty), 1899; "Martin et Martine" (music by Trépard), 1900; "Rhéa" (music by Spiro Samara), 1910; "La Découverte du Docteur Mallory"; "La Vie Crève" (music by De Falla); "Madame Sans-Gêne" (music by Giordano); "Forfaiture" (with André de Lorde, music by Camille Erlanger); "L'Ombre de la Croix" (with Jerome and Jean Tharaud), etc.; has also adapted to the French stage " André Chenier," " Siberia," " L'Ami Fritz," " Méphistophelès," " Adrienne Lecouvreur," " Le Roi d'Argent," " Chopin," " Cavalleria Rusticana " (from the Italian), " Electra " (from the Spanish), and " La Fille Prodigue " (" The Prodigal Daughter "), from the English ; is also the author of many historical and biographical works ; is a Chevalier of the Legion of Honour, Officer of Public Instruction, Commander of the Order of Charles III (of Spain), and is director of *Le Monde artiste illustré* ; Vice-President of the Society of Dramatic Authors and Composers. *Address :* 2 Rue Saint Didier, Paris.

MILLS, A. J., author and lyrist ; *b.* Richmond, Surrey, 24 Nov., 1872 ; *s.* of John William Mills and his wife Marie (Yorke) ; *e.* Richmond Grammar School ; was for some time engaged as an entertainer ; has written many hundreds of songs, some of which have achieved enormous success ; among them may be mentioned " By the side of the Zuyder Zee " ; " All the nice girls love a sailor " ; " Just like the Ivy " ; " Wonderful Rose of Love " ; " I wonder if you miss me sometimes " ; " My heart is with you to-night " ; " When love creeps in your heart " ; " Fall in and follow me," etc. ; mostly writes in collaboration with Bennett Scott ; is a director of the Star Music Publishing Co., Ltd. *Recreations :* Motoring, fishing, and golf. *Address :* 51 High Street, New Oxford Street, W.C. *Telephone No. :* Gerrard 8446. *Telegraphic Address :* " Songonia," London.

MILLS, Mrs. Clifford, dramatic author ; has written " Where the Rainbow Ends " (with Reginald Owen), 1911 ; " The Basker," 1916 ; " The Luck of the Navy," 1918 ; " In Nelson's Days," 1922 ; " The Man from Hong-Kong," 1925. *(Died 2 July, 1933; age 70)*

MILLS, Florence, actress and vocalist ; *b.* 1901 ; made her first appearance on the stage at the age of four ; appeared at the Vanderbilt Theatre, New York, 18 Nov., 1919, as Mrs.

Marshall in " Irene " ; at the Sixty-third Street Music Hall, during 1921, made a success, when she played in " Shuffle Along " ; at the Forty-eighth Street Theatre, July, 1922, scored a great success when she played in " The Plantation Revue " ; made her first appearance in London, at the London Pavilion, 31 May, 1923, in " Dover Street to Dixie," which included the Plantation revue ; at the Greenwich Village Theatre, New York, Sept., 1923, played in " The Greenwich Village Follies " ; at the Broadhurst Theatre, Oct., 1924, in " Dixie to Broadway."

MILLS, Frank (Frank Ransom), actor ; *b.* Kendal, Michigan, 1870 ; *s.* of Ephraim and Helen Ransom ; *e.* Kalamazoo, Mich. ; *m.* Helen Macbeth ; made his first appearance on the stage in 1888 ; in 1890, appeared in William Gillette's play " Held by the Enemy," subsequently playing a long " stock " engagement at San Francisco ; in 1892, played in " Men and Women " under the management of Charles Frohman ; in 1893, with the late Mrs. John Drew, played Captain Absolute in " The Rivals," Harry Dornton in " The Road to Ruin," etc. ; next played in " Poor Girls," and subsequently toured as Ned Annesley in " Sowing the Wind " ; joined Mrs. Fiske in 1895 ; appeared with her at the Garden Theatre, New York, Mar., 1896, playing Pierre in " Marie Deloche," Dr. Rank in " A Doll's House," and Cantagnac in " Cesarine " ; next joined the Lyceum company, New York, under Daniel Frohman, appearing there in 1896-8, as Geoffrey Moray and Jack Dane in " The Courtship of Leonie," Gerald in " The Wife of Willoughby," Lord Carisbrook in " The First Gentleman of Europe," the Hon. Charles Denstroude in " The Princess and the Butterfly," and Brian Hollingsworth in " The Tree of Knowledge," also in " The Late Mr. Castello," " The Mayflower," " The Prisoner of Zenda," and " Dangerfield '95 " ; made his first appearance on the London stage, at the Adelphi, 9 Apr., 1898, as Captain Alan Kendrick in " The Heart of

Maryland"; at the Garrick, June, 1898, played Jim Wynd in " Sue "; was then engaged by Beerbohm Tree at Her Majesty's Theatre, and in Nov., 1898, he appeared there as Athos in " The Musketeers "; in Apr., 1899, played in " Carnac Sahib "; next appeared at the Prince of Wales's, Sept. to Oct., 1899, in " The Moonlight Blossom," and " The Sacrament of Judas "; at the Royalty, Feb., 1900, played Von Keller in " Magda "; in June, 1900, played Golaud in " Pelléas and Mélisande "; Dec., 1900, played Lord George Hell in " The Happy Hypocrite "; at the Comedy, Apr., 1901, appeared as Captain Valeski in " Count Tezma," and May, 1901, as the Count of Kervern in " The Sacrament of Judas "; returned to New York, and at the Victoria Theatre, Nov., 1901, played Mr. Croyden in " The Way of the World "; at the Garrick, London, July, 1903, played Monsignor Campden in " The Bishop's Move "; and Captain Hugh Austin in " The Soothing System "; in Sept., 1903, appeared as Randolph Carlingby in " The Golden Silence "; in Dec., 1903, played Edward in " The Cricket on the Hearth "; in Feb., 1904, played Vagret in " The Arm of the Law "; at the Duke of York's, June, 1904, appeared as Bayonki Ferenz in " The Edge of the Storm "; at the Coronet, Sept., 1904, played Neuville in " Marguerite "; returning to New York, appeared at the New Amsterdam Theatre, Dec., 1904, as Lancelot in " Merely Mary Ann "; played Lord Cardew in " The Perfect Lover," at Imperial, Oct., 1905 ; went to America as leading man with Olga Nethersole, 1906, and again in 1907-8, playing in " The Awakening," " Adrienne Lecouvreur," " I Pagliacci," " The Enigma," etc.; subsequently appeared in " vaudeville," in " The Submarine "; at the Savoy, New York, Nov., 1908, played Valbrand in " The Winterfeast "; during 1908-9, toured as Robert Smith in " The Servant in the House "; at the Savoy, New York, Jan., 1910, played Richard Sidney in " The Heights "; at the Comedy, New York, Mar., 1910, appeared as Malcolm Gaskell in " A Man's World "; subsequently toured

in " Ambition," " Shadows," and " A Fool there Was "; at Atlantic City, July, 1911, played Richard Grayson in " The Real Thing," playing the same part at Maxine Elliott's Theatre, Aug., 1911 ; at Concord, R.H., Feb., 1912, played in " The Night to be Happy "; at St. Louis, Apr., 1912, appeared as Dr. Eric McKay in " The Glass House "; in Sept., 1912, went on tour, playing Robert Stafford in " Bought and Paid For "; during 1913-4, toured in the same part ; at the Longacre Theatre, New York, Nov., 1914, played Warren Grieves in " What It Means to a Woman "; at the Columbia, Washington, D.C., Feb., 1915, appeared in " A Girl of To-Day." *Recreations :* Tennis, golf, collecting old furniture. *Clubs :* Lambs', New York ; Players', New York ; Green Room, Leicester Square, W.C.

(Died 12 June, 1921; age 51)

MILLS, Horace, actor and dramatic author ; *b.* Portsmouth, 1 Sept., 1864 ; *s.* of Colonel H. J. Mills, C.B. ; *e.* private school at Halifax, Nova Scotia ; *m.* Jessie Julia Raynes ; was engaged in the offices of the Guardian Assurance Company for a few years, and had had some experience as an amateur prior to making his first appearance on the London stage, at the Gaiety, 4 Oct., 1890, as Remendado in " Carmen Up-to-Data " ; subsequently toured as Lord Arthur Pomeroy in " A Pantomime Rehearsal," and with Cissy Grahame ; appeared at the Criterion, 1895, as Mr. Beaver in " All Abroad " ; Prince of Wales's, 1896, Sergeant Struggles in " On the March " ; then toured under George Edwardes' management as Biggs in " The Circus Girl," 1897 ; Heliodorus in " A Greek Slave," 1898 ; Li in " San Toy," 1899-1900 ; appeared at Wyndham's, 1906, as Adolphus Dudd in " The Girl behind the Counter " ; at the Globe Theatre, 1908, as Buckle in " The Hon'ble Phil " ; at the Queen's, 1909, Swaak in " The Persian Princess " ; in 1912-13 toured as Brissard in " The Count of Luxembourg " ; at the London Opera House,

May, 1916, played Cupid in "The Miller's Daughters"; in Aug., 1916, toured as Walter in "The Happy Day"; played the part of Mrs. Tutt in the pantomime "Goody Two-Shoes," at Leeds, 1914; Manchester, 1915; Bristol, 1916; Leeds, 1917; Manchester, 1918; during 1920 toured as Mrs. Lillywhite in "Any Lady"; at Christmas, 1920, played in "Mother Goose" at the Theatre Royal, Birmingham; during 1923–4 toured as Christian Veit in "Lilac Time"; was part-author with the late Fred Leslie of "Miss Esmeralda," 1887; and of several one-act plays, and pantomimes in which he has played at Manchester, Bristol, Birmingham, Liverpool, Glasgow, etc. *Recreations :* Cricket, golf, tennis, and riding. *Hobby :* Gardening. *Clubs :* Green Room, Thespid C.C., and the George Edwardes Golfing Society.

(Died 14 Aug., 1941; age 76)

MILLWARD, Jessie, actress; *b.* 14 July, 1861; *d.* of Charles Millward, well known in the 'sixties and 'seventies of the last century as a successful writer of many pantomimes; *m.* John Glendinning; she acted as an amateur with the Carlton Amateur Dramatic Club, and made her first appearance on the professional stage at the Folly Theatre (subsequently Toole's), in July, 1881, as Constance in "The Love Chase"; she next went on tour with the St. James's company, and at Manchester, 7 Sept., 1881, appeared as Mrs. Mildmay in "Still Waters Run Deep"; subsequently played at the same theatre Mabel Meryon in "Coralie"; at the St. James's, 27 Oct., 1881, she played the part of Mary Preston in "The Cape Mail," this being her first original part; at the same theatre, 29 Dec., 1881, she played the part of Florence in "Cousin Dick"; and on 17 May, 1882, appeared as Mary Sullivan in "A Quiet Rubber"; in June, 1882, she went on tour with Miss Geneviève Ward, playing Alice Verney in "Forget-Me-Not," in which she made a big hit; on the strength of this success was engaged by the late Sir Henry Irving at the Lyceum, and on 11 Oct.,

1882, she appeared there as Hero in "Much Ado About Nothing"; at the Lyceum she also played the following parts: Julie Lesurques in "The Lyons Mail," Annette in "The Bells," Jessica in "The Merchant of Venice," Lady Dolly Touchwood in "The Belle's Stratagem," and Marie in "Louis XI"; she then accompanied the Lyceum company to America, where, in addition to the foregoing, she also played Lady Anne in "King Richard III"; on the conclusion of her engagement with Sir Henry Irving she appeared at Stetson's Fifth Avenue Theatre, New York, 1 Sept., 1884, as Pauline in "Called Back," subsequently touring in the same part; at Madison Square Theatre, 13 Apr., 1885, she appeared as Katherine Ray in "Sealed Instructions," and subsequently appeared as Ada in the same play; she then returned to London, and appeared at the Adelphi, on 19 Sept., 1885, succeeding Cissy Grahame as Fanny Power in "Arrah-Na-Pogue"; on 24 Oct. played Anne Chute in "The Colleen Bawn"; 23 Dec., 1885, appeared as Dora Vane in "The Harbour Lights," at the Adelphi, which was the first of the series of popular melodramas at that house, in which she appeared with the late William Terriss; at the Vaudeville Theatre, 30 June, 1886, she played Hazel Kirke in the play of that name; at the Adelphi she played in "The Bells of Haslemere," "The Union Jack," "The Silver Falls," and "The Shaughraun"; in 1889 accompanied Terriss to America on a joint starring tour, appearing at Niblo's Garden, 8 Oct., 1889, as Julie de Noirville in "Roger La Honte" ("A Man's Shadow"), and 6 Nov., 1889, as Pauline in "The Lady of Lyons"; she also played in "Ingomar," "Frou-Frou," "Othello," and "The Marble Heart"; she reappeared in England at the Grand Theatre, Islington, 5 Apr., 1890, as Dora in "The Harbour Lights"; at Drury Lane, 12 May, 1890, she played Diane de Beaumont in "Paul Kauvar"; 6 Sept., 1890, Mary Maythorne in "A Million of Money"; at the Avenue, 7 Feb., 1891, she played Mercédès in "Monte Cristo"; and at the Vaudeville, 18 Mar., 1891, appeared as Miss Young in " Diamond Deane " ; returning to Drury Lane, in Apr., she played Susan Merton in " It's Never Too Late to Mend " ; in May she appeared as Jenny Boker in " Formosa " ; and in June as Gervaise in " Drink " ; in Sept., she was again at Drury Lane, playing Marie Delaunay in " A Sailor's Knot " ; and in May, 1892, she returned to the Lyceum to play Julie de Mortemar in " Richelieu " ; she next toured with William Terriss in costume recitals of " Romeo and Juliet," " The Lady of Lyons," " The Hunchback," and " The Taming of the Shrew " ; at Drury Lane, Sept., 1892, she played the part of Rose Woodmere in " The Prodigal Daughter " ; and at the Lyceum, 22 Apr., 1893, appeared as Jeannette in " The Lyons Mail " ; at the Grand, Islington, 5 June, 1893, she played Alma Dunbar in " For England " ; returned to the Lyceum in June, and played Queen Eleanor in " Becket " ; and in Sept. accompanied Sir Henry Irving and company to the United States ; on her return she appeared at the Lyceum, 5 May, 1894, as Margaret in " Faust " ; in Sept., 1894, she returned, with William Terriss, to the Adelphi, and continued to play there until the tragic death of that popular actor ; she appeared there in the following plays : " The Fatal Card," " The Girl I Left Behind Me," " The Swordsman's Daughter," " One of the Best," " Boys Together," " Black Eyed Susan," " Secret Service," and " In the Days of the Duke " ; in 1898 she went to America, and appeared at the Empire under Charles Frohman ; on 26 Dec., 1898, she appeared as Euphrosine in " Phroso " ; and subsequently appeared as Lady Algernon Chetland in " Lord and Lady Algy," Stella de Gex in " His Excellency the Governor," Lady Doura in " My Lady's Lord," Eleanor Ainslie in " A Man and His Wife," Lady Eastney in " Mrs. Dane's Defence," and the Comtesse Zicka in " Diplomacy " ; at the Garrick, New York, 15 Sept., 1902, she played the Comtesse D'Autreval in " There's Many a Slip," and at the Savoy, 30 Mar., 1903, appeared as Helen in

" The Taming of Helen " ; at Madison Square, 3 Nov., 1903, played Mrs. Tracy Auberton in " A Clean Slate " ; at the Princess, 14 Mar., 1904, Beatrice in " Much Ado About Nothing " ; and at Proctor's, 23 May, 1904, in " A Queen's Messenger" ; she reappeared in London, after nearly nine years' absence, at the Scala Theatre (which she leased for a time), on 10 Mar., 1906, as Lady Manners in " A School for Husbands " ; after a short tour with the same play she again returned to America, and at the Hudson Theatre, 30 Aug., 1906, she played the part of Mrs. Wilmore in " The Hypocrites " ; during 1907, she toured in the same play ; at the Hudson Theatre, Nov., 1908, played Lady Mereston in " Lady Frederick " ; at the Court Theatre, Chicago, Jan., 1910, played Clara Stewart in " The Girl in the Taxi," appearing in the same part at the Astor Theatre, New York, Oct., 1910 ; during 1911 played in various music halls in " As a Man Sows" ; and during 1912 in " Reaping the Whirlwind " ; reappeared in London, at the Chelsea Palace, 10 Feb., 1913, when she played Kate Kerrigan in " In the Grey of the Dawn " ; subsequently toured in a playlet, " The Laird and the Lady " ; at Brixton Theatre, 3 Aug., 1914, played Vera Wilton and Alice Marsh in " The Rosary " ; during 1914–15 toured in the same part ; in 1923 published her reminiscences under the title of " Myself and Others."

(Died 11 July, 1932; age 71)

MILNE, Alan Alexander, dramatic author ; *b.* London, 18 Jan., 1882 ; *s.* of John Vine Milne ; *e.* Westminster School, and Trinity College, Cambridge ; *m.* Dorothy de Sélincourt ; was formerly a journalist ; assistant editor of *Punch* from 1906–14 ; served in the Royal Warwickshire Regiment, 1915–18 ; is the author of the following plays : " Wurzel-Flummery," 1917 ; " Belinda," 1918 ; " The Boy Comes Home," 1918 ; " Make-Believe," 1918 ; " The Camberley Triangle," 1919 ; " Mr. Pim Passes By," 1919 ; " The Romantic Age," 1920 · " The Truth

About Blayds," 1921 ; " The Dover Road," 1922 ; " The Lucky One," 1922 ; " The Great Broxopp," 1923 ; " Success," 1923 ; " To Have the Honour," 1924 ; " Ariadne," 1925 ; " Portrait of a Gentleman in Slippers," 1926 ; " The Ivory Door," 1927 ; " Miss Marlow at Play," 1927 ; " The Fourth Wall," 1928 ; " Michael and Mary," 1929 ; "Toad of Toad Hall" (adaptation), 1930 ; "Other People's Lives," 1932 ; "Miss Elizabeth Bennet," 1936 ; "Sarah Simple," 1937 ; "Gentleman Unknown," 1938 ; his autobiography, "It's Too Late Now," was published 1939. *Clubs :* Athenaeum, Beefsteak, and Garrick.

(Died 31 Jan., 1956; age 74)

MILTERN, John E., actor ; *b.* New Britain, Conn., U.S.A. ; made his first appearance on the stage under the management of Sullivan, Harris, and Woods ; appeared at the American Theatre, New York, Mar., 1906, as Buck Harris in "Chinatown Charlie" ; made his first success at the Fourteenth-street Theatre, New York, 23 Dec., 1907, as Buck Farren in " Deadwood Dick's Last Shot " ; was next seen at the Liberty Theatre, Nov., 1908, when he played Edward Pinckney in " Via Wireless," and Dec., 1908, Mr. Quayle in " Ticey " ; subsequently toured with William Gillette in " Clarice," etc. ; appeared with Gillette at the Empire, New York, Dec., 1910, as Professor Moriarty in " Sherlock Holmes," Benton Arrelsford in " Secret Service," and Leon Dathis in " Too Much Johnson" ; Lyceum, Feb., 1912, James Stracey in "Lydia Gilmore" ; at Chicago, 1912, played Alfred Wilson in "Officer 666," and made his first appearance on the London stage, at the Globe Theatre, Oct., 1912, in the same part ; at the Criterion, New York, Nov., 1913, played Josh Hayes in " The Man Inside " ; at the Maxine Elliott Theatre, Feb., 1914, appeared as George Stuart in " Help Wanted " ; at the Eltinge Theatre, Sept., 1914, as Bela Memzetti in " Innocent " ; at Belasco, Washington, Dec., 1914, played in " The Fallen Idol " ; at the La Salle Theatre, Chicago, Aug., 1915, in

" Molly and I " ; at the Lyceum, New York, Feb., 1916, played John Hardin in " The Heart of Wetona " ; at Maxine Elliott's, Jan., 1917, John Leighton in " Gamblers All " ; at the Plymouth, New York, Nov., 1917, Dr. Richard Long in " Barbara " ; at the Republic, Nov., 1918, Lewis Marsh and Grantland Lewis in " Roads of Destiny " ; at the Playhouse, New York, Jan., 1920, Bill Bruce in " The ' Ruined ' Lady " ; at the Punch and Judy Theatre, Oct., 1922, Harry Sheridan in " Persons Unknown " ; at the Henry Miller, Jan., 1924, Major Fowler in " The Merry Wives of Gotham " ; Lyceum, Sept., 1925, John Weldon in " Canary Dutch " ; National, Sept., 1928, Inspector Manning in " Trapped " ; Belmont, Feb., 1929, Philip Latimer in "Be Your Age" ; New Amsterdam, Nov., 1929, again played Professor Moriarty in "Sherlock Holmes" ; Martin Beck, Mar., 1934, Major Walter Reed in "Yellow Jack" ; Empire, Oct., 1934, Mr. Corwin in "Allure" ; Martin Beck, Dec., 1934, Montague in "Romeo and Juliet" ; in May, 1935, toured with Mary Pickford in "Coquette."

(Died 15 Jan., 1937; age 67)

MILTON, Billy, actor ; *b.* London, 8 Dec., 1905 ; *s.* of Harry Harmon Milton and his wife Hilda Eugene (Jackson) ; *e.* Lancing College ; was formerly a wine merchant at Rheims, France ; made his first appearance on the stage at the Regent Theatre, King's Cross, Mar., 1926, in "The Devil's Disciple" ; appeared at His Majesty's, May, 1927, in "White Birds" ; London Hippodrome, July, 1927, in "Shake Your Feet" ; Prince of Wales, Oct., 1927, in "The Bow-Wows" ; Shaftesbury, Apr., 1928, in "Will o' the Whispers" ; he then went to the United States, and made his first appearance in New York, at the Selwyn Theatre, 7 Nov., 1928, in "This Year of Grace" ; on his return, appeared at His Majesty's Theatre, July, 1929, as Vincent Howard in "Bitter Sweet" ; at the Cambridge, June, 1931, appeared in "The Sign of the Seven Dials" ; went to Paris, and appeared at the Casino de Paris, with Mistinguett, in "Paris qui-Brille,"

1708

1931-2; at the London Hipprodrome, June, 1932, played in "Bow Bells"; Alhambra, Nov., 1932, played Florimond in "A Kiss in Spring"; went to Australia, 1933, starring at the King's, Melbourne, Dec., 1933, as Guy in "Gay Divorce"; at the Playhouse, New York, Dec., 1934, appeared in "Fools Rush In"; Gate, Dec., 1937, appeared in "Members Only"; during 1938, appeared in New York at the Rainbow Room, Rockefeller Center; Saville, London, Feb., 1939, played Alan Paddock in "Worth a Million"; during the War, joined the R.A.F., as A.C.2; took part in nearly 2000 performances for troops; discharged from R.A.F., 1944; Coliseum, May, 1944, on tour and again at the Coliseum, Feb., 1945, played Tony Chute in "The Quaker Girl"; toured, Nov., 1946, in "The Red Mill"; Boltons, Dec., 1947, and St. James's, Mar., 1948, produced and played in "The Boltons Revue," of which he was the author; Torch, Dec., 1948, appeared in "Revue for Two"; appeared in cabaret, from Apr., 1949, with Daphne Barker; Boltons, July, 1949, produced and appeared in "Billy Milton's Party"; King's, Hammersmith, Dec., 1949, played Sarah in "Dick Whittington"; toured, 1950, in the *revue* "Touch Wood and Whistle"; Richmond, Aug., 1958, played Professor Armand Dubois in "Love a la Carte"; toured, 1960, in "No, No, Nanette"; toured in England, Scotland, and South Africa, 1963–6, as Mr. Veidt in "Lilac Time"; films include: "Heavens Above," "Licence to Kill" and "Hot Millions"; has written a number of television *revues*, and has appeared in many television productions; has also appeared in radio series and many other sound programmes. *Recreations:* Songwriting, piano-playing and walking. *Address:* 23 Holland Street, London, W.8. *Telephone No.:* 01-937 6687.

MILTON, Ernest, actor; *b.* San Francisco, 10 Jan., 1890; *m.* Naomi Royde-Smith (dec.); made his first appearance on the stage at the Grand Theatre, Newport News, Oct., 1912, as Pietro Golfanti in "The Climax,"

followed by a tour in the same play; made his first appearance in New York, at the Century Theatre, 11 Jan., 1913, as the First Camel Driver in "Joseph and his Brethren"; in Jan.; 1914, played in repertory in the New England States; made his first appearance in London, at the Queen's Theatre, 14 Apr., 1914, as Boris Andrieff in "Potash and Perlmutter"; returned to America, Nov., 1915; returned to London, 1916, and at the Queen's, Sept., 1916, played Boris in "Potash and Perlmutter in Society"; toured the camp theatres, May, 1917, playing in "Bought and Paid For," "A Butterfly on the Wheel," "Caste," etc.; at the Kingsway, June, 1917, succeeded Basil Sydney as Oswald Alving in "Ghosts," subsequently touring in the same part; at the Gaiety, Manchester, Christmas, 1917, played Captain Carey and the Geni of the Carpet in "Where the Rainbow Ends"; at the Court, Apr., 1918, Jokanaan in "Salome"; subsequently played Romeo, Eugene Marchbanks in "Candida," Tom Kemp in "The Mollusc," in a repertory season with the Players of the Gate, at the Kennington Theatre, and at Brighton, appeared as Bassanio in the trial scene from "The Merchant of Venice," with Ellen Terry; in Sept., 1918, joined the Old Vic company, playing a long round of leading parts, including Shylock. Benedick, Macbeth, Ferdinand in "The Tempest," Orsino in "Twelfth Night," Biron in "Love's Labour's Lost," the title-*rôle* in "Everyman," "Hamlet," etc.; St. James's, Sept., 1919, Artemyev in "Reparation," and Jan., 1920, Decius Brutus in "Julius Caesar"; rejoined the Old Vic Company, Sept., 1920–1, to play a number of leading parts, including "Hamlet," Don Pedro, King John, King Richard II, Romeo, Mark Antony, Cleon in "Pericles," etc.; in June, 1921, appeared with the company at the Théâtre du Parc, Brussels, as Hamlet, Shylock, Romeo, etc.; at the Old Vic, Nov., 1921, played John Ball in "Wat Tyler," and Parolles in "All's Well that Ends Well"; at the St. Martin's, Mar., 1922, Ferdinand de Levis in "Loyalties"; in 1923, played a season with the People's Theatre, Whitechapel, played leads in "The Witch," "You Never Can Tell," "Ghosts," "Thérèse Raquin"; at the Criterion, Nov., 1923, played Vincent Leach in "Dulcy"; at the Shaftesbury, Apr., 1924, Pettigrew in "A Perfect Fit"; at the Regent, June, 1924, Romeo in "Romeo and Juliet"; at the Court, July, 1924, Paul Kosloff in "A Surplus Man"; in Sept., 1924, toured as Count Beppo in "The Lonely House"; Lyric, Feb., 1925 (for the Independent Players), played Lyngstrand in "The Lady from the Sea," which he also produced; Old Vic, Apr., 1925, again played "Hamlet," and June, 1925, Tom Wrench in "Trelawny of the 'Wells'"; Everyman, July, 1925, the name part in Pirandello's "Henry IV"; Oct., 1925, Oswald in "Ghosts"; Ambassadors', Nov., 1925, Mr. Windlesham in "The Madras House"; Scala (or Renaissance Society), Dec., 1925, Thomas Arden in "Arden of Feversham"; Everyman, Aug., 1926, Evan in "A Balcony"; "Q," Feb., 1927, Daniel Deronda in a play of that name; Royalty, Apr., 1927, Channon in "The Dybbuk"; toured in Egypt, Oct.-Dec., 1927, playing a round of Shakespearean parts with Robert Atkins's Company; rejoined the Old Vic Company, Feb.-May, 1928, playing Mercutio, Shylock, King Lear, Palamon in "The Two Noble Kinsmen," and Joseph in "The School for Scandal"; Garrick, Aug., 1928, played Li Hung in "The Moving Finger"; entered on a short period of management at the Queen's, Jan.-Mar., 1929, playing Pirandello's "Henry IV," under the title of "The Mock Emperor," and Mafro in "Mafro, Darling"; Ambassadors', Apr., 1929, played Rupert Cadell in "Rope"; subsequently went to New York to play the same part, at the Masque Theatre, Sept., 1929, when the play was called "Rope's End"; after returning to London, appeared at the Everyman, July, 1930, as Pierrot in "Prunella"; Arts, Oct., 1930, played Alfred Allmers in "Little Eyolf"; Phoenix (for Repertory Players), Jan., 1931, Roger Aslan in "John Brown's Body"; Savoy, June, 1931, The Prince in "Death Takes a Holiday"; Adelphi, Sept., 1931, Doctor Otternschlag in "Grand Hotel"; en-

tered on the management of the St. James's Theatre, Apr., 1932, and appeared as Othello and Shylock; Westminster Theatre, Oct., 1932, played Lord Beaconsfield in "Dizzy"; "Q" and Royalty, Mar., 1933, Francis Thompson in the play of that name; Cambridge, Mar., 1933 (for Jewish Drama League), Shylock in "The Lady of Belmont"; Fulham, May, 1933, and Queen's, Sept., 1933, Lorenzino de Medici in "Night's Candles"; Morosco, New York, Nov., 1933, Marcus Blaine in "The Dark Tower"; Fulham, Sept., 1934, Sir Charles Knightley in "Death at Court Lady"; Whitehall, Jan., 1935, Nicolo Paganini in his own play "Paganini"; Comedy, Mar., 1935, Ivan Tsarakov in "Delusion"; Westminster, Nov., 1935, Timon in "Timon of Athens"; Old Vic., Sept., 1936, Don Adriano in "Love's Labour's Lost"; Lyric, June, 1937, Earl of Beaconsfield in "Victoria Regina"; Globe (for the Group Theatre), Feb., 1939, The Guidanto in "On the Frontier"; Globe (for London International Theatre), Apr., 1939, Mordecai in "Scandal in Assyria"; Vaudeville, Oct., 1940, King of France in "All's Well That Ends Well"; toured, 1941, with the Old Vic company, as Sir Andrew Aguecheek, King John and Svengali, and later, in industrial areas, as Shylock; New, July, 1941, played King John; Ambassadors', Oct., 1942, Kynaston Carver in "Murder from Memory"; Open Air, May, 1944, Leontes in "The Winter's Tale"; Lyric, Hammersmith, July, 1944, Macbeth; Citizen's, Glasgow, Oct., 1944, Sir Giles Overreach in "A New Way to Pay Old Debts"; King's, Hammersmith, May, 1945, Mr. Dombey in "Dombey and Son"; Garrick, Altrincham, Aug., 1945, Quintus in his own play, "Mary of Magdala"; Lindsey Theatre, Oct., 1945, The Tsar in "Red Horizon"; Lyric, Hammersmith, June, 1946, Father Zossima in "The Brothers Karamazov"; Arts, Feb., 1947, played Sylvester Tiffney in "The Wise Have Not Spoken"; Duchess, June, 1947, Count Mancini in "He Who Gets Slapped"; Torch, Sept., 1948 Simeon Barr in "Ten Shilling Doll"; New Lindsey, Feb., 1949, Hugo von

Gerhardt in "The Compelled People"; Saville, Oct., 1950, Manasseh da Costa in "The King of Schnorrers"; at the Old Vic, during the 1951–52 season, played Lodovico in "Othello"; Court, Aug., 1952, Solinus in "The Comedy of Errors"; Arts, Salisbury, May, 1954, played Merlin in "The Knights of the Round Table"; Piccadilly, Nov., 1955, appeared as Lorenzo Querini in "The Strong Are Lonely," and played the same part when this production was revived at the Haymarket, Jan., 1956; Lyric, Hammersmith, Mar., 1957, played Pope Paul in "Malatesta"; Sadler's Wells, June, 1960, appeared as the Narrator in "The Finsbury Story"; Pembroke, Croydon, Oct., 1960, played the Ghost and Player King in "Hamlet"; Dublin Festival, Sept., 1961, and Vaudeville, London, Oct., 1961, played Philip II in "Teresa of Avila"; for the Royal Shakespeare Company, New Arts, July, 1962, Lord Cardinal in "Women, Beware Women"; Mermaid, Oct., 1963, played Bishop Tibon in "The Possessed"; toured, Feb., 1964, as Mr. Lapham in "Mother's Boy"; 1966, in Westminster Cathedral, played Nicodemus in "This is For Now," first play to be performed in a Roman Catholic Church in England; Savoy, Apr., 1967, Joseph Millet in "The Deadly Game"; entered films, 1935, and has appeared in "The Scarlet Pimpernel," "It's Love Again," etc.; has also made a number of television appearances; is a naturalized British subject; is also the author of a play, "Christopher Marlowe" (Constable, 1924), produced at East London College, 1931; and a novel, "To Kiss the Crocodile," Duckworth, 1928. *Address:* c/o Barclay's Bank, Ltd., 52 Regent Street, London, W.1.

MILTON, Harry, actor and vocalist; *b.* London, 26 June, 1900; *s.* of Harry Harmon Milton and his wife Hilda Eugene (Jackson); *e.* Aldenham; *m.* Dorothy Bouchier; from 1924–8, served as an officer with the Royal Air Force (29th Squadron); made his first appearance on the stage in 1928, touring with "The Bow-Wows"; at the Victoria Palace, 4 June, 1929, appeared in "The Show's the Thing"; subsequently toured with "The Co-Optimists," 1930; Piccadilly, Sept., 1930, played Redwick Clarke in "Open Your Eyes"; he then toured in "Lavender"; Gaiety, Dec., 1931, played Robert Crayne in "Hold My Hand"; Gaiety, Oct., 1932, appeared in "After Dinner"; Gaiety, Mar., 1934, Freddy Croome in "Sporting Love"; Palace, May, 1935, appeared with "The Co-optimists"; Victoria Palace, Oct., 1943, Johnnie Stanton in "The Love Racket"; commenced film career 1931, and has appeared in several pictures.

(Died 8 Mar., 1965; age 64)

MILTON, Maud, actress; *b.* Gravesend, 24 Mar., 1859; *d.* of a captain in the merchant service; *e.* at home; was originally trained for a dancing-mistress; prepared for the stage by the late John Ryder; made her first appearance on the stage, at the Royal Aquarium Theatre, 15 Apr., 1876, as Rosa in "Jo"; at the Queen's, Dec., 1876, played Hero in "Much Ado About Nothing"; at the St. James's, Apr., 1877, played Maria Surefoot in "The Wandering Heir"; at the Gaiety, June, 1877, appeared as Juliet in "Romeo and Juliet"; at the Queen's, Jan., 1878, played Inez in "Fatherland," subsequently playing Isabel Markham in "'Twixt Axe and Crown," Nerissa in "The Merchant of Venice," Irene in "Madelaine Morel"; at the Princess's, June, 1878, played the Fairy Queen in "Elfinella," also appearing there in "Queen's Evidence," and as Josephs in "It's Never too Late to Mend"; at the same theatre, 1880, with Edwin Booth, played the Player Queen in "Hamlet," Desdemona in "Othello," Cordelia in "King Lear," Nerissa in "The Merchant of Venice"; at Leeds, in 1881, played Louise in "The Two Orphans," Adrienne in "Proof," Eliza in "After Dark," and Pauline in "The Lady of Lyons"; in 1882 joined Wilson Barrett's touring company, and remained with him, playing lead in "The Lights o' London" and "The Silver King"; in 1882-3 toured in the United States with Madame Modjeska ; returned to Barrett's company in the autumn of 1883, playing in "The Silver King," "The Lights o' London," etc., for some years ; appeared at the Olympic, June, 1887, as Ellen Grandison in "The Golden Band," and Aug., 1887, as Lizzie in "The Pointsman" ; at Drury Lane, Sept., 1888, appeared as Fame in "The Armada" ; in 1889 toured as Sybil Tilney in "The Armada" ; in 1890, toured as Henriette in "A Man's Shadow" ; in 1891, toured with F. R. Benson's Shakespearean Company ; in 1891–2 toured as Gloriana in the play of that name ; in 1892 appeared at the Haymarket, as Sylvia in "The Waif" ; at the Strand as Alalanta Woodcock in "A Lucky Dog" ; at the Lyric as Lady Dedlock in "Jo" ; at the Opéra Comique, as Greta in "The Goldfish" ; she then joined Henry Irving at the Lyceum, in Nov., 1892, and remained with him until 1902 ; during this period she played Regan in "King Lear," Lady Eleanor in "Charles I," Mrs. Primrose in "Olivia." Catherine in "The Bells," Margaret in "Much Ado About Nothing," the Spirit of the Lake in "King Arthur," Guinevere in the same play, Maria in "Don Quixote," Bessy in "Faust," Nerissa in "The Merchant of Venice," Martha in "Louis XI," Jeannette in "The Lyons Mail," Coralie in "The Corsican Brothers," Lady Elizabeth in "Richard III," La Rousotte in "Madame Sans-Gêne," the Empress Catherine in "Peter the Great," Lady Agatha Warrington in "The Medicine Man," Madame de Narbonne in "Robespierre," Valeria in "Coriolanus," the Queen of Naples in "Madame Sans-Gêne" ; also played Clarisse in "Robespierre," and Portia in "The Merchant of Venice," during Miss Terry's illness in America ; appeared at Drury Lane, Apr., 1902, as the Mother of Ben Hur in "Ben Hur" ; in 1903, toured in Australia and New Zealand as Helena in "A Midsummer Night's Dream," and Maria in "Twelfth Night" ; in 1904 toured with Martin Harvey as Gertrude in "Hamlet" ; appeared in the same part at the Adelphi, Apr., 1905, with Oscar Asche and H. B. Irving, and again

at the Lyric, May, 1905, with Martin Harvey ; in Aug., 1905, appeared in New York as Lady Caterham in "The Catch of the Season" ; toured America with H. B. Irving, 1906 ; at the Court, Apr., 1907, she played Lady John Wynnstay in "Votes for Women" ; at the Adelphi, in June, played Rachel in "Great Possessions," and Madame dei Franchi in "The Corsican Brothers" ; at the Aldwych, Dec., 1907, played Janet McLeod in "The Gay Gordons" ; in Apr., 1908, toured as Ellen in "Sweet and Twenty" ; at the Hicks Theatre, Feb., 1909, played the Duchesse de Noailles in "The Dashing Little Duke" ; in Sept., 1909, toured with Marie Tempest as Mrs. Golightly in "Penelope," and appeared at the Lyceum, New York, with her, in the same part, Dec., 1909 ; at the Empire, New York, Apr., 1910, played the Marquise de St. Maur in "Caste," and Jan., 1911, Mrs. Telfer in "Trelawny of the Wells" ; returning to England, toured as Rosalie in "The Marriage of Kitty," and Mrs. Clifton in "Lily, the Bill-topper" ; subsequently returned to America and toured in "Pomander Walk," 1911–2 ; at the Garrick, London, Mar., 1913, appeared as the Reverend Mother in "The Greatest Wish" ; in 1914 appeared in the United States in "Damaged Goods" ; at the Teck Theatre, Buffalo, Aug., 1915, played Lady Tollhurst in "The Ragged Messenger" ; at the New Amsterdam Theatre, New York, Mar.-May, 1916, played the Old Lady in "King Henry VIII," and Mistress Quickly in "The Merry Wives of Windsor," with Sir Herbert Tree ; at the Lyceum, New York, Aug., 1916, Lady Lethbridge in "Please Help Emily" ; at the Empire, New York, Oct., 1916, the Duchess of Cheviot in "The Basker '; at the Thirty-ninth Street Theatre, Oct., 1917, appeared as Mrs. Fountain in "The Old Country" ; at the Punch and Judy Theatre, Feb., 1918, as Mrs. Munroe in "Her Country" ; at the Lyceum, New York, Sept., 1918, played Lady Susan Delamothe in "Humpty-Dumpty" ; in the autumn of 1919 toured in "Scandal" ; at the Morosco Theatre, Feb., 1920, Marie

Sardis in " Sacred and Profane Love " ; at the Cort Theatre, Feb., 1921, Mrs. Chichester in " Peg o' My Heart " : returned to England, 1921 ; at the Garrick, Feb., 1923, played Everyman's Mother in " Via Crucis."

(Died 19 Nov., 1945; age 90)

MILTON, Robert, producer and stage director; *b.* Dinaburg, near St. Petersburg, Russia; *s.* of Michael Davidor; was formerly an actor and gained his first experience with Richard Mansfield, for whom he produced "The Devil's Disciple," "The Misanthrope," etc.; was associated with Mrs. Fiske, as stage-director, for four years, and later with William Harris; has produced many plays in New York, among which may be mentioned "The Return from Jerusalem," 1911; "The Cinderella Man," 1916; "A Pair of Queens," 1916; "Bosom Friends," 1917; "Leave It to Jane," 1917; "Oh, Boy!" 1917; "Oh, Lady, Lady," 1918; "The Five Million," 1919; "Crooked Gamblers," "The Charm School" (of which he was part-author), "The Unwritten Chapter," 1920; "Bluebeard's Eighth Wife," 1921; "He Who Gets Slapped," "Madame · Pierre," "A Serpent's Tooth," "Banco," "The Lady Cristilinda," 1922; "You and I," 1923; "The Far Cry," "The Youngest," 1924; "The Dark Angel," "The Enemy," 1925; "Bride of the Lamb" (with Alice Brady), "Sandalwood," "Peggy-Ann," 1926; "Revelry," "Paradise," 1927; "Napoleon," 1928; "The Marriage Bed," 1929; "Dark Victory," 1934; "Black Limelight," 1936; "The Seagull," "Here Come the Clowns," 1938; has also directed several pictures since 1929.

(Died 13 Jan., 1956; age 70)

MILWARD, Dawson, actor ; *b.* Woolwich, 13 July, 1870; *s.* of Colonel T. W. Milward, R.A., C.B.; was a pupil of the late Carlotta Leclercq, and had had much experience as an amateur before making his first professional appearance on the stage at the Avenue Theatre, 5 July, 1894, as Mr. Greville in " Such is Love " ; he then went on tour, commencing at Southport, Aug., 1894, as Lord Mountsorrell in " A Bunch of Violets " ; in 1895 toured as Aubrey Tanqueray in " The Second Mrs. Tanqueray " ; made his next appearance on the London stage, at the Haymarket, 17 Oct., 1896, as Sir Thomas Brunt in " Under the Red Robe " ; appeared at Drury Lane, Sept., 1897, as Captain Alec Maclintock in " The White Heather," and Sept., 1898, as Captain Clive Dalrymple in " The Great Ruby " ; toured with Kate Rorke in " The Squire " ; has appeared in prominent parts in " Wheels Within Wheels," Criterion, 1901 ; " The Undercurrent," Criterion, 1901 ; " The Heel of Achilles," Globe, 1902 ; " My Lady Virtue," Garrick, 1902 ; " Caste," Criterion, 1903 ; " The Man Who was," His Majesty's, 1903 ; " The Rich Mrs. Repton," Duke of York's, 1904 ; " Business is Business," His Majesty's, 1905 ; " Lights Out," Waldorf, 1905 ; " Major Barbara," Court, 1905 ; at the St. James's, Feb., 1906, played Major Maurewarde in " His House in Order " ; at the Comedy, Apr., 1907, appeared as Fred Lindon in " The Truth " ; Oct., 1907, The Marquis of Studland in " The Barrier " ; at the St. James's, Nov., 1908, played Arnold Faringay in " The Builder of Bridges " ; during 1909 appeared at the St. James's, in May, as Raymond Leyton in " The Thief " ; at the Hicks, in July, as Major Sumner in " His Borrowed Plumes " ; at the Haymarket, Sept., as Edmund in " King Lear," and in Oct., as General Sinclair in " Don " ; at the Globe, Nov., 1909, played Lord Glaverhouse in " The Great Mrs. Alloway " ; at the Queen's Theatre, Sept., 1910, played Mark Averill in " The Man from the Sea," and in Oct., Major John Skeffington in " Mrs. Skeffington " ; at the Comedy, Jan., 1911, appeared as Reginald Stulkeley, M.P., in " Preserving Mr. Panmure " ; at the Criterion, May, 1911, Major Sergius Saranoff in " Arms and the Man " ; at the St. James's, Oct., 1911, Lord Windermere in " Lady Windermere's Fan " ; at the Palace, Dec., 1911, played the Husband in " How He Lied to Her Husband " ; at the Lyric, May, 1912, The Prince of

Klausthal-Agordo in "The Five Frankforters"; at Wyndham's, Oct., 1912, Captain Harding in "Doormats"; at the Kingsway, Mar., 1913, Lord Leonard Alcar in "The Great Adventure"; at the Duke of York's, Sept., 1914, played the Earl of Rintoul in "The Little Minister"; at the St. James's, Oct., 1914, re-appeared as Major Maurewarde in "His House in Order"; at the New Theatre, Apr., 1915, played Colonel Hildebrand in "The Joker"; at the St. James's, May, 1915, Colonel Wallingford in "The Day Before the Day"; at His Majesty's, July, 1915, Dr. Seraskier in "Peter Ibbetson"; at Wyndham's, Sept., 1915, Sir Harry Egerton in "The Ware Case"; at the St. James's, May, 1916, played Captain Victor Goby in "Pen," and Mahmoud Baroudi in a revival of "Bella Donna"; at the Haymarket, Sept., 1916, Arthur Paraday in "Mr. Jubilee Drax"; in 1917 toured as Sir Dennys Broughton in "General Post"; at the Royalty, June, 1917, played Lord William Dromondy in "The Foundations"; Aug., 1917, Colonel Preedy in "Billeted"; at the Haymarket, May, 1918, Mr. Floyer in "Uncle Anyhow"; at the Globe, June, 1918, Brooke Stanway in "Nurse Benson"; at Wyndham's, June, 1918, Major Armitage in "A Well-Remembered Voice"; Nov., 1918, the Emperor of Austria in the "all-star" production of "L'Aiglon"; at the Criterion, Apr., 1919, the Earl of Lamberhurst in "Our Mr. Hepple-white"; at the Little Theatre, Feb., 1920, appeared as Colonel Armytage in "Mumsee"; Apr., 1920, as Mr. Lorimer in "Other Times"; at the Globe, May, 1920, as the General in "A Marriage of Convenience"; at the Kingsway, Sept., 1920, as the Rt. Hon. Lord Henry Markham in "The Grain of Mustard Seed"; at the St. Martin's, Nov., 1920, played Mr. Hillcrist in "The Skin Game"; at the Globe, Feb., 1921, the Duke of Rockingham in "The Hour and the Man"; at the Royalty, Jan., 1922, Sir Noel Barchester in "The Eleventh Commandment"; at the St. Martin's, Mar., 1922, General Carynge in

"Loyalties"; Mar., 1923, Sir Roger Tenterden in "The Great Broxopp"; at the St. James's, May, 1923, Jasper Sturdee in "The Outsider"; at Wyndham's, Jan., 1924, Lord Blantyre in "The Flame"; at the Adelphi, Mar., 1924, Henry Beauclerc in "Diplomacy"; June, 1924, in aid of King George's Pension Fund for Actors, Sir Henry Egerton in "The Ware Case"; is the author of "Cornered" and "Jealousy," both produced in 1919. *(Died 15 May, 1926; age 60)*

MINER, Worthington C., producer; *b.* Buffalo, New York, U.S.A., 13 Nov., 1900; *s.* of Worthington Miner and his wife Margaret (Willard); *e.* Kent School, Cambridge, England; *m.* Frances Fuller; has produced the following, among other plays: "Week-End," "Top o' the Hill," 1929; "Up Pops the Devil," "Five Star Final," 1930; "The House Beautiful," "Reunion in Vienna," 1931; "I Loved You Wednesday," "Both Your Houses," 1932; "Her Master's Voice," 1933; "Revenge with Music," "On to Fortune," 1934; "Blind Alley," "Let Freedom Ring," 1935; "Bury the Dead," "Prelude," "On Your Toes," "Two Hundred Were Chosen," 1936; "Excursion," "Father Malachy's Miracle," 1937; "Stop-Over," "Washington Jitters," "Dame Nature," 1938; "Jeremiah," 1939; adapted "The Inner Light," 1938, and was part-author of "Jeremiah," 1939. *Recreation :* Gardening. *Address :* 1 West 72nd Street, New York City, U.S.A. *Telephone No. :* Endicott 2–6844.

MINETTI, Maria, actress; during 1918, was touring the provinces in the title-*role* in "Carminetta"; made her first appearance in London, at the Wimbledon Theatre, 8 Dec., 1919, as Maria in "Gay Bohemia"; subsequently toured in "The Fun of the Fayre"; at the Gaiety, Apr., 1922, played Ninette in "His Girl"; toured in "The Nine o'Clock Revue"; at Daly's, May, 1926, played Lolotte in "Yvonne"; Drury Lane, Apr., 1927, Clementina in "The Desert Song"; subsequently toured in

"Lilac Time"; at Daly's, Dec., 1928, played Signorina Marini in "Lilac Time"; Piccadilly, Feb., 1930, Maria in "Here Comes the Bride"; Lyceum, July, 1931, Corinna in "Nina Rosa"; in July, 1934, toured as Frieda Hatzfeld in "Music in the Air"; Westminster, Feb., 1935, played Valentine in "They Do These Things in France"; appeared in the film "The Hate Ship." *Address :* 190 Spring Grove Road, Isleworth, Middlesex. *Telephone No.:* Hounslow 0428.

MINIL, Renée du (Séveno), French actress ; *b.* Bourges, France, 15 Oct., 1868 ; *d.* of Lesuer du Minil and Hippolyte Séveno, Army officer, Lieut.-Colonel 41*e* ; studied at the National Conservatoire under Delaunay, obtaining first prize for comedy and second prize for tragedy, 1886 ; made her first appearance on the stage at the Comédie Française, 22 Sept., 1886, in " Denise " ; elected *sociétaire* of the Comédie Française, Jan., 1895 ; played one hundred and twenty-two different parts at the theatre, until the date of her retirement ; created leading parts in " La Dédale," " La Loi de l'Homme," " La Vassale," " Les Mouettes," " L'Autre," " La Plus Faible," etc.; since May, 1914, has been a Professor of Music and Elocution at the Conservatoire ; appeared at the Nouveau Théâtre-Libre, Mar., 1920, as Madame Delarbre in " La Maison en flammes " ; made her first appearance on the London stage at the Royalty Theatre, Apr., 1889, in " Pepa " ; has toured France and Austria ; is a professor of elocution, has been decorated with various medals, and has been elected an Officer of Public Instruction. *Address :* 4 Rue Benouville, Paris.

MINNEY, Rubeigh James, critic and author; *b.* Calcutta, 29 Aug., 1895; *e* King's College, London; *m.* Edith Anne Murielle Fox; has had much journalistic experience in England and in India, where he was on the editorial staffs of *The Pioneer,* Allahabad, and *The Englishman,* Calcutta; has written dramatic criticism for *The Daily Chronicle, Sunday News,* and *Everybody's Weekly,* of which he was also editor; Managing Editor of *The Sunday Referee,* 1935 to 1939; author (with W. P. Lipscomb) of the play, "Clive of India," 1933, which was also made into a film; "They Had His Number " (with Juliet Rhys-Williams), 1942; "The Red Horizon" (with Osbert Sitwell), 1943 ; is the author of several books on Indian life; his book "Shiva; or the Future of India," published 1929, was banned; issued a biography of "Clive," 1931 ; also the author of "Distant Drums," 1935 ; "Hollywood by Starlight," 1935 ; "Governor General," the love story of Warren Hastings, 1935 ; "How Vainly Men," 1940 ; "A Woman of France," 1945 ; has also written and produced films, including "Madonna of the Seven Moons," "A Place of One's Own," "The Wicked Lady," etc. *Club :* Savage. *Address :* Lawford House, Manningtree, Essex. *Telephone No.:* Manningtree 35.

MINSTER, Jack, actor, manager, and director; *b.* London, 11 June, 1901; *s.* of Robert Frederick Minster Schipper and his wife Sybil Violet (Pitt-Tayler); *e.* Seaford and privately; *m.* (1) Faith Liddle (mar. dis.); (2) Barbara Cochran-Carr; made his first appearance on the stage at the Grand Theatre, Croydon, 4 Mar., 1920, as Fred in "Pygmalion"; subsequently toured in "Three Wise Fools" and "If Winter Comes"; St. James's Jan., 1923, played Harold Twyning in "If Winter Comes"; Princes, Oct., 1923, Froggie in "The Return of Sherlock Holmes"; toured with Mrs. Patrick Campbell, 1924; was engaged with the Liverpool Repertory Company, at the Playhouse, Liverpool, 1926–28; Wyndham's, June–July, 1929, appeared in "Exiled" and "The Skin Game"; toured as Falder in "Justice," and De Levis in "Loyalties"; Globe, Sept., 1930, played Harry Easter in "Street Scene"; Phoenix, Jan., 1931, Harris in "The Last Mile"; St. Martin's, May, 1931, Jack Crabb in "Lean Harvest"; subsequently toured in Canada, with Sir Barry Jackson's company; Garrick, London, Aug., 1932, played Graviter in "Loyalties"; Nov., 1932. toured in

Canada, with his own company, as Clive Popkiss in "Rookery Nook" and Major Bone in "A Cuckoo in the Nest"; Garrick, London, Apr., 1933 played Peter Randall in "Beggars in Hell"; Cambridge, Feb., 1934, Raymond Merritt in "Success Story"; Little, May, 1934, Sir James Beddington in "Once Upon a Time"; Lyric June, 1934, Dr. Mitchelson in "Men in White"; Westminster, Sept., 1934, the Earl of Warwick in "Rose and Glove"; Victoria Palace, May, 1935, Harry in "The Miracle Man"; from 1935-8, was engaged as director at the Little Theatre, Hull; returning to London, 1938, directed several plays at the "Q," Intimate and Richmond Theatres, including "Weights and Measures," 1938 and "I am the King," 1939; in 1940, was engaged with the Windsor Repertory company, acting and directing; was engaged with the B.B.C., 1941-2; he has since directed the following plays: "An Ideal Husband," 1943; "Not So Fast, my Pretty," "Emma," "Perchance to Dream," 1945; "The Guinea Pig," "Our Betters," "The Gleam," "Lady Windermere's Fan" (New York), 1946; "Wonders Never Cease," 1948; "The Mountain," 1949; "Larger than Life," 1950; "Harvest Time," "Years Ago," 1951; "Sweet Madness," "The Step Forward," "When In Rome," 1952; "Two In the Bush," "Little Idiot," "The Summerhouse," 1953; "The Whirligig of Time," "Lucky Strike," "The Reluctant Debutante," "Patience," 1955; in 1955, joined E. P. Clift in management as Minster Productions, Ltd., presenting "The Reluctant Debutante," May, 1955; this was followed by "The Rainmaker," (co-directed with Sam Wanamaker), "Plaintiff in a Pretty Hat," (also directed), "The Touch of Fear," (also directed) 1956; "The Iron Duchess" (also directed), "Dear Delinquent" (also directed), "Head of the Family" (also directed), "The Happy Man" (also directed) 1957; transferred "At the Drop of a Hat" from the New Lindsey to the Fortune, 1957; during 1958, E. P. Clift resigned from the Company, and Minster Productions, Ltd., then presented "The Brass Butterfly," "Rose-

land," "The Velvet Shotgun" (with Frith Banbury, Ltd.), "The Grass is Greener" (with Anna Deere Wiman, and also directed), "The Bright One," 1958; also directed "Auntie Mame" for David Pelham, 1958; presented and directed "The Woman on the Stair" (with Anna Deere Wiman), "The Darling Buds of May," 1959; "Double Yoke" (co-directed with Celia Johnson), "The Warm Peninsula," 1960; "The Irregular Verb to Love" (with Anna Deere Wiman, also directed), "The Bad Soldier Smith" (also directed), 1961; "Boeing-Boeing" (with John Gale, also directed), "The Hot Tiara" (with Martin Landeau, also directed), 1962; "Domino" (directed), "The Shot in Question," "The Gentle Avalanche" (with Linnit and Dunfee), 1963; "The Dark Stranger" (directed), "The Easter Man" (with H. M. Tennent Ltd.), "Rookery Nook" (with David Kitchen—Henry Velez, Ltd., also directed), 1964; "Boeing-Boeing" (New York, directed), "Dual Marriageway" (also directed), 1965.
(Died 1 Aug., 1966; age 65)

MINTER, Mary Miles, actress; *b.* Shreveport, La., U.S.A., 1 Apr., 1902; *m.* Commander H. H. Ridder, U.S.N.; formerly known as Juliet Shelby; made her first appearance on the stage as a small child, in 1908, in "Cameo Kirby," with the late Nat Goodwin; during 1909 appeared with Robert Hilliard in "A Fool There Was," and in 1910 with Bertha Kalich in "A Woman of To-day," and in "The Master Key"; at the Liberty Theatre, New York, 14 Nov., 1911, made a great success as Virgie in "The Littlest Rebel," and for three and a half years continued to play the same part on tour; at the Longacre Theatre, Nov., 1914, played Helen in "What it Means to a Woman"; in the same year she turned her attention to the cinema stage, on which she has taken a prominent place, "starring" in such pictures as "The Fairy and the Waif," "The Amazing Impostor," "South of Suva," "Drums of Fate," "The Trail of the Lonesome Pine," "Peggy Leads the Way," "The Mate of Sally Ann," etc.

MINTO, Dorothy, actress; *b.* London, 21 Feb., 1891; *m.* (1) Shiel Barry, (2) Robert Geoffrey Buxton; made her first appearance on the stage at the age of thirteen with F. R. Benson's company, playing among other parts that of the Second Gravedigger in " Hamlet "; appeared at the Royalty, Dec., 1904, as Nan in " The Power of Darkness "; at the St. George's Hall, Apr., 1905, played the Peasant Girl in " The First Franciscans "; first attracted attention by her performance of the part of Juliet in " Romeo and Juliet," at the Royalty May, 1905, under the auspices of the Elizabethan Society; appeared at the Court, Sept., 1905, in " The Wild Duck "; next appeared as Jenny Hill in " Major Barbara," at the Court Theatre, Nov., 1905; at the Scala, Mar., 1906, played Clarissa Huntleigh in " The School for Husbands," and at the Court, Apr., 1906, played Prunella in a revival of that play; at the Haymarket, May, 1906, appeared as Kitty in " Olf and the Little Maid "; at the Court, July, 1906, as Dolly Clandon in " You Never Can Tell "; and at the Lyric, Oct., 1906, as Adela in " Robin Hood "; at the Court, played Sylvia Craven in " The Philanderer " (Feb., 1907), Ernestine Blunt in " Votes for Women " (Apr., 1907), and Stella Faringford in " The Return of the Prodigal " (Apr., 1907); at His Majesty's, June, 1907, appeared as Nora in " Mr. Steinmann's Corner "; at the Imperial, June, 1907, as Mercy Hainton in " David Ballard "; and at the Court, Sept., 1907, as Joy in the play of that name; at His Majesty's, Apr., 1908, played Nerissa in " The Merchant of Venice "; at the Lyric, Sept., 1908, played Flora in " The Duke's Motto "; at Duke of York's, Dec., 1908, played in " Peter Pan "; appeared at same theatre, Mar., 1910, as Carry in " Old Friends," and in May, 1910, as Sybil Frost in " Chains "; joined Gertrude Kingston at the Little Theatre, Oct., 1910, and appeared as Myrrhina in " Lysistrata "; subsequently appeared there as Daphne Grayle in " Just to Get Married," Fiordelisa in " The Merciful Soul," Bianca in " An Episode," Dora Delaney in " Fanny's

First Play "; at the Kingsway, May, 1911, played Kitty Clive in " The First Actress "; at the Apollo, Sept., 1912, played Betty Baker in " The Grass Widows "; at the Criterion, Nov., 1912, Dolly Graham in " Where there's a Will—— "; at the Hippodrome, Dec., 1912, appeared in the *revue* " Hullo, Ragtime ! "; at the Garrick, Aug., 1913, played Lulu in " The Real Thing "; at the Apollo, Mar., 1914, Dorothy Gedge in " Things We'd Like to Know "; at the Prince of Wales's, June, 1914, Ursula in " An Indian Summer "; at the Strand, Oct., 1914, Kiki in " The Glad Eye "; at the Prince of Wales's, Jan., 1915, Fifi in " A Chinese Honeymoon "; at the Empire, May, 1915, appeared in " Watch Your Step "; at the Ambassadors', Mar., 1916, appeared in " More," and June, 1916, in " Pell-Mell "; at the Apollo, Apr., 1917, played Miena in " Double Dutch "; at the Strand, Oct., 1917, Dolly Thompson in " Wild Heather "; Dec., 1917, Melisande in " The Happy Family "; at the Savoy, Feb., 1918, appeared as Mabel Jackson in " Nothing But the Truth "; at the Little Theatre, May, 1920, Jemima in " Husbands for All "; in Sept., 1920, at the Little Theatre, joined the Grand Guignol Company, appearing in " G.H.Q. Love," " Oh! Hell !! " and " What did her Husband Say ? "; in Dec., 1920, appeared in " A Man in Mary's Room," and " Punch and Judy "; at the Queen's Theatre, Mar., 1921, played Trixie Lorraine in " Nightie Night "; at the Queen's, Oct., 1921, Mauricette in " The Hotel Mouse "; at the Shaftesbury, Mar., 1922, Trixie in a revival of " Nightie Night "; at the Ambassadors', May, 1923, Alice in " The Piccadilly Puritan"; at the Duke of York's, June, 1923, Eliza in " Eliza Comes to Stay "; at the Prince's, Oct., 1924, Rosie Callaghan in " The Blue Peter "; Comedy, May, 1925, succeeded Olga Lindo as Nettie in " Tarnish "; London Pavilion, June, 1925, succeeded Hermione Baddeley in " On With the Dance "; Portsmouth, Nov., 1926, played Dou Dou Delville in " His Wild Oat "; Savoy, June, 1927, Hetty in " Wild-Cat Hetty "; Duke of York's, Nov., 1927,

Lottie in "Good Morning, Bill"; Vaudeville, May, 1928, Zita Lorton in "Who's Who?"; July, 1929, toured as Philippa in "The Third Party"; Aug., 1929, toured as the Girl in "Damaged Goods"; in Jan., 1930, toured as Ivy in "The Double Man"; Everyman, Apr., 1930, played Stella Dallas in "Fourth Floor Heaven"; "Q," Nov., 1930, Ginger Hopkins in "The Great Silence"; Feb., 1931, toured as Rosemary in "Two Deep"; Wyndham's, Nov., 1931, played Edith in "Port Said"; Sept., 1932, went to Canada, with Barry Jones and Maurice Colbourne's company, to play the Nurse in "Too True to be Good," and Amanda in "The Apple Cart"; after returning to London, appeared at the Embassy, July, 1933, as Edith in "Vessels Departing."

MIRAMOVA, Elena, actress; *b.* Czaritjyn, Russia; *e.* Michigan University and University of California; *m.* Frederic Theodore Rolbein; studied for the stage under private tutors and at the Corinsh School of Art, Seattle, U.S.A.; has been on the stage since childhood; appeared at the leading theatres in San Francisco, Los Angeles, and Hollywood, playing in 1923, Ginevra in "The Jest," Martha Bernick in "The Pillars of Society"; in 1924, Liza Doolittle in "Pygmalion," Sydney Fairfield in "A Bill of Divorcement," 1925, Madame Butterfly in Belasco and Long's play of that name; 1926 Sister Beatrice in Maeterlinck's play, etc.; made her first appearance on the New York stage, at the Lyceum Theatre, 16 Jan., 1931, as Bianca in "Anatol"; at the National Theatre, Apr., 1931, succeeded Eugenie Leontovitch as Grusinskaja in "Grand Hotel"; made her first appearance in London, at the Adelphi Theatre, 3 Sept., in the same part, and in Feb., 1932, toured the English provinces in the same part; Garrick, Oct., 1932, played Vera Levine in "The Bear Dances"; Forrest, New York, Jan., 1934, Theodora in "Theodora, the Quean"; National, Feb., 1935, Marianne Pentland in "Times Have Changed"; again appeared in London at the St. Martin's, June, 1935, when she played Sally in "The Two Mrs. Carrolls"; returned to the United States, 1936, and appeared at the National, Washington, Dec., 1936, in "The Two Mrs. Carrolls," and toured 1937, in the same play; at Ogunquit, Maine, July, 1938, played Fay in "Fata Morgana"; Golden, New York, Mar., 1939, Liesa Bergman in "Close Quarters"; Belasco, Jan., 1943, played Tonia Karpova in "Dark Eyes," which she wrote, in collaboration with Eugenie Leontovitch. *Recreations:* Reading and horseback-riding.

MIRANDE, Yves (A. Charles Le Querrec); French dramatic author; author of the following, among other, plays: "Excelsior" (with Fernand Nozière), 1910; "Les Jeux sont Faits"? (with Guillaume Wolff), 1910; "Champion de Boxe," 1912; "Le Partenaire Silencieux" (with Henri Géroule), 1913; "La Première Idée" (with Géroule), 1913; "Amour quand Tu Nous Tiens!"; "La Gare Régulatrice" (with Gaston Leroux); "Un Homme en Habit" (with André Picard), 1920; "La Femme de mon Ami" (with H. Géroule), 1920; "Un Petit Trou pas Cher" (with Henri Cain), 1920; "Le Chasseur de Chez Maxim" (with Gustave Quinson), 1920; "Peg de Mon Coeur" (adaptation with Maurice Vaucaire), 1921; "Simone est Comme ca" (with A. Madis), 1921.

MIRBEAU, Octave, French novelist and dramatic author; *b.* Travières, Calvados, France, 16 Feb., 1848, has written the following, among other plays: "Les Mauvais Bergers," "Le Portefeuille," 1902; "L'Epidémie," "Vieux Ménage," "Scrupules," and "Les Affaires sont les Affaires," which was staged at the Comédie Française, 1903; an adaptation of this piece (by Sydney Grundy) was produced at His Majesty's, by Sir Herbert Tree, 1905, under the title of "Business is Business"; his play, "Le Foyer," written in collaboration with M. Thadée Natanson, was produced at the Comédie Française, Dec., 1908,

after several postponements. *Recreation :* Motoring.
(Died 16 Feb., 1917; age 69)

MISTINGUETT, (*née* Jeanne Bourgeois); actress and dancer; *b.* La Pointe de Raquet, near Enghien and Montmorency (S. et O.) France; *e.* Enghien and Paris; made her first appearance on the stage at the Trianon Concert-hall, Paris; subsequently appeared at the Gaîté-Rochechouart, and from 1899–1907, appeared at the Eldorado music-hall; at the Folies-Dramatiques, 1907, made her first appearance in "straight" plays, playing comedy parts in "Le Coup de Jarnac," and "Le Millième Constat"; subsequently appeared at the Moulin-Rouge, when she first presented La Valse Chaloupée; appeared at the Bouffes-Parisiens, in the *revue* "Aux Bouffes on pouffe"; at the Gymnase 1909, appeared in "L'Ane de Buridan," and at the Palais-Royal, 1910, in "Tais-toi, mon cœur"; Variétés, 1911, in "Les Midinettes," "Le Bonheur sous la main," and "La Vie Parisienne"; subsequently appeared in the United States; on her return, appeared at the Folies-Bergère, where she appeared in numerous sensational dances, and when her dancing-partner was Maurice Chevalier, with whom she danced the famous "Valse Renversant"; she then appeared at the Casino de Paris, where she was seen in numerous *revue* sketches, and introduced her famous song "Mon Homme"; in 1920, she was again at the Folies-Bergère and Casino de Paris, with Chevalier; in 1921, she appeared in a revival of "Madame Sans-Gêne"; again appeared at the Casino de Paris, in "Paris en l'air," where she launched her famous "J'en ai marre," and in 1924, appeared there in "Bonjour Paris"; at the Moulin Rouge, 1928, appeared in "Le Salon de la Dubarry," which was subsequently banned by the French Government; Casino de Paris, 1929, in "Paris-Miss," and 1933, in "Voilà Paris"; has since appeared at intervals in several of her original creations, and in 1944, was appearing at l'Etoile de Paris, in

revue; made her first appearance on the London stage at the Casino, 8 Dec., 1947; her book "Mistinguett and her Confessions," was translated into English, and published in 1938; was for some years, part-proprietor of the Moulin-Rouge.
(Died 5 Jan., 1956; age 82)

MITCHELHILL, J. P., manager and theatre proprietor; *b.* London, 27 May, 1879; entered management when, in conjunction with Lt.-Col. E. S. Halford and Cecil Halford, he purchased the Duchess Theatre in 1930; his first production at that theatre was "An Object of Virtue," 4 Nov., 1930; with Nancy Price, produced "A Rose Without a Thorn," 1932; then produced "Children in Uniform," 1932; "Eight Bells," "Laburnum Grove" (with J. B. Priestley), 1933; "Eden End" (with Priestley), 1934, "Cornelius" (with Priestley), 1935; "Night Must Fall," 1935; "Springtide" (with Priestley), "Murder in the Cathedral," 1936; "Mile Away Murder," "Time and the Conways" (with Priestley), "I Killed the Count," 1937; "Glorious Morning," 1938; disposed of the Duchess, 1938; he also produced "Anthony and Anna" at the Whitehall Theatre, 1935, soon after production presenting the play to the company, who continued the run on communal lines until 1937; at the St. James's, Dec., 1938, produced "Let's Pretend"; is now Chairman of the London Mask Theatre, Ltd. *Recreations:* Lawn tennis and squash.
(Died 6 Aug., 1966; age 87)

MITCHELL, Dodson, actor; *b.* 23 Jan., 1868; made his first appearance on the New York stage, at the Grand Opera House, 20 Nov., 1885, as Didier Barbeau in "Fanchon the Cricket," with his aunt, the famous Maggie Mitchell; subsequently he appeared in her company in "Jane Eyre"; for thirteen seasons, 1888–1900, he appeared in Julia Marlowe's company; he then joined John Drew, and appeared at the Empire Theatre, Sept., 1900, as Captain Lewis in "Richard

Carvel"; with John B. Mason, he appeared in 1901, in "The Altar of Friendship," and later, he appeared in "Arizona"; during 1902–03, played Simonides in "Ben Hur"; from 1903–06, appeared with Arnold Daly in "Major André," "Candida," "How He Lied to Her Husband," "You Never Can Tell," "John Bull's Other Island," etc.; at the American Theatre, May, 1905, appeared in "The Merchant of Venice," with Jacob P. Adler, and in "Fédora," with Bertha Kalich; at the Princess Theatre, 1906–7, appeared with Madame Nazimova in "Hedda Gabler" and "A Doll's House"; at the Manhattan, Mar., 1907, appeared as Mr. Praed in "Mrs. Warren's Profession"; Liberty, Sept., 1907, as John Westervelt in "Lola from Berlin"; Bijou, 1907–08, with Madame Nazimova, appeared in "The Comtesse Coquette," "The Master Builder," and "The Comet"; New York Theatre, Aug., 1909, played Morris in "The Sins of Society"; Stuyvesant, Dec., 1909, Emile Plock in "The Lily"; Criterion, Mar., 1912, Ira Corbus in "The Bargain"; Eltinge, Sept., 1912, Edward Gilder in "Within the Law"; Fulton, Mar., 1913, Loches in "Damaged Goods"; Booth, Oct., 1914, Hartridge Senior in "The Money Makers"; 39th Street, Mar., 1915, Henri Blondeau in "Taking Chances"; Longacre, Apr., 1915, Pastor Manders in "Ghosts"; 44th Street, Sept., 1915, Ralph Knight in "Husband and Wife"; Fulton, Oct., 1915, Captain Hartwig in "Sherman Was Right"; 48th Street, Dec., 1916, in "The Eternal Magdalene"; Princess, Jan., 1917, Smoot in "'Ception Shoals"; Plymouth, Mar., 1918, Werle in "The Wild Duck"; Booth, Sept., 1918, Comrade Nagel in "Watch Your Neighbour"; Belasco, Apr., 1919, Sandy McKillop in "Dark Rosaleen"; Maxine Elliott Theatre, Nov., 1919, Mr. Warrington in "The Unknown Woman"; Cohan, May, 1920, G. W. Parker in "Honey Girl"; Sept., 1920, the Tavern-Keeper in "The Tavern"; Playhouse, Aug., 1921, John C. Kent in "Personality"; 39th Street, Oct., 1921, George W. Grubble in "Like a King"; Henry Miller, Jan., 1922, John K. Carlton in "The National Anthem"; Frazee, Apr.,

1922, George Dodge in "The Night Call"; Bijou, Dec., 1922, Jonathan Cumberland in "Listening In"; 39th Street, Aug., 1923, Dana Roberts in "Home Fires"; Broadhurst, Sept.–Oct., 1924, David Schussell in "Izzy," and Gifonetto in "The Red Falcon"; Cherry Lane, Apr., 1925, John Slag in "Wild Birds"; Ritz, Apr., 1926, Tom Beale in "Beau Gallant"; Fulton, Oct., 1926, succeeded Robert Haines as Peter Rankin in "The Donovan Affair"; Cort, Oct., 1927, John Strickler in "Behold This Dreamer"; Royale, Oct., 1929, Mr. Gray in "First Mortgage"; Biltmore, May, 1931, Henry Duncan in "Her Supporting Cast"; Longacre, Nov., 1931, David Benson in his own play "In Times Square"; Morosco, Oct., 1932, Henry Porter in "Black Sheep"; Vanderbilt, Nov., 1932, Jonathan Schorr in "Jamboree", Selwyn, Dec., 1932, Senator Thompson in "The Little Black Book"; Civic Repertory, Apr., 1934, Walcott in "Stevedore"; Fulton, Sept., 1934, Ned Kirchwey in "Errant Lady"; National, Oct., 1934, a Platform Speaker in "Within the Gates"; 49th Street, Mar., 1935, Dr. Wade in "A Woman of the Soil"; Biltmore, Oct., 1935, Charles Franker in "Good Men and True"; Booth, Jan., 1936, Doc Tanner in "Mid-West"; St. James, Oct., 1936, Otto von Kruif in "Ten Million Ghosts"; 48th Street, Dec., 1936, Ephraim Clark in "Around the Corner"; Hudson, Feb., 1937, Morten Kiil in "An Enemy of the People"; is also the author of "Paul Revere," 1903, and "Cornered," produced at the Astor, 1920.

(Died 2 June, 1939; age 71)

MITCHELL, Grant, actor; *b.* Columbus, Ohio, U.S.A., 17 June, 1874; *s.* of General John Grant Mitchell and his wife Laura (Platt); *e.* public schools, Columbus, Ohio State University, Phillips Academy, Andover, Yale College, and Harvard Law School; commenced life as a newspaper reporter; subsequently, for three years, practised law; then became a student at the American Academy of Dramatic Arts; made his first appearance on the stage at the Grand Opera House, Chicago, 14 Oct., 1902, in "Julius Caesar," with the late Richard Mansfield; made his first appearance in New York, Dec., 1902, in the same play, at the Herald Square Theatre; he next appeared at the Savoy, New York, 1903, in "The Girl with the Green Eyes," later, playing in "Glad of It"; was with Francis Wilson in "Cousin Billy," at the Criterion, New York, Jan., 1905, and "The Mountain Climber," at the same theatre, Mar., 1906; at the Savoy, New York, in Oct., 1906, played in "The House of Mirth," subsequently touring in "The Butterfly"; at the Garrick, New York, Nov., 1907, played the Lamplighter in "The Toymaker of Nuremberg"; at the Hudson, Aug., 1908, the Rev. Archibald Crane in "The Call of the North"; at Daly's, New York, Oct., 1908, Charlie Hope in "Myself—Bettina"; at the Maxine Elliott Theatre, Dec., 1908, the Native in "The Chaperon"; at the Hudson, Sept., 1909, played in "An American Widow"; at Rochester, N.Y., Oct., 1909, in "A Man's World"; at the Hudson, Dec., 1909, played Harry Parkes in "The Next of Kin"; at the Gaiety, New York, Sept., 1910, Edward Lamb in "Get-Rich-Quick Wallingford"; at the Belasco, Dec., 1912, Farrel Howard, Jun., in "Years of Discretion"; at the Cohan Theatre, Sept., 1914, Rodney Martin in "It Pays to Advertise"; at the Cohan and Harris, Aug., 1917, John Paul Bart in "A Tailor-Made Man"; in 1919 Charles Martin in "A Prince There Was"; at the Longacre, Jan., 1921, William Burroughs in "The Champion"; Mar., 1921, Andrew Lane in "The Hero"; at the Belmont, May, 1922, "Duke" Merrill in "Kempy"; at the Bijou, Aug., 1923, Chester Binney in "The Whole Town's Talking"; at the Forty-eighth Street Theatre, Dec., 1924, Rodney Kingsley in "The Habitual Husband"; June, 1925, Douglas Blackwell in "Spooks"; 49th Street Theatre, Dec., 1925, Henry Adams in "One of the Family"; Henry Miller Theatre, Sept., 1927, Joseph Meadows in "Baby Cyclone"; Fulton, Feb., 1929, Walter Fairchild in "All the King's Horses"; at Boston,

May, 1929, Andrew Gillis in "Andrew Takes a Wife"; Lyceum, New York, Feb., 1937, Jim Cogswell, in "Tide Rising"; Guild, Nov., 1938, Orrin Sturgis in "Ringside Seat"; in summer theatres, 1948, appeared in "The Late George Apley"; commenced film career, 1930, and has appeared in innumerable pictures. *Clubs:* Players', Lambs, Century, Yale, and Town Hall, New York, and The Masquers, Hollywood. *(Died 1 May, 1957; age 82)*

MITCHELL, Julien, actor; *b.* Glossop, Derbyshire, 13 Nov., 1888; *s.* of Julien Mitchell and his wife Helen (Vose); *e.* Glossop Grammar School; *m.* Sofia Buchanan; made his first appearance on the stage at the Theatre Royal, Blackburn, 1906; during the War served with the Royal Fusiliers; toured in the provinces for twenty years; including several years with his own repertory company; made his first appearance in London at the Apollo Theatre, 29 May, 1928, as Field in "The Squeaker"; made a notable success at the Garrick Theatre, Jan., 1935, when he played Mr. Hardcastle in "Love On The Dole," which ran for a year; "Q," Apr., and Duke of York's, June, 1936, played Marden in "Miss Smith"; Savoy, Dec., 1937, Norman Merridew in "Bulldog Drummond Hits Out"; Savoy, Apr., 1938, the Father in "Power and Glory"; Duke of York's, Nov., 1938, Thomas Cromwell in "Traitor's Gate"; Westminster, Apr., 1939, Mr. Burgess in "Candida"; Globe, May, 1939, Big Mog in "Rhondda Roundabout"; Lyric, Aug., 1942, Lieut.-Commander Hopkins in "Escort"; Piccadilly, Oct., 1942, Benjamin Hubbard in "The Little Foxes"; Arts, June, 1943, Dr. Johnson in "The Judgment of Doctor Johnson"; Lyric, Mar., 1944, Mr. Carfax in "A Murder for a Valentine"; Aldwych, Aug., 1944, Fred Miller in "To-morrow the World"; New, Oct., 1946, played Arthur Birling in "An Inspector Calls"; toured in Germany, 1947, as Boanerges in "The Apple Cart"; Criterion, Sept., 1947, played Hamilton Hardy in "School for Spinsters"; St. James's, Nov., 1947, Arthur Selby in "Private

Enterprise"; Strand, Nov., 1949, Uncle Stanley in "Queen Elizabeth Slept Here"; entered films, 1935, and has appeared in numerous pictures. *Recreation:* Golf. *Clubs:* Savage, Green Room, and Stage Golfing Society. *(Died 4 Nov., 1954; age 65)*

MITCHELL, Langdon Elwyn, author and dramatist; *b.* Philadelphia, 17 Feb., 1862; *s.* of Silas Weir Mitchell, the eminent physician and author; *e.* St. Paul's School, U.S.A., Dresden, and Paris; courses at the Harvard Law School and the Columbia Law School, and admitted to the New York Bar in 1886; *m.*, 1892, Marion Lea, actress; his first play was " In the Season," produced at the St. James's Theatre, London, 1893, besides which he has made a dramatization of Thackeray's " Vanity Fair," under the title of " Becky Sharp," and produced an original comedy of American life called " The New York Idea," both plays in the *répertoire* of Mrs. Fiske; his other plays include " A Kentucky Belle " and a dramatization of " The Kreutzer Sonata," played by Madame Bertha Kalich, " Step by Step," " The New Marriage," " Major Pendennis "; in addition, Mr. Mitchell is the author of " Sylvian, and other Poems," 1884; "Poems," 1894; "Love in the Backwoods," 1896; "Understanding America," 1927; his play, "The New York Idea," was produced at the Apollo Theatre, London, 27 Nov., 1907, by Mr. Herbert Sleath. *Club:* The Players'. *(Died 20 Oct., 1935; age 73)*

MITCHELL, Thomas, actor and dramatic author; *b.* Elizabeth, New Jersey, U.S.A., 11 July, 1895; *s.* of James Mitchell and his wife Mary (Donnelly); *e.* public schools, New Jersey; *m.* Anne Stuart Brewer; formerly engaged as a newspaper reporter; made his first appearance on the stage at Madison Square Garden Theatre, New York, Jan., 1913, as Trinculo in "The Tempest," with the Ben Greet Players; in 1913–15, was a member of Charles D. Coburn's Shakespearean company, touring all over the United States; at the

Harris Theatre, 2 Oct., 1916, played Tony in "Under Sentence"; Bandbox, Mar., 1917, played the Waiter and the Florist in "Nju"; Belmont, Sept., 1918, Ray Parcher in "Crops and Croppers"; Plymouth, Oct., 1918, Artemyev in "Redemption"; Belasco, Apr., 1919, Martin Donagh in "Dark Rosaleen"; Booth, May, 1920, Sam Robinson in "Not So Long Ago"; Bramhall Playhouse, Apr., 1921, Christopher Mahon in "The Playboy of the Western World"; Belasco, Nov., 1921, Adolphe in "Kiki"; Little, Feb., 1926, Bemis in "The Wisdom Tooth"; Hudson, Aug., 1927, James Bolton in "Blood Money"; Selwyn, Nov., 1927, Tommy Glennon in "Nightstick"; Morosco, Oct., 1928, Norman Overbeck in "Little Accident"; subsequently played John Mears in "The Last Mile"; Morosco, Sept., 1931, Peter Hammil in "Cloudy With Showers"; John Golden Theatre, Feb., 1932, McKinley in "Riddle Me This"; Times Square, Sept., 1932, Buckley Joyce Thomas in "Clear All Wires"; Little, Dec., 1932, Bob Taylor in "Honeymoon"; 48th Street, Jan., 1935, James Masters in Fly Away Home"; Nov., 1935, Paw Meriwether in "Stick-in-the-Mud"; Booth, Oct., 1947, Inspector Goole in "An Inspector Calls"; Mansfield, Mar., 1949, Bert Hutchins in "The Biggest Thief in Town"; at Chicago, during the 1949 season, and at the Morosco, New York, Sept., 1950, played Willy Loman in "Death of a Salesman"; in summer theatres, 1952, played Mr. Burnham Wicks in "The Other Foot," which he also directed; at the Mark Hellinger, New York, Feb., 1953, played Dr. Downer in "Hazel Flagg"; at the Ambassador, N.Y., Feb., 1960, played Rollie Evans in "Cut of the Axe"; has also staged many successful productions; part author (with Floyd Dell) of "Little Accident," and "Cloudy With Showers"; commenced film career, 1936, and has appeared in innumerable films since that date. *Clubs:* Lambs, and Players', New York. *(Died 17 Dec., 1962; age 70)*

MITZI-DALTY, Mdlle., French actress; appeared at the Odéon in 1903, in " Les Appeleurs " ; joined the

Comédie Française in 1904, making her first appearance, 15 Mar., 1904, as Mdlle. Hackendorf in "L'Ami des Femmes"; also appeared there as Fortunata in "Le Dieu Terme," Le Baronne de Ligneuil in "La Rivale," Marcelle Renaud in "Chacun sa Vie," "Paraître," etc.; at the Théâtre de Sarah Bernhardt, 1919, played in "L'Aiglon," "Napoléonette"; appeared at the Garrick, London, July, 1921, with M. Louis Verneuil in "Monsieur Beverley," "Le Traité d'Auteuil," "La Charrette Anglaise," etc. *Address* : 41 Rue Boissy d'Anglais, Paris.

MOELLER, Philip, dramatic author and producer; *b.* New York City, 26 Aug., 1880; *s.* of Frederick Moeller and his wife Rachael Kate (Phillips); *e.* New York public and high schools, New York University, and Columbia University; made his first production at the Bandbox Theatre, New York, 1913, when he produced "Helena's Husband"; was one of the founders and a director of the Washington Square Players, 1914-17; a founder and director of the Theatre Guild; among his productions may be mentioned "Saint Joan," 1923; "Fata Morgana," 1924; "The Guardsman," 1924; "They Knew What They Wanted," 1924, etc.; as director and producer for the Theatre Guild of New York, from 1925–37 he produced over seventy plays; he also directed films, from 1934; is the author of "The Roadhouse in Arden," 1916; "Sisters of Susanne," 1916; "The Beautiful Legend of Pokey," 1918; "Madame Sand," 1918; "Molière," 1919; "Sophie," 1920; "Fata Morgana" (adaptation, with J. L. A. Burrell), 1924; "Caprice" (adaptation), 1928. *Recreations*: Travel and book collecting. *(Died 26 Apr., 1958; age 78)*

MOFFAT, Graham, actor and dramatic author; *b.* Glasgow, 21 Feb., 1866; *s.* of William Moffat and his wife Helen (Dobson); *e.* St. Stephen's Parish School, Hampton Court Academy and Rosemount Academy, Glasgow; *m.* Maggie L. Linck; was for many years a platform enter-

tainer; made his first appearance on the regular stage at the Athenaeum, Glasgow, 26 Mar., 1908, as John Snodgrass in "Till the Bells Ring"; same theatre, Apr., 1909, played Bob Dewar in "The Concealed Bed," and Mattha Inglis in "A Scrape o' the Pen"; at the Royalty, Glasgow, Dec., 1910, played M'Tavish in "Colin in Fairyland"; made his first appearance on the London stage, at the London Pavilion, 10 Apr., 1911, as Bob Dewar in "The Concealed Bed"; next appeared at the Playhouse, June, 1911, in "Till the Bells Ring," and 4 July as Tammas Biggar in "Bunty Pulls the Strings," which was transferred to the evening bill at the Haymarket on 18 July, and ran over 600 performances, finishing in Oct., 1912; at the Comedy, Sept., 1912, appeared as Mattha Inglis in "A Scrape o' the Pen"; in Apr., 1914, sailed for Australia, where he appeared in "Bunty Pulls the Strings," "A Scrape o' the Pen," "Till the Bells Ring"; Alhambra, Glasgow, Mar., 1920, appeared as Baillie John Cameron in "Don't Tell"; subsequently went to the United States, and at the Nora Bayes Theatre, New York, Sept., 1920, appeared in the same part; subsequently toured in South Africa; reappeared in London, at the Garrick, Jan., 1924, as Tammas Biggar in a revival of "Bunty Pulls the Strings"; Mar., 1924, played Mattha Inglis in a revival of "A Scrape o' the Pen"; Apr., 1924, played Jeems Gibb in "Susie Knots the Strings"; appeared at the Coliseum, Apr., 1925, in "Till the Bells Ring"; Royalty, Dec., 1926, played Andra Beddle in "Granny"; subsequently toured in the same part; during 1929, toured as Wull Todd in "Susie Tangles the Strings"; at the Saville Theatre, Jan., 1933, again played Tammas in "Bunty Pulls the Strings"; is the author of all the above-mentioned plays, with the exception of "Colin in Fairyland"; appeared at the Theatre Royal, Glasgow, June, 1932, in connection with the centenary of Sir Walter Scott, as David Deans in "Jennie Deans," Bailie Nicol Jarvie in "Rob Roy," and Dominie Sampson in "Guy Mannering." *Favourite part* :

Bailie Nicol Jarvie.
(Died 12 Dec., 1951; age 85)

MOFFAT, Mrs. Graham, actress; *b.* Spital, 7 Jan., 1873; *d.* of Frederick William Linck and his wife Margaret (Dowie); *e.* Glasgow; *m.* Graham Moffat; made her first appearance on the stage at the Athenaeum, Glasgow, 26 Mar., 1908, as Janet Struthers in her husband's first play " Till the Bells Ring "; made her first appearance on the London stage, at the London Pavilion, 10 Apr., 1911, as Mrs. Dewar in " The Concealed Bed "; at the Playhouse, June, 1911, played Ellen Dunlop in " Bunty Pulls the Strings," and played the same part at the Haymarket for five months of the run of that play; Comedy, Oct., 1912, played Leezie Inglis in " A Scrape o' the Pen "; during 1914-5 toured in these plays in Australia and New Zealand; at the Alhambra, Glasgow, Mar., 1920, played Cousin Tibbie in " Don't Tell," subsequently touring in the same part in Canada and America; during 1921 toured in South Africa; at the Garrick, Jan. to Apr., 1924, appeared in revivals of " Bunty Pulls the Strings," " A Scrape o' the Pen," and as Susie in " Susie Knots the Strings "; Alhambra, Glasgow, Mar., 1926, played Granny in a play of that name, appearing in the same part at the Royalty, Dec., 1926; in 1930, toured as Leezie in " A Scrape o' the Pen"; at the Saville Theatre, Jan., 1933, played Susie in "Bunty Pulls the Strings"; appeared 1934, in the film "Rolling Home."
(Died 19 Feb., 1943; age 70)

MOFFAT, Kate, actress; *b.* Glasgow; *d.* of William Moffat and his wife Helen (Dobson); sister of Graham Moffat; made her first appearance on the stage at Glasgow, 1896, in concert platform work, with her brother Graham Moffat, and remained in that class of entertainment until 1908; appeared at the Athenaeum, Glasgow, 26 Mar., 1908, as Annie Laurie in a play of that name, written by Graham Moffat; appeared at the same theatre, Apr., 1909, as Madge Dewar in " The Concealed Bed," and Mrs. Dashwood in " A Scrape o' the Pen "; made

her first appearance on the London stage at the London Pavilion, 10 Apr., 1911, as Madge Dewar in " The Concealed Bed "; at the Playhouse 4 July, 1911, appeared as Bunty Biggar in " Bunty Pulls the Strings," and played the same part at the Haymarket, when the play was transferred to that theatre; at the Playhouse, Nov., 1911, played Mary Brown in " The Price of Coal "; June, 1912, Kate Mercer in " The Starling "; at the Duke of York's, Feb., 1913, appeared as Kate in " The Twelve Pound Look "; at the Playhouse, June, 1913, appeared in her original part in a revival of " Bunty Pulls the Strings "; in Sept., 1913, toured as Minnie Gilfillian in " Sweet Lavender "; at the Savoy Theatre, Sept., 1916, played Effie in " The Professor's Love Story "; at the Saville Theatre, Jan., 1933, played Ellen Dunlop in " Bunty Pulls the Strings." *Address :* The Oasis, Sandhurst, by Camberley, Berks.

MOFFAT, Margaret, actress; *b.* Edinburgh, 11 Oct., 1882; *d.* of Thomas Bury, sculptor, and his wife Christine (Shierlaw); *e.* public schools and University of Toronto, Canada; *m.* Sewell Collins; was engaged as a journalist prior to making her first appearance on the stage, at the Savoy Theatre, New York, 1903, as Suky in a revival of " Janice Meredith "; she then played in " stock," appearing in a great variety of parts, from Shakespeare to farce; in 1904 sang the part of Contrary Mary in " Babes in Toyland," and she next played in " The Wizard of Oz " ; she then left the stage for two years, during which she was engaged as a newspaper reporter, and as editor of the woman's page of *The New York Evening Mail*; returned to the stage, 1906, with Robert Edeson, as Molly Livingstone in " Strongheart "; subsequently played in " vaudeville "; made her first appearance in London, at the Royalty, 7 Dec., 1911, as Millicent in her husband's one-act play " Tuppence, Please " ; at the Coliseum, Apr., 1912, played in " Just Like a Woman," in which she appeared by command at Sandringham before H.M. the King, on 2 Dec., 1912; Daly's, New York, Dec., 1912, played Mary Murray in " The Drone "; returned to London, and at the Coliseum, Mar., 1913, played the Charwoman in " The Scrub Lady "; subsequently appeared at the London Hippodrome, in " Hullo Ragtime "; at the Globe, Apr., 1916, Sadie in " The Show Shop "; in 1917 toured in " The Girl from Ciro's "; at the Duke of York's, Oct., 1917, played Mary Eastwood in " The Thirteenth Chair "; at the Royalty, May, 1918, Martha in " The Man from Toronto "; appeared for several years in sketches in variety theatres; at the Shaftesbury, Apr., 1923, played the Casting Director in " Merton of the Movies "; at the Vanderbilt Theatre, New York, Nov., 1923, Sarah in " The Camel's Back "; at the Everyman, London, Nov., 1924, Fanny Simister in " Clogs to Clogs "; at the Little Theatre, Dec., 1924, Nancy White in " You and I "; Ambassadors', Oct., 1925, Mrs. Baxter in " Growing Pains "; Comedy, Dec., 1925, Margaret Clancy in " 9.45 "; subsequently toured in the same part; Globe, Apr., 1928, succeeded Clare Greet as Bridget O'Rourke in " Square Crooks "; then toured in " Mother's Brother "; Prince's, July, 1928, played Anna in " Contraband "; Embassy, Oct., 1928, Katie in " The Seventh Guest," in which she also toured; Globe, Sept., 1930, played Emma Jones in " Street Scene "; Ambassadors', Sept., 1932, Lillian Garfield in "The Left Bank"; Phoenix, Oct., 1932, Mrs. Linkley in "Never Come Back"; St. Martin's, Oct., 1933, Mrs. McFee in "The Wind and the Rain," which ran over two years; Strand, Apr., 1936, Amy Oxley-Dobbins in "Baby Austin"; Queen's, Feb., 1937, Maggie in "Retreat from Folly"; Globe, Nov., 1938, Mrs. Jones in "Robert's Wife," which ran for eighteen months; has appeared in films and since 1936, has played in "The End of the Road," "Keep Your Seats, Please," "Farewell Again," etc.

(Died 19 Feb., 1942; age 50)

MOFFAT, Winifred, actress; *b.* Glasgow, 2 May, 1899; *d.* of Graham

Moffat and his wife Maggie (Linck); *e.* Girls' High School, Glasgow, and London; made her first appearance on the stage at the Athenaeum Hall, Glasgow, 1909, as Eppie in " A Scrape o' the Pen "; made her first appearance in London at the Haymarket, July, 1911, as a child in " Bunty Pulls the Strings" during 1914--15 toured in Australia, as Teenie in the same play; at the Alhambra, Glasgow, in 1920, played Jessie Bella Cameron in " Don't Tell," and then toured; went to America, Canada, and South Africa, 1920-23, playing Jean in " A Scrape o' the Pen," Madge in " The Concealed Bed," Nell in " The Days of Robbie Burns," Jessie Bella in "Don't Tell," Bunty in "Bunty Pulls the Strings," and Janet in "Aldersyde"; on returning to England, toured in "Till the Bells Ring," and as Bunty; at the Garrick, London, Jan.–Apr., 1924, played Bunty, Jean Menzies in " A Scrape o' the Pen," and Nannie Ormiston in " Susie Knots the Strings "; Royalty, Dec., 1926, Jenny Forsyth in " Granny," subsequently touring in the same part; during 1929, toured as Nannie Ormiston, jun., in "Susie Tangles the Strings"; at the Saville Theatre, Jan., 1933, again played Bunty in "Bunty Pulls the Strings." *Address:* The Oasis, Sandhurst, by Camberley, Berks.

MOFFATT, Alice, actress; *b.* Berlin, 23 July, 1890; *d.* of Alfred Moffatt; *e.* Edinburgh; *m.* Max Montesole; was a pupil at the Royal College of Music; she made her first public appearance at His Majesty's Theatre, Feb., 1908, as Gretel in the second act of " Hansel and Gretel," to the Hansel of Viola Tree; she then appeared at the Prince's, Manchester, Dec., 1908, as Dulcie Dobbins in " The Dollar Princess "; in 1910 toured as Princess Marie in " The King of Cadonia "; during 1910-11 she toured as Mollie in " Pinkie and the Fairies "; subsequently she went to America, and toured in " The Pink Lady " and " Oh ! Oh ! Delphine "; she made her first appearance in New York, at the Casino Theatre, 25 Dec., 1914, as Maude Draper-Cowles in " Lady Luxury "; subsequently was a member of the company at the Toy Theatre, Boston, where, in the autumn of 1915, she played in " Independent Means " and " A Place in the Sun " ; appeared at the Wimbledon Theatre, Dec., 1917, as Colin in " The Babes in the Wood " ; at the Lyric Theatre, July, 1918, played Laurette in " The Purple Mask " ; at the Prince's, Apr., 1919, Lucy in " Monsieur Beaucaire " ; at the St. James's, Sept., 1919, Masha in " Reparation " ; Mar., 1920, Helen Graham in " Uncle Ned " ; at the Playhouse, Aug., 1920, appeared as Marcia Hunter in " Wedding Bells " ; at the St. James's, Jan., 1921, as Suzanne Girard in " Daniel " ; Mar., 1921, as Myrtle Davis in " Polly with a Past " ; at the Apollo, Dec., 1922, played Millicent in " Hawley's of the High Street " ; during 1923 toured as Lavender in " Sweet Lavender," and as Jenny in " The Gentle Shepherd " ; at the Ambassadors'Theatre, New York, Aug., 1924, played Elinor Levison in " The Dream Girl " ; at Newark, N.J., Nov., 1924, Rachel Levi in " The Money Lender "; Little, New York, Oct., 1927, played Mary Beal in " If "; Empire, May, 1928, Ada in " The Happy Husband." *Recreations :* Swimming and walking.

MOFFATT, Margaret, actress ; *b.* Edinburgh, 11 Oct., 1882 ; *d.* of Thomas Bury, sculptor, and his wife Christine (Shierlaw) ; *e.* public schools and University of Toronto, Canada ; *m.* Sewell Collins ; was engaged as a journalist prior to making her first appearance on the stage, at the Savoy Theatre, New York, 1903, as Suky in a revival of " Janice Meredith " ; she then played in " stock," appearing in a great variety of parts, from Shakespeare to farce ; in 1904 sang the part of Contrary Mary in " Babes in Toyland," and she next played in " The Wizard of Oz " ; she then left the stage for two years, during which she was engaged as a newspaper reporter, and as editor of the woman's page of *The New York Evening Mail* ; returned to the stage, 1906, with Robert Edeson, as Molly Livingstone in " Strongheart " ; subsequently played in " vaudeville " ;. made her first appearance in London, at the Royalty, 7 Dec.,

1911, as Millicent in her husband's one-act play " Tuppence, Please " ; at the Coliseum, Apr., 1912, played in " Just Like a Woman," in which she appeared by command at Sandringham before H.M. the King, on 2 Dec., 1912 ; at the Coliseum, Mar., 1913, played the Charwoman in " The Scrub Lady " · at the Globe, Apr., 1916, Sadie in " The Show Shop " ; in 1917 toured in " The Girl from Ciro's " ; at the Duke of York's, Oct., 1917, played Mary Eastwood in " The Thirteenth Chair " ; at the Royalty, May, 1918, Martha in " The Man from Toronto " ; appeared for several years in sketches in variety theatres ; at the Shaftesbury, Apr., 1923, played the Casting Director in " Merton of the Movies " ; at the Vanderbilt Theatre, New York, Nov., 1923, Sarah in " The Camel's Back " ; at the Everyman, London, Nov., 1924, Fanny Simister in " Clogs to Clogs " ; at the Little Theatre, Dec., 1924, Nancy White in " You and I." *Address :* 18 Boundary Road, St. John's Wood, N.W.8. *Telephone No. :* Hampstead 5116.

MOFFET, Harold, actor ; *b.* Chicago, Illinois, U.S.A., 9 Aug., 1892 ; *s.* of Edgar Donald Moffet and his wife Sarah Alberta (Feemster) ; *e.* Central High School, Kansas City, and Universities of Wisconsin and Pennsylvania ; *m.* Sylvia Field ; formerly engaged as an engineer, and golf-course instructor ; made his first appearance on the stage at the Klaw Theatre, New York (for the Theatre Guild), 23 Nov., 1925, as a Gladiator in " Androcles and the Lion"; Playhouse, Jan., 1927, played Carthalo in " The Road to Rome"; Longacre, Jan., 1929, Andrew in " Judas"; Erlanger, Mar., 1929, Nosebag in " Buckaroo"; Music Box, Apr., 1929, appeared in " The Little Show"; Selwyn, Oct., 1930, in " Three's a Crowd"; Music Box, Dec., 1931, played Francis X. Gilhooley in " Of Thee I Sing"; Imperial, Oct., 1933, Gilhooley in " Let 'Em Eat Cake"; Martin Beck, Mar., 1934, Roger P. Ames in " Yellow Jack"; Music Box, Sept., 1934, George Niles in " Merrily

We Roll Along"; Cort, May, 1935, A. J. Lamb in "The Hook-Up"; Plymouth, Sept., 1935, Sergeant Jonnart in "Paths of Glory." *Recreation :* Golf. *Club :* Players.

(Died 7 Nov., 1938; age 46)

MOLESWORTH, Ida, actress and manageress; *b.* near Calcutta, India; *d.* of William Molesworth, of the Indian Civil Service; *e.* at convents in the Himalayas, the Continent, and London ; *m.* (1) Mark Blow, actor and manager ; (2) Templer Powell ; was trained for the stage by Hermann Vezin, Emil Behnke, and Odoardo Barri ; made her first public appearance at the old St. James's Hall, as a reciter ; as an actress, received her first engagement from Mark Melford in " Flying from Justice," making her first appearance at Morton's Theatre, Greenwich, in 1893; after playing a "stock" season at Croydon, secured a three-years' engagement from Augustus Daly, making her first appearance at Daly's, 8 Jan., 1894, as a Player in "Twelfth Night"; also appeared there, 30 Apr., 1894, as Phoebe in "As You Like It "; she then went to America, playing second parts to Ada Rehan; making her first appearance in New York, at Daly's, 15 Dec., 1894, as Berta in " Love on Crutches "; Jan., 1895, played Tika in " The Heart of Ruby "; she also played Lady Sneerwell, Maria, Sylvia, etc.; on returning to England, toured as Lady Harding in " The Idler," Theophila Fraser in " The Benefit of the Doubt," and Mrs. Ralstan in " Jim the Penman," 1896; then toured as Berenice in " The Sign of the Cross," and in 1897 toured with Forbes-Robertson as Bazilide in " For the Crown," Janet Preece in " The Profligate," and Emilia in " Othello "; appeared at the **St.** James's, Apr., 1898, as Anita in " **The** Conquerors "; appeared at the Lyceum, under the late Sir Henry Irving, 1899, as Jessica in " The Merchant of Venice," and the Princess Elisa **in** " Madame Sans-Gêne "; toured for 500 nights in " The Adventure of Lady Ursula "; appeared at the Duke of York's, 1901, as Loretta in

" The Swashbuckler "; toured for some time in England and America as Cigarette in " Under Two Flags "; appeared in " The Sword of the King," Wyndham's Theatre, 1904 ; during 1909 toured as the Princess Flavia in " The Prisoner of Zenda," and during 1910 as Julie Alardy in " The Little Damozel " ; in conjunction with Templer Powell, assumed the management of the Playhouse, May, 1924, producing " White Cargo," which secured a run of over 800 performances ; in Nov., 1924, in conjunction with Templer Powell, assumed the management of the new Fortune Theatre, which they opened on 8 Nov., 1924, with " Sinners "; toured " White Cargo," 1925-8 ; " Escape," 1927 ; "S.O.S.," 1928 ; revived "White Cargo" at the Cambridge Theatre, Nov., 1935. *Favourite parts :* Lady Ursula, and Theo Fraser in " The Benefit of the Doubt." *Hobby :* Collecting antique furniture.
(Died 14 Oct., 1951)

MOLLISON, Henry, actor; *b.* Broughton Ferry, Dundee, 21 Feb., 1905 ; *s.* of the late William Mollison and his wife Evelyn (McNay) ; *e.* St. Paul's School, London, and Caen, France; *m.* (1) Jane Welsh (mar. dis.) ; (2) Lina Basquette ; made his first appearance on the stage at the age of three, in his father's company and his grown-up *début* in 1924, with the Benson company ; made his first appearance in London at the New Theatre (for the 300 Club), 12 Feb., 1928, as Vining in " Young Woodley," and played the same part at the Savoy, Mar., 1928, and at the Queen's, July, 1929 ; at Golders Green, Oct., 1929, played Wheeler in "I'm Wise"; London Hippodrome, June, 1930, the French Officer in "Sons O' Guns"; London Pavilion, Mar., 1931, appeared in "Cochran's 1931 Revue"; Duke of York's, Apr., 1931, played Eric Brewer in "London Wall"; Garrick, June, 1932, Swann in "Hocus-Pocus"; Comedy, Dec., 1932, appeared in "Ballyhoo"; New, Feb., 1933, played the Earl of Derby in "Richard of Bordeaux"; went to America, 1934, and at the Empire, New York, Feb.,

1934, appeared in the same part; spent the next five years in films; went to Australia, 1939, to tour as Harry Van in "Idiot's Delight": was a prisoner of War for five years; reappeared on the stage at the Court, Liverpool, July, 1945, as Arthur Waring in "Under the Gooseberry Bush"; Piccadilly, May, 1947, played Alec D'Urberville in "Tess of the D'Urbervilles"; Wimbledon, Oct., 1947, appeared as Nick Helmar in "Jassy," which he also produced; Royal Court, Liverpool, Apr., 1952, played Norman Farrell in "Shadow Of a Man"; Opera House, Manchester, Aug., 1952, Miles Lamprey in "Hanging Judge"; Royal, Newcastle, Aug., 1955, Marcus Saintsbury in "Postman's Knock!"; commenced film career, 1931, in "Third Time Lucky," and has since appeared in numerous pictures. *Address:* 43 William Mews, Knightsbridge, S.W.1.

MOLLISON, William, producer; *b.* London, 24 December, 1893; *s.* of the late William Mollison, actor, and his wife Evelyn (McNay); *e.* privately; *m.* Joan Clarkson (mar. dis.); formerly an actor; made his first appearance on the stage as a child, at Drury Lane Theatre, 30 Apr., 1903, in "Dante"; made his grown-up *début* at the Theatre Royal, Nottingham, 1910, in "Strife"; toured with his father in "Rob Roy," 1911; in 1912 was engaged by Sir Herbert Tree on a three years contract at His Majesty's Theatre; appeared Sept., 1913, as Issachar in "Joseph and His Brethren"; also appeared with Tree in "The Darling of the Gods," "David Copperfield," "Drake," "King Henry IV" (Part II), etc.; appeared at the Garrick, 1914, in "Grand Guignol" plays; on the outbreak of War joined the Army, and served four years in Central Africa, Congo, Nyasaland, etc., in the King's African Rifles; after leaving the Army, was engaged by the South African Theatre Trust as leading actor and producer; from 1921-24 toured in South Africa and Australia with Gertrude Elliott, playing leading parts and producing; he was then engaged by Herbert Clayton and Jack Waller, and staged the following plays

for that firm, 1925-30: "No, No, Nanette," "Mercenary Mary," 1925; "The Best People," "Princess Charming," "The Gold Diggers," 1926; "The Garden of Eden," "The Girl Friend," "Hit the Deck," 1927; "Sauce for the Gander," "Baby Cyclone," "Good News," "Virginia," 1928; "Merry Merry," "Hold Everything," "Dear Love," "Murder on the Second Floor," 1929; "Silver Wings," "Sons o' Guns," "Little Tommy Tucker," 1930; during 1930-1, produced "Meet My Sister," "Wonder Bar," "Everybody's Welcome," in New York; has since produced "The Cat and the Fiddle," "Tell Her the Truth," "Business with America," 1932; "Jolly Roger," "He Wanted Adventure," "Give Me a Ring," "Command Performance," 1933; "Richard of Bordeaux" (New York), "Lucky Break," "Jill, Darling," 1934; "Gay Deceivers," "Accidentally Yours," "Seeing Stars," 1935; "Going Places," "O Mistress Mine," 1936; "The Laughing Cavalier," "Thank You, Mr. Pepys" (with Miles Malleson), 1937; "Bobby Get Your Gun," 1938; "Magyar Melody," 1939; "French for Love," 1939; "No, No, Nanette," "The Duchess of Dantzic," 1942; "The Merry Widow," "The Love Racket," "Panama Hattie," 1943; "Happy Few," 1944; "Irene," "Merrie England," 1945; "Can-Can," 1946; "Romany Love," "Off the Record," "The Girl Who Couldn't Quite," 1947; "Diamond Lil," "Written for a Lady," "The Kid from Stratford," 1948; "Top Secret," 1949; has produced over one hundred plays; in Apr., 1926, produced "No, No, Nanette," in Paris, in French. *Recreations:* Boxing, cricket, and golf. *Clubs:* Reform, Savage, Stage Golfing Society, and Green Room.
(Died 19 Oct., 1955; age 64)

MOLNAR, Ferencz, dramatic author; *b.* Budapest, Hungary, 12 Jan., 1878; *e.* Universities of Budapest and Geneva, where he studied Law; *m.* Lilli Darvas; commenced life as a journalist; his first play was "Der Doctor," 1902; subsequent plays were "Der Teufel" ("The Devil"), "Der Herr Verteidiger," "Der Liebgarddist," ("Playing with

Fire"), "Der Gardeoffizier" ("The Guardsman"), "Die Rote Mühle" ("The Red Mill"), "Spiel in Schloss" "Der Schwan" ("The Swan"), "Die Fee" ("The Good Fairy"), "Liliom" ("The Daisy"), "Harmonia," also others which have been translated as "The Glass Slipper," "Fashions for Men," "Husbands and Lovers," "The Play's the Thing," "Mina," "The Phantom Rival," "Where Ignorance is Bliss," "Intermezzo in the Office," "Great Love," "Girl Unknown," etc.; at the Playhouse, New York, Apr., 1947, staged the production of his own play, "Miracle in the Mountains."
(Died 1 Apr., 1952; age 74)

MOLYNEUX, Eileen, actress; *b.* Pietermaritzburg, Natal, South Africa, 26 Aug., 1893; *d.* of Herbert Molyneux and his wife Emmie Mary (Kenny); *e.* privately and at Dresden and Paris; made her first appearance on the stage at Daly's Theatre, 1 June, 1912, in the chorus of " Gipsy Love," where she remained ten months; she played her first part at Daly's, May, 1913, when she appeared as Dolly in " The Marriage Market " ; at the Alhambra, Oct., 1913, appeared as Commere in " Keep Smiling," and May, 1914, in " Not Likely " ; she then went to the United States, making her first appearance in New York, at the Winter Garden, Oct., 1914, as Ethel in " Dancing Around," subsequently touring all over the States in the same piece; at the Century Music Hall, New York, Sept., 1915, played in " Town Topics " ; on returning to London appeared at the Empire, July, 1916, in " We're All in It " ; at the Comedy, Sept., 1916, in " This and That," and Dec., 1916, in " See-Saw " ; next appeared at the Alhambra, July, 1917, in " Round the Map " ; at the Ambassadors', Oct., 1918, in " Telling the Tale " ; in Nov., 1918, toured in various music halls; at the Strand, June, 1919, appeared in " Laughing Eyes " ; at the Duke of York's, Sept., 1923, appeared in " London Calling." *Hobby:* Housekeeping. *Recreations :* Dancing and motoring.
(Died 13 Apr., 1962; age 68)

MONCK, Nugent, O.B.E., F.R.A.M., actor and producer; *b.* Welshampton, Salop, 4 Feb., 1877; *s.* of the Rev. G. G. Monck and his wife Hester Isabella (Nugent); *e.* Royal Institution School, Liverpool, and the Royal Academy of Music, where he studied under the late William Farren; made his first appearance on the stage at the Royalty Theatre, 7 Nov., 1901, as Pastor Jensen in " Beyond Human Power " ; was an actor for many years, and appeared in New York, at the Maxine Elliott Theatre, 1911, with the Irish Players; in the same year founded the Norwich Players; served in the Army from 1914–19; from 1919 produced over 280 different plays at Norwich, where, in 1921, he reconstructed the Maddermarket Theatre as an Elizabethan playhouse; he also produced " The Machine Wreckers," for the Stage Society, 1923; The Norwich Pageant, 1926; The Northampton Pageant, 1930; Cardinal Wolsey Pageant, Ipswich, 1930; "The Force of Conscience," Grafton Theatre, 1931; has written and adapted several plays, including "The Heavens Shall Laugh," for the twenty-first birthday of the Norwich Players, 1932, and a version of "The Pilgrim's Progress," 1932; staged "Timon of Athens," at the Westminster Theatre, 1935; in June, 1936, in celebration of the Silver Jubilee at Norwich revived "The Shoemaker's Holiday"; at Stratford-on-Avon, 1946, produced "Cymbeline," and in 1947, "Pericles"; at the King's, Hammersmith, Oct., 1953, produced "King Lear"; he has revived all of Shakespeare's plays and also works of nearly every Elizabethan dramatist of note, besides many modern works. *Favourite parts :* Touchstone and Feste. *Recreation :* Travelling. *(Died Oct., 1958; age 81)*

MONCKTON, Lionel, musical composer and critic; *b.* London, 1862; *e.s.* of the late Sir John Monckton, Town Clerk of the City of London, and of the late Lady Monckton, actress; *e.* Charterhouse School, and at Oxford; *m.* Gertie Millar; was a prominent amateur actor at Oxford, where he was associated with the Philo-Thespian

Club and the O.U.D.S.; his first compositions were heard in public at the Gaiety and other theatres under the management of George Edwardes, and he contributed many popular songs to "Cinder-Ellen Up Too Late," "The Shop Girl," "Claude Duval," "The Geisha," "The Greek Slave," "San Toy," "The Cingalee," etc.; he was part composer of "The Toreador," 1901; "The Orchid," 1903; "The Spring Chicken," 1905; "The New Aladdin," 1906; "The Girls of Gottenburg," 1907; "Our Miss Gibbs," 1909; "The Arcadians," 1909; "The Mousmé," 1911; "Bric-a-Brac," 1915; "We're All In It," 1916; "Airs and Graces," 1917; "The Boy," 1917; he was the sole composer of "The Quaker Girl," 1910; and "The Dancing Mistress," 1912. *Recreation:* Motoring. *Address:* 69 Russell Square, W.C.1. *Telephone:* Museum 7833. *Clubs:* Conservative, Eccentric, Green Room.

MONCRIEFF, Gladys, actress and vocalist; *b.* Bundaberg, Queensland, Australia, 13 Apr., 1893; *d.* of Robert Edward Moncrieff and his wife Amy (Wall); *e.* Convent of Mercy, Townsville, Queensland; *m.* Thomas H. Moore; made her first appearance on the stage, in 1915, at Her Majesty's Theatre, Sydney, N.S.W., as Josephine in "H.M.S. Pinafore," under the management of J. C. Williamson, Ltd., with which she remained several years; in 1916, toured in South Africa in "So Long, Letty"; returned to Australia, where she played the leading parts in all the Gilbert and Sullivan operas, also Teresa in "The Maid of the Mountains," Mariana in "The Lady of the Rose," "Katinka," Yvette in "The Street Singer," Dolores in "The Southern Maid," Lucienne in "Kissing Time," Ottillie in "Maytime," Claudine in "The Pink Lady," also appeared (in revivals) as Sonia in "The Merry Widow," Nadina in "The Chocolate Soldier," Violet Gray in "The Belle of New York," Rosette in "Ma Mie Rosette," etc.; made her first appearance in London at the Gaiety, 16 Apr., 1926, as Riki-Tiki in the play of that name; at Daly's, Feb., 1927, played

Bianca in "The Blue Mazurka"; returned to Australia, 1928, and appeared as Rio Rita in the play of that name; at Melbourne, May, 1930, again appeared as Sonia in "The Merry Widow"; during 1933, again played Teresa in "The Maid of the Mountains"; played Amelia in "Jolly Roger," and Dianella Watson in "The Cedar Tree," 1934; during 1936, again appeared in "The Merry Widow" and in "The Gypsy Princess"; has appeared in revivals of her old successes continuously, and in 1944, was seen as Katinka, and 1945, as Rio Rita: in 1949, again played Teresa in "The Maid of the Mountains." *Favourite parts:* Ottillie in "Maytime" and Sonia in "The Merry Widow." *Recreation:* Surf riding.

MONKHOUSE, Allan, dramatic critic, journalist, novelist, and dramatic author; *b.* Barnard Castle, Durham, 7 May, 1858; *s.* of John W. S. Monkhouse and his wife Mary (Brown); *e.* privately; *m.* Elisabeth Dorothy Pearson; was originally engaged in the Manchester cotton trade; was for many years one of the dramatic critics of the *Manchester Guardian*; has had the following plays produced; "Reaping the Whirlwind," 1908; "The Choice," 1910; "Mary Broome," 1911; "Resentment," 1912· "The Education of Mr. Surrage," 1912; "Nothing Like Leather," 1913; "The Conquering Hero," 1924· "The Hayling Family," 1924; "Sons and Fathers," 1926; "First Blood," 1926; "The Rag," 1928; "Paul Felice," 1930; "Cecilia," 1932; "The Grand Cham's Diamond," 1933; issued a volume of essays, "Farewell Manchester," 1931; has also had several other plays published.
(*Died 10 Jan., 1936; age 77*)

MONKMAN, Phyllis, actress and dancer; *b.* London, 8 Jan., 1892; *d.* of Jack Harrison and his wife Florence (Young); *e.* Newton House College, Tunbridge Wells; *m.* Laddie Cliff; studied dancing under Madame Sismondi; made her first appearance on the stage as a child at the Prince of Wales's Theatre, 17 Dec., 1904, appearing as a dancer in " Lady Madcap "; at the Vaudeville, Apr., 1906, danced in " The Belle of Mayfair "; at the Duke of York's played the First Twin in " Peter Pan "; at the Apollo, May, 1908, appeared as principal dancer in " Butterflies "; at the Prince of Wales's, Sept., 1909, played Elsa in " Dear Little Denmark "; at the Vaudeville, June, 1910, appeared in " The Girl in the Train "; at the Adelphi, Nov., 1910, in " The Quaker Girl "; at the Duke of York's, Feb., 1912, in " The ' Mind-the-Paint ' Girl "; July, 1912, appeared at the Coliseum as Claire in " The Dancing Viennese "; at the Victoria Palace, Oct., 1912, as Lady Margery in " The Monte Carlo Girl "; in May, 1913, commenced an engagement as principal dancer at the Alhambra, which lasted until the end of 1916, during which period she appeared in " Eightpence a Mile," " Keep Smiling," " Not Likely," " 5064 Gerrard," " Now's the Time," and " The Bing Boys are Here "; she was next seen at the Comedy, where she appeared from Dec., 1916, until 1920, in " See-Saw," " Bubbly," " Tails Up," and " Wild Geese "; at the Prince of Wales's, June, 1920, played in " Bran Pie "; at the Winter Garden, Sept., 1920, played Victorine in " A Night Out"; at the Royalty, June, 1921, was one of " The Co-Optimists " : she remained with " The Co-Optimists " for three years, and was then seen at the Prince of Wales's, Sept., 1924, in " Charlot's Revue "; Shaftesbury, Aug., 1925, played Billie Brent in " Dear Little Billie "; Queen's, June, 1926, Julia Blue in " Down Hill "; Carlton, Apr., 1927, Jane Juste in " Lady Luck "; during 1928 toured as Letty Robbins in " Oh! Letty! "; Vaudeville, July, 1929, appeared with the revived " Co-Optimists "; London Hippodrome, Apr., 1930, appeared with " The Co-Optimists of 1930 "; Prince of Wales's, May, 1932, played in "The Jack-Pot"; Winter Garden, Sept., 1932, in "Rhyme and Rhythm"; Gaiety, Dublin, Christmas, 1932, Aladdin; Queen's, Nov., 1933, Ruby Sunshine in "Sunshine Sisters"; Daly's, Mar., 1934, Lottie in "Good Morning, Bill"; autumn, 1934, toured as Sybil Grant in "Cut for Partners"; Adelphi, Feb., 1935, appeared in "Stop Press," and in the autumn, toured in the same piece; toured, 1936, in "Uneasily to Bed"; London Hippodrome, July, 1936, played Lucille in "No, No, Nanette"; Ambassadors', Mar., 1939, succeeded Joyce Barbour as Mrs. Gill in "The Two Bouquets"; His Majesty's, Mar., 1938, played Maisie Welbey in "Operette"; King's, Hammersmith, Apr., 1939, Sadie Thompson in "Rain"; Prince of Wales's, May, 1940, Babette in "Present Arms"; Stoll, July, 1942, Lady Jane in "Rose Marie"; Palace, Aug., 1944, appeared in "Keep Going"; toured, 1944, as Mrs. Miller in "Flare Path"; Duke of York's, May, 1947, appeared as Phyl Perriman in "We Proudly Present"; entered films, 1935, and appeared in "The King of Paris."

MONKS, James, actor; *b.* New York City, U.S.A., 10 Feb., 1917; *s.* of John Monks; *e.* Pleasantville High School; made his first appearance on the stage on tour, in "Captain Applejack"; first appeared in New York, at the Biltmore Theatre, 16 Dec., 1936, as a Member of the Guard in "Brother Rat"; played in various "stock" companies; at the National Theatre, 1939–40, understudied in "The Little Foxes"; toured, 1940, as Leo Hubbard in "The Little Foxes"; was engaged in films in Hollywood, 1941–2; at the Guild Theatre, New York, Apr., 1942, played Bevan in "Yesterday's Magic"; Cort, Oct., 1942, Private Francis Marion in "The Eve of St. Mark"; Shubert, Oct., 1943, appeared as Cassio in "Othello," with Paul Robeson; first appeared in films, 1941, in "How Green Was My Valley." *Favourite part:* Private Marion in "The Eve of St. Mark." *Recreation:* Swimming. *Address:* c/o Actors' Equity Association, 45 West 47th Street, New York City, U.S.A.

MONKS, Victoria, comedienne; *b.* Manchester, 1 Nov., 1884; *d.* of Charles Monks; *e.* England and Belgium; *m.* Karl F. Hooper; made her first appearance on the stage in 1899, as Little Victoria; made her first appearance in London, at the Oxford, 9 Mar., 1903; has appeared at all the leading halls in London and the provinces; among a number of popular songs associated with her name, may be mentioned "Ain't the old place good enough for you?"; "Ain't yer gwine to say 'How do'?"; "Buy me a home in London"; "Give my regards to Leicester Square"; "Take me back to London Town"; "Ain't I no use, Mr. Jackson?"; "If you want to have a row, wait till the sun shines"; "Won't you come home, Bill Bailey?"; "Brown Eyes and Blue Eyes"; "I'm going home to Jacksonville," etc.

MONNA-DELZA, Mdlle., French actress; has appeared at the Vaudeville, 1907, as Clémence in "La Veine"; at the Vaudeville, 1908, as Nodia Meynard in "La Patronne"; at the Gymnase, 1910, as Diane de Charance in "La Vierge Folle," and Miquette Grandier in "Miquette et sa Mère"; at the Théâtre Femina, 1912, played Lucienne in "L'Enjóleuse"; at the Comédie des Champs-Elysées, 1913, appeared as Jacqueline de Teroines in "Exilée"; at the Porte-St.-Martin, 1914, played Chouquette in "Madame."
(Died 5 May, 1921)

MONTAGU, Elizabeth, actress; *b.* London, 26 Sept., 1909; *d.* of Lord Montagu of Beaulieu and his wife Lady Cecil (Kerr); studied for the stage at the Royal Academy of Dramatic Art; made her first appearance on the stage at the Playhouse, Jesmond, 29 Dec., 1932, as Joan in "Well Caught," with the Newcastle Repertory Company, where she played a number of parts; made her first appearance in London, at the Garrick Theatre, 17 Apr., 1933, as Nadine Browning in "Beggars in Hell"; Wyndham's, July, 1933, succeeded Leonora Corbett as Lola Waite in "Other People's Lives"; Westminster, Feb., 1934, played the Young Lady in "Private Room"; Daly's, Apr., 1934, Jessica Lane in "Dark Horizon"; Arts, May, 1934,

Henriette in "Viceroy Sarah"; Whitehall, Feb., 1935, Mary in "Viceroy Sarah"; King's, Glasgow, May, 1935, Baroness Hareczky in "Mesmer." *Recreations:* Sailing, motoring and tennis. *Address:* 20 Hallam Street, London, W.1. *Telephone No.:* Langham 2554.

MONTAGUE, Bertram, manager; *b.* London, 13 Nov., 1892; *s.* of Moss Montague Marks and his wife Dinah (Hyams); *e.* London; *m.* (1) Helen Moray (dec.); (2) Lalla Dodd (mar. dis.); (3) Iris Kirkwhite; engaged in a commercial career, 1906–13; was engaged in variety agency work from 1913–24; his first production was a *revue,* "Rat-a-Tat," Empire, Swansea, 1925; has since produced over 100 *revues,* in the English provinces, South Africa, Australia, New Zealand, etc.; produced his first pantomime, "Aladdin," at the Chiswick Empire, 1933, and has since produced over a hundred others; toured "To-Night's the Night," 1943, and "The Gypsy Baron," 1945; occupied the Prince's Theatre, 1947–52, and presented five pantomimes there; King's, Hammersmith, Dec., 1951, produced "Mother Goose"; at the Coliseum, Harrow, Dec., 1954, presented "Dick Whittington," and at the King's, Southsea, presented "Aladdin"; assumed the name of Montague by deed-poll. *Recreations:* Golf and chess. *Address:* 43 Circus Road, London, N.W.8.

MONTAGUE, Charles Edward, dramatic critic and author; *b.* Ealing, 1 Jan., 1867; *s.* of Francis Montague and his wife Rosa; *e.* City of London School, and Balliol College, Oxford; *m.* Madeline Scott; has been a journalist since 1890, when he joined the staff of the *Manchester Guardian;* subsequently leader-writer to the same paper; appointed dramatic critic of the paper, 1897; is the author of "A Hind Let Loose," novel, 1910; "Dramatic Values" (criticism), 1911; "The Morning's War," 1913; "Disenchantment," 1922; "Fiery Particles" (short stories), 1923; "The Right Place," 1924. *Favourite play:*

" Twelfth Night.' *Recreation :* Mountaineering. *Clubs :* Alpine, Architecture, and Reform, Manchester.
(Died 28 May, 1928; age 61)

MONTAGUE, Harold, entertainer and author ; *b.* Exeter, 1874 ; *s.* of Harold Smith ; *e.* privately ; *m.* Ethel Burney ; was engaged in the City for four years, during which period he appeared as a concert entertainer ; in 1897, he launched out as a professional entertainer ; from 1898-1901, appeared as the Jester with " The Scarlet Mr. E's " ; in Mar., 1905, accompanied Sir (then Mr.) George Alexander on a recital tour ; in Oct., 1905, appeared at Wyndham's Theatre, taking the place of the ordinary curtain-raiser; in the same year, he started " The Vagabond's " Concert party, which he still runs ; subsequently started " Montague's Mountebanks " ; has many popular songs to his credit, among which may be mentioned " The Artful Coon " ; " A handy little thing to have about you " ; " Do you follow me ? " ; " Castles in Spain " ; " My beastly eyeglass " ; " Never Mind " ; " Posers " ; " Someone should speak to him gently," etc. ; has written over a hundred songs, also several one-act plays. *Recreations :* Sailing and billiards. *Address :* 4 Northcote Mansions, Hampstead, N.W. *Telephone No. :* Hampstead 6823.

MONTEFIORE, Eade, press representative, former manager and producer ; *b.* Charmouth, 6 Feb., 1866 ; *s.* of the Rev. Thomas Law Montefiore, M.A., Rector of Chideock, Dorset, and Rural Dean, and his wife Katharine (Brice) ; *e.* Chardstock College, Somerset ; made his first appearance on the stage at the Lyric Theatre, 17 Dec., 1888, in " Dorothy" ; in 1892, was manager for the late Harry Monkhouse on tour ; in Aug., 1893, was appointed resident manager of the Paisley Theatre, of which he became lessee and manager in 1894 ; he was also Managing Editor of the *Paisley Mirror* and *Paisley Magazine*; inaugurated a series of " stock" seasons, which he carried on at Paisley, Newcastle-on-Tyne, Birmingham, Bradford,

Bath, Dundee, Aberdeen, Edinburgh, Kennington, Camden, and Coronet, London; in all was responsible for over thirty " stock" seasons; lessee and manager of the Amphitheatre, Newcastle-on-Tyne, 1894-5 ; toured several well-known plays, 1895-9, including Pinero's plays, " The Second Mrs. Tanqueray," " The Profligate," " The Magistrate," " Dandy Dick," " The Schoolmistress," " Sweet Lavender," " The Amazons," and " The Hobby Horse"; toured " The Streets of London," for over a thousand performances; in 1899 was engaged by Milton Bode and Edward Compton to manage the Dalston Theatre; in 1901, engaged by Robert Arthur to control Her Majesty's, Dundee, and Her Majesty's, Aberdeen; resigned in 1904; in Dec., 1904, opened the Grand Theatre, Edinburgh, which he also managed; from 1908-11, was manager of the Coronet Theatre; joined Robert Courtneidge, as general manager at the Shaftesbury, July, 1911, and remained until 1914; in 1915, was engaged by Frederick Harrison to manage tours of "Quinney's" and "Who is He?"; from 1917-19, toured his own companies in Haymarket plays, "Quinney's," "Fishpingle," "The Widow's Might," and "Mr. Jubilee Drax"; in 1920, directed the tours of the Compton Comedy Company, and founded the Nottingham Repertory Theatre, for Mrs. Edward Compton; subsequently produced "Columbine," at the Prince's Theatre, 1921; was one of the six organizers for England of the "Warrior's Day Fund"; manager of the Grand Theatre, Croydon, 1922-23; was press representative, St. Martin's Theatre, 1926; manager, Playhouse, Cardiff, 1927; engaged with Jevan Brandon-Thomas, at Edinburgh and elsewhere, 1931; supervised building of the Garrick Theatre, Southport, 1932; manager, Manchester Repertory Theatre, 1933-34; general manager of "The Greeks had a Word for It," Duke of York's and Cambridge, 1935; toured "Red Night" with Robert Donat, 1936; was with J. P. Mitchellhill at the Duchess and Whitehall Theatres, 1936-9; was secretary of the London International Theatre; has

edited and published several publications, including "Robertsoniana," "Dickensiana," and edited the Farewell Souvenir of J. P. Mitchelhill's management of the Duchess Theatre, 1938, etc. *Hobby:* Collecting theatrical engravings and books. *Recreation:* Seeing plays.
(Died 26 Sept., 1944; age 78)

MONTGOMERY, Douglass (*né* Robert Douglass Montgomery), actor; *b.* Los Angeles, 29 Oct., 1909; *s.* of Chester Arthur James Montgomery and his wife Leona (Smith); *e.* Los Angeles; *m.* Kathleen Young; first appeared on the stage as a child in Pasadena, Cal.; made his professional *début* at the Orange Grove Theatre, Los Angeles, Dec., 1925, as Sid Hunt in "Hell Bent for Heaven" subsequently appeared in Los Angeles and San Francisco, in "The Copperhead," "Silence," "Desire Under the Elms," and "Kempy"; made his first appearance in New York, at the Maxine Elliott Theatre, 18 Oct., 1926, as Tommy in "God Loves Us"; Eltinge, Feb., 1927, played Tommy Brown in "Crime"; Forrest, Sept., 1927, Harry in "Women Go on Forever"; Selwyn, Sept., 1927, Richard Lamont in "The Garden of Eden"; Guild, July, 1928, succeeded Alfred Lunt as Mosca in "Volpone"; Guild, Oct., 1928, played Gabriel and Valentine in "Faust"; Dec., 1928, Robert in "Caprice"; came to London, where he made his first appearance at the St. James's Theatre, 4 June, 1929, as Robert in "Caprice"; on returning to New York, appeared at the Guild Theatre, Dec., 1929, as Douglas Carr in "Meteor"; Little, Feb., 1930, Jerry Brooks in "Many a Slip"; Longacre, Sept., 1931, Shep Lambart in "Nikki"; Royale, Dec., 1931, George in "Fata Morgana"; Lyceum, Oct., 1932, Robert Seward in "Men Must Fight"; Guild, Feb., 1933, Daniel Pingree in "An American Dream"; at Pasadena, Cal., June, 1933, played lead in "The Playboy of the Western World," "Peer Gynt," "Volpone," etc.; and toured California in "Merrily We Roll Along"; Ford's, Baltimore, Nov., 1937, played Kenneth Vereker in "Merely Murder";

Empire, Oct., 1939, Joe in "They Knew What They Wanted"; toured the U.S. and Canada, 1941, as Danny in "Night Must Fall"; King's, Edinburgh, Oct., 1945, played Charlie Randall in "Now the Day is Over"; Apollo, London, May, 1946, played the Captain in "The Wind Is Ninety"; Embassy, Feb., 1948, appeared as the Prosecutor in "The Vigil," and played the same part at the Prince of Wales's, May, 1948; "Q," Apr., 1949, played Dick Dudgeon in "The Devil's Disciple," and July, 1949, Peter Standish in "Berkeley Square"; Princes, Mar., 1950, Detective McLeod in "Detective Story"; Embassy, June, 1951, Oswald in "Ghosts"; toured the British Isles in all his London performances, except "Detective Story"; at the 54th Street Theatre, N.Y., Feb., 1959, played District Attorney Sewell in "The Legend of Lizzie"; in summer theatres in New England, has played in "Young Woodley," "The Butter and Egg Man," "Men in White," "High Tor," "Berkeley Square," "The Playboy of the Western World," "Night Must Fall," "The Petrified Forest," "To-Night at 8.30," "Romeo and Juliet," "The Wind and the Rain," "The Firebrand," "Autumn Crocus," "Brief Moment," "The Devil's Disciple," etc.; entered films, 1933, and under the name of Kent Douglass appeared in "Paid," "Waterloo Bridge," and "A House Divided"; under his own name has also appeared in numerous pictures, including "Little Women," "Little Man, What Now?," "The Way to the Stars," "Everything Is Thunder," "Johnny in the Clouds," etc.; for his contribution to Anglo-Saxon solidarity was awarded an Honorary Citizenship in England. *Recreation:* Breeding and raising Irish wolfhounds, and swimming. *Address:* "Eagle Rock," Tokeneke, Darien, Conn., U.S.A.
(Died 23 July, 1966; age 56)

MONTGOMERY, James, dramatic author; *b.* 27 Apr., 1882; was formerly an actor and made his first appearance on the stage in 1902, and followed this profession for seven years; appeared at the Gaiety, New York,

Sept., 1909, in " The Fortune Hunter ";
is the author of the following plays :
" The Native Son," 1909 ; " The
Aviator," 1910 ; " Take My Advice "
(with William Collier), 1911 ; " Ready
Money," 1912 ; " Bachelors and
Benedicts " (with Jackson D. Haag),
1912 ; " Me and Grant " (from novel),
1914 ; " Come Home, Smith," 1914 ;
" Irene O'Dare," 1916 ; " Nothing
But the Truth " (from a novel), 1916 ;
" Drafted," 1917 ; " Oh, Look ! "
(musical version of " Ready Money "),
1918 ; " Irene," 1919 ; " Glory," 1922 ;
" The City Chap " (on " The Fortune
Hunter "), 1925 ; " Yes, Yes, Yvette "
(with W. Cary Duncan), 1927 ; "Stella
Brady," 1931.
(Died 17 June, 1966; age 84)

MONTGOMERY, Robert, actor; *b.*
Beacon, N.Y., U.S.A., 21 May, 1903;
s. of Henry Montgomery and his wife
Mary (Bernard); *e.* Pawling preparatory school, N.Y.; *m.* Elizabeth Allen;
made his first appearance on the stage
at the Bijou Theatre, 10 Sept., 1924,
as Tito in "The Mask and the Face,"
with William Faversham; he then
went to Rochester, N.Y., where he
joined the "stock" company, and
played innumerable parts during a
stay of seventeen months; Sam H.
Harris, Nov., 1924, Louis Rhodes
in "Dawn"; at the Booth Theatre, New York, Mar., 1925, played
Blink in "The Complex"; Sam H.
Harris, Nov., 1925, Captain Shenstone
in "The Carolinian"; Greenwich Village, Apr., 1926, appeared in "Bad
Habits of 1926"; subsequently toured
in "One of the Family," and "The
Garden of Eden"; Booth Theatre,
New York, Oct., 1928, played Edward Whiteman in "Possession";
during the War, served with the U.S.
Navy; commenced film career, 1926,
in "College Days," and has since
played in innumerable pictures. *Recreations :* Tennis, golf, riding, fencing,
and flying. *Address :* c/o Metro-Goldwyn-Mayer Studio, Culver City, Hollywood, Cal., U.S.A.

MONTGOMMERY, David Craig,
actor ; *b.* St. Joseph, Mo., 21 Apr.,
1870 ; *e.* St. Joseph ; made his first

appearance on the stage in Mar.,
1886 ; subsequently appeared with
Haverley's Minstrels ; met his present
partner, Fred A. Stone, in 1894,
and appeared with him for the first
time at Keith's Theatre, Boston ;
appeared at the Palace Theatre,
London, 1900 ; engaged by Charles
Frohman and appeared at the Herald
Square Theatre, 7 Jan., 1901, as
Solomon Scarlet in " The Girl from
Up There," subsequently appearing
in London, at the Duke of York's
Theatre, Apr., 1901, in the same
part ; next engaged by Robert Arthur
for pantomime at Liverpool ; on his
return to America played The Wood-
man in " The Wizard of Oz," 1903,
" Kid " Conner in " The Red Mill,"
1906, and Archibald Hawkins in
" The Old Town," 1909 ; toured in the
last-mentioned play from 1910-12 ;
at the Globe, New York, Oct., 1912,
played Punks in " The Lady of the
Slipper " ; subsequently touring in
the same part ; at the Globe, New
York, Oct., 1914, played Chin Hoop Lo
in " Chin-Chin." *Recreation :* Horses.
Club : The Lambs'.
(Died 20 Apr., 1917; age 47)

MONTROSE, Muriel, actress and
dancer; *b.* Stapleford, Cambridge; *d.*
of Walter Andrews and his wife Bertha
(Bouttell); *e.* London; *m.* Group-
Captain W. A. B. Savile; studied for
the stage at the Ben Greet Academy
of Acting; appeared at the Prince of
Wales's, Oct., 1921, in "A to Z";
Vaudeville, Dec., 1921, in "Pot Luck";
Aug., 1922, in "Snap"; and Feb.,
1923, in "Rats"; Little, Aug., 1923,
in the "Nine O'Clock Revue," and
Oct., 1923, in the "Little Revue Starts
at Nine"; Gaiety, Sept., 1924, played
Molly in "Poppy"; Apollo, Jan.,
1925, in "By the Way," and at the
Gaiety, New York, Dec., 1925, and
Gaiety, London, Aug., 1926, in the
same *revue*; Gaiety, Dec., 1926,
played Mollie Doone in "Lido Lady";
Theatre Royal, Birmingham, Dec.,
1927, Kitty in "Robinson Crusoe";
Selwyn, New York, Nov., 1928, in
"This Year of Grace"; Dominion,
Jan., 1930, succeeded Elsie Randolph
as Ruth Vanning in "Follow Through";

1735

Strand, Oct., 1930, played Peters in "It's a Boy"; Strand, Dec., 1931, Cynthia Snape in "It's a Girl"; Hippodrome, Dec., 1932, played for Fay Compton as Dick in "Dick Whittington"; Aldwych, Nov., 1933, Lola in "Ladies' Night"; Palace, May, 1935, in "The Co-Optimists"; Shaftesbury, June, 1935, Angele Bertin in "Accidentally Yours"; Gaiety, Oct., 1935, Miss Walton in "Seeing Stars"; Ambassadors', Jan., 1946, in "Sweeter and Lower"; toured, May, 1949, as Gussi in "Bitter Sweet." *Address:* 3 Douglas House, The Avenue, Beckenham, Kent. *Telephone No.:* Beckenham 5166.

MOORE, A. P., theatre manager; *b.* Sligo, Co. Sligo, Ireland, 11 Oct., 1906; *s.* of Thomas Charles Moore and his wife Elizabeth Eleanor (L'Estrange); *e.* Stowe School, Bucks; *m.* Joan White; commenced his career as business manager to Charles Dillingham in New York, Nov., 1928, and remained there until 1931; became business manager at the Duke of York's Theatre, London, Sept., 1933; licensee since 1935; was one of the founders of the London International Theatre Club, 1937, and is on the committee. *Recreations:* Playgoing and bridge. *Clubs:* Royal Automobile and Overseas. *Address:* 5 Raphael Street, Knightsbridge, S.W.7. *Telephone No.:* Kensington 8450.

MOORE, Carrie, actress; *b.* Albury, New South Wales, 20 July, 1883; *m.* John Wyatt; distinguished in Australia as the youngest singer who ever appeared in leading parts in Sydney and Melbourne, with J. C. Williamson's Royal Comic Opera Company; appeared as a girl of fourteen in the Sydney pantomime, "Djin-Djin," 1896, and at the end of 1899 sang Maid Marian in De Koven's opera, "Robin Hood," with Florence Perry, the Savoy soprano, as Annabel; during a stay of four years with Williamson's company she appeared chiefly in soubrette characters, but also as Yum-Yum, Phyllis, and other Gilbert and Sullivan characters, and in second parts in

"Paul Jones," and "The Old Guard"; also played Suzette in "The French Maid," and Ruth in "The Gay Parisiennes"; in Aug., 1903, came to England, and under the management of George Edwardes went on tour in "San Toy"; made her first appearance on the London stage, at the Apollo Theatre, Sept., 1903, when she succeeded Letty Lind as Ellen in "The Girl from Kay's"; she next appeared at Daly's, Mar , 1904, as Natooma in "The Cingalee," and at Christmas, 1904, appeared in pantomime at Liverpool; at the Lyric, Aug., 1905, played Millicent Leroy in "The Blue Moon"; at the Apollo, Apr., 1906, played Peggy in "The Dairymaids"; at the Apollo Theatre, Apr., 1907, appeared as Honour in "Tom Jones"; at Christmas, 1907, played the Prince in "Cinderella," at Birmingham; returned to Australia, 1908, where she toured as Sonia in "The Merry Widow"; returned to England in Dec., and appeared at the Adelphi Theatre, as the Prince in "Cinderella," at Christmas; at the Queen's, Apr., 1909, played Zingarie in "A Persian Princess"; at Christmas, 1909, played Dick in "Dick Whittington," at the Shakespeare, Liverpool; during 1910, toured as Mary Gibbs in "Our Miss Gibbs"; at Christmas, 1910, played Aladdin at the Theatre Royal, Birmingham; subsequently appeared at various music halls in songs; at Christmas, 1911, played the Prince in "Cinderella" at the Court Theatre, Liverpool; returned to Australia, 1912; during 1913 appeared in Australia in various comedies, including "Oh, Jemima" ("Jane"); in 1917 toured in Australia, as Mamie Scott in "A Little Bit of Fluff," subsequently touring as Lolotte in "Mr. Manhattan." 189 Macquarie Street, Sydney *(Died 5 Sept., 1956; age 74)*

MOORE, Decima, C.B.E., actress and vocalist; *b.* at Brighton, 11 Dec., 1871; *d.* of the late Edmund Henry Moore and his wife Emily (Strachan); sister of Eva Moore; *e.* Boswell House College, Brighton; *m.* the late Brig.-Gen. Sir F. Gordon Guggisberg, R.E.,

K.C.M.G., D.S.O., F.R.G.S.; Governor and Commander-in-Chief of British Guiana; winner of Victoria Scholarship for Singing, at Blackheath Conservatoire of Music; made her first appearance on the stage, 7 Dec., 1889, as Casilda in "The Gondoliers" at the Savoy; she has also played leading parts in "Miss Decima," Prince of Wales's, 1892; "A Pantomime Rehearsal" and "Rosencrantz and Guildenstern," Court, 1892; "Dorothy," and "The Wedding Eve," at Trafalgar Square, 1892–3; "Jane Annie," Savoy, 1893; "La Fille de Madame Angot," Criterion, 1893; "A Gaiety Girl," Prince of Wales's, 1893; in 1895, toured in Australia in "The Shop Girl" "In Town," etc.; appeared in "The White Silk Dress," Prince of Wales's, 1896; "The Scarlet Feather," Shaftesbury, 1897; "Great Caesar," Comedy, 1899; "Florodora," Lyric, 1900; "The Wrong Mr. Wright," Strand, 1899; "My Lady Molly," Terry's, 1903; has toured through Australia and America; during 1906, she toured in "All-of-a-Sudden Peggy"; during 1907 toured as Becky Warder in "The Truth"; during 1908 toured as Mrs. Worthley in "Mrs. Dot"; at the Court, May, 1910, played Nimble in "A Likely Story"; during 1910 also toured as Lady Frederick in the play of that name; at the Kilburn Empire, Oct., 1910, played in "A Black Mark"; during 1912 toured as Muriel Glayde in "John Glayde's Honour"; at the Court, June, 1914, played Katharine Mayne in "Vantage Out"; created C.B.E., June, 1918; was also a favourite concert singer, and has sung at the Albert Hall, St. James's Hall, etc.; engaged on War work in France, 1914-21; was Hon. Director-General of the British Empire Leave Club, Cologne, during the occupation by the British Army; was Hon. Exhibition Commissioner for the Gold Coast, at the British Empire Exhibition, 1923-6; Chairman of the Play Actors, 1927-9; Chairman of the Overseas Section of the Forum Club, 1928-32; appeared in the film "Nine Till Six," 1931. *Recreations:* Riding, driving, and golf. *Club:* Ladies' Army and Navy. *(Died 2 Feb., 1964; age 93)*

MOORE, Dennie, actress; *b.* New York City, 31 Dec., 1907; *e.* Sacred Heart Convent, New York; studied for the stage at the American Academy of Dramatic Arts; as a child sat as a model to many well-known artists; made her first appearance on the stage at the New Amsterdam Theatre, New York, July, 1925, in "The Ziegfeld Follies"; at the 48th Street Theatre, Apr., 1926, succeeded Justine Johnstone as Kathleen Forest in "Hush Money"; has since appeared at Lyceum, Feb., 1927, as Moll in "A Lady in Love"; National, Sept., 1927, May Harris in "The Trial of Mary Dugan"; Longacre, Sept., 1928, Sallie in "Jarnegan," and in Nov., 1928, Velma in the same play; Fulton, Mar., 1929, Mary Bishop in "Conflict"; Morosco, Nov., 1929, The Girl in "Cross Roads"; Plymouth, Aug., 1930, Edna Kinsey in "Torch Song"; Lyceum, Jan., 1931, Hilda in "Anatol"; Manhattan, Oct., 1931, Lorraine Fortier in "East Wind"; Broadhurst, Sept., 1932, Chonchon in "The Man Who Reclaimed His Head"; Selwyn, Dec., 1932, Jackie in "The Great Magoo"; Broadhurst, Dec., 1932, Anita Highland in "Twentieth Century"; Lyceum, Apr., 1933, Renée in "Man Bites Dog"; Avon, Oct., 1933, Meg in "The Pursuit of Happiness"; Imperial, Nov., 1934, Aimee Bates in "Say When"; toured 1935-6, in "Three Men on a Horse"; Booth, New York, Oct., 1936, played Cookie McGinn in "Swing Your Lady"; 48th Street, Apr., 1937, Miss Schwartz in "Hitch Your Wagon"; Vanderbilt, Oct., 1937, Polly in "In Clover"; Guild, Oct., 1941, Belle in "Ah, Wilderness!"; Music Box, Jan., 1944, Mrs. Foley in "Over 21"; Ziegfeld, Dec., 1944, appeared in the *revue*, "The Seven Lively Arts"; Biltmore, Apr., 1945, played Gwen Purchase in "Star Spangled Family"; first appeared in films, 1936, in "Sylvia Scarlett." *Address:* c/o Actors' Equity Association, 45 West 47th Street, New York City, U.S.A.

MOORE, Eva, actress; *b.* Brighton, 9 Feb., 1870; *d.* of the late Edmund Henry Moore and his wife Emily

1737

(Strachan) ; sister of Decima and Bertha Moore ; *m.* H. V. Esmond, has two children, Jack and Jill ; was educated at Brighton ; made her first appearance on the stage at the Vaudeville Theatre, 15 Dec., 1887, as Varney in " Proposals " ; she next joined the late John L. Toole, and appeared at Toole's Theatre, 26 Dec., 1887, as the Spirit of Home in " Dot " ; at the Vaudeville, Feb., 1888, played in " The Red Rag"; rejoined Toole and appeared in the provinces with him as Dora in " The Don," and on returning to London appeared in that part at Toole's Theatre, Dec., 1888 ; she also played in " Artful Cards " and " A Broken Sixpence " ; at the Shaftesbury, Aug., 1889, she played Felicia Umfraville in " The Middleman " ; she was next engaged at the Court, playing the Countess of Drumdurris in " The Cabinet Minister," Apr., 1890 ; she appeared at the Strand, 1891, as Mrs. Richard Webb in " The Late Lamented," and at the Lyric, 1892, played Minestra in " The Mountebanks " ; she was then seen at the Vaudeville, 1892, and appeared as Violet Melrose in a revival of " Our Boys " ; she appeared at the Court, Jan., 1893, in " The Pantomime Rehearsal," and at the Opéra Comique, played Margery Knox in " Man and Woman "; she appeared at the Lyric, Oct., 1893, as Pepita in " Little Christopher Columbus " ; at the Court, 1894, was playing in " The Gay Widow " ; at the Gaiety, Mar., 1895, played Bessie Brent in " The Shop Girl " ; at the St. James's, 1895, she played Fairy in " Bogey " ; at Terry's, 1896, in " The Sunbury Scandal " ; at the Comedy, 1897, played Maysie in " One Summer's Day " ; at Her Majesty's, 1899, played Ellice Ford in " Carnac Sahib " ; Prince of Wales's, 1899-1900, Lucie Manette in " The Only Way," Grown-up Christina in " Ib and Little Christina," and Lily Eaton-Belgrave in " A Pantomime Rehearsal " ; at Drury Lane, 1900, appeared as Louise in " Marsac of Gascony " ; at the St. James's, 1901 she played Mabel Vaughan in " The Wilderness," afterwards touring in the same part ; at the Garrick, 1902, played Lady Hetty in " Pilkerton's Peerage," and Lady

Ernestone in " My Lady Virtue " ; at the St. James's, 1903, played Kathie in " Old Heidelberg " ; at the Criterion, 1903, appeared as Wilhelmina Marr in " Billy's Little Love Affair " ; and in 1904, played there as Lady Henrietta Addison in " The Duke of Killicrankie " ; at the Imperial, 1904, played Lady Mary Carlyle in " Monsieur Beaucaire " ; at the Waldorf, 1905, appeared as Klara Volkhardt in " Lights Out " ; at the Comedy, 1906, played Miss Blarney in " Josephine " and Judy in " Punch " ; at the St. James's, Mar., 1907, played Muriel Glayde in " John Glayde's Honour " ; at the Haymarket, Oct., 1907, appeared in the name part of " Sweet Kitty Bellairs " ; at the Lyric, June, 1908, played Mrs. Crowley in " The Explorer " ; at Drury Lane, Sept., 1908, appeared as Dorothy Gore in " Marriages of Mayfair " ; at the Court, Dec., 1908, played Mrs Errol in " Little Lord Fauntleroy " ; during 1909 played at the Afternoon (His Majesty's) Theatre, as Lady Joan Meredith in " The House of Bondage," at the St. James's, Kathie in " Old Heidelberg," at Wyndham's, the Hon. Mrs. Bayle in " The Best People," and at the Queen's, the Hon. Mrs. Rivers in " The House Opposite " ; at the Kingsway Theatre, Oct., 1910, played Gay Birch in " Company for George " ; appeared at the Palladium, Apr., 1911, as Christine in " A Woman's Wit " ; at the Aldwych, May, 1912, played Kate Bellingham in " Looking for Trouble " ; at His Majesty's, May, 1912, Minna in " In Haarlem there Dwelt— " ; at the Prince of Wales's, July, 1912, succeeded Marie Tempest as Mollie Blair in " At the Barn " ; in Sept., 1912, toured as Dorothy in " Sandy and his Eliza " ; at the Criterion, Feb., 1913, played the same part, when the play was called " Eliza Comes to Stay " ; at the Lyceum, Edinburgh, Dec., 1913, played Betty Dunbar in " The Dear Fool " ; then went to America, and appeared at the Garrick, New York, Jan., 1914, as Eliza in " Eliza Comes to Stay," and Betty Dunbar in " The Dear Fool"; reappeared in London, at the Vaudeville, May, 1914, as Betty Dunbar in the last-mentioned play, which was then re-named "The Dangerous Age"; subsequently appeared in a revival of "Eliza Comes to Stay"; during 1914-15 toured in the same part; in Aug., 1915, toured as Phyllis in "When We were Twenty-one"; at the Royalty, July, 1918, played Mrs. Culver in "The Title"; Mar., 1919, Mrs. Etheridge in "Caesar's Wife"; in the autumn toured in variety theatres as Cynthia Gates in "The Punctual Sex," in which she appeared at the Coliseum, Dec., 1919; at the Little, Feb., 1920, appeared as Marie Symonds in "Mumsee"; at the Comedy, June, 1920, as Olive Gresham in "The 'Ruined' Lady"; in Oct., 1920, accompanied her husband on a Canadian tour; at the Comedy, Apr., 1921, played Lady Marlow in "A Matter of Fact"; at the St. James's, Jan., 1922, Miss Cornelia Van Gorder in "The Bat"; at Eastbourne, Aug., 1923, appeared as Mary Westlake in "Mary, Mary, Quite Contrary"; appeared at the Brixton Theatre, Sept., 1924, in the same part, and toured throughout the provinces; appeared at the Savoy, June, 1925, in the same part; she then toured as Judith Bliss in "Hay Fever"; at the Savoy, Dec., 1925, succeeded Henrietta Watson as Helen Delisse in "The Unfair Sex"; Apollo (for Play Actors), May, 1926, played Mrs. Brabazon in "Getting Mother Married"; Garrick, July, 1926, Mrs. Dawn in "Cock o' the Roost"; Lyric, May, 1927, Rosa in "The Garden of Eden"; Garrick, Feb., 1928, Mrs. Drake in "Tin Gods"; Arts, Sept., 1928, Mrs. Culverwell in "Payment"; Vaudeville, Jan., 1929, Lady Tankerton in "He Walked in Her Sleep"; in July, 1929, toured in "Getting Mother Married"; St. James's, Aug., 1930, succeeded Irene Vanbrugh as the Princess Maria in "The Swan"; Embassy, June, 1931, played Aunt Ottillie in "Delicate Question"; at the Duke of York's, Nov., 1932, played the Marchesa in "To-Night or Never"; Lyric, Feb., 1933, Mrs. Watson in "The Holmeses of Baker Street"; Ambassadors', Nov., 1933, Agnese in "Cabbages and Kings"; St. James's, Feb., 1936, Lady Catherine de Bourgh in "Pride and Prejudice"; Embassy, Mar., 1937, Cornelia Van

Gorder in a revival of "The Bat"; Garrick, Jan., 1939, Duchess of Wickham in "Hundreds and Thousands"; Richmond, June, 1939, Marjory Marlow in "Without Motive?"; toured Mar., 1941, as Mrs. Simmons in "Wasn't it Odd?"; St. James's, Dec., 1942, played Aunt Ella in "It Happened in September"; has appeared also in numerous films; published her reminiscences, under the title of "Exits and Entrances," Oct., 1923. *Club:* Bath. *(Died 27 Apr., 1955; age 85)*

MOORE, Florence, actress; *m.* (2) William Montgomery; (3) John O. Kerner; appeared at the Broadway Theatre, New York, 5 Aug., 1912, as Clorinda Scribblem in "Hanky-Panky"; at the Winter Garden, Nov., 1913, played Violet Bliffkins in "The Pleasure Seekers"; June, 1916, Lady Bluff Gordon in "The Passing Show of 1916"; at Chicago, Aug., 1917, appeared as Polly Hathaway in "Parlour, Bedroom, and Bath," and played the same part at the Republic, New York, Dec., 1917; continued to play this part on tour until 1919; at the Eltinge Theatre, Feb., 1920, appeared as Emily Duval in "Breakfast in Bed"; at the Music Box Theatre, Sept., 1921, played in "The Music Box Revue," and again in Sept., 1923; 46th Street Theatre, Dec., 1925, appeared in "The Greenwich Village Follies"; Booth, Aug., 1926, played Alice Hinsdale in "She Couldn't Say No"; Winter Garden, Nov., 1927, played in "Artists and Models"; Majestic, Feb., 1930, in "The International Review"; at Cincinnati, Sept., 1932, in "The Passing Show of 1932"; has also appeared successfully in "talking" pictures on the cinema stage.
(Died 23 Mar., 1935; age 49)

MOORE, George, dramatic author, poet, and novelist; *b.* 24 Feb., 1852; *s.* of the late George Henry Moore, M.P.; is the author of the following plays: "The Strike at Arlingford," 1891; "The Bending of the Bough," 1900; "Esther Waters," 1911; "Elizabeth Cooper," 1913; "The Coming of Gabrielle" (revised version of "Eliza-

beth Cooper ''), 1923; '' The Making of an Immortal,'' 1928; ''The Passing of the Essenes,'' 1930; among his literary works may be mentioned '' Flowers of Passion,'' '' A Modern Love,'' '' A Mummer's Wife,'' '' Literature at Nurse,'' '' Confessions of a Young Man,'' '' Vain Fortune,'' '' Ideals in Ireland,'' '' Esther Waters,'' '' Celibates,'' '' Evelyn Innes,'' '' Sister Teresa,'' '' Memoirs of My Dead Life,'' '' Hail and Farewell,'' '' Lewis Seymour and Some Women,'' '' A Storyteller's Holiday,'' ''The Book Kerith,'' ''The Untilled Field,'' ''The Lake,'' ''Heloise and Abelard,'' ''Conversations of Ebury Street,'' ''Celibate Lives,'' ''Ulick and Soracha,'' ''Aphrodite in Aulis,'' ''A Communication to My Friends,'' etc.
(Died 21 Jan., 1933; age 80)

MOORE, Grace, actress and vocalist; *b.* Del Rio, Cocke Co., Tennessee, U.S.A., 5 Dec., 1901; *d.* of Colonel Richard L. Moore and his wife Tessie Jane Stokeley; *e.* Jellico, and Ward Belmont School, Nashville, Tenn.; *m.* Valentin Parera; studied singing under Dr. P. M. Marafioti and Albert Carré; made her first appearance on the stage at the Colonial Theatre, Boston, 7 Sept., 1920, in ''Hitchy-Koo 1920,'' and made her first appearance in New York, at the New Amsterdam Theatre, 19 Oct., 1920, in the same piece; at the Lyric, New York, Jan., 1922, played Jean Jones in ''Above the Clouds''; Music Box, Sept., 1923, appeared in ''The Music Box Revue''; Dec., 1924, appeared in the second ''Music Box Revue''; after appearing in Concert work, made her *début* as an operatic vocalist at the Metropolitan Opera House, 7 Feb., 1928, as Mimi in ''La Bohème,'' subsequently appearing as Juliette in ''Romeo et Juliette,'' Marguerite in ''Faust,'' Micaela in ''Carmen,'' and title-*rôle* in ''Manon''; appeared at the Metropolitan Opera House from 1928–31, and in various seasons, since that date as Floria in ''La Tosca,'' ''Madame Butterfly,'' and in ''The Love of Three Kings,'' etc.; in 1929 appeared at the Opéra Comique, Paris, as Louise in the opera of that name, and at the Opera

House, Monte Carlo, etc.; at the George M. Cohan Theatre, New York, Nov., 1932, played Jeanne in ''The Dubarry''; first appeared on the London stage at Covent Garden, 6 June, 1935, as Mimi in ''La Bohême,'' when she created a furore; her autobiography, ''You're Only Human Once,'' was published in 1944; commenced film career 1930, and has appeared in ''A Lady's Morals'' ('' Jenny Lind''), ''New Moon,'' ''One Night of Love,'' ''Love Me Forever '' (''On Wings of Song''), ''The King Steps Out,'' ''When You're in Love,'' ''I'll Take Romance,'' ''Louise,'' etc.; is a Chevalier of the Legion of Honour (France), and has received decorations from twelve countries. *Hobby*: Cooking. *(Died 25 Jan., 1947; age 45)*

MOORE, Hilda, actress; *d.* of Oscar and Alice M. Moore; *m.* Austin Fairman; was a pupil at the Academy of Dramatic Art, 1904–5; made her first appearance on the stage at the Shakespeare Theatre, Liverpool, Nov., 1905, as Rose Maylie in '' Oliver Twist,'' with Sir Herbert Tree; made her first appearance in London, at His Majesty's, 25 Jan., 1906, as Myrrha in '' Nero ''; remained at His Majesty's, till 1908, playing several small parts, including the Nurse in '.' Colonel Newcome ''; the First Lady in '' Richard II ''; Iras in '' Antony and Cleopatra,'' Player Queen in '' Hamlet,'' First Lady in '' The Winter's Tale,'' Alice in '' A Woman of No Importance,'' etc.,; in May, 1908, toured as Beatrice Ebernoe in '' The Liars,'' and as Gwen in '' Raffles,'' with Leonard Boyne; in May, 1909, went to Germany to play in ' A Florentine Tragedy ''; returned to His Majesty's, Sept., 1909, to play Nagaou in '' False Gods ''; subsequently appeared at the same theatre as Mimi in '' Trilby,'' the First Symphony and Giuletta in '' Beethoven,'' Jessica in '' The Merchant of Venice,'' Calpurnia in ''Julius Caesar,'' Lady Belinda and Fancy Free in '' The O'Flynn ''; joined Charles Hawtrey at Prince of Wales's, Oct., 1910, and appeared at that theatre as Vivette Lambert in '' Inconstant

George," Madame Grenelle in "Better Not Enquire," Apr., 1911; Lady Roderick in "The Great Name," Sept., 1911; Louise Carnot in "The Uninvited Guest" Oct., 1911; at the Duke of York's, Feb., 1912, played Enid Moncrieff in "The 'Mind-the-Paint' Girl"; appeared at the Tivoli, June, 1912, as Delia in "Fancy Free"; in Aug., 1912, toured as Mrs. Chepstow in "Bella Donna"; at the St. James's Theatre, Jan., 1913, played Adelma in "Turandot"; at the Tivoli, Mar., 1913, played in "Stolen Fruit,"; in Sept., 1913, toured with Sir George Alexander, as Mrs. Chepstow in "Bella Donna"; at the Playhouse, Feb., 1914, played Mdme. de Semiano in "The Marriage of Kitty"; at the St. James's, May, 1914, Mrs. Cheveley in "An Ideal Husband"; at Wyndham's, Nov., 1914, Miriam in "Outcast"; Dec., 1914, Mrs. Vidal in "Raffles"; at the Playhouse, May, 1915, the Terrorist in the play of that name; at Wyndham's, June, 1915, Millicent Hope in "Gamblers All"; at the St. James's, Jan., 1916, appeared as Mrs. Radford in "The Basker"; at the Savoy, Apr., 1916, as Ellen Young in a play of that name; at the Royalty, Mar., 1917, as Manon in "Remnant"; at the Strand, July, 1917, played the Countess Valeski in "Three Weeks"; at Wyndham's, Oct., 1917, Mrs. Dearth in "Dear Brutus"; in 1918, served in France with the F.A.N.Y.; from Sept., 1919-20, toured in the United States as Mrs. Dearth in "Dear Brutus"; on returning to London, appeared at the St. James's, July, 1920, succeeding Sybil Thorndike as Mathilde Sangerson in "The Mystery of the Yellow Room"; at the Gaiety, Manchester, Nov., 1920, played Marguerite Arnaut in "Daniel"; at the Royalty, Feb, 1921, Millicent Hannay in "A Social Convenience"; at the Criterion, July, 1921, Anna Valeska in "Ambrose Applejohn's Adventure"; at the Everyman Theatre, Jan., 1923, Julia Craven in "The Philanderer"; Feb., 1923, Laura Pasquale in "At Mrs. Beam's"; at the Duke of York's, Mar., 1923, Madame de Semiano in "The Marriage of Kitty"; at the Prince's, Oct., 1923, Cecilia in "The Return of Sherlock Holmes."
(Died 18 May, 1929; age 43)

MOORE, Maggie, actress and vocalist; b. San Francisco, Cal., U.S.A., 1847; m. (1) J. C. Williamson; (2) Harry R. Roberts; made her first appearance on the stage in San Francisco, 1871; while playing in "stock" in that city, met and married J. C. Williamson; in 1873, she appeared as Lizzie Stofel in "Struck Oil," which met with instantaneous success; in 1874, went to Australia, and made her first appearance there, at Sydney, July, 1874, in the same part; coming to England, she appeared, with her husband, at the Adelphi, 17 Apr., 1876, in the same part, repeating her success, and the play ran over one hundred nights; she also appeared at the Adelphi, in Apr., 1876, in "Fool of the Family"; May, 1876, as Eily O'Connor in "The Colleen Bawn"; Aug., 1876, as Arrah Meelish in "Arrah-Na-Pogue"; returning to America again played "Struck Oil"; subsequently played in "The Chinese Question," "Yulie; or Kindes-Liebe," and "Our Boarding House"; again visited Australia 1879, and from that date onward, settled there; at the Theatre Royal, Melbourne, Feb., 1880, she played Josephine in "H.M.S. Pinafore"; at the Opera House, May, 1881, Ruth in "The Pirates of Penzance"; July, 1881, Buttercup in "H.M.S. Pinafore"; Dec., 1882, Bettina in "La Mascotte"; subsequently played innumerable parts in every class of performance, drama, comedy, burlesque, opera-bouffe, musical comedy, farce and pantomime; in 1886, played Katisha in "The Mikado"; in 1892, "starred" in "Meg, the Castaway"; at Her Majesty's Theatre, Sydney, July, 1924, was the recipient of a testimonial benefit (realising nearly £1,500), to celebrate the fiftieth anniversary of her first appearance in Australia, on which occasion she again played Lizzie Stofel in an act of "Struck Oil."
(Died 15 Mar., 1926; age 79)

MOORE, Mary, actress; b. London, 3 July, 1861; d. of late Charles Moore, Parliamentary agent; e. Warwick

Hall, Maida Vale; *m.* (1) James Albery, 1878 (*d.* 1889) ; (2) Sir Charles Wyndham, 1916 (*d.* 1919) ; made her first appearance on the stage at the Gaiety Theatre, under the management of the late John Hollingshead; after her marriage she quitted the stage and was not seen again until she appeared at the Theatre Royal, Bradford, 30 Mar., 1885, as Lady Dorothy in "The Candidate," under the management of Charles Wyndham ; she continued to appear under the same management until 1912, when Wyndham discontinued acting ; she first appeared at the Criterion, 26 Oct., 1885, as Lady Oldacre in "The Candidate" ; she then appeared there as Violet Greenwood in "The Man with Three Wives," Jan., 1886, and she next made quite a "hit" when she played Lady Amaranth in "Wild Oats," May, 1886 ; since that date she has made many notable successes, and among the parts she played at the Criterion was Ada Ingot in "David Garrick," Nov., 1886, in which she appeared at Sandringham, before the late King Edward (then Prince of Wales) on 7 Jan., 1887, and in the same year played the part in Germany and Russia, and using the German language; she reappeared in the same part at the Criterion, Feb., 1888 ; then played Emma Thornton in "The Bachelor of Arts," May, 1888 ; Mrs. Mildmay in "Still Waters Run Deep," Jan., 1889 ; Pauline in "Delicate Ground," Apr., 1890 ; Julia in "Sowing and Reaping," June, 1890 ; Grace Harkaway in "London Assurance," Nov., 1890 ; Maria in "The School for Scandal," Apr., 1891 ; Effie Remington in "Brighton," Dec., 1891 ; Marion Carslow in "The Fringe of Society," Apr., 1892 ; Jessie Keber in "The Bauble Shop," Jan., 1893 ; Alice, Countess of Forres, in "An Aristocratic Alliance," Mar., 1894 ; Lady Susan Harabin in "The Case of Rebellious Susan," Oct., 1894 ; Mrs. Thorpe Didsbury in "The Home Secretary," May, 1895 ; Adeline Dennant in "The Squire of Dames," Nov., 1895 ; Dorothy Cruickshank in "Rosemary," May, 1896 ; Edana Hinde in "The Physician," Mar., 1897 ; Lady Jessica Nepean in "The Liars" ; Fiorella in "The Jest," Nov., 1898 ; Mrs. Parbury in "The Tyranny of Tears," Apr., 1899 ; at Wyndham's, Roxane in "Cyrano de Bergerac," Apr., 1900 ; Lady Eastney in "Mrs. Dane's Defence," Oct., 1900 ; Mrs. Ruth Thornton in "The Mummy and the Humming Bird," Oct., 1901 ; Lady Barbara O'Hagan in "The End of a Story," Apr., 1902 ; Mrs. Gorringe in "Mrs. Gorringe's Necklace," May, 1903 ; at the New Theatre, Lady Mordaunt in "My Lady of Rosedale," Feb., 1904 ; Lady Allison in "The Bride and Bridegroom," May, 1904 ; Miss Mills in "Captain Drew on Leave," Oct., 1905 ; at the Criterion, appeared in a revival of "The Liars," as Lady Jessica, Apr., 1907 ; Mrs. Baxter in "The Mollusc," Oct., 1907 ; Lady Epping in "Lady Epping's Lawsuit," Oct., 1908 ; Mrs. Gorringe in a revival of "Mrs. Gorringe's Necklace," Jan., 1909 ; Lady Susan in a revival of "The Case of Rebellious Susan," June, 1910 ; Lady Jessica Nepean in a revival of "The Liars," Oct., 1910 ; at the Gala performance at His Majesty's, 27 June, 1911, played Ada Ingot in the second act of "David Garrick" ; at the New Theatre, May, 1912, appeared as Lady Eastney in a revival of "Mrs. Dane's Defence"; at the Criterion, Oct., 1914, played Gertrude Vyse in "Sir Richard's Biography"; made her first appearance on the variety stage, at the Coliseum, 10 May, 1915, as Mrs. Gorringe in a condensed version of "Mrs. Gorringe's Necklace"; at the Criterion, July, 1917, for a benefit performance, reappeared as Mrs. Baxter in "The Mollusc"; at the Criterion, Apr., 1919, played Lady Bagley in "Our Mr. Hepplewhite"; she accompanied Sir Charles Wyndham on all his American tours from 1885 ; appeared by Command at Windsor Castle, 19 Nov., 1903, before the late King Edward in "David Garrick," and 16 Nov., 1907, in "Still Waters Run Deep"; was partner with Sir Charles Wyndham in Criterion from 1897, and with him built the New and Wyndham's Theatres, and is still proprietor (with the executors of her late husband) of the two last-mentioned theatres, and co-lessee (with Sir Charles Wyndham's executors) of the Criterion ; is the President of the Actors' Benevolent Fund. *Recreations :* Reading, walking, and driving. *(Died 6 Apr., 1931; age 69)*

MOORE, Victor Frederick, actor ; *b.* Hammonton, New Jersey, 24 Feb., 1876 ; *s.* of Orville E. and Sarah A. Moore ; *e.* at Hammonton and Boston ; *m.* (1) Emma Littlefield ; (2) Shirley Page ; made his first appearance in a non-speaking part in "The Babes in the Wood," at Boston Theatre, 1893 ; served as a "super" for two years ; then followed a season in "A Summer Shower" ; with John Drew in "Rosemary," 1896 ; subsequently played in "A Romance of Coon Hollow," "The Real Widow Brown," "The Girl From Paris" ; played four years in "vaudeville," in "Change Your Act, or Back to the Woods" ; two seasons playing Kid Burns in "45 Minutes from Broadway" ; during the autumn of 1907 played in "The Talk of New York," appearing in this piece in New York, at the Knickerbocker Theatre, 3 Dec., 1907 ; during 1910 toured in "The Happiest Night of his Life," and appeared in this play at the Criterion, New York, Feb., 1911 ; in 1911-12 toured in "Shorty McCabe" ; subsequently appeared in "vaudeville," in "Change Your Act," from 1913-15 ; in 1918, toured in "Patsy on the Wing" ; in 1919 toured in "See You Later" ; at the Cohan Theatre, Oct., 1925, played Jim Bailey in "Easy Come, Easy Go" ; Imperial, Nov., 1926, "Shorty" McGee in "Oh, Kay!" ; Earl Carroll, Aug., 1927, played in "Allez-Oop" ; Alvin, Nov., 1927, Herbert in "Funny Face" ; Broadhurst, Oct., 1928, Nosey Bartlett in "Hold Everything" ; Alvin, Nov., 1929, Skippy Dugan in "Heads Up" ; Imperial, Oct., 1930, Irving Huff in "Princess Charming" ; Longacre, Feb., 1931, Captain O'Leary in "She Lived Next to the Firehouse" ; Music Box, Dec., 1931, Alexander Throttlebottom in "Of Thee I Sing," which ran throughout 1932 ; Imperial, Oct., 1933, Throttlebottom in "Let 'Em Eat Cake" ; Alvin, Nov., 1934, the Rev. Dr. Moon in "Anything Goes," which ran a year ; on the Pacific Coast, July, 1938, played Gramps in "On Borrowed Time" ; Imperial, New York, Nov., 1938, Alonzo P. Goodhue in "Leave It to Me!" ; and May, 1940, Senator Loganberry in "Louisiana Purchase" ; Alvin, May, 1945, Joseph W. Porter in "Hollywood Pinafore" ; Adelphi, Jan., 1946, Phineas T. Fogarty in "Nellie Bly" ; 48th Street, Feb., 1953, played his old part of Gramps in a revival of "On Borrowed Time" ; at the City Center, N.Y., Sept., 1957, played Starkeeper in "Carousel" ; entered films 1934, and has appeared in numerous pictures. *Recreations :* Hunting, fishing, and automobiling. *Club :* Lambs.
(Died 23 July, 1962; age 86)

MORAN, Lois, actress and vocalist; *b.* Pittsburgh, Pa., U.S.A., 1 Mar., 1907 ; *d.* of Roger Dowling and his wife Gladys (Evans) ; *e.* Greensburgh, Pa., and the Lycée de Tours, France; *m.* Clarence M. Young ; made her first appearance on the stage as a dancer, at the Paris Opera House, 1922, and remained there until 1924 ; she appeared in pictures, in Paris, 1924, and returning to America, appeared in pictures in 1925 ; in 1926, she toured in "The Wisdom Tooth," and again returned to pictures ; at the Plymouth Theatre, New York, 28 Nov., 1930, played Emma Krull in "This is New York" ; at the Music Box, Dec., 1931, made a great success when she appeared as Mary Turner in "Of Thee I Sing," which ran throughout 1932 ; Imperial, Oct., 1933, played Mary in "Let 'Em Eat Cake" ; at the Geary, San Francisco, 1935, played in "The Petrified Forest" ; commenced film career in France in 1924, and appeared in "La Galerie des Monstres," and "Feu-Mathias Pascal" ; returning to America, she played in "Stella Dallas," and subsequently appeared in innumerable pictures. *Recreations :* Dancing, singing, book-collecting, and writing.

MORAND, Eugène, French dramatic author and librettist ; *b.* Petrograd, Russia, 17 Mar., 1855; has written the following works: " Les Dossiers," " Jaunes," " Raymonde " (with A. Theuriet), 1887; " Griselidis " (with Armand Silvestre), 1891; " Les Drames Sacrés " (with Silvestre, music by Gounod), 1893; " Izeyl " (with Silvestre), 1894; " Kosacks ! " (with Silvestre), 1898; " La Tragique Histoire d'Hamlet " (" Hamlet," with Marcel Schwob), 1899; " Messaline " (with Silvestre, music by Isidore de Lara), 1903; is also the author of a number of books and poems; is a Chevalier of the Legion of Honour. *(Died Jan., 1930; age 75)*

MORAND, Marcellus Raymond, actor; *b.* Bury, Lancs., 17 Dec., 1860; made his first appearance on the stage in the provinces in Dec., 1883; made his first appearance on the London stage at the Avenue, Sept., 1889, as Domino in " The Brigands "; appeared at the Savoy, Dec., 1894, as José in " The Chieftain "; subsequently toured in leading parts in Gilbert and Sullivan opera, also in " The Emerald Isle," and " Merrie England "; at the Savoy, Jan., 1903, Yapp in " A Princess of Kensington "; Adelphi, Dec., 1903; Downham in " The Earl and the Girl ", Lyric, Jan., 1905, Ernest English in " The Talk of the Town "; Criterion, Aug., 1905, Sin-Chong in " The White Chrysanthemum "; Adelphi, Dec., 1907, No Fang in " Aladdin "; at the Queen's Theatre, Apr., 1909, played King Khafilah in "A Persian Princess "; played a " repertory " season at the Royalty, Glasgow, 1910; at the Haymarket, 1911-2, played Tammas Biggar in " Bunty Pulls the Strings "; Criterion, Nov., 1912, William Burchell in " Where's there's a Will—"; Strand, Apr., 1913, Admiral Peter Maxwell in " The Chaperon "; at the Playhouse, June, 1913, played Tammas in a revival of " Bunty Pulls the Strings "; at the Lyceum, June, 1914, played Ichabod Bronson in " The Belle of New York "; at the Duke of York's, Sept., 1914, Snecky Hobart in " The Little Minister "; at the Apollo, July, 1915, appeared in the *revue* " All Scotch "; in 1916, accompanied Miss

Ethel Irving to South Africa, where he appeared in " Dame Nature," " Lady Frederick," " The Ware Case," " The Witness for the Defence," " The Turning Point," " Caroline," " What Every Woman Knows," " Tiger's Cub "; at the St. James's, Nov., 1917, played David Macfarlane in " Loyalty "; at the Ambassadors', Apr., 1918, Sir Robert McCorbel in " Too Much Money "; at the St. Martin's, Nov., 1918, Mr. Tinkerton in " The Officers' Mess "; at the Garrick, Mar., 1919, Lignière in " Cyrano de Bergerac "; at the Duke of York's, Dec., 1919, General Petkoff in " Arms and the Man "; at the Globe, July, 1920, Brigadier-General Sir Archibald Root in " French Leave." *(Died 5 Mar., 1922; age 62)*

MORE, Unity, actress, dancer, and vocalist; *b.* Galway, Ireland, 27 July, 1894; *m.* Captain Nigel E. Haig, M.C., R.A.; made her first appearance on the stage at the Empire, 9 Oct., 1909, in the ballet, " Round the World "; subsequently appeared at the Midland Theatre, Manchester, Dec., 1909, as Bluebell in " Bluebell in Fairyland "; returned to the Empire, and appeared there, Nov., 1910, as Kathleen in " Ship Ahoy ! "; Dec., 1910, as Jane in " Widow's Weeds "; Feb., 1911, in " By George ! "; May, 1911, as Fros in " Sylvia "; Oct., 1911, as Celia Van Buren in " New York "; Feb., 1912, as Bunty and Kiki in " Everybody's Doing It "; Apr., 1913, as Patsy in " All the Winners "; Sept., 1913, as Dahlia in " The Gay Lothario "; Oct., 1913, as Puck in " Titania "; at Daly's Theatre, 7 Jan., 1914, played the Maid in " The Marriage Market "; at the Hippodrome, 16 Nov., 1914, appeared in " Business as Usual "; at the Comedy Theatre, Aug., 1915, played in " Shell Out "; at the New Theatre, Dec., 1915, appeared as Peter Pan; at Daly's, May, 1916, played Ma Petite in " The Happy Day "; at the New Theatre, Dec., 1916, again played Peter Pan; at the Empire, Mar., 1917, appeared in " Hanky-Panky," and Aug., 1917, in " Topsy-Turvey "; retired from the stage on the occasion of her marriage, 1918.

MOREAU, Emile, French dramatic author; *b.* Brienon-sur-Armançon, Yonne, 8 Dec., 1852; *e.* Auxerre; has written the following works : " Parthenice," 1877 ; " Les Mineurs," 1878 ; " Camille Desmoulins," 1879 ; " Le Gladiateur," 1883 ; " Matapan," " Manfred," 1886 ; " Pallas-Athéné," " Protestation," 1887 ; " Le Procès de Ravaillac," "La Peur de l'Étre " (with P. Valdagne), 1889 ; "Le Gaul de Conradin," 1889 ; "Le Drapeau " (with Ernest Depré), " Cléopâtre " (with Victorien Sardou), 1890 ; " L'Auberge des Mariniers," 1891 ; " Madame Sans-Gêne " (with Sardou), 1893 ; " Le Capitaine Floréal " (with Ernest Depré), 1895 ; " La Montagne Enchantée " (with Albert Carré), 1897 ; " Madame de Lavalette," 1899 ; " Le Secret de Saint-Louis," 1900 ; " Quo Vadis ?" (from the novel, with music by F. Thomé), 1901 ; " Dante " (with Sardou, for Sir Henry Irving) ; " Eglé," " Le Vert Galant," 1907 ; " Le Procès de Jeanne D'Arc," 1909 ; " Manfred " (translated from Byron), 1909 ; " Madame Margot " (with Charles Clairville), 1909 ; " La Boniche " (with Marc Sonal), 1911 ; " Le Deserteur " (with M. Villard), 1911 ; "La Reine Elisabeth," 1912 ; is a Chevalier of the Legion of Honour ; Laureate of the French Academy ; member of the Societies of Dramatic Authors, and Authors and Composers of Music. *Recreations :* Painting and cycling. *Address :* 43 Rue de Maubeuge, Paris.

MOREHOUSE, Ward, dramatic critic, author, and journalist; *b.* Savannah, Georgia, U.S.A., 24 Nov., 1899; *s.* of Augustus Ward Morehouse and his wife Sarah (McIntosh); *e.* Savannah High School and North Georgia College, Dahlonega, Ga.; *m.* (1) Ruth Nisbet; (2) Jean Dalrymple; (3) Joan Marlowe; (4) Rebecca Franklin; has been a theatre journalist since 1916, having been a reporter on the *Savannah Press*; subsequently reporter and sub-editor on the *Atlanta Journal*; reporter for the *New York Tribune*; joined the staff of the *New York Sun,* 1926; appointed dramatic critic, 1943; on the amalgamation of the *New York Sun* with the *World Telegram,* Jan., 1950, continued as theatre columnist; currently drama critic and theatre columnist for the S.I. Newhouse Newspapers and for General Features Corporation; author of the plays: "Gentlemen of the Press," 1928; "Miss Quis," 1937; "U.S. 90," 1941; author of numerous film scenarios; author of "Forty-five Minutes Past Eight" (semi-autobiographical), 1939; "George M. Cohan—Prince of the American Theatre," 1943; "Matinée To-morrow," 1949; "Just the Other Day," 1953; is a member of the Authors' League of America and the New York Drama Critics' Circle; is an Hon. Overseas Member of the Critics' Circle, London. *Recreations :* Duck-shooting and motoring. *Clubs :* Lambs. *(Died 7 Dec., 1966; age 67)*

MORETON, Ursula, dancer; *b.* Southsea, Hants, 13 Mar. 1903; *d.* of Captain J. A. Moreton, C.M.G., D.S.O., R.N., and his wife Catherine Beatrice (Hirtzel); *e.* Byculla School Portsmouth; *m.* Gerald V. Stevens; studied dancing under Enrico Cecchetti; made her first appearance on the stage at the London Coliseum, 15 Mar., 1920, as one of the bridesmaids in "The Truth About the Russian Dancers," with Tamara Karsavina; danced with the Diaghileff ballet company, 1921–2, and with Leonide Massine's company, 1923 ; His Majesty's, Sept., 1923, was principal dancer in "Hassan"; Drury Lane, June, 1924, principal dancer in "London Life" and Dec., 1924, principal dancer in "A Midsummer Night's Dream"; joined Ninette de Valois, and assisted in the inauguration of the Old Vic. ballet company, Oct., 1929; assistant ballet mistress and soloist with the Vic.-Wells company at Sadler's Wells, from Jan., 1931; after her marriage, retired for a time, but returned to the theatre, in 1945, as Assistant Director of Ballet, for Sadler's Wells Ballet. *Favourite parts :* The Young Girl in "Spectre de la Rose," Prélude in "Les Sylphides," and the dancer in "The Rake's Progress." *Recreation :* Gardening. *Address :* Whyte Friars, Pitstone Green, near Leighton Buzzard, Beds. *Telephone No. :* Cheddington 243.

MORGAN, Charles Langbridge, novelist, dramatist and critic; M.A. (Oxford); LL.D. (Hon. St. Andrews); Docteur (Hon. Caen); Docteur (Hon Toulouse); F.R.S.L. (Vice-President); *b.* Kent, 22 Jan., 1894; *s.* of Sir Charles Morgan, C.B.E.; *e.* R.N. Colleges, Osborne and Dartmouth, and Brasenose College Oxford; President Oxford University Dramatic Society, 1920; *m.* Hilda Campbell Vaughan; served in the R.N. Division in the First World War and in the Naval Intelligence Division in the Second World War; was appointed assistant dramatic critic to *The Times,* Dec., 1921, and on the death of A. B. Walkley, 1926, was dramatic critic to that paper until Sept., 1939; President of the Critics' Circle, 1932–33; author of the novels, "The Gunroom," "My Name is Legion," "Portrait in a Mirror," "The Fountain," "Sparkenbroke," "The Voyage," "The Empty Room," "The Judge's Story," "The River Line," and "A Breeze of Morning"; also the author of "Epitaph on George Moore," "The House of Macmillan," "Reflections in a Mirror," and "Second Reflections in a Mirror," "Ode to France," and "Liberties of the Mind"; his work is translated into seventeen languages; his novel "Portrait in a Mirror" gained the *Femina Vie Heureuse* prize, 1929–30, "The Fountain" gained the Hawthornden prize, 1933, and "The Voyage" gained the James Tait Black Memorial Prize, 1940; is author of the plays "The Flashing Stream," 1938; "The River Line," 1952; "The Burning Glass," 1954; after London production, each has been performed throughout Europe; "The Flashing Stream," presented in Paris, 1945, ran for a year; "The Burning Glass" was outstandingly successful in Germany, 1955; is Officier de la Légion d'Honneur; is a member of the French Académie des Sciences Morales et Politiques, and of the Institut de France; is a member of the Academy of Lucca (Italy) and is an Honorary Citizen of Lucca; President of the English Association 1953–54; International President of P.E.N., 1954–56. *(Died 6 Feb., 1958; age 64)*

MORGAN, Claudia (*née* Wuppermann), actress; *b.* Brooklyn, N.Y., U.S.A., 12 June, 1912; *d.* of Ralph Morgan and his wife Georgiana (Iverson); *e.* Greenwich, Conn., and Briarcliff, N.Y.; *m.* (1) Talbot Cummings (mar. dis.); (2) Robert Shippee (mar. dis.); (3) Ernest Chappell (mar. dis.); (4) Kenneth Loane; studied for the stage with her father, and Professor George P. Baker of Yale, and Fanny Bradshaw; made her first appearance on the stage on tour, as April in "Gypsy April," 1928, with Margaret Anglin; made her first appearance in New York, at the Eltinge Theatre, 26 Nov., 1929, as Sally Lawrence in "Top o' the Hill"; she then played "stock" in Philadelphia, with the "Play of the Week" company; Belasco, New York, Aug., 1930, played Gwendolyn Davenham in "Dancing Partner"; went to London, where she made her first appearance, at the Lyric Theatre, 3 Feb., 1931, as Madeline Arnold in "Strange Interlude"; on returning to New York, at the Booth, May, 1931, played Mina Gutherie in "A Modern Virgin"; Comedy, Sept., 1931, Fan Arndt in "People on the Hill"; Bijou, Nov., 1931, Marie in "Marriage for Three"; spent 1932–3, in Hollywood, in films and in three plays; Vanderbilt, New York, Nov., 1933, played Mary in "Thoroughbred"; Little, Jan., 1934, Joan Arden in "False Dreams Farewell"; Cort, Mar., 1934, Connie Blane in "Gentlewoman"; Ambassador, Apr., 1934, Antonia Wayne in "Are You Decent?"; Biltmore, Oct., 1934, Cathleen Barton in "Bridal Quilt"; Adelphi, Nov., 1934, Barbara Kemble in "The Lord Blesses the Bishop"; Ambassador, Jan., 1935, Joan Palmer in "A Lady Detained"; Booth, Feb., 1935, Janny Travis in "De Luxe"; Plymouth, June, 1935, succeeded Constance Cummings as Linda Brown in "Accent on Youth"; Mansfield, Oct., 1935, Sheila Danforth in "On Stage"; Morosco, Jan., 1936, Beatrice Gwynne in "Call It a Day"; Ritz, Apr., 1936, Sylvia Farren in "Co-Respondent Unknown"; Guild, Oct., 1936, Lucy Trenchard in "And Stars Remain"; Shubert (for the Guild), Feb., 1937, Countess Larisch in "The Masque of Kings";

Guild, Mar., 1937, Victoria Thomson in "Storm over Patsy"; Vanderbilt, Oct., 1937, Harriet Freeman in "In Clover"; Playhouse, Dec., 1937, Tony Vereker in "Merely Murder"; Guild, Feb., 1938, Wilda Doran in "Wine of Choice"; in summer theatres, July, 1940, played in "The Bat"; Music Box, Nov., 1940, played Maggie Cutler in "The Man Who Came to Dinner"; toured, 1942, as Linda Easterbrook in "No Time for Comedy"; Biltmore, Dec., 1942, played Judith Winthrop in "The Sun Field"; Broadhurst, June, 1944, Vera Claythorne in "Ten Little Indians": in summer theatres, 1951, played Barbara Lomax in "Background," and appeared in "The Philanderer"; at the New Century, New York, Feb., 1952, played Jessie Dill in "Venus Observed"; in summer theatres, 1952, appeared as Judith in "Jezebel's Husband"; Plymouth, N.Y., Oct., 1956, played Amanda in "The Apple Cart"; Gramercy Arts, June, 1961; Mrs. Patrick Campbell in "A Fig Leaf in Her Bonnet"; Bucks County Playhouse, July, 1961, Rosella in "Two Queens of Love and Beauty"; in summer theatres, 1962, played the Countess de la Brière in "Maggie"; in summer theatres, 1965, Alicia in "Gigi"; has also broadcast, notably as Nora Charles in *The Thin Man*, 1942–8, and Carolyn Kramer in *The Right to Happiness*, 1943–60; has appeared frequently on the major dramatic television programs including *Kraft Television Theatre, Armstrong Circle Theatre, The Way of the World* (serial, 1954–5), *Edge of Night* (serial, 1958–9), *The Doctors*; entered films, 1932, and has appeared in "Once in a Lifetime," "The World of Henry Orient" (1963), etc. *Recreations:* Gardening and crossword puzzles. *Address:* 50 East 83rd Street, New York, N.Y. 10028, U.S.A.

MORGAN, Frank, actor; *b.* 1 June, 1890; *s.* of George Wupperman; studied for the stage at the American Academy of Dramatic Arts, 1913-14; made his first appearance on the stage at the Lyceum Theatre, New York, Mar., 1914, in a revival of "A Woman Killed With Kindness"; he next appeared at the same theatre, Sept., 1914, as Remi in "The Beautiful Adventure"; Hudson, Aug., 1915, played Lieut. Baum and Dr. Charles in "Under Fire"; Harris, Oct., 1916, Kid in "Under Sentence"; in 1917, played leads in the stock company at the Academy of Music, Northampton, Mass.; Astor, May, 1918, Alfred Hardy in "Rock-a-Bye Baby"; Comedy, Dec., 1919, Edward Early in "My Lady Friends"; Lyric, Dec., 1920, Tom Craddock in "Her Family Tree"; Eltinge, Feb., 1921, Joergan Malthe in "The White Villa"; Comedy, Aug., 1921, Robert Knowles in "The Triumph of X"; Empire, Nov., 1921, Geoffrey Cliffe in "The Dream Maker"; Booth, Oct., 1922, Brissac in "Seventh Heaven"; Knickerbocker, Sept., 1923, Count Carlo Beretti in "Lullaby"; Morosco, Oct., 1924, Allessandro in "The Firebrand"; Ritz., Jan., 1926, Henri Fournier in "A Weak Woman"; Times Square, Sept., 1926, Henry Spoffard in "Gentlemen Prefer Blondes"; Masque, Feb., 1927, the Gentleman in Grey in "Puppets of Passion"; Morosco, Apr., 1927, Raoul de Trembly-Matour in "Hearts Are Trumps"; Eltinge, Aug., 1927, Guy Peters in "Tenth Avenue"; New Amsterdam, Jan., 1928, King Cyril in "Rosalie"; Bijou, Oct., 1929, Jack Mills in "Among the Married"; Masque, Dec., 1929, Harlow Balsam in "The Amorous Antic"; Music Box, Feb., 1930, Topaze in the play of that name; New Amsterdam, June, 1931, appeared in "The Band Wagon"; Shubert, June, 1932, in "Hey, Nonny, Nonny"; originally appeared in silent films, 1915; since his reappearance in 1930, has played in innumerable pictures. *Clubs:* Lambs and Players.
(Died 18 Sept., 1949; age 59)

MORGAN, Helen, actress and vocalist; *b.* Danville, Ill., U.S.A., 1900; *e.* Crane High School, Chicago; *m.* Maurice Maschke, jun. (mar. dis.); studied singing at the Metropolitan Opera School; made her first appearance on the stage at the Green Mill, Chicago, 1918; made her first appearance in New York at the New Amsterdam Theatre, 21 Dec., 1920, in the chorus of "Sally"; in 1922, returned to Chicago, and appeared in cabaret at the Café Montmartre; while fulfilling an engagement at the Back Stage Club, New York, 1925, was engaged by George White, and appeared at the Apollo, June, 1925, in "George White's Scandals"; at the Belmont, July, 1926, appeared in "Americana"; subsequently appeared at Greenwich Village, in a short season of "Grand Guignol" plays; after appearing in "vaudeville," appeared at Ziegfeld Theatre, Dec., 1927, as Julie in "Show Boat," in which she continued, 1928–29; at the Ziegfeld Roof, New York, July, 1929, appeared in the cabaret entertainment; Hammerstein's, Sept., 1929, played Addie in "Sweet Adeline"; Ziegfeld Theatre, July, 1931, appeared in "Ziegfeld's Follies of 1931"; Casino, May, 1932, again played Julie in "Show Boat"; at the Biltmore. Los Angeles, May, 1934, played in "Memory"; Grand Opera House, Chicago, June, 1936, played in "George White's Scandals"; appeared at the Victoria Palace, London, Apr., 1937, in a programme of Songs; has also appeared in London in cabaret; has also appeared in films since 1929. *(Died 8 Oct., 1941; age 41)*

MORGAN, Ralph, actor; *b.* New York City, 6 July, 1888; *s.* of George Wupperman; *e.* Columbia University; *m.* Grace Arnold; originally studied Law; made his first appearance on the stage at the Hudson Theatre, New York, 23 Mar., 1908, as Lind in "Love's Comedy"; he then played a "stock" season at Richmond, Va.; was then seen in "The Blue Mouse," and appeared in several other plays written by the late Clyde Fitch; appeared at the Thirty-ninth Street Theatre, New York, Aug., 1912, as Harry in "The Master of the House"; Harris, Nov., 1912, played Matthew Plummer, jun., in "A Rich Man's Son"; at the Cort, Aug., 1914, Monty Vaughn in "Under Cover"; Longacre, May, 1915, Ned Pembroke, Jun. in "A Full House"; Maxine Elliott's, Sept., 1915, Theodore in "Our Children"; Gaiety, Aug., 1918, John Marvin in "Lightnin'"; Lyric, July, 1919, Douglas Adams in "The Five Million"; Hudson, Aug., 1921, Stanley Bennett in "The Poppy

God"; Henry Miller, July, 1922, Arthur Carlton in "The National Anthem"; Ritz, Aug., 1923, Jack Gardner in "In Love With Love"; Hudson, Apr., 1924, Tony Dorning in "Cobra"; Longacre, Sept., 1925, Pierre in "The Dagger"; Maxine Elliott's, Nov., 1925, Dick Hamill in "The Joker"; Ritz, Jan., 1926, Serge Paveneyge in "A Weak Woman"; Garrick, Jan., 1927, Buckland Steele in "Damn the Tears"; Lyric, June, 1927, Paddy Griggs in "The Woman of Bronze"; Little, Oct., 1927, Quartermaster Henry Cowboy in "Romancin' Round"; Belmont, Nov., 1927, Bradley Clement in "Take My Advice"; Forrest, Feb., 1928, Gordon in "The Clutching Claw"; at Chicago, Jan., 1930, succeeded Tom Powers, as Charles Marsden in "Strange Interlude"; Court, Oct., 1930, played Albert Rustin in "Sweet Stranger"; appeared at the Lyric, London, 3 Feb., 1931, as Charles Marsden in "Strange Interlude"; Hudson, Nov., 1940, played Hugh Linton in "Fledgling"; Martin Beck, Apr., 1942, Mayor Orden in "The Moon is Down"; Belasco, Apr., 1946, Dr. Steven Alexander in "This, Too, Shall Pass"; Mark Hellinger, Mar., 1952, played Father Kerrigan in "Three Wishes For Jamie"; commenced film career, 1931, in "Charlie Chan's Chance," and since played in innumerable pictures; since 1953 has played leading parts in innumerable television productions. *Clubs:* Lambs and Players'.
(Died 11 June, 1956; age 67)

MORGAN, Sydney, actor; *b.* Dublin, 21 Oct., 1885; *e.* Belvedere College, Dublin; was formerly an engineer; made his first appearance on the stage at the Abbey Theatre, Dublin, 20 Sept., 1908, as Pat Denehey in "The Piper"; made his first appearance in London at the Court Theatre, June, 1909, as Old Mahon in "The Playboy of the Western World"; he remained a member of the Irish Players for nearly twenty years, appearing in nearly one hundred and fifty different parts; of late years has played at the Little, Mar., 1925, Brian O'Connor in "Persevering Pat"; Royalty, Nov., 1925,

" Joxer " Daly in " Juno and the Paycock "; Fortune, May, 1926, The Young Covey in " The Plough and the Stars "; Vaudeville, Mar., 1927, James Kilroy in " Professor Tim "; Court, May, 1927, Adolphus Grigson in " The Shadow of a Gunman "; New, June, 1928, Riordan in " Spread Eagle "; Haymarket, Feb., 1929, the Recruiting Sergeant in " Quality Street." *Favourite part :* " Joxer " Daly in " Juno and the Paycock." *Recreations :* Motoring and golf. *(Died 5 Dec., 1931; age 46)*

MORISON, Patricia, actress and singer; *b.* New York City, 19 Mar., 1915; *d.* of William R. Morison and his wife Selena (Carson); studied acting at the Neighborhood Playhouse School of the Theatre and design at the Ecole des Beaux Arts, Paris; was a dress designer; made her first appearance in New York, at the Ambassador, Nov., 1933, as Helen in "Growing Pains"; was an understudy in "Victoria Regina," 1935; at the Windsor Theatre, 31 May, 1938, Laura Rivers in "The Two Bouquets"; in the same year, she went to Hollywood to appear in films, first appearing in " Persons in Hiding "; she remained there, appearing in numerous pictures until 1942, when she went overseas with the first U.S.O. group to entertain the American troops; on returning to America, again went to Hollywood to make more films; on her return to New York, appeared at the Adelphi, Apr., 1944, as Marcia Mason Moore in "Allah Be Praised !"; New Century, Dec., 1948, Lilli Vanessi and Katherine in "Kiss Me Kate," in which she continued until 1950; made her first appearance in London at the Coliseum, 8 Mar., 1951, making a great success in the same parts; took over as Anna Leonowens in "The King and " at the St. James, N.Y., Feb., 1954; toured the U.S., Mar., 1954-5, as Anna Leonowens in "The King and "; toured, July, 1958, in "The Song of Norway"; toured, 1959, in the *revue* "Gay 90's Night"; Opera House, Seattle, Washington, Apr., 1965, Lilli Vanessi and Katherine in "Kiss Me Kate"; City Center, New York, May, 1965, again played in " Kiss Me Kate"; among her films are "The

Song of Bernadette," "The Fallen Sparrow," "Song Without End," etc.; on television has played in "The King and I," "Kiss Me, Kate," *The Voice of Firestone,* etc. *Recreation:* Painting.

MORLAY, Gaby, actress; *b.* Biskra, Algeria, 1896; made her first appearance on the stage at the Théâtre de la Gaîté, 1912, in "Les Cloches de Corneville"; Capucines, 1912, appeared in "Potins et Pantins," and "Paris fin de règne"; Renaissance, 1913, in "Pour faire son chemin," "Le Zèbre," and "Fred"; Châtelet, 1915, in "Les Exploits d'une petite Française"; Theatre Michel, 1916, in *revue,* "Bravo" and "Bis"; Renaissance, 1917, in "Le Minaret"; Bouffes-Parisiens, 1917, "Le Scandale de Monte-Carlo," and "Le Poulailler"; Théâtre Marigny, 1917, in "La Mariée du Touring Club," and Théâtre Edouard VII, 1917, in "La Petite Bonne d'Abraham"; Gymnase, 1918, in "La Petite Reine," and Théâtre Antoine, 1918, in "Le Traité d'Auteuil"; Théâtre Femina, 1920, in "Mademoiselle ma mère"; Capucines, 1921, in "Simone est comme ça"; Théâtre de Paris, 1922, in "Miquette et sa Mère"; Gymnase, 1925, appeared as Jeanne in "La Discorde," and Athenée, as Suzanne in "Les Nouveaux Messieurs"; Gymnase, Feb., 1931, played in "Le Jour"; Ambassadeurs, Apr., 1932, appeared in "Il Etait une Fois "; Madeleine, Sept., 1937, played Paulette in "Quadrille," and Apr., 1938, appeared in "Une Femme et un Roi"; Théâtre Saint-Georges, Mar., 1939, played Marthe in "La Maison Monestier"; Gymnase, in "Charlotte et Maximilien"; of late years has frequently appeared in films, notably in "Le Bois Sacré," "Son Dernier Rôle," etc. *(Died 4 July, 1964; age 71)*

MORLEY, Malcolm, actor, manager, and director; *b.* Aldershot, 20 May, 1890; *s.* of Captain Frederick Morley and his wife Angelina Mary; *e.* Harvard University, U.S.A.; was formerly engaged in journalism; made his first appearance on the stage at the Garden Theatre, New York, with John E. Kellerd, in " Hamlet "; spent many years in the United States as an actor, under the management of George Arliss, Nat Goodwin, Grace George, William Faversham, etc.; was managing director of the Arts Theatre, Cincinnati; first appeared in London, at the Ambassadors', 7 Feb., 1921, in "Moleskin Joe"; at the Kingsway, Mar., 1922 played Lee Sin in "The Yellow Jacket"; June 1922, Pencho in "Spanish Lovers"; Ambassadors', Sept., 1922, Ireton in "Charles I"; Nov., 1922, Michaelis in "The Secret Agent"; New, Aug., 1923, Rama Dass in "The Eye of Siva"; was general manager for Leon M. Lion, 1924-5; from 1926-31 was associated with the management of the Everyman Theatre; among the fifty plays he produced there were "The Father," "The Master Builder," "The Silver Box," "Little Eyolf," "Pleasure Garden," "The Ship," "L'Invitation au Voyage," "The Storm," "Masks and Faces," "Ghosts," "Charles and Mary," "The Wild Duck," "91 Miles from Colombo," "The Wild Asses Skin," etc.; directed "The Ship," at the Fortune, 1931; "The Master Builder," and "Windows," at the Duchess, 1931, etc.; "Pay the Piper," Birmingham, 1932; subsequent productions included "It's a Wise Wife . . . ," "Bargains in Brides," "Stormy Passage," "Midsummer Fires," "Wedding Night," "Spring Symphony," "The Green Phantom," "Happiness," "The Fisher of Shadows," "The Emperor of Make Believe" (of which he was the author), "Climbing," etc.; in 1940, was directing and acting at the Memorial Theatre, Stratford-on-Avon; St. Martin's Theatre, Apr., 1941, played Alex Minster in "Under One Roof"; in 1941–2, was manager at the Birmingham Repertory Theatre, and later, in 1942, was director at the Richmond Theatre, and touring with his own play, "The Crimson Vulture"; in 1943, was director at Watford; from Feb., 1944–7, was director at the Oxford Playhouse; on several occasions has visited Canada to act as adjudicator in the amateur productions made under the auspices of Earl Bessborough, former Governor-General of Canada; was in Canada, 1947-50, and established the only

professional resident playhouse in the country, at Ottawa; also directed Shakespearean plays for the Open Air Playhouse, Montreal; in London subsequently directed "Isn't Life Wonderful," "Three Were Waiting," 1951; "Knight of Love" (author, with Madge Pemberton), "The Bamboo Curtain," 1952; at the New Torch, Feb., 1952, played Tossil Munn in "A Sigh For Solitude"; Palace, Mar., 1956, author (with Philip Phillips), and directed "Trevallion"; St. Pancras Town Hall, May, 1957, directed Glinka's opera "Russlan and Ludmilla"; has also directed "Everyman" and "The Boy With a Cart" in various churches; since 1960, has adjudicated at numerous Drama Festivals, and also given Talks on the theatre in Great Britain; author of "The Theatre," "Canadian Journey," "The Old Marylebone Theatre," "The Royal West London Theatre," "Margate and its Theatres," etc. *Favourite parts:* John Brown in "Victoria Regina," Jones in "The Silver Box," Adolf in "The Father." *Recreations:* Swimming, motoring, reading, and chess. *Clubs:* Authors', London; Players, New York.
(*Died 10 Feb., 1966; age 75*)

MOROSCO, Oliver, manager; *b.* Logan, Utah, U.S.A., 1876; *s.* of Walter Morosco; *e.* San Francisco; *m.* (2) Selma Paley (mar. dis.); (3) Helen Mitchell (mar. dis.); was originally an acrobat in his father's troupe; in 1892, was assistant manager of the San José Theatre, Cal.; was engaged as Press agent and business manager at the Grand Opera House, San Francisco, and the Burbank Theatre, Los Angeles; since 1899 has presented many notable productions at the last-mentioned theatre; in 1908 acquired the Majestic Theatre, Los Angeles; subsequently took over six other theatres in California, and became a producing manager in 1909; his first production was "The Fox"; was responsible for the production of "The Bird of Paradise," "Peg o' My Heart," "The Tik Tok Man of Oz," "The Truth Wagon," "Sadie Love," "The Cinderella Man," "Mile-a-Minute Kendal," "Upstair

1750

and Down," "Canary Cottage," "Cappy Ricks," "Civilian Clothes," "Please Get Married," "The But," "Beyond the Horizon," "Mama's Affair," "Letty Pepper," "Mike Angelo," "The Sporting Thing to Do," "Pride," "Across the Street," "Pretty Mrs. Smith," "So Long, Letty," "The Unchastened Woman," "Love Dreams," "Artistic Temperament," "His Queen," "Head First," etc.; is the author of the following plays: "The Judge and the Jury" (with H. D. Cottrell), 1906; "The Society Plot" (with C. W. Backman), 1908; "Canary Cottage" (with Elmer B Harris), 1916; "So Long, Letty" (with Harris), 1916; "Pamela," 1917; "What Next?" (with Harris), 1917; "Gosh! We're All Friends" (a *revue*), 1918; "Merely Mary Brown" (with Harris), 1919; lyrics of "Love Dreams," 1921; "Letty Pepper" (with G. V. Hobart), 1922; "Myrtie," 1924; "The Morning After the Night Before," 1927; was the proprietor of the Morosco Theatres, New York, and Los Angeles.
(Died 25 Aug., 1945; age 69)

MORRIS, Chester, actor; *b.* New York City, U.S.A., 16 Feb., 1901; *s.* of William Morris, actor, and his wife Etta (Hawkins); *e.* Lincoln School, Mt. Vernon, N.Y.; *m.* Susie Kilborn; for a time studied Art at the N.Y. School of Fine Applied Arts; made his first appearance on the stage with the Westchester "stock" company, Mount Vernon, 1917; made his first appearance on the New York stage at the Shubert Theatre, 18 Feb., 1918, as Sam Carter in "The Copperhead"; he then toured in "Turn to the Right," and subsequently, for a short time, appeared at the Gaiety, New York, in "Lightnin'," 1919; at the Criterion, Sept., 1919, played Sam Disbrow in "Thunder"; appeared in stock at Providence, Washington, and Baltimore; Maxine Elliott Theatre, New York, Dec., 1921, played Carey in "The Mountain Man"; Times Square, Sept., 1922, Lexington Dalrymple in "The Exciters"; Longacre, Jan., 1923, Wallace King in "Extra"; he then toured in "So This is London," and subse-

quently appeared in "vaudeville," for two years, in a sketch, "All the Horrors of Home": next toured in "The Home Towners"; at the National, New York, Sept., 1926, played "Val" Parker in "Yellow"; at the Eltinge, New York, Feb., 1927, Rocky Morse in "Crime"; Hudson, Feb., 1928, Al Wheeler in "Whispering Friends"; Ambassador, Sept., 1928, Chester Palmer in "Fast Life"; commenced film career 1929, in "Alibi" ("The Perfect Alibi"), and has played in innumerable pictures, since 1936, has appeared in "Three Godfathers," "Moonlight Murder," "Frankie and Johnnie," "Counterfeit," "They Met in a Taxi," "Devil's Playground," "I Promise to Pay," "Flight from Glory," "Law of the Underworld," "Sky Giant," "Smashing the Rackets," "Blind Alley," "Five Came Back," etc.
(Died 1970; age 69)

MORRIS, Clara, actress; *b.* Toronto, Canada, 17 Mar., 1846; *m.* F. C. Harriott; made her first appearance on the stage at the age of thirteen, at the Academy of Music, Cleveland, Ohio, in "The Seven Sisters"; she remained at that theatre and at Columbus under the management of the late John A. Ellsler for a number of years; made her first appearance in New York at the Fifth Avenue Theatre, under the management of the late Augustin Daly, on 13 Sept., 1870, when she played the part of Anne Sylvester in "Man and Wife," and scored an instantaneous success; remained a member of Daly's company until 1873, playing the following among other parts: Lucy Carter in "Saratoga," Madame D'Artignes in "Jezebel," Magdalen in "No Name," Fanny Ten Eyck in "Divorce," Cora in "Article 47" (in which her acting furnished the sensation of the day), Herminie in "Diamonds," Oriana in "The Inconstant," and Magdalen in "New Year's Eve, or False Shame"; at Daly's Fifth Avenue Theatre, 21 Jan., 1873, she played the part of Alixe in a play of that name, and, 20 May, appeared as Pervenche in

"Madeleine Morel"; she was next seen at the Union Square Theatre, 17 Nov., 1873, as Selene in "The Wicked World"; at Fourteenth Street Theatre (then Lyceum), 16 Mar., 1874, as Camille; at Union Square, 21 Sept., 1874, as Blanche in "The Sphinx," and 26 Oct., 1874, as Julia in "The Hunchback"; at Booth's, 10 May, 1875, as Evadne; same theatre, 17 May, 1875, as Lady Macbeth, and 22 May, 1875, as Jane Shore; she then appeared at Daly's New Fifth Avenue Theatre, on 22 Nov., 1875, as Esther in "The New Leah," and at Union Square, 20 Nov., 1876, as Sara Multon in "Miss Multon"; at Broadway Theatre, 11 Feb., 1878, she played Jane Eyre; at Union Square, 17 Mar., 1881, was Constance in "Conscience"; 25 Apr., 1881, Raymonde in the play of that name, and 5 Jan., 1882, Mercy Merrick in "The New Magdalen"; for many years she "starred" in these plays all over the United States and Canada; her appearances in new plays or productions since that date have been very intermittent, but notable among them was her performance at Daly's, 21 Mar., 1885, as Denise in the play of that name; at the Grand Opera House, 20 Oct., 1887, as Renée de Moray in "Renée"; at the Union Square Theatre, 29 Oct., 1889, as Helene Buderoff in "Helene," and at the Fourteenth Street Theatre, 4 Apr., 1894, as Claire in a play of that name, adapted by herself from a novel by Richard Voss, entitled "Eva"; after a long retirement she reappeared on the New York stage, at the New Amsterdam Theatre, 28 Mar., 1904, as Sister Geneviève in the "all-star" revival of "The Two Orphans"; in May, 1905, appeared in "vaudeville" at the Colonial Theatre, New York; at the Columbia, Washington, 30 Apr., 1906, she appeared as Judith Grange in "The Indiscretion of Truth"; is the author of "A Silent Singer," 1899; "My Little Jim Crow," 1900; "A Pasteboard Crown," 1902; "Stage Confidences," 1902; "The Story of My Life," 1904; and "The Trouble Woman," 1904.
(Died 20 Nov., 1925; age 79)

MORRIS, Margaret, dancer; *b.* London, 10 Mar., 1891; *d.* of the late William Bright Morris, artist; studied dancing under John D'Auban, from the age of seven years to seventeen, and then under Raymond Duncan; made her first appearance on the stage at the Theatre Royal, Plymouth, Christmas, 1899, when she appeared as Twinkle Star (solo dancer) in the pantomime of "Red Riding Hood"; made her first appearance in London, with Ben Greet's company, at the Botanical Gardens, July, 1901, as Puck in "A Midsummer Night's Dream"; remained a member of Greet's Company until 1906, when she joined F. R. Benson's company, and remained for three years; in 1909 commenced operations at her school of dancing, and which she has conducted ever since; at the Haymarket, June, 1910, appeared as Water in "The Blue Bird"; she trained the dancers and was responsible for the dances in Miss Marie Brema's revival of Gluck's "Orpheus," at the Savoy, 1910; was responsible for the dances in Sir Herbert Tree's revival of "Henry VIII," at His Majesty's, Sept., 1910; appeared at the Haymarket, Dec., 1910, as Water in the revival of "The Blue Bird"; at the Royalty, Jan., 1912, appeared as Guinevere Megan in Galsworthy's fantasy "The Pigeon"; at the Court Theatre appeared in "The Little Dream," with her own company of dancers, subsequently touring in the provinces, after which she quitted the stage, in order to devote herself to her school; at the Kingsway, Mar., 1912, produced the dances in Granville Barker's revival of "Iphigenia in Tauris"; she established the Margaret Morris Club, 1914; appeared at the Comédie Marigny, Paris, 1915; in 1918 started a school for general education for children of from three to sixteen years of age, the main idea being to make the unity of the Arts the foundation of education; appointed a member of the National Advisory Council for Physical Training and Recreation 1937. *Address:* 31 Cromwell Road London, S.W.7. *Telephone No.:* Kensington 7237–8.

MORRIS, Mary, actress; *b.* Swampscott, Mass., U.S.A., 24 June, 1895 *d.* of George Perry Morris and his wife Martha Sophia (Turner); *e.* Brookline public schools, and Radcliffe College; had had amateur experience before making her first appearance on the stage at the Bandbox Theatre, 10 Jan., 1916, with the Washington Square Players, as the Woman in "The Clod"; subsequently spent five years in "stock" and repertory, playing many leading parts in Shaw, Barrie, and Galsworthy plays, etc.; during 1918, toured with George Arliss in "Alexander Hamilton"; Provincetown Theatre, Jan., 1924, played the Dark Lady in "The Spook Sonata"; Feb., 1924, Gertrude in "Fashion"; Oct., 1924, Miss Streetfield in "The Crime in the Whistler Room"; Greenwich Village, Nov., 1924, Abbie Putman in "Desire Under the Elms," which she continued to play 1925–6; Lyceum, Oct., 1927, Ellen Faring in "Hidden"; Civic Repertory, Oct., 1928, Dorimene in "The Would-Be Gentleman"; Morosco, Nov., 1929, Barbara in "The Cross Roads"; Waldorf, Jan., 1930, Vasilisa in "At the Bottom"; Feb., 1930, Irina in "The Sea Gull"; Little, Dec., 1930, Elizabeth Courtney in "Life is Like That"; Martin Beck (for the Guild), Sept., 1931, Mrs. Connelly in "The House of Connelly"; Mansfield (for the Group), Dec., 1931, appeared in "1931"; 48th Street (for the Group), Mar., 1932, Doña Vera in "Night Over Taos"; Morosco, Nov., 1932, Nanine in "Camille"; Ritz, Sept., 1933, made a big success when she played Victoria Van Bret in "Double Door"; National, Oct., 1934, the Old Woman in "Within the Gates"; during the summer of 1935, at various theatres, played Lady Lebanon in "Criminal at Large"; 58th Street, New York, Nov. 1935, Sarah Schermer in "Mother Sings"; Vanderbilt, Jan., 1936, Judith Morris in "Granite"; 46th Street, Nov., 1936, Mrs. Clemm in "Plumes in the Dust"; Mansfield, Jan., 1937, Emma Good in "Behind Red Lights"; made her first appearance in London, at the St. Martin's, 16 Feb., 1937, as Mrs. Smith in "Suspect"; Queen's, July, 1937, the Mother of Niskavuori in "Women of Property"; Lyceum, New York, Feb., 1938, Mrs. Schuster

in "Roosty"; St. James, Mar., 1938, Empress Elizabeth in "Empress of Destiny"; summer theatres, 1938, played in "George and Margaret" and "Uncle Harry"; Ann Arbor, Mich., May, 1939, in "No War in Troy"; Booth, Jan., 1941, Mrs. Sawters in "The Cream in the Well"; Woodstock, N.Y., July, 1942, Britina Day in "Storm"; Cort, Nov., 1949, played the Nurse in "The Father"; appeared in films, in "Double Door," 1934. *(Died 16 Jan., 1970; age 74)*

MORRIS, McKay, actor; *b.* Fort Sam Houston, Texas, U.S.A., 22 Dec., 1891; *s.* of Louis Thomson Morris and his wife Susan Frances (Reese); *e.* Germantown Academy, Penn., U.S.A.; studied for the stage under the late David Belasco; made his first appearance on the stage at the Broad Street, Philadelphia, 1 May, 1912, as Waiter No. 7 in "The Governor's Lady"; first appeared in New York at the Republic Theatre, Sept., 1912, in "The Governor's Lady"; at the Booth, Oct., 1914, played Blue Blood in "Experience"; at the 39th Street Theatre, Nov., 1916, appeared with Stuart Walker's Portmanteau Theatre company, and he remained with that organization for three years; appeared at the Punch and Judy Theatre, Jan.–Mar., 1919, with the same company; at the Century, Nov., 1919, played Demetrius in "Aphrodite"; National, Oct., 1931, Dr. Kennicott in "Main Street"; 39th Street, Aug., 1922, Alvin Bruce in "The Monster"; Longacre, Sept., 1922, Arthur Streckmann in "Rose Bernd"; Dec., 1922, Romeo in "Romeo and Juliet," to the Juliet of Ethel Barrymore; Feb., 1923, Sir Hector Colladine in "The Laughing Lady"; 48th Street, May, 1923, Faulkland in "The Rivals"; Lyceum (for the Players), June, 1923, Joseph Surface in "The School for Scandal"; Klaw, Aug., 1923, Dick in "The Breaking Point"; Broadhurst, Oct., 1924, the Red Falcon and Adriano in "The Red Falcon"; Ambassador, Feb., 1925, Holophernes in "The Virgin of Bethulia"; Broadhurst, Apr.,1925, Lieut. von Lauffen in "Taps"; May, 1925, Jan in "Man or Devil"; Martin

Beck, Feb., 1926, Sir Guy Charteris in "The Shanghai Gesture"; Guild, Mar., 1926, Parakleta in "The Chief Thing"; Belmont, Feb., 1927, Kenneth Reynolds in "Off-Key"; Guild, Apr., 1928, Leone in "Volpone"; Ethel Barrymore, Dec., 1928, Enrique in "The Kingdom of God"; appeared at the Théâtre Femina, Paris, as Hannibal in "The Road to Rome"; Fulton, Feb., 1931, Colonel Aaron Burr in "Colonel Satan"; Ritz, Feb., 1931, Paolo Vanni in "A Woman Denied"; Ethel Barrymore, Nov., 1931, Joseph Surface in "The School for Scandal"; Ritz, Feb., 1933, Dr. Gruelle in "Before Morning"; Guild, Feb., 1935, The Priest, Pra, in "The Simpleton of the Unexpected Isles"; Music Box (for the Guild), Sept., 1935, John Gordon in "If This Be Treason"; subsequently toured with Nazimova as Pastor Manders in "Ghosts," and appeared in the same part at the Empire, New York, Dec., 1935; Longacre, Nov., 1936, Judge Brack in "Hedda Gabler"; Mount Kisco, N.Y., June–Aug., 1937, Maurice in "Retreat from Folly" and the Emperor in "Princess Turandot"; toured, 1937–38, as Prince Mikail in "Tovarich"; toured with Helen Hayes, 1938, as the Duke of Venice in "The Merchant of Venice" and Sohemus in "Herod and Mariamne"; Center, New York, Jan., 1939, Samuel Brockton in "The American Way"; Cort, Nov., 1939, Isaac Gerart in "Farm of Three Echoes"; National, Feb., 1940, Pastor Reisinger in "Another Sun," and May, 1940, the Governor in "The Return of the Vagabond"; Henry Miller, Jan., 1941, Ivan Godden in "Eight o'clock Tuesday"; Playhouse, Nov., 1941, Ralph Sherry in "Ring About Elizabeth"; Ethel Barrymore, Dec., 1942, Captain Solyony in "The Three Sisters," and Mar., 1945, Edward Moulton-Barrett in "The Barretts of Wimpole Street"; toured, Dec., 1945, as Prince Nisou in "Lute Song." *Recreations*: Swimming riding, and dancing. *(Died 3 Oct., 1955; age 64)*

MORRIS, William, actor ; *b*. Boston, U.S.A., 1 Jan., 1861 ; *s*. of Maria M. (Lloyd) and Henry Morris ; *e*. Boston ; *m*. Etta Hawkins ; made his first appearance on the stage 28 Aug., 1876, at the Boston Museum in " Ferreol " ; subsequently fulfilled engagements with W. H. Crane, Signor Rossi, Augustin Daly, Madame Modjeska, etc. ; first appeared at Daly's, 1882, in " Mankind," subsequently played in " The Passing Regiment," and with Modjeska in "Odette " ; during 1883-4 toured as the " Spider," in " The Silver King " ; at Madison Square Theatre, New York, during 1884-5, appeared in " Called Back," and " Hazel Kirke " ; during 1886-7 toured with Mrs. Fiske ; during 1887-8 with Mdme. Modjeska ; during 1889-90 played " stock " at San Francisco ; at Proctor's Twenty-third Street Theatre, New York, Oct., 1890, played William Prescott in " Men and Women " ; at same theatre, Nov., 1891, played Reuben Warner in " The Lost Paradise " ; at the Empire, Jan., 1893, appeared as Lieutenant Hawksworth in " The Girl I Left Behind Me " ; at the American Theatre, Feb., 1894, played Frank Drummond in " A Woman's Revenge " ; during the same year " starred " as Reuben Warner in " The Lost Paradise " ; subsequently " starred " as Gil de Berault in " Under the Red Robe," and as George Sylvester in " The Adventure of Lady Ursula " ; entered into partnership with Edward E. Rice, 1901, and toured as Richard Carewe in " When We Were Twenty-one " ; during 1903 toured in " When Rueben Comes to Town " ; at the Princess Theatre, 1904, played a number of parts with the Century Players ; at Madison Square Theatre, 1905, played Frank Fuller in " Mrs. Temple's Telegram " ; appeared in this part at the Waldorf Theatre, London, 10 Sept., 1906 ; during 1908 toured in " A Kentucky Boy " ; during 1909 toured with Olga Nethersole, and appeared at the Savoy, New York, Apr., 1909, as Irving Laurence in " The Writing on the Wall," with her ; at the Belasco Theatre, Aug., 1909, played Paul Barton in " Is Matrimony a Failure ? " ; same theatre, Oct., 1910, played Dr. Dallas in " The Concert " ; at the Forty-eighth Street Theatre, Aug., 1912, Richard Dennison in " Little Miss

Brown "; Oct., 1912, played Howard Trennery in "The Point of View"; at the Playhouse, New York, Aug., 1913, Charles Nelson in "The Family Cupboard"; at Springfield, Nov., 1913, played Jim Wakeley in "Miss Jenny O'Jones"; at the Liberty Theatre, New York, Sept., 1914, William Bartlett in "He Comes Up Smiling"; at the Gaiety, New York, Nov., 1915, Detective Maloney in "Sadie Love"; at the Eltinge Theatre, Aug., 1916, George Brockton in "Cheating Cheaters"; at the Belasco Theatre, New York, Apr., 1917, Philip Cramner in "The Very Minute"; at Chicago, Nov., 1917, played in "Mr. Jubilee Drax"; at Philadelphia, Sept., 1918, appeared as Dicky Foster in "Not with My Money"; at the Bijou, New York, Feb., 1919, as Talbot Chandler in "A Sleepless Night"; at the Harris Theatre, Sept., 1919, as Richard Peneld-Clark in "The Dancer"; at the Empire, New York, Aug., 1920, played Howard Mowbray in "Call the Doctor"; toured in the same part, 1921; at the Henry Miller Theatre, Aug., 1921, played Daniel G. Talbot in "The Scarlet Man"; at the Empire, New York, Nov., 1921, Charles Freak Farrar in "The Dream Maker"; at the Playhouse, New York, Sept., 1923, John Maury in "Chains"; at the Charles Hopkins Theatre, Oct., 1928, the Elderly Man in "The Unknown Warrior"; at San Francisco, 1931-32, played Augustus Merrick in "The Vinegar Tree."
(Died 11 Jan., 1936; age 75)

MORRISON, George E., dramatic critic, author, and journalist; *b.* Cheshunt, Herts., 8 Jan., 1860; *s.* of Christina (McLaren) and Joseph Robert Morrison; *e.* St. John's Wood School, and Scoones's, Garrick Street; *m.* Rose Emilie Jackson; dramatic critic of *The Pall Mall Gazette,* 1900-7; dramatic critic of *The Morning Post* to 1924; author of "Sixteen Not Out" (with Robert Stewart), produced at Prince of Wales's, 1892, "Don Quixote," produced by F. R. Benson, 1907; "The Shortest Story of All," 1921; and of a pamphlet, "On the

Reconstruction of the Theatre" (1919); is a barrister-at-law, a Fellow of the Institute of Journalists, and was President of The Critics' Circle, 1918-20. *Hobby:* Friendship. *Club:* Whitefriars. *(Died 19 Nov., 1930; age 70)*

MORRISON (Howard) Priestly, producer; *b.* Baltimore, Md., U.S.A.; 5 July, 1871; *s.* of Robert Dighton Morrison and his wife Mary Frances (Mulley); *e.* Baltimore; *m.* Mary Florence Horne: was educated for the Law, which he practised for a time: formerly an actor, he made his first appearance on the stage at Opera House, Wellsville, N.Y., Sept., 1894, in "Fate"; the first production which he staged in New York, was at the Bijou Theatre, Oct., 1910, when he produced "New York"; produced "The Girl of the Golden West" and "An Englishman's Home," in Australia, 1908–09; "The Fascinating Widow," New York, 1910; "Smilin' Through," 1919; "Mama's Affair," 1920; "Like a King," 1921; "For Goodness Sake," 1922; "Queen Victoria," "Thumbs Down," 1923; "Stella Dallas," "The Locked Door," 1924; "The Piker," "Alias the Deacon," "Easy Come, Easy Go," 1925; "One Man's Woman," "The Challenge of Youth," 1926; "The Barker," 1927; "Best Years," 1932; "Errant Lady," "So Many Paths," 1934; "Triumph," 1935; at the Broadhurst, New York, Sept., 1935, appeared as J. M. Badcock in "Life's Too Short." *Recreations:* Fishing, shooting, and wild life conservation. *Clubs:* Lambs', Players', and Actors' Equity. *(Died 26 Jan., 1938; age 66)*

MORRISON, Jack, actor and vocalist; *b.* Newcastle-on-Tyne, 6 Apr., 1887; *s.* of Ralph Morrison and his wife Phoebe (Blake); *e.* Rutherford College, Newcastle-on-Tyne; *m.* Gwen Yates, *g.d.* of the late Edmund Yates; made his first appearance on the stage at the Aquarium, Great Yarmouth, 3 Aug., 1907, in the chorus of "See-See"; made his first appearance in London at the Shaftesbury, 28 Apr., 1909, in the chorus of "The Arcadians " ; appeared at the Alhambra, May, 1913, in the *revue* " Eightpence-a-Mile " ; subsequently appeared at the same theatre in " Keep Smiling," " Not Likely," " 5064 Gerrard," " Now's the Time," " The Bing Boys are Here " ; at Wyndham's, June, 1919, played Jack Grayson in " His Little Widows " ; at the Palace, Dec., 1919, appeared in " The Whirligig " ; at the Alhambra, Oct., 1920, in " Johnny Jones " ; at the Royalty, May, 1921, in " Pins and Needles " ; went to America the following year, and in 1925, to Australia ; toured in England, 1930, as Gustave Fayard in " The Red Dog"; Feb., 1931, toured as Tom Carter in " The Last Coupon " ; Garrick, Dec., 1931, played Susan, the Cook, in " Dick Whittington " ; Jan., 1932, Tom Carter in " The Last Coupon"; Kingsway, Dec., 1933, Private Bill Grant in " Alf's Button " ; at the Theatre Royal, Newcastle-on-Tyne, Dec., 1934, played the Baron in " The Babes in the Wood "; in 1935–36, toured as Tony in " Yes, Madam ? " ; toured, 1937, as Detective-Sergeant Elk in " The Frog"; 1938, as Sir Roger Boyne in " Crazy Days"; 1939, Robert Ramsden in " Man About the House "; London Hippodrome, Nov., 1939, appeared in " Black Velvet"; Prince's, Aug., 1942, played Diamond Jim Brady in " Wild Rose"; toured, 1944, as Joachim in " A Waltz Dream " ; Winter Garden, Dec., 1944, played the Baron in "Cinderella"; toured, 1945, as Harry Q. Conder in " The Dollar Princess"; Empire, Newcastle-on-Tyne, Dec., 1945, the Dame in " Red Riding Hood"; toured again in 1946, in "A Waltz Dream."

MORRITT, Charles, illusionist ; *b.* Saxton, Yorks,, 13 June, 1860; *s.* of William Morritt and his wife Maria ; *e.* Higher Grade School, Leeds ; was a music-hall proprietor, previous to making his first appearance in a thought transmission entertainment, at the Prince's Hall, Piccadilly, 5 Aug., 1886 ; has since appeared at the old Aquarium, Egyptian Hall, St. James's Hall, Crystal Palace, St. George's Hall, Polytechnic, Empire, London Pavilion, Oxford, Tivoli, and all the leading halls in London and the provinces, playing all the principal tours and circuits ; has also toured in the United States and Australia ; during 1915, appeared at the Polytechnic. *Recreations :* Billiards, cricket, driving, and sketching. *Club :* Magicians. *Address :* Polytechnic, Regent Street, W.

MORROW, Doretta, actress and vocalist; *m.* Albert E. Hardman; first appeared on the New York stage when she succeeded Ann Andre at the 46th Street Theatre, June, 1946, as Gretchen in "The Red Mill"; subsequently appeared in "The Chocolate Soldier"; St. James, Oct., 1948, played Kitty Verdun in "Where's Charley?"; at the same theatre, Mar., 1951, Tuptin in "The King and I"; Ziegfeld, Dec., 1953, played Marsinah in the musical version of "Kismet," and made her first appearance on the London stage in the same part at the Stoll, 20 Apr., 1955; toured in the U.S., 1957, in the title-part of "Fanny"; Shubert, Washington, D.C., Jan., 1959, played Evelyn in "The Poker Game"; Coliseum, London, Dec., 1959, played the Princess in "Aladdin." *(Died 28 Feb., 1968; age 42)*

MORSE, Barry, actor; *b.* London, 10 June, 1919; *s.* of Charles Hayward Morse and his wife Mary Florence (Hollis); *e.* elementary school; *m.* Sydney Sturgess; studied for the stage at the Royal Academy of Dramatic Art (held Leverhulme Scholarship, 1935–6); made his first appearance on the stage at the People's Palace, 28 Dec., 1936, as Mountjoy in "If I Were King"; from 1937 to 1941, played over two hundred parts in repertory companies at Croydon, Leeds, Bradford, Coventry, York, Sunderland, Newcastle, and Harrogate; toured, May, 1941, as Ninian Fraser in "The First Mrs. Fraser," with Dame Marie Tempest; Westminster, Mar., 1942, played Richard in "School for Slavery"; Lyric, Aug., 1942, Lieut. Fladgate in "Escort"; Phoenix, Aug., 1943, Andrey in "War and Peace"; Lyric, May, 1944, Alexander Pushkin in "Crisis In Heaven"; "Q,"

Jan., 1945, Gyles Flemyng in "Not So Fast, My Pretty"; Savoy, Mar., 1945, Robert de Mauny in "The Assassin"; at the "Q," between Oct., 1947, and Apr., 1948, appeared as Lord Henry Wootton in "The Picture of Dorian Gray," Sir Cosmo Leigh in "Clouded Vision," Mephistopheles in "Faust"; Garrick, July, 1948, played Sam in "Written For a Lady"; Duchess, Feb., 1950, Stan Roberts in "Flowers for the Living"; first appeared in films, 1942, in "Thunder Rock." *Address:* 21 De Vere Gardens, Kensington, W.8. *Telephone No.:* Western 8853.

MORTIMER, Charles, actor; *b.* 1885; *s.* of Charles Mortimer, actor; has been on the stage since early childhood and appeared at the Middlesex Music Hall, 1894, in sketches with his father in Brien McCullough and Mrs. Bennett's company; in Nov., 1894, played Willie Carlyle in "East Lynne"; spent many years in the provinces playing innumerable parts in all kinds of plays; in more recent years, at the Everyman, Dec., 1925, played Prince Palugay in "Sweet Pepper"; Savoy, May, 1927, Marsh in "Anne, One Hundred Per Cent"; Savoy, Mar., 1928, Mr. Woodley in "Young Woodley"; Garrick, Aug., 1928, Mr. Howard in "The Moving Finger"; Apollo, Nov., 1928, Dr. Wangel in "The Lady from the Sea"; Palace, June, 1929, O'Keefe in "Hold Everything"; Phoenix, Jan., 1931, Dr. Lawes in "John Brown's Body" and Mr. Paunceforth in "Frailties"; Phoenix, June 1931, Hinchecliffe in "Late Night Final"; Little, Oct., 1932, Snow in "The Silver Box"; Lyric, Nov., 1932, Paul Hallam in "Another Language"; Kingsway, Apr., 1933, Kiasso in "The Voice"; Fortune, Sept., 1933, Dr. Bristol in "What Happened Then?"; Shaftesbury, Sept., 1933, Eric Klamroth in "Before Sunset"; Lyric, Nov., 1933, Hyperbolus in "Acropolis"; Strand, June, 1934, Detective-Inspector Webster in "Living Dangerously"; Embassy, Nov., 1935, Supt. Stainer in "Murder Gang"; St. Martin's, Jan., 1936, Herr Kappell in "Sauce for the Goose"; Embassy, Apr., 1936, Captain

Hardy in "England Expects ——?"; Haymarket, Aug., 1936, Benny Kellerman in "The Amazing Dr. Clitterhouse"; Garrick, Nov., 1937, G. A. Appleby in "It's a Wise Child"; Arts, Oct., 1938, the Solicitor-General in "Oscar Wilde"; Aldwych, Jan., 1940, Mr. Nelson in "As You Are"; Vaudeville, May, 1940, Inspector Weston in "Peril at End House"; Wyndham's, July, 1940, and again in May, 1941, Chief Constable Gennett in "Cottage to Let"; New, Feb., 1942, Commander Copley in "Goodnight Children"; Lyric, Aug., 1942, Vice-Admiral Sir Frederick Wood in "Escort"; has appeared on numerous occasions for the Repertory Players, etc.; appeared in the films "Aren't Men Beasts!" "Someone at The Door," "Dead Men Are Dangerous," "Poison Pen," etc. *Clubs:* Green Room and Stage Golfing Society. *(Died 1 Apr., 1964; age 79)*

MORTLOCK, Charles Bernard, F.S.A., Hon. A.R.I.B.A., Hon. C.F., drama film, and ballet critic; *b.* London, 27 Feb., 1888; *e.* Jesus College, Cambridge (M.A.); formerly dramatic critic to *The Weekly Dispatch*; later, on the dramatic staff of *The Daily Telegraph*, ballet critic to *Punch*, dramatic and film critic to *The Church Times*; President of The Critics' Circle, 1946, and is a member of the Council; author of "Inky Blossoms," 1949; is a Member of the Grand Council of the Royal Academy of Dancing, and the Imperial Society of Dance Teachers; a Governor of The Royal Ballet School, and a Fellow of the Institute of Journalists. *Clubs:* Athenæum and Garrick.
(Died 31 Oct., 1967; age 79)

MORTON, Clive, actor; *b.* London, 16 Mar., 1904; *s.* of Francis Morton and his wife Ingeborg Marie (Becker); *e.* Bradfield College; *m.* (1) Joan Harben (dec.); (2) Frances Rowe; studied for the stage at the Royal Academy of Dramatic Art; was formerly engaged in the offices of a firm of East India Merchants in the City, for four years; made his first appearance on the stage at the Barnes

Theatre, 23 Aug., 1926, as a Russian peasant in "The Idiot"; Little, Sept., 1926, played General Epanchin in the same play; from May, 1927, to Aug., 1928, was engaged at the Bristol Repertory Theatre, where he played over sixty parts; St. Martin's, Oct., 1928, played Angus in "77 Park Lane"; Apollo (for the 300 Club), May, 1929, Cyril Greenwood in "After All"; Apollo, Oct., 1929, in "The Silver Tassie"; Strand, Dec., 1929, Joe Purdie in "The Sport of Kings"; in Aug., 1930, toured as Captain Stanhope in "Journey's End"; Haymarket, Feb., 1931, played Dicky Greig in "Supply and Demand"; His Majesty's, May, 1931, Leonard Oakroyd in "The Good Companions," which ran for a year; Aldwych, Sept., 1932, Viscomte la Coste in "Fifty-Fifty"; Jan., 1933, Jim Boyd in "A Bit of a Test"; Wyndham's, Sept., 1933, Albert in "Sheppey"; Globe, June, 1934, Pressman in "Meeting at Night"; Westminster, July, 1934, Noel Hutt in "French Salad"; Duke of York's, Nov., 1934, David in "The Greeks Had a Word for It"; Globe, June, 1935, David Oldham in "Grief Goes Over"; Whitehall, Nov., 1935, Hubert Dunwoody in "Anthony and Anna," which he played for two years; Embassy, Mar., and Duke of York's, Apr., 1938, Henry Trowbridge in "Three Blind Mice"; Duke of York's, Apr., and Whitehall, June, 1938, Mr. Angell in "Lot's Wife"; Wyndham's, Oct., 1938, Denys Royd in "Quiet Wedding"; toured, 1939, as Gurney in "Spotted Dick," playing the same part at the Strand, Dec., 1939; from Apr.–Aug., 1940, played leading parts with the H. M. Tennent Players at Lyceum, Edinburgh and Theatre Royal, Glasgow; joined the Army, Aug., 1940, and served in the Royal Norfolk Regiment, until Sept., 1945; appeared at the Salisbury Garrison Theatre, 1944, in leading parts in "The Late Christopher Bean," "The Power and the Devil," and "On Approval"; Lyric, May, 1946, played Desmond Curry in "The Winslow Boy"; Arts, Oct., 1947, Charles Poulter in "Cupid and Mars"; Wyndham's, July, 1948, Harold Carter in "People Like Us"; Duchess, Nov.,

1948, the Lawyer in "Miss Mabel"; Vaudeville, June, 1949, Lt.-Com. Rogers in "French Without Tears"; Embassy, Jan., 1950, Christopher in "Party Manners"; Lyric, Hammersmith, May, 1950, Dr. David Moore in "If This Be Error"; Wyndham's, Nov., 1950, succeeded Sir Ralph Richardson as David Preston in "Home at Seven"; Arts, Feb., 1951, played Paul Kirsanov in "Spring at Marino"; Criterion, Dec., 1951, Charles Lane-Roberts in "Indian Summer"; toured, Feb., 1952, as The General in "Under the Sycamore Tree"; Comedy, Nov., 1952, played Richard Maybury in "Tomorrow's Too Late"; St. James's, May, 1953, Dr. Robert Stevens in "The Uninvited Guest"; Duke of York's, Dec., 1953, Antoine Villardier in "Thirteen for Dinner"; Duchess, Mar., 1955, Carlo Bombas in "Misery Me"; at the same theatre, Sept., 1955, appeared as George Kettle in "Mr. Kettle and Mrs. Moon"; Comedy, Sept., 1959, played Stanley Harrington in the second production of "Five Finger Exercise", and subsequently toured with the play; Assembly Hall, Edinburgh, Aug., 1960, played King Edward I in "The Wallace"; Savoy, May, 1961, played Wilfred Gantry in "The Bird of Time"; Aldwych, Aug., 1962, George Selincourt in "A Penny for a Song"; Ipswich, June, 1963, appeared as Guest-artist as James Tyrone in "Long Day's Journey Into Night"; Phoenix, Aug., 1963, took over the part of Ezra Fitton in "All in Good Time"; joined the Royal Shakespeare Company, Stratford-on-Avon, Apr.–Nov., 1964, to play the following parts: Bishop of Carlisle in "Richard II," Earl of Worcester in "Henry IV" (Part I), Davy in "Henry IV" (Part II), and Lord Talbot in "Henry VI" ("Wars of the Roses"); Royal Court, June, 1965, Lt.-Col. Ludwig von Mohl in "A Patriot For Me"; Piccadilly, Dec., 1968, the Earl of Clincham in "The Young Visiters"; Arnaud, Guildford, Feb., 1970, Sir George Crofts in "Mrs. Warren's Profession"; began film career, 1932, in "The Fires of Fate," and has since appeared in over sixty films; he has also played in over a hundred television productions, and made numerous radio broadcasts.

Recreations: Sport, music and entertaining. *Club:* Garrick. *Address:* Flat 34, 17 Airlie Gardens, London, W.8. *Telephone No.:* 01-727 2452.

MORTON, Edward, dramatic author and critic, " Mordred," late of *The Referee* ; *m.* Rosamond, *d.* of Captain Thomas Devereux Bingham ; author of " Miss Impudence," Terry's, 1892 ; " San Toy, or The Emperor's Own," Daly's, 1899 ; author of " Travellers' Tales," 1892 ; part author with Israel Zangwill of " Man and Beast."
(Died 6 July, 1922)

MORTON, Hugh (see McLellan, C. M. S.).

MORTON, Leon, actor ; appeared at La Scala, Paris, Sept., 1912, in " Si t'étais roi " ; made his first appearance in London, at the Ambassadors' Theatre, 17 Oct., 1914, as Dauberthier in " L'Ingénue," and in the *revue* " Odds and Ends " ; he appeared at the same theatre, June, 1915, in " More," and Apr., 1917, in " £150 " ; at the Prince of Wales's, Aug., 1917, played Panelli in " Carminetta " ; at the London Pavilion, June, 1918, appeared as Zedekiah Dubois in " The Profiteers " ; Aug., 1918, in " As You Were " ; at the Palace, Paris, Apr., 1919, in " Hullo ! Paris ! " ; at the Adelphi, Oct., 1920, played Gospodar in " The Naughty Princess " ; at the Porte-St.-Martin, Paris, Nov., 1921, appeared as Bertrand and Quincampoix in " Robert Macaire et cie." *Address :* 54 Fitzroy Road, N.W.1. *Telephone No. :* Hampstead 5339.

MORTON, Martha, dramatic author ; *b.* New York City, 10 Oct., 1870 ; *e.* New York ; sister of Michael Morton ; *m.* Hermann Conheim ; has written the following among other plays : " Helene," 1888, also known as " The Refugee's Daughter " ; " The Merchant," 1890 ; " Geoffrey Middleton, Gentleman," 1892 ; " Brother John," 1893 ; " Christmas," 1894 ; " His Wife's Father," 1895 ; " The Fool of Fortune," 1896 ; " A Bachelor's Romance," 1897 ; " The Sleeping Partner," 1897 ; " Her Lord and Master," 1902 ; " The Diplomat," 1902 ; " The Triumph of Love," 1904 ; " A Four-Leaf Clover," 1905 ; " The Truth Tellers," 1905 ; " The Illusion of Beatrice," 1906 ; and " The Movers," 1907 ; " On the Eve " (from the German), 1909 ; " The Senator Keeps House," 1911 ; " The Three of Hearts," 1915.
(Died 18 Feb., 1925; age 59)

MORTON, Michael, dramatic author ; brother of Martha Morton ; author of the following among other plays : " Miss Francis of Yale," 1897 ; " Taming a Husband," 1898 ; " A Rich Man's Son," 1899 ; " Caleb West," 1900 ; " Resurrection " (Tolstoy's novel), 1903 ; " Marguerite " (from the French), 1904 ; " Colonel Newcome " (from Thackeray's novel, " The Newcomes "), 1906; " The Little Stranger," 1906 ; " My Wife " (from the French), 1907 ; " Charlie the Sport " (from the French), 1907 ; " Her Father " (from the French), Jan., 1908 ; " The Richest Girl " (with Paul Gavault), Sept., 1908 ; " The Heart of the City " (with Julian Wellesley), 1909 ; " Detective Sparks," 1909 ; " Tantalising Tommy " (with Paul Gavault), 1910 ; " The Impostor " (with Leonard Merrick), 1910 ; " The Runaway " (from the French), 1911 ; " What a Game ! " 1913 ; " The Yellow Ticket," 1914 ; " The Prodigal Husband " (with Dario Nicodemi), 1914 ; " The Shadow " (with Nicodemi), 1914 ; " My Superior Officer," 1916 ; " Jeff," 1916 ; " Remnant " (with Nicodemi), 1917 ; " On With the Dance," 1917 ; " In the Night Watch " (from the French), 1918 ; " Woman to Woman," 1921 ; " The Talking Shop," 1921 ; " The Guilty One " (with Peter Traill), 1922 ; " Fallen Angels " (with Traill), 1924 ; " Five Minutes Fast," 1925 ; " By Right of Conquest " (with Traill), 1925 ; " Salvage " (with Traill), 1926 ; " Riceyman Steps " (from Arnold Bennett's novel), 1926 ; " The Stranger in the House " (with Traill), 1928 ; " Alibi " (from a novel by Agatha Christie), 1928 ; " Because of Irene " (with Traill), 1929; "Beauty" (from the French), 1929; for some time connected with Sir Herbert Tree at His Majesty's Theatre, as literary adviser and producer. *Club:* Authors'. *(Died 11 Jan., 1931; age 76)*

MOSCOVITCH, Maurice, actor; *b.* Odessa, Russia, 23 Nov., 1871; *s.* of Nathaniel Maaskoff and his wife Miriam (Rostow); *e.* Odessa and Moscow; *m.* Rosa Baumar; made his first appearance on the stage at the National Theatre, Odessa, in 1885; spent many years touring in Russia, Germany, Roumania, Austria, etc.; made his first appearance in New York, at the Windsor Theatre, in 1893, as Samson in "Samson and Delilah"; subsequently with his own company toured the United States, Canada, Argentine, Brazil, Russia, Roumania, Austria, etc.; made his first appearance in London, at the Pavilion Theatre, Mile End, in 1908, playing the title-rôle in "The Devil"; in 1913 played a repertory season at the same theatre, playing in "Thorns," "The Jewish King Lear," etc., and again in 1915, when he appeared in "Ikele Mazik," "Solomon Caus," "Bought and Paid For," etc.; at the New Queen's Theatre, Manchester, June, 1919, played an extended season in "The Return of Faith," "The Great Question," "Blind Youth," "Edmund Kean," "A Mother's Heart," "Two Mothers," "The Power of Nature," etc.; made his English-speaking *début* at the Gaiety, Manchester, 15 Sept., 1919, as Shylock in "The Merchant of Venice," and made his first appearance in the West End of London, in the same part, at the Court Theatre, 9 Oct., 1919, scoring an immediate success; at the Duke of York's, Apr., 1920, played Anton Anton'itch in "The Government Inspector"; at the Shaftesbury, Oct., 1920, made a further success, when he appeared as Jean Paurel in "The Great Lover"; made his first appearance in variety theatres, at Glasgow, May, 1921, when he appeared in "Don Carlos," in which he also appeared at the Palladium, London; entered on the management of the Apollo Theatre, Sept., 1922,

opening as Jurg Winkelreid in "The Torch," and Nov., 1922, played Richard Bolger in "Devil Dick"; at Drury Lane, Mar., 1923, played Maestro Angelo in "Angelo"; subsequently toured in South Africa; and in 1924-5 toured in Australia in "The Merchant of Venice," "The Outsider," "The Great Lover," etc.; returned to London, and appeared at the Shaftesbury, Apr., 1926, in a revival of "The Great Lover"; again returned to Australia, 1926-9, and appeared there in "They Knew What They Wanted," "The Fake," "Trilby," "Arms and the Man," "The Ringer," "The Terror," "The Silent House"; returned to London, 1929; at Erlanger's, New York, Jan., 1930, played Josef-Süss Oppenheimer in "Josef Süss"; Times Square, Dec., 1930, Shylock in "The Merchant of Venice"; has played in five different languages; has appeared in films since 1936, in "Winterset," "Make Way for To-Morrow," "Lancer Spy," "Gateway," "Suez," "Love Affair," "Susannah of the Mounties," etc. *Favourite part:* Iago. *Hobby:* Collecting old violins. *Recreation:* Motoring. *(Died 18 June, 1940; age 69)*

MOSES, Montrose J., author, dramatic editor, and critic; *b.* New York City, U.S.A., 2 Sept., 1878; *s.* of Montefiore Moses and his wife Rose (Jonas); *e.* New York; *m.* (1) Lucille Dorothy Herne (dec.), (2) Leah Agnes Houghtaling; was dramatic editor of *The Reader Magazine*, 1903–07; dramatic critic of *The Independent*, and of *The Book News Monthly*, 1908–18; edited "The Plays of Clyde Fitch," 1915; "Representative Plays by American Dramatists" (three volumes); "Representative British Dramas"; "Representative Continental Dramas"; "Clyde Fitch and His Letters"; "Representative American Dramas"; "British Plays from the Restoration to 1820"; "Dramas of Modernism and Their Forerunners"; contributed to "The Green Room Book," 1908; translated The Passion Play of Oberammergau, 1909; is a prolific author, and has written the following among other notable books, "Francesca da Rimini," "Famous Actor-Families in

America"; "Henrik Ibsen: the Man and His Plays"; "The American Dramatist," "Maurice Maeterlinck: a Study"; "The Fabulous Forrest—The Record of an American Actor"; has also contributed articles and verse to leading periodicals.

(Died 29 Mar., 1934; age 55)

MOSHEIM, Grete, actress; *b.* Berlin, 8 Jan., 1907; *d.* of Marcus Mosheim, M.D., and his wife Clara (Hilger); *e.* Victoria Lyceum, Berlin; *m.* Howard Gould; studied for the stage at the Deutsches Theater School, Berlin; she was placed under a three years contract with Max Reinhardt, and made her first appearance on the stage at the Deutsches Theater, 1925, in "Des Esels Schatten"; taking over the leading part in "Der Sprechende Affe" at the Komodie Theatre, in 1925, she made a substantial success, and with few exceptions was engaged at Reinhardt's theatres from that date until 1932, when Reinhardt retired from Berlin; she appeared at the Deutsches Theater, 1926, in "We Moderns" and "You Never Can Tell"; at the Komodie, 1926, in "The Captive"; in 1927, in "Widower's Houses" and Noel Coward's "This Was a Man," and in 1928 in "Marcelin Fradelin"; her performances in the last two-mentioned plays put her in the front rank of German actresses; later, in 1928, at the Deutsches, starred in Reinhardt's "Artisten"; subsequently appeared as Rose in "Street Scene," 1930; Lu in "The Good Fairy" and Jill in "Mr. Cinders," 1931; "Phaea" and Myra in "Waterloo Bridge," 1932; played Marguerite in "Faust," Eliza Doolittle in "Pygmalion" and Beatrice in "Much Ado About Nothing," 1933; she then toured Germany with her own company, playing "Pygmalion," "Waterloo Bridge," and Nora in "A Doll's House"; after leaving Germany, toured with her own company in Switzerland, Austria, and Czechoslovakia in "Pygmalion" and "Katz im Sack"; came to England and, after studying the language, appeared in a film, "The Car of Dreams," 1935; made her first appearance on the London stage at the St. James's,

8 Oct., 1935, as Lilia Verrick in "Two Share a Dwelling"; subsequently went to America; made her first appearance on the New York stage, at the Cort Theatre, Dec., 1941, as Erna Schmidt in "Letters to Lucerne"; National, Mar., 1945, played Mary Gaylord in "Calico Wedding."

MOSS, Sir (Horace) Edward, D.L., J.P., cr. 1905; director of variety theatres; *b.* Manchester, 1854; *s.* of James Moss; theatrical manager and *impresario ; e.* Edinburgh and Glasgow; *m.* Florence Nellie Craig; opened the Gaiety, Edinburgh, 1877; the first of the now famous Moss Empires; subsequently managing director of the Moss and Thornton Theatres, and later of the Moss, Thornton and Stoll Theatres; is a Justice of the Peace and Deputy Lieutenant for Midlothian. *Address :* Middleton Hall, Gorebridge, near Edinburgh. *Clubs :* Junior Constitutional, Royal Automobile, and Conservative Club, Edinburgh.

MOSS, W. Keith, editor of *The Spotlight,* producer, and stage director; *b.* Manchester, 29 Mar., 1892; *e.* Manchester; *m.* (1) Patricia O'Carroll (dec.); (2) Carlotta Mossetti; formerly an actor and made his first appearance on the stage at the Gaiety Theatre, Manchester, as a member of Miss Horniman's company; subsequently gained wide experience in all kinds of plays, both as actor and stage-manager; toured in Australia in 1914, but returned to England on the outbreak of War, and in the Royal Flying Corps (R.A.F.) until 1919; after being demobilized mainly devoted himself to stage-management and production; was stage-manager at various times with Leon M. Lion, Robert Loraine, Milton Rosmer, and Theodore Komisarjevsky; in 1924, was for a time business manager of the "Q" Theatre, and later was appointed stage-director at the same theatre; in 1926, was associated with the Komisarjevsky-Tchekov Season, at the Barnes Theatre as stage-director; founded *The Spotlight,* 1927, and is now joint-director of the company controlling that pub-

lication; has also had great experience in film production.
(Died 16 Aug., 1935; age 43)

MOSSETTI, Carlotta, dancer and ballet mistress; *b.* London, 23 Sept., 1890; *d.* of Victorio Mossetti and his wife Eugenie (McQuinn); *e.* London; *m.* (1) S. V. Etheridge (dec.); (2) W. Keith Moss; was apprenticed to the school of dancing at the Alhambra, when she was ten years of age, and made her first appearance at that theatre, on 12 Oct., 1908, in the ballet "Paquita"; subsequently appeared there in "On the Square," "Psyche," "On the Heath," "Femina," "The Dance Dream," "1830," "Carmen," etc.; was for some time ballet mistress at the Alhambra, where she also acted as producer; subsequently appeared at the Empire, Sept. 1914, as Alexis in "Europe"; produced "Lilac Time" at the Coliseum, and was responsible for the dances and ballet in "Angelo," at Drury Lane, Mar., 1923. *Recreations :* Motoring, swimming, sculling, and tennis. *Address :* c/o "The Spotlight," 43 Cranbourn Street, W.C.2.

MOUËZY-EON, André, French dramatic author; *b.* Nantes, 9 June, 1880; has written the following, among other plays: "Tire au Flanc" (with André Sylvane), 1904; "Le Major Ipéca," 1906; "Panachot, Gendarme," 1907; "Les Amours d'Ovide," 1908; "L'Enfant de ma Soeur" (with R. Francheville), 1908; "Moulard S'Emancipe," 1908; "L'Année en l'air" (with H. Bataille), 1908; "Il ? . . . ou Elle ?" 1908; "Monsieur Zéro" (with Paul Gavault), 1909; "Le Papa du Régiment" (with J. Durieux), 1909; "Le Grand Ecart" (from the German), 1910; "L'Amour en Manoeuvres," 1911; "On opère sans doleur," 1911; "La Pavillon" (with Sylvane), 1911; "La part du feu" (with M. Nancey), 1912; "La Folle Nuit" (with Félix Gandera," 1917; "La Marraines de l'escouade," "Malikoko, roi négre," 1919; "La Filon,' 1919; "La Liason dangereuse (with Gandéra), 1919; "Rue et Place (with Sylvane),

1919; "Les Potaches" (with A. Machard), 1920; "T'auras pas sa," 1920; "Les Degourdis du 11e Escadron" (with M. Daveillans), 1920; "Le Crime du Bouif" (with A. La Fouchardière); "La Pucelle du rat mort," "Madame Lebureau" (with Marséle), 1920; "La petite bonne d'Abraham" (with Gandera), 1921; "T'auras pas sa fleur," 1921; "Qu'en mariage seulement" (with M.M. Nancey and Pierrefeux), 1921. *Address :* 8 Cité Malesherbes, Paris.

MOUILLOT, Gertrude, actress; *d.* of Robert Davison, sculptor; *m.* Frederick Mouillot (*d.* 1911); first appeared professionally in "The Dark Continent," Plymouth, followed by tours as Niobe in the play of that name, Lucy White in "The Professor's Love Story," Hester Worsley in "A Woman of No Importance," title-*rôles* in "Jane" and "Sophia," Princess Elizabeth in "The Prince and the Pauper," the Princess of Pannonia in "My Friend the Prince"; with Hermann Vezin she played Rosalind, Ophelia, Portia, Desdemona, Lady Macbeth, etc.; she next toured in "Miss Hobbs" and "Madame Butterfly," playing the title-*rôles ;* this was succeeded by a tour in the principal part in "Becky Sharp," following which came an engagement by Beerbohm Tree to play Katusha in "Resurrection," in Glasgow, Dublin, Belfast, and Leeds; appeared at Comedy as Clara Hunter in "The Climbers"; in Judge Parry's and F. Mouillot's comedy, "What the Butler Saw," played Kitty Barrington, Wyndham's, 1905; appeared at the Gaiety, Dec., 1910, as Mrs. Bessie Higgins in "The Captain of the School"; is the proprietor of the Palace Theatre, Westcliff, and lessee of theatres at Bournemouth, Southampton and Swansea.
(Died 24 Nov., 1961; age 91)

MOULAN, Frank, actor and vocalist; *b.* New York City, U.S.A., 24 July, 1875; *m.* Maud Lillian Berri; as a boy, gained a great reputation as a soloist, and sang in various churches in New York and New Jersey; made his first appearance on the stage with the Calhoun Opera company, and subsequently joined the company of the Castle Square Opera company, Boston; made his first appearance on the New York stage with this company, at the American Theatre, 25 Dec., 1897, as Don Quixote in a revival of "The Queen's Lace Handkerchief"; at the same theatre, 1898, played Scalza in "Boccaccio," and Nakid in "A Trip to Africa"; scored a big success, when he appeared at the Studebaker Theatre, Chicago, Mar., 1902, in "The Sultan of Sulu," which was repeated when the play was produced at Wallack's, New York, Dec., 1902; at the New Amsterdam Theatre, Mar., 1907, played George Washington Barker in "The Grand Mogul," in which he appeared for two seasons, in New York and on tour; Liberty Theatre, Jan., 1910, played James Smith and Simplicitas in "The Arcadians"; Knickerbocker, Aug., 1911, Baron Siegfried and Bazilos in "The Siren"; New Amsterdam, Sept., 1912, the Grand Duke Rutzinov in "The Count of Luxembourg"; Globe, Jan., 1914, Professor Clutterbuck in "The Queen of the Movies"; Knickerbocker, Mar., 1915, Professor Glum in "Fads and Fancies"; Broadhurst, Nov., 1917, Blanquet in "Her Regiment"; Belmont, Sept., 1920, "Fingers" Clay in "Little Miss Charity"; Central, May, 1921, Hiram Demarest in "Princess Virtue"; Earl Carroll Theatre, Mar., 1922, Mr. Cummings in "Just Because"; after a lengthy absence from New York, reappeared at Erlanger's Theatre, and from May–Aug., 1931, played Ko-Ko in "The Mikado," Sir Joseph Porter in "H.M.S. Pinafore," Duke of Plaza-Toro in "The Gondoliers," Reginald Bunthorne in "Patience," Major-Gen. Stanley in "The Pirates of Penzance," the Lord Chancellor in "Iolanthe," the Judge in "Trial by Jury," and Robin Oakapple in "Ruddigore"; appeared in the same parts 1932–35; Adelphi, New York, July, 1935, played Jack Point in "The Yeomen of the Guard." *(Died 13 May, 1939; age 63)*

MOULD, Raymond Wesley, theatre Press-representative; *b.* Nottingham,

16 Sept., 1905; *s.* of Walter Henry Mould and his wife Alice (Weatherington); *e.* Foster School, Nottingham; commenced his career as a journalist, at the age of sixteen, and was engaged on the *Nottingham Journal* and *Nottingham Evening News*; came to London, 1926, and was engaged as publicity agent for Carl Brisson; then joined Robert Jorgensen, and, in 1937, joined the firm of George Elliot and Anthony Vivian, and has represented several important managements, including Gilbert Miller, Lee Ephraim, Alec Rea, O'Bryen, Linnit and Dunfee; joined the R.A.F., July, 1941; served as A.C.2, for over two years, until commissioned; served as Squadron-Leader in the Directorate of Public Relations, carrying on with publicity, representing Linnit and Dunfee, Henry Sherek, and Bernard Delfont; demobilized Oct., 1945; represented Sir Charles Cochran at the Adelphi and Vaudeville, from 1947. *Hobby:* Finding old pubs. *Address:* 25 Shaftesbury Avenue, London, W.1. *Telephone No.:* Gerrard 6881.

MOUNET, Jean Paul, French actor; *b.* Bergerac, Dordogne, 5 Oct., 1847; *br.* of Jean Mounet-Sully; *e.* Bergerac, Bordeaux, and Paris; *m.* Andrée Barbot; *sociétaire* of the Comédie Française, 1891, professor at the Paris Conservatoire; was originally intended for the medical profession, and is a fully qualified doctor of medicine; made his first appearance on the stage at the Odéon Theatre, in "Horace," 1880; subsequently appeared in "Andromaque," "Iphigénie," "L'Arlésienne," "Numa Roumestan," "Les Jacobites," etc.; made his first appearance at the Comédie Française, 15 July, 1889, as Don Salluste, in "Ruy Blas"; his principal successes have been Severo Torelli, Oreste in "Les Erynnyes," Balthazar in "L'Arlésienne," Iago in "Othello," Latro in "Martyre," Marat in "Charlotte Corday," the Duc d'Albe in "Patrie," Ghost in "Hamlet," Le Père Remy in "Claudie," Monte Prade in "L'Aventurière," Marquis de Nangis in "Marion Delorme," Talma in "L'Ame des

Héros," Herakles in "La Furie," Tiresias in "Antigone," Count de Roqueville in "Un Cas de Conscience"; Corneille in "Le Ménage de Molière"; D'Hervey in "Antony"; Un Messager in "Andromaque," Macbeth in "Macbeth," etc.; has also appeared in "Le Roi," "L'Enigme," "Le Dédale," "Oedipe Roi," "Hernani," etc.; is a Chevalier of the Legion of Honour, and an Officer of Public Instruction. *(Died 10 Feb., 1922; age 74)*

MOUNET-SULLY, Jean, French actor; *b.* at Bergerac, 27 Feb., 1841; *br.* of Jean Mounet; *e.* at Paris Conservatoire under Bressant; sociétaire 1874; made his first appearance on the stage at Odéon in 1868; after the war of 1870-1, appeared at the Comédie Française, where he made his first appearance, 4 July, 1872, as Oreste in "Andromaque"; played lead in "Le Cid," "Athalie," "Iphigénie," "Hamlet," "Phèdre," "Horace," "Zaïre," "Amphitryon," "Hernani," "Ruy Blas," "Œdipe Roi," "L'Etrangère," "L'Aventurière," "Antigone," "Le Roi s'amuse," "Othello," "Le Fils de l'Arétin," "Les Burgraves," "Marion Delorme," "Polyeucte," "Andromaque," "Les Erynnyes," "Patrie"; author of "La Vieillesse de Don Juan"; Officer of the Academy; Officer of the Legion of Honour; Officer of Public Instruction; is the *doyen* of the Comédie Française.
(Died 1 Mar., 1916; age 75)

MOYA, Natalie, actress; *b.* Tipperary, 25 Dec., 1900; *d.* of William Thomas Mullaly, M.D., and his wife Alice (Harvey); *e.* Ursuline Convent, Waterford, Ireland and Lausanne, Switzerland; *m.* George Rikard Schjelderup; studied for the stage under Kate Rorke and at the Royal Academy of Dramatic Art; made her first appearance on the stage at the Memorial Theatre, Stratford-on-Avon, Apr., 1921, as the Prince of Wales in "Richard III"; played two seasons at Stratford-on-Avon, appearing as Phoebe in "As You Like It," Nerissa, Titania, Desdemona, Maria in "The School for Scandal," etc.; made her first appearance in London at the Ambassadors' Theatre, 2 Nov., 1922, as the First Lady Guest in "The Secret Agent"; in 1924 toured in South Africa with Maurice Moscovitch, playing *ingénues*; at the Haymarket, Dec., 1924, played a Court Lady in "A Kiss for Cinderella"; at Barnes, Sept., 1925, and Garrick, Nov., 1925, played Sarah in "Tess of the D'Urbervilles"; at the Regent (for the Fellowship of Players), Feb., 1926, played the Queen in "King Richard II"; at the Royalty, July, 1926, Viera Aleksandrovna in "A Month in the Country"; Fortune, Nov., 1926, Teresa in "The Cradle Song"; Duke of York's, Apr., 1927, Jean Rankin in "The Donovan Affair"; Strand, Oct., 1927, Lulu in "The Kingdom of God"; Strand, May, 1928, Meta in "The Road to Rome"; autumn of 1928, played lead at the Festival Theatre, Cambridge; in Jan., 1929, went to Australia, to play Laura Simmons in "Young Woodley" and Nora Blake in "Lombardi Ltd."; after returning to London, appeared at the Everyman and Criterion, Sept., 1930, with the Irish Players, as Marian in "The Far-off Hills"; Criterion, Oct., 1930, played Pegeen Mike in "The Playboy of the Western World"; Embassy, Apr., 1931, Irene in "The Romantic Young Lady"; with the Birmingham Repertory Company, played Kunie in "See Naples and Die"; then joined the Hull Repertory Company, and played a round of leading parts; Globe (for the Players, Theatre), May, 1932, played Maureen Elliott in "Ourselves Alone"; Ambassadors', Sept., 1932, Sonya Dalachek in "The Left Bank," and Oct., 1932, Lilian Garfield in the same play; Fulham, Jan., 1933, Mary in "Juno and the Paycock"; "Q," Mar., 1933, Mary Thompson in "Francis Thompson"; Grafton, May, 1933, Eleonora in "Easter"; at New Brighton, May, 1934, played a repertory season; then left the stage for two years; St. James's, Feb., 1936, played Maggie in "Pride and Prejudice"; Gate, Nov., 1937, Vera in "Distant Point"; Torch, Sept., 1938, Sophie in "The Game of Love and Death" (which she translated) and

Nov., 1938, Katie in "Katie Roche"; toured, Feb., 1939, as Eleanor Pound in "Banana Ridge"; Torch, May, 1939, played Mary Byrne in "A Tinker's Wedding"; Chanticleer, Dec., 1939, Miss Joyce in "Hyacinth Halvey," and Biddy Lally in "The Unicorn and the Stars"; Gaiety, Dublin, July, 1941, the Lady in "The Man with a Load of Mischief"; subsequently, Sept.–Oct., 1941, played leading parts at the Opera House, Belfast; Mercury Theatre, Sept., 1942, Mrs. Elvsted in "Hedda Gabler," and Nov., 1942, Mrs. Fainall in "The Way of the World"; toured for E.N.S.A., Nov., 1944–May, 1945, as Olivia in "Twelfth Night"; appeared in the Parks at Birmingham, May–Aug., 1945, as Janet in "The First Mrs. Fraser," Mrs. Clandon in "You Never Can Tell," and Mrs. Lothian in "The Light of Heart." *Recreations:* Walking, reading, talking, and dancing. *Address:* 2 Holly Place, Hampstead, London, N.W.3. *Telephone No.:* Hampstead 3609.

MOZART, George, comedian; *b.* Great Yarmouth; as a boy was a member of the Prince of Wales's Own Norfolk Military band; made his first appearance on the professional stage in 1890; for some years appeared as a musical entertainer, with a partner, as the Mozarts, making their first appearance in 1892; made their first appearance in London, at the Queen's, Poplar, 6 Mar., 1893, followed by engagements at the Middlesex, Washington, Collins's, and all the leading music halls; subsequently appeared by himself, as a comic vocalist, and of late years has presented a series of humorous character sketches, such as "Callers"; "Colonel Nutty of the Nuts"; "A Day at the Races"; "The Flash-Light Express"; "Old Hats," etc., at the principal variety theatres throughout the United Kingdom; visited Australia, 1914-15; reappeared in England at the Brighton Hippodrome, Aug., 1915, in "A Smart Wedding"; in Oct., 1915, appeared at the Alhambra, Leicester Square, in "Now's the time!"; is a skilful musician and instrumentalist. *Ad-*

dress : 24 Ashworth Mansions, Maida Vale, W. *Telephone No. :* Hampstead 6412.

MUDIE, Leonard, actor; *b.* 11 Apr., 1884; *m.* (1) Beatrice Terry (mar. dis.); (2) Gladys Lennox; a prominent member of Miss Horniman's Company, at the Gaiety Theatre, Manchester, where he first appeared in 1908; he appeared there in a number of parts, including Mr. Thompson in "Makeshifts," Humphrey in "The Knight of the Burning Pestle," Porter in "Cupid and the Styx," Albert in "The Three Barrows," Saemund Halldorsson in "The Feud," Ben Jordan in "The Dear Departed," Dr. Fawcett in "Woman's Rights," Verges in "Much Ado About Nothing," Tom Naylor in "The Purse of Gold," August Grant in "The Tallyman," Herbert Bingham in "Spring in Bloomsbury," The Great Horn in "The Little Dream," Hubert Norton in "Revolt," Alan Jeffcoate in "Hindle Wakes," Joseph Surface in "The School for Scandal," Timpson in "Garside's Career," James Durham in "Loving as We Do," Freddie Fincham in "Consequences," Leslie Fyfe in "The Waldies," Gordon Jayne in "The Second Mrs. Tanqueray," Walter How in "Justice," the Dean of Stour in "The Mob," Amos Guppy in "Love Cheats," etc.; has appeared at the Coronet and Court Theatres, London, with Miss Horniman's Company, also in America; appeared at the Comedy Theatre, New York, 1 Oct., 1914, as Freddie Fincham in "Consequences"; at the Opera House, Boston, Mass., 1914-15, appeared in "The Merry Wives of Windsor," "Julius Caesar," "The Merchant of Venice," and "Twelfth Night," and at the Plymouth Theatre, Boston, in "The Sin of David"; at the New Amsterdam Theatre, New York, 1916, played Shallow in "The Merry Wives of Windsor," with Sir Herbert Tree; at the Astor Theatre, Aug., 1916, appeared as the Counsel for the Defence in "The Guilty Man"; at the Maxine Elliott Theatre, Feb., 1917, played in "The Little Man" and "Magic"; at the Globe, New York, Mar., 1917, played the Cockney in "Out There"; at the Liberty, Nov., 1917, Cyril Parriscourt in "The Wooing of Eve"; at the Empire, New York, Dec., 1917, Gaston Rieux in "The Lady of the Camellias"; at the Forty-fourth Street Theatre, Mar. 1918, Captain Eric Lowndes in "A Pair of Petticoats"; during 1919, toured in "Why Marry?"; in 1920, toured in the title-*rôle* of "Abraham Lincoln"; at the Garrick, New York, Feb., 1921, played Brian Strange in "Mr. Pim Passes By"; at the Eltinge Theatre, Sept., 1922, Henry Anderson in "East of Suez"; at the Knickerbocker, Sept., 1923, Claudet in "The Lullaby"; Henry Miller, Feb., 1926, Edward in "Embers"; Daly's, Jan., 1928, Jacques Guidon in "Red Rust"; Garrick, Mar., 1928, The Elder Brother in "12,000"; Knickerbocker, Nov., 1928, Lennox and the First Witch in "Macbeth"; Ritz, Sept., 1929, Captain Luke Arnold in "Soldiers and Women"; Assembly, Nov., 1929, Richard Legrange in "A Ledge"; Dec., 1929, Claudio in "The Novice and the Duke" ("Measure for Measure"); Guild, May, 1930, succeeded Eliot Cabot as Mikhail Rakitin in "A Month in the Country"; Forrest, Oct., 1931, played Steven in "Lean Harvest"; Fulton, Sept., 1948, Mr. McPherson in "Time for Elizabeth"; at Hollywood, 1950, appeared as Arthur Winslow in "The Winslow Boy," and Professor Tobias Emanuel in "The Traitor"; has also appeared in innumerable films. *Address*: 2028 North Beachwood Drive, Hollywood, 28, Calif., U.S.A.

MUIR, Jean, actress; *b*. New York City, U.S.A., 13 Feb., 1911; *d*. of George Knox Fullarton and his wife Ida Eagleton (Hanson); *e*. Dwight School, Englewood, New Jersey; *m*. Henry Jaffe; made her first appearance on the stage under her real name of Jean Fullarton at Hartford, Conn., Oct., 1930, as Joan Greenleaf in "Bird in Hand"; made her first appearance in New York at the Ethel Barrymore Theatre, 27 Dec., 1930, as Atkins in "The Truth Game"; Shubert, Apr., 1931, played Mdme. Pasquier de la Marière in "Peter Ibbetson"; Selwyn, Mar., 1932, Mrs. Brown in "Life Begins"; Broadway,

June, 1932, a Trojan Woman in "Troilus and Cressida"; Music Box, Oct., 1932, understudied several parts in "Dinner at Eight"; Lyceum, Jan., 1933, played Nadja Nikolaivna in "Saint Wench"; then spent four years in films, when she appeared for the first time as Jean Muir; returned to the regular theatre at Ogunquit, Maine, Aug., 1937, as Arabella Love in "Dearly Beloved"; she then went to England and made her first appearance on the London stage at the Apollo Theatre, 24 Nov., 1937, as Diana Lismore in "People at Sea"; on returning to America, played in summer theatres, 1938, as Lise in "High Tor," Beatrice in "Much Ado About Nothing," Raina in "Arms and the Man," etc.; Dec., 1938, commenced touring as Lorna in "Golden Boy"; at the County Theatre, Suffern, July, 1941, played in "Once in a Lifetime," and "The Play's the Thing"; entered films, 1933, in "The World Changes," and has since appeared in innumerable pictures.

MULCASTER, G. H., *b*. London, 27 June, 1891; *m*. (1) Mollie Ellis (mar. dis.); (2) Lola de Laredo; first appeared on the stage, at the West Pier, Brighton, 25 July, 1910, as one of the students in "Old Heidelberg"; from 1910-17 was engaged touring in the provinces, appearing in such plays as "The Chorus Lady," "The Prisoner of Zenda," "Alias Jimmy Valentine," etc.; he toured with Olga Nethersole in "The Awakening of Helena Ritchie," appeared in variety theatres, as Everyman in the morality play of that name; toured in the leading parts in "The Story of the Rosary," "The Witness for the Defence," "The New Clown," "Sowing the Wind," etc.; in 1916 toured as Stuart Randolph in "Her Husband's Wife," and Captain Bagnall in "A Pair of Silk Stockings"; made his first appearance in London, at the New Theatre, 8 Feb., 1917, as Frank Taylo in the revival of "The Land of Promise"; at the same theatre, appeared as Private Dowey in "The Old Lady Shows her Medals"; Captain River in "His Excellency the Governor"

Captain Rattray in "Seven Women"; and at the Globe Theatre, Jan., 1918, played Dr. Bell in "Love in a Cottage"; at the Devonshire Park, Eastbourne, Nov., 1918, Prince Alfred in "His Royal Happiness"; at the St. Martin's, Apr., 1919, Joe Garvin in "The Very Idea"; at the Haymarket, Sept., 1919, William Rivers in "Daddies"; at the Savoy, Oct., 1919, Bruce Norton in "Tiger Rose"; at the Globe, Apr., 1921, played Lucas Errol in "The Knave of Diamonds"; at the Royalty, June, 1922, Lucas Chadacre in "The Green Cord"; in Feb., 1923, went to Australia, where he played the title-*rôle* in "Bull-Dog Drummond" and Waverley Ango in "The Faithful Heart"; on returning to London, appeared at the St. James's, Jan., 1924, succeeding George Relph as Dr. Basil Traherne in "The Green Goddess"; at the Scala (for the Play Actors), Nov., 1924, played Geoffrey Allen in "Dear Father"; New Oxford, June, 1925, Arthur Marsden in "The Gorilla"; St. Martin's, Nov., 1925, Richard Winthrop in "The Ghost Train," which he played throughout the long run of that play; Savoy, May, 1927, Peter Nixon in "Anne, One Hundred"; New, Dec., 1927, Roger Doyle in "The Wrecker"; Comedy, Mar., 1929, Hon. John St. Clair in "Big Fleas ——"; Arts, Nov., 1929, Leslie Dale in "Chinese White"; Comedy, Jan., 1930, Lawrence Trent in "The Way Out"; "Q," June, 1930, Henry Kimball in "Motives"; Sept., 1930, toured as Captain William Trent in "The Cheat"; Savoy, July, 1931, played Gabriel Utterson in "Dr. Jekyll and Mr. Hyde"; Nov., 1932, toured as John Summers in "Recipe for Murder," and appeared in the same part at the Duke of York's, Dec., 1932; Kingsway, Feb., 1934, Sir Anthony Knevett in "The Queen Who Kept her Head"; "Q," Aug., 1934, Hawley Trenmore in "Strangers in Paradise"; Criterion, Dec., 1934, Richard Winthrop in "The Ghost Train"; Phoenix, Mar., 1935, Rev. James Garland in "Glory Be ——"; Ambassadors', Mar., 1936, Jim Malton in "Her Last Adventure"; Arts, June, 1936, Charles Ashton in "When the Bough Breaks"; Winter Garden, Sept., 1936, Howard Scott and Robert Wainwright in "Murder on Account"; Whitehall, Oct., 1937, Sir Temple Brooks in "The Dead Hand"; Duke of York's, Jan., 1938, Count Gathy in "Gentlemen's Agreement"; toured, 1938, as Charles in "Eden End"; Apollo, June, 1941, played Emmerich Hoetzler in "Actresses Will Happen"; St. Martin's, June, 1942, Rev. Alfred Davidson in "Rain"; Opera House, Manchester, Mar., 1943, Sir Philip Durward in "Devil's Own"; has frequently appeared in films. *Recreations:* Tennis and boxing. *Club:* Green Room.
(Died 19 Jan., 1964; age 72)

MULHOLLAND, J. B., manager; *b.* 11 Nov., 1858; made his first appearance on the stage at the Queen's Theatre, Dublin, 1879, in "The Vicar of Wakefield"; in 1880 toured all over Ireland with Charles Wybert; in 1881 joined Miss Maggie Morton; during 1883-4 toured with "The Unknown"; made his first venture into management Aug., 1884, when he took "The Unknown" on tour, commencing at Burnley, also played the leading part, Harold; at Great Grimsby, Jan., 1885, produced "Mizpah," a play written by himself, and toured with it nearly 1,000 nights, the play running altogether over twelve years; at Glasgow, 1887, produced "Disowned," also written by himself; in the spring of 1888 he succeeded to the management of the Grand Theatre, Nottingham, which he retained several years; about 1890 he finally gave up acting; his first venture into London management was made at the Princess's Theatre, Dec., 1891, when, under his management and the stage direction of Henry Neville, he produced "The Swiss Express"; he was the pioneer of the suburban playhouse as we know it to-day, and when he opened The Metropole Theatre, Camberwell, on 29 Oct., 1894, it was the first suburban house to prove successful; its success was so pronounced that no fewer than fourteen new suburban theatres were built within the next six years; among the stars who appeared at the Metropole were the late Sir Henry Irving, John L. Toole, Edward Terry, Sir H. Beerbohm Tree, Forbes-Robertson, Lewis Waller, Mr. and Mrs. Kendal, Ellen Terry, Arthur Bourchier, Seymour Hicks; he was for a period tenant of the Comedy Theatre, where he presented Arthur Roberts and Ada Reeve, and " A Lady of Quality," etc.; in 1903 he opened the King's Theatre, Hammersmith; in 1906 became chairman of the Marlborough Theatre Company; in 1910 opened the theatre at Wimbledon; was Vice-President of the Theatrical Managers' Association. (*Died 2 June, 1925; age 66*)

MUNDIN, Herbert, actor; *b.* St. Helen's, Lancs, 21 Aug., 1898; *s.* of William Mundin and his wife, Elizabeth; *e.* St. Albans Grammar School; *m.* Hilda Hoyes (mar. dis.); was formerly in the Royal Navy (Wireless Section); commenced his stage career with a concert party, at Boulogne, Apr., 1919; made his first appearance, on the regular stage in the provinces when he toured as Dr. Pym in " The Kiss Call "; while appearing with a concert party at Devonshire Park, Eastbourne, was seen by André Charlot, who engaged him, and he made his first appearance in London; at the Prince of Wales's Theatre, 11 Oct., 1921, in " A to Z "; at the Vaudeville, Dec., 1921, played in " Pot Luck "; Aug., 1922, in " Snap "; Feb., 1923, in " Rats "; Sept., 1923, in " Yes "; he then went to America, and at the Times Square Theatre, New York, 9 Jan., 1924, played in, " André Charlot's Revue of 1924 "; reappeared in London at the Prince of Wales's, Mar., 1925, in " Charlot's Revue "; played a further engagement in the same piece in the United States, Oct., 1925; appeared at the Prince of Wales's Oct., 1926, in " The Charlot Show of 1926 "; appeared at the Alhambra in May, 1927; Daly's, Feb., 1928, played Waghorn in " Lady Mary "; went to Australia, 1928, and appeared there in " Hit the Deck," " The Desert Song," etc.; after returning to London, appeared at the London Hippodrome, Apr., 1930, with " The Co-Optimists of

1930 "; Piccadilly, Sept., 1930, played Detective Montague in " Open Your Eyes"; Playhouse, Hollywood, Mar., 1932, Johnny Jelliwell in "Springtime for Henry"; commenced film career, 1930, and has appeared in " East Lynne on the Western Front," " The Wrong Mr. Perkins," " Peace and Quiet," " We Dine at Seven," " The Silent Witness," " The Devil's Lottery," " The Trial of Vivienne Ware," " Bachelor's Affairs," " Life Begins," " Almost Married," " Chandu the Magician," " One Way Passage," " Sherlock Holmes," " Cavalcade," " Dangerously Yours," " Pleasure Cruise," " Adorable," " It's Great to be Alive," " Arizona to Broadway," " The Devil's in Love," " Shanghai Madness," " Hoopla," " Orient Express," " Ever Since Eve," " Bottoms Up," " All Men Are Enemies," " Such Women are Dangerous," " Springtime for Henry," " Call it Luck," " Lovetime," " Hell in the Heavens," " David Copperfield," " Black Sheep," " Ladies Love Danger," " Mutiny on the Bounty," " The Imperfect Lady" (" The Perfect Gentleman"), etc. *Recreations:* Cricket and Association football.
(*Died 5 Mar., 1939; age 40*)

MUNDY, Meg, actress; *b.* London; *d.* of John Mundy and his wife Clytie (Hine); *e.* Dublin, Wadleigh High School, and Institute of Musical Art, New York; *m.* Dino Yannopoulos (mar. dis.); formerly a singer, appearing with several symphony orchestras as soloist, including the New York Philharmonic, under Sir John Barbirolli; made her first appearance on the New York stage, at the St. James Theatre, 23 Oct., 1936, as the secretary in " Ten Million Ghosts"; Winter Garden, Dec., 1937, was in the chorus of " Hooray for What!"; Broadhurst, Oct., 1938, in " The Fabulous Invalid "; Adelphi, Mar., 1946, appeared in the *revue*, " Three to Make Ready"; Hudson, Sept., 1947, played Lisa in " How I Wonder "; Cort, Mar., 1948, Lizzie McKaye in " The Respectful Prostitute"; Hudson, Mar., 1949, Mary McLeod in " Detective Story"; City Center, Feb., 1953, played Rosaline in "Love's Labour's Lost"; Helen

Hayes, Apr., 1958, played Laurie Trumbull in "Love Me Little"; toured, Mar., 1959, as Lizzie in "The Rainmaker"; East 74th Street Theatre (off Broadway), May, 1959, played the title-rôle in "Lysistrata"; has appeared also in summer theatres; has also appeared extensively on television. *Recreations:* Music and cooking.

MUNI, Paul, actor; *b.* Lemberg, Austria, 22 Sept., 1895; *s.* of Philip Weisenfreund and his wife Sally (Weisberg); *e.* Chicago, Ill., U.S.A.; *m.* Bella Finkel; made his first appearance on the stage in 1908, in the Yiddish Theatre "stock" company in New York, and subsequently was a member of the Jewish Art Theatre company in New York; he toured all over the United States and remained on the Yiddish stage until 1926; made his first appearance on the London stage, at the Scala Theatre, 17 Apr., 1924, as Nehamia Kohn in "Sabbethai Zvi," with Maurice Schwartz and his Yiddish Art Theatre company, and subsequently appeared at the Prince of Wales's Theatre; made his first appearance in an English-speaking part, when he appeared at the Eltinge Theatre, 12 Oct., 1926, as Morris Levine in "We Americans"; at the John Golden Theatre, Sept., 1927, played Benny Horowitz in "Four Walls"; Morosco, Oct., 1930, Saul Holland in "This One Man"; Royale, Feb., 1931, Steven Moorhead in "Rock Me, Julie"; Plymouth, Nov., 1931, made a great success as George Simon in "Counsellor-at-Law"; reappeared in the same part at the Plymouth, Sept., 1932; Ethel Barrymore, Nov., 1939, played King McCloud in "Key Largo"; Guild, Apr., 1942, Maddoc Thomas in "Yesterday's Magic," ("The Light of Heart"); Royale, Nov., 1942, again played George Simon in "Counsellor-at-Law"; Alvin, Sept., 1946, played Tevya in "A Flag Is Born"; Music Box, Feb., 1949, Tony in "They Knew What They Wanted"; reappeared in London at the Phoenix, July, 1949, as Willy Loman in "Death of a Salesman"; at the National, New York, Apr., 1955, played Henry Drummond in "Inherit the Wind"; toured, July, 1958, as Kringelein in "At the Grand"; commenced film career, 1929, and has appeared in numerous films, including: "Scarface," "The Story of Louis Pasteur," "The Good Earth," "The Life of Emile Zola," "Commandos Strike at Dawn," "Stage Door Canteen," "The Last Angry Man," etc. *Recreation:* Boxing.
(Died 25 Aug., 1967; age 71)

MUNRO, C. K., dramatic author; *b.* Portrush, Co. Antrim, Ireland, 17 Feb., 1889; *s.* of Samuel James MacMullan and his wife Anne (Marshall Weir); *e.* Harrow and Pembroke College, Cambridge; *m.* Mary Sumner; is the author of "Wanderers," 1915; "The Rumour," 1922; "At Mrs. Beam's," 1923; "Progress," 1924; "Storm," 1924; "The Mountain," 1926; "Cocks and Hens," 1927; "Veronica," 1928; "Mr. Eno, His Birth, Death, and Life," 1930; "Bluestone Quarry," "Bletheroe," 1931; "The True Woman," 1932; "Veronica," 1933; "Ding and Co.," 1934; "Coronationtime at Mrs. Beam's," 1938; also the author of "Watching a Play," 1933. *Favourite play:* Tchekoff's "Uncle Vanya." *Recreations:* Walking and cycling. *Address:* 2 Newtining, Calcott, near Bridgwater, Somerset.

MUNSON, Ona, actress and vocalist; *b.* Portland, Oregon, U.S.A., 16 June, 1906; *d.* of Owen Munson and his wife Sallie (Gore); *e.* Portland; *m.* (1) Eddie Buzzell (mar. dis.); (2) Stewart McDonald; (3) Eugene Berman; made her first appearance on the stage in 1922, appearing on the Keith-Orpheum Vaudeville Circuit in "The Manly Revue"; in 1924 toured in "No Other Girl"; at the Garrick, Philadelphia, Jan., 1925, played Nanette in "No, No, Nanette"; made her first appearance in New York, at the Globe Theatre, 24 May, 1926, succeeding Louise Groody as Nanette in "No, No, Nanette"; at San Francisco, Sept., 1926, played Tip-Toes Kaye in "Tip-Toes"; Liberty, New York, Nov., 1926, Alice James in "Twinkle, Twinkle"; Apollo, Sept., 1927, Mary

Brennan in "Mercenary Mary"; Broadhurst, Oct., 1928, Sue Burke in "Hold Everything"; Columbia, San Francisco, Aug., 1931, played in "As Husbands Go"; El Capitan, Hollywood, Oct., 1931, in "The Silver Cord"; National Washington, Apr., 1932, in "A Church Mouse"; Garrick, Philadelphia, Dec., 1932, appeared in "Pardon My English"; Winter Garden, Sept., 1933, played Marjory Ellis in "Hold Your Horses," with Joe Cook; Chestnut Philadelphia, Dec., 1934, played Clara Wilson in "Petticoat Fever," and played the same part at the Ritz, New York, Mar., 1935; at Carmel, N.Y., July, 1935, Hester Grantham in "The Bishop Misbehaves," Bunty in "The Vortex," Linda Brown in "Accent on Youth"; subsequently toured with Nazimova, as Regina in "Ghosts," and at the Empire, New York, Dec., 1935, played the same part; at Elitch's Gardens, Denver, June, 1937, appeared in "Reflected Glory," and "Hitch Your Wagon"; commenced film career, 1928, and has appeared in numerous pictures. (Died 11 Feb., 1955; age 48)

MURDOCK, Ann, actress (née Irene Coleman); b. Port Washington, Long Island, N.Y., 10 Nov., 1890; d. of John J. Coleman and his wife Teresa (Deagle); e. Philadelphia; m. (1) Harry Carson Powers (mar. dis.); (2) Hallam Keep Williams; made her first appearance on the stage at the Grand Opera House, Pittsburgh, 6 Sept., 1908, as Ardminter Nesbitt, in "The Lion and the Mouse"; made her first appearance in New York, at the Hudson Theatre, 28 Sept., 1908, as Margy North in "The Offenders"; the same year she toured with Robert Edeson as Virginia Albret in "The Call of the North"; at the Criterion, New York, Sept., 1909, appeared as Lucy in "The Noble Spaniard"; at the Lyceum, New York, Oct., 1910, played Ruth Draycott in "Electricity"; at the Gaiety, New York, Feb., 1911, Marjorie Newton in "Excuse Me"; at the Garrick, New York, Oct., 1911, Mrs. Abrams in "The Sign of the Rose"; at Thirty-ninth Street Theatre, Feb., 1913, Natalie Marshall in "The Bridal Path"; at the

Harris Theatre, Nov., 1913, Gertrude in "Miss Phoenix"; at the Longacre, Mar., 1914, appeared as Florence Cole in "A Pair of Sixes"; at the Lyceum, New York, Sept., 1914, as Hélène de Trevillac in "The Beautiful Adventure"; at the Empire, New York, Apr., 1915, played Adrienne in the "all-star" revival of "A Celebrated Case"; at Utica, N.Y., Apr., 1916, played Suki in a play of that name; at the Lyceum, New York, Aug., 1916, appeared as Emily Delmar in "Please Help Emily"; at the Empire, New York, Nov., 1917, as Sylvia Weston in "The Three Bears."

MURFIN, Jane, dramatic author; b. Quincy, Mich., U.S.A.; e. Ypsilanti, Mich., and in France and Italy; m Donald Crisp; in collaboration with Jane Cowl is the author of "Lilac Time," 1917; "Information Please," 1918; "Smilin' Through," 1919; and "Daybreak"; author of "Stripped," 1929; subsequently became a scenario writer for films. (Died 10 Aug., 1955)

MURRAY, Alma, actress; b. London, 21 Nov., 1854; d. of Leigh Murray, actor; e. privately; m. Alfred Forman; made her first appearance on the stage at the Olympic Theatre, 8 Jan, 1870, as Saccharissa in "The Princess"; in 1872 appeared at the Royalty in "High Life Below Stairs," "The Blue Faced Shore," "As You Like It," "Janet's Ruse," etc.; appeared at Drury Lane, 1872, in pantomime; at the Adelphi, 1873, in "The Wandering Jew"; at the Princess's, 1874, in "Beauty and the Beast"; in 1875 appeared there in "The Lancashire Lass," "Round the World in Eighty Days," etc.; from 1875 to 1877, toured in the provinces; at the Adelphi, 1877, played in "The Golden Plough"; at Drury Lane, 1877, in "England"; at Adelphi, 1877, in "After Dark," "Formosa," and "The Deal Boatman"; in 1879, toured as Esther in "Caste"; in June, 1879, appeared with Henry Irving at Lyceum as Julie de Mortemar in "Richelieu," Jessica and Portia in "Merchant of Venice," Annette in "Bells," Julie in "The Lyons

Mail," Daisy and Ruby in Pinero's "Daisy's Escape," and "Bygones"; from 1881 to 1883, appeared at the Vaudeville, as Sophia in "The Road to Ruin," Julia in "The Rivals," Grace Harkaway in "London Assurance," Clara Douglas in "Money"; at the Olympic, 1883, played in "The Spider's Web"; in 1884, at the Prince's Hall, she appeared in Browning's play "In a Balcony," in the same year played Juliet at Edinburgh; at the St. George's Hall, Nov., 1885, appeared as Colombe in Browning's "Colombe's Birthday"; at the Grand, Islington, May, 1886, secured a triumph, when she played Beatrice in the single performance of Shelley's play "The Cenci"; at Hengler's Circus, 1886, played Helena in "Helena in Troas"; at the Crystal Palace, in the same year, played Titania in "A Midsummer Night's Dream"; at Drury Lane, Aug., 1886, played Daisy Copsley in "A Run of Luck"; at the Princess's, Apr., 1887, appeared as Rachel McCreery in "Held by the Enemy"; at Drury Lane, Sept., 1887, played Jessie Newland in "Pleasure"; at the Olympic, Mar., 1888, played the title-*rôle* in "Christina," and gained another triumph, as Mildred in Browning's drama, "A Blot in the 'Scutcheon"; at the Globe, Oct., 1888, played Eleanor in "The Monk's Room"; in 1889, appeared at the Adelphi, as Violet Chester in "London Day by Day"; during 1890, played at various *matinées*; at the Vaudeville, July, 1891, played Clarissa in "The Sequel"; at the Avenue, Apr., 1894, played Raina in Bernard Shaw's "Arms and the Man"; at the Comedy, Sept., 1894, played Mrs. Sylvester in "The New Woman"; in 1897, appeared at the Metropole, Camberwell, as Rosalind in "As You Like It"; in 1902, appeared at the Criterion, in her old part in "The Sequel"; at the Pavilion, 1903, played Marion Grey in "The Woman from Gaol"; at His Majesty's, July, 1905, played Mrs. Maylie in "Oliver Twist"; in 1906, toured as Anna in "The Prodigal Son"; at the Aldwych Theatre, Oct., 1908, played Jane Bennett in "Fanny and the Servant

Problem"; at the Garrick, Sept., 1910, played Kerry in "The Bishop's Son"; at the Lyceum, July, 1911, appeared as Queen Geneviève in "Pelleas and Mélisande"; appeared at His Majesty's, June, 1912, in her old part of Mrs. Maylie in "Oliver Twist"; at the Court Theatre, Sept., 1913, played Mrs. Dedmond in "The Fugitive"; at His Majesty's, June, 1914, Mrs. Eynsford-Hill in "Pygmalion"; at the St. James's, Jan. 1915, Baroness de Lisle in "Kings and Queens"; at His Majesty's, Apr., 1915, again played Mrs. Maylie in "Oliver Twist"; for many years was one of the best exponents of poetical drama and tragedy in England; is one of the pensioners of King George's Pension Fund for Actors. *Recreations :* Reading, country walks, and observing character. *(Died 3 July, 1945; age 90)*

MURRAY, Douglas, dramatic author; has written the following, among other plays: "A Sentimental Cuss," 1907; "The Great Mrs. Alloway," 1909; "Kit," 1911; "The New Duke," 1913; "A Fine Bit o' Work," 1916; "Burgess Decides," 1917; "The Man from Toronto," 1918; "Uncle Ned," 1919; "Sarah of Soho," 1922; "The Eternal Quest," 1925; "What Fools We Are," and "Time and the Hour," 1929; "Gingerbread's Partner," 1933; "The King's Highway," 1934.
(Died 6 Aug., 1936; age 73)

MURRAY, George Gilbert Aimé, O.M., LL.D., Lit.D., F.B.A.; litterateur and dramatist; *b.* Sydney, New South Wales, 2 Jan., 1866; *s.* of the late Sir Terence Aubrey Murray, President of the Legislative Council, New South Wales; *e.* Merchant Taylors' School, and St. John's College, Oxford; Fellow of New College, Oxford, 1888; Professor of Greek, Glasgow University 1889-99; Regius Professor of Greek, Oxford University, 1908–36; *m.* Mary *e.d.* of the Earl of Carlisle (dec.); author of plays: "Carlyon Sahib," 1899; "Andromache," 1900; translated the "Hippolytus" of Euripides, produced at Court 1904;

WHO WAS WHO IN THE THEATRE

" The Trojan Women," Court, 1905 ; the " Electra " of Euripides, Court, 1906, and " Medea " of Euripides, Savoy, 1907 ; " The Bacchæ " of Euripides, Court, 1908 ; " Œdipus Rex," Covent Garden, 1912 ; " Iphigenia in Tauris," Kingsway, 1912 ; has also translated many other plays, and reconstructed Menander's fragmentary comedies, "The Rape of the Locks," 1943, and "The Arbitration," 1946 ; translated "The Wife of Heracles," 1948 ; has also written a History of Greek Literature ; published "Collected Plays of Euripides," 1955. *Clubs :* Athenæum and National Liberal. *(Died 20 May, 1957; age 91)*

MURRAY, J. Harold, actor and vocalist; *b.* South Berwick, Maine, U.S.A., 17 Feb., 1891 ; *e.* Boston, Mass., U.S.A. ; made his first appearance in public as a boy ballad-vocalist; was subsequently employed in a music-publishing business; in 1918, entered " vaudeville," and remained two years ; made his first appearance on the regular stage at the Winter Garden, New York, 29 Dec., 1920, in "The Passing Show of 1921"; at the Century Promenade, Feb., 1921, played in "The Midnight Rounders of 1921"; Winter Garden, June, 1921, Harry Bronson in "The Whirl of New York"; Apr., 1922, appeared there in "Make It Snappy"; Broadhurst, Oct., 1922, played Richard Stokes in "The Springtime of Youth"; Ambassador, Jan., 1923, Captain Robert Langdon in "Caroline"; Shubert, Mar., 1924, played in "Vogues of 1924"; at the Martin Beck Theatre, Jan., 1925, played Cha-Ming in "China Rose"; Sept., 1925, Captain Robert Jinks in "Captain Jinks"; Selwyn, Sept., 1926, John Brown in "Castles in the Air"; Ziegfeld, Feb., 1927, Jim in "Rio Rita," in which he played two years; Manhattan, Oct., 1931, Captain Paul Beauvais in "East Wind"; New Amsterdam, Feb., 1932, Pat Mason Jun. in "Face the Music"; St. James, Dec., 1934, appeared in "Thumbs Up"; at Pittsburgh, Oct., 1935, played the Stranger in "Venus in Silk"; commenced film career 1929, and has appeared in "Married in Hollywood,"

"Cameo Kirby," "Happy Days," "Women Everywhere," "Under Suspicion," etc. *(Died 11 Dec., 1940; age 49)*

MURRAY, Paul, manager; *b.* Cork, Ireland, 15 July, 1885; *e.* St. Malachy's College, Belfast; has presented the following plays in London: " The Charm School," 1920; with Andre Charlot presented " A to Z," " Pot Luck," 1921 ; " Dédé," " Snap," 1922 ; with Jack Hulbert, presented "By-the-Way," 1924; "Lido Lady," 1926; "Clowns in Clover," 1927 ; "Follow a Star," 1930 ; "Folly to be Wise," 1931 ; has since interested himself in films. *Recreation :* Golf. *Club :* Stage Golfing Society. *(Died 17 Oct., 1949; age 64)*

MURRAY, Peter, actor; *b.* London, 19 Sept., 1925; *s.* of Henry James and his wife Violet Carolyn (Reece); *e.* St. Paul's, Hammersmith; studied for the stage at the Royal Academy of Dramatic Art, 1942–3, and was Bronze Medallist, 1943; made his first appearance on the stage, at the "Q" Theatre, Apr., 1943, as Bobbie Townsend in "Marigold"; the following month, appeared at the Arts Theatre, Cambridge, in "The Idiot"; at the Savoy, Aug., 1943, played Richard Stanley in "The Man Who Came to Dinner"; after the War, appeared at the "Q," June, 1945, as Charles in "Oflag 3," and Aug., 1946, as Léon Dupuis in "Madame Bovary"; made his first appearance in New York, at the Shubert Theatre, 13 Jan., 1948, as Cliff in "Power Without Glory"; on his return, appeared at the Embassy, May, 1948, as Slim in "Symphony in Violence"; Duchess, Nov., 1948, Peter in "Miss Mabel"; "Q," Sept., 1949, played Tom Gillies in "Marriage Playground"; first appeared in films, 1945, in "Caravan." *Recreations :* Swimming, cricket, and theatre-going. *Club :* Albany. *Address :* c/o Herbert de Leon, Ltd., 30 South Audley Street, W.1.

MURRAY, T. C., dramatic author ; *b.* County Cork; *e.* St. Patrick's Train-

ing College, Dublin; is the author of the following plays produced by the Irish National Theatre Society: "The Wheel of Fortune," 1909; "Birthright," 1910; "Maurice Harte," 1912; "Sovereign Love," 1913; "Spring," 1918; "The Briery Gap," 1917; "Aftermath," 1922; "Autumn Fire," 1924; "The Pipe in the Fields," 1927; "The Blind Wolf," 1928; "A Flutter of Wings," 1930; "Michaelmas Eve," 1932; "A Spot in the Sun," 1938; "Illumination," 1939; was Headmaster of Inchicore Model Schools, Dublin; now retired; President of the Irish Playwrights' Association; Member of the Irish Academy of Letters; Member of the Film Censorship Appeal Board (Ireland).
(Died Apr., 1959; age 86)

MUSGROVE, Gertrude, actress and vocalist; *b.* London, 9 Sept., 1912; *d.* of Octavius Archibald Musgrove and his wife Anne Ethel (Harrison); *e.* Seaford Ladies' College; *m.* Vincent Korda; studied for the stage at the Royal Academy of Dramatic Art; made her first appearance on the stage at the Savoy Theatre, 1931, succeeding Ethel Baird as Electra Pivonka in "Wonder Bar"; Globe, June, 1932, played Greta Galla in "Men About the House"; His Majesty's, Nov., 1934, Mrs. Richards in "Mary Read"; Comedy, May, 1935, appeared in "Shall We Reverse?"; Vaudeville, Sept., 1935, in "Stop—Go!"; Dec., 1935, Queen Arabella in "What a Witch!"; Mar., 1936, in "The Town Talks"; Ambassadors', Aug., 1936, played Patty Moss in "The Two Bouquets"; Vaudeville, Dec., 1936, again played in "What a Witch!"; Westminster (for the Stage Society), Apr., 1937, Angelica in a play of that name; Piccadilly, Dec., 1937, Hazel Campbell in "Talk of the Devil"; Whitehall, Dec., 1939, Observa in "Who's Taking Liberty?"; subsequently went to New York; made her first appearance in New York at the Henry Miller Theatre, Feb., 1942, as Judy in "Heart of a City"; Ethel Barrymore, Dec., 1942, Irina in "The Three Sisters"; Belasco, Jan., 1944, Lt. Thomasina Grey in "Storm Opera-

tion"; entered films, 1933, and has appeared in numerous pictures in England and in Hollywood. *Recreation:* Swimming.

"MY FANCY," dancer (*née* Mae Rose Baker); *b.* St. Louis, Mo., U.S.A., 23 May, 1878; *m.* Harry Bawn; commenced dancing, when a small child of eight years of age, joining a travelling company, and appearing with another child as "The Macumber Sisters"; was subsequently a trapeze artiste, acrobat, and illusionist; made her first appearance in London, under her own name, at the London Pavilion, 17 Dec., 1894; was subsequently engaged at the Oxford, where she first assumed the title of "My Fancy," 25 Mar., 1895; has since appeared at the principal variety theatres all over the world; appeared at the opening of Hammerstein's Olympia, New York, 1896; toured in Australia, 1897-8 and 1912-13, and also fulfilled engagements at the Folies Bergères, Paris; has visited Egypt, Ceylon, India, South Africa, and Australia; is considered one of the finest sand-dancers in the world. *Address:* Empire Buildings, Edmonton. *Telephone No.:* Museum 608.

MYERS, Richard, producer and composer; *b.* Philadelphia, Pa., 25 Mar., 1901; *s.* of Milton Myers and his wife Alice (Foster); *e.* William Penn Charter School; *m.* (1) Carolyn Preble Smith (dec.); (2) Suzanne Royer (dec.); (3) Countess Suzanne de Gozaloff (mar. dis.); (4) Henriette Bisserier; contributed music to the following among other productions: "Greenwich Village Follies," 1925 and 1926; "Allez-Oop," 1927; "Night Hostess," "Hello, Yourself," 1928; "The Street Singer," 1929; "Ruth Selwyn's 9:15 Revue," "Garrick Gaieties," 1930; "Here Goes the Bride," 1931; "Earl Carroll Vanities," "Americana," 1932; "Murder at the Vanities," 1933; "Ziegfeld Follies," "The Pure in Heart," 1934; "The Ziegfeld Follies," 1957; presented "I Want a Policeman" (with Francis Curtis), 1936; in conjunction with Richard Aldrich, presented "Tide Rising," "Be So Kindly!", 1937;

"Lorelei," 1938; "The Importance of Being Earnest," "Margin for Error," 1939; "My Dear Children," "Cue for Passion," 1940; "Plan M.," 1942; with Max Reinhardt and Norman Bel Geddes presented "Sons and Soldiers," 1943; alone he presented "Mrs. January and Mr. Ex," 1944; in conjunction with Lester Meyer presented "Calico Wedding," 1945; with Richard Aldrich presented the Dublin Gate Theatre Company, 1948; "Goodbye, My Fancy," 1948; "Caesar and Cleopatra," 1949; "The Devil's Disciple," 1950; "Four Twelves Are 48," 1951; with Julius Fleischmann presented "The Moon Is Blue," 1951; "A Girl Can Tell," and, with Richard Aldrich, "The Love of Four Colonels," 1953; "Dear Charles," 1954; co-produced the following: "Little Glass Clock," 1956; "Hotel Paradiso," 1957; "Interlock," 1958; "Requiem for a Nun," 1959; "Jack Be Nimble!" at the Ogunquit, Maine, Playhouse, 1966. *Clubs:* Piping Rock, Regency Coffee House, New York; The Travellers', Paris, France. *Address:* 156 East 79th Street, New York City, N.Y., 10021, U.S.A.

MYRTIL, Odette, actress and violinist; *b.* Paris, 28 June, 1898; *d.* of Charles Quinguard; *e.* France; *m.* (1) Bob Adams of the Two Bobs (mar. dis.); (2) Stanley Logan (dec.); made her first appearance on the stage at Olympia, Paris, in 1911, as a violinist, subsequently touring the principal European cities; made her first appearance in New York at the New Amsterdam Theatre, Sept., 1914, in "The Follies of 1914"; at the Winter Garden, June, 1915, appeared in "The Ziegfeld Follies of 1915"; made her first appearance in London, at the Alhambra, 28 Feb., 1916, as a singer and violinist; at the same theatre, Apr., 1916, played in "The Bing Boys Are Here"; during 1917 toured in "Ciro's Frolics"; at the Vaudeville,

June, 1918, appeared in "Tabs"; appeared at the Comedy, 1918, in "Bubbly" and "Tails Up"; at the St. Martin's, Nov., 1918, played Cora Merville in "The Officers' Mess"; at the Prince of Wales's, Aug., 1919, played in "Bran-Pie"; at the Apollo, Paris, Dec., 1920, played Venus in "La Ceinture de Vénus"; during 1921 toured in "Bran-Pie"; at the Court Theatre, Mar., 1923, played in "Carte Blanche"; at the London Pavilion, May, 1923, in "Dover Street to Dixie"; at the Shubert Theatre, New York, Mar., 1924, in Vogues "of 1924"; New Century, Jan., 1925, Hortense in "The Love Song"; Shubert, Sept., 1926, Manja in "Countess Maritza," in which she continued until 1928, appearing in a revival of the piece at the Century, Apr., 1928; at the Shubert, Sept., 1928, played Madame George Sand in "White Lilacs"; 44th Street Theatre, July. 1929, played Marian La Varve in "Broadway Nights"; Globe, Oct., 1931, Odette in "The Cat and the Fiddle," in which she continued, 1932; at the New Amsterdam, July, 1934, succeeded Lyda Roberti as Clementina in "Roberta"; Ziegfeld, Oct., 1945, played Madame La Fleur in "The Red Mill"; at the Greek Theatre, Los Angeles, in the summer of 1950, played the Countess in "Miss Liberty"; during 1951 appeared as an entertainer in night clubs; at the Majestic, New York, Jan., 1952, succeeded Musa Williams as Bloody Mary in "South Pacific"; National, Feb., 1953, played Mme. Marstonne in "Maggie"; Winter Garden, Dec., 1959, Belle Piquery in "Saratoga"; in summer theatre, June, 1960, played Madame La Four in "Operation Mad Bull"; films include: "Dodsworth," 1936; "I Married an Angel," 1942; "Rhapsody in Blue," 1945; "Here Comes the Groom," 1951; since 1961 has been proprietress of the Inn Chez Odette in New Hope, Pa.; was a well-known dress designer in Beverly Hills. *Address:* Sugan Road, New Hope, Pennsylvania, U.S.A.

NAGEL, Conrad, actor; *b.* Keokuk, Iowa, U.S.A., 16 Mar., 1897; *s.* of Frank Nagel, Mus.D., and his wife Frances (Murphy); *e.* Des Moines, Iowa; *m.* (1) Ruth Helms (mar. dis.); (2) Lynn Merrick (mar. dis.); made his first appearance on the stage with the Peerless "stock" company at Des Moines, 1914; appeared in "Experience," "The Natural Law," and in 1917 in Chicago played in "The Man Who Came Back"; subsequently, during the latter part of the War, served in the U.S. Navy; at the Central, New York, 9 Sept., 1918, played Ted in "For Ever After"; spent the next fourteen years in films; reappeared on the stage in the autumn of 1933, when he toured as Gilbert Carey in "The First Apple"; appeared at the Booth Theatre, New York, Dec., 1933, in the same part; in Feb., 1934, toured as Kenneth Bixby in "Good-Bye, Again," and in Apr., 1934, as David Linden in "The Shining Hour"; at the Geary, San Francisco, 1935, played Alan Squier in "The Petrified Forest"; Pilgrimage Bowl, Hollywood, Sept., 1938, Faust in Max Reinhardt's production of that play; toured, 1941, in "The Male Animal," and 1942, as Colonel Lanser in "The Moon Is Down"; Plymouth Theatre, New York, May, 1943, succeeded Fredric March as Mr. Antrobus in "The Skin of Our Teeth"; N.Y. City Center, Dec., 1943, Barrie Trexel in "Susan and God"; Ethel Barrymore, Mar., 1944, succeeded Ralph Bellamy as Michael Frame in "To-Morrow the World": Playhouse, Jan., 1945, played David in "A Goose for the Gander": toured, 1945, in "To-Morrow the World"; toured, 1946–7, as Grant Matthews in "State of the Union," and at the Hudson, New York, May, 1947, succeeded Ralph Bellamy in the same part; in summer theatres, 1947, played Alan Squier in "The Petrified Forest"; Henry Miller Theatre, June, 1948, succeeded John Loder as Preston Mitchell in "For Love or Money"; Morosco, Nov., 1948, played James Merrill in "Goodbye, My Fancy"; Ziegfeld, Oct., 1951, played Ernst Webber in a revival of "Music in the Air"; 48th Street, Jan., 1953, played Eliot Spurgeon in "Be Your Age"; Cort, Sept., 1957, played Gage in "Four Winds"; in summer theatres, 1958, played Anthony Drexel-Biddle in "The Happiest Millionaire"; toured in Canada and the U.S., 1959–60, as Jim Dougherty in "The Pleasure of His Company"; Bucks County Playhouse, New Hope, Pa., Aug., 1960, John Nichols in "Happy Ending"; Playhouse, Jan., 1962, Admiral Bradley in "The Captain and the Kings"; President of Associated Actors and Artistes of America; first appeared in films, 1919, in "Little Women," and has since played in innumerable films, including: "Tess of the D'Urbevilles," 1924; "Three Weeks," 1926; "The Jazz Singer," 1927; "Forever Yours," 1937; "The Adventures of Rusty," 1945; "Ride a Tiger," 1954; "Stage Struck," 1958. *Recreations:* Reading and collecting books. *Clubs:* Lambs, New York; Masquers' and Beach, Los Angeles.
(Died 24 Feb., 1970; age 72)

NAINBY, Robert, actor; *b.* Dublin, 14 June, 1869; made his first appearance on the stage at the Pier Theatre, Hastings, in 1887, in the pantomime " Blue Beard "; made his first appearance on the London stage at the Strand Theatre, 4 Apr., 1888, as Archdeacon Grimm in " Airey Annie "; he remained at this theatre under Willie Edouin until 1891, appearing in " His Wives," " Kleptomania," " Run Wild," " Aladdin," " Our Flat," etc.; next appeared at the Royalty Theatre, Jan., 1892, as Jakes in " The Showman's Daughter "; at the Court Theatre, 1892–4, played in " The Guardsman," " The Amazons," " The Other Fellow," " Faithful James," " Good-Bye," and " Under the Clock "; was next engaged by George Edwardes for the Gaiety and appeared there from 1894–8, in " Don Juan," " The Shop Girl," " My Girl," " The Circus Girl," and " The Runaway Girl "; appeared at the Comedy, Sept., 1898, in " The Topsy-Turvy Hotel," and at the Avenue, June, 1899, in " Pot-Pourri "; returned to the Gaiety, Feb., 1900, to appear in " The Messenger Boy "; subsequently playing in

"The Toreador," 1901 ; "The Orchid," 1903 ; "The Spring Chicken," 1905 ; "The New Aladdin," 1906 ; "The Girls of Gottenburg," 1907 ; appeared at Daly's, Dec., 1908, as Novikovitch in "The Merry Widow " ; from 1909–11 toured in "The Merry Widow," " Our Miss Gibbs," and " The Quaker Girl " ; again returned to the Gaiety, Feb., 1912, when he played Stepneyak in "The Sunshine Girl " ; Apr., 1913, Doddie in "The Girl on the Film " ; at the Shubert Theatre, New York, Dec., 1914, played Archibald in " To-Night's the Night," and Apr., 1915, at the Gaiety, London, played the same part (re-named Alphonse) when the play was produced there ; at the Gaiety, Sept., 1916, played Crump in " Theodore and Co." ; at the Prince of Wales's, Dec., 1917, appeared as Diablo Casablanca in "Yes, Uncle " ; at the Shaftesbury, Sept., 1919, as Proop in "Baby Bunting " ; at the Gaiety, Mar., 1920, appeared in his original part of Count St. Vaurien in the revival of "The Shop Girl " ; at Daly's, May, 1921, succeeded Leonard Mackay as The Governor in " Sybil " ; at the Empire, Sept., 1922, played the Prime Minister in "The Smith Family " ; at the Lyric, Dec., 1922, Novotny in " Lilac Time " ; Shaftesbury, June, 1925, Chablis in " Clo-Clo " ; then toured as M. Gaudet in " Fivers " ; Lyric, Dec., 1925, again played Novotny in " Lilac Time " ; Gaiety, Nov., 1927, M. Renaud in " The Girl from Cook's " ; Daly's, Dec., 1927, again appeared in " Lilac Time " ; Palace, June, 1928, played Mr. Burke in " The Girl Friend " ; Oct., 1928, Bournet in "Virginia" ; Palace, Nov., 1929, Mr. Scantlebury in "Dear Love"; Daly's, Sept., 1930, General de Arredondo in "Eldorado"; Prince's, Nov., 1930, Rupert Boddy in "Oh, Daddy !"; Alhambra, Aug., 1931, Ferdinand Wesseley in "Waltzes from Vienna"; "Q," Dec., 1934, Robin Turgis and Petit Jean in "If I Were King"; Shaftesbury, June, 1935, Celestine Maraval in "Accidentally Yours"; Savoy, Oct., 1936, Thomas Bax in "Going Places ——"; commenced film career, 1934, in "My Old Dutch"; since 1936, has appeared in "All In," "Wise Guys,"

"Crackerjack," "Public Nuisance No. 1," "When Knights Were Bold," "Chick," "Land Without Music," "Mademoiselle Docteur," "We're Going To Be Rich," etc.
(Died 17 Feb., 1948; age 78)

NAISH, Archie, entertainer ; *b.* Huntingdonshire, 12 Apr., 1878 ; *s.* of Ebenezer John Naish and his wife Ada Sarah (Clark) ; *e.* Kent College, Canterbury ; formerly engaged as an organist ; made his first professional appearance, Jan., 1904, as an entertainer at the piano ; in Oct., 1908, was engaged by Maskelyne and Devant at the St. George's Hall ; during 1909, appeared at the Coliseum and Hippodrome, and has since appeared at a number of West End theatres and music halls, and some of the principal variety houses in the provinces ; has several successful songs to his credit, and is the author and composer of "The Village Pump " ; "Won't you waltz with me ? " ; " Sybil " ; " The Employment Bureau " ; " The Duck Pond " ; "Made in England," etc. *Address :* 106 Great Russell Street, W.C. *Telephone No. :* Museum 2347.

NAPIER, Alan, actor ; *b.* Harborne, Birmingham, 7 Jan., 1903 ; *s.* of Claude Gerald Napier-Clavering and his wife Millicent Mary (Kenrick) ; *e.* Packwood Haugh, and Clifton College ; *m.* Emily Nancy Bevill (Pethybridge) ; studied for the stage at the Royal Academy of Dramatic Art ; made his first appearance on the stage at the Playhouse, Oxford, May, 1924, as the Policeman in "Dandy Dick," under J. B. Fagan ; made his first appearance in London at the Ambassadors', 13 Aug., 1924, as Professor Bolland in "Storm"; Mar., 1925, played the Rev. John Williams in "A Comedy of Good and Evil"; Lyric, Hammersmith, May, 1925, Leonid Gayef in "The Cherry Orchard"; in 1926, was a member of the repertory company, at the Theatre Royal, Huddersfield; Queen's, Sept., 1926, played the Pick-purse in "And So to Bed"; Globe, June, 1927, The Colonel in "The Spook Sonata"; during 1927, appeared at Glasgow ;

Vaudeville, May, 1928, Boris Waberski in "The House of the Arrow"; Arts, July, 1928, Colonel Tripp in "Down Wind"; Everyman, Sept., 1928, the Episcopal Vicar in "Ginevra"; Strand, Nov., 1928, Ernie Dunstan in "Out of the Sea"; Dec., 1928, Dr. Knock in a revival of the play of that name; in 1929, toured in "Loyalties," and "Justice"; at His Majesty's, July, 1929, played the Marquis of Shayne in "Bitter Sweet"; Daly's, Jan., 1930, Everard Webley in "This Way to Paradise"; Savoy, Apr., 1930, the Professor in "Brain"; Arts, July, 1930, Pharmaceutis in "The Devil and the Lady"; New, Sept., 1930, Edward IV in "Richard III"; Gate, Jan., 1931, the Earl of Dorincourt in "Little Lord Fauntleroy"; Haymarket, June, 1931, Claude Spencer in "Marry at Leisure"; Royalty, Oct., 1931, the Venetian Ambassador in "The Immortal Lady"; Savoy (for Repertory Players), Nov., 1931, Sir Henry Cosham in "A-Hunting We Will Go"; Grafton, Nov., 1931, Nasmyth Sheldon in "The Home Front"; Wyndham's, Feb., 1932, Mark Elliott in "The Green Pack"; Playhouse, Aug., 1932, Lovasdy in "Firebird"; Little, Feb., 1933, Absalon in "The Witch"; Arts, Mar., 1933, and Westminster, Apr., 1933, John Clayne in "The Lake"; Shaftesbury, Nov., 1933, Richard Greatham in "Hay Fever"; Westminster, Feb., 1934, Mr. Wise in "Private Room"; Fulham, May, 1934, Sir John Craig in "Forsaking All Others"; Embassy, May, 1934, Mr. Lennox in "The Roof"; Wyndham's, Oct., 1934, Lord Farrington in "Sweet Aloes"; New, Oct., 1935, the Prince of Verona in "Romeo and Juliet"; Vaudeville, Sept., 1936, Gray Blackett in "Gentle Rain"; Westminster, Nov., 1936, Hialmar Ekdal in "The Wild Duck"; Wyndham's, Feb., 1937, Sir Basil Graham in "Because We Must"; Westminster, Mar., 1937, Hector Hushabye in "Heartbreak House"; Strand, June, 1937, General Rakovski in "Judgment Day"; Westminster, Feb.–Mar., 1938, Hugh Gifford in "Land's End" and Michael in "The Zeal of Thy House"; Savoy, June, 1938, Boris Rachinoff in "No Sky So Blue"; Playhouse, Nov., 1938, The

King in "The Shoemaker's Holiday"; Haymarket, Dec., 1938, Sir Francis Chesney in "Charley's Aunt"; at the Martin Beck Theatre, New York, Mar., 1940, played Sir William Warring in "Lady in Waiting"; Las Palmas, Los Angeles, 1948, appeared as Charles II in "And So To Bed"; at the Plymouth, New York, Jan., 1952, played Mr. Ritchie in "Gertie"; at Boston, Dec., 1952, appeared as Insp. Hubbard in "Dial 'M' For Murder"; Phoenix, New York, Jan., 1954, played Menenius Agrippa in "Coriolanus"; Belasco, New York, Oct., 1956, played Captain Massingham in "Too Late the Phalarope"; has also appeared in numerous films; has appeared frequently for the Stage Society. Repertory Players, etc. *Favourite parts:* Captain Shotover in "Heartbreak House," and Marquis of Shayne in "Bitter Sweet." *Recreations:* Reading, gardening, and motoring. *Address:* c/o *The Spotlight*, 43 Cranbourn Street, London, W.C.2.

NAPIERKOWSKA, Stanislawa, or **Stasia** ; *danseuse ;* b. Constantinople ; studied dancing at the National Academy, Paris ; made her first appearance on the stage in the ballet at the Opéra Comique, Paris, 18 Dec., 1907, in "Jeux Athlétiques"; next appeared 1909, at the Folies Bergères, Dossiers," "Jaunes," "Raymonde" (with A. Theuriet), 1887 ; "Griselidis" (with Armand Silvestre), 1891 ; "Les Drames Sacrés" (with Silvestre, music by Gounod), 1893 ; "Izeyl" (with Silvestre), 1894 ; "Kosacks !" (with Silvestre), 1898 ; "La Tragique Histoire d'Hamlet" ("Hamlet," with Apr., 1910, appeared in "Le Mariage de Télémaque"; Sept., 1910, in "La Reine Fiammette"; in 1911, appeared at the Folies Bergères in "Les Ailes"; made her first appearance in London at the Palace Theatre, 6 Nov., 1911 ; at the Folies Bergères, Mar., 1912, appeared in "Enfin ... une Revue ! ! !"

NARES, Geoffrey, actor and designer; b. London, 10 June, 1917; s. of Owen Nares and his wife Marie (Polini) ; e. Westminster School; made his first appearance on the stage at the Adelphi

Theatre, 17 Dec., 1934, as the Stable Boy in "The Winning Post," with an "all-star" cast, in aid of King George's Pension Fund for Actors; Globe Theatre, June, 1935, played Kim Oldham in "Grief Goes Over"; Globe, Oct., 1935, Martin Hilton in "Call It A Day," which ran over a year; Globe, Oct. 1937, Smith in "Blondie White"; has designed scenery and settings for "Girl Unknown," 1936; "Candida," "The Road to Rome," "George and Margaret," "The Constant Wife," "Time and the Conways," "Blondie White," 1937; "Gaily We Set Out," 1938. *Recreations:* Tennis and painting. *(Died 20 Aug., 1942; age 25)*

NARES, Owen, actor and producer; *b.* Maiden Erleigh, 11 Aug., 1888; *s.* of William Owen Nares and his wife, Sophie Marguerite (Beverley); *g.s.* of William Roxby Beverley, the famous scene-painter; *e.* Reading School; *m.* Marie Polini; studied for the stage under Rosina Filippi, for a period of six months; made his first appearance on the stage at the Haymarket Theatre, 28 Jan., 1908, walking on in the production of "Her Father"; toured for a year as Harry Leyton in "The Thief"; appeared at the St. James's, May, 1909, in "Old Heidelberg," and Sept., 1909, in "Mid-Channel"; in 1910 toured as Karl Heinrich in "Old Heidelberg"; appeared at the Little Theatre, Jan., 1911, as Bobby Lechmere in "The Saloon," and at the Court, Jan., 1911, in "John Gabriel Borkman"; at the Comedy, June, 1911, Kenyon Shrawardine in "The Crucible"; at the St. James's, Sept., 1911, Tony Sitgrave in "The Ogre"; Oct., 1911, Cecil Graham in "Lady Windermere's Fan"; at the Little Theatre, Jan., 1912, appeared as the Hon. Archibald Graham in "The Blindness of Virtue"; at the Royalty, Mar., 1912, played Lord Monkhurst in "Milestones"; at the Prince's, Mar., 1912, Hugo Haist in "The Fool and the Wise Man"; at the Haymarket, Mar., 1912, Noel Frobisher in "An Object Lesson"; at the Royalty, May, 1912, Peter Grieve in "Peter's Chance"; at the Court, Nov., 1912,

Braun in "Lonely Lives"; at Wyndham's, Mar., 1913, Julian Beauclerc in "Diplomacy"; at His Majesty's, 22 May, 1914, played Frank Selwyn in the "all-star" revival of "The Silver King," given in aid of King George's Actors' Pension Fund; at the Haymarket, June, 1914, Captain Furness in "Driven"; at the Vaudeville, Oct., 1914, John Woodhouse in "The Cost"; at His Majesty's, Nov., 1914, Henry, Prince of Wales, in "King Henry IV" (part I); Dec., 1914, the title-*rôle* in "David Copperfield"; at Covent Garden, 2 Feb., 1915, Sir Toby in the "all-star" revival of "The School for Scandal," given in aid of the Actors' Benevolent Fund; at the St. James's, Apr., 1915, Geoffrey Annandale in "The Panorama of Youth"; May, 1915, 2nd Lieut. Robert Cresfield in "The Day Before the Day"; at the Little Theatre, May, 1915, Louis in "Foolery"; at the Coliseum, June, 1915, Gerald in "The Way to Win"; at the Haymarket, 2 July, 1915, The Prince in "The Princess and the Pea"; at His Majesty's, 5 July, 1915, Thomas Cromwell in the "all-star" revival of "King Henry VIII," given in aid of King George's Actors' Pension Fund; 23 July, 1915, Peter in "Peter Ibbetson"; at the Duke of York's, Oct., 1915, played the Bishop and Thomas Armstrong in "Romance"; at the Globe, Oct., 1917, Edward Hamilton in "The Willow Tree"; at the Palace, Dec., 1917, Guy Tremayne in "Pamela"; at the Victoria Palace, Sept., 1918, Philip in "The Boy Comes Home"; at the Palace, Sept., 1918, appeared in "Hullo! America"; in conjunction with Sir Alfred Butt entered on the management of the Queen's Theatre, opening 8 Mar., 1919, as the Count Paul de Virieu in "The House of Peril"; June, 1919, appeared as Anthony Quintard in "The Cinderella Man'; Jan., 1920, as Arthur John Carrington in "Mr. Todd's Experiment"; then retired from management, and at the Playhouse, Aug., 1920, played Reginald Carter in "Wedding Bells"; at the Comedy, Dec., 1920, Peter Bevans in "The Charm School"; at the Aldwych, May, 1921, Kit Harwood in " Love Among the Paint Pots," and Larry Darrant in " The First and the Last " ; subsequently toured in " The Charm School " ; at the Aldwych, July, 1921, played Jim Chevrell in " James the Less " ; at the Duke of York's, Mar., 1922, Oliver Bashforth in " The Enchanted Cottage " ; he then entered into partnership with Bertie Meyer, and in Aug., 1922, toured the provinces as Mark Sabre in " If Winter Comes " ; they entered on the management of the St. James's, Jan., 1923, when he played the same part ; at His Majesty's, Feb., 1923, in aid of King George's Pension Fund for Actors, played Hugh Paton in " Half-an-Hour " ; at the Queen's, Nov., 1923, Rev. Gavin Dishart in " The Little Minister " ; at the Adelphi, Mar., 1924, again played Julian Beauclerc in " Diplomacy " ; at the same theatre, June, 1924, in aid of King George's Pension Fund for Actors, played Marston Gurney in " The Ware Case " ; in Aug., 1924, went on tour with his own company, playing Julian Beauclerc in " Diplomacy " ; St. James's, Jan., 1925, played Maurice Sorbier in " Grounds for Divorce " ; June, 1925, Anthony Walford in " The River " ; in the same year went to South Africa with a repertory of plays, including " Diplomacy," " Grounds for Divorce," " Romance," and " The Last of Mrs. Cheyney " ; reappeared in London, at the Playhouse, Oct., 1926, as Thomas Armstrong and the Bishop in a revival of " Romance " ; St. Martin's, Mar., 1927, played Jeremy Dairiven in " No Gentlemen " ; Queen's, Apr., 1927, succeeded Nicholas Hannen as John Freeman in " The Fanatics " ; Drury Lane (for King George's Pension Fund), May, 1927, Pietro Morelli in " The Wandering Jew " ; Ambassadors', Jan., 1928, Cary Liston in " Two White Arms " ; June, 1928, Georges Duhamel in " The Man They Buried " ; then toured in " Two White Arms " ; Wyndham's, Jan., 1929, Tony Ambersham in " Living Together " ; Duke of York's, Apr., 1929, Kenneth Vail in " These Few Ashes " ; Palace, June, 1929, Jim Brooks in " Hold Everything " ; Wyndham's, Sept., 1929, Garry Anson in " The Calendar " ; New, May, 1930, Victor Gresham in

"The Last Chapter," July, 1930, Désiré Tronchais in " Désiré," which he also produced ; Ambassadors', Aug., 1930, succeeded Raymond Massey as Raymond Dabney in " The Man in Possession " ; during 1931, toured as Jim Warlock in " Cynara " ; Embassy, June, 1931, Peter in " Delicate Question " ; Strand, Aug., 1931, Logan in " Counsel's Opinion " ; Apollo, Apr., 1932, Andrew Poole in " Pleasure Cruise " ; Haymarket, Oct., 1932, Gerald Graham in " Once a Husband " ; Haymarket, Jan., 1933, John Rockingham in " Double Harness " ; Lyric, Apr., 1933, Jimmie Lee in " When Ladies Meet " ; Wyndham's, Nov., 1933, Toby Strang in " Man Proposes " ; Globe, Mar., 1934, Robert Van Brett in " Double Door " ; Comedy, May, 1934, Henry in " All's Over Then ? " ; at the Criterion, May, 1934, succeeded Godfrey Tearle as Sir John Corbett in " Sixteen " ; Vaudeville, Oct., 1934, played Roger Storer in " Lovers' Leap " ; Globe, Feb., 1935, Randolph Warrender in " Youth at the Helm " ; Globe, Oct., 1935, played Roger Hilton in " Call it a Day," which ran for 15 months ; Globe, July, 1937, John Fothergil in " They Came By Night " ; Globe, Nov., 1937, the Rev. Robert Carson in " Robert's Wife," which ran for 18 months ; produced " Nina," Criterion, 1935 ; " Our Own Lives," Ambassadors', 1935 ; " Girl Unknown," New, 1936, and " Give Me Yesterday," Comedy, 1938 ; commenced film career, 1913, in " Just a Girl," and appeared in numerous films, silent and talking ; since 1936, has played in " Head Office," " The Show Goes On," etc. *Recreations :* Motoring, golf, cricket and water-colour painting. *Clubs :* Bath, and Stage Golfing Society. *(Died 31 July, 1943; age 54)*

NASH, Florence, actress ; *b.* Troy, Albany, N.Y., U.S.A., 2 Oct., 1888 ; *d.* of Philip F. Nash and his wife Eileen (MacNamara) ; made her first appearance on the stage in 1906, in a " stock " company ; made a substantial hit when she made her first appearance in New York, at the Lyceum Theatre, 8 Apr., 1907, as Madge Blake in " The Boys of Company B." ; at the Criterion,

New York, Dec., 1907, played Gretchen in " Miss Hook of Holland " ; at the Broadway, Aug., 1908, Mrs. Billings F. Cooings in " Algeria " ; during 1908–9 toured with De Wolf Hopper in " The Pied-Piper " ; at the Stuyvesant Theatre, Dec., 1909, appeared as Lucie in " The Lily " ; at the Nazimova Theatre, Aug., 1910, as Clara Gilroy in " Miss Patsy " ; during 1911 toured in " When Sweet Sixteen," and 1911–12, with Thomas W. Ross in " An Everyday Man " ; subsequently appeared in " vaudeville," in " 1999 " ; at the Eltinge Theatre scored a great success, Sept., 1912, as Aggie Lynch in " Within the Law," and after the termination of the long run of the play in New York toured in the same part, 1914 ; at the Playhouse, New York, Jan., 1915, played Polly Cary in " Sinners " ; at Schenectady, Nov., 1915, Elsie Darling in " Very Good, Eddie " ; at the Palace, New York, Apr., 1916, appeared in " Pansy's Particular Punch " ; at the Forty-eighth Street Theatre, Oct., 1917, played Sonya Marinoff in " The Land of the Free " ; at the Morosco Theatre, Nov., 1918, played Remnant in the play of that name ; at Wilkes-Barre, Feb., 1920, appeared in " Cornered " ; at the Times Square Theatre, Sept., 1920, appeared as Betty Bond in " The Mirage " ; at the Cort Theatre, Nov., 1922, played the Montagu Girl in " Merton of the Movies " ; Bijou, Nov., 1925, Sally Halstead in "A Lady's Virtue " ; Cosmopolitan, Apr., 1926, Marianne in " The Two Orphans " ; Booth, Apr., 1930, Clara Gibbings in " Lady Clara."

(Died 2 Apr., 1950; age 60)

NASH, George Frederick, actor ; *b.* Philadelphia ; *m.* Julia Hay ; had had experience as an amateur before making his first professional appearance on the stage as Pierre in " The Two Orphans," under the management of M. B. Leavitt ; subsequently toured with Frank Mayo in " Nordeck," and with W. J. Florence and Joseph Jefferson, with whom he made his first appearance in New York, at Tompkins' Fifth Avenue Theatre, 29 Oct., 1888, when he played Faulk-

land in " The Rivals " ; at the Star Theatre, Aug., 1891, played Percival in " The Club Friend " ; at Palmer's Theatre, Sept., 1894, played the Rev. Ferguson Clark in " New Blood," and Oct., 1894, Gerald Hurst in " The Transgressor," and De Varville in " Camille " ; at the Standard, New York, Sept., 1895, Gunther Hartmann in " Honour," and Feb., 1896, Small Bottles in " Chimmie Fadden " ; at Wallack's, Sept., 1900, played Baron von Gondremark in " Prince Otto " ; in 1901 toured as Sir Percival Lovelace in " Tom Moore " ; at the Criterion, New York, Apr., 1904, played Colonel Bowie in " The Dictator " ; made his first appearance in London, at the Comedy Theatre, 3 May, 1905, in the same part, and Sept., 1905, played McGeachey in " On the Quiet " ; during 1906 toured in the United States as Martinac in " The Heart of a Sparrow " ; at Wallack's, Oct., 1907, played Nathan Hargrave in " The Silver Girl " ; at the Hackett, Nov., 1907, Frank Hardmuth in " The Witching Hour " ; at Maxine Elliott's Sept., 1909, Henry Van Cleve in " The Revellers " ; at the Garrick, New York, Oct., 1909, M. Vavin in " The Harvest Moon " ; at the Maxine Elliott, Oct., 1910, Wilbur Emberson in " The Gamblers " ; at the Gaiety, New York, Jan., 1912, Alfred Wilson in " Officer 666 " ; at the Union Square, Jan., 1914, appeared in " The Reckoning " ; at the Booth, Mar., 1914, appeared as Baron de Duisitort in " Panthea " ; at the Astor, Sept., 1914, as John Madison in " The Miracle Man " ; at Atlantic City, May, 1915, as Harry Hamilton in " The Three of Hearts " ; at the Princess Theatre, Oct., 1915, as Robert Ormsby in " The Mark of the Beast " ; at the Harris Theatre, Oct., 1916, played Blake in " Under Sentence " ; at the Longacre Theatre, Aug., 1918, Stephen Drake in " The Blue Pearl " ; at the Astor Theatre, Dec., 1918, Charlie Yong in " East is West " ; reappeared in London, in the same part, at the Lyric Theatre, June, 1920 ; at the National Theatre, New York, Dec., 1921, played Talbot Wynne in a revival of " Trilby "; Guild Theatre, Dec., 1925, Pigal in " Merchants of

Glory"; Hudson, Oct., 1926, Buck Gordon in "The Noose"; Klaw, Sept., 1927, M. Merluche in "Creoles"; Little, Feb., 1928, Captain Aaron Bowditch in "La Gringa"; Shubert-Riviera, Oct., 1928, Father Wilks in "Marooned"; Hammerstein's, Sept., 1930, Captain Hatch in "Luana"; Ambassador, Sept., 1931, the Chief of Gendarmes in "If I Were You"; Biltmore, Oct., 1932, Mr. Flood in "The Other One"; Martin Beck, Mar., 1934, Major Gorgas in "Yellow Jack"; Empire, Jan., 1935, Dr. Lanskell in "The Old Maid"; Empire, Oct., 1936, First Gravedigger in "Hamlet"; Guild, Nov., 1937, Senator Callory in "The Ghost of Yankee Doodle"; Martin Beck, Feb., 1938, Eldridge in "How To Get Tough About It."
(Died 31 Dec., 1944; age 71)

NASH, Mary, actress; *b.* Troy, N.Y. State, U.S.A., 15 Aug., 1885; *d.* of Philip F. Nash and his wife Eileen (MacNamara); *e.* Convent of St. Anne, Montreal; *m.* José Ruben; was a pupil at the American Academy of Dramatic Art, 1900; made her first appearance on the stage with Sam Bernard in "The Girl from Kay's," 1904; she made her first appearance in New York, at the Criterion Theatre, 25 Dec., 1905, as Leonora Dunbar in "Alice-Sit-by-the-Fire"; during 1906 toured in the same part; at the Empire, New York, Feb.-May, 1907, played the First Ballet-lady in "Captain Jinks"; the Unknown Lady in "The Silver Box," Ethel Carlton in "His Excellency the Governor," and Amy Spencer in "Cousin Kate"; at the Lyric, New York, Nov., 1907, appeared as Freda in "The Girls of Holland"; during 1908 toured as leading lady with Andrew Mack, playing Arrah Meelish in "Arrah-na-Pogue," and in "Sergeant Devil-may-Care"; at the Majestic, New York, Dec., 1908, succeeded Grace Cameron as Lizzie Dizzy in "The Pied Piper"; at Washington, Apr., 1909, appeared as Pamela Gray in "The Truants"; at the Lyric, New York, Dec., 1909, scored a great success when she appeared as Cicely Rand in "The City," in which she also toured during 1910-11; made a further success at the Republic Theatre, Sept.,

1911, as Wanda Kelly in "The Woman," in which she also toured during 1912-13; at Maxine Elliott's, Aug., 1913, played the Girl in "The Lure"; in 1914 appeared in "vaudeville" in "The Watch Dog"; at the Longacre Theatre, Dec., 1914, played Jeannette in "Secret Strings"; at the Playhouse, New York, Sept., 1915, Mrs. Vida Phillimore in "The New York Idea"; Nov., 1915, Lady Rosamund Tatton in "The Liars"; and Dec., 1915, Jenny Hill in "Major Barbara"; during 1916 toured as Nancy Price in "The Ohio Lady," subsequently re-named "The Country Cousin"; at the Playhouse, New York, Sept., 1916, played Marcelle in "The Man who Came Back," in which she continued to play throughout 1917-18; at the Belmont Theatre, Oct., 1918, appeared as "Bobo" Hardy in "I.O.U."; at the Forty-eighth Street Theatre, Oct., 1918, as Mary Delano in "The Big Chance"; at Wilkes-Barre, Pa., Feb., 1920, played the Woman in "Man and Woman"; made her first appearance in London at the Oxford, 8 Apr., 1920, as Marcelle in "The Man who Came Back," scoring an immediate success.; at the Playhouse, New York, Nov., 1920, played the Woman in "Thy Name is Woman" (formerly "Man and Woman"); at the Cort Theatre, Dec., 1921, played Anna Valeska in "Captain Applejack" ("Ambrose Applejohn's Adventure"); at the Empire, New York, Dec., 1923, Polly Pearl in "The Lady"; at the Knickerbocker, Sept., 1924, Yasmin in "Hassan"; Bijou, Nov., 1925, Madame Sisson in "A Lady's Virtue"; Cosmopolitan, Apr., 1926, Henriette in "The Two Orphans"; Longacre, Sept., 1927, Manuela in "The Command to Love"; Ambassador, Sept., 1929, Janet Hale in "A Strong Man's House"; Longacre, Dec., 1929, Diana in a play of that name; Ritz, Feb., 1931, Barbara in "A Woman Denied"; Selwyn, Jan., 1932, Dorothy Lister in "The Devil Passes"; entered films, 1934, and has appeared in "Uncertain Lady," "College Scandal" ("The Clock Strikes Eight"), "Come and Get It," "The King and the Chorus Girl," "Easy Living," "Heidi," "Wells Fargo," "The Little Princess," etc.

NATANSON, Jacques, dramatic author; has written the following among other plays: "The Lady of the Orchids," "L'Été," "Le Greluchon Delicat," "L'Infidéle Eperdu," "Les Amants Saugrenus," "La 40 C.V. du Roi," "Knock-Out" (with Théry), "I Was Waiting for You," etc.

NATHAN, Ben, comedian and manager; *b.* Glasgow, 26 June, 1857; was well known for some years as an actor, and made his first appearance on the London stage, at the Gaiety Theatre, Sept., 1889, in " Ruy Blas, or the Blasé Roué "; made his first appearance on the variety stage at the Empire and Royal, 7 April, 1890, while still appearing at the Gaiety; subsequently was manager for Hugh Jay Didcott, the late well-known variety agent, and later became a director of the firm when it was turned into a limited company; was founder of the firm of Nathan and Somers, agents, and was manager of the variety branch of Ashton's Agency; was manager of the London Opera House, and produced the *revue* " Come Over Here ! "; re-appeared on the theatrical stage at the Lyric, Feb., 1915, as Tweedlepunch in revival of " Florodora "; for over twenty years, gave an annual reading at Birmingham Town Hall, of Dickens's story, " A Christmas Carol " *Address :* 81 Corringham Road, Golder's Green, N.W. *Telephone No. :* Finchley 906.

NATHAN, George Jean, dramatic critic and author; *b.* Fort Wayne, Ind., U.S.A., 14 Feb., 1882; *s.* of Charles Nathan and his wife Ella (Nirdlinger); *e.* Cornell University, where he took his B.A. degree; while at the University, was one of the editors of the Cornell *Daily Sun*; for three years he was engaged on the staff of the New York *Herald*, and subsequently became dramatic editor of *The Bohemian*; contributed articles on theatrical subjects to *Harper's Weekly, Munsey Magazine, Theatre Magazine*, and *The Green Book*; subsequently dramatic critic of the *Burr Mc Intosh Magazine*; was for many years co-editor and dramatic editor of the *Smart Set*

Magazine; dramatic critic of *Judge*, and *The American Mercury*, and co-editor of the latter publication; dramatic critic of *Vanity Fair, Life, Newsweek*, and *Esquire*; founder, co-editor, and dramatic critic of *The American Spectator*; author of " Comedians All," " The Critic and the Drama," " Materia Critica," " The Popular Theatre," " The World in Falseface," " Another Book on the Theatre," " Art of the Night," " The House of Satan," " The Theatre, The Drama, and The Girls," " Testament of a Critic," " Friends of Mine," " Mr. George Jean Nathan Presents," " The Intimate Notebooks of George Jean Nathan," " Since Ibsen," " Passing Judgments," " The Theatre of the Moment," " The Morning After the First Night," " The Entertainment of a Nation," " Theatre Book of the Year," for 1942–3, and on : in June, 1931, joined *The Daily Express*, London, for a fortnight, as guest critic; contributed the article on American Drama to *Encyclopaedia Britannica*; in Sept., 1943, joined the staff of *Journal-American*, as drama critic; received the honorary degree of Lit.D., University of Indiana, 1954; was President of the N.Y. Drama Critics' Circle; is an honorary member of the London Critics' Circle.
(Died 8 Apr., 1958; age 76)

NATION, **W. H. C.,** manager, author, and composer; *b.* Exeter, 1843; *e.* at Eton and Oriel College, Oxford; has been identified with numerous theatrical enterprises, and first entered into management in 1866, when Sadler's Wells Theatre passed under his control, and where he produced, among other plays, " The Golden Dustman," the original adaptation of Charles Dickens's work " Our Mutual Friend "; he next became sole manager of Astley's, 1866-7; the Royalty came under his charge in 1871-2, the old Holborn in 1873, and the Charing Cross in 1873-4, his next appearance as a manager being at Terry's, which he took for a six months' season in Oct., 1906; opened the Scala Theatre, 26 Oct., 1907, with " Stemming the Stream " and a revival of " Weighed in the Balance "; undertook the management of the Royalty Theatre, 1908-9, and again in 1910-11 ; and the Scala in 1910 ; at one time edited the defunct *Covent Garden Magazine ;* he also edited *The London* and *The Weekly Companion ;* author of a number of farces, comedies, and other pieces, and has delivered public addresses on the Drama ; was Vice-President of the Dramatic College, Dramatic and Musical Sick Fund, and Royal General Theatrical Fund.

(Died 17 Mar., 1914; age 71)

NATIONAL THEATRE COMPANY, The, producing managers; National Theatre Board: The Rt. Hon. Viscount Chandos, P.C., D.S.O., M.C. (*Chairman*), Mr. Hugh Beaumont, Sir Kenneth Clark, C.H., K.C.B., Sir Ashley Clarke, G.C.M.G., G.C.V.O., Sir Douglas Logan, D.C.L., LL.D., Mr. Victor Mishcon, D.L., Mr. Henry Moore, O.M., C.H., Alderman Sir Maurice Pariser, M.A., Mr. J. B. Priestley, LL.D., D.Litt., Mr. Hugh Willatt, Mr. Kenneth Rae (*Secretary*); Director: Sir Laurence Olivier; in July, 1962, the Chancellor appointed the National Theatre Board, and an agreement was reached with the Governors of the Old Vic whereby the Old Vic Theatre became the temporary home of the National Theatre; the inaugural production of "Hamlet" took place on 22 Oct., 1963; the Company has since presented the following productions at the Old Vic: "Saint Joan," "Uncle Vanya," "The Recruiting Officer," 1963; "Hobson's Choice," "Andorra," "Play," and "Philoctetes" (double-bill), "Othello," "The Master Builder," *Amleto* (Proclemer-Albertazzi Company), "The Dutch Courtesan," "Hay Fever," "The Royal Hunt of the Sun," 1964; "The Crucible," "Much Ado About Nothing," "Mother Courage," (*Berliner Ensemble* in "The Resistible Rise of Arturo Ui," "Coriolanus," "The Days of the Commune," "The Threepenny Opera") Armstrong's Last Goodnight" "Love for Love," Trelawny of the Wells," 1965; The National Theatre Company has also presented the following plays at the Chichester Festival: "The Royal Hunt of the Sun," "The Dutch Courtesan," "Othel-

lo," 1964; "Armstrong's Last Goodnight," "Trelawny of the 'Wells'," "Miss Julie," and "Black Comedy" (double-bill), 1965; the Company has also undertaken short provincial tours, and made its first overseas appearance at the Kremlevsky Theatre, Moscow, Sept., 1965. *Address:* National Theatre Offices, The Archway, 10a Aquinas Street, London, S.E.1. *Telephone No.:* Waterloo 2033.

NAYLOR, Robert, actor and vocalist; *b.* Luddenden Foot, Yorks., 15 Apr., 1899; *s.* of Robert Sutcliffe Naylor and his wife Sarah (Clayton); *e.* Heath Grammar School, Halifax; *m.* Cecilia Farrar; was formerly engaged in a woollen manufacturer's business; studied singing in his spare time and appeared at concerts and in oratorios; made his first appearance on the stage at the Hippodrome, Todmorden, Feb., 1921, as Colonel Fairfax in "The Yeomen of the Guard"; made his first appearance in London, at the Chelsea Palace, June, 1923, with the Old Vic. vacation company, in the title-*rôle* of "Faust"; sang for three years at the Old Vic., appearing as Rudolfo in "La Bohéme," Othello in Verdi's opera, etc.; sang with the Carl Rosa Opera company as a guest artist, appearing in "Madame Butterfly," "Faust," "Rigoletto," "Cavalleria Rusticana," "La Bohème," "Carmen," "Bronwen," "Martha," "The Bohemian Girl," "La Traviata," "Il Trovatore," etc.; has sung Faust over 200 times; at the Adelphi, Nov., 1929, appeared in "The House that Jack Built"; Drury Lane, May, 1930, succeeded Webster Booth, as the Duke of Buckingham in "The Three Musketeers"; Palace, Oct., 1930, deputized for Joseph Hislop as Goethe in "Frederica"; made a signal success at Drury Lane, May, 1931, when on the third night of "The Land of Smiles" he deputized for Richard Tauber, in the leading part of Prince Sou Chong, which he subsequently sang for five weeks; during 1931–32, appeared in variety theatres with Edith Day in a scene from Drury Lane musical plays; appeared in "variety" theatres, Aug., 1932, with Annie Croft; London Hippodrome, Feb., 1933, Dick in "The

One Girl "; Prince's, Feb., 1935, Yussuf in " The Rose of Persia "; *Recreations:* Golf and cricket. *Clubs:* Savage and Stage Golfing Society. *Address:* Savage Club, 1 Carlton House Terrace, London, S.W.1.

NAZIMOVA, Alla, actress ; *b.* Yalta, Crimea, Russia, 4 June, 1879 ; *e.* at Zurich, Switzerland ; at Odessa studied the violin, and entered a dramatic school at Moscow, where she remained four years ; subsequently played in various provincial companies, and was leading lady at St. Petersburg, in 1904 ; joined Paul Orleneff's company, visiting Berlin, London, and New York ; first appeared in London, at the Avenue Theatre, 21 Jan., 1905, as Lia in " The Chosen People "; proceeding to America, made her *début* in New York, at the Herald Square Theatre, 23 Mar., 1905, in the same part ; subsequently played a season of some months with Paul Orleneff ; entered into a contract with Messrs. Shubert Bros. in May, 1906, to play in English by Nov., 1906 ; received her first lesson in English on 23 June, and made her English-speaking *début* at the Princess's Theatre, 13 Nov., 1906, as Hedda Tesman in " Hedda Gabler " ; she then gave a series of *matinée* performances ; commenced regular evening performances at the Princess's Theatre, 14 Jan., 1907, when she played Nora Helmer in " A Doll's House " ; in Mar. she migrated to the Bijou Theatre, appearing in " Hedda Gabler " and " A Doll's House," and on 12 Apr., 1907, as the Comtesse Nina de Lorenzo in " The Comtesse Coquette " ; same Theatre, 23 Sept., 1907, appeared as Hilda Wangel in " The Master Builder"; and 30 Dec., 1907, as Lona in " The Comet " ; during 1908 toured all over the United States ; at Albany, New York, Nov., 1909, played in " The Passion Flower " ; appeared at the Nazimova Theatre (now 39th Street Theatre) New York, Apr., 1910, as Rita Allmers in " Little Eyolf " ; at New Haven, Conn., Sept., 1910, played Fannie Theren in " The Fairy Tale " ; at Utica, New York, Sept., 1911, appeared in " The Other Mary " ; at the Lyceum, New York, Dec., 1911, appeared as the Marquise de Monclars in " The Marionettes " ; at the Empire, New York, Nov., 1912, played Mrs. Chepstow in " Bella Donna," subsequently touring in the same part ; at the Harris Theatre, New York, Nov., 1914, Diana Laska in " That Sort " ; at the Palace, New York, Jan., 1915, played Joan in " War Brides " ; at the Princess Theatre, New York, Jan., 1917, Eve in " 'Ception Shoals " ; at the Plymouth Theatre, New York, Mar.-Apr., 1918, played Nora in " A Doll's House," Hedda Tesman in " Hedda Gabler," Hedvig in " The Wild Duck," and Hilda Wangel in " The Master Builder " ; subsequently turned her attention to the cinema stage, on which she achieved great success, and appeared in " Revelation," "A Doll's House," " The Red Lantern," " War Brides," " Toys of Fate," " Eye for Eye," " The Brat," " Salome," " The Redeeming Sin," " Heart of a Child," " The Madonna of the Streets," " Camille," " My Son," etc. ; reappeared on the New York Stage, at the Selwyn Theatre, Jan., 1923, when she played Countess Dagmar in " Dagmar " ; at the Frolic Theatre, Oct., 1923, appeared with the French Grand Guignol Players ; re-appeared in London, at the Coliseum, 30 May, 1927, as Azah in " A Woman of the Earth " ; at the Civic Repertory Theatre, New York, Oct., 1928, played Mdme. Ranevsky in " The Cherry Orchard " ; Feb., 1929, Katerina Ivanovna in " Katerina "; joined the company of the Theatre Guild, and appeared at the Guild Theatre, Mar., 1930, as Natalie Petrovna in " A Month in the Country " ; Oct., 1931, played Christine in " Homecoming," and " The Hunted " (" Mourning Becomes Electra "); Oct., 1932, O'—Lan in " The Good Earth " ; Playhouse, Nov., 1933, Monica in " Doctor Monica " ; Guild, Feb., 1935, The Priestess Prola in " The Simpleton of the Unexpected Isles " ; in the autumn of 1935, toured as Mrs. Alving in " Ghosts," appearing in the same part at the Empire, New York, Dec., 1935 ; Longacre, Nov., 1936, played Hedda Tesman in " Hedda Gabler " ; Lyceum, Apr., 1939, the title-*rôle* in " The Mother " ; in 1938, assisted in the pro-

duction of the film "Zaza."
(Died 13 July, 1945; age 66)

NEAL, Patricia (Louise), actress; *b.* Packard, Kentucky, 20 Jan., 1926; *d.* of William Burdette Neal and his wife Eura Mildred (Petrey); *e.* Knoxville Public School (Tennessee) and Northwestern University; *m.* Roald Dahl; studied for the stage at the Barter Theatre, Virginia, and Actors' Studio; made her first appearance in New York at the Morosco Theatre, 1946, when she played Olive, the part she was understudying, in "The Voice of the Turtle"; Fulton, Nov., 1946, played Regina in "Another Part of the Forest"; Theatre De Lys, N.Y., June, 1953, played Lady Teazle in a revival of "The School for Scandal"; Coronet, Dec., 1953, played Martha in a revival of "The Children's Hour"; Playhouse, Oct., 1955, played Nancy Fallon in "A Roomful of Roses"; Morosco, Mar., 1956, took over the part of Margaret in "Cat on a Hot Tin Roof" for three weeks, while Barbara Bel Geddes was on holiday; made her first appearance in London, at the Arts, Sept., 1958, when she played Catherine Holly in "Suddenly Last Summer," one of two plays by Tennessee Williams, entitled "Garden District"; Playhouse, N.Y., Oct., 1959, played Mrs. Keller in "The Miracle Worker"; first appeared in films, 1949, and principal pictures include: "The Fountainhead," "The Hasty Heart," "A Face in the Crowd," "In Harm's Way," "Breakfast at Tiffany's," "Hud" (receiving the Academy Award, 1963, for this performance), "Psyche 59"; made her first appearance on television, 1954, in New York, and has also appeared in television plays in England, notable successes include: "Royal Family," "Biography," "Clash By Night," "Tonight," and "The Days and Nights of Beebee Fenstermaker," 1962. *Favourite parts:* All—especially Catherine Holly. *Recreations:* Her children, cooking, breeding free-flying parakeets. *Address:* Gipsy House, Great Missenden, Bucks., England. *Telephone No.:* Great Missenden 2757.

NEDELL, Bernard, actor and director; *b.* New York City, U.S.A., 14 Oct., 1899; *s.* of William Louis Nedell and his wife Rose Mary (Speyer); *e.*

Western Reserve University, Cleveland, Ohio, U.S.A.; *m.* Olive Blakeney; born of theatrical parents, made his first appearance on the stage at Hartford, Conn., as a small child playing Little Willie in "East Lynne"; from 1915 to 1926, was engaged in "stock" companies at New York City, Trenton, Cleveland, Omaha, Boston, Des Moines, Chicago, Birmingham (Alabama), etc.; made his first appearance in New York at the Playhouse, in 1916, as Henry Potter in "The Man Who Came Back," succeeding Henry Hull, whom he understudied; during 1916–18, served in the U.S. Army, in France; toured in the Orient, 1921–3, with T. D. Frawley's Company; made his first appearance in London, at the Strand Theatre, 22 Dec., 1926, as Steve Crandall in "Broadway"; at the Prince of Wales's, Mar., 1928, played Eddie Ellison in "Square Crooks"; Prince's, Sept., 1929, Michael Marlow in "The Flying Fool"; during 1929–30, appeard in variety theatres with Tallulah Bankhead, in "The Snob"; Prince Edward Theatre, Apr., 1930, played General Romero Esteban in "Rio Rita"; Wyndham's, Dec., 1930, Perryfeld in "Smoky Cell"; King's, Hammersmith, Aug., 1931, and tour, played Gresh in "The Lady Known as 'Lu'"; Embassy, Jan., 1932, and Little, Mar., 1932, Charles Carroll in "See Naples and Die"; Little, Feb., 1933, George McAuliffe in "Cock Robin"; Piccadilly, Apr., 1933 (for Repertory Players), and Garrick, June, 1933, Buckley Joyce Thomas in "Clear All Wires"; in June, 1934, toured in variety theatres, in "The Snob"; "Q," Sept., 1934, played Mark Antoine in "Romantic Ladies"; Wyndham's, Feb., 1936, Patsy in "Three Men on a Horse"; Phoenix, Nov., 1936, Cliff Bellamy in "Hell-for-Leather"; directed "Speed Limit," 1929; "Appearances," 1930; "Who Knows?" 1930; "The Lady Known as 'Lu,'" 1931; "See Naples and Die," 1932; "Money for Jam," 1932; "It's a Wise Child," 1935; "And the Music Stopped," 1937; since 1938, mainly engaged in Hollywood, in films, although he has played several stock engagements; New York City Center, Jan., 1951, appeared as Herbert Dean in a revival of "The Royal Family"; adapted "Piccadilly," 1934; commenced film career, in America, 1916, in "The Serpent," and has since appeared in innumerable pictures. *Favourite parts:* Steve in "Broadway," and Henry Potter in "The Man Who Came Back." *Recreations:* The violin and baseball. *Clubs:* Players', and Lambs, New York. *Address:* 333 West 56th Street, New York City, U.S.A.

NEILSON, Francis, M.P., dramatic author; *b.* Birkenhead, 26 Jan., 1867 ; *s.* of Isabel (Neilson) and Francis Butters; *e.* privately and at Liverpool High School ; *m.* Catherine Eva O'Gorman ; was formerly a journalist and critic ; was stage director to Charles Frohman at the Criterion, Vaudeville and Duke of York's Theatres, 1898-1901, producing among other plays "The Dovecot," "The Masked Ball," "Self and Lady," "The Christian," "The Swashbuckler," "The Lackey's Carnival," etc. ; also produced "My Mother-in-Law" and "Sherlock Holmes" for Mr. Frohman ; was stage director of the Royal Opera, Covent Carden, 1900, where he produced "La Tosca," "Der Wald," "Much Ado About Nothing," "Princess Osra," etc.; superintended the alterations to the stage at Covent Garden, 1901 ; part author (with E. G. Hemmerde) of "A Butterfly on the Wheel," 1911, and "The Crucible," 1911 ; is the author of the following books : "Madame Bohemia," "Manabozo," "The Bath Road," etc., also pamphlets on Economics, Taxation and Industry ; is Radical M.P., for the Hyde division of Cheshire. *Recreation:* Golf.
(Died 13 Apr., 1961; age 94)

NEILSON, Harold V., actor and manager ; *b.* Manchester, 8 Jan., 1874 ; *e.* Manchester Grammar School ; *m.* Esmé Biddle ; made his first appearance on the stage with F. R. Benson's company at the Theatre Royal, Manchester, Nov., 1897, as the groom in "Richard II" ; subsequently toured with Louis Calvert, Edmund Tearle, Hermann Vezin, and William Haviland ; during 1901 was playing

in "The Little Minister" and "The Second in Command " ; entered into management on his own account 1901, and toured with various plays, including Shaw's "Captain Brassbound's Conversion," "The Admirable Bashville" (first public performances), "The Devil's Disciple," "Arms and the Man," and Ibsen's "A Doll's House," "Pillars of Society," "Rosmersholm," "An Enemy of the People," "John Gabriel Borkman," and "Ghosts " ; in 1907 gave the first public performance of Maeterlinck's "Death of Tintagiles," at the Royal Court Theatre, Liverpool ; subsequently toured many other plays ; at the Garrick, Mar., 1917, produced "Wonderful James " ; at the conclusion of the War reorganised the Benson Shakespearean Company, and directed it until 1921 ; at the St. Martin's, 1920, produced "Pompey the Great " and "Hamlet," with Sir Frank Benson in the leading parts ; at the Royalty, Jan., 1922, produced "The Eleventh Commandment"; during 1922 was Director of the Exeter Repertory Theatre; during 1923 produced "Mary, Mary, Quite Contrary," "The Lord of Death," etc. ; at the Aldwych, Dec., 1923, revived "Bluebell in Fairyland"; Regent, 1924, "From Morn to Midnight"; Apollo, 1927, "Puss in Boots"; for three years managed and directed Sir Frank Benson's tours; has directed Shakespearean Festivals at leading provincial cities; Ambassadors', 1932, presented "The Price of Wisdom," with Irene Vanbrugh; Arts, 1934, presented "The Springtime of Others"; since 1933, has directed the Benson Shakespearean Company, Covent Garden Opera company, and other ventures. *Favourite parts:* Dr. Stockmann, Brutus, and Dick Dudgeon. *Recreations:* Swimming, water-polo, and tennis. *Clubs:* Authors', Arts Theatre, and M.C.C.
(Died 17 Feb., 1956; age 82)

NEILSON, Julia, actress ; *b.* London, 12 June, 1868; *d.* of the late Alexander Ritchie Neilson and his wife Emily (Davis) ; *e.* Wiesbaden ; *m.* Fred Terry ; at the age of fifteen became a student at the Royal Academy of Music, where she secured the Llewellyn Thomas Gold Medal, 1885, the Westmoreland Scholarship, 1886, and the Sainton Dolby Prize, 1886; studied elocution under the late Walter Lacy; while still a student at the Academy, she appeared with success at the St. James's Hall, 1 Apr., 1887, singing "Der Tod Jesu," as a mezzo-soprano; under the advice of the late Sir W. S. Gilbert she abandoned the musical profession for the stage, and made her first appearance at the Lyceum Theatre, on 21 Mar., 1888, as Cynisca in " Pygmalion and Galatea," with Mary Anderson; at the Savoy, 16 May, 1888, she played Galatea to the Pygmalion of Lewis Waller, and she played Lady Hilda in " Broken Hearts," at the Crystal Palace, 31 May, with Waller as Florian, Selene in " The Wicked World," at the Savoy, 4 July, to the Ethais of George Alexander; she was then engaged by Rutland Barrington for his season at the St. James's, and on 29 Nov. played Ruth Redmayne in Gilbert's " Brantinghame Hall "; she was next engaged by Beerbohm Tree and toured with him as Stella in " Captain Swift," Olga in " The Red Lamp " and Anne Page in " The Merry Wives of Windsor "; she appeared at the Haymarket, 12 Sept., 1889, as Julie de Noirville in " A Man's Shadow," and remained there five years, playing Clarice in " Comedy and Tragedy," Marguerite in " A Village Priest," Pauline in " Called Back," Olga in " The Red Lamp," Loyse in " The Ballad Monger," Drusilla Ives in " The Dancing Girl," Lady Ormond in " Peril," Hypatia in the play of that name, Hester Worsley in " A Woman of No Importance," Lady Isobel in " The Tempter," and Magdalena in " Once Upon A Time "; she then went to the Adelphi Theatre, where she appeared on 20 June, 1894, as Grace West in " Shall We Forgive Her ? "; at the Haymarket, under Messrs. Lewis Waller and H. H. Morrell, 3 Jan., 1895, she played Lady Chiltern in " An Ideal Husband "; at the Criterion, with Messrs. Waller and Wyndham, 7 May, 1895, she played Rhoda Trendel in " The Home

Secretary "; in Dec., she accompanied John Hare to America, and made her first appearance in New York at Abbey's Theatre, 23 Dec., 1895, as Agnes in " The Notorious Mrs. Ebbsmith "; during the tour she also played in " Comedy and Tragedy "; on her return to England, she joined George Alexander; she appeared at the St. James's, 20 Oct., 1896, as the Princess Flavia in " The Prisoner of Zenda," and she remained until 1898, playing Rosalind in " As You Like It," Princess Pannonia in " The Princess and the Butterfly," Belle in " The Tree of Knowledge," Beatrice in " Much Ado About Nothing," and Yvonne de Grandpré in " The Conquerors "; she was then seen at the Adelphi, 31 Aug., 1898, playing Naomi Lovell in " The Gipsy Earl "; at the Garrick, 25 Apr., 1899, she played Celia in " Change-Alley "; she rejoined Beerbohm Tree, this time at Her Majesty's, and appeared there on 20 Sept., 1899, as Constance in " King John "; she also played Oberon in " A Midsummer Night's Dream," 10 Jan., 1900; she then toured in conjunction with William Mollison, as Rosalind in " As You Like It," and then with her husband entered on London management for the first time, opening at the Haymarket, 30 Aug., 1900, as Nell Gwyn in " Sweet Nell of Old Drury "; their joint management continued until 1930, and she has played the following parts since that date : Lady Leslie Hartington in " The Heel of Achilles, " Globe, 6 Feb., 1902 ; Count Vladimir in " For Sword or Song," Shaftesbury, 21 Jan., 1903 ; Sunday in the play of that name, Comedy, 2 Apr., 1904 ; Lady Blakeney in " The Scarlet Pimpernel," New, 5 Jan., 1905 ; Dorothy Vernon in " Dorothy o' the Hall," New, 14 Apr., 1906 ; she again visited America, in Oct., 1910, playing in "The Scarlet Pimpernel," and "Henry of Navarre"; played Queen Frédérique in " The Popinjay," New, 2 Feb., 1911 ; at the Strand, 2 Jan., 1915, Margaret Goodman in " Mistress Wilful "; 22 Apr., 1915, Mrs. Martin in " The Argyle Case "; 11 Sept., 1915, again played Lady Blakeney in " The Scarlet Pimpernel "; from that date she frequently toured with her husband ; in 1920 toured in " Sweet Nell of Old Drury," " The Scarlet Pimpernel," " Much Ado About Nothing," " Henry of Navarre " ; during 1921 toured as Queen Mary in " The Borderer," and appeared in the same part, at the King's, Hammersmith, Mar., 1923 ; during 1924 toured as Sarah, Countess of Marlborough in " The Marlboroughs," appearing in that part at Wimbledon, Mar., 1925 ; in 1926 toured as Katherine in " The Wooing of Katherine Parr," and appeared in the part at the Borough, Stratford, Feb., 1927 ; at the Palace (for King George's Pension Fund), May, 1928, again played Lady Blakeney in " The Scarlet Pimpernel " ; at the Strand, Dec., 1928, played the same part; during 1930, toured in "Sweet Nell of Old Drury," and "Henry of Navarre"; at Daly's, May, 1934, appeared as Josephine Popinot in "Vintage Wine," and played the same part when the play was revived at the Victoria Palace, June, 1935 ; was the recipient of a testimonial luncheon, Mar., 1938, in celebration of her Jubilee on the stage; reappeared on the stage, at the "Q" Theatre, Nov., 1944, when she played Lady Rutven in "The Widow of 40." *(Died 27 May, 1957; age 88)*

NEILSON-TERRY, Dennis, actor, manager, and producer; *b.* London, 21 Oct., 1895; *s.* of Fred Terry and his wife Julia (Neilson) ; *e.* Felixstowe and Charterhouse ; *m.* Mary Glynne ; made his first appearance on the stage at Drury Lane, 12 June, 1906, when he walked on as a Page in " Much Ado About Nothing," on the occasion of the performance to commemorate Ellen Terry's Jubilee ; made his first regular appearance on the stage under the name of Derrick Dennis, at the New Theatre, 11 May, 1911, when he played Silvius in " As You Like It " ; subsequently played Armand St. Just in " The Scarlet Pimpernel " ; next toured with F. R. Benson's company for a year, playing Lorenzo, Silvius, Rosencrantz, Paris, Octavius Caesar, Demetrius in " A Midsummer Night's Dream," Malcolm in " Macbeth,"

etc. ; at His Majesty's, May, 1912, played Sebastian in " Twelfth Night," to his sister's Viola ; at Eastbourne, July, 1912, appeared as Julian Ross in " Big Game " ; was then engaged by Lillah McCarthy and Granville Barker, for the Savoy, and in Sept., 1912, played Florizel in "The Winter's Tale," and Nov., 1912, Sebastian in " Twelfth Night " ; at the New Theatre, Manchester, Feb., 1913, played Romeo in " Romeo and Juliet " ; at the Gaiety, Manchester, Apr., 1913, played Pierrot in " Prunella " ; at the New Theatre, Aug., 1913, played Julian Ross in " The Big Game " ; at the St. James's, Oct., 1913, Martin in " The Witch " ; Dec., 1913, Louis Dubetat in " The Doctor's Dilemma " ; at the Savoy, Feb., 1914, Oberon in " A Midsummer Night's Dream " ; at the Little Theatre, Sept., 1914, Barrato in " Forget-Me-Not " ; subsequently joined the 4th Batt. Royal West Surrey Regt. ; after his discharge from the Army, appeared at the St. James's, Jan., 1917, as Gautier Lalance in " The Aristocrat " ; at the Prince of Wales's, Aug., 1917, Ensign O'Hara in " Carminetta " ; at the New, Apr., 1918, Claude Devenish in " Belinda " ; at the Kingsway, Sept., 1918, Eric Keats in " A Week-End " ; during 1919, toured with Matheson Lang as Count Andrea Scipione in " Carnival," and appeared in the same part at the New Theatre, Feb., 1920; at the Theatre Royal, Manchester, Nov., 1920, played Viscount Hambledon in " The Honourable Mr. Tawnish " ; at the Empire, Dec., 1922, played Pierrot in " Arlequin " ; at the Lyceum, Feb., 1923, the Chevalier de Vaudrey in " The Orphans " ; Apr., 1923, Paul Azario in " A Night of Temptation " ; Sept., 1923, Rev. Denzil Norton in " What Money Can Buy " ; during 1924 toured in " The Honourable Mr. Tawnish " ; at the Coliseum, Jan., 1925, played Walter in " Then and Now " ; New, Feb., 1925, again played Count Andrea in " Carnival " ; Comedy, May, 1925, Michael Tristan in " The Crooked Friday " ; went to New York, and at the Bijou, 8 Oct., 1925, appeared in the same part; Ritz, Nov., 1925, played Martin Stapleton in " The

Offense "; in 1926 took his own company to South Africa, playing " The Man With a Load of Mischief," " The Honourable Mr. Tawnish," " The Crooked Friday," etc.; on his return appeared at Golder's Green, Apr., 1927, and Lyceum, May, 1927, as Ferdinand Fane in " The Terror "; Strand (for Play Actors), Nov., 1927, played Tony Matthews in " Fear "; in Oct., 1928, toured as Archie Clutter in " No Other Tiger," and appeared in the same part at the St. James's, Dec., 1928; at the Queen's, Mar., 1929, played Campbell Edwards in " The Man at Six." *Recreations:* Cricket, tennis, music, and fencing.
(Died 14 July, 1932; age 36)

NEILSON-TERRY,Phyllis,F.R.A.M., actress; *b.* London, 15 Oct., 1892; *d.* of Fred Terry and his wife Julia (Neilson); *e.* Westgate-on-Sea, Paris, and Royal Academy of Music; *m.* (1) Cecil King (dec.); (2) Heron Carvic; made her first appearance on the stage at the Opera House, Blackpool, Oct., 1909, as Marie de Belleforêt, in "Henry of Navarre," under the name of Phillida Terson; she made her first appearance on the London stage, at the New Theatre, 3 Jan., 1910, in the same part; in Feb., 1910, during the indisposition of her mother, she played the part of Marguerite de Valois in the same play; at His Majesty's Theatre, 7 Apr., 1910, she assumed the part of Viola in "Twelfth Night," her father appearing on that occasion as Sebastian; at the Haymarket Theatre, June, 1910, she played Princess Priscilla of Lothen Kunitz in "Priscilla Runs Away," and at the same theatre, Feb., 1911, she played Olive Kimber in "All that Matters"; New Theatre, May, 1911, played Rosalind in "As You Like It," and same theatre, Sept., 1911, she played Juliet in "Romeo and Juliet"; at His Majesty's Theatre, 19 Feb., 1912, Trilby in the play of that name; 9 Apr., 1912, appeared as Desdemona in "Othello"; 20 May, 1912, as Portia in "The Merchant of Venice"; at the Duke of York's, 14 June, 1912, played Lady Noeline Belturbet in a revival of "The Amazons"; at His Majesty's, 3 Sept., 1912, appeared as

Queen Elizabeth in "Drake"; 24 Mar., 1913, as Clair Remmington in "The Happy Island"; 12 Apr., 1913, as Lady Teazle in "The School for Scandal"; 27 May, 1913, Madame Jourdain in "The Perfect Gentleman"; during June, 1913, played Portia in "The Merchant of Venice," Viola in "Twelfth Night," Portia in "Julius Caesar" (23 June), and Juliet in "Romeo and Juliet"; at the St. James's, 27 June, 1913, appeared as Grace Harkaway in the "all-star" revival of "London Assurance," given in aid of King George's Actors' Pension Fund; at the Garrick, 29 Aug., 1913, appeared as Paulette Vannaire in "The Real Thing "; at the St. James's, 14 May, 1914, as Lady Chiltern in "An Ideal Husband "; at His Majesty's, 19 Aug., 1914, reappeared as Queen Elizabeth in "Drake"; made her first appearance in New York, at the Liberty Theatre, 23 Nov., 1914, as Viola in "Twelfth Night "; at Maxine Elliott Theatre, 1 Mar., 1915, played Lady Ursula Barrington in "The Adventure of Lady Ursula "; at the Shubert Theatre, 3 Apr., 1915, played the title-rôle in "Trilby "; in Aug., 1915, went on tour, playing the same part; appeared at the Palace, New York, in "vaudeville," Nov., 1915, giving songs, recitations, and excerpts from "Romeo and Juliet "; at the Shubert Theatre, New York, Mar., 1916, played Lady Harding in "The Great Pursuit" ("The Idler "); during 1917 toured in "vaudeville" over the Orpheur i Circuit; at His Majesty's, Montreal, Jan., 1918, played Maggie in a play of that name, subsequently touring in the same part; at Vancouver, Apr., 1918, played Nora Marsh in "The Land of Promise "; returned to England in 1919; appeared at the Coliseum, Oct., 1919, and subsequently toured in the leading provincial variety theatres; at Wolverhampton, Feb., 1920, played Trilby, and toured in the same part during 1920-1; entered on the management of the Apollo Theatre, Jan., 1922, when she played Ruth Dangan in "The Wheel "; in May, 1922, revived "Trilby," playing the title-*rôle*; in the autumn of 1922, toured in "The

Wheel"; returning to the Apollo, Jan., 1923, played Mrs. Stenning in "A Roof and Four Walls"; toured the provinces in the autumn of 1923 with the same play; during 1924 toured as Gemma dei Savorigi in "Stigmata," and as Mrs. Chepstow in "Bella Donna"; in 1925 toured as Victoria Burgesse in "The Folly of Youth"; in 1926 toured as Helen de Castelotte in "Honour," and 1927, in "Trilby"; in Oct., 1927, went to South Africa, and during 1927-8 played Nell Gwyn in "Sweet Nell of Old Drury," Trilby, Leslie Crosbie in "The Letter," Lady Ursula in "The Adventure of Lady Ursula," Gringoire in "The Ballad Monger," Mrs. Stenning in "A Roof and Four Walls," etc.; on her return to England, toured Nov., 1928, as Mrs. Craig in "Craig's Wife," appearing in that part at the Fortune, Jan., 1929; Strand, Feb., 1929, took up her mother's part of Lady Blakeney in "The Scarlet Pimpernel"; Feb., 1929, played Queen Mary in "The Borderer"; Prince of Wales's (for the Sunday Play Society), Mar., 1929, played Alaine d'Estoile in "Hunter's Moon"; Strand, Sept., 1929, Ann in "Devil in Bronze"; St. James's, Oct., 1929, Phillipa March in "Heat Wave"; Apr., 1930, toured as Valerie Merryman in "The Crime at Blossoms"; Malvern Festival, Aug., 1930, Candida in the play of that name; Cambridge, Sept., 1931, played Elizabeth in "Elizabeth of England"; Victoria Palace, Mar., 1932, She in "Business Before Pleasure"; New, May, 1932, Olivia in "Twelfth Night"; Trocadero, Sept., 1932, appeared in Cabaret; Ambassadors', Nov., 1932, played Stella Floyd in "Philomel"; Winter Garden, Dec., 1932, Mistress Page in "The Merry Wives of Windsor"; in Jan., 1933, went on tour, playing Irela in "Evensong"; Open Air Theatre, June–Sept., 1933, Olivia and Viola (alternatively) in "Twelfth Night"; Rosalind in "As You Like It"; Oberon in "A Midsummer Night's Dream"; at the Palace, Manchester, Dec., 1933, made her first appearance in pantomime, when she played Prince Charming in "Cinderella"; Prince's, Mar., 1934, played Nell Gwyn in "Sweet

Nell of Old Drury"; Open Air Theatre, June, 1934, again played Oberon; July, 1934, Queen Phillipa in "The Six of Calais"; Drury Lane, Dec., 1934, again played Prince Charming in "Cinderella"; Open Air Theatre, June–Sept., 1935, again played Countess Olivia, Rosalind, the Lady in "Comus," Oberon, and also played the Princess of France in "Love's Labour's Lost"; Westminster, Oct., 1935, Lady Patricia Cosway in "Lady Patricia"; toured, 1936, as Mary Tudor in the play of that name; Open Air, June–Sept., 1936, played Oberon, Olivia, Queen Katharine in "Henry VIII," and the Princess in "Love's Labour's Lost"; "Q," Dec., 1936, Lady Blakeney in "The Scarlet Pimpernel"; Open Air, June–Sept., 1937, Oberon, Olivia, Portia in "Julius Caesar," Hermione in "The Winter's Tale," Adriana in "A Comedy of Errors"; toured Oct., 1937, with Donald Wolfit's company, playing the Queen in "Hamlet," Portia in "The Merchant of Venice," Katherine in "The Taming of the Shrew," Lady Macbeth, and Olivia; "Q," Dec., 1937, Nell Gwyn in "Sweet Nell of Old Drury"; Stratford-on-Avon Memorial Theatre, 1938 season, Lady Macbeth, and Queen Katharine; toured, 1939, as June Harding in "To Have and to Hold," and Mellie in "Then and Again"; toured, 1939–40, as Miss Moffat in "The Corn is Green"; toured, 1941, as Mrs. Gordon Peel in "The Luck of the Navy"; at the "Q," May, 1944, played Epifania in "The Millionairess," and Nov., 1944, Raina Everleigh in "The Widow of 40," in which she again toured in 1946; toured. 1946, as Lynne and Julie in "Beggars' Union"; Embassy, July, 1949, played Lady Wimpole in "Fit for Heroes"; Saville, May, 1954, appeared in the *revue* "Cockles and Champagne"; St. James's, Sept., 1954, played Mrs. Railton-Bell in "Separate Tables"; Wyndham's, June, 1956, appeared for The Repertory Players as Marion Yorke in "More Things in Heaven"; Music Box, N.Y., Oct., 1956, again played Mrs. Railton-Bell in "Separate Tables"; Cambridge, London, May, 1959, Lady Bletchley in "Let Them Eat Cake"; Royal, Windsor, Feb.,

1960, Lady Godolphin in "Off a Duck's Back"; recent films include "Doctor in the House," "Look Back in Anger," "Conspiracy of Hearts," etc.; she has also made many television appearances; made her début on the concert platform as a singer at the Queen's Hall, 6 Feb., 1913. *Recreations:* Reading and playgoing. *Address:* Upton, Appledore, Kent. *Telephone No.:* Appledore 355.

NEIMAN, John M., M.I.P.R., theatre press-representative; *b.* Edgware, Middlesex, 25 May, 1935; *s.* of Adolph Joseph Neiman and his wife Betsy Jane (Woolf); *e.* London; *m.* Enid Mary Darwent; began his career in a theatre agency at the age of sixteen, and remained until he was called up for National Service in 1953; after demobilization, he joined Moss' Empires, 1955, as assistant press-representative; press representative to Moss Empires, Jan., 1958–65; member of the Institute of Public Relations, Dec., 1964. *Recreations:* Swimming and reading.

NEMCHINOVA, Vera, dancer; studied dancing in Moscow under Nelidova; joined the Diaghileff company 1915, and went with the company to the United States in the same year, making her first appearance there on 5 June, 1915; first appeared in London at the Coliseum, 18 Sept., 1918, and during the following year, appeared with the company at the Coliseum, Alhambra, and the Empire; Covent Garden, 1920; Prince's, 1921; Alhambra, 1921, where she appeared in "The Sleeping Princess"; joined forces with Anton Dolin, 1927, and with their own company, appeared at the Coliseum in "The Nightingale and the Rose," and the following year appeared with him in Paris, in "Rhapsody in Blue," "Espagnol," and "Revolution"); she has danced with outstanding success in "Soleil de Nuit," "Pulcinella," "La Boutique Fantasque," "Cimarosiana," "Giselle," "Le Lac des Cygnes," "Coppélia," "L'Epreuve d'Amour," "Les Biches," "Les Matelots," "Raimonda," etc.; is reputed to have a repertory of over 300 ballets.

NESBITT, Miriam Anne; daughter of George Laurence Skancke and Alice C. (Norton) Skancke; *b.* Chicago, Ill., 14 Sept., 1879; *e.* in public schools of Chicago, St. Mary's Convent, Notre Dame, Ind., and Mary Sharpe College, Winchester, Tenn.; made her first appearance on the stage at Madison Square Theatre, New York, 20 Jan., 1897, in "The Cup of Betrothal"; subsequently appeared with J. K. Hackett, in 1898, as Monica in "The Tree of Knowledge"; then played the part of Attille in "At the White Horse Tavern" at Wallack's Theatre, 1899; in the summer of the same year played leading business with the Bond Stock Company (Albany, New York); during 1900-1 appeared with the late Joseph Haworth in "Robert of Sicily"; next appeared with Miss Ada Rehan in "Sweet Nell of Old Drury," 1901, and during the summer months was the leading woman with Dean's Stock Company, Teledo, Ohio; subsequently appeared with W. H. Crane in "David Harum," 1901; with Chauncey Olcott in "Old Limerick Town," 1902, and with Henry E. Dixey in "Facing the Music," 1903, after which joined "The County Chairman" company, 1903; made her first appearance in London, at the Duke of York's Theatre, Dec., 1904, as Tiger Lily in "Peter Pan"; during 1905 she joined Henrietta Crosman's company, playing in "Mary, Mary, Quite Contrary," and, subsequently, with Lawrance D'Orsay played in "The Embassy Ball"; then assumed the *rôle* of Eleanor in "The Road to Yesterday," 1906-7; during 1909-10 toured as Beth Elliott in "The Travelling Salesman"; at Chicago, Nov., 1910, played Helen in "The Seventh Daughter"; since 1911 has devoted herself to acting in "film" plays. *Recreations :* Reading, country life, and travel. *Clubs :* Actors' Society, Actors' Church Alliance, Actors' Fund. *Business Address :* 133 West 45th Street (Actors' Society). *Residence :* Hotel Chelsea, New York City.

NESMITH, Ottola, *b.* Washington, 1893; *d.* of Captain Otto A. Nesmith and his wife Blanche (Vaughan); made her first appearance on the stage at San Diego, in 1910, in " Under Southern Skies," in a " stock " company, where she remained some time ; she subsequently played in " stock " companies at Los Angeles, Kansas City, and Washington, D.C. ; made her first appearance in New York, at Daly's Theatre, 19 Dec., 1912, as Dorothy Stuart in " The Question " ; during 1913-14 appeared with the Fulton Stock Company, at Lancaster, Pa., in the leading parts of " Sapho," " Madame X," " A Butterfly on the Wheel," " What Happened to Mary," " The Third Degree," " The White Sister," " Dorothy Vernon of Haddon Hall," etc. ; subsequently appeared as Eva in " The Vanishing Bride " ; at the Gaiety, New York, Aug., 1915, played Gloria in " Just Outside the Door " ; at the Fulton Theatre, Apr., 1916, Mrs. Hester Worsley in " A Woman of No Importance." *Recreations :* Music and piano-playing.

NETHERSOLE, Olga Isabel, C.B.E., actress ; *y.d.* of the late Henry Nethersole, solicitor ; *b.* Kensington, 18 Jan., 1866 ; *e.* London and on the Continent ; had some experience as an amateur before making her first appearance on the professional stage, at the Theatre Royal, Brighton, 5 Mar., 1887, as Lettice Vane in " Harvest " ; after touring with this play for some months was engaged by the late Arthur Dacre and Amy Roselle, and with their company played the parts of Blanche Maitland in " 'Twixt Kith and Kin," Claire in " A Double Marriage," and Alice Pengelly in " Our Joan " ; made her first appearance on the London stage, at the Grand Theatre, Islington, 3 Oct., 1887, in this last-mentioned part ; she next toured in the late Willie Edouin's company as Agatha in " Modern Wives " ; she appeared at the Strand Theatre, 9 June, 1888, as Nelly Busby in " The Paper Chase," and was then engaged for the Adelphi, where she appeared on 19 July, 1888, as Ruth Medway in " The Union Jack " ; she was next seen at the St. James's, 29 Nov., 1888, as Miriam St. Aubyn in " The Dean's Daughter," and she then returned to the Adelphi,

22 Dec., 1888, to play Lola Montez in " The Silver Falls " ; she was then engaged by John Hare for the Garrick Theatre, and appeared there on the opening night, 24 Apr., 1889, as Janet Preece in Pinero's play " The Profligate," in which she made quite a success ; on 31 Dec., 1889, in consequence of the illness of Mrs. Bernard Beere, she played Floria Tosca in " La Tosca " with complete success ; she then joined Charles Cartwright and went to Australia on a joint-starring tour, opening at the Garrick Theatre, Sydney, 20 Dec., 1890, as Vera in " Moths " ; other parts played on the Australian tour were, Mary Blenkarn in " The Middleman," Lady Harding in " The Idler," Leslie Brudenell in " The Profligate," Marguerite in " A Village Priest," Susan Hartley in " A Scrap of Paper " and Miriam in " The Ambassador " (" The Dean's Daughter ") ; she made her reappearance in London at the Garrick Theatre, 2 Jan., 1892, as Beatrice Selwyn in " A Fool's Paradise " ; at the Criterion, 24 May, she made a great success by her playing of the part of Mercede da Vigno in " Agatha" (" The Silent Battle "), playing the same part in Dec. of the same year ; at the Garrick, 18 Feb., 1893, she further increased her reputation by her performance of the Comtesse Zicka in " Diplomacy," when the cast included John Hare, the Bancrofts, Arthur Cecil, Forbes-Robertson and Kate Rorke ; the following year, she entered on the management of the Court Theatre, opening on 27 Jan., 1894, with A. W. Gattie's play, " The Transgressor," in which she played the part of Sylvia Woodville, subsequently touring in the same play in the provinces and in America ; she made her first appearance on the American stage at Palmer's Theatre, 15 Oct., 1894, in the same part, subsequently playing Marguerite Gauthier in "Camille," Juliet in "Romeo and Juliet," and Gilberte in "Frou-Frou" ; on her return she made her reappearance in London at the Garrick, 15 May, 1895, as Agnes in " The Notorious Mrs. Ebbsmith " ; she then toured the provinces, playing Juliet, Gilberte in " Frou-Frou," Denise in the play

of that name, Marguerite in " Camille," Sylvia in " The Transgressor " and Clarice in " Comedy and Tragedy " ; she again visited America in 1895, when she produced and played Carmen in the play of that name; she next appeared in London, at the Gaiety, June, 1896, as Carmen ; a further American tour followed, during which she appeared as Emma in " The Wife of Scarli " ; she produced " The Termagant," at Her Majesty's Theatre, 1 Sept., 1898, playing the part of Beatrix, and during a tour in the United States, 1899, appeared as Paula in " The Second Mrs. Tanqueray " ; at Wallack's Theatre, New York, 16 Feb., 1900, she appeared as Fanny Legrand in Clyde Fitch's play "Sapho"; subsequent to that date her appearances in London became very infrequent, but she produced "Sapho" at the Adelphi, 1 May, 1902; appeared at His Majesty's, 20 May, 1903, as Gabrielle Melville in "The Gordian Knot," and produced "The Flute of Pan" at the Shaftesbury, 12 Nov., 1904, when she played the part of the Princess Margaret of Siguria; in America, she has produced, and toured in " Magda," 1904 ; " The Labyrinth," 1905, in which she appeared as Marianne ; " Adrienne Lecouvreur," 1906, adapted by herself, in which she played the title-*rôle* ; " The Awakening," 1907, playing the part of Thérèse de Megee ; " I Pagliacci," playing Nedda, and " The Enigma," 1908 ; " The Writing on the Wall," 1909, in which she appeared as Barbara Lawrence, and " Luck of Wall Street," 1909 ; appeared at the New Theatre, New York, 5 Dec., 1910, as Mary Magdalene in Maeterlinck's play of that name ; at Richmond, Va., Jan., 1911, produced " The Redemption of Evelyn Vaudray," playing the leading part ; at San Francisco, Apr., 1911, appeared in the title-*rôle* of " Sister Beatrice"; reappeared in England, at the Prince of Wales's, Birmingham, Oct., 1912, when she played Helena in " The Awakening of Helena Ritchie" ; in Sept., 1913, toured in America, in "vaudeville," playing the third act of Daudet's "Sapho"; after many years absence from the stage, reappeared for a single performance, at Wyndham's

July, 1923, playing Barbara Lawrence in " The Writing on the Wall " ; she appeared with great success at the Théâtre Sarah Bernhardt, Paris, in the spring of 1907, when she played "The Second Mrs. Tanqueray," "Camille," "Sapho," "Adrienne Lecouvreur," "Magda," and "Carmen."
(Died 9 Jan., 1951; age 84)

NETTLEFOLD, Archibald, manager ; *b.* London, 1870 ; *s.* of Frederick Nettlefold and his wife Mary (Warren) ; his first managerial venture was made in association with Marian Wilson, Oct., 1921, when they staged The British Ballet season, at the Kingsway Theatre ; was next associated with J. H. Benrimo, when he revived " The Yellow Jacket " at the Kingsway, Mar., 1922; followed by " Spanish Lovers," in both of which he also acted under the name of R. Chee; at the Ambassadors', produced " Charles I," " The Secret Agent," 1922; subsequently became lessee and manager of the Comedy Theatre, where he produced, among other plays, " Lavender Ladies," " The Ring o' Bells," 1925 ; " The Rescue Party," 1926 ; " The Silent House," 1927 ; " The Devil's Host," 1928 ; " The Devil in the Cheese," " Secrets," 1929 ; " Lucky Dip," 1930 ; " Paris in London," 1932. *Recreation :* Farming.
(Died 29 Nov., 1944; age 74)

NETTLEFOLD, Frederick John, actor and manager ; *b.* Hastings, 1867 ; *s.* of Frederick Nettlefold and his wife Mary (Warren) ; *e.* Eastbourne College, Corpus Christi, Oxford, Heidelberg, and Berlin; *m.* Judith Kyrle (dec.) ; studied for the stage under Hermann Vezin and Henry Neville ; made his first appearance on the stage at the Opéra Comique Theatre, 9 Feb., 1893, as Jack Poyntz in " School " ; during the same year toured in " In the Ranks " ; at Toole's, 1893, was engaged understudying " Mrs. Othello " ; subsequently toured with Miss Fortescue, 1894 ; Edmund Tearle, 1894-5 ; Osmond Tearle, 1895-7 ; " The Sorrows of Satan," 1897 ; with Kate Vaughan's repertory company, 1898-9, appeared at Terry's under his own management, with Kate Vaughan; appeared at the Garrick, under Arthur Bourchier; has also toured with Willie Edouin and Ben Greet; assumed the management of the Scala Theatre, May, 1919, and appeared there as Dick Kent in " The Black Feather," Pygmalion, Claude Melnotte, Othello, and Major Vivian Addingham in " The Net "; assumed the management of the Apollo, Mar., 1921, appearing as Don Caesar in " Don Q "; Sept., 1921, played John Daunt in " Crooked Usage "; Nov., 1921, Phillips in " Thank You, Phillips ! " *Club :* Garrick. *Recreations :* Motoring, swimming and walking. *(Died 25 Nov., 1949; age 82)*

NEWALL, Guy, actor; *b.* Isle of Wight, 25 May, 1885; *s.* of Col. M. G. Newall, R.H.A.; *m.* (2) Ivy Duke (mar. dis.); (3) Dorothy Batley; first appeared at the Prince of Wales's, Oct., 1911, as J. K. Ainslie in "Same Lodge"; in 1912 joined the London Film Company and played in several film productions; was engaged with Marie Tempest at the Playhouse, May, 1914, appearing as Adrian Harper in " The Wynmartens," subsequently touring with her in the United States and Canada, playing Harvey Betts in " Mary Goes First," William Lewis in " At the Barn," etc.; during the War, served with the Royal Garrison Artillery; after the War was managing director of George Clark Film Productions, writing, producing, and acting in many of the company's productions; reappeared on the regular London stage at the Grand, Putney, Nov., 1924, as Jim Valentine in his own play " Husband Love "; at the Criterion, June, 1925, played Howell James in " Mixed Doubles "; Sept., 1927, Vivian Essex in " When Blue Hills Laughed "; at the Comedy, May, 1928, Herb in " Our Little Wife "; subsequently toured as Joseph Meadows in " Baby Cyclone " and Teddy Deakin in " The Ghost Train "; sailed for South Africa, May, 1929, with his own company, to play " Just Married," " When Blue Hills Laughed," "77 Park Lane"; on his return, appeared at the Everyman, Aug., 1930, as Toby Heron in " The

Bond "; Fortune, Nov., 1930, played Lord Strathpeffer in "The Man from Blankley's"; in 1931, toured as Dionysius Woodbury in "Never Say Die"; Royalty, Aug., 1932, succeeded Sir Nigel Playfair as Colonel Hammond in "While Parents Sleep"; Playhouse, Oct., 1933, Sir George O'Gorman in "So Good! So Kind!!"; at the Playhouse, June, 1934 succeeded Sir Nigel Playfair as Sir Wilfred Kelling in "Libel"; King's, Hammersmith, Feb., 1935, played Victor Saltmarsh in "All Rights Reserved"; among recent films in which he has appeared are "The Ghost Train," "The Eternal Feminine," "Potiphar's Wife," "Rodney Steps In," "The Marriage Bond," "The Admiral's Secret," etc. *(Died 28 Feb., 1937; age 52)*

NEWBERRY, Barbara, actress and dancer; *b.* Boston, Mass., U.S.A., 12 Apr., 1910; *d.* of M. N. Newberry and his wife Elizabeth Foy (Wiley); *e.* Kenwood School, Chicago; *m.* (1) Eddie Foy, Jun. (mar. dis.); (2) R. B. Foster; as a child studied dancing at the Metropolitan Opera House, New York, and subsequently at the Merriel Abbott School, Chicago; made her first appearance on the stage at the Globe Theatre, New York, 1918, succeeding to the part of Marjorie Jones in "Penrod," and at the Shubert Theatre, Nov., 1918, appeared as one of the children in "The Betrothal"; she also appeared as a child in several operas at the Metropolitan Opera House; at the New Amsterdam, New York; 1 June, 1925, appeared in "The Ziegfeld Follies"; Globe, June, 1926, in "No Foolin'"; played her first part at the New Amsterdam, Dec., 1926, as May Meadow in "Betsy"; Royale, May, 1927, Pollyanna Montague in "Oh, Ernest!"; Hammerstein's, Nov., 1927, Ann Milford in "Golden Dawn"; Sept., 1928, Betty Summers in "Good Boy"; Ziegfeld, Jan., 1929, appeared as Ellie in "Show Boat"; July, 1929, appeared in "Show Girl"; Alvin, Nov., 1929, played Mary Trumbell in "Heads Up"; subsequently toured in "Pyjama Lady"; 44th Street Theatre, Jan., 1932, played Alberta in "A Little

Racketeer"; Majestic, Jan., 1933, Gerry Martin in "Pardon My English"; Apollo, June, 1933, Toni Ray in "Take a Chance"; in 1933, appeared at the Dorchester Hotel, London, with Carl Randall, in "Monte Carlo Follies," which they produced, and again appeared there, 1934–35; made her first appearance on the London stage at the London Hippodrome, 27 June, 1935, as Eve Crawley in "Love Laughs ——"; with Carl Randall arranged all the dance numbers in "Gay Divorce," New York and in London, 1932–33; produced the dance numbers in "Take a Chance," 1933. *Recreations :* Swimming, riding and reading. *Address :* 145 West 58th Street, New York City, U.S.A. *Telephone No. :* Circle 7–7740.

NEWCOMB, Mary, actress; *b.* North Adams, Mass., 21 Aug., 1897; *d.* of Josiah T. Newcomb and his wife Sophie (De Wolfe); *e.* privately, at home; *m.* (1) Robert Edeson (mar. dis.); (2) Alexander Henry Higginson; made her first appearance on the stage at the Pitt Theatre, Pittsburg, 22 Jan., 1918, as Constance Weems in " Sick-a-Bed," and appeared at the Gaiety, New York, 25 Feb., 1918, in the same part; at Atlantic City, Jan., 1919, played in " The Dislocated Honeymoon "; at Maxine Elliott's, New York, Sept., 1919, played Annabelle in " First is Last "; at the Comedy, Jan., 1920, appeared in " My Lady Friends "; she then went to California, and played on the Western Coast of America for three years; at Chicago, 1923, played in " Kelly's Vacation "; at the Eltinge Theatre, Aug., 1923, made a distinct success when she appeared as Betty Brown in " The Woman on the Jury "; at Chicago, May, 1924, and Thirty-ninth Street Theatre, New York, Aug., 1924, played Agnes Sheridan in " Easy Street "; at Chicago, 1924, played Maisie Buck in " The Lady of the Streets "; at the Bijou, New York, Feb., 1925, appeared in the same part when the play was renamed " The Night Hawk "; Morosco, Sept., 1925. played Lady Susan Herryot in " The Bridge of Distances "; she then left the stage and was not seen again until she appeared at the Hudson Theatre, Jan., 1928, as Lynn Wilson in " A Distant Drum "; made her first appearance on the London stage at the Fortune Theatre, 5 Dec., 1928, as Valerie in " Jealousy," scoring an instantaneous success; at the Arts Theatre, Apr., 1929, scored a further success when she played Mary in " The Infinite Shoeblack," subsequently transferred to the Comedy and Globe Theatres; at the New, Sept., 1929, played the title-*rôle* in " Emma Hamilton"; Mar., 1930, Philippa Woodall in "Healthy, Wealthy, and Wise"; Arts, June, 1930, and Little, July, 1930, appeared in a revival of " Jealousy"; Little, Aug., 1930, played Marceline in " John o' Dreams"; Royalty, Dec., 1930, Irene in "A Marriage has been Disarranged"; Haymarket, Feb., 1931, Kit Kennedy in "Supply and Demand"; Arts, Sept., 1931, Antoinette Lyle in "Behold, the Bridegroom"; St. James's, Apr., 1932, Portia in "The Merchant of Venice";

Lyric, Apr., 1933, Claire Woodruff in "When Ladies Meet"; Vaudeville, Dec., 1933, Angel in a play of that name; Shaftesbury, Apr., 1934, Lady Carlingford in "There's Always To-Morrow"; in Sept., 1934, joined the Old Vic.-Sadler's Wells company, and during the season appeared as Cleopatra in "Antony and Cleopatra," the Duchess of York in "Richard II," Beatrice in "Much Ado About Nothing," Joan in "Saint Joan," Emilia in "Othello," Phaedra in "Hippolytus" (of Euripides), and Barbara Undershaft in "Major Barbara"; "Q," Jan., 1936, Judith Coventry in "The Prickly Pear"; Duke of York's, Mar., 1936, Stella Harringway in "Children to Bless You"; "Q," Nov., 1936, Princess Dolores in "Storm Over Europe"; Mercury, Aug., 1942, the Lady in "A Man With a Load of Mischief," and Feb., 1943, Elsa in "Days Without End," in which she also appeared at the Arts Theatre, June, 1943; in 1939, founded the Mary Newcomb Players Mobile Theatre for the free entertainment of H.M. Forces, under Southern Command, playing "The Man With a Load of Mischief," "Gaslight," "French Leave" and "Jealousy"; in 1943, her company was taken over by C.E.M.A.; in 1944-5, toured France, Belgium and Holland, for E.N.S.A., in "Jealousy"; has since devoted her time to work for the Dorset Drama League, of which she has been President since 1947, and the Dorset Music Society, of which she is Chairman. *Recreations:* Golf, fishing and croquet.

(Died 26 Dec., 1966; age 69)

NEWELL, Raymond, actor and vocalist; *b.* Malvern, Worcestershire, 28 Apr., 1894; *s.* of John Newell and his wife Maria Phoebe (Porter); *e.* Lyttelton School, Malvern; *m.* Muriel Chandler; formerly engaged in the Civil Service; studied for the stage at the Guildhall School of Music, 1919-23; on the outbreak of War, 1914, joined the Royal Engineers (Signal Service), and served until 1918, in the German East African campaign; was invalided from the Army, May, 1919; commenced his musical career as a concert artist, and appeared at the Queen's Hall, Albert Hall, etc., 1923-6; toured in variety theatres, 1927; made his first appearance on the regular stage, Jan., 1928, when he toured as Francis Moray in "That's a Good Girl"; made his first appearance on the London stage at the London Hippodrome, 5 June, 1928, in the same part; from May to Sept., 1929, toured in South Africa; at the Alhambra and Coliseum, Oct.–Nov., 1929, appeared in "Melodies and Memories"; Drury Lane, Mar., 1930, played Aramis in "The Three Musketeers"; Jan., 1931, The Hillman and the Fisherman in "The Song of the Drum"; Cambridge Theatre, June, 1931, appeared in "The Sign of the Seven Dials"; in Aug., 1931, toured as Monsieur Beaucaire in the opera of that name, and appeared in the same part at Daly's, Nov., 1931; Jan., 1932, toured as Stefan in "Viktoria and Her Hussar"; Sept., 1932, toured as André D'Aubigny in "The Lilac Domino"; Saville, Mar., 1933, Petrolski in "He Wanted Adventure"; during 1934-5, engaged in broadcasting; London Palladium, Sept., 1937, appeared in "London Rhapsody," and also appeared there at the Royal Variety performance; Prince's, Dec., 1939, and again in May, 1941, appeared in "Shephard's Pie"; Stoll, July, 1942, played Jim Kenyon in "Rose Marie"; Cambridge Theatre, Feb., 1944, appeared in "The Gay Follies"; Stoll, Oct., 1944, played the Fisherman and the Wine Seller in "The Lisbon Story," in which he also toured, 1945. *Favourite parts:* Aramis and Beaucaire. *Recreations:* Golf and motoring. *Club:* Savage. *Address:* The Third Green, Church Road, Wimbledon Park, London, S.W.19. *Telephone No.:* Wimbledon 1238.

NEWMAN, Claude, dancer; *b.* Plymouth, 20 Apr., 1903; *e.* privately; studied dancing under Phyllis Bedells; made his first appearance on the stage at Drury Lane Theatre, 26 Dec., 1924, in Fokine's ballet in "A Midsummer Night's Dream"; Apollo, Jan., 1925, appeared in "By the Way"; during 1926, toured in "The Three Graces," and at the Winter Garden, Aug., 1926, appeared in "Tip-Toes"; was engaged by C. B. Cochran, 1927, appearing at the Trocadero in cabaret, and at the London Pavilion, May, 1927, in "One Dam Thing After Another"; Daly's, Feb., 1928, danced in "Lady Mary"; His Majesty's, Sept., 1928, in "Song of the Sea"; London Pavilion, Mar., 1929, in "Wake Up and Dream," and in Dec., 1929, appeared at the Selwyn Theatre, New York, in the same piece; in 1930, danced in "Coppélia"; on returning to England, joined Idzikowsky for a short period; Adelphi, Dec., 1930, appeared in "Ever Green"; joined the Vic.-Wells Ballet company, 1931; Adelphi, Jan., 1932, danced in "Helen!", and was again seen in cabaret at the Trocadero; Vaudeville, July, 1933, appeared in "After Dark"; appeared at the Open Air Theatre, 1934; he appeared at Sadler's Wells throughout the seasons, 1932-9; during the War, served five years in the Royal Navy; returned to Sadler's Wells, 1946, as ballet-master and mime; is an examiner for the Royal Academy of Dancing. *Favourite parts:* The Tailor in "The Rake's Progress," Dr. Coppelius, "Buffon" and Drosselmayer in "Casse-Noisette." *Recreation:* Gardening. *Address:* 63 Oakley Street, London, S.W.3. *Telephone No.:* Flaxman 5263.

NEWMAN, Greatrex, lyric writer and librettist; *b.* Manchester, 3 July, 1892; commenced writing in 1914, when he contributed sketches and lyrics to " The Passing Show "; contributed sketches and lyrics to " Joy-Bells," 1919; " Midnight Follies," " Poppy," 1924; " Patricia," 1924; author of " Patches," " Records," " Notions," " Headlights," " Designs," " Chimes," 1925; contributed sketches and lyrics to " The Punch Bowl," 1925; contributed lyrics to " The Blue Kitten," 1925; sketches and lyrics " R.S.V.P.," 1926; " Vaudeville Vanities " (second edition), 1926; part-author of " Palladium Pleasures," 1926; " C.O.D.," 1927; contributed scenes and lyrics to "Lady Luck," 1927; "Rhyme and Rhythm," "Here We Are Again," 1932; part-author of "Shake Your Feet," "The Girl from Cook's," "False Faces," 1927; author of the programme for "The Optimists" (New York), 1928; part-author (with Clifford Grey) of "Mr. Cinders," 1929; "Mr. Whittington," 1934; "Love Laughs" (with Grey), 1935; contributed sketches and lyrics to seven programmes of "The Co-Optimists," (1921–6); "Fine and Dandy," 1942; "Africa Stars," 1944; "Gaieties," 1945; co-presented "Ye Good Olde Days," 1964; proprietor and principal author of the revived "Co-Optimists," 1929; also of "The Fol-de-Rols," at various seaside resorts, from 1911 to date. *Recreations:* Cricket and tennis. *Club:* Savage. *Address:* c/o Fol de Rols Ltd., Ashleigh, Little London, Heathfield Sussex. *Telephone No.:* 04-353 2478.

NEWMAN, Paul, actor; *b.* Cleveland, Ohio, 26 Jan., 1925; *s.* of Arthur S. Newman and his wife Theresa (Fetzer); *e.* Kenyon College and Yale University; *m.* (1) Jackie Witte (mar. dis.); (2) Joanne Woodward; studied for the stage at Yale University Graduate School and at the Actors Studio, N.Y.; began his career in summer "stock," 1949; made his first appearance on Broadway, at the Music Box, Feb., 1953, as Alan Seymour in "Picnic," which ran for more than a year; Ethel Barrymore, Feb., 1955, played Glenn Griffin in "The Desperate Hours"; Martin Beck, Mar., 1959, played Chance Wayne in "Sweet Bird of Youth"; Little, Apr., 1964, Emil in "Baby Want a Kiss"; notable films in which he has appeared include "Cat on a Hot Tin Roof," "The Long Hot Summer" (Cannes Film Festival best actor Award), "Exodus," "From the Terrace," "Young Philadelphian," "The Hustler," "Hud," "The Outrage," "Cool Hand Luke," "Hombre," "Butch Cassidy and the Sundance Kid," etc.; made his first appearance on television in 1952. *Recreations:* Reading, and all sports in general.

NEWNHAM - DAVIS, Nathaniel, Lieut.-Col.; *b.* London, 6 Nov., 1854; *e.s.* of Henry Newnham-Davis; *e.* Harrow; joined the Buffs, 1873; served with the Imperial Mounted Infantry in the Zulu War, and was twice mentioned in despatches 1877 to 1879, receiving medal and clasp; retired from Service in 1894; was on the staff of *The Sporting Times*, 1894-1912; was also Editor of *The Man of the World*, 1894-1900; is dramatic critic of *Town Topics*, and was elected to the Committee of the Critics' Circle, on the formation of that body, 1913; author of " An Ideal," Palace Theatre, 1896; " A Charitable Bequest," Criterion, 1900; part-author of " Lady Madcap," Prince of Wales's, 1904; also responsible for the ballets, " Round the Town Again," " A Day in Paris," and " New York," at the Empire; author of several books. *Recreation :* Amateur theatricals (member of Old Stagers and Windsor Strollers). *Address :* 32 Clarence Gate Gardens, N.W. *Telephone :* 3722 Paddington. *Clubs :* Naval and Military, Beefsteak, Garrick, Royal Eastern, Eccentric.

(Died 28 May, 1917; age 62)

NEWTON, Henry Chance, dramatic critic, dramatic author, etc.; " Carados " of *The Referee*; *b.* London, 13 Mar., 1854; *m.* Margaret Reid; in his younger days was an actor; was on the staff of *Fun*, 1875; was one of the original staff of *The Referee*, 1877, and is still one of the chief contributors on the staff of that famous journal; for some years

was on the staff of *The Sketch*; for over twenty years London Correspondent of *The New York Dramatic Mirror*, under the *nom de plume* of "Gawain," resigning in June, 1911; with Richard Butler (under the joint name of "Richard-Henry") is the author of the burlesques, "Monte Cristo, Junior," "Frankenstein," "Jaunty Jane Shore," and "Lancelot the Lovely"; of the plays: "First Mate," "Queer Street," "A Silver Honeymoon," "Adoption," "A Happy Day," and "Crime and Christening"; also the author of the following plays: "Letters Addressed Here," "Weatherwise," "The Newest Woman," "The House-That Jack Built," "The Maid of Athens" (with Charles Edmund), "Honour or Love," "The A.B.C., or Flossie the Frivolous," "Cartouche and Co.," "Mr. Gull's Fortune," "Giddy Ostend," "The Nut Brown Maid," "Don Quixote," "Are You a Smoker?" (with Walter Stephens), "Gelert," "The Up-River Girl," "Wellington," "Keep to the Right," "Home from Home" (with Fred Karno), "A Celestial Bride"; part-author of "The Life of Charles Morton"; author of "The Old Vic," 1923; contributed his reminiscences, under the title of "True Stories of the Stage," to *The Referee*, and music-hall reminiscences to *The Performer*; author of "Cues and Curtain Calls," 1927; "Idols of the Halls," 1928; "Crime and the Drama," 1928. *Recreations*: Playgoing and fishing. *Clubs*: National Sporting, Eccentric, Irish, Savage, and Arts Theatre.
(Died 2 Jan., 1931; age 76)

NEWTON, Robert, actor; *b.* Shaftesbury, Dorset, 1 June, 1905; *s.* of Algernon Newton, A.R.A., and his wife Marjorie Balfour (Ryder); *e.* Newbury Grammar School and in Switzerland; *m.* Nathalie Newhouse; made his first appearance on the stage at the Birmingham Repertory Theatre, Nov., 1920, walking on in "Henry IV" (Part I); spent three years with that company and was assistant stage manager there from Aug., 1921 to July, 1923; he appeared there as Fabian in

"Twelfth Night," Jesse Redvers in "The Secret Woman," Balthasar in "Romeo and Juliet," etc.; dur ng 1923-4, toured in South Africa; made his first appearance in London, at Drury Lane, 3 June, 1924, in "London Life"; Comedy, Nov., 1925, played George Bristow in "The Ring O' Bells"; toured the provinces for three years; Lyric, July, 1928, played Jacko Blaker in "My Lady's Mill"; Aug., 1928, Paul Guisard in "Her Cardboard Lover"; Jan., 1929, John Murray and the Regent in "Byron"; His Majesty's, July, 1929, Hugh Devon in "Bitter Sweet," which ran over a year; went to America, and made his first appearance in New York at the Times Square Theatre, 11 May, 1931, succeeding Laurence Olivier as Victor Prynne in "Private Lives"; Prince of Wales's, London, Mar., 1932, played Mort in "I Lived With You"; Duchess, June, 1932, Jesse Redvers in "The Secret Woman"; he then assumed the management of the Grand Theatre, Fulham, which he ran as the Shilling Theatre for two years, and played there, among other parts, Pietro Strozzi in "Night's Candles," Boris Feldman in "The Greeks Had a Word For It," etc.; Little Theatre, May, 1934, Patrick O'Leary in "Once Upon a Time"; Duke of York's, Nov., 1934, Boris in "The Greeks Had a Word For It"; Arts, Jan., 1935, Jean in "Miss Julie"; Duke of York's, May, 1935, Mark Gresham in "Roulette"; Little, Apr., 1936, Renny in "Whiteoaks"; subsequently toured in "Saturday's Children"; Old Vic., Jan., 1937, Horatio in "Hamlet"; spent the next five years in films; Prince of Wales's, July, 1942, played Slim Grisson in "No Orchids for Miss Blandish"; appeared in films again from 1943-5; toured, Oct., 1945, as Randy Jollifer in "So Brief the Spring," and appeared in this at the Wimbledon Theatre, Feb., 1946; Vaudeville, June, 1950, played Mr. Manningham in "Gaslight"; entered films, 1937 in "Fire Over England." *Recreations*: Fishing and shooting. *(Died 25 Mar., 1956; age 51)*

NEY, Marie, actress; *b.* Chelsea, 18 July, 1895; *d.* of William Fix;

e. St. Mary's Convent, Wellington, New Zealand; *m*. (1) Thomas H. Menzies (mar. dis.); (2) Thomas H. Menzies, (dec.); on leaving school was trained for Kindergarten work; made her first appearance on the stage at the Princess's, Melbourne, 4 Nov., 1916, as The Widow in "The Taming of the Shrew," with Allan Wilkie's Shakespearean Company; subsequently played Nerissa, Phoebe, Player Queen, Valentine in "Twelfth Night," etc.; she then appeared as Lady Mary in "Seven Days Leave," Princess Venetia in "The Story of the Rosary," etc.; during 1919 played leading parts in "stock" at Perth, Western Australia; subsequently, 1919–20, played under J. N. Tait's management in "Peg o' My Heart," "The Little Damozel," "Kindling," etc.; was then engaged by Marie Tempest in Aug., 1921, to play Dinah in "Mr. Pim Passes By"; under the J. C. Williamson management, July, 1922, played Liza and Mrs. Collinson in "My Lady's Dress," and Lucy Shale in "The Lie"; she then came to England, and made her first appearance on the English stage at Brixton Theatre, 27 Aug., 1923, as Rosalie in "The Marriage of Kitty," with Marie Tempest; in Feb., 1924, went on tour playing Lucy Shale in "The Lie"; was then engaged for the Old Vic., opening there in Oct., 1924, as Desdemona in "Othello," followed by Helena in "A Midsummer Night's Dream," Martha in "Hannele," Lady Macbeth, Ophelia; Rose Trelawny in "Trelawny of the 'Wells'," Kate Hardcastle, Queen in "Richard II," Beatrice in "Much Ado About Nothing," Hermione in "The Winter's Tale," Viola in "Twelfth Night"; Ambassadors', Nov., 1925, played Emma Huxtable in "The Madras House"; Regent (for the Repertory Players), Jan.–Mar., 1926, Ruth Atkins in "Beyond the Horizon," and Miss Jubb in "The Rescue Party"; New, Sept., 1926, Kate and Millicent Gregory in "The Constant Nymph"; Holborn Empire, Dec., 1926, Mrs. Carey in "Where the Rainbow Ends"; Oct.–Dec., 1927, was in Egypt with Robert Atkins' Shakespearean Company, playing lead; Lyric, Hammersmith, Aug., 1928, played Kate Hardcastle in "She Stoops to Conquer";

Oct., 1928, Tilburina in "The Critic"; Strand (for Repertory Players), Dec., 1928, Mrs. Myra Lewis in "Wrongs and Rights"; Strand (for the Venturers), Jan., 1929, Marquise de Pommeraye in "La Marquise D'Arcis"; Kingsway, Jan., 1929, Jane Moonlight in "Mrs. Moonlight"; Everyman, Feb., 1929, Jessica in "The Offence"; Arts, Sept., 1929, Veronica in a play of that name; Lyric, Hammersmith, Oct., 1929, Dorothy Musgrave in "Beau Austin"; Strand (for Repertory Players), Nov., 1929, Ethel in "People Like Us"; Lyric, Jan., 1930, Sylvia in "Murder on the Second Floor"; Drury Lane, Mar., 1930, Lady de Winter in "The Three Musketeers"; Strand (for Repertory Players), May, 1930, Claire Blanchard in "How to be Healthy, though Married"; Arts, Nov., 1930, Joyce Willoughby in "Machines"; Old Vic., Feb., 1931, Raina in "Arms and the Man"; Duke of York's, May, 1931, Miss Janus in "London Wall"; Lyric, May, 1932, Freda Caplan in "Dangerous Corner"; Arts and Westminster, Mar., 1933, Stella in "The Lake"; Alhambra, Mar., 1934, Portia in "The Merchant of Venice"; Haymarket, May, 1934, Sylvia Herriot in "Touch Wood"; at the Comedy, Feb., 1935, produced under her own management, "Mrs. Nobby Clark," in which she appeared as Anne Taylor; Ambassadors', Mar., 1935, Knowledge in "Everyman"; Criterion, July, 1935, Mary Penshott in "This Desirable Residence"; Old Vic., Nov., 1935, Olga in "The Three Sisters"; New, Mar., 1936, Cecily Harrington in "Love from a Stranger," and Feb., 1937, Celia in "As You Like It"; Haymarket, June, 1937, June Harding in "To Have and to Hold"; Old Vic., Oct., 1937, Isabella in "Measure for Measure"; Vaudeville, Nov., 1937, Mrs. Alving in "Ghosts"; Westminster, Mar., 1938, the Lady Ursula in "The Zeal of thy House"; toured, 1938, in "Love from a Stranger"; Gaiety, Dublin, June, 1938, Epifania in "The Millionairess"; Wyndham's, Aug., 1938, Emily Treowain in "She, Too, Was Young"; Piccadilly (for the Sunday Theatre), Dec., 1938, Princess Elizabeth in "Sanctity"; toured in Holland, Mar., 1939, with the London

Mask Theatre, as Candida; appeared with the Old Vic company, at Buxton Festival, Aug., 1939, and at Streatham Hill, Oct., 1939, as the Duchess of Marlborough in "Viceroy Sarah," the Nurse in "Romeo and Juliet," and Mrs. Croaker in "The Good-Natured Man"; went to Australia, 1940, and from Sept., 1940–May, 1941, appeared in Melbourne and Sydney in "Ladies in Retirement," "No Time for Comedy," "Private Lives," and a one-woman show, "Shakespeare's Women," which she gave in aid of various War funds; engaged in broadcasting in Malaya, 1941–2; toured in South Africa, 1942, subsequently proceeding to the Middle East under the auspices of the British Council; toured for E.N.S.A., in Italy and Middle East; returned to England, 1945; appeared in Holland and the Channel Islands in "Shakespeare's Women"; reappeared in London, at the Lyric, Hammersmith, Nov., 1945, when she played Hecuba in "The Trojan Women"; Boltons, between Apr., 1947, and Feb., 1948, appeared as Marie Louise in "King of Rome," Lady Blair in "A Fish in the Family," Ellen Dalton in "Native Son"; New, June, 1948, played Nurse Braddock in "The Gioconda Smile"; Aldwych, Aug., 1948, Lady Corbel in "Rain on the Just"; St. Martin's, June, 1949, Sara Cantry in "The Young and Fair"; Arts, Aug., 1949, Doña Barbarita in "The Romantic Young Lady"; Haymarket, Aug., 1950, Mrs. Cortelyon in "The Second Mrs. Tanqueray"; Old Vic, Apr., 1952, played Marthe in "The Other Heart"; Court, Aug., 1952, Aemilia in "The Comedy of Errors"; also Oct., 1952, Lady Windermere in "Lord Arthur Savile's Crime"; Royal, Brighton, Nov., 1952, Lady Caroline in "We Have Company"; at the Grand, Blackpool, Jan., 1953, played Mrs. Armstrong in "The Man Upstairs"; at the Edinburgh Festival, Aug., 1953, appeared as Mary Stuart in "Fotheringhay"; toured, 1954, as Gerda Verity in "All Night Sitting"; Arts, Apr., 1954, played Alice Makepeace in "The Sun Room"; Court, Mar., 1955, Mrs. Coleridge in "The Burning Boat"; Royal, Bristol, Sept., 1955, Cora Fellowes in "The Mulberry

Bush"; Lyceum, Edinburgh, Mar., 1958, Mrs. Logan in "The Last Word"; appeared as a Guest Artist at the Salisbury Playhouse, June, 1960, as Mrs. Alving in "Ghosts"; first appeared in films, 1930, in "Escape," and has since appeared in numerous pictures, radio and television plays. *Recreations:* Walking and reading. *Address:* c/o London Artists Ltd., 25 Gilbert Street, London, W.1.

NICANDER, Edwin, actor; *b.* New York City, U.S.A., 23 Dec., 1876; *s.* of Arnold Rau and his wife Elizabeth (Dotzert); *e.* New York City; made his first appearance on the stage at Spec's Opera House, Philadelphia, 24 Sept., 1894, as Gustave in "Vendetta"; made his first appearance on the New York stage, at the Murray Hill Theatre, 27 Aug., 1898, as Private Perry in "The New South," with Henry V. Donelly's "stock" company, and remained there two seasons; at the Garrick, Sept., 1900, played Walter Hochstuhl in "All on Account of Eliza"; subsequently played numerous "stock" engagements in various parts of the United States; at Wallack's Theatre, Oct., 1906, played Guy Hoggenheimer in "The Rich Mr. Hoggenheimer"; Oct., 1907, played Richard Hunter in "The Silver Girl"; Savoy, Jan., 1908, Albert in "Twenty Days in the Shade"; Empire, Sept., 1908, Vincent in "Jack Straw"; Garrick, Aug., 1909, Alick Forbes in "Detective Sparkes"; Mar., 1910, Arthur Greenfield in "The Girl He Couldn't Leave Behind Him"; Lyric, Oct., 1910, Samuel Twimbley in "Electricity"; Knickerbocker, Apr., 1911, Donald Houston in "Dr. de Luxe"; Lyceum, Oct., 1911, Alcide Pingo in "The Runaway"; Park, Sept., 1912, Samuel Brown in "My Best Girl"; Comedy, Sept., 1914, Robert in "A Modern Girl"; Gaiety, May, 1915, Leslie Tarton in "She's In Again"; Booth, Jan., 1916, Bertie Sayre in "The Fear Market"; Republic, Oct., 1916, George Wimbledon in "Good Gracious, Annabelle"; Comedy, Feb., 1917, played in "The Iron Cross"; Gaiety, Feb., 1918, played Reginald Jay in "Sick-a-Bed"; 39th Street, Dec.,

1918, Edouarde Chaumet in "Keep It To Yourself"; Morosco, May, 1919, Captain John Dasent in "Pretty Soft"; Plymouth, Dec., 1919, The Actor in "Night Lodging"; Fulton, Apr., 1920, Robert Campbell in "The Bonehead"; Booth, Sept., 1922, Adonis Duckworth in "The Plot Thickens"; National, Dec., 1922, The Count in "Fashions for Men"; Astor, Feb., 1924, The Baron in "The Moon-Flower"; 49th Street, Aug., 1924, Florencio in "The Werewolf"; Playhouse, Aug., 1925, Albert La Garde in "Oh! Mama"; Comedy, Nov., 1925, Herr Beermann in "Morals"; Henry Miller, Feb., 1926, Martelet in "Embers"; Sam H. Harris, Sept., 1926, Guy Warren in "No Trespassing"; Princess, Oct., 1926, Ronald Bradford in "Buy, Buy, Baby"; Republic, Oct., 1927, Edgar Worth in "The Mulberry Bush"; Music Box, Dec., 1927, Peter Cope in "Paris Bound." *(Died 1 Jan., 1951; age 74)*

NICHOLLS, Harry, actor ; *b.* London, 1 Mar., 1852 ; *e.* City of London School ; *m.* a sister of the late Henry Pettitt, dramatic author ; made his first appearance on the stage in 1870 ; made his first appearance in London, at the Surrey Theatre, 3 Oct., 1874, as Honeybun in " Did you ever send your wife to Camberwell ? " ; remained at that theatre for two years ; then went to the Grecian where he remained for nearly five years, and where he first formed his connection with the late Herbert Campbell, with whom for so many years he appeared in Drury Lane pantomimes ; he appeared at the Folly Theatre, 1879, in " Heavy Fathers," " La Périchole," " Lord Mayor's Day," and " The First Night " ; he first joined the Drury Lane Company, under Augustus Harris, on 31 July, 1880, when he played in his own farce " Timson's Little Holiday," which subsequently became " Jane " ; he appeared at Drury Lane, almost without intermission until 1893, playing the principal comedy parts in the various dramas and pantomimes produced there during that period ; among the more noted plays in which he successfully took part may be mentioned, " Youth," 1881 ; " Pluck," 1882 ; " Human Nature," 1885 ; " A Run of Luck," 1886 ; " Pleasure," 1887 ; " The Armada," 1888 ; " The Royal Oak," 1889 ; " A Million of Money," 1890 ; " A Sailor's Knot," 1891 ; " The Prodigal Daughter," 1892 ; " A Life of Pleasure," 1893 ; during the autumn of 1887, appeared at the Princess's, as Jim Farren in " Shadows of a Great City " ; in 1894, he became a member of the Adelphi Theatre, and appeared there in " The Fatal Card," 1894 ; " The Swordsman's Daughter," 1895 ; " One of the Best," 1895 ; " Boys Together," 1896 ; " Black Eyed Susan," 1896 ; " All that Glitters is not Gold," 1896 ; " Secret Service," 1897 ; " In the Days of the Duke," 1897 ; " The Gipsy Earl," 1898 ; " With Flying Colours," 1899 ; then appeared at the Gaiety, Feb., 1900, as Hooker Pacha in " The Messenger Boy " ; toured in South Africa for six months under the management of Leonard Rayne, 1902 ; he appeared at the Adelphi, Aug., 1903, as Micawber in " Em'ly " ; at the Waldorf, Mar., 1906, as Zekiel Homespun in " The Heir-at-Law " ; at the Royalty, Nov., 1906, as Walter Everest in " The Electric Man " ; at the Grand, Fulham, Sept., 1908, as Samuel Scarper in " If We Only Knew !"; at the Aldwych Theatre, May, 1909, as Private Jupp in a revival of " One of the Best " ; at the Empire, Sept., 1909, as Marmaduke Mountjoy in " The Superior Sex," and at the Comedy, Mar., 1910, as Bill Avery in " Alias Jimmy Valentine " ; at the Little Theatre, Oct., 1912, played Felix Drinkwater in " Captain Brassbound's Conversion " ; is the author of " Jane " (with W. Lestocq), " A Runaway Girl " (with Seymour Hicks), " The Toreador " (with James T. Tanner), " If We Only Knew ! " (with Charles Ross), and innumerable pantomimes and songs ; is a prominent Freemason (P. M. of Drury Lane, Jubilee Masters, and Green Room Lodges, Past Grand Standard Bearer of England) ; Treasurer and member of Executive Committee of the Actors' Benevolent Fund ; Trustee (with Arthur Bourchier and Charles Cruikshanks) of the

Actors' Orphanage Fund; Past-Master of the Drury Lane Fund; is a Past-Master of the Worshipful Company of Joiners. *(Died 29 Nov., 1926; age 74)*

NICHOLS, Anne, dramatic author and producing manager; was formerly an actress; has written the following plays: " Heart's Desire " (with Adelaide Matthews); " Down Limerick Way," 1919; " Seven Miles to Arden," 1919; " Linger Longer, Letty," 1919; " The Gilded Cage," 1920; " Love Dreams," 1921 ; " Just Married " (with Adelaide Matthews), 1921; " The Happy Cavalier," 1921; "Abie's Irish Rose," produced at Stamford, Conn., 6 Mar., 1922, and at the Fulton Theatre, New York, 23 May, 1922, ran continuously until 1927, 2,327 performances; "The Land of Romance," 1922; as manager was responsible for the production of French Repertory with Madame Simone, 1924; "Puppy Love," 1926; "Howdy, King," 1926; "Sam Abramovitch," 1927; "Pre-Honeymoon," of which she was part-author with A. van Ronkel. *(Died 15 Sept., 1966; age 75)*

NICHOLS, Beverley, author, composer, and dramatic critic; *b.* 9 Sept., 1898; *s.* of John Nichols; *e.* Marlborough and Balliol College (B.A.), Oxford; while at Oxford was President of the Union, and Editor of *The Isis* and *The Oxford Outlook*; in 1926 was dramatic critic of *The Weekly Dispatch*; composed music for the *revue* "Picnic," 1927; editor of *The American Sketch*, New York, 1928–9; part-composer of "Many Happy Returns," 1929; author of "The Stag," 1929; "Cochran's 1930 Revue," for which he also composed part of the music; "Avalanche," 1931; "Evensong" (with Edward Knoblock), 1932; "When the Crash Comes," 1933; "Mesmer," 1935; "Floodlight," 1937; "Song on the Wind," an operette, of which he also composed the score, 1948; "La Plume de ma Tante," "Shadow of the Vine," 1950; is the author of many books, notably "25," "Evensong," "Down the Garden Path," "Cry Havoc," "The Fool Hath Said," "Revue," "Verdict on India," "All I Could Never Be," "Merry Hall," "A Pilgrim's Progress," "No Man's Street," "Beverley Nichols Cats' ABC.," "Beverley Nichols Cats' XYZ," "Forty Favourite Flowers," and also "Murder by Request," and other detective novels. *Recreation:* Music. *Address:* c/o Jonathan Cape, Ltd., 30 Bedford Square, London, W.C.1.

NICHOLS, Lewis, dramatic critic; *b.* Lock Haven, Penna., U.S.A., 1 Sept., 1903; *s.* of Lewis Nichols and his wife Fanny (Lowther); *e.* Harvard University; *m.* Helen R. Malone; for several years was dramatic editor of the *New York Times*; dramatic critic to the paper, Nov., 1942 to 1946. *Club:* Harvard. *Address: New York Times*, 229 West 43rd Street, New York City, U.S.A. *Telephone No.:* Lackawanna 4–1000.

NICHOLSON, H. O., actor; *b.* Gothenburg, Sweden, 5 Jan., 1868; *s.* of the Rev. Dr. John A. Nicholson, of Leamington, and his wife Editha Caroline (Hunt); *e.* Leamington College and Jesus College, Cambridge, where he gained a classical scholarship in 1887, and took a second-class degree in the Classical Tripos of 1890; was formerly engaged as a schoolmaster; made his first appearance on the stage at the Opera House, Cork, 26 Dec., 1896, in F. R. Benson's company; he remained with Benson practically without a break from that date until 1911; he made his first appearance on the London stage, at the Lyceum Theatre, 15 Feb., 1900, as Nym in " Henry V "; he also appeared with Benson's company at the Comedy, 1901; Adelphi, 1905; on leaving the Benson company appeared at the Savoy, under Granville Barker and Lillah McCarthy's management, Sept., 1912, as the Old Shepherd in " The Winter's Tale "; Nov., 1912, as Fabian in " Twelfth Night "; at the St. James's, Sept., 1913, the Centurion in " Androcles and the Lion," and Pantaloon in " The Harlequinade "; subsequently appeared in " Nan," " The Witch," and " The Silver Box "; at the Savoy, Feb., 1914, played Starveling in " A Midsummer Night's Dream " ; at the Criterion, June, 1914, Professor Horatio Titmouse in " A Scrap of Paper " ; subsequently rejoined F. R. Benson's company, and appeared at the Court, Dec., 1915, as Starveling in " A Midsummer Night's Dream " ; at the Court, Mar., 1919, played Sir Oliver Surface in " The School for Scandal " ; June, 1919, James Clancy in " The Lost Leader " ; at Covent Garden Theatre, Dec., 1919, Polonius in " Hamlet " ; Jan., 1920, Mr. Lorry in " The Only Way " ; at the Little Theatre, Apr., 1920, Edgar Symonds in " Mumsee " ; Apr., 1920, Jaikes in " Other Times " ; at the Comedy, Oct., 1920, Gentleman Susan in " The Romantic Age " ; at the Court, Dec., 1920, Starveling in " A Midsummer Night's Dream " ; Feb., 1921, Justice Shallow in " King Henry IV " (part II) ; Sept., 1921, Matt Haffigan in " John Bull's Other Island " ; Oct., 1921, Mazzini Dunn in " Heartbreak House " ; Dec., 1921, Old Hardcastle in " She Stoops to Conquer " ; at the Everyman Theatre, May, 1922, Fergus Crampton in " You Never Can Tell " ; Sept., 1922, Andrew Boyd in " Mary Stuart " ; at the New Theatre, Mar., 1923, Henry Smith in " The Bad Man " ; at the Haymarket, Nov., 1923, the Rev. Canon Chasuble in " The Importance of Being Earnest " ; at Wyndham's, Apr., 1924, Simon Battersby in " To Have the Honour " ; at Drury Lane, Dec., 1924, Starveling in " A Midsummer Night's Dream " ; Comedy, Nov., 1925, Joe Dunkerton in " The Ring o' Bells " ; Kingsway, Apr., 1926, the Prior of Aosta in " The Marvellous History of St. Bernard " ; Haymarket, Nov., 1926, Mr. Baslow in " Yellow Sands " ; Garrick, Nov., 1928, Benjamin Borlase in " The Runaways " ; Lyric, Mar., 1929, The Ambassador in " Berkeley Square " ; Little, June, 1929, Saul in " Water " ; Playhouse, Feb., 1930, Joseph Munday in " Devonshire Cream " ; Embassy, June, 1930, Polonius in " Hamlet " ; Prince of Wales's, Sept., 1930, Manoah in " Delilah " ; Fortune, Nov., 1930, Mr. Toomer in " The Man from Blankley's " ; Embassy, Apr., 1931, and Playhouse, May, 1931, the Rev. Charles Stern in " The Crime at

Blossoms " ; Duchess, Nov., 1931, Knut Brovik in " The Master Builder " ; Globe, Feb., 1932, the Old Actor in " Punchinello " ; New, Apr., 1932, Dr. de Beauregarde in " Napoleon " ; Shaftesbury, Jan., 1934, Augustin Philips in " Spring 1600 " ; Lyric, Oct., 1936, Dr. Harvey in " Charles the King " ; Adelphi, Nov., 1938, Adam in " As You Like It." *Club :* Green Room. *Address :* Green Room Club, 46 Leicester Square, W.C.2.

NICHOLSON, Kenyon, dramatic author; *b.* Crawfordsville, Ind., U.S.A., 21 May, 1894; *s.* of Thomas B. Nicholson and his wife Anne (Kenyon); *e.* Crawfordsville, New York, and Columbia University; *m.* Lucile Nikolas; studied playwriting at Columbia University; is the author of " Honor Bright " (with Meredith Nicholson), 1921; " Bedside Manners " (with S. N. Behrman), 1923; " The Barker," 1927; " Love is Like That " (with Behrman), 1927; " Little Eva," 1928; " Before You're Twenty-five," 1929; " Torch Song," " Stepdaughters of War " (from a novel), 1930; " Sailor, Beware! " (with Charles Robinson), 1933; " Swing Your Lady " (with Robinson), 1936; " Dance Night," 1938; " The Flying Gerardos " (with Robinson), 1940; " Apple of his Eye " (with Robinson), 1946; is also the author of several books. *Address :* Raven Rock, New Jersey, U.S.A.

NICHOLSON, Nora, actress; *b.* Leamington, Warwickshire, 7 Dec., 1889; *d.* of Rev. John Aldwell Nicholson, LL.D, and his wife Editha (Hunt); *e.* Leamington High School, and in Germany; studied for the stage in the Frank Benson Dramatic School, and made her first appearance on the stage at the Memorial Theatre, Stratford-on-Avon, Apr., 1912, as Dolly Clandon in " You Never Can Tell "; remained with the Benson company, 1912–13, and during 1914–15, was at the Old Vic., playing Ariel, Titania, Jessica, Celia, etc.; during 1916–17, toured as Sally in " The Scarlet Pimpernel," and then, 1918–19, served with the W.R.N.S.; first appeared in the West-end of London, at the St. Martin's, 22 Dec., 1919, as the Little Grey Man, and Fishface in "Once Upon a Time"; Queen's, Mar., 1920, played Miss Plum in "The Fold"; toured in Canada, 1921-2, as Mrs. Jackman in "The Skin Game"; toured, 1924, in "The Fake"; Royalty, June, 1925, played Charlotta in "The Cherry Orchard"; Comedy, Apr., 1926, the Maid in "The Rescue Party"; was engaged at the Haymarket, 1927-8, understudying in "Yellow Sands," and subsequently touring as Minnie Masters in the play; made her first appearance in New York, at the Masque Theatre, Sept., 1929, as Mrs. Debenham in "Rope's End" ("Rope"); Potinière, Paris, Sept., 1930, played Miss Puddleton in "The Well of Loneliness"; toured in Canada, 1931-2, with Sir Barry Jackson's company; Fulham, May, and Queen's, Sept., 1933, played the Duenna in "Night's Candles"; Queen's, Nov., 1933, Mrs. Clutch in "Sunshine Sisters"; Savoy, Oct., 1934, Hodo in "Two Kingdoms"; Lyric, Hammersmith, Nov., 1935, the Third Witch in "Macbeth"; during 1936-7, toured with Lewis Casson and Sybil Thorndike; Old Vic., Sept., 1938, Miss Gower in "Trelawny of the 'Wells' "; St. James's, Nov., 1938, Mrs. Andrew in "Gentleman Unknown"; Old Vic., Feb., 1939, Mrs. Stockman in "An Enemy of the People"; Shaftesbury, Jan., 1940, Mrs. Queen in "Behind the Schemes"; from 1940-5, engaged at the Playhouse, Oxford, and 1946, at the Bristol Old Vic; New Theatre (for Bristol Old Vic), Nov., 1946, played Mrs. Brooks in "Tess of the D'Urbervilles"; Lyric, Hammersmith, Oct., and St. Martin's, Dec., 1947, Miss Loder in "Dark Summer"; New Lindsey, May, 1948, Miss Malleson in "Corinth House"; Globe, Nov., 1948, Mrs. Pratt in "The Return of the Prodigal," and May, 1949, Margaret Devize in "The Lady's Not For Burning"; toured, May, 1950, as Mrs. Helseth in "Rosmersholm," appearing in the same part, at the St. Martin's, Aug., 1950; Royale, New York, Nov., 1950, again played Margaret Devize in "The Lady's Not for Burning"; at the "Q," and Embassy, June, 1951, played Catherine Petkoff in "Arms and the Man"; Criterion, Dec., 1951, Lucy

Bagot in "Indian Summer"; Westminster, Jan., 1952, Mrs. Sholto in "Sunset in Knightsbridge"; Arts, Mar., 1952, Marina in "Uncle Vanya"; New, June, 1952, played the Woman in "The Millionairess," and appeared in this part at the Shubert, New York, Oct., 1952; Arts, London, Feb., 1953, appeared as the Nurse in "The Father," and June, 1953, again played Catherine Petkoff in "Arms and the Man"; Vaudeville, Sept., 1953, played Gertrude in "Trial and Error"; Duke of York's, May, 1954, Rachel in "The Facts of Life"; at the Henry Miller, New York, Nov., 1954, appeared as Miss Teresa Browne in "The Living Room"; Arts, Dec., 1955, Grandmother in "Listen to the Wind"; Mar., 1956, toured as Mrs. Chillingworth in "Love Affair"; Phoenix, June, 1956, played Ivy in "The Family Reunion"; toured Mar., 1958, as Cornelia Brigham in "Come Rain, Come Shine"; Westminster, Jan., 1959, Mrs. Temple in "The Woman on the Stair"; Duke of York's, Sept., 1960, played Sarita Myrtle in "Waiting in the Wings"; Connaught, Worthing, Nov., 1961, Grandma, in "Death and All That Jazz"; Lyric, Hammersmith, May, 1962, Marfa Timofeyevna in "Come Back With Diamonds"; Hampstead Theatre Club, Feb., 1964, Hester Fortescue in "The Tower"; Ashcroft, Croydon, Sept., 1964, Lady Meanwell and Mistress Quickly in "No Bed For Bacon"; Yvonne Arnaud Theatre, Guildford, Aug., 1965, and Phoenix, Sept., 1965, played Ardotya Nazarovna in "Ivanov"; Apollo, Oct., 1968, Miss Nisbitt in "Forty Years On"; has written several short stories, and with Angela Green, is the author of the play, "To-Morrow Never Comes," St. Martin's (for the R.A.D.A. Players), Nov., 1932; first entered films, 1934; recent pictures include "Raising a Riot," "A Town Like Alice," "Diamonds for Breakfast," "Captain's Table," "Run a Crooked Mile"; television plays in which she has appeared, since 1955, include "Corinth House" (Canada), "Law and Disorder," "The Whisperers," "That Woman," "The Forsyte Saga," "The Dead" and "Kate." *Favourite parts:* Mrs. Jones in "The Silver Box," Margaret in "The

Lady's Not for Burning," and Juno in "Juno and the Paycock." *Club:* Arts Theatre. *Recreations:* Reading and writing. *Address:* 28 Eaton Mansions, Cliveden Place, London, S.W.1.

NICODEMI, Dario, French dramatic author; is an Italian by birth; has written the following plays, all produced at the Théâtre Réjane: "Raffles" (from the English), 1907; "Le Refuge," 1909; "La Flamme," 1910; "L'Aigrette," 1912; "The Prodigal Husband" (with Michael Morton), New York, 1914; during the War, resumed his Italian Nationality; his latest plays are "L'Ombra," "Il Titano," "Scampolo," "La Nemica," "Remnant."
(Died 24 Sept., 1934; age 60)

NIELSEN, Alice, operatic vocalist; *b.* Nashville, Tenn., U.S.A., 1876; *d.* of Erasmus Ivarius and Sarah A. Nielsen; *e.*, musically, at San Francisco, under Mdlle. Ida Valerga; *m.* (1) Benjamin Nentwig · (2) J. F. Leffler; (3) Le Roy R. Stoddard (mar. dis.); her first appearance on the regular stage was made in 1893, at Oakland, California, as Yum-Yum in "The Mikado"; in 1896 was a member of the Bostonians; created a most favourable impression in 1897, with this company, as Yvonne, in a comic opera called "The Serenade"; at Wallacks's, New York, in 1898, played Muset and Irma in "The Fortune Teller," and Maid Marian in "Robin Hood"; at the Casino, Oct., 1899, appeared in "The Singing Girl"; made her first appearance in London at Shaftesbury as Muset and Irma in "The Fortune Teller," 9 Apr., 1901, in which she achieved a great success; she determined on a course of hard musical study with a view to appearing in grand opera; she accordingly went to Italy, placing herself under the best masters, and Dec., 1903 made her *début* at The Bellini Opera House, Naples, as Marguerite in "Faust"; coming to London, 1904, she was engaged at Royal Opera, Covent Garden, appearing as Zerlina in "Don Giovanni," Suzanne in "The Marriage of Figaro";

Mimi in "La Bohème," with Caruso, and Gilda in "Rigoletto," with Victor Maurel; appeared at the Waldorf with the San Carlo company, 1905-6, as Mimi in "La Bohème" and Norina in "Don Pasquale"; she remained with this opera company throughout 1907; appeared at Boston, 1909, in "Madame Butterfly"; during 1910 appeared in "Rigoletto," "Faust," "L'Enfant Prodigue"; at Boston, 1911, appeared as Chonitain in "The Sacrifice"; during 1912 appeared in "The Secret of Suzanne"; at the Casino, New York, Nov., 1917, appeared as Mistress Kitty Bellairs in "Kitty Darlin'"; at the Royal Alexandra Theatre, Toronto, June-July, 1918, played Jenny Lind in "Mr. Barnum," and Carolina in "The Gentleman from Mississippi."
(Died 8 Mar., 1943; age 66)

NIESEN, Gertrude, actress and vocalist; *b.* at sea, 8 July, 1910; *e.* Brooklyn and New York public schools; *m.* Albert Greenfield; made her first professional appearance in New York, in cabaret, at the 300 Club; subsequently appeared at St. Louis, with the Municipal Opera company, in "The Vagabond King," "Sonny," "Good News," etc.; subsequently appeared in vaudeville with Lou Holtz; made her first appearance on the regular stage at the Hollywood Theatre, New York, 13 Dec., 1934, in "Calling All Stars"; at the Winter Garden, Jan., 1936, appeared in "The Ziegfeld Follies"; made her first appearance in London, at the Savoy Theatre, 8 June, 1938, as the Countess Petkoff in "No Sky So Blue"; at the Adelphi, Oct., 1938, played Lupe in "Bobby Get Your Gun"; made a great success, when she appeared at the Century Theatre, Apr., 1944, as Bubbles La Marr in "Follow the Girls," which ran for two years; entered films, 1938, in "The Top of the Town." *Address:* c/o Actors' Equity Association, 45 West 47th Street, New York City, U.S.A.

NIGHTINGALE, Joe, actor; *m.* Maud Prenton; had had provincial experience extending over a number of years, in drama, comedy, and pantomime, before attracting considerable attention by his performance at the Apollo Theatre, 22 June, 1916, of the part of William Mossop in " Hobson's Choice " ; he appeared at the Empire, Mar., 1917, in " Hanky-Panky " ; at the Prince of Wales's, Mar., 1918, played Lucas Whittle in " Flora " ; during 1919 toured as Hu-Du in " Shanghai " ; at the Ambassadors', Dec., 1919, played Jacquot in " Sylvia's Lovers " ; at the Gaiety, Manchester, May, 1920, William Mossop in " Runaway Will " (a sequel to " Hobson's Choice ") ; subsequently toured as Walter Wex in " A Southern Maid " ; at the Vaudeville, Dec., 1922, played in " Snap " ; in 1926-7 toured in " The Mirthquake."

NIJINSKA, Bronislava, dancer and choreographist; *b.* St. Petersburg, 8 Jan., 1891 ; a sister of Vaslav Nijinsky; studied under Cecchetti, privately, and in 1900 entered the Imperial Ballet School, where she also studied under Michel Fokine and Nicholas Legat; made her first appearance with the Imperial Ballet, 1908; she achieved notable success in "Le Réveil de Flore," "The Sleeping Princess," "Le Carnaval," etc.; joined Diaghileff in Paris, 1909, where she appeared, subsequently, in "Petrouchka" and "Narcisse"; appeared at the Palace Theatre, London, 1914, with her brother; returned to Russia, where she opened her own school; rejoined Diaghileff, 1921, and appeared at the Alhambra, London, Nov., 1921, in "The Sleeping Princess," to which she contributed several numbers; subsequently composed several ballets for Diaghileff: "Le Renard," 1922; "Les Noces," 1923; "Les Biches," "Le Train Bleu," "Les Fâcheux," 1924; "Romeo and Juliet," 1926; was *maîtresse-de-ballet* at the Colon Theatre, Buenos Aires, 1926-7; in 1928-9, was engaged with Ida Rubinstein, for whom she made several productions; 1930-1, with the Russian Opera, Paris; 1931, at Covent Garden, London; in 1932 founded her own company, and also arranged the dances

for Max Reinhardt's film production of "A Midsummer Night's Dream," 1934; in 1935, became producer for Colonel de Basil's Ballet Russe de Monte Carlo, producing "Les Cents Baisers," "Les Noces," etc.; in 1937 was engaged with the Markova-Dolin ballet company.

NIJINSKY, Vaslav, ballet-dancer and choreographer; *b.* Kieff, Russia, 28 Feb., 1890; *s.* of Thomas Nijinsky and his wife Eleanora (Bereda); *e.* Imperial School of Dancing, St. Petersburg; *m.* Romola Marcus de Pulszky; his parents were both ballet-dancers; admitted to the Imperial School, 1899, and remained until he was seventeen; made his first appearance, while still a student, at the Maryinski Theatre, St. Petersburg, 1907, as the Marquis in "Le Pavillon d'Armide"; made his professional *début* at that theatre, in the same year, in "Don Giovanni," in company with Matilde Khessinskaya, Preobrajenskaya, Anna Pavlova, and Tamara Karsavina, and was an immediate success; first appeared in Paris, at the Châtelet, 17 May, 1909, in "Le Pavillon d'Armide"; appeared in Rome, 1911; first appeared in London, at Covent Garden, 26 June, 1911, in "Le Pavillon d'Armide," the Royal Command performance, given to celebrate the Coronation of H.M. King George V; during the ballet season which followed, appeared in 'Cleopatre," "Le Spectre de la Rose," "Prince Igor," etc.; appeared in Berlin, 1912; during the first World War was for a time a prisoner of war; released in 1916, he went to the United States; made his first appearance in New York, at the Metropolitan Opera House, 12 Apr., 1916, in "Le Spectre de la Rose"; he was probably the greatest male ballet-dancer of the twentieth century, and was almost generally acclaimed as such, all over the world, until his retirement, through ill-health, in 1919; his repertory included "Le Pavillon d'Armide," "Giselle," "Carnaval," "Le Festin," "Scheherazade," "Petrouchka," "Le Spectre de la Rose," "Narcisse," "L'Aprés-midi d'un

Faune," "Jeux," "Sacre du Printemps," "Cleopatre," "Les Orientales," "Le Talisman," "Prince Igor."
(Died 8 Apr., 1950; age 60)

NIKITINA, Alice, dancer; *b.* Russia; studied dancing and joined the Diaghileff Ballet company, eventually filling leading *rôles* in classical repertory; appeared in "La Chatte," "Les Biches," "Zephyr et Flora," "Les Sylphides," etc.; appeared with the Russian Ballet, at His Majesty's Theatre, June, 1928, as Flora in "Pulcinella," also appearing in "Les Sylphides," "Aurora's Wedding," etc.; in Dec., 1929, appeared at the Atélier Theatre, Paris, in a series of dance recitals; appeared at the London Pavilion, Mar., 1930, with Serge Lifar in "Cochran's 1930 Revue"; subsequently studied singing in Italy with Madame Tetrazzini; made her *début* in opera at Palermo, 1937, as Gilda in "Rigoletto"; subsequently appeared as Lucia di Lammermoor.

NILLSON, Carlotta, actress; *b.* Sweden; was taken to the United States when ten years of age; made her first appearance on the stage, with Madame Modjeska's company, in a minor capacity in "Marie Stuart"; first appeared in New York, at Daly's Theatre; then toured in "The Private Secretary" and "The Crust of Society," three years in all; was next seen in "Shenandoah," on tour, after which she went to England; for three years studied with William Farren and Geneviève Ward, and made her reappearance on the stage at the St. James's Theatre, June 2, 1898, as Mrs. Dasney in "The Ambassador"; also appeared at Terry's Theatre, 13 Nov., 1899, as Evelyn in "The Happy Life"; on her return to America, was engaged to play Eunice in "Quo Vadis?"; at the Garden Theatre, 10 Nov., 1902, played in "Among Those Present"; then made a substantial success at the Manhattan Theatre, 5 Oct., 1903, when she played Mrs. Elvsted in "Hedda Gabler"; at the Criterion, 8 Feb., 1904, appeared as Miriam Selwyn in "The Triumph of Love"; at Wallack's, 14 Apr., 1904, played Dorothy Graydon in "Love's

Pilgrimage"; made another success, at the Hudson Theatre, 12 Sept., 1904, when she played Letty in Pinero's play of that name; this was followed by her appearance at Madison Square Theatre, 3 Oct., 1905, as Elizabeth Annesley in "The Man on the Box"; at the same theatre, 17 Oct., 1906, made her greatest success, so far, as Rhy Macchesney in "The Three of Us"; at the Savoy, New York, 5 Sept., 1908, played Diana Massingberd in "Diana of Dobson's"; at the Maxine Elliott Theatre, New York, 22 Feb., 1909, played Thekla Muellet in "This Woman and this Man"; subsequently toured as Elsie in "For Better, For Worse"; at Atlantic City, July 1911, played in "Thyra Avery"; at Toronto, May, 1913, produced "Deborah," in which she played the title-*rôle*; this play caused some sensation, and was stopped by the local authorities.
(Died 31 Dec., 1951)

NISSEN, Brian, actor; *b.* Wimbledon, 20 Oct., 1927; *s.* of Einar Nissen and his wife Eva Maria (Lavendt); *e.* Walmer House School, Kensington; studied for the stage under Marion Ross; made his first appearance on the stage at the Adelphi Theatre, 24 Dec., 1941, as Nibs in "Peter Pan"; Aldwych, Apr., 1942, played Joshua Miller in "The Watch on the Rhine"; Lyric, Dec., 1944, made a great success when he played Michael Brown in "Love in Idleness," with Alfred Lunt and Lynn Fontanne; joined the R.A.F., Feb., 1946; reappeared on the stage at the Duchess, Aug., 1948, as Wilfred Kirby in "Eden End"; Wyndham's, Feb., 1949, Lt. Tony Harding in "Sweethearts and Wives"; Duke of York's, Feb., 1950, Roger Gosselyn in "Larger than Life"; "Q," July, 1950, Nigel Forbes in "Dr. Morelle"; Aug., 1950, Dick Franz in "Give Me Yesterday"; Embassy, May, 1951, played David in "A Matter of Fact"; Piccadilly, June, 1952, Leslie Gowland in "The Gay Dog"; New (for Repertory Players), Feb., 1953, Mark Pearson in "The King's Son"; Her Majesty's, Brighton, Apr., 1953, appeared as Tuffy Mann in "The

Miraculous Miss Mann"; first appeared in films, 1943, in "Demi-Paradise," and subsequently in "Henry V," and "They Were Sisters." *Recreations:* All sports and reading. *Address:* c/o Marion Ross, 66–8 Brewer Street, W.1. *Telephone No.:* Gerrard 6182.

NISSEN, Greta (*née* Grethe Ruzt-Nissen), actress and dancer; *b.* Oslo, Norway, 30 Jan., 1906; *e.* Copenhagen; *m.* (1) Weldon Heyburn (mar. ann.); (2) Stuart D. Eckert, studied dancing as a child and made her first appearance on the stage in ballet, at the early age of six; subsequently studied under Michel Fokine, and toured extensively in Europe; went to America 1923, and made her first appearance on the New York stage at the Broadhurst Theatre, 12 Feb., 1924, as the Crown Princess of Xanadu in the interlude "A Kiss in Xanadu" in "Beggar on Horseback"; Globe, New York, June, 1926, under Ziegfeld, appeared in "No Foolin'"; spent ten years in films in Hollywood; reappeared on the stage, when she made her first appearance in London, at the Palace Theatre, 24 Apr., 1934, in "Why Not To-Night?"; at the Comedy, Dec., 1934, succeeded June in "Hi-Diddle-Diddle"; in Aug., 1935, commenced a tour of the English provinces as Cavallini in "Romance"; Theatre Royal, Brighton, June, 1937, played Linda Tor in "Borrow the Moon"; Ambassadors', Sept., 1937, Hélène in "People in Love"; entered films, 1925, in "In the Name of Love," and appeared in numerous pictures. *Recreations:* Sculpture, music and swimming.

NOBLE, Dennis, actor and vocalist; *b.* Bristol, Glos., 25 Sept., 1898; *s.* of William Vernon Noble and his wife Elizabeth Guard (Titcombe); *e.* Bristol Cathedral; *m.* (1) Kathleen Marjorie Bain; (2) Miriam Ferris; was specially trained for an operatic career by Dinh Gilly; made his first appearance on the stage at the Adelphi Theatre, 8 Sept., 1923, as the Hon. Montague Jepson in "Head Over Heels"; subsequently appeared at

Covent Garden, and on the Continent, singing principal baritone parts in Grand Opera; at the Alhambra, Aug., 1931, appeared as Leopold Wessely in "Waltzes from Vienna," and continued in this until 1932, when he went on tour in the same piece; Streatham Hill, Dec., 1932, played Dick in "The One Girl"; Open Air Theatre, Sept., 1933, Adrian in "The Tempest"; went to New York, where he made his first appearance at the Center Theatre, 22 Sept., 1934, as Leopold in "The Great Waltz" ("Waltzes from Vienna"); appeared at the Royal Opera House, Covent Garden, 1936, 1937, 1938, as Sam Weller in "Pickwick," Sharpless in "Madame Butterfly," Lescaut in "Manon Lescaut," Valentine in "Faust," Rigoletto, Marcello in "La Bohème," Peter in "Hansel and Gretel," Figaro in "The Barber of Seville," Frank in "Die Fledermaus," etc.; Palace, July, 1940, Nur Al-Huda Ali in "Chu-Chin-Chow"; Piccadilly, Aug., 1943, Jean Gervais in "Sunny River"; Cambridge Theatre, May, 1944, Caramello in "A Night in Venice"; Prince's, Sept., 1945, the Earl of Essex in "Merrie England." *Favourite parts:* Rigoletto, and Elder Germont in "La Traviata." *Recreations:* Cricket and motoring. *Club:* Savage. *(Died 14 Mar., 1966; age 67)*

NOLAN, Doris, actress; *b.* New York City, 14 July, 1916; *d.* of Frank J. Nolan; *e.* Washington; *m.* Alexander Knox; studied for the stage at the Provincetown Playhouse Dramatic School; made her first appearance on the stage, 1934, in "The Late Christopher Bean"; subsequently appeared in summer "stock" companies; first appeared in New York, at the Ambassador Theatre, 16 Sept., 1935, as Karen Andre in "The Night of January 16th"; National, Sept., 1936, played Marie Smith in "Arrest That Woman"; Mansfield, Dec., 1937, Margo Dare in "Tell Me, Pretty Maiden"; Longacre, Nov., 1938, Karen von Singall in "Lorelei"; Royale, Dec., 1940, Vivienne Ames in "Cue for Passion"; toured, 1941, as Lorraine Sheldon in "The Man Who Came to Dinner"; Martin Beck,

June, 1942, Gwen Reid in "The Cat Screams"; Lyceum, Dec., 1942, Nan in "The Doughgirls," which ran through 1943; Empire, Dec., 1949, Norma Trahern in "The Closing Door"; first appeared in films, 1936, in "The Man I Marry."

NOLAN, Lloyd, actor; b. San Francisco, California, U.S.A., 11 Aug., 1902; s. of James Charles Nolan and his wife Margaret (Shea); e. Santa Clara, Preparatory School, California and Stanford University; m. Mell Efird; following a trip round the world (as a cadet) in the "President Polk," he made first professional appearance on the stage in vaudeville, on the Keith-Albee Circuit, in 1924, in "The Radio Robot"; he subsequently performed in twenty-eight plays at the Pasadena Playhouse; next appeared at the Dennis Theatre on Cape Cod, Massachusetts, as a Pirate in the *revue* "Cape Cod Follies"; made his Broadway début when this transferred to the Bijou in 1929, at which time he played various parts; thereafter toured in the plays "The Blue and the Gray, or War Is Hell," and "High Hat"; returned to New York, 1931, to play an Office Boy in "Sweet Stranger"; Martin Beck, Nov., 1931, played with Alfred Lunt and Lynn Fontanne in "Reunion in Vienna"; also in New York, 1932, played various parts in "The Third American *Revue*"; Little, Feb., 1933, played Biff Grimes in "One Sunday Afternoon" for 322 performances; in New York, 1934, played in "Ragged Army" and "Gentlewomen"; went to Hollywood in 1934, where he remained filming until 1950; toured in 1950 as Oliver Erwenter in "The Silver Whistle"; toured, April–May, 1951, as Samuel Rilling in "Courtin' Time," but had to relinquish his rôle because of a throat infection; returned once more to Hollywood; at the Plymouth, New York, Jan., 1954, played Lt.-Commander Philip Queeg in "The Caine Mutiny Court Martial" for one year, for which he won the Donaldson and the New York Drama Critics' Awards; following the N.Y. run, he toured with the production; made his London début at the Hippodrome, in June, 1956,

in the same play, which he also directed; Ambassador, New York, March, 1960, played Johnny Condell in "One More River"; films in which he has appeared include "The House on 92nd Street," "A Tree Grows in Brooklyn," "A Hatful of Rain," and "Peyton Place"; first appeared in television in 1949 and has since made regular appearances, notably in "The Caine Mutiny Court Martial," 1955, for which he received American television Emmy Award, and "Ah, Wilderness" with Helen Hayes, also the series "Martin Kane, Private Eye," and "S.A. 7." *Favourite parts:* Biff Grimes and Lt.-Commander Queeg. *Address:* 239 North Bristol Avenue, Los Angeles, 10049, California. *Telephone No:* Crestview 4–7633.

NORDSTROM, Frances, dramatic author; d. of Captain E. Nordstrom, U.S. Army; was formerly an actress, and commenced her career in Mrs. Fiske's company, in 1902, in "Mary of Magdala"; she played lead in various "stock" companies, and had a varied experience; commenced writing in 1912, when her farce, "Room 44," was produced; since then has written nearly sixty sketches for "vaudeville," a number of which have proved highly successful; is also the author of "It Pays to Flirt" (with Joseph McManus), 1918; "The 'Ruined' Lady" (in which she also played Olive Gresham), 1919; "Some Lawyer," 1919; "On the Ragged Edge," 1919; "All Wrong," 1919; "Snapshots of 1921" (with Glen MacDonough), 1921; "Lady Bug," 1922; "Her Market Price," 1924.

NORFOLK, Edgar, actor; b. Bradford, Yorks., 5 Nov., 1893; m. (1) Dorothie Helen Saintsbury (mar. dis.); (2) Marie Gregory; was formerly employed as a textile analyst in woollen industry; had had some experience as an amateur, before making his first appearance on the professional stage, at the Spa Theatre, Scarborough, June, 1912, in "Nell Gwynne"; made his first appearance in London, at the New Theatre, 23 Dec., 1916, as one of the Pirates in "Peter

Pan"; at the Strand, Mar., 1920, played Randolph Weeks in "Come Out of the Kitchen"; next toured in "Mary Rose"; Kingsway, Sept., 1920, played the Policeman in "The Daisy"; Aldwych, Nov., 1920, Malcolm in "Macbeth"; St. James's, May, 1921, Montague Leroy in "Emma"; Haymarket, Dec., 1921, appeared in "Quality Street"; Aug., 1923, Horace Glyn in "The Prisoner of Zenda"; during 1923–4, was a member of the Birmingham Repertory company, and during 1924–5, toured as the Man in "The Man With a Load of Mischief"; Savoy, Oct., 1926, played Chandler in "Love's a Terrible Thing"; Prince of Wales's, Jan., 1928, Hugh Lennox in "Regatta," and the Rev. William Duke in "Outward Bound"; subsequently accompanied Margaret Bannerman on her Australian tour; on his return, appeared at the Holborn Empire, Dec., 1928, as the Dragon King in "Where the Rainbow Ends"; His Majesty's, Mar., 1929, Pointer in "The Berg"; Duchess, Dec., 1929, Renard-Beinsky in "Typhoon," and Frank Pine in "The Man at Six" Comedy, Jan., 1930, Tony Cartwright in "The Way Out"; Kingsway, Mar. 1930, Peter Ingram in "The Artist and the Shadow"; New, May, 1930, Fletcher in "The Last Chapter"; Comedy, Jan., 1931, Donald Parish in "Hawk Island"; Prince of Wales's, May, 1931, Earl of Chasemore in "The Unforeseen"; appeared at the Malvern Festival, Aug., 1931, in "A Woman Killed With Kindness," "A Trip to Scarborough," and "The Switchback"; St. James's, Sept., 1931, Colonel Townly in "A Trip to Scarborough"; Lyceum, Oct., 1931, Peter Mostyn in "Sensation"; St. Martin's, May, 1932, Attridge in "Somebody Knows"; "Q," Aug., 1932, Frederick Curtis in "Time's Fool"; Arts, Oct., 1932, Bernard Shaw in "Spacetime Inn"; Dec., 1932, Nicholas Harnigan in "Silver Wedding"; "Q," Jan., 1933, Simon Ledbury in "Trust Berkely"; Mar., 1933, Horace in "Francis Thompson"; Apollo, Sept., 1933, Gilbert Baize in "The Distaff Side"; Lyric, Oct., 1933, Christopher Marlowe in "This Side Idolatry"; Shaftesbury, May, 1934, Ben Weston in "The Dark Tower";

Wyndham's, Sept., 1934, James Ralston in "No More Ladies"; Plymouth, New York, Nov., 1934, Michael in "Dark Victory"; Ambassadors', London, Feb., 1935, Sydney in "Family Affairs"; Masque, New York, Oct., 1935, Charlie Appleby in "Eden End"; Phoenix, Nov., 1936, Dal Morgan in "Hell-for-Leather"; New, Mar., 1937, the Lord in "The Taming of the Shrew," and June, 1937, Alfred de Vigny in "The Great Romancer"; Embassy, Jan., 1938, Colonel Cashelton in "Poison Pen"; Haymarket, June, 1938, Julian Harvey in "Comedienne"; from 1939–43, was engaged with the B.B.C. repertory company; Playhouse, Mar., 1945, played Major Ellis in "Great Day"; Arts, July, 1945, Nils Krogstad in "A Doll's House"; Embassy, Sept., 1945, and Whitehall, Dec., 1945, James in "Fit for Heroes"; Westminster, May, 1946, Rev. Francis Munroe in "Frieda"; Westminster, Aug., 1946, Stephen Austin in "Message for Margaret"; Aldwych, Aug., 1948, Dr. Robert Strachan in "Rain on the Just"; Embassy, Dec., 1952, played the Chancellor in "The Dancing Princesses." *Favourite parts:* Renard-Beinsky in "Typhoon," and the Man in "The Man With a Load of Mischief." *Club:* Green Room. *Address:* Green Room Club, 8–9 Adam Street, London, W.C.2.

NORMAN, Norman J., manager; *b.* Pennsylvania, U.S.A., 12 Nov., 1870; *m.* Marie George; gained his early training in the theatrical business at the Casino Theatre, New York, of which his uncle, G. W. Lederer, was the lessee; came to London as manager for "The Belle of New York," at the Shaftesbury Theatre, Apr., 1898; followed by "The American Beauty," and "The Casino Girl"; was associated with the building of the Apollo Theatre, 1901, and the opening attraction, "The Belle of Bohemia"; subsequently appointed European manager to the Shubert Bros.; in 1903 brought to the Shaftesbury Theatre, the coloured comedians, Williams and Walker, in "In Dahomey"; in 1905 was manager for the Henry Russell Opera Company at the opening of the Waldorf (now Strand) Theatre, to which he also brought Eleonora Duse and her company; in 1907-8 was manager of the Shaftesbury, where he produced "Lady Tatters," "The Christian," and presented several foreign companies, including Madame Bartet, Suzanne Després, Tariol Baugé, the Sicilian Players, and the Grand Guignol; for several years was interested in the cinematograph business; at the Criterion, 1919, presented "Oh, Don't, Dolly"; at the New, 1920, "Little Women"; at the Comedy, 1921, "By all Means, Darling"; at the Strand, 1922, "Angel Face"; at the Shaftesbury, 1926, "Just a Kiss"; toured "Two Little Girls in Blue," 1927; "Peg o' Mine" (with Peggy O'Neil), 1928; presented "Apron Strings," Vaudeville, 1931; manager for Ronald Squire, at Playhouse and Apollo, 1932; appointed manager of the Apollo Theatre, 1932; manager at Shaftesbury, for Mary Newcombe, 1934; Criterion, for Ronald Squire, 1935; Daly's, for Ronald Squire and Yvonne Arnaud, 1935; Duke of York's, 1936–37; has been manager of Vaudeville, 1937–39. *Club:* Eccentric. *(Died 10 Oct., 1941; age 70)*

NORMAN, Norman V., actor and manager; *b.* Somerset, 24 Oct., 1864; *s.* of John Norman-Burt; *e.* at Clifton, Bristol; *m.* Beatrice Wilson; was originally intended for the Army; made his first appearance on the stage at the New Theatre Royal, Bristol, 10 Mar., 1884, as Chouser in "The Flying Scud"; subsequently toured with Roberts, Archer and Bartlett, Barry Sullivan, Marie Litton, Alice Lingard, etc.; in 1885 toured as Compton Kerr in "Formosa"; he toured with his own company in "Moths," 1886; subsequently toured with Herman Vezin, and also toured in "New Babylon"; at the Strand, Nov., 1893, produced "A Vain Sacrifice"; in 1895, toured in "Lord Allangford"; in 1896 was the Marcus Superbus in the first provincial tour of "The Sign of the Cross"; has toured in conjunction with Ben Greet, and since 1897 has toured his own companies; has produced several plays

in London; in 1917 played in "Pygmalion and Galatea," and "Comedy and Tragedy," with Mary Anderson; at the Lyric, Hammersmith, Feb., 1924, played Petulant in "The Way of the World"; at the Strand (for the Fellowship Players), Nov., 1924, played Philip Faulconbr dge in "King John"; Lyric, Hammersmith, Mar., 1925, played Sir Anthony Absolute in "The Rivals"; Century, Sept., 1925, Ilam Carve in "The Great Adventure"; Empire, Dec., 1925, King Henry in "Henry VIII"; Everyman, June, 1926, Meadows in "Down on the Farm"; Wyndham's, Nov., 1927, again played Petulant in "The Way of the World"; New, Apr., 1928, Sir Septimus Bifulco in "Come With Me"; Prince of Wales's, May, 1928, Sir Roger Ackroyd in "Alibi"; Royalty (for the International Theatre), Feb., 1929, Menelaus in "Peace, War, and Revolution"; Wyndham's, Apr., 1929, Sir Elijah Impey in "Warren Hastings"; Players, Dec., 1930, Archdeacon Brandon in "The Cathedral"; Duke of York's, Feb., 1931, General Von Neidschutz in "The Rocklitz"; Comedy, Dec., 1936, Bunter in "Busman's Honeymoon"; has produced several of the plays given by the Fellowship Players; has played cricket and football for Gloucester County. *Recreations:* Cricket, football, and hockey. *Clubs:* Savage, Mid-Surrey, and M.C.C. *(Died 26 Feb., 1943; age 78)*

NORMAN, Thyrza, actress; *b.* London, 9 Oct., 1884; *d.* of Robert Neeves; *e.* privately; *m.* J. V. Bryant; studied voice production under Mrs. Emil Behnke; made her first appearance on the stage at the Prince of Wales's Theatre, 1900, as Puck in "A Midsummer Night's Dream"; at the St. George's Hall, Apr., 1902, played Louise Vernière in "An Interrupted Rehearsal"; first came into prominence when she appeared at the Court Theatre, Oct., 1903, as Miranda in "The Tempest"; at the same theatre, Jan., 1904, played Leonida in "Bohemos"; Feb., 1904, Juliet in "Romeo and Juliet"; Apr., 1904, Julia in "The

Two Gentlemen of Verona "; June, 1904, Sabina Silver in " Where there is Nothing "; same theatre under the Vedrenne-Barker management, appeared in Nov., 1904, as Selysette in " Aglavaine and Selysette," and Dec., 1904, as Prunella in the play of that name; at the Adelphi, 1906, played Titania in " A Midsummer Night's Dream," with Oscar Asche and Lily Brayton; at the Court, June, 1908, played a Novice in " Guinevère," and July, 1909, Thalia Twickenham in " Thalia's Teacup "; played two seasons with the Repertory Theatre company, Glasgow, 1911; at the Court, Jan., 1912, appeared as Mary in " Rutherford and Son "; played the same part at the Little Theatre, when the piece was placed in the evening bill in Mar., 1912; went to the United States, and appeared in the same part, at the Little Theatre, New York, Dec., 1912; has also appeared as Rosalind in " As You Like It," and as Ophelia in " Hamlet," with F. R. Benson. *Recreations :* The river and reading.

NORRIS, William (William Norris Block), actor; *b.* New York City, 15 June, 1872; *s.* of Elias M. and Harriet Block; *e.* North Cosmopolitan School, and Boys' High School, San Francisco; *m.* Mabel Mordaunt; made his first appearance on the stage at the Standard Theatre, New York, 21 December, 1891, in " The Girl from Mexico "; appeared at the Bijou Theatre, in 1893, in " Delmonico's at Six," and subsequently in " Miss Dynamite "; he appeared at the Garrick, New York, Sept., 1895, as Charles Ingle in " The Man with a Past," and as Livingston Remsen in " The Social Highwayman," subsequently touring in the same plays; at the Garrick in 1896 he played Bertie Nisril in " Thoroughbred," and at the Casino he appeared for a time as " The Polite Lunatic " in " The Belle of New York "; appeared at the Herald Square Theatre in 1898 as Muscadel in " A Normandy Wedding," and, at the Casino, as Panagl in " A Dangerous Maid "; at the Lyceum, New York, 9 May, 1899,

played Baverstock in " His Excellency the Governor," and at Herald Square, 16 Oct., 1899, appeared as Pinchas in " The Children of the Ghetto "; made his first appearance in London, at the Adelphi, 11 Dec., 1899, in the same part; in 1900 he appeared at the Republic Theatre, as Miguel de Antona in " In the Palace of the King," and since that date has played Pepe in " Francesca da Rimini," Peter in " The Burgomaster," Barry in " The Country Girl," Alan in " Babes in Toyland," Pincus Meyer in " A Business Man," Chambuddy Ram in " The Cingalee," the Man in the Moon in " The Land of Nod," and Tom Harrington in " A Strenuous Life "; at the Savoy Theatre, New York, Nov., 1906, he played the part of Clarence Chope in " Sir Anthony "; in 1907, toured as Partridge in " Tom Jones," and appeared in this part at the Astor Theatre, New York, Nov., 1907; at the Majestic, Sept., 1908; played " Doc " Filkins in " Father and Son "; in Nov., toured with Adeline Genée, as Mephisto in " The Soul Kiss "; at Daly's, New York, Jan., 1910, played the Duke of Alasia in " King of Cadonia," and The Parson in " The Wishing Ring "; at Chicago, Apr., 1910, played in " My Cinderella Girl "; in 1911 toured as Theophilus Sherry in " Madame Sherry "; at Daly's, Sept., 1911, played Jefferson Todd in " When Sweet Sixteen"; at Chicago, Apr., 1912, played in " A Modern Eve "; at the Republic Theatre, New York, Jan., 1913, appeared as Mrs. McMiche in " The Good Little Devil "; appeared in " vaudeville," 1914, in " The Lavender Lady "; appeared at the Knickerbocker Theatre, Feb., 1914, in " The Laughing Husband "; at the Casino, New York, May, 1915, played Casimir Cascadier in " A Modern Eve "; at the New Amsterdam Theatre, New York, Nov., 1915, appeared as Impikoff and the Maharajah of Gginggs Gaboo in " Around the Map "; at the Shubert Theatre, Aug., 1917, as Matthew Van Zandt in " Maytime "; he continued to tour in this piece until 1920; at the Lyric, New York, Oct., 1920, played Polydore Cliquot in " Kissing Time," and toured

in the same part, 1921.
(Died 20 Mar., 1929; age 56)

NORTHCOTT, Richard, archivist of the Royal Opera, Covent Garden; *b.* London, 1 Aug., 1871; *e* King's College (where he was a choral exhibitioner) and Heidelberg University; author of " Records of Covent Garden," " Covent Garden and the Royal Opera," " Parsifal and Wagner's other operas "; " Beethoven's Fidelio in London "; " Opera Chatter "; " A Tribute to Algarotti," " Musical Freemasons," and biographies of Donizetti, Bizet, Offenbach, Gounod and Sir Henry Bishop; " Royal Performances in London Theatres "; has numerous compositions to his credit; organist and choirmaster of the Swiss Church, London, 1889–1903; Hon. Sec., Old Neuenheimers Society, 1890–1913; was formerly musical critic and assistant dramatic critic of *The Daily Chronicle*; is a Fellow of the Institute of Journalists, and of the Royal Philharmonic Society, and a member of The Critics' Circle. *Clubs:* Constitutional, Royal Automobile, Junior Carlton, and Savage.
(Died 22 Jan., 1931; age 59)

NORTON, Frederic, composer; *b.* Manchester; *e.* Manchester Grammar School; formerly engaged in an insurance office; studied singing under Paolo Tosti; joined the Carl Rosa Opera Company, singing baritone parts; next toured as the Monk in " La Poupée"; subsequently appeared in variety theatres, including the London Pavilion; is the composer of "The Water Maidens," 1901; " Pinkie and the Fairies," 1908; " Orpheus in the Underground," 1912; " What, Ho ! Daphne," 1913; certain numbers in " The Passing Show," 1915; " Chu-Chin-Chow," 1916, which secured the longest run of any play on record in England; "Pamela," 1917; during 1916, on several occasions sang the *rôle* of Ali Baba in "Chu-Chin-Chow," at His Majesty's, during the absence of Courtice Pounds. *Clubs:* Beefsteak, and St. John's Wood Arts.
(Died 15 Dec., 1946)

NORWOOD, Eille, actor; *b.* York; 11 Oct., 1861; *e.* St. John's College, Cambridge University (B.A.); *m.* Ruth Mackay; had some experience as an amateur before making his first appearance on the professional stage with F. R. Benson's Shakespearean Company, as Paris in " Romeo and Juliet" in 1884; later on, he played Romeo to Marie de Grey's Juliet; then toured in "Fédora" and " Masks and Faces "; his next important engagement was with Edward Compton, 1886-7, playing Young Marlow, Joseph Surface, Captain Absolute, Harry Dornton, etc.; appeared at the Globe, 1888, as Capt. Gilchrist in " Bootle's Baby "; then came a three years' engagement in Australasia, with incessant change of parts, and on his return to England he took Terry's Theatre and produced his three-act farce, " The Noble Art," May, 1892; for seven years he had to retire from the stage owing to illness, but after a successful operation he reappeared at the Strand, Aug., 1901, in his own play " The Talk of the Town " (" The Noble Art "); appeared at the Avenue, Apr., 1902, in " The Little French Milliner"; his opportunity came when he played Arthur Bourchier's part of Bramley Burville in Esmond's play, " My Lady Virtue," at the Garrick in 1902, where he was seen and engaged by Sir Charles Wyndham, with whom he has played the leading heavy parts in " My Lady of Rosedale," 1904; "Captain Drew on Leave," 1906; " The Liars," 1907; toured in America and Canada with Nat Goodwin for ten months as leading man; appeared at the Waldorf, 1906, as Lieutenant-Colonel Anstruther in " The Second in Command "; the following autumn he toured with Miss Winifred Emery as Burchell in " Olivia," and created the part of Dick Gascoyne in " Her Son " at Glasgow; he was then once more with Sir Charles Wyndham, and Louis Calvert secured him for his production of " Sweet Kitty Bellairs," at the Haymarket; during 1908 played in " The Greater Glory," and at Terry's Theatre, appeared as Rosmer in " Rosmersholm "; during 1909 toured as Raffles in the play of that name, and as Gerald Merriam in "Idols"; joined H. B. Irving at the Queen's, Jan., 1910, and played Dr. Lanyon in "Dr. Jekyll and Mr. Hyde," subsequently appearing there as Horatio in "Hamlet," Nemours in "Louis XI," The Prisoner in "Judge Not," and James Stuart in "The Princess Clementina"; at the Duke of York's, Apr., 1911, played Georges Arnaud in "The Lily"; appeared at the Palladium, June, 1911, in "The King's Ransom"; in Sept., 1911, toured in "The Quality of Mercy"; at the Queen's Theatre, Oct., 1911, played the part of George Admaston, M.P., in "A Butterfly on the Wheel"; appeared in the same part at the Thirty-ninth Street Theatre, New York, Jan., 1912, subsequently touring in the United States and Canada in the same play; appeared at the Grand, Croydon, Apr.-May, 1913, in connection with the repertory season, playing Charlie Wilson in "Chains" Mr. Parbury in "The Tyranny of Tears," George Yonge in "The Situation at Newbury," Hilary Cutts in "The New Sin," and Philip Lowe in "Dropping the Pilot"; at the Haymarket, May, 1913, played Joe Garson in "Within the Law"; at the Criterion, June, 1914, played Lord Icebrook in "A Scrap of Paper"; July, 1914, Robert Orde in "A Working Man"; at the Comedy, Oct., 1914, Christian Brent in "Peg o' My Heart"; at the Globe, Mar., 1917, appeared as William Meyer in "The Man Who Went Abroad"; at the Apollo, May, 1917, as Captain Woodhouse in "Inside the Lines"; at the New Theatre, July, 1918, as Paul Marketel in "The Chinese Puzzle"; in addition he has acted as producer of several plays, among which may be mentioned "The Man Who Stayed at Home," 1914; "The Clock Goes Round," 1916; "The Man Who Went Abroad," 1917; "French Leave," 1920; "A Pair of Sixes," 1920; in 1920, was engaged by the Stoll Film Company, for the title-*rôles* in the cinema versions of "The Tavern Knight," "A Gentleman of France," and "Sherlock Holmes," "starring" in forty-seven "Adventures"; at the Prince's Theatre, Oct.,

1923, played Sherlock Holmes in "The Return of Sherlock Holmes"; during 1924 toured in the same part; at the Fortune, Apr., 1925, played Sir Hugh Symonds in "Yetta Polowski"; Arts and Garrick, Jan., 1929, Lord Palmerston in "The Lady With a Lamp"; Arts, Oct., 1929, Lord Deering in "Time and the Hour"; Vaudeville, Jan., 1930, succeeded Charles Laughton as Brig.-General Root in "French Leave"; "Q," Dec., 1930, Sir Philip Chown in "Gamble"; after an absence of some years, reappeared at Daly's, Dec., 1934, as Sir John Marley in "The Moon is Red"; produced the revival of "French Leave," Vaudeville, 1930; he is the author of several plays, "Hook and Eye," "Chalk and Cheese," "The Noble Art," "One Good Turn" (with Martin Swayne), "The Grey Room" (with Max Pemberton), 1917, and the composer of many published songs and pianoforte pieces; compiled over 2,000 crossword puzzles for *The Daily Express. Club:* Savage. *(Died 24 Dec., 1948; age 87)*

NORWORTH, Jack, actor; *b.* Philadelphia, 5 Jan., 1879; *m.* (1) Louise Dresser; (2) Nora Bayes; (3) Mary Johnson; made his first appearance on the stage in 1898, as a "blackfaced" comedian on the "vaudeville" stage, and continued in this line for seven years; he also toured in a drama, "The Californian"; made his first appearance on the regular stage, at Herald Square Theatre, New York, 30 Aug., 1906, when he played the part of Jack Doty in "About Town," and scored an immediate success by his singing of the topical song "The Great White Way"; at the Jardin de Paris, New York, June, 1909, played Kermit in "The Follies of 1909"; at the Broadway, Jan., 1910, Howson Lot in "The Jolly Bachelors"; appeared at the Globe Theatre, New York, Apr., 1911, as Buddie Arnold in "Little Miss Fix-It"; at Weber and Fields' Music Hall, New York, Nov., 1912, played Percy Fitzsimmonds in "Roly-Poly" and Robert Pilfer in "Without the Law"; subsequently appeared at the leading variety theatres in the United States, and making a pronounced success with such songs as " Naughty Boy " ; " I'm a Nut," etc. ; coming to London, he made his first appearance at the London Hippodrome, 2 June, 1914, in " Hullo ! Tango " ; subsequently appeared at the London Pavilion and elsewhere ; appeared at the Duke of York's Theatre, Mar., 1915, in " Rosy Rapture," with great success ; later he toured in variety theatres in " A Syncopated Romance " ; appeared at the Garrick, Nov., 1915, in " Looking Around," and at the Queen's, Dec., 1915, in " Oh ! La, La " ; on returning to America, again played in " vaudeville " ; at the Bijou Theatre, New York, Nov., 1917, played in " Odds and Ends " ; during 1919 again in " vaudeville " ; at Atlantic City, July, 1920, played in " My Lady Friends," and at Chicago, continued to play in this piece 1920-21 ; during 1923-4 played in " Honeymoon House," in Chicago ; subsequently returned to the " vaudeville " stage ; Ritz, New York, Sept., 1937, played Father Kennedy in " On Location " ; Broadhurst, Oct., 1938, the Doorman in " The Fabulous Invalid " ; he introduced several songs of the " tongue-twisting type " to the public, among which may be mentioned " Sister Susie's sewing shirts for soldiers " ; " Mother's sitting knitting little mittens for the Navy"; "Which switch is the switch, Miss, for Ipswich," etc. ; also sang " Private Michael Cassidy, V.C." *(Died 1 Sept., 1959; age 80)*

NOVELLO, Ivor, actor, manager, dramatic author, and composer; *b.* Cardiff, 15 Jan., 1893; *s.* of David Davies and his wife, Clara Novello (Davies) ; *e.* Magdalen College School, Oxford, made his first appearance on the stage, at the Ambassadors' Theatre, 3 Nov., 1921, as Armand Duval in " Deburau " ; at the Kingsway, Mar., 1922, played Wu Hoo Git in " The Yellow Jacket"; June, 1922, Javier in " Spanish Lovers " ; at the Playhouse, Aug., 1923, Victor Leroux in " Enter Kiki ! " ; at the Prince of Wales's, June, 1924, Pierre Boucheron in " The Rat " ; Garrick, Feb., 1925, played Karl Heinrich in a revival of

" Old Heidelberg " ; Adelphi, Apr., 1925, Laurence Trenwith in the revival of " Iris "; Adelphi, May, 1925, in aid of King George's Pension Fund, played Peo in " My Lady's Dress " ; Palace, Manchester Dec., 1925, Roddy Berwick in " Down Hill " ; Wyndham's, Feb., 1926, Benvenuto Cellini in " The Firebrand " ; Queen's, June, 1926, Roddy in " Down Hill " ; Duke of York's, Dec., 1926, Liliom in the play of that name ; Prince of Wales's, Feb., 1927, appeared in a revival of " The Rat " ; Daly's, Nov., 1927, played Sirio Marson in " Sirocco " ; appeared at the Palladium, Sept., 1928, in " The Gate Crasher " ; Globe, Oct., 1928, played Max Clement in " The Truth Game"; New, Oct., 1929, David Kennard in " Symphony in Two Flats " ; went to Canada, and appeared at Montreal, Sept., 1930, in the same part, and also appeared in it, at the Shubert Theatre, New York, Sept., 1930 ; at the Ethel Barrymore Theatre, New York, Dec., 1930, again played Max in " The Truth Game"; after returning to London, appeared at the Prince of Wales's, Mar., 1932, as Felix in " I Lived With You"; Strand, Aug., 1932, played Lord Bay Clender in " Party"; Sept., 1932, toured in " I Lived With You" Playhouse, Jan., 1933, Seraphine in " Flies in the Sun " ; Globe, June, 1933, Lt.-Col. Sir Geoffrey Bethel and Gray Raynor in " Proscenium"; Sept., 1934, Jacques Clavel in " Murder in Mayfair"; Drury Lane, May, 1935, Anthony Allen in " Glamorous Night"; Nov., 1935, at the Shakespeare *matinée*, Romeo in the balcony scene from " Romeo and Juliet"; His Majesty's, Apr., 1936, Lord George Hell in " The Happy Hypocrite"; Drury Lane, Sept., 1936, Michael in " Careless Rapture"; Sept., 1937, the Duke of Cheviot and Otto Fresch in " Crest of the Wave"; Winter Garden, Dec., 1937, in aid of King George's Pension Fund, Charles Surface in " The School for Scandal"; Drury Lane, Sept., 1938, King Henry in " Henry V"; Mar., 1939, Rudi Kleber in " The Dancing Years"; toured, Oct., 1939, as Justin in " Second Helping," and at the Lyric, Apr., 1940, played the same part, when the play was renamed " Ladies into Action"; toured, June, 1940, as Felix in "I Lived With You"; toured from Sept., 1940–Feb., 1942, as Rudi in "The Dancing Years," which he again played at the Adelphi, from Mar., 1942–June, 1944; toured, Aug., 1944, in Normandy and Belgium, for the troops, as Bruce Lovell in "Love from a Stranger"; again toured from Oct., 1944, in "The Dancing Years"; London Hippodrome, Apr., 1945, played Sir Graham Rodney, Valentine Fayre and Bay, in "Perchance to Dream," which ran until 1947; toured in South Africa, 1947, in "Perchance to Dream"; at the Palace, London, Sept., 1949, played Niki in "King's Rhapsody," which was still running at the end of 1950; commenced film career, 1919, in "The Call of the Blood"; has since appeared in numerous films, silent and talking; he was part-composer of "Theodore and Co.," 1916; "See-Saw," 1916; "Arlette," 1917; "Who's Hooper?"' 1919; "A to Z," 1921; "Our Nell," 1924; composer of "Tabs," 1918; "The Golden Moth," 1921; "Puppets," 1924; "The House That Jack Built," 1929; some of his more notable song compositions are "Keep the Home Fires Burning," "Laddie in Khaki," "Dreamboat," "The Little Damozel," "The Valley," "Megan," "We'll Gather Lilacs"; composed the song-cycle "The Valley of Rainbows"; is the author of "The Rat" (with Constance Collier), 1924; "Down Hill" (with Constance Collier), 1925; "The Truth Game," 1928; "A Symphony in Two Flats," 1929; "I Lived With You," "Party," 1932; "Fresh Fields," "Flies in the Sun"; "Proscenium," "Sunshine Sisters," 1933; "Murder in Mayfair," 1934; "Glamorous Night" (for which he also composed the music), "Full House," 1935; composer of "How Do, Princess!", and author and composer of "Careless Rapture," 1936; "Crest of the Wave," 1937; author of "Comedienne," and composer of incidental music to "Henry V," 1938; author and composer of "The Dancing Years," 1939; author of "Second Helping" ("Ladies into Action"), 1940; "Breakaway," 1941; author and composer of "Arc de Triomphe,"

1943; author, composer and lyrist of "Perchance to Dream," 1945; "We Proudly Present," 1947; "King's Rhapsody" (author and composer), 1949; "Gay's the Word" (author and composer), 1950; also wrote the film version of "The Truth Game" ("But the Flesh is Weak"), and dialogue for "Tarzan of the Apes," etc.

(Died 6 Mar., 1951; age 58)

NOZIERE, Fernand (Weyl) ; French dramatic author and critic ; is the author of the following, among other, plays : " Les Hasards du Coin du Feu " ; " Les Liaisons Dangereuses " ; " Un Episode Sous la Terreur," 1908 ; " La Maison des Danses " (with Muller), 1909 ; " Excelsior " (with Yves Mirande), 1910 ; " La Sonate à Kreutzer " (with A. Savoir), 1910 ; " Le Baptème " (with Savoir), 1913 ; " La Saignée " (with Lucien Descaves), 1913 ; " Gabrielle a Découché," 1919 ; " Le Tour du Cadran," 1919 ; " La Vie est Belle," 1920 ; " Musard," 1920 ; " Les Quatre Coins," 1920 ; " Marie Gazelle," 1920 ; " Les Trois Voleurs " (from the Italian), 1920 ; " La Raquette," 1921 ; " On n'en Sortira Pas " (with M. Wilned), 1921 ; " Bethsabée," 1921 ; " Elvire," 1921 ; " Madame Durand," 1921 ; is dramatic critic of *Le Matin* and *Gil Blas ;* is a Chevalier of the Legion of Honour.

(Died 25 Mar., 1931)

NUGENT, Elliott, actor, dramatic author, director, and producer; *b.* Dover, Ohio, U.S.A., 20 Sept., 1899; *s.* of John Charles Nugent and his wife Grace Mary (Fertig); *e.* Ohio State University; *m.* Norma Lee; has been on the stage since he was four years of age, appearing with his parents in vaudeville, at the Orpheum Theatre, Los Angeles, in 1904; made his first appearance in New York, at the Frazee Theatre, 13 Aug., 1921, as Tom Sterrett in "Dulcy"; at the Belmont, May, 1922, played "Kempy" James in "Kempy"; Belmont, Nov., 1923, played in "The Dumb-Bell"; Frazee, Dec., 1923, Eddie Hudson in "The Wild Westcotts"; Klaw, Oct., 1924; Ted Alamayne in "The Rising Son"; Henry Miller, Apr., 1925, John Miller in "The Poor Nut"; Liberty, Sept., 1925, played in "Human Nature"; 52nd Street, Mar., 1926, played in "The Trouper"; Hudson, May, 1927, again played "Kempy" James in "Kempy"; at Chicago and on tour, 1927, played in "Hoosiers Abroad"; Klaw, Apr., 1928, played Jim Dolf in "The Breaks"; Hudson, Sept., 1928, William Abbott in "By Request"; Hammerstein's, Nov., 1928, Walter Meakin in "Good Boy"; Selwyn, Nov., 1931, Bing Allen in "Fast Service"; after a lengthy absence in Hollywood, reappeared on the New York stage, at the Cort Theatre, Jan., 1940, as Tommy Turner in "The Male Animal"; St. James (for the Guild), Nov., 1942, Patrick Jamieson in "Without Love"; Morosco, Dec., 1943, Bill Page in "The Voice of the Turtle"; in summer theatres, 1949, George Hunter in "The Fundamental George"; at the Coronet, New York, Feb., 1951, appeared as Ambrose Atwater in "Not for Children"; City Center, Apr., 1952, played Tommy Turner in a revival of "The Male Animal"; at the Fulton, Nov., 1952, presented with Courtney Burr "The Seven Year Itch," and succeeded Tom Ewell as Richard Sherman in this play in 1954; Cort, Feb., 1955, presented with Courtney Burr and John Byram "The Wayward Saint"; Shubert, New Haven, Nov., 1956, played Dr. Brothers in "Build with One Hand"; Ethel Barrymore, New York, May, 1957, co-produced and directed "The Greatest Man Alive!"; is part-author, with his father, of the following plays: "A Clean Town," 1922; "Kempy," 1922; "The Dumb-Bell," 1923; "The Rising Son," 1924; "The Poor Nut," 1925; "Human Nature," 1925; "The Trouper," 1926; "By Request," 1928; "Fast Service," 1931; "The World's My Onion," 1935; also the author of "Nightstick" (with John Wray), 1927; "The Fight's On" (with Hagar Wilde and Ernest V. Heyn), 1937; "The Male Animal" (with James Thurber), 1940; "A Place of Our Own," 1945; directed the following plays: "All in Favor," 1942; "To-Morrow the World," 1943;

"A Place of Our Own," 1945; "The Big Two," "Darling, Darling, Darling," "Message for Margaret," 1947; in 1929 joined the Metro-Goldwyn-Mayer Company in Hollywood, as actor, author, and director; appeared in several films, and has directed "Three Cornered Moon," "The Cat and the Canary," "Welcome Stranger," "The Great Gatsby," etc.; author of "Of Cheat and Charmer," 1962, and the autobiography "Events Leading Up to the Comedy," 1965. *Recreations:* Tennis, golf, and swimming. *Clubs:* Players and Lambs, New York; Masquers, Hollywood. *Address:* Players Club, 16 Gramercy Park, New York City, U.S.A. 10003.

NUGENT, John Charles, actor and dramatic author; *b.* Niles, Ohio, U.S.A., 6 Apr., 1878; *s.* of Michael N. Nugent and his wife Bessie (Brennan); *e.* Reeves University, Ohio; *m.* Grace Mary Fertig; made his first appearance on the stage as a child, at the Somerset Theatre, Somerset, Ohio, Apr., 1888, as the child in "The Danites"; made his first appearance in New York, Oct., 1900, at the Union Square Theatre, as Jim Blair in "The Veteran," a vaudeville sketch; continued in vaudeville for many years, playing in his own and other sketches; at the Belmont Theatre, May, 1922, played "Dad" Bence in "Kempy"; Nov., 1923, Romeo in "The Dumb-Bell"; Klaw, Oct., 1924, Jim Alamayne in "The Rising Son"; Fifty-second Street, Mar., 1926, Larry Gilbert in "The Trouper"; Maxine Elliott Theatre, Oct., 1926, Hector Midge in "God Loves Us"; Masque Theatre, Apr., 1927, The Comedian in "The Comic"; Wallack's, Sept., 1927, Carleton Hazleton in "Mister Romeo"; Klaw, Apr., 1928, Jed Willis in "The Breaks"; Hudson, Sept., 1928, John Hector Henry in "By Request"; Lyceum, Jan., 1929, Mr. Ewing in "The Skyrocket";. Selwyn, Nov., 1931, John Blair in "Fast Service"; Waldorf, June, 1932, Thomas Maxwell in "That's Gratitude"; Pittsburgh, Sept., 1932, played in "Humpty Dumpty"; Biltmore, Jan., 1934, Herbert Kalness in "Big Hearted

Herbert"; Vanderbilt, Sept., 1934,
"King Tut" Jones in "Dream Child";
at Dennis, Mass., Sept., 1935, appeared
in "Ah! Wilderness"; Bijou, New
York, Feb., 1936, succeeded James
Bell as John J. Jennings in "The Sap
Runs High"; Lyceum, Dec., 1939,
Henry Ormonroyd in "When We Are
Married"; Golden, June, 1941, Mr.
West in "Snookie"; Cort, Sept.,
1941, Senator Broderick in "The
More the Merrier"; Henry Miller,
Jan., 1942, Bixby in "All in Favor";
Playhouse, June, 1944, Jim Blair in
"That Old Devil"; Royale, Apr.,
1945, Sam Reddy in "A Place of
Our Own"; in 1929 went to Holly-
wood with the Metro-Goldwyn-Mayer
Company, as actor, author, and di-
rector; has played in numerous pic-
tures; is part-author with his son
of the following plays: "A Clean
Town," "Kempy," 1922; "The
Dumb-Bell," 1923; "The Rising Son,"
1924"; The Poor Nut," "Human
Nature," 1925; "The Trouper," 1926;
"By Request," 1928; "Fast Service,"
1931; "The World's My Onion," 1935;
also author of "Dream Child" ("Live
Dangerously"), 1934; "Mr. Shaddy,"
1936; "That Old Devil," 1944; part-
author "Nightstick" (with Elliott
Nugent and John Wray), 1927; is
a well-known public speaker, and
author of many articles on theatrical and allied subjects. *Recreations:*
Swimming and dancing. *Club:* The
Lambs. *(Died 21 Apr., 1947; age 79)*

NUGENT, Moya, actress; *b.* 1901;
made her first appearance on the stage
at the Playhouse, 21 Sept., 1911, as
Meenie in "Rip Van Winkle"; she
next appeared at the Duke of York's
Theatre, Dec., 1911, as the Baby Mermaid and Liza in "Peter Pan," which
parts she also played in the three
succeeding annual revivals of that
play; at the Aldwych Theatre, Sept.,
1913, played Maggie in "The Ever-
Open Door"; at the Duke of York's,
Nov., 1913, appeared as Isabella in
"Quality Street"; at the Ambassadors', Oct., 1915, appeared in "More,"
and June, 1916, in "Pell-Mell"; at
the Playhouse, May, 1917, appeared
as Emily in "Wanted a Husband";

at the Grand Opera House, Belfast,
Christmas, 1918, and at the Gaiety,
Dublin, Christmas, 1919, played the
Princess in "Old King Cole"; at the
New Theatre, July, 1920, played Joyce
in "I'll Leave it to You"; at the
Theatre Royal, Edinburgh, Christmas,
1920, played Cinderella; at the
Queen's, Aug., 1921, Sarah in "My
Nieces"; at the Lyric, Dec., 1922,
Tilli in "Lilac Time"; Golder's Green,
Aug., 1926, played in "Bits and
Pieces"; Opera House, Manchester,
Dec., 1926, played Polly Perkins in
"Robinson Crusoe"; Apollo, Sept.,
1927, Charlotte in "The Music
Master"; London Pavilion, Mar.,
1928, appeared in "This Year of
Grace"; Mar., 1929, in "Wake Up
and Dream"; Drury Lane, Mar., 1930,
played Zoe in "The Three Musketeers";
Apollo, Apr., 1931, Sally Hamil in
"The New Gossoon"; Drury Lane,
Oct., 1931, Daisy Devon in "Caval-
cade"; Adelphi, Sept., 1932, played in
"Words and Music"; Adelphi, Oct.,
1933, Miss Pratt in "Nymph Errant";
His Majesty's, Feb., 1934, Martha
James in "Conversation Piece," and
played the same part at the 44th
Street Theatre, New York, Oct., 1934;
after returning to England, in Oct.,
1935, toured in a variety of parts with
Noel Coward and Gertrude Lawrence
in "To-Night at 7.30"; Phoenix, Jan.,
1936, appeared in the same plays,
when the programme was known as
"To-Night at 8.30"; appeared at the
National, New York, Nov., 1936, in
"To-Night at 8.30"; Morosco, New
York, Sept., 1937, played Gladys in
"George and Margaret"; St. James's,
London, Dec., 1937, Essie in "You
Can't Take It With You"; His
Majesty's, Mar., 1938, Blanche Wal-
lace in "Operette"; Music Box, New
York, Jan., 1939, played in "Set to
Music" ("Words and Music"); on
returning to London, appeared at the
Queen's, Dec., 1939, in "All Clear";
Piccadilly, July, 1941, played Mrs.
Bradman in "Blithe Spirit," which
ran nearly five years; "Q," June,
1946, Mrs. Finch in "Through the
Door"; Drury Lane, Dec., 1946, Miss
Scobie in "Pacific 1860"; Palace,
May, 1947, Countess Adelaide in "The
Bird Seller"; Lyric, Hammersmith,

Feb., 1948, May Carey in "Castle Anna"; Wimbledon, and at the Playhouse, May, 1948, played Miss Dennington in "Calypso"; Saville, Feb., 1950, Miss Ranklin in "The Schoolmistress"; Phoenix, Oct., 1950, Mary Willoughby in "Dear Miss Phoebe." *(Died 26 Jan., 1954; age 52)*

OAKER, Jane, actress (*née* Minnie Dorothy Peper); *b.* St. Louis, Mo., U.S.A., 17 June, 1880 ; *s.* St. Louis ; *m.* Hale Hamilton (mar. dis.) ; was a student at the American Academy of Dramatic Art prior to making her first professional appearance in 1900, when she appeared as Hermia in " A Midsummer Night's Dream," with Louis James and Kathryn Kidder, on tour ; in the same year toured with J. K. Hackett as Maritana in " Don Caesar's Return," and Princess Alicia in " A Chance Ambassador " ; at the Lyric, New York, Feb., 1904, played Laura Dearborn in " The Pit " ; at the New Amsterdam, May, 1905, appeared as Trilby O'Farrell in " Trilby " ; subsequently played a " stock " engagement, at Denver, with her own company ; in 1907 toured with George Fawcett as Annie Hunter in " The Silver Girl," and appeared in this part at Wallack's, New York, Oct., 1907 ; during 1908-9 toured as Olga in " The Devil " ; at the Garrick, New York, Aug., 1910, played Lorana de Castro in " Love Among the Lions " ; at the Lyceum, New York, Nov., 1910, the Hon. Gwendolen Fairfax in " The Importance of Being Earnest " ; at Chicago, 1911, appeared as Everywoman in the play of that name ; at the Hudson, June, 1914, played Agnes Meredith in " The Dummy " ; at the Cohan Theatre, Aug., 1915, Queeny in " Cousin Lucy," and during 1916-17, toured in the same part ; at the Gaiety, New York, Aug., 1918, played Margaret Davis in " Lightnin'," which ran for 1291 performances ; at the Garrick, Aug., 1927, played Fanny Lehman in " The Butter and Egg Man " ; Hudson, Dec., 1927, Mrs. Canfield in " Los Angeles."

OBER, Philip, actor ; *b.* Fort Payne, Alabama, U.S.A., 23 Mar., 1902 ; *s.* Frank Willis Ober and his wife Emily Kendrick (Nott) ; *e.* Roger Ascham School, Hartsdale, N.Y., and Princeton University ; *m.* (1) Phyllis Roper ; (2) Vivian Vance (mar. dis.) ; formerly engaged as a salesman ; before entering the professional theatre, played for six seasons with the Beechwood Players, Scarborough-on-Hudson ; made his first appearance on the professional stage at the Empire Theatre, New York, 9 June, 1932, as Jo Fisk in " The Animal Kingdom" ; 46th Street, Nov., 1933, played Henry Broughton in " She Loves Me Not" ; Henry Miller, Oct., 1934, Chester (Bud) Norton in " Personal Appearance," which he played for over a year in New York and on tour for six months ; Empire, Aug., 1936, Walter Beckett in " Spring Dance" ; National, May, 1937, Mr. Jevries in " Without Warning" ; in the summer of 1937, played a twelve-week " stock" engagement at Elitch's Gardens, Denver ; Little Theatre, New York, Mar., 1938, played Brent in " The Hill Between" ; Vanderbilt, May, 1938, Ted Strong in "Eye on the Sparrow" ; Henry Miller, Sept., 1938, Horace Rand in " Kiss the Boys Goodbye" ; Biltmore, May, 1940, Humphrey Williams in " Out from Under" ; Belasco, Jan., 1941, Lieut. Weigand in "Mr. and Mrs. North" ; Lyceum, Nov., 1941, Harry Graves in " Junior Miss," which he played for twenty months ; Fulton, Oct., 1943, Michael Fox in " Another Love Story" ; Bijou, Dec., 1943, Dr. William Lathrop in "Doctors Disagree" ; went overseas, Apr., 1944, for U.S.O., with the first play sent to the combat zone, "Over 21" ; toured in United States, from Sept., 1945, as Judge Wilkins in "Dear Ruth": Playhouse, New York, Feb., 1947, played Walter Craig in "Craig's Wife" ; appeared in summer theatres, 1947, as Grant Matthews in "State of the Union" ; Royale, Nov., 1948, played Owen Turner in "Light Up the Sky" ; first entered films, 1933, and since 1949 has played only in that medium and on television, including the films "From Here to Eternity," "North by Northwest," "Beloved Infidel," etc. ; elected a Councillor of Actors Equity Association, 1947 ; elected a Member of the Board of Directors, Screen Actors' Guild, 1954. *Address:* 11451 Albata Street, Los Angeles 49, California, U.S.A. *Telephone No.:* Granite 2–5780.

OBEY, André, dramatic author ; *b.* Douai, 8 May, 1892 ; *s.* of Oscar Obey and his wife Elisabeth (Hisette) ;

e. Lycée de Douai; the author of the following among other plays: "La Souriante Madame Beudet" (with Denys Amiel), 1921; "La Carcasse" (with Amiel), 1926; "Noé" ("Noah"), "Le Viol de Lucrèce," 1931, "La Bataille de la Marne," 1931; "Vénus et Adonis," "Loire," "Richard III" (adaptation), 1933; "Don Juan," 1934; "Le Trompeur de Séville," 1937; "Maria," 1946; "Œdipe-Roi" (adaptation), 1947; "L'Homme de Cendres," 1949; "Lazare," 1951; "Une Fille pour du Vent," 1953; "Orestie" (adaptation), 1955; "La Chatte sur un Toit Brûlant" (adaptation), 1956; "Les Trois Coups de Minuit," 1958; joined Jacques Copeau's Company, "Les Copiaus," at Lyons, May, 1929; "Noé" and "Le Viol de Lucrèce," were the first plays presented by La Compagnie des Quinze at the Théâtre du Vieux Colombier, Jan., 1931; "La Bataille de La Marne," gained the Eugène Brieux prize, 1932; director of the Comédie-Française, 1945–6; Officier de la Légion d'Honneur. *Address:* 32, rue de Sévigné, Sucy-en-Brie, S-et-O, France.

OBRAZTSOV, Sergei Vladimirovich, chief producer and director of the State Central Puppet Theatre; *b*. 5 July, 1901; *e*. secondary technical school; studied painting, and then graphic art, at the Higher Art Technical Workshop for five years; in 1922, made his first appearance as an actor at the Music Studio of the Moscow Art Theatre (later Nemirovich–Danchenko Theatre), as Terapot in "La Périchole," and remained a member of the company for eight years; during this time, he played, among other parts, the Leader of the Old Men in "Lysistrata," and Pompon in "Madame Angot's Daughter"; 1930–6, at No. 2 Studio, Moscow Art Theatre, he played the following parts: Volgin in Afinogenov's "The Eccentric," Tsarevich Alexei in "The Death of Ivan the Terrible," by Tolstoy, Feste in "Twelfth Night," and Professor Dossa in Deval's "Prayer for Life"; in 1923, began presenting puppets at concerts, and since 1931, has been chief director of the State Central Puppet Theatre; included among the 40 productions he has

presented (*for children*) are Speransky's "Kashtanka" (based on Chekhov), 1935, E. Tarakhovskaya's "As if by Magic," 1936, Polivanova's "Happy Bear-Cubs," 1945, Marshak's "Pussy's House," 1947, N. Gernet's "Mowgli," based on Kipling, 1954, V. Kurdyumov's "Little Hump-Backed Horse" (based on Yershov), 1955; "A Tale of Time Lost," by E. Shvarts, 1958; (*for adults*), Gernet's "Aladdin's Magic Lamp" from "The Thousand and One Nights," 1940, Speransky's "King Deer" (based on Carlo Gozzi), 1943, "An Unusual Concert," 1946, Speransky's "To the Flutter of Your Lashes," 1949, "The Devil's Mill" (by Jan Drda and I. Shtok), 1953, Speransky's "Divorce Case," 1954, A. Barto's "A Marriageable Daughter," 1956, B. Tuzlukov's "Mine, Only Mine," N. Erdman's "The Straw Hat," based on Labiche, 1958; author of the following books: "Actor and Puppet," 1938; "My Profession," 1950; "London, A Traveller's Notebook," 1955; "What I Learnt and Understood during My Two Visits to London," 1956; "Theatre of the Chinese People," 1957; awarded the State Prize (2nd class) for outstanding work in the Puppet Theatre, 1946; Order of the Red Banner of Labour, 1946 and 1961. *Hobby:* Breeding aquarium fish. *Address:* Flat 97, 5 Nemirovich-Danchenko Street, Moscow, U.S.S.R.

O'BRIEN, Barry, producing manager and dramatic agent; *b*. London, 23 Dec., 1893; *s*. of Richard Barry O'Brien and his wife Kathleen (Teevan); *e*. St. Paul's School; was formerly an actor; in 1925 opened a dramatic agency, became active as producing manager in 1925, when he revived "The Young Person in Pink"; has since toured many notable London successes, with star artists, including Jessie Matthews, Evelyn Laye, Eva Moore, Zena Dare, Violet Vanbrugh, Ethel Irving, Oscar Asche, Marie Löhr, Iris Hoey, Fay Compton, Ivor Novello, Gladys Cooper, Dame Sybil Thorndike, José Collins, Marie Burke, Frances Day, Alice Delysia, Phyllis Neilson-Terry, Ruth Draper, Ralph Lynn, Henry Kendall, Yvonne

Arnaud, Alastair Sim, Rosalinde Fuller, Francis L. Sullivan, Franklin Dyall, etc.; made his first London production at the St. Martin's, June, 1927, with "Meet the Wife"; subsequent London productions were "The Flying Squad," "The Squeaker," "The Man Who Changed His Name," "Passing Brompton Road" (with Alban Limpus), "The Mollusc," 1928; "The Lad," "Persons Unknown," "The Calendar," 1929; "Bees and Honey" (with Limpus), "Her Shop" (with Limpus), 1930; "A Pair of Trousers," "Blue Sky Beyond," "The Merry Widow," 1931; "The Outsider," "Lilac Time," 1932; in 1936, took over the lease of the Palace Theatre, Westcliff, Southend-on-Sea, and in 1937, of the Shanklin (I.O.W.) Theatre; in 1938 and 1939, ran repertory seasons at the Pier, Eastbourne; during 1939, presented seasons of repertory at the Chiswick and Wood Green Empires for Sir Oswald Stoll, and again presented Ruth Draper in a short provincial tour; London Coliseum, 1940, presented a season of repertory; from 1940–5, has toured "Chu-Chin-Chow," "Rookery Nook," "Tons of Money," "Thark," "Nap Hand," "How Are They at Home?" "Geneva," "What Say They," "Flare Path," "While the Sun Shines," "Is Your Honeymoon Really Necessary?," "Pink String and Sealing Wax," "Rebecca," "Peril at End House," "Gaslight," "Quiet Weekend," etc.; in 1945, re-opened the theatres at Shanklin and Ventnor; from 1946–50 ran repertory seasons at Bournemouth, Southsea, Shanklin and Ryde, and during these years toured "Duet for Two Hands," "No Medals," "The Years Between," "The Perfect Woman," "Lady From Edinburgh," "Young Mrs. Barrington," "Fools Rush In," "A Man About The House," "The Winslow Boy," "The Chiltern Hundreds," "White Cargo," "The Paragon," "The Happiest Days of Your Life," "Breach of Marriage," "Dr. Angelus," "Little Lambs Eat Ivy," "Edward, My Son," "The Late Edwina Black," "One Wild Oat," and "Black Chiffon"; in 1946, at the Ambassadors', presented (with Alec L. Rea and E. P. Clift), "Murder on

the Nile"; Winter Garden, 1947 (with Linnit and Dunfee), "Outrageous Fortune"; toured (with Jack Hylton), 1947–9, "No Room at the Inn"; from 1947–50, arranged tours for the International Ballet, with seasons at Casino and Coliseum; toured, 1950, "The Day After To-Morrow," "September Tide," "The Late Edwina Black," "One Wild Oat," "Black Chiffon," and "Castle in the Air"; from 1951–60 continued running repertory seasons each year at Bournemouth, Shanklin, and Ryde, and during 1953 ran repertory seasons at the People's Palace in East London and at the Royal, Exeter; commenced presenting The New Malvern Company at Torquay, 1955; during all this period toured "Home At Seven," "Desire In the Night," "The Holly and the Ivy," "A Streetcar Named Desire," "Say It With Flowers," "Will Any Gentleman?," 1951; "Passionate Youth," "The Seventh Veil," 1952; "Women of Twilight," 1953; "Escapade," "A Call on the Widow," "Seagulls Over Sorrento," 1954; "Reluctant Heroes," 1955; arranged tour for International Ballet, 1956; toured "Doctor in the House" (with Jack Hylton) 1957–58; presented repertory at Southampton, 1958; toured "Housemaster," "The Reluctant Debutante," "Not in the Book," "The Perfect Woman," "The Bride and the Bachelor," "The Marquise," 1958–60; presented Alicia Markova, and Ram Gopal at the Princes, 1960. *Recreations:* Fishing and motoring. *Address:* 18 Charing Cross Road, W.C.2. *Telephone No.:* Temple Bar 6447 and 2602.

(Died 25 Dec., 1961; age 69)

O'BRIEN, David, actor; *b.* Coventry, 20 Aug., 1930; *s.* of James Herd and his wife Kathleen May (Mackay); *e.* Park Lane School, Wembley, and King's School, Harrow; made his first appearance on the stage at the Theatre Royal, Brighton, 21 Aug., 1944, as Emil Bruckner in "To-Morrow the World," first appeared in London at the Aldwych, 30 Aug., 1944, in the same part; Stratford-on-Avon, Apr.–Sept., 1946, appeared with the Memorial Theatre company; Lyric, Hammersmith, Feb., 1949, Michael Randall in "The Damask Cheek"; Strand, Sept., 1949, Robin Spender in "Master of Arts"; Palace, July, 1955, with the Shakespeare Memorial Theatre Company, played Verges in "Much Ado About Nothing" and the Fool in "King Lear"; Ambassador, New York, Jan., 1962, played Lieutenant in "A Passage to India"; Delacorte, N.Y., July, 1967, King of France in "King John." *Hobbies:* Photography, toy-engines and tracks, golf.

O'BRIEN, Kate, dramatic author, novelist, and journalist; *b.* Limerick, 1897; *d.* of Thomas O'Brien and his wife Catherine (Thornhill); *e.* Laurel Hill Convent, Limerick, and University College, Dublin; is the author of the following plays: "Distinguished Villa," 1926; "The Bridge," 1927; "The Ante-Room" (with W. A. Carot and Geoffrey Gomer), 1936; "The Schoolroom Window," 1937; "The Last of Sur..mer" (with John Perry), 1944; "That Lady," 1949; her first novel was "Without My Cloak," which gained the Hawthornden Prize and the James Tait Black Memorial Prize, 1931; other novels are "The Ante-Room," "Mary Lavelle," "Pray for the Wanderers," "The Land of Spices," "The Last of Summer"; has also been actively engaged in literary criticism. *Address:* The Fort, Roundstone, Co. Galway, Ireland.

O'BRIEN, Terence actor; *b.* Dublin, 25 Oct., 1887; *s.* of Terence O'Brien and his wife Marion Lorna (Preston); *e.* Highfield, Chertsey, and Godwin College, Margate; was formerly engaged in the City for a few years; made his first appearance on the stage at the Public Hall, Woking, in 1908, as the Sea Captain in " Twelfth Night"; made his first appearance in London, at the Lyceum Theatre, 1909, as the First Player in " Hamlet "; subsequently appeared at the same theatre in " The Prisoner of the Bastille," " The Proud Prince " and " East Lynne "; in 1911 accompanied Matheson Lang on his South African tour, subsequently touring with him

in India, China, and the Philippines; on returning to London, appeared at the Haymarket, 1913, in " The Pretenders "; returned to South Africa, with the Stratford-on-Avon Players, playing juveniles; on returning to London, fulfilled several engagements as understudy; subsequently joined the British Army; at the St. James's, Dec., 1915, played Morocco and Tubal in " The Merchant of Venice "; at the Strand, 1916, played Holman in " Mr. Wu," and Black Tom in " Pete," and as understudy to Matheson Lang, played Shylock, and Wu Li Chang in " Mr. Wu," in one day; in Sept., 1916, joined the Old Vic. company as leading man, playing Othello, Hamlet, Benedick, Brutus, Henry V, etc.; in 1917 toured as Oswald in " Ghosts "; subsequently played a season at the Liverpool Repertory Theatre; at the Court Theatre, under J. B. Fagan, Oct., 1918, played Orsino in " Twelfth Night," and Mar., 1919, Trip in " The School for Scandal "; Oct., 1919, Bassanio in " The Merchant of Venice "; Dec., 1920, Demetrius in " A Midsummer Night's Dream "; Feb., 1921, Prince John in " King Henry IV " (Part II); then for nearly three years toured as leading man in the Bernard Shaw Repertory Company, playing John Tanner, Henry Higgins, Eugene Marchbanks, Valentine, Juggins, Andrew Undershaft, and Louis Dubedat; at the Court, Feb., 1924, played Burge Lubin in part III, and Martellus in part V, of " Back to Methuselah "; at the Savoy, July, 1924, played Sergeant Flynn in " In the Snare," and subsequently, Sir Terence O'Moy in the same play; at the Everyman, Nov., 1924, Joshua Wilson in " Clogs to Clogs "; at " Q," Jan., 1925, played Horace Parker in " A Message from Mars "; Kingsway, Apr., 1925, the Centurion in " Caesar and Cleopatra "; Lyric, July, 1925, Captain Kaschumowsky in " The Czarina "; Kingsway, Aug., 1925, the First Player in " Hamlet " (in modern dress); Scala (for the Renaissance Society), Oct., 1925, Monticelso in " The White Devil "; " Q," Dec., 1925, to Feb., 1926, played in " The Lifting," " Rust," and " The Joy-

1824

Ride," and also produced several plays there, 1925–7; toured, under his own management, 1928, as Adolf in "The Father," and other plays; Arts, Sept., 1927, played Jo Howard in "Master"; subsequently with the Birmingham Repertory Company; in Nov., 1928, went to India and the Far East, with the Macdona Players, in Shaw repertory; on returning to England, produced several plays at the Players' Theatre, 1929–30; during 1931, again toured with the Macdona Players; St. James's, Apr., 1932, played Montano in "Othello," and Gratiano in "The Merchant of Venice"; Garrick, June, 1933, Sozanoff in "Clear All Wires;" subsequently left the stage for some years; Old Vic., Apr., 1938, played Cominius in "Coriolanus"; Duchess and Whitehall, 1938–9, Leman in "Glorious Morning"; Duchess, June, 1939, Joce in "The Jews of York"; Chanticleer, Dec., 1939, Father John in "The Unicorn from the Stars"; Comedy, June, 1943. Mr. O'Brien in "Case 27 V.C."; toured for E.N.S.A., in "The Father," "Man and Superman," "Jeannie," "Tobias and the Angel," etc.; is producer and principal actor of the Rock Theatre Company Productions. *Address:* 37 Charles Street, London, S.W.
(Died 13 Oct., 1970; age 82)

O'BRIEN, Virginia, actress and vocalist; *b.* Trenton, New Jersey, U.S.A., 14 Dec., 1896; *d.* of William O'Brien and his wife Mary Teresa (Dowd); *e.* St. Joseph Convent, and New England Conservatory, Boston; *m.* Donald Brian; studied music at the Conservatory, under Charles Bennett, Yeatman Griffith, and Arthur Laurason; made her first appearance on the stage at Parson's Theatre, Hartford, Conn., 5 Nov., 1917, in the chorus, in "Her Regiment"; made her first appearance on the New York stage, at the Broadhurst Theatre, 12 Nov., 1917, in the same piece; at the New Amsterdam, 16 Sept., 1918, played Zellie in "The Girl Behind the Gun"; during 1919, toured in "The Royal Vagabond," and at the Selwyn Theatre, succeeded Peggy Wood as Julie in "Buddies"; during 1920, appeared as

Mary Howells in "Mary"; at the Century, Dec., 1921, played Mascha in a revival of "The Chocolate Soldier"; in 1922, appeared in "vaudeville" with Donald Brian, and in "Sue, Dear," and "Marjolaine," at the Globe, Mar., 1923, played Jill Malone in "Jack and Jill"; Liberty, Dec., 1923, Rosie in "The Rise of Rosie O'Reilly"; Shubert, Apr., 1925, Lady Psyche in "Princess Ida"; during 1925–6, toured as Pauline in "No, No, Nanette," and during 1927, as Evelyn Devine in "Castles in the Air"; at the Vanderbilt, Nov., 1929, played Helen McCoy in "How's Your Health?"; Erlanger's, Sept., 1931, Sonia in a revival of "The Merry Widow"; in Sept., 1932, toured in the same part; is a member of Actors' Equity Association and Catholic Actors' Guild. *Address:* 30 Arleigh Road, Great Neck, Long Island, U.S.A. *Telephone No.:* Great Neck 1725.

O'BRIEN-MOORE, Erin, actress; *b.* 2 May, 1908; *d.* of J. B. L. O'Brien-Moore and his wife Agnes (Jenkins); *m.* Mark Barron; originally intended to become an artist, and was trained in painting and modelling; made her first appearance on the New York stage at the Charles Hopkins Theatre, 21 Jan., 1926, as the Maid in "The Makropoulos Secret"; at Chanin's 46th Street, Aug., 1926, played Marianna in "My Country"; Greenwich Village, Feb., 1927, Elsa Lally in "Lally"; joined Harry Green's company and accompanied him to London, where she made her first appearance, at the Apollo, 6 Sept., 1927, as Helen Stanton in "The Music Master"; after her return to New York, appeared at the Provincetown Theatre, Apr., 1928, as Me in "Him"; Bijou, June, 1928, succeeded Marguerite Churchill as Marion Hardy in "Skidding"; Playhouse, Jan., 1929, played Rose Moran in "Street Scene," and returned to London, Sept., 1930, to play the same part, at the Globe Theatre; returned to America, 1931, and toured in the same part; at the John Golden Theatre, Feb., 1932, played Vera Marsh in "Riddle Me This!"; at Magnolia, Mass., July, 1932, played in the Magnolia "stock" company; Lyceum, New York, Oct., 1932, played Peggy Chase in "Men Must Fight"; at Jackson Heights, July, 1933, appeared in "Strictly Dynamite"; National, New York, Dec., 1933, played Malkele in "Yoshe Kalb"; at the Biltmore, Los Angeles, May, 1934, appeared in "Memory"; Curran, San Francisco, Jan., 1935, in "Merrily We Roll Along"; Henry Miller, New York, Jan., 1938, played Sweets Ramirez in "Tortilla Flat"; in summer theatres, 1938, played the leading parts in "High Tor," "Penny Wise," "Private Lives," "Night Must Fall," and "Outward Bound"; was absent from the stage for two years, 1939–40, owing to an accident; at Newport, 1941, played lead in "The Little Foxes"; during 1942, at the Alexandra, Toronto, in "Little Women," and "Smilin' Through," and in summer theatres, in "Ladies in Retirement," and "Without Love"; Mansfield Theatre, New York, Mar., 1943, played Betty in "Apology"; toured, 1944, overseas for U.N.O., in "Over 21," the first play sent to the combat zone in North Africa, and in 1945, on the European continent, in "The Night of January 16th"; toured, Aug., 1946, as Sister Margaret in "The Hasty Heart"; Hudson, New York, June, 1947, played Mary Matthews in "State of the Union"; toured, 1949, as Catherine Sloper in "The Heiress"; entered films, 1934, and has appeared in numerous pictures. *Address:* 400 East 49th Street, New York City, U.S.A.

O'BRYEN, W. J. (*né* Wilfrid James Wheeler–O'Bryen), manager; formerly agent; *b.* London, Mar., 1898; *s.* of James Wheeler O'Bryen, M.D., J.P., and his wife Maude (Gandon) *e.* Ladycross School, Seaford, and The Oratory School, Edgbaston; *m.* Elizabeth Allan; during 1914–18 War, served with the Royal Warwickshire Regiment and Lancashire Fusiliers, retiring as Captain; awarded M.C. with two bars, and was decorated with the Croix de Guerre; was twice wounded and mentioned in dispatches; after the war, joined the film and dramatic de-

partment of Curtis Brown, Ltd.; subsequently represented them in New York and then became production manager of Atlantic Union Films; subsequently casting and publicity director to Gainsborough Pictures; commenced business on his own account as publicity agent, 1930; business developed into representation as sole agents of a number of actors and actresses, film directors and writers, cameramen, etc., first, in partnership with S. E. Linnit, and subsequently with S. E. Linnit and Jack Dunfee; the firm was also very active in the presentation of numerous plays, including "Aren't Men Beasts!" 1936; "A Spot of Bother," "The Phantom Light," 1937; "Elizabeth, La Femme Sans Homme," "Banana Ridge," "Golden Boy," "Good-bye Mr. Chips," 1938; "Gas Light," "The Jealous God," 1939; the firm was also associated with the production of "French Without Tears," 1936; "George and Margaret," "Judgment Day," 1937; "Death on the Table," "Can We Tell?" "Quiet Wedding," 1938; the partnership was dissolved in Sept., 1939; rejoined the Army, Sept., 1939, and was demobilized, Aug., 1945. *Recreation:* Riding. *Address:* 8 Hertford Street, London, W.1. *Telephone No.:* Grosvenor 1781.

O'CASEY, Sean (*né* Shaun O'Cathasaigh), dramatic author; *b.* Dublin, 31 Mar., 1880; *s.* of Michael O'Cathasaigh and his wife Susanna; *e.* Dublin; *m.* Eileen Carey (Katherine Reynolds); was formerly in succession, a builder's labourer, railway labourer, and general labourer; his first play was "The Shadow of a Gunman," 1922; "Cathleen Listens In,"was produced at the Abbey Theatre, Dublin, Oct., 1923; has since written "Nannie's Night Out," Abbey, Sept., 1924; "Juno and the Paycock," which was his first big success, produced at the Royalty, Nov., 1925; "The Plough and the Stars," Abbey Theatre, Dublin, Feb., 1926, and Fortune, London, May, 1926; "The Shadow of a Gunman," Court, May, 1927; "The Silver Tassie," 1929; "Within the Gates," 1934; "The End of the Beginning," 1939, was first performed at the Théâtre de l'Œuvre, Paris, 17 May, 1939, and at the "Q" Theatre, London, in Oct., 1939; later plays are "The Star Turns Red," 1940; "Red Roses for Me," 1943; "Purple Dust," 1945; "Oak Leaves and Lavender," 1946; "Cockadoodle Dandy," 1949; "Time to Go," "Bedtime Story," "Hall of Healing," 1951; "The Bishop's Bonfire," 1955; adapted "Pictures in the Hallway" and "I Knock at the Door," 1956; author of a book "The Flying Wasp," 1937; has published six volumes of autobiography, "I Knock at the Door," 1939, which was banned in Eire, followed by "Pictures in the Hallway," "Drums Under the Window," "Inishfallen, Fare Thee Well," "Rose and Crown," and "Sunset and Evening Star"; he is also the author of "The Green Crow" (essays), 1957; gained the Hawthornden Prize, 1926. *Address:* Flat 3, 40 Trumlands Road, St. Marychurch, Torquay, Devon.

(Died 18 Sept., 1964; age 84)

O'CONNELL, Hugh, actor; *b.* New York City, U.S.A., 4 Aug., 1898; *s.* of Hugh O'Connell and his wife Jane (Butler); *e.* Appleton, Wisconsin, and Chicago Musical College; was engaged as an usher in a Chicago theatre, before he made his first appearance on the stage; joined a small travelling company, and gained much experience, prior to appearing in Chicago in 1920, in "Toto"; made his first appearance on the New York stage, at the 49th Street Theatre, 26 Dec., 1921, as Harry Stewart in "Face Value"; 48th Street, Aug., 1923, played James Cartier in "Zeno"; Central Park, Dec., 1925, Maurice Burr in "Cousin Sonia"; Little, Feb., 1926, Everett in "The Wisdom Tooth"; Waldorf, Oct., 1926, Alfred Lowell in "Sure Fire"; 49th Street, Jan., 1927, Texas Dan in "Ballyhoo"; National, Feb., 1927, Darcy in "Fog"; Ambassadors', Nov., 1927, Miller in "The Racket"; Henry Miller Theatre, Aug., 1928, Charlie Haven in "Gentlemen of the Press"; John Golden, Oct., 1929, Chris Chapman in "Week-End"; Sam H. Harris, Jan., 1930, Littleton Looney in "A Sap from

Syracuse" ("So Was Napoleon!"); Music Box, Sept., 1930, George Lewis in "Once in a Lifetime"; New Amsterdam, Feb., 1932, Martin Van Buren Mashbesher in "Face the Music"; Playhouse, Feb., 1933, Jim Langdon in "A Saturday Night"; at Long Branch, N.J., July, 1933, played "The Phantom" in "American Plan"; Cort, May, 1934, Burleigh Sullivan in "The Milky Way"; El Capitan, Los Angeles, Aug., 1935, Billy Crocker in "Anything Goes"; Winter Garden, New York, Jan., 1936, appeared in "Ziegfeld Follies"; Windsor, Nov., 1938, played Wilkes Potter in "Run, Sheep, Run"; has appeared in films since 1931, and since 1936 has played in "The Affair of Susan," "Ready, Willing, and Able," "That Certain Woman," "Marry the Girl," "The Perfect Specimen," "Swing Your Lady," "Women are Like That," "Accidents Will Happen," "Penrod's Double Trouble." *Clubs:* Lambs, and Players, New York. *Address:* Players Club, 16 Gramercy Park, New York City, U.S.A. *(Died 19 Jan., 1943; age 44)*

O'CONNOR, Bill, actor and vocalist; *b.* Sault Ste. Marie, Ontario, 3 Oct., 1919; *s.* of William Jennings O'Connor and his wife Augusta (La Haye); *e.* Sault Ste. Marie Collegiate Institute; *m.* June van Alstyne; originally employed as a lumberjack and car salesman, later becoming a commercial broadcaster; studied singing at the Toronto Conservatory of Music, and with Albert Garcia and Madame Mabel Corran in London; first appeared on the stage at the Royal Victoria, Toronto, Aug., 1943, in "Meet the Navy"; made his first appearance in London at His Majesty's, Feb., 1946, when he took over the part of Bob Munroe in "Follow the Girls"; Strand, June, 1948, played Mercury in "Cage Me a Peacock"; His Majesty's, Apr., 1949, Charlie Cameron in "Brigadoon"; toured, 1951, as Count Max in "Goodnight Vienna"; Saville, Sept., 1952, played Jervis Pendleton in "Love From Judy," which ran for nearly eighteen months. *Favourite parts:* Mercury in "Cage Me a Peacock," and Jervis Pendleton in "Love From

Judy." *Recreations:* Squash, base ball, and ice hockey. *Address:* 29 Marlborough Mansions, Cannon Hill, London, N.W.6. *Telephone No.:* Hampstead 1759.

O'CONNOR, Charles Wm., theatrical Press representative and journalist; *b.* Roscommon, Ireland, 15 Feb., 1878; *e.* High School, Islington; Dramatic Critic of *Military Mail* since 1905, and Burton *Daily Mail*, 1908; Press representative at Lyceum, Dec., 1905; Press representative to Palace Theatre since 1906; Press representative to the De Freece Vaudeville Circuit, 1907; and National Sunday League, 1908; officiated in similar capacity at Ambassadors' Theatre, 1913; Queen's Theatre, 1914; on the outbreak of war, Aug., 1914, joined the 9th Bedfordshire Regt.; is a member of the Institute of Journalists. *Clubs:* Press, and Canonbury Tower. *Address:* New Kinema Gallery, Regent Street, W.
(Died 28 Nov., 1955; age 77)

O'CONNOR, John J., dramatic critic; *b.* New York City, 10 July, 1933; *e.* City College of New York and Yale University; previously engaged as a college instructor; became the drama critic for *The Wall Street Journal* in 1969, succeeding Richard Cooke; in 1971 joined *The New York Times* as television reviewer and general writer on the arts; also reviews films, ballet, opera, and art, as well as reportorial stories on business and the arts. *Recreation:* Rock music. *Address: The New York Times*, New York, N.Y., U.S.A. 10036.

O'CONNOR, Una, actress; *b.* Belfast, Ireland, 23 Oct., 1893; *e.* Omagh, Belfast, and London; studied for the stage at the Abbey Theatre School, Dublin; made her first appearance on the stage at the Abbey Theatre, Dublin, in 1911, as Jessie in "The Shewing-up of Blanco Posnet"; went to New York, and made her first appearance there, at the Maxine Elliott Theatre, 23 Nov., 1911, in the same part; made her first appearance in

London at the Court Theatre, 28 June, 1913, as Aunt Jug in "The Magic Glass"; at the Kingsway, Dec., 1915, played Grannie in "The Starlight Express"; during 1917-18 toured for two years as the Mother in "Damaged Goods"; at the Savoy, Apr., 1920, appeared as Miss O'Hara in "Paddy the Next Best Thing," which she played for two years; at the Haymarket, Jan., 1923, played Mrs. Plumbridge in "Plus Fours"; scored a great success when she appeared at the Apollo, Mar., 1924, as the Waitress in "The Fake," and went to New York to play the same part at the Hudson Theatre, Oct., 1924; on returning to London, appeared at the St. Martin's, July, 1925, as the Cook in "The Show"; at the Lyceum, July, 1925, again played in "The Fake"; Comedy, Nov., 1925, Miss Bibby in "The Ring o' Bells"; Everyman, Jan., 1926, the Barmaid in "The Man Who Was Thursday"; at the "Q," Mar., 1926, and Little, Apr., 1926, made a big success when she appeared as Ellen Keegan in "Autumn Fire"; at the Little, July, 1926, played Mabel Hemworth in "Distinguished Villa"; Klaw, New York, Oct., 1926, played Ellen in "Autumn Fire"; on her return, appeared at the Globe, July, 1927, as Martha in "The Village"; Criterion, Nov., 1927, played Miss Cathcart in "Chance Acquaintance"; Adelphi, Nov., 1927, Mrs. Jowett in "The Big Drum"; Court, Feb., 1928, the Third Witch in "Macbeth" (in modern dress); Lyric, Hammersmith, Apr., 1928, Aunt Deborah in "Love in a Village"; Everyman, Nov., 1928, Mrs. Jones in "The Silver Box"; Dec., 1928, Miss Kite in "The Passing of the Third Floor Back"; Wyndham's, June, 1929, The Woman in "Exiled"; Apollo, Oct., 1929, Mrs. Foran in "The Silver Tassie"; Everyman, Dec., 1929, Miss Kite in "The Passing of the Third Floor Back"; Sept., 1930, Ellen Nolan in "The Far-off Hills"; St. James's, Feb., 1931, Cousin Valérie in "Etienne"; Drury Lane, Oct., 1931, Ellen Bridges in "Cavalcade"; commenced film career, 1929, in "Dark Red Roses"; went to Hollywood, 1932, for the film of "Cavalcade," and has since appeared in innumerable pic-

tures; reappeared on the New York stage, at the Plymouth Theatre, Sept., 1945, as Weavy Hicks in "The Ryan Girl"; Music Box, Mar., 1948, Mrs. Cotton in "The Linden Tree"; Booth, Jan., 1949, Mrs. Catt in "The Shop at Sly Corner"; Lyceum, Jan., 1950, Leonide Mangebois in "The Enchanted"; Royale, Jan., 1954, Ellen in "The Starcross Story"; Henry Miller Theatre, Dec., 1954, Janet MacKenzie in "Witness For the Prosecution"; appeared in a number of parts for the Repertory Players, Play Actors, etc.; has made frequent appearances in radio and television programmes in New York. *Favourite parts:* Mrs. Jones in "The Silver Box," Ellen in "Autumn Fire," and the Waitress in "The Fake." *Recreation:* Modelling in clay. *Address:* Hotel Windsor, 100 West 58th Street, New York City, 19, U.S.A.
(Died 4 Feb., 1959; age 65)

O'DEA, Denis, actor; *b.* Dublin, 26 Apr., 1905; *s.* of Michael O'Dea and his wife Catherine (Neilan); *e.* St. Mary's College, Dublin; *m.* Siobhan McKenna; studied for the stage at the Abbey Theatre School of Acting, Dublin; made his first appearance on the stage, at the Abbey Theatre, Dublin, 1930, in "The Woman"; has played with the Abbey Theatre Company throughout his career, and has also directed innumerable plays there; first appeared in New York, at the Martin Beck Theatre, 17 Oct., 1932, as Terrence Noonan in "Things That Are Caesar's," and subsequently appeared there in nearly a dozen plays from the Abbey company's repertory; appeared for a further season of repertory, at the Golden Theatre, New York, from Nov., 1934; Belmont Theatre, New York, Jan., 1936, played Francis Ferriter in "The Puritan," and Masque Theatre, Nov., 1936, Michael Fraser in "Green Waters"; appeared in another repertory season, with the Abbey Company, at the Ambassador, New York, from Oct., 1937; made his first appearance in London, at the Embassy Theatre, 3 Mar., 1947, as Father Shaughnessy in "The White Steed," and played the same part at the Whitehall Theatre,

later in the month; New Lindsey, Aug., 1950, played Stephen Marston in "Sayonara"; Gaiety, Dublin, Dec., 1962, played Dame Mulligan in "Goody Two-Shoes"; first entered films, 1934, in Hollywood, in "The Informer." *Recreation:* Golf. *Address:* The Abbey Theatre, Dublin. *Telephone No.:* Dublin 53139.

ODELL, George C. D., dramatic historian and professor of dramatic literature; *b.* Newburgh, New York, U.S.A., 19 Mar., 1866; *s.* of Benjamin B. Odell and his wife Ophelia (Bookstaver); *e.* Columbia University, M.A., and Ph.D.; appointed instructor, 1895, and later professor of English at Columbia University; succeeded the late Brander Matthews as professor of dramatic literature in 1924; is the author of "Shakespeare, from Betterton to Irving," 1920; "Annals of the New York Stage," of which the first volume was issued in 1927, and the fourteenth (to 1891), in July, 1945; has also edited editions of Shakespeare's plays. *Clubs:* Players, and Century. *Address:* Hotel Seymour, West 45th Street, New York City, U.S.A *(Died 17 Oct., 1949; age 83)*

ODETS, Clifford, actor, dramatic author and director; *b.* Philadelphia, Pa., U.S.A., 1906; *s.* of Louis J. Odets and his wife Pearl; *m.* (1) Luise Rainer (mar. dis.); (2) Betty Grayson (dec.); made his first appearance in "stock," and played with various companies for five years; at the Guild Theatre, New York, 29 Dec., 1930, played Arthur Weldon in "Midnight"; Sept., 1931, Reuben in "The House of Connelly"; Dec., 1931, in "1931";· Group, Mar., 1932, played Mateo in "Night Over Taos"; Maxine Elliott (for the Group), Jan., 1933, Eugene in "By Night"; Lyceum, May, 1933, Andrey Brikin in "They All Come to Moscow"; Broadhurst (Group), Sept., 1933, Houghton in "Men in White"; Morosco (Group), Nov., 1934, Burns and Jolais in "Gold Eagle Guy"; Longacre (Group), Mar., 1935, Dr. Benjamin in "Waiting for Lefty" (which he also directed); A.N.T.A. Playhouse, Mar., 1952, directed a

revival of "Golden Boy"; Belasco, Dec., 1954, directed "The Flowering Peach"; is the author of "Awake and Sing," "Waiting for Lefty," "Till the Day I Die," "Paradise Lost," 1935; "Golden Boy," 1937; "Rocket to the Moon," 1938; "Night Music," 1940; "Clash by Night," 1941; "The Russian People" (adaptation), 1942; "The Big Knife," 1949; "The Country Girl" ("Winter Journey"), which he also directed, 1950; "The Flowering Peach," 1954; has also written and directed motion pictures, notably "None But the Lonely Heart," 1943, and "Story on Page One," 1960. *Recreation:* Music. *Address:* Actors' Equity Association, New York City.
(Died 14 Aug., 1963; age 57)

ODETTE, Mary, actress; *b.* Dieppe, 10 Aug., 1901; *d.* of Gustave Goimbault and his wife Mary Amelia (Lorimare); *e.* privately; *m.* John Hardacre; formerly known as Odette Goimbault; made her first appearance on the stage at the Garrick Theatre, 11 Dec., 1912, as an Elf in the revival of "Where the Rainbow Ends"; during the following September, appeared at the Birmingham Repertory Theatre, as Tintagiles in Maeterlinck's "Death of Tintagiles," and at the St. James's Theatre, 17 Dec., 1913, appeared in the same part; at the Savoy, 6 Feb., 1914, played Peas-Blossom in "A Midsummer Night's Dream"; at the Garrick, 4 Sept., 1914, Lady Jane Grey in "Bluff King Hal"; and at the Lyric, 29 Apr., 1915, scored a great success when she played the part of Doris Strickland in "On Trial"; at His Majesty's, May, 1916, played Cordeil in "King Lear's Wife"; subsequently turned her attention to the cinema stage, with considerable success; reappeared on the regular stage at the Comedy, Nov., 1921, when she played Blacky in "The Faithful Heart"; at the Court, Apr., 1922, Faith Bly in "Windows"; Apr., 1924, toured as Anne Latter in "The Man in the Wheel Chair"; "Q," Dec., 1926, played Odette in "A Night in Montmartre"; commenced film career, 1916, and has appeared in "Dombey

and Son," "The Way of an Eagle,'" "A Spinner of Dreams," "Lady Clare," "The Shadow of the Mosque," "If Youth But Knew," "The Woman Who Squandered Men," "Eugene Aram," "The Lion and the Mouse," "She," "Not for Sale," "The Emerald of the East," etc. *Recreations:* Reading, dancing, and the promotion of kindness to animals. *Address:* 132 Hamilton Road, N.W.11. *Telephone No.:* Speedwell 5171.

O'DOHERTY, Eileen (Anna Walker); *b.* Dublin, Sept., 1891; *d.* of Eileen (O'Doherty) and Matthew Walker; *e.* Dublin; studied for the stage under W. G. and F. J. Fay; made her first appearance on the stage with the Irish National Theatre Society, at the Abbey Theatre, Dublin, 1905, as the child in "The Hour Glass"; made her first appearance on the London stage, at the Court Theatre, 7 June, 1909, as Mamie in "Dervorgilla"; during her career she has played the following parts either at the Abbey Theatre, Dublin, or at the Court Theatre, London: Babsy in "The Shewing-up of Blanco Posnet," the old Woman in "Deirdre," Bridget Twomey in "Harvest," Mary Kate in "The Eloquent Dempsey," Mrs. Desmond in "The Cross Roads," Mrs. Pender in "The Casting Out of Martin Whelan," Maura Morrissey in "Birthright," Margaret in "The Piedish," Nerine in "The Rogueries of Scapin," Miss Joyce in "Hyacinth Halvey," Mary Brien in "The Clancy Name," Mary Mulroy in "The Mineral Workers," Maria Donnelly in "Family Failing," Mrs. O'Connor in "Maurice Harte," Mrs. Keegan in "The Supplanter," Mrs. Hickey in "Sovereign Love," Mrs. Sullivan in "Patriots," Kate Moran in "Crusaders," Mrs. Geoghegan in "The White Headed Boy"; she toured with the company in England, Scotland, and the United States. *Recreation:* Boating.

O'DOHERTY, Mignon, actress; *b.* Brisbane, Queensland, Australia, 30 Jan., 1890; *d.* of Edward O'Doherty and his wife Maud (French); *e.* Royal School, Bath, and Paris; *m.* Tom Nesbitt; was a student at the Academy of Dramatic Art; made her first appearance on the stage at the Globe Theatre, 26 Apr., 1913, as Angélique in "Lady Frederick"; later in the year toured with Leonard Boyne in "General John Regan"; in 1914 toured as Emily Rhead in "Milestones"; at the Haymarket, Jan., 1915, played Lucy in "The Recruiting Officer"; at the Royalty, July, 1916, played Miriam Leigh in "The Man who Stayed at Home"; at the St. Martin's, 1917, played The Nurse in "Damaged Goods"; subsequently toured in the same part; at the Ambassadors', Feb., 1918, played Bridget in "The Little Brother"; at the Court, Oct., 1918, appeared as Maria in "Twelfth Night"; June, 1919, Kate Buckley in "The Lost Leader"; at the Duke of York's, Apr., 1920, Madame Klopoff in "The Government Inspector"; June, 1920, Rosalie in "Madame Sand"; at the Ambassadors', Sept., 1920, Baby in "The White-Headed Boy"; at the Aldwych, Apr., 1922, Mrs. Geoghegan in the same play; she then went to America; at the Fulton Theatre, New York, Dec., 1922, played Audrey Carlton in "Secrets"; Cathy Donovan and Widow Gorman in "The Merry Wives of Gotham"; at the Cort Theatre, Dec., 1924, played in "Carnival"; returned to London, and appeared at the Adelphi, Sept., 1925, as Mrs. Armitage and Sister Virginia in "The Green Hat"; Queen's, Sept., 1926, played Julia in "And So To Bed"; Globe, Mar., 1927, the Janitress in "The Spook Sonata"; subsequently toured with Edna Best, as Linda, in "The Constant Nymph"; Arts, Sept., 1928, Lena in "Diversion"; St. James's, Feb., 1929, Mrs. Prew in "Fame"; Haymarket, June, 1931, Joanna Sleath in "Marry at Leisure"; Arts, Oct., 1931, Mrs. Crump in "Vile Bodies"; Ambassadors', Feb., 1932, Sally in "So Far and No Father"; Royalty, Mar., 1935, Mrs. Murat-Blood in "Frolic Wind"; Westminster (for the Charta Theatre), May, 1935, Lady Margaret Tatler in "Disturbance"; Royalty, June, 1936, Maggie

Jones in "Winter Sunshine"; Duke of York's, Sept., 1936, Madame Dumontier in "No Ordinary Lady"; toured, 1937, as Muriel Weston in "Call It a Day"; Haymarket, June, 1937, Roberta in "To Have and to Hold"; toured, autumn, 1937, as the Duchess in "Me and My Girl"; Phoenix, May, 1938, Jane Latimer in "Married Unanimously"; Malvern Festival, Aug., 1938, Mrs. Bebb in "Coronationtime at Mrs. Beam's," and Mrs. Bucklyvie in "The Last Trump"; Duke of York's, Sept., 1938, again played the last-mentioned part; Intimate, Palmer's Green, June, 1940, Lady Wilson in "Wasn't it Odd?"; "Q," Dec., 1940, Mildred in "A Lass and a Lackey"; St. James's, Apr., 1942, succeeded Maire O'Neill as Mary in "The Nutmeg Tree"; Wimbledon, Oct., 1942, and Vaudeville, July, 1943, Madgie in "Lottie Dundass"; Apollo, May, 1944, Commodore Pentworthy in "How Are They at Home?"; His Majesty's, Mar., 1945, Mrs. O'Dare in "Irene"; Embassy, Oct., 1947, Mrs. Pratt in "Deliver My Darling"; Boltons, Mar., 1948, Miss Maebelle Finn in "Hog's Blood and Hellebore"; Nov., 1948, Mrs. Murat-Blood in "Frolic Wind"; Wyndham's, Feb., 1949, Lady Agincourt in "Sweethearts and Wives"; Boltons, Feb., 1950, Mrs. O'Farrel in "Lady Patricia";

toured, 1951, as Lady Winslow in "Daddy Wore Velvet Gloves"; Criterion, Oct., 1951, played Lady Wilson in "And This Was Odd," (previously entitled "Wasn't It Odd?"); at the "Q," Feb., 1952, Sophinesba Leaton-Knowles in "Not Proven"; King's, Hammersmith, Apr., 1952, Mrs. Entwistle in "Beggar My Neighbour"; Lyric, Hammersmith, June, 1952, Ruby Bottomley in "The Pink Room";

Ambassadors', Nov., 1952, played Mrs. Boyle in "The Mousetrap," and continued to appear in this part until 1955; commenced film career, 1932, in "The Faithful Heart," and has since appeared in numerous pictures; has made frequent appearances in radio and television programmes. *Address:* 30 Hans Road, S.W.3. *Telephone No.:* Kensington 3237. (*Died*, Mar., 1961.)
(Died Mar., 1961; age 71)

O'DONOVAN, Fred, actor; *b.* Dublin, 14 Oct., 1889; s. of Robert Henry O'Donovan and his wife Lilian (Oakes); *e.* Diocesan Intermediate School, Dublin; *m.* Joyce Chancellor; was originally employed in a land agent's office; made his first appearance on the stage, at the Abbey Theatre, Dublin, with the Irish National Theatre Society, 13 Feb., 1908, in the title-*rôle* of "The Man Who Missed the Tide"; made his first appearance on the London stage, at the Court Theatre, 7 June, 1909, as the Playboy in "The Playboy of the Western World," and the Wandering Songmaker in "Dervorgilla"; has since played the following among other parts: Blanco Posnet in "The Shewing-up of Blanco Posnet," Naisi in "Deirdre of the Sorrows," Hyacinth Halvey in the play of that name, Aleel in "The Countess Cathleen," Robert Donnelly in "Family Failing," Denis in "The White Headed Boy," Lucius Lenihan in "The Lost Leader"; appeared at the Hicks Theatre, July, 1909, as John Waterbury, M.P., in "His Borrowed Plumes," and at the Palace and Coliseum in one-act plays; has also toured through the United States in "The Playboy of the Western World," which was stopped by rioters on the occasion of its first performance at the Maxine Elliott Theatre, New York, Nov., 1911; was producer and manager of the Abbey Theatre, Dublin, 1917-19; at the Ambassadors', Sept., 1920, played John Duffy in "The White Headed Boy"; again appeared in "The Playboy of the Western World," and as Peter Keegan in "John Bull's Other Island," at the Court Theatre, 1921; at the Aldwych, Apr., 1922, again appeared in "The White Headed Boy"; at the Everyman Theatre, Jan., 1923, played Doctor Perron in "Medium," and Mr. Joseph Cuthbertson in "The Philanderer"; Feb., 1923, Mr. Durrows in "At Mrs. Beam's," and the same part at the Royalty, Apr., 1923; at the Everyman, Dec., 1923, played Sir William Meadows in "Love in a Village"; at the Prince's, Oct., 1924, James Callaghan in "The Blue Peter"; at the Everyman, Dec., 1924, Randal

in "The Tyranny of Home," and Cuthbertson in "The Philanderer"; Little, Mar., 1925, Peter O'Hare in "Preserving Pat"; Lyric, Hammersmith, May, 1925, Lopahin in "The Cherry Orchard"; Regent (for the Phoenix Society), July, 1925, Johnson in "The Rehearsal"; Royalty, Oct., 1925, again played Christopher Mahon in "The Playboy of the Western World"; in the same month went to South Africa with Franklin Dyall, to play in "Sacred and Profane Love," "At Mrs. Beam's," and "Smilin' Through"; subsequently toured through Portuguese East Africa, and Kenya Colony; at the Vaudeville, Mar., 1927, played Hugh O'Cahan in "Professor Tim"; he then toured as Mr. Pepys in "And So To Bed," and went to America to play the same part; returned in 1928, and again toured as Mr. Pepys; "Q," Dec., 1928, played Tom Weeden in "High Tide—Low Tide"; Court, Jan., 1929, Jimmy Craig in "The Eternal Flame"; "Q," Jan.-Mar., 1929, played in "The Local Rag," and "The Far-off Hills"; Everyman and Criterion, Sept., 1930, again played in "The Far-off Hills"; Criterion, Oct., 1930, played in a revival of "The Playboy of the Western World"; Nov., 1930, Dr. Lucius O'Grady in a revival of "General John Regan"; Aug., 1931, toured with Angela Baddeley in South Africa in "Marigold," "Autumn Crocus," "The Truth Game," etc.; on returning to London, appeared at the Savoy, Apr., 1932, as Charles Murfree in "Old Man Murphy"; Aug., 1932, toured as Sean Macaward in "Pay the Piper," and Mike Duddy in "Mountain Dew"; Arts, Jan., 1933, Rev. Father Duffy in "Things That Are Caesar's"; "Q," June, 1933, Corrigan in "The Haunted Legacy"; Gate, Sept., 1933, Salesio in "As You Desire Me"; Fulham, Dec., 1933, and Little, Feb., 1934, Dan Deegan in "Paul Twyning"; Embassy, June, 1934, Mr. Blaney in "Mrs. McConaghy's Money"; "Q," July, 1934, Ryan in "Line Engaged"; Westminster, Sept., 1934, Commandant Lanigan in "The Moon in the Yellow River," playing the same part at the Haymarket, Nov., 1934; Westminster, July, 1934, Count Wolfsberg in

"Marriage Makes It Easy"; Playhouse, Dec., 1935, the White King in "Alice Through the Looking-Glass"; Arts, Jan., 1936, Michael O'Byrne in "Glory"; Westminster, Mar., 1936, Leclercq in "Toussaint Louverture"; Little, Nov., 1936–Jan., 1937, General Wei in "Lady Precious Stream," The White King in "Alice Through the Looking-Glass," and Bill Casey in "Curse It, Foiled Again!"; Playhouse, Nov., 1937, Commissioner of Police in "Orphée," and Dec., 1937, again played the White King; Phoenix, June, 1944, Uncle Corney in "The Last of Summer"; has also produced many plays; in Mar., 1938, was appointed a producer of television at the Alexandra Palace. *Favourite part:* Blanco Posnet. *Recreations:* Walking, motoring, and cycling. *Address:* 2 Brookland Garth, N.W.11. *Telephone No.:* Speedwell 4837.

(Died 19 July, 1952; age 62)

OENSLAGER, Donald, designer; *b.* Harrisburg, Pa., U.S.A., 7 Mar., 1902; *s.* of John Oenslager, Jun., and his wife Jane (Connely); *e.* Phillips' Exeter Academy, and Harvard University; *m.* Mary Osborne Polak; formerly an actor, and appeared at Greenwich Village, 11 Nov., 1924, in "Desire Under the Elms"; designed his first work for a ballet, "Sooner or Later," 1925; productions he has since designed are "Morals," "A Bit o' Love," 1925; "Pinwheel," "Good News," 1927; "Anna," "L' Histoire du Soldat," "The New Moon," 1928; "Follow Thru'" (also co-directed), "Stepping Out," "Heads Up," 1929; "Girl Crazy," "Overture," 1930; "The Winter's Tale" (Yale), "Free for All," "Singin' the Blues," "East Wind," "The Emperor Jones," 1931; "Whistling in the Dark," "Adam Had Two Sons," "A Thousand Summers," 1932; "Forsaking All Others," "Keeper of the Keys," "Jezebel," "Uncle Tom's Cabin," 1933; "Salome," "The Lady from the Sea," "Dance with Your Gods," "Divided by Three," "Tristan and Isolde," "Rosenkavalier," "The Farmer Takes a Wife," "Anything Goes," "Gold-Eagle Guy," 1934; "Something Gay,"

"Sweet Mystery of Life," "First Lady," "Tapestry in Gray," 1935; "Stage Door," "Ten Million Ghosts," "Sweet River," "Red, Hot and Blue!", "200 Were Chosen," "Johnny Johnson," "Russet Mantle," "Matrimony Pfd.," "You Can't Take It with You," 1936; "Miss Quis," "Robin Landing," "Edna, His Wife," "Otello" (opera), "Of Mice and Men," "A Doll's House," "I'd Rather Be Right," 1937; "The Circle," "The Fabulous Invalid," "Amelia Goes to the Ball," "I Am My Youth," "Spring Thaw," "The Good," "A Woman's a Fool to Be Clever," 1938; "From Vienna," "The American Way," "Off to Buffalo," "Skylark," "The Man Who Came to Dinner," "Margin for Error," "I Know What I Like," 1939; "Young Couple Wanted," "My Dear Children," "Beverly Hills," "Retreat to Pleasure," "The Old Foolishness," "My Sister Eileen," 1940; "The Lady Who Came to Stay," "Claudia," "The Doctor's Dilemma," "Mr. Big," "Theatre," "Spring Again," "Pie in the Sky," 1941; "The Flowers of Virtue," 1942; "Hairpin Harmony," 1943; "Pygmalion," 1945; "Born Yesterday," "Three to Make Ready," "On Whitman Avenue," "Loco," "La Traviata," "Present Laughter," "The Abduction from the Seraglio," "Park Avenue," "The Fatal Weakness," "Years Ago," "Land's End," "Lovely Me," 1946; "The Eagle Has Two Heads," "Message for Margaret," "Portrait in Black," "Fidelio," "How I Wonder," "Eastward in Eden," "Angel in the Wings," 1947; "The Men We Marry," "Cosi Fan Tutte," "Town House," "The Leading Lady," "Life with Mother," "Goodbye, My Fancy," 1948; "The Smile of the World," "At War with the Army," "The Father," "The Rat Race," "The Velvet Glove," 1949; "The Liar," "Springboard to Nowhere," "The Live Wire," 1950; "Second Threshold," "The Small Hours," "Peer Gynt," "The Constant Wife," 1951; "Paris '90," "Candida," "To Be Continued," "La Bohème," 1952; "Horses in Midstream," "Dido and Aeneas," "Sabrina Fair," "Escapade," "Madam Will You Walk," "The Prescott Proposals," 1953; "Coriolanus," "Dear Charles," 1954; "The

Wooden Dish," "Janus," "A Roomful of Roses," 1955; "Major Barbara," "The Ballad of Baby Doe," 1956; "Four Winds," "Mary Stuart," "Nature's Way," "A Shadow of My Enemy," 1957; "The Girls in 509," "The Pleasure of His Company," "The Man in the Dog Suit," "The Marriage-Go-Round," "J.B." (Yale), 1958; "A Majority of One" (which won the Antoinette Perry Award), "The Mikado," "The Pink Jungle," "The Highest Tree," "Orpheus and Eurydice," 1959; "Dear Liar," and the operas "Orfeo" and "The Prisoner," 1960; "A Far Country," "A Call on Kuprin," "Blood, Sweat and Stanley Poole," "The Wings of the Dove," "First Love," 1961; "Venus at Large," 1962; "The Irregular Verb to Love," "A Case of Libel," 1963; "One by One," and the operas "Madame Butterfly" and "Lady from Colorado," 1964; "Carmen," "The Italian Lady from Algiers," "La Tosca" (all operas), 1966; "Love in E Flat," "Der Rosenkavalier," "Antigone," "The Merry Widow," "Don Pasquale," "The Masked Ball," "Spofford," 1967; "Avanti!" "The Mikado," "Don Carlos," 1968; "The Wrong Way Light Bulb," 1969; author of the books "Scenery Then and Now," 1936; "The Theatre of Bali," 1941; edited "Notes on Scene Painting," 1952; President of the Board of Directors of the Neighborhood Playhouse School of the Theatre, 1930–63; First Vice-President of A.N.T.A.; is a Member of the Board of Trustees of Brooklyn Institute of Arts and Sciences, American Academy of Dramatic Arts, The Museum of the City of New York; member of Drama Panel of the Department of State's Cultural Presentations Program; member of the U.S. National Commission of U.N.E.S.C.O., 1963–8; is on the Advisory Committee of the High School of Performing Arts; received Pennsylvania Ambassador Award, 1950; D.F.A., Colorado College, 1953; Honorary Member Phi Beta Kappa, Harvard University, 1954; served as Captain, later Major, in U.S. Air Force, 1942–5; taught scenic design at Middlebury, Vermont, 1925; appointed to faculty of School of Drama at Yale University in 1925, and is currently Professor Emeritus; instructor at American Academy of Dramatic Arts, New York, 1926, and Trustee, 1966–7; has lectured extensively in America, and has received various State Department grants to lecture and consult on the theatre in Latin America 1950, Yugoslavia 1953, Iceland, Ireland, and Finland, 1955; has served as consultant on theatre architecture and design, most notably for American Pavilion Theatre, Brussels World Fair, 1958, for the Montreal Cultural Center, 1961, Broadmoor International Center, 1961; Design Consultant for Philharmonic Hall of Lincoln Center, 1962, 1969, and New York State Theatre, 1964; designed the lighting and fountains for the New York World's Fair, 1964–5; designer and consultant for Scott Theatre of the Fort Worth Performing Arts Center, Spingold Theatre at Brandeis University, Wilkes College Fine Arts Center in Wilkes-Barre, Pa., John F. Kennedy Center for the Performing Arts in Washington, D.C., and the Meeting Center of the Albany South Mall Project; Ford Foundation Grant for Theatre Research in 1960; member of Board of Directors, Pratt Institute; member of Board of Directors of the Brooklyn Museum; member of the Art Commission of the City of New York, 1965 to present, and served as President in 1970; member of the Board of Trustees, American Federation of Arts, London, 1969; member of the Board of Trustees of The MacDowell Colony, 1961–8; member of Association Internationale de Bibliophilie, 1970 to present; experimented with first designs for television in 1931. *Recreations:* Collector of works of Adolph Appia and Gordon Craig; and drawings, paintings, manuscripts of 17th, 18th, 19th century European stage designers. *Clubs:* The Century Association, Harvard, Grolier, and Coffee House. *Address:* Suite 1915, 1501 Broadway, New York City, U.S.A. *Telephone No.:* Longacre 3–1531.

O'FARRELL, Mary, actress; *b.* London, 27 May, 1892; *d.* of James

O'Farrell and his wife Joanna (Murphy) ; *e.* Convent of Ladies of Mary, London ; made her first appearance on the stage at the Criterion, 6 July, 1911, walking on in " The Girl Who Couldn't Lie " ; at Drury Lane, Sept., 1911, appeared in " The Hope " ; her first part of any importance was Mrs. Thynne in " Mrs. Skeffington," in which she toured from Dec., 1911 ; at the Whitney Theatre (now Strand), Feb., 1912, played Nancy in " A Member of Tattersall's " ; at the Little Theatre, Nov., 1912, Barbara Morrison in " Barbara Grows Up " ; was engaged at the Royalty, 1912-13, during the run of " Milestones," as understudy, and appeared on several occasions as Emily Rhead ; at the New Theatre, Aug., 1913, played Lizzie Hopton in " The Big Game " ; at the Globe, Oct., 1913, Lady Morecambe in " People Like Ourselves " ; at the Prince of Wales's, June, 1914, appeared as Mabel Lamson in " The Bill " ; subsequently played sketches in variety theatres ; at the Comedy, June, 1915, appeared as Mrs. Trevor in " Mr. and Mrs. Ponsonby " ; she then toured as Peg in " Peg o' My Heart," 1915–16 ; early in 1916 was engaged as understudy at Wyndham's Theatre, in " The Ware Case," and " A Kiss for Cinderella " ; at Wyndham's, Aug., 1916, played Dorothy Marston in " The Sister-in-Law " ; at the Globe, Oct., 1916, Peg in " Peg o' My Heart " ; Apr., 1917, toured as Betty in " General Post," and appeared at the Haymarket, Aug., 1917, in the same part ; at the St. James's, Sept., 1917, appeared as Lady Jessica Nepean in " The Liars " ; at the Palace, Dec., 1917, as Kitty O'Malley in " Pamela " ; at the Strand, Mar., 1918, succeeded Shirley Kellogg as Nan Carey in " Cheating Cheaters " ; at the Haymarket, June, 1918, played Patricia O'Brien in " Marmaduke " ; at the Gaiety, Manchester, Nov., 1918, Rosamund in " The Farringdon Case " ; at the Lyceum, Sheffield, Mar., 1919, Helen Graham in " Uncle Ned," and toured in this part ; during 1920 toured as Paddy in " Paddy the Next Best Thing " ; at the Duke of York's, May, 1921, played Mary Hudson in " The Tartan Peril ; at His Majesty's, May,

1923, played Bridget Cromwell in " Oliver Cromwell " ; during 1924 again toured in " Peg o' My Heart " ; Lyric, May, 1925, played Val Chantess in " Just a King " ; " Q," July, 1925, Mrs. Baxter in " The Mollusc " ; Sept., 1925, Angela Fane in " The Life Line " ; Scala (for the Playmates), July, 1926, Phyllis Brabeson in " Quicksands of Youth " ; in May, 1930, toured as Lady Angela Leigh in " The Silent Flyer " ; Everyman, June, 1931, Nancy Flynn in " Facing the Shadow " ; Sept., 1931, Ellen Keegan in " Autumn Fire " ; Westminster, Nov., 1932, Madeleine in " Follow Me " ; Embassy, Jan., 1933, Ellen Croy in " The Young Huntress " ; Westminster, Mar., 1933, and Piccadilly, May, 1933, Claudia Procula in " Caesar's Friend." *Recreations :* Music, reading, golf, tennis, and billiards. *Address :* 7 Chalcot Gardens, N.W.3. *Telephone No. :* Primrose 2063.
(Died 10 Feb., 1968; age 75)

OGILVIE, Glencairn Stuart, J.P., dramatic author ; *b.* Haslemere, Surrey, 27 Mar., 1858 ; *e.* at Rugby and Oxford, called to Bar, 1882 ; J.P., Surrey, 1887 ; *m.* Helen Emmeline Davidson ; author of the following plays : " Knowledge," 1883 ; " Hypatia," 1892 ; " The Sin of St. Hulda," 1896 ; " The White Knight," 1898 ; " The Master," 1898 ; " John Durnford, M.P.," 1901 ; and (with Louis N. Parker) the English version of " Cyrano de Bergerac," 1900 ; the first Episode of the Bury St. Edmunds Pageant, 1907 (by invitation of Louis N. Parker, Master of the Pageant). *Address :* Sizewell Hall, near Leiston, Suffolk. *Clubs :* Garrick, Beefsteak, etc. *Telephone No. :* 23 Leiston.
(Died 7 Mar., 1932; age 73)

O'HIGGINS, Harvey J., dramatic author ; *b.* London, Ont., Canada, 14 Nov., 1876 ; *s.* of Joseph P. O'Higgins and his wife Isabella (Stephenson) ; *e.* University of Toronto ; *m.* Anna G. Williams ; in collaboration with Harriet Ford, has written the following plays : " The Argyle Case," 1912 ; " The Dummy," 1913 ; " Polygamy," 1914 ;

1835

"The Dickey Bird," 1915; "Mr. Lazarus," 1916; "When a Feller Needs a Friend," 1918; "On the Hiring Line," 1918, produced in London as "The Wrong Number," 1921; "Main Street," 1921; "Sweet Seventeen," 1924; is the author of the following books: "The Smoke Eaters," 1905; "Don-a-Dreams," 1906; "A Grand Army Man," 1908; "Old Clinkers," 1909; "Silent Sam," 1914; "From the Life," 1919; "The Secret Springs," 1920; "Some Distinguished Americans," 1922; "The American Mind," 1924; "Julie Cane," 1924. *Address* Martinsville, N.J., U.S.A. *(Died 28 Feb., 1929; age 53)*

OHNET, Georges, French novelist, and dramatic author; *b.* Paris, 3 Apr., 1848; *e.* St. Barbe and Paris; *m.* Mdlle. Schaffer; is the author of dramatic versions of many of his novels, notably "Le Maître de Forges," "Dernier Amour," "La Grande Marnière," "Serge Panine," and "La Comtesse Sarah"; has also written the following original plays: "Régina Sarpi," "Marthe," "Le Colonel de Roquebrune," "Les Rouges et les Blancs"; is the author of nearly thirty novels; member of the Societies of Dramatic Authors and Men of Letters; is an Officer of the Legion of Honour. *Address:* 14 Avenue Trudaine, Paris.

(Died 5 May, 1918; age 70)

OKHLOPKOV, Nikolai Pavlovich, actor, and theatre director; *b.* Irkutsk, 6 May, 1900; *s.* of Pavel Iosafovich Okhlopkov and his wife Yuliya Filippovna Okhlopkova; *e.* Irkutsk Gymnasium, higher education; graduate of the State Experimental Theatre Workshop; *m.* Elena Zotova; studied for the theatre with Vsevolod Meyerhold at the Meyerhold Theatre; made his first appearance on the stage at the Irkutsk Municipal Theatre in 1918, as Golub in "Tsar Fyodor Ioannovich"; 1930–5, was Chief Director at the Realistic Theatre, Moscow, where he directed the following plays: "A Running Start" (V. Stavsky), "Mother" (M. Gorky), "The Iron Flood" (A. Serafimovich), "Othello" (Shakespeare), "Aristocrats" (N. Pogodin), and "Colas Breugnon" (R. Rolland); at the Vakhtangov Theatre, Moscow, 1939–43, directed among other plays, "Cyrano de Bergerac" (E. Rostand), and "Kutuzov" (V. Soloviev); 1943–60, Chief Director of the Drama Theatre and the Mayakovsky Theatre, Moscow, and has directed the following: "Young Guard" (A. Fadeev), "The Law of Honour" (A. Shtein), "Hamlet," "Storm" (Ostrovsky), "Astoria Hotel" (A. Shtein), and "The Irkutsk Story" (A. Arbuzov); in 1949, he toured Poland and Czechslovakia with the following plays: "Momentous Days" (N. Virta), "Young Guard," "The Law of Honour," "The Dog in the Manger" (Lope de Vega); he attended the International Shakespeare Conference, Stratford-on-Avon, England, Sept., 1955, when his paper on his own production of "Hamlet" was read by George Rylands (in translation); at the Small Opera House, Leningrad, 1950, he directed the opera "Young Guard" (Y. Meitus); at the Bolshoi Theatre, Moscow, 1952, directed the operas "The Decembrists" (Y. Shaporin); and 1957, "Mother" (T. Khrennikov); films in which he has appeared, since 1924, include "Mitya," 1926; "Lenin in October," 1938; "Kutuzov," 1944; "Story of a Real Man," 1949. *Favourite parts:* Prince Calaf in "Princess Turandot," Kachala in "Tarelkin's Death," General Berkovets in "Teacher Bubus," and Old Chinese Man in "Roar, China." *Recreations:* Travelling. *Clubs:* Central House of Art Workers, All-Russian Theatrical Society, and Cinema House. *Address:* Mayakovsky Theatre, 19 Herzen Street, Moscow, U.S.S.R.
(Died Jan., 1967; age 66)

OLAND, Warner, actor; *b.* Umea, Sweden, 3 Oct., 1880; *s.* of Jonas J. Oland and his wife Maria (Fosberg); *e.* Boston, Mass., U.S.A.; *m.* Edith Shearn; made his first appearance on the stage at the Garden Theatre, New York, 28 Nov., 1898, in a minor *rôle* in "The Christian"; toured all over the United States, and appeared in Shake-

spearean repertory with E. H. Sothern and Julia Marlowe; appeared at the Victoria, New York, 1902, as Captain Cavalli in "The Eternal City"; appeared at the Bijou, New York, Sept.-Dec., 1907, with Nazimova, as Ragnar Brovik in "The Master Builder," in "A Doll's House," "Comtesse Coquette," etc.; Hudson, Mar., 1908, played Falk in "Love's Comedy"; Hudson, Nov., 1911, Stanard Dole in "The Price"; Berkeley, Apr., 1912, the Captain of Cavalry in "The Father," which he also adapted; in 1913, toured as John Schuyler in "A Fool There Was"; in 1916, toured as Baron André in "The Yellow Ticket"; commenced film career 1920, and has appeared in "Sin," "The Jewels of the Madonna," "Patria," "The Cigarette Girl," "The Naulakha," "Mandarin Gold," "The Avalanche," "The Witness for the Defense," "Twin Pawns," "The Third Eye," "The Phantom Fox," "Convict 993," "His Children's Children," "East is West," "The Pride of Palomar," "Don Q," "The Marriage Clause," "Don Juan," "The Mystery Club," "Infatuation," "The Jazz Singer," "Tong War," "Love's Dream," "The Scarlet Lady," "The Wheel of Chance," "The Faker," "Chinatown Nights," "The Mighty," "The Mysterious Dr. Fu Manchu," "The Studio Murder Case," "A Dangerous Paradise," "Paramount on Parade," "The Return of Dr. Fu Manchu," "The Vagabond King," "Charlie Chan Carries On," "Dishonored," "The Black Camel," "The Shanghai Express," "The Daughter of the Dragon," "Charlie Chan's Chance," "The Big Gamble," "Passport to Hell" ("Burnt Offering"), "The Son-Daughter," "Before Dawn," "Chan's Greatest Case," "As Husbands Go," "Mandalay," "Bull-Dog Drummond Strikes Back," "Charlie Chan's Courage," "Charlie Chan in London," "The Painted Veil," "Charlie Chan in Paris," "The Werewolf of London," "Charlie Chan in Egypt," "Shanghai," etc.
(Died 6 Aug., 1938; age 57)

OLCOTT, Chauncey, actor and vocalist; *b.* Buffalo, New York, July 21, 1860; *e.* at Public Schools, Buffalo,

where he made his first appearance, at the Academy of Music, as a ballad singer, in 1880; *m.* Margaret O'Donovan; made his first appearance on the regular stage at the Union Square Theatre, New York, 16 Mar., 1886, as Pablo in "Pepita; or the Girl with the Glass Eyes"; at the Academy of Music, 30 Aug., 1888, he appeared as Frank Hopkins in "The Old Homestead," and continued to play in this piece until 1890; in May, 1890, he appeared at the Academy of Music as Ralph Rackstraw in "H.M.S. Pinafore," and in June as Nanki-Poo in "The Mikado"; he then came to London, where he studied music under Holland and Randegger; he made his first appearance on the London stage at the Criterion Theatre, 23 July, 1891, as the Chevalier O'Flanagan in "Miss Decima," and at the Prince of Wales's, 6 Feb., 1892, he played Gnatbrain in "Blue Eyed Susan"; returning to the United States, he toured in "Mavoureen"; he appeared in the following parts at the Fourteenth Street Theatre: Maurice Cronin in "The Irish Artist," 1894; the Minstrel in "The Minstrel of Clare," 1896; Gerald O'Carroll in "Sweet Inniscarra," 1897; Dick R nyane in "A Romance of Athlone," 1899; and Garret O'Magh in an opera of that name, 1901; and also in "Old Limerick Town," 1902: at the New York Theatre, 5 Jan., 1904, he appeared as Terence in an Irish opera of that name; at the Majestic, 2 Oct., 1905, he played the title-*rôle* in "Edmund Burke," and at Saratoga, 17 Aug., 1906, he appeared as Richard Temple in "Eileen Asthore"; at the New York Theatre, 22 Oct., he appeared in the same part; at Saratoga, 16 Aug., 1907, he played the title-*rôle* in "O'Neill of Derry," subsequently playing the same part, at the Liberty Theatre, New York, 25 Nov., 1907; at Saratoga, Aug., 1908, appeared in "Ragged Robin," playing the same part at the Academy of Music, 24 Jan., 1910; same theatre, 30 Jan., 1911, played Thomas Barry in "Barry of Ballymore"; at San Francisco, 9 July, 1911, played Sir Bryan Fitzgerald in " Macushla " ; appearing in the same part at the Grand Opera House, New York, 5 Feb., 1912 ; at Minneapolis, 25 Aug., 1912, played in " The Isle o' Dreams," and appeared in the same play at the Grand Opera House, New York, 28 Jan., 1913 ; at St. Louis, Mo., Oct., 1913, played Dave O'Donnell in " Shameen Dhu," appearing in the same part at the Grand Opera House, New York, 2 Feb., 1914 ; in Oct., 1914, toured as Dennis O'Malley in " The Heart of Paddy Whack," playing the same part at the Grand Opera House, New York, 23 Nov., 1914 ; continued to tour in this part until 1916.; at Detroit, Dec., 1916, played John O'Brien in " Honest John O'Brien " ; during 1917 toured as Terry in " Once Upon a Time," and played the same part at the Fulton, New York, Apr., 1918 ; at the Century Theatre, New York, May, 1918, played The Irish Soldier in " Out There " ; at the Manhattan Opera House, New York, Dec., 1918, Tom McConnell in " The Voice of McConnell " ; during 1919-20 played Sir Brian Fitzgerald in " Macushla," and played the same part at the Park Theatre, New York, May, 1920 ; again toured in the same piece, 1920-21. *Recreations :* Golf, tennis, and riding. *Clubs :* Players', Lambs', New York ; Buffalo Club, and Eccentric Club, London. *Address :* c/o Guaranty Trust C ..., 44th Street, and Fifth Avenue, New York City, U.S.A. *(Died 18 Mar., 1932; age 71)*

OLDHAM, Derek, actor and singer; *b.* Accrington, Lancs, 29 Mar., 1892; *s.* of Thomas Oldham and his wife Harriett Elizabeth (Stephens) ; *e.* privately in Lancashire ; *m.* Winnie Melville (dec.); formerly engaged as a bank clerk ; made his first appearance on the stage at the London Pavilion, Apr., 1914, as Julien in an operetta, " The Daring of Diane " ; at the Lyric Theatre, Sept., 1914, appeared as Bumerli in " The Chocolate Soldier " ; in Nov., 1914, joined the Scots Guards ; received a commission in East Lancs Regiment, Dec., 1915 ; mentioned in dispatches, France, 1917 ; awarded the Military Cross, in Macedonia, 1918 ;

demobilized July, 1919, and joined the D'Oyly Carte Opera Company, Aug., 1919 ; at the Princes Theatre, with this company, Sept., 1919, to Jan., 1920, appeared as Marco in " The Gondoliers," Lord Tolloller in " Iolanthe," Nanki-Poo in " The Mikado," Colonel Fairfax in " The Yeomen of the Guard," Ralph Rackstraw in " H.M.S. Pinafore," Cyril in " Princess Ida," Alexis in " The Sorcerer " ; subsequently toured with the company when he also appeared as Richard in " Ruddigore " ; returned to London for the season at the Princes Theatre, 1921–2; in July, 1922, at the Lyric Theatre, succeeded Austin Melford as Horace Wigg in " Whirled Into Happiness " ; at Daly's, May, 1923, played the Viscomte Camille de Jolidon in the revival of " The Merry Widow " ; Dec., 1923, the Comte D'Estrades in " Madame Pompadour " ; Drury Lane, Mar., 1925, Jim Kenyon in " Rose Marie " ; Winter Garden, Apr., 1927, François Villon in " The Vagabond King " ; appeared at the Coliseum, Sept., 1928, with a repertory of songs ; Dec., 1928, toured as Captain James Wynegate in " Winona " ; rejoined the D'Oyly Carte Company, 1929, and appeared in all his old parts at the Savoy, 1929-30 ; during 1930, toured as Sir George Fairmount in " Blue Eyes " ; Drury Lane, Jan., 1931, played Captain Anthony Darrell in " The Song of the Drum " ; during 1931-2, appeared at variety theatres ; London Hippodrome, Sept., 1932, played the Viscomte de Jolidon in the revival of " The Merry Widow " ; during 1933, toured as Pierre Birabeau in " The Desert Song " ; Alhambra, Dec., 1933, played Baron Franz Schober in " Lilac Time " ; rejoined the D'Oyly Carte Opera Company, at the Martin Beck Theatre, New York, Sept., 1934, singing all his old parts, also Frederic in " The Pirates of Penzance," and Hilarion in " Princess Ida " ; on returning to London, appeared at the Coliseum, May, 1935, as Franz in " Dancing City " ; in Aug., 1935, toured as Baron Schober in " Lilac Time " ; again appeared at the Martin Beck, New York, 1936–7, with the D'Oyly Carte company and subsequently toured ; appeared at the Royal Albert

Hall, London, 1938, as Chibiabos in "Hiawatha"; toured, 1939, as Jim Kenyon in "Rose Marie"; Coliseum, Mar., 1940, played Leopold in "White Horse Inn"; Stoll, Oct., 1942, Franz Schober in "Lilac Time"; toured, 1943, as Beaucaire in "Monsieur Beaucaire," and in "The Windmill Man"; during 1944, toured as Prince Niki in "A Waltz Dream," and Pierre in "I Call it Love," and 1945, as Captain Dick in the first English production of "Naughty Marietta"; after 1946, developed as a lieder singer and lecture-recitalist; Apr., 1950, toured as Nathaniel Jeffcote in "Hindle Wakes"; toured, 1952, as James Winter in "The White Sheep of the Family"; St. Martin's, May, 1953, played Mr. Gill in a revival of "The Two Bouquets"; Sadler's Wells, July, 1954, Lord Mount Severn in "East Lynne"; Piccadilly, Nov., 1955, André Cornellis in "The Strong Are Lonely"; Strand, May, 1958, played Dr. Stoner in "Verdict"; entered films, 1934, and has appeared in numerous pictures; since 1958 has appeared on television, and also broadcast in radio programmes. *Recreations:* Gardening and photography. *Address:* Gillan, St. Mary's Road, Hayling Island, Hants. *Telephone No.:* Hayling Island 72003. *(Died Mar., 1968; age 75)*

OLDLAND, Lilian, actress; *b.* Gloucester, 7 Feb., 1905; *d.* of Ernest Oldland; *m.* Reginald Denham; studied for the stage at the Royal Academy of Dramatic Art; made her first appearance on the stage at the Ambassadors' Theatre, 15 Sept., 1924, as Thérèse in "Fata Morgana"; at Oxford, Feb., 1925, for the O.U.D.S., played Ingrid in "Peer Gynt"; subsequently, at the Aldwych, 1925, succeeded Madge Saunders for a time as Barbara Wykeham in "A Cuckoo in the Nest"; she then appeared in several films, including "The Secret Kingdom," "Bindle," etc.; at the Savoy, Mar., 1926, played Lucienne de la Tour in "The Snow Man"; subsequently returned to the films, appearing in "The Flag Lieutenant," "Passion Island," "A Daughter in Revolt," "Virginia's Husband," "Further Adventures of the Flag

Lieutenant," and "The City of Youth"; reappeared on the regular stage at the Ambassadors', Apr., 1929, when she played Leila Arden in "Rope." *Recreations:* Riding, motoring, swimming, and walking. *Club:* Arts Theatre. *Address:* 21A Well Walk, Hampstead, N.W.3. *Telephone No.:* Hampstead 6557.

OLIFFE, Geraldine, actress; *m.* Otway Compton; made her first appearance on the stage at the Globe Theatre, 16 Mar., 1889, as one of the Queen's attendants in "Richard III," under Richard Mansfield; appeared at Drury Lane, Sept., 1890, as Mrs. Marlowe in "A Million of Money"; in 1893 toured as Mrs. Allonby in "A Woman of No Importance"; subsequently went to Australia, where she played a number of parts under the management of Brough and Boucicault; on her return appeared at the Duke of York's, Dec., 1895, as Margaret Maitland in "Tommy Atkins"; at the Princess's, Sept., 1896, played Marion Thornton in "Two Little Vagabonds"; Dec., 1897, Lady Ferrers in "How London Lives"; at the Strand, Aug., 1898, Lady Rollestone in "As a Man Sows"; in Feb., 1899, toured as Lizzie Medwin in "The Power and the Glory"; at the Garrick, Apr., 1899, played Madame Moody in "Change Alley," and June, 1899, Mrs. William Dawson in "Halves"; since then she has appeared on tour with Charles Warner, 1901, as Toinette in "Eve"; at Wyndham's, Mar., 1902, as Marie Marex in "Heard at the Telephone"; Duke of York's, Sept., 1904, the Countess of Foxwell in "Merely Mary Ann"; at the Court, Nov., 1905, Honor Voysey in "The Voysey Inheritance"; Comedy, Oct., 1907, Mrs. Pethick in "The Barrier"; Lyceum, May, 1909, Anne of Austria in "The Prisoner of the Bastille"; Duke of York's, Mar., 1910, Miss Chancellor in "The Madras House"; Kingsway, Feb., 1911, Odette in "The Lily"; Criterion, May, 1911, Madame Petkoff in "Arms and the Man"; Duke of York's, Oct., 1912, Mrs. Luna in "Overruled"; His

Majesty's, Apr., 1914, Mrs. Pearce in "Pygmalion." *Address :* c/o *The Era* or *The Stage.*

OLIPHANT, Jack, theatre press-representative; *b.* Leeds, Yorks, 5 Feb., 1895; *s.* of Morris Oliphant and his wife Rebecca (Cooper); *e.* Leeds Grammar School; *m.* Julie Olan; was formerly a journalist, and commenced his career on the *Daily Citizen,* 1914; subsequently on staff of *Daily Mirror* and *Sunday Pictorial;* during the first World War, served from 1915–18, in the R.N.A.S., in France, Italy and the Middle East; after demobilization, returned to journalism, in which he remained until 1925; in that year became press-representative at the Aldwych Theatre. under Tom Walls, remaining until 1929; held similar appointments at numerous West-end theatres, for several years; subsequently became personal press agent to a number of well-known theatrical artistes, also representing many American notabilities; appointed press-representative to Mr. Jack Waller for his productions, 1945. *Recreations :* Swimming and boxing (was bantam-weight champion Egyptian Expeditionary Force, 1917–18).

OLIVE, Edyth, actress ; *e.* at Newton Abbot, Devon ; *m.* Arthur Applin, actor and author ; studied at the Guildhall School of Music ; made her first appearance on the stage at the Strand Theatre, 9 Jan., 1892, as Louisa Dexter in " The New Wing," under Willie Edouin ; subsequently toured in " A Broken Melody " ; was for some time in Ben Greet's company, and then joined F. R. Benson, and with him appeared as Rosalind, Viola, Hermione, Beatrice, Ophelia, and Desdemona ; in 1897 toured as Militza in " For the Crown," and also as Princess Flavia in " The Prisoner of Zenda," Elcia in " The Daughters of Babylon " ; she also toured as Lady Marchant in " A Bunch of Violets," Olive de Carteret in " Sporting Life " ; appeared at the Globe, 1902, with Fred Terry

and Julia Neilson in " Sweet Nell of Old Drury," " The Heel of Achilles," etc. , at the Comedy, Apr., 1904, played the Nun in " Sunday," and at the Court, May, 1904, Mrs. Marwood in " The Way of the World " ; played Cassandra in " The Trojan Women," Medea in " Medea in Corinth," Clytemnestra in " Electra," Phædra in " Hippolytus," Aglavaine in " Aglavaine and Selysette," at the Lyric and Court Theatres, 1904-6 ; at the St. James's, 1905, played Edith in " A Maker of Men " ; at the Imperial, 1904, appeared as Martha in " The Perfect Lover " ; at the Scala, Jan., 1906, played the title-*rôle* in " Lady Inger of Osträt " ; during 1907 toured in the United States, as Ruth Jordan in " The Great Divide " ; at the Scala, Apr., 1908, appeared as the Sister of Mercy in " Hannele " ; at the Court, 1909, played in " The Test," and " John Malone's Love Story " ; at the Coliseum music hall, in " A Loyal Traitor," and " The Attic " ; at the Duke of York's, Feb., 1910, played Ruth in " Justice " ; at the Queen's, May, 1910, appeared as the Prisoner's Wife in " Judge Not " ; at the Court, Feb., 1911, played Herodias in " Salomé " ; at the Lyceum, July, 1911, played Marie Louise in " A Royal Divorce " ; at the Court Theatre, Jan., 1912, played Janet in " Rutherford and Son," subsequently appearing in the same part at the Little and Vaudeville, and in America ; at the Coronet, Dec., 1913, played Mrs. Rüs in " A Gauntlet " ; at the Ambassadors', May, 1914, Dido in " Dido and Æneas " ; at the Lyric, Oct., 1914, Sarah Ehrlich in " The New Shylock " ; at the Little, Apr., 1915, Evelyn Pallant in " The Blow " ; at the London Pavilion, June, 1915, Margery Silchester in " The Rub " ; during 1919-20 toured with Louis Calvert as Cora Bliss in " Bo'sun 'Enery," and Jeannie in " Daddalums " ; at Wyndham's, June, 1920, appeared in the last-mentioned part ; at the Aldwych (for the Play Actors), Oct., 1924, played Mrs. Hayling in " The Hayling Family." *Hobby :* Working. *Address :* 18 Addison Avenue, W.11. *Telephone No. :* Park 3750.
(Died 7 Nov., 1956; age 84)

OLIVER, Barrie, actor and dancer; *b.* West Point, Mississippi, U.S.A., 12 Jan., 1900; *s.* of Isaac Augustus Oliver and his wife Eleanor (Ellis); *e.* St. Bernard's College, Cullman, Ala.; was formerly engaged with the Hearst publications in New York; made his first appearance on the stage in vaudeville, appearing at the Alhambra, New York, Mar., 1923; at Chicago, 1924, appeared in " The Greenwich Village Follies "; came to London in 1925, and appeared at the Café de Paris, in dances, Aug., 1925; made his first appearance on the London stage at the Shaftesbury, 8 Sept., 1926, as Charles Crawford in " Just a Kiss "; in Apr., 1927, toured as Robert Barker in " Two Little Girls in Blue "; appeared at the London Pavilion, Nov., 1927, in " One Dam Thing After Another "; at the Vaudeville, Aug., 1928, played in " Charlot, 1928 "; subsequently returned to America; at the Broadway, New York, Dec., 1930, played James Livingstone in " The New Yorkers "; San Francisco, May, 1932, appeared in " Love Time "; has appeared in films, including " The Musical Beauty Shop," " The Jerry Builders," " The New Waiter," etc; has also appeared in *revue* in France. *Recreations :* Tennis, motoring, and swimming. *Clubs :* Embassy and " 500."

OLIVER, Edna May (*née* Nutter), actress; *b.* Boston, Mass., U.S.A., Sept., 1885; *e.* Boston; *m.* D. W. Pratt (mar. dis.); originally intended to follow a musical career; made her first appearance on the stage in Boston, 1911; first appeared in New York, at the Fulton Theatre, 5 Dec., 1916, as Juliet in " The Master "; at the Princess, Feb., 1917, played Penelope Budd in " Oh, Boy! "; Lyric, Nov., 1919, Mrs. Hobson in " The Rose of China "; Nora Bayes Theatre, Feb., 1920, Mrs. Judson Mitchell in " My Golden Girl "; Liberty, Nov., 1920, Mrs. Francis Jarvis in " The Half-Moon "; Playhouse, Sept., 1921, Aunt Meridian in " Wait Till We're Married "; Cort, Nov., 1921, Mrs. Sophie Perkins in " Her Salary Man "; Broadhurst, Sept., 1922, June in " Wild Oats Lane "; Sam H. Harris, Feb., 1923,

Hannah in " Icebound "; Fulton, Oct., 1924, Mrs. John Clarendon in " In His Arms "; Empire, Jan., 1925, Aunt Olivia in " Isabel "; Music Box, Sept., 1925, Ethel Drake in " Cradle Snatchers "; Ziegfeld, Dec., 1927, Parthy Ann Hawks in " Show Boat," which she continued to play until 1929, when she went into pictures for three years; at the Casino, May, 1932, again appeared as Parthy Ann in a revival of " Show Boat"; commenced film career 1923, and appeared in " Icebound "; returned to the stage, and reappeared in films in 1929; since that date she has played in innumerable pictures; since 1936, has appeared in " Romeo and Juliet," " Parnell," " My Dear Miss Aldrich," " Rosalie," " Paradise for Three." " Little Miss Broadway," " The Story of Vernon and Irene Castle," etc. *Recreations :* Swimming and music. *(Died 9 Nov., 1942; age 59)*

OLIVER, Vic., actor and musician; *b.* Vienna; *s.* of Baron Victor von Samek and his wife Josephine (Rauch); *e.* University of Vienna; *m.* (1) Sarah Churchill, *d.* of the Rt. Hon. Winston Churchill, P.C., C.H., M.P. (mar. dis.); (2) Natalie Frances Conder; was formerly engaged successively in banking, in the business of a cloth manufacturer, and as a conductor; went to the United States, 1926, where he abandoned his career as a conductor to become a comedian; made his first appearance in "vaudeville," at the Lyric, Indianapolis, July, 1926, subsequently touring all over the United States; first appeared in New York, at the Palace Theatre, June, 1929; made his first appearance in London at the Palladium, July, 1931; first appeared on the regular stage in London, at the Adelphi Theatre, 4 Feb., 1936, in C. B. Cochran's *revue,* "Follow the Sun"; July–Dec., 1938, toured as Harry Van in "Idiot's Delight"; London Hippodrome, Mar., 1939, appeared in "Black and Blue"; Nov., 1939, in "Black Velvet"; toured, 1940, in "To-Night at 8.30," and "Plays and Music"; Nov., 1941, played Vic Vandyke in "Get a Load of This"; Coliseum, May, 1945, appeared in

"The Night and Music," which ran for fifteen months; at the Albert Hall, Jan., 1946, conducted a classical concert; Hippodrome, Oct., 1947, appeared in the *revue* "Starlight Roof"; Casino, Dec., 1948, King Yolk of Eggville in "Humpty-Dumpty"; Mar., 1950, appeared in the *revue* "Latin Quarter, 1950"; toured, Dec., 1950, in "Let Yourself Go"; Casino, Mar., 1953, appeared in the *revue* "Three Cheers"; Grand, Leeds, Dec., 1954, played King Cole in "Old King Cole"; Newcastle Empire, Dec., 1957, appeared as King Cole in the Christmas pantomime; Dublin, Dec., 1958, again played King Cole; is also a highly popular turn in cabaret and variety theatres, and during 1937–8, played fourteen engagements in twelve months at the Holborn Empire; featured in many regular programmes with the B.B.C., notably in "Hi Gang!" etc.; entered films, 1933; has appeared successfully in numerous pictures, and also in television programmes; in 1945 became Director and Conductor of the British Concert Orchestra, and since that date has divided his time between stage appearances and concert work; has published an autobiography, "Mr. Showbusiness"; elected President of the Stage Golfing Society for 1956. *Recreation:* Golf. *Club:* Wentworth. *Address:* 66 Westminster Gardens, S.W.1. *Telephone No.:* Victoria 2640. *(Died 15 Aug., 1964; age 66)*

OLSEN, Ole (*né* John Siguard Olsen), actor; *b.* Peru, Indiana, 6 Nov., 1892; *e.* North Western University, Chicago; made his first appearance on the vaudeville stage, 1914; in 1915, joined Chic Johnson, and appeared all over the United States, also visiting England and Australia; while in Australia, 1926, appeared in "Tip Toes" and "Tell Me More"; on returning to America, 1926, appeared on the Pacific Coast, at Los Angeles, and elsewhere, in "Monkey Business"; subsequently toured in "Atrocities of 1932," and "Everything Goes"; first appeared on the regular stage in New York, at the Apollo Theatre, June, 1933, when he succeeded Jack Haley as Duke Stanley in "Take a Chance," subsequently touring all through the country, in the same piece; in 1938, with Johnson, presented "Hellzapoppin" on the Pacific Coast, which was so successful, that it was taken to New York and produced at the 46th Street Theatre, Sept., 1938; it again proved such an attraction, that it was played there and at the Winter Garden, over 1400 times in succession; at the Broadhurst Theatre, June, 1939, they presented "The Streets of Paris," without appearing in it; at the Golden Theatre, June, 1941, they presented "Snookie," but did not appear in this play; Winter Garden, Dec., 1941, they appeared together in "Sons O'Fun," which was performed nearly 800 times; Ethel Barrymore, Oct., 1942, they presented "Count Me In," without appearing in it; Winter Garden, Dec., 1944, they appeared in "Laffing Room Only"; first appeared on the London stage, Casino Theatre, 23 Feb., 1948, in "Hellzapoppin"; Madison Square Garden, New York, July, 1949, appeared in "Funzapoppin"; Broadway, Sept., 1950, appeared in "Pardon Our French"; they first appeared in films, 1930, in "Oh, Sailor Behave," and have since appeared in "Fifty Million Frenchmen," "Hellzapoppin," "Crazy House," "The Ghost Catchers," "See My Lawyer," etc. *Address:* c/o Actors' Equity Association, 226 West 47th Street, New York City, U.S.A. *(Died 26 Jan., 1963; age 70)*

O'MALLEY, Ellen, actress; *b.* Malahide, co. Dublin, Ireland; *d.* of the late Captain Charles Gray Jones, R.N.; *e.* privately; *m.* Major John Evelyn Thornhill; studied for the stage under the late Sarah Thorne, with whom she made her first appearance on the stage at the Theatre Royal, Margate, 1898; after leaving Miss Thorne, she became leading lady of the Compton Comedy Company, playing Lady Teazle, Kate Hardcastle, Lydia Languish, Sophia in "The Road to Ruin," Doris Maddison in "The Scarlet Coat," Amy Bellair in "Edmund Kean," Violet Gresham in "Davy

Garrick," Countess Thekla in " An Emperor's Romance," etc.; during 1901-2 toured in the United States as leading lady with E. S. Willard, playing Ada Ingot in " David Garrick," Lucy White in " The Professor's Love Story," Mary Blenkarn in " The Middleman," Ruth in " Tom Pinch," Filiberta in " The Cardinal "; made her first appearance on the London stage at the Comedy Theatre, 11 Dec., 1902, as Marthe de Moisand in " The Mouse "; at the Imperial, Mar., 1903, played Margaret in " The Two Mr. Wetherbys "; at the Queen's, Manchester, under Mr. Richard Flanagan, June, 1903 appeared as Beatrice Portinari in " Dante," and Jan., 1904, as Elizabeth Woodville in " Richard III "; at the Court Theatre. Apr., 1904, played Sylvia in " The Two Gentlemen of Verona "; at the Queen's, Manchester, May, 1904, appeared in the title-*rôle* in " Ygraine," and July, 1904, played the title-*rôle* in " Joan of Arc "; at the Court Theatre, under the Vedrenne-Barker management, Nov., 1904, played Nora in " John Bull's Other Island "; at the Avenue, Feb., 1905, appeared as Lady Thyra Egglesby in " Mr. Hopkinson "; toured in Germany as Candida in the play of that name; at the Court, Sept., 1907, played Gloria in " You Never Can Tell "; at the Duke of York's, Mar., 1909, played Enid Underwood in " Strife "; at the Haymarket, Sept., 1909, appeared as Cordelia in " King Lear," and Oct., 1909, as Ann Sinclair in " Don "; at the Queen's, Oct., 1910, played Mrs. Thynne in " Mrs. Skeffington "; at the Haymarket, Dec., 1910, Light in " The Blue Bird," and June, 1911, Madame d'Orbesson in " Above Suspicion "; subsequently joined F. R. Benson and appeared at Stratford-on-Avon and on tour as Portia in " The Merchant of Venice," Juliet, Lady Macbeth, Rosalind in " As You Like It," and Katherine in " The Taming of the Shrew," appearing in the last-mentioned part at the King's, Hammersmith, Sept., 1911; at the Kingsway Theatre, Nov., 1912, played Mabel Lanfarne in " The Eldest Son "; at the Haymarket,

Dec., 1912, Hannah Waldie in " The Waldies "; at the Kingsway, Dec., 1912, again played Nora in " John Bull's Other Island "; at the King's Hall, Covent Garden, Mar., 1913, appeared as Ophelia in " Hamlet "; at the Court, Mar., 1913, Eve Michelmore in " The Morning Post "; and June, 1913, Irene Martin in " The Cage "; at the Little Theatre, July, 1913, played Dame Julian in " Dame Julian's Window "; at the Criterion, Feb., 1914, Irene Maitland in " A Pair of Silk Stockings "; at the Prince of Wales's June, 1914, Kitty Melville in " An Indian Summer "; at the Court, June, 1914, Cecily Warren in " His Duty "; at the Kingsway, Apr., 1915, Rose Appleyard in " Advertisement "; at the St. James's, Jan., 1916, Philippa de Lacorfe in " The Basker "; at the Savoy, Apr., 1917, the Queen in " Hamlet "; at the Globe, Jan., 1918, appeared as Jane Raymond in " Love in a Cottage "; at the New Theatre, July, 1918, as Victoria Cresswell in " The Chinese Puzzle "; at the Globe, June, 1919, as the Archduchess Sophia in " L'Aiglon "; Aug., 1919, as Miss Rodd in " The Voice from the Minaret "; at the Aldwych, Aug., 1920, played Sylvia Bullough in " The Unknown "; at the Court, Sept., 1921, again appeared as Nora Reilly in " John Bull's Other Island "; Oct., 1921, Ellie Dunn in " Heartbreak House "; at the Shaftesbury (for the Phoenix Society), Mar., 1922, Octavia in " All for Love "; at the Everyman Theatre, June, 1923, Candida in the play of that name; re-appeared on the stage after an absence of eleven years, at the Webber-Douglas Theatre, Oct., 1934, in " L'Arlésienne." *Recreation*: Sailing. *Address*: 6 Gloucester Road, South Kensington, S.W.7. *Telephone No.*: Western 0280
(*Died 30 May, 1961*)

O'MALLEY, Rex (Sean Rex Patrick O'Malley), actor; *b.* London, 2 Jan., 1901; *s.* of William Thomas O'Malley and his wife Emily Anne (Whyte); *e.* Llandaff House, Cambridge, and Bishop's Palace, Oxford; made his first appearance on the stage at the Garrick Theatre, 28 Mar., 1919, as

Aramis in "Cyrano de Bergerac," in Robert Loraine's original production; Court, Apr., 1920, succeeded Frank Vosper as Charles in "The Young Visitors"; from 1921–2, toured in "The Man from Toronto," "Gabrielle," and "The Gypsy Princess"; Vaudeville, Feb., 1923, appeared in Charlot's *revue*, "Rats"; Regent (with Birmingham Rep. Co.), May, 1924, played Paris in "Romeo and Juliet"; then toured in South Africa, 1925, with Iris Hoey, in "The Pelican," "Clothes and the Woman," "The Man from Toronto," etc.; Prince of Wales, London, Feb., 1926, played Maurice in "Wet Paint"; Comedy, Apr., 1926, Robert Gilmour in "The Man from Toronto"; made his first appearance in New York at the Booth Theatre, 7 Dec., 1926, as Prince Lyov Myshkin in "The Strange Prince" ("The Idiot"); Masque, Apr., 1927, played the Pupil in "The Comic"; Biltmore, Nov., 1927, Miguel in "The Marquise"; Belasco, Feb., 1928, Geoffrey Trent in "The Bachelor Father," appearing in the same part at the Globe, London, Sept., 1929; returning to New York, appeared at the Martin Beck (for the Theatre Guild), Feb., 1930, as Sempronius in "The Apple Cart"; Selwyn, May, 1930, played Eric Bailey in "Lost Sheep"; Bayes, Mar., 1931, Ramon Colmano in "Wonder Bar"; Longacre, Dec., 1931, Winthrop Allen in "Experience Unnecessary"; Broadhurst, Dec., 1932, Claude Hope in "The Mad Hopes"; Morosco, June, 1933, Gilbert Marechal in "Best Sellers"; Booth, Jan., 1934, James Salston in "No More Ladies"; Broadhurst, Sept., 1934, the Marquis de Lac in "The Red Cat"; New Amsterdam, Nov., 1934, Pablo in "Revenge with Music"; Guild, Feb., 1935, the Emigration Officer in "The Simpleton of the Unexpected Isles"; subsequently toured for Theatre Guild as Tranio in "The Taming of the Shrew"; Playhouse, New York, Nov., 1936, Dr. Robert Levy-de-Coudray in "Matrimony Pfd."; Playhouse, Dec., 1937, Kenneth Vereker in "Merely Murder"; Winter Garden, Sept., 1938, Baron de Romer in "You Never Know"; in the spring of 1940, toured in "Private Lives," and as Beverly

Carlton in "The Man Who Came to Dinner," appearing in the last-mentioned part, at the Music Box, Aug., 1940; toured, Aug., 1941, as Daffodil in "The Yellow Jacket"; Curran, San Francisco, autumn, 1942, played Adhemar in "Adamant Eve"; Plymouth, New York, Oct., 1943, Frederic in "The Naked Genius"; National, Jan., 1944, Epihodov in "The Cherry Orchard"; Playhouse, Jan., 1945, Charles Barrows in "Many Happy Returns"; Royale, Sept., 1945, Atamar in "Devils Galore"; Plymouth, Feb., 1946, Youen-Kong in "Lute Song"; Cort, Dec., 1946, succeeded Cecil Beaton as Cecil Graham in "Lady Windermere's Fan"; in 1947, appeared in summer theatres, as Lord Goring in "An Ideal Husband," and directed productions of "Best of Friends," and "Private Lives"; in 1948–9, in summer theatres, appeared in "O Mistress Mine," and "Light Up the Sky," etc.; in 1950, toured as Beverly Carlton in "The Man Who Came to Dinner," and appeared in summer theatres in "To-Night at 8.30," and "Light Up the Sky"; McCarter Theatre, Princeton, Jan., 1951, played Gaisceen in "The King of Friday's Men"; New York City Center, Dec., 1953, played Brasset in "Charley's Aunt"; Coronet, Nov., 1956, Northbrook in "The Sleeping Prince"; Theatre East, N.Y., 1957, the Priest in "The Tinker's Wedding"; Madison Avenue Playhouse, Jan., 1963, Lane in "The Importance of Being Earnest"; Winter Garden, Mar., 1963, Augusto in "The Lady of the Camelias"; Curran, San Francisco, and Hartford, Los Angeles, Oct.–Nov., 1963, Dr. Clayton in "The Time of the Barracudas"; Jan Hus Playhouse, New York, Jan., 1965, Joshua in "Say Nothing"; has also directed and played in summer stock and on tours, including "O Mistress Mine," "Private Lives," "The Little Hut," "Visit to a Small Planet," "The Circus of Dr. Lao," "Captain Brassbound's Conversion," "Look Out, Sailor," "Life with Father," etc.; has also made frequent appearances in radio and television programmes; first entered films in England, 1924, subsequent films include "The Thief," 1952, and "Taxi,"

1953. *Recreations:* Gardening and writing. *Hobby:* Animals.

O'NEAL, Zelma, actress and vocalist; *b.* Rock Falls, Indiana, U.S.A., 29 May, 1907; *d.* of August Schroeder and his wife Grace Herlihy; *e.* Chicago; *m.* (1) Raymond Buffington (mar. dis.); (2) Henry Burns (mar. dis.); (3) Anthony Bushell (mar. dis.); made her first appearance on the stage in Chicago, as a singer and dancer; subsequently appeared in "vaudeville" on the Orpheum circuit; attracted attention in New York, when she appeared at 46th Street Theatre, 6 Sept., 1927, as Flo in "Good News"; went to London, and made her first appearance there, at the Carlton Theatre, 15 Aug., 1928, in the same part; on returning to New York, appeared at 46th Street, Jan., 1929, as Angie Howard in "Follow Thru"; Imperial, Feb., 1931, played "Willy" Wilson in "The Gang's All Here"; at the El Capitan, Hollywood, July, 1931, played Jackie Sampson in a revival of "Oh, Boy!"; Strand, Sept., 1933, Tutti in "Nice Goings On"; Gaiety, Feb., 1935, Peggy Turner in "Jack o' Diamonds," and Sept., 1936, Miami in "Swing Along"; Richmond, Oct., 1938, Bunty Potter in "Guests at Random"; has also appeared in pictures, notably in "Follow Thru," "Peach o' Reno," "Freedom of the Seas," "Give Her a Ring," "There Goes Susie," "Mister Cinders," "Spring in the Air," "Joy Ride," "Let's Make a Night of It," etc. *Recreations:* Bridge and golf. *Address:* 49 Cambridge Court, W.2. *Telephone No.:* Paddington 7669.

O'NEIL, Nancy, actress; *b.* Sydney, N.S.W., Australia, 25 Aug., 1911; *d.* of Stewart Arthur Smith and his wife Muriel (Pitt); *e.* Sydney; *m.* Dermot George Crosbie Trench; studied for the stage at the Royal Academy of Dramatic Art, 1929–30; made her first appearance on the stage, in the Repertory Company, at the Palace Theatre, Salisbury, 26 Jan., 1931, as Sadie in "The Chinese Bungalow," subsequently playing Jodie in "Plus

Fours," Blanny Wheeler in "Fair and Warmer," etc.; in Aug., 1931, toured as Judy in "The Breadwinner"; returned to Australia, 1932, and in Aug., 1932, toured there as Evelyn in "Doctor Pygmalion"; made her first appearance in London, on the variety stage, 1932, with Donald Calthrop, in "The Man in the Street"; she then understudied Helen Spencer at the Playhouse, 1933, in "The Rats of Norway"; made her first appearance on the West End stage, at Wyndham's, 29 Nov., 1933, as Shirley Norton in "Man Proposes"; Daly's, May, 1934, played Blanche Popinot in "Vintage Wine"; New, May, 1935, Sally Martin in "Someone at the Door"; "Q," Jan., 1938, Madge Stevenson in "The Prodigal Mother"; entered films, 1933, and has appeared in numerous pictures. *Address:* 41 First Street, S.W.3. *Telephone No.:* Kensington 9651.

O'NEIL, Peggy, actress; *b.* Gneeveguilla, Co. Kerry, Ireland, 16 June, 1898; *d.* of Frederick A. O'Neil and his wife Mary (Buckley); *e.* Loretta Convent, Niagara Falls; made her first appearance on the stage, at the La Salle Opera House, Chicago, 29 Aug., 1910, as a child dancer in "The Sweetest Girl in Paris"; subsequently appeared in "Honeymoon Land"; was next engaged in cinema acting, followed by her appearance in "The Deadlock," 1912; in 1913 appeared in "The Top o' the Morning," and after another engagement for the cinema, played Peg in "Peg o' My Heart" during the longest run in Chicago; in 1916 played Lady Patricia O'Brien in "Mavoureen"; made her first appearance in New York, at the Lyric Theatre, 4 Sept., 1916, as Maya in "The Flame"; in 1917 was seen in "vaudeville" with her own sketch "The Crossways"; at His Majesty's, Montreal, Jan., 1918, appeared as Maggie in a play of that name, which was subsequently re-named "Patsy on the Wing"; at Washington, Apr., 1918, played Doris Grieg in "The Laughter of Fools"; at the George M. Cohan Theatre, Nov., 1918, appeared as Margot Latour in "By

Pigeon Post," subsequently playing Marie in the same play; at the Selwyn Theatre, Mar., 1919, played Anne Wilson in "Tumble In"; was then engaged by Robert Courtneidge for England, and made her first appearance at the Queen's, Manchester, 24 Feb., 1920, as Paddy in "Paddy the Next Best Thing," in which part she made her first appearance in London at the Savoy, 5 Apr., 1920, meeting with great success; this piece ran over 800 performances; at the Haymarket, Jan., 1923, played Josephine Nuthall in "Plus Fours"; at the Savoy, Dec., 1923, appeared in a revival of "Paddy the Next Best Thing"; at Cardiff, Mar., 1924, played in "Special Licence," and then toured as Maggie Wylie in "What Every Woman Knows"; in Aug., 1924, toured for Basil Dean as Lady Babbie in "The Little Minister"; Strand, Mar., 1925, played Fay in "The Sea Urchin"; London Hippodrome, Oct., 1925, Mary in "Mercenary Mary"; Savoy, Oct., 1926, Marjorie in "Love's a Terrible Thing"; Oct., 1927, toured as Peg in "Peg o' Mine"; Lyceum, June, 1928, played Ann Perryman in "The Flying Squad"; Palladium, Dec., 1928, Molly in "Out of the Rain"; Carlton, Feb., 1929, Sadie la Salle in "Merry Merry"; subsequently toured in variety theatres in "The Honeymoon," and "It Must Be Love"; at the Garrick, Dec., 1929, played Tony Flagg in "The Bachelor Father," and Paddy in "Paddy the Next Best Thing"; during 1930, toured in "The Bachelor Father," and as Jeannine in "When Dreams Come True"; Grand, Blackpool, Sept., 1931, played the Woman in "Two's Company"; Aug., 1932, toured as Nellie Fitzpatrick in "Pay the Piper," and Anna Moylen in "Mountain Dew"; in Aug., 1933, toured as Kitty Hamble and Bella Tout in "Road House"; in Feb., 1934, toured in "No Surrender"; Arts, Oct., 1934, played Tishy Merz in "No Greater Crime"; at the Garrick, Dec., 1934, played Margot Gresham in "First Episode"; at Theatre Royal, Bournemouth, Jan., 1935, played Lydia Languish in "The Rivals," and Lady Teazle in "The School for Scandal"; at the Grand Theatre,

Southampton, Sept., 1938, played Peg in "Peg O' My Heart," Belle Tout in "Road House," Susan Martin in "Sauce for the Gander" and Elizabeth in "Mrs. Christopher Columbus."*(Died 7 Jan., 1960; age 61)*

O'NEILL, Eugene Gladstone, dramatic author; *b.* New York, 16 Oct., 1888; *s.* of James O'Neill, actor, and his wife Ella (Quinlan); *e.* Princeton and Harvard Universities; *m.* (1) Kathleen Jenkins (mar. dis.); (2) Agnes Boulton (mar. dis.); (3) Carlotta Monterey; formerly engaged in commerce, and also spent two years at sea; was for a time engaged as an actor, and also as a journalist; is the author of the following plays: "Thirst," 1914; "In the Zone," 1917; "The Rope," 1918; "'Ile,'" 1918; "The Moon of the Carribes," 1919; "Beyond the Horizon," 1919; 'Diff'rent," 1920; "The Emperor Jones," 1920; "The Straw, 1921; "Gold," 1921; "Anna Christie," 1921; "The First Man," 1922; "The Hairy Ape," 1922; "The Fountain," 1923; "Welded," 1924; "All God's Chillun Got Wings," 1924; "Desire Under the Elms," 1924; "The Great God Brown," 1926; "Lazarus Laughed," 1926; "Before Breakfast," 1927; "Where the Cross is Made," 1927; "Marco Millions," 1928; "Strange Interlude," 1928; "Dynamo," 1929; "Mourning Becomes Electra," a triology, including "Homecoming," "The Hunted," and "The Haunted," 1931; "Ah, Wilderness!," 1933; "Days Without End," 1934; "The Iceman Cometh," 1946; associated with Kenneth Macgowan and Robert Edmond Jones in the production of several plays at the Greenwich Village Theatre, New York, from 1925 onwards; he was awarded the 1936 Nobel Prize, for Literature. *Address:* Sea Island, Georgia, U.S.A. *(Died 27 Nov., 1953; age 65)*

O'NEILL, Frank B., business manager; *b.* Cranbrook, Kent, 31 Oct., 1869; *s.* of G. B. O'Neill, artist; *e.* Haileybury College and Trinity College, Oxford (M.A., 1894), where

he took honours in classics and history ; *m.* Mary (Vincent) Gray ; business manager to Sir John Martin Harvey from July, 1901, to date, his only engagement. *Recreations :* Athletics, breeding of dogs, and gardening. *Address :* "The Tuns," Ockley, Surrey. *Telephone No. :* Oakwood Hill 36.
(Died 28 Dec., 1959; age 90)

O'NEILL, Henry, actor ; *b.* Orange, New Jersey, U.S.A., 10 Aug., 1891 ; made his first appearance on the stage in his native town in the local "stock" company, 1919 ; made his first appearance in New York, with the Celtic Players, at the Provincetown Playhouse, 24 May, 1920, in "Birthright"; remained with the company three years, and played Philly Cullen in "The Play-boy of the Western World," Dr. Sheldon in "The Spring," Tom Edgeworthy in "The Verge," Paddy in "The Hairy Ape," Dean Davis in "Chains of Dew," also in "Riders to the Sea," "The Great God Brown," "John Ferguson," etc. ; at Daly's, Sept., 1925, played Sir Sampson Legend in "Love for Love"; Greenwich Village, Nov., 1925, the Statue of the Commander in "The Last Night of Don Juan"; Dec., 1925, Christopher Columbus in "The Fountain"; Provincetown, Jan., 1926, the Voice of Indra in "The Dream Play"; 48th Street, Nov., 1926, Don Diego in "The Squall"; Longacre, Sept., 1928, Patsy Brady in "Jarnegan"; Sept., 1929, Paul Cooper in "Hawk Island"; Sam. H. Harris, Feb., 1930, Father O'Connors in "The Last Mile"; Royale, May, 1931, Charles Murfree in "Old Man Murphy"; Alvin, Oct., 1931, George Kelly in "Wonder Boy"; Harris, Feb., 1932, George La Tour in "Trick for Trick"; Oct., 1932, Philip Fletcher in "I Loved You Wednesday"; Times Square, Jan., 1933, Dr. Harrold in "Foolscap"; Plymouth, Feb., 1933, Frederick Nolte, Sen., in "Conquest"; Selwyn, June, 1933, Carl Hoffman in "Shooting Star"; entered films, 1933, in "I Loved a Woman"; has since appeared in innumerable productions. *Address :* c/o Warner Bros., Olive Avenue,

Burbank, Cal., U.S.A.
(Died 18 May, 1961; age 69)

O'NEILL, James, actor ; *b.* Kilkenny, 15 Nov., 1849 ; *m.* Ella Quinlan ; made his *début* at the age of fifteen at Cleveland, Ohio, in 1865, with the late John Ellsler's stock company in "The Colleen Bawn"; in 1872 was at National Theatre, Cincinnati, in Edwin Forrest's Company ; then proceeded to McVicker's Theatre, Chicago ; Hooley's, Chicago, and thence to California ; subsequently appeared with Adelaide Neilson and Edwin Booth ; with Booth he alternated several parts ; appeared in "The Passion Play" at San Francisco ; "starred" jointly with W. H. Crane ; has appeared most successfully as Enoch Arden, Montaiglin in "Raymonde," Julian Gray in "The New Magdalen," D'Artagnan and Monte Cristo, Robert Landry in "The Dead Heart," Jean in "A Celebrated Case," Pierre in "The Two Orphans," Maurice in "Miss Multon," Vladimir in "The Danischeffs," Monsieur Florion in "The Mother's Secret," George Lovell in "The Man of Success," Henri Lavelle in "When Greek Meets Greek," Pete in "The Manxman," Gerard in "The Adventures of Gerard," John the Baptist in "The Voice of the Mighty," Virginius, etc., etc. ; he appeared in the last-mentioned part in a revival of that play at the Lyric Theatre, New York, 16 Sept., 1907 ; at Asbury Park, Sept., 1908, appeared in the title-*rôle* of "Abbé Buonaparte"; during 1909, toured with Viola Allen, as Monsignor Saracinesca in "The White Sister," and appeared in that part at Daly's Theatre, New York, Sept., 1909 ; during 1910, toured in the same part ; at the Century Theatre, New York, Jan., 1913, appeared as Jacob and Pharaoh in "Joseph and His Brethren"; toured in the same part, 1913-4. *Address :* New London, Conn., U.S.A.
(Died 10 Aug., 1920; age 73)

O'NEILL, Maire, actress ; *b.* Dublin ; *y. d.* of George Allgood and his **wife**

Margaret (Harold); sister of Sara Allgood; *m.* (1) G. H. Mair (dec.); (2) Arthur Sinclair; made her first appearance on the stage as a member of the Irish National Theatre Society, at the Abbey Theatre, Dublin ; made her first appearance in London at the Great Queen Street (now Kingsway) Theatre, 10 May, 1907, as Margaret Flaherty in " The Playboy of the Western World "; during her connection with the Irish company played the following, among other parts ; Fand in the play of that name, Mary Cushin in " The Gaol Gate," a Woman in " On Bailie's Strand," Bridget in " The Hour Glass," Min and Maryanne in " The Country Dressmaker," Biddy Lally in " The Unicorn from the Stars," Mona in " Dervorgilla," Mrs. Donohoe in " The Workhouse Ward," the Woman in " The Shewing-up of Blanco Posnet," Deirdre in " Deirdre of the Sorrows," Conal's Wife in " The Green Helmet," Anna Crilly in " Thomas Muskerry," Mary Hurley in " Harvest," Peggy Mahon in " The Image," Mrs. McCarthy in " The Cross Roads," Ellen Barton in " The Casting Out of Martin Whelan," Dan's Wife in " The Deliverer," Queen Cahafra in " King Argimines," Mrs. Rainey in " Mixed Marriage," Johanna in " The Piedish," Cracked Mary in " The Full Moon," Mrs. Shillane in " The Clancy Name," Countess Cathleen in the play of that name, and Maggie Cather in " The Magnanimous Lover "; quitting the Irish company, she appeared at the St. James's Theatre, Jan., 1913, as Zerlina in " Turandot " ; next joined the company of the Repertory Theatre, Liverpool, Mar., 1913, and with that company appeared as the Mother of Hannele in " Hannele," Kalleia in " The Perplexed Husband," Freida Conyngham in " The Conynghams," Candida in the play of that name, and Nora Burke in " The Shadow of the Glen " ; at His Majesty's Theatre, June, 1913, during Sir Herbert Tree's Shakespearean Festival, appeared as Nerissa in " The Merchant of Venice "; in the autumn of 1913 crossed to America, and at the Hudson Theatre, New York, 10 Nov., 1913, played

Mary Ellen in " General John Regan "; after returning to London, appeared at the Haymarket, Feb., 1914, as Catherine Botal in " The Comedy of the Man Who Married a Dumb Wife " ; at the Court Theatre, Feb., 1914, played Portia in " The Merchant of Venice " ; at the Little Theatre, May, 1915, Genevieve in " Foolery "; at the Abbey Theatre, Dublin, Dec., 1916, appeared as Aunt Helen in " The White Headed Boy " ; at the Court, Jan., 1917, as Mary Byrne in " The Tinker's Wedding "; Feb., 1918, as Anna in " The Dead City " ; at the King's Hall, Covent Garden, May, 1919, as Decima in " The Player Queen " ; at the Lyric, Hammersmith, Feb., 1920, played Sarah Ferguson in " John Ferguson " ; at the Ambassadors', Sept., 1920, Aunt Ellen in " The White Headed Boy " : at the Court, July, 1921, again played Margaret Flaherty in a revival of " The Playboy of the Western World " ; later in the year, went to New York, and at the Henry Miller Theatre, Sept , 1921, again played Aunt Ellen in " The White Headed Boy " ; at the Regent, Apr., 1923, played Mrs. Beetle and the Flag Seller in " The Insect Play " ; at the Criterion, July, 1923, Mrs. Kerrigan in " Send for Dr. O'Grady " ; at the St. James's, Dec., 1924, Nancy in " Pollyanna "; Little, Mar., 1925, played Widow Dougherty in " Preserving Pat "; Bristol, Aug., 1925, Biddy in a play of that name; Royalty, Oct., 1925, again played Margaret in " The Playboy of the Western World"; Nov., 1925, Mrs. Maisie Madigan in " Juno and the Paycock "; Fortune, May, 1926, Mrs. Gogan in " The Plough and the Stars "; Vaudeville, Mar., 1927, Mrs. Kilroy in " Professor Tim "; Court, May, 1927, Mrs. Grigson in " The Shadow of a Gunman "; went to America and played in " The Plough and the Stars," and " Juno and the Paycock "; returned to England and toured as Rose Ann McKoy in " The Real McKoy," appearing in this part at the Theatre Royal, Hammersmith, Aug., 1928; during 1929, toured in " Juno and the Paycock," " The Plough and the Stars," and " The Shadow of a Gunman"; at the Broadhurst, New York, Sept., 1930, played

Cissy in "Mr. Gilhooley"; Royale, May, 1931, Widow Donovan in "Old Man Murphy"; at the Savoy, London, Apr., 1932, played the last-mentioned part; in Aug., 1932, toured as Cissy in "Pay the Piper," and Mrs. Moylen in "Mountain Dew"; Arts, Jan., 1933, Josephine Noonan in "Things That Are Caesar's"; Little, Feb, 1934, Daisy Mullan in "Paul Twyning"; at New Brighton, May, 1934, played in "Other Men's Wives," "The Yellow Streak"; Embassy, June, 1934, Mrs. McConaghy in "Mrs. McConaghy's Money"; "Q," Aug., 1934, and Vaudevill Sept., 1934, Mrs. Hayes in "The N.ght Hawk"; Lyric, Hammersmith, July, 1935, Matilda Murphy in "Matilda Goes A-Cruising"; Garrick, July, 1936, succeeded Sara Allgood as Honoria Flanagan in "Storm in a Teacup"; Haymarket, Aug., 1937, Mrs. Madigan in "Juno and the Paycock"; Ambassadors', Mar., 1938, Mrs. Fogarty in "Moonshine"; "Q," Dec., 1938, Aunt Judy in "John Bull's Other Island"; Mercury, Jan., 1939, Widow Quin in "The Playboy of the Western World"; "Q," June, 1939, Mrs. Gogan in "The Plough and the Stars"; Duchess, Jan., 1940, Mrs. Vanderbilt in "The Golden Cuckoo"; Strand, Apr., 1941, The Nurse in "Under One Roof"; Lyric, Oct., 1941, Mary in "The Nutmeg Tree"; Prince's, Feb., 1943, Mistress Murphy in "Old Chelsea"; St. Martin's, Feb., 1945, Bessie Clary in "Laura"; Phoenix, Aug., 1945, Louise in "Kiss and Tell"; toured, 1946, in "The Shop at Sly Corner"; Embassy, Mar., 1948, played Nellie the Post in "The Righteous Are Bold"; Watergate, July, 1950, Maurya in "Riders to the Sea" and Mary Byrne in "The Tinker's Wedding"; entered films, 1934, in "Sing As We Go," and has since appeared in numerous pictures. *Address:* 40 Redcliffe Square, S.W.10. *Telephone No.:* Flaxman 3436. (*Died 2 Nov., 1952*)

O'NEILL, Nance, actress (*née* Gertrude Lamson); *b.* Oakland, California, 8 Oct., 1874; *m.* Alfred Hickman; made her first appearance on the stage, at the Alcazar Theatre, San Francisco, under the management of McKee Rankin, 16 Oct., 1893, in "Sarah"; subsequently toured in "The Danites"; after playing "stock" engagements at Los Angeles and Denver, went on tour in "The Snowball," and "The Private Secretary"; made her first appearance in New York, at Weber and Fields' Theatre, 7 Dec., 1896, in "The Long Strike"; at Murray Hill Theatre, 21 Dec., 1896, she played Anna Dunning in "True to Life"; during 1897 she appeared at this house, playing the leading parts in "The Danites," "Leah," "Led Astray," "Camille," "East Lynne," "Jim the Penman," etc., etc.; in 1898 she toured in California as Juliet, Rosalind, Viola, etc.; made her first appearance on the London stage, at the Shaftesbury Theatre, 27 June, 1899, as Leah in "The Jewess" ("Leah"), meeting with great success; she returned to America and subsequently played such parts as Magda, Fédora, and La Tosca; in Mar., 1900, she started on a tour of the world, and opened in that month at Sydney, N.S.W.; subsequently she proceeded to England, and made her reappearance on the London stage at the Adelphi, on 1 Sept., 1902, as Magda; subsequently she played here in "Camille" and "Elizabeth, Queen of England," but was not successful, and shortly afterwards returned to America; she has since played successfully in the principal cities of the United States in such plays as "Judith of Bethulia," "Magda," "Hedda Gabler," "The Fires of St. John," "Macbeth," "The Jewess," "The Sorceress," "Monna Vanna," etc., etc.; at Atlantic City, Apr., 1907, appeared in the title-*rôle* of "Cleo," and in May opened a six weeks engagement at San Francisco, where, among other parts, she played Magda, Parthenia in "Ingomar," etc., etc.; during 1907 she also appeared in "vaudeville," in a condensed version of "The Jewess"; at the Majestic Theatre, New York, Oct., 1908, played Agnes in a play of that name; at the Stuyvesant Theatre, New York, Dec. 1909, played Odette de Maigny in "The Lily"; during 1910 played in a number of English music halls, as Lady Macbeth in the sleep-walking scene from " Macbeth " ; during 1912 played a " stock " season at Boston, appearing as Nancy in " Oliver Twist," Leah, Trilby, and Thaïs in the plays bearing those names ; appeared in " vaudeville," in " Joan of Arc," in Sept., 1912 ; at Wallack's, New York, Mar., 1913, played the title-*rôle* in " Anne Boyd " ; at the Fifth Avenue Theatre, Apr., 1913, appeared in " The Worth of a Man " ; at Richmond, Va., May, 1913, played in " The Lily " ; during 1913-14, toured in " vaudeville," in " Self-defence " ; at Pittsburgh, Oct., 1914, played lead in " Bella Donna," " Cousin Kate," " Her Own Money," etc. ; at the Manhattan Opera House, New York, Feb., 1917, played Huldah in " The Wanderer " : at the Palace, New York, Jan., 1919, played in " The Common Standard " ; at the Greenwich Village, New York, Jan., 1920, appeared as Raimunda in " The Passion Flower," and toured in this, 1920-1 ; at the Greek Theatre, California University, Aug., 1924, played Hamlet, with great success ; at the Belasco, New York, Dec., 1925, played Anne de Bernois in " Stronger than Love " ; Belmont, Apr., 1927, Hester Penny in " Fog-Bound " ; Maxine Elliott Theatre, Oct., 1927, Julia Shane in "The House of Women" ; during 1931-2, toured in "Lysistrata " and "The Passion Flower" ; at the Mayan Theatre, Hollywood, Feb., 1934, appeared as Victoria Van Brett in "Double Door" ; Lyceum, Feb., 1935, the Mother in "Bitter Oleander" ; Westport, Conn., July, 1935, Abigail Adams in "The Long Frontier" ; Booth, New York, Nov., 1935, Agatha Payne in "Night in the House" ("The Old Ladies") ; at summer theatres, July, 1937, Comtesse Rochecourt in "The Lady of La Paz " and Mrs. Dudgeon in "The Devil's Disciple" ; Opera House, Central City, Denver, July, 1938, the Duchesse du Albuquerque in " Ruy Blas" ; Ogunquit, Maine, July, 1938, Mrs. Conway in " Time and the Conways" ; at summer theatres, 1939, Marty Owen in " Anna Christie" ; toured, July, 1946, as Queen Margaret in " Richard III " ; commenced

film career 1929, in " The High Road," and has appeared in numerous pictures since that date.
(Died 7 Feb., 1965; age 90)

O'NEILL, Norman, composer and conductor ; *b.* London, 14 Mar., 1875 ; *s.* of G. B. O'Neill and his wife Emma Stuart (Callcott) ; *e.* London and Frankfort-on-Main ; *m.* Adine Ruckert ; his first composition for the theatre, was the incidental music to " After All," at the Avenue Theatre, 1902 ; also composed the incidental music for Martin Harvey's production of " Hamlet," 1905 ; " King Lear," Haymarket, 1909 ; " The Blue Bird," Haymarket, 1909 ; " The Gods of the Mountain," Haymarket, 1911 ; " The Golden Doom," Haymarket. 1912 ; " The Pretenders," Haymarket, 1913 ; " Through the Green Door " (fairy play) ; " Julius Caesar," St. James's, 1920 ; " Mary Rose," Haymarket, 1920 ; " Macbeth," Aldwych, 1920 ; " The Merchant of Venice," New York, 1922 ; " Punch and Judy " Ballet, Duke of York's, 1924 ; " R.S.V.P." Vaudeville, 1926 ; " Potinière Revue," Little, 1926 ; " The Ivory Door," Haymarket, 1929 ; was musical conductor at the Haymarket, 1908-19 ; St. James's 1919-20, Haymarket 1921 to 1932. *Club :* Savage. *Address :* 4 Pembroke Villas, W.8. *Telephone No. :* Western 3069.
(Died 3 Mar., 1934; age 58)

OPENSHAW, Charles Elton, dramatic author ; has written the following plays: " Three Days," 1924 ; " Blessed Are the Rich " (with James Agate), 1925 ; " All the King's Horses," 1926 ; " Payment," 1928 ; "Scapegoat," 1931 ; "The Shadow Princess," 1933 ; "The Convict" (adaptation of "Great Expectations "), 1935.

OPP, Julie ; *b.* New York City, 28 Jan., 1871 ; *e.* in a convent at New York ; *m.* William Faversham ; was originally a journalist in New York, and contributed articles to a number of magazines ; coming to London in 1896, she was engaged by George

Alexander for the St. James's, and made her first appearance on the stage at that theatre, 2 Dec., 1896, as Hymen in " As You Like It "; she was also engaged as understudy to Julia Neilson, and had the opportunity of playing Rosalind during the run of " As You Like It "; she appeared at the St. James's on 29 Mar., 1897, as Mrs. Ware in " The Princess and the Butterfly," subsequently playing the Princess Pannonia in the same play; she crossed to America to play the latter part, and made her first appearance in New York at the Lyceum, 23 Nov., 1897; at the same theatre, 8 Mar., 1898, she appeared as Adelaide in a play of that name; she returned to England, and re-appeared at the St. James's on 1 Feb., 1900, as Rosa Holf in " Rupert of Hentzau," she subsequently appeared at this theatre in a number of parts, among them the following: Antoinette de Mauban in " The Prisoner of Zenda," Mrs. Egerton in " The Man of Forty," Annabel East in " The Wisdom of the Wise," Mrs. Herbertson in " The Awakening," and Edith Thorold in " The Wilderness "; returning to New York in 1901, she appeared at the Criterion Theatre, August 19th, 1901, as Marita in " A Royal Rival "; at the Criterion, New York, 22 Oct., 1901, as Eleanor Laird in " Prince Charlie "; returned to London, and re-appeared at the St. James's, Sept., 1902, as Katharine in " If I Were King "; again returned to America and since then she has played Lady Algernon Chetland in " Lord and Lady Algy," Hilda Gunning in " Letty," and during the autumn of 1906 appeared with her husband in " The Squaw Man "; at Boston, 12 Feb., 1907, she played Donna Teodora in " The World and his Wife "; appeared at Daly's, New York, 2 Nov., 1908, in the same part; on 15 Jan., 1909, played Antoinette in " The Barber of Orleans "; at the Lyric, New York, 26 Oct., 1909, played Marianne in " Herod "; at Daly's, New York, 16 Jan., 1911., appeared as Lady Alexandra Vancey in " The Faun "; subsequently toured in the same play; at the

Lyric, New York, 4 Nov., 1912, played Portia in " Julius Cæsar," and subsequently toured in the same part. Is the authoress (with Kate Jordan) of a one-act play, entitled " The House of Pierre," produced by Mr. Martin Harvey, at Dublin, Nov., 1907. *Recreations :* Riding and farming. *Address :* 214 East 17th Street, New York City; or The Old Manor Chiddingfold, Surrey, England. *(Died 8 Apr., 1921; age 50)*

O'RAMEY, Georgia, actress; *b.* Mansfield, Ohio, 31 Dec., 1886; *e.* Oberlin College; *m.* Robert B. Griffin; made her first appearance on the stage as a violinist, in " vaudeville," Dec., 1905; subsequently appeared at Fischer's Theatre, San Francisco, 1906, in the " stock " company, where she remained eighteen months: at Broad Street, Philadelphia, 1907, played in " Spangle," subsequently toured with Richard Golden in " The Tourists "; made her first appearance in New York, at the Circle Theatre, 20 Jan., 1908, as Hazy Fogg in " Lonesome Town "; appeared at Maxine Elliott's Theatre, Dec., 1908, as Alithea de Morelos in " The Chaperon "; at the Astor Theatre, Nov., 1909, played Kit McNair in " Seven Days," and subsequently toured in this, 1910–11; at the Liberty Theatre, 1911, played in " Uncle Sam "; at Daly's, New York, Nov., 1912, played Polly Gasford in " The Point of View "; at the Princess, Mar., 1913, the Operator in " The Switchboard "; at the Winter Garden, Oct., 1914, appeared as Tillie in " Dancing Around "; at Atlantic City, May, 1915, as Martha Gardner in " See My Lawyer "; at the New Amsterdam, New York, Nov., 1915, as Lulu Cachou in " Around the Map "; Sept., 1916, as Maimie Stone in " Miss Springtime "; at the Longacre Theatre, Aug., 1917, as Flora Wiggins in " Leave it to Jane "; at Chicago, Mar., 1919, played in " The Velvet Lady "; at Philadelphia, Apr., 1920, played Pansy in " Oui, Madame "; made her first appearance in London, at the London Pavilion, 4 Sept., 1920, in " London, Paris, and New York," scoring an immediate success; at the Apollo, New York, Aug., 1922, played Gertie in " Daffy Dill " ; at the Globe, New York, Mar., 1923, Mrs. Malone in " Jack and Jill " ; at Chicago, 1924, Lucille in " No, No, Nanette ! " *(Died 2 Apr., 1928; age 42)*

ORCZY, Emmuska, Baroness, dramatic author and novelist ; *b.* Tarnäors, Hungary ; *d.* of Baron Felix Orczy ; *e.* Paris and London ; *m.* Montagu Barstow ; author of " The Scarlet Pimpernel " (with her husband), 1905 ; " The Sin of William Jackson," 1906 ; " Beau Brocade," 1908 ; " The Legion of Honour," 1920 ; is the author of several romantic novels. *Address :* Villa Bijou, Monte Carlo, France. *(Died 12 Nov., 1947; age 80)*

ORD, Robert, dramatic author ; penname of Mrs. W. Gayer Mackay ; collaborated with her late husband in the following plays : " Dr. Wake's Patient," 1904 ; "The Port Arms," 1909 ; " A Midnight Visitor," 1911 ; " A Thief," 1914 ; " The Prize," 1915 ; " Paddy the Next Best Thing " (from Gertrude Page's novel), 1920 ; was for many years an actress, under her maiden name of Edith Ostlere.

ORD, Simon, manager ; *b.* Muirhouselaw, Scotland, 15 Feb., 1874 ; *s.* of the late John Ord and his wife Jane Reid (Dodd) ; *e.* preparatory schools, and at Monkton Combe and Geneva ; was formerly engaged in ranching, prospecting, and mining in British Columbia ; entered the theatrical profession in 1898, as manager for Ben Greet's Company ; subsequently engaged in a managerial capacity with the late Frank Curzon, Laurence Irving, Arthur Bourchier, etc. ; was manager of the Lyceum Theatre, Edinburgh, 1912-14 ; served in the Army, 1915-21 in Mesopotamia, France, and after the Armistice, in India ; awarded the M.C. ; was chief stage-manager for the Pageant of Empire and tattoos at Wembley ; subsequently entered into the management of the Kingsway Theatre, Apr., 1927, when he produced " Marigold," followed by " Thunder on

the Left," 1928 ; " Mrs. Moonlight," 1928 ; " The Autocrat," 1929 ; " The Rising Sun," 1929 ; " The School for Scandal," 1929. *Recreation :* Fly fishing. *Address :* Wendover. Bucks. *(Died 11 May, 1944; age 70)*

ORDONNEAU, Maurice, French dramatic author and librettist ; *b.* Saintes, Charente Inférieure, 18 June, 1854 ; Versailles ; *m.* Hortense Pirotte ; formerly contributed theatrical articles to *Le Gaulois* and *Clarion,* and was for some time dramatic critic to *Le Matin, La Libre Parole,* etc. ; has written the following plays and operas : " L'Heure du Berger," " Les deux Chambres," " Les Parisiens en province," 1883 ; " Les Petites Godin," 1884 ; " Cherchons Papa," " Mon Oncle," 1885 ; " Sergeant d'Amour " (music by Audran), " Maître Corbeau," " La Princesse Columbine " (music by Planquette), 1886 ; " Durand et Durand " (with Valabrégue), " La Fiancée des Verts-Poteaux " (music by Audran), 1887 ; " Miette," " Les Noces de Mdlle. Gamache," 1888 ; " Les Boulinards " (with Valabrégue and Kéroul), 1890 ; " La Plantation Thomassin " (" Too Much Johnson "), " L'Oncle Celestin " (" Baron Golosh," with Kéroul, music by Audran), " La Petite Poncette " (with Hennequin, music by Pugno), " La Vertu du Lolotte," 1891 ; " La Cocarde Tricolore " (music by Planquette), " La Femme du Commissaire " (with Hennequin), 1892 ; " Madame Suzette " (with André Sylvane, music by Audran), " Le Voyage de Berluron " (with Grenet-Dancourt and Kéroul), " Mademoiselle ma femme," 1893 ; " Cousin-Cousine " (with Kéroul, music by Serpette), 1893 ; " Le Marraine de Charley " (adapted from " Charley's Aunt "), " Le Pélerinage," " Fanoche," " L'Article 214 " (with Sylvane), 1894 ; " La Saint-Valentin," " La Perle du Cantal," " L'Ablette," 1895 ; " La Grand Via," " Paris quand-même," " La Falote," " La Poupée " (music by Audran), 1896 ; " Niobe " (adapted from Paulton's play), " L'Auberge du Tohu-Bohu," 1897 ; " L'Agence Crook and

Co.," 1898 ; " Les Sœurs Gaudichard,"
" Les Saltimbanques," 1899 ; " La
Dame du 23," " Le Bon Pasteur "
(" What Happened to Jones "),
" L'Etude Tocasson " (with Vala-
brégue), " Le Curé Vincent " (music by
Audran), 1901 ; " Une Affaire Scan-
daleuse " (with Gavault), 1904 ; " Les
Filles Jackson et Cie " (music by
Clerice), 1905 ; " Les Hirondelles "
(music by Hirschmann), 1907 ; " Le
Jockey Malgre-lui " (with Gavault) ;
" L'Heure de la Bergère," 1908 ;
" La Mome Flora," (with A. Prodels),
1908 ; " La D'Moiselle du Tabarin "
(with A. Alexandre, music by Edmond
Missa), 1910 ; " Trois Amoureuses,"
1912 ; member of the Society of Dra-
matic Authors and Composers ; is a
Chevalier of the Legion of Honour.
Hobby : Motoring. *Address* : 37 Rue
d'Amsterdam, Paris.
(Died Dec., 1916; age 62)

O'REGAN, Kathleen, actress; *b.*
Ireland, 11 Nov., 1903; *d.* of Owen
Melville; *m.* Lieut.-Col. K. A. Plimp-
ton, D.S.O.; made her first appearance
on the stage at Sheffield in 1921, as
Paddy in "Paddy the Next Best
Thing"; toured, 1923, as Maggie
in "Baby Mine," and 1924, as Geral-
dine in "Up in Mabel's Room"; made
her first appearance on the London
stage at the Little Theatre, Mar., 1925,
as Mary O'Connor in " Persevering
Pat "; at Theatre Royal, Bristol, Aug.,
1925, played Kathleen O'Grady in
" Biddy "; Royalty, Oct., 1925, Sara
Tansey in " The Playboy of the West-
ern World "; Nov., 1925, Mary Boyle
in " Juno and the Paycock "; at the
New, June, 1926, succeeded Eileen
Carey as Nora Clitheroe in " The
Plough and the Stars "; Vaudeville,
Mar., 1927, Peggy Scally in " Professor
Tim "; Strand, Oct., 1927, Margarita in
" The Kingdom of God "; Everyman,
Jan., 1928, Mona Mannering in "A
Night in June "; at the New (for the
300 Club), Feb., 1928, made a great
success when she played Laura Sim-
mons in " Young Woodley "; at the
Royalty, Mar., 1928, played Nora in
" Tinker, Tailor ——"; Lyric, Apr.,
1928, Jessie Hurley in " Baby Cy-

clone "; Savoy, July, 1928, took up
her original part of Laura Simmons in
" Young Woodley "; at the Queen's,
June, 1929, appeared in the same part.
at the Criterion, Sept., 1929, succeeded
Yvonne Arnaud as Elizabeth in " By
Candle Light "; Everyman, May, 1930,
played Evelyn Cruise in "The Blue
Coast"; July, 1930, Lady Windermere
in "Lady Windermere's Fan"; Roy-
alty, 1931, Mary Chalfont in "Black
Magic"; Vaudeville, Dec., 1931, Betty
in "Max and Mr. Max"; "Q," May,
1932, Barbara Hanbury in "An
Average Man"; Duchess, June, 1933,
Marjorie Dale in "Eight Bells"; Duke
of York's, Apr., 1935, Joan Gilson in
"And a Woman Passed By"; Royalty,
May, 1936, Mrs. John Farquhar in
"Marriage Settlement"; Arts, Jan.,
1938, Jacqueline in "Beloved"; Strand,
Apr., 1938, Eleanor Pound in "Banana
Ridge"; "Q.," Apr., 1939, Yvonne
Ducroix in "Prison Without Bars";
toured, 1940, in Garrison theatres,
playing Min Lee in "On the Spot,"
Marjorie Dale in "Eight Bells," Betty
Findon in "Ten Minute Alibi," and
Renee in "I Killed the Count";
in 1942, toured as Mrs. Davidson in
"Rain" and made a production of
"Young Woodley," for British National
Films; at Cairo Opera House, 1943,
and 1944, appeared as Pamela Dark
in "Ladies in Waiting," and Julia
Jelliwell in "Springtime for Henry,"
subsequently touring Egypt, in theatres
and in camps; Comedy, London, July,
1947, appeared as Margaret Foley in
"The Crime of Margaret Foley";
commenced film career, 1929, in "Juno
and the Paycock." *Recreations*:
Riding and swimming. *Address*: 25
Cheyne Place, Chelsea, London, S.W.3.
Telephone No.: Flaxman 2262.

ORME, Denise, vocalist, actress;
b. 26 Aug., 1884 ; *o.d.* of Alfred
Smither ; *m.* John Yarde-Buller, 3rd
Baron Churston ; received musical
training at Royal Academy of Music
(scholarship for violin) and Royal
College of Music (scholarship for singing) ; made her first appearance on the
stage at Daly's Theatre, 29 Apr.,
1905, in the chorus of " The Little
Michus " ; in July, 1905, appeared as

Blanche-Marie in the same piece; created title-*rôle* in "See-See," Prince of Wales's Theatre, 20 June, 1906; returned to Daly's, 27 Oct., 1906, to play Illyrine in "Les Merveilleuses"; subsequently appeared at the Palace Theatre, after which she went on tour; at the Hicks Theatre, 3 Oct., 1908, appeared as Marie Marinet in "The Hon'ble Phil"; at the Gaiety, 23 Jan., 1909, played Lady Elizabeth Thanet in "Our Miss Gibbs." *Address:* Hall Place, Bexley. *Telephone:* Bexley Heath 162. *(Died 20 Oct., 1960; age 76)*

ORME, Michael, dramatic author and producer; pen-name of Alice Augusta Greeven; *m.* J. T. Grein, dramatic critic; has written or adapted the following sketches and plays: "Maternité," 1906; "Midsummer Fires" (with J. T. Grein), 1906; "Wedding Bells," 1911; "La Pompadour," 1911; "The Widow and the Waiter," 1915; "Those who Sit in Judgment," 1915; "The Eternal Snows," 1916; "The Woman on the Window-Sill," 1917; "Great Aunt Elizabeth," 1919; "Life's a Game," 1922; "Tiger Cats" (from the French), 1924; "The Folly of Youth," 1925; "Enchantress" (adaptation), 1926; "The Lady of the Camellias" (adaptation), 1926; "The Lonely Road," 1927; "The Eternal Snows," 1928; "Samson and the Philistines" (adaptation), 1928; "Out of the Blue" (adaptation), 1930; has also had much experience as an actress and producer; is film critic to the *Illustrated London News* and *The Sketch*; author of the biography of her late husband, "J. T. Grein," 1936. *Address:* 63 Courtfield Gardens, S.W.5. *Telephone No.:* Frobisher 3654. *(Died 16 July, 1944)*

O'RORKE, Brefni, actor; *b.* Dublin, Eire, 26 June, 1889; *s.* of Frederick O'Rorke and his wife Jane Caroline (Morgan); *e.* Dublin; studied for the stage under his mother; made his first appearance on the professional stage at the Gaiety Theatre, Dublin,

1912, as Broadbent in "John Bull's Other Island"; first appeared in London, at the Court Theatre, 30 June, 1921, as Mike O'Reilly in "Mr. Malatesta"; toured, and appeared in innumerable films during the next eighteen years; at the "Q," June, 1939, played Fluther Good in "The Plough and the Stars"; Mercury, Sept., 1939, Old Mahon in "The Playboy of the Western World," and the same part at the Duchess when the play was transferred; Chanticleer, Dec., 1939, James Quirke in "Hyacinth Halvey," and Thomas Horne in "The Unicorn and the Stars"; Duchess, Jan., 1940, Mr. Bullock in "The Golden Cuckoo"; Golder's Green, Mar., 1940, Dan McEntee in "What Say They?"; Apollo, Aug., 1940, Dr. Jennings in "Margin for Error"; then returned to films; at the Criterion, Sept., 1945, played Sir Lucius O'Trigger in "The Rivals"; first appeared in films, 1918, and has appeared in innumerable pictures. *Favourite parts:* Myles-na-Coppaleen in "The Colleen Bawn," and Dick Dudgeon in "The Devil's Disciple." *Hobby:* Collecting foreign stamps. *Address:* 39 Fairway Avenue, London, N.W.9. *Telephone No.:* Colindale 7267.

OSBORN, Paul, dramatic author; *b.* Evansville, Indiana, U.S.A., 4 Sept., 1901; *s.* of Edwin Faxon Osborn and his wife Bertha (Judson); *e.* University of Michigan (A.B., M.A.,) and Yale University; was formerly engaged as English Master at the University of Michigan; studied playwriting with Prof. George Pierce Baker at Workshop 47; is the author of the following plays: "Hotbed," 1928; "A Ledge," 1929; "The Vinegar Tree," 1930; "Oliver Oliver," 1934; "On Borrowed Time," 1938; "Mornings at Seven," 1939; "Maiden Voyage," 1957; adapted "The Innocent Voyage," 1943; "A Bell for Adano," 1944; "Point of No Return," 1951; "The World of Suzie Wong," 1958; "La Contessa," 1965; author of the films "The Young in Heart," "The Yearling," "Mme. Curie," "East of Eden," "Cry Havoc," "Homecoming," "Portrait of Jennie,"

"Sayonara," "South Pacific," "Wild River," and many others. *Address:* 1165 Park Avenue, New York, N.Y. 10028, U.S.A.

OSBORN, E. W., dramatic critic; *b.* Winthrop, Maine, U.S.A., 24 Oct., 1860; *s.* of Thomas A. Osborn and his wife Marie Frances; *e.* Winthrop, Ashland, Mass., and Auburn, N.Y.; *m.* Ida Birdsall; has been a journalist from the age of twenty, when he joined the staff of the local newspaper at Auburn, and remained there seven years; joined the staff of the *New York Evening World,* 1888; was dramatic editor, 1896-98; literary editor, *New York World,* 1893; dramatic critic of *The Evening World,* 1923-9. *Club:* Newspaper. *(Died 4 May, 1930; age 69)*

OSBORNE, Vivienne, actress; *b.* Des Moines, Iowa, 10 Dec., 1905; *m.* Francis Worthington Hine (mar. dis.); has been on the stage since she was five years of age; appeared in the "stock" company at Spokane, Washington Terr., for five years; at the Belasco, Washington, May, 1917, played in "Dollars and Sense"; appeared at the Standard Theatre, New York, Dec., 1919, as Bessie Van Ashton in "The Whirlwind"; at the Fulton, Apr., 1920, Jean Brent in "The Bonehead"; Maxine Elliott's, Sept., 1921, Frankie Turner in "The Silver Fox"; Cohan, Nov., 1922, Aline de Mar in "The Love Child"; Morosco, Oct., 1923, Climene in "Scaramouche"; Fulton, Feb., 1924, Ruth Webb in "New Toys"; Vanderbilt, June, 1924, The Girl in 'The Blue Bandanna'; Hudson, Feb., 1925, Miss Kane in "Houses of Sand"; Lyric, Apr., 1925, Aloma in "Aloma of the South Seas"; made her first appearance on the London stage, at the Adelphi, 21 May, 1926, in the same part; at the National, New York, Feb., 1927, played Eunice in "Fog"; Selwyn, Apr., 1927, Maria in "One Glorious Hour"; Lyric, Apr., 1928, Lady De Winter in the musical version of "The Three Musketeers"; John Golden, Oct., 1929, Marga Chapman in "Week-End"; Booth,

Mar., 1930, Countess of Rutland in "The Royal Virgin"; Times Square, Oct., 1930, Mrs. Violet Hargrave in "As Good as New"; Playhouse, Oct., 1934, Phoebe Watson in "Order, Please"; commenced film career, 1931, and has appeared in numerous pictures. *Address:* 1324 Miller Drive, Hollywood, Calif., U.S.A.

OSCAR, Henry, actor and director; *b.* Hornsey, 14 July, 1891 ; *s.* of Henry Montague Wale and his wife Florence Emily (Hyatt); *e.* Enfield Grammar School; *m.* Elizabeth Dundas; formerly engaged in the City; made his first appearance on the stage at the Memorial Theatre, Stratford-on-Avon, 1 Sept., 1911, as Snug in "A Midsummer Night's Dream" with the Benson company; the following year joined the Alexander Marsh Shakespearean Company, and 1914 the Edward Compton Comedy Company; during 1915 was engaged with the Paisley Repertory Company; made his first appearance on the West End stage, at the Lyric Theatre, Aug., 1916, as Frank Burroughs in "Romance"; at the St. James's, Jan., 1917, played Renaud in "The Aristocrat"; June, 1917, Mr. Davies in "Sheila"; subsequently, at the Criterion, took up the part of John Ayers in "A Little Bit of Fluff"; at the Coliseum, Feb., 1918, played Antonio in an excerpt from "The Merchant of Venice," with Ellen Terry; during 1918 toured as David Ebbing in "Trimmed in Scarlet," and in a tour of the British Camp Theatres as Richard Chelford in "The Thief": at the New Oxford, Dec., 1918, played Dr. Ribot in "In the Night Watch"; at the St. James's, Jan., 1920, Metellus in "Julius Caesar"; at the New Oxford, Apr., 1920, Binksie in "The Man Who Came Back"; subsequently played Tybalt in "Romeo and Juliet," at the Everyman, and Daniel in the play of that name, at the Gaiety, Manchester, Dec., 1920; at the Globe, Apr., 1921, Bertie Errol in "Knave of Diamonds": joint-organizer with W. Edward Stirling, of the London Players, 1921, and as director and leading man organized and directed Repertory seasons since that date; appeared with the company at the Comédie des Champs-Elysées, Paris, for three months; became joint-director and partner in the Ben Greet Players, 1922; at the Comedy, June, 1924, played John Weston in " Peter Weston "; at the Princes, Oct., 1924, Harold Plevin in " The Blue Peter "; Everyman, Aug., 1925, Fabrizio in " Mirandolina "; St. Martin's, Apr., 1927, The Chronicler in " The White Château "; Globe, Aug., 1927, Geoffrey Stanforth in " Potiphar's Wife "; New, Apr., 1928, Hugo Pash in " Come With Me "; Strand, Nov., 1928, Arthur Logris in " Out of the Sea "; Arts and Garrick, Jan., 1929, Dr. Sutherland in " The Lady With a Lamp "; Haymarket, Aug., 1929, Philip Logan in " The First Mrs. Fraser "; at the Arts, Mar., 1930, and Criterion, Apr., 1930, Torvald Helmer in " A Doll's House "; Arts, July, 1930, Hidoux in " S.S. Tenacity "; Fortune, July, 1931, the Duke in " Measure for Measure "; New, Nov., 1931, Alfred Perry in " The Red Light "; Westminster, Feb., 1932, the Father in " Six Characters in Search of an Author "; St. James's, Apr., 1932, Iago in " Othello "; at the Westminster, Dec., 1932, appeared as the Whale in " Jonah and the Whale "; Lyric, Hammersmith, Apr., 1933, Gabriel Perry in " Wild Justice "; Embassy, July, 1934, the Prince in " My Lady Wears a White Cockade "; Whitehall, Nov., 1934, Lewis Jacklin in " Flowers of the Forest "; Arts, Dec., 1934, Llewellyn Evans in " Glory Be! "; His Majesty's, Feb., 1935, Worcester in " Henry IV " (Part I); Aldwych (for Repertory Players), Nov., 1935, Henry Ross in " Legend of Yesterday "; Ambassadors', Feb., 1936, Derek Huntley in " Out of the Dark," and Apr., 1936, Enoch in " The Future that Was "; Open Air Theatre, July, 1936, the Duke in " As You Like It "; Royalty, May, 1937, Dr. Sporum in " The Good Fairy "; Shaftesbury, Nov., 1937, Earl of Shaftesbury in " Thank You, Mr. Pepys "; Drury Lane, June, 1938, Abdul Hajiz in " The Sun Never Sets "; Playhouse, Aug., 1938, Laurent in " Thou Shalt Not ——"; Hudson, New York, Nov.,

1938, Count Von Laidi in " Waltz in Goose Step "; " Q," London, May, 1939, Lenkheim in " Jitta's Atonement "; Gate, May, 1940, Georges in " Les Parents Terribles "; Phoenix, Aug., 1943, Paroshin in " War and Peace "; Savoy, Mar., 1945, Victor Malassie in " The Assassin "; Apollo, May, 1946, Doc Ritchie in " The Wind is Ninety "; St. Martin's, July, 1946, succeeded Keneth Kent as Descius Heiss in " The Shop at Sly Corner "; Aldwych, Oct., 1946, played Don John in " Much Ado About Nothing "; " Q," Nov., 1946, Sir Daniel Carteret in " Mrs. Dane's Defence "; Embassy, Dec., 1946, Sir Hugh Croft in " Drake's Drum "; Richmond, Jan., 1949, played Graham Blayne in " The White Cliffs," which he also directed; Phoenix, July, 1949, Uncle Ben in " Death of a Salesman "; Saville, Mar., 1950, Manuel Benavente in " The Platinum Set "; St. James's, May, 1951, appeared as Pothinus in "Caesar and Cleopatra," and Philo Canidius in " Antony and Cleopatra "; Saville, May, 1952, played Edmund Taylor in " The Moonraker "; Her Majesty's, Brighton, Sept., 1953, Dr. Charles Baird in " A Chance of Happiness "; Adelphi, July, 1958, acted as *compère* for the six week visit of The Classical Theatre of China; has played on numerous occasions for the Repertory Players, Stage Society, Renaissance Society, etc., and has also directed numerous plays; was on the Council of the Actors' Association in 1919, and assisted in the reorganization of the Association as a Trade Union; subsequently represented the A.A. as delegate at the Trades Union Congress; is a Governor of the Central School of Speech Training and Dramatic Art, N.W.3; was elected to the Council of British Actors' Equity, June, 1939; from 1939–45, was Drama Director of E.N.S.A., and was responsible for all dramatic entertainment in all theatres of war; among the plays he has staged are " Jonah and the Whale," 1932; " Cecilia," " The Brontës," " House of Jealousy," " The Lady of Belmont," " Up in the Air," 1933; " Saturday's Children," " Double Door," " My Lady Wears a White Cockade," " Invitation to a Murder," 1934; " Glory Be! ," " Legend of Yesterday," "Duet by Accident," 1935; "Out of the Dark," "The Future that Was," "Green Waters," 1936; "Climbing," 1937; "Lottie Dundass," "The House of Jeffreys," 1942; "The Man in Possession," 1951; entered films, 1932, in "After Dark," and has played in innumerable pictures including: "Lawrence of Arabia," "The Long Ships," etc.; has frequently appeared on television including: "Wild Justice," "The Makropoulos Secret," "Hamlet," "Epitaph For a Spy," "Front Page Story," and in many series; he has also broadcast on sound radio; author of "Flowers for Two," 1932. *Favourite parts:* Hamlet, and Gabriel Perry in "Wild Justice." *Recreations:* Rambling, painting, and sports. *Club:* Savage. *Address:* 48 Esmond Road, Bedford Park, W.4. *Telephone No.:* Chiswick 1725.

(Died 28 Dec., 1969; age 78)

OUGHTON, Winifred, actress; *b.* London, 1890; *d.* of David Oughton and his wife Anna (Edwards); *e.* James Allen's Girls' School; was formerly engaged as a schoolmistress; made her first appearance on the stage at the Old Vic., Sept., 1915, walking on in "The Merchant of Venice"; remained at that theatre until Mar., 1920, and during the war period had the unique experience of playing over seventy men's parts in most of Shakespeare's plays, including Justice Shallow, Osric, Gonzalo, Bishop of Carlisle in "Richard II," etc.; first appeared in the West End at the Comedy (for the Play Actors), July, 1921, as Mrs. Wippell in "The Parish Watchman"; from 1924–30 was engaged almost continuously with Dame Sybil Thorndike and Lewis Casson, beginning at the New Theatre, 1924, with "Saint Joan"; appeared at Ambassadors', Mar., 1925, as Minnie Huxtable in "The Madras House"; Wyndham's, May, 1925, as Bee Drennan in "The Round Table" and Miss Pinsent in "The Lie"; at the Empire, Dec., 1925, in "Henry VIII"; Lyceum, Mar., 1926, in "Saint Joan"; Prince's, Dec., 1926, in "Macbeth"; Lyric, Hammersmith, Sept., 1927–Jan., 1928, played the Widow in "The Taming of the Shrew," Margaret in "Much Ado

About Nothing," Alice in "Henry V"; Strand, Feb., 1928, Miriam in "Judith of Israel"; in 1928 toured in South Africa; Wyndham's, Apr., 1929, Miss Pym in "Mariners"; Arts, July, 1930, Mrs. Marling in "Dance With No Music"; Globe, Jan., 1931, Gunning in "The Improper Duchess"; Nov., 1931, Julia in "And So To Bed"; Lyric, Nov., 1932, Helen in "Another Language"; Adelphi, Oct., 1933, Edith Sandford and Feliza in "Nymph Errant"; Shaftesbury, May, 1934, Dolly in "The Dark Tower"; Globe, June, 1935, Lady Maddox in "Grief Goes Over"; Playhouse, Dec., 1935, Katharine Ashley in "Mary Tudor"; Cambridge, July, 1936, Mrs. Terence in "Night Must Fall"; Aldwych, June, 1937, Mrs. Fairfax in "Jane Eyre"; Lyceum, Aug., 1937, Janet in "Wanted for Murder"; "Q," June, 1938, Daisy in "The Little Stranger"; toured in Scandinavia, 1938, as Lady Bracknell in "The Importance of Being Earnest"; Old Vic., Mar., 1939, the Hostess in "The Taming of the Shrew"; Criterion, May, 1939, Mary Sandeman in "Grouse in June"; Lyric, Oct., 1941, Griffin in "The Nutmeg Tree"; Playhouse, Liverpool (for the Old Vic), 1942–3, played the Actress in "Six Characters in Search of an Author," Megaera in "Androcles and the Lion," and Mrs. Lincoln in "Abraham Lincoln"; Lyric, Oct., 1944, Mrs. Proudie in "Scandal at Barchester"; Embassy, Feb., 1945, Miss Willoughby in "Quality Street"; Piccadilly, May, 1947, Mrs. Durbeyfield in "Tess of the D'Urbervilles"; St. Martin's, Oct., 1949, Nanny in "Before the Party"; Duchess, Aug., 1958, Miss Bennett in "The Unexpected Guest"; part-author of two plays, "Wuthering Heights" and "Little Women," 1948; a teacher of acting at the Royal Academy of Dramatic Art, 1935–58; has also appeared in numerous films and made frequent radio and television appearances. *Recreation:* Gardening. *Address:* Hathaway, Surrey Gardens, Effingham, Surrey. *Telephone No.:* East Horsley 445.

(Died 26 Dec., 1964; age 74)

OULD, Hermon, F.R.S.L., dramatic author, poet, and journalist; *b.* 14

Dec., 1885; has written the following among other plays: "Between Sunset and Dawn," 1913; "Christmas Eve," 1919; "The Dance of Life," 1925; "The Moon Rides High," 1929; "Hoppla" (translated from the German), 1929; "The Light Comedian," 1930; "The Shadow and the Substance," 1934; "New Plays from Old Stories"; has also published many other plays, verse, and books, and has contributed freely to the periodical Press; author of "The Art of the Play," 1938 (revised edition, 1948); general-secretary of the P.E.N., the International Association of Writers; was joint-editor of "Theatre Craft," and was a co-founder of the Curtain Group and Peoples' Theatre Society. *Clubs:* Savile, English Speaking Union, and P.E.N.; is a Fellow of the Royal Society of Literature, and Chevalier de la Légion d'Honneur. *Address:* 1 Saint John's Gardens, London, W.11. *Telephone No.:* Park 5868. *(Died 21 Sept., 1951; age 65)*

OUSPENSKAYA, Maria, actress; *b.* Tula, Russia, 29 July, 1876; made her first appearance on the stage with the Moscow Art Theatre company, under Stanislavsky; appeared in many famous Russian plays, including "The Three Sisters," "The Cherry Orchard," "The Brothers Karamazov," "The Lower Depths," etc.; made her first appearance in New York, with the Moscow Art Theatre company, at the 59th Street Theatre, Jan, 1923, in "Tsar Fyodor Ivanovitch"; subsequently appeared with Richard Boleslawsky at the Laboratory Theatre; first appeared in an English-speaking part, at the Greenwich Village Theatre, 11 Oct., 1924, as Paris Pigeons in "The Saint"; Plymouth Theatre, Feb., 1926, played Fiametta in a revival of "The Jest"; Greenwich Village, Nov., 1926, Herlofs-Marte in "The Witch"; Garrick, Oct., 1927, Curtis in "The Taming of the Shrew"; Ethel Barrymore, Dec., 1931, played Fraulein in "The Passing Present"; Shubert, Feb., 1934, Baroness von Obersdorf in "Dodsworth"; Ritz, Nov., 1935, Emma in

"Abide With Me"; 44th Street, Oct., 1936, Polymnia in "Daughters of Attreus"; 48th Street, Nov., 1943, played Mrs. Harris in "Outrageous Fortune"; first appeared in films, 1936, in "Dodsworth"; founded her school of acting in New York, 1931, and in Hollywood, 1939. *(Died 3 Dec. 1949; age 62)*

OVEREND, Dorothy, actress; *b.* Melbourne, Victoria, Australia; *d.* of Dr. E. K. Overend and his wife Effie (Caldwell); *e.* Melbourne; *m.* Claud Allister; studied for the stage at the Royal Academy of Dramatic Art; made her first appearance on the stage at Sunderland, Nov., 1912, as Laura Murdoch in "The Easiest Way"; toured in "Passers-By," "Raffles," "Nobody's Daughter," 1913–14, under her own management, in conjunction with her husband; during the war, toured for the N.A.C.B. through all the camps, playing lead in "Outcast," "Billeted," "French Leave," "Oh! I Say," "A Pair of Silk Stockings," etc.; made her first appearance on the London stage, at Wyndham's Theatre, 29 Mar., 1921, as Irma Peterson in "Bull-Dog Drummond"; at the Strand, May, 1922, played Constance Damer in "Tilly of Bloomsbury"; at the Haymarket, Mar., 1923, Lady Massingham in "Isabel, Edward, and Anne"; at Drury Lane, Sept., 1923, Rose Collett in "Good Luck"; went to New York, 1925, and appeared at the Ritz, Nov., 1925, as Lucy Stapleton in "The Offense"; Forrest, Jan., 1927, Kathryn Peters in "Lady Alone." *Recreations:* Motoring and tennis.

OVERMAN, Lynne, actor; *b.* Maryville, Missouri, U.S.A., 19 Sept., 1887; *s.* of William James Overman and his wife Dora Alice (Johnson); *e.* Blees Military Academy, and Missouri University; *m.* Emily Helen Drange; was formerly engaged as a jockey; had had some amateur experience prior to making his first appearance on the professional stage at the Academy of Music, Milwaukee, 4 Nov., 1907, as Toby in "Out of the Fold"; subsequently toured with Ward and

Wade's Minstrels; for two years toured as Chick Sewell in "The Boys of Company B"; subsequently toured in "The Wolf," and with Robert Edeson in "Classmates"; played "stock" engagements at New Haven, Milwaukee, Providence, Denver, San Francisco, Jersey City, Brooklyn, etc.; made his first appearance in New York, at the Harris Theatre, 1916, succeeding John Cumberland as Billy Bartlett in "Fair and Warmer"; subsequently played in "A Prince of To-night," "The Honeymoon Trail," "A Stubborn Cinderella," "Oh! Boy"; at the Forty-eighth Street Theatre, Apr., 1919, played Charley Carter in "Come On, Charley"; at the Cohan and Harris Theatre, May, 1920, played David Graham in "Honey Girl"; also played in "Top Hole," "The School Belles"; at the Comedy, New York, Apr., 1921, played Robert Adams in "Just Married"; played for two years in "vaudeville," both in sketches and as a single turn; made his first appearance in London, at the Comedy, 15 Dec., 1924, as Robert Adams in "Just Married"; at the Queen's, Feb., 1926, played Sam Harrington in "The Hottentot"; at the Mansfield, New York, Apr., 1927, Danny Grundy in "The Gossipy Sex"; 48th Street Theatre, Nov., 1927, Jeffrey Osborne in "People Don't Do Such Things"; Imperial, Feb., 1928, Maurice Vane in "Sunny Days"; again appeared in London, at the Apollo, Apr., 1929, when he played Norman Beckwith in "Little Accident"; on returning to America, appeared at Syracuse, July, 1929, as Slim Sherman in "Slim Sherman, U.S.A."; Bijou, New York, Oct., 1929, played Button in "Button, Button"; Belasco, Aug., 1930, Lord Robert Brummell in "Dancing Partner"; Lyceum, Apr., 1931, Mr. Janney in "Company's Coming"; at Providence, Oct., 1931, Thomas Madison in "Stella Brady"; Ziegfeld, Mar., 1932, Hap. Wilson in "Hot-Cha!"; at Baltimore, Sept., 1932, Peter Harper in "The Budget"; during 1933, toured in "Peggy, Be Careful," and "Beware of the Bull"; at Newark, N.J., Sept., 1933, played Peter in "Farewell Performance"; entered films, 1934, in "Midnight," and has since played in innumerable pictures; since 1936, has appeared in "The Charm School" ("Collegiate"), "Poppy," "Yours for the Asking," "Three Married Men," "Jungle Princess," "Don't Tell the Wife," "Hotel Haywire," "Partners in Crime," "Night Club Scandal," "True Confession," "Her Jungle Love," "Hunted Men," "Spawn of the North," "Men with Wings," "Persons in Hiding," "Union Pacific," etc.; author (with Le Roy Clemens) of "After the Rain," 1923. *Recreations:* Horses and Riding, and Hockey. *Address:* c/o Paramount Pictures Inc., 5451 Marathon Street, Hollywood, Cal., U.S.A.

(Died 19 Feb., 1943; age 55)

OWEN, Catherine Dale, actress; *b.* Louisville, Kentucky, U.S.A., 28 July, 1900; *d.* of Robert Owen and his wife Reba (Dale); *e.* Nashville, Tenn., and Chestnut Hills, Pa.; studied for the stage at the American Academy of Dramatic Art; made her first appearance on the stage at the Lyceum, New York, 1920, in "Little Women"; Sept., 1921, toured as Tillie Welwyn in "Happy-Go-Lucky"; Maxine Elliott Theatre, Dec., 1921, played Delaney McCloud in "The Mountain Man"; appeared at the Thirty-ninth Street Theatre, New York, Nov., 1922, as Nina Rossmore in "The Bootleggers"; at the Punch and Judy, Mar., 1923, played Gertrude Lamont in "The Love Set"; Bijou, Aug., 1923, Letty Lythe in "The Whole Town's Talking"; Knickerbocker, May, 1925, Clara de Foenix in "Trelawney of the Wells"; Lyceum, Sept., 1925, Mrs. John Weldon in "Canary Dutch"; Little, Jan., 1926, Tze-Chi and Evelyn in "The Love City"; made her first appearance on the London stage, at the Strand Theatre, 7 Sept., 1926, as Norma Lythe in "The Whole Town's Talking"; at the Henry Miller, New York, Nov., 1926, played Ilona Szabo in "The Play's the Thing"; during 1927, toured in "The Silent House"; Liberty, Oct., 1928, Glory in "Mr. Moneypenny"; 46th Street Theatre, Mar., 1932, played Norma Landis in "Happy Landing"; at the Capitol, Albany, May, 1933, Lura Roland in

"Hard-Boiled Angel"; commenced film career, 1927, in "The Forbidden Woman," and has since appeared in "His Glorious Night," "The Rogue Song," "Strictly Unconventional," "Such Men Are Dangerous," "To-day," "Behind Office Doors," "Born Reckless," "In Defence of the Law," etc. *Address:* 316 West 79th Street, New York City, U.S.A. *Telephone No.:* Endicott 2–8417.
(Died 7 Sept., 1965; age 65)

OWEN, Harold, dramatic author; *b.* Burslem, Staffs, 3 May, 1872; has written the following plays : " A Little Fowl Play," 1912 ; " Mr. Wu " (with H. M. Vernon), 1913 ; " Such is Life," 1916 ; " Loyalty," 1917 ; " The Man who Missed the War," 1918 ; " Father-hood," 1925 ; " A Man Unknown," 1926 ; was a journalist for many years, and for some time was engaged on the *Manchester Guardian, Daily Despatch,* and *Daily Mail. Address:* 47 Norbiton Avenue, Norbiton. ˮ *phone No.:* Kingston 2533.
(Died 10 May, 1930; age 58)

OWEN, Harrison, dramatic author; *b.* Geelong, Victoria, Australia, 24 June, 1890; *s.* of Albert Thomas Owen and his wife Elizabeth Ann (Swin-dells); *e.* privately; *m.* Esther Dyson; was dramatic critic of the *Daily Herald,* Melbourne; went to London 1920; has written the following plays: "The Gentleman in Waiting," 1925; "The Happy Husband," 1927; "Dr. Pygmalion," 1932; author of "The Mount Marunga Mystery," "Tommy-rot Rhymes," etc. *Recreations:* The theatre, reading, and golf. *Address:* Gloucester Cottage, Collingham Road, S.W.5. *Telephone No.:* Frobisher 4909.

OWEN, Reginald, actor; *b.* Wheat-hampstead, 5 Aug., 1887; *s.* of J. Fenwick Owen; *m.* (1) Lydia Bil-brooke (mar. dis.); (2) Mrs. Harold Austin (dec.); (3) Mrs. Barbara Haveman; prepared for the stage at Tree's Academy of Dramatic Art; win-ner of the first Bancroft Gold Medal for acting, 1905; made his first appear-ance professionally at His Majesty's, Jan., 1905, in " The Tempest " : subsequently played Guildenstern in " Hamlet," Oatcake in " Much Ado About Nothing," Sebastian in " Twelfth Night," Harry Seabrook in " Captain Swift," Simple in " The Merry Wives of Windsor," Tom Chit-ling in " Oliver Twist," Cyril Jackson in " The Man Who Was," The Slave in " Nero," Sebastian in " The Tempest," Francis in " King Henry IV" (Part I), Henry Percy in "Richard II," Captain Hallock in " Colonel Newcome," etc., under the same management; next joined F. R. Benson's company for a time, gaining further experience in Shakespearean repertoire; at the St. James's, Nov., 1907, appeared as Harry Leyton in "The Thief"; at the same theatre, May, 1908, played Rev. Mr. Trist in "The Thunderbolt"; at the Duke of York's, Dec., 1908, played Mr. Darling in "Peter Pan"; at the St. James's, Feb. 1909, played Horace Glyn and Fritz von Tarlenheim in " The Prisoner of Zenda "; in Apr., 1909, appeared as Henry Steele in " Colonel Smith," and in May, 1909, as Von Weddel in " Old Heidelberg " ; at the Globe, Nov., 1909, played Patrick Moore in " The Great Mrs. Alloway "; was next engaged at His Majesty's, Apr., 1910, as Sir Andrew Aguecheek in " Twelfth Night," and Sept., 1910, to play Cromwell in " King Henry VIII "; at the Little Theatre, Apr. 1911, appeared first as Mr. Gunn in " Fanny's First Play," and subsequently as Bobby ; at the Haymarket. June, 1911, played Thahn in " The Gods of the Mountain "; at the Play-house, June, 1911, appeared as Lieutenant John Sayle, R.N., in " Pomander Walk "; at the Coronet, Sept., 1911, played Raymond in " Madame X "; at the Prince of Wales's, Oct. 1911, played Pedro Gonzalez in " The Uninvited Guest " ; at the Savoy, Dec., 1911, appeared as St. George of England in " Where the Rainbow Ends "; at Drury Lane, Apr., 1912, played Messala in " Ben Hur "; at the Queen's, Nov., 1912, Captain Harte in " Sylvia Greer ˮ ;

at the Shaftesbury, Feb., 1913, Louis Gigoux in " Oh ! Oh !! Delphine !!! " ; at the Haymarket, June, 1913, Sebastian Dayne in " Elizabeth Cooper " ; at the Comedy, Nov., 1913, Stuart Capel in " A Place in the Sun " ; at the St. James's, Mar., 1914, Tommy Owen in " A Social Success " ; Sept., 1914, Tom Forbes in " Those Who Sit in Judgment " ; in Nov., 1914, toured as Roderick Collingwood in " A Butterfly on the Wheel " ; at the Savoy, Feb., 1915, Harry Blaine in " Searchlights " ; at the Coliseum, June, 1915, played in " Always Tell Your Wife " ; at His Majesty's, Oct., 1915, appeared as Sidney Montague in " Mavourneen " ; at the Strand, May, 1916, as Charles in " The Girl from Upstairs " ; served in the Army, 1916-19 ; after the war appeared at the Kingsway Theatre, Dec., 1919, as George Guerand in " In the Night " ; at Wyndham's, May, 1920, succeeded Leon Quartermaine as Robert Dalman in "The Choice"; New, Dec., 1922, played Major Arnold Darenth in " The Great Well " ; at the Haymarket, June, 1923, Bertie Capp in " Success " ; at the Globe, Sept., 1923, Gilbert Paxton in " Our Betters"; at the Blackstone Theatre, Chicago, Oct., 1924, played Prince Albert in "The Swan"; Sam H. Harris Theatre, New York, Nov., 1925, played Captain Manderville in "The Carolinian"; Guild Theatre, Feb., 1926, Alfred Allmers in " Little Eyolf " ; in Mar., 1926, toured with Cyril Maude in " These Charming People " ; Comedy, May, 1926, Algernon Moncrieff in " The Importance of Being Earnest " ; Henry Miller, Nov.. 1926, Almady in " The Play's the Thing "; Liberty, Oct., 1927, Parrish Weston in " Skin Deep" ; Biltmore, Nov., 1927, Esteban in " The Marquise "; Lyric, Mar., 1928, Cardinal Richelieu in " The Three Musketeers "; reappeared in London, at the Globe Theatre, Apr., 1929, as Victor Conway in "The Stag"; on returning to New York, appeared at the Empire, Sept., 1929, as Prince Rudolf in "Candle Light"; Booth, Feb., 1930, played Dr. Neumann in "Out of a Blue Sky"; subsequently, in San Francisco, played Von Echart in "Caprice," and also played in "The

Crimson Hour" ; at the Opera House, Providence, Nov., 1930, appeared in his own play, " Jack's Up " ; Empire, New York, Dec., 1930, played Reggie Melcombe in "Petticoat Influence"; Manhattan, Jan., 1932, John Carteret, in "Through the Years"; Fulton, Mar., 1932, Otto Vanderkill in "Child of Manhattan"; commenced film career, 1929, in "The Letter," and has since appeared in innumerable pictures, recent films include: "Five Weeks in a Balloon," 1962; "The Thrill of It All," 1963; "Mary Poppins," 1964; after an absence of 17 years, reappeared on the stage at New Haven, Aug., 1950, as Philip Russell in "Affairs of State," and played the same part at the Royale, New York, Sept., 1950; toured, Mar., 1959, as Colonel Barstow in "Not in the Book"; at the Shubert, New Haven, Mar., 1960, played Sir Robert Balchion in "Goodwill Ambassador"; is part-author of "Where the Rainbow Ends," 1911; "The Joker," 1915; "The Jolly Family" (with Bertha Hope), 1929. *Address:* 488 Saint Pierre Road, Bel Air, Los Angeles, Cal., U.S.A. *Telephone No.:* 472-7713.

OYRA, Jan, dancer ; *b.* Warsaw, Poland, 8 Mar., 1888 ; *s.* of Josef Wojcieszko ; *e.* Russian ballet school, Warsaw ; made his first appearance at the age of six at the Eldorado, Warsaw, as Cupid in ballet ; first appeared in London at Daly's Theatre, 17 Jan., 1911, in the revival of " A Waltz Dream " ; also appeared at the Gaiety, Apr.. 1913. and toured in the United States as Doddie in " The Girl on the Film " ; first appeared on the variety stage at the Palace Theatre, and has also appeared at the Coliseum, etc. ; at the Adelphi Theatre, Nov., 1915, played in " Tina " ; appeared at the Alhambra, Jan., 1916, in " Now's the Time " ; at the Palace, Nov., 1916, in " Vanity Fair " ; June, 1917, in " Airs and Graces " ; at the Gaiety, Dec., 1917, appeared as the Spirit of Hashish in " The Beauty Spot " ; subsequently went to Paris; appeared at the Casino de Paris, New York,

Jan., 1926, in " A Night in Paris "; Winter Garden, Nov., 1927, in " Artists and Models "; is a teacher of dancing. *Recreations :* Inventing and sports.

PAGE, Austin, dramatic author; has written the following plays: "By Pigeon Post," 1918; "The Beating on the Door," 1922; "The Devil in Bronze," 1929; "Hocus Pocus," 1932.

PAGE, Norman, actor and producer; *b.* Nottingham; *s.* of Alice (Barker) and Arthur Page, F.R.C.O.; *e.* Trent College, Nottingham; *m.* Amy Lamborn; was formerly engaged as an artist; prepared for the stage by the late Sarah Thorne, at the Theatre Royal, Margate; made his first appearance on the stage at the Opera House, Chatham, 7 Mar., 1896, walking on in "The Green Bushes"; with Miss Thorne he played over two hundred parts, of every description; made his first appearance on the London stage at the Court Theatre, under the Vedrenne-Barker management, 23 Dec., 1904, as the Gardener's Boy in "Prunella"; played in nearly all the pieces produced under that management 1904-8; was engaged at His Majesty's, 1908-9, playing Launcelot Gobbo in "The Merchant of Venice," the Clown in "Twelfth Night," Sir Hugh Evans in "The Merry Wives of Windsor," Gravedigger in "Hamlet," Hans in "Faust," Charles in "The Dancing Girl," etc.; at the Haymarket, Dec., 1909, played the Cat in "The Blue Bird"; June, 1910, played Mr. Price in "Priscilla Runs Away"; Feb., 1911, Mr. Twidle in "All that Matters"; Mar., 1911, John in "Lady Patricia"; Nov., 1912, Mr. Leadbitter in "The Younger Generation"; at this theatre he produced "The Gods of the Mountain," "James and John," etc., went to Australia, 1912, to produce "The Blue Bird"; after returing to London, appeared at the Shaftesbury, Dec., 1913, as Thomas Salter in "In and Out"; at the Comedy, May, 1914, as Zacharias in "The Holy City"; at the Haymarket, May, 1914, Alfred in "The Silver Lining"; at the Kingsway,. Nov., 1914, as Private Cantle in "The Dynasts"; Feb., 1915, Bobby in "Fanny's First Play"; at the New Theatre, Apr., 1915, Arthur Smith in "The Joker"; at His Majesty's,

Jan., 1916, Herbert Dix in "Mrs. Pretty and the Premier"; at the Garrick, June, 1916, Aaron Kelp in "Bluff"; at the Coliseum, July, 1916, Hiram Bennett in "The Great Redding Street Burglary"; during 1917 produced several playlets at the Coliseum, and several plays for Miss Horniman, at the Gaiety, Manchester; at the Comedy, Aug., 1918, played Ellis in "The Knife"; during 1919 principally engaged with acting for the cinema stage; at the Gaiety, Manchester, Dec., 1919, appeared in "Through the Green Door"; in Apr., 1920, appointed producer to Arthur Bourchier at the Strand Theatre; produced "Tiger! Tiger!" June, 1920; "At the Villa Rose," July, 1920, in which he played Perrichet; "The Storm," Nov., 1920, in which he played Jacques Fachard; "A Safety Match," Jan., 1921, playing Jacob Entwhistle and Bob Atkinson; "The Trump Card," Aug., 1921, playing Colonel Brimston-Gower; Dec., 1921, at the King's, Hammersmith, again appeared as Tylette in "The Blue Bird"; at the Comedy, Sept., 1922, played Bob in "Secrets"; at the Duke of York's, Dec., 1922, and Garrick, Dec., 1923, again played in "The Blue Bird"; Duke of York's, Sept., 1925, played Cyrus Monroe in "De Luxe Annie"; Garrick, Dec., 1925, again played Tylette in "The Blue Bird"; Apollo, Dec., 1926, Billycat in "Puss in Boots"; Kingsway, Mordan in "Marigold"; Royalty, Mar., 1928, Andrew Bligh in "Tinker, Tailor ——"; Vaudeville, May, 1928, Moreau in "The House of the Arrow"; "Q," Aug., 1929, Humphrey Temple in "Portrait of a Lady"; Comedy, Sept., 1929, again played Bob in "Secrets"; Lyric, Hammersmith, Apr., 1930, Samuel Dummidge, in "Out of the Blue"; Haymarket, Mar., 1931, the Second Gravedigger in "Hamlet"; Daly's, Apr., 1931, Karl Von Pumpernick in "The Belle of New York"; Cambridge (for the "G" Club), Oct., 1932, Mr. Whitty in "Well, Gentlemen ——?"; is a well-known producer, and in this capacity was responsible for "Running Water," 1922; "Secrets," 1922; "The Piccadilly Puritan," 1923; "The Flame," 1924; "Bachelor Husbands," 1924; "Clogs to Clogs," 1924; "The Thief," "The Lavender Ladies," "De Luxe Annie," 1925; "Summer Lightning," "This Woman Business," "The White Witch," 1926; "Marigold," "Fresh Fruit," 1927; "Tinker, Tailor ——," "The House of the Arrow," 1928; "The Autocrat," "Portrait of a Lady," 1929; "A Christmas Carol " and " A Pantomime Rehearsal," 1930; "Cock Robin," 1931; "Common Folk," "Well, Gentlemen ——?," 1932; is also engaged as instructor at the Royal Academy of Dramatic Art. *Recreations*: Work, billiards, and scene painting.

(Died 4 July, 1935; age 59)

PAGE, Philip P., dramatic and musical critic and author; *b.* St. Alban's, Herts, 17 July, 1889; *s.* of Thomas Gowland Page and his wife Frances (Major); *e.* Brasenose College, Oxford (Classical Scholar, and Bridgeman Essay Prize); *m.* Olive Cherry (mar. dis.); while at Oxford, took part in several O.U.D.S. productions, and was on the staff of the *Isis*; was appointed musical critic of *Daily Graphic*, 1910; dramatic critic, *Daily Graphic*, 1911; joined *Daily Sketch* as dramatic critic and social and literary editor, 1913; musical critic and writer of theatrical notes, *Evening Standard*, 1922; dramatic critic, *Sunday Express*, 1923; dramatic critic, *Evening Standard*, 1931–34, *The Sphere*, 1931; *Sunday Referee*, 1936; *Daily Mail*, 1938–45; *Truth*, 1945; literary critic, *Daily Mail*, 1939; has done much general journalism and has acted as Paris correspondent; part-author of "The Smith Family," 1922; composer of "Mr. and Mrs. M.P.," 1923; author of "Life of Chopin," 1924; has composed music for several pantomimes; is an Hon. Member of the Critics' Circle. *Recreations*: Music, and long voyages in cargo boats. *Clubs*: Carlton, Garrick, Buck's, and Savage. *Address*: Savage Club, 1 Carlton House Terrace, London S.W.1.

PAGE, Rita, actress and vocalist; *b.* London, 16 Aug., 1906; *d.* of James Francis Leighton Page and his wife Louise (Petersen); *e.* St. Mary's College, Barnes; *m.* G. Melville Cooper; studied for the stage at the Royal Academy of Dramatic Art; made her first appearance on the stage at the Prince's Theatre, 2 Dec., 1916, as Winnie in "Bluebell in Fairyland"; at the Scala, Dec., 1919, appeared as one of the children in "Fifinella"; having completed her education, and studied at the R.A.D.A., where she was a Silver Medallist, at the Ambassadors', May, 1923, understudied Dorothy Minto in "A Piccadilly Puritan"; at His Majesty's, Sept., 1923, played Alder in "Hassan"; Kingsway, June, 1924, appeared in "Yoicks"; at the London Hippodrome, Oct., 1925, understudied June in "Mercenary Mary," and at the Palace, performed the same office for Binnie Hale in "No, No, Nanette"; Prince of Wales's, Dec., 1926, played Susan Remington in "Happy-Go-Lucky"; in 1927, toured the provinces as Peggy Ann in the play of that name; Prince's, Nov., 1928, played Dora Wynne in "Funny Face"; Dominion, Oct., 1929, Babs Bascomb in "Follow Through," and subsequently succeeded Ada May as Angie in the same piece; Comedy, Mar., 1930, played Betty Strange in "Odd Numbers"; Prince Edward, Apr., 1930, Dolly in "Rio Rita"; Streatham, Aug., 1930, Lolette in "The Red Dog"; New, Oct., 1930, Ernestine Muche in "Topaze"; Daly's, Nov., 1930, Judy Blair in "Little Tommy Tucker"; Coliseum, Apr., 1931, Ottoline in "White Horse Inn," which she played for a year; Daly's, Feb., 1932, Dudley in "San Toy"; Little, June, 1932, Molly Mellish in "Intimate Relations"; at the Empire, Liverpool, Dec., 1933, played Alice in "Dick Whittington"; Saville, London, Aug., 1934, Peggy Rivers in "She Shall Have Music —"; has also appeared in pictures, notably in "Let's Love and Laugh" and "Aren't We All?" *Recreations*: Swimming, golf, motoring, and dancing.

(Died 19 Dec., 1954; age 48)

PAGE, Tilsa, actress; *b.* Stoke Poges, Bucks., 14 Apr., 1926; *d.* of Edwin Harold Stubbs and his wife Joyce Adeline (Satow); *e.* Cranley

Court, Gerrard's Cross; *m.* Donald Duff Mackay; studied for the stage at the Cone-Ripman College, where she trained as a dancer; made her first appearance on the stage at the Strand Theatre, 24 Dec., 1941, as Pease-blossom in "A Midsummer Night's Dream"; toured, 1942, with Donald Wolfit's company; Prince's, Feb., 1943, appeared as a dancer in "Old Chelsea"; Phoenix, Nov., 1943, in "Arc de Triomphe"; Stoll, Oct., 1944, in "The Lisbon Story"; toured, 1944, as Corliss Archer in "Kiss and Tell," and appeared in that part at the Phoenix Theatre, Aug., 1945; Saville, Feb., 1946, played Susan Paige in "Stage Door"; Embassy, Apr., 1946, Velvet Brown in "National Velvet"; "Q," Sept., 1946, Judy in "The Rocking Horse"; during 1947, appeared at the Theatre Royal, Windsor; Duchess, Aug., 1947, played Dinah Linden in "The Linden Tree," which ran for a year; Wyndham's, Feb., 1949, Penelope in "Sweethearts and Wives"; St. Martin's, June, 1949, Nancy Gear in "The Young and Fair"; Bedford, Camden Town, Mar., 1950, Elsie Nixon in "Craven House"; Duke of York's, Nov., 1950, Susan Hubbard in "Return to Tyassi"; New Lindsey, May, 1951, played Suzanne Beaker in "The Lonely Heart," and June, 1951, Caroline in "Hand in Glove"; Arts, July, 1951, Jenny in "Poor Judas"; Criterion, Oct., 1951, Margot Kemp in "And This Was Odd"; appeared with the Birmingham Repertory Company at the Alexandra Theatre during the seasons 1952–53; has also appeared in several television plays; first appeared in films, 1948, in "Edward, My Son." *Favourite parts:* Velvet Brown and Dinah Linden. *Recreations:* Music, reading and mountain-climbing. *Address:* c/o M.C.A. (London), Ltd., 139 Piccadilly, London, W.1.; or, Laburnam Cottage, Ruscombe, Stroud, Glos.

PAGET, Cecil, manager; in 1896 was acting-manager at the Grand Theatre, Islington; was manager of the Crown Theatre, Peckham, at its opening in 1898, and remained there several years; in 1913 was business manager at the Queen's Theatre;

subsequently became general manager at Daly's Theatre, and was subsequently licensee of the same house until 1937, when the theatre was demolished.

PAGNOL, Marcel, dramatic author; *b.* Aubagne, Bouches-du-Rhône, France, 1895; was formerly a schoolmaster and professor of English; is the author of the following among other plays: "Les Marchands de Gloire" (with Paul Nivoix), 1925; "Jazz," 1926; "To-paze,"1928; "Marius," 1929; "Fanny," 1931; "Phaëton," 1932; "César," 1946; films include: "Topaze," "Marius," "Fanny," "César," "La Femme du Boulanger," "La Belle Meunière," etc.; was elected a Member of the French Academy, 1947.

PAINTER, Eleanor, actress and vocalist; *b.* Walkerville, Iowa, 1890; *e.* Germany; *m.* Louis Graveure (Wilfred Douthitt) (mar. dis.); made her first appearance on the stage at the Deutsches Opera House, Charlottenberg, as Fatima in "Oberon," and remained in Germany for two years; when "Der Rosenkavalier" was first produced in New York she played the leading part; abandoning grand opera, she appeared at the Forty-fourth Street Theatre, 28 Oct., 1914, as Georgine de Brissac in "The Lilac Domino"; at the Cort Theatre, Sept., 1915, played the Princess di Montaldo in "Princess Pat"; at the Knickerbocker Theatre, Nov., 1917, Pauline Chaverelle in "Art and Opportunity"; at the Liberty Theatre, Oct., 1918, Glorianna Grey in "Glorianna"; at the Century Theatre, Apr., 1920, Dolores in "Florodora"; May, 1921, Vera Lizaveta in "The Last Waltz"; at the George M. Cohan Theatre, Apr., 1923, played Berenice Millet in "The Exile"; at the Lyric, New York, Feb., 1924, Tonita Rovelli in "The Chiffon Girl"; Jolson Theatre, Jan., 1927, Jenny Lind in "The Nightingale." *(Died 4 Nov., 1947; age 57)*

PALADINI, Ettore, Italian actor and manager; *b.* Florence, 1849; *s.* of Francesco Palladini and his wife,

Clotilde (Sacchi) ; has appeared successfully as Lamberti in " Romantismo," " I Buffoni," " Fiamme nell'Ombra," etc. ; formerly toured with his own company ; subsequently director of the Compagnia Argentina, at Buenos Ayres.

PALADINI-ANDÓ, Celestina, Italian actress ; *m.* Flavio Andò ; as far back as 1863, was a leading actress, and for some time conducted her own company ; has appeared successfully with Eleonora Duse and Tina di Lorenzo, in the following, among other plays : " Marcelle," " Le Monde ou l'on s'ennuie," " Dora," " Frou-Frou," " Amants," " Niobe," " Le Moglie d'Arturo," " Adrienne Lecouvreur," " La Bataille des dames," " Andréa," " I Disertori," " I Figli d'Ercole," etc.

PALERME, Gina, actress and dancer ; first came into prominence in London when she appeared at the Adelphi Theatre, 5 Nov., 1910, as Toinette in " The Quaker Girl," followed by her performance of Lili in " The Dancing Mistress," Oct., 1912 ; at the Ambassadors', May, 1914, played in " Plantons les Capucines " ; at the Prince's, Manchester, Dec., 1914, played Chiquette in " Betty " ; at the Palace, Sept., 1915, appeared in " Bric-a-Brac," and Nov., 1916, in " Vanity Fair " ; at the Court Theatre, Feb., 1917, appeared as Benjamine Lapistoke in " La Petite Chocolatière " ; entered on a short period of management at the Duke of York's, Sept., 1919, when she appeared as Jacqueline in " The Girl for the Boy," an adaptation of the previously mentioned play.

PALFREY, May Lever, actress ; *b.* 1 May, 1867 ; *d.* of Dr. James Palfrey ; is a direct descendant of Charles Lever, the famous novelist ; *m.* Weedon Grossmith ; prepared for the stage by Miss Florence Haydon, made her first appearance on the stage at Drury Lane Theatre, 26 Dec., 1889, as the Fairy Peach Blossom in the pantomime " Jack and the Beanstalk " ; appeared at the same theatre, Sept., 1890, as Madame Ribob in

" A Million of Money " ; subsequently appeared at the Shaftesbury, Aug., 1891, in " A Pantomime Rehearsal " ; at the Court, Dec., 1891, played Parker in " A Commission," and appeared at the same theatre in " Rosencrantz and Guildenstern," " Faithful James," " The Guardsman," " Over the Way," etc. ; she then appeared at Terry's, 1894, in " The New Boy " ; at the Vaudeville, she played the leading juvenile parts in " The New Boy," " The Strange Adventures of Miss Brown," " The Ladies' Idol," " The Shopwalker," " Poor Mr. Potton " ; appeared at the Strand, Royalty, Comedy, Globe and Avenue, respectively, in " The Prodigal Father," " Young Mr. Yarde," " A Lady of Quality," " Miss Francis of Yale," and " The Night of the Party," in which she played over 500 times, in London, New York, and the provinces ; in conjunction with Mr. Fred Kerr she produced " Three Blind Mice " on tour, 1906, appearing in the same play, at the Criterion Theatre, Feb., 1907 ; at the St. James's, May, 1908, appeared as Mrs. Ponting in " The Thunderbolt " ; subsequently toured, with her own company, as Mrs. Worthley in " Mrs. Dot " ; at the St. James's, 1909, played in " The Blessings of Balaam " ; at the Shaftesbury, 1910, in " How It's Done " ; at the Kingsway, Oct., 1910, produced " Company for George," but took no part in the piece ; at the Theatre Royal, Bournemouth, Feb., 1918, played Lady Emma Jones in " Lady Emma's Romance " ; at the Coliseum, Apr., 1918, appeared in the same part in an abridged version of the same piece, entitled " Stopping the Breach " ; revived the longer play at the St. James's, May, 1921, when it was re-named " Emma " ; revived " The Night of the Party," at the St. James's, June, 1921 (*Died* 31 Oct., 1929, *age 62*)

PALMER, Barbara, actress ; *b.* Reading, Berks, 22 May, 1911 ; *d.* of Charles Eric Palmer and his wife Gwenllian Salier (Jones) ; *e.* Eastbourne and in France ; *m.* Godfrey Tearle ; for a time studied medicine at London University; studied for the stage at the Royal Academy of Dramatic Art; made her first appearance on the stage on tour, 1934, playing Helen Norton in "Living Dangerously"; "Q," Dec., 1934, played Katherine de Vaucelles in "If I Were King," and during 1936 in "The Great Adventure; Mercury Theatre, May, 1936, appeared as Fountain in "Reverie of a Policeman"; during 1938 toured with Godfrey Tearle as Nurse Ann in "The Amazing Dr. Clitterhouse," and 1939, as Karen Selby in "The Flashing Stream." *Recreations:* Riding and reading. *Address:* Busker's End, Tring, Herts. *Telephone No.:* Tring 251.

PALMER, Charles, dramatic critic; *b.* 9 Sept., 1869; dramatic critic of *The Sun* 1903-6; succeeded the late W. Davenport Adams as the writer of "Plays and Players" in *The Globe,* 1904; appointed dramatic critic of *The Globe,* 1910; also dramatic critic of *The People;* appointed Editor of *The Globe,* 1912.
(Died 25 Oct., 1920; age 51)

PALMER, John, former dramatic critic and author; *b.* 4 Sept., 1885; *s.* of Charles Palmer and his wife Agnes (Wells); *e.* Balliol College, Oxford; *m.* Mildred Hodson Woodfield; was the Dramatic critic of *The Saturday Review* and *The Evening Standard;* author of "The Censor and the Theatres," 1912, and of the one-act play, "Over the Hills," produced at His Majesty's 1912; during the autumn of 1913 published two works, "The Comedy of Manners," and "The Future of the Theatre"; author of "Studies in the Contemporary Theatre," 1926; also author of "Peter Paragon," "The King's Men," "The Happy Fool," "Looking After Joan," "Jennifer"; now attached to the permanent Secretariat of the League of Nations. *Club:* Junior Carlton.
(Died 5 Aug., 1944; age 59)

PALMER, Minnie, actress and vocalist; *b.* in Philadelphia, Pa., U.S.A., 31 Mar., 1857; *e.* at the Convent of the Sacred Heart, Manhattanville, New York; *m.* John R. Rogers; made her first appearance on the stage at the Park Theatre, Brooklyn, 8 June, 1874, in "Le Pavilion Rouge"; first appeared on the New York stage, at the old Lyceum, 13 Mar., 1876, in "Off the Stage"; also appeared at this theatre in "The Pique Family," "The Day After the Wedding," and "Black Eyed Susan" (burlesque); in 1876, at Booth's Theatre, she played the part of Dorothy in "Dan'l Druce"; in 1877, at the Fifth Avenue Theatre, she was Laura in "The Little Rebel"; also played Louise in "The Two Orphans," Gertrude in "The Little Treasure," and Dot in "The Cricket on the Hearth"; at the Park Theatre, Jan., 1878, she appeared in "Risks"; at the Fifth Avenue, June, 1879, she played Minnie Symperson in "Engaged"; and in May, 1880, at the San Francisco Music Hall, Jessie in "The Boarding House"; she played the last-mentioned part for two years; she next appeared as Tina in "My Sweetheart," the play with which she is chiefly identified; she made her first appearance on the English stage in this part at the Princess's Theatre, Glasgow, 4 June, 1883, and made her *début* on the London stage, at the Grand Theatre, Islington, 17 Sept., 1883, in the same part; 14 Jan., 1884, she appeared at the Strand Theatre in the same play; at Tompkins' Fifth Avenue, 29 Apr., 1889, she appeared as Nadine in "My Brother's Sister," and at Her Majesty's Theatre, London, at Christmas, 1889, she appeared as Cinderella; at the Gaiety, 15 Feb., 1890, she played in "My Brother's Sister," subsequently returning to America; at Hermann's, New York, 11 Oct., 1890, she played the title-*rôle* in "Suzette"; at the Grand, Cardiff, 2 Sept., 1895, and at the Standard, London, 14 Oct., 1895, she played Loo in "The School Girl," subsequently touring in the same piece for some considerable period; subsequently she was seen in sketches in the principal variety theatres; returned to America, 1908; reappeared on the stage, after many years absence, at the Gaiety

Theatre, New York, 26 Aug., 1918, when she played Mrs. Jordan in " Lightnin'," which was performed continuously 1,291 times. *(Died 21 May, 1936; age 79)*

PANTER, Joan, actress; *b.* Boreham Wood, Herts, 29 Sept., 1909; *d.* of Gilbert Godfrey Panter and his wife Henrietta Lillian May (Gibbons); *e.* Southwood Hall, Highgate; studied for the stage under Italia Conti, Gwladys Dillon and Mdme. Micklass-Kempmer; made her first appearance on the stage at the Gaiety Theatre, 8 Jan., 1921, as one of the five little ones in "The Betrothal"; Regent, Dec. 1922, played the Fairy in "The Christmas Party"; Victoria Palace, Dec., 1923, the Rose Queen in "The Windmill Man"; His Majesty's, May, 1927, appeared in "White Birds"; Adelphi, Dec., 1927, in "Clowns in Clover"; during 1928 toured in "The Rat"; His Majesty's, July, 1929, in "Bitter Sweet"; Daly's, Sept.–Dec., 1931, Miss Eckroyd in "A Country Girl," and Gudulina in "La Poupée"; during 1933, toured as Catherine in "Casanova," and Kitty Packard in "Dinner at Eight"; Gaiety, Feb., 1935, played Phyllis Featherstone in "Jack O' Diamonds"; Garrick, Oct., 1935, in "Don't Spare the Horses"; Fortune, Dec., 1935, played Lady Rowena in "When Knights Were Bold"; New Theatre, Cardiff, Dec., 1936, Jack in "Jack and the Beanstalk"; Lyceum, May, 1937, Bella in "Paganini"; Adelphi, Oct., 1937, Annette in "The Laughing Cavalier." *Favourite parts.* Kitty in "Dinner at Eight" and Bella in "Paganini." *Recreations:* Swimming, reading, sewing and knitting. *Address:* "Grovelands," Southgate, N.14. *Telephone No.:* Palmer's Green 3636.

PARISH, James, dramatic author; *b.* Northington, Hampshire, 15 Feb.; *s.* of Charles James Parish and his wife Ada Maria (Clouting); *e.* King Alfred's School, Wantage; was an actor for ten years, prior to directing plays at the Rusholme Repertory Theatre, Manchester, and subsequently at the Prince of Wales, Cardiff; commis-sioned in the Intelligence Corps, 1943, and demobilized with the rank of Major, 1946, being mentioned in dispatches; directed a production of "The Apple Cart" for E.N.S.A.; he is also the author of the following plays: "The Flight of the Arrow," "Hangman's Farm," 1932; "Cheapside," 1933; "Distinguished Gathering," 1935; "Goodbye to Yesterday," 1937; "Forty-eight Hours Leave," 1941; "Letters to a Lady," 1945; "Message for Margaret," 1946; "Truant in Park Lane," 1947; "The Lady Asks for Help," 1948; (he also directed the three last-mentioned plays); "Mrs. Inspector Jones," 1950; "The Distant Hill," 1953; "The Night of the Leopard," 1957; "The Woman on the Stair" (originally presented on television under the title "The Witness"), 1959; he also writes for broadcasting and television; is the author of a novel, "The Hour of the Unicorn." *Recreations:* Travel, and talking to strangers.

PARISYS, Marcelle, French actress; made her first appearance on the stage, at the Concert Mayol, Paris, 1916, in the *revue,* "Tout va bien"; has appeared successfully at the Comédie-Marigny, May, 1919, as Lodoiska in "Aladdin"; at the Michel, 1919, in "Saison d'Amour"; at the Capucines, Oct., 1919, in "C.G.T. Roi!"; at the Jeunesse," 1904; "L'amour veille," 1907; "La joie fait peur," "Le Marquis de Villemer," "Le Monde ou l'on s'ennuie," "Les deux Hommes," 1908; "Sire," 1909; "Bagatelle," 1912, etc.; has now retired. *Recreations:* Painting and country life.

PARKER, Anthony, director and author; *b.* Hull, 4 Aug., 1912; *s.* of John Leslie Tull and his wife Margaret Elsa (Parker); *e.* Clifton College; *m.* Diana Marguerite Crosby; formerly an actor, and made his first appearance on the stage at the Devonshire Park Theatre, Eastbourne, 1930, in "Bandits"; first appeared in London, at the Embassy, 1930, as the Third Player in "Hamlet"; in 1939, was Master of the Pageant at Kenilworth Castle; served in the Army, Sept., 1939, to Feb., 1946; demobilized with the rank of Brigade-Major; was acting-manager at the Haymarket Theatre, 1946–7; directed "The Man from the Ministry," 1946; was associated with Peter Mather in the presentation of "The Man from the Ministry," 1946; "1066 and All That," 1947, "Bob's Your Uncle," 1948, and with Molly May, in "Wonders Never Cease," 1948; at the "Q" Theatre, from July, 1949, directed thirteen plays; subsequently, 1950, director at the Theatre Royal, Stratford; in 1953, was Pageant Master of the Warwickshire Coronation Pageant; has adjudicated at numerous Drama Festivals; author of "The Morning After," 1938; "Strange Reality," 1939; "Return My Love," 1949; "Pageants: Their Presentation and Production," 1954; "Let's Do Some Acting," "Great Men of Warwickshire," 1955; "Theatrecraft," 1959; etc. *Recreation:* Writing. *Address:* 18 Pembroke Gardens, W.8. *Telephone No.:* Western 4024.

PARKER, Cecil, actor; *b.* Hastings, Sussex, 3 Sept., 1897; *s.* of Charles Augustus Schwabe and his wife Kate (Parker); *e.* St. François Xavier College, and at Bruges, Belgium; *m.* Muriel Anne Randell-Brown; after being demobilized at the end of the War, made his first appearance on the stage at Devonshire Park Theatre, Eastbourne, Sept., 1922, as Lorenzo in "The Merchant of Venice," with Charles Doran's company, with which he remained until 1924; subsequently played a short engagement with Huddersfield Repertory company, and also at the Abbey Theatre, Dublin; from 1924–6, playing leading parts at the Liverpool Repertory Theatre; made his first appearance on the London stage, at the Everyman Theatre, 28 Dec., 1925, as Holden in "Inheritors," with the Liverpool Repertory company; at the New Theatre, Sept., 1926, played Dr. Churchill in "The Constant Nymph"; during 1927–8, toured in "Interference" and "The Crooked Billet"; appeared at the opening of the Embassy Theatre, Sept., 1928, as David Latimer in "The Yellow Streak" and also played Jack Morris in "The

Seventh Guest"; Vaudeville, Nov., 1928, Justin Kerr in "Clara Gibbings"; Arts, Jan.–Feb., 1929, Gordon in "Full Moon," and George Miles in "The Likes of 'Er"; Arts and Comedy, Apr., 1929, Captain Chesney in "The Infinite Shoeblack"; during 1929–30, toured in South Africa with Mary Clare, in "The Matriarch," "The Squall," and "The Lonely House"; on his return,appeared at the Everyman, July, 1930, as Lord Windermere in "Lady Windermere's Fan"; Lyceum, July, 1930, played Det.-Insp. Osborne in "Traffic," and Nov., 1930, Maurice Hargreaves in "The House of Danger"; Savoy, Dec., 1930, Erbach in "Wonder Bar"; St. Martin's, Aug., 1931, George Brent in "The Young Idea"; Embassy, Sept., 1931, Albert Gregor in "The Makropulos Secret"; St. Martin's, Nov., 1931, Conrad Hanitz in "Lady-in-Waiting"; Embassy, Nov., 1931–Feb., 1932, appeared in a number of productions, and played Mercutio in "Romeo and Juliet"; in Feb., 1932, toured as Preysing in "Grand Hotel"; Comedy, Apr., 1932, Richard Morris in "Faces"; Globe, June, 1932, Bertram Varda in "Men About the House"; Arts, June, 1932, Bill Goring in "As It Was in the Beginning"; in Aug., 1932, toured as Rex Garnett in "Dr. Pygmalion"; Duke of York's, Nov,, 1932, His Excellency in "To-Night or Never"; Haymarket, Jan., 1933, Colonel Livingstone in "Double Harness"; Playhouse, Apr., 1933, Robin Claydon in "The Rats of Norway"; Lyric, Jan., 1934, Dr. Anton Krug in "Reunion in Vienna"; Queen's, Sept., 1934, Gilbert in "Moonlight is Silver"; Comedy, Feb., 1935, Nobby Clark in a play of that name; Whitehall, May, 1935, Philippe Fayard in "Golden Arrow"; Criterion, Sept., 1935; Stephen Buchanan in "Nina"; Playhouse, Apr., 1936, Ralph Dexter in "The Shadow"; Wyndham's, Sept., 1936, Lucien Galvoisier in "Mademoiselle"; Globe, May, 1937, John Middleton in "The Constant Wife"; New, Sept., 1937, Sir Rupert Morellian in "Bonnet Over the Windmill"; St. James's, Jan., 1938, Peter Bingham in "The Innocent Party"; Whitehall, June, 1938, Mr. Lot in "Lot's Wife"; New, Sept., 1938, Colonel Cairns in "Official

Secret"; Savoy (for Repertory Players), Dec., 1938, Digby Grant in "Two Roses"; Strand, Feb., 1939, Sir John Brent in "Little Ladyship"; Criterion, Oct., 1939, Victor in "French for Love"; Piccadilly, July, 1941, York stage at the Music Box, 18 Sept., 1950, as Sir Joseph Pitts in "Daphne Laureola"; at the Globe, London, June, 1953, played Menelaus in "The Private Life of Helen"; has also appeared frequently for the Repertory Players; entered films, 1933, in "The Silver Spoon," and recent films include: "The Man in the White Suit," "Father Brown," "The Constant Husband," "The Court Jester," "The Lady-Killers," "Twenty-three Paces to Baker Street," "A Tale of Two Cities," "Indiscreet," "The Pure Hell of St. Trinian's," "The Amorous Prawn," etc.; television appearances include "The Browning Version" (New York), 1959. *Favourite part:* Charles Condamine in "Blithe Spirit." *Recreations:* Swimming, golf, and gardening. *Club:* Green Room.
(Died 21 Apr., 1971; age 73)

PARKER, Frank, producer and stage director; late equestrian and stage director, London Hippodrome; *b.* 17 Feb., 1864; originally call-boy at the Adelphi Theatre; subsequently stage manager and producer at Drury Lane Theatre, Terry's Theatre, etc.; on the opening of the London Hippodrome, was appointed general producing manager, and remained there until 1909. *Recreations:* Country life, boating. *Club :* Eccentric.
(Died 20 Dec., 1926; age 64)

PARKER, John, editor of "Who's Who in the Theatre," dramatic critic and theatrical journalist; *b.* New York City, 28 July, 1875; *e.* London; *m.* (1) Edith Maud Pizey, *y.d.* of the late Montague Belfield Pizey (*d.* 1942); (2) Doris Mary Sinclair, *y.d.* of George Sinclair; commenced writing in 1892; has contributed numerous articles on theatrical matters to *The Era, Illustrated London News, The Theatre, The Free Lance, New York Dramatic Mirror,*

New York Dramatic News, The Stage, etc.; London manager, critic and Correspondent of *New York Dramatic News,* 1903–20; on the celebration of their stage jubilees by the late Lionel Brough, 1905, and Ellen Terry, 1906, designed and executed in gold, illuminated vellums detailing every part played by those artistes; contributed American biographies to 1907 edition of "The Green Room Book"; Editor "The Green Room Book," 1908-9; compiled "Who's Who in the Theatre," 1912; has compiled and edited each edition to date; has contributed a number of theatrical biographies to each of the supplemental issues of the "Dictionary of National Biography," 1910–49; member of the Society of Dramatic Critics, 1907; member of The Critics' Circle, 1913; Hon. Secretary of the Critics' Circle since 1924; President, 1937–8; represented the Critics' Circle as British Delegate, at the International Congress of Critics, Paris, 1937; Hon. Editor of *The Critics' Circular. Hobby :* Collecting theatrical literature. *Clubs :* Savage, Green Room, and Surrey County Cricket. *(Died 18 Nov., 1952; age 77)*

PARKER, Joy, actress; *b.* London, 22 Feb., 1924; *d.* of Henry Edward Parker and his wife Evelyn Alice (Day); *e.* Surbiton; *m.* Paul Scofield; was a student at the Birmingham Repertory Theatre, where she made her first appearance in 1941; during 1942, appeared with the Windsor Repertory Company; returning to Birmingham, 1943–5, she appeared with the Parks company, in "The Devil's Disciple," "Pygmalion," "The Constant Wife," etc.; during 1946-7, played two seasons with the Shakespeare Memorial company, Stratford-on-Avon, playing Ariel in "The Tempest," the Queen in "Richard II," Jessica in "The Merchant of Venice," Celia in "As You Like It," and Maria in "Love's Labour's Lost"; made her first appearance in London, at His Majesty's Theatre, 2 Oct., 1947, as the Queen in "Richard II," with the Stratford company; Cambridge Theatre, Nov., 1948, played Rosa Olacca in "Home is To-

Morrow"; St. James's, Mar., 1949, Roxana in "Adventure Story"; Arts, Aug., 1949, Rosario in "The Romantic Young Lady"; Oct., 1949, Mashenka in "The Diary of a Scoundrel," and Mar., 1950, Belinda in "The Provoked Wife"; Duke of York's, May, 1950, played Prudence Fenton in "The Hat Trick"; Arts, Dec., 1950, Precious Stream in "Lady Precious Stream"; Lyric, Hammersmith, Apr., 1952, played Felisa in "Montserrat"; at the same theatre, Dec., 1952, the Queen in "Richard II"; Cambridge, Feb., 1954, Miriam Oppenheim in "The Fifth Season"; Fortune, Dec., 1954, the Princess Isobel in "The Marvellous Story of Puss In Boots"; Royal, Brighton, Mar., 1955, Fanny in "The Art of Living"; Arts, Apr., 1958, played The White Princess in "The Imperial Nightingale"; Stratford Shakesperean Festival, Ontario, Canada, June, 1961, played the Princess of France in "Love's Labour's Lost"; appeared in the *Theatre of Performing Arts* television programme (New York), 1962; is the author of a children's book, "The Story of Benjamin Scarecrow." *Recreations:* Painting and writing. *Address:* The Gables, Balcombe, Sussex. *Telephone No.:* Balcombe 378.

PARKER, Lew (*né* Austin Lewis Jacobs), actor; *b.* Brooklyn, N.Y., U.S.A., 29 Oct., 1906; *s.* of Lewis John Jacobs and his wife Florence (Nightingale); *e.* Erasmus Hall, Brooklyn; *m.* Betty Kean; made his first appearance in New York, at the Lyric Theatre, 30 Sept., 1926, in "The Ramblers"; Gallo, Nov., 1928, danced in "The Rainbow"; Alvin Theatre, Nov., 1929, appeared as James Clarke in "Heads Up," and Oct., 1930, as Jake Howell in "Girl Crazy"; directed the national tour of "Girl Crazy," 1931; Alvin Theatre, Oct., 1936, played Deputy Warden Mulligan in "Red, Hot and Blue"; toured, 1940–2, in "Hellzapoppin"; 1944–5, was playing for U.S.O. in the Pacific, entertaining troops; Century Theatre, New York, Nov., 1945, played "Goldie" in "Are You with It?"; Royale, Sept., 1945, Hildy Johnson in a revival of "The Front Page"; made his first

appearance in London, at the King's Theatre, Hammersmith, 7 Apr., 1948, in the *revue*, "Maid to Measure," and appeared in the same piece at the Cambridge Theatre, May, 1948; London Hippodrome, Dec., 1948, played Harrison Floy in "High Button Shoes"; returned to America, 1949, and toured in "Inside U.S.A."; Mark Hellinger, New York, Apr., 1955, appeared as Dinky in "Ankles Aweigh"; Broadway, Mar., 1956, took over as Fred Campbell in "Mr. Wonderful"; East 78th Street Playhouse, Feb., 1964, Arnolphe in "The Amorous Flea"; Las Palmas, Los Angeles, Nov., 1965, again played Arnolphe in "The Amorous Flea." *Address:* c/o Actors Equity Association, 165 West 46th Street, New York, City, N.Y. 10036, U.S.A.

PARKER, Lottie Blair, American dramatic author; *b.* Oswego, N.Y.; *d.* of George Blair and his wife Emily (Hitchcock); *e.* Oswego Normal School; *m.* Harry Doel Parker; was formerly an actress; has written the following among other plays : " White Roses," 1897 ; " 'Way Down East," 1897 ; " Under Southern Skies,' 1901 ; " The Lights of Home," 1903 ; " The Redemption of David Corson " (founded on the novel of that name, 1906).

(Died 5 Jan., 1937; age 78)

PARKER, Louis Napoleon, F.R.A.M., F.R.Hist.S.; Officier de l'instruction publique; dramatic author and composer; *b.* Calvados, France, 21 Oct., 1852; *m.* Georgiana Calder; *e.* Freiburg and Royal Academy of Music (F.R.A.M.), 1898; was Director of Music at Sherborne School, Dorset, for nineteen years, during which period composed numerous cantatas, songs, etc.; resigned in 1892 in order to devote himself to playwriting; has written, translated or collaborated in the following dramatic works: " A Buried Talent," Vaudeville, 1890 ; " Taunton Vale," Manchester, 1890 ; " Love in a Mist," 1890 ; " The Sequel," 1891 ; " Chris," subsequently known as " A Broken Life," and " Captain Burchell's Luck," Vaudeville,

1892 ; " A Bohemian," Globe, 1892 ; " The Love Knot," York, 1892 ; " David," Garrick, 1892 ; " Gudgeons," Terry's, 1893 ; " The Man in the Street," Avenue, 1894 ; " Once Upon a Time," Haymarket, 1894 ; " The Blue Boar," Terry's, 1895 ; " Rosemary," Criterion, 1896 ; " Magda," Lyceum, 1896 ; " Love in Idleness," Terry's, 1896 ; " The Spell-Bound Garden," Brixton, 1896 ; " The Mayflower," Lyceum, New York, 1897 ; " The Vagabond King," Metropole, Camberwell, 1897 ; " The Happy Life," Duke of York's, 1897 ; " Ragged Robin," Her Majesty's, 1898 ; " The Termagant," Her Majesty's, 1898 ; " The Jest," Criterion, 1898 ; " Change Alley," Garrick, 1899 ; " Man and His Makers," Lyceum, 1899 ; " The Sacrament of Judas," Prince of Wales's, 1899 ; " The Bugle Call," Haymarket, 1899 ; " Cyrano de Bergerac," Wyndham's, 1900 ; " The Masque of War and Peace," Her Majesty's, 1900 ; " L'Aiglon," Knickerbocker, New York, 1900 ; " The Swashbuckler," Duke of York's, 1900 ; " The Cardinal," Montreal, 1901 (St. James's, 1903) ; " The Twin Sister," Duke of York's, 1902 ; " The Heel of Achilles," Globe, 1902 ; " Burnside and Co.," Dublin, 1903, produced at Terry's, 1904, as " The House of Burnside " ; " The Optimist," Philadelphia, 1903 ; " The Monkey's Paw," Haymarket, 1903 ; " The Sorceress," Washington, D.C. 1904 ; " Beauty and the Barge," New, 1904 ; " Agatha," His Majesty's, 1905 ; " Everybody's Secret," Haymarket, 1905 ; " The Creole," Haymarket, 1905 ; " The Harlequin King," Imperial, 1906 ; " The Duel," Garrick, 1907 ; " Mr. George," Vaudeville, 1907 ; " Jemmy," Adelphi, 1907 ; " Pete," Lyceum, 1908 ; " Beethoven," His Majesty's, 1909 ; " Pomander Walk," Toronto, 1910 (Playhouse, 1911) ; " Chantecler," Knickerbocker, New York, 1911 ; " Sire," New York, 1911 ; " Disraeli," Montreal, 1911 ; " The Redemption of Evelyn Vaudray," Richmond, Va., 1911 ; " The Woman and the Sheriff," New York, 1911 ; " The Lady of Coventry," New York, 1911 ; " Drake," His Majesty's, 1912 ; " The

Paper Chase," New York, 1912 ; " Joseph and his Brethren," New York, 1913, and His Majesty's, London, 1913 ; " Bluff King Hal," Garrick, 1914 ; " The Highway of Life," New York, 1914, produced at His Majesty's, 1914, as " David Copperfield " ; " Mavourneen," His Majesty's, 1915 ; " The Aristocrat," St. James's, 1917 ; " L'Aiglon " (from the French), Globe, 1918 ; " The Great Day " (with George R. Sims), Drury Lane, 1919 ; " Summertime," Royalty, 1919 ; " Johannes Kreisler " (adapted from the German), 1922, and performed at Drury Lane as " Angelo," 1923 ; " Mr. Garrick," 1922 ; " Arlequin " (adapted from the French), 1922 ; " Our Nell " (with Reginald Arkell), 1924 ; " The Lost Duchess," 1924 ; " The Lily of France," 1936 ; organised pageants at Sherborne, 1905 ; Warwick, 1906 ; Bury St. Edmunds, 1907 ; Dover, 1908 ; York and Colchester, 1909 ; the Pageant of the "Edwards'," in the Lord Mayor's procession, 1907 ; the Pageant of the "City's Men of Letters," in the Lord Mayor's procession, 1908 ; author of the Pageants "Through Toil to Victory," Drury Lane, 1916 ; "The Treasures of Britain," Shaftesbury, Apr., 1918 ; "The Pageant of Freedom," Queen's Hall, 1918 ; "The Pageant of Drury Lane," Drury Lane, 1918 ; also the author of "The Lady of Dreams" and "The Masque of Life"; published his reminiscences, under the title of " Several of My Lives," 1928. *Clubs :* Garrick, R.A.M., Tatlers', Omar Khayyám. *(Died 21 Sept., 1944; age 91)*

PARKER, Thane, manager ; *b.* Long Buckby, Northamptonshire, 25 Sept., 1907; *s.* of George Dancer Thane Parker and his wife Gertrude Elisabeth (Skinner) ; *m.* (1) Dorothy Peacock Drover (mar. dis.) ; (2) Elspeth Dorothea Currie ; was formerly engaged, successively, in the Mercantile Marine, as an interior decorator, and in journalism ; began theatre career as an actor, 1927, and was stage-manager over a period of two years, for Prince Littler, Edgar Wallace and also with Gilbert Miller ; subsequently engaged as stage-manager at the Shaftesbury, Apr., 1934, for " There's Always To-morrow," and was later at the Comedy, Alhambra, and Lyric; Westminster, Sept., 1936, engaged as stage-manager; subsequently appointed the General Manager of the Westminster Theatre, under Anmer Hall, until Apr., 1938; founder member and general manager of the London Mask Theatre, at the Westminster, from Sept., 1938, and was a director of the Company; during the late War, served in the Royal Navy; demobilized, Apr., 1946 with the rank of Lieut.-Commander; he subsequently joined the Arts Council, and was general manager of the Sadler's Wells Ballet at Covent Garden, until the London Mask Theatre was revived in 1947, where he remained as managing director for seven years; at the Westminster, May, 1952, presented "The Trial of Mr. Pickwick"; Lyric, Hammersmith, June, 1960, presented "Innocent As Hell." *Recreations:* Gardening and painting. *Address:* Shepherd's Cottage, Stow-on-the-Wold, Gloucestershire.

PARKS, Larry, actor; *b.* Olathe, Kansas, 13 Dec., 1914; *s.* of Frank Parks and his wife Leona (Klausman); *e.* University of Illinois (B.S.); *m.* Betty Garrett; formerly an usher at Carnegie Hall, a guide at Radio City, and a train inspector for the New York Central Railroad; made his first stage appearance in stock at the Lake Whalom Playhouse, Fitchburg, Massachusetts, summer, 1936; made his New York début at the Belasco, 4 Nov., 1937, in "Golden Boy"; entered films in "Mystery Ship," 1941; reappeared on the stage at the Playhouse, Worcester, Massachusetts, July, 1947, in "A Free Hand"; performed in vaudeville, 1949; made his London début with his wife at the Palladium, 1950, and subsequently played in Glasgow; played in vaudeville at the Casino, Toronto, Canada, May, 1952; Playhouse, Worcester, Massachusetts, July, 1952, played John Moreland in "The Anonymous Lover"; toured, 1955–6, as Sakini in "Teahouse of the August Moon"; Shubert, N.Y., 1958, took over from Sydney Chaplin as Jeff Moss in "Bells Are Ringing";

Royale, 1958, took over from Johnny Carson as Augie Poole in "The Tunnel of Love"; Martin Beck, Feb., 1960, Rafe in "Beg, Borrow, or Steal"; Music Box, Dec., 1963, Jeff Pringle in "Love and Kisses"; toured, 1964–5, as John Cleves in "Any Wednesday"; toured, 1969–70, as Sam Nash, Jesse Kiplinger, and Roy Hubley in "Plaza Suite"; among his numerous films may be noted "Sing for Your Supper," "Blondie Goes to College," "You Were Never Lovelier," "The Jolson Story," "Down to Earth," "Jolson Sings Again," "Freud," etc.; has appeared on television in "The Happiest Day," 1953, "A Smattering of Bliss," 1956, *Suspicion*, etc. *Address:* Actors Equity Association, 165 West 46th Street, New York, N.Y. 10036, U.S.A.

PARNELL, Val (Valentine Charles), manager; *b.* London, 14 Feb., 1894; *s.* of Frederick Thomas Parnell (Fred Russell) and his wife Elizabeth (White); *e.* Godwin College, Margate; *m.* Helen Howell; began his career with the late Sir Walter de Frece in 1907, in a junior capacity, on the managerial side of the De Frece circuit of music-halls; and was subsequently assistant booking manager to the Variety Theatre Controlling Company; was later appointed booking manager, a position he retained with the General Theatre Corporation, Ltd., in 1928, when that company absorbed the Variety Theatre Controlling Company; solely responsible for the policy and all bookings at the London Palladium, 1928–58; appointed general manager of Moss Empires, Ltd., 1931, and in 1941, joined the board of directors; was appointed managing-director, Mar., 1945, in succession to the late George Black; appointed chief executive of Associated Television, Jan., 1956; Managing Director, 1957–62; resigned as managing director of Moss Empires, Ltd., Dec., 1958. *Recreation:* Golf. *Address:* 36 Chester Terrace, London, S.W.1.

PARRY, Sir Edward Abbott (His Honour Judge Parry); dramatic author; *m.* Helen Hart (dec.); called to the Bar 1885; judge of Manchester

County Court from 1895 to 1911; Lambeth County Court, 1911; retired 1927; is the author of the following plays: "England's Elizabeth" (with Louis Calvert), 1901; "Katawampus" (with Louis Calvert), 1901; "What the Butler Saw" (with the late Frederick Mouillot), 1905; "The Captain of the School" (with Mouillot), 1910; "The Tallyman," 1910; "Disraeli," 1916; has also written a number of books, including "Letters of Dorothy Osborne to Sir William Temple," "Life of Macklin," "Katawampus," "The Scarlet Herring," "The Story of Don Quixote," "Pater's Book of Rhymes," etc. *Clubs:* Garrick and Green Room.

(Died 1 Dec., 1943; age 80)

PARSONS, Alan, dramatic critic and journalist; *b.* London, 6 Mar., 1888; *e.* Eton and Magdalen College, Oxford (B.A.); *m.* Viola Tree; was engaged in the Civil Service from 1912-25; was appointed dramatic critic to the *Daily Sketch,* 1925; dramatic critic *Daily Mail,* 1929; author of " A Winter in Paradise." *(Died 15 Jan., 1933 age 44)*

PARSONS, Donovan, lyric writer; *b.* 24 Dec., 1888; *e.* Christ's Hospital; has written lyrics for " Dédé," 1922; " Charlot's Revue," "The Whirl of the World," 1924; " P's and Q's," " 9-11 Revue," " Wildfire," 1925; " Cochran's Revue " (1926), " The Charlot Show of 1926 "; " Jumbles," " Clowns in Clover," 1927; " The House That Jack Built," 1929; author of the book of " Will o' the Whispers," 1928, and, with Mary Parsons, of the *revue* "Paris in London," 1932; author of the film, "East Lynne on the Western Front," 1931. *Club:* Stage Golfing Society. *Address:* 60 Greencroft Gardens, N.W.6. *Telephone No.:* Maida Vale 2822.

PARSONS, Nancie, (née Lady Mercy Greville), actress; *b.* 1904; *d.* of the fifth Earl of Warwick and his wife Frances Evelyn (Maynard); *m.* Basil Dean (mar. dis.); made her first appearance on the stage at the Ambas-

sadors' Theatre, 5 June, 1923, as the Maid in "The Lilies of the Field"; at the Queen's, Nov., 1923, played Felice in "The Little Minister"; Drury Lane, June, 1924, Miss Mountaspen in "London Life"; St. Martin's, Jan., 1925, Connie Gillies in "Spring Cleaning"; New, Apr., 1928, Honor Sandland in "Come With Me"; Wyndham's, Aug., 1928, Lady Adela in "Loyalties"; Garrick, Sept., 1928, Antonia Sanger in "The Constant Nymph."

PARSONS, Percy, actor and vocalist; *b.* Louisville, Kentucky, U.S.A., 12 June, 1878; *s.* of Edward Young Parsons and his wife Mary (Story Belknap); *e.* Louisville; *m.* Natalie Lynn; was formerly a Church and concert singer; studied for the stage at the American Academy of Dramatic Arts; made his first appearance on the stage at Wallack's Theatre, New York, 1904, as General Kee-Otori in "The Sho-Gun," which he played for two years at that theatre, and on tour; at the Garden Theatre, Dec., 1906, played Frederick in "The Student King"; next toured as Colonel Osten in "The Yankee Tourist," and played the same part at the Astor Theatre, Aug., 1907; then devoted four years to concert work; returned to the stage as leading basso, at the New York Hippodrome, where he remained for two seasons, 1912-14; subsequently played Captain Corcoran and Dick Deadeye in "H.M.S. Pinafore"; toured for two years throughout the United States as Nobody in "Everywoman," 1916-17; at the Casino, New York, 1918, played in "Sometime"; made his first appearance in London at the Savoy, 16 Oct., 1919, as Dr. Cusick in "Tiger Rose"; at the Empire, Feb., 1920, played Rustom Khan in "Sunshine of the World," subsequently touring as Nadir, Shah, in the same play; at the Queen's, Apr., 1921, played Huggins in "Mary"; at the Kingsway, Dec., 1922, Vanderbluff in "Polly"; Feb., 1924, Sir Gregory Galhouse in "Kate"; at the New Oxford, Nov., 1924, Zu-far in "The First Kiss"; Adelphi, Feb., 1925, Lurgan in "Love's Prisoner"; Drury Lane, Mar., 1925, Black Eagle in " Rose Marie "; His Majesty's, Sept., 1927, Revenue Officer Jansen in " Oh, Kay! "; Wyndham's, Feb., 1928, Washington Vaughan in " Listeners "; Drury Lane, May, 1928, Vallon in " Show Boat "; Palace, June, 1929, Murphy in " Hold Everything"; Drury Lane, Sept., 1929, again played Black Eagle in "Rose-Marie"; Criterion, Nov., 1930, Horace P. Billing in "General John Regan"; Wyndham's, Dec., 1930, Lieut. Lavine in "Smoky Cell"; Phoenix (for the Venturers), Jan., 1931, Red Kirby in "The Last Mile"; Phoenix, June, 1931, Brannegan in "Late Night Final"; Wyndham's, Aug., 1931, Gilder in "The Case of the Frightened Lady"; Nov., 1931, Ibrahim Abdou Ali in "Port Said"; Lyceum, May, 1934, Mocha in "King of the Damned"; Prince's, Apr., 1936, Joshua Broad in "The Frog," and July, 1937, Valentine in "The Gusher"; Kingsway, Oct., 1938, Bertoldo in "An Elephant in Arcady"; Saville, Feb., 1939, Barney in "Worth a Million"; commenced film career, 1930, in "Suspense," and has appeared in innumerable pictures; since 1936, has played in "Twelve Good Men," "The Gay Adventure," "Everybody Dance," "Blondes for Danger," "Song of the Road," "Victoria the Great," "Climbing High," "The Citadel," etc. *Favourite parts:* Nobody, Dr. Cusick, and Vanderbluff. *Recreations:* Experimental wireless. *Club:* Actors' Equity Association.

(Died 3 Oct., 1944; age 65)

PASSEUR, Stève, dramatic author; *b.* Sedan, 24 Sept., 1899; author of the following plays: "Un Bout de Fil Coupé en Deux," 1925; "Pas Encore," 1927; "L'Acheteuse" ("A Measure of Cruelty"), 1930; "La Chaine," 1931; "Les Tricheurs," "Je vivrai un Grand Amour," "Une Vilaine Femme," 1932; "L'Amour Gai," "La Bête Noire," 1934; "Le Témoin," 1935; "Suzanne," "Le Normand," "La Folle du Ciel," 1936; "Le Château de Cartes"; "Pacifique," 1937; "Vin du Souvenir," 1946; "N'Importe Quoi Pour Elle." *Address:* 25 Avenue Matignon, Paris VIII, France.

(Died Oct., 1966; age 67)

PASSMORE, Walter; actor and vocalist; *b.* London, 10 May, 1867; *m.* Agnes Fraser; *e.* privately; made first professional appearance in 1881, at Sunderland with the Majiltons, as "Cinderella"; was for some years engaged as a pianist, etc., with travelling concert parties; in 1888–9 was with Lieutenant Walter Cole's concert party; subsequently appeared in the provinces in "Round the Clock," and "A Gay City"; also toured with the Milton-Rays in "Kindred Souls," etc.; toured abroad in "Carmen Up-to-Date"; made his first appearance on the London stage, at the Standard Theatre, Bishopsgate, 24 May, 1890, in "The Flying Scud"; first appeared in the West End, at the Savoy, 13 May, 1893, as Greg in "Jane Annie"; remained at the Savoy for ten years, during which period he built up a solid reputation as a singing comedian of the first class; appeared there as Tarara in "Utopia, Ltd.," Bobinet in "Mirette," Grigg in "The Chieftain," General Boom in "The Grand Duchess," The Devil in "The Beauty Stone," Boodel in "His Majesty," Hassan in "The Rose of Persia," King Ouf in "The Lucky Star," Rudolph in "The Grand Duke," Professor Bunn in "The Emerald Isle," Walter Wilkins in "Merrie England," Puck in "A Princess of Kensington," besides playing the following parts in revivals of the famous Gilbert-Sullivan operas; Koko in "The Mikado," Jack Point in "The Yeomen of the Guard," Don Alhambra in "The Gondoliers," John Wellington Wells in "The Sorcerer," the Usher in "Trial by Jury," Sir Joseph Porter in "H.M.S. Pinafore," the Sergeant of Police in "The Pirates of Penzance," Bunthorne in "Patience," the Lord Chancellor in "Iolanthe"; on quitting the Savoy, he appeared at the Adelphi, Dec., 1903, as Jim Cheese in "The Earl and the Girl"; at the Lyric, Jan., 1905, played Jerry Snipe in "The Talk of the Town"; Aug., 1905, Private Charlie Taylor in "The Blue Moon"; appeared at Drury Lane, Dec., 1905, as the Baroness in "Cinderella"; at the Apollo, Apr., 1906, played Sam Brudenell in "The Dairymaids"; at Drury Lane, Dec.,

1906, as Sinbad in the pantomime ; at the Shaftesbury, May, 1907, appeared as Seth Lewys in " Lady Tatters " ; at the Apollo, Aug., 1909, Garibaldi Pimpinello, in " The Three Kisses," and at Drury Lane, at Christmas, 1907, the Boy Babe, Reggie, in " The Babes in the Wood " ; at the Queen's Theatre, Oct., 1908, played Baptiste Boubillon in " The Belle of Brittany " ; in 1909, toured as Walter Wilkins in " Merrie England," and as John Smith and Simplicitas in " The Arcadians " ; at His Majesty's, with the Beecham Opera Company, July, 1910, played Frank in " Die Fledermaus " ; at the Hippodrome, Dec., 1910, played Baron Bantam Bad-Egg in " The Chicks in the Wood " ; at the Whitney Theatre, Apr., 1911, appeared as Nikola in " Baron Trenck " ; subsequently toured in " Sweet Williams," and 1912, in " Queer Fish " ; at the Shaftesbury, Feb., 1913, played Alphonse Bouchotte in " Oh ! Oh !! Delphine !!! "; at the Woolwich Hippodrome, July, 1914, played Private Adam Blinder in " The Soldiers' Mess," of which he was also the composer ; during 1914-15 toured in the same part in variety theatres, and in " Ducks and Quacks " ; at Daly's, Dec., 1916, played Tom Moon in " Young England " ; at the Empire, New Cross, May, 1917, appeared in " Follow the Flag " ; at the St. James's, Jan., 1918, played Gastricus in " Valentine"; subsequently toured as Jotte in " Betty " ; at the Hippodrome, Newcastle-on-Tyne, Dec., 1918, played Tom in " Petticoat Fair," and toured in this during 1919 ; at the Hippodrome, Liverpool, Dec., 1919, appeared as Tim Grogan in " Too Many Girls," and toured in this during 1920 ; subsequently toured as Mooney in " The Purple Lady " ; at the Empire, Mar., 1921, played Solomon Hooker in " The Rebel Maid " ; in 1922, toured with his own *revue* " Titbits " ; during 1923 toured as Bené Ben in " The First Kiss " ; at the Gaiety, Apr., 1924, played Jericho Mardyke in " Our Nell " ; in July, 1924, went on tour playing Calicot in " Madame Pompadour "; during 1928 toured as Chubby in " Princess Charming " ;

during 1929 toured as Count Theodore Volny in "The Damask Rose," and appeared at the Savoy, Mar., 1930, in the same part.

(Died 29 Aug., 1946; age 79)

PASTON, George (Miss Emily Morse Symonds), dramatic author and novelist ; d. of the Rev. Henry Symonds ; has written the following plays : " The Pharisee's Wife," 1904 ; " Clothes and the Woman," 1907 ; " Feed the Brute," 1908 ; " Tilda's New Hat," 1908 ; " The Parents' Progress," 1910 ; " The Naked Truth " (with W. B. Maxwell), 1910 ; " Nobody's Daughter," 1910 ; " Stuffing," 1910 ; " The Kiss " (adapted from the German), 1910 ; " Colleagues," 1911 ; " The Conynghams," 1913 ; " In and Out " (from the French), 1913 ; " Divorce While You Wait (with Francis Coutts), 1915 ; " A Great Experiment," 1916 ; " The Dawn," 1916 ; " Gold-Fields " (from the French), 1920 ; " When Adam Delved," 1927 ; " The Theatre of Life " (from the French), 1929 ; is the author of the following, among other novels : " A Modern Amazon," " A Bread and Butter Miss," " The Career of Candida," " A Study in Prejudices," " A Writer of Books," etc. ; also author of "Lady Mary Wortley Montague and Her Times," "Mr. Pope, His Life and Times," "At John Murray's." *Recreations :* Motoring and reading.

(Died 11 Sept., 1936)

PATCH, Wally, actor ; b. London, 26 Sept., 1888 ; s. of James Edward Vinnicombe and his wife Mary ; e. St. Augustine's School, Kilburn ; m. Emmeline Bowmer ; made his first appearance, on the music-hall stage, 1912, appearing in numerous acts and sketches for many years ; first appeared on the regular stage in London, at Drury Lane Theatre, 9 June, 1938, as Sergeant Hopkins in "The Sun Never Sets"; toured, 1939, as Bill Grant in "Alf's Button"; Duchess, July, 1942, played 'Oppy Parker in "Lifeline"; again toured, 1943, in "Alf's Button"; toured, 1944, as Henry Blore in "Ten Little Niggers"; Cambridge, Oct., 1944, played Private

Bronson in "Happy Few"; toured, 1946, as Bates in "The Sport of Kings"; Embassy, July, 1946, Wally Etheridge in "Grim Fairy Tale"; "Q," Apr., 1947, Sergt. Bell in "Those Were the Days"; toured, 1947–8, as George Palfrey in "Peace Comes to Peckham"; Richmond, Jan., 1949, Drake in "The White Cliffs"; toured, 1950, as Bill Summertop in "The Magic Cupboard"; Whitehall, Sept., 1950, Sergt. Bell in "Reluctant Heroes" (previously entitled "Those Were the Days"), in which he continued to appear until 1953; toured, from Apr., 1953, as Sgt. Mild in "Tell the Marines"; subsequently returned to the cast of "Reluctant Heroes"; toured, from June, 1954, as Dusty Bates in "Not So Dusty," which he wrote in collaboration with Frank Atkinson; toured, 1955, in "Tropical Fever"; toured, 1956, as Jim Drew in "This Happy Home," and also toured as Dugdale in "Time, Murderer, Please"; Victoria Palace, June, 1958, played Pringle in "You, Too, Can Have a Body"; Theatre Royal, Stratford, Oct., 1959, Sparta in "Make Me An Offer," subsequently transferring with the production to the New, Dec., 1959, and later touring with the company; Garrick, 1961, took over the part of Tubby in "Fings Ain't Wot They Used T'Be," which he played for one year; first appeared in films, 1919; first appeared on television, 1937. *Recreation:* Swimming. *Club:* Stage Golfing Society. *(Died 27 Oct., 1970; age 82)*

PATEMAN, Robert, actor; *b.* 17 Oct., 1840; *m.* (1862) Bella Theodore; made his first appearance on the stage in 1841, at the age of six months, at the Theatre Royal, Cork, being carried on in the farce, "Mr. and Mrs. Peter White"; for some years played children's parts in the provinces, and acted with Macready, Charles Kean, Charles Dillon, Charles Pitt, Barry Sullivan, etc.; subsequently played "stock" seasons at Birmingham, Bristol, Manchester, Hull, York, etc., prior to sailing for the United States in 1869; made his first appearance in New York at the Theatre Comique, 14 June, 1869, as Ivan in "Tiddle-

winki," and in the farce "Turn Him Out"; subsequently appeared with the late Edwin Booth and Dion Boucicault at Booth's Theatre, where he played in the "stock" company for four years; in Sept., 1874, opened at the California Theatre, San Francisco, as Harvey Duff in "The Shaughraun," remaining there two years; made his first appearance in London, at the Olympic Theatre, 30 Sept., 1876, as Carrigue in "The Duke's Device"; also appeared at this theatre, as "Scum" Goodman in "Lady Clancarty," in "Sli Slocum," "Raising the Wind," "The Scuttled Ship," "Lady Audley's Secret," "The Moonstone," etc.; at the Adelphi, 1878-80, played with Adelaide Neilson, Dion Boucicault, etc.; rejoined Edwin Booth in America the next year, and also appeared with him at the Adelphi, 1882; in 1884, at the Opéra Comique, with Lotta, played Quilp in "The Old Curiosity Shop," Mr. Grimstone in "Old Flames," Tulkinghorne in "Lady Dedlock's Secret," The Major in "Nitouche"; at the Olympic, 1885, played Sigurd in "The White Pilgrim"; at the Adelphi, 1885, appeared as Michael Feeney in "Arrah-Na-Pogue"; at the Haymarket, 1885, played in "Dark Days"; in 1886, played in "Nadjesda"; at Drury Lane, Apr., 1886, appeared as Joe Lambkin in "Human Nature," and at Christmas played Cassim in "The Forty Thieves"; at the Comedy, Apr., 1887, appeared as Ivan Zazzulic in "The Red Lamp"; toured as Jagon in "The Grip of Iron," 1888; at Manchester, July, 1888, played Jean de Lussac in "Hands Across the Sea," also playing the same part at the Princess's; during 1889 toured as Humpy Logan in "Master and Man"; played the same part at Princess's, Dec., 1889; during 1891 toured as Cyrus Blenkarn in "The Middleman"; during 1892-3 toured in "Master and Man"; at the Gaiety, Dec., 1893, played the Lieutenant in "Don Juan"; at the Avenue, Mar., 1895, appeared as Koko Gaga in "Dandy Dick Whittington"; at the Duke of York's, Jan., 1896, appeared in "The Fool of the Family"; at the Princess's, Apr., 1896, played

Aleem Khan in " The Star of India " ; during 1896-7 toured with Olga Nethersole in " Carmen," " Camille," " The Wife of Scarli," " Denise," etc. ; at Drury Lane, Sept., 1898, played Morris Longman in " The Great Ruby " ; at the Adelphi, Aug., 1899, appeared as Lotan Hackett in " With Flying Colours " ; and May, 1900, as Chilo Chilonides in " Quo Vadis ? " during 1901 toured in the United States with Charles Hawtrey as the Tramp in " A Message from Mars " ; at the Prince of Wales's, 1902, played Don Pedro in " The President " ; in 1904, was engaged by Beerbohm Tree to play Zakkuri in " The Darling of the Gods," on tour ; at the Court, Feb., 1905, appeared as A Tramp in " The Pot of Broth " ; in 1905, toured as Kleschna in " Leah Kleschna " ; at the Lyric, Aug., 1906, played Tomasso Alfieri in " The Sin of William Jackson " ; at Terry's, Feb., 1908, played John Reeves in " The Lord of Latimer Street " ; subsequently appeared at the Empire, Leicester Square as Lawrence Devas in " After the Opera " ; in 1909, toured as Mr. Brown in " An Englishman's Home " ; at the Duke of York's, Feb., 1910, played Moaney in " Justice " ; in Aug., 1910, toured with Edward Terry, playing Colonel Lukyn in " The Magistrate," the Sergeant in " The Toymaker of Nuremberg," also in " Sweet Lavender," " Fiander's Widow," and " Liberty Hall " ; in Dec., 1910, toured in Canada and the United States with Edward Terry ; in the autumn of 1911, toured as Colonel Sapt in " The Prisoner of Zenda " ; at the Apollo, Dec., 1912, again appeared in " After the Opera " ; at the Metropolitan, Mar., 1913, played Mr. Hulton in " Our Mutual Wife " ; at the Repertory Theatre, Birmingham, Dec., 1914, played John Anthony in " Strife." *Club :* Green Room.
(Died 8 June, 1924; age 83)

PATRICOLA, Tom, actor and vocalist ; *b.* New Orleans, La., U.S.A., 22 Jan., 1891 ; *s.* of Louis Patricolo and his wife Catarina (D'Angelo) ; *e.* Chicago and San Francisco grammar schools ;

has been on the stage since childhood, having first appeared at Tony Pastor's, New York, 1901, as one of the Patricolo Family ; remained with the Keith and Orpheum circuits eighteen years ; and then at the Globe and Apollo Theatres, New York, from 1923 to 1928, appeared annually in " George White's Scandals " ; with George White was responsible for the introduction of the well-known dances, the Charleston and the Black-Bottom ; at the Palace, Chicago, Sept., 1932, played in " Stepping Around " ; appeared at the London Palladium, Nov., 1932 ; re-appeared in New York, 1933, in " Music Hall Varieties " ; Winter Garden, New York, Sept., 1933, played Kid Hogan in " Hold Your Horses " ; commenced film career 1929, and has appeared in " Si-Si Signor," " Moonlight Cactus," " Three Sisters," " Fox Follies," " Frozen Justice," " The Children of Dreams," " Happy Days," " Words and Music," " Married in Hollywood," " South Sea Rose," " The Romance of the Rio Grande," " Seven Faces," " One Mad Kiss," " Anybody's Woman." *Recreation :* Motoring. *Clubs :* National Variety Association and The Friars, New York.
(Died 1 Jan., 1950; age 58)

PATTERSON, Neva, actress ; *b.* Nevada, Iowa, 10 Feb., 1922 ; *d.* of George Louis Patterson and his wife Marjorie Zoa Marie (Byers) ; *e.* Nevada High School, Nevada, Iowa ; *m.* James Lee ; formerly a secretary and also a singer with a dance band ; first appeared on the stage in Brewster, Minnesota, 1929, as a Bluebell in "Goldilocks" ; U.S. tour, 1946, appeared as a Soubrette in "Cyrano de Bergerac" with José Ferrer ; first appeared in New York at the Morosco, Oct., 1947, as Brenda Maddox in "The Druid Circle" ; Morosco, 1948, took over the rôle of Clarissa Blynn Cromwell in "Strange Bedfellows" ; Lyceum, Apr., 1949, Baroness Angela Burdett-Coutts in "The Ivy Green" ; Martin Beck, Nov., 1950, Diana Messerschmann in "Ring Round the Moon" ; Empire, Apr., 1951, Ann Adams in "The Long Days" ; Booth, Sept., 1951, Faith McNairn in "Lace on Her Petticoat" ; U.S. tour, 1952, took over Celia Coplestone in "The Cocktail Party" ;

Fulton, Nov., 1952, Helen Sherman in "The Seven Year Itch," in which she appeared for two years; John Golden, Oct., 1956, Nan Waterhouse in "Double in Hearts"; Royale, Dec., 1956, Connie Barnes Ashton in "Speaking of Murder"; Playhouse, Apr., 1958, Claire Manning in "Make a Million"; Bucks Country Playhouse, New Hope, Pa., Sept., 1961, played Octavia Weatherwax and Grace Fitzgerald in "The Beauty Part"; has appeared in many films including "The Solid Gold Cadillac," "The Desk Set," "David and Lisa," "The Out-of-Towners," etc.; first appeared on television in 1947 and has since made many appearances in *Playhouse 90*, *The U.S. Steel Hour*, *Kraft Playhouse*, "The Best of Broadway," etc. *Favourite part:* Faith McNairn in "Lace on Her Petticoat." *Recreation:* Sewing. *Address:* 12 Blind Brook Road, Westport, Conn., U.S.A. *Telephone No.:* 203–227–4609.

PAUL, Betty, actress; *b.* Hendon, London, 21 May, 1921; *d.* of Henri Arthur Percheron and his wife Jane Ellen (Neale); *e.* South Hampstead High School, and Institut Français; *m.* (1) Hartley Power (mar. dis.); (2) Peter Lambda; studied for the stage at the Cone-Ripman College, under Italia Conti, and Margaret Craske; made her first appearance on the stage at the Birmingham Repertory Theatre, 1936, as Adele Varens in " Jane Eyre "; made her first appearance in London at the Queen's Theatre, 13 Oct., 1936, in the same part; subsequently one of C. B. Cochran's "Young Ladies," at the Trocadero Restaurant, 1938–40; His Majesty's, July, 1941, appeared as Minnie Masters in "Lady Behave"; Princes, Feb., 1943, played Christine in "Old Chelsea"; during 1943–5, appeared in variety and on radio programmes with Vic Oliver; Coliseum, May, 1945, appeared in "The Night and the Music"; Adelphi, Apr., 1947, played Suzanne Valdis in "Bless the Bride," which ran over two years; toured, 1949, as Manon in "Bitter Sweet"; Whitehall, June, 1950, played Désirée in "The Dish Ran Away"; New, Oct., 1951, played Mistress Pepys in the musical play "And So To Bed"; Winter Garden, Oct., 1952, Ilena de Faucon in "Husbands Don't Count"; made her first appearance on the New York stage at the National, 18 Feb., 1953, as Maggie Wylie in "Maggie"; Savoy, London, Dec., 1953, played Nora Parker in "Down Came a Blackbird"; Duke of York's, Sept., 1954, Mary Millar in "All For Mary"; at the same theatre, July, 1955, played Yvette Leroux in "Wild Thyme"; Royal, Windsor, Oct., 1955, appeared as Polly Eccles in a musical version of "Caste"; Coliseum, Mar., 1957, played Meg in "Damn Yankees"; New Shakespeare, Liverpool, Sept., 1958, Grace in Sam Wanamaker's production of "Bus Stop"; first appeared in films, 1947, in "Oliver Twist." *Favourite parts:* Suzanne in "Bless the Bride," and Manon in "Bitter Sweet." *Recreations:* Painting, cooking and sewing. *Address:* c/o Betty Farmer, 97 Charing Cross Road, London, W.C.2.

PAULINE, Princess, comedienne ; *b.* 3 Sept., 1873 ; *m.* M. Serpentello ; commenced her stage career at the early age of four, as a member of the Jennins family, with Ginnett's Circus ; she then toured with Pindar's Circus for seven years, and with Sanger's Circus for a further five years ; made her first appearance on the variety stage at Sadler's Wells, under G. E. Belmont ; she then went to America, opening at Tony Pastor's, New York ; on her return to England, appeared at the Theatre Royal, Manchester, in " Sinbad the Sailor " ; she next appeared at the Canterbury, Paragon, Middlesex, and other halls, and has since appeared at leading halls all over the kingdom ; toured in South Africa, 1899 ; among some of the more popular songs which she has introduced to the public may be mentioned, " A Sporting Girl " ; " Little Tottie Brown Shoes " ; " I've got 'em " ; " Maggie Ryley " ; " A Yankee Girl," etc.

PAULL, Harry Major, dramatic author ; *b.* Monmouth, 6 Jan., 1854 ; *s.* of Rev. William Major Paull ; *e.* privately ; is a retired civil servant ;

has written the following among other plays : " His Own Guest " (with Arthur Ayres), 1881 ; " The Great Felicidad," 1887 ; " Tenterhooks," at the Comedy, 1889 ; " The Gentleman Whip," Terry's, 1894 ; " Hal the Highwayman," Vaudeville, 1894 ; " Poor Mr. Potton " (with C. Hamlyn), Vaudeville, 1895 ; " Merrifield's Ghost," Vaudeville, 1895 ; " The Spy," 1896 ; " The New Clown," Terry's, 1902 ; " The Fortunes of Fan," 1908 ; "The Painter and the Millionaire," 1912 ; " The Lady Cashier," 1912 ; author of " Literary Ethics," 1928 ; late Hon. Secretary of the Dramatists' Club. *Recreations :* Golf, chess, and music. *Club :* Dramatists'.
(Died 29 Nov., 1934; age 80)

PAULTON, Harry, actor and dramatic author ; *b.* Wolverhampton, 16 Mar., 1842 ; made his first appearance on the stage in 1861, at Wolverhampton ; subsequently played " stock " engagements at Wakefield, Derby, Leeds, York, etc.; from 1864-7, was engaged as " low " comedian at the Theatre Royal, Glasgow ; made his first appearance on the London stage, at the Surrey Theatre, 23 June, 1867, as Wormwood in " The Lottery Ticket " ; subsequently he fulfilled engagements at the Theatre Royal, Birmingham, and Prince of Wales's, Liverpool ; he returned to London in 1870, and joined the Strand Theatre company under Mrs. Swanborough ; here he appeared with great success as Blueskin in " The Idle 'Prentice," the Archduke in " Cœur-de-Lion," Uncle Sedley in " Up in the World," Aristæus in " Eurydice," Quasimodo in " Esmeralda," Zekiel Homespun in " The Heir-at-Law," Danny Mann in " Miss Eily O'Connor," Athos in " The Three Musket-Dears," Isaac of York in " Ivanhoe," Molasses in " Arion," The King in " Pygmalion," and Humphrey Harrowby in " The Poor Gentleman " ; he then went to the Alhambra, making his first appearance there on 1 Apr., 1872, as Robin Clodhopper in " Clodhopper's Fortune " ; he remained here for some years, playing the leading comedy parts in the various comic operas produced during that period ; he made notable successes as King Carrot in " Le Roi Carotte," Dandelion in " The Black Crook," Menelaus in " La Belle Hélène," Leporello in " Don Juan," La Cocadière in " La Jolie Parfeumeuse," Filastenish in " The Demon Bride," the 'Prentice in " Whittington," the Court Physician in " Chilperic," Rhadamanthus John in " Lord Bateman," the King in " Le Voyage dans la Lune," Sancho Panza in " Don Quixote," also in " Orphée aux Enfers," as King Indigo in the opera of that name, Kit in " Wildfire " ; in 1878, he appeared at the Philharmonic, as Frimousse in " The Little Duke," returned to the Alhambra in Oct., 1879, appearing in " La Petite Mademoiselle," and " Rothomago " ; appeared at the Globe, 1880, as Don Prolixia in " The Naval Cadets," Abbé Bridaine in " Les Mousquetaires," Flam in " La Boulangère " ; again appeared at the Alhambra, in 1881, as the Great Bamboo in " The Bronze Horse," in " The Black Crook," and as Auricomos in " Babil and Bijou " ; in 1882, appeared at the Avenue, as Dromez in " Les Manteaux Noirs," at the Strand, Mar., 1883, played Arthur in " Cymbia " ; at the Comedy, Sept., 1883, played Nick Vedder in " Rip Van Winkle " ; at the Empire, Apr., 1884, re-appeared in " Chilperic " ; at the Gaiety, in Nov., 1884, played Professor Roscius Muggeridge in " Lillies " ; at the Comedy, Nov., 1885, played Cadeau in " Erminie " ; Mar., 1886, Thomaso Aniello in " Masse-en-Yell-Oh " ; next appeared at Vaudeville, July, 1886, as Sulky in " The Road to Ruin " ; at the Royalty, Oct., 1886, played Noah Winter in " Noah's Ark " ; at the Comedy, Feb., 1887, appeared as Hans in " Mynheer Jan " ; and in Mar., 1887, as MacAlister in " The Mormon " ; at the Royalty, Aug., 1887, played Soperius in " The Quack " ; was absent from the London stage for the next three years ; re-appeared at the Globe, Jan., 1891, as Theodore Bender in " All the Comforts of a Home," also played Ledger in " The Parvenu " ; at the Vaudeville, July, 1891, he played Tapperton in " The

Mischief Maker " ; at the Globe, Nov., 1891, Timothy Chadwick in " Gloriana " ; he next appeared at the Strand, Apr. 1892, as Peter Amos Dunn in " Niobe (all Smiles)," which had a run of nearly six hundred performances, and which is still being toured in the provinces ; since that date his appearances in London have not been numerous, but he has played at the Strand, 1895, in " In a Locket," and " The Lord Mayor " ; at the Trafalgar Square, 1895 in " Baron Golosh " ; on tour, 1896, in " Dorcas " ; at the Strand, 1897, in " The Prodigal Father " ; at the Metropole, 1898, in " A Bad Lot " ; at the Court, 1900, played Touchstone in " As You Like It " ; at the Shakespeare, Clapham, 1901, in " Smith, Brown, Jones and Robinson " ; at the New, 1903, in " Rosemary " ; at the Court, May, 1904, Launce in " Timon of Athens " ; at the Lyric, May, 1905, appeared as the First Gravedigger in " Hamlet " ; at the Waldorf, 1906, in " Noah's Ark " ; at Daly's, May, 1908, Père Olier in " The Chalice " ; at the Strand, 1910, in " The Raven's Cry " ; at the Gala performance at His Majesty's, 27 June, 1911, appeared as Smith in Act II of " David Garrick " ; at Hull, Mar., 1913, with Martin Harvey, appeared as Grumio in " The Taming of the Shrew " ; at His Majesty's, 22 May, 1914, appeared in the " all-star " revival of " The Silver King," given in aid of King George's Actors' Pension Fund ; was the first actor to be granted a pension from King George's Actors' Pension Fund, 1912 ; has written many successful comic operas and plays, mostly in collaboration ; among these may be mentioned, " Don Quixote," " Wedded Bliss," " The Black Crook," " Cymbia," " The Babes," " The Japs," " Mynheer Jan," " Niobe," " In a Locket," " The Lord Mayor," " Dorcas," " A Bad Lot," " Meredith Marriages," " The Old Firm," "A Double Woman." *Club :* Green Room.
(Died 17 Apr., 1917; age 75)

PAUMIER, Alfred, actor and manager ; *b.* Liverpool, 14 Nov., 1870 ; *s.* of Alfred Richard Hodgson and his wife Diana (Peck Boadle) ; *e.* Tattenhall, Cheshire ; *m.* (1) Lilian Bridle ; (2) Eva White ; name changed to Paumier by deed-poll ; made his first appearance on the stage as a child in 1878, at the Theatre Royal, Burnley, as the little Count in " The Stranger " ; made his first appearance in London at the Standard Theatre, 1 Aug., 1887, as Walter Briscoe in " Passion's Slave " ; at the Princess's, Apr., 1888, appeared as The Inspector in " The Mystery of a Hansom Cab " ; in 1889 and for many years was a member of the Edmund Tearle Shakespearean Company, and he appeared at the New Olympic, May, 1892, with that company playing Cauis Claudius in " Virginius," Montano in " Othello," etc. ; in 1899 he went to South Africa to produce (for the first time in South Africa) " Julius Caesar," playing Brutus, and in partnership with Leonard Rayne played most of the classical plays out there ; in 1901 entered into partnership with Walter Howard, the dramatic author, and has toured his plays in England, South Africa, and the United States ; appeared at the Prince's, Dec., 1913, as Paul Romain in " The Story of the Rosary," and made his first appearance in New York, at the Manhattan Opera House, 7 Sept., 1914, in the same part ; on returning to England, appeared at the Prince of Wales's, Feb., 1916 as Pascal in " The Silver Crucifix " ; at the Lyceum, Feb., 1917, appeared as Captain Terence Fielding in " Seven Days' Leave," which ran over seven hundred performances ; at the Apollo, Dec., 1917, played the Man in " Master Wayfarer " ; at the New Theatre, Sept., 1919, played Lord Seton Replington in " Jack o' Jingles " ; in Dec., 1920, engaged by Leonard Rayne for another South African tour, when he played " Mr. Wu," " Dear Brutus," " The Skin Game," " The Right to Strike," " Seven Days' Leave," "The Wandering Jew," " Carnival," etc. ; at the Ambassadors', Sept., 1924, played Blazy in " Fata Morgana "; Barnes, June, 1925, Mr. Hardcastle in " Jungle Law " ; Gaiety, Oct., 1925, Bumble Bunting in " The Good Old Days "; Duke of York's, Mar., 1926, Inspector Purcell in " Life Goes On "; New

Oxford, Apr., 1926, Richard Maitland in " Temptation "; in 1927 produced his own comedy " Pat," with which he toured the provinces; during 1928 toured as Dr. Seward in " Dracula "; during 1929 toured as Paul Gouffet in " The Face at the Window," and played the same part at the Little, July, 1929. *Recreations :* Landscape painting and writing. *Clubs :* Savage, Green Room.

(Died 25 Jan., 1951; age 80)

PAVLOVA, Anna, *danseuse ; b.* Petrograd, 31 Jan., 1885 ; *m.* M. V. Dandré ; was trained for the ballet at the Imperial Ballet School, attached to the Marianski Theatre, Petrograd ; subsequently became *prima ballerina* of that theatre, subsequently appearing at the Imperial Opera House, Petrograd ; made her first appearance in London, at the Palace Theatre, 1910, assisted by Michael Mordkin, scoring an immediate success in " Le Cygne," " Les Papillons," " Valse Caprice," etc. ; appeared in Paris with Diaghileff's Russian Ballet in " Les Sylphides," " Pavillon d'Armide," and " La Nuit Egyptienne "; made her first appearance in New York, 1 Mar., 1910, in the ballet " Coppelia "; appeared regularly at the Palace, London, for some years ; subsequently toured in the United States ; during 1920 appeared at Drury Lane Theatre, and 1921 at the Queen's Hall ; appeared at Covent Garden, with her own company, Sept., 1923, and again in Sept., 1924, and Sept., 1925 ; subsequently went to South Africa and thence to Australia, 1925-6 ; again appeared at Covent Garden, Sept., 1927 ; returned to Australia, where she appeared, 1928-9 ; returned to London, 1929 ; has toured all through the provinces, and all over the world.

(Died 23 Jan., 1931; age 48)

PAWLE, J. Lennox, actor ; *b.* London, 27 Apr., 1872 ; *s.* of John Christopher Pawle ; *e.* France, and Berkhampstead ; *m.* Dorothy Parker, *d.* of Louis N. Parker ; was a pupil at Sarah Thorne's Dramatic School at Margate, and made his first appearance

on the stage at the Theatre Royal, Margate, 1890, in "Ticklish Times"; made his first appearance on the London Stage at the Royalty Theatre, 11 June, 1892, as Norfolk Howard in "Moses and Son"; appeared at the Adelphi, 10 Mar., 1894, as the Rev. Mr. Ponder in "The Cotton King"; at the Lyceum, 21 Sept., 1895, as Sampson in "Romeo and Juliet," with Forbes-Robertson; at the Duke of York's, Dec., 1895, as Ebenezer Skindle in a revival of "Tommy Atkins"; was for some time comedian at the Pavilion, Mile End, from 1895, appearing there in "Saved from the Sea," "Tommy Atkins," etc.; joined Sir George Alexander at the St. James's, in 1901, to play Todman in "Liberty Hall "; appeared at the Duke of York's, Mar., 1902, as Mr. Malpas in " The Princess's Nose "; at the Avenue, 1902, in " The Little French Milliner "; at the New Theatre, Aug., 1904, played Tom Codd in " Beauty and the Barge "; appeared at the Criterion, 1905, in " What Pamela Wanted "; at the Prince of Wales's, Jan., 1906, as Algernon Southdown in " The Little Cherub "; at Daly's, 1906, played in " Les Merveilleuses "; same theatre, June, 1907, played the Marquis de Cascada in " The Merry Widow "; appeared at Drury Lane, Christmas, 1907, as the Baron in " The Babes in the Wood "; at His Majesty's (Afternoon Theatre), Jan., 1909, played Mellish in " The Admirable Bashville "; in Sept., 1909, toured with Hayden Coffin, as Jabez Gover in " The Man in the Street "; at the Playhouse, Dec., 1909, appeared as Horace Eglamore in " Tantalising Tommy "; at the Savoy, Mar., 1910, appeared as King Utops in " Two Merry Monarchs "; at the New Theatre, Aug., 1910, played Canuche in "The Crisis "; subsequently went to America, and at Wallack's, New York, Dec., 1910, played Jerome Brooke-Hoskyn in " Pomander Walk "; continued in that part 1910-11 ; at Atlantic City, Apr., 1912, and at the Criterion, New York, Aug., 1912, played Loulou in " The Girl from Montmartre "; at the Empire, New York, Mar., 1913, appeared as William Todman in

"Liberty Hall"; at Chicago, Apr., 1913, played in "The Money Moon"; in the autumn of 1913 joined Cyril Maude for his Canadian and American tour; on his return to London, appeared at the New Theatre, May, 1914, as Isaac Wolfe in "Grumpy"; at Wallack's, New York, Oct., 1914, played Wilkins Micawber in "The Highway of Life"; on returning to London appeared at the New Theatre, Mar., 1915, as James Wilson in "Seven Days"; at the Vaudeville, July, 1915, as Sir Daniel Dollary in "Enterprising Helen"; in Aug., 1915, toured as Montagu Lovitt-Lovitt in "To-Night's the Night"; at the Globe, Oct., 1916, played Willie Piggott in "When the Clock Goes Round"; at the St. James's, Jan., 1917, the Marquis de Béassac in "The Aristocrat"; Sept., 1917, Weech in "The Pacifists"; Nov., 1917, Ernest Stuchbury in "Loyalty"; at the Prince of Wales's, Mar., 1918, appeared as Hamilton P. Brapwick in "Flora"; at the Comedy, Aug., 1918, succeeded the late Arthur Playfair in "Tails Up!"; at the Criterion, Mar., 1919, played Hyacinth Steddall in "Oh! Don't Dolly"; at the Prince's, Apr., 1919, Frederick Bantison in the opera, "Monsieur Beaucaire"; in the same year played the same part in the United States, and toured there in 1920; during 1921 toured as Jerome Brooke-Hoskyn in "Marjolaine" (musical version of "Pomander Walk"), and played the same part at the Broadhurst Theatre, New York, Jan., 1922; at the Globe, New York, Mar., 1923, played the Duke of Dippington in "Jack and Jill"; at the Lyceum, New York, May, 1923, Horatio Bakkus in "The Mountebank"; at the Belasco, Sept., 1923, Mr. Beeby in "Mary, Mary, Quite Contrary"; at the Forty-ninth Street Theatre, Aug., 1924, Eliphas Leone in "The Were-wolf"; at the Belasco, Dec., 1924, Petri in "The Harem"; at "Q," and Garrick, London, July, 1926, Major Knapshott in "None But the Brave"; Ambassador, New York, Oct., 1927, Auguste in "The Matrimonial Bed"; Winter Garden, London, Mar., 1928, The Manager in "The Spider"; Belasco, New York, Dec., 1928, The

Adjutant in "Mima"; Ziegfeld, Feb., 1930, Olee King in "Simple Simon"; Gaiety, Feb., 1932, The Author in "Collision"; commenced film career, 1929, and has appeared in "Married in Hollywood," "Hot for Paris," "Sky Hawk," "Lullaby" ("The Sin of Madelon Claudet"), "David Copper-field," etc. (*Died* 22 Feb., 1936 *age 63*)

PAWLEY, Nancy, actress; *b.* Aner-ley, Surrey, 21 Dec., 1901; *d.* of Ernest Frederick Pawley and his wife Edith (Perry); *m.* Bertram S. Can-nell; made her first appearance on the stage at the Vaudeville The-atre, 21 Dec., 1912, as one of the little Guests in "Shockheaded Peter"; Duke of York's, Nov., 1913, played in "Quality Street," and Dec. 1913, in "Peter Pan"; His Majesty's (for King George's Pension Fund), May, 1914, was one of the school children in "The Silver King"; for several years ap-peared at the Duke of York's and New Theatre, each Christmas, in "Peter Pan," eventually playing Tiger Lily; Apollo, July, 1920, played the Hon. Agatha Byefleet in "Cherry"; sub-sequently toured with Mrs. Patrick Campbell in "The Second Mrs. Tan-queray," "Madge," etc.; His Maj-esty's, Apr., 1923, played Miss Claridge in "The Gay Lord Quex"; Prince of Wales's, June, 1924, Madeline Sornay in "The Rat"; Globe, June, 1926, Betty Royer in "There's No Fool"; Lyric, 1927, played Eleanor in "The Gold Diggers"; London Hippodrome, Nov., 1927, Pamela Carr in "Hit the Deck"; Garrick, Dec., 1928, again played Tiger Lily in "Peter Pan"; Lyric, Mar., 1929, the Maid in "Ber-keley Square," subsequently play-ing Kate; toured as Lady Panniford in "The Calendar," 1929; Lyric, Apr., 1930, played Babe Otway in "De-bonair"; Fortune, Jan., 1931, Wheeler in "The Silver Box"; Duke of York's, Feb., 1931, Anna in "The Rocklitz"; Wyndham's, Apr., 1931, the Lady and Regina in "Charles the Third"; Kingsway, June, 1931, Daphne in "The Age of Youth"; next toured as Anita Gunn in "It's a Boy"; Strand, May, 1932, played Eva in "Party"; London Hippodrome, June, 1933, Lucille in

"Give Me a Ring"; then toured in S. Africa, 1933–4, in "A Murder has Been Arranged," and "Mr. What's His Name?"; on returning to London appeared at the Lyric, June, 1934, as Nurse Jameson in "Men in White"; Arts, May, 1935, played ' Polly in "Rosetti"; Drury Lane, Sept., 1936, Lady Triplex in "Careless Rapture"; toured, Feb., 1938, as Geraldine Burke in "Back Your Fancy," and subsequently in "Toss of a Coin." *Recreations:* Riding and dancing.

PAWSON, Hargrave, actor; *b.* 6 Dec., 1902; *s.* of William Hargrave Pawson and his wife Violet (Gaskell); *e.* Eton and Grenoble University, France; *m.* Irene Russell; made his first appearance on the stage at the Opera House, Harrogate, Aug., 1930, as Murdo Fraser in "The First Mrs. Fraser"; made his first appearance in London, at the Criterion Theatre, 23 Dec., 1930, as the Hon. Evelyn Vane in "A Pair of Trousers"; Wyndham's, Apr., 1931, played Conrad in "Charles the Third"; subsequently toured as Marston Gurney in "The Ware Case," and as Sir Philip Bay-Clender in "Party"; Shaftesbury, Nov., 1931, Lieutenant Merrivale in "Orders are Orders"; Globe, June, 1933, Geoffrey Worth in "Proscenium"; St. Martin's, Oct., 1933, Roger Cole in "The Wind and the Rain"; Shaftesbury, Nov., 1933, Sandy Tyrell in "Hay Fever"; Feb., 1934, toured as Julian in "The Green Bay Tree"; Shaftesbury, Apr., 1934, played Ian George Stanley in "There's Always To-Morrow." *Recreation:* Riding. *Club:* Cavalry.

(Died 26 Jan., 1945; age 42)

PAXINOU, Katina, actress; *b.* Piraeus, Athens, Greece, 1900; *d.* of Basil Constantopoulos; *e.* Geneva Conservatoire (Gold Medallist and First Prize); *m.* (1) Ivannis Paxinou (mar. dis.); (2) Alexis Minotis; studied singing in Geneva, Berlin, and Vienna; first appeared, in opera, in Athens; first appeared on the dramatic stage, 1924, in "La Femme Nue," and played in repertory for two-and-a-half years; she became leading lady at the Royal Theatre, Athens, where she appeared for many years in all the dramas of ancient Greeec, many translations of Shakespeare, and in a number of English and American plays, which she translated into Greek and produced, including "Anna Christie," "Desire Under the Elms," etc.; in 1934, she revived Ibsen's "Ghosts," playing Mrs. Alving, and played it annually for six years; made her first appearance in New York, at the New Yorker Theatre, 26 Dec., 1930, as Clytemnestra in the "Electra" of Sophocles; first appeared in London, at His Majesty's Theatre, 19 June, 1939, in "Electra," and the following evening appeared as Queen Gertrude in "Hamlet"; at the Duchess, May, 1940, playing in English for the first time, appeared as Mrs. Alving in "Ghosts"; at the Longacre Theatre, New York, Jan., 1942, played Hedda Tesman in "Hedda Gabler"; Playhouse, New York, Dec., 1944, Sophie Halenczic in "Sophie"; Mark Hellinger, Nov., 1952, played the title-*rôle* in "Electra," and Jocasta in "Œdipus Tyrannus"; A.N.T.A., Oct., 1961, Ana Zachariadis in "The Garden of Sweets"; Aldwych, Apr., 1966, in the World Theatre Season, played the name part in "Hecuba" and Jocasta in "Oedipus Rex," also composing the music for both plays; first appeared in films, 1943, in "For Whom the Bell Tolls," receiving the Academy (Oscar) Award for this performance; made her first television appearance in England, June, 1959, as the Mother in "Blood Wedding," and has since played in "Ghosts" and "The Old Ladies". *Address:* c/o Larry Dalzell Associates Ltd., 14 Clifford Street, London, W.1.

PAXTON, Sydney (Sydney Paxton Hood), actor and manager ; *b.* London, 25 June, 1860; *s.* of Rev. Edwin Paxton Hood ; *e.* London and Bremen ; *m.* Lillie Leicester ; made his first appearance on the stage in 1880, at Southport ; toured for some time with the late Arthur Lloyd ; fulfilled a seven years' engagement with Edward Compton (1885 to 1892) ; in the latter year toured in " Walker, London " ;

joined W. S. Penley at the Globe, 1894, and played Spettigue in " Charley's Aunt," over a thousand times ; appeared at Lyceum, Feb., 1899, as Stryver in " The Only Way " ; from 1903 to 1905, was manager of the Southampton and Boscombe Hippodromes ; reappeared on London stage in " The Electric Man," Royalty, 1906 ; engaged as business manager for the Zancigs on their British tour ; after an interval of eleven years, was re-engaged by Brandon Thomas, to play his old part of Spettigue in ' Charley's Aunt," at the Royalty, Christmas, 1907 ; at the Playhouse, June, 1908, appeared as General Gough Bogle in " The Flag Lieutenant " ; June, 1909, played Messer Marco Ricci in " A Merry Devil " ; at the Garrick, Dec., 1909, played Dr. Garlick in " Where Children Rule " ; at His Majesty's, Feb., 1910, appeared as the Duke of Tyrconnel in " The O'Flynn " ; in Aug., 1911, toured with Evelyn Millard as the Rev. Mr. Blimboe in " The Adventure of Lady Ursula," also managing the business of the company ; in Sept., 1912, went to the United States to appear in " Fanny's First Play," as Mr. Robin Gilroy ; at the Apollo, Sept., 1914, played Elijah Quimby in " Seven Keys to Baldpate " ; Jan., 1915, Mr. Spencer Garrington in " A Busy Day " ; at the Lyric, Apr., 1915, Mr. Summers in " On Trial " ; at the New, Oct., 1915, Mr. Jamison in " Stop Thief ! " ; at the Apollo, June, 1916, Timothy Wadlow in " Hobson's Choice " ; at the Prince of Wales's, Feb., 1917, Rev. John Hopply in " Anthony in Wonderland " ; at the Royalty, June, 1917, Poulder in " The Foundations " ; at the St. James's, Nov., 1917, Albert Stapleton Dunt in " Loyalty " ; at the Ambassadors', Feb., 1918, appeared as Isaac Elkantrovitch and Vanderlinde in " The Little Brother " ; Aug., 1919, as the Rev. Edward Chase in " Green Pastures and Piccadilly " ; at the New, Nov., 1919, as Mr. Lawrence in " Little Women " ; at the Queen's, Mar., 1920, as Mr. Perkins in " The Fold " ; at the Duke of York's, Dec., 1920, as the Dean in " When Knights Were Bold " ; at the St. James's,

June, 1921, as Alderman Harzen in " The Night of the Party " ; at the Lyric, Oct., 1921, played Seth Trimble in " Welcome Stranger " ; in 1924 went to America and at the Forty-ninth Street Theatre, New York, Aug., 1924, played The Priest in " The Werewolf " ; 49th Street Theatre, May, 1925, Schigolch in " The Loves of Lulu " ; Little, Oct., 1925, Sir Oliver Surface in " The School for Scandal " ; Selwyn, Dec., 1926, Sir Bartlemy Pugh in " The Constant Nymph " ; Ambassador, Mar., 1928, James in " The Great Necker " ; during the past few years has devoted much time to the cinema stage ; was Hon. Sec. of the Actors' Association for twelve months, 1917-18 ; with the late Sydney Valentine was instrumental in forming the Actors' Union ; served on the Executive Committee of the Actors' Benevolent Fund for many years ; in 1917 published his reminiscences, " Stage See-Saws ; or the Ups and Downs of an Actor's Life."

(Died 13 Oct., 1930; age 70)

PAYNE, Ben Iden, actor and director ; *b.* Newcastle-on-Tyne, 5 Sept., 1888 ; *s.* of the Rev. Alfred Payne and his wife Sarah (Glover) ; *m.* (1) Mona Limerick (mar. dis.) ; (2) Barbara Rankin Chiaroni ; made his first appearance on the stage, Nov., 1899, at the Theatre Royal Worcester, as Diggory in " She Stoops to Conquer," with F. R. Benson's company ; first appeared in London, at Lyceum, 15 Feb., 1900, in " King Henry V" ; General Manager of Abbey Players, Dublin, where he directed "Interior" and "Fand" ; resigned and subsequently was prominently connected with Miss A. E. F. Horniman's management at the Midland and Gaiety Theatres, Manchester, and was first director and producer of the company, 1907–11, for more than 200 plays ; in 1907, appeared as Owen Ford in "The Street" ; 1908, as Mr. Ebton-Smith in "The Few and the Many" ; Victor Meux in "The Three Barrows," Oscar Eckersley in "Trespassers Will Be Prosecuted" ; Godfrey Rawlings in "When the Devil Was Ill" ; Lickcheese in " Widowers' Houses,"

Eugene Marchbanks in "Candida," etc.; toured with Miss Mona Limerick and organized repertory seasons at Sheffield, Leeds, Glasgow and Edinburgh, 1911–13, producing "The Tragedy of Man," "Man and Superman," "The Philanderer," etc.; went to America, and at the Fine Arts Theatre, Chicago, Nov., 1913, directed "The Master of the House," "Phipps," "A Florentine Tragedy," "Press Cuttings," directed and played Lucio in "Measure for Measure," etc.; returned to England and directed tours of "The Younger Generation" and "Arms and the Man," 1914; in 1914 was appointed Art Director of the Little Theatre, Philadelphia, and played Bob Acres and directed "The Rivals," directed "The Silver Box," "Courage," etc.; at the Princess Theatre, New York, Jan., 1915, played Puff in "The Critic"; in Nov., 1915, directed "Hobson's Choice," at the Shubert Theatre, New York; was subsequently appointed General Producer to Charles Frohman Inc.; from 1916–21, he directed "Justice," "The Guilty Man," "The Case of Lady Camber," "The Old Lady Shows Her Medals," "Pendennis," "At the Villa Rose," "The Lady of the Camellias,"' "The Off-Chance," "The Grasshopper,"' "The New World," "Rambler Rose,"' "Crops and Croppers," "Dear Brutus,"' "Blood and Love," "Déclassée," and "Caesar's Wife"; from 1919–34, was visiting Professor at the School of the Drama of the Carnegie Institute of Technology; in May, 1920, his play (with Thomas Wood Stevens) "Poe," was produced at the Institute; at the Punch and Judy Theatre, New York, Nov., 1921, played James Broxopp in "The Great Broxopp," which he also directed; directed "That Day," 1922; "Dagmar," "Hail and Farewell," "Children of the Moon," 1923; Producer and Director of the Copley Repertory Company, and produced "Hobson's Choice," "Wallpapers," "A Successful Calamity," and "Candida," also played Marchbanks, and directed "A Weak Woman" and "Service for Two"; in 1926 was director at the Goodman Repertory Theatre, Chicago, appearing in and directing principally Shakespeare's plays; during 1928–9 directed

for the Theatre Guild, New York; Guild Theatre, New York, May, 1931, directed "The Way of the World," for the Players' Club; at the Casino, Newport, June, 1932, played Henry Straker in "Man and Superman"; in July, 1934, was appointed Director of the Shakespeare Memorial Theatre, Stratford-on-Avon, in succession to Bridges Adams; he commenced his direction in Apr., 1935, with a revival of "Antony and Cleopatra," personally directing from three to five plays annually; during the War, directed the Memorial Theatre seasons of 1941–2; returned to the United States, 1943, and became Visiting Professor, and subsequently Head of Drama, at the Carnegie Institute of Technology, and the Universities of Washington, Iowa, Missouri, Colorado and Michigan, directing plays at each; directed "Embezzled Heaven," for the Theatre Guild of New York, 1944, and "The Winter's Tale," 1945; since 1946 has been guest Professor of Drama at the University of Texas, where he directed "Arms and the Man," 1946, "The Taming of the Shrew," 1947, "She Stoops to Conquer" and "Romeo and Juliet," 1948, "The Critic" and "Richard II," 1949, "Dear Brutus" and "The Merchant of Venice," 1950, "Much Ado About Nothing," 1951, "Henry IV" (Parts I and II), 1952, "Hobson's Choice" and "Cymbeline," 1953, "A Midsummer Night's Dream," 1954, "Hamlet," 1955, "Love's Labour's Lost," 1956, "Richard III," 1957, "King Lear," 1958, "The Taming of the Shrew," 1959, "The Winter's Tale," 1960, "Macbeth," 1961, "Merry Wives of Windsor," 1962, "Othello," 1963, "As You Like It," 1964, "Measure for Measure," 1965; director of the Summer Shakespeare Festival at the Old Globe Theatre, San Diego, 1949–52, 1955, 1957, and 1964; Director of Oregon Shakespeare Festival, 1956 and 1961; Visiting Professor of Drama, Banff School of Fine Arts, Alberta, Canada, 1957–64; directed Shakespeare Productions at University of Alberta, 1958–60, and 1962; is the author of "Dolly Jordan," directed at Daly's Theatre, New York, Oct., 1922; "The Saint's Husband" (with Rosemary Casey), 1934; "Mary Goes to See" (with Rosemary Casey), produced at The Haymarket, London, 1938; received Fifth Annual Award of American National Shakespeare Festival and Academy, 1959; Rodgers and Hammerstein Award for distinguished services to the theatre, 1962; in 1962 a fund was established in his name at the University of Texas to aid Shakespeare production; LL.D., University of Alberta, Canada, 1963; Consular Law Society Award of Merit, 1968. *Clubs:* Players, New York, and Savage, London. *Address:* Players Club, 16 Gramercy Park, New York City, U.S.A.

PAYNE, Edmund, actor; *b.* 1865; made his first appearance on the stage, at Market Harborough, in 1880, as Man Friday in " Robinson Crusoe "; played stock engagements at Oxford and Newport; toured in " Forbidden Fruit," and appeared with the Milton-Rays, succeeding the late George Stone; made his first appearance on the London stage, at the Gaiety, 29 July, 1889, as Mephistopheles in " Faust Up-to-Date," with Auguste Van Biene's company; subsequently toured in the same part, and as Don Juan in " Carmen Up-to-Data "; spent the next three years touring; reappeared in London, at the Gaiety, July, 1892, in " Faust Up-to-Date ", in Dec., 1892, he made a " hit ' when he played Shrimp in " In Town " at the same theatre; he has since appeared at the Gaiety, as the Lieutenant in " Don Juan," 1893; Miggles in " The Shop Girl," 1894; Biggs in " The Circus Girl," 1896; Flipper in " The Runnaway Girl," 1898 Tommy Bang in " The Messenger Boy," 1900; Sammy Gigg in " The Toreador," 1901; Meakin in " The Orchid," 1903; Girdle in " The Spring Chicken," 1905; Tippin in " The New Aladdin," 1906 Max Moddelkopf in " The Girls of Gottenberg," 1907; Timothy in " Our Miss Gibbs," 1909; Albert Umbles in " Peggy," 1911; at His Majesty's Gala performance, 27 June, 1911 played Sir Christopher Hatton in " The Critic." *Recreation :* Cycling *(Died 1 July, 1914; age 49)*

PAYNE, Laurence, actor; *b.* London, 5 June, 1919; *s.* of Ernest George Payne and his wife Emily Mary (Gooding); *e.* Tottenham Grammar School; *m.* (1) Sheila Burrell (mar. dis.); (2) Pamela Alan; was originally a clerk in the city; studied for the stage at the Old Vic. Dramatic School; made his first appearance on the stage, at the Old Vic., 21 Feb., 1939, walking-on in " An Enemy of the People "; remained with the Old Vic company, until 1944, touring, and appearing at the New Theatre, during their London seasons in " King John," as the Messenger, 1941; Cassio in " Othello," 1942; Dr. Caius in " The Merry Wives of Windsor," 1942; at the Chanticleer Theatre, 1944–5, played Richard II, and the Earl of Warwick in " St. Joan," also producing various plays; appeared at the Arts Theatre, Oct., 1944 to Mar., 1945, as Patrick in " The Breadwinner," Larry in " Anna Christie," Leonce in " Leonce and Lena," etc.; Chanticleer, Mar., 1945, Professor Rubeck in " When We Dead Awaken "; toured in Germany, 1946, for E.N.S.A., playing Essex in " Elizabeth "; Lyric, Hammersmith, July, 1946, Maurice in " Summer at Nohant "; subsequently with the B.B.C. repertory company; joined the company of the Shakespeare Memorial Theatre, Stratford-on-Avon,

for the 1947 season, playing Romeo, Berowne in "Love's Labour's Lost," Bassanio, Henry Percy in " Richard II," and Sebastian in " Twelfth Night "; His Majesty's, London, Oct., 1947, played Percy, Romeo and Sebastian; Arts, May, and Playhouse, July, 1948, Joseph Schindler in " Musical Chairs "; Embassy, Mar., 1949, Cherea in "Caligula"; July, 1949, Horace Barnett in " Fit for Heroes"; Arts, Mar., 1950, Constant in " The Provoked Wife"; New Boltons, Apr., 1951, appeared as He in "Happy and Glorious"; New Lindsey, July, 1951, and at the Embassy the following month, played Georg von Hartnig in "Fires of Midsummer Eve," which he also directed; joined the Bristol Old Vic Company, 1951, and appeared in "The Traveller Without Luggage," "The Prodigious Snob," etc.; joined the Old Vic Company in London, 1952, and during the year played

Proteus in "The Two Gentlemen of Verona," Tybalt in "Romeo and Juliet," Fadinard in "An Italian Straw Hat"; at the Embassy, between Dec., 1952, and May, 1953, produced "The Dancing Princesses," "The Herald Angels," "Twelfth Night," and "Hamlet," playing the title-*rôle* in the last-named production; St. James's, Aug., 1953, appeared as Piotr Petrovsky in "Anastasia"; first appeared in films, 1946, in "Train of Events," and recent pictures include "Ill Met by Moonlight," "Ben Hur," and "The Tell Tale Heart"; he has played in numerous television plays, including "The Three Musketeers," "The Ivor Novello Story," and "The Trial of Spencer Cowper." *Recreations:* Music, painting, writing, golf. *Address:* Walter Jokel Management, 39 St. James's Place, London, S.W.1. *Telephone No.:* Hyde Park 5126.

PAYNE, Millie, comedienne; made her first appearance in London, at the Standard Music Hall, Pimlico, 1905, singing " The old log cabin down the lane "; " Jenny Jones," etc.; has since appeared at every hall of importance throughout the kingdom.

PAYNE, Walter, O.B.E., director and manager; *b.* London; *s.* of the late George Adney Payne and his wife Mary (Maisterson-Ford); *e.* City of London School and Heidelberg University; *m.* (1) Phyllis Lytton (mar. dis.); (2) Claire Beatrice Bauer (*née* Wissinger); is the President of the Society of West End Theatre Managers; joint Vice-Chairman of the London Theatre Council; Chairman and Managing-Director of London Pavilion, Ltd.; Variety Theatres Consolidated, Ltd.; Director of Moss Empires, Ltd.; Chairman of Theatres National Committee; Chairman United Trustees Investment Company, Ltd.; Life-Governor and member of the Council of the Chelsea Hospital for Women; Associate of the Institute of Chartered Accountants; Barrister-at-Law, Middle Temple; from 1915-18 was Director of Outside Organization and Munitions Tribunals, Ministry of Munitions; during 1918-19 was Chief Re-settlement Officer, London and South of England Demobilization and Re-settlement Dept.; during 1919-20 Deputy-Controller, Civil Liabilities (military service) Dept., Ministry of Labour. *Recreations:* Golf, riding, and the theatre. *Clubs:* Bath and Savile.
(Died 30 Oct., 1949; age 76)

PAYNE-JENNINGS, Victor, manager; *b.* Ashstead, Surrey, 2 May, 1900; *s.* of John Payne-Jennings and his wife Mary (Heald); *e.* Cranleigh School, Surrey; *m.* (1) Sheelagh Young; (2) Nancy Cobleigh; has been engaged in management since June, 1927, when in conjunction with C. Egerton Killick acquired a lease of the Savoy Theatre; relinquished this in 1932; subsequently they acquired a lease of the Comedy Theatre from 1932–5; acquired various other leases and in 1939 controlled the Comedy, Playhouse, Savoy, etc.; went to the United States, 1939; at the Cort, New York, Nov., 1939, presented (with Arthur Hopkins) "Farm of Three Echoes"; presented "Rebecca," "Happily Ever After" (with Bernard Klawans), and "Thérèse" (with Klawans), 1945. *Recreations:* Yachting, aviation and shooting.
(Died 17 June, 1962; age 62)

PEACOCK, Kim, actor; *b.* Watford, Herts, 24 Mar., 1901; *s.* of Charles Herbert Peacock and his wife Melicent (Calcutt); *e.* Haileybury; formerly engaged in journalism; made his first appearance on the stage at the Theatre Royal, Edinburgh, Mar., 1925, as Basil Owen in "The Outsider"; made his first appearance in London, Queen's, 7 May, 1925, in "The Beggar on Horse-back"; subsequently toured in repertory; St. James's, Dec., 1926, played Charles Wykeham in "Charley's Aunt"; London Hippodrome, July, 1927, in "Shake Your Feet"; New, Apr., 1928, Alan Tweedie in "Come With Me"; went to America, and made his first appearance in New York, at the Fulton Theatre, 20 May, 1929, as Harold Huggins in "Stepping Out"; Prince's, London, Dec., 1929, played Bertrand Vallé in "A Warm Corner"; Haymarket, Sept., 1931, Mario in "Two from One"; Dec., 1931, Nicholas Waterlow in "Can the Leopard . . .?" Little, Feb., 1933, Hancock Robinson in "Cock Robin"; Queen's, May, 1933, John Lambert in "Spendlove Hall"; Fortune, Sept., 1933, Jeremy in "Disharmony"; toured as Elyot Chase in "Private Lives"; His Majesty's, Feb., 1934, played Lord St. Mary's in "Conversation Piece"; Westminster, Nov., 1934, Dr. Alan Stevens in "Three-Cornered Moon"; Ambassadors', Mar., 1936, Ronnie Trent in "Children to Bless You"; Daly's, July, 1937, Rev. Thomas Rawleigh in "The First Legion"; at the outbreak of War, served full-time as a fireman in the A.F.S.; entered the Royal Navy, July, 1940, volunteering as an ordinary seaman; commissioned in the R.N.V.R., Feb., 1941; served in H.M.S. "Queen Elizabeth," Mar., 1941, to Feb., 1942; subsequently appointed Flag Lieutenant, and served in South Africa; subsequently engaged with radio and stage entertainment with Admiralty; demobilized 1946, with rank of Lieut.-Commander; has appeared on several occasions at the Arts Theatre; author of the play "Battle Royal," Embassy, 1934; produced and played lead in "Sail Away," Arts Theatre, Dec., 1935; produced and presented his own play "Under One Roof," Richmond, Mar., 1940, and St. Martin's, Apr., 1941; played the title-*rôle* in the B.B.C. serials of "Paul Temple," 1946–50; commenced film career, 1930, in "A Warm Corner," and has since appeared in numerous pictures. *Recreations:* Tennis, photography, piano and violin.

(Died 26 Dec., 1966; age 65)

PEARCE, Alice, actress; *b.* New York City, 16 Oct., 1917; *d.* of Robert E. Pearce and his wife Margaret (Clark); *e.* Collège Montmorency, Paris; Dobbs College; and Sarah Lawrence College, where she prepared for the stage; *m.* (1) John J. Rox (dec.); (2) Paul Davis; made her first appearance on the stage at the Ritz, New York, Dec., 1942, in the *revue* "New Faces of 1943"; Adelphi, Dec., 1944, played Lucy Schmeeler in "On the Town"; Adelphi, Jan., 1948, Dusty Lee in "Look Ma, I'm Dancin'"; Coronet, Sept., 1948, appeared in the *revue* "Small Wonder"; Ziegfeld, Dec., 1949, Mrs. Ella Spofford in "Gentlemen Prefer Blondes"; Martin Beck, Mar., 1952, Miss Baby Love Dallas in "The Grass Harp"; Imperial, 1954, took over various rôles in the *revue* "John Murray Anderson's Almanac"; Morosco, Sept., 1954, played Madame Bouchemin in "Dear Charles"; Playhouse, Jan., 1956, Jasmine Saunders in "Fallen Angels"; Martin Beck, Oct., 1957, The Principal in "Copper and Brass"; Shubert, 1958, took over the rôle of Sue in "Bells Are Ringing," and subsequently toured with the production; Martin Beck, New York, Feb., 1961, played Dorothy Plunkett in "Midgie Purvis"; Broadhurst, Oct., 1961, Elinor Spencer-Bollard in "Sail Away!"; first entered films in "On the Town," 1949, and has since appeared in "Belle of New York," "How to Be Very Very Popular," "Bus Riley Is Back in Town," "Tammy and the Doctor," etc.; first appeared on television, 1947, in the *Ed Sullivan Show*, recent appearances include the series "Bewitched," 1965–6. *Favourite part:* Gladys Kravitz in the television series "Bewitched." *Recreations:* Painting and writing. *Address:* 8272 Hillside Avenue, Los Angeles 10069, California, U.S.A. *(Died 4 Mar., 1966 age 47)*

PEARCE, Vera, actress and vocalist: *b.* Australia; had considerable and varied experience in Australia, having first appeared on the stage at the age of four; was touring in England prior to the War in 1914, when she returned to Australia; at the Tivoli, Sydney, Nov., 1915, appeared in "The Tivoli Follies," and during 1917, appeared in "The Beauty Shop"; at His Majesty's, Melbourne, Christmas, 1918, played Dick in "Dick Whittington"; at the Tivoli, Sydney, 1919, played in "My Lady Frayle" and "The Officers' Mess"; subsequently appeared as Zahrat-al-Kulub in "Chu-Chin-Chow," "As You Were," "His Little Wives," etc.; has appeared in London at the Empire, Apr.,

1922, as Marietta in "Love's Awakening"; London Hippodrome, Mar., 1924, in "Leap Year"; Palace, Mar., 1925, as Flora in "No, No, Nanette"; at the Shaftesbury, Nov., 1926, as Clare in "My Son John"; June, 1927, played Madame Joujou Durant in "Castles in the Air"; London Hippodrome, June, 1928, Sunya Berata in "That's a Good Girl"; Drury Lane, Apr., 1929, Clotilde Lombaste in "The New Moon"; Empire, Edinburgh, Aug., 1929, Mrs. Rosalie Symes in "Open Your Eyes"; at the Palace, London, Nov., 1929, played Jeannette in "Dear Love": Strand (for Venturers), Feb., 1930, the Duchess in "Camille in Roaring Camp"; went to New York, and appeared at the Majestic, June, 1930, as Jeannette in "Artists and Models" ("Dear Love"); London Hippodrome, Mar., 1931, played the Princess Amaris in "Stand Up and Sing"; in 1932, toured in the same part; from Dec., 1932-4, toured as Augusta in "Wild Violets"; London Hippodrome, Sept., 1934, Pansy Beresford in "Yes, Madam?"; Oct., 1935, Miss Trundle in "Please, Teacher!"; Feb., 1937, Annabelle Ray in "Big Business"; Prince's, Apr., 1938, Maria Cloppitt in "Wild Oats"; Aug., 1939, Clementina Tuttle in "Sitting Pretty"; Dec., 1939, and again in May, 1941, appeared in "Shephard's Pie"; toured, 1944, as Miriam in "Staff Dance"; Saville, Sept., 1944, played Sister in "Three's a Family"; London Palladium, Sept., 1946, succeeded Tessie O'Shea in "High Time"; Saville, May, 1948, played Mrs. Edgoose in "Bob's Your Uncle"; Stoll, Sept., 1951, played "Countess" Winkler in "Rainbow Square"; toured, 1954, as Mrs. Violet Binder, M.P., in "Liberty Bill," and appeared in this part at the Piccadilly, Sept., 1954, in a revised version of the play entitled "The Party Spirit"; at the Henry Miller, N.Y., Apr., 1957, played Madame Boniface in "Hotel Paradiso"; in 1932, appeared in the film, "Yes, Mr. Brown," and has since appeared in numerous pictures. *(Died 18 Jan., 1966)*

PEARL, Jack, actor; *b.* New York City, U.S.A., 29 Oct., 1895; *e.* New York public schools and De Witt Clinton High School; *m.* Winifred Desborough; made his first appearance on the stage with Gus Edwards in "School-Days," in which he played for some time in one-night stands, and subsequently toured in "Seven Hours in New York"; in 1913–1915, was playing in vaudeville and burlesque, in "The Peacemakers" and "The Powder-Puff Revue"; appeared at the New Amsterdam, New York, Oct., 1920, in "Hitchy-Koo, 1920"; Winter Garden, June, 1921, in "The Whirl of New York"; Jan., 1923, in "The Dancing Girl"; Broadhurst, Nov., 1923, in "Topics of 1923"; Casino de Paris, Jan., 1926, in "A Night in Paris"; Winter Garden, Nov., 1927, in "Artists and Models"; Majestic, Feb., 1929, in "Pleasure Bound"; Feb., 1930, in "The International Review"; Ziegfeld, July, 1931, in "Ziegfeld Follies of 1931"; Majestic, Jan., 1933, played Commissioner Bauer in "Pardon My English"; Maryland, Baltimore, Dec., 1937, Jaro in "One Flight Down"; Shubert, Boston, June, 1939, appeared in "Yokel Boy"; Bijou, Sept., 1943, John Bauer Sen. in "All for All"; has also appeared in films. *Recreation:* Reading.

PEARSON, Beatrice, actress; *b.* Denison, Texas, U.S.A., 27 July, 1920; *e.* Pasadena High School, Calif.; made her first appearance on the stage at the Pasadena Playhouse; first appeared in New York, at the 44th Street Theatre, 25 Mar., 1940, walking-on in "Liliom"; toured, 1941, in "Life With Father"; Cort, Nov., 1943, played Martha Harper in "Get Away, Old Man"; Music Box, Jan., 1944, Jan Lupton in "Over 21"; Empire, Nov., 1945, Dee Matthews in "The Mermaids Singing"; Morosco, 1946, Sally Middleton in "The Voice of the Turtle"; Booth, Oct., 1950, Mary Flemin in "The Day After To-Morrow." *Address:* c/o Actors' Equity Association, 45 West 47th Street, New York City, U.S.A.

PEARSON, Lloyd, actor; *b.* Yorkshire, 13 Dec., 1897; *s.* of William Edward Pearson and his wife Ada (Farrar); *e.* Whitcliffe Mount Grammar

School, and Owen's College; formerly a clerk in the Midland Bank; immediately after being demobilized from the Army, 1919, studied for the stage at Lady Benson's Dramatic School; made his first appearance on the stage at the Palace Pier, Brighton, 1919, as the Police Officer in "Diana of Dobson's"; made his first appearance in London at the St. Martin's Theatre, 21 Jan., 1920, as Lentulus in "Pompey the Great," with Sir Frank Benson; remained with the Benson Company for seven years, eventually playing the leading comedy parts in Shakespeare, Sheridan, Goldsmith, etc.; then played a short season with the Birmingham Repertory Company, where he appeared as Launce in "The Two Gentlemen of Verona"; in 1927, joined the company of the Playhouse, Liverpool, under William Armstrong, and remained until 1937, playing leading parts; returned to London 1937, and appeared at the "Q," Nov., 1937, as Viscount Pascal in "The Switchback"; Palace, Feb., 1938, played Tubby Pearson in "Dodsworth"; Fortune, June, 1938, Harper in "Nanny"; St. Martin's, Oct., 1938, Alderman Helliwell in "When We Are Married"; Savoy (for Repertory Players), Dec., 1938, Mr. Furnival in "Two Roses," and Feb., 1939, Charles Pemberton in "At Night We Play"; Strand, July, 1940, Major Gaunt in "Women Aren't Angels"; Duchess, Mar., 1942, Ned Franklin in "Skylark," and July, 1942, Fred Judd in "Lifeline"; Garrick, June, 1943, Sam Morrow in "Living Room"; Lyric, May, 1944, Aristophanes in "Crisis in Heaven," and June, 1944, Professor Mallory in "Zero Hour"; Strand, June, 1944 succeeded Frank Pettingell as Teddy Brewster in "Arsenic and Old Lace"; toured, April, 1946, as Rev. Alfred Prescott in "The Poltergeist," and played the same part at the Vaudeville, July, 1946; St. James's, Oct., 1946, Sir Edward Harkalong in "The Man in the Street"; Aldwych, June, 1948, appeared as M. Baski in "Ambassador Extraordinary"; Embassy, Feb., 1949, Joey Wright in "The Passing of the Third Floor Back"; Phoenix, May, 1949, Gibbet in "The Beaux' Strata-

gem," which ran for over a year; toured, Oct., 1950, as Udolphus McCluskey in "The Chuckeyhead Story"; at the "Q," Jan., 1951, played the Marquis of Malford Christian in "High Life"; Grand, Blackpool, Nov., 1951, Col. Brion in "Something In the Cellar"; toured, Feb., 1952, as Horace Logan in "Treasure on Pelican"; Royal, Brighton, Oct., 1952, played Wilfred Hackforth-Barnes in "A Fiddler at the Wedding"; "Q," Sept., 1953, John Clarke in "The Gentle Maiden"; Grand, Blackpool, Apr., 1953, Baron Klopp in "Happy As a King"; "Q," Nov., 1953, Insp. Hailstone in "The Summerhouse"; Arts, Feb., 1954, Mr. Marsland in a revival of "The Private Secretary"; Duke of York's, July, 1954, Sir Gregory Uppshot in "Meet a Body"; Strand (for Repertory Players), Oct., 1954, Commodore Hawser in "The Adventures of Peregrine Pickle"; Grand, Leeds, June, 1955, J. G. Van Velt in "Three Times a Day"; Arts, Nov., 1956, played the Fire Brigade Captain in "The Bald Prima Donna"; Vaudeville, June, 1957, took over The Tramp in "Salad Days" for two and a half years; Haymarket, Nov., 1962, played Doctor Lennon in "The Tulip Tree"; entered films, 1937, in "The Challenge," and has since appeared in numerous pictures, and on television. *Favourite parts:* Falstaff, Sir Toby Belch, Bob Acres, Shotover in "Heartbreak House," Hornblower in "The Skin Game." *Recreations:* Cricket, golf, and motoring. *Club:* Green Room.

(Died 1 June, 1966; age 68)

PEARSON, Molly, actress; *b.* Edinburgh; *e.* England, France, and Germany; *m.* Ethelbert Hales; made her first appearance on the stage in England on a provincial tour, in a minor part in "The Little Minister," and her first hit in the part of Lady Babbie in the same play, in which part she toured for some time; she has toured in South Africa, Egypt, Australia, India, and China; at the Duke of York's, 12 July, 1904, played Rosamond in "The Pharisee's Wife"; at the Shaftesbury, Nov., 1904, appeared in "The Flute of Pan";

she made her first appearance in America with Olga Nethersole, playing the part of Dolores in a revival of "Carmen" at the Alvin Theatre, Pittsburgh, 10 Nov., 1906; at Maxine Elliott's Theatre, Oct., 1909, played Stasia in "The Passing of the Third Floor Back"; at the Comedy, New York, Oct., 1911, Bunty Biggar in "Bunty Pulls the Strings," in which she also toured for some time; at the Longacre, Sept., 1914, appeared as Bella in "Tipping the Winner"; at the Princess, Nov., 1915, as Maggie Hobson in "Hobson's Choice"; at the Knickerbocker, Feb., 1917, played Effie Proctor in "The Professor's Love Story"; at the Nora Bayes Theatre, Apr., 1920, Meg Duncan in "Lassie"; at the Bijou, New York, Dec., 1921, played Eustatia in "The Dover Road"; Longacre, Feb., 1925, Miss Smallwood in "The Dark Angel"; Globe, Mar., 1925, Nanny Webster in "The Little Minister"; Knickerbocker, June, 1925, Sarah in "Trelawney of the Wells"; for the Theatre Guild, 1927-28, toured as Mrs. Phelps in "The Silver Cord," Catherine Petkoff in "Arms and the Man," "Mama" in "The Guardsman," and Lady Marden in "Mr. Pim Passes By"; Vanderbilt, Nov., 1929, played Aunt Dora in "White Flame"; Longacre, Dec., 1929, Mistress Brewster in "The Unsophisticates"; Forrest, Oct., 1931, Mrs. Trent in "Lean Harvest"; Charles Hopkins Theatre, Feb., 1932, Mrs. Tilling in "They Don't Mean Any Harm"; Apr., 1932, Martha Sedgwick in "Housewarming"; Bijou, Oct., 1932, Jessie Ann in "The Anatomist"; Ritz, Oct., 1934, Sweeney in "Good-Bye Please"; Booth, Jan., 1935, Mrs. Dorothy Radfern in "Laburnum Grove," and Jan., 1936, Madam Wang in "Lady Precious Stream"; toured, autumn of 1936, in "Pride and Prejudice"; Fulton, Nov., 1937, Maria Disraeli in "Young Mr. Disraeli"; John Golden, Dec., 1937, Mrs. Wingate in "Love of Women"; Martin Beck, Feb., 1938, Kirsten in "Save Me the Waltz"; 51st Street, Oct., 1938, Queen Victoria in "Knights of Song"; Henry Miller Theatre, 1940, for a time, played Ellen Creed in "Ladies in Retirement." *Address :* Walnut

Tree Hill, Sandy Hook, Conn., U.S.A. *(Died 26 Jan., 1959; age 83)*

PECK, Gregory, actor; *b.* La Jolla, California, U.S.A., 5 Apr., 1916; *e.* University of California; first attracted attention in New York, when he appeared at the Morosco Theatre, Sept., 1942, as Cliff Parrilow in "The Morning Star"; Windsor, Dec., 1942, played Robin and Kirkland Todd in "The Willow and I"; Morosco, May, 1943, Andrew Tadlock in "Sons and Soldiers"; appeared in films in Hollywood, 1944, in "Days of Glory."

PEDGRIFT, Frederic Henchman, son of the late Dr. Frederic Woodcock Pedgrift, of Halesworth, Suffolk; educated for a schoolmaster; manager of *The Era ;* hon. treasurer to numerous theatrical charitable funds; founder of the Showmen's Guild; vice-president of the Music Hall Home, a member of the Scenic Artists' Association, the Amalgamated Musicians' Union, and hon. member of the Stage Operatives' Society; a baritone singer and teacher of singing. *Hobbies :* Gardening, photography, the art of making friends. *Address :* 21 Hillbury Road, Streatham, S.W. *Telephone :* 827 Streatham.

PEDRICK, Gale, dramatic author and critic; *b.* London, 15 June, 1905; *s.* of John Gale Pendrick, F.R. Hist. Society, and his wife Hilda Beatrice (Perkins); *e.* St. Anne's School, Redhill, and Sir Roger Manwood's School, Sandwich; *m.* Doris Pattison; commenced his career, 1924, as music critic to the *Western Morning News*, Plymouth; music critic, 1927, to *Daily Dispatch*, Manchester; joined *The Star*, London, 1929, and became theatre correspondent, and later radio and television critic; he was second dramatic critic on *The Star*, 1930–9; has been associated with broadcasting since 1925, and has written and produced many radio features and plays; has written many sketches for leading radio artists; was part-author of "The Little Dog Laughed," Palladium, 1939; joined the Queens Royal Regiment as a private, 1940; commissioned in the Devon Regiment; became Intelligence Officer, and was promoted Major, 1942; was subsequently appointed Officer-in-charge of Entertainments, Western Command, and founded the Western Command Symphony Orchestra, and produced his radio-play, "The Fingers of Private Spiegel," 1942; appointed Chief of the Army Broadcasting Service in North Africa, Nov., 1943, with the rank of Lieut.-Colonel; was mentioned in dispatches; returned to England, 1945; demobilized, 1946; rejoined *The Star*, 1946, as radio correspondent and critic, but resigned after a few months, to take up the appointment of Script Editor of the B.B.C. *Hobby:* Study of "fan"-worship in all its forms.

(Died 23 Feb., 1970; age 63)

PEEL, David, actor; *b.* London, 19 June, 1920; *e.* St. Paul's School, Hammersmith; studied for the stage at the Royal Academy of Dramatic Art; made his first appearance on the stage at the Holborn Empire, 23 Dec., 1934, as Black Bear in "Where the Rainbow Ends"; Kingsway, Mar., 1937, played Ryan in "Come Out to Play"; Savoy, June, 1938, in "No Sky So Blue"; Shaftesbury, Sept., 1938, in "Goodbye, Mr. Chips"; Richmond, Feb., 1939, played John Fortescue in "Ill Blows the Wind"; served in H.M. Forces, 1939–42, when he was invalided out; he then appeared at the Piccadilly, Aug., 1942, as Lennox in "Macbeth"; Westminster, Oct., 1943, David in "Landslide"; Aldwych, Dec., 1943, Frank Olmstead in "There Shall Be No Night"; joined the Shakespeare Memorial Theatre company, Stratford-on-Avon, for 1945 season, and played Romeo, Orsino, Claudio in "Much Ado About Nothing," Eros in "Antony and Cleopatra," Hastings in "She Stoops to Conquer," Fenton in "The Merry Wives of Windsor," and Chorus in "Henry VIII"; St. James's, May, 1946, Duke of Clarence in "The Kingmaker," and July, 1946, Leonidas in "Marriage à la Mode"; Arts, Apr., 1947, Alan in "Less Than Kind"; Wyndham's, Oct., 1947, Philip Clandon

in "You Never Can Tell"; Whitehall, Apr., 1948, produced "Bates Wharf"; "Q," Apr., 1949, played Roy Kane in "House on the Sand"; Arts, Aug., 1949, Pepe in "The Romantic Young Lady"; produced "Fallen Angels" for provincial tour, 1949; first appeared in films, 1934. *Hobby:* Collecting pictures. *Address:* 61a Cadogan Square, London, S.W.1. *Telephone No.:* Sloane 6435.

PEILE, Frederick Kinsey, dramatic author and actor; *b.* Allahabad, India, 20 Dec., 1862; *s.* of Sarah (Oman) and Frederick Weston Peile; *e.* Wimbledon; was formerly a Lieutenant in the Second Battalion of the Welsh Regiment; first appeared on the stage at the Prince of Wales's Theatre, 1892, as the White Admiral in "Blue Eyed Susan"; subsequently toured with George Alexander, and also appeared at the St. James's Theatre in "Liberty Hall," "The Importance of Being Earnest," etc.; after a lengthy absence from the stage, reappeared during 1908, when he toured with Miss May Palfrey as Blenkinsopp in "Mrs. Dot"; at the Garrick, 1910, played in "Dame Nature"; at the Strand, 1910, in "The Man from Mexico"; at the Royalty, 1911, played in "The Career of Nablotsky," at the Kingsway, played George Tesman in "Hedda Gabler," at the Royalty, Du Mesnil in "The Parisienne," and at the Kingsway in "The Great Young Man"; at the Garrick, May, 1913, appeared as Rochebrune in "Croesus"; on the outbreak of war, 1914, received a commission as Lieutenant of the Welsh Regiment; at the Globe, May, 1918, played Lord Anthony Fitzurse in "Press the Button"; Nov., 1918, the Marquis of Bombelles in "L'Aiglon"; at the Lyric, Hammersmith, Dec., 1918, played in "Make Believe"; at the Globe, July, 1919, Archer Kingston in "Trimmed in Scarlet"; at the Kingsway, Mar., 1923, played Colonel Yarborough in "Love in Pawn"; at the Regent, Apr., 1923, Otho in "The Insect Play"; June, 1923, General Scott in "Robert E. Lee"; at the Court,

Nov., 1923, Bishop of Chelmgate in " Our Ostriches " ; at the Everyman, Nov., 1924, and the Royalty, Dec., 1924, Pauncefort Quentin in " The Vortex " ; New, Sept., 1925, Richard Twining in " The Moon and Sixpence " ; Little, Feb., 1926, Duke D'Azollo in " The Forcing House " ; Savoy, Mar., 1926, Baron de Lisle in " The Snow Man " ; Court (for Renaissance Society), June, 1926, Béraide in " Le Malade Imaginaire " ; " Q," Sept., 1926, Sir Marcus Voigt in " Trust O'Brien " ; New (for Stage Society), Feb., 1927, Horace Tiptree in " One More River " ; Haymarket, Feb., 1928, Major Fothergill in " The Fourth Wall " ; Royalty, May, 1930, the Bishop of Chelmsgate in " Our Ostriches"; St. James's, June, 1930, Caesar in "The Swan"; Prince of Wales's (for Stage Society), Dec., 1930, the Comte de Laumont in "The Borrowed Life"; Playhouse, Feb., 1932, Edgar Mervyn in " King, Queen, Knave"; Globe, Apr., 1932, Lord Cossington in "Wings Over Europe"; has also appeared in films, including "The Face at the Window," "The Vortex," "The Burgomaster of Stilemonde," "Three Live Ghosts," "High Society," etc. ; has written the following plays : "The Belle of Cairo," 1896 ; " Solomon's Twins," 1897 ; " An Interrupted Honeymoon," 1899 ; " Lyre and Lancet," 1902 ; " The Man Who Was," 1903 ; " Money and the Girl," 1910 ; " Biff," " Twelve o'clock," " The Shooting Star," 1912 ; " The Pink Nightgown," 1913 ; " Who Laughs Last," 1919 ; wrote his reminiscences, under the title of "Candied Peel." *Recreations :* Golf and motoring. *Club :* Naval and Military.
(Died 13 Apr., 1934; age 72)

PÉLISSIER, Harry Gabriel, composer and entertainer ; *b.* Finchley, 1874 ; *s.* of Frederic Anton Pélissier, of French origin on his father's side, his mother being English ; a descendant of the famous Marshal Pélissier ; *e.* Folkstone, Highgate, and Scarborough ; *m.* Fay Compton ; on leaving school went to Switzerland to study French, being destined by his father, a diamond merchant, for a business career in his own office ; his tendencies, however, were towards music and the stage ; acquired considerable popularity on the concert platform and in drawing-rooms ; founded " The Follies," and of late years has appeared mainly at the Apollo Theatre, with this company.
(Died 25th September, 1913 ; age 39)

PEMBERTON, Brock, producing manager; *b.* Leavenworth, Kansas, U.S.A., 14 Dec., 1885; *s.* of Albert Pemberton and his wife Ella (Murdock); *e.* College of Emporia and University of Kansas (B.A.); *m.* Margaret McCoy; formerly engaged as a journalist, and was engaged on the *Emporia Gazette*, 1908-10; dramatic editor *New York Evening Mail*, 1910-11; assistant dramatic editor *New York World* and *New York Times*, 1911-17; assistant producer to Arthur Hopkins, 1917-20; commenced producing on his own account in 1920, when he presented " Enter Madame " ; has since produced " Miss Lulu Bett," 1920 ; " Swords," 1921 ; " Six Characters in Search of an Author," " The Plot Thickens," 1922; " Rita Coventry," " The Love Habit," " The White Desert," 1923 ; " The Living Mask," " Mr. Pitt," " The Marionette Man," "The Mask and the Face," 1924 ; " Puppets," 1925 ; "The Masque of Venice," " Loose Ankles," "The Ladder," "Say It With Flowers," 1926; " Goin' Home," " Hotbed," 1928; with Antoinette Perry, produced "Strictly Dishonorable," 1929; "Three Times the Hour," 1931; "Christopher Comes Across," 1932; "Personal Appearance," 1934 ; "Ceiling Zero," 1935; "Now You've Done It," "Chalked Out," "Red Harvest," 1937 ; " Kiss the Boys Goodbye," 1938; "Lady in Waiting,"" Out from Under," "Glamour Preferred," 1940; "Cuckoos on the Hearth," 1941; "Janie," 1942; "Pillar to Post," 1943; "Harvey," 1944. *Recreation :* Tennis.
(Died 11 Mar., 1950; age 64)

PEMBERTON, John Wyndham, manager; *b.* Gwalior, India, 31 Oct., 1883; *s.* of Colonel A. R. Pemberton and his wife Mary Frances (Cockerell); *e.* Eton; *m.* (1) Ana Duggan (dec.);

(2) Suzy Primerose; originally intended for the Army, but failed medically; commenced his theatrical career as a touring manager in the provinces, 1914; produced "Extra Special," Kingsway, 1916; "Telling the Tale," Ambassadors', 1918; subsequently had considerable managerial experience on the Continent; presented "Fritzi," Adelphi, 1935; acquired a 21 years lease of the Ambassadors' Theatre, 1937, also an interest in the St. Martin's; in 1939 acquired the lease of the Shaftesbury Theatre; produced "Sweet and Low," Ambassadors', 1943; "Sweeter and Lower," 1944, which ran over two years, longer than any other *revue*; "Sweetest and Lowest," 1946; in addition, produced "A House in the Square," St. Martin's, 1940; "Other People's Houses," Ambassadors', 1941; "Scoop," Vaudeville, 1942. *Address:* 5 Lancaster Gate, London, W.2. *Telephone No.:* Ambassador 1679.
(Died 6 Aug., 1947; age 63)

PEMBERTON, Sir Max (cr. 1928); dramatic author and novelist; *b.* Birmingham, 19 June, 1863; *s.* of Thomas Joshua Pemberton and his wife Katherine Jane (Fisher); *e.* Merchant Taylors' School and Caius College, Cambridge, where he took his M.A. degree; *m.* Florence Bertha Pemberton; his first work, "The Diary of a Scoundrel," was published in 1891; was Editor of *Chums*, 1892–3, and for ten years, 1896–1906, was Editor of *Cassell's Magazine*; has written the following plays or sketches: "The Finishing School," 1904; "The Lady of the Pageant" (with Cyril Wentworth Hogg), 1908; "The Woman of Kronstadt" (with George Fleming, from his own novel "Kronstadt"), 1908; "The Grey Room," 1911; "Diane's Diamonds," 1912; "Hullo, Ragtime!" (part author), 1912; "Hullo, Tango!" (part author), 1913; "Come Over Here!" (part author), 1913; "Garrick," 1913; "The Belles of St. Valoir," 1914; "The Haunted Husband," 1915; "Vivien" (with Arthur Wimperis), 1915, subsequently renamed "My Lady Frayle"; "Oh, Caesar!" (with A. M. Thompson),

1916; "Oh! Don't, Dolly!" (with Eustace Ponsonby, founded on "Betsy"), 1919; among his novels are: "The Iron Pirate," "Queen of the Jesters," "Féo," "The Giant's Gate," "The Diamond Ship," "Kronstadt," etc.; wrote "The Life of Sir Henry Royce"; Founder of the London School of Journalism. *Clubs:* Garrick and Leander.
(Died 22 Feb., 1950; age 86)

PENLEY, Arthur, business manager; *b.* London, 24 July, 1881; *s.* of the late W. S. Penley and his wife, Mary Ann (Ricketts); *e.* at Margate and King Edward VI Grammar School, Guildford; *m.* Doris Mansell; his first connection with the theatre was in the capacity of advance agent to a provincial company, and subsequently as business manager; business manager at the Royalty, 1899; Kingsway, 1909; Garrick, 1910; subsequently he became manager for the late Laurence Irving, Marie Tempest, and J. E. Vedrenne; The Little, 1911-13; served in R.F.A. during the war; demobilised 1919; business manager at the Comedy, 1920-24; Gaiety, 1925; London Pavilion, 1925-7; subsequently went to South Africa; on his return, was appointed Dramatic Manager to the I.V.T.A. *Recreations:* Fishing, swimming, and outdoor sports.
(Died 2 July, 1954; age 72)

PENLEY, W. S., actor and manager; *b.* St. Peter's, Margate, 19 Nov., 1851; *s.* of a schoolmaster; *e.* Westminster; in his youth, was a chorister at the Chapel Royal, Savoy and at Westminster Abbey; was for some time in the wholesale drapery business, as a clerk; made his first appearance on the professional stage at the Court Theatre, 1871, as Tim in "My Wife's Second Floor"; subsequently appeared at the Holborn, May, 1872, in "Doctor Faust," and the Opéra Comique, Nov., 1874, in "Ixion Re-Wheeled"; in Mar., 1875, appeared at the Royalty, as the Foreman of the Jury in "Trial by Jury," and subsequently played in "The Dumb Belle" and "La Périchole"; appeared at the Opéra Comique, Jan., 1876, in " Madame L'Archiduc," " Geneviève de Brabant," etc. ; at the Strand, Sept., 1876, played Zapeter in " Princess Toto " ; subsequently played there in " The Maid and the Magpie," " Old Soldiers," " Family Ties," " The Red Rover," " Dora and Diplunacy," etc. ; at the Royalty, in Apr., 1879, made a " hit " as Grinder in " The Zoo," and Jellicoe in " Crutch and Toothpick " ; subsequently toured in " H.M.S. Pinafore " ; in Mar., 1880, was at the Gaiety, playing Matthew Popperton in " La Voyage in Suisse," with the Hanlons, subsequently touring with them in the United States ; later in the year was at the Alhambra, understudying Fred Leslie in " Mefistofele II," and the following year appeared there as Valentine in that opera, and as the Prince in " Jeanne, Jeannette and Jeanneton " ; during 1882, appeared at the Globe, in " The Vicar of Bray " ; and at the Comedy in " Rip Van Winkle " ; in 1883, made a great " hit," as Lay Brother Pelican in " Falka " ; then 19 May, 1884, came his performance of the Rev. Robert Spalding in " The Private Secretary," at the Globe, a part with which his name was identified for years, and in which he was the successor of Beerbohm Tree ; in 1886, he played in " The Pickpocket," and subsequent successes at the Globe were achieved in " The Doctor " and " The Arabian Nights " ; at the Comedy, 1888, appeared in " Uncles and Aunts," and the following year, in " Merry Margate " ; at the Strand, 1889, played in " Æsop's Fables " ; at Terry's, Feb., 1890, played in " New Lamps for Old," and later in " The Judge " ; in 1891, appeared at Toole's in " Our Regiment," and at the Savoy in " The Nautch Girl " ; on 29 Feb., 1892, he produced the famous " Charley's Aunt," at Bury St. Edmunds, appearing as Lord Fancourt Babberley ; the piece was produced at the Royalty Theatre, on 21 Dec., 1892, and transferred to the Globe, in the following year ; the piece was performed no fewer than 1,466 times in succession, and holds the record for the largest number of successive performances :

the play was withdrawn in Dec., 1896, but has been revived on several occasions since ; Dec., 1898, he appeared at the Royalty, as Lord Markham in " A Little Ray of Sunshine " ; rebuilt the old Novelty Theatre, opening it as the Great Queen Street Theatre, 24 May, 1900, with " A Little Ray of Sunshine " ; in July, 1900, revived " The Private Secretary," and Dec., 1900, " Charley's Aunt " ; since 1901, has practically retired from the stage.

(Died 11 Nov., 1912; age 59)

PENN, Bill, actor, producer, director; *b.* Reading, Pennsylvania, 15 June, 1931; *e.* Franklin and Marshall College; studied drama at the University of California at Los Angeles; first appeared in New York at the Cort, July, 1953, when he took over as Marty Goodwin in "The Fifth Season"; toured, 1953, in "Stalag 17"; founded the Broadway Chapel Players and, at the Broadway Tabernacle Church, played Cuthman in "The Boy with a Cart," Oct., 1954, Japheth in Andre Obey's "Noah," and, Mar., 1955, the Guide in "In April Once"; Broadway Congregational Church, Oct., 1955, played the Angel in Yeats's "The Hour-Glass"; Tempo Playhouse, May, 1956, directed Jean Genet's "The Maids," and, June, 1956, directed "By Hex"; Broadway Congregational Church, Oct., 1957, directed "Tobias and the Angel," and, Feb., 1958, produced and directed "The Marvelous History of Saint Bernard"; Phoenix, Feb., 1958, played the Messenger from Corinth in "The Infernal Machine"; since then has concentrated on directing and producing, and directed "The Potting Shed," 1958; "Fugue for Three Marys," "The Women at the Tomb," "Susannah and the Elders," 1959; "The Bible Salesman," "Tobacco Road," "Medium Rare" (Chicago), "The Miracle," 1960; "Double Entry," "Bartleby," "Sing Muse," 1961; "Put It in Writing" (Chicago), 1962; "Like Other People," "Put It in Writing," "Three Cheers for the Tired Businessman" (Chicago), 1963; "That Thing at the Cherry Lane," 1965; "By Hex" (Lancaster, Philadelphia), 1966. *Ad-*

dress: 219 East 69th Street, New York, N.Y., U.S.A. *Telephone No:* UN 1-0646.

PENNINGTON, Ann, dancer; *b.* Camden, N.J., U.S.A., 23 Dec., 1892; *e.* Cooper's School, Camden; was well-known as an amateur dancer in Philadelphia before making her first appearance, professionally, at Aston, New York, Nov., 1911, in "The Red Widow," in which she subsequently toured all over the United States; at the Grand Opera House, Chicago, Sept., 1912, played Hansel in "A Polish Wedding"; first attracted attention when she appeared at the New Amsterdam Theatre, New York, 16 June, 1913, in "The Ziegfeld Follies of 1913"; she appeared regularly with the Follies until 1918; also appeared at the Century Theatre, Nov., 1917, in "Miss 1917"; at the Liberty, June, 1919, appeared in "Scandals of 1919"; at the Globe, June, 1920, in "Scandals of 1920"; Liberty, July, 1921, in "George White's Scandals"; Globe, Mar., 1923, played Gloria Wayne in "Jack and Jill"; at the New Amsterdam, June, 1924, re-appeared in "The Ziegfeld Follies"; Apollo, June, 1926, returned to "George White's Scandals"; Apollo, July, 1928, again appeared with "George White's Scandals"; Broadway, Dec., 1930, played Lola McGee in "The New Yorkers"; Brighton Beach, June, 1931, played in "Broadway Personalities"; Shubert, Oct., 1931, Louella May Carroll in "Everybody's Welcome"; at the Chicago Theatre, Oct., 1933, appeared in "Crazy Quilt"; at the Blackstone, Chicago, Oct., 1934, played Prudence Kirkland in "The Pursuit of Happiness"; Plymouth, Boston, Nov., 1938, Blossom in "The Flying Ginsburgs"; in 1939, appeared World's Fair, Florida, in George Jessel's "Gaieties"; subsequently appeared at various night clubs; toured, 1942–3, in "Hell-zapoppin," and 1943, in "Blossom Time"; Broadway Theatre, New York, June, 1943, played Gretchen in "The Student Prince," in which she subsequently toured; at Chicago, July, 1944, appeared in "The Merry Widow"; first appeared in films, 1916, in "Susie's Snowflake," and has appeared in numerous pictures since that date. *Address:* Hotel Lincoln, 44th and 45th Streets, at Eighth Avenue, New York City, U.S.A.

PENROSE, John, actor; *b.* Southsea, Hants., 5 May, 1917; *s.* of Commander J. S. Edward Penrose, R.N., and his wife Irene Hester (Graham-Smith); *e.* Diocesan College, Rondebosch, Cape Town, South Africa; studied sculpture at the School of Applied Art, Cape Town; studied for the stage at the Royal Academy of Dramatic Art, where he won the Lawrence prize for stage design; made his first appearance on the stage at the Barn Theatre, Oxted, Oct., 1936, as Squire Ulfheim in "When We Dead Awaken"; in Dec., 1936, founded and directed the Amersham Repertory company; made his first appearance in London, at the St. James's, 18 Aug., 1937, as a Footman in "Old Music"; Arts, Jan., 1938, played Brian Calthorpe in "But For the Grace," and Nov., 1938, Eustace in "Oscar Wilde"; Kingsway, Apr., 1939, Bill Ferguson in "A Woman's Privilege"; Richmond, Oct., 1939, and later, in the same month at the Criterion, played Robin in "French for Love"; joined the Royal Navy, June, 1940, as a stoker; during the War, directed nearly forty plays with professional actors serving in the Navy; "Q," Jan., 1947, played Algernon in "The Day After To-Morrow," and Apr., 1947, Leonard in "Quiet in the Forest"; played leading parts at Southsea, June–July, 1948; toured, Apr., 1949, as Beecham in "The Chiltern Hundreds"; in Sept., 1949, with Pat Nye, purchased the Bedford Theatre, Camden Town, opening with a revival of "Lady Audley's Secret," Oct., 1949, subsequently transferred to the Prince's Theatre; played several parts in various revivals, at the Bedford, Nov., 1949 to June, 1950; New Boltons, June, 1952, played Oscar Wilde in "Whistler's Mother"; first appeared in films, 1938. *Recreations:* Squash and swimming, drawing and stage design. *Club:* Stage Golfing Society. *Address:* 25 Iverna Court, Kensington, W.8. *Telephone No.:* Western 5928.

PEPLE, Edward H.; dramatic author; *b.* Richmond, Va., 10 Aug., 1867; *s.* of Gustavus Adolphus and Sarah Bell (Lowndes) Peple; *e.* Richmond, Va.; originally engaged in business on the Chesapeake and Ohio Railway, and subsequently on the Southern Pacific; his first play was "The Broken Rosary"; then followed "The Prince Chap," produced in 1904, followed by "A Woman's Way," 1906; "The Mallet's Masterpiece," 1906; "The Love Route," 1906; "The Silver Girl," 1907; "Vasta Herne," 1909; "The Call of the Cricket," 1910; "The Spitfire," 1910; "The Littlest Rebel," 1911; "Taken on Credit," 1912; "The Charity Girl," 1912; "A Pair of Sixes," 1914; "Friend Martha, 1916; "Maggie" ("Patsy on the Wing"), 1918; "Ladies' Day," 1920; "Her Birthright," 1921.

PERCEVAL-CLARK, Perceval, actor; *b.* London, 25 Nov., 1881; *o.s.* of the late Captain P. Perceval-Clark, 9th Lancers; *e.* Aldenham School and Wellington College; *m.* Jean Cadell; served in the South African War, 1901–2, as 2nd Lieut. in the 4th East Surrey; made his first appearance on the stage at the Court Theatre, 17 Sept., 1906, walking on in "John Bull's Other Island"; at the Haymarket, May, 1907, appeared as M. Potin in "My Wife"; for two years played with the Glasgow Repertory Company, appearing as Kit French in "Admiral Guinea"; Octavius Robinson in "Man and Superman," Philip Clandon in "You Never Can Tell," George D'Alroy in "Caste," Walter How in "Justice," etc.; at the Court, Sept., 1912, played Edward Hargreaves in "Ann"; at the Queen's, Nov., 1912, Bertie Channing in "Sylvia Greer"; Nov., 1913, Reggie Moody in "If We had only Known"; at the Court, Jan., 1914, Quincy Davenport, junr., in "The Melting Pot"; in 1914 joined the 8th East Surrey Regiment; invalided out, 1915; joined the War Trade Intelligence Dept., 1916; at the Apollo, Mar., 1916, played Percival Pennicuik in "The Man who Stayed at Home"; at the Royalty, Oct., 1916, Eric Carrington in "Home on Leave";

at the St. James's, Nov., 1917, appeared as Harry Craig in "Loyalty"; at the Savoy, Feb., 1918, as Richard Donnelly in "Nothing But the Truth"; at the St. James's, May, 1920, as Le Candeur in "The Mystery of the Yellow Room"; at the Aldwych, July, 1921, played Tom Quest in "James the Less"; at the Everyman, Oct., 1921, Jack Crosby in "Diff'rent"; at the Queen's, Apr., 1922, the Hon. Ian Maxwell in "Lass o' Laughter"; at the Aldwych (for the Play Actors), Mar., 1924, and at the Queen's, Apr., 1924, Stephen Rokeby in "The Conquering Hero"; at the Grand, Fulham, Sept., 1924, James Sharman in "The Letter of the Law"; Nov., 1924, Tom in "Marigold"; Ambassadors', Mar., 1925, Edward Waters in "Anyhouse"; Kingsway, Apr., 1927, St. Leger Carington in "Marigold"; Everyman, Oct., 1928, Ragnar Brovik in "The Master Builder"; Apollo, Apr., 1932, Mr. Purefoy in "Pleasure Cruise"; is a member of the Salters' Company, and a Freeman of the City of London. *Club :* Green Room. *(Died 6 June, 1938; age 57)*

PERCY, Edward (*né* Edward Percy Smith), dramatic author; *b.* London, 5 Jan., 1891; *y.s.* of Benjamin Figgis Smith and his wife Emily Elizabeth (Judson); *e.* Haileybury and in France; *m.* (1) Gertrude Ethel Glazebrook (mar. dis.); (2) Lilian Mary Denham (*née* Oldland); was engaged in East Indian and Colonial produce business, 1909–30; subsequently a miller and corn merchant, and a director of several companies; is the author of the following, among other, plays: "If Four Walls Told," 1922; "Trespasses," 1923; "Ancient Lights," 1923; "A Magdalen's Husband" (with Milton Rosmer), 1924; "The Rigordans," 1926; "The Misdoings of Charley Peace," 1929; "Mary Darling," 1936; "Suspect" (with Reginald Denham), 1937; "The Last Straw" (with Reginald Denham), 1937; "Give Me Yesterday" (with Reginald Denham), 1938; "Ladies in Retirement" (with Reginald Denham), 1939; "Dr. Brent's Household," 1940; "Play With Fire" (subsequently "The Shop at Sly Corner"), 1941, and produced in London under the latter title, 1945; "The House on the Bridge," 1944; "Dogs Delight" (with Reginald Denham), 1946; "My Wives and I," 1947; "The Man They Acquitted" (with Reginald Denham), 1949; "Angels Don't Wear Wedding Rings," 1950; "Lords of Creation" (with Lilian Denham), 1952; "The Man With Expensive Tastes" (with Lilian Denham), 1953; "The Old Gentleman," 1956; "Stranger in the Tea" (with Lilian Percy), 1957; "Major Road Ahead" (with Lilian Percy), 1958; has also written novels, prose, and verse; Conservative M.P. for the Ashford Division of Kent, 1943–50, and is a Freeman of the City of London. *Recreations:* Gardening and fishing. *Hobby:* Cooking. *Club:* Garrick. *Address:* Selmeston House, Selmeston, Sussex. *Telephone No.:* Ripe 323.

PERCY, S. Esmé, actor and producer; *b.* London, 8 Aug., 1887; *e.* at Windsor and Brussels; studied for the stage at the Brussels Conservatoire, and in Paris, under MM. Georges Berr and Maurice Leloir and Mdme. Sarah Bernhardt; made his first appearance in England, at the Theatre Royal, Nottingham, Feb., 1904, in F. R. Benson's company; first appeared in London at the Royalty, 5 May, 1905, as Romeo in " Romeo and Juliet," under the auspices of the Elizabethan Stage Society; appeared at His Majesty's, Jan., 1906, as Britannicus in " Nero "; also appeared at same theatre as the Earl of March in " King Henry IV " (Part I), Apr., 1906, and as Lucius in "Julius Caesar," Apr., 1906; toured in South Africa, 1907, with Mrs. Brown-Potter, playing Orlando, Armand Duval, Charles Surface, etc.; on his return to England, joined F. R. Benson's Midland Company, playing Hamlet, Shylock, Macbeth, etc.; at the Court Theatre, Nov., 1908, played Pentheus in " The Bacchae " of Euripides; subsequently joined Miss Horniman's company at the Gaiety, Manchester, remaining until July, 1911; subsequently toured as John Tanner in " Man and Superman"; at the King's Hall, Covent Garden,

Dec., 1912, played Troilus in " Troilus and Cressida "; formed a travelling repertory company with Miss Kirsteen Graeme, 1913, and produced the following, among other plays : " The Awakening Woman," " Joy," " The Orangeman," " The Master," " Cupid and Commonsense," " The Honeymoon," " The Voysey Inheritance," " The Doctor's Dilemma," " The Melting Pot," " The Importance of Being Earnest," " The Little Man," " Lies that Fester," " The Cloister," " Man and Superman," " Birds of Passage," " The Philanderer," " Merely Mary Ann," " The Silver Box," " A Life of Man "; appeared at the Little Theatre, London, Jan., 1914, and played Hamlet; enlisted in the London Scottish, Dec., 1915; granted a commission in the Highland Light Infantry, 1916; served in France and with the Army of Occupation in Germany, until 1923; whilst with the Army of the Rhine was Officer-in-charge of the Dramatic company, and produced over 140 plays; in Apr., 1923, joined Reandean as assistant producer; at the St. Martin's July, 1923, played Lonny Copshrews in " Melloney Holtspur "; Aug., 1923, produced " The Likes of Her "; at His Majesty's, Sept., 1923, played Selim in " Hassan "; at the St. Martin's, Nov., 1923, produced " Fledglings "; at the Regent (for the Phoenix Society), June, 1924, played Bellmour in " The Old Bachelor "; was then appointed general producer to Charles Macdona's " Bernard Shaw Repertory Company," and besides producing the various plays has appeared at various times as Don Juan Tenorio in " Don Juan in Hell," Blanco Posnet, Androcles, Louis Dubedat, Professor Higgins, John Tanner, St. John Hotchkiss, Valentine, etc.; at the Regent, Oct., 1925, played John Tanner and Don Juan in " Man and Superman " in its entirety, and repeated the performance at the Little Theatre, Jan., 1928; at the New Oxford, Oct., 1924, played Hamlet in " Fratricide Punished "; Court, Feb., 1925 (for 300 Club), de Bomph in " Smaragda's Lover "; Scala, Oct., 1925 (for the Renaissance Society), Duke of Brachiano in " The White Devil "; Kingsway, Dec., 1926,

Rev. Robert Spalding in "The Private Secretary"; Lyric, Jan., 1929, Lord Byron in "Byron"; Arts, Apr., 1929, Harlequin in "The Theatre of Life"; Prince of Wales's (for Stage Society), Dec., 1929, the Soldier in "Douamont"; Royalty, Dec., 1929, Rex Appellini in "The Amorists"; at the Court, Dec., 1929–Mar., 1930, played lead and produced in a season of Shaw revivals, and Feb., 1930, played Hamlet; with the Masque Theatre Company, at Edinburgh, in 1930, played in "Back to Methuselah"; Haymarket, Jan., 1931, played Bobiche in "Colonel Satan"; Kingsway, May, 1931, again appeared in "Pygmalion," and "Man and Superman"; June, 1931, played the Marquis of Sark in "The Heir"; July, 1931, rejoined the Masque Theatre Company at Edinburgh as producer and leading man, and appeared by Royal Command at the Lyceum, Edinburgh, 11 July, 1931, as Crichton in "The Admirable Crichton"; at the Duchess, Jan., 1932, played Geoffrey March in "Windows"; Fortune, Mar., 1932, Archbishop Cranmer in "Fire"; Vaudeville, Apr., 1932, Miles Malpractise in "Vile Bodies"; went to America, and at Buffalo, N.Y., Nov., 1932, played the Lord Chancellor in "Red Planet"; after returning to London, appeared at the Garrick, June, 1933, as Prince Tomofsky in "Clear All Wires"; Lyric, Aug., 1933, Lemmle in "The Ace"; Lyric, Oct., 1933, Robert Greene in "This Side Idolatry"; Playhouse, Dec., 1933, Mr. Gray in "The World of Light"; Fulham, Jan., 1934, and Cambridge, Feb., 1934, Sol Ginsburg in "Success Story"; Westminster, Sept., 1934, Dobelle in "The Moon in the Yellow River"; Little, Nov., 1934, His Excellency Wang Yun in "Lady Precious Stream"; Westminster, Feb., 1935, Samson Toublanc in "They Do These Things in France"; Grafton (for Stage Society), Mar., 1935, Tiresias in "The Machine of the Gods"; at the Cambridge, Aug., 1935, again played lead in Shaw repertory, also producing the plays; in Aug., 1935, again played in the full-length version of "Man and Superman"; Sept., 1935, played King Magnus in "The Apple Cart"; Playhouse, Dec., 1935, Humpty

Dumpty in "Alice Through the Looking Glass"; Comedy, Nov., 1936, appeared in "To and Fro"; Little, Dec., 1936, again played Humpty-Dumpty; Strand, Jan., 1937, Adam Adams in "Behind Your Back"; Arts, Apr., 1937, Peter Petrous in a play of that name; Lyceum, May, 1937, Bartucci in "Paganini"; toured, Feb., 1938, as Mr. Duirky in "Back Your Fancy"; Wyndham's, Aug., 1938, Sir Eustace Lestrange in "She, Too, Was Young"; "Q," Dec., 1938, Peter Keegan in "John Bull's Other Island"; Embassy, Dec., 1938, Chauvelin in "The Scarlet Pimpernel"; Playhouse, Feb., 1939, Blanco Posnet in "The Shewing-up of Blanco Posnet"; Old Vic., Mar., 1939, Baptista in "The Taming of the Shrew"; Open Air, July, 1940, Quince in "A Midsummer Night's Dream"; Vaudeville, Oct., 1940, Parolles in "All's Well That Ends Well," and Hotspur in "King Henry IV" (Part I); Westminster, Aug., 1941, Vlas Fillipovich in "Distant Point"; Strand, Mar., 1942, Cochinele, Franz and Menelaus in "Tales of Hoffman"; Wimbledon, Oct., 1942, Mr. Porphory in "Lottie Dundass"; Playhouse, Aug., 1943, Maestro Servandoni in "Blow Your Own Trumpet"; Westminster, Nov., 1943, Earl of Caversham in "An Ideal Husband"; "Q," Jan., 1945, Colonel Gregg in "Not So Fast, My Pretty"; Gateway, Apr., 1945, The Linguist in "Easter"; Piccadilly, June, 1945, The Tragic Gentleman in "Jacobowsky and the Colonel"; Torch, Aug., 1945, Ulric Brendel in "Rosmersholm"; Lindsey, Nov., 1945, Antonio in "To-Morrow Will Be Different," and Mar., 1946, Ahab in "The Fountain of Youth"; "Q," Dec., 1947, played Humpty-Dumpty in "Alice Through the Looking-Glass"; Globe, May, 1949, Matthew Skipps in "The Lady's Not For Burning," of which he was also co-producer; Watergate, Sept., 1950, played the Commissioner and Herm in "Farfetched Fables," which he also produced; at the Royale, New York, Nov., 1950, again appeared as Matthew Skipps in "The Lady's Not For Burning"; produced "The Sowers," 1933; "Success Story," "Once Upon a Time," 1934; "The

Machine of the Gods," 1935; "Serena Blandish," 1938; "Jerusalem," 1939; "Circe," "Too True to be Good," "Gog and MacGog," 1948; "Widowers' Houses," "Buoyant Billions," 1949; "MacAdam and Eve," "Exiles," 1950; at the Prince's, June, 1951, with John Clements produced the full version of "Man and Superman," appearing as Mendoza and The Devil; New Lindsey, Sept., 1951, produced "No Strings"; New, Dec., 1951, played Emile Robert in "Colombe"; at the "Q," Mar., 1954, produced "The Praying Mantis"; Lyric, Hammersmith, May, 1954, played Gayeff in "The Cherry Orchard"; Salisbury Playhouse, Nov., 1954, appeared as Cardinal Zampi in "Bacchus"; Arts, Sept., 1955, played Nicholas in "The Burnt Flower Bed"; of late years has also frequently broadcast in many notable plays; in 1949, was elected President of the Shaw Society; has appeared in numerous films. *Clubs:* Savage, Savile, and Arts Theatre. *(Died 16 June, 1957; age 69)*

PERCY, William Stratford, actor; *b.* Melbourne, Australia, 23 Dec., 1872; *s.* of William Percy and his wife Christina (Lawrenson); *m.* Jessie Ramsay; made his first appearance on the stage as the Pirate King in the children's production of "The Pirates of Penzance"; subsequently joined J. C. Williamson's Royal Comic Opera Company, and made his grown-up *début* at the Princess Theatre, Dunedin, N.Z., 23 July, 1891, in "The Pirates of Penzance"; since then has played over two hundred comedy parts in comic opera, musical comedy, comedy, drama, and pantomime, including the light French operas such as "Rip Van Winkle," "Paul Jones," "Madame Favart," "Olivette," "La Mascotte," "La Vie," "La Fille du Tambour Major," "La Fille de la Madame Angot," etc.; all the Gaiety musical comedies, in which he played the Edmund Payne parts; all the Daly Theatre musical productions, such as "The Geisha," "San Toy," "A Country Girl," "The Merry Widow," in which he played both Popoff and Nish; also Captain Coddington in

"In Town," the polite lunatic in "The Belle of New York," etc.; toured in South Africa, 1903–4, with J. C. Williamson's Company, in comic opera and in pantomime; in 1914 was in the United States, and at the New Amsterdam Theatre, New York, Mar., 1914, played Dyke Green in "Maids of Athens"; made his first appearance in London, at the Oxford, 1 Nov., 1915, in "Who's Who?"; at the Hippodrome, Mar., 1916, appeared in "Joyland"; during 1917–18 toured as Dr. Wilkie Thorne in "High Jinks," and Mr. Meebles in "The Boy"; at the Criterion, Mar., 1919, made a great success, when he played Washington Pollock in "Oh! Don't, Dolly!"; at the Duke of York's, Sept., 1919, played Parkinson in "The Girl for the Boy"; at the Alhambra, Jan., 1920, Dadoohlah in "Medorah"; subsequently toured as Mooney in "The Love Girl," and Madame Lucy in "Irene." *Recreations:* Reading, painting, and philately. *(Died 19 June, 1946; age 73)*

PERCYVAL, T. Wigney, actor and dramatic author; *b.* Yorkshire, 29 Dec., 1865; made his first appearance on the stage at the Princess's Theatre, 18 Feb., 1886, in "The Lord Harry"; accompanied Wilson Barrett to America, 1886; at the Globe Theatre, Dec., 1887, played the Rev. Mr. Stanley in "The Golden Ladder"; subsequently appeared there in "Hamlet," "The Lady of Lyons," "The Silver King"; returning to the Princess's, May, 1888, with Wilson Barrett, he appeared as Jim Curphey in "Ben-My-Chree"; Jan., 1889, played Colonel Wayne in "The Good Old Times"; in Apr., 1889, appeared in "Claudian"; at the New Olympic, 1890–1, played in "The People's Idol"; "The Stranger," "The Lights o' London," "The Acrobat," "Theodora," "A Royal Divorce"; subsequently appeared at the Globe, 1891–2, in "Gloriana" and "A Bohemian"; at the Royalty, Dec., 1892, played Sartorius in "Widowers' Houses"; at Terry's, Feb., 1893, played in "Flight," and then rejoined Wilson Barrett for his American tour, playing Cassio, Osric, Governor Harcourt in "Ben-My-Chree," etc. ; at Grand, Leeds, Aug., 1894, was the original Philip Christian in " The Manxman " ; on another American tour with Barrett, played Laertes, the " Spider " in " The Silver King," Theorus in " Claudian " ; at St. Louis, Mo., U.S.A., first performance of " The Sign of the Cross," Mar., 1895, played Favius, and appeared in the same part at the Lyric, London, Jan., 1896 ; Apr., 1897, played Philip in " The Christian " ; May, 1897, Caius Claudius in " Virginius," and Cassio in " Othello " ; he then accompanied Barrett to Australia ; he also toured with him in South Africa in 1901 ; of late years has been mainly identified with the American stage, though he appeared at the Scala Theatre, Mar., 1906, as Lord Foppington in " The School for Husbands " ; at Wallack's, New York, Dec., 1910, played the Rev. Jacob Sternroyd in " Pomander Walk " ; at the Empire, New York, Mar., 1913, Mr. Pedrick in " Liberty Hall " ; at the Booth Theatre, Oct., 1913, Dr. Pascoe in " The Great Adventure " ; at the New Amsterdam, Sept., 1915, The Professor in " Moloch " ; at the Gaiety, New York, Dec., 1917, Albert Smith in " General Post " ; at the Liberty, Nov., 1919, Richard Appleby in " Caesar's Wife " ; at the Globe, New York, Nov., 1922, Foxhall Davidson and the Earl of Torwood in " The Bunch and Judy " ; at the Lyceum, New York, May, 1923, Anthony Hylton in " The Mountebank " ; Jan., 1924, Dr. Rodson in " The Way Things Happen " ; at the Forty-ninth Street Theatre, Feb., 1924, Sir Montague Tollemache in " The Outsider " ; Eltinge, Sept., 1925, James Collester in " All Dressed Up " ; Bijou, Dec., 1926, Dr. Felix Burn in " Slaves All " ; Plymouth, Mar., 1927, Dr. Ludlow Bell in " Mariners " ; Selwyn, Sept., 1927, Count de L'Esterel in " The Garden of Eden " ; Mansfield, Dec., 1927, Reginald Walter Willett in " Caste " ; Booth, Apr., 1930, the Earl of Drumoor in " Lady Clara " ; Morosco, Mar., 1931, Sir John Lawson, K.C., in " The Silent Witness " ; is the author, with Horace Hodges and Edward Irwin, of " When the Devil Drives," 1901, and " Sunday," 1904 ; and with Horace Hodges, of " The Little Admiral,"

1907 ; " Grumpy," 1913 ; " The Little Lady in Blue," 1916 ; " One Wife or Another " (with Percy Shaw), 1933.

PERKINS, Osgood, actor ; *b.* West Newton, Mass., U.S.A., 16 May, 1892 ; *s.* of Henry Phelps Perkins and his wife Helen Virginia (Anthony) ; *e.* Newton High School and Harvard University (B.A.) ; *m.* Janet Esselstyn Rane ;. during the War, served with the U.S Army in France ; subsequently engaged in motion picture production with the Film Guild ; made his first appearance on the stage at the Broadhurst Theatre, New York, 12 Feb., 1924, as Homer Cady in " Beggar on Horseback," and played the same part when the play was revived at the Shubert, Mar., 1925 ; Booth Theatre, Oct., 1925, played Siegfried Strong in " Weak Sisters " ; Mansfield, Mar., 1926, Joshua Cox in " The Masque of Venice " ; Longacre, Apr., 1926, Trebus Hemingway in " Pomeroy's Past " ; Biltmore, Aug., 1926, Andy Barton in " Loose Ankles " ; Garrick, Dec., 1926, Professor Paolino in " Say It With Flowers " ; Martin Beck, Apr., 1927, Joe Cobb in " Spread Eagle " ; Forrest, Sept., 1927, Pete in " Women Go On Forever " ; Empire, Jan., 1928, Whittaker in " Salvation " ; Times Square, Aug., 1928, Walter Burns in " The Front Page " ; Cort, Apr., 1930, Michael Astroff in " Uncle Vanya " ; Henry Miller, Jan., 1931, Samuel Gillespie in " To-Morrow and To-Morrow " ; Plymouth, Apr., 1931, Bruce Ingram in " The Wiser They Are " ; Times Square, Feb., 1932, Mitch Gratwick in " Wild Waves " ; Avon, Apr., 1932, Otto Zeigen in " Foreign Affairs " ; Selwyn, May, 1932, Laurence Hereford in " A Thousand Summers " ; at the Maryland, Baltimore (for the Theatre Guild), Oct., 1932, played Doctor Goshen in " Pure In Heart " ; at the Martin Beck, Nov., 1932, Michael Haverill in " Chrysalis " ; Masque, Dec., 1932, Kenneth Bixby in " Good-Bye Again " ; Empire (for the Guild), Oct., 1933, Sganarelle in " The School for Husbands " ; Ethel Barrymore, Jan., 1935, Mortimer Quinn in " Point Valaine " ; Music Box, Apr., 1935, Jake Lee in " Ceiling Zero " ; Mansfield, Oct., 1935, Morgan

1902

Crawford in "On Stage"; commenced film career in 1920; has appeared in the following, among other, films: "Syncopation," "Wild, Wild Susan," "Knock-Out Reilly," "Love 'Em and Leave 'Em," "The Front Page," "To-Morrow and To-Morrow," "Mother's Boy," "Tarnished Lady," "Scarface," "Madame Du Barry," "Kansas City Princess," "The President Vanishes," "The Secret of the Château." *Recreations:* Golf, tennis, and painting. *Club:* Harvard.
(Died 21 Sept., 1937; age 45)

PERREY, Mireille, actress and vocalist; *b.* Paris, France; studied for the stage at the Paris *Conservatoire*, where she gained first prize for comedy; made her first appearance on the stage at the Odéon Theatre, Paris, where she remained some time; subsequently appeared in the Oscar Straus operette "Theresina," and in 1929, at the Folies Wagram, appeared in "Rosey"; made her first appearance on the London stage at the London Hippodrome, 26 June, 1930, as Yvonne in "Sons O' Guns"; at the Prince's, Oct., 1931, played Jeanne in "Henry the Ninth"; at the Savoy, Mar., 1932, appeared as Paulette in the piece of that name; has also appeared in pictures, in "Just a Kiss," etc. *Address:* 42 Rue des Acacias, Paris, XVII, France.

PERRINS, Leslie, actor; *b.* Moseley, Birmingham; studied for the stage at the Royal Academy of Dramatic Art; made his first appearance on the stage at the Shaftesbury Theatre, 10 Jan., 1922, in "The Rattlesnake"; Little Theatre, Apr., 1922, played Nathaniel Niven in "Amelia's Suitors," and Pierrot in "Columbine"; at the Kingsway, Aug., 1922, Spence in "The Limpet"; at the St. Martin's, Apr., 1923, a Robot in "R.U.R."; at the Criterion, Nov., 1923, Clyde Rowlands in "Three Birds"; during 1924, toured with Dennis Eadie, as Pat in "The Eternal Spring"; in 1925, toured with Violet Vanbrugh in "The Letter of the Law"; at Barnes, June, 1925, played Geoffrey Farnell in "Jungle Law"; Vaudeville, Aug., 1925, Oliver Sheldon

in "Blessed Are the Rich"; Prince of Wales's, Jan., 1926, James Burke in "The House of Glass"; Savoy, Mar., 1926, M. Saverac in "The Snow Man"; Strand, Dec., 1926, Dr. Livesay in "Treasure Island"; Adelphi, Jan., 1927, Nuitane in "Aloma"; Duke of York's, Feb., 1927, Neil Lindsey in "The Donovan Affair"; Prince of Wales's, Jan., 1928, Ian Farr in "Regatta," and Henry in "Outward Bound"; Strand, May, 1928, Scipio in "The Road to Rome"; Shaftesbury, Aug., 1928, Steve Tolman in "The Skull"; Apollo, Sept., 1928, Jim Bridge in "The Lord of the Manor"; Apollo, June, 1929, Stanley Wentworth in "Coquette"; New, Dec., 1929, M. de Beauvais in "Madame Plays Nap"; Little, Apr., 1930, Hans Hartman in "Insult"; went to New York, and appeared at the 49th Street Theatre, Sept., 1930, in the same part; on his return to London, appeared at the Cambridge Theatre, Sept., 1931, as Essex in "Elizabeth of England"; Palace, Jan., 1933, played Ricci in "Dinner at Eight"; Prince's, Dec., 1943, Tony Abbott in "Halfway to Heaven"; Savoy, Mar., 1945, General Lacapelle in "The Assassin"; during the War, was engaged for nearly four years with the B.B.C. European Services; since the end of the War has been engaged in many radio programmes, notably in "Ray's a Laugh," and "P.C. 49"; first broadcast in 1927.
(Died 13 Dec., 1962; age 60)

PERRY, Antoinette, actress, manager and producer; *b.* Denver, Col., U.S.A., 27 June, 1888; *d.* of William R. Perry and his wife Minnie Betsy (Hall); *m.* Frank Wheatcroft Freauff; made her first appearance on the stage at Power's Theatre, Chicago, 26 June, 1905, as Dorothy in "Mrs. Temple's Telegram"; made her first appearance in New York, Madison Square Theatre, 1905, as Mrs. Frank Fuller in the same play; Weber's, New York, Aug., 1906, appeared in "Lady Jim"; Bijou, Sept., 1906, in "The Music Master," with David Warfield, and toured in the same play, 1906-7; Stuyvesant (now Belasco) Theatre, Oct., 1907, played Hallie in "A Grand Army Man," with

Warfield; toured 1908–9, in "The Music Master"; she left the stage on the occasion of her marriage, Nov., 1909; reappeared on the stage at 39th Street Theatre, New York, Jan. 1924, when she played Rachel Arrowsmith in "Mr. Pitt," with Walter Huston; Booth, Sept., 1924, Lil Corey in "Minick"; Daly's, Apr., 1925, Ma Huckle in "The Dunce Boy"; 52nd Street, June, 1925, Belinda Treherne in "Engaged"; 39th Street, Oct., 1925, Judy Ross in "Caught"; Mansfield, Mar., 1926, Sophia Elphinstone Weir in "The Masque of Venice"; Mansfield, Oct., 1926, Margaret in "The Ladder"; Gallo, Dec., 1927, Clytemnestra in "Electra," with Margaret Anglin; since 1928, with Brock Pemberton, has produced and staged "Goin' Home," "Hotbed," 1928; "Strictly Dishonorable," 1929; "Three Times the Hour," "Divorce Me, Dear," 1931; "Christopher Comes Across," 1932; "Personal Appearance," 1934; "Ceiling Zero," 1935; "Now You've Done It," "Chalked Out," "Red Harvest," 1937; "Kiss the Boys Goodbye," 1938; in 1937, was appointed Chairman of the American Theatre Council's Committee of the Apprentice Theatre, in which capacity she inaugurated auditions for theatre aspirants; in May, 1939, was the recipient of a Testimonial Dinner, in recognition of her work in this connection; is a member of the League of New York Theatres, Dramatists' Guild and Actors' Equity Association; is an Officer of the American Theatre Council and Stage Relief Fund. *Clubs:* National Arts, Twelfth Night, Atlantic Beach and Cosmopolitan, New York; Cherry Hills and Denver Country, Denver. *(Died 28 June, 1946; age 58)*

PERRY (Arthur), John, dramatic author; *b.* Woodrooff, Clonmel, Co. Tipperary, Eire, 7 May, 1906; *s.* of William Perry and his wife Emily Dorothea Clare (Boyce); *e.* Cheltenham College; was formerly an actor, and made his first appearance on the stage at the Princes Theatre, Manchester, Sept., 1928, as Jack Chesney in "Charley's Aunt"; toured, 1929, as Captain Winsford in "The Silent

House"; toured, 1930–1, in Canada and the West Indies with the Florence Glossop-Harris company; subsequently left the stage for seven years; at the Ambassadors', 1938, appeared as Fox-Collier in "Spring Meeting"; Piccadilly, Nov., 1939, played Roger in the revival of "George and Margaret"; joined the R.A.F., 1940, and served for five years; is the author of "Spring Meeting" (with M. J. Farrell); "The Last of Summer" (with Kate O'Brien), 1944; "A Man About the House" (adapted from Francis Brett Young's novel), 1945; "Castle Anna" (with Elizabeth Bowen), 1948; "Treasure Hunt" (with M. J. Farrell), 1949; "Dazzling Prospect" (with M. J. Farrell), 1961; from 1947, was Administrator of "The Company of Four," at the Lyric Theatre, Hammersmith; director of H. M. Tennent, Ltd. *Recreations:* Riding and tennis. *Clubs:* Queen's, and International Sportsmen's. *Address:* 15 Lord North Street, London, S.W.1.

PERRY, Margaret, actress; *b.* Denver, Colorado, U.S.A., 23 Feb., 1913; *d.* of Frank W. Frueauff and his wife Antoinette (Perry); *e.* privately in New York City; *m.* (1) Winsor Brown French (mar. dis.); (2) Burgess Meredith (mar. dis.); (3) Paul Fanning; studied for the stage under her mother; she made her first appearance on the stage at the Avon Theatre, 16 Dec., 1929, when she succeeded Muriel Kirkland in the leading part of Isabelle Parry in "Strictly Dishonorable," making a striking success; went to London, where she made her first appearance at the Phoenix Theatre, 10 Mar., 1931, in the same part; on returning to New York, appeared at the Booth Theatre, Dec., 1931, as Phyl in "After All"; at Playhouse, Cleveland, Jan., 1934, appeared as Isla in "Criminal at Large"; Music Box, New York, Apr., 1935, played Tommy Thomas in "Ceiling Zero"; Miller, Mar., 1937, Grace Dosher in "Now You've Done It"; at Suffern, N.Y., Sept., 1937, Ellen Hope in "Worse Things Happen at Sea"; Playhouse, New York, Jan., 1938, Kitty in "The Greatest Show on

Earth." *Recreation:* Reading. *Address:* 510 Park Avenue, New York City, U.S.A. *Telephone No.:* Volunteer 5-0448.

PERTWEE, Roland, dramatic author; *b.* Brighton, 15 May, 1885; *s.* of Ernest Pertwee and his wife Emily (Moore); *m.* (1) Avice Scholtz (mar. dis.); (2) Mrs. Dorothy Colbourne; (3) Mrs. K. D. Butler; was formerly an actor; made his first appearance on the stage at the old Globe, Feb., 1902, walking on in "The Heel of Achilles"; during 1910 was engaged with the late H. B. Irving at the Queen's Theatre, playing small parts in "Louis XI," "Robert Macaire," "The Lyons Mail," "Princess Clementina"; subsequently fulfilled engagements at the Criterion, Garrick, Court, and Scala theatres; Garrick, 1914, played in "Bluff King Hal," "The Double Mystery"; Haymarket, 1915-16, in "Quinney's," "Who is He?" "The Mayor of Troy"; His Majesty's, 1915, in "Peter Ibbetson"; Kingsway, Sept., 1922, played Shirley Terrell in his own play, "I Serve"; is the author of numerous plays, including "Postal Orders," 1916; "Out to Win" (with Dion Clayton Calthrop), 1921; "I Serve," 1922; revised "The Creaking Chair," 1924; author of "Interference" (with Harold Dearden), 1927; "The Spider" (adaptation), 1928; "Heat Wave" (from a novel), 1929; "Honours Easy," 1930; "This Inconstancy" (with John Hastings Turner), 1933; "Further Outlook" (with Denise Robins), 1935; "Independence" ("To Kill a Cat"), with Harold Dearden, 1939; "Pink String and Sealing Wax," 1943; "School for Spinsters," 1947; "The Paragon" (with Michael Pertwee), 1948; "House on the Sand," 1949; "Many Happy Returns" (with Noel Streatfield), 1950; with Michael Pertwee wrote "Rough Shooting," 1950; "In the Bag," "Tell the Marines," 1951; "Give Them a Ring," 1954; has also written numerous short stories and novels; was part-author of the television series "The Grove Family."
(Died 26 Apr., 1963; age 77)

PETERS, Rollo, actor and designer; *b.* Paris, 25 Sept., 1892; *s.* of Charles Rollo Peters and his wife Kathleen (Murphy); *e.* in California, and at art schools in England, Germany, and France; was formerly a portrait painter and scenic designer; designed the production, scenery and costumes for various New York productions, including "The Prince and the Pauper," "Salome," "Camille," "One Night in Rome," "Josephine," "Madame Sand," "Little Men," "Bonds of Interest," "John Ferguson," "Romeo and Juliet," "Antony and Cleopatra," "Pelleas and Melisande," "The Depths," etc.; was director of The Theatre Guild, 1919-20, for which he designed and produced several plays; designed and produced all the plays presented by the Washington Square Players, 1917-18; as an actor made his first appearance on the stage at the Comedy Theatre, New York, Apr., 1918, as the Syrian Captain in "Salome"; at the Garrick, New York, Apr., 1919, played Leander in "Bonds of Interest"; May, 1919, Andrew Ferguson in "John Ferguson"; Oct., 1919, Asano in "The Faithful"; at the Bramhall Playhouse, Dec., 1920, Hugh Rainey in "Mixed Marriage"; at the Hudson, Dec., 1921, Richard and John Garrison in "The Varying Shore"; at the Henry Miller Theatre, Jan., 1923, Romeo in "Romeo and Juliet"; at the Times Square, Dec., 1923, Pelleas in "Pelleas and Melisande"; at the Lyceum, New York, Feb., 1924, Antony in "Antony and Cleopatra"; at the Selwyn, Boston, June, 1924, played Karl in "The Depths," and appeared in the same part at the Broadhurst, New York, June, 1925; Eltinge, Oct., 1925, Count Philippe in "Stolen Fruit"; New Amsterdam, Jan., 1927, Tom Wrench in "Trelawny of the Wells"; Eltinge, Dec., 1927, John Marstin in "Out of the Sea"; Erlanger's, May, 1928, Julian Beauclerc in "Diplomacy"; Empire, Nov., 1928, Newland Archer in "The Age of Innocence"; Erlanger's, Mar., 1930, Jack Absolute in "The Rivals"; Ritz, Aug., 1930, Maurice Larned in "Café"; at the 48th Street Theatre, Oct., 1931, played

Mark Livingston in a revival of "The Streets of New York," and Johan Tonnesen in a revival of "The Pillars of Society," and designed the settings for both productions; also designed the settings for "The Bride the Sun Shines On," 1931; at Detroit, Dec., 1932, Peter Ibbetson in the play of that name; at the Studebaker, Chicago, Jan., 1934, Andreas Steiner in "Autumn Crocus"; at Milwaukee, May, 1934, David Linden in "The Shining Hour"; Erlanger, Philadelphia, Oct., 1934, Paul Ebony in "Home Chat"; at Berkeley, California, July, 1935, Petruchio in "The Taming of the Shrew," and the Dreamer in "Within the Gates." *Favourite parts:* Andrew in "John Ferguson," and Romeo. *Recreations:* Country life, swimming, and draughtsmanship.

(Died 21 Jan., 1967; age 74)

PETIT, Roland, dancer and choreographer; *b.* Villemomble, near Paris, 1924; *s.* of Edmund Petit; *m.* Renée Jeanmaire; at the age of ten, joined the Paris Opera Ballet, and for some years, danced in the *corps de ballet;* created his first ballet, 1941, with Janine Charrat, "Paul et Virginie"; he quitted the Opera House, in 1944, and in the same year he staged "The Nightingale and the Rose," and "Les Forains," at the Theatre Sarah Bernhardt; he then founded Les Ballets des Champs-Elysées, and produced "Le Bal des Blanchisseuses," "Le Jeune Homme et la Mort," "Les Amours de Jupiter," "Jeu de Cartes"; founded his own company, May, 1948, at the Marigny Théâtre; here he has produced "Le Rendez-vous," "Le Combat," "L'Œuf à la Coque," "Carmen," "Pas d'Action," etc.; played seasons in London, at the Prince's, Feb., 1949; New York, Winter Garden, Oct., 1949 National Theatre, New York, Oct., 1950; during 1950, in Paris, produced "La Croqueuse de Diamants."

PETLEY, Frank E., actor; *b.* Old Charlton, Kent, 28 Mar., 1872; *s.* of John Edward Petley and his wife Caroline (Gibson); *e.* Streatham; *m.* Gertrude Price; was formerly a shipping clerk; made his first appearance on the stage at the Pavilion Theatre, Mile End, Feb., 1894, in "Deadwood Dick"; spent many years touring and in "stock" companies, both in London and the provinces; made his first appearance in the West End of London at the St. James's, 6 Mar., 1902, as Matteo in "Paolo and Francesca"; has played all sorts of parts in the provinces, ranging from Jack Hearne in "The Romany Rye" to Marcus Superbus in "The Sign of the Cross," Othello, Shylock, Drake, "The White Man," and the Doctor in "Damaged Goods"; made his first appearance in New York at the Lincoln Square Theatre, 13 Sept., 1909, as Jim Carston in "The Squaw Man" ("A White Man"); at the Garrick, London, Dec., 1915, played the Dragon King in "Where the Rainbow Ends"; at His Majesty's, Mar., 1916, Sir John Unthank in "Stand and Deliver"; at the Queen's, Sept., 1916, B. Gans in "Potash and Perlmutter in Society"; at the Globe, Mar., 1917, Ernest Hyman in "The Man who Went Abroad"; next toured as the Doctor in "Damaged Goods"; at Kennington, Mar., 1919, played Daniel Slade in "The Governor's Lady"; at the Ambassadors', June, 1919, Laurence Trench in "The Storm"; at the Savoy, June, 1919, Robert Blanchford in "Business Before Pleasure"; at the Lyric, June, 1920, Lo Sang Kee in "East is West," and July, 1920, Jim Carston in "A White Man"; at the Lyric, Oct., 1921, Ichabod Whitson in "Welcome Stranger"; at the Strand, July, 1922, Professor Godefroy in "The Risk"; Dec., 1922, George Merry in "Treasure Island"; at Drury Lane, May, 1923, Capt. Gaskell in "Ned Kean of Old Drury"; at the Strand, Dec., 1923, again played George Merry in "Treasure Island"; in Sept., 1924, went on tour with Phyllis Neilson-Terry, playing Dr. Meyer Isaacson in "Bella Donna"; Duke of York's, Sept., 1925, Steve Cronin in "De Luxe Annie"; Globe, Jan., 1927, Thomas Craig in "Give and Take"; Apollo, Dec., 1927, Delaney in "Whispering Wires"; "Q," Jan., 1928, Captain Villiers in "The Temptation of Eve"; Duke of

York's, Apr., 1928, Rev. Arthur Stanes in "Thunder in the Air"; went to America, 1929, and appeared at Booth Theatre, New York, Apr., 1929, as Ambrose Godolphin in "Bird in Hand"; 49th Street, Nov., 1930, played in a revival of "Bird in Hand"; on returning to London, appeared at the Grafton, June, 1931, as Sir Samuel Rich in "I Want"; 44th Street, New York, Oct., 1931, played Ridvers in "The Good Companions"; in the autumn of 1932, toured in English provinces as James Haydon in "Dr. Pygmalion"; Wyndham's, Jan., 1934, Admiral Watson in "Clive of India"; New, May, 1935, Kapel in "Someone at the Door"; Aldwych (for Repertory Players), Nov., 1935, Rev. Archibald Ffoulkes in "Legend of Yesterday"; Whitehall, Oct., 1937, Sir Henry Bickerton in "The Dead Hand"; Vaudeville, June, 1938, Martin Everton in "Sexes and Sevens." *Recreations:* Golf, motoring, and sea-fishing. *Club:* Green Room.

(Died 12 Jan., 1945; age 72)

PETRASS, Sari, actress and vocalist; *b.* Budapest, 5 Nov., 1890; *d.* of Istvande Petrass and his wife Cecilie (de Kiss); *e.* Budapest; *m.* (1) F. A. Sommerhoff (mar. dis.), (2) Gordon Crocker; made her first appearance on the stage at the People's Theatre, Budapest, 1906, as Hippolit in "The Two Hippolits"; was a singer of repute in light opera in her own country before making her first appearance on the London stage at Daly's Theatre, 1 June 1912, as Ilona in "Gipsy Love," when she scored an immediate success; at the same theatre, May, 1913, played Mariposa Gilroy in "The Marriage Market," and at the termination of the run of that piece went to the United States; at the New Amsterdam Theatre, New York, Sept., 1916, played Rosika Wenzel in "Miss Springtime"; at Hartford, Conn., Jan., 1917, played in "The Beautiful Unknown"; reappeared in London, at the Prince of Wales's, May, 1921, as Sylva in "The Gipsy Princess"; at Welbeck Palace Hotel (with the Guild Players), Nov., 1928, played Erginie in "Those Foreigners." *(Died 7 Sept., 1930; age 39)*

PETRIE, David Hay, actor; *b.* Dundee, Scotland, 16 July, 1895; *s.* of David Mathers Petrie and his wife Jessie Ann (Hay); *e.* Harris Academy, Dundee, and St. Andrew's University (M.A.); *m.* Muriel Eleanor Stevens; studied for the stage for a short period, with Rosina Filippi; made his first appearance on the stage at the "Old Vic.," 18 Feb., 1920, as Starveling in "A Midsummer Night's Dream"; he remained a member of that company until 1924, during which period he played a great number of parts; among his more notable impersonations during this period may be mentioned Sir Hugh Evans in "The Merry Wives of Windsor," Dromio of Syracuse in "The Comedy of Errors," Puck in "A Midsummer Night's Dream," Old Gobbo, Lancelot, Tubal and Shylock in "The Merchant of Venice," Touchstone in "As You Like It," Christopher Sly in "The Taming of the Shrew," Sir Andrew Aguecheek in "Twelfth Night," Costard in "Love's Labour's Lost," Launce in "The Two Gentlemen of Verona," Bob Acres in "The Rivals," Bob Cratchit in "A Christmas Carol," Caleb Plummer in "The Cricket on the Hearth," Justice Greedy in "A New Way to Pay Old Debts," etc.; at the Regent (for the Phoenix Society), June, 1924, played Fondlewife in "The Old Bachelor"; at the New Oxford, June–July, 1924, appeared with the "Old Vic." company in "The Taming of the Shrew," "Hamlet" (as the First Gravedigger), "Twelfth Night," and "As You Like It"; at the Vaudeville, Oct., 1924, appeared in "The Looking Glass"; at Drury Lane, Dec., 1924, played Puck in "A Midsummer Night's Dream" Golder's Green, Aug., 1925, and St. Martin's, Sept., 1925, Percival Custard in "Easy Money"; Duke of York's (for Stage Society), Dec., 1925, Kosich in "Ivanoff"; Criterion, Aug., 1926, Wilfred Bulstrode-Smith in "Thy Name is Woman"; Little, Oct., 1926, in "The Potinière Revue"; Royalty, Dec., 1926, Herbert Nicolson in "Granny"; Royalty, Mar., 1927, The Scholar in "Cocks and Hens"; Arts, May, 1927, Launcelot Gobbo in "The Lady of Belmont"; rejoined the Old

Vic. Company, at the Lyric, Hammersmith, Sept. to Dec., 1927, playing Christopher Sly, Launcelot, Dogberry, etc.; Arts, Apr., 1928, Jack Fold in "The Making of an Immortal"; Everyman, Apr., 1928, Clodd in "Queen Elizabeth"; in May, 1928, toured in "Riverside Nights"; Lyric, Hammersmith, Aug., 1928, Hardcastle in "She Stoops to Conquer"; Oct., 1928, Dangle in "The Critic," and Lord Withers in "Two Gentlemen of Soho"; Haymarket and Apollo, July, 1929, Parson Hugh Evans in "The Merry Wives of Windsor" (in modern dress); Playhouse, Sept., 1929, Lob in "Dear Brutus"; Duchess, Dec., 1929, Joshua Atkinson in "The Man at Six"; Victoria Palace, Dec., 1930, played in "Chelsea Follies"; Lyric, Hammersmith, Apr., 1931, played Isaac Mendoza in "The Duenna"; Sept., 1931, Setter in "The Old Bachelor"; Adelphi, Jan., 1932, Mercury in "Helen!"; Westminster, Feb., 1933 (for the Stage Society), The Burglar in "Oh, Hang!"; "Q" and Royalty, Mar., 1933, Saul Right in "Francis Thompson"; Little, Apr., 1933, the Cockney in "Overture"; Nov., 1933, Crockson in "Will You Play With Me?"; Alhambra, Jan., 1934, Captain Fluellen in "Henry V"; Embassy, Apr., 1934, Feodor Debinsky in "The Drums Begin"; Savoy, June, 1935, Zimenez in "A Kingdom for a Cow"; Drury Lane, May, 1936, Count Bruzzi in "Rise and Shine"; Ambassadors', Feb., 1937, Goldfinch in "The Road to Ruin"; commenced film career, 1931, in "Gipsy Blood"; since 1936, has appeared in "Men of Yesterday," "Hearts of Humanity," "Secret Lives," "Knight Without Armour," "The Last Barricade," "Keep Smiling," "The House of the Spaniard," "Not Wanted on Voyage," "Q Planes," "The Spy in Black," "Trunk Crime," "Twenty-one Days," "Jamaica Inn," etc.; has played on numerous occasions for the Fellowship of Players, Stage, Phoenix, and Renaissance Societies. *Recreations :* Tennis and golf. *(Died 30 July, 1948; age 53)*

PETROVA, Olga (Muriel Harding), actress and dramatic author; *b.* Liverpool, 1886; *e.* Brussels, Paris and London; *m.* John D. Stewart, M.D.; made her first appearance on the stage, 1906, in London; subsequently toured the English provinces; then went to the United States where she appeared in "vaudeville"; appeared at the Folies Bergères, New York, 1910; at the Park Theatre, New York, Oct., 1911, played Diane in "The Quaker Girl"; at the Booth Theatre, Mar., 1914, appeared as Panthea in the play of that name, subsequently touring in the same part; at the Park Theatre, Oct., 1915, played Anna in "The Revolt," in which she also toured for some time; she then devoted herself for some years to the cinema stage, appearing in such film-plays as "The Undying Flame," "The Law of the Land," "The Soul of a Magdalen," "Daughter of Destiny," "The Orchid Lady," "Bridges Burned," "More Truth than Poetry," "The Life Mask," "The Panther Woman," "The Soul Market," "My Madonna," etc.; returned to the regular stage at the Comedy Theatre, New York, Dec., 1921, when she played Rivette di Ribera in "The White Peacock"; at the Frolic Theatre, New York, Dec., 1923, played Ilka in "Hurricane"; Wallack's, Dec., 1927, Kasha in "What Do We Know?"; is the author of several plays for the cinema, and also "The White Peacock," "Hurricane," "What Do We Know?" etc.; is a fairly frequent contributor to periodical press, and has also composed songs, etc.; author of "The Black Virgin," 1930. *Address :* 1035 Park Avenue, New York City, U.S.A. *Telephone No. :* Sacramento 2-7676; and Les Colombes Grises, St. Jean, Cap Ferrat, A.M., France.

PETTINGELL, Frank, actor; *b.* Liverpool, 1 Jan., 1891; *s.* of Frank Ernest Pettingell and his wife Harriet Helen Beatrice (Hart); *e.* Manchester University; *m.* Ethel Till; was formerly an artist and journalist; made his first appearance on the stage, with Allan Wilkie's Shakespearean company, at the Winter Gardens, Blackpool, Nov., 1910, as the Tailor in "The Taming of the Shrew"; had an extensive experience in repertory companies, touring dramas and concert-parties; during World War I, served with the King's Liverpool (25th) Regiment; after being demobilized, toured in his own version of "Les Misérables" and in "East is East": made his first appearance on the London stage at the Queen's Theatre, 29 Apr., 1922, as Davie Nicholson in "Lass o' Laughter"; at the Apollo, May, 1923, played James Wylie in "What Every Woman Knows," and in 1924, toured in the same play as John Shand; subsequently played in several repertory companies, and as director, staged many productions; Ambassadors', Dec., 1927, played Inspector Dixon in "9.45"; at the Court, Feb.-Oct., 1928, played the Porter in "Macbeth" (in modern dress), Burge-Lubin and Badger Bluepin in "Back to Methuselah," Gamel in "Harold," Christopher Sly in "The Taming of the Shrew" (in modern dress), and Richard Varwell in "Yellow Sands"; subsequently toured as Pancho in "The Bad Man," Baron Andreyeff in "The Yellow Ticket," Simon Hardy in "The Stranger Within," etc.; Player's, Mar., 1930, played William Bromley in "Every Mother's Son"; subsequently played a "stock" season at the Alexandra Theatre, Birmingham; at the Duchess, Dec., 1930, played Sergeant Chugg in "Jane's Legacy"; scored a big success when he appeared at His Majesty's, May, 1931, as Sam Oglethorpe in "The Good Companions"; Apollo, Apr., 1932, played Mr. Crum in "Pleasure Cruise"; New, Oct., 1932, John Arnold in "My Hat!"; Shaftesbury, Dec., 1933, John Torrent in "A Present from Margate"; Jan., 1934, Ned Pope in "Spring, 1600"; Adelphi, Mar., 1934, Steve Townie in "Magnolia Street"; Haymarket, May, 1934, Fred McCrossan in "Touch Wood"; Queen's, Dec., 1934, Det.-Inspector Grimshaw in "Inside the Room"; Shaftesbury, Oct., 1935, A Serious Person in "The Black Eye"; Adelphi, Feb., 1936, appeared in "Follow the Sun"; Prince's, Apr., 1936, Philo Johnson in "The Frog"; Queen's, May, 1937, Mr. Leroy in "He Was Born Gay"; Duke of York's, Oct., 1937, Bel Kabbittu in "Susannah

and the Elders"; Vaudeville, Dec 1937, Count Mariassy in "A Lady's Gentleman"; Royalty, Apr., 1938, Charles Mollison In "April Clouds"; Malvern Festival, Aug., 1938, Buchlyvie in "The Last Trump" and de Stogumber in "Saint Joan"; St. Martin's, Oct., 1938, Henry Ormonroyd in "When We Are Married"; Duchess, Jan., 1940, Mr. Dotheright in "The Golden Cuckoo"; Embassy, May, and Criterion, June, 1940, appeared in "Come Out of Your Shell"; St. Martin's, Feb., 1942, played Hubert Benson in "Jam To-day"; Duchess, July, 1942, Jim Lloyd in "Lifeline"; Strand, Dec., 1942, Teddy Brewster in "Arsenic and Old Lace," which he continued to play until June, 1944; Strand, Mar., 1946, Albert Biggleswade in "Fifty-Fifty"; Covent Garden, July, 1948, Talkative in "The Pilgrim's Progress"; Boltons, Aug., 1948, appeared as Oscar Wilde in a play of that name; Wyndham's, Mar., 1949, Mr. Gooch in "Daphne Laureola"; Duke of York's, Oct., 1951, played Roger Manifold in "All the Year Round"; Phoenix, Sept., 1953, the Doctor in "Bruno and Sidney"; Cambridge, Sept., 1953, followed Wilfrid Hyde-White as Philip Russell in "Affairs of State"; Winter Garden, May, 1956, played Monsieur Cot in "Hotel Paradiso"; St. Martin's, Feb., 1958, Liam Shaughnessy in "Roseland"; Westminster, Feb., 1960, General Tom Powers in "Visit to a Small Planet"; Duke of York's, Sept., 1962, played Basil Smythe in "Big Fish, Little Fish"; Duchess, Jan., 1964, Beecham in "The Reluctant Peer"; television appearances include Falstaff, in the Shakespeare historical series, "An Age of Kings"; has written and adapted several historical plays and sketches, and is the author of several theatrical treatises; commenced film career, 1931, in "Jealousy" and has since appeared in innumerable pictures. *Recreations:* Reading, drawing, writing, and walking.
(Died 17 Feb., 1968; age 75)

PHILIPS, F. C., dramatic author and novelist; *b.* Brighton, 3 Feb., 1849; *s.* of Rev. G. Washington

Philips, of Ruxley Park, Surrey; *e.* at Brighton College and Sandhurst; *m.* Eva Kevill-Davies; served some years in the Army, before being called to the Bar in 1884; in the 'seventies was known as "Francis Fairlie," and was manager of several theatres; has written the following plays: "As in a Looking Glass," 1887; "The Dean's Daughter" (with Sydney Grundy), 1888; "Husband and Wife" (with Percy Fendall), 1891; "Margaret Byng" (with Fendall), 1891; "Godpapa" (with Charles Brookfield), 1891; "The Burglar and the Judge" (with Brookfield), 1892; "Papa's Wife" (with Seymour Hicks), 1895; "A Woman's Reason" (with Brookfield), 1895; "The Fortune of War," 1896; "The Free Pardon" (with Leonard Merrick), 1897; "Lady Paddington" (with Walter Parke), 1902; author of nearly thirty novels, among them "As in a Looking Glass," "The Dean and his Daughter," "Margaret Byng," "Little Mrs. Murray," "A Devil in Nun's Veiling," "A Lucky Young Woman," "Jack and Three Jills," "One Never Knows," "Social Vicissitudes," etc.

(Died 21 Apr., 1921; age 71)

PHILIPS, Mary, actress; *b.* New London, Conn., 23 Jan., 1901; *d.* of Charles Ellsworth Philips and his wife Anne (Hurley); *e.* public schools and St. Mary's, New Haven, Conn.; *m.* (1) Humphrey Bogart (mar. dis.) (2) Kenneth MacKenna; made her first appearance on the stage at the Globe Theatre, New York, 6 Oct., 1919, in the chorus of "Apple Blossoms"; at the Plymouth, Aug., 1922, played Ina Heath in "The Old Soak"; Comedy, Sept., 1924, Jane in "Nerves"; 49th Street, Nov., 1925, Irene Adams in "One of the Family"; Little, Feb., 1926, Sally Field in "The Wisdom Tooth"; Sept., 1926, Miss Timoney in "Two Girls Wanted"; Lyceum, Jan., 1929, Del Ewing in "Skyrocket"; Fulton, Aug., 1929, Mazie in "Gambling"; May, 1930, the Woman in "The Tavern"; June, 1930, Jane Rosemond in "The Song and Dance Man"; Apollo, Mar., 1931, Jennifer Davis in "The House Beau-

tiful"; Royale (for the Guild), Mar., 1933, Bus Nillson in "Both Your Houses"; Henry Miller, Dec., 1933, Cassie Bond in "All Good Americans"; Plymouth, May, 1934, Eve Hayward in "Come What May"; Music Box, Sept., 1934, Julia Glenn in "Merrily We Roll Along"; Golden, Sept., 1935, Janet Faber in "A Touch of Brimstone"; Martin Beck, Mar., 1938, Edie in "Spring Thaw"; Henry Miller, Apr., 1944, Emily Blachman in "Chicken Every Sunday"; in summer theatres, 1949, appeared in "The Heiress"; La Jolla Playhouse, July, 1954, played Kay Davis in "Time For Elizabeth"; has appeared in films in "Farewell to Arms," "Lady in the Dark," etc. *Recreations:* Golf, sailing, and bridge.

PHILLIPS, Cyril L., manager; *b.* Edgbaston, Birmingham, 12 Feb., 1894; *s.* of James Berriman Phillips and his wife Florence (Underwood); *e.* Coleshill Grammar School, King Edward's School, and privately; *m.* Yvette Olive Eugenie Pienne; during the War served in R.N.V.R. and Tank Corps; formerly engaged as a private secretary; joined the staff of Birmingham Repertory Theatre in 1920; in 1921 was appointed Assistant Secretary; in 1923, appointed Business Manager; from 1925–38, General Manager of Birmingham Repertory Theatre and for Sir Barry Jackson's various theatrical enterprises, which also included seasons at the Court, Kingsway, Haymarket, Queen's, Comedy, Playhouse, Garrick, Globe and New Theatres, London; is now a director of the Repertory Theatre; was manager also for the Malvern Festivals, 1929–38, and tours in Canada and United States. *Recreations:* Horticulture, billiards and water-colour painting. *Address:* 10 Lambolle Road, Hampstead, London, N.W.3. *Telephone No.:* Primrose 5226.

PHILLIPS, Kate, actress; *b.* in Essex, 28 July, 1856; *d.* of the late Phillip Goldney, of Bradleigh Hall, Essex; *m.* H. B. Conway; made her first appearance on the stage at the Lyceum Theatre, 22 Jan., 1870, as William in "Chilperic"; subsequently appeared at the same theatre in "Little Faust"; at the Globe, in 1871, played in "Fal-sac-ap-pa"; in 1873, at the Holborn, played in "The Daughter of the Danube," "A Restless Night," "The Ticket-of-Leave Man" (as Sam Willoughby), "The Home Wreck," etc.; at the Court in 1873-74, played in "The Wedding March," "The White Pilgrim," "Peacock's Holiday," "Calypso," "Playing with Fire," "Brighton," etc.; appeared at the Strand, 1874, in "Loo," subsequently playing Phoebe in "Paul Pry," De Boissy in "The Field of the Cloth of Gold," Zidon de Filoselle in "Nemesis"; at the Vaudeville, 1875, played Baccharia in "Romulus and Remus"; at the Holborn, 1875, Gwynneth in "The Hidden Hand"; at the Queen's, 1876, made a "hit" as the Boy in "King Henry V"; at the Gaiety, played in "The Man in Possession" and "William Tell"; at the Opéra Comique, 1877, in "Bachelors' Hall"; joined the Haymarket company in Sept., 1877, and played Phoebe in "Paul Pry," Maria in "Twelfth Night," Lucy in "The Rivals," etc.; at the Court, 1879, played Jenny in "The Queen's Shilling," also appearing at the St. James's, 1880, as Polly in "William and Susan," Dorinda in "The Money Spinner"; in 1881, appeared at the Vaudeville, as Dolly Beck in "The Half-Way House"; at the same theatre played Lucy in "The Rivals," Maria in "Confusion," Lady Franklin in "Money," Lydia in "Saints and Sinners," Timpson in "Open House," Lottie in "Loose Tiles," Louisa Linwood in "Under Fire," Miranda in "Plebeians"; in 1886, appeared at Toole's, as Lavinia Muddle in "The Butler," in 1888, as Mrs. Coventry Sparkle in "The Don," and Mrs. Pomfret in The Paper Chase"; at the Crystal Palace, 1888, appeared as Mistress Quickly in "The Merry Wives of Windsor"; during 1889 appeared at *matinées* at the Gaiety and Crystal Palace, as Lady Gay Spanker in "London Assurance"; at the Lyceum, Sept., 1889, played Cerisette in "The Dead Heart";

at the Avenue, Sept., 1890, appeared as the Maréchale de Séléney in "The Struggle for Life"; returning to the Lyceum, played Sozel in "The Bells," Margaret in "Much Ado About Nothing," Susan Oldfield in "Nance Oldfield," Martha in "Louis XI," Coralie in "The Corsican Brothers"; at the Vaudeville, 1892, appeared in revivals of "Saints and Sinners" and "Sophia" (as Honour); at the Lyceum, 1893, played Margery in "Becket," the Postmaster's Niece in "The Lyons Mail," Nerissa in "The Merchant of Venice," Polly in "Olivia," etc.; in 1894, played Bessy in "Faust"; at the Garrick, Dec., 1894, played Mrs. Winterbottom in "Slaves of the Ring"; at the Comedy, Mar., 1895, Mrs. Fretwell in "Sowing the Wind"; at the Royalty, 1895, appeared as Honor Bliss in "The Chili Widow," and at the Shaftesbury, as Nancy in "The Manxman"; appeared at the Olympic, 1896, in "True Blue"; at the Haymarket, 1896, as Mrs. Quickly in "King Henry IV" (part I); at the Shaftesbury played in "The Little Genius"; at the St. James's, Dec., 1896, appeared as Audrey in "As You Like It"; at the Avenue, 1897, played in "On Leave"; at the Globe, 1897, in "The Wild Duck"; at the Strand, 1897, in "The Purser," "The Fanatic," and "The Triple Alliance"; at the Lyric, 1900, played in "The Ring Mistress"; at Great Queen Street, 1901, in "The Lady From Texas"; at Wyndham's, 1901, in "My Bachelor Past," and "Little Lord Fauntleroy"; at the Avenue, 1902, appeared in "The Little French Milliner"; at Wyndham's, 1903, played Mrs. Mac-Taggert in "Just Like Callaghan"; appeared at His Majesty's as Maria in "Twelfth Night," etc., 1903; specially engaged by Lewis Waller to appear before their Majesties as Marton in "A Marriage of Convenience," Sandringham, 1903; engaged by Messrs. Leibler to play in "The Prince Consort," New York, 1905; in 1907 toured for a time in "Moths"; and in Dec. fulfilled engagements at various music halls; appeared at His Majesty's 1908, as

Mistress Quickly in "The Merry Wives of Windsor"; at the Kingsway, Dec., 1908, played Lady Culthorne in "Management"; at Terry's, Apr., 1909, played Lady Bun in "Artful Miss Dearing"; at the Nazimova Theatre, New York, Dec., 1910, appeared as Lady Katherine Greenop in "We Can't Be So Bad As All That"; at Croydon, Sept., 1916, played the same part; subsequently toured as the Dowager Lady Pomeroy in "Mrs. Pomeroy's Reputation," and appeared in the same part at the Queen's, July, 1917; at the Garrick, Mar., 1918, appeared as Madame Chalfont in "By Pigeon Post"; at the New Theatre, Nov., 1919, as Aunt March in "Little Women"; at the Strand, Oct., 1922, played Mrs. Larkins in "Angel Face"; at the New Theatre, Aug., 1923, Mrs. Marsh in "The Eye of Siva"; at Drury Lane, June, 1924, Lady Coningsby in "London Life"; at the Playhouse, Nov., 1925, Anna in "A Doll's House."
(Died 9 Sept., 1931; age 82)

PHILLIPS, Stephen, dramatic author and poet; *b.* Somertown, near Oxford, 28 July, 1866; *s.* of Rev. Dr. Stephen Phillips of Peterborough Cathedral; *e.* Peterborough Grammar School; *m.* May Lidyard; joined F. R. Benson's company and remained with him some time; appeared at the Globe, Dec., 1889, as Flute in "A Midsummer Night's Dream"; subsequently playing Gremio in "The Taming of the Shrew," the Ghost in "Hamlet," the Duke in "Othello"; for some years was an army tutor but subsequently adopted literature as his profession; is the author of the following plays: "Herod," 1900; "Paolo and Francesca," 1902; "Ulysses," 1902; "The Sin of David," 1904; "Nero," 1906; "Faust" (with J. Comyns Carr), 1908; the English version of "Everywoman," Drury Lane, 1912; "Armageddon," 1915; re-appeared on stage as the Ghost in Martin Harvey's revival of "Hamlet," at the Lyric, in May, 1905. *(Died 9 Dec., 1915; age 49)*

PHILLPOTTS, Adelaide, dramatic author; *b.* 23 Apr., 1896; *d.* of Eden Phillpotts and his wife Emily (Topham); *m.* Nicholas Ross; part-author of "Yellow Sands" (with her father), "Akhnatou," 1926; "My Lady's Mill" (with her father), 1928; "The Good Old Days" (with her father), 1930; "The Wasp's Nest" (with Jan Stewer), 1935; "Laugh With Me," 1938; "A Song of Man," 1959; is also author of "The Mayor," 1929, and over twenty other novels. *Address:* "Cobblestones," Kilkhampton, Bude, Cornwall.

PHILLPOTTS, Eden, dramatic author and novelist; *b.* Mount Aboo, India, 4 Nov., 1862; *s.* of Captain Henry Phillpotts; *e.* Plymouth; *m.* (1) Emily Topham (dec.); (2) Lucy Robina Webb; was for ten years a clerk in the Sun Fire Insurance Company, and later studied for the stage; commenced writing in 1890; is the author of the following plays: "A Breezy Morning," 1895; "The Golden Wedding" (with Charles Groves), 1898; "The Secret Woman" (from his novel), 1912; "Hiatus," 1913; "The Point of View," 1913; "The Carrier Pigeon," 1913; "The Mother," 1913; "The Shadow," 1913; "The Angel in the House" (with B. Macdonald Hastings), 1915; "Bed Rock" (with Hastings), 1916; "The Farmer's Wife," 1916, produced at the Court, London, Mar., 1924, when it ran for 1,329 performances; "St. George and the Dragons," 1919; "Devonshire Cream," 1924; "Comedy Royal," "Jane's Legacy," "The Point of View," 1925; "The Mother," "The Purple Bedroom," "The Blue Comet," "Yellow Sands" (with Adelaide Phillpotts), 1926; "My Lady's Mill" (with Adelaide Phillpotts), "The Runaways," 1928; "The Good Old Days" (with Adelaide Phillpotts), 1930; "Buy a Broom," 1931; "A Cup of Happiness," 1932; "The Orange Orchard," 1950; is the author of many successful novels; published a volume of reminiscences, "One Thing and Another," 1954. *(Died 29 Dec., 1960; age 98)*

PICARD, André, French dramatic author; *b.* Paris, 1874; has written

the following, among other plays:
" La Cuivre" (with Paul Adam),
1896; " La Confidante," 1898;
" Franchise," 1899; " Un amant
délicat," 1900; " Bon Fortune," 1903;
" Monsieur Malézieux," 1904; " Jeu-
nesse " (" Mauricette "), 1905; " Le
Protecteur," 1904; " L'Ange Gardien,"
1910; " La Fugitive," 1910;
" Dozulé," 1912; " Kiki," " Mon
Homme " (with Francis Carco,) 1920;
" Un Homme en Habit " (with Yves
Mirande), 1920; is a Chevalier of
the Legion of Honour. *Address:* 31
Boulevard Pereire, Paris.
(Died 25 Feb., 1926; age 51)

PICKARD, Helena, actress; *b.*
Handsworth, Sheffield, 13 Oct., 1900;
d. of Percy Pickard and his wife
Jennie (Skelton); *e.* Convent of
Mercy; *m.* (Sir) Cedric Hardwicke
(mar. dis.); studied for the stage
at the Royal Academy of Dramatic
Art; made her first appearance on
the stage at the Repertory Theatre,
Birmingham, Dec., 1915; she remained
a member of that company until
1917, and played, among other parts,
Robin in "The Merry Wives of
Windsor," Ellen in "The Tragedy
of Nan," Sophy Smerdon in " The
Farmer's Wife," Jenny in " The
Fountain," etc.; made her first appear-
ance in London at the Kennington
Theatre May, 1918, as Ruth in " The
Just Impediment "; toured for two
years with Armitage and Leigh's
repertory company; toured in the
West Indies with Florence Glossop-
Harris repertory company; subse-
quently toured as Lady Sloane in
" Brown Sugar "; at the Court Theatre,
June, 1924, succeeded Phyllis Shand as
Sibley Sweetland in " The Farmer's
Wife," which she played for six months;
at the Aldwych (for the Interlude
Players), Nov., 1925, played Azema
in " The Palace of Truth "; Royalty,
Apr., 1926, the Nurse in " Doctor
Knock "; subsequently toured in
" Ask Beccles "; at the Coliseum, Jan.,
1927, played in " The Purple Bedroom";
at the Lyric, Hammersmith, with the
Old Vic. Company, Oct.-Nov., 1927,
played Jessica in " The Merchant of
Venice " and Hero in " Much Ado

About Nothing "; in 1928, at the Gate
Theatre, played in " The Hairy Ape ";
Duke of York's, Apr., 1928, Anna in
" Thunder in the Air "; Lyric, July,
1928, Dolly Quick in " My Lady's
Mill "; Strand, Oct., 1928, the English
Girl in " The Beetle "; at the Gate,
Oct.-Nov., 1928, Lala in " Rampa "
and Ella Downey in " All God's
Chillun Got Wings "; Court, Jan.,
1929, Esther in " The Eternal Flame ";
at the Gate, Jan., 1929, and Kingsway,
Feb., 1929, Seraphina Tiffany in
" Fashion "; Coliseum, May, 1929,
played in "The Point of View";
Garrick, Nov., 1929, Harriet Marsh
in "The Woman in Room 13";
Everyman and Criterion, Sept., 1930,
played Anna in "The Far Off Hills";
Criterion, Oct., 1930, Susan Brady
in "The Playboy of the Western
World "; Nov., 1930, Mrs. Gregg in
"General John Regan "; Grafton, Dec.,
1930, played Cinderella; in May, 1931,
in conjunction with Beatrix Thomson,
entered on the management of the
Grafton Theatre, opening as Catherine
in "Lilies of the Field"; after appearing in half a dozen plays, relinquished
the management at the end of the year;
Royal Artillery Theatre, Woolwich,
Dec., 1931, again played Cinderella;
Little, Oct., 1932, played Ann Leslie
in "Alison's House"; Royalty, Apr.,
1933, Anne Brontë in "The Brontës";
May, 1933 (for "G" Club), Eileen Kay
in "The Call of Youth"; Little, Jan.,
1934, Lady Isabel in "East Lynne";
Gate, Feb., 1934, Ophelia in "The
Marriage of Hamlet"; in 1934, toured
as Ada in "The Late Christopher
Bean"; Little, May, 1934, played
Ellen and Mary Starling in "Once
Upon a Time"; King's, Hammer-
smith, Apr., 1935, Rose Smithers in
"The Magic Cupboard"; Strand,
Aug., 1935, succeeded Clarice Hard-
wicke in "1066 and All That"; West-
minster, June, 1936, played Jenny
Lind in "The Emperor of Make
Believe"; Miller Theatre, New York,
Dec., 1936, Mrs. Squeamish in "The
Country Wife"; Malvern Festival,
July, 1937, Grace Carey in "Return
to Sanity"; Ritz Theatre, New York,
Jan., 1938, Joan Helford in "Time
and the Conways"; Malvern Festival,
Aug., 1938, Katherine Shiel in "Music

at Night"; St. Martin's, London, Oct., 1938, Annie Parker in "When We Are Married"; Malvern Festival, Aug., 1939, played in "The Professor from Peking," and "Big Ben"; Richmond, June, 1940, Penny in "Penny Wise"; Henry Miller Theatre, New York, Dec., 1942, Mrs. Miller in "Flare Path"; then toured Canada, with "Celebrity Parade," also lecturing and broadcasting; on returning to England, toured for C.E.M.A., 1944, as Charlotte Brontë in "The Brontës"; toured on the Continent, 1945, in "Yellow Sands"; toured, Sept., 1945, as Carol Mayne in "Thirteen to the Gallows"; "Q," Apr., 1947, Lucy in "Quiet in the Forest"; Apollo, Sept., 1947, Thirza Tapper in "The Farmer's Wife"; New Chepstow, Nov., 1949, Christina Rossetti in "Rossetti"; Bedford, Camden Town, Mar., 1950, Mrs. Spicer in "Craven House"; Arts, Apr., 1950, Marfa Yegorovna Babakina in "Ivanov"; Nov., 1950, Mrs. Panmure in "Preserving Mr. Panmure," and appeared in this part at the Aldwych, Feb., 1951; King's, Glasgow, Nov., 1951, appeared as Helen Poulter in "A Multitude of Sins"; Strand (for Repertory Players), Feb., 1952, played Lady Caroline Stoke-Furness in "Mr. Sartorius"; New, Bromley, Sept., 1953, Sylvia Young in "La Plume de ma Tante"; Adelphi, Jan., 1955, appeared for the Repertory Players as Mrs. Calyton in "The Yellow Curtains"; New, May, 1955, played Aunt Jane Pennypacker in "The Remarkable Mr. Pennypacker"; since 1950 has acted in a number of television plays and has also appeared in numerous films. *Favourite part:* Ella in "All God's Chillun." *Recreations:* Reading, walking and entertaining young people. *(Died 27 Sept., 1959; age 58)*

PICKARD, Margery, actress; *b.* Sheffield, Yorks, 17 Dec., 1911; *d.* of Percy Pickard and his wife Jennie (Skelton); *e.* Montrose, Cliftonville, and Ursuline Convent, Belgium; *m.* Dr. Leonard Woods; studied for the stage at the Royal Academy of Dramatic Art; her first engagement was to understudy her sister, Helena, at the Gate Theatre, 1929, in "Fashion"; Garrick, Mar.,

1931, played Sally in "My Wife's Family," and appeared in this for eighteen months; Grafton, June, 1931, Vera Hurst in "Shall We Say Grace?"; Nov., 1931, Betty Clifton in "The Home Front"; Duchess, June, 1932, Simone Foresti in "Beginner's Luck"; "Q," Jan., 1933, Peggy Maxwell in "Trust Berkeley"; Royalty, Feb., 1933, Joan Manning in "The Synthetic Virgin"; Little, Apr., 1933, Rosie in "Overture"; Duchess, Nov., 1933, Elsie Radfern in "Laburnum Grove," which she played throughout 1934; went to America, and made her first appearance in New York, at the Booth Theatre, 14 Jan., 1935, in the same part; Royalty, London, June, 1936, played Daphne in "A Comedy of Crooks"; Aldwych, Dec., 1937, Ellen Jones in "Man at Liberty"; appeared at the Malvern Festival, Aug., 1939; during the War, 1939–45, served as an Ambulance driver in the Civil Defence Corps; Westminster Theatre, Mar., 1945, played Minnie Masters in "Yellow Sands"; Alexandra, Stoke Newington, Feb., 1947, Sue in "Cry Havoc"; St. Martin's, Oct., 1947, Alice in " . . . And Seem a Saint"; has appeared in films. *Recreations:* Sailing, swimming, reading and writing. *Address:* 204 Raleigh House, Dolphin Square, London, S.W.1. *Telephone No.:* Victoria 3800; extension, Raleigh 204.

PICKERING, Edward A., business manager; *b.* London, 6 June, 1871; *s.* of James Mark Pickering and his wife Sarah J. (Halford); *e.* Harlow and Mitcham; *m.* Mary Lissney Gurney; made his first appearance on the stage at the Theatre Royal, Brighton, 1878, as the Midshipmite in "H.M.S. Pinafore," and subsequently came to the Opéra Comique, to make his first appearance in London, in the same part; was subsequently engaged as a choir-boy with the Moore and Burgess Minstrels; and later with the D'Oyly Carte Opera Company; quitting the stage, he was engaged in the office at the Savoy Theatre, and subsequently at the Empire; was acting-manager at the Alhambra, 1898–1903;

travelled in South Africa, 1903–6 ; acting-manager at the Palace Theatre, 1906–11 ; Alhambra, 1911–12 ; again travelled in Africa, 1912–14 ; officiated as manager of various London Theatres, 1914–17 ; appointed manager of the Gaiety Theatre, 1917, where he remained until 1921 ; in 1921, became a partner in a Theatrical and Variety Agency ; relinquished this in 1921, and was appointed General Manager to Jack Buchanan's enterprises, 1922 ; subsequently resigned ; manager at Little Theatre, for Maurice Browne, 1930 ; appointed acting-manager Stoll's Picture Theatre, Kingsway, 1931. *Recreation :* Walking. *Address :* 129 Bedford Court Mansions, W.C.1. *Telephone No. :* Museum 1186.

PICKFORD, Mary, actress (*née* Gladys Mary Smith) ; *b.* Toronto, 9 Apr., 1893 ; *e.* Toronto ; *m.* (1) Owen Moore (mar. dis.) ; (2) Douglas Fairbanks (mar. dis.) ; (3) Charles ("Buddy") Rogers ; made her first appearance on the stage in 1898, with the Valentine Stock Company at Toronto, as Cissy Denver in "The Silver King" ; she next appeared in "The Little Red School House" ; in 1902 she was "starring" as Jessie, the child, in "The Fatal Wedding," followed by a "star" tour as Mignon in "Bootles' Baby," also in "In Convict Stripes" ; she then played Eva in "Uncle Tom's Cabin" and Willie Carlyle in "East Lynne" ; she subsequently toured with Chauncey Olcott in "Edmund Burke," 1906 ; made her first appearance in New York, at the Belasco Theatre, 3 Dec., 1907, when she played Betty in "The Warrens of Virginia," in which she also toured ; at the Republic Theatre, New York, Jan., 1913, she was "starred" by David Belasco, as Juliet in "A Good Little Devil," in which she continued for some time ; at Chicago, Jan., 1934, appeared in a sketch, "The Church Mouse" ; re-appeared on the legitimate stage, at Seattle, Washington, May, 1935, playing Norma Besant in "Coquette," in which she subsequently toured ; in 1913, she turned her attention to the cinema stage, and made her first appearance for the Biograph Company, under the direction of David W. Griffith in "The Violin Maker of Cremona" ; next appeared with Harold Lockwood in "Hearts Adrift," and "Tess of the Storm Country"; she achieved remarkable success on the cinema stage in such films as "Stella Maris," "In the Bishop's Carriage," "Fanchon the Cricket," "Rebecca of Sunnybrook Farm," "Cinderella," "Mistress Nell," "Little Pal," "The Poor Little Rich Girl," "Madame Butterfly," "Such a Little Queen," "Daddy Long-Legs," "Pollyanna," "Suds," "Little Lord Fauntleroy," "Rosita," "Dorothy Vernon of Haddon Hall," "Sparrows," "My Best Girl," "Coquette," "The Taming of the Shrew," "Kiki," "Secrets," etc. ; is the author of the following books: "Why Not Try God ?," 1934 ; "The Demi-Widow" (a novel), 1935 ; "My Rendezvous with Life," 1935. *Address :* 1041 North Formosa Avenue, Hollywood, Cal., U.S.A. *Telephone No. :* Granite 5111.

PIÉRAT, Marie Thérèse (*née* Pelletier), French actress ; *b.* Paris ; entered the Conservatoire at the end of 1900, and gained first prize for comedy ; made her first appearance at the Odéon, 1901, in "Brignole et sa fille" ; subsequently played Élise in "L'Avare," Madeleine in "L'Autre Danger" and in "Les Noces Corynthiennes" ; at the Comédie Française, where she first appeared 22 Dec., 1902, as Madeleine in "L'Autre Danger"; has played in "Ames en peine," Yvonne in "L'Irrésolu," Lucienne in "Notre Jeunesse," Juliette in "Paraître," Pauline Clermain in "Chacun Sa Vie," Simone de Montagnes in "La Rivale," Alice in "On n'oublie pas," La Duchesse de Chailles in "Le Duel," Blanchette, La Reine in "Le Bon Roi Dagobert," Ginette Ménard in "Comme ils sont tous," Lise Lortay in "Le Goût du Vice," Simone in the play of that name, Fernand de Monclars in ' Les Marionettes," ; also lead in "I 'Elevation," "La Princesse Georges," "Amoureuse, "La Marche Nuptiale," "Juliette et Romeo," "Les Soeurs d'Avril,"

"L'Indiscret," "Françillon," "Les Femmes Savantes," "Aimer," etc.; is a *sociétaire* of the Comédie Française, 1905. *Recreations* : Horses, music, and reading. *Address* : 91 Avenue de Villiers, Paris.
(Died 30 May, 1934; age 48)

PIFFARD, Frederic, manager; *b.* Deoghurr, India, 6 Aug., 1902; *s.* of Frederick Eyre Piffard and his wife Gertrude (Schorr); *e.* St. Paul's School, Hammersmith; *m.* Mary Sutton; formerly an acrobatic dancer, cabaret and music-hall entertainer; from 1926–35, performed an Adagio Act in cabaret and music-halls with a partner, as Vanda and Vladimir; partner in the Piffard and Robinson Productions Ltd., managing the Duke of York's Theatre from 1944; founded the New Lindsey Theatre, 1946, and was responsible for the productions there until July, 1948; productions included: "Pick-Up Girl," "Gingerbread House," "Golden Rain," "Flowers for the Living," "Georgia Story," and others; presented "We Proudly Present," at the Duke of York's, 1947; "The Queen Came By," Duke of York's, 1949; "Flowers For the Living," Duchess, 1949; at the Stoll, Dec., 1950, presented a new production of "Where the Rainbow Ends"; Winter Garden, Dec., 1951, again presented "Where the Rainbow Ends"; resumed direction of the New Lindsey Theatre, 1952, when he presented "Intimacy at Eight"; "Blame It On Adam," 1954, "Malice Domestic," 1956; "Tropical Heatwave," "At the Drop of a Hat," 1957; with Bertie Meyer presented "Noddy In Toyland," Stoll Theatre, 1954, and again at the Princes, Dec., 1955; London Hippodrome, Dec., 1956, presented (with Bertie Meyer) "The Famous Five," and "Noddy In Toyland" at the Stoll Theatre; presented "This Is Your Wife" (tour), 1964; between 1947–60 presented (with Alan Miles) a number of productions at the Richmond Theatre; became sole lessee and licensee of Richmond Theatre, 1960; plays presented by him at Richmond which were subsequently produced in the West End include: "Goodnight Mrs. Puffin,"

"Rattle of a Simple Man," "One for the Pot," "Chase Me Comrade," "Diplomatic Baggage," "Big Bad Mouse," "Not Now Darling," "Let Sleeping Wives Lie," "She's Done It Again"; led film expedition into Western Ethiopia and found site of Queen Sheba's Mines; variety producer (B.B.C.) 1936–52. *Recreations:* Chess and gardening. *Address:* Old Rickhurst, Dunsfold, Surrey. *Telephone No.:* Dunsfold 356.

PIGOTT, A. S., business manager; *b.* Somerset ; *e.* Clifton and Stratford-on-Avon ; is a nephew of the late E. F. Pigott, Examiner of plays; joined F. R. Benson as business manager in Jan., 1901, and remained with him several years ; has fulfilled similar duties at the Kingsway, Haymarket, Court, Queen's, New, Garrick, and Savoy Theatres ; has also toured various plays from time to time under his own management. *Recreations :* Shooting and rowing. *Address :* The Playhouse, Liverpool.

PILBEAM, Nova, actress; *b.* Wimbledon, Surrey, 15 Nov., 1919; *d.* of Arnold William Pilbeam and his wife Margery Cecilia (Stopher); *e.* Wimbledon and Blackheath; *m.* (1) Frederick Penrose Tennyson (dec.); (2) Alexander Whyte; studied for the stage under Gertrude Burnett; made her first appearance on the stage at the Savoy Theatre, 22 Dec., 1931, as Marigold in "Toad of Toad Hall," which she also played at the same theatre, Dec., 1932; "Q" and Royalty, Mar., 1933, played Rosie in "Francis Thompson"; Croydon, Apr., 1933, and Shaftesbury, May, 1933, Ellen Brown in "Gallows Glorious"; Palladium, Dec., 1935, appeared as Peter Pan in Barrie's play, subsequently touring in the same part; at Oxford, for the O.U.D.S., June, 1936, played Rosalind in "As You Like It"; Criterion, July, 1936, Felicia in "The Lady of La Paz"; Palladium, Dec., 1938, again played Peter Pan; "Q," Nov., 1941, Anna in "School for Slavery"; Playhouse, Liverpool (with the Old Vic. company), from Mar., 1943, played Shirley in the play of that name, Nina in "The Seagull," Susannah in "Susannah and the Elders," Belle in "Ah, Wilderness!", and Juliet in "Romeo and Juliet"; Comedy, Mar., 1944, Fenella in "This Was a Woman"; appeared with the Dundee repertory company, June, 1945; toured, 1946, as Anne in "Day After To-Morrow"; Duchess, Feb., 1950, played Lily Holmes in "Flowers for the Living"; first appeared in films, 1934, in "Little Friend," and has since played in numerous pictures. *Recreations:* Riding, swimming, tennis, and badminton. *Address:* 4 Cheyne Row, London, S.W.3, or c/o Al Parker, Ltd., 50 Mount Street, London, W.1.

PILCER, Harry, dancer; *b.* New York; *s.* of Samuel Pilcer; is chiefly known through his association with Gaby Deslys, with whom he appeared as dancing partner for several years; he appeared at Blaney's, Lincoln Square, New York, Nov., 1907, as Percy Harrington in "The Bad Boy and his Teddy Bears"; at the Folies Bergères, New York, Aug., 1911, played Johnnie Sikes in "Hello, Paris!"; at the Winter Garden, New York, Nov., 1911, Andrew Mason in "Vera Violetta," with Gaby Deslys; at the Palace, London, Aug., 1912, played Billy in "Mdlle. Chic"; at the Winter Garden, New York, Feb., 1913, Baudry in "The Honeymoon Express"; at the Palace, London, Sept., 1913, Carolus in "A la Carte"; at the Shubert Theatre, New York, Mar., 1914, Jack Richley in "The Belle of Bond Street"; during 1915 appeared at the London Pavilion, with Miss Teddie Gerard, in various dances; rejoined Gaby Deslys and appeared at the Alhambra, June, 1915, in "5064 Gerrard"; subsequently again returned to the United States, and at the Globe Theatre, New York, Dec., 1915, played in "Stop! Look! Listen!"; at the Shubert Theatre, Jan., 1922, played in "Pins and Needles"; inventor and composer of "The Gaby Glide"; was subsequently proprietor of a school of dancing in Paris.

(Died 14 Jan., 1961; age 75)

PINERO, Sir Arthur Wing, *cr.* 1909; dramatic author; *b.* London, 24 May, 1855; *s.* of John Daniel Pinero, solicitor, and his wife Lucy (Daines); *m.* Myra Emily Holme (*d.* 1919); *d.* of Beaufoy A. Moore, widow of Captain John Angus L. Hamilton.; on leaving school, was for a period in his father's office; made his first appearance on the stage at the Theatre Royal, Edinburgh, 22 June, 1874, under the management of Mr. and Mrs. R. H. Wyndham; in 1875 he was engaged at Liverpool, at the Alexandra Theatre, under Edward Saker; made his first appearance on the London stage, at the Globe Theatre, 15 Apr., 1876, as Mr. Darch in "Miss Gwilt"; in Sept., he joined the Lyceum company on tour, playing Claudius to the Hamlet of Henry Irving on the latter's first "Hamlet" tour; he appeared at the Lyceum Theatre, first under Mrs. Bateman and subsequently under Irving, from 1876 to 1881; he made his first appearance there on 16 Dec., 1876, in "Diamond Cut Diamond"; he appeared there as Lord Stanley in "Richard III," 1877; the Senator in "Fazio," 1877; Master Heartwell in "The Hunchback," 1887; Shrowle in "The Dead Secret," 1887; Dr. Zimmer in "The Bells," 1878; the Marquis of Huntly in "Charles I," 1877; Alderman Jorgen in "Vanderdecken," 1878; Perker in "Jingle," 1878; Scriven in "Mary Warner," 1878; Rosencrantz in "Hamlet," 1878; Oliver in "Louis XI," 1879; Courriol in "The Lyons Mail," 1879; Fainwould in "Raising the Wind," 1879; Guildenstern in "Hamlet," 1879; Salarino in "The Merchant of Venice," 1879; Alfred Meynard in "The Corsican Brothers," 1880; Saville in "The Belle's Stratagem," 1881; and Roderigo in "Othello," 1881; besides playing in his own one-act plays, "Daisy's Escape" and "Bygones"; from the Lyceum he went to the Haymarket under the Bancrofts, first appearing there on 26 Nov., 1881, as the Marquis de Cevennes in "Plot and Passion"; he also appeared there as Sir Alexander Shendryn in "Ours," 1882; Mr. Hanway in "Odette," 1882; and Sir Anthony

Absolute in "The Rivals," 1884; he retired from acting after that date, but appeared as Dolly Spanker in a scene from "London Assurance," on the occasion of the final performance of the Bancroft management at the Haymarket, 20 July, 1885; of course, it is as dramatic author that Pinero stands predominant, and it is interesting to note that his first play, in one act, entitled "£200 a Year," was produced at the Globe Theatre, 6 Oct., 1877, by R. C. Carton, who at that time was also an actor; since that date he has written the following plays : "Two Can Play at that Game," Lyceum, 26 Dec., 1877; "La Cométe, or Two Hearts," Theatre Royal, Croydon, 22 Apr., 1878; "Daisy's Escape," Lyceum, 20 Sept., 1879; "Hester's Mystery," Folly, 5 June, 1880; "Bygones," Lyceum, 18 Sept., 1880; "The Money Spinner," Prince's, Manchester, 5 Nov., 1880, and St. James's, 8 Jan., 1881, which was his first play to attract serious attention; "Imprudence," Folly, 27 July, 1881; "The Squire," St. James's, 29 Dec., 1881; "Girls and Boys," Toole's, 31 Oct., 1882; "The Rector," the Court, 24 Mar., 1884; "Lords and Commons," Haymarket, 24 Nov., 1883; "The Rocket," P.O.W., Liverpool, 30 July, 1883, and Gaiety, 10 Dec., 1883; "Low Water," Globe, 12 Jan., 1884; "The Ironmaster," adapted from Georges Ohnet's play, "Le Maître de Forges," St. James's, 17 Apr., 1884; "In Chancery," Lyceum, Edinburgh, 19 Sept., 1884, and Gaiety, 24 Dec., 1884; "The Magistrate," Court, 21 Mar., 1885; "Mayfair," adapted from Sardou's play "Maison Neuve," St. James's, 31 Oct., 1885; "The Schoolmistress," Court, 27 Mar., 1886; "The Hobby Horse," St. James's, 25 Oct., 1886; "Dandy Dick," Court, 27 Jan., 1887; "Sweet Lavender," Terry's, 21 Mar., 1888; "The Weaker Sex," T. R., Manchester, 28 Sept., 1888, and Court, 16 Mar., 1889; "The Profligate," Garrick, 24 Apr., 1889; "The Cabinet Minister," Court, 23 Apr., 1890; "Lady Bountiful," Garrick, 7 Feb., 1891; "The Times," Terry's, 24 Oct., 1891; "The Amazons," Court, 7 Mar., 1893; "The

Second Mrs. Tanqueray," St. James's, 27 May, 1893; "The Notorious Mrs. Ebbsmith," Garrick, 13 Mar., 1895; "The Benefit of the Doubt," Comedy, 16 Oct., 1895; "The Princess and the Butterfly," St. James's, 29 Mar., 1897; "Trelawney of the Wells," Court, 20 Jan., 1898; "The Beauty Stone," comic opera, written in collaboration with J. Comyns Carr, with music by Sir Arthur Sullivan, Savoy, 28 Mar., 1898; "The Gay Lord Quex," Globe, 8 Apr., 1899; "Iris," Garrick, 21 Sept., 1901; "Letty," Duke of York's, 8 Oct., 1903; "A Wife without a Smile," Wyndham's, 12 Oct., 1904; "His House in Order," St. James's, 1 Feb., 1906; "The Thunderbolt," St. James's, 9 May, 1908; "Mid-Channel," St. James's, 2 Sept., 1909; "Preserving Mr. Panmure," Comedy, 19 Jan., 1911; "The 'Mind-the-Paint' Girl," Duke of York's, 17 Feb., 1912; "The Widow of Wasdale Head," Duke of York's, 14 Oct., 1912; "Playgoers," St. James's, 31 Mar., 1913; "The Big Drum," St. James's, 1 Sept., 1915; "Mr. Livermore's Dream," Coliseum, 15 Jan., 1917; "The Freaks," New, 14 Feb., 1918; "Monica's Blue Boy" (wordless play, with music by Sir Frederic Cowen), New, 8 Apr., 1918; "Quick Work," Springfield, Mass., U.S.A., 17 Nov., 1919; "A Seat in the Park," a sketch, Winter Garden, 21 Feb., 1922; "The Enchanted Cottage," Duke of York's, 1 Mar., 1922; "A Private Room," Little, May, 1928; "A Cold June," Duchess, 20 May, 1932; was created a Knight by the late King Edward on the occasion of His Majesty's birthday, 1909. *Clubs* : Athenaeum and Garrick.
(*Died 23 Nov., 1934; age 79*)

PINK, Wal (Walter Augustus Pink), author; *b*. London; *s*. of George and Martha Pink; commenced his career by appearing at various smoking concerts; made his first appearance on the music-hall stage at the Metropolitan Music Hall, 27 Dec., 1886, as a comic vocalist; subsequently wrote and produced many sketches, and for many years appeared with the Pink and Collinson Sketch Combination; subsequently appeared with his own sketch combination, playing his own productions; appeared at all the leading halls in the United Kingdom, and toured in the United States; retired from the stage in 1907, to devote his entire time to authorship; is the author of hundreds of sketches and specialty acts, and most of the successful sketches produced by Joe Elvin and Harry Tate are from his pen; among his pieces of late years may be mentioned " The King of the Castle "; " Bustown by the Sea "; " The Missing Miss "; " Sky High "; " The Taxi "; " The Rocket "; " The Confidence Trick "; " A Doubtful Policy "; " Enquire Within "; " Who sez so ? "; " Say Nothing "; " Irish, and proud of it "; part-author of the following *revues* : " Shell Out," 1915 ; " Joyland," 1915 ; " Fun and Beauty," 1916 ; " Razzle-Dazzle," 1916 ; " Flying Colours," 1916 ; " The Big Show," 1917 ; " Good By-ee," 1917 ; " Mr. Mayfair," 1917 ; " Here and There," 1917 ; " Ocean Waves," 1917 ; " Smile," 1917 ; " Zig-Zag," 1917 ; " Box o' Tricks," 1918 ; " Happy-Go-Lucky," 1918 ; " Hotch-Potch," 1918 ; " Joy-Bells," 1919 ; " Keep 'Em Alive," 1919 ; " The Whirligig," 1919 ; " Rat-tat-tat," 1920 ; " Twinkles," 1920 ; " Jig-Saw," 1920 ; " Pins and Needles," 1921 ; is one of the founders of the Variety Artistes' Federation, and proposed the resolution which called it into existence; represented the V.A.F., as " expert witness " before the Board of Conciliation formed to settle the music-hall strike, also at the subsequent Arbitration and revisionary proceedings; represented the V.A.F., with the late W. H. Clemart on the committee of the Royal Command performance at the Palace Theatre, 1912. *Recreations :* Motoring and angling.

(Died 27 Oct., 1922; age 60)

PINO, Rosario, Spanish actress; made her first appearance on the stage in 1897, in the company of Maria Tubau ; has appeared in *ingénue* parts with much success in plays by Jacinto Benaventa and the Brothers Quin-

teros ; has played in " Los Conejos," " Casa de Banos," " El Marido de la Tellez," also in " Fédora," " Zaza," " Madame Flirt," etc. ; toured in South America, 1905; formerly connected with the Teatro Lara, Madrid, now a member of the company of the Teatro de la Comedia.
(Died 15 July, 1933)

PIPER, Franco, banjo expert; *b.* Redbourn, Herts. ; made his first appearance on the stage at Pietermaritzburg, Natal, with his own company of minstrels ; coming to England he appeared at the Alhambra, and made an immediate success; has since appeared at most of the leading halls in London and the provinces.

PIRANDELLO, Luigi, dramatic author, poet and novelist; *b.* Girgenti, Sicily, 28 June, 1867; *e.* Rome and Bonn University; formerly a teacher in the Girls' High School, Rome; commenced his career in literature as a poet, subsequently turning to novel and short-story writing; his first play, "La Morsa," was produced in 1912; has since written nearly fifty plays, many of which have been translated into English; among his plays produced in London are "Six Characters in Search of an Author," "Naked," "And That's the Truth," "The Vice," "The Mock Emperor," "The Man with a Flower in His Mouth," "The Game as He Played It," "The Life that I Gave Him," "As You Desire Me"; they have also been performed in the United States; in 1925, he opened his own theatre in Rome, and in the same year toured his company in several European capitals; the company appeared at the New Oxford, London, June, 1925, playing "Six Characters in Search of an Author," "Henri IV," etc. ; in Nov., 1934, was awarded the Nobel Prize for Literature.
(Died 10 Dec., 1936; age 69)

PITOËFF, Georges, actor and manager; *b.* Tiflis, Russia, 1886; made his first appearance on the stage at St. Petersburg, 1912, and produced plays by Tchekov, Shaw, Henry Becque and others; in 1915, formed his own company and appeared in Geneva and Paris; after the War returned to Paris, where he has made nearly two hundred productions at Théâtre des Arts, Comédie des Champs Élysées, Vieux Colombier, Mathurins, etc.; among his productions have been "Le Temps est un Songe," 1919; "Les Ratés," 1920; "Le Mangeur des Rêves," 1922; "La Dame aux Camélias," "Salome," "Candida," "Hamlet," "Romeo and Juliet," "Measure for Measure," "Macbeth," "Au Seuil du Royaume," "Les Epoux d'Hen-le-Port," Comédie Champs-Élysées, 1924; "La Puissance des Ténèbres," Vieux Colombier, 1924; "Saint Jeanne," "Henri IV," "Le Lâche," Théâtre des Arts, 1925; "Comme Ci ou Comme Ca," "Sardanapale," "Mdlle. Bourat," "Jean le Maufranc," "L'Âme en Peine," "Hamlet," 1926; "Mixture," Mathurins, 1927, etc.; made his first appearance in London, at the Globe Theatre, 10 June, 1930, as Le Dauphin in "Saint Jeanne," and also produced "La Dame aux Camelias"; again appeared in London, at the Arts Theatre, Feb., 1933, when he played Jean in "Mademoiselle Julie," Le Mari and Le Comte in "La Ronde," Dr. Rank in "Maison de Poupée," and Joë Meng in "Joë et Cie"; at the Mathurins, in 1933, produced "Gants Blancs," and revived "Hamlet" and "Saint Jeanne"; produced "Ce Soir On Improvise," "Merveilleux a. ge," and "Le Chocolat Soldat," 1935; "Le Canard Sauvage," "La folle du Ciel," "Poucette," "Revanants" ("Ghosts"), in which he played Oswald Alving, and "Tu ne m'echapperas jamais" ("Escape Me Never"), in which he played Caryl Sanger, 1936; "Le Voyageur Sans Baggage," "Kirika," 1937.

(Died 17 Sept., 1939; age 53)

PITOËFF, Ludmilla, actress; *b.* Tiflis, Russia, 1896; she appeared in Georges Pitoëff's company from 1917; appeared with him at the Théâtre des Arts, Comédie des Champs-Elysées, Vieux Colombier, Mathurins, etc.; at the Comédie des Champs-Elysées, 1924, appeared in "Au Seuil du Royaume";

Vieux Colombier, 1924, "La Puissance des Ténèbres," which she adapted from Tolstoy; Théâtre des Arts, 1925, in "Saint Jeanne"; "Comme Ci ou Comme Ça," "Sardanapale," "Mdlle. Bourat," "Jean le Maufranc," "Hamlet," 1926; Mathurins, 1927, "Mixture"; visited London with her husband, and made her first appearance, at the Globe Theatre, 10 June, 1930, as Jeanne in "Saint Jeanne," subsequently playing Marguerite Gautier in "La Dame Aux Camélias"; again visited London, Feb., 1933, and appeared at the Arts Theatre, as Mademoiselle Julie, in the play of that name; played five parts in "La Ronde," Nora Helmer in "Maison de Poupée," Mary Meng in "Joë et Cie"; at the Mathurins, 1933, played in "Gants Blancs," and revivals of "Hamlet," and "Saint Jeanne"; in 1935, played Mimi in "Ce Soir On Improvise," and Nadina in "Le Chocolat Soldat," also appearing in "Merveilleux alliage"; during 1936, appeared in "La folle du Ciel," "Poucette," and as Gemma in "Tu ne m'échapperas jamais" ("Escape Me Never"); during 1937, in "Amal et la Lettre du Roi" and "Le Voyageur Sans Bagage"; after the death of her husband, 1939, went to the United States; Fulton Theatre, New York, 20 Mar., 1944, played Madame Fisher in "The House in Paris." *(Died 16 Sept., 1951; age 55)*

PITOU, Augustus, manager and playwright; *b.* New York City, 26 Feb., 1843; made his first appearance on the stage in Edwin Booth's company at the Winter Garden Theatre, New York, 18 Mar., 1867, as the Priest in "Hamlet"; subsequently supported Booth in "Ruy Blas," "Richelieu," "The Apostate," "Brutus," etc.; at Booth's Theatre, on the opening night, 3 Feb., 1869, he played Prince Escalus in "Romeo and Juliet"; his connection with Booth lasted many years; at Booth's in 1870 he supported John S. Clarke, as Charles Fenton in "Toodles"; his first experience as manager was with "The Danischeffs"; subsequently leased the Grand Opera House, Toronto; was manager of the Fifth Avenue and Booth's Theatres for John Stetson; among the "stars" who have played under his management have been W. J. Scanlan, Chauncey Olcott, Rose Coghlan, etc.; was the manager of the Grand Opera House from 1895 to 1900; is the author of "Sweet Inniscara," "A Romance of Athlone," "Garrett O'Magh," "The Irish Artist," "The Adventurers," "Old Limerick Town," "The Power of the Press" (with Geo. H. Jessop), "Across the Potomac" (with E. M. Alfriend), etc. *Recreations :* Fishing and shooting. *Clubs :* The Players', Green Room, American Dramatists'. *(Died 4 Dec., 1915; age 72)*

PITT, Archie, actor, author, and manager; *b.* 1885; *s.* of the late Morris Selinger; *m.* Gracie Fields (mar. dis.); made his first appearance on the stage in 1900, at the Greenwich Hippodrome, in variety; appeared at the old Oxford Music Hall, 1909, in variety; appeared in several pantomimes, in London, and the provinces; subsequently started his own revue company, and in 1915 toured with "Yes, I Think So," appearing at the Middlesex, July, 1915, in this piece; in Feb., 1916, produced "It's a Bargain," with which he toured for two years; in 1918 produced "Mr. Tower of London," which was extraordinarily successful, and toured it for seven years, producing it at the Alhambra, London, in July, 1923; has since produced "By Request," "A Week's Pleasure," 1925; "False Alarms," "Two Many Cooks," 1926; "Orders is Orders," "Safety First," 1927; "All at Sea," "Boys Will be Boys," "The Lido Follies," and "The Show's the Thing," 1928; at the Victoria Palace, June, 1929, produced "The Show's the Thing," and played the leading part; subsequently produced "Making Good"; Winter Garden, Dec., 1931, wrote and produced "Walk This Way"; was managing director of Archie Pitt, Ltd., lessees of the Alexandra Palace Theatre; entered films, 1934, and has appeared in "Danny Boy," "Barnacle Bill," "Excuse My Glove," etc. *Favourite part:* Cockney character. *Recreations:* Golf and fishing. *(Died 12 Nov., 1940; age 55)*

PITT, Tom, business manager; *b.* Ashton-under-Lyne; *s.* of John Pitt; *e.* Sunderland's private school, Ashton-under-Lyne; commenced his connection with the theatrical profession, as private secretary to the late Carl Rosa, with whom he remained until the date of his death in 1889; was the acting manager at the Prince of Wales's Theatre, 1889-91, during the productions of "Paul Jones," "Marjorie," and "Captain Thérèse"; was manager of "The Sign of the Cross" company in the United States, for William Greet, for seven years, and from 1891, officiated as acting manager for William Greet at the Lyric Theatre, until his death in 1914, and since his death, represents his interests as executor. *Recreations :* Fishing and croquet.

(Died 30 Dec., 1924; age 68)

PITTS, ZaSu, actress (née Eliza Susan Pitts); *b.* Parsons, Kansas, U.S.A., 3 Jan., 1900; *m.* (1) Thomas Gallery (mar. dis.); (2) Edward Woodall; began her career in films, in "The Little Princess"; has appeared in nearly 400 pictures; made her first appearance on the stage, 1942, when she toured in "Her First Murder"; in Apr., 1943, at Wilson, Detroit, appeared in "The Bat"; first appeared on Broadway, at the Royale Theatre, 3 Jan., 1944, as Belinda in "Ramshackle Inn," and toured in this 1944-5; in summer theatres, 1947-9, played Gwenny in "The Late Christopher Bean"; summer theatres, 1950, appeared in "Post Road"; National, N.Y., Jan., 1953, again played Lizzie in "The Bat"; Pasadena Playhouse, Feb., 1957, starred in "The Curious Miss Caraway." *(Died 7 June, 1963; age 63)*

PIXLEY, Frank, librettist; *b.* Richfield, Ohio, 21 Nov., 1867; *e.* Ohio State University, and Buchtell Coll., Akron, Ohio; *m.* Isabel MacRoy; was engaged as managing editor of the *Chicago Mail,* 1892-9; editor of the *Chicago Times-Herald,* 1899-1902; author of "The Carpet-Bagger," "Thoughts and Things"; has furnished the libretti for the following among other musical plays, the music to which has been composed by Gustav Luders : " The Burgomaster," " King Dodo," " The Prince of Pilsen," " Woodland," " The Grand Mogul," " Marcelle," " The Gypsy," " The Enchanted Isle." *Clubs :* Press, Chicago, Lambs', Players', and American Dramatists', New York.

(Died 30 Dec., 1919; age 52)

PLEASANTS, Jack, comedian ; *b.* Bradford, Yorks., 27 Aug., 1874 ; made his first appearance on the stage, at the Gaiety, Chatham, Jan., 1901 ; has appeared at most of the leading halls in the kingdom ; among some of his more popular songs may be mentioned " I'm twenty-one to-day " ; " To cheer him up and help him on his way " ; " I deserve a good slapping I do ! " ; " I'll be cross, Arabella, I'll be cross " ; " I'm shy, Mary Ellen, I'm shy " ; " She makes me walk in Ragtime " ; " I felt so awfully shy," etc. *Address :* 189 Brixton Hill, S.W. *Telephone No. :* Brixton 821.

PLEYDELL, GEORGE, dramatic author and novelist ; *b.* London, 1 Nov., 1868 ; *s.* of Sir Squire and Lady Bancroft ; *e.* at Eton and Brasenose College, Oxford, taking B.A. degree with honours in law in 1892, and afterwards M.A. ; called to the Bar in 1893 ; *m.* Effie, elder daughter of Sir John Hare, 1893 ; appeared on the stage at the St. James's under George Alexander, in 1896, as Lord Topham in " The Prisoner of Zenda " ; afterwards in Pinero's " The Princess and the Butterfly," as Adrian Mylls ; author of the following plays : " The Birthday," 1894 ; " Teresa," 1898 ; " What Will the World Say ? " 1899 ; " The Little Countess," 1903 ; " Lady Ben," 1905 ; " The Princess Clementina " (with A. E. W. Mason), 1910 ; " One of the Dukes," 1911, and of the novel, " The Ware Case," 1913 ; appointed in 1906 Administrator of the Academy of Dramatic Art by its Council ; resigned 1910. *Recreation :* Golf. *Club :* Garrick. *Address :* 6 Burwood Place, W. *Telephone :* 6507 Paddington

PLANCHON, Roger, actor, dramatic author, and director; *b.* Saint Chamond, Loire, 22 Sept., 1931; *s.* of Emile Planchon and his wife Maria Augusta (Nogier); *e.* Collège des Frères des Écoles Chrétiennes; formerly employed in a bank; between 1949–57, at the Théâtre de la Comédie, Lyons, directed among other plays: "Ballade du Grande Macabre," "Sens de la Marche," "Le Professeur Taranne," "Les Coréens," "Paolo Paoli," "La Bonne Âme de Se-Tchouan," "Grande Peur et Misères du IIIe Reich," also many burlesques, and classical plays; at the Théâtre de la Cité, Villeurbanne, has directed the following productions: "Henry IV" (Parts I and II) (also played the Prince of Wales), "Les Trois Mousquetaires" (also played D'Artagnan), "Georges Dandin," 1957–8; "La Bonne Âme de Se-Tchouan" (also played Soun), "La Seconde Surprise de L'Amour" (also played Hortensius), 1958–9; "Les Âmes Mortes" (also played Nozdriev), "Edouard II" (also played Gaveston), 1959–60; "Schweyk dans la IIe Guerre Mondiale," "La Remise" (also played Old Chausson), 1960–1; "Le Tartuffe" (also played Tartuffe), "O M'man Chicago," 1962–3; "Troilus et Cressida," 1963–4; at the Edinburgh Festival, Aug., 1960, directed and played D'Artagnan in "Les Trois Mousquetaires," subsequently making his first appearance in London, at the Piccadilly, Sept., 1960, in the same production; since 1960, with the Compagnie Théâtre de la Cité, he has toured extensively visiting Paris, Berlin, Athens, Venice, Zurich, Holland, Hungary, Poland, Rumania, and Bulgaria; author of the following plays: "La Remise," "O M'man Chicago," "Patte Blanche," and also adapted "Les Trois Mousquetaires" from the novel of Alexandre Dumas. *Address:* Théâtre de la Cité, Place de la Libération, Villeurbanne (Rhône), France.

PLATT, Agnes, theatrical journalist and author; *b.* London, *d.* of James Platt and his wife Emma Jane (Holman) ; *e.* privately at Hampstead ; her father was a well-known author, and her mother was the daughter of Emma Elizabeth Boden, a former leading lady with Macready ; studied for the stage with Hermann Vezin ; was a contributor to *The Daily Express* in 1900, and her first book, *The Stage in 1902*, was a reprint of her dramatic criticisms ; she next joined James Welch as play-reader, for some years, and later filled a similar post with Marie Tempest and with Herbert Jay ; started a School for Dramatists, 1916 ; undertook the management of the Ambassadors' Theatre, Aug., 1919, producing " Green Pastures and Picca- dilly " ; is the author of " Practical Hints on Playwriting," 1920 ; " Prac- tical Hints on Training for the Stage," 1921 ; " Practical Hints on Acting for the Cinema," 1921; " Film Plays: How to Write and Sell Them," 1929; " Merle," a story of the stage, 1922; is a skilful translator and a well-known " play-doctor." *Address:* 1 Carrington Court, Mayfair, W.1.

PLATT, Livingston, designer ; de- signed the settings and costumes for the following among other plays in New York: "Dinner at Eight," "Mademoiselle," "For Services Ren- dered," "Domino," "Lilly Turner," 1932; "Hangman's Whip," "Her Tin Soldier," "A Saturday Night," "$25 an Hour," "The Pursuit of Happiness," "Three and One," "A Party," 1933.

PLAYFAIR, Arthur, actor ; *b.* Elichpoor, India, 20 Oct., 1869 ; *m.* Laurie Stevens ; made his first appearance on the stage at the Grand Theatre, Douglas, Isle of Man, Aug., 1887, as Chapstone in " Jim the Penman " ; first appeared on the London stage at the Opéra Comique, 5 Dec., 1887, as the Butler in " As in a Looking Glass " ; in 1888 toured with Mr. and Mrs. Kendal, and subsequently in " Captain Swift," " The Union Jack," " A Man's Shadow," etc. ; in 1891, appeared at the Prince of Wales's in " The Prancing Girl " ; in 1892, played Giorgo in " The Mountebanks," at the Gaiety in, and in 1892 was at the Gaiety in " Cinder-Ellen," subsequently ap- pearing there in " In Town " ; at the Lyric, 1894, played in " His Ex- cellency " ; at the Comedy, 1895,

in " The Prude's Progress," and at the Vaudeville, in " The Strange Adven- tures of Miss Brown " ; produced " The Eiderdown Quilt," under his own management, at Terry's, 1896, and " On Leave," at the Avenue, 1897 ; at the Comedy, 1898, played in " The Seaflower," and " The Topsy- Turvey Hotel " ; in 1900, toured as Jim Blagden in " Wheels Within Wheels " ; from 1901-4 fulfilled a long engagement with Charles Hawtrey at the Prince of Wales's, etc., and accompanied him to the United States ; has also appeared at various music halls as a mimic ; one of his biggest successes was gained as the Butler in " The Man from Blankley's " on its original production at the Prince of Wales's, and on its revival at the Haymarket in 1906 ; during 1904, appeared in America as Bernard Mandeville in " Letty " ; appeared at the Comedy, 1906, in " The Alabaster Staircase " ; at the Vaudeville, 25 Apr., 1907, played Charles Vulliamy in " Mr. George " ; subsequently ap- peared at the various music halls in sketches ; at the Empire, 1908, played in the *revue* " Oh, indeed ! " and, in 1909, in " Come Inside " ; at Wyndham's, Aug., 1909, appeared as Walter Angel in " The Little Damozel " ; in Apr., 1910, played James Darrell in " The Naked Truth " ; at the Comedy, Nov., 1910, played Dr. Grimstone in " Vice-Versâ," and Jan., 1911, appeared as St. John Panmure in " Preserving Mr. Pan- mure " ; at the Prince of Wales's, Sept., 1911, played Isaac Manhard in " The Great Name," and Oct., 1911, he appeared as Barthazar in " The Uninvited Guest " ; at the Lyric, Sept., 1912, appeared as Baron Dauvray in " The Girl in the Taxi " ; in 1914, toured in the same part ; appeared at the Palace, Apr., 1914, in the *revue,* " The Passing Show," and remained there, 1914-15.

(Died 28 Aug., 1918; age 49)

PLAYFAIR, Sir Nigel (*cr.* 1928,) actor, producer, and manager; *b.* Lon- don, 1 July, 1874; *s.* of William Playfair, physician, and his wife, Emily (Kitson), cousin of Arthur

Playfair, actor; *e.* Winchester, Harrow, and University College, Oxford (B.A.); *m.* May Martyn, actress, July, 1905; was formerly occupied as a barrister; his early dramatic experience was gained with the O.U.D.S., the Old Stagers, and the Windsor Strollers, all famous amateur societies; first appeared on the professional boards at the Garrick, 30 July, 1902 as Mr. Melrose in " A Pair of Knickerbockers "; at the Apollo, 1903, played Mac Sherry in " Madame Sherry "; in 1903, appeared at His Majesty's, as Dr. Caius in " The Merry Wives of Windsor "; toured in the West Indies, with F. R. Benson's company; at the Court, Nov., 1904, played Hodson in " John Bull's Other Island "; May, 1905, Bohun in " You Never Can Tell "; at the St. James's, Feb., 1906, Dr. Dillnott in " His House in Order "; at His Majesty's, 1907, played Stephano in " The Tempest," Clown in " The Winter's Tale," First Gravedigger in " Hamlet "; at the Imperial, May-June, 1907, played in " Les Hannetons," and " David Ballard "; in 1907, toured with Laurence Irving; appeared at the Savoy, Sept., 1907, as Finch Mc-Comas in " You Never Can Tell "; at the Haymarket, Dec., 1908, as the Rev. Mr. Brown in " The Last of the De Mullins "; appeared at His Majesty's, Feb., 1910, as Tulpin in " The O'Flynn "; and in Mar., 1910, as the Host of the Garter in " The Merry Wives of Windsor "; at the Queen's, Dec., 1910, appeared as the Prince of Baden in " The Princess Clementina "; at the Palace in Feb., 1911, and at the Little Theatre in Mar., 1911, supported Granville Barker as Max in the " Anatol " dialogues; at the Little Theatre, Apr., 1911, appeared as Mr. Flawner Bannel in " Fanny's First Play "; at the Palace, Oct., 1911, played Hector Allen in " The Man in the Stalls "; at the Duke of York's, Feb., 1912, played Sam de Castro in " The ' Mind-the-Paint ' Girl "; at the Savoy, Sept., 1912, appeared as Paulina's Steward in " The Winter's Tale "; at the Haymarket, Nov., 1912, as Thomas Kennion in " The Younger Generation "; at His Majesty's, Mar.,

1913, as Mortimer Hunt in " The Happy Island "; Apr., 1913, Sir Benjamin Backbite in " The School for Scandal "; at the St. James's, June, 1913, played Cayley Drummle in " The Second Mrs. Tanqueray "; at the Court, Sept., 1913, played General Sir Charles Dedmond, K.C.B., in " The Fugitive "; at the St. James's, Oct., 1913, Master Klaus in " The Witch "; Dec., 1913, Sganarelle in " Le Marriage Forcé," and Cutler Walpole in " The Doctor's Dilemma "; at the Savoy, Feb., 1914, Bottom in " A Midsummer Night's Dream "; at the Apollo, May, 1914, Henri Lafitte in " The Little Lamb "; at the St. James's, Sept., 1914, Frank Mears in " Those Who Sit in Judgment "; Oct., 1915, Dr. Dilnott in " His House in Order "; at His Majesty's, Dec., 1914, Mr. Dick in " David Copperfield "; at the Haymarket, Jan., 1915, Sergeant Kite in " The Recruiting Officer "; at the Queen's, Mar., 1915, Thomas in " Wanderers "; at the St. James's, Apr., 1915, Clifford Carstairs in " The Panorama of Youth "; May, 1915, Ludwig Grunau in " The Day Before the Day "; Sept., 1915, Bertram Filson in " The Big Drum "; at the Shaftesbury, Jan., 1916, played Dangle in the operatic version of " The Critic "; at the Playhouse, Jan., 1916, Hubert Threadgold in " Please Help Emily "; at the Ambassadors', Sept., 1916, succeeded Mr. Morris Harvey in " Pell-Mell "; at the New Theatre, Apr., 1917, played Robert Crawshaw, M.P., in " Wurzel-Flummery "; at the London Pavilion, Oct., 1917, James Whibley in " A Kiss or Two "; at the New, Feb., 1918, Edward Waterfield in " The Freaks "; at the Royalty, July, 1918, Sampson Straight in " The Title "; in Dec., 1918, assumed the management of the Lyric Theatre, Hammersmith, opening with " Make Believe "; in Feb., 1919, produced John Drinkwater's " Abraham Lincoln," which ran for a year; produced " John Ferguson," 1920; " As You Like It," 1920, and revived " The Beggar's Opera," 1920, which ran for 1,463 performances, and has been frequently revived since; he appeared at the Lyric, Hammersmith, Apr., 1920, as Touchstone in " As You Like It " ; he revived " The Knight of the Burning Pestle," at the Kingsway, Nov., 1920, and in Dec., played the part of Ralph, for a time ; appeared at the Royalty, Feb., 1921, as Mr. Prothero in " A Social Convenience " ; at the Lyric, Hammersmith, Dec., 1923, played the Host of the Garter in " The Merry Wives of Windsor " ; Feb., 1924, Witwoud in " The Way of the World " ; Oct., 1924, Don Jerome in " The Duenna " ; Mar., 1925, Bob Acres in " The Rivals " ; Sept., 1925, Lamberto Landisi in "And That's the Truth " ; Oct., 1925, Colonel Oldboy in " Lionel and Clarissa " Apr., 1926, in " Riverside Nights " ; Nov., 1926, M. Jourdain in " The Would-Be Gentleman " ; Jan., 1927, Gibbett in " The Beaux' Stratagem " ; at the Ambassadors', Apr., 1927, The Hon. George Telford in " The Transit of Venus " ; Little, Oct., 1927, General Cottam in " Their Wife " ; Lyric, Hammersmith, Apr., 1928, Old Meadows in " Love in a Village " ; Aug., 1928, Tony Lumpkin in " She Stoops to Conquer " ; Oct., 1928, spoke the Prologue to " The Critic " ; Nov., 1928, Alonso in "A Hundred Years Old " ; Oct., 1929, Menteith in " Beau Austin "; Jan., 1930, Very Rev. Augustin Judd in " Dandy Dick " ; Apr., 1930, Mr. Fratton in "Out of the Blue," and Tony Lumpkin in " She Stoops to Conquer " ; at the St. Martin's, June, 1930, played the Earl of Darnaway in "Petticoat Influence"; Vaudeville, Mar., 1931, Clive Champion-Cheney in " The Circle " ; Criterion, Aug., 1931, Mr. Wilder in "Those Naughty Nineties"; Royalty, Jan., 1932, Colonel Hammond in " While Parents Sleep "; in addition to the greater majority of these plays, he has produced " Body and Soul " at the Regent, Sept., 1922, "Polly" at the Kingsway, Dec., 1922; " The Insect Play," at the Regent, Apr., 1923 ; "Robert E. Lee," Regent, June, 1923 ; " The Merry Wives of Windsor," Dec., 1923 ; "The Way of the World," Feb., 1924 ; "Midsummer Madness," June, 1924 ; "The Duenna," Oct., 1924, all at the Lyric, Hammersmith ; "Prisoners of War," Playhouse, Aug., 1925 ; " The Green Hat," Adelphi, Sept., 1925 ; "Mr. Godly

Beside Himself" (for the 300 Club), Feb., 1926 ; " When Crummles Played," Lyric, Hammersmith, June, 1927 ; "The Duchess of Elba," Arts, Oct., 1927 ; "Give a Dog ——" (for Repertory Players), Strand, Jan., 1929 ; "La Vie Parisienne," Lyric, Hammersmith, Apr., 1929 ; "The Lady of the Camellias," Garrick, May, 1930 ; "The Beaux' Stratagem," June, 1930 ; "The Importance of Being Earnest," July, 1930 ; "Marriage á la Mode," Oct., 1930 ; "Tantivy Towers," Jan., 1931 ; "The Piper," and "The Fountain of Youth," July, 1931 ; "The Old Bachelor," Sept., 1931 ; all at the Lyric, Hammersmith ; "Vile Bodies," Arts, Oct., 1931 ; "The Red Light," New, 1931 ; "Aladdin," Lyric, Hammersmith, Dec., 1931 ; "Derby Day," Lyric, Hammersmith, Feb., 1932 ; relinquished the active management of the theatre at the conclusion of "Derby Day"; adapted Capek's "R.U.R.," St. Martin's, Apr., 1923, and (with Clifford Bax) "The Insect Play," 1923 ; author of "Shock-headed Peter," and "Amelia," both produced at Garrick, part author with Paul Rubens of various children's plays; part-author of "Riverside Nights"; published "The Story of the Lyric Theatre, Hammersmith," 1925 ; "Hammersmith Hoy," 1930 ; during 1932, appeared in the film, "Perfect Understanding"; was a frequent contributor to leading London periodicals. *Favourite part :* Ralph in "The Knight of the Burning Pestle." *Clubs :* Garrick, and Stage Golfing Society.

(Died 19 Aug., 1934; age 60)

" PLINGE, Walter," actor; was discovered by the late H. O. Nicholson, and first appeared with F. R. Benson's Shakespearean Company about 1898; was well-known in connection with minor parts in most of the plays in the extensive Benson repertory, and occasionally in other companies; is related to "Mr. Bart" and "Mr. F. Anney" of the Benson Company, to "George Spelvin" (U.S.A.) and "A. N. Other" (Sport).

PLUNKETT, Patricia, actress; *b.* Streatham, London, 17 Dec., 1926; *d.*

of Captain Gunning Francis Plunkett and his wife Alice (Park); *e.* St. Martin's-in-the-Fields High School, Tulse Hill; specialized in dramatic study at school, and attended the Royal Academy of Dramatic Art, 1944; made her first appearance on the stage, at the Saville Theatre, 21 Feb., 1946, as Ann Braddock in "Stage Door"; New Lindsey, May, and Prince of Wales's, July, 1946, made a great success, when she played Elizabeth Collins in "Pick-Up Girl"; St. Martin's, Aug., 1947, played Ruth Taylor in "The Girl Who Couldn't Quite"; New Lindsey, Mar., 1949, Vicki King in "Foxhole in the Parlor"; Vaudeville, June, 1949, Jacqueline Maingot in "French Without Tears"; Watergate, Feb., 1951, Rosa in "The Brothers"; Embassy, Sept., 1951, Louise Heller in "The Family Upstairs"; Strand, Nov., 1951, Mary White in "Mary Had a Little . . .''; at the "Q," June, 1954, played Judy Mills in "Spring Model"; toured, 1959, as Antiope in "Rape of the Belt"; entered films, 1947 in "It Always Rains on Sunday." *Address:* 12 Dorland Court, Putney, London, S.W.15.

PLYMPTON, Eben, actor; *b.* Boston, Mass., 7 Feb., 1853; *s.* of Elizabeth Priscilla (Williams) and John Bradlee Plympton; *e.* Boston public schools; made his first appearance on the stage at Stockton, California, Sept., 1871; subsequently appeared at Sacramento, San Francisco, Brooklyn, etc.; at Wallack's Theatre, New York, 17 Aug., 1874, supported the late John L. Toole as James Strickett in "Wig and Gown," and Darville in "The Spitalfields Weaver"; in 1875 he appeared at Wallack's as Beauseant in "The Lady of Lyons," and at Union Square Theatre as André in "Rose Michel," and Clay Hawkins in "The Gilded Age"; he then toured with Adelaide Neilson, playing Romeo, Sebastian in "Twelfth Night," Leonatus Posthumous in "Cymbeline," etc.; subsequently appeared at Wallack's in "Marriage," "Won at Last," "A Sheep in Wolf's Clothing," etc.; at the Fifth Avenue Theatre, Nov., 1877, supported Mary Anderson as Claude in "The Lady of Lyons," subsequently appearing there with her in "Romeo and Juliet," and "Evadne"; at Madison Square, 4 Feb., 1880, played Lord Travers in "Hazel Kirke," also playing Dave Hardy in "Esmeralda," etc.; in 1881, toured in the English provinces as chief support to Miss Bateman (Mrs. Crowe); then joined Edwin Booth, and made his first appearance in London with that actor at the Adelphi Theatre, 26 July, 1882, playing Du Mauprat in "Richelieu," also appearing in "Don Cæsar de Bazan"; after his return to New York appeared at the Bijou Opera House, in 1883, as George D'Alroy in "Caste" and Jack Wyatt in "The Two Roses"; rejoined Booth, and played with him in "Othello," "Hamlet," "The Merchant of Venice," "The Taming of the Shrew," "The Fool's Revenge," etc.; subsequently played Louis de Ferrière in "Justine," George Brand in "The Wages of Sin," Victor in "Lynwood," Carol Glendenning in "In Spite of All"; next supported Clara Morris in "Miss Multon"; re-visited London in 1886, appearing at the Royalty Theatre in June, as Jack Beamish in "Jack"; toured all over the United States in the same play; appeared at Wallack's, New York, May, 1887, as Walter Leslie in "Deacon Brodie," and at Madison Square, as Captain Demalquez in "Fashion"; appeared at the Bijou, Oct., 1887, as Ingomar, when Julia Marlowe made her *début* in that play; supported Mary Anderson on her farewell tour, 1888; was a "co-star" with the late Madame Modjeska in 1888, playing Benedick in "Much Ado About Nothing," Romeo and Armand Duval in "Camille," etc.; at the Metropolitan Opera House, 21 May, 1888, on the occasion of Lester Wallack's testimonial benefit, played Laertes in "Hamlet"; toured with Julia Marlowe as Ingomar, Orlando, Pygmalion, Sir Thomas Clifford in "The Hunchback," Romeo, Claude Melnotte, etc.; at Palmer's, April, 1894, played Giles Corey in "Giles Corey, Yeoman"; at the Academy of Music, played Jack in "The Cotton King"; at Palmer's,

May, 1895, played Count Marcy in "Gossip"; has since played Philip, King of Spain, in "In the Palace of the King" (Republic, Dec., 1900); Mercutio in "all star" cast of "Romeo and Juliet," 1903; Sir Harcourt Courtley in "all star," "London Assurance," 1905; Monseigneur Bolene in "The Duel" (Hudson, 1906); Grand Duke Vassili Vasilivitch in "The Man from Home" (Louisville, 1907); toured with Marion Terry in "Divorce," 1908; in 1909, toured in "The Man from Home," and "The Debtors"; at the Lyric, New York, Nov., 1909, played Pere Euvrard in "Divorce"; at the Century Theatre, Oct., 1911, appeared as Count Anteoni in "The Garden of Allah." *Club:* Lotos.

(Died 12 Apr.,1915; age 62)

POEL. William (Pole). actor and stage director; *b.* London, 22 July, 1852; *s.* of William Pole, F.R.S.; *m.* Ella Constance Locock; made his first appearance on the stage in 1876; was, for two years, manager of the Royal Victoria Hall, Waterloo Road; for ten years, 1887-97, was general instructor to the Shakespeare Reading Society; founded the Elizabethan Stage Society, 1895, and in connection with which he made many notable revivals, notably Marlowe's "Dr. Faustus," Shakespeare's part of the play, "Edward III," "Arden of Faversham," "Edward II," "The Broken Heart," "Samson Agonistes," "Everyman," etc.; in connection with the Independent Theatre, revived Webster's tragedy, "The Duchess of Malfi," at the Opéra Comique, 1892, also "Measure for Measure" and "Troilus and Cressida"; author or adaptor of the following plays: "Priest or Painter," 1884; "Mehalah," 1886; "The Wayside Cottage" (from Kotzebüe), "The Man of Forty" (from the same source), etc.; during 1909 toured as Keegan in "John Bull's Other Island"; at the Gaiety, Manchester, Oct., 1910, played Dom Balthazar in "The Cloister"; at the Little Theatre, Mar., 1911, revived and acted in "The Historie of Jacob and Esau"; at the Kings-

way Theatre, Dec., 1912, again played Keegan in "John Bull's Other Island"; in Aug., 1924, produced for the first time in England, at the Oxford Playhouse, Oxford, the old Hamlet play "Fratricide Punished," and the performance was repeated at the New Oxford Theatre, London, 11 Oct., 1924; in Dec., 1925, produced "Arden of Feversham" at the Scala (for the Renaissance Society); on the platform stage, at Holborn Empire (for the Elizabethan Stage Circle), presented "When You See Me, You Know Me," July, 1927, and "Sejanus, His Fall," Feb., 1928; revived Fletcher's "Bonduca," at the King's Hall, Jan., 1929, and Chapman's "The Duke of Byron," at the Royalty, July, 1929; at the Mary Ward Settlement, Nov., 1932, revived George Peele's old play "David and Bethsabe" (first performance since 1599); President of the London Shakespeare League, 1925; author of "Shakespeare in the Theatre," "What is Wrong with the Stage?"

(Died 13 Dec., 1934; age 82)

POLAIRE, Mdlle. (Emilie Zouzé), French actress; *b.* Agha, Algiers, 13 May, 1879; appeared at the Bouffes-Parisiens, 1902, in "Claudine à Paris"; at the Gymnase, 1904, in "Le Friquet"; at the Renaissance, 1906, in "Les Hannetons"; at the Gymnase, 1907, in "La Revue de Centenaire," also in "La Glu"; at the Vaudeville, 1910, played Estrella in "La Maison de Danses," and Marie-Claire in "Montmartre"; at Olympia, 1910, appeared in "Le Visiteur"; at the Vaudeville, 1912, played Mioche in the play of that name; at the Théâtre Réjane, 1912, Suzanne Granger in "Les Yeux ouverts"; at the Porte-St,-Martin, Oct., 1917, Marie-Claire in "Montmartre"; at the Théâtre Réjane, Dec., 1918, Estrella in "Maison de Danse"; at the Montparnasse, Sept., 1920, Marie Gazelle in the play of that name; at the Theatre-Marjal, May, 1921, again played Claudine in "Claudine à Paris" appeared at the London Opera House, June, 1913, in the *revue* "Come Over Here!" at the Bouffes-Parisiens, May, 1914, played Suzy in " La Sauvageonné " ; at the London Coliseum, Mar., 1915, played Agathe in " Agathe à Petrograd " ; July, 1915, appeared there as Louisette in " Le Mannequin Amoureux." *(Died 14 Oct., 1939; age 59*

POLIAKOFF, Vera, actress *(see* LINDSAY, VERA).

POLINI, Marie, actress ; *b.* Shoreham, Sussex ; *d.* of G. M. Polini ; *e.* Convent of Our Lady of Zion, Bayswater ; *m.* Owen Nares ; made her first appearance on the stage at the Lyric Theatre, 1896, when she walked on in Wilson Barrett's production of " The Sign of the Cross " ; at the Princess's, July, 1897, played Elsie Wilson in " Tommy Atkins," then toured as Ruth in " When the Lamps are Lighted," . and in 1898, toured as Mrs. Tudway in " Lord and Lady Algy'' ; spent several years touring, playing such parts as Nellie Denver in " The Silver King," Madame de Semiano in " The Marriage of Kitty," Sunday in the play of that name, Nancy in " Oliver Twist," Donna Roma in " The Eternal City," Lady Marion in " Robin Hood," Nina in " His House in Order," Marise in " The Thief," Muriel Glayde in " John Glayde's Honour," etc. ; appeared at Haymarket, Sept., 1909, as Regan in " King Lear " ; at the Strand, Feb., 1910, Julie de Mortemar in " Richelieu " ; at the Lyceum, Edinburgh, Apr., 1911, played Poland in " Lily, the Bill-Topper " ; at the Duke of York's, June, 1911, Madame de Semiano in " The Marriage of Kitty," Lyceum, Feb., 1912, Liane in " The Monk and the Woman " ; Prince of Wales's, Jan., 1913, Joselyn Penbury in " Esther Castways " ; subsequently succeeded Gladys Cooper as Dora in " Diplomacy," at Wyndham's Theatre ; reappeared on the stage, at the Queen's Theatre, Jan., 1920, as Alice Desborough in " Mr. Todd's Experiment " ; in Aug., 1922, toured with her husband in " If Winter Comes " ; in Aug., 1924, toured with her husband as the Comtesse Zicka in " Diplomacy."

Favourite parts : Nancy in " Oliver Twist," Marise in " The Thief." *Recreation :* Motoring and reading. *(Died May, 1960)*

POLLARD, Daphne, actress ｜ *b.* Melbourne, Australia, 19 Oct., 1890 ; *m.* Ellington K. Bunch ; had considerable experience in "vaudeville," on the Pacific coast of America in the Pollard Lilliputian Opera Company, in which she figured as a " star," from the time she was eight years of age ; she made her first appearance in New York, at the Casino Theatre, 23 Dec., 1908, as Cymbaline Bustle in " Mr. Hamlet of Broadway " ; from 1909–14 was mainly engaged in " vaudeville " ; in 1914 appeared at San Francisco in " A Knight for a Day," and subsequently toured in " The Candy Shop " ; at the Winter Garden, New York, May, 1915, played Ruby in " The Passing Show of 1915," and she toured in this during 1915–16 ; came to England and made her first appearance in London, at the London Hippodrome, 31 Jan., 1917, in " Zig-Zag " ; subsequently appeared there in " Box o' Tricks," 1918 ; " Joy-Bells," 1919 ; " Jig-Saw," 1920 ; appeared at the Lyric, 1921, in " After. Dinner " ; subsequently returned 'o America ; on returning to London, appeared at the Empire, Apr., 1923, in " The Rainbow " ; again returned to New York, and at the Greenwich Village Theatre, Sept., 1923, appeared in " The Greenwich Village Follies " ; reappeared in London, at variety theatres, Mar., 1926 ; appeared on the vaudeville stage, 1928-29 ; commenced film career, 1927, and has appeared in numerous pictures ; in 1936, appeared in " Our Relations," with Laurel and Hardy.

POLLOCK, Arthur, dramatic critic ; *b.* Brooklyn, N.Y., 19 May, 1886 ; *s.* of William Pollock and his wife Lucretia Jane (Denton) ; *e.* Richmond Hill, Long Island, Cornell and Columbia Universities ; *m.* Mabel Sondheim ; has contributed articles on the drama to various magazines since 1912 ; dramatic critic to the *Brooklyn Eagle*

1928

from 1917 to 1948; New York theatre correspondent to *The Christian Science Monitor*, 1937–8; dramatic critic *The Daily Compass*, from 1948; adapted "Melo," from the French, 1931. *Address :* 470 West 24th Street, New York City, U.S.A. *Telephone No. :* Watkins 9–3650.

POLLOCK, Channing, dramatic author and lecturer; *b.* Washington, D.C., 4 Mar., 1880; *s.* of Alexander L. Pollock and his wife, Verona E. (Larkin); *e.* Warrington, Va., and the Polytechnic, Prague, Bohemia; *m.* Anna Marble; general manager for William A. Brady (1899–1903); general representative for the Shuberts (1903–06); from 1895 to 1897 Mr. Pollock was dramatic critic for the Washington *Post,* and in 1897 joined the staff of *The New York Dramatic Mirror* ; during 1898–1899 was dramatic critic for the Washington *Post* and *Times* ; during this period he published a volume of "Stage Stories," and a novel, "Behold the Man"; has contributed stories, articles, and theatrical data to *Ainslee's Magazine, Smith's Monthly, Saturday Evening Post, Collier's Weekly, Munsey's Magazine,* and *The Smart Set* ; his plays are as follows : " The Stepping Stones," " A Game of Hearts," " The Pit," " The Little Gray Lady," " Napoleon the Great," " In the Bishop's Carriage," " Clothes " (in collaboration with Avery Hopwood), " The Secret Orchard," " The Traitor " (with Thomas Dixon, jun.), " Such a Little Queen," " The Red Widow " (with Rennold Wolf), " My Best Girl " (with Rennold Wolf), " Her Little Highness " (with Wolf), " The Inner Shrine," " The Beauty Shop " (with Wolf), " A Perfect Lady " (with Wolf), " It Doesn't Happen," " The Follies of 1915 " (with Wolf) ; " The Grass Widow " (with Wolf), " The Crowded Hour " (with Edgar Selwyn), "Roads of Destiny," "The Sign on the Door," "The Ziegfeld Follies of 1921 " ; "The Fool," 1922 ; "The Enemy," 1925 ; "Mr. Moneypenny," 1928; "The House Beautiful," 1931 ; "The Stranglehold," 1932; "Winner, Lose All," "The Captains and the Kings," 1939; of the above mentioned, the following have

been performed in London : "In the Bishop's Carriage," Waldorf (now Strand) Theatre, 1907 ; "The Sign on the Door," Playhouse, 1921 ; "The Fool," Apollo, 1924 ; "The Enemy," Strand, 1928 ; is the author of a book "The Footlights—Fore and Aft," and "Star Magic" (a novel), 1933 ; "Synthetic Gentleman" (novel), 1934 ; "The Adventures of a Happy Man" (essays), 1939 ; is a director of the British Society of Authors, Playwrights, and Composers; a director of the Authors' League of America; is well known as a lecturer, and has received the Hon. Degree of LL.D. from Colgate University. *Club :* Players, New York; was one of the founders of the organisation known as The Friars. *(Died 17 Aug., 1946; age 66)*

POLLOCK, Elizabeth, actress ; *b.* London, 3 Aug., 1898 ; *d.* of Sir Adrian Pollock and his wife the Hon. Norah (Gully) ; *m.* James Cecil Irving McConnel; studied for the stage under Rosina Filippi ; made her first appearance on the stage at Wyndham's Theatre, 16 Mar., 1916, as the Probationer in " A Kiss for Cinderella " ; at the Criterion, Nov., 1919, played Evelyn Lovejoy in " Lord Richard in the Pantry " ; at the Prince of Wales's, Oct., 1921, appeared in " A to Z " ; at the Criterion, Jan., 1923, played Rachel Shaw in " Advertising April " ; at Wyndham's, Feb., 1924, Jennie in " Not in Our Stars " ; at the Ambassadors, Oct., 1924, Hermione Blundell in " The Pelican "; Court (for 300 Club), Feb., 1925, Maud Torrent in " Smaragda's Lover "; Everyman, Nov., 1925, Lady Violet Beaumont in " The Dark Angel "; Court (for 300 Club), Apr., 1926, Lady Isabella in " Don Juan "; Everyman, Oct., 1926, Naomi in " The Rat Trap "; Arts and Duke of York's, Apr., to June, 1928, appeared in " Many Happy Returns"; Playhouse, Sept., 1929, Lady Caroline in " Dear Brutus"; Cambridge, June, 1931, appeared in "The Sign of the Seven Dials"; Strand, May, 1932, played Betty in "Party"; Little, Jan., 1938, appeared in "Nine Sharp"; is a clever mimic, and has given impersonations at several theatres; has also broadcast her "impressions" from the B.B.C. on several occasions. *(Died 6 Jan., 1970; age 71)*

POLLOCK, John, M.A., dramatic author ; *b.* 26 Dec., 1878 ; *s.* of the Rt. Hon. Sir Frederick Pollock, Bart., and his wife Georgina (Deffell) ; *e.* Eton, and Trinity College, Cambridge ; *m.* Lydia Yavorska ; studied law, and was called to the Bar, 1906 ; is the author or adaptor of the following plays : " The Invention of Dr. Metzler," 1905 ; " Rosamond," 1910 ; " The Parisienne " (from the French), 1911 ; " The Great Young Man " (from the Russian), 1911 ; " The Lower Depths " (from the Russian, with Frank Collins), 1911 ; " The Man who was Dead " (from the Russian), 1912 ; " I Love You " (from the Italian, with Collins), 1913 ; " Mademoiselle Fifi " (from the French, with Collins), 1913 ; " Anna Karenina " (from the Russian), 1913 ; " Lolotte " (from the French), 1913 ; " Damaged Goods " (from the French), 1914 ; " For Russia," 1915 ; " In the Darkness of the Night," 1920. *Clubs :* Savile, Athenaeum, and London Fencing. *(Died 22 July, 1963; age 84)*

POLLOCK, William, theatrical journalist and author ; *b.* Eastbourne, 21 Nov., 1881 ; *s.* of William Pollock, M.B., C.M., and his wife Elizabeth (Watkins) ; *e.* Eastbourne ; *m.* Mercia Gregori ; was formerly engaged as a schoolmaster at various preparatory schools for about six years ; was appointed dramatic critic of the *Daily Mail*, 1921, and continued to represent that paper until 1923 ; dramatic critic, *Weekly Dispatch*, 1922-23 ; theatrical correspondent to the *Daily Mail* 1923-29 ; dramatic critic *Sunday Express*, 1929-30 ; invented the " Five o'Clock Follies," at the Prince's Restaurant, 1924 ; author of " Kimono," 1926 ; "Cheated," "Say It With Music" (film), etc. ; is a frequent contributor to contempory magazines ; also writes on Cricket. *Favourite play :* " Henry V." *Recreation :* Watching cricket and trying to play it. *Clubs :* Middlesex County Cricket, and Savage. *(Died 27 Oct., 1944; age 62)*

POLUSKIS, The (Will and Sam), comedians ; Will Poluski made his first appearance as a child of three years of age ; for several years, the brothers appeared together, but eventually parted for ten years, Sam going into the circus business, and Will remaining on the variety stage with another partner ; after rejoining forces, they produced several comedy scenes, among which may be mentioned " The Schemers " ; " The Tipster " ; " The Bo'sun " ; " Late on Parade " ; " The Tallyman," etc. ; have appeared at all the leading halls all over the kingdom. *Address :* " The Lindens," Effra Road, Brixton, S.W. *Telephone No. :* Brixton 1365.

POMEROY, Jay (*né* Joseph Pomeranz), director ; *b.* Theodosia, Crimea, Russia, 13 Apr., 1895 ; *e.* Theodosia and University of Geneva, Switzerland ; originally studied medicine at Geneva ; came to England, 1915, and became a naturalized British subject in 1929 ; organized regular Saturday concerts at the Albert Hall, and Sunday concerts at the Cambridge Theatre, where he also organized an International Festival of Music ; gave two Festivals of Russian Music at the Royal Albert Hall in 1943 and 1944 ; was also responsible for nearly forty Popular Symphony Concerts at the Stoll Theatre, 1944 ; produced "Sorochintzi Fair," Savoy, 1941 ; "Wonderland," Cambridge, 1942 ; "What Every Woman Knows," Lyric, 1943 ; "A Night in Venice," Cambridge, 1944 ; in May, 1943, acquired the Court Theatre ; is director of The Music Art and Drama Society. *(Died 1 June, 1955; age 60)*

POOLEY, Olaf, actor, writer and director ; *b.* Parkstone, Dorset ; *s.* of Hugh Pooley and his wife Michaela (Krohn) ; *e.* Dane Court, Pyrford, and at Gresham's Holt, and Freiburg University ; *m.* Irlin Hall ; studied décor, and painting for a year in Paris ; subsequently became a designer in films; first acted at the Freiburg University theatre, Germany, in 1935; first appeared in London at the Westminster, 2 Sept., 1943, as Telyegin in "Uncle Vanya"; Open Air Theatre, May, 1944, played Antigonus in "The Winter's Tale"; Lyric, Hammersmith, July, 1944, Macduff in "Macbeth"; Piccadilly, June, 1945, played the Street Musician in "Jacobowsky and the Colonel"; Arts, Aug., 1945, appeared in "The Circle of Chalk"; Whitehall, Dec., 1945, played Horace Barnett in "Fit For Heroes"; Piccadilly, Dec., 1946, Mardian in "Antony and Cleopatra"; Lyric, July, 1947, Charley Bannister in "Peace In Our Time"; New Lindsey, Jan., 1949, Max Pabst in "Here Come the Clowns"; St. Martin's, Sept., 1949, Dr. Bahru in "Summer Day's Dream"; Saville, Mar., 1950, Neville Cavendish in "The Platinum Set"; Westminster, June, 1952, played Capt. Lesgate in "Dial 'M' For Murder," which ran for over a year; toured, Nov., 1956, as Alan Coles in "Oh, Men! Oh, Women!"; Cambridge, London, Mar., 1957, played Mr. Sass in "The Iron Duchess"; Queen's, Aug., 1959, played Pasquale in "The Aspern Papers," which ran for nearly a year; Mermaid, July, 1963, played the Cardinal Inquisitor in "The Life of Galileo"; May Fair, Dec., 1963, took over the Director in "Six Characters in Search of An Author"; Queen's, July, 1964, played Juror No. 2 in "12 Angry Men"; Saville, May, 1965, played Clifford Snell in "The Solid Gold Cadillac"; Richmond, Sept., 1965, President Bernardo Garcia in "Flashpoint"; Bromley, Oct., 1965, Dr. Philip Hillman in "A Murder of Crows"; first appeared in films in 1945, and has also written the film-scripts "Velvet House," and "Johnstown Monster" in which he made his début as a director; has also appeared on television in a variety of parts. *Favourite parts:* Horace Barnett in "Fit For Heroes," Charley Bannister in "Peace In Our Time," Tony Lumpkin in "She Stoops To Conquer," and Alan Coles in "Oh, Men! Oh, Women!" *Hobbies:* Painting and collecting paintings and prints. *Address:* c/o Derek Glynne, 65 Knightsbridge, London, S.W.1.

POPE, Muriel, actress; *b.* in India; *d.* of John Pope, I.C.S.; *e.* Brussels; *m.* Clifford Mollison; had had much experience as an amateur before making her first appearance on the professional stage at Theatre Royal, Bournemouth, Mar., 1905, as Violet Aynsley in "A Country Mouse"; made her first appearance on the London stage, at the Criterion Theatre, 6 July, 1911, as Pauline in "The Girl who Couldn't Lie"; she spent two years with Alfred Wareing at the Glasgow Repertory Theatre, and three years with Miss Horniman at the Gaiety Theatre, Manchester, playing a very great number of parts, playing lead during her last season in 1916; she appeared with Miss Horniman's company at the Duke of York's, Jan., 1916; in May, 1916, she was engaged by Dennis Eadie to succeed Mdlle. Dorziat as Mrs. Travers in "Disraeli"; at the Court, Jan., 1917, appeared as Lady Thomasin in "The Amazons"; at the Royalty, Mar., 1917, as Emilie in "Remnant"; subsequently went to France during the latter part of the war, acting in Y.M.C.A. huts; at the Haymarket, June, 1918, played Beatrice Wyley in "Marmaduke"; at the St. Martin's Theatre, July, 1919, Gertrude Enderwick in "The Bantam V.C."; Dec., 1919, Muriel Williams in "A Dear Little Lady"; at the New Theatre, July, 1920, Evangeline in "I'll Leave it to You"; in Sept., 1920, toured as Maggie Black in "The Heart of a Child"; at the Strand, Jan., 1921, Nina Tallentyre in "A Safety Match"; at the Kingsway, Mar., 1921, Maggie in "The Heart of a Child"; at the Strand, Aug., 1921, Diana Simpson in "The Trump Card"; at the Comedy, June, 1922, Pamela Josephs in "Quarantine"; at the Savoy, Jan., 1923, Cicely Brent in "The Young Idea"; at the Gaiety, Apr., 1924, Louise de Kerouailles in "Our Nell"; appeared at the Everyman, 1925-26, as Mrs. Martin in "The Painted Swan," Miss Nathan in "I'll Tell the World," and Helen Periplot in "The Gift Horse." *Recreations:* Tennis and music. *Club:* New Victorian. *Address:* 191 Queen's Gate, S.W.7. *Telephone No.:* Kensington 3731.

POREL, Paul (Paul Désiré Parfouru), French actor and manager; *b.* St. Lô, 25 Aug., 1843; *m.* Gabrielle Reju (Madame Réjane), marriage dissolved; studied at the Conservatoire, Paris, where he gained a second prize in 1862; after completing his military training, appeared at the Gymnase, 1867; was especially successful in " Idées de Mdme. Aubray," " Le Monde où l'on s'ennuie," " Le Bel Armand," " Le Mari," " Joseph Balsamo "; was for some years, stage-manager at the Odéon, and became manager of the Odéon Theatre, Paris, in 1885; has since managed the Eden Theatre, and with M. Albert Carré, the Gymnase and Vaudeville Theatres; has written the History of the Odéon Theatre, in collaboration with M. Monval, in two volumes; in 1908 contributed his Memoirs to *Figaro Illustré*; is a Chevalier of the Legion of Honour.

(Died 4 Aug., 1917; age 73)

PORTEOUS, Gilbert, actor; *b.* London, May 19th, 1868; *s.* of Captain Laurie Porteous; *e.* King's College; *m.* Ethel Irving; originally intended for the medical profession, but studied singing under Signor Mezzoni with a view to adopting the concert stage; made his first appearance as an operatic singer, at the Theatre Royal, Birmingham, 1888, as Lucien in " Nanon "; made his first appearance in London, at the Lyric Theatre, 1891, as William in " La Cigale "; played at the Prince of Wales's Theatre, 1893, in " A Gaiety Girl "; at Daly's, 1895, in " An Artist's Model "; 1896 in " The Geisha "; 1899, in " San Toy "; 1902 " A Country Girl "; at the Prince of Wales's, 1903, in " The School Girl "; at the Strand, 1904, in " Sergeant Brue "; etc., etc.; at the Garrick, 1908, appeared in " Lady Frederick "; at the Haymarket, Nov., 1908, appeared as Criddle in " Dolly Reforming Herself "; Feb., 1909, played Stingo in " She Stoops to Conquer "; in 1911 toured in " Dame Nature "; accompanied his wife on her Australian tour, 1911 on his return to London, 1913, assumed the management of the Globe Theatre,

producing " Vanity," Apr., 1913; revived " Lady Frederick," Apr., 1913; produced " Years of Discretion," Sept., 1913; in Aug., 1915, in conjunction with Messrs. Gatti, presented " Kick In," at the Vaudeville; at the Ambassadors', June, 1917, played M. Pouchelet in " The Three Daughters of M. Dupont "; at the Royalty, Mar., 1918, Galloway in " The Prime Minister "; at the Aldwych, Sept., 1920, Eusebe and Paisiello in " La Tosca "; at the Garrick, Jan., 1921, again played Pouchelet in " The Three Daughters of M. Dupont." *Favourite parts :* Yen-How in " San Toy," and William in " La Cigale." *Recreations :* Fishing, shooting, and hunting. *Club :* Savage. *(Died 6 Sept., 1928; age 60)*

PORTER, Caleb, actor; *b.* London, 1 Sept., 1867; *s.* of Caleb Porter and his wife Elizabeth (Tidcomb); *e.* Walpole House, Chiswick, and privately; *m.* (1) Jessie Hannah Neil; (2) Kitty de Legh; was formerly a medical student; studied for the stage with Sarah Thorne at Margate; made his first appearance on the stage at the Theatre Royal, Margate, 1887, in " The Colleen Bawn"; made his first appearance in London at the Grand, Islington, 1890, as Talbot in " Mary, Queen of Scots "; was stage-manager at the Adelphi Theatre, 1894–7, and also appeared there as Hiram Webster in " The Fatal Card," 1894; Prevot in " The Swordsman's Daughter," 1895; the Arab Messenger in " Boys Together," 1896; subsequently went to Australia to produce " The Sign of the Cross "; was associate several years with Wilson Barrett, and toured with him as Nero in " The Sign of the Cross "; also acted as private secretary to Barrett; during 1901 played Prince Moskowski in " The Green Goddess "; subsequently fulfilled engagements with John Hare and Mrs. Patrick Campbell; joined Oscar Asche at the Adelphi, Apr., 1905, and played Bernardo in " Hamlet "; June, 1905, Simon in " Under Which King ? "; Nov., 1905, Egeus in " A Midsummer Night's Dream "; Mar., 1906, Abhorson in " Measure for Measure "; May, 1906, Vincentio in " The Taming of

the Shrew " ; Sept., 1906, The Sailor in " Tristram and Iseult " ; at His Majesty's, Sept., 1907, the Soothsayer in " Attila " ; Oct., 1907, Corin in " As You Like It " ; Nov., 1907, Brabantio in " Othello " ; at the Aldwych, June, 1908, Detrichstein in " The Two Pins " ; June, 1908, Gremio in " The Taming of the Shrew " ; at Prince's, Bristol, Mar., 1909, Father Pezeley in " Count Hannibal ' ; then accompanied Oscar Asche to Australia, 1909–10 ; on returning to London, appeared at the New Theatre, Oct., 1910, in " Count Hannibal " ; at the Garrick, Feb., 1911, played Dr. Caius in " The Merry Wives of Windsor " ; Apr., 1911, the Sheik Jawan in " Kismet " ; in 1912–13 again visited Australia with Oscar Asche, subsequently proceeding to South Africa ; on his return appeared at the Globe, Mar., 1914, as the Sheik Jawan in " Kismet " ; Sept., 1914, played Mapita in " Mameena " ; at the Apollo, Dec., 1915, Pedro Malorix in " The Spanish Main " ; in 1916 concluded his long association with Oscar Asche, which had lasted from 1905 ; at the Globe, Mar., 1917, played Inspector O'Reilly in " The Man Who Went Abroad " ; at the Vaudeville, Dec., 1918, played in " Buzz-Buzz ; at Drury Lane, June, 1920, played The Sand Diviner in " The Garden of Allah " ; at the Shaftesbury, Oct., 1922, Patterson in " The Cat and the Canary " ; during 1924 toured as Petulant in " The Way of the World " ; at the St. Martin's, Nov., 1925, played Saul Hodgkin in " The Ghost Train " ; in 1927 went to South Africa with Percy Hutchison, playing in " The Joker," " The Silent House," " Cock o' the Roost," and " The Ghost Train " ; on returning to England, toured, Apr., 1928, as Phil Merton in " The House With the Purple Stairs " ; Lyceum, Edinburgh, Apr., 1929, appeared in "Betty at Bay" ; Comedy, Dec., 1929, again played Saul Hodgkin in " The Ghost Train"; Fortune, Oct., 1931, McJamieson in "The Glory of the Sun." *Clubs :* Savage, Authors', and Wigwam.
(Died 13 Mar., 1940; age 72)

PORTER, Cole, composer; *b.* Peru, Indiana, U.S.A., 9 June, 1893; *s.* of

Samuel Fenwick Porter and his wife Kate (Cole); *e.* East Worcester, and Yale and Harvard Universities; studied music under Vincent d'Indy; *m.* Linda Lee Thomas (dec.) during the first World War served in the Foreign Legion, subsequently transferring to the French Army; one of his early lyrics, "A Little Flat in Washington Square," was purchased by C. B. Cochran for one of his *revues*; has composed the scores and written the lyrics of "See America First," 1916; "Hitchy-Koo 1919," 1919; "Hitchy-Koo, 1922," 1922; "Greenwich Village Follies," 1924; "Paris," "*Revue* des Ambassadeurs," 1928; "Wake Up and Dream," 1929; "Fifty Million Frenchmen," 1929; "The New Yorkers," 1930; "Gay Divorce," 1932; "Nymph Errant," 1933; "Anything Goes," 1934; "Jubilee," 1935; "Red Hot and Blue!" 1936; "Rosalie," 1937; "You Never Know" (part lyrics and music), "Leave It to Me" (part lyrics and music), 1938; "Du Barry Was a Lady," 1939; "Broadway Melody of 1940," "Panama Hattie," 1940; "Let's Face It," 1941; "Something for the Boys," "Mexican Hayride," 1943; "Seven Lively Arts," 1944; "Around the World in 80 Days," 1946; "Kiss Me, Kate" (lyrics and music), 1948; "Out of this World" (lyrics and music), 1950; "Can-Can," 1953; "Silk Stockings," 1955; "Aladdin" (which was originally written for American television in 1958), 1959; contributed additional numbers to "Mayfair and Montmartre," and "Phi-Phi," 1922; and "The Sun Never Sets," 1938; has also composed the scores of several notable films, including "Born To Dance," 1936; "Something to Shout About," 1942; "You'll Never Get Rich," 1942; "Night and Day" (his film "biography"), 1945; "The Pirate," 1947; "High Society," 1956; "Les Girls," 1957; as well as many films of his stage musicals.
(Died 5 Oct., 1964; age 71)

PORTER, Neil, actor and producer; *b.* London, 10 Jan., 1895; *s.* of Caleb Porter and his wife Jessie Hannah (Neil); *e.* Ardingly; *m.* Marjorie Clayton; was employed in the Submarine Cable Service for ten years, prior to making his first appearance on the stage, at the Opera House, Perth, Nov., 1918, as Sir Charles Fellowes in "Betty at Bay"; toured for nearly two years with Charles Doran's Shakespearean company, and spent two more years touring, and in repertory companies; made his first appearance in London at the Old Vic., 25 Oct., 1924, as Cassio in "Othello," subsequently appearing there as Theseus in "A Midsummer Night's Dream," Bolingbroke in "Richard II," Macduff, Benedick, Claudius, Orsino, etc.; during the two following seasons played nearly thirty parts; for short periods in 1926–27, toured as Dr. Syn in the play of that name; remained at the Old Vic. until May, 1927; during 1927 toured in Bernard Shaw repertory, playing John Tanner in "Man and Superman," Professor Higgins in "Pygmalion," Bluntschli in "Arms and the Man," etc.; at the Strand (for the Repertory Players), Dec., 1927, played J. G. Swither in "Sadie Dupont"; "Q," Sept., 1928, John Strange in "Earthbound"; Arts, Oct., 1928, Rubio in "The Fountain Head"; Arts and Garrick, Jan., 1929, Sidney Herbert in "The Lady With a Lamp"; Wyndham's, Apr., 1929, Captain Palmer in "Warren Hastings"; Arts, July, 1929, Rodney Ash in "Gentlemen of the Jury"; at the Court, Feb.–Mar., 1930, with the Macdona Players, appeared as Horatio in "Hamlet," etc.; Everyman, July, 1930, Love in "Prunella"; Arts, Oct., 1930, Mathias in "The Passing of the Essenes"; Embassy, Oct., 1930, Ralph Morland in "Rich Man, Poor Man"; Prince of Wales's, Dec., 1930, Israel Hands in "Treasure Island"; Arts and New, Feb., 1931, Meyerburg in "Who Goes Next?"; Arts, May, 1931, Guillaume Erard in "The Trial of Jeanne D'Arc"; in the autumn of 1931, toured as Von Mark in "The Student Prince"; appointed director and producer of the Sheffield Repertory Theatre, Dec., 1931; appeared there, May, 1932, as the Rev. Patrick Brontë in "The Brontës"; subsequently appeared as Othello; at the Memorial Theatre, Stratford-on-Avon, from Apr. 1934, played Prospero, Don John, Marc Antony in "Julius Caesar," Exeter in "Henry V," Tybalt, Biron

in "Love's Labour's Lost"; Westminster, Oct., 1934, the Earl of Kent in "King Lear"; Nov., 1934, played De Sylva in "Two Kingdoms"; Arts, Dec., 1934, Soranzo in "'Tis Pity She's a Whore"; Embassy, Jan., 1935, the Cardinal in "The Duchess of Malfi"; Grafton (for Stage Society), Feb., 1935, Loving in "Days Without End"; Stratford-on-Avon, Aug., 1935, Petruchio in "The Taming of the Shrew"; Embassy, Nov., 1935, Inspector Hoggett in "Murder Gang"; Ring, Blackfriars, Nov., 1936, Pistol in "Henry V"; New, Feb., 1937, Frederick in "As You Like It"; Royalty, Apr., 1937, Dr. Okanovitch in "Ride a Cock-Horse"; Westminster (for the Stage Society), May, 1937, the Doctor in "The Road to Damascus"; Open Air Theatre, June–July, 1937, Ford in "The Merry Wives of Windsor," Snout in "A Midsummer Night's Dream," and Julius Caesar; Old Vic., Nov., 1937, Duncan in "Macbeth," also at the New, Dec., 1937; Drury Lane, Sept., 1938, Archbishop of Canterbury in "Henry V"; St. Martin's, June, 1939, Lieutenant Cristeneck in "Bridge of Sighs"; appointed to the teaching staff of the R.A.D.A., Sept., 1936; appointed Shakespeare producer to the L.C.C. Schools, 1937; appeared in the film, "The Four Just Men," 1939. *Recreation*: Cricket. *Clubs*: Savage, and Exiles. *(Died 21 Apr., 1944; age 49)*

PORTERFIELD, Robert (Huffard) actor, director, and manager; *b.* Austinville, Virginia, 21 Dec., 1905; *s.* of William Breckenridge Porterfield and his wife Daisy (Huffard); *e.* Saltville High School, Hampden-Sydney College, and the University of Virginia; studied for the stage at the American Academy of Dramatic Arts; made his first appearance in New York at the Charles Hopkins Theatre, Oct., 1927, in "The Ivory Door," subsequently appearing at the Belasco, 1928, in "Mima"; at the Forrest, 1930, in "The Blue Ghost," and at the Broadhurst, 1935, in "The Petrified Forest"; Broadhurst, Nov., 1935, Jesse Macdonald in "Let Freedom Ring"; National, Dec., 1938 played Cyrus McCormick in "Everywhere I Roam"; founder and managing director of the Barter Theatre in Abingdon, Virginia, since 1932; entered films, 1941, and has since appeared in the following pictures: "Army Chaplain," "The Yearling," "Sergeant York," "Thunder Road," etc.; gave a Drama Survey Report to Virginia State Board of Education, and the Rockefeller Foundation, 1940; received the Antoinette Perry ("Tony") Award for outstanding contribution to the theatre, 1948; acclaimed First Citizen of Abingdon, Virginia, 1957; Thomas Jefferson Award, 1958, for cultural activities in Virginia; Suzanne Davis Award, 1967, for contribution to theatre in the South; Vice-Chairman, Virginia Commission of the Arts and Humanities; in Apr., 1946, the Barter Theatre received recognition from the Virginia Conservation Commission, and became the first theatre to receive state support in the United States. *Club:* Players. (*Died 28 Oct., 1971.*)

PORTMAN, Eric, actor; *b.* Yorkshire, 13 July, 1903; *s.* of Matthew Portman and his wife Alice (Harrison); *e.* Rishworth School, Yorks.; made his first appearance on the stage at the Victoria Theatre, Sunderland, 1924, with Henry Baynton, in Robert Courtneidge's Shakespearean company; made his first appearance on the London stage at the Savoy Theatre, Sept., 1924, as Antipholus of Syracuse in "The Comedy of Errors," subsequently appearing as Mowbray in "Richard II"; at the Strand, 1925, played Worthing in "White Cargo"; in 1926, toured in a repertory of modern plays; Rudolf Steiner Hall, Feb., 1927, played Orestes in "Electra," of Euripides; appeared at the Old Vic, Apr., 1927, as Horatio in "Hamlet"; joined the Old Vic. company at the Lyric, Hammersmith, and Sept., 1927–Jan., 1928, played Lucentio in "The Taming of the Shrew," Bassanio, the Dauphin in "Henry V," and Claudio in "Much Ado About Nothing"; at the Old Vic, Feb.–May, 1928, played Romeo, Charles Surface, Edmund in "King Lear," Arcité in "The Two Noble Kinsmen," Laertes, and Strength in "Everyman"; Arts, Oct.–Nov., 1928, Erhard Bork-

man in "John Gabriel Borkman," and Kaleve in "Caravan"; Queen's, Jan., 1929, Berthold in "The Mock Emperor"; Wyndham's, Mar., 1929, Stephen Undershaft in "Major Barbara"; Arts, July, 1929, Robert in "The Hell Within"; "Q," Aug., 1929, Edward Adishan in "Portrait of a Lady"; Vaudeville, Nov., 1929, Tony in "The Roof"; Court, Feb., 1930, Laertes in "Hamlet"; Gate, Mar., 1930, Le Vicomte in "The Lion Tamer"; Court, Mar., 1930, Joseph Percival in "Misalliance"; Lyric, Hammersmith, Apr., 1930, Crowley Tukes in "Out of the Blue," and Young Marlow in "She Stoops to Conquer"; Royalty, June, 1930, Aimwell in "The Beaux' Stratagem"; Embassy, Oct., 1930, Lelio in "The Liar"; Gate, Feb., 1931, Eben in "Desire Under the Elms"; Lyric, Hammersmith, Sept., 1931, Bellmour in "The Old Bachelor"; Duchess, Nov., 1931, Ragnar Brovik in "The Master Builder"; Gate, Feb., 1932, Paul in "Which . . .?"; Embassy, Oct., 1932, George D'Alroy in "Caste"; May, 1933, Captain Absolute in "The Rivals," and Georg von Hartwig in "Midsummer Fires"; Prince's, May, 1933, Count Orloff in "Diplomacy"; Wyndham's, Sept., 1933, Ernest Turner in "Sheppey"; Apollo, Nov., 1933, Thomas Lawrence in "Mrs. Siddons"; Playhouse, Dec., 1933, Hubert Capes in "The World of Light"; New, 1934, for a time, played Robert de Vere in "Richard of Bordeaux"; Embassy, Sept., 1934, Murat in "Napoleon"; Piccadilly (for Repertory Players), Nov., 1934, Carlo Monreale in "Our Mutual Father"; Shaftesbury, Nov., 1934, Dante Alighieri in "For Ever"; Westminster, Mar., 1935, and Daly's, May, 1935, Adrian Adair in "Chase the Ace"; Criterion, July, 1935, Edward Tramley in "This Desirable Residence"; Arts, Jan., and St. Martin's, May, 1936, Lord Byron in "Bitter Harvest"; New, June, 1937, Victor Brun in "The Great Romancer"; Open Air Theatre, July, 1937, Brutus in "Julius Caesar"; Broadhurst, New York, Nov., 1937, Rodolph Boulanger in "Madame Bovary"; Gate, London, Apr., 1938, Crown Prince Rudolph in "The Masque of Kings"; Comedy, Aug., 1938, Richard Dahl in "Give Me

1935

Yesterday"; Guild, New York, Oct., 1938, Oliver Farrant in "I Have Been Here Before"; Wyndham's, May, 1939, Blaise Lebel in "The Intruder"; Embassy, Nov., and His Majesty's, Dec., 1939, played Mark Antony in "Julius Caesar" (in modern dress); Torch, Feb., and Wyndham's, Apr., 1940, Stanley Smith in "Jeannie"; toured, Feb., 1943, as Harry Quincey in "Uncle Harry"; Duke of York's, May, 1944, played Stephen Marlowe in "Zero Hour"; Phoenix, Sept., 1948, played Andrew Crocker-Harris in "The Browning Version," and Arthur Gosport in "A Harlequinade"; Princes, May, 1950, appeared as His Excellency the Governor in "His Excellency"; Adelphi, Nov., 1951, appeared as The Marshall in "The Moment of Truth"; Opera House, Manchester, Sept., 1952, Sir Robert Briston in "The Guilty Party"; Wyndham's, Apr., 1953, Father James Brown in "The Living Room"; Wyndham's (for Repertory Players), Feb., 1954, Mark Heath in "Shadow of the Vine"; St. James's, Sept., 1954, appeared in Terence Rattigan's two plays, "Separate Tables," playing Mr. Martin in "The Window Table," and Major Pollock in "Table Number Seven"; played the same parts on Broadway at the Music Box, Oct., 1956, and also on tour in America, until Jan., 1958; Belasco, N.Y., May, 1958, played Mr. Rochester in "Jane Eyre"; Helen Hayes, Oct., 1958, Cornelius Melody in "A Touch of the Poet"; Lyceum, Oct., 1959, appeared as Cherry in "Flowering Cherry"; Ambassador, Jan., 1962, played Mr. Fielding in "A Passage to India"; on returning to England he appeared at the Comedy, Apr., 1964, in the title-part in "The Claimant"; St. Martin's, July, 1965, Edward Kimberley in "The Creeper"; has appeared in numerous television productions in London, New York, and in Canada, including "The Elder Statesman" (London), "Oliver Twist" (New York); has also appeared in numerous films, including: "49th Parallel," "One of Our Aircraft is Missing," "We Dive at Dawn," "A Canterbury Tale," "Wanted for Murder," "Dear Murderer," "Cairo Road," "His Excellency," "The Colditz Story," "The Good Companions," etc.

Favourite part: Romeo. *Recreations:* Reading, walking, swimming, and talking. *(Died 7 Dec., 1969; age 66)*

PORTO-RICHE, Georges de, French poet and dramatic author; *b.* Bordeaux, 20 May, 1849; author of the following plays : " Le Vertige," 1873 ; " Un Drame sous Philippe II," 1875 ; " Les Deux Fautes," 1878 ; " La Chance de Françoise," 1889 ; " L'Infidèle," 1891 ; " Amoureuse," 1891 ; " Le Passé," 1897 ; " Les Malefilatres," 1904, etc. ; " Le Vieil Homme," 1911 ; " Zubiri," 1912 ; " Le Marchand d'Estampes," 1918 ; is a Commander of the Legion of Honour.
(Died 5 Sept., 1930; age 81)

POSFORD, George, composer; *b.* Folkestone, Kent, 23 Mar., 1906; *s.* of Benjamin Ashwell Posford and his wife Cécile Marguerite Emma Georgette (Pigâche); *e.* Downside and Christ's College, Cambridge; *m.* Evelyn Mary Thorne; originally studied Law; began his career in 1930, writing music for radio productions; composed the music for "Goodnight Vienna," 1932; "Invitation to the Waltz," "The Gay Hussar," 1933; "Balalaika," 1936; "Paprika" ("Magyar Melody"), 1938; "Full Swing," 1942; "Masquerade," 1948; "Zip Goes a Million," 1951; "Happy Holiday," 1954; also composed music for many films; has also composed several symphonic poems; was a member of the London Fire Service, 1940–41, and served in the Royal Corps of Signals, 1942–45. *Recreations:* Tennis, golf, swimming, and all sports. *Club* · Queen's. *Address:* "Kingston Corner," Kingston Gorse, Angmering, Sussex. *Telephone No.:* Rustington 1390.

POSSART, Ernst, Ritter von, German actor and manager; *b.* Berlin, 11 May, 1841; made his first appearance on the stage at Breslau in 1860 ; was engaged at Bern in 1862, and at the Stadt Theater, Hamburg, in 1863 ; in 1864 proceeded to München, where he became stage-manager in 1872 ; and general director in 1875 ;

from 1887 to 1892, toured throughout Germany, Russia, Holland, the United States of America, etc. ; Intendant General of the Royal Theatres in Munich since 1893 ; founder of the Prinz Regent Theater, and of festivals in commemoration of Wagner and Mozart, 1893 to 1905 ; appeared in New York, 1910-1, in " Nathan the Wise," " The Learned Woman," " By Command of the King," " Friend Fritz," " The Merchant of Venice," " The Failure " ; has dramatised various works for the stage, including versions of " Faust," " Don Juan," " King Lear," " Coriolanus," " The Magic Flute," " Andromache," etc. ; his principal *rôles* are, Nathan the Wise, Gessler in " William Tell," Mephistopheles, Iago, Manfred, Antonio in " Tasso," Franz Moor, Marinelli, etc. *Address :* Maria Theresiastrasse, 25 München, Germany.

(Died 8 Apr., 1921; age 70)

POST, Guy Bates, actor ; *b.* Seattle, Wash., 22 Sept., 1875, his father, John James Post, being English, and his mother, Mary Annette Post, of French and Dutch extraction ; *e.* Trinity School in San Francisco, and the State University ; *m.* (1) Jane Peyton ; (2) Adele Ritchie (mar. dis.) ; began his career by studying law in Seattle ; made his first professional appearance in " Charlotte Corday " with Mrs. James Brown-Potter and Kyrle Bellew (1893) ; subsequently appeared in " She Stoops to Conquer," " Camille," " Thérèse Raquin," " Francillon," " The Queen's Necklace," " Romeo and Juliet," etc. ; after this engagement he supported William Owen in Shakespearean *répertoire* ; then played with Otis Skinner in " Hamlet," " Romeo and Juliet," " Richard III," " Much Ado About Nothing," " The Lady of Lyons," " A Soldier of Fortune," " The Merchant of Venice," " His Grace de Grammont," etc. ; joined Marie Wainwright in " Shall We Forgive Her ? " ; played Denton in Augustus Thomas's " Arizona," and in " My Lady Dainty " with Herbert Kelcey and Effie Shannon ; he made his first appearance in New York in this play, produced at Hoyt's, Madison

Square, 8 Jan., 1901 ; after this he appeared in " Manon Lescaut " ; he then supported Sadie Martinot in Clyde Fitch's " The Marriage Game," and assumed a dual *rôle* in a dramatization of Cooper's " The Spy " ; also appeared in " Children of the Ghetto," " Soldiers of Fortune," and " A Rose o' Plymouth Town " ; he was next seen in " The Bird in the Cage," 1903 ; and in " Major Andre," 1903 ; subsequently played with Gertrude Coghlan in " Bleak House," " Hamlet," etc. ; his next appearance was with Dustin Farnum in " The Virginian," 1904 ; after which he created the leading *rôle* in " The Heir of the Hoorah," 1905, in which he played for two years ; during 1907-8 was leading man with Mrs. Fiske, playing in a *répertoire* which included " Leah Kleschna," " Tess of the D'Urbervilles," and " Hedda Gabler " ; during 1909 toured in " Paid in Full " and " The Bridge " ; at the Majestic, New York, Sept., 1909, played John Stoddard in " The Bridge " ; at the New Theatre, New York, Dec., 1909, appeared as Philip Morrow in " The Nigger," and Feb., 1910, as Gabriel Hathorne in " The Witch " ; during 1911 appeared in " The Challenge," and " The Bird of Paradise " ; at Daly's, New York, Jan., 1912, appeared as " Ten-Thousand Dollar " Dean in " The Bird of Paradise " ; at the Lyric, New York, Jan., 1914, played Omar Khayyam in " Omar the Tentmaker " ; he continued playing this part until 1916, performing the part 959 times without a break ; at New Haven, Conn., Nov., 1916, played John Chilcote, M.P., and John Loder in " The Masquerader," and appeared in the same parts at the Lyric, New York, Sept., 1917 ; in 1918 toured in Australia in " The Masquerader," and " The Nigger " ; returned to the United States, 1918, and resumed touring in the same plays ; again toured in Australia, 1925-7, playing " The Climax," " The Bad Man," " The Masquerader," " The Nigger," " The Green Goddess," etc.; then came to London, making his first appearance at the Little Theatre, 26 Aug., 1927, as Luigi Golfanti in " The Climax " ; after returning to America, produced

"The Wrecker" at the Cort, New York, Feb., 1928, and "The Play's the Thing," at San Francisco, Sept., 1928; at Los Angeles, 1931, appeared in "A Lady in Pawn," and "Typhoon"; at San Francisco, 1931-2, appeared in "Three Men and a Woman"; Bijou, June, 1933, again played Luigi in "The Climax"; Maxine Elliott, Mar., 1934, Professor Fritz Opal in "The Shatter'd Lamp"; Biltmore, Los Angeles, July, 1945, played Wynton Haggard in "Good Morning, My Son"; of late years has appeared principally in films. *(Died 16 Jan., 1968; age 92)*

POTTER, Cora Urquhart (Mrs. Brown-Potter), actress; *b.* New Orleans, 15 May, 1857; *d.* of Colonel David Urquhart; *m.* James Brown-Potter, of New York (mar. dis. 1903); *e.* privately; made her first appearance on the professional stage, at the Theatre Royal, Brighton, Mar., 1887, as Faustine de Bressier in "Civil War"; made her first appearance on the London stage, at the Haymarket, 29 Mar., 1887, as Ann Sylvester in "Man and Wife"; was next seen at the Gaiety, June, 1887, as Faustine in "Civil War," and in Aug., 1887, as Inez in "Loyal Love"; she returned to America, Oct., 1887, and in conjunction with the late Kyrle Bellew, appeared at the Fifth Avenue Theatre, 31 Oct., 1887, in "Civil War"; her association with Mr. Bellew continued until 1898, and during this period she appeared as Juliet, Pauline in "The Lady of Lyons," Kate Hardcastle in "She Stoops to Conquer," Rosalind, Cleopatra, Françillon, Camille, Floria in "La Tosca," Hero in "Hero and Leander," etc.; and toured in India, Australia, China, and America; reappeared in London, at the Shaftesbury Theatre, 2 June, 1892, as Hero in "Hero and Leander"; more touring followed; appeared at the Duke of York's Theatre, Sept., 1897, in "Françillon"; at the Adelphi, Jan., 1898, played Charlotte Corday, in a play of that name, subsequently appearing there in "The Lady of Lyons"; was next engaged by Beerbohm Tree at Her Majesty's Theatre, appearing there in Nov.,

1898, as Miladi in "The Musketeers"; in Apr., 1899, appeared at the same theatre, as Olive Arnison in "Carnac Sahib"; rejoining Kyrle Bellew, appeared at the Comedy, Sept., 1899, as Rosa in "The Ghetto"; at the Avenue, Apr., 1901, played Nicandra in a play of that name; at the Theatre Royal, Brighton, May, 1901, appeared as Mrs. Willoughby in "Mrs. Willoughby's Kiss"; rejoined Beerbohm Tree at His Majesty's, 1902, to play Calypso in "Ulysses"; at Yarmouth, June, 1903, played Stella in "For Church or Stage"; at the King's, Hammersmith, Oct., 1903, appeared as Stephanie in "Forget-Me-Not," and as Santuzza in "Cavalleria Rusticana"; assumed the management of the Savoy Theatre, Sept., 1904, opening as Clare in "The Golden Light"; in Oct., revived "Forget-Me-Not," and "Cavalleria Rusticana"; in Nov., revived "For Church or Stage"; in Nov., 1904, appeared with Beerbohm Tree, at Windsor Castle, as Julie de Noirville in "A Man's Shadow"; at the Savoy, Dec., 1904, appeared as Nedda in "Pagliacci"; in Mar., 1905, produced "Du Barri"; and played the title-*rôle*; subsequently toured in various music halls, playing "Mary Queen of Scots, and the Murder of Rizzio"; toured in South Africa, 1907, in "La Belle Marsellaise"; during 1908 toured in English provinces as Lady Frederick in the play of that name; during 1909 toured as Helene Vaillant in "The Devil"; during 1910 toured as Jacqueline in "Madame X"; subsequently returned to America; returning to England, appeared at the Court Theatre, Feb., 1912, as the Prologue in "Buddha"; after several years' absence from the stage, reappeared for a single performance, at a benefit *matinée*, at St. Julian's, Guernsey, Feb., 1919; published her reminiscences, "The Age of Innocence and I," 1933. *(Died 12 Feb., 1936.)*

POTTER, H. C., director; *b.* New York City, U.S.A., 13 Nov., 1904; *e.* Yale University, where he also studied in "47" workshop; com-

1938

menced his theatrical career with the Hampton Players, Southampton, L.I.; went to New York, where he was engaged in stage-management, 1928–30; produced "Button Button" (with George Haight and Herman Shumlin), 1929–30; his first appointment as director, was for "Overture," New York, 1930; other plays which he has staged include "Double Door," "Wednesday's Child," 1933–4; "Post Road," "Kind Lady," 1934–5; went to Hollywood, 1935, where he directed many motion pictures; returned to New York to direct "A Bell for Adano," 1943; "Anne of the Thousand Days," 1948; "Point of No Return," 1951; "Sabrina Fair," 1953; is a member of the producing firm of Myers, Potter, Fleischman; among the motion pictures he has directed are "The Story of Vernon and Irene Castle," "The Time of Your Life," "The Farmer's Daughter," "Mr. Blandings Builds His Dream House," etc. *Address:* 22 East 60th Street, New York 22, New York. *Telephone No.:* Plaza 5–1503.

POTTER, Paul, American dramatic author; *b.* Brighton, England, June 3rd, 1853; his father was headmaster of King Edward's School, Bath; from 1876 to 1883, he was the foreign editor of the *New York Herald*; was London correspondent of the same paper from 1883 to 1884; and dramatic critic from 1885 to 1887; joined the editorial staff of the *Chicago Tribune* in 1888; has written the following, among other plays: " The Chouans," 1886; " The City Directory," 1889; " The Ugly Duckling," 1890; " The World's Fair," 1891; " The American Minister," 1892; " Sheridan, or the Maid of Bath," 1893; " Our Country Cousins," 1894; " The Victoria Cross," 1894; " Trilby," adapted from Du Maurier's novel, 1895; " A Stag Party " (with Bill Nye), 1895; " The Conquerors," 1898; " Under Two Flags," from Ouida's novel, 1901; " The Red Kloof," 1901; " Notre Dame," from Victor Hugo's romance, 1902; " The School Girl " (with Henry Hamilton), 1903; " Nancy Stair," 1905; " Barbara's Millions " (from the French), 1906; " The Honour of the Family " (adapted from Emile Fabre's play, founded on one of Balzac's stories, 1907); " Twenty Days in the Shade " (from the French, 1908); " The Queen of the Moulin Rouge " (from the French, 1908); " The Girl from Rectors " (from the French), 1909; " Parasites " (from the French), 1910; " The Zebra " (from the French), 1911; " Half Way to Paris," 1911.

(Died 7 Mar., 1921; age 67)

POULTON, A. G. (Arthur Gordon Lane Plews), actor; *b.* Malton, Yorks, 5 Dec., 1867; first appeared on the stage in Australia with the late George Rignold in " Henry V," and in 1893 he appeared at the Theatre Royal, Melbourne, in " The Double Event," and " Life for Life "; he played also in most of Shakespeare's plays, and in " The Hypocrite," " The Country Girl," " The Busybody," " The Rivals," " The School for Scandal," etc.; also Simeon Strong in " The Idler," with Charles Cartwright, and many other modern dramas; appeared at the Garrick, Sept., 1897, as the Marquis de Santarem in " La Périchole "; at the Adelphi, Dec., 1897, played Marat in " Charlotte Corday "; appeared at Terry's, 1898, with Kate Vaughan in " She Stoops to Conquer " and " The School for Scandal "; subsequently appeared at the Vaudeville, in " Never Again "; at the Adelphi, May, 1900, played Nero in " Quo Vadis ? "; at the Globe, Dec., 1901, played Sergeant Macrelle in " Hidenseek "; toured in 1903 as Caesar Q. Anthony in " Bill Adams "; at the Court, Apr., 1904, Launce in " The Two Gentlemen of Verona," and Mr. Burgess in " Candida "; at the Royalty, Aug.-Sept., 1904, Frank Cardwin in " The Chetwynd Affair," and Haldor Eriksson in " Eriksson's Wife " · at the Court, Feb., 1905, the Husband in " How he Lied to her Husband "; toured with Sir John Hare, autumn 1905; toured with Mrs. Patrick Campbell, 1906, in " The Whirlwind "; appeared at the Criterion, 1906, as Sir Henry Laughan in " The Whirlwind," the Fisherman in " Undine," and David in " The Macleans of Bairness ";

at the Lyric, Jan., 1908, played Sir John Applegate in " A White Man " ; at Wyndham's, 1909, succeeded Mr. E. W. Garden as Captain Finch in " An Englishman's Home " ; at the Kingsway, Apr., 1909, played Michael Dickson in " The Earth " ; at the Royalty, May, 1909, James Brindley in " What the Public Wants " ; at the Royalty, Feb., 1912, and Criterion, May, 1912, played David Llewellyn Davids in " The New Sin " ; at the Kingsway, Mar., 1913, Peter Horning in " The Great Adventure " ; at the Vaudeville, Oct., 1913, Prosper in " The Green Cockatoo " ; at the Kingsway, Nov., 1914, the First Sentinel, and A Citizen in " The Dynasts " ; at the Kingsway, Feb., 1915, Cecil Savoyard in " Fanny's First Play " ; at the Haymarket, Apr., 1915, Sam Tomlin in " Quinneys "; at the New, Dec., 1915, Gentlemen Starkey in " Peter Pan " ; at the Queen's, Feb., 1917, James Weir in " The Double Event " ; at the Coliseum, Mar., 1917, Jake Samuels in the " all-star " cast of " The Passing of the Third Floor Back " ; at the Apollo, May, 1917, Mr. Reynolds in " Inside the Lines " ; at the Shaftesbury, Sept., 1917, the Chancellor in " Arlette " ; at the Gaiety, Manchester, May, 1918, Mr. Westmacott in " Phyl " ; toured 1918 as E. M. Ralston in " Nothing But the Truth," and appeared at the Savoy, Jan., 1919, in the same part ; at the Lyric, July, 1920, appeared as Sir John Applegate in " A White Man " ; at The Duke of York's, Oct., 1920, as Mr. Macready in " Priscilla and the Profligate " ; at the St. Martin's, Feb., 1921, as Sir John Gotch in " The Wonderful Visit " at the Garrick, Nov., 1922, played Edward de Burg in " Biffy " ; at the Criterion, Nov., 1923, Sir Ralph Warne in " Three Birds " ; Haymarket, Feb., 1925, Francisco in " Hamlet " ; Adelphi, May, 1926, Hongi in " Aloma " ; Playhouse, Feb., 1927, Chung Hi in " The Letter " ; Sept., 1928, toured as P.C. Merkes in " Mister Cinders " ; Little, Sept., 1928, played David Llewellyn Davids in a revival of " The New Sin "; June, 1929, Ernest Gregory in " Water "; " Q," Nov., 1929, Legg in " The Hours

Between " ; Playhouse, Aug., 1932, the Hall-Porter in " The Firebird."

POUNDS, Charles Courtice, actor and vocalist ; b. London, May 30th, 1862 ; s. of Charles Pounds and his wife, Mary (Curtice), a well-known singer ; brother of Louie Pounds ; e. St. Mark's College, Chelsea, was for some years studying music at the Royal Academy of Music ; as a child, was a chorister at St. Stephen's, Kensington, and later, at the Italian Church, Hatton Garden ; still later returned to St. Stephen's as solo tenor ; made his first appearance on the stage at the Savoy, 10 Oct., 1881, in the chorus of " Patience " ; subsequently appeared there in " Mock Turtles " ; in Nov., 1882, appeared in " Iolanthe " ; subsequently touring in the same piece as Lord Tololler ; he also toured as Hilarion in " Princess Ida " ; in 1885 went to America, and at the Fifth Avenue Theatre, 19 Aug., 1885, appeared as Nanki-Poo in " The Mikado " ; returning from America played the same part in Berlin, Hamburg, and Vienna ; again went to the United States and remained in America for three seasons, playing Richard Dauntless in " Ruddigore " ; Hilarion in " Princess Ida," etc. ; he appeared at the Casino, New York, Sept., 1887, in " The Marquis " (" Jeanne, Jeannette and Jeanneton") ; Dec., 1887, as Jolivett in " Madelon," and returned to England in 1888 ; appeared at the Savoy, 1888-1892, as Colonel Fairfax in " The Yeomen of the Guard," Marco in " The Gondoliers," Indru in " The Nautch Girl," the Rev. Henry Sandford in " The Vicar of Bray," and John Manners in " Haddon Hall " ; appeared at the Globe, Nov., 1892, as Vincent in " Ma Mie Rosette " ; in 1893 toured with his own company in a triple bill ; at the Criterion, July, 1893, played Ange Pitou in " Madame Angot," and at the Princess's, Oct., 1893, Connor O'Kennedy in " Miami " ; returned to the Savoy in 1894 and played Picorin in " Mirette," Count Vasquez in " The Chieftain " ; in 1895 toured in Australia ; on his return appeared at the Prince of Wales's, Feb., 1897, as Lancelot in " La Poupée," also playing there, Jack Hooton in " The Royal Star," 1898, and Michéle in " The Coquette," 1899 ; at the Lyceum, Dec., 1899, appeared as Franz in " The Snowman "; made a fresh departure when he appeared at Her Majesty's Theatre, Feb., 1901, as Feste, the Clown in " Twelfth Night " ; appeared at the same theatre, Oct., 1901, as Ferdinand in " The Last of the Dandies," Feb., 1902, as Phemius in " Ulysses," and June, 1902, as Sir Hugh Evans in " The Merry Wives of Windsor " ; at the Prince's, Manchester, played Touchstone in " As You Like It " ; at the Coronet, Mar., 1903, played the title-*rôle* in "Chilperic"; at the Lyric, Oct., 1903, appeared as Papillon in " The Duchess of Dantzic "; played the same part in New York in 1904 ; on returning to London appeared at the Coliseum, in " Fritz " ; appeared at the Lyric, Aug., 1905, as Major Vivian Callabone in " The Blue Moon " ; at the Vaudeville, May, 1906, played Hugh Meredith in " The Belle of Mayfair " ; accompanied Sir Herbert Tree to Berlin, Apr., 1907 ; appeared at His Majesty's during the Shakespearean Festival of 1907, also appeared at that theatre in October, 1907, as Touchstone in " As You Like It " ; at the Shaftesbury in May, 1907, appeared as Dick Harrold in " Lady Tatters," and subsequently was seen at the Coliseum and elsewhere in a sketch entitled " Charles, His Friend " ; appeared at the Gaiety, 1908, in " Havana," subsequently again played at various music halls ; at the Hicks Theatre, Feb., 1909, appeared as the Abbé de la Touche in " The Dashing Little Duke " ; at the Strand, Oct., 1909, played Mattheus Roiter in " The Merry Peasant " ; subsequently again appeared in the music halls in " A Very Modern Othello," etc. ; at the Gala performance at His Majesty's, 27th June, 1911, played Herr Schillinkz in " The Critic " ; at the Whitney Theatre, Sept., 1911, played Prince Nepomuk in " The Spring Maid "; at His Majesty's, Dec., 1911, appeared as Orpheus in " Orpheus in the Underground " ; at the Shaftesbury, May, 1912, played Jasomir in " Princess Caprice " ; Feb., 1913, Colonel Pomponnet in " Oh ! Oh !!

Delphine !!! " ; at the New Theatre, Oct., 1913, played Otto Brückner in " The Laughing Husband " ; at the Knickerbocker Theatre, New York, Feb., 1914, played the same part ; in 1915, toured in English variety theatres in " Chez Nous " ; at the Garrick, June, 1915, played Bruno Richard in " Oh ! Be Careful " ; at the Shaftesbury, Jan., 1916, played Harry Benn in " The Boatswain's Mate " ; Mar., 1916, the Canon of Dorcaster in " My Lady Frayle " ; at His Majesty's, Aug., 1916, appeared as Ali Baba in " Chu-Chin-Chow," and continued to play this part almost throughout the record run of nearly five years ; at the same theatre, Oct., 1921, played Aba Yaksan in " Cairo " ; at the Lyric, Dec., 1922, Franz Schubert in " Lilac Time " ; at the New Oxford, Nov., 1924, Ben Ib-Ben in " The First Kiss." *Recreation :* Golf. *Clubs :* Savage, Green Room.

Died 21 Dec., 1927; age 65)

POUNDS, Louie, actress ; *b.* Kensington ; *d.* of Charles Pounds and his wife Mary (Curtice) ; youngest sister of Courtice Pounds ; made her first appearance on the stage in 1890, in the provinces, under George Edwardes ; made her first appearance on the London stage at the Opéra Comique Theatre, 17 Jan., 1891, in " Joan of Arc " ; next appeared at the Prince of Wales's Theatre, 6 Feb., 1892, as Daisy Meadows in " Blue Eyed Susan " ; understudied Kate Cutler in " In Town," Oct., 1892, and subsequently appeared in the part of Lady Gwendoline in that piece ; appeared at the same theatre, 14 Oct., 1893, as the Hon. Daisy Ormsbury in " A Gaiety Girl " ; appeared at Daly's, Feb., 1895, as Amy Cripps in " An Artist's Model " ; toured in the United States in the same piece ; appeared at Terry's, Apr., 1897, as Dorothy Travers in " The French Maid " ; same theatre, Dec., 1897, played in " The Princess and the Swineherd," " The Emperor's New Clothes," and " The Soldier and the Tinderbox " ; at the Vaudeville, Sept., 1898, appeared as Prince Rollo in " Her Royal Highness " ; at the

Crystal Palace, June, 1899, played Lady Lila in " The Dream of Whitaker's Almanac " ; at the Savoy, Nov., 1899, appeared as Heart's Desire in " The Rose of Persia " ; at the Coronet, July, 1900, played in " The Great Silence " and " Ib and Little Christina " ; at the Savoy, Apr., 1901, played Molly in " The Emerald Isle " ; Dec., 1901, appeared in the title-*rôle* in " Iolanthe " ; Apr., 1902, Jill-all-Alone in " Merrie England " ; Jan., 1903, Joy in " A Princess of Kensington " ; was next seen at the Adelphi, Dec., 1903, as Daisy Fallowfield in " The Earl and the Girl " ; at the Vaudeville, 1904, appeared in " The Catch of the Season " ; during 1905 toured as Mrs. Robinson in " The Golden Girl " ; subsequently succeeded Marie George as Cornelia Vanderdecken in " The White Chrysanthemum," at the Criterion ; at the Vaudeville, May, 1906, played the Princess Carl in " The Belle of Mayfair " ; at the Shaftesbury, May, 1907, appeared as Isabel Scraby in " Lady Tatters " ; at the New Theatre, Dec., 1908, played Lydia Hawthorn in " Dorothy " ; at the Hicks Theatre, Feb., 1909, played the Duchesse de Burgoyne in " The Dashing Little Duke " ; at the Knickerbocker Theatre, New York, Sept., 1909, appeared as Olga Labinska in " The Dollar Princess " ; during 1910 toured the English provinces as Sonia in " The Merry Widow," and 1910-11 as Jana Van Buren in " The Girl in the Train " ; in 1912 toured as Alix Luttrell in " Autumn Manoeuvres " ; in 1913 toured in South Africa ; on her return to London, appeared at the Duke of York's, Nov., 1913, as Patty in " Quality Street " ; at the Duke of York's, Apr., 1916, played Madame Jolette in " Toto " ; at the Chelsea Palace, May, 1918, Lily Lancaster in " The Absent-Minded Husband " ; in 1919 toured as Mrs. Culver in " The Title " ; in Nov., 1920, went to Australia, where she appeared in " Chu-Chin-Chow " ; returned to England, 1921 ; at the Adelphi, Oct., 1922, played Lady Baynham in " The Island King " ; during 1923, toured in " Be My Friend " ; retired from the

stage, 1923-6 ; reappeared, Aug., 1926, when she toured in " Lionel and Clarissa " ; during 1927, toured in " The Blue Kitten " ; subsequently appeared in film plays ; at Wimbledon, Sept.' 1928, played Mrs. Lorraine in " The Lad " ; during 1929, toured in " Square Crooks" ; at Wimbledon, Dec., 1929, played Mamma in " Shock-Headed Peter."

POVAH, Phyllis, actress ; *b.* Detroit. Mich., U.S.A. ; first attracted attention in New York, at the Lyric, 6 Jan., 1920, when she played Margot Haser in " The Light of the World " ; at the Garrick (for the Theatre Guild), Feb., 1921, played Dinah in " Mr. Pim Passes By " ; Forty-eighth Street Theatre, Nov., 1922, Muriel Humphrey in " Hospitality " ; Sam H. Harris Theatre, Feb., 1923, Jane Crosby in " Icebound " ; Garrick (for the Guild), Oct., 1923, Faith Bly in " Windows " ; Booth, Sept., 1924, Nettie Minick in " Minick " ; Dec., 1924, Francesca in " Paolo and Francesca " ; Empire, Oct., 1925, Vilma in " A Tale of the Wolf " ; Maxine Elliott, Feb., 1926, Ruth Whipple in " The Virgin " ; made her first appearance in London, at the Apollo, 29 Nov., 1926, as Grace Livingstone in " The First Year " ; at the Hudson, New York, Aug., 1927, played Julia Jones in " Blood Money " ; Wallack's, Mar., 1928, Marie Tobin in " Marriage on Approval " ; Erlanger's, Jan., 1929, Ann Carter in " Vermont" ; Martin Beck (for the Guild), Apr.,1930, Hope Ames in " Hotel Universe" ; Forrest, Jan., 1934, Grace Manning in " Re-Echo" ; Ritz, Feb., 1936, Claire Hammond in " Co-Respondent Unknown" ; Ethel Barrymore, Dec., 1936, Edith Potter in " The Women," which ran until 1938 ; Broadhurst, Jan., 1939, Margery Harvey in " Dear Octopus" ; Music Box, Oct., 1941, Ellen Kincaid in " The Land is Bright" ; Henry Miller, June, 1942, Belle Newell in " Broken Journey" ; Plymouth, Oct., 1943, Pansy in " The Naked Genius" ; Henry Miller, Dec., 1944, Edith Wilkins in " Dear Ruth" ; Royale, Nov., 1948, Stella Livingston in " Light Up the Sky" ; Playhouse, Oct., 1953, Monica Bare in " Gently

Does It"; Broadhurst, Apr., 1954, Mrs. Gans in "Anniversary Waltz." *Address:* Beacon Hill Road, Port Washington, Long Island, N.Y., U.S.A. *Telephone No.:* Port Washington 1567.

POWELL, Eleanor, actress and dancer; *b.* Springfield, Mass., U.S.A., 21 Nov., 1912; *d.* of Clarence Gardener Powell (dec.) and his wife Blanche Helen (Torrey); *e.* Springfield; *m.* Glenn Ford; studied dancing under the late Jack Donahue; as a child appeared with Gus Edwards children's company; made her grown-up *début* at the Casino de Paris, New York, 29 Jan., 1928, in "The Optimists," under Melville Gideon; 46th Street, Jan., 1929, played Molly in "Follow Thru"; Fulton, Mar., 1930, supported Maurice Chevalier; Erlanger's, Sept., 1930, played Miss Hunter in "Fine and Dandy"; Ziegfeld, Mar., 1932, appeared in "Hot-Cha"; Casino, Nov., 1932, in "George White's Music Hall Varieties"; subsequently toured in "The Crazy Quilt"; Winter Garden, Sept., 1935, appeared in "At Home Abroad"; made her first appearance in London, at the Palladium, 21 Mar., 1949; entered films, 1934, and has appeared in numerous pictures. *Recreations:* Reading and collecting gramophone records. *Address:* 727 North Bedford Drive, Beverly Hills, Cal., U.S.A.

POWELL, Peter, director; *b.* London, 19 Aug., 1908; *s.* of Claud Forbes Powell and his wife Jessie (Chapman); *e.* Mill Hill School; *m.* (1) Jean Anderson; (2) Julia Lang; directed seasons at Guildford, 1934; Festival Theatre, Cambridge, 1935; Leeds, 1936; Gate Theatre, Dublin, 1937–9; his first London productions took place at the Westminster Theatre, Sept.–Nov., 1937, for the Earl of Longford's season, when he directed the plays "Carmilla," "The Moon in the Yellow River," "Youth's the Season?" "Anything But the Truth," and "Yahoo"; during the War, served in the R.N.V.R., 1940–6; since demobilization, has directed "Exercise Bowler," "The Dove and the Carpenter," and "Don Juan in Hell," at the Arts, 1946; "Othello," and "Candida,"

Piccadilly, 1947, and at the Arts, 1947–8, "Cupid and Mars," "Smith," "Invitation to a Voyage," "Rosmersholm," "Tartuffe," and "The Cherry Orchard"; at the "Q," Apr., 1949, directed "House on the Sand"; 1949–59, director of the Repertory Company, at the Alexandra Theatre, Birmingham; Embassy, Feb., 1951, directed "The Late Christopher Bean"; at the Saville, Apr., 1957, co-directed "Zuleika"; Artistic Director of the new Everyman, Cheltenham, 1960; is the author of "The Parson Said No.," 1938; "Here's Your Uncle George," 1939; "Young To-day," 1939; "The Two Children," 1944; "The Smooth Faced Gentleman," 1950; "Running Wild," 1956; book and lyrics for "Johnny the Priest," 1960. *Recreations:* Cricket and fishing.

POWELL, William, actor; *b.* Kansas City, Mo., U.S.A., 29 July, 1892; *s.* of Horatio Powell and his wife Hattie; *e.* Kansas; *m.* (1) Eileen Wilson (mar. dis.); (2) Carole Lombard (mar. dis.); (3) Diana Lewis; studied for the stage at the American Academy of Dramatic Arts; made his first appearance on the stage at the Lyric Theatre, New York, 2 Sept., 1912, walking on in "The Ne'er Do Well"; spent eight years in various stock and touring companies, including a tour, 1913–14, in "Within the Law," and 1918, in "The Judge of Zalamea," and "The King," with Leo Ditrichstein; his last appearance on the New York stage was at the Maxine Elliott Theatre, Aug., 1920, when he played Javier in "Spanish Love"; entered films 1920, in "Sherlock Holmes," and has played lead in innumerable pictures since that date, and notably in "One Way Passage," "Lawyer Man," "The Thin Man" series, "Escapade," "The Great Ziegfeld," "Libelled Lady," "The Ex-Mrs. Bradford," "My Man Godfrey," "The Last of Mrs. Cheyney," "The Emperor's Candlesticks," "Crossroads," etc. *Address:* c/o Metro-Goldwyn-Mayer Studios, Culver City, Cal., U.S.A.

POWER, Hartley, actor; *b.* New York City, U.S.A.. 14 Mar., 1894; *s.* of

Henry C. Power and his wife Katherine (Kolb); *e.* New York; *m.* (1) Iris Leslie Williamson; (2) Betty Paul (mar. dis); was trained as an electrical engineer at Woolwich, London; made his first appearance in the stage at the Theatre Royal, Belfast, Ireland, Sept., 1911, as Herbert Cheswell in " Her Past Redeemed "; made his first appearance on the London stage, at the Garrick Theatre, in the same year, playing small parts in " Kismet "; after returning to America, made his first appearance at the Cort Theatre, Boston, May, 1914, in "Phyllis"; made his first appearance in New York, at the New Amsterdam Theatre, 14 Sept., 1914, as Chow San and Poole in "The Dragon's Claw"; during 1915 played David in " Kitty Mackay "; Comedy, New York, Aug., 1915, Horace Myd in "Mr. Myd's Mystery "; Astor, Oct., 1916, The Waster in " His Majesty Bunker Bean "; served during the War, 1916-19, with the French Army; after the War went to Australia, and during 1919-20 played leading parts with J. C. Williamson, Ltd. ; returning to New York, appeared at the Astor Theatre, Oct., 1920, as Captain Jack Madison in " The Unwritten Chapter "; at the Globe, Atlantic City, Feb., 1921, played Jack Floyd in " Tangerine "; 1921–2, played in "vaudeville," appearing as Romeo to the Juliet of Josephine Victor; at Daly's, New York, Oct., 1922, played George Inchbald in " Dolly Jordan "; Empire, Mar., 1923, Bigo in " Pasteur "; at the Booth, 1923, succeeded Frank Morgan as Brissac in "Seventh Heaven"; Sam H. Harris, Nov., 1924, played Robert Carter in "Dawn"; Eltinge, Mar., 1925, "Nifty" Frank Herman in "The Fall Guy"; Garrick, Philadelphia, Oct., 1925, Phil Corning in "The Wolf at the Door"; Ritz, Aug., 1926, Kent Goldstein in "Potash and Perlmutter, Detectives "; returned to London, to appear at the Strand, Dec., 1926, as Dan McCorn in " Broadway "; at the same theatre, Sept., 1927, staged " Seventh Heaven "; at the Apollo, Mar., 1928, played Jerry Muller in " The Man Who Changed His Name," subsequently succeeding Robert Loraine as Selby Clive in the

same play; at the same theatre, May, 1928, played Captain Leslie in " The Squeaker"; Adelphi, Sept., 1929, Robert Naughton and Eddie Connelly in "Brothers"; during 1930, toured as Robert Brand in "Virtue for Sale"; Playhouse, May, 1930, played Richard Wadsworth in "Dishonoured Lady"; Globe, Jan., 1931, Senator Corcoran in "The Improper Duchess "; Wyndham's, Oct., 1934, Jim Baker in "Sweet Aloes," which ran for eighteen months, subsequently touring in the same part; Strand, Mar., 1937, Captain Leslie in "The Squeaker"; Haymarket, June, 1937, Max Harding in "To Have and To Hold"; Strand, Dec., 1937, Gordon Miller in "Room Service," and Mar., 1938, Mark Ryder in "Death on the Table"; toured, Feb., 1939, as Steve Ferguson in "The Bowery Touch"; Wyndham's, July, 1939, played Harry Conway in "Alien Corn"; Apollo, Dec., 1939, Alan Herst in "You, of all People," and Aug., 1940, Officer Finklestein in "Margin for Error"; His Majesty's, July, 1941, Jimmie Blake in "Lady Behave"; Prince of Wales's, July, 1942, Dave Fenner in "No Orchids for Miss Blandish"; Globe, Dec., 1942, Duke Mantee in "The Petrified Forest," touring in the same part, 1943; Lyric, June, 1944, played Tracy in "Zero Hour"; Phoenix, Nov., 1945, Sir Alec Dunne in "Under the Counter"; Garrick, Jan., 1947, played Harry Brock in "Born Yesterday"; 1948–9, toured in Australia as Harry Brock in "Born Yesterday"; returned to England, 1949, and at the Garrick, Sept., 1949, succeeded Arthur Riscoe as Alfred Gilbey in "One Wild Oat"; toured, 1950, as Connor in "Don't Lose Your Head"; New Boltons, July, 1951, and at the Duchess the following month, played Bert Hutchins in "The Biggest Thief in Town"; Drury Lane, Nov., 1951, Capt. George Brackett, U.S.N., in "South Pacific"; toured, Mar., 1952, as Doc in "Come Back, Little Sheba"; toured, Mar., 1953, as Pokey Thompson in "To-morrow Is a Secret"; St. Martin's, Apr., 1954, played Harry Lancaster in "Marching Song"; Globe, May, 1955, Walter Karp in "Into Thin Air"; at the Devonshire Park Theatre,

Eastbourne, Aug., 1955, played Hank Endicott in "Double Crossing"; Piccadilly, May, 1956, played Hooper Moulsworth in "Romanoff and Juliet"; in 1932, appeared in the film "Yes, Mr. Brown," and has since appeared in numerous pictures. *Recreations:* Tennis, motor-boating, and writing short stories. *Clubs:* Lambs, New York; Green Room, National Sporting, Roehampton, and Savage, London.

(Died 29 Jan., 1966; age 71)

POWER, Tyrone, actor; *b.* London, England, 2 May, 1869; *s.* of Harold and Ethel Power; *e.* Dover College; *m.* (1) Ethel Crane; (2) Emma Reaume; (3) Bertha Knight; made his first appearance on the stage at St. Augustine, Florida, 26 Nov., 1886, as Gibson in "The Private Secretary"; played for four seasons with the late Madame Janauscheck, 1888-9; at the Bijou Theatre, New York, Aug., 1889, appeared as Captain Kill Gory in "The Lion and the Lamb"; from 1890 until 1898 was principally connected with the late Augustin Daly's company, with which he appeared in numerous parts; among these may be noted Frederick in "As You Like It," Brooke Twombley in "The Cabinet Minister," Old Much in "The Foresters," Recberg in "The Transit of Leo," Antonio in "Much Ado About Nothing," Poskett in "The Magistrate," Caliban in "The Tempest," the Host of the Garter in "The Merry Wives of Windsor," etc., etc.; at the Princess's Theatre, London, 21 June, 1894, played the leading part in his own play, "The Texan"; subsequently toured with Beerbohm Tree, in "A Bunch of Violets," "The Red Lamp," etc.; in 1898 appeared with Beerbohm Tree at Her Majesty's Theatre, London; on his return to America joined Mrs. Fiske's Company, and appeared with her as Michele in "Little Italy," Marquis of Steyne in "Becky Sharp," etc.; toured in Australia, 1900-2, with Edith Crane; subsequently played an engagement with the late Sir Henry Irving; on returning to America appeared with Mrs. Fiske as Judas in "Mary of Magdala"; next appeared at the Garden Theatre, New York, Sept., 1903, as Ulysses in the play of that name; in the spring of 1904 toured with Julia Marlowe as Charles Brandon in "When Knighthood was in Flower," Ingomar in the play of that name, etc.; in May, 1904, played at the Knickerbocker Theatre as Leon Saval in "Yvette"; at the Empire, in May, appeared as Ingomar; next joined Mrs. Leslie Carter, and appeared at the Belasco Theatre, 11 Jan., 1905, as Kaeso of Noricum in "Adrea"; during 1906 played James Dexter in "The Trancoso Trail," Lonawonda in "The Redskin," Mr. Adams in "The Strength of the Weak"; at the Garrick, Philadelphia, 8 Oct., 1907, played Beelzebub in "The Christian Pilgrim," with Henrietta Crosman; also played the same part at the Liberty Theatre, New York, in Nov., 1907; at the Savoy, New York, Mar., 1908, played Mr. Robert Smith in "The Servant in the House," and continued in this during 1909; at the Criterion, New York, Mar., 1911, appeared as Daniel in "Thaïs"; at the Lyric, Nov., 1912, played Brutus in William Faversham's revival of "Julius Caesar"; subsequently toured as Mark Antony in the same play; at the Manhattan Opera House, New York, Oct., 1917, played Abu Hasan in "Chu-Chin-Chow"; at the Cort Theatre, Mar., 1918, Brutus in "Julius Caesar"; at the Belmont Theatre, Nov., 1918, Father Petrovitch in "The Little Brother"; during 1919-20 toured in the same play, and in a revival of "The Servant in the House"; at the Knickerbocker, Oct., 1921, played Matathias in "The Wandering Jew"; at the Empire, New York, June, 1922, Sir Anthony Absolute in "The Rivals"; at the Sam H. Harris Theatre, Nov., 1922, Claudius in "Hamlet"; New Amsterdam, June, 1927, Brutus in "Julius Caesar"; Masque, Dec., 1927, Herbert Beveridge in "Venus"; Erlanger's, May, 1928, Markham in "Diplomacy." *Recreation:* Yachting. *Clubs:* Lambs' and Players', New York.

(Died 30 Dec., 1931; age 62)

POWER, Tyrone, actor; *b.* Cincinnati, Ohio, U.S.A., 5 May, 1914; *s.* of

Frederick Tyrone Edmond Power and his wife Patia Emma (Reaume); *e.* public schools in Cincinnati, Dayton Preparatory School and St. Xavier University; *m.* (1) "Annabella" (Suzanne Georgette Charpentier) (mar. dis.); (2) Linda Chrisitan (mar. dis.); before adopting the stage professionally, worked as an usher, and soda fountain dispenser; studied for the stage under his father; made his first appearance on the professional stage at Chicago, in the summer of 1931, in a small part in "The Merchant of Venice"; made his first appearance in New York at the Royale Theatre, 19 Nov., 1931, as a page in "Hamlet," with the Chicago Civic Shakespeare Co.; towards the end of 1934, appeared at the Blackstone Theatre, Chicago, as Fred Livingstone in "Romance," with Eugenie Leontovitch; during Apr., 1935, was engaged as understudy to Burgess Meredith in "The Flowers of the Forest," at the Martin Beck Theatre; he appeared at that theatre, Dec., 1935, as Benvolio in "Romeo and Juliet," and Mar., 1936, as Bertrand de Poulengy in "Saint Joan"; made his first appearance on the London stage at the Coliseum, 19 July, 1950, as Lieut. Roberts in "Mister Roberts"; New Century, New York, Feb., 1953, was engaged in "John Brown's Body," a dramatic reading; A.N.T.A. Playhouse, Feb., 1955, appeared as Richard Gettner in "The Dark Is Light Enough"; entered films, 1932, in "Tom Brown of Culver"; has since appeared in innumerable pictures. *Recreations:* Tennis, bowling, swimming, golf, and riding. *Clubs:* Players', Hollywood Athletic and Screen, Stage and Radio Guild.
(Died 15 Nov., 1958; age 44)

POWERS, Eugene, actor; *b.* Houlton, Maine, U.S.A., 21 May, 1872; *s.* of Cyrus Mathews Powers and his wife Ann Eliza (Doyle); *e.* Ricker Classical Institute; made his first appearance on the stage at Boothbay Harbor, Maine, Sept., 1891, as Don André in "British Born"; then played seven years in repertory and "stock" companies; made his first appearance on the New York stage at the 14th Street Theatre,

14 Nov., 1898, as Silas Toner in "The Village Postmaster"; same theatre Aug., 1902, played Lord Norbury in "Robert Emmet"; spent many more years in repertory and "stock" companies, and in touring melodramas; at the Playhouse, New York, Mar., 1913, played Long Rogers in "The Painted Woman"; Manhattan Opera House, Oct., 1914, Father O'Connor in "Life"; at the Frazee, Sept., 1920, played James in "The Woman of Bronze," with Margaret Anglin, and appeared with her at the Manhattan Opera House, Apr., 1921, as Agamemnon in "Iphigenia in Aulis," and at the Shubert Theatre, Apr., 1921, Winchester in "The Trial of Joan of Arc"; Neighbourhood Theatre, Oct., 1921, Eustace in "The Madras House"; Mar., 1922, Mark Sheffield in "The First Man"; Punch and Judy, Oct., 1922, Inspector Danby in "The Ever Green Lady"; Broadhurst, Dec., 1922, Sir Julius Samoon in "The Lady Cristilinda"; Bijou, Feb., 1923, Herman Krauss in "Rita Coventry"; 39th Street, Aug., 1923, Abner in "Home Fires"; Ritz, Nov., 1923, Jefferson Davis in "Robert E. Lee"; Jan., 1924, Mr. Lingley in "Outward Bound"; Bijou, Feb., 1925, Alfred Leadbeater in "Episode"; Broadhurst, Sept., 1925, Sir Maurice Harpenden in "The Green Hat"; Bijou, Oct., 1927, Bishop of Avila in "Immortal Isabella"; Broadhurst, Mar., 1928, John Collier in "The Buzzard"; Hampden's, Oct., 1928, King of the Sakyas in "The Light of Asia"; Royale, Feb., 1929, James Livingston in "Kibitzer"; Biltmore, Jan., 1930, Lord Wainwright in "Children of Darkness"; Cort, Apr., 1930, Alexander Serebrakoff in "Uncle Vanya"; Hudson, Dec., 1930, Lyapkin-Tyapkin in "The Inspector General"; Bijou, Apr., 1931, The Father in "Six Characters in Search of an Author"; Guild, Sept., 1931, Professor Coq in "He"; Booth, Jan., 1932, the Detective in "Jewel Robbery"; Broadway (for the Players Club), June, 1932, Pandarus in the revival of "Troilus and Cressida"; has been a councillor of Actors' Equity Association since 1922. *Hobby:* Collecting postage stamps. *Recreations:* Auction bridge and swimming. *Club:* Players'. *Address:*

Players' Club, 16 Gramercy Park, New York City, U.S.A.

POWERS, James T., actor and vocalist; b. in New York, 26 Apr., 1862; m. Rachel Booth; made his first appearance on the stage, at the Park Theatre, Boston, 1880, as Chip in "Dreams; or Fun in a Photographic Gallery"; first appeared in New York at the Bijou Theatre, 30 Aug., 1880, as Bob in the same play; subsequently toured in "Evangeline"; he made his first appearance on the London stage at the Avenue Theatre, with Willie Edouin, 16 July, 1883, as Bob Bibbity and Chip Cheekly in "A Dream," and also appeared there 25 Aug., 1883, as Jonas Grimes in "A Bunch of Keys"; next played with the Vokes Family, at Her Majesty's, 26 Dec., 1883, in "Little Red Riding Hood"; he then went to the Empire Theatre, which was opened on 17 Apr., 1884, and appeared as Toc in "Chilperic"; at Drury Lane, Christmas, 1884, he played the Emperor in "Dick Whittington"; returning to America, he played Rats in "A Tin Soldier"; he then went to the Casino, New York, and appeared in "The Marquis"; played Taboureau in "Madelon," and subsequently appeared in "Nadgy," "The Drum Major," and "Erminie"; he "starred" for four years as Dick Dasher in "A Straight Tip," and was seen in this part at Harrigan's Park Theatre, for the first time in New York, on 26 Jan., 1891; at the Bijou Theatre, 27 Feb., 1893, played Arthur Jones in "A Mad Bargain"; at Harrigan's Park Theatre, 26 Feb., 1894, was Jasper in "Walker, London"; at the Standard, Oct., 1894, played Archibald in "The New Boy"; at the Bijou, in 1896, played Gentleman Joe, and at Hammerstein's Lyric, 1896, played Moccarelli in "Santa Maria"; he appeared at Daly's Theatre, New York, from 1897 to 1902, in "The Circus Girl," "The Geisha," "La Poupée," "A Runaway Girl," "San Toy," and "The Messenger Boy"; during 1903 he played in "The Jewel of Asia," and "The Princess of Kensington"; at the Star, Buffalo, 31 Dec., 1903, appeared as Simon Pentweazle in "The Medal and the Maid," subsequently in "vaudeville" in "Dreaming"; and in Aug., 1906, he played Moolraj in "The Blue Moon," appearing in this part at the Casino, New York, on 3 Nov., 1906; at the Casino, 11 Feb., 1909, played Samuel Nix in "Havana," subsequently touring in the same part, 1909; at the Casino, 29 Apr., 1912, played Polycarp Ivanowitch in "Two Little Brides"; at the Forty-fourth Street, Theatre, 27 Mar., 1913, reappeared as Wun-Hi in "The Geisha"; after three years' absence from the stage, reappeared at Washington, June, 1916, as Alfred Hopper in "Somebody's Luggage," and played the same part at the Forty-eighth Street Theatre, Aug., 1916; at the Century Theatre, May, 1918, played Monty in "Out There"; of late years, his appearances have been confined to the "all-star" revivals given in New York annually, and at the Empire, New York, June, 1922, he played David in "The Rivals," and the same part at the Forty-eighth Street Theatre, May, 1923; Knickerbocker, May, 1926, Francis in "King Henry IV" (Part I); New Amsterdam, June, 1927, the Cobbler in "Julius Caesar"; Hampden's, June, 1928, Scrub in "The Beaux' Stratagem"; Knickerbocker, June, 1929, Sir Pitt Crawley in "Becky Sharp"; Erlanger's, Mar., 1930, Bob Acres in "The Rivals"; Oct., 1931, Wun-Hi in "The Geisha"; National (for the Players' Club), May, 1935, Peters in "Seven Keys to Baldpate"; his autobiography, "Twinkle Little Star," was published in 1939. *Address:* Players Club, 16 Gramercy Park, New York City, U.S.A.

POWERS, Leona, actress; b. Salida, Colorado, U.S.A., 13 Mar., 1898; d. of Walter Osgood Powers and his wife Emily Margaret (Macpherson); e. privately; m. Howard Miller; made her first appearance on the stage as a small child at McVicker's Theatre, Chicago, as Dick in "Lovers' Lane"; made her first appearance in New York, at the New Star Theatre, 31 Aug., 1903, as Ruth in "The Charity Nurse";

appeared at the New Amsterdam Theatre, Mar., 1905, as the little Duke of York in "Richard III," with Richard Mansfield; Criterion, New York, Dec., 1905, played the Child in "Pantaloon"; Empire, Sept., 1906, Derek Jesson in "His House In Order"; she then retired from the stage to outgrow the "awkward age" and when she returned, reappeared with Woodward's "stock" company at the Denham Theatre, Denver; subsequently played lead in numerous "stock" companies all over the United States; reappeared in New York at the Bijou Theatre, Sept., 1932, as Floss Reynolds in "Best Years"; Alvin (for Theatre Guild), Jan., 1934, played Lady Fleming in "Mary of Scotland"; Fulton, Sept., 1934, Clara Jessup in "Errant Lady"; Biltmore, Nov., 1935, Mrs. Sweeney in "Whatever Goes Up"; Guild, June, 1936, Leonie in "End of Summer"; Booth, Sept., 1936, Violet Freely in "The Golden Journey"; Lyceum, Dec., 1936, Mrs. Brawne in "Aged 26"; National, Mar., 1937, Zinna Meek in "Red Harvest"; 46th Street, Jan., 1938, Flora Baldwin in "Right This Way"; Windsor, Mar., 1938, Julia Wetherby in "There's Always A Breeze"; Windsor, Oct., 1938, Norma Babcock in "The Good"; Lyceum, Dec., 1939, Lottie Grady in "When We Are Married"; Golden, Nov., 1940, Carlotta Faulkner in "Return Engagement," and Nov., 1941, Louise Montfavet in "Little Dark Horse"; Playhouse, Dec., 1941, Sylvia Kent in "Pie in the Sky"; Martin Beck, Apr., 1942, Madame Orden in "The Moon is Down"; Guild, Nov., 1942, Myrtle Staines in "Mr. Sycamore"; Cort, Jan., 1944, Dixie James in "Wallflower"; at Chicago, 1945–6, Edith Wilkins in "Dear Ruth," and succeeded Helen McKellar in the same part at the Henry Miller, New York, May, 1946; National, Feb., 1949, played Patty Benedict in "The Big Knife"; entered films, 1935, in "Sweet Surrender," and has appeared in several pictures; has also made frequent appearances in television. *Recreations:* Motoring, golf.

(Died 7 Jan., 1967; age 73)

POWERS, Tom, actor; *b.* Owensboro', Kentucky, U.S.A., 7 July, 1890; *s.* of Colonel Joshua De Vere Powers and his wife Clara Galatin (Hawes); *e.* High School, Louisville, and Portland College, Texas; studied for the stage at American Academy of Dramatic Art; made his first appearance on the stage at Lancaster, Pa., Feb., 1911, as Dave in "In Mizzoura"; made his first appearance in New York, at the Portmanteau Theatre, 21 July, 1915, as the Ballad Singer in "Six Who Pass, While the Lentils Boil"; appeared at the Shubert Theatre, 5 Sept., 1916, as William Booth in "Mr. Lazarus"; at the Lyceum, Nov., 1916, played Jack Kendall in "Mile-a-Minute Kendall"; at the Princess, Feb., 1917, George Budd in "Oh, Boy!"; made his first appearance on the London stage, at the Kingsway, 27 Jan., 1919, in the same part, when the play was renamed "Oh, Joy!"; at the Park Theatre, New York, Oct., 1920, played Carter Brooks in "Bab"; at Chicago, Feb., 1921, played in "Cognac"; Times Square, New York, Oct., 1921, Larry Pell in "Love Dreams"; Belmont, Jan., 1922, Segard in "S.S. Tenacity"; Princess, Mar., 1922, Martin Wells in "The First Fifty Years"; Forty-eighth Street, Nov., 1922, Peter Wells in "Hospitality"; Dec., 1922, Leonard Chadwick in "Why Not?"; Belmont, Oct., 1923, Emmett Carr in "Tarnish"; Earl Carroll, Oct., 1924, Erik Fane in "Great Music"; Forty-eighth Street, Feb., 1925, Gregers Werle in "The Wild Duck"; Klaw Theatre (for the Theatre Guild), Nov., 1925, The Captain in "Androcles and the Lion," Napoleon in "The Man of Destiny," and Bluntschli in "Arms and the Man"; Gaiety, Apr., 1926, Count Scipione Varelli in "Love in a Mist"; Booth, Oct., 1926, Archie Inch in "White Wings"; Mansfield, Jan., 1927, George Parsons in "For Better or Worse"; Longacre, Apr., 1927, The Professor in "The House of Shadows"; John Golden Theatre (for the Guild), Charles Marsden in "Strange Interlude," which he played 1928-9; Martin Beck (for the Guild), Feb., 1930, King Magnus in "The Apple Cart"; Empire, June, 1930, John Rhead in "Milestones"; Guild, Sept., 1931, He in a play of that name; at Louisville, Kentucky, 1932, appeared in his own play, "The Handy Man"; at Newport, June, 1932, played Elyot Chase in "Private Lives"; Harris, Chicago, Sept., 1932, Victor Hallam in "Another Language"; at Ann Arbor, May-June, 1933, played leads in "Design for Living," "Springtime for Henry," and "The Mad Hopes"; Playhouse, New York, Jan., 1934, played Mr. Kubeck in "Mackerel Skies"; Longacre, Mar., 1934, Dr. Martin Goshen in "The Pure in Heart"; Biltmore, Oct., 1934, produced his own play "Bridal Quilt"; Masque, Oct., 1934, played Louis Von Alchek in "Waltz in Fire"; Civic Repertory, Dec., 1934, Franz Rasch in "Sailors of Catarro"; at Westport, July, 1935, played Pinchwife in "The Country Wife," Professor Hertz in "The Coward," and Koye in "If This Be Treason"; White Plains, N.Y., Aug., 1935, the Bishop in "The Bishop Misbehaves"; Music Box, New York (for the Guild), Sept., 1935, Yato in "If This Be Treason"; Guild, Feb., 1936, Count Mirsky in "The End of Summer"; White Plains, N.Y., Aug., 1936, The Prince in "Death Takes a Holiday"; Vanderbilt, New York, Jan., 1937, Frankie Lotzgazel in "A House in the Country"; Brighton Beach, Brooklyn, Aug., 1937, Hilary Shaw in "Never Trouble Trouble"; Mercury, New York, May, 1938, succeeded Orson Welles as Brutus in "Julius Caesar" (in modern dress); Maplewood, N.J., Aug., 1938, Colin Derwent in "Ten Minute Alibi"; Little, New York, Nov., 1938, Francis Bacon in "Gloriana"; White Plains, N.Y., 1939, appeared in "Goodbye Again," and "Springtime for Henry"; Henry Miller, Nov., 1939, Durward Nesbitt in "Ring Two"; Lyceum, Dec., 1939, Joseph Helliwell in "When We Are Married"; Hudson, Nov., 1940, Richard Dennis in "Fledgling"; toured, 1941, in "The Man Who Came to Dinner"; Henry Miller, June, 1942, Hale Thatcher in "Broken Journey"; Forrest, Philadelphia, Aug., 1942, appeared in "Candida"; Ethel Barrymore, Dec., 1942, Kuligin in "The Three Sisters"; Adelphi, Apr., 1944, the Merchant in "Allah, Be Praised"; in addition to the plays already

mentioned, is the author of "He Knew Them All," and "Life Studies" (1939). *Recreations*: Painting and sculpture (both exhibited), music, and poetry and verse. *(Died 9 Nov., 1955; age 65)*

POWYS, Stephen (*née* Virginia de Lanty), dramatic author; *b*. Los Angeles, Cal., 1907; *d*. of John Mark de Lanty and his wife Mary Virginia (Durnal); *e*. Ward Seminary, Nashville, Tenn.; *m*. Guy Bolton; was formerly engaged in the United States as a dancer and also appeared in various plays; later, wrote several short stories for American magazines; author of "Wise To-Morrow," produced at the Lyric, London, 1937; "Three Blind Mice," Embassy and Duke of York's, 1938; "There's Always To-Morrow," 1940; "Don't Listen," (with Guy Bolton), 1948; "The Girl in the Swing," 1965. *Address*: Remsenberg, Long Island, New York.

PRAGA, Marco, Italian dramatic author; *b*. Milan, 1862; has written the following, among other plays: "Le Vergini," 1889; "La Moglie ideale," 1890; "Il canzoniere del Timbo," "Le Due case," "Mater dolorosa," "La Biondina," "L' amico," "L'Ereder," "L'Alleluia," "Giuliana," "L'Ondina," "L'Innamorata," "La Morale della favola," "L'Atto unico," "Storie di Palcoscenio," "La Crisi," "La Porta Chinsa"; since 1914, has devoted himself to management.

(Died 31 Jan., 1929; age 66)

PRATT, Muriel, actress; *b*. Nottingham; *d*. of W. Dymock Pratt; studied for the stage under Rosina Filippi; had had amateur experience prior to making her first appearance on the professional stage at Cheltenham, in 1909, as Portia in "The Merchant of Venice"; the following year she joined Miss Horniman's Company, at the Gaiety Theatre, Manchester, and remained four years, playing nearly ninety parts; made her first appearance in London with this company at the Coronet Theatre, 22 Feb., 1911, in the title-*rôle* in " Red 'Ria " ; appeared at the Coronet, in 1912, also at the Playhouse, 1912, with the same company, where she succeeded Edyth Goodall as Fanny Hawthorn in " Hindle Wakes " ; in 1914–15 she was director and leading lady of the repertory seasons at the Theatre Royal, Bristol ; at the Kingsway Theatre, Oct., 1915, played Muriel Hudson in " Iris Intervenes " ; next became director and leading lady of the Liverpool Repertory Theatre, 1916 ; at the New Theatre, June, 1918, played Blanchefleur in " The Loving Heart " ; at the Court, Sept., 1918, Countess de Clermont in " Philip II " ; subsequently, at the Garrick, took up the part of Dr. Marie Latour in " By Pigeon Post " ; at the Winter Garden Theatre, Nov., 1919, played Priyamvada in " Sakuntala " : at the Court Theatre, Dec., 1919, played Portia in " The Merchant of Venice," succeeding Miss Mary Grey ; in Sept., 1920, joined the repertory company at the Everyman Theatre, Hampstead, where among other parts she played Juliet in " Romeo and Juliet " ; at the Queen's, Oct., 1921, played Laurina Coote in " The Hotel Mouse " ; at the Court, Feb., 1922, Guinevere Megan in " The Pigeon " ; at the St. Martin's, Mar., 1922, Lady Wrathie in " Shall We Join the Ladies ? " ; at the Palace, May, 1922, Cassandra in " The Trojan Women " ; at the Little, Oct., 1922, Chihaya in " The Toils of Yoshitomo "; at the Apollo, Nov., 1922, Elsie in " Devil Dick " ; Dec., 1922, Mother in " Through the Crack " ; Scala (for the Renaissance Society), June, 1925, Estifania in " Rule a Wife and Have a Wife " ; Court (for the same), Mar., 1926, Dorine in " Tartuffe " ; Arts, Mar., 1928, Sonia in " Flies and Treacle " ; July, 1928, Alma in " Down Wind " ; Dec., 1928, Arabella in " The Lion Tamer."

(Died 15 Jan., 1945; age 54)

PREEDY, George R. (*née* Gabrielle Margaret Vere Campbell), dramatic author ; *b.* Hayling Island, Hants, 1888 ; *d.* of Vere Campbell, and his wife Josephine Elizabeth (Ellis) ; *e.* privately in Paris, Rome, and **London** ; *m.* (1) Emilio Costanzo (*d.* 1916) ; (2) Arthur L. Long ; as Marjorie Bowen wrote many novels ; since 1928, under the name of George R. Preedy, has also written a dozen novels, and has been a frequent contributor to the contemporary Press ; author of the following plays : "The Rocklitz," "General Crack," "Captain Banner," 1931 ; "Rose Giralda," 1933 ; "Court Cards," 1934. *Recreations :* Painting, reading, needlework, travel and the theatre. *(Died 23 Dec., 1952; age 68)*

PRENTICE, Charles W. ("Jock"), Mus.Bac. ; musical director, composer and orchestrator ; *b.* Prestonpans, Scotland, 15 Jan., 1898 ; *s.* of Adam Prentice, M.A., J.P. and his wife Mary (Whitecross) ; *e.* George Watson's Boys' College, Edinburgh, and Edinburgh University ; *m.* Phyllis Zimmerman Cartwright ; studied violin under William Waddell and graduated in Music at Edinburgh University under Sir Donald Tovey ; was conductor of the Edinburgh University Choral and Orchestral Society and composed and orchestrated music for the University *revues* ; his first appointment as musical director was at the Gaiety, 1922, when he took over during the run of "His Girl" ; subsequently conducted at the Empire, Adelphi, Prince of Wales's, Daly's, London Hippodrome, London Pavilion, Coliseum and Palace ; appointed musical director of Drury Lane Theatre, 1932, and remained there until the outbreak of War, Sept., 1939 ; was musical director at the Palace, 1940, for the revival of "Chu-Chin-Chow," and at the Coliseum, Dec., 1940, for the pantomime "Aladdin"; served in the Army 1941–5, as Captain in the Royal Artillery ; musical director for "Big Ben," Adelphi, 1946; "The Wizard of Oz," Winter Garden, 1946–7, and Strand, 1948 ; "Brigadoon," His Majesty's, 1949 ; "Can-Can," Coliseum, 1954 ; orchestrated the music for several of Andre Charlot's *revues,* "Streamline," 1934 ; "Jill Darling," 1934 ; Noel Coward's "Conversation Piece," 1934, and "Operette," 1938 ; and Ivor Novello's "Glamorous Night," 1935 ; "Care-

1950

less Rapture," 1936; "Crest of the Wave," 1937; "The Dancing Years," 1939; "Big Ben," 1946; "Harlequinade Ballet," for Festival Ballet company, 1950; has also composed incidental music and numbers for several West End productions, also ballets, suites, etc.; has conducted, composed and orchestrated for several films and B.B.C. feature productions, etc. *Recreations:* Tennis, fishing, and shooting. *Club:* Savage. *Address:* 27 Roman Road, Steyning, Sussex. *Telephone No.:* Steyning 2318.

PRENTICE, Herbert M., director and designer; *b.* Marple, Cheshire, 15 June, 1890; *s.* of William Prentice and his wife Elizabeth (Ashworth); *e.* Marple, and Manchester School of Commerce, Manchester University; *m.* Marion Smith; gained special scholarship training on Railway, in competitive examination; left Railway work and became director in 1920; his first production, "The Silver Box," was at the Little (Repertory) Theatre, Sheffield, Dec., 1918, and subsequently he formed the Sheffield Repertory Company, and directed there for seven years; then went to the Festival Theatre, Cambridge, directing for several years; spent four and a half years with the Repertory Theatre, Northampton, and was then engaged by Sir Barry Jackson for the Birmingham Repertory Theatre, and remained there until 1940, directing many interesting plays and first productions; among first productions, he has staged "The Adding Machine," "Progress," "The Crooked Cross," "Once in a Lifetime," "Merciless Lady," "When the Crash Comes," "The Brontës of Haworth Parsonage," "Counsellor-at-Law," "The Immortal Hour" (as a play), "Each in His Own Way," "1066 and All That," "The Simpleton of the Unexpected Isles," "The Composite Man," "The Year of the Locusts," "Jane Eyre," "The Millionairess," "Laugh With Me," "The Iron Road," "The Wooing of Anne Hathaway," "The Swiss Family Robinson," and numerous others; has directed, in all, over nine hundred plays; his first production in London

was at the Queen's, Feb., 1933, "Once in a Lifetime"; also directed "Counsellor-at-Law," Piccadilly, 1934; "1066 and All That," Strand, 1935; produced the plays at Malvern Festivals, 1934–7, including "St. Joan," on the occasion of Shaw's 80th birthday; directed for Roy Limbert, 1940; returned to the Sheffield Repertory company as director-producer, 1941, at Southport, and subsequently, 1944, back to Sheffield, as director and producer for both companies; in 1946, directed "As You Like It," at Stratford-on-Avon, also "1066 and All That"; returned to Birmingham, 1948, where he directed the first English productions of "The Merchant of Yonkers," "Jonathan Wild," and "The Bears of Bay-Rum"; directed "The Firstborn" at the Civic Theatre, Chesterfield, and remained there for two years; directed for the Pitlochry Festival, 1953–54; he has acted as adjudicator for the British Drama League, and is a member of the Guild of Adjudicators; became a Fellow of the Royal Society of Arts, 1949; adapted and directed "Alice in Wonderland," and "Through the Looking Glass." *Recreations:* Handicrafts, gardening, and motoring. *Address:* "The Beehive," Chipping Campden, Glos.

PRESBREY, Eugene Wyley, dramatic author; *b.* Williamsburg, Mass., U.S.A., 13 Mar., 1853; was formerly an actor, and made his first appearance on the stage at the Boston Theatre, Boston, 1874; remained there until 1879, when he went to New York, and was engaged at the Madison Square Theatre, 1880, during the run of "Hazel Kirke"; was stage-director for A. M. Palmer, from 1883-1896; has written the following, among other plays: "Squirrel Inn" (with Frank R. Stockton), 1893; "Giles Covey," 1894; "The Courtship of Miles Standish," 1895; "A Ward of France" (with Franklin Fyles), 1897; "A Virginia Courtship," 1898; "Worth a Million," 1898; "Marcelle," 1900; "New England Folks," 1903; "Personal," 1903; "Raffles" (from E. W. Hornung's novel), 1904; "Terence,"

1904 ; " Mary, Mary, Quite Contrary " (an adaptation of " A Scrap of Paper"), 1905 ; " The Adventures of Gerard " (from Conan Doyle's story), 1905 ; " A Fool's Wisdom," 1906 ; " The Garden of Eden," 1906 ; " Susan in Search of a Husband " (from a story of Jerome K. Jerome), 1906 ; " The Right of Way " (from Sir Gilbert Parker's story), 1906 ; " The Three Graces," 1907 ; " The Coast of Chance " (from the novel), 1908 ; " The Barrier " (from Rex Beach's novel), 1908 ; " The Other Man," 1912. *Recreations :* Painting, yachting, freemasonry. *Clubs :* Lambs' and Players'.
(Died 9 Sept., 1931; age 78)

PREVOST, Marcel, French dramatic author ; *b.* Paris, 1 May, 1862 ; was formerly an engineer ; has written the following plays : " Les Demi-Vierges," 1895 ; " La Plus Faible," 1904 ; " Les Anges-Gardiens," " Pierre et Thérèse," 1909 ; " L'Abbe Pierre " ; has also written numerous novels and literary works ; is a Commander of the Legion of Honour, a Member of the French Academy, a former president of the Société des Gens de Lettres, and literary editor of *La Revue de France ;* was decorated with the Croix de Guerre. *(Died 8 Apr., 1941; age 78)*

PRICE, Dennis, actor; *b.* Twyford, Berks, 23 June, 1915; *s.* of Brigadier-General T. Rose-Price and his wife Dorothy (Verey); *e.* Radley College, Berks, and Worcester College, Oxford; *m.* Joan Schofield (*née* Temperley); acted as an amateur while at Oxford; studied for the stage under Ronald Adam and Eileen Thorndike, at the Embassy Theatre School of Acting; made his first appearance on the stage at the Croydon Repertory Theatre, June, 1937, as Dick in "Behind Your Back"; first appeared in London, at the Queen's Theatre, 6 Sept., 1937, as Green and Exton's servant in "Richard II"; at the Arts, Jan., 1938, played Marcellus in "Hamlet"; returned to Croydon Repertory, Apr.–Sept., 1938; at the Arts and Haymarket, Oct., 1938, played Michael

Firbanks in "A Party for Christmas"; Chanticleer, Oct., 1939, appeared in "September Rain"; played a season of repertory at the Playhouse, Oxford, Nov., 1939–Feb., 1940; served in the Royal Artillery, Mar., 1940–June, 1942; reappeared on the stage at the Arts Theatre, Aug., 1942, in "The Springtime of Others"; toured, 1942, in "This Happy Breed," and "Present Laughter," with Noel Coward; Haymarket, Apr., 1943, played Morris Dixon in "Present Laughter," and Sam Leadbitter in "This Happy Breed"; Duchess, Aug., 1943, Charles Condamine in "Blithe Spirit"; New, Feb., 1944, Horatio in "Hamlet"; Lyric, Oct., 1944, Major Henry Grantley in "Scandal at Barchester"; Duchess, Mar., 1945, again played Charles Condamine in "Blithe Spirit"; went to the United States, and at the Playhouse, Wilmington, Dec., 1951, appeared as Shepherd Henderson in "Bell, Book and Candle"; Winter Garden, London, Oct., 1952, played Leon Lebrun in "Husbands Don't Count"; Grand, Blackpool, Sept., 1953, Cyrus Armstrong in "The Man Upstairs"; St. Martin's, Oct., 1953, Dr. Frank Chevasse in "Blind Man's Buff"; Fortune, June, 1956, Pedro in "To My Love"; made his first appearance in South Africa, Feb., 1957, when he played Mr. Malcolm in "Table by the Window," and Major Pollock in "Table Number Seven" ("Separate Tables"); Winter Garden, London, Dec., 1957, Bruce Wickson in "Be My Guest"; Billy Rose, N.Y., Oct., 1959, played Hector Hushabye in "Heartbreak House"; Apollo, London, Aug., 1965, played John in "Any Wednesday"; Little, St. Peter Port, May, 1966, Mr. Andrew Bennett in "Not in the Book"; first appeared in films, 1944, in "A Canterbury Tale," and further films include "Tunes of Glory," "The Amorous Prawn," "I'm Alright Jack," "The Millionairess," "Victim," etc.; television appearances include Jeeves in "The World of Wooster," 1965, and the Somerset Maugham series. *Favourite parts:* Noah in the play of that name, and Condamine in "Blithe Spirit." *Recreation:* Riding. *Address:* c/o A.L.S. Management Ltd., 67 Brook Street, London, W.1.

1952

PRICE, Evadne (Helen Zenna Smith); dramatic author, actress, novelist, etc.; *b.* at sea, in the Indian Ocean, 1896; *e.* West Maitland, N.S.W., and in Belgium; *m.* (1) Captain C. A. Fletcher (dec.); (2) Ken A. Attiwell; made her first appearance on the stage at the Theatre Royal, Sydney, N.S.W., 1906, as the First Twin in "Peter Pan"; during 1914, toured in English provinces as Nang Ping in "Mr. Wu"; toured in South Africa, 1915, and on her return, toured in "Oh, I Say" and "Within the Law"; then left the stage during remainder of the War, working on munitions and clerical work in the Air Ministry; during 1919, toured as Suzee in "Five Nights"; made her first appearance in London at the Lyric Theatre, 11 Sept. 1919, as Liliha in "The Bird of Paradise" and on occasions played Luana; Aldwych, Nov., 1920, Sua-See in "The Dragon"; Garrick, Jan., 1922, Liliha in "The Bird of Paradise"; subsequently appeared at the Coliseum and Alhambra in sketches; Shaftesbury, Apr., 1923, played Tessie Kearns in "Merton of the Movies"; Wyndham's, Dec., 1923, Princess Angelica in "The Rose and the Ring"; she then left the stage and devoted herself to writing; was a regular contributor to *The Sunday Chronicle, The Daily Sketch, The People,* and various magazines; author of the plays "The Haunted Light" (with Joan Byford), 1928; re-written as "The Phantom Light," 1937; "Red for Danger," 1938; "Big Ben" (with Ruby Miller), 1939; "Once a Crook" (with Ken Attiwell), 1940; "Who Killed My Sister?" (with Attiwell), 1942; "Three Wives Called Roland" (with Attiwell), 1943; "Through the Door" (with Attiwell), 1945; "Blonde for Danger," 1949; "Wanted on Voyage" (with Attiwell), 1949; author of several novels, including "Not So Quiet," "Women of the Aftermath," "Luxury Ladies," "They Lived With Me," "Society Girl," "Probationer," "Married to a Star," "Glamour Girl," the Jane Turpin books; has also written for the films. *Recreations:* Motoring and gardening. *Clubs:* P.E.N., Automobile Assn. *Address:*

17 Eccleston Square, London, S.W.1. *Telephone No.:* Victoria 4387.

PRICE, Nancy, C.B.E., actress; *b.* Kinver, Worcestershire, 3 Feb., 1880; *d.* of William Henry Price and his wife Sarah Julia (Mannix); *e.* Malvern Wells, Worcester; *m.* Charles Maude (dec.); made her first appearance on the stage at Birmingham, Sept., 1899, as a member of F. R. Benson's company in a non-speaking part; made her first appearance on the London stage at the Lyceum, 15 Feb., 1900, as one of the Pickers in "Henry V," and during the Lyceum engagement played Olivia in "Twelfth Night"; after leaving the Benson company was engaged at the Haymarket Theatre, as understudy; toured as Constance in "The Trumpet Call," and the Duchess of Strood in "The Gay Lord Quex"; at the Court Theatre in 1901, appeared in "John Durnford, M.P.," and "The Strange Adventures of Miss Brown"; first came into prominence in the part of Calypso in "Ulysses," at His Majesty's, Feb., 1902, the part originally designed for Mrs. Brown-Potter; subsequently appeared at the same theatre as Olivia in "Twelfth Night," and Princess Bellini in "The Eternal City"; next appeared at the Adelphi, in Aug., 1903, as Rosa Dartle in "Em'ly"; Duke of York's, 8 Oct., 1903, played the part of Hilda Gunning in Pinero's "Letty"; at the Garrick, in Aug., 1904, played in "The Chevaleer"; at Wyndham's, Feb., 1905, appeared as the heroine of Marshall's comedy, "The Lady of Leeds"; returned to His Majesty's, 1905, to play Mrs. Ford in "The Merry Wives of Windsor," Calpurnia in "Julius Cæsar," etc.; at Drury Lane, Sept. of the same year, appeared as Helga in "The Prodigal Son"; and at the Duke of York's, Sept., 1906, played the part of Mrs. Bowler in "Toddles"; at the Playhouse, Jan., 1907, appeared in "The Drums of Oude," and at the Garrick, 6 Mar., 1907, played Kitty Montmorency in "Mr. Sheridan"; at the Garrick, April, 1908, appeared as Sophie Fullgarney in Sir John Hare's farewell performances of "The

Gay Lord Quex " ; at the Aldwych, May, 1909, played Esther Coventry in " One of the Best " : in June, 1909, appeared there as Muriel Meredith in " A Modern Aspasia " : at Drury Lane, Sept., 1909, played Mrs. D'Aquila in " The Whip " ; at the Garrick, Jan., 1910, played the Princess de Chabran in " Dame Nature " ; at the Playhouse, Nov., 1910, appeared as Louise Parker in " A Single Man " ; at Stratford-on-Avon, Apr., 1911, played Portia in " The Merchant of Venice " : at the Kingsway, May, 1911, played Margaret Hughes in " The First Actress " ; at the Hippodrome, Oct., 1911, played in " Some Showers " ; at His Majesty's, Nov., 1911, played Mrs. Mineral in " The Borstal Boy " ; at the Coliseum, Mar., 1912, appeared as India in Sir Edward Elgar's " Crown of India " ; at the Coronet, Dec., 1913, played Mdme. Nérisse in " Woman on Her Own " ; at the Vaudeville, Feb., 1914, Helen Rathbone in " Helen with the High Hand " ; at the Comedy, May, 1914, Mary Magdalene in " The Holy City " ; in conjunction with Lyn Harding directed "A Scrap of Paper," at the Criterion, June, 1914, playing Susan Lawless, also appearing as Matka in " The Receipt " ; July, 1914, played Mrs. Cordingway in " A Working Man " ; during 1915 appeared in variety theatres, in " Not a Bad Judge " ; at His Majesty's, May, 1916, with Martin Harvey, played Queen Elizabeth in " Richard III " ; at Stratford-on-Avon, Aug., 1916, played Hermione in " The Winter's Tale," and Lady Macbeth in " Macbeth " at the Haymarket, Nov., 1916, Rebecca Gluckstein in " The Widow's Might " ; during the latter part of the war, worked with the blind ; gave several performances at Worthing, 1917–18 for war charit es, playing Viola in " Twelfth Night," and Titania in " A Midsummer Night's Dream " ; in 1920 went on tour, playing Zahratal-Kulub in " Chu-Chin-Chow " ; at the New Theatre, Dec., 1921, played Encarnacion in " Blood and Sand " ; at the Garrick, Oct., 1923, Harriet Nichols in " Ambush " ; subsequently illustrated a series of Shakespeare lectures with eight of the plays, at the

Royal Society of Arts ; at Golder's Green, Jan., 1924, played Mrs. Cliveden-Banks in " Outward Bound " ; at the Grand, Fulham, Sept., 1924, played Lady Rorke in " The Letter of the Law " ; Jan., 1925, Agnes Haldenstedt in " Jitta's Atonement " ; Everyman, Apr.–July, 1925, Mrs. Bagleigh in " Overture " and the Marchioness Matilda in Pirandello's " Henry IV " ; Lyric, Hammersmith, Sept., 1925, Signora Frola in " And That's the Truth " ; Little, Dec., 1925, The Princess and Queen Elizabeth in " Gloriana " ; Garrick, July, 1926, Hon. Honoria Tankerdown in " None But the Brave " ; Kennington, Dec., 1926, Time in " The Blue Bird " ; during 1927, appeared at " Q," in " Open Spaces," " Daniel Deronda," " The Village," and " Old Mrs. Wiley " ; Lyric, Jan., 1928, played Ethel Drake in " Sauce for the Gander " ; Everyman, Apr., 1928, Queen Elizabeth in a play of that name ; " Q," Sept.-Oct., 1928, played in " The House of Women," " Fetters," and " John Gabriel Borkman " ; Everyman, Dec., 1928, played the Rat-Wife in " Little Eyolf " ; Court, Feb., 1929, Madame Raquin in " Thérèse Raquin " ; Little, June, 1929, Janet in " Water " ; Vaudeville, Apr., 1930, Anne Collins in "Down Our Street" ; New, Sept., 1930, Queen Margaret in "Richard III" ; founded The People's National Theatre, and commenced at the Fortune Theatre, Nov., 1930, with a revival of "The Man from Blankley's" ; since that date has produced 82 plays at the Fortune, Duchess, Little, Duke of York's and Savoy Theatres, and the Playhouse ; at the Fortune, Jan., 1931, played Mrs. Jones in " The Silver Box" ; Apr., 1931, Martha in " Bush Fire" ; June, 1931, Old Mrs. Thurlow in " The Ship" ; Savoy, Oct., 1931, Herodias in " Salome" ; Duchess, Dec., 1931, Mistress Page in " The Merry Wives of Windsor" ; Feb., 1932, Mrs. Hale in " Trifles" ; June, 1932, Ann Redvers in " The Secret Woman" ; Little, Oct., 1932, Miss Agatha in " Alison's House," and Mrs. Jones in " The Silver Box" ; Feb, 1933, Merete Beyer in " The Witch, and Alice Montgomery in " Cock Re bin" ; Apr., 1933, Mrs. Bagleigh in 'Overture" ;

May, 1933, Annie Roberts in "Strife";
"Q," Feb., 1934, and Vaudeville,
Mar., 1934, Edith Cavell in "Nurse
Cavell"; Vaudeville, Mar., 1934, the
Blind Beggar in "Good Friday"; Open
Air Theatre, June, 1934, Queen Mar-
garet in "King Richard III"; Little,
Oct., 1934, Donn' Anna Luna in "The
Life that I Gave Him"; Little, Nov.,
1934, with the author, directed "Lady
Precious Stream"; Little, July, 1935,
played Mrs. Alving in "Ghosts"; at
the Duke of York's, Oct., 1935, dir-
ected "The Hangman"; Little, Apr.,
1936, played Adeline in "Whiteoaks,"
which ran for two years; Playhouse,
Aug., 1938, Madame Raquin in "Thou
Shalt Not ——" ("Thérèse Raquin");
Playhouse, Mar., 1939, Mrs. Van
Kleek in a play of that name; at the
Tavistock Little Theatre, Jan., 1940,
directed "The Child of Kensington,"
and "The Widow of Windsor," and
also played Annie Collins in a revival
of "Down Our Street"; subsequently
toured as Madame Popinot in "Vintage
Wine"; Comedy, Apr., 1942, again
appeared in "Whiteoaks"; "Q,"
Aug., 1942, played Edith Cavell in
"Nurse Cavell"; Wimbledon, Oct.,
1942, Mrs. Dundass in "Lottie Dundass"; Playhouse, Liverpool (for
the Old Vic), Aug.–Sept., 1944,
played Mrs. Borkmann in "John
Gabriel Borkmann," and Marfa Pestof
in "Lisa"; St. Martin's, Feb., 1948,
played Mrs. Hardlestone in "Gathering
Storm"; New Lindsey, Apr., 1950,
Martha Blanchard in "The Orange
Orchard," which she adapted and
directed; June, 1950, in association
with Fred O'Donovan, directed "The
Family Honour"; has appeared fre-
quently in films; adapted "Alice in
Wonderland," 1932; "Alice Through
the Looking Glass," 1935; is the
author of the following books: "Be-
hind the Nightlight," "Vagabond's
Way," "Shadows on the Hills," "The
Gull's Way," "Nettles and Docks,"
"Hurdy Gurdy," "Jack by the Hedge,"
"I Had a Comrade," "Tails and
Tails," "The Wonder of Wings,",
"Acquainted with Night," "Where
the Skies Unfold," "Tamera," "Bright
Pinions," "Into an Hourglass," "Pa-
gan's Progress," "The Heart of a
Vagabond," "Feathered Outlaws," "I

Watch and Listen," "In Praise of
Trees," "Winged Builders"; received
the C.B.E. in the Birthday Honours,
1950. *Recreations:* Music, tennis,
painting, climbing, riding, and walking.
(Died 31 Mar., 1970; age 90)

PRINCE, Adelaide, actress; *b.* London, 14 Dec., 1866; *d.* of Solomon
Rubinstein and his wife Mary (Stevenson); *e.* Millican, Texas, U.S.A.;
m. Creston Clarke; made her first
appearance on the stage, at Portland,
Maine, in 1888, as Ethel Sorrero in
" A Possible Case "; from 1889 to
1893, was a member of the Augustin
Daly Company; with this company
she played a great variety of parts,
notably Mdlle. Agatha in " The Great
Unknown," Mistress Coupler in " Miss
Hoyden's Husband," Lady Sneerwell
in " The School for Scandal," Maria in
" Love's Labour's Lost," Celia in " As
You Like It "; Lady Twombley in
" The Cabinet Minister," Madame
Lauretta in " Love in Tandem," Mrs.
Rackett in " The Belle's Stratagem,"
Olivia in " Twelfth Night," etc.; made
her first appearance in London, with
the Daly Company, at the Lyceum
Theatre, 10 June, 1890, as Dora Holly-
hock in " Casting the Boomerang ";
she also appeared at the Lyceum, as
Celia in " As You Like It "; after
quitting the Daly company, appeared
at the American Theatre, New York,
1893, as Rose Woodmere in " The
Prodigal Daughter "; she then became
joint-star with her husband, Creston
Clarke, playing Shakespearean and
standard repertory from 1893–1900,
and including among her parts Ophelia,
Juliet, Beatrice, Portia, Galatea, Pau-
line Deschappelles, etc.; in 1901–2
toured with Viola Allen, as Princess
Eboli in " In the Palace of the King ";
in 1903, as Lady Sylvia in " A Country
Mouse," with Ethel Barrymore; at the
Garden Theatre, New York, Sept.,
1903, appeared as Pallas Athene in
" Ulysses "; at Daly's, New York,
Feb., 1904, as Mrs. Jack James in
" Glittering Gloria "; at the Duke of
York's, London, Sept., 1905, and
Garrick, New York, Oct., 1906, as
Mrs. Trent in " Clarice "; at the Lyric,
New York, Dec., 1907, played the

Duchess of Cluny in "The Secret Orchard"; at the Empire, New York, Sept., 1908, Lady Wanley in "Jack Straw," and Sept., 1909, Odette de Versannes in "Inconstant George"; at the Hudson Theatre, Nov., 1910, Betty Jackson in "Nobody's Widow," and toured in this, 1911–12; after a lengthy absence from the stage, appeared at the New Amsterdam Theatre, Apr., 1917, with Sir Herbert Tree, as Madame de Florac in "Colonel Newcome"; at the Bijou, Aug., 1917, played Mrs. Burns in "Mary's Ankle"; at the Lyceum Theatre, Sept., 1919, Aunt Abby Rocker in "Adam and Eva"; Bijou, Apr., 1926, Comtesse de la Bière in "What Every Woman Knows"; Mansfield, Oct.. 1927, Mrs. Hazen in "The Springboard"; Playhouse, Jan., 1928, Mrs. Deborah Ashe in "A Free Soul"; Little, Nov., 1930, Judith in "Mr. Samuel"; is the authoress of the play, "The Power that Governs," 1907.

PRINCE, Arthur, ventriloquist; *b.* London, 17 Nov., 1881; *e.* London; *m.* Ida Rene; made his first appearance as an entertainer, at *al-fresco* concerts at Llandrindod Wells, where he played four seasons; first appeared in London, in 1902; has appeared at most of the principal halls in London, including the Palace, London Pavilion, Tivoli, Oxford, etc., and all the leading halls in the United Kingdom; has also toured in the United States; after the outbreak of War, during 1915, took up a commission in the Royal Field Artillery. *Address:* 27 Maresfield Gardens, Hampstead, N.W.

PRINCE, Elsie, actress and vocalist; *b.* London, 27 Nov., 1902; *d.* of Reginald Prince; made her first appearance on the stage at the Queen's Theatre, Dublin, 15 Dec., 1913, as Little Miss Nobody in the pantomime, "Jack and Jill"; subsequently appeared in variety theatres, and played in pantomime each Christmas; in 1917, visited Australia, and appeared in "The Jinker"; while singing in a pierrot entertainment at Blackpool was "discovered" by Mr. J. M. Glover, and was engaged to understudy Ella Retford; appeared at

the London Hippodrome, Dec., 1920, as Aladdin in the pantomime; toured 1921-23, in Julian Wylie's productions; returned to London, to appear at the London Hippodrome, Mar., 1923, in "Brighter London"; was then engaged by Hugh J. Ward, and in 1925 went to Australia, where she appeared successfully as Nanette in "No, No, Nanette" and Jack in "Jack and the Beanstalk," 1926; Mary in "Mercenary Mary," Susie Trevor in "Lady, Be Good," and Billie Cobb in "Archie," 1927; Constance Lane in "Good News," 1928; toured through New Zealand in the title-*rôle* of "Sunny"; appeared in Australia as Peggy Bassett in "Lido Lady," 1929; returned to England 1929, and appeared at the Theatre Royal, Birmingham, Dec., 1929, as Roland in "Goldilocks"; again returned to Australia, 1930, and appeared as Jill Kemp in "Mrs. Cinders," Yvonne in "Sons O' Guns," Rita Payne in "The Love Race," Angy in "Follow Through," etc.; returned to England, 1931, and in 1932, toured as Yvonne in "Sons O' Guns"; at the Duke of York's, June, 1932, played in "Frills"; Prince of Wales's, Sept., 1932, in "Folies Bergère Revue" ("De la Folie Pure"); at the Hippodrome, Newcastle-on-Tyne, Christmas, 1932, played Robin Hood in "The Babes in the Wood"; during 1933, toured in "By George," "Folies Bergère," and "I'm Telling You"; Grand, Leeds, Dec., 1933, played Robinson Crusoe in the pantomime; Lyceum, Dec., 1934, Dick in "Dick Whittington"; Grand Opera House, Belfast, 1935, Robinson Crusoe; Empire, Newcastle-on-Tyne, 1936, Aladdin; Grand Opera House, Belfast, 1937, Dick Whittington; Feldman's, Blackpool, June, 1938, appeared in "Rockin' the Town." *Address:* 114 Falkland Road, Hornsey, N.8. *Telephone No.:* Mountview 3538.

PRINSEP, Anthony Leyland, manager; *b.* London, 21 Sept., 1888; *s.* of Val Prinsep, R.A., and his wife Florence (Leyland); *e.* Eton and Trinity College, Cambridge; *m.* (1) Marie Löhr (mar. dis.); (2) Margaret Bannerman (mar. dis.); was formerly

engaged as an underwriter at Lloyd's; entered into the management of the Globe Theatre, with Marie Löhr, Jan., 1918, opening with "Love in a Cottage"; other productions which he made, were, "Press the Button," "Nurse Benson," "L'Aiglon," 1918; "Victory," "Trimmed in Scarlet," "The Voice from the Minaret," 1919; "Birds of a Feather," "A Marriage of Convenience," "French Leave," "Every Woman's Privilege," "Fedora," 1920; "The Hour and the Man," "Her Husband's Wife," "The Knave of Diamonds," "Woman to Woman," "The Truth About Blayds," 1921; "Mr. Pim Passes By," "Eileen," "Belinda," "The Return," "The Laughing Lady," 1922; "Aren't We All?" "Reckless Reggie," "Our Betters," 1923; "Camilla States Her Case," "The Grand Duchess," "Beginner's Luck," "Lullaby," 1925; "By-Ways," "Engaged," "Our Dogs," "There's No Fool ——," "Trelawney of the Wells," 1926; "A Hen Upon a Steeple," "The Golden Calf," 1927; he then relinquished the management of the theatre; in 1928 went to Australia, returning in 1929; at the Haymarket, Dec., 1932, produced "Business With America"; also produced "Bluebeard's Eighth Wife," at the Queen's, 1922; "The Prisoner of Zenda," at the Haymarket, 1923; "Orange Blossom," Queen's, 1924; was responsible for the Italian season with Ruggero Ruggeri at the Globe, 1926, and the French season with Louis Verneuil and Elvire Popesco; received the Order of Chevalier de Legion d'Honneur from the French Government, 1926; played lawn-tennis for Cambridge, 1909–10–11. *Recreation:* Lawn tennis. *Clubs:* Arts, Green Room, and Stage Golfing Society.
(Died 26 Oct., 1942; age 54)

PRINTEMPS, Yvonne, actress and singer; *b.* Ermont, Seine-et-Oise, France, 25 July, 1895; *m.* (1) Sacha Guitry (mar. dis.); (2) Pierre Fresnay; made her first appearance on the stage at the Théâtre Cigale, Paris, 8 June, 1908, as Lison, La Marchande de Plaisirs and Le Petit Chaperon Rouge, in the *revue* "Nue! Cocotte!!";

she then went to the Folies-Bergère, where she appeared, Dec., 1908, in the annual *revue*, and again in Dec., 1909; at the Alcazar, June, 1911, played Le Hollandais and Cyrano in "Ah! les Beaux Nichan!"; at the Folies-Bergère, Dec., 1911, appeared in "La Revue des Folies-Bergère; Apr., 1912, in "La Revue de Printemps des Folies-Bergère"; at the Scala, Sept., 1912, in "Si j'étais Roi"; Folies-Bergère, Oct., 1912, in "La Revue des Folies-Bergère; Capucines, Apr., 1913, in "Et Patati et Patata"; Olympia, Oct., 1913, in "La Revue d'Olympia," and as Trouhanowa in "La Romanichelle"; Gaîté, Dec., 1913, played Prince Charmant in "Les Contes de Perrault"; Olympia, Mar., 1914, appeared in "Miousic"; she was then seen at the Palais-Royal, Apr., 1915, in the *revue* "1915"; Théâtre Antoine, Oct., 1915, in "La Nouvelle Revue"; Palais-Royal, Nov.. 1915, in "Il faut l'avoir"; Jan., 1916, played Suzanne Letillois in "Le Poilu"; Théâtre Antoine, June, 1916, appeared in "La Revue du Théâtre Antoine"; Gymnase, Oct., 1916, in "Tout avance!" and "La Petite Dactylo"; she then joined Sacha Guitry's Company at the Bouffes-Parisiens, and appeared there Dec., 1916, as Mdlle. Certain, in "Jean de la Fontaine"; at the same theatre, Aug., 1917, appeared as Miss Hopkins in "L'Illusionniste"; at the Vaudeville, Feb., 1918, played Marie Duplessis in "Deburau"; June, 1918, Nono in a revival of the play of that name; Oct., 1918, appeared in "La Revue de Paris"; Apr., 1919, played Janine Audoin in "Le Mari, La Femme et l'Amant"; at the Porte-St.-Martin, Oct., 1919, Loulou in "Mon Père avait Raison," with Lucien and Sacha Guitry, and Jan., 1920, Lisette in "Béranger"; at the Théâtre Edouard VII, Oct., 1920, appeared as Elle in "Je t'aime," and at the Sarah-Bernhardt, Mar., 1921, as Paulette Vannaire in a revival of "La Prise de Berg-Op-Zoom"; at the Edouard VII, Apr., 1921, played Marie Vermillion in "Le Grand Duc," with Lucien Guitry; Nov., 1921, Suzette in "Jacqueline," with Lucien Guitry, and Elle in a revival of "Faisons un Rêve"; May, 1922, Marie-Louise in "Une petite main qui se place"; Feb., 1923, Elle in "L'Amour Masqué"; at the Etoile, Dec., 1923, appeared as Andrée in "L'Accroche-Cœur," and May, 1924, in "La Revue de Printemps"; at the Edouard VII, Dec., 1924, played Jeanne de Canigou in "Une étoile nouvelle"; Mar., 1925, Maggy Gérard in "On ne joue pas pour s'amuser"; Dec., 1925, the title-*rôle* in "Mozart"; at the Sarah-Bernhardt, Aug., 1926, appeared in a revival of "Deburau"; at the Edouard VII, Apr., 1927, played Odette Cléry in "Désiré"; Apr., 1928, Mariette Fleury in "Mariette"; at the Madeleine, Mar., 1931, Annette in "Franz Hals"; June, 1931, appeared in "Une Revue de Sacha Guitry"; Oct., 1931, played Sophie Arnould in "Chagrin d'Amour"; Nov., 1931, Caroline Linsel in "Monsieur Prud-homme," and Elle in "Le S.A.D.M.P."; Mar., 1932, Françoise in a play of that name, and Nias in "Le Voyage de Tchong-Li"; Gymnase, Apr., 1933, Clara Stuart in "Le Bonheur"; made her first appearance on the London stage, at the Aldwych Theatre, 11 May, 1920, as Nono in the play of that name, and also appeared during the same month as Paulette in "La Prise de Berg-Op-Zoom," Mdlle. Certain in "Jean de la Fontaine," Miss Hopkins in "L'Illusionniste," and Loulou in "Mon Père avait Raison"; at the Princes, June–July, 1922, as Miss Hopkins in "L'Illusionniste," Suzette in "Jacqueline," Elle in "Un Monsieur attend une Dame," and Marie Ver-million in "Le Grand Duc"; New Oxford, June, 1923, as Mariette de Ronceray in "Comment on Ecrit l'Histoire," Elle in "Le Veilleur de Nuit," and Nono in "Nono"; Gaiety, June, 1926, Mozart in the operetta of that name; His Majesty's, June, 1929, Mariette Fleury in "Mariette"; His Majesty's, Feb., 1934, Melanie in "Con-versation Piece," in which she played in English for the first time; St. James's, Dec., 1936, Sophia in "O Mistress Mine"; made her first appear-ance in New York, at the 46th Street Theatre, 27 Dec., 1926, as Mozart in the play of that name; 44th Street Theatre, Oct., 1934, played Melanie in "Conversation Piece" (in English); at the Marigny, Paris, Nov.,

1935, played the title-*rôle* of "Margot"; at the Bouffes-Parisiens, 1937, ap-peared in "Trois Valses"; also in 1937 she took over the management of the Théâtre de la Michodière, and in 1939 appeared there in a revival of "Trois Valses"; Michodière, 1940, appeared in "Léocadia"; at the Athénée, 1941, played in "Comédie en trois actes"; subsequently at the Michodière appeared in "Père," 1942–44; "Vient de paraître," 1945; "Auprès de ma blonde," 1946–47; "Du côté de chez Proust," 1948; "Le Moulin de la Galette," 1951; "Hyménée," 1952; "Voici le Jour," 1954; "Le Voyage à Turin," 1956; "Père," 1958; in 1934, appeared in the film "La Dame Aux Camélias," and has since ap-peared in "Adrienne Lecouvreur," "Les Trois Valses," "Le Duel," "Je Suis Avec Toi," "Les Condamnés," "Le Valse de Paris," "Le Voyage en Amérique," etc.; Chevalier de la Légion d'Honneur. *Address:* 4 bis, Rue de la Michodière, Paris, France.

PRIOR, Allan, actor and vocalist; first attracted attention in New York, when he appeared at the Broadhurst Theatre, Nov., 1923, in "Topics of 1923"; at the Winter Garden, Sept., 1924, appeared in "The Passing Show of 1924"; Century, Jan., 1925, played Offenbach in "The Love Song"; made his first appearance in London, at His Majesty's Theatre, 3 Feb., 1926, as Prince Karl Franz in "The Student Prince"; at the Forty-fourth Street Theatre, Oct., 1926, played Prince Carl in "Katja"; Casino, Dec., 1927, Captain James Wynnegate in "White Eagle"; Gallo Theatre, New York, Nov., 1928, Harry Stanton in "Rain-bow"; Cosmopolitan, Oct., 1929, Jim Brent in "The Great Day"; Curran Theatre, San Francisco, Nov., 1930, Paul Delacroix in "Paris in Spring"; during 1933, in Australia, appeared in "The Student Prince," and 1934, in "Jolly Roger"; in 1930, appeared in the film "The Bride of the Regiment."

PROVOST, Jeanne, French actress; studied at the Conservatoire, and gained first prize in 1907; made her first appearance on the stage at the

Comédie Française, 1 Oct., 1907, as Lucienne de Morfontaine in " L'Amour veille " ; from 1907-11, appeared as Colette Mertal in " L'Imprévu," Alida in "La Fleur Merveilleuse." Baronne de Chanceney in " Comme ils sont tous," Madame de Lancey in " Les Marionettes " ; Jeanne in " Le Monde ou l'on s'ennuie," Casilda in " Ruy Blas," Agatha in " Les Folies Amoureuses," Armande in " Les Femme Savantes," Mdme. de Santis in " Le Demi-Monde," Cherubin in " Le Mariage de Figaro," etc.; in 1911, appeared at the Théâtre Michel, St. Petersburg, in a round of parts ; in Apr., 1912, appeared as Madame de Léry in " Le Caprice," before the late German Emperor, at the French Embassy, in Berlin, during 1912, toured in South America ; at the Gymnase, 1912, appeared as Thérèse in " La Femme seule " ; in 1913, appeared at the Comédie Royale, in " Le Garde Du Corps " ; at the Porte-St,-Martin, 1913, in " Le Ruisseau " ; at the Porte-St,-Martin, Feb., 1914, played Mdlle. Germer in " Madame " ; at the London Coliseum, Aug., 1915, played Rafaëli in " Le Brésilien," and Suzanne in " Le Bureau de Poste " ; from 1916-18, toured in France, Switzerland, Algiers and Tunis ; at the Marigny, Feb., 1919, played Lysistrata ; in July, 1919, played Suzanne in " Le Mariage de Figaro," at Mayence, Wiesbaden, Coblenz, etc. ; at the Vaudeville, Oct., 1920, played Jacqueline Remon in " Les Aisles Brisées " ; at Brussels, Apr., 1921, played Marthe in " La Tendresse " ; at the Théâtre de Paris, May, 1921, appeared as Chloé in " Cherubin " ; subsequently toured in Holland and Belgium in " Le Secret," " Amants," and " Le Rubicon " ; at the Gymnase, Dec., 1921, appeared as La Duchesse de Valore in " Lorsqu'on aime." *Address :* 22 Quai du Louvre, Paris.

PRUSSING, Louise, actress; *b.* Chicago, Illinois, U.S.A., 11 Jan., 1897; *d.* of Eugene E. Prussing and his wife Louise; *e.* Chicago and Stamford, Conn.; was formerly a dancer and also appeared on the cinema stage; made her first appearance on the legitimate stage at the Gaiety Theatre, New York, 3 Sept., 1917, as Athalie Wainwright in " The Country Cousin "; during 1919 appeared at the Knickerbocker Theatre as Vittoria in " The Maid of the Mountains "; toured 1921 as Theodora in " Nice People "; at the Sam H. Harris Theatre, New York, 1921, succeeded Hedda Hopper as Margaret in " Six-Cylinder Love " ; at the Broadhurst, 1922, succeeded Juliet Crosby as Suzanne in " The Nest "; during the seasons 1922-4 toured with Eugene O'Brien in " Steve "; made her first appearance in London, at the Garrick Theatre, 24 Dec., 1924, as Margaret in " Six-Cylinder Love ' ; at Wyndham's, Mar., 1925, played Lady Greyshott in " A Man With a Heart "; Lyceum, July, 1925, Mrs. Hesketh Pointer in " The Fake "; Ambassadors' Oct., 1925, Lola Pratt in " Growing Pains " ; " Q," May, 1926, Liane in " The Prince's Harem "; June, 1926, toured as Diana Trawley in " Three for Diana "; Barnes, Sept., 1926, played Lucetta in " The Mayor of Casterbridge "; Wyndham's, Nov., 1926, Cora Ann Milton in " The Ringer "; Arts, Oct., 1927, Hildegonde in " Yolande and Sylvain "; during 1927 toured as Marini in " Lilac Time," and appeared in the same part at Daly's Theatre, Dec., 1927; during 1928, toured in the United States in " Whispering Friends"; Lyceum, New York, Nov., 1929, played the Duchess of Devonshire in "Berkeley Square"; during 1930-1, toured in the same play, in the part of Kate Pettigrew; during a summer "stock" season at Elitch's Gardens, Denver, July, 1931, Lady Violet Hardy in "The Whistler"; at the Plymouth, New York, Nov., 1931, Cora Simon in "Counsellor-at-Law"; 48th Street Theatre, Nov., 1932, played Hilda Armstrong in "Singapore"; Ritz, Feb., 1933, Mrs. Nichols in "Before Morning"; at Scarsborough-on-Hudson, N.Y., July, 1935, appeared in "The Naked Man," Lady Marriot in "Beginners' Luck," Ethel Gower in "The Closed Door"; retired from the stage for ten years, returning to tour, 1943, as Mrs. Aldrich in "What a Life!"; toured, 1944, in South America, and went to

South Africa, for U.S.O., playing Mrs. Ralston in "Nothing but the Truth"; toured in Europe, 1945, for U.S.O., as Mrs. Archer in "Kiss and Tell"; has also appeared successfully in several films. *Address:* c/o Actors' Equity Association, 45 West 47th Street, New York City, U.S.A.

PRYCE, Richard, dramatic author and novelist; *b.* Boulogne, France; *s.* of Sarah (Hamilton) and the late Colonel Pryce; *e.* Leamington; has written the following plays: "A Scarlet Flower" (with Frederick Fenn), 1903; "Saturday to Monday" (with Fenn), 1904; "'Op o' Me Thumb" (with Fenn), 1904; "A Privy Council" (with Major W. P. Drury), 1905; "His Child" (with Fenn), 1906; "The Dumb Cake" (with Arthur Morrison), 1907, "Little Mrs. Cummin," 1910; "The Visit," 1910; "Helen with the High Hand" (from Arnold Bennett's novel), 1914; "The Old House" (from Mary E. Mann's novel "Candle Light"), 1920; "The Love Child" (with Frederick Fenn), 1921; "Thunder on the Left" (from Christopher Morley's novel), 1928; "Frolic Wind" (from Richard Oke's novel), 1935; is the author of the following, among other novels: "An Evil Spirit," "Just Impediment," "The Quiet Mrs. Fleming," "The Burden of a Woman," "Jezebel," "Elementary Jane," "The Successor," "Towing-Path Bess," "Christopher," "The Statue in the Wood," "David Penstephen," "Romance and Jane Weston," "Morgan's Yard," etc. *Club:* Royal Aero.

(Died 30 May, 1942; age 79)

PRYDE, Peggy (*née* Letitia Matilda Woodley), comedienne; *b.* 19 July, 1869; *d.* of the famous Jenny Hill; made her first appearance on the stage at the Mechanics' Hall, Hull, Oct., 1877; she then appeared at the Star, Bradford; in 1878-9, appeared in pantomime at the Theatre Royal, Dublin, and also played two seasons in pantomime at the Grand Theatre, Leeds, under the late Wilson Barrett; made her first appearance on the music-hall stage in London, at Gatti's, West-minster Bridge Road; has appeared at most of the leading halls in the United Kingdom; in 1891, visited the United States, and has also toured in Australia; for some time sang some of the songs identified with her mother's name, and among other songs she sang may be mentioned "Monte Carlo"; "Italiano Sarah"; "And lots of other things," etc.

PRYOR, Roger, actor; *b.* Asbury Park, New Jersey, 27 Aug., 1901; *s.* of Arthur Pryor, composer and conductor, and his wife Maud (Russell); *e.* New York City; *m.* (1) Priscilla Mitchell (mar. dis.); (2) Ann Sothern (mar. dis.); made his first appearance on the New York stage at the Hudson Theatre, 11 Apr., 1925, as Douglas Lane in "The Backslapper"; Little Theatre, Aug., 1925, played the Engineer in "The Sea Woman"; Booth, Nov., 1925, John Ramsey Jun. in "Paid"; Booth, Jan., 1927, Rims O'Neil in "Saturday's Children"; at Times Square, 1928, succeeded Lee Tracy as Hildy Johnson in "The Front Page," and also toured in the part; Vanderbilt, Sept., 1929, Charles Carroll in "See Naples and Die"; Bijou, Feb., 1930, Daniel Curtis in "Apron Strings"; Masque, Sept., 1930, Steve Merrick in "Up Pops the Devil"; Booth, May, 1931, Hazard in "A Modern Virgin"; Longacre, Feb., 1932, Alvin Roberts in "Blessed Event"; subsequently played "stock" at Denver; at the Ethel Barrymore Theatre, Oct., 1932, played Dwight Houston in "There's Always Juliet"; at the Princess, Chicago, Apr., 1933, played McKinley in "Riddle Me This"; Los Angeles, Feb., 1934, George Ferguson in "Men in White"; El Capitan, Hollywood, Dec., 1934, Ned Farrar in "Her Master's Voice"; Geary, San Francisco, 1935, Alan Squier in "Petrified Forest"; toured, Aug., 1945, as Peter Grayson in "Windy Hill"; Plymouth, New York, Apr., 1947, played Stephen Austin in "Message for Margaret"; in summer theatres, 1947, appeared in "Goodbye Again"; during the War was a Flight Instructor in the U.S. Air Corps;

entered films 1933, in "Moonlight and Melody," and has appeared since in innumerable pictures. *Recreations:* Golf, music, and swimming. *Address:* c/o M.C.A. Artists, Ltd., 9300 Burton Way, Beverly Hills, Cal., U.S.A.

PRYSE, Hugh (*né* John Hwfa Pryse), *b.* London, 11 Nov., 1910; *s.* of Albert Edward Pryse and his wife Rosetta Mary (Thomas); *e.* Kent College, Canterbury, and Xaverian College, Bruges; studied for the stage at the Royal Academy of Dramatic Art; made his first appearance on the stage at the Festival Theatre, Malvern, 24 Aug., 1929, walking-on in "Caesar and Cleopatra"; first appeared in London, at the New Theatre, 4 Nov., 1936, as Mr. Stanley in "Parnell"; spent two years playing at the "Q," and Richmond Theatres in a number of plays; at the Whitehall, 1937–8, played Fred in "Anthony and Anna"; was engaged at the Westminster Theatre, May, 1939 to Apr., 1940, in "Bridge Head," "Music at Night," "Major Barbara," "Desire Under the Elms," and "Abraham Lincoln"; served with the Armed Forces, 1940–5; reappeared on the stage, at the Granville Theatre, 26 Dec., 1945, as Ben Gunn in "Treasure Island"; New Lindsey, Apr., 1946, played Thomas Williams in "The Long Mirror," and Doctor Prentice in "For Services Rendered"; May, 1946, played Mr. Collins in "Pick-Up Girl," and also when the play was transferred to the Prince of Wales's and the Casino; Boltons, Oct., 1947, Mr. Ireland in "The Hidden Years"; Lyric, Hammersmith, May, and Globe, June, 1948, Dr. Jim Baylis in "All My Sons"; Lyric, ·Hammersmith, Mar., and Ambassadors', Apr., 1949, Conjur Man in "Dark of the Moon"; Mercury, Dec., 1949, Mr. Hodge, the Wizard, in "Beauty and the Beast"; Arts, Apr., 1950, Count Shabelsky in "Ivanov," July, 1950, Mazzini Dunn in "Heartbreak House," and Sept., 1950, Pier Zanotti in "The Mask and the Face"; toured, Nov., 1950, as Dr. Douche in "The Gay Invalid"; first appeared in films, 1929, in "Escape," and has appeared in numerous pictures. *Favourite parts:* Shabelsky in "Ivanov."

and Thomas in "The Long Mirror,"
(Died 11 Aug., 1955; age 44)

PURCELL, Charles, actor and vocalist; *b.* Chatanooga, Tenn., U.S.A., 1883; *m.* Ilona Bauer; made his first appearance on the stage as a ballad vocalist, 1904, in London; made his first appearance in the United States in 1905; at the Broadway, New York, 12 Oct., 1908, played Count Androssy and Lazlov in "The Golden Butterfly"; Casino, Sept., 1914, Forest Smith in "Pretty Mrs. Smith"; during 1915, played Bumerli in "The Chocolate Soldier," and appeared in "The Ziegfeld Follies"; Casino, Sept., 1916, played Prince Nicholas in "Flora Bella"; Lyric, June, 1917, Captain Poildeau in "My Lady's Glove"; Shubert, Aug., 1917, Richard Wayne in "Maytime"; Broadhurst, Dec., 1918, Dr. John Moore in "The Melting of Molly"; Winter Garden, Feb., 1919, played in "Monte Cristo Jun."; Shubert, Nov., 1919, Beppo Corsini and Captain Arthur Stanley in "The Magic Melody"; Central, July, 1920, William Pembroke in "The Poor Little Ritz Girl"; Ambassador, Feb., 1921, Victor in "The Rose Girl"; Knickerbocker, Sept., 1925, Sir John Copeland in "Dearest Enemy"; Fulton, Dec., 1926, Robert Vandeleur in "Oh, Please"; Royale, Feb., 1927, Jack Lethbridge in "Judy"; Jolson, Jan., 1930, Bumerli in "The Chocolate Soldier"; Shubert, July, 1933, Richard Brandt in "Shady Lady"; St. James, May, 1934, again played Bumerli in "The Chocolate Soldier"; Shubert, Nov., 1946, played Reggie Fox in "Park Avenue."

(Died 20 Mar., 1962; age 78)

PURCELL, Harold, dramatic author, librettist, and lyric writer; *b.* London, 9 Dec., 1907; *s.* of Joseph George Purcell and his wife Mary Ann Isabella (Lord); *e.* Brockley School, and Worcester College, Oxford (M.A.); *m.* Iris Boon; was formerly a schoolmaster, and journalist; author of the lyrics (with Eric Maschwitz) for "Magyar Melody," 1939; contributed lyrics to "Diversion," 1941; "Rise Above

It," "The New Ambassadors' Revue," "Orchids and Onions," "Apple Sauce," "Hulbert Follies,"1941; "Full Swing," "Big Top," 1942; "Something in the Air," 1943; author of book and lyrics of "The Lisbon Story," 1943; author of "The Rest is Silence," 1944; author of lyrics of "Jenny Jones," 1944; "Under the Counter," 1945; author of lyrics of "Here Come the Boys," "The Shephard Show," 1946; "The Red Mill," 1947; book and lyrics of "Her Excellency," 1949; lyrics for "Music at Midnight," "Blue for a Boy," 1950; with Guy Bolton, book and lyrics of "Rainbow Square," 1951; book and lyrics of "The Glorious Days," 1952; film script and screen play "The Lady is a Square"; has contributed certain lyrics to numerous other productions. *Address:* "Carriage and Pair," Portsmouth Road, Camberley, Surrey. *Telephone No.:* Camberley 372.

PURCELL, Irene, actress; *b.* Hammond, Indiana, U.S.A., 7 Aug., 1903; *e.* St. Mary's Convent, Wisconsin, and the Ann Morgan School, Chicago; *m.* Herbert F. Johnson Jun.; made her first appearance on the stage in Otis Skinner's company, in "Mister Antonio"; appeared at the Playhouse, New York, 7 Jan., 1924, as Constance Wellby in "The New Poor"; at the Henry Miller, Apr., 1924, played Tot Raymond in "Helena's Boys"; Mansfield, Oct., 1926, Betty in "The Ladder"; Klaw, Dec., 1927, Ann in "Sisters"; Ambassador, Mar., 1928, Pansy Hawthorne in "The Great Necker"; Morosco, Nov., 1929, Tony in "Cross Roads"; Belasco, Aug., 1930, Roxy in "Dancing Partner"; at the Playhouse, Hollywood, Mar., 1932, Julia Jelliwell in "Springtime for Henry"; Belasco, Los Angeles, Sept., 1932, played in "The Bride the Sun Shines On"; Avon, New York, Jan., 1933, played Leila in "A Good Woman, Poor Thing"; Booth, Dec., 1933, Sylvia Carson in "The First Apple"; Broad Street, Philadelphia, Mar., 1934, Marion Froude in "Biography"; Plymouth, New York, Dec., 1934, Genevieve Lang in "Accent on Youth"; Elitch's Gardens, Denver, June, 1936,

played Belinda Warren in "Sweet Aloes," and Lady Loddon in "Libel!"; Morosco, New York, Apr., 1937, Tina in "Penny Wise"; toured, 1937, as Lucy in "First Lady"; toured in Australia, 1938, in "The Women"; commenced film career 1930, and has appeared in numerous pictures since that date.

PURDELL, Reginald, actor; *b.* Clapham, London, 4 Nov., 1896; *s.* of Charles William Grasdorff and his wife Miriam (Purdell); *e.* London; *m.* May Watson; made his first appearance on the stage as a child entertainer at the Camberwell Palace of Varieties, May, 1911; made his first appearance on the regular stage at the New Theatre, 2 Sept., 1911, as a Page in "Romeo and Juliet"; Savoy, Dec., 1911, played the Hyena in the first production of "Where the Rainbow Ends"; during 1912, played in "A Member of Tattersall's" at the Strand, and "A Winter's Tale," at Savoy; His Majesty's, Mar., 1913, played Midshipman Merryweather in "The Happy Island"; in 1913, was at the Liverpool Repertory Theatre, in "Shock-Headed Peter"; went to America, and made his first appearance in New York, at the Garrick Theatre, 26 Jan., 1914, as Bill Dunbar in "The Dear Fool"; on his return, appeared at the Vaudeville, May, 1914, in the same part, when the play was called "The Dangerous Age"; July, 1914, appeared in "Eliza Comes to Stay"; during the War (1915–18) served as second lieutenant with the South Wales Borderers, in Gallipoli and France; 1917, in Royal Flying Corps, as observer; after the War, appeared at the Garrick, Mar., 1919, as D'Antignac-Juzet in "Cyrano de Bergerac"; St. Martin's, July, 1919, Martin Kittering in "The Bantam V.C."; subsequently toured in "Tilly of Bloomsbury," "The Maid of the Mountains," "Yes, Uncle"; went to Australia, Oct., 1922, and played in musical comedy, until 1924; reappeared in London, Queen's, May, 1924, in "Come In"; toured in "Little Nelly Kelly," "The Shingled Honeymoon," "Is Zat So?" and "The First Year"; was then producer and leading man at Southend Repertory Theatre for one

year; at the New, Aug., 1928, played Mac in "A Damsel in Distress"; Arts and Garrick, Jan., 1929, Bamford in "The Lady With a Lamp"; Comedy, Mar., 1929, Horace in "Big Fleas——"; Shaftesbury, Aug., 1929, Ah Fong and Corporal Duckett in "The Middle Watch"; Prince Edward, Oct., 1930, Anthony Cheshire in "Nippy"; Palace Sept., 1931, Janczi in "Viktoria and Her Hussar"; Shaftesbury, Aug.,1932, Waggermeyer in "Orders is Orders"; Saville, Aug., 1934, Freddie Baines in "She Shall Have Music ——"; Gaiety, Feb., 1935, Chick Osborne in "Jack o' Diamonds"; Alhambra, Feb., 1936, succeeded Steve Geray as "Piggy" in "Tulip Time"; Whitehall, Dec., 1939, Gretchen in "Who's Taking Liberty?"; Wimbledon, Aug., 1942, Chick Osborne in "Susie"; Embassy, Oct., 1945, Joe in "Zoo in Silesia"; has also appeared in numerous performances for Repertory Players, Arts Theatre Club, etc.; part-author of "I'll Tell the World," 1925; "Wild Violets," 1932; commenced film career in "The Middle Watch," and has appeared in innumerable pictures. *Recreations:* Golf, walking and swimming. *Clubs:* Green Room, Savage, and Stage Golfing Society. *Address:* Savage Club, 1 Carlton House T(London, S.W.1.
(Died 21 Apr., 1953; age 56)

PURDOM, C. B., author and dramatic critic; *b.* London, 15 Oct., 1883; *s.* of Benjamin Purdom and his wife Margaret (Newington); *m.* Lilian Antonia Cutlar; was appointed dramatic critic of *Everyman,* 1912; editor of *Everyman,* 1928–32; editor of *New Britain,* 1933–4; editor of *The Theatregoer,* 1935; was formerly finance director of Welwyn Garden City, where he built the Welwyn Theatre, 1928; has directed several plays at the Arts Theatre, London, Festival Theatre, Cambridge, etc.; has done much adjudication at Drama Festivals, etc.; General Secretary of British Actors' Equity Association, 1939–40; author of "Producing Plays," 1928; "Producing Shakespeare," 1950; "Drama Festivals and Their Adjudication," 1952; "Harley Gran-

ville Barker," 1955; "Letters of Bernard Shaw to Granville Barker," 1956; was the editor of the Swan Edition of Shakespeare, 1930; has also written works on town planning and literary subjects; is a Critics' Circle councillor. *Recreations:* Books and the theatre. *(Died 8 July, 1965; age 81)*

PUSEY, Arthur, actor; *m.* Adrienne Brune (mar. dis.); was a pupil at the Academy of Dramatic Art, prior to making his first appearance on the professional stage, 1913; appeared at the Empress, Brixton, Mar., 1915, in "The Playgoers"; in the autumn of 1915 joined the Liverpool Repertory Company, playing a number of small parts; at the Strand as Monty Vaughan in "Under Cover"; at the Royalty Theatre, Oct., 1919, played Harry Davenport in "Summertime"; at the Little Theatre, Feb., 1920, scored a hit as Noël in "Mumsee"; at the same theatre, Apr., 1920, played Tony Stiles in "Other Times"; at the St. James's, May, 1920, Joseph Rouletabille in "The Mystery of the Yellow Room"; in Sept., 1920, toured as Gilbert Burnarsham, Lord Kidderminster in "The Heart of a Child," and played the same part at the Kingsway, Mar., 1921; at the Ambassadors', Feb., 1922, played Kenneth Holloway in "My Son"; at the Adelphi, Sept., 1923, Dick Bythesea in "Head Over Heels"; at the Ambassadors', Aug., 1924, Dennis Welch in "Storm"; Strand, Mar., 1925, Guy Trebarrow in "The Sea Urchin"; Everyman, Sept., 1925, Dick in "The Limpet"; Nov., 1925, Gerald in "The Dark Angel"; Kingsway, Dec., 1925, Fritz Lobeheimer in "Light o' Love"; Globe, Jan., 1926, Roger Elrington in "All the King's Horses"; Daly's, May, 1926, Maurice de Fremond in "Yvonne"; Apollo (for the Play Actors), May, 1926, Robin Brabazon in "Getting Mother Married"; Strand (for the same), Mar., 1927, Michael Horton in "Two and Two"; "Q," Jan., 1928, Frank Pine in "The Man at Six"; Everyman, Apr., 1928, Earl of Leicester in "Queen Elizabeth";

Queen's, Mar., 1929, Frank Pine in "The Man at Six"; Arts, Feb., 1930, Gaston in "The Command to Love"; Duchess, Jan.–Feb., 1932, played Blunter in "Windows," George Henderson in "Trifles," and Francis Derham in "The Rose Without a Thorn"; Globe, May, 1932, Captain Wiltshire in "Ourselves Alone"; Piccadilly, Oct., 1932, Clifford Barton in "All for Joy"; Little, Mar., 1933, J. G. Lockhart in "Scott of Abbotsford"; Apr., 1933, Joe in "Overture"; May, 1933, Edgar Anthony in "Strife"; Queen's, Dec., 1933, David Remington in "The Old Folks at Home"; Duke of York's, Oct., 1935, the Young Hangman and the Airman in "The Hangman"; toured, 1937, as Titus Jaywood in "Yes, My Darling Daughter"; Tavistock Little Theatre, Jan., 1940, Lord Conyngham and Ludovic Cart in "The Child of Kensington"; Playhouse, Dec., 1942, Theodore Rudd in "The House of Jeffreys"; King's, Hammersmith, Nov., 1943, Maurice Holmes in "Pretty as Paint"; toured, 1944, in "Flare Path," and 1946, in "Three Waltzes"; has also frequently appeared in films.